WORLD ATLAS
OF
TRAVEL

ISBN: 1 900341 55 7

©1998 Thomas Cook Publishing Ltd/Columbus Press Ltd *

* General Maps
ICA Bokförlag, AB, Sweden © 1997/8, designed and produced by AND Map Graphics Ltd
* Specialist Maps & Index
Columbus Press Ltd © 1998 (information for Skiing Maps on Pages 70 & 116 © Snow-Hunter, Inverness)
* Relief Maps
Mountain High Maps © 1993 Digital Wisdom Inc.
* Transport Maps
Thomas Cook Publishing © 1998
* Statistics & Appendices
Columbus Press Ltd © 1998 from various sources as credited

Thomas Cook Publishing · PO Box 227 · Thorpe Wood · Peterborough · PE6 6PU
Tel: (01733) 503571/2 · Fax: (01733) 503596 · Email: books@thomascook.com

Editor
Mike Taylor of the University of Brighton
Original Cartography
David Burles
Researchers
Kate Meere, Nonke Beyer, Nick Ryan, Dr Margaret Penston, Barbara Bentele,
Nick Dent, Pedro Machado, Tony Peisley, Patrick Thorne
Design and Production
Space Design and Production Services Ltd, London N1
Project Co-ordinators
Stephen Collins, Bernard Horton
Publisher
Stephen York
Printed in the United Kingdom by
Thanet Press Ltd, Margate
Colour Reproduction by
Kingswood-Steele, London N1; Derek Croxson Ltd, Chesham

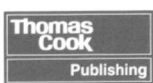

The publishers and Columbus Press Ltd would like to thank all the tourist offices, embassies, airlines, cruise and ferry operators, sporting bodies and other organisations and individuals who assisted in the preparation of this edition, with particular thanks to UNESCO, the World Tourism Organisation, the British Tourism Authority, the English Tourist Board, the World Health Organisation, Snow-Hunter, the Travel Industry Association of America, the Automobile Association, the Royal Automobile Club, the Royal Grenwich Observatory, the Tidy Britain Group and the National Maritime Museum.

GENERAL CONTENTS

STATISTICS IV-VIII

World	iv-v
USA	vi
UK	vii
Countries A-Z	viii

GENERAL MAPS 1-46

Key & Introduction	1
World Political	2-3
Europe	4
Benelux	5
British Isles	6-7
Germany	8-9
France	10
Spain & Portugal	11
Italy	12
Central Europe	13
The Balkans	14
Greece & Turkey	15
Scandanavia	16
European Russia	17
Middle East	18
Africa	19
Northwest Africa	20
Northeast Africa	21
West Africa	22
Central Africa	23
Southern Africa	24
Asia	25
Northwest Asia	26
Northeast Asia	27
South Asia	28
East Asia	29
Japan & Korea	30
South-East Asia	31
Malaysia & Indonesia	32
Oceania	33
Australia	34
New Zealand & New Guinea	35
North America	36
Central America	37
Canada	38-39
USA	40-41
South America	42
Northern South America	43
Central South America	44
Southern South America	45
Polar Regions	46

SPECIALIST MAPS 47-127

Key & Introduction	47

World 48-64

Climate	48
Time	49
Health	50
National Income	51
Tourism	51
Sport	52
Driving	53
Airports	54-56
IATA Areas	54-56
International Flight Times	57
Cruising	58-59
Natural Heritage Sites	60-61
Cultural Heritage Sites	62-64

Europe 65-97

Climate	65
Railways	66-67
Ferries	66-67
Blue Flag Beaches	68-69
Skiing	70
Historical	71
National Parks	72
Leisure Parks	73
UK	74
UK Beaches	75
UK National Parks	75
UK Motorways	76
UK Airports	76-77
UK Ferries	78
Ireland	79
Benelux	80
Germany	81-82
German Spas	83
France	84-85
Spain	86-87
Portugal	88
Switzerland	89
Austria	89
Italy	90-91
Greece	92-93
Turkey	92-93
Malta	93
Cyprus	93
Scandanavia	94-95
Central Europe	96-97
Former Soviet Union	96-97

Africa 99-103

Climate	99
Languages	100
South Africa	100
Morocco	101
Egypt	101
Tunisia	101
Kenya	101
Tanzania	102
Zimbabwe	102
Parks & Game Reserves	102-103

Asia 98 & 104-110

The Holy Land	98
Ancient Trade Routes	98
Climate	104
India	105-106
Sri Lanka	106
Maldives	106
Seychelles	106
China, Hong Kong & Macau	107
Malaysia	108
Singapore	108
Vietnam	108
Thailand	109
Indonesia	110

Australasia 111-112

Australia	111-112
New Zealand	112

The Americas 113-127

Climate	113
Railways	114
Airports	114-115
Skiing	116
USA	117-119
US National Parks	120-121
US Theme Parks	120-121
Canada	122-123
Mexico	123
Caribbean Languages	124
Bahamas	124
Jamaica	124
Cuba	124
Puerto Rico	125
Antigua	125
St Kitts & Nevis	125
Barbados	125
St Lucia	125
Trinidad & Tobago	125

South America Climate   126
South America   127

RELIEF MAPS   128-136

World   128
Europe   129
Africa   130
Asia   131
North America   132
South America   133
Australia & New Zealand   134
Polar Regions   135
The Earth from Space   136
Pacific & Atlantic Oceans   136

TRANSPORT MAPS   137-168

British Isles   137
France   138
Germany   139
Scandanavia   140
Benelux   140
Iberia   140
Italy   141

The Balkans   141
Austria   142
Switzerland   142
Central & Eastern Europe   143
The Middle East   144
Arabia   145
Northeast Africa   145
Northwest Africa   146
West Africa   147
Central & East Africa   148
Southern Africa   149
South Africa   150
Northern Asia   151
China   152
Pakistan   153
Northern India   154
Southern India   155
The Asian Islands   156
Bangladesh   156
Southeast Asia   157
Japan   158
Central Japan   159
Australia   160

Southeast Australia   161
New Zealand   161
Western Canada   162
Eastern Canada   163
Western USA   164
Eastern USA   165
Mexico & Central America   166
Northern South America   167
Southern South America   168

APPENDICES   169-172

1 Geographical Definitions 169
2 US States   170
3 Canadian Prov's/Terr's   170
4 Australian Prov's/Terr's   170
5 French Départements   170
6 Major Urban Areas   171
7 Longest Rivers   171
8 Highest & Lowest   171
9 Conversion Chart   171
10 Glossary   171-172

INDEX   173-216

THEMATIC CONTENTS

The specialised nature of the World Atlas of Travel means that the a country or theme may be featured in more than one place. There are, for instance, four sets of maps – General (global); Specialist (selected countries and themes); Relief (global); and Transport (selected countries) – as well as a statistical section and several appendices. To assist in locating all references to countries or themes which may be of interest, we've chosen some of the more important and listed the pages where a significant reference to each may be found. Remember also that there is a comprehensive index at the back of the book: in general, this gives a reference to the entry where the location is shown at the largest scale.

Airports: iv, 54, 55, 56, 57, 76, 77, 114, 115.

Australia: v, viii, 34, 57, 61, 111, 112, 134, 160, 161, 170, 171.

Beaches: 68, 69, 73, 79, 80, 84, 85, 86, 87, 88, 90, 91, 92, 93, 94, 95, 97, 100, 101, 102, 105, 106, 107, 108, 109, 110, 111, 112, 117, 118, 119, 123, 124, 125, 127.

Canada: iv, v, viii, 38, 39, 54, 58, 60, 62, 113, 114, 115, 122, 123, 132, 162, 163, 170, 171.

Caribbean: iv, viii, 37, 54, 57, 58, 60, 62, 124, 125, 132, 166.

Climate: 48, 65, 99, 104, 113.

Cruises & Ferries: 58, 59, 66, 67, 78, 137-168.

Driving: 53, 76, 144-168.

France: v, viii, 10, 52, 56, 57, 61, 64, 65, 66, 68, 70, 71, 72, 73, 84, 85, 129, 138, 170, 171.

Germany: iv, v, viii, 8, 9, 52, 56, 57, 61, 64, 65, 66, 68, 70, 71, 72, 73, 81, 82, 83, 129, 139, 171.

Greece: viii, 15, 52, 56, 57, 59, 61, 64, 65, 67, 69, 71, 72, 92, 93, 129, 141.

History & Heritage: 19, 60, 61, 62, 63, 64, 71, 75, 82, 84, 86, 98.

India: viii, 28, 52, 55, 57, 59, 61, 63, 98, 105, 106, 131, 154, 155, 171.

Italy: v, viii, 12, 52, 56, 57, 59, 61, 64, 65, 66, 68, 70, 71, 72, 73, 90, 91, 129, 141, 171.

Japan: iv, v, viii, 30, 51, 52, 53, 55, 57, 59, 61, 63, 131, 158, 159, 171.

Languages: 80, 89, 100, 124, 139, 140.

National Parks: 72, 75, 101, 102, 103, 120, 121, 122, 123.

Railways: 66, 67, 77, 97, 105, 109, 112, 114, 137-168.

Scandanavia: iv, viii, 16, 51, 52, 53, 56, 57, 59, 61, 63, 64, 65, 94, 95, 129, 140.

Skiing: 52, 70, 116.

Spain: v, viii, 11, 52, 56, 57, 59, 61, 64, 65, 66, 68, 71, 72, 73, 86, 87, 129, 140.

Statistics: iv, v, vi, vii, viii, 51, 52, 118, 120, 138, 171.

Theme Parks: vii, 73, 120, 121.

UK: iv, vii, viii, 6, 7, 52, 56, 57, 59, 61, 64, 65, 66, 71, 72, 73, 74, 75, 76, 77, 78, 129, 137, 139, 171.

USA: iv, v, vi, viii, 40, 41, 54, 57, 58, 60, 62, 113, 114, 115, 116, 117, 118, 119, 120, 121, 132, 138, 139, 164, 165, 170, 171.

WORLDWIDE

Figures 1a-e
TOURISM PAYMENTS – RECEIPTS AND EXPENDITURE

Figure 1a **US tourism payments**
Source: World Tourism Organization 1995 statistics

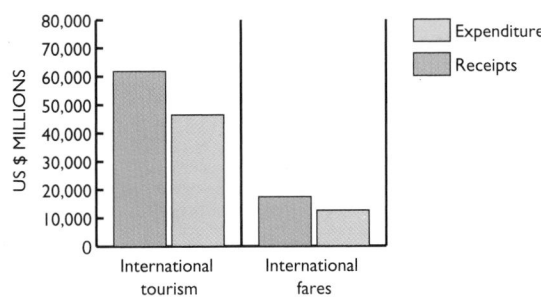

Figure 1b **Canada tourism payments**
Source: World Tourism Organization 1996 statistics

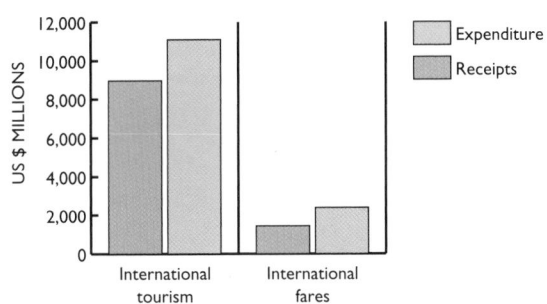

Figure 1c **UK tourism payments**
Source: World Tourism Organization 1995 statistics

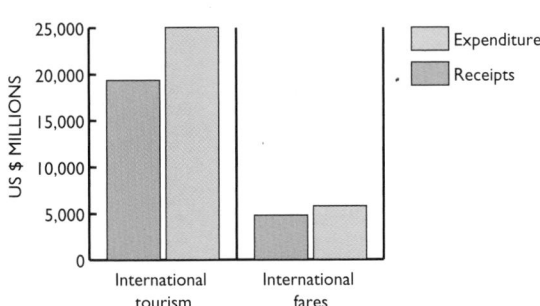

Figure 1d **Germany tourism payments**
Source: World Tourism Organization 1996 statistics

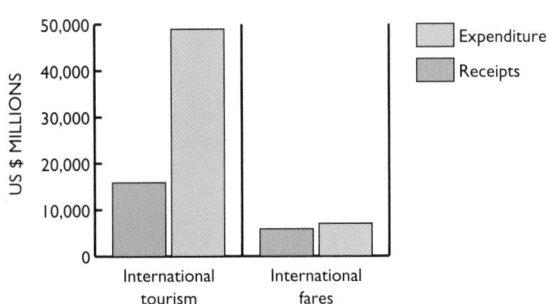

Figure 1e **Japan tourism payments**
Source: World Tourism Organization 1996 statistics

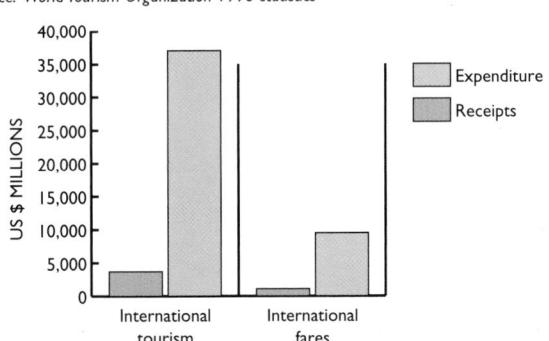

Figure 2 **TOURIST ARRIVALS BY REGION (1996)**
Source: World Tourism Organization

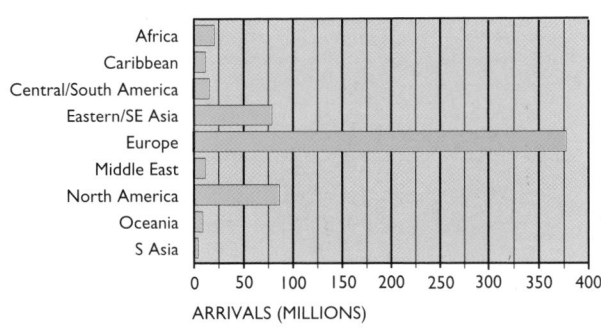

Figure 3 **TOURIST ARRIVALS BY REGION % CHANGE 96/95**
Source: World Tourism Organization

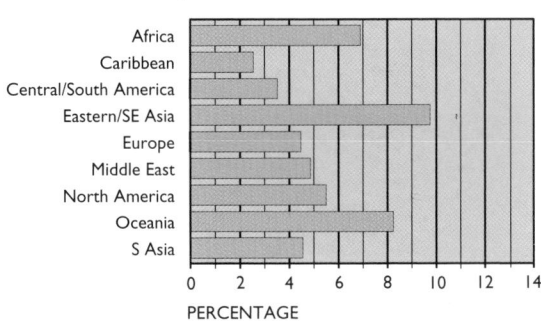

Figure 4
THE TOP 50 AIRPORTS
Source: Annual Airport Traffic Statistics, Airports Council International (ACI), 1996

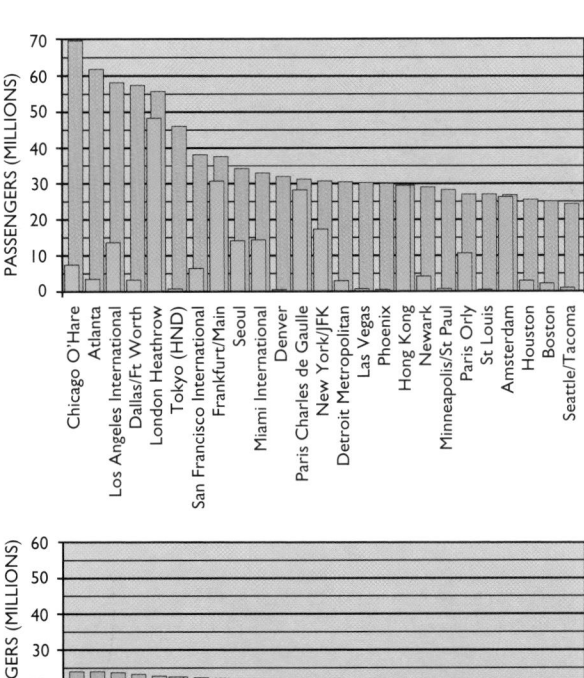

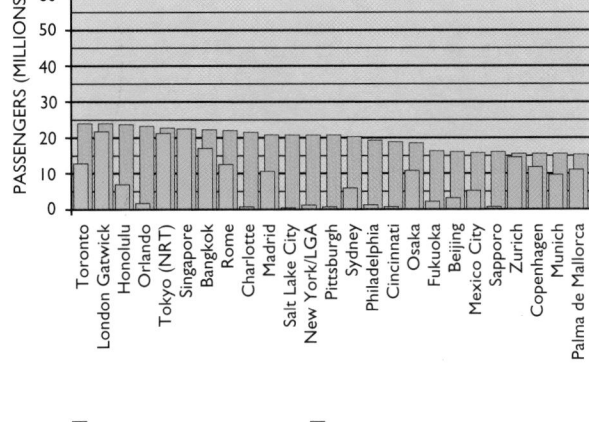

WORLDWIDE

Figures 6a-j
WORLDWIDE DESTINATIONS – WHO GOES WHERE

Figure 6a **United States – destinations by region, 1996**
Source: World Tourism Organization

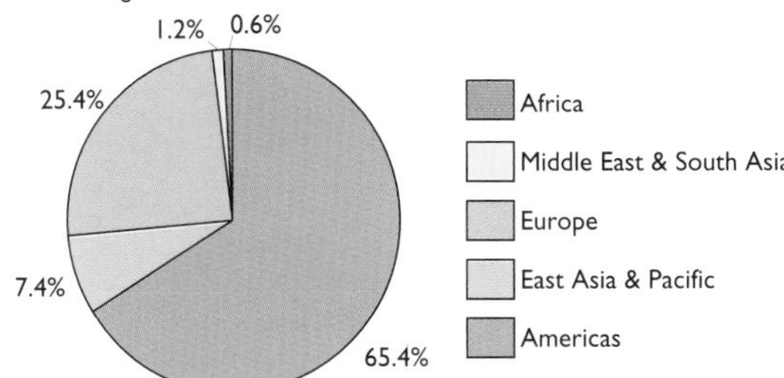

Figure 6b **Canada – destinations by region, 1996**
Source: World Tourism Organization

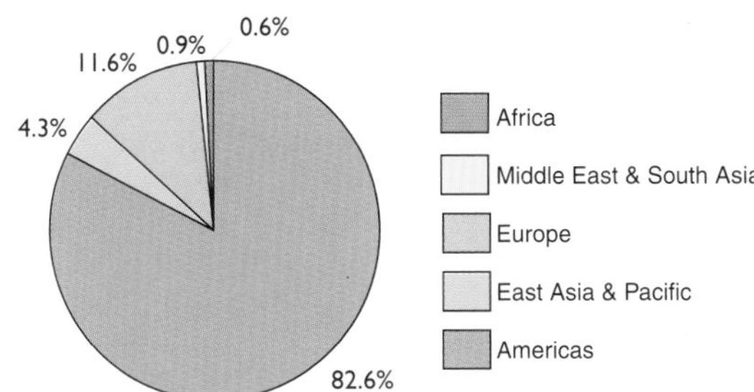

Figure 6c **United Kingdom – destinations by region, 1996**
Source: World Tourism Organization

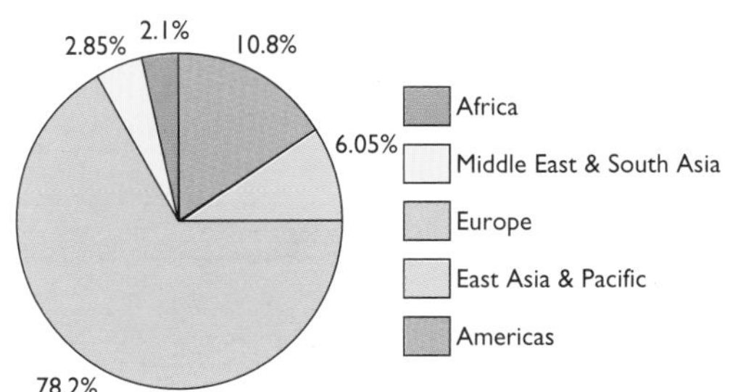

Figure 6d **Germany – destinations by region, 1996**
Source: World Tourism Organization

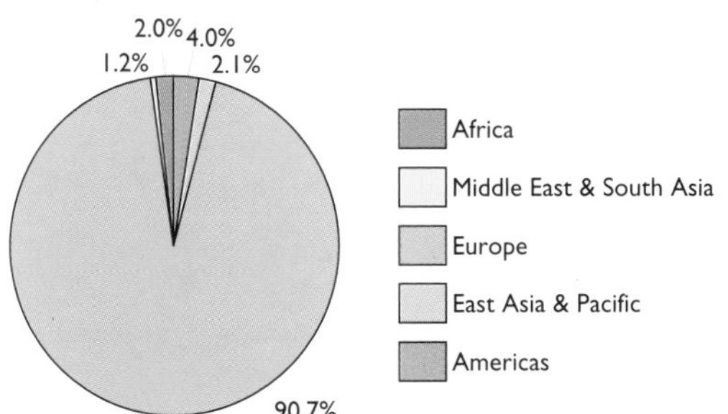

Figure 6e **Japan – destinations by region, 1996**
Source: World Tourism Organization

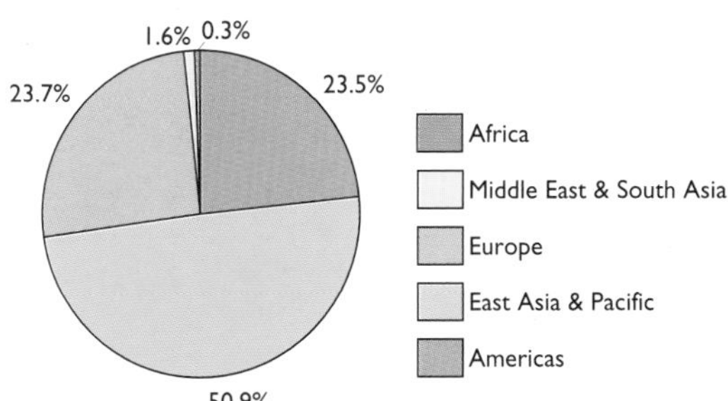

Figure 6f **Australia – destinations by region, 1995**
Source: World Tourism Organization

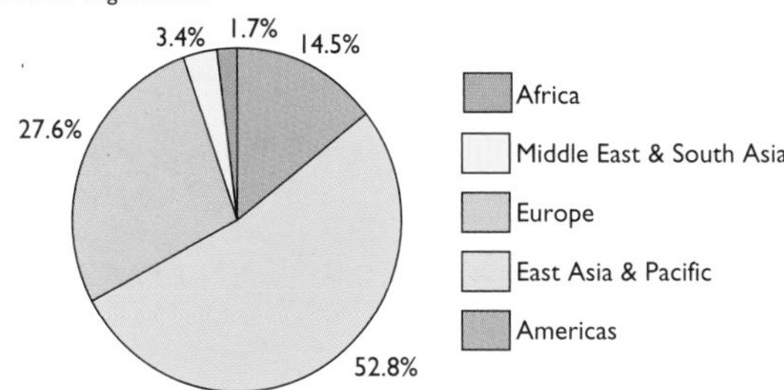

Figure 6g **Netherlands – destinations by region, 1995**
Source: World Tourism Organization

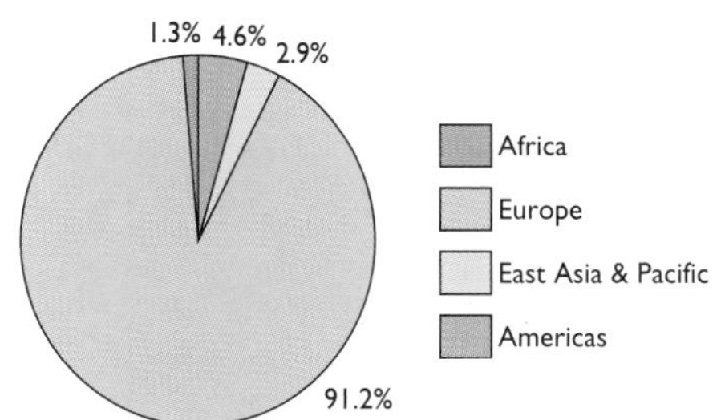

Figure 6h **France – destinations by region, 1996**
Source: World Tourism Organization

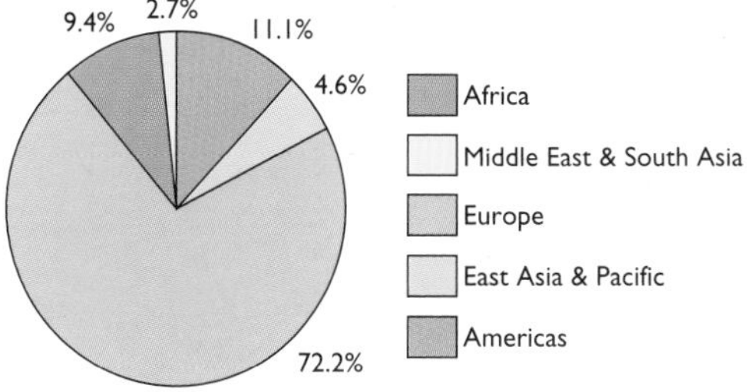

Figure 6i **Spain – destinations by region, 1995**
Source: World Tourism Organization

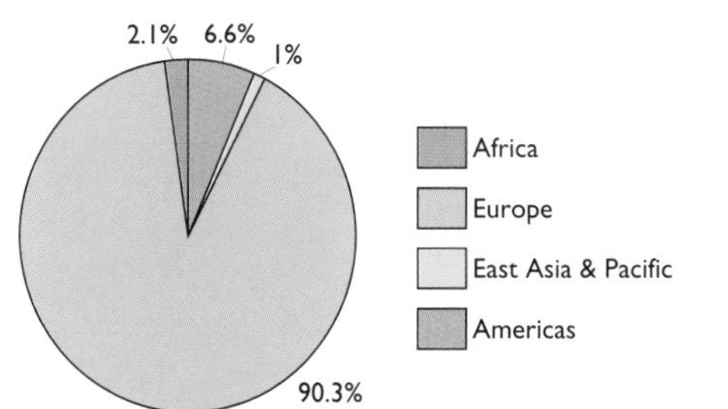

Figure 6j **Sweden – destinations by region, 1995**
Source: World Tourism Organization

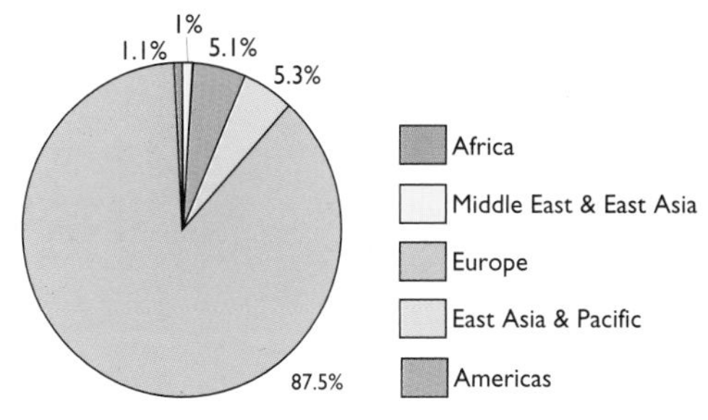

USA

Figure 7
DOMESTIC TRAVEL – EXPENDITURE BY STATE, 1994
Source: Travel Industry Association of America

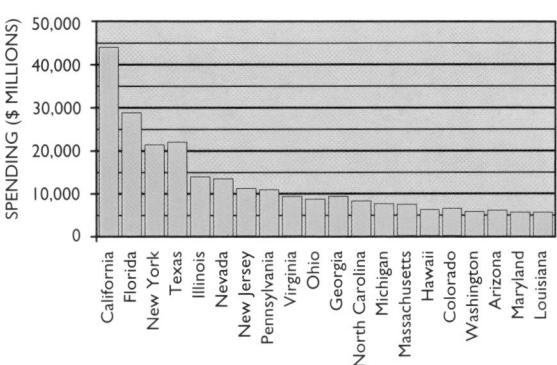

Figure 8
DOMESTIC TRAVEL – EMPLOYMENT BY STATE, 1994
Source: Travel Industry Association of America

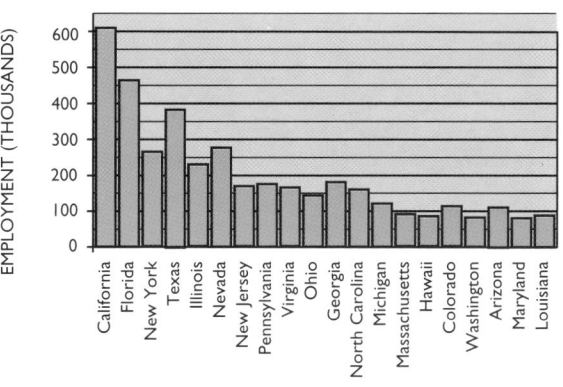

Figure 9
INTERNATIONAL VISITORS TO THE USA, 1996
Source: International Trade Administration Tourism Industries

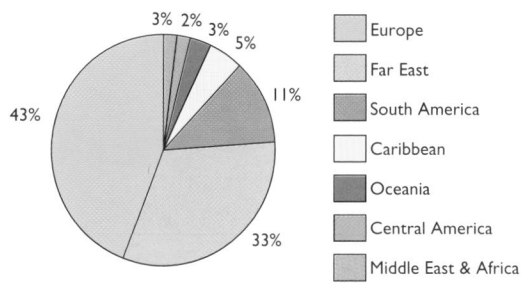

Figure 10
OVERSEAS VISITORS TO THE USA, 1996
Source: International Trade Administration Tourism Industries

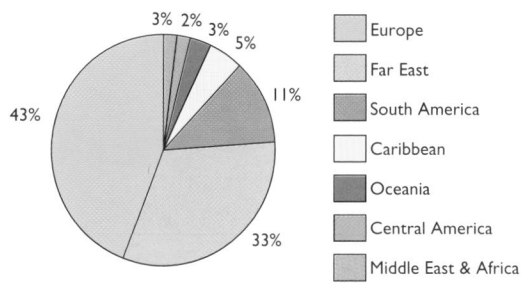

Figure 11
TOP STATES VISITED BY OVERSEAS TRAVELLERS TO THE U.S. 1995
Source: Survey of International Air Travelers to the United States (In-Flight Survey)

Figure 12
ARRIVALS BY MODES OF TRANSPORT, 1995
Source: World Tourism Organization

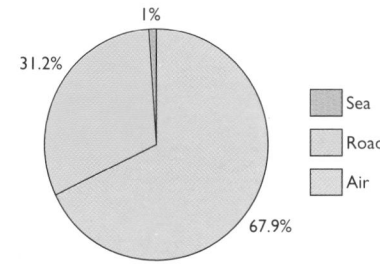

Figure 13
TOP CITIES VISITED BY OVERSEAS TRAVELLERS TO THE U.S. 1995
Source: Survey of International Air Travelers to the United States (In-Flight Survey)

Figure 14
US TOURISM RECEIPTS
Source: World Tourism Organization

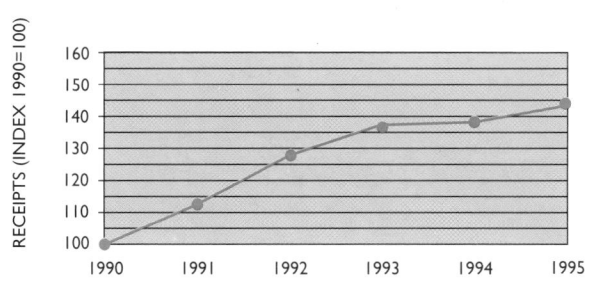

UNITED KINGDOM

Figure 14
OVERSEAS VISITS TO THE UK BY AREA OF RESIDENCE, 1996
Source: British Tourist Authority 1997

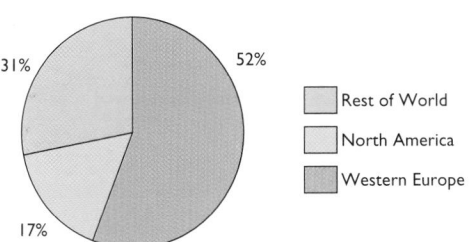

Figure 15
OVERSEAS VISITS TO THE UK BY PURPOSE OF VISIT, 1995
Source: British Tourist Authority 1996

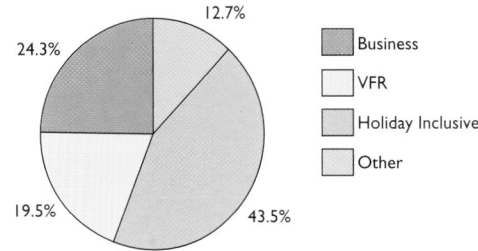

Figure 16
TOP FIVE COUNTRIES OF ORIGIN OF VISITORS TO UK
Source: British Tourist Authority 1997

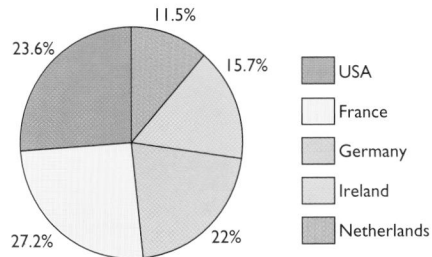

Figure 17
ENGLAND – TYPES OF LOCATION
Source: British Tourist Authority/English Tourist Board 1996

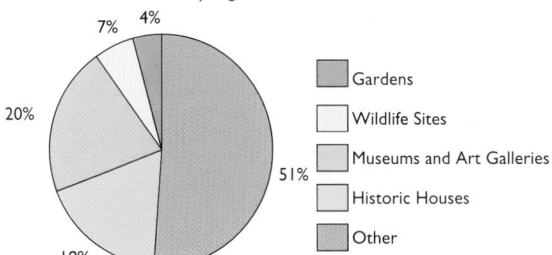

Figure 18
VISITS TO TOP TWENTY ATTRACTIONS CHARGING ADMISSIONS
Source: Statistics supplied to British Tourist Authority/English Tourist Board 1997

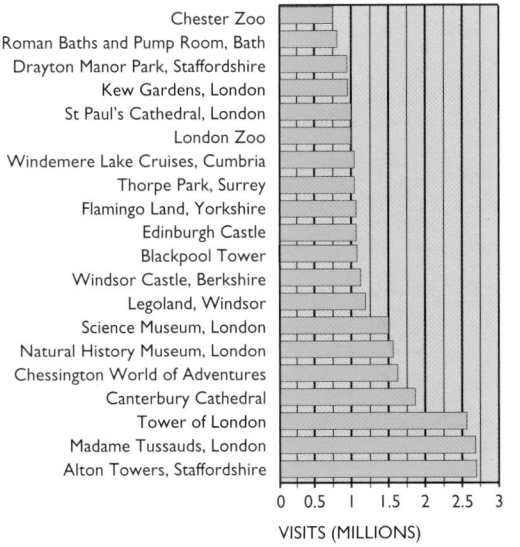

Figure 19
DISTRIBUTION OF OVERSEAS TOURISM, 1996
Source: Statistics supplied to British Tourist Authority/English Tourist Board 1997

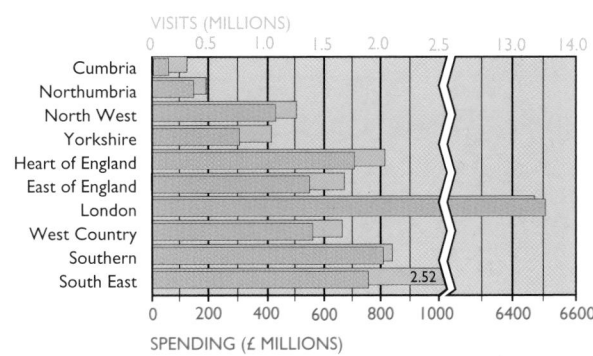

Figure 20
OVERSEAS SPENDING IN THE UK, 1985-1995
Source: Statistics supplied to British Tourist Authority/English Tourist Board 1996

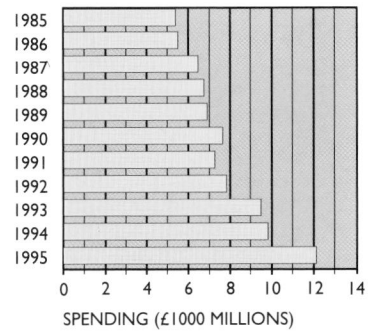

Figure 21
TOURISM SPENDING BREAKDOWN, 1996
Source: Statistics supplied to British Tourist Authority/English Tourist Board 1997

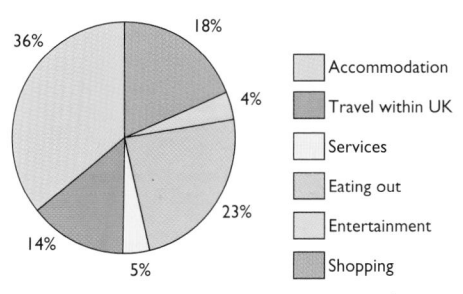

COUNTRIES A-Z

The list below gives information on all the world's independent states. Many countries have dependencies, overseas possessions, colonies, offshore island groups etc and with the exception of a few common-sense exceptions (such as Réunion and Gibraltar), these have not been listed. The matter of defining what is and what is not a state is by no means clear-cut, but no political or other subjective stance has been adopted. For more information on states and territories worldwide, please consult the relevant pages of your *World Travel Guide.*
Some **Country** names have been shortened for reasons of space. **Area** is given in 1,000s of square kilometres, **Population** in 1,000s and **Population Density** as the latter divided by the former. Population figures are based on the most up-to-date information available (usually census returns or official estimates), some being as recent as 1996. In general, refugees are not included. Please see the notes at the foot of the chart regarding **Capitals**, as some countries have more than one, or are in the process of changing over from one to another.

Country	Area	Pop.	Pop. Den.	Capital
Afghanistan	652	17,080	28.5	Kabul
Albania	28.7	3,363	117	Tirana
Algeria	2,382	26,581	11.2	Algiers
American Samoa	0.19	53	272.1	Pago Pago
Andorra	0.47	65	130.6	Andorra la Vella
Angola	1,247	10,609	8.5	Luanda
Anguilla	0.1	10.3	107.3	The Valley
Antigua & Barbuda	0.4	64.1	145.3	St John's
Argentina	2,767	34,180	12.4	Buenos Aires
Armenia	29.8	3,754	126	Yerevan
Aruba	0.19	80	416.2	Oranjestad
Australia	7,682	17,657	2.3	Canberra
Austria	84	8,031	95	Vienna
Azerbaijan	87	7,499	86.6	Baku
Bahamas	14	269	19.3	Nassau
Bahrain	0.7	568	817	Manama
Bangladesh	148	117,787	798	Dhaka
Barbados	0.4	264	614.0	Bridgetown
Belarus	208	10,297	49.6	Minsk
Belgium	31	10,101	330.9	Brussels
Belize	23	209	9.1	Belmopan
Benin	113	5,215	46.3	Porto Novo
Bermuda	0.05	59.5	1124	Hamilton
Bhutan	47	600	12.9	Thimphu
Bolivia	1,085	7,237	6.6	La Paz [1]
				Sucre [1]
Bonaire	0.3	10.2	35.4	Kralendijk
Bosnia-Herzegovina	51	3,527	69	Sarajevo
Botswana	582	1,450	2.5	Gaborone
Brazil	8,512	155,822	18.3	Brasília
British Virgin Is.	0.2	19	124.2	Road Town
Brunei	6	284.5	49.3	Bandar Seri Begawan
Bulgaria	111	8,427	75.9	Sofia
Burkina Faso	274	9,889	36.1	Ouagadougou
Burundi	28	6,134	220.4	Bujumbura
Cambodia	181	9,568	52.9	Phnom Penh
Cameroon	475	11,540	24.3	Yaoundé
Canada	9,958	29,248	2.9	Ottawa
Cape Verde	4	341	84.7	Praia
Cayman Is.	0.2	32	123.5	George Town
Central African Rep.	623	2,463	4	Bangui
Chad	1,284	6,214	4.9	Ndjaména
Chile	757	14,210	18.8	Santiago
China, People's Rep. [2]	9,572	1,204,690	125.8	Beijing (Peking)
Colombia	1,142	34,520	30.2	Bogotá
Comoro Is.	2	484	259.9	Moroni
Congo	342	1,843	5.4	Brazzaville
Congo, Dem. Rep [3]	2,345	36,672	15.6	Kinshasa
Cook Is.	0.2	19	80	Avarua
Costa Rica	51	3,500	68.5	San José
Côte d'Ivoire	322	13,695	42.5	Yamoussoukro [4]
				Abidjan [4]
Croatia	57	4,779	84.4	Zagreb
Cuba	111	10,901	98.3	Havana
Curaçao	0.4	144	324.5	Willemstad
Cyprus	9	730	78.9	Nicosia
Czech Rep.	79	10,333	131.0	Prague
Denmark	43	5,216	121	Copenhagen
Djibouti	23	520	22.4	Djibouti
Dominica	0.7	71	94.9	Roseau
Dominican Rep.	48	7,769	160.4	Santo Domingo
Ecuador	272	11,460	42.1	Quito
Egypt	998	57,851	58	Cairo
El Salvador	21	5,048	239.9	San Salvador
Equatorial Guinea	28	356	12.7	Malabo
Eritrea	121	3,436	28.4	Asmara
Estonia	45	1,476	33	Tallinn
Ethiopia	1,133	56,677	50.0	Addis Ababa
Falkland Is.	12	2	0.2	Stanley
Fiji	18	797	42.6	Suva
Finland	338	5,098	15.1	Helsinki
France	544	57,903	106.4	Paris
French Guiana	91	114	1.3	Cayenne
French Polynesia	4	212	50.9	Papeete
Gabon	268	1,011	3.8	Libreville
Gambia, The	11	1,038	91.9	Banjul
Georgia	70	5,471	78.5	Tbilisi
Germany	357	81,338	227.9	Berlin [5]
				Bonn [5]
Ghana	239	17,000	71.3	Accra
Gibraltar	0.007	28	4319.2	Gibraltar
Greece	132	10,368	78.5	Athens
Greenland	2,176	55	0.03	Nuuk
Grenada	0.3	95	276.9	St George's
Guadeloupe	2	387	217.4	Basse-Terre [6]
				Pointe-à-Pitre [6]
Guam	0.5	146	265.9	Agaña
Guatemala	109	10,322	97.5	Guatemala City
Guinea Rep.	246	5,600	22.8	Conakry
Guinea-Bissau	36	1050	26.1	Bissau
Guyana	215	738	3.4	Georgetown
Haiti	28	7,041	253.7	Port-au-Prince
Honduras	112	5,770	51.5	Tegucigalpa
Hungary	93	10,277	110.5	Budapest
Iceland	103	268	2.6	Reykjavík
India	3,287	920,000	279.9	New Delhi
Indonesia	1,904	194,440	102	Jakarta
Iran	1,648	59,778	36.3	Tehran
Iraq	438	17,903	40.8	Baghdad
Ireland	70	3,582	52.0	Dublin
Israel	22	5,462	249.4	Jerusalem
Italy	301	57,269	190.1	Rome
Jamaica	11	2,374	216	Kingston
Japan	378	125,200	331.4	Tokyo
Jordan	98	5,198	53.2	Amman
Kazakhstan	2,717	16,763	6.2	Akmola [7]
Kenya	580	29,292	50.5	Nairobi
Kiribati	1	78	96	Bairiki
Korea, DPR (N)	121	23,483	194.8	Pyongyang
Korea, Rep. (S)	99	44,850	451.3	Seoul
Kuwait	18	1,576	88.4	Kuwait City
Kyrgyzstan	199	4,476	22.6	Bishkek
Laos	237	4,581	19.3	Vientiane
Latvia	65	2,530	39.2	Riga
Lebanon	10	2,745	262.6	Beirut
Lesotho	30	1,700	56	Maseru
Liberia	98	2,700	27.6	Monrovia
Libya	1,776	4,899	2.8	Tripoli
Liechtenstein	0.2	31	191	Vaduz
Lithuania	65	3,717	56.9	Vilnius
Luxembourg	3	407	157.2	Luxembourg-Ville
Macau	0.02	400	20,250	Macau
Macedonia (FYR)	26	1,937	75.3	Skopje
Madagascar	587	12,092	20.6	Antananarivo
Malawi	118	10,033	84.7	Lilongwe
Malaysia	330	20,103	61	Kuala Lumpur
Maldives	0.3	245	821	Malé
Mali	1,240	8,156	6.6	Bamako
Malta	0.3	369	1169	Valletta
Marshall Is.	0.2	52	287	Majuro
Martinique	1	371	328.7	Fort-de-France
Mauritania	1,031	2,211	2.1	Nouakchott
Mauritius	2	1,113	565.1	Port Louis
Mayotte	0.4	94	252.4	Dzaoudzi
Mexico	1,958	93,008	47.5	Mexico City
Micronesia, Fed. States	0.7	105	149.6	Pohnpei
Moldova	34	4,350	129.1	Chisinău
Monaco	0.002	30	15,370	Monaco-Ville
Mongolia	1,567	2,317	1.5	Ulan Bator
Montserrat	0.1	11	103.7	Plymouth [8]
Morocco	711 [9]	26,024 [9]	36.7 [9]	Rabat
Mozambique	799	17,423	21.8	Maputo
Myanmar	677	41,550	61.4	Yangon [10]
Namibia	824	1,500	1.8	Windhoek
Nauru	0.02	10	465.7	Yaren District
Nepal	147	19,280	131	Kathmandu
Netherlands	34	15,385	453	Amsterdam
New Caledonia	19	183	9.6	Nouméa
New Zealand	271	3,592	13.3	Wellington
Nicaragua	120	4,500	37.4	Managua
Niger	1,267	8,361	6.6	Niamey
Nigeria	924	88,515	95.8	Abuja [11]
Niue	0.3	2	8.8	Alofi
N. Mariana Is.	0.5	53	115.8	Saipan
Norway	324	4,348	13.4	Oslo
Oman	310	2,096	6.8	Muscat
Palau	0.5	17	34	Koror
Pakistan	796	126,610	159	Islamabad
Panama	76	2,631	34.8	Panama City
Papua New Guinea	463	3,997	8.6	Port Moresby
Paraguay	407	4,642	11.4	Asunción
Peru	1,285	23,088	18	Lima
Philippines	300	67,038	223.5	Manila
Poland	313	38,609	123.4	Warsaw
Portugal	92	9,902	107.3	Lisbon
Puerto Rico	9	3,720	415.2	San Juan
Qatar	11	593	51.8	Doha
Réunion	3	642	255.7	Saint-Denis
Romania	238	22,731	95.4	Bucharest
Russian Federation	17,075	148,100	8.7	Moscow
Rwanda	26	7,165	272	Kigali
Saba	0.01	1	86.9	The Bottom
St Eustatius	0.02	2	87.6	Oranjestad
St Kitts & Nevis	0.3	44	166.9	Basseterre
St Lucia	0.6	140	227	Castries
St Maarten	0.03	32	947.7	Philipsburg
St Vincent & the Gren.	0.4	111	285	Kingstown
Samoa [12]	3	164	57.9	Apia
San Marino	0.06	25	414	San Marino
São Tomé e Príncipe	1	125	124.9	São Tomé
Saudi Arabia	2,240	16,929	7.6	Riyadh
Senegal	197	8,152	41.4	Dakar
Seychelles	0.5	74	163	Victoria
Sierra Leone	72	4,509	62.9	Freetown
Singapore	0.6	2,986	4612.4	Singapore
Slovak Rep.	49	5,368	109.5	Bratislava
Slovenia	20	1,989	98.2	Ljubljana
Solomon Is.	28	366	13.3	Honiara
Somalia	638	7,114	11.2	Mogadishu
South Africa	1,219	41,245	33.8	Pretoria [13]
				Cape Town [13]
				Bloemfontein [13]
Spain	505	39,188	78.4	Madrid
Sri Lanka	66	18,000	274.3	Colombo
Sudan	2,506	24,940	10	Khartoum
Suriname	163	418	2.6	Paramaribo
Swaziland	17	879	50.6	Mbabane
Sweden	450	8,839	19.6	Stockholm
Switzerland	41	7,019	170	Bern
Syria	185	15,000	81	Damascus
Taiwan	36	21,126	586.8	Taipei
Tajikistan	143	5,751	40.2	Dushanbe
Tanzania	945	30,340	32.1	Dodoma
Thailand	513	60,000	115.2	Bangkok
Togo	57	3,928	69.2	Lomé
Tonga	0.7	98	131	Nuku'alofa
Trinidad & Tobago	5	1,250	243.7	Port of Spain
Tunisia	164	8,947	57.9	Tunis
Turkey	779	61,644	79.1	Ankara
Turkmenistan	488	4,483	9.2	Ashgabat
Turks & Caicos Is.	0.4	14	32.6	Cockburn Town
Tuvalu	0.03	9	346	Funafuti
Uganda	241	16,671	69.1	Kampala
Ukraine	604	51,728	85.7	Kyyiv (Kiev)
United Arab Emirates	78	2,378	30.6	Abu Dhabi
United Kingdom	242	58,394	241.5	London
United States	9,809	264,648	27	Washington DC
US Virgin Is.	0.3	102	293.3	Charlotte Amalie
Uruguay	176	3,167	18	Montevideo
Uzbekistan	447	22,098	49.4	Tashkent
Vanuatu	12	165	13.5	Port Vila
Vatican City	0.0004	0.8	1741	Vatican City
Venezuela	912	21,377	23.4	Caracas
Vietnam	331	70,983	214.4	Hanoi
Yemen	537	14,561	27.1	San'a
Yugoslavia	102	10,482	102.6	Belgrade
Zambia	753	8,210	10.9	Lusaka
Zimbabwe	391	11,215	28.7	Harare

Notes:

1 *La Paz (administrative), Sucre (legislative).*
2 *Including Hong Kong.*
3 *Formerly Zaïre.*
4 *Yamoussoukro (administrative), Abidjan (commercial).*
5 *Berlin is the capital and Bonn the administrative capital. Berlin will also become an administrative capital by 2002.*
6 *Basse-Terre (administrative), Pointe-à-Pitre (commercial).*
7 *The former capital was Almaty (Alma Ata).*
8 *Plymouth was destroyed during the recent volcanic activity. Discussions are currently being held concerning the site and name of the new capital.*
9 *Including the area of Western Sahara.*
10 *Formerly known as Rangoon.*
11 *The former capital was Lagos.*
12 *Formerly known as Western Samoa.*
13 *Pretoria (administrative), Cape Town (legislative), Bloemfontein (judicial). This arrangement is currently under review.*

GENERAL MAP SECTION

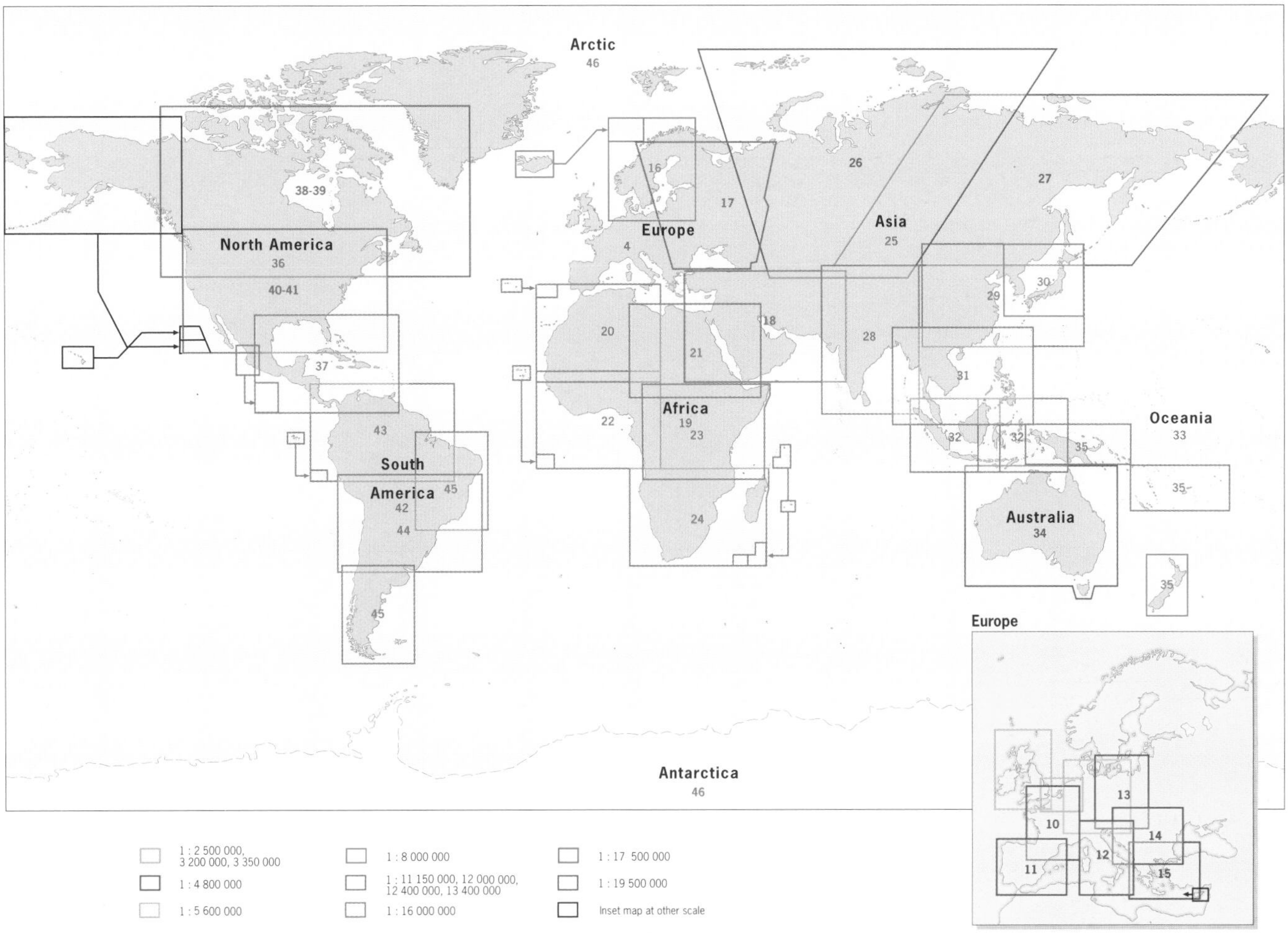

Arctic
46

North America
36

38-39

40-41

37

South
America
42
44

43

45

45

45

Europe
4

16

17

Asia
25

26

27

20

21

18

22

Africa
19
23

28

29

30

31

24

32

32

35

Oceania
33

35

Australia
34

35

Antarctica
46

Europe

1

10

13

14

11

12

15

☐ 1 : 2 500 000, 3 200 000, 3 350 000	☐ 1 : 8 000 000	☐ 1 : 17 500 000
☐ 1 : 4 800 000	☐ 1 : 11 150 000, 12 000 000, 12 400 000, 13 400 000	☐ 1 : 19 500 000
☐ 1 : 5 600 000	☐ 1 : 16 000 000	☐ Inset map at other scale

KEY TO MAP SYMBOLS

Hydrography

River
Intermittent river
Canal
Lake / Reservoir
Intermittent lake
Salt lake
Intermittent salt lake
Marsh / Swamp
Salt marsh

Other symbols

+ + + + International Dateline
National Park boundary
Pass
Mountain peak (metres)
Depression (metres)
Ruin/Ancient Site
Oasis
Desert
✈ Airport

Limit of ice shelf
Limit of pack ice
Limit of drift ice
▼ Sea Depth (metres)
) Dam
/ Waterfall

Communications

Motorway
Principal road
Other main road
Track
Railway

Population

Extent of urban area
■ City of over 1 000 000 people
● 250 000 - 1 000 000 *
● 100 000 - 250 000 *
○ ● 25 000 - 100 000 *
○ ● < 25 000 *

* Size of spot determined by approximate population of settlement

Administration

International boundary
International boundary (Disputed)
State boundary
TASHKENT National capital
Abakan State capital
Hahitševan Other administrative centre

Land Height (metres)

land above 4000
2000 - 4000
1000 - 2000
500 - 1000
200 - 500
0 - 200
land below sea level

Sea Depth (metres)

0 - 200
200 - 1000
1000 - 2000
2000 - 4000
4000 - 6000
below 6000

WORLD - POLITICAL

ICA Förlaget AB

CANADA
NORTH AMERICA
UNITED STATES
MEXICO
Greenland (Den.)
Alaska
Anchorage
Aleutian Islands
Arctic Circle
Banks Island
Victoria Island
Melville Island
Baffin Island
NUUK
ICELAND
REYKJAVIK
Faroe Is. (Den.)
IRELAND
DUBLIN
Vancouver
Winnipeg
Newfoundland
St. Pierre et Miquelon (Fr.)
OTTAWA
Montréal
Toronto
Detroit
Chicago
Cleveland
Boston
New York
Baltimore
Philadelphia
WASHINGTON D.C.
Salt Lake City
San Francisco
Los Angeles
Dallas
Atlanta
Houston
Azores (Port.)
PORTUGAL
LISBON
RABAT
Madeira (Port.)
Canary Islands (Sp.)
LA'YOUNE
Western Sahara
Bermuda (U.K.)
Gulf of Mexico
ATLANTIC OCEAN
Tropic of Cancer
Hawaiian Islands (U.S.)
Miami
HAVANA
CUBA
DOMINICAN REPUBLIC
Guadalajara
MEXICO CITY
BELIZE
BELMOPAN
JAMAICA
KINGSTON
HAITI
PORT-AU-PRINCE
SANTO DOMINGO
Puerto Rico (U.S.)
SAN JUAN
ANTIGUA AND BARBUDA
Guadeloupe (Fr.)
DOMINICA
Martinique (Fr.)
ST. LUCIA
ST. VINCENT AND THE GRENADINES
BARBADOS
GRENADA
TRINIDAD AND TOBAGO
PORT OF SPAIN
Aruba (Neth.)
Curaçao (Neth.)
GUATEMALA
GUATEMALA CITY
HONDURAS
Caribbean Sea
SAN SALVADOR
EL SALVADOR
TEGUCIGALPA
NICARAGUA
MANAGUA
COSTA RICA
SAN JOSE
PANAMA CITY
PANAMA
CARACAS
VENEZUELA
GEORGETOWN
PARAMARIBO
GUYANA
SURINAME
CAYENNE
French Guiana
BOGOTA
COLOMBIA
MAURITANIA
NOUAKCHOTT
CAPE VERDE
DAKAR
SENEGAL
BANJUL
GAMBIA
BISSAU
G.B.
GUINEA
CONAKRY
FREETOWN
MONROVIA
LIBERIA
PACIFIC OCEAN
Polynesia
Equator
KIRIBATI
Tokelau (N. Z.)
WESTERN SAMOA
APIA
TONGA
Cook Islands (N. Z.)
Marquesas Islands (Fr.)
French Polynesia
Tuamotu Islands (Fr.)
Tropic of Capricorn
Pitcairn Islands (U.K.)
Galapagos Islands (Ecuador)
QUITO
ECUADOR
SOUTH AMERICA
BRAZIL
PERU
LIMA
Recife
LA PAZ
BOLIVIA
SUCRE
BRASILIA
Belo Horizonte
Rio de Janeiro
São Paulo
PARAGUAY
ASUNCION
Porto Alegre
URUGUAY
MONTEVIDEO
BUENOS AIRES
ARGENTINA
SANTIAGO
CHILE
Easter Island (Chile)
Ascension (U.K.)
St. Helena (U.K.)
Tristan da Cunha (U.K.)
Gough I. (U.K.)
Chatham Islands
Falkland Islands (U.K.)
South Georgia (U.K.)
South Sandwich Islands (U.K.)
Cape Horn
South Orkney Islands (U.K.)
South Shetland Islands (U.K.)
Arctic Circle
Bellingshausen Sea
Antarctic Peninsula
Weddell Sea
Ross Sea
ANT
ICA Forlaget AB

WORLD - POLITICAL

ALB. - Albania
AR. - Armenia
AZ. - Azerbaijan
B. - Burundi
B.H. - Bosnia-Herzegovina
BEL. - Belgium
BH. - Bhutan
BULG. - Bulgaria
CR. - Czech Republic
CZ. - Croatia
EQ.G. - Equatorial Guinea
G.B. - Guinea-Bissau
GE. - Georgia
HGY. - Hungary
L. - Lesotho
LEB. - Lebanon
LIE. - Liechtenstein
LUX. - Luxembourg
MA. - Former Yugoslav Republic of Macedonia
NETH. - The Netherlands
R. - Rwanda
S. - Swaziland
SL. - Slovenia
SLO. - Slovak Republic
U.A.E. - United Arab Emirates
YUG. - Federal Republic of Yugoslavia

Robinson Projection

0	1000	2000	3000 km
0	1000	2000	3000 miles

EUROPE

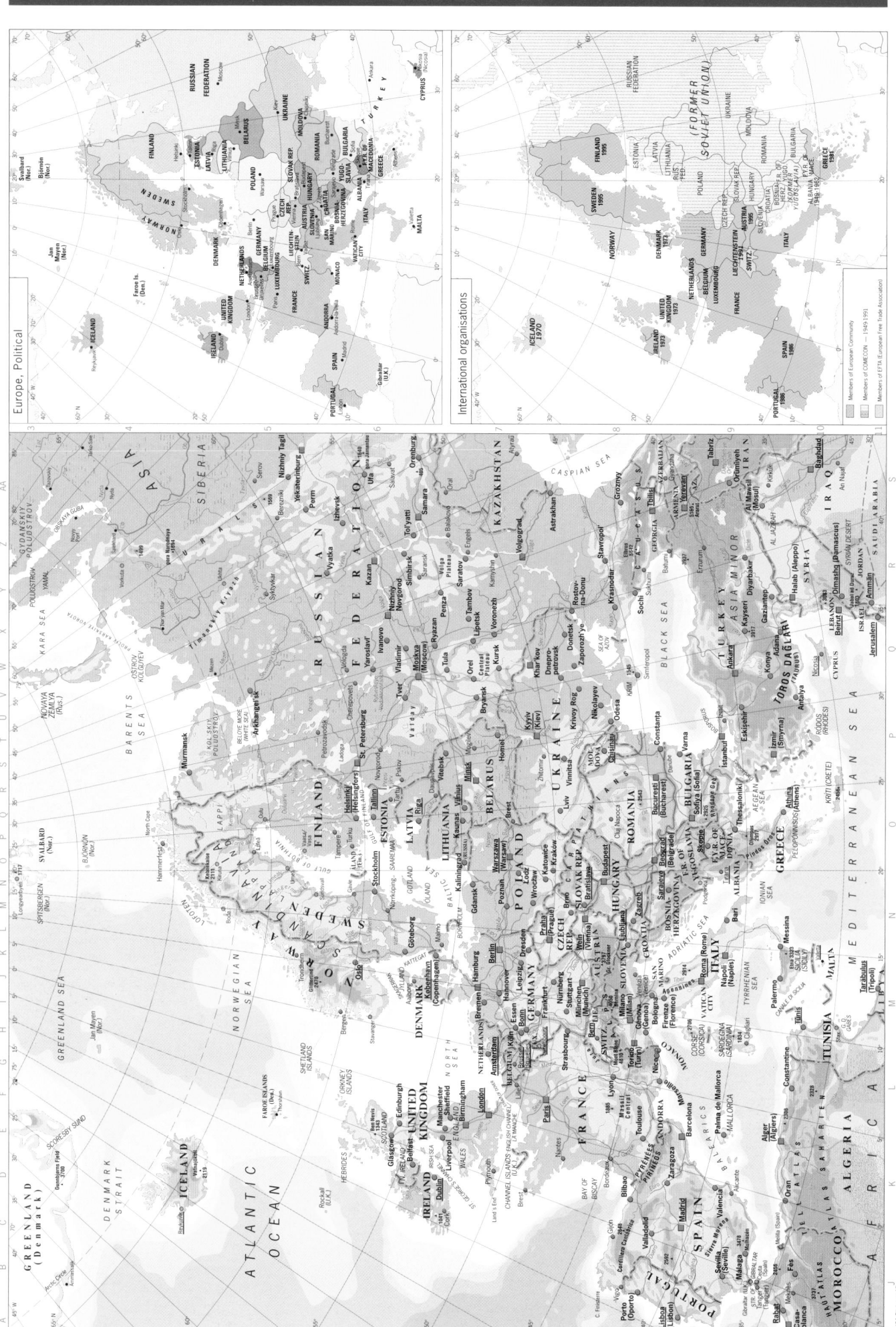

Europe, Political

International organisations

Members of European Community
Members of COMECON — 1949-1991
Members of EFTA (European Free Trade Association)

© ICA Förlaget AB

Scale 1 : 28 000 000

0   250   500   750   1000 km

BENELUX AND SURROUNDING AREA

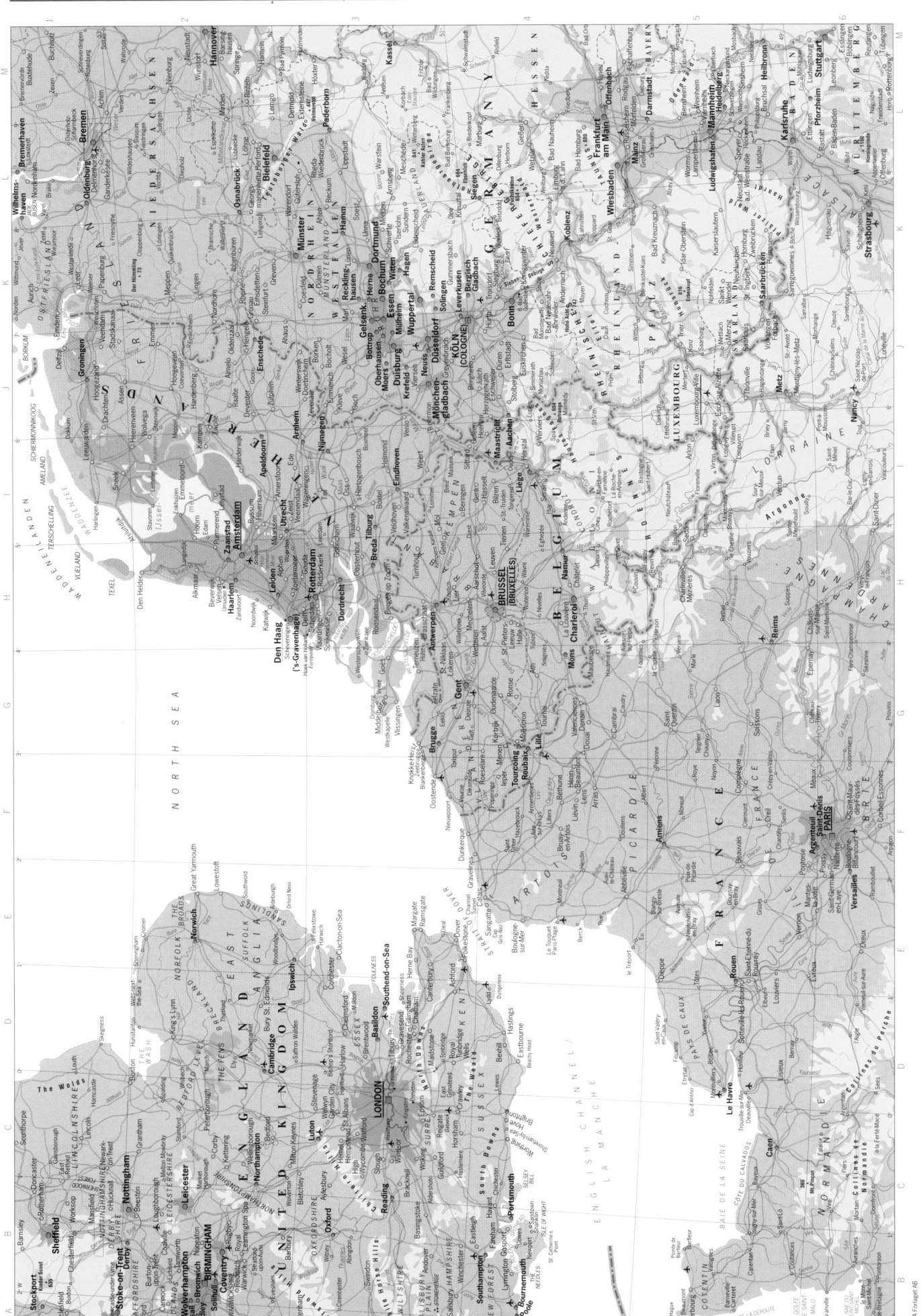

Scale 1 : 3 200 000

© ICA Förlaget AB

BRITISH ISLES

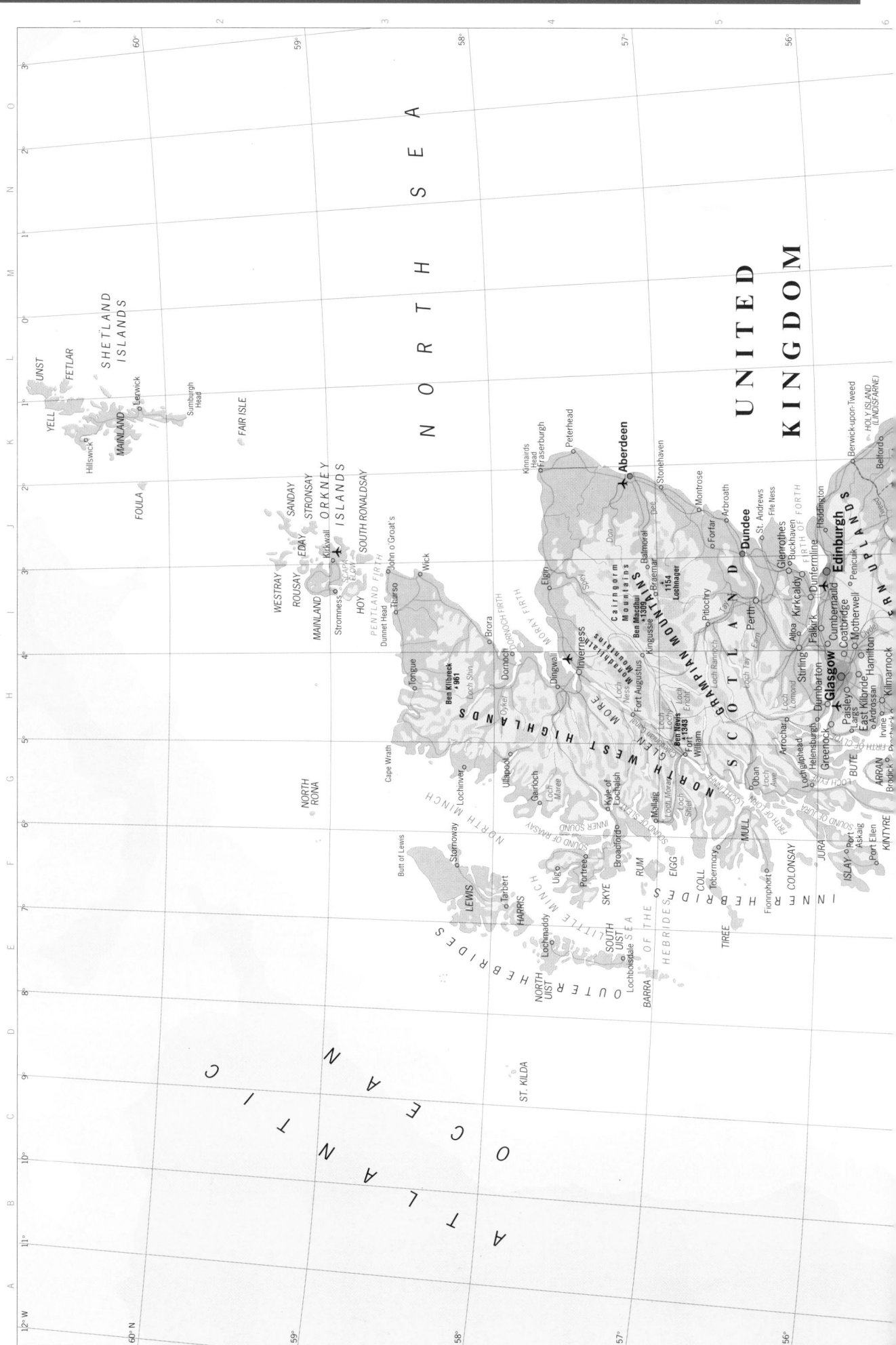
NORTH SEA
UNITED KINGDOM
ATLANTIC OCEAN
SHETLAND ISLANDS
UNST
FETLAR
YELL
MAINLAND
Lerwick
Hillswick
Sumburgh Head
FOULA
FAIR ISLE
ORKNEY ISLANDS
SANDAY
STRONSAY
EDAY
WESTRAY
ROUSAY
MAINLAND
Kirkwall
Stromness
HOY
SOUTH RONALDSAY
PENTLAND FIRTH
John o Groat's
Dunnet Head
Thurso
Wick
Cape Wrath
NORTH RONA
Butt of Lewis
Stornoway
LEWIS
Tarbert
HARRIS
NORTH UIST
Lochmaddy
SOUTH UIST
Lochboisdale
BARRA
OUTER HEBRIDES
NORTH MINCH
LITTLE MINCH
SEA OF THE HEBRIDES
ST. KILDA
SKYE
Uig
Portree
Broadford
RUM
EGG
COLL
TIREE
Tobermory
MULL
Oban
Fionnphort
COLONSAY
JURA
ISLAY
Port Askaig
Port Ellen
KINTYRE
ARRAN
BUTE
INNER HEBRIDES
Tongue
Ben Klibreck 961
Lochinver
Ullapool
Gairloch
Kyle of Lochalsh
Mallaig
Fort William
Ben Nevis 1343
Fort Augustus
Inverness
Dingwall
Dornoch
Brora
Elgin
Kingussie
Ben Macdhui 1309
Braemar
Balmoral
Lochnagar 1154
Cairngorm Mountains
Monadhliath Mountains
NORTH WEST HIGHLANDS
GLEN MORE
GRAMPIAN MOUNTAINS
SCOTLAND
MORAY FIRTH
DORNOCH FIRTH
Kinnairds Head
Fraserburgh
Peterhead
Aberdeen
Stonehaven
Montrose
Arbroath
Forfar
Dundee
St. Andrews
Fife Ness
Pitlochry
Perth
Glenrothes
Buckhaven
Kirkcaldy
Dunfermline
Alloa
Stirling
Falkirk
Edinburgh
Haddington
Penicuik
Cumbernauld
Coatbridge
Motherwell
Hamilton
Glasgow
Dumbarton
Paisley
East Kilbride
Kilmarnock
Largs
Ardrossan
Irvine
Greenock
Helensburgh
Lochgilphead
Arrochar
Brodick
FIRTH OF FORTH
FIRTH OF CLYDE
SOUTHERN UPLANDS
Berwick-upon-Tweed
HOLY ISLAND (LINDISFARNE)
Belford
60° N
59°
58°
57°
56°
12° W

BRITISH ISLES

DOGGER BANK
NORTH CHANNEL
IRISH SEA
ST. GEORGE'S CHANNEL
CELTIC SEA
ATLANTIC OCEAN
BRISTOL CHANNEL
ENGLISH CHANNEL
LA MANCHE
STRAIT OF DOVER
CHANNEL ISLANDS
ENGLAND
WALES
IRELAND
NORTHERN IRELAND
ULSTER
CONNACHT (CONNAUGHT)
LEINSTER
MUNSTER
ISLE OF MAN
ISLE OF WIGHT
ISLES OF SCILLY
ANGLESEY
ALDERNEY
GUERNSEY
JERSEY
SARK
NORMANDIE
LONDON
BIRMINGHAM
Dublin (Baile Átha Cliath)
Belfast
Cork (Corcaigh)
Limerick (Luimneach)
Galway (Gaillimh)
Cardiff
Bristol
Liverpool
Manchester
Leeds
Sheffield
Newcastle upon Tyne
Kingston upon Hull
Nottingham
Leicester
Coventry
Plymouth
Southampton
Portsmouth
Brighton
Norwich
Ipswich
Cambridge
Oxford
Reading
Swansea
Le Havre
Caen
Cherbourg
Calais
Dieppe
Boulogne-sur-Mer
Scale 1 : 3 350 000
0 50 100 150 200 km
0 50 100 miles
© ICA Förlaget AB

GERMANY

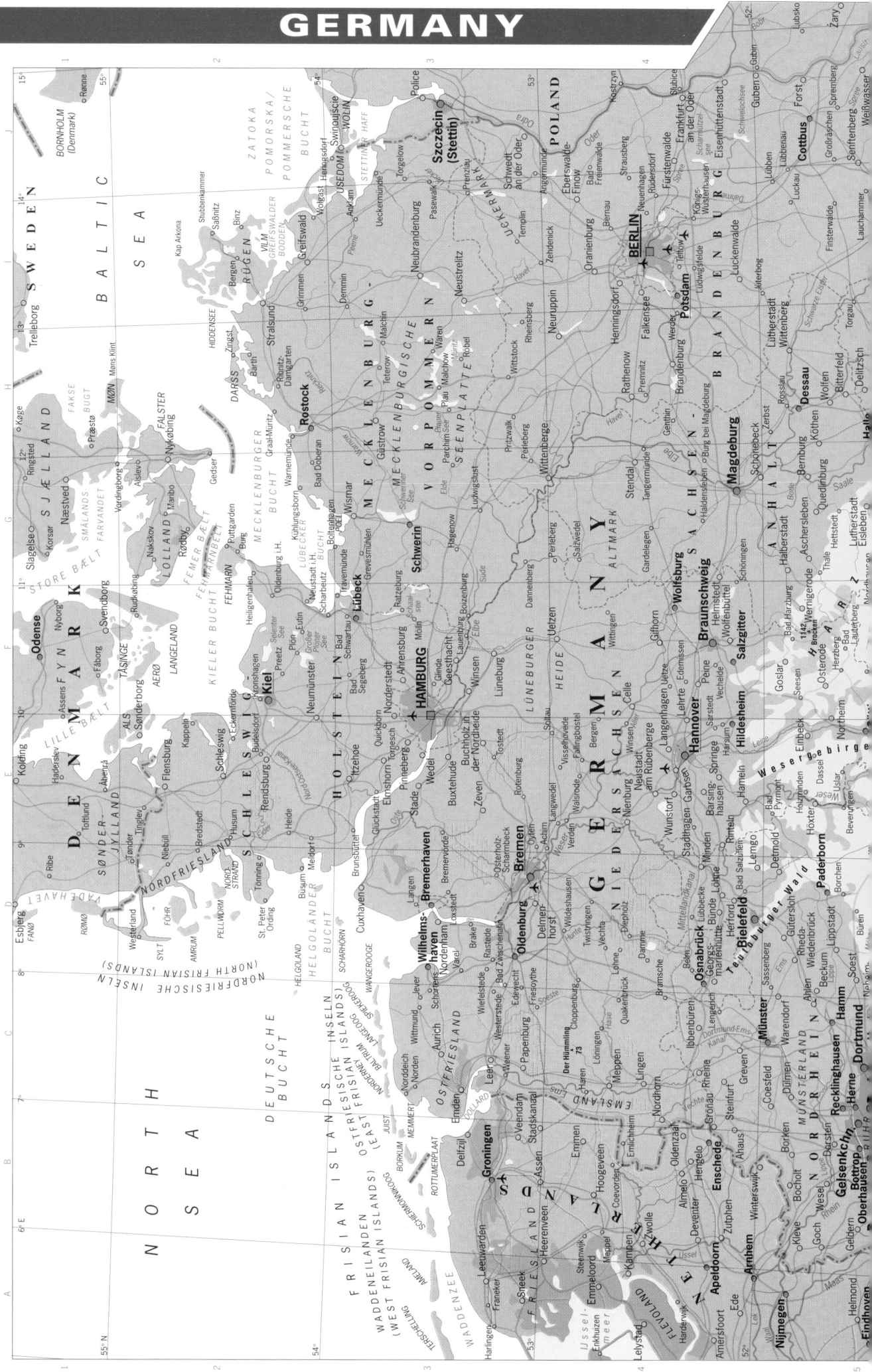

NORTH SEA
BALTIC SEA
DENMARK
SWEDEN
POLAND
NETHERLANDS
GERMANY
BORNHOLM (Denmark)
DEUTSCHE BUCHT
FRISIAN ISLANDS
NORDFRIESISCHE INSELN (NORTH FRISIAN ISLANDS)
OSTFRIESISCHE INSELN (EAST FRISIAN ISLANDS)
WADDENEILANDEN (WEST FRISIAN ISLANDS)
WADDENZEE
HELGOLÄNDER BUCHT
KIELER BUCHT
MECKLENBURGER BUCHT
LÜBECKER BUCHT
ZATOKA POMORSKA/ POMMERSCHE BUCHT
STETTINER HAFF
SJÆLLAND
FYN
SØNDERJYLLAND
LOLLAND
FALSTER
MØN
RÜGEN
FEHMARN
USEDOM
WOLIN
SCHLESWIG-HOLSTEIN
MECKLENBURG-VORPOMMERN
MECKLENBURGISCHE SEENPLATTE
NIEDERSACHSEN
SACHSEN-ANHALT
BRANDENBURG
NORDRHEIN-WESTFALEN
LÜNEBURGER HEIDE
ALTMARK
UCKERMARK
OSTFRIESLAND
EMSLAND
FRIESLAND
MÜNSTERLAND
HARZ
Wesergebirge
Teutoburger Wald
Odense
Kolding
Esbjerg
Flensburg
Kiel
Lübeck
Rostock
Stralsund
Greifswald
Schwerin
HAMBURG
Bremerhaven
Wilhelmshaven
Bremen
Oldenburg
Neubrandenburg
Szczecin (Stettin)
BERLIN
Potsdam
Frankfurt an der Oder
Hannover
Braunschweig
Wolfsburg
Magdeburg
Dessau
Cottbus
Osnabrück
Bielefeld
Münster
Paderborn
Hildesheim
Salzgitter
Groningen
Leeuwarden
Enschede
Apeldoorn
Arnhem
Nijmegen
Recklinghausen
Gelsenkirchen
Dortmund
Herne
Hamm
Bottrop
Oberhausen

GERMANY

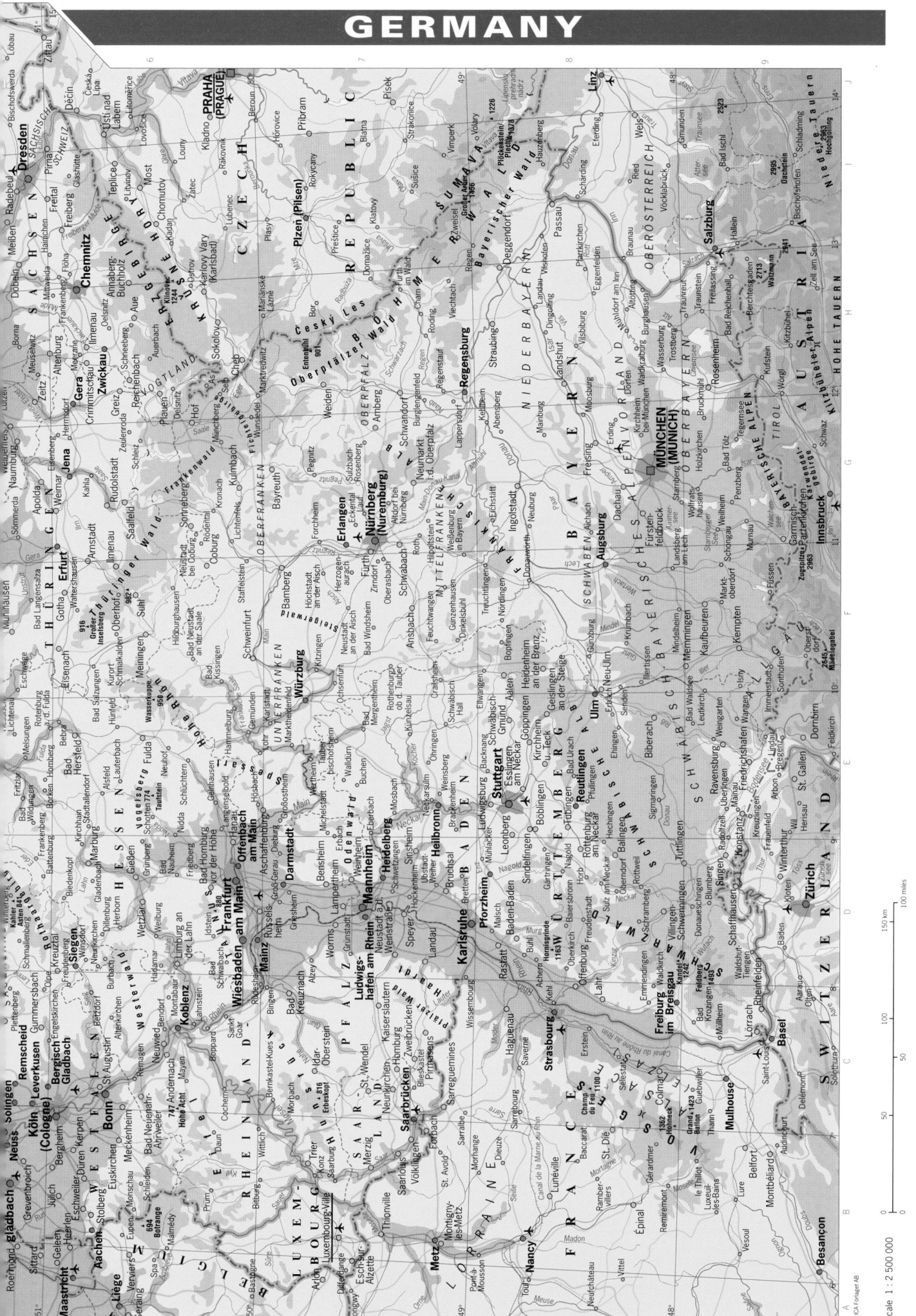
Dresden
Chemnitz
Leipzig
Erfurt
Jena
Gera
Zwickau
PRAHA (PRAGUE)
Plzeň (Pilsen)
Köln (Cologne)
Bonn
Koblenz
Wiesbaden
Frankfurt am Main
Offenbach am Main
Mainz
Darmstadt
Würzburg
Erlangen
Nürnberg (Nuremburg)
Regensburg
Mannheim
Heidelberg
Heilbronn
Karlsruhe
Pforzheim
Stuttgart
Ulm
Augsburg
MÜNCHEN (MUNICH)
Salzburg
Innsbruck
Linz
Passau
Strasbourg
Saarbrücken
Freiburg im Breisgau
Basel
Zürich
Mulhouse
Metz
Nancy
Luxembourg-Ville
Besançon
SACHSEN
THÜRINGEN
HESSEN
RHEINLAND-PFALZ
SAARLAND
BADEN-WÜRTTEMBERG
BAYERN
CZECH REPUBLIC
AUSTRIA
SWITZERLAND
FRANCE
LUXEMBOURG
BELGIUM
LORRAINE
© ICA Förlaget AB
Scale 1 : 2 500 000
0 50 100 150 km
0 50 100 miles

FRANCE

© ICA Förlaget AB

Scale 1 : 4 800 000

0   50   100   150   200 km

0   50   100 miles

SPAIN AND PORTUGAL

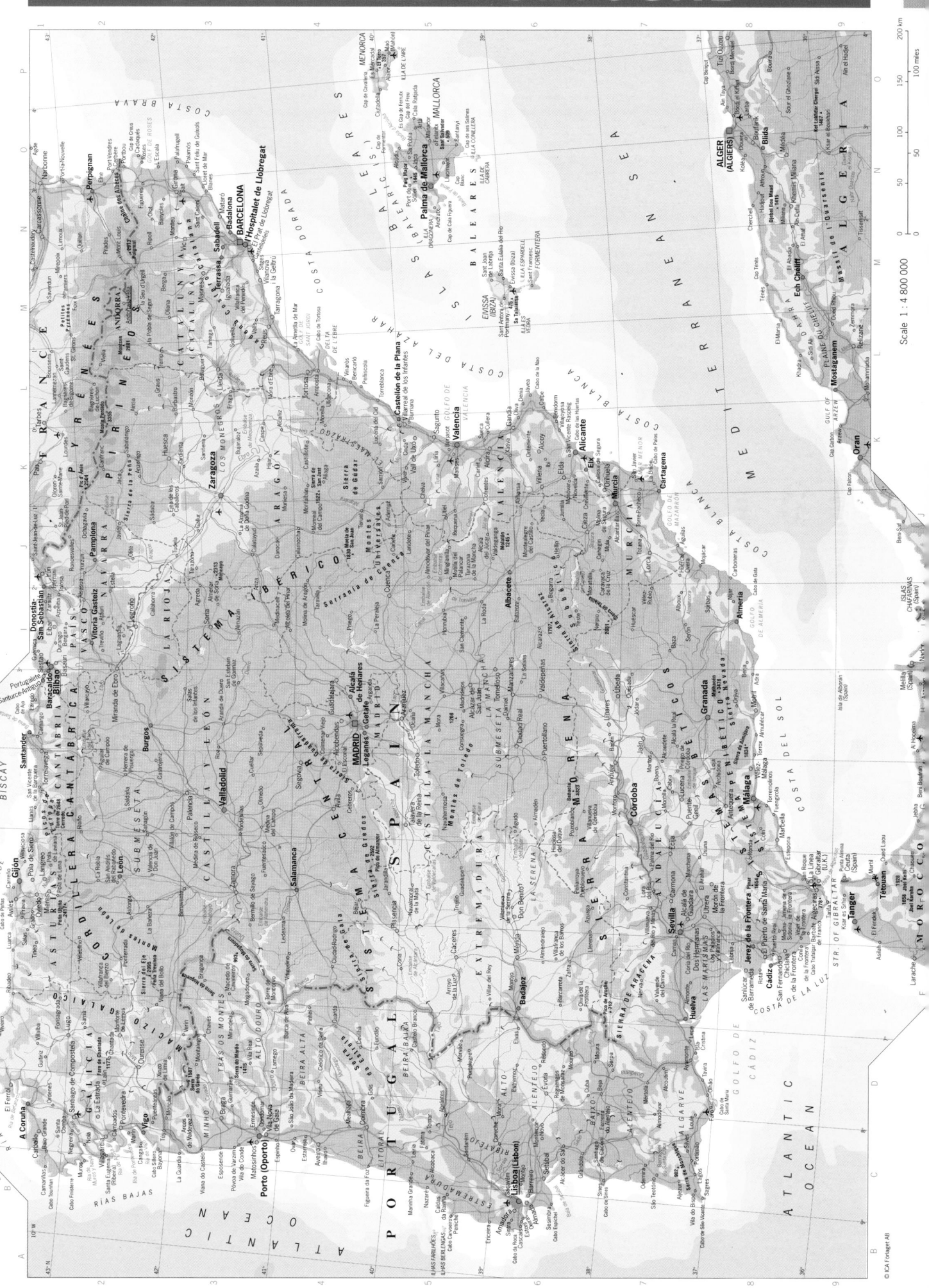

Scale 1 : 4 800 000

© ICA Förlaget AB

ITALY

© ICA Förlaget AB

Scale 1 : 4 800 000

0   50   100   150   200 km

0   50   100 miles

CENTRAL EUROPE

© ICA Förlaget AB

Scale 1 : 4 800 000

0   50   100   150   200 km

0   50   100 miles

THE BALKANS

Scale 1 : 4 800 000

© ICA Forlaget AB

UKRAINE
MOLDOVA
ROMANIA
HUNGARY
SLOVAK REP.
AUSTRIA
SLOVENIA
CROATIA
BOSNIA-HERZEGOVINA
SRBIJA (SERBIA)
CRNA GORA (MONTENEGRO)
KOSOVO
ALBANIA
F.Y.R. OF MACEDONIA
BULGARIA
GREECE
TURKEY
ITALY
BLACK SEA
ADRIATIC SEA
SEA OF MARMARA
BUCUREŞTI (BUCHAREST)
BEOGRAD (BELGRADE)
BUDAPEST
SOFIYA (SOFIA)
WIEN (VIENNA)
Zagreb
Ljubljana
Sarajevo
Skopje
Tiranë (Tirana)
Chişinău
ISTANBUL
0 50 100 150 200 km
© ICA Förlaget AB

GREECE AND TURKEY

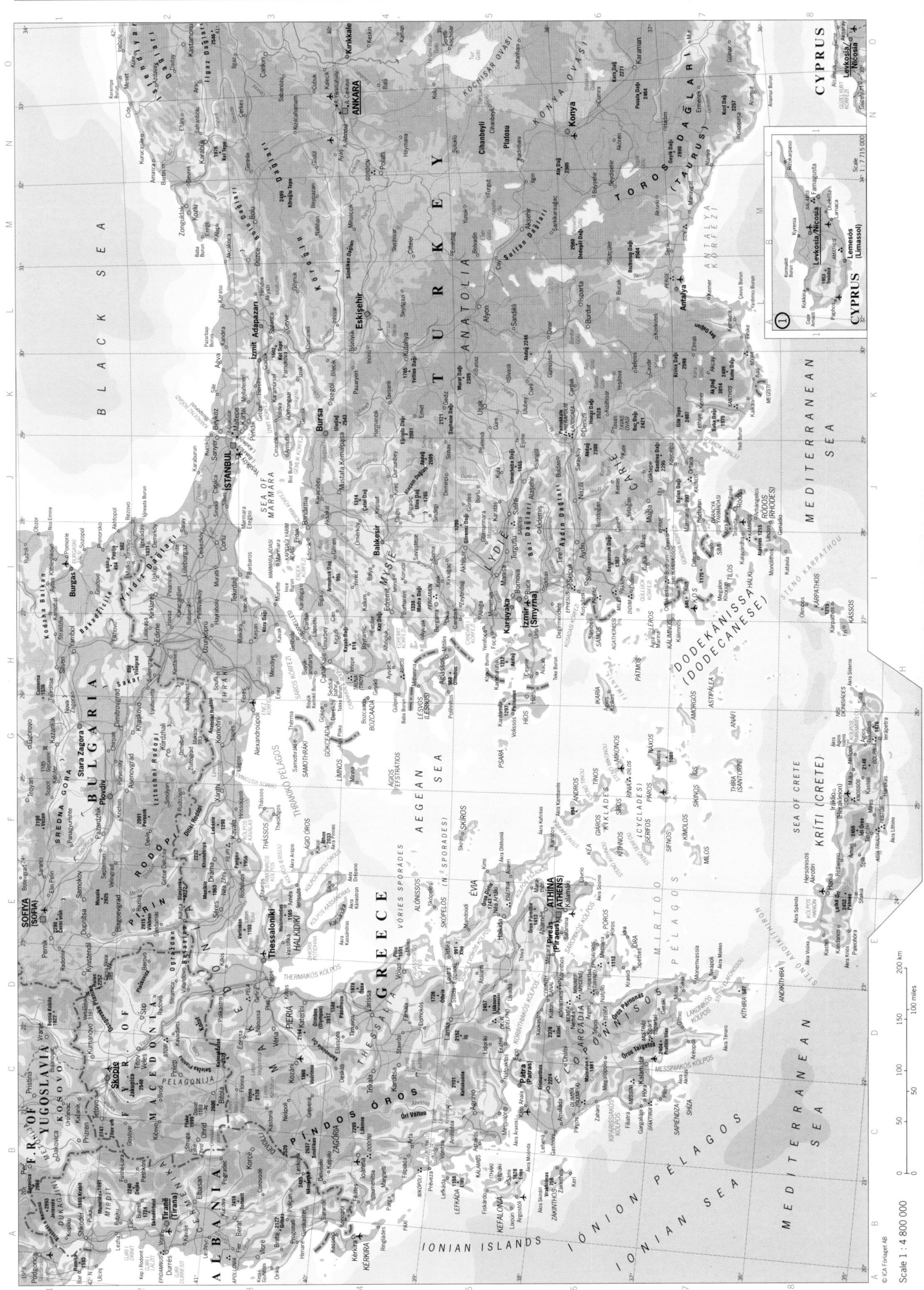

Scale 1 : 4 800 000

© ICA Förlaget AB

SCANDINAVIA

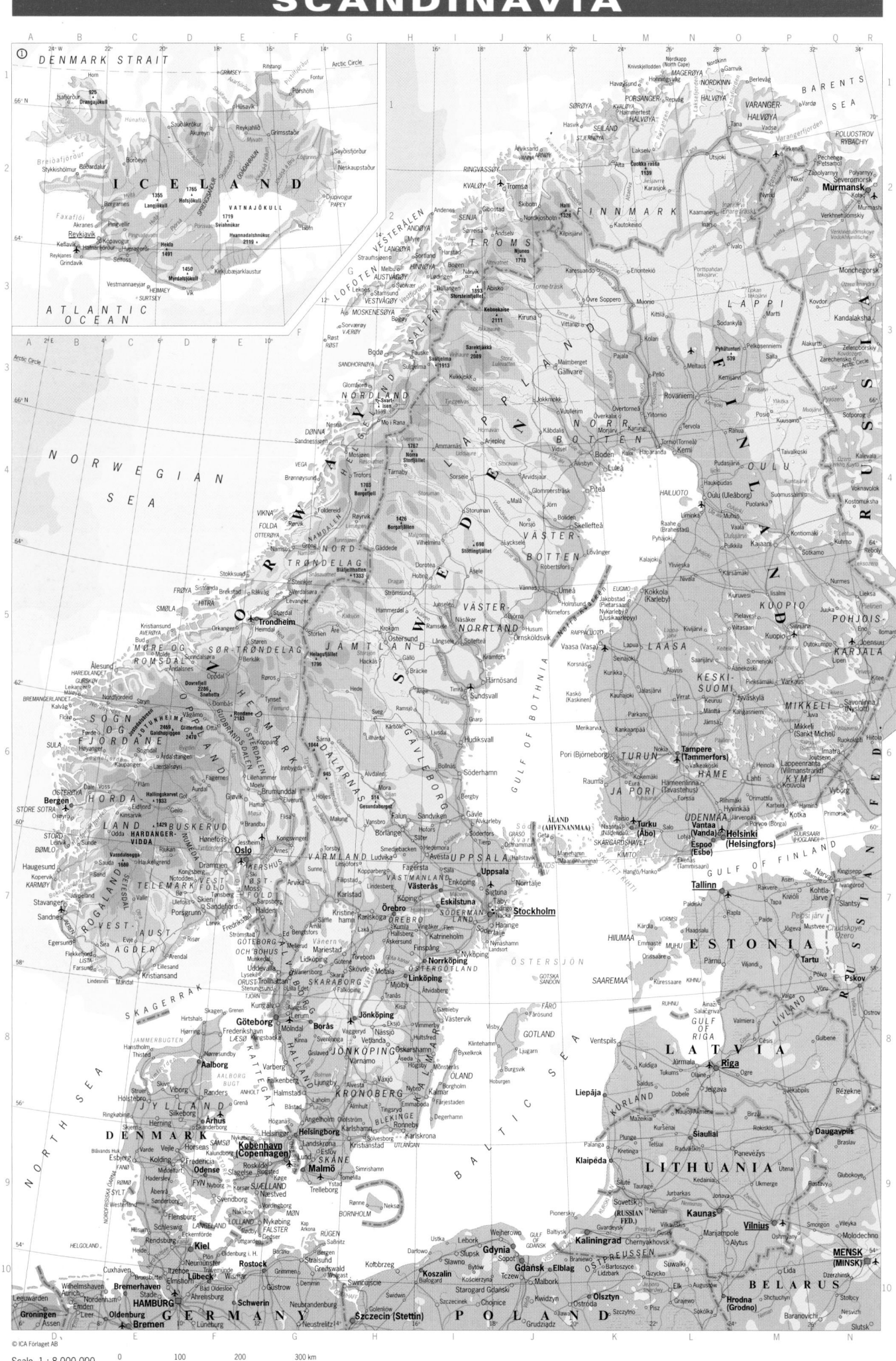

© ICA Förlaget AB

Scale 1 : 8 000 000

0   100   200   300 km

0   100   100 miles

EUROPEAN RUSSIA

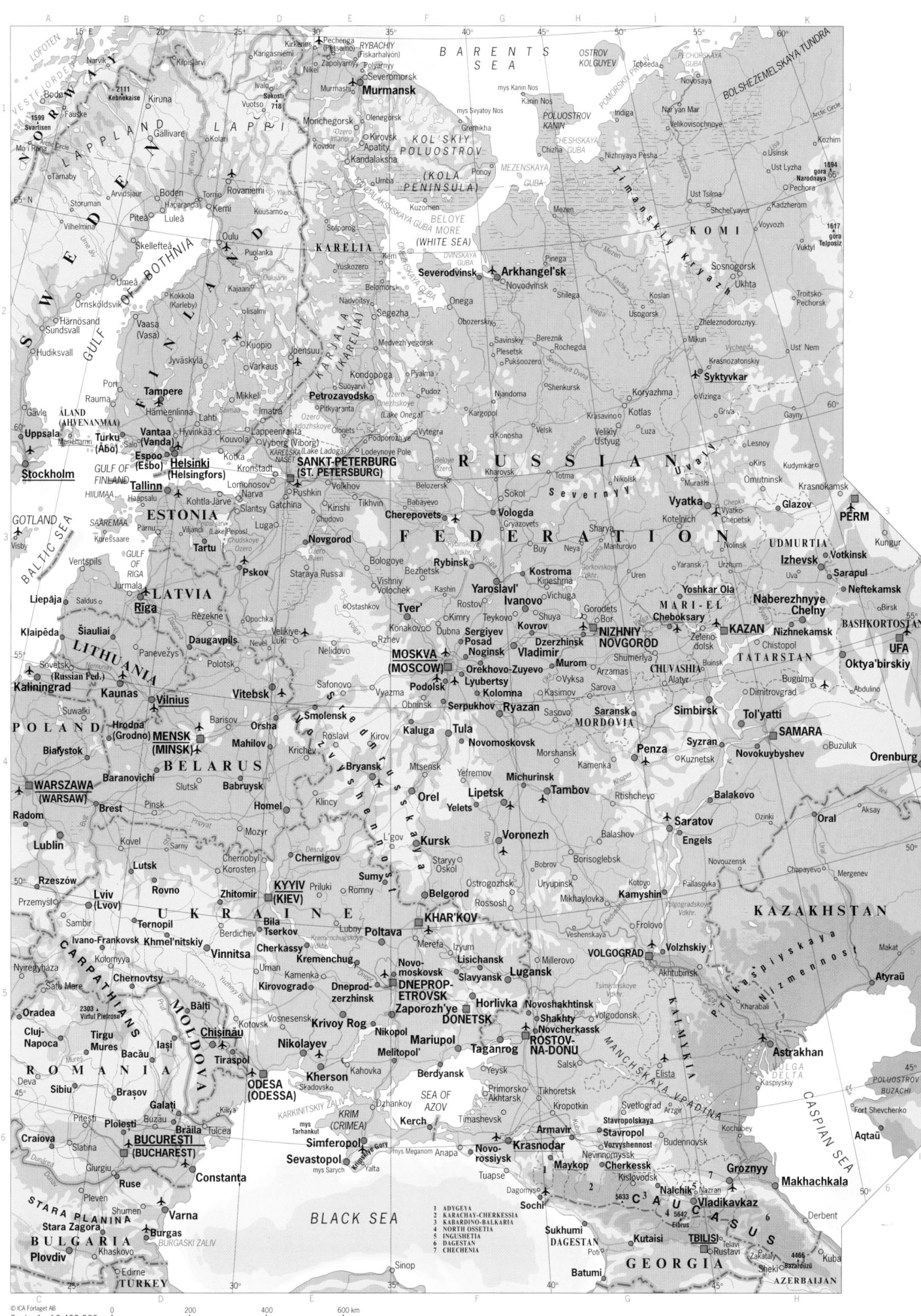

© ICA Förlaget AB

Scale 1 : 12 400 000

0   200   400   600 km
0   200   400 miles

MIDDLE EAST

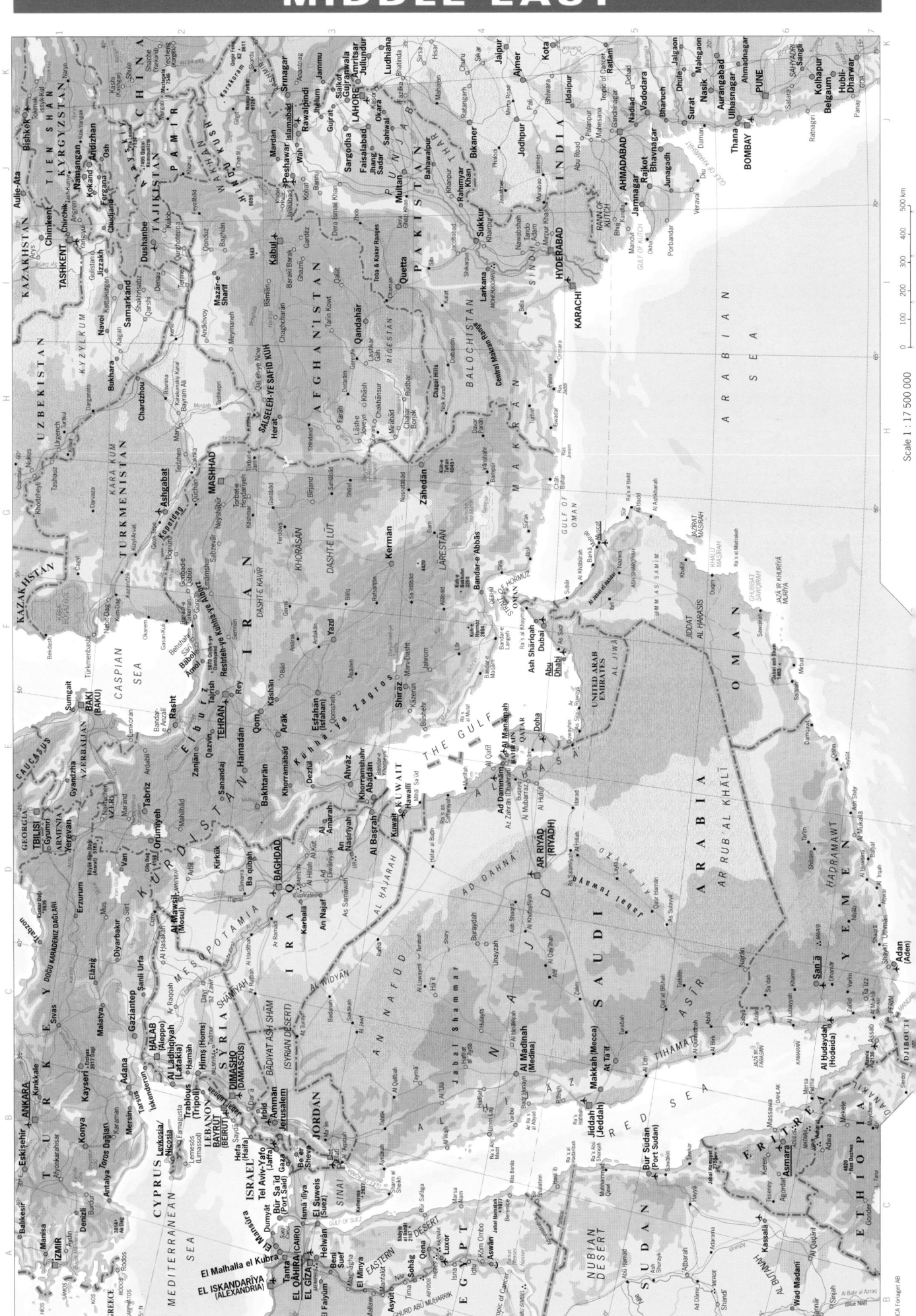

Scale 1 : 17 500 000

0   100   200   300   400   500 km

©ICA Förlaget AB

AFRICA

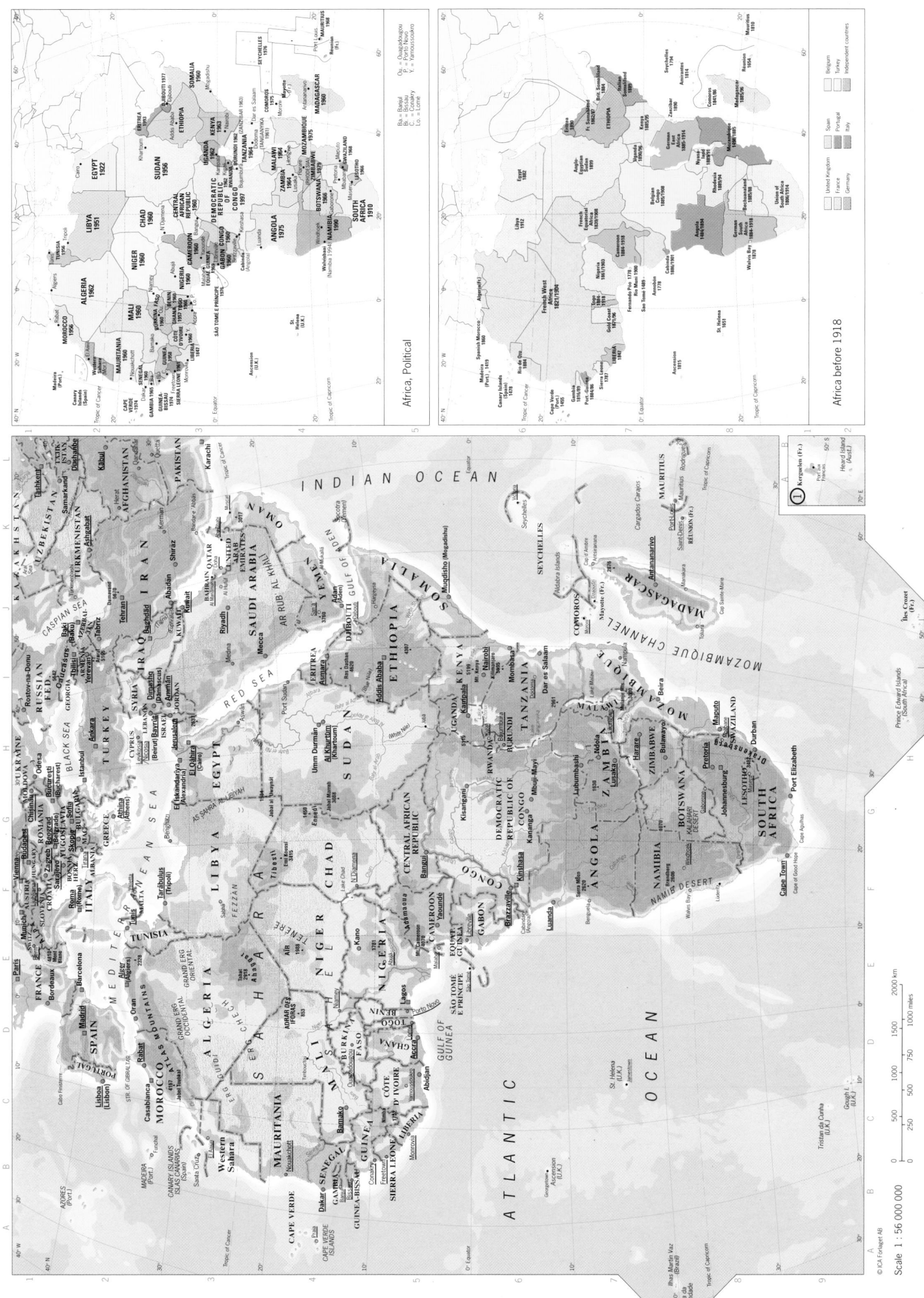

Africa, Political

Africa before 1918

Scale 1 : 56 000 000

NORTHWEST AFRICA

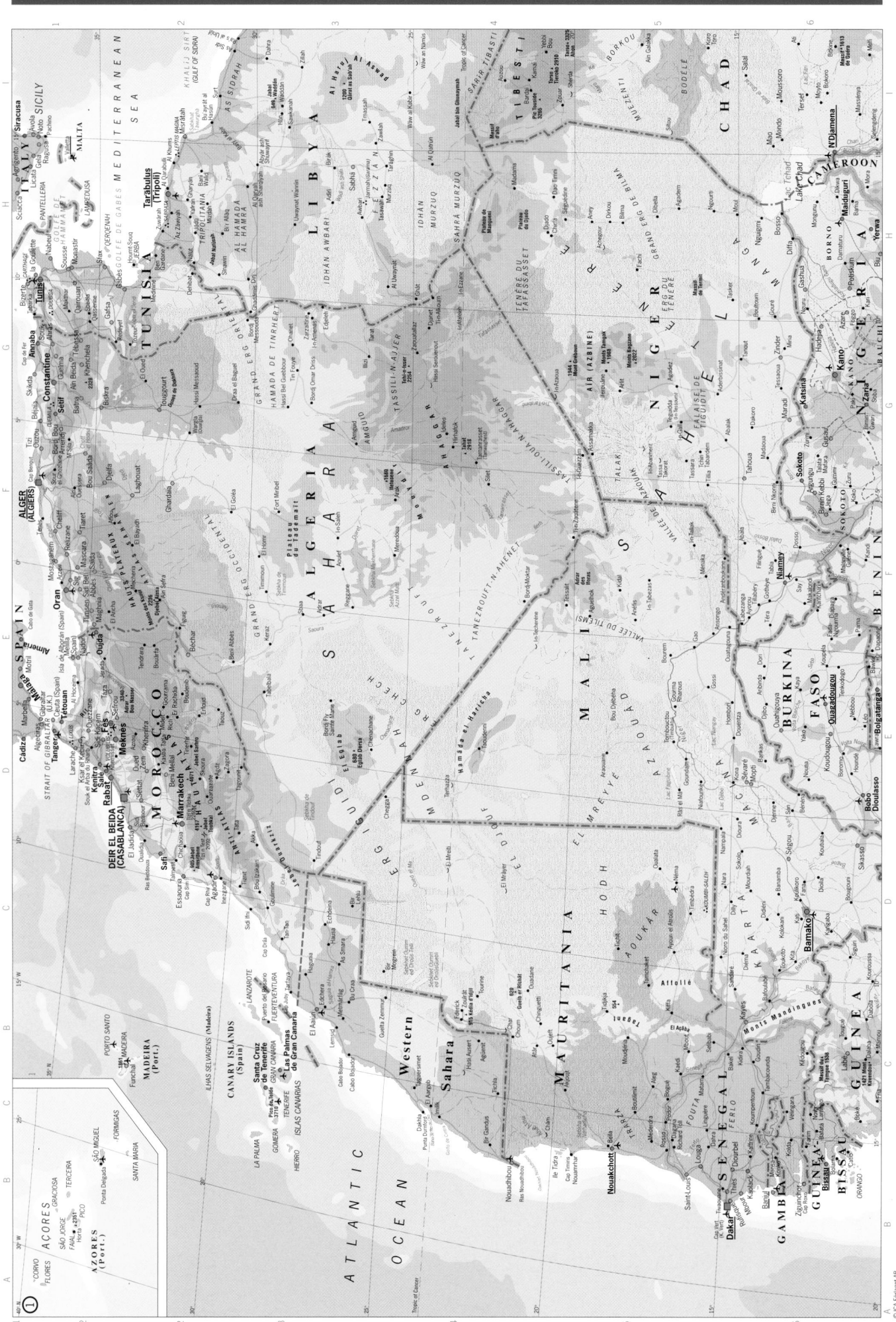

MOROCCO
ALGERIA
TUNISIA
LIBYA
MAURITANIA
MALI
NIGER
CHAD
SENEGAL
GAMBIA
GUINEA-BISSAU
GUINEA
BURKINA FASO
NIGERIA
BENIN
CAMEROON
SPAIN
ITALY
MALTA
SICILY
Western Sahara
ATLANTIC OCEAN
MEDITERRANEAN SEA
S A H A R A
CANARY ISLANDS (Spain)
MADEIRA (Port.)
AÇORES (Port.)
ALGER (ALGIERS)
Tunis
Tarābulus (Tripoli)
Rabat
DEIR EL BEIDA (CASABLANCA)
Marrakech
Fès
Meknès
Oran
Constantine
Annaba
Nouakchott
Dakar
Bamako
Niamey
Ouagadougou
N'Djamena
Kano
Las Palmas de Gran Canaria
Santa Cruz de Tenerife
STRAIT OF GIBRALTAR
© ICA Förlaget AB

NORTHEAST AFRICA

Scale 1:16 000 000

© KA Förlaget AB

WEST AFRICA

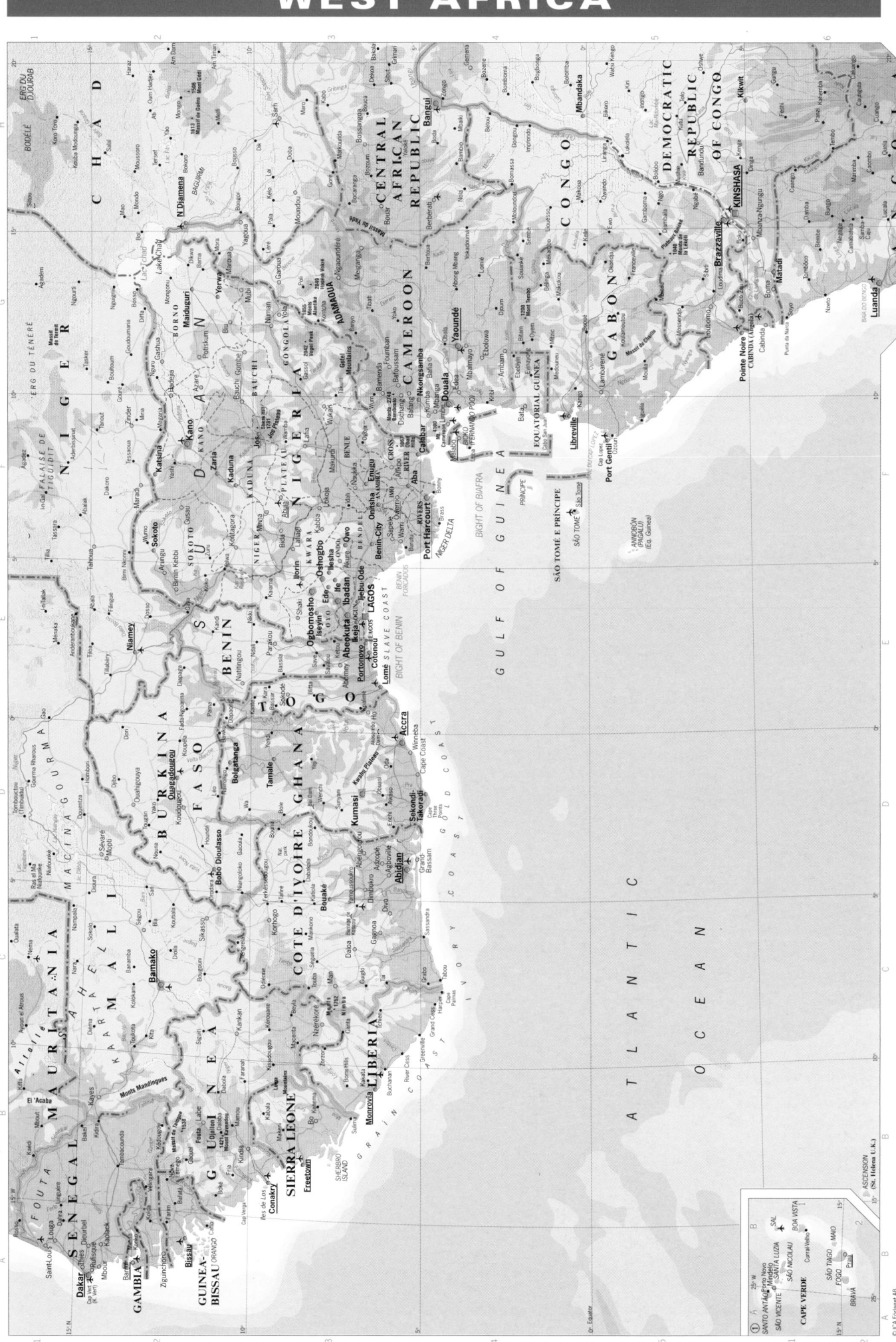
MAURITANIA
SENEGAL
GAMBIA
GUINEA-BISSAU
GUINEA
SIERRA LEONE
LIBERIA
MALI
BURKINA FASO
COTE D'IVOIRE
GHANA
TOGO
BENIN
NIGER
NIGERIA
CHAD
CAMEROON
CENTRAL AFRICAN REPUBLIC
EQUATORIAL GUINEA
GABON
CONGO
DEMOCRATIC REPUBLIC OF CONGO
ANGOLA
SÃO TOMÉ E PRÍNCIPE
CAPE VERDE
GULF OF GUINEA
BIGHT OF BENIN
BIGHT OF BIAFRA
ATLANTIC OCEAN
Dakar
Bamako
Niamey
Ouagadougou
Conakry
Freetown
Monrovia
Abidjan
Accra
Lomé
Portonovo
LAGOS
Abuja
N'Djamena
Yaoundé
Bangui
Libreville
Malabo
Brazzaville
KINSHASA
Luanda
ASCENSION (St. Helena U.K.)
© ICA Förlaget AB
0 200 400 600 km

CENTRAL AFRICA

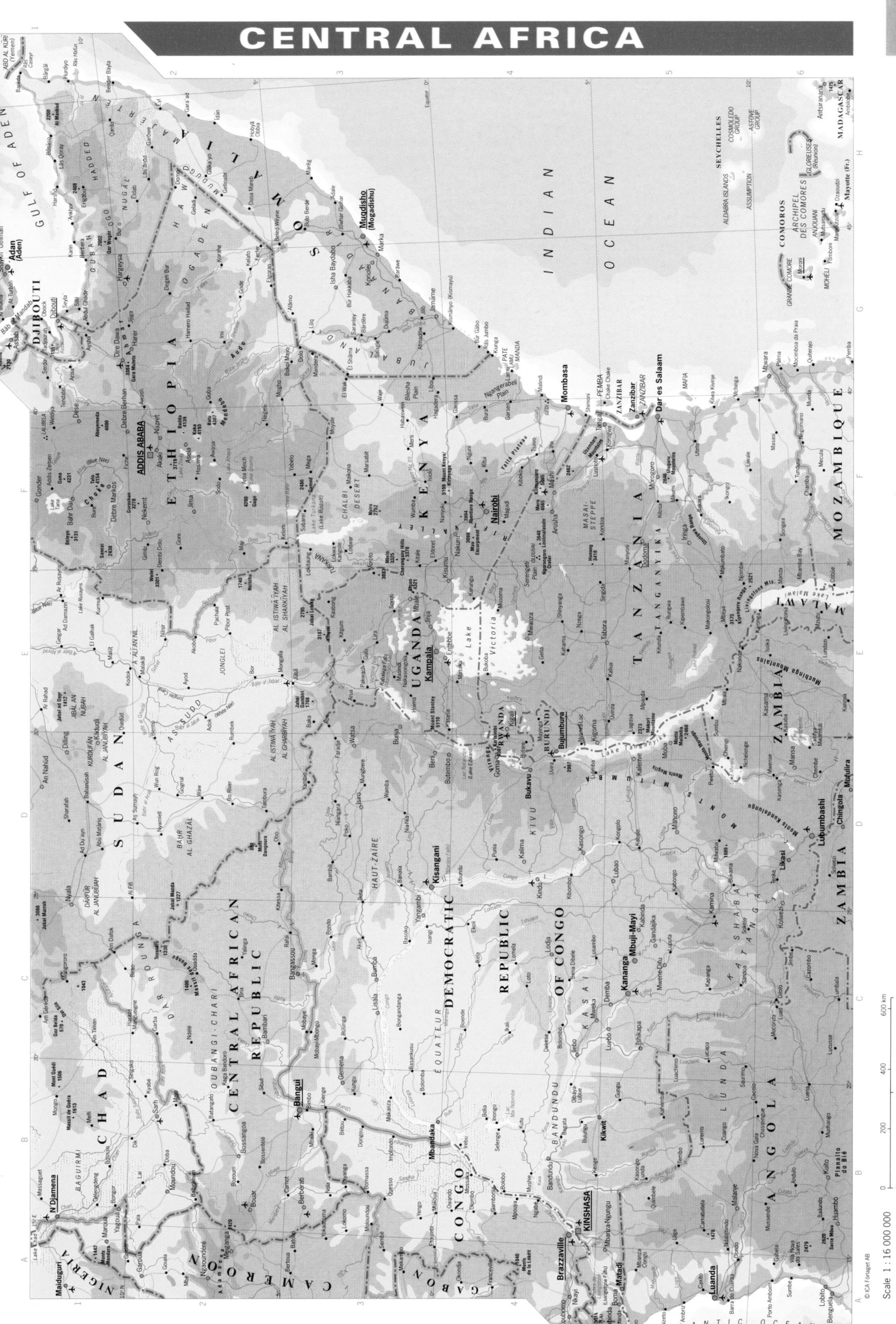

GULF OF ADEN
DJIBOUTI
ETHIOPIA
SOMALIA
KENYA
UGANDA
RWANDA
BURUNDI
TANZANIA
SUDAN
CHAD
CENTRAL AFRICAN REPUBLIC
CAMEROON
GABON
CONGO
DEMOCRATIC REPUBLIC OF CONGO
ANGOLA
ZAMBIA
MALAWI
MOZAMBIQUE
NIGERIA
INDIAN OCEAN
ATLANTIC OCEAN
SEYCHELLES
COMOROS
MADAGASCAR
ADDIS ABABA
Mugdisho (Mogadishu)
Nairobi
Kampala
Kigali
Bujumbura
Dar es Salaam
Mombasa
Zanzibar
Kinshasa
Brazzaville
Bangui
N'Djamena
Luanda
Lubumbashi
Kisangani
Lake Victoria
Lake Tanganyika
Lake Malawi
Scale 1 : 16 000 000
© ICA Förlaget AB

SOUTHERN AFRICA

ATLANTIC OCEAN

INDIAN OCEAN

ANGOLA

NAMIBIA

BOTSWANA

ZAMBIA

ZIMBABWE

MOZAMBIQUE

MALAWI

TANZANIA

DEMOCRATIC REPUBLIC OF CONGO

SOUTH AFRICA

LESOTHO

SWAZILAND

MADAGASCAR

SEYCHELLES

COMOROS

NAMIB DESERT

KALAHARI DESERT

SKELETON COAST

MOZAMBIQUE CHANNEL / CANAL DE MOÇAMBIQUE / CANAL DE MOZAMBIQUE

Tropic of Capricorn

Luanda
Windhoek
Walvis Bay
Cape Town
Cape of Good Hope
Port Elizabeth
East London
Durban
Maputo
Mbabane
Pretoria
JOHANNESBURG
Bloemfontein
Kimberley
Harare
Bulawayo
Lusaka
Lilongwe
Blantyre
Beira
Quelimane
Nampula
Antananarivo
Lubumbashi
Ndola
Kitwe-Nkana
Likasi
Gaborone
Vereeniging
Springs
Benoni
Welkom
Pietermaritzburg
Richard's Bay
Moroni
Port-Louis
Saint-Denis

MAURITIUS

Réunion (France)

© ICA Förlaget AB

ASIA

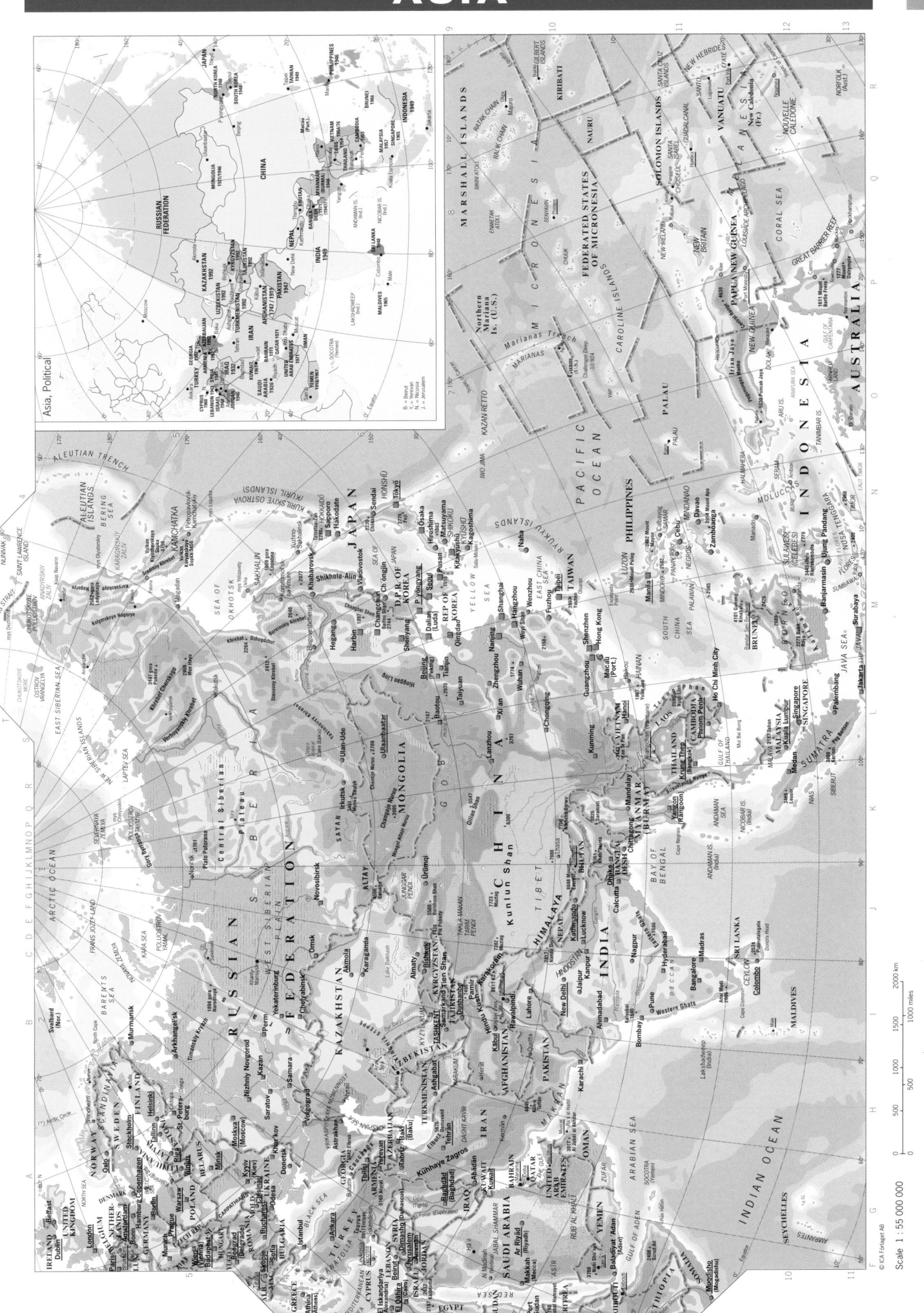

Asia, Political

B = Beirut
Y = Yerevan
N = Nicosia
J = Jerusalem

Scale 1 : 55 000 000

© ICA Förlaget AB

N. W. ASIA

© ICA Förlaget AB

Scale 1 : 19 150 000

0   200   400   600 km

0   200   400 miles

NORTHEAST ASIA

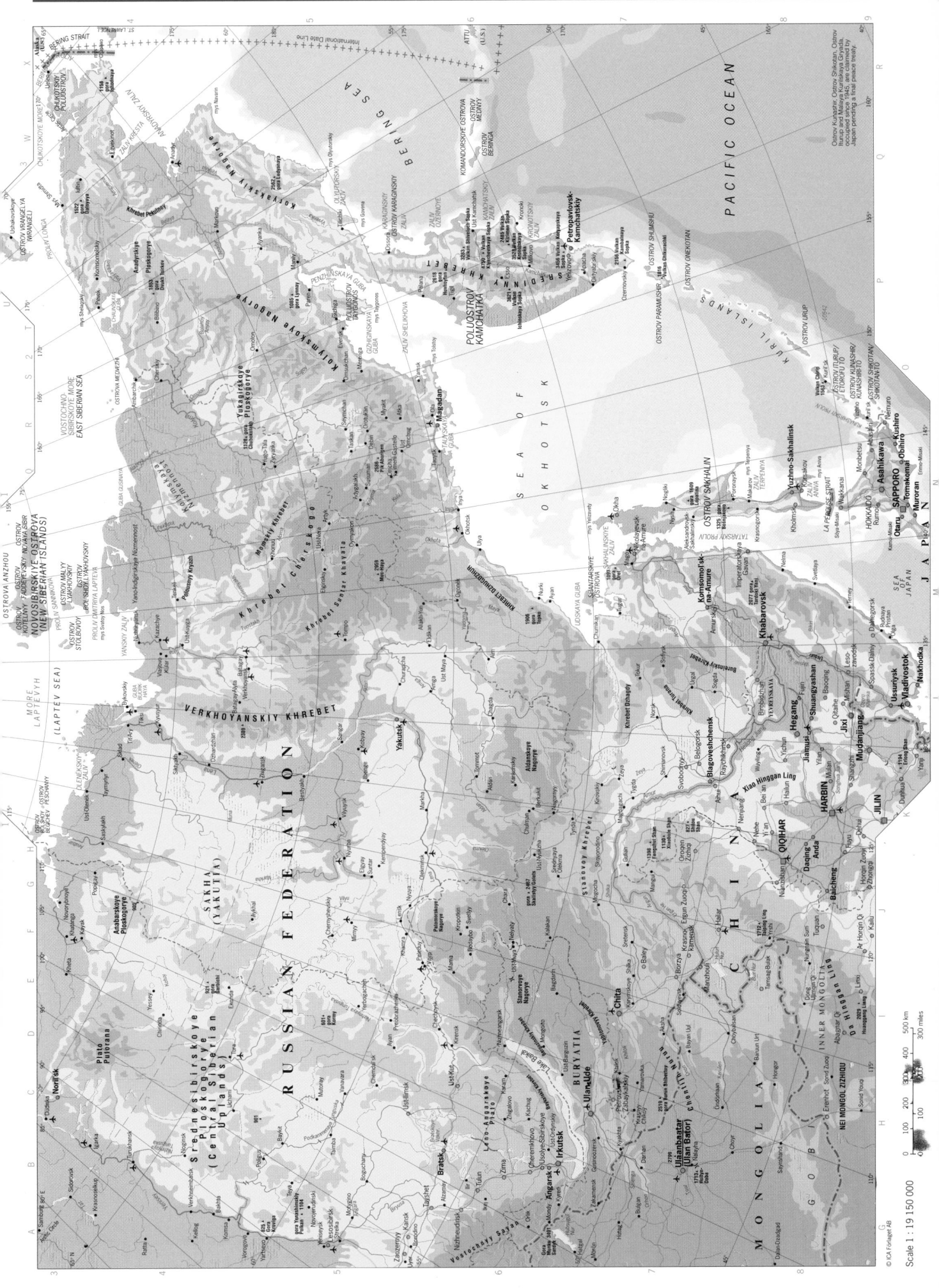
RUSSIAN FEDERATION
SAKHA (YAKUTIA)
BURYATIA
CHINA
MONGOLIA
JAPAN
INNER MONGOLIA
NEI MONGOL ZIZHIQU
GOBI
PACIFIC OCEAN
BERING SEA
SEA OF OKHOTSK
SEA OF JAPAN
MORE LAPTEVYH (LAPTEV SEA)
VOSTOCHNO-SIBIRSKOYE MORE EAST SIBERIAN SEA
KURIL ISLANDS
POLUOSTROV KAMCHATKA
OSTROV SAKHALIN
HOKKAIDO
NOVOSIBIRSKIYE OSTROVA (NEW SIBERIAN ISLANDS)
OSTROV VRANGELYA (WRANGEL)
BERING STRAIT
International Date Line
Koryakskoye Nagorye
Kolymskoye Nagorye
Khrebet Cherskogo
VERKHOYANSKIY KHREBET
Srednesibirskoye Ploskogorye (Central Siberian Uplands)
Plato Putorana
Stanovoy Khrebet
Xiao Hinggan Ling
Da Hinggan Ling
Lake Baikal
Yakutsk
Magadan
Petropavlovsk-Kamchatskiy
Khabarovsk
Vladivostok
Irkutsk
Ulan-Ude
Chita
Bratsk
Norilsk
Ulaanbaatar (Ulan Bator)
HARBIN
QIQIHAR
JILIN
Yuzhno-Sakhalinsk
SAPPORO
Asahikawa
Blagoveshchensk
Komsomol'sk-na-Amure
Ostrov Kunashir, Ostrov Shikotan, Ostrov Iturup and Malaya Kurilskaya Gryada, occupied since 1945 are claimed by Japan pending a final peace treaty.
Scale 1 : 19 150 000
0 100 200 300 400 500 km
0 100 200 300 miles
© ICA Förlaget AB

SOUTH ASIA

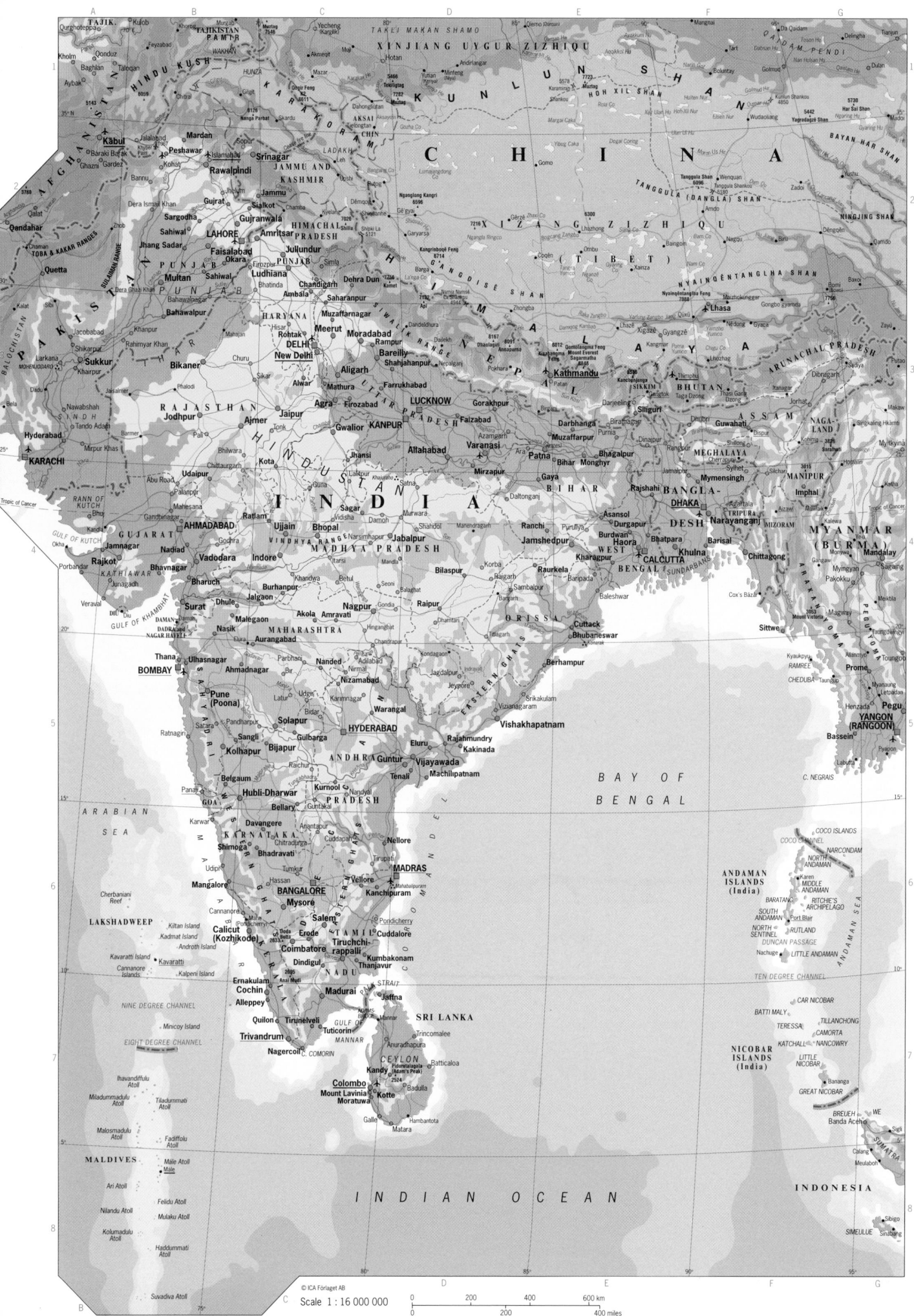

TAKLI MAKAN SHAMO
XINJIANG UYGUR ZIZHIQU
KUNLUN SHAN
HINDU KUSH
KARAKORAM
C H I N A
TANGGULA (DANGLA) SHAN
XIZANG ZIZHIQU
(TIBET)
NYAINQÊNTANGLHA SHAN
GANGDISÊ SHAN
HIMALAYA
AFGHANISTAN
PAKISTAN
Kābul
Peshawar
Islamabad
Rawalpindi
JAMMU AND KASHMIR
Srinagar
Jammu
Sialkot
Gujranwala
LAHORE
Amritsar
Faisalabad
Multan
Quetta
Qandahar
Sukkur
Hyderabad
KARACHI
HIMACHAL PRADESH
PUNJAB
Ludhiana
Chandigarh
Dehra Dun
HARYANA
DELHI
New Delhi
Meerut
Moradabad
Bareilly
Aligarh
Agra
Gwalior
KANPUR
LUCKNOW
Allahabad
Varanasi
Patna
NEPAL
Kathmandu
Lhasa
SIKKIM
BHUTAN
Thimphu
ARUNACHAL PRADESH
ASSAM
NAGALAND
MEGHALAYA
MANIPUR
TRIPURA
MIZORAM
BANGLADESH
DHAKA
Chittagong
Khulna
CALCUTTA
WEST BENGAL
BIHAR
RAJASTHAN
Jodhpur
Jaipur
Ajmer
Bikaner
THAR
HINDUSTAN
I N D I A
GUJARAT
AHMADABAD
Rajkot
Vadodara
Surat
GULF OF KUTCH
GULF OF KHAMBHAT
MADHYA PRADESH
Bhopal
Indore
Ujjain
Jabalpur
UTTAR PRADESH
ORISSA
Cuttack
Bhubaneswar
MAHARASHTRA
BOMBAY
Pune (Poona)
Nagpur
Nasik
Aurangabad
Solapur
HYDERABAD
ANDHRA PRADESH
Vijayawada
Vishakhapatnam
Guntur
KARNATAKA
BANGALORE
Mysore
Mangalore
GOA
Hubli-Dharwar
MADRAS
KERALA
Calicut (Kozhikode)
Cochin
Trivandrum
TAMIL NADU
Coimbatore
Madurai
Tiruchchirappalli
Pondicherry
EASTERN GHATS
WESTERN GHATS
SRI LANKA
CEYLON
Colombo
Kandy
Jaffna
Trincomalee
PALK STRAIT
GULF OF MANNAR
ARABIAN SEA
BAY OF BENGAL
INDIAN OCEAN
LAKSHADWEEP
MALDIVES
Male
NINE DEGREE CHANNEL
EIGHT DEGREE CHANNEL
ANDAMAN ISLANDS (India)
NICOBAR ISLANDS (India)
ANDAMAN SEA
TEN DEGREE CHANNEL
MYANMAR (BURMA)
Mandalay
YANGON (RANGOON)
Pegu
Bassein
INDONESIA
SUMATRA
Tropic of Cancer
© ICA Förlaget AB
Scale 1 : 16 000 000
0 200 400 600 km
0 200 400 miles

EAST ASIA

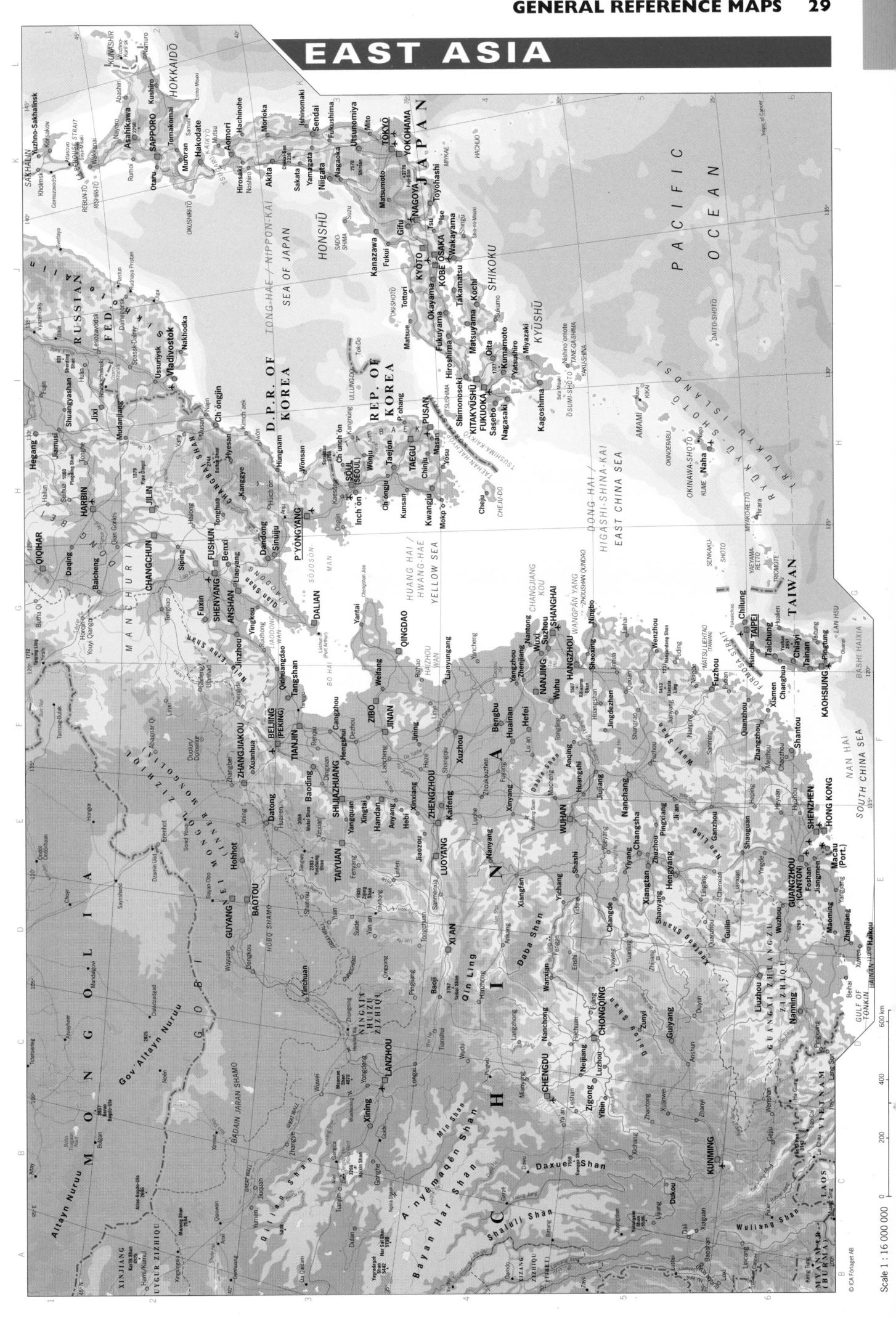

PACIFIC OCEAN

RUSSIAN FED.

MONGOLIA

CHINA

JAPAN

D.P.R. OF KOREA

REP. OF KOREA

TAIWAN

SEA OF JAPAN
TONG-HAE / NIPPON-KAI

YELLOW SEA
HUANG HAI / HWANG-HAE

EAST CHINA SEA
DONG HAI / HIGASHI-SHINA-KAI

SOUTH CHINA SEA
NAN HAI

Scale 1 : 16 000 000

0   200   400   600 km

© ICA Förlaget AB

JAPAN AND KOREA

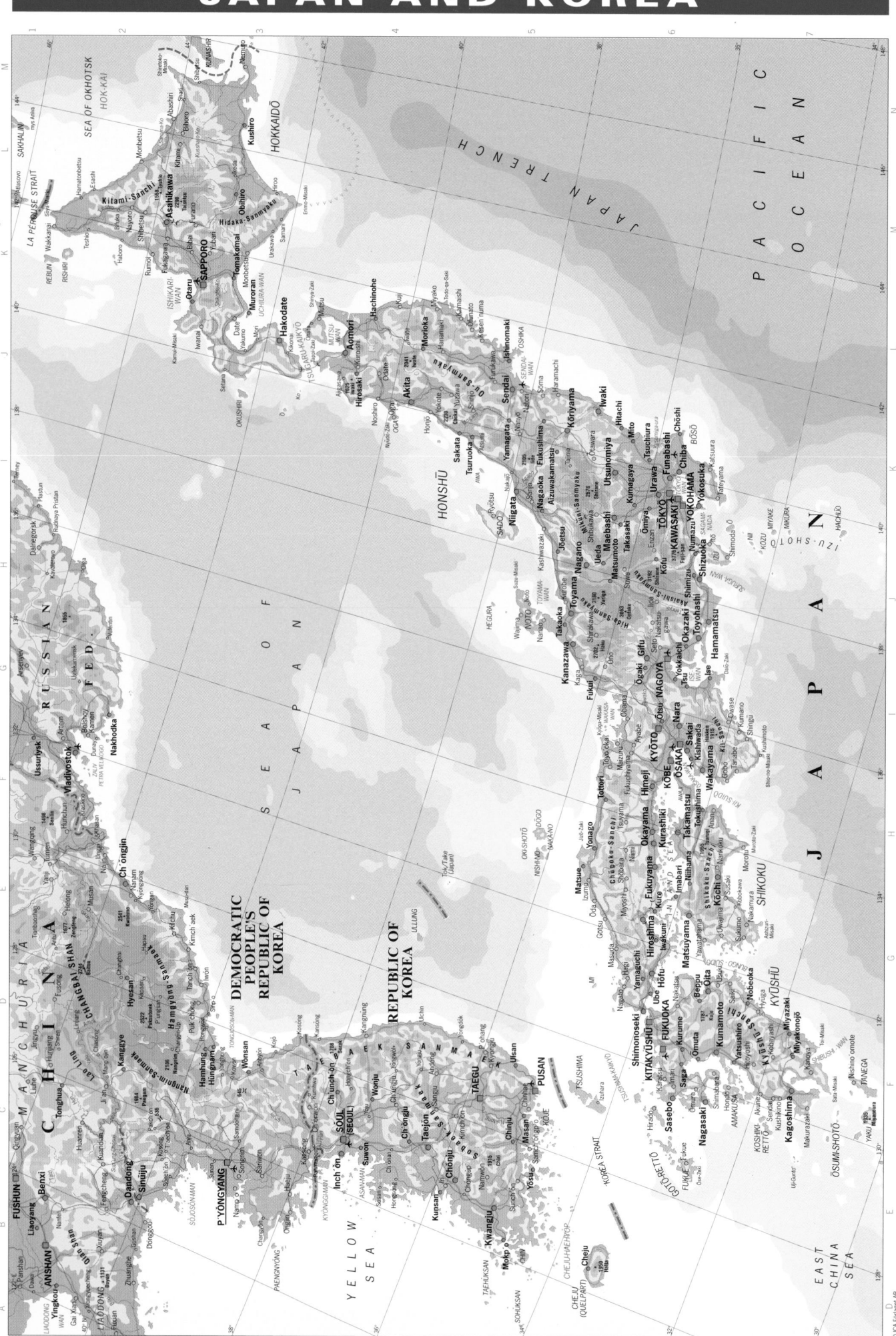

Scale 1 : 8 000 000

0   100   200   300 km

© ICA Förlaget AB

SOUTH-EAST ASIA

Scale 1 : 16 000 000

© ICA Förlaget AB

0   200   400   600 km

MALAYSIA AND INDONESIA

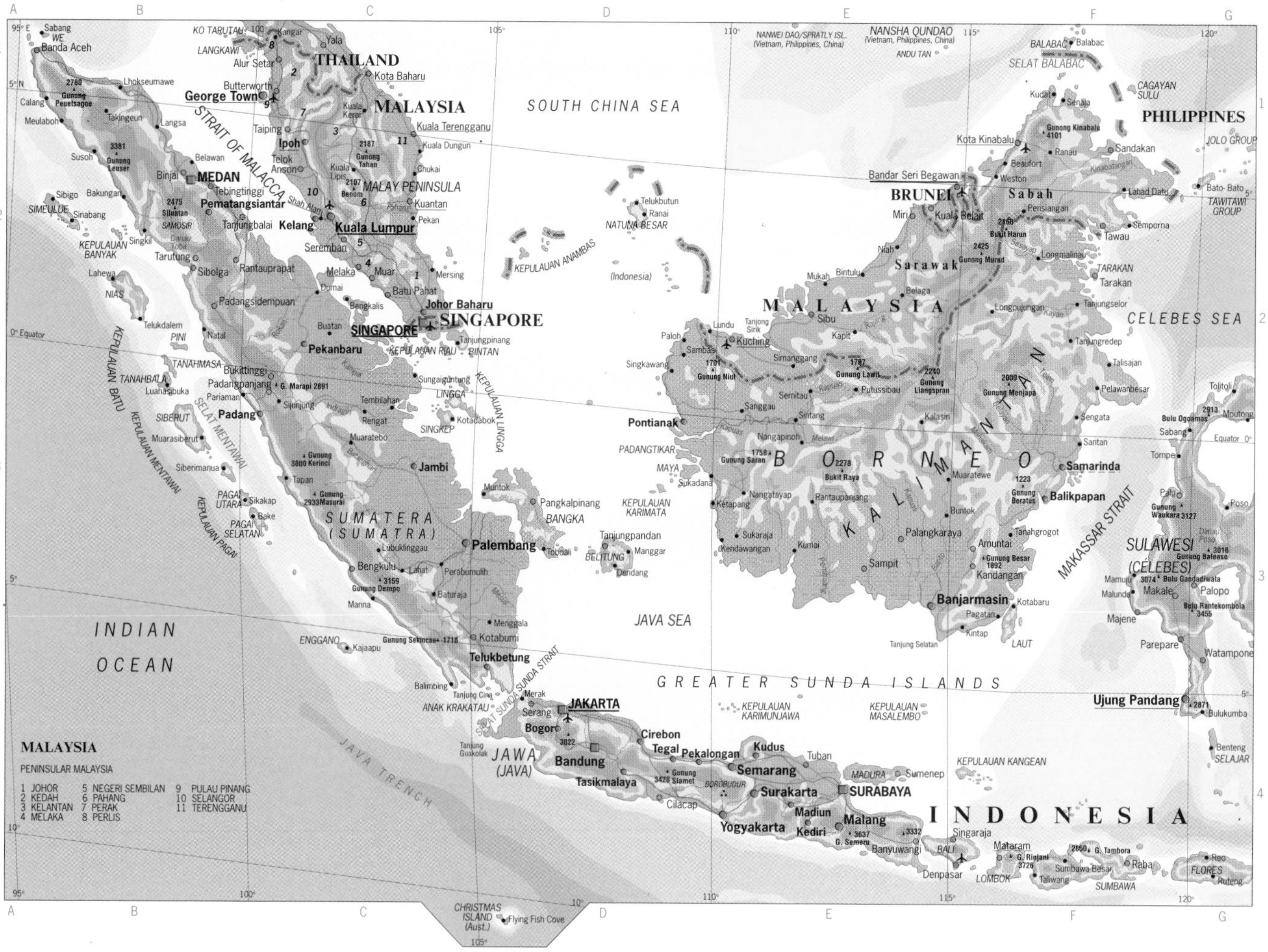

Top map labels

THAILAND
MALAYSIA
George Town
Butterworth
Kota Baharu
Kuala Terengganu
Medan
Kelang
Kuala Lumpur
Singapore
SINGAPORE
Johor Baharu
Pekanbaru
Padang
Jambi
Palembang
SUMATERA (SUMATRA)
Pontianak
BORNEO
KALIMANTAN
BRUNEI
Bandar Seri Begawan
Sabah
Kota Kinabalu
MALAYSIA
Sarawak
Kuching
Sibu
PHILIPPINES
Balikpapan
Samarinda
Banjarmasin
MAKASSAR STRAIT
SULAWESI (CELEBES)
Ujung Pandang
SOUTH CHINA SEA
NATUNA BESAR
KEPULAUAN ANAMBAS
CELEBES SEA
JAVA SEA
GREATER SUNDA ISLANDS
INDIAN OCEAN
JAVA TRENCH
JAKARTA
Bogor
Bandung
Cirebon
Tegal
Pekalongan
Semarang
Surakarta
SURABAYA
Yogyakarta
Madiun
Kediri
Malang
JAWA (JAVA)
Denpasar
BALI
LOMBOK
SUMBAWA
FLORES
INDONESIA

MALAYSIA — PENINSULAR MALAYSIA

1 JOHOR
2 KEDAH
3 KELANTAN
4 MELAKA
5 NEGERI SEMBILAN
6 PAHANG
7 PERAK
8 PERLIS
9 PULAU PINANG
10 SELANGOR
11 TERENGGANU

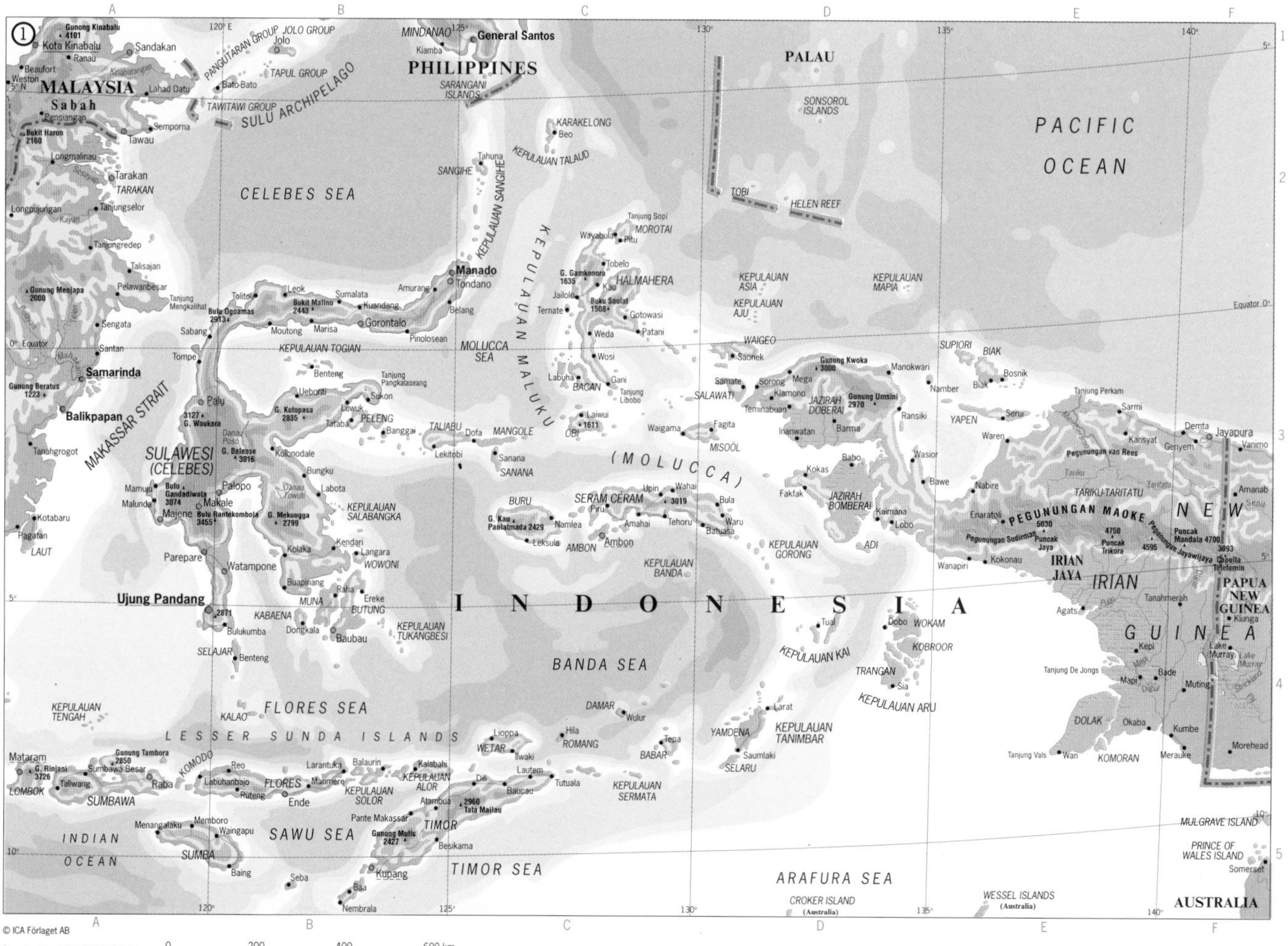

Bottom map labels

MALAYSIA
Sabah
Kota Kinabalu
PHILIPPINES
MINDANAO
General Santos
PALAU
SULU ARCHIPELAGO
CELEBES SEA
Manado
Tondano
HALMAHERA
MOLUCCA SEA
SULAWESI (CELEBES)
Samarinda
Balikpapan
MAKASSAR STRAIT
Palu
Palopo
Makale
Ujung Pandang
Kendari
SERAM CERAM
(MOLUCCA)
BURU
AMBON
MISOOL
WAIGEO
IRIAN JAYA
PEGUNUNGAN MAOKE
Jayapura
Puncak Jaya
IRIAN
PAPUA NEW GUINEA
NEW GUINEA
INDONESIA
PACIFIC OCEAN
BANDA SEA
FLORES SEA
LESSER SUNDA ISLANDS
KEPULAUAN TANIMBAR
KEPULAUAN ARU
TIMOR
SUMBA
SAWU SEA
TIMOR SEA
ARAFURA SEA
AUSTRALIA
PRINCE OF WALES ISLAND
INDIAN OCEAN

© ICA Förlaget AB

Scale 1 : 16 000 000

0 200 400 600 km
0 200 400 miles

OCEANIA

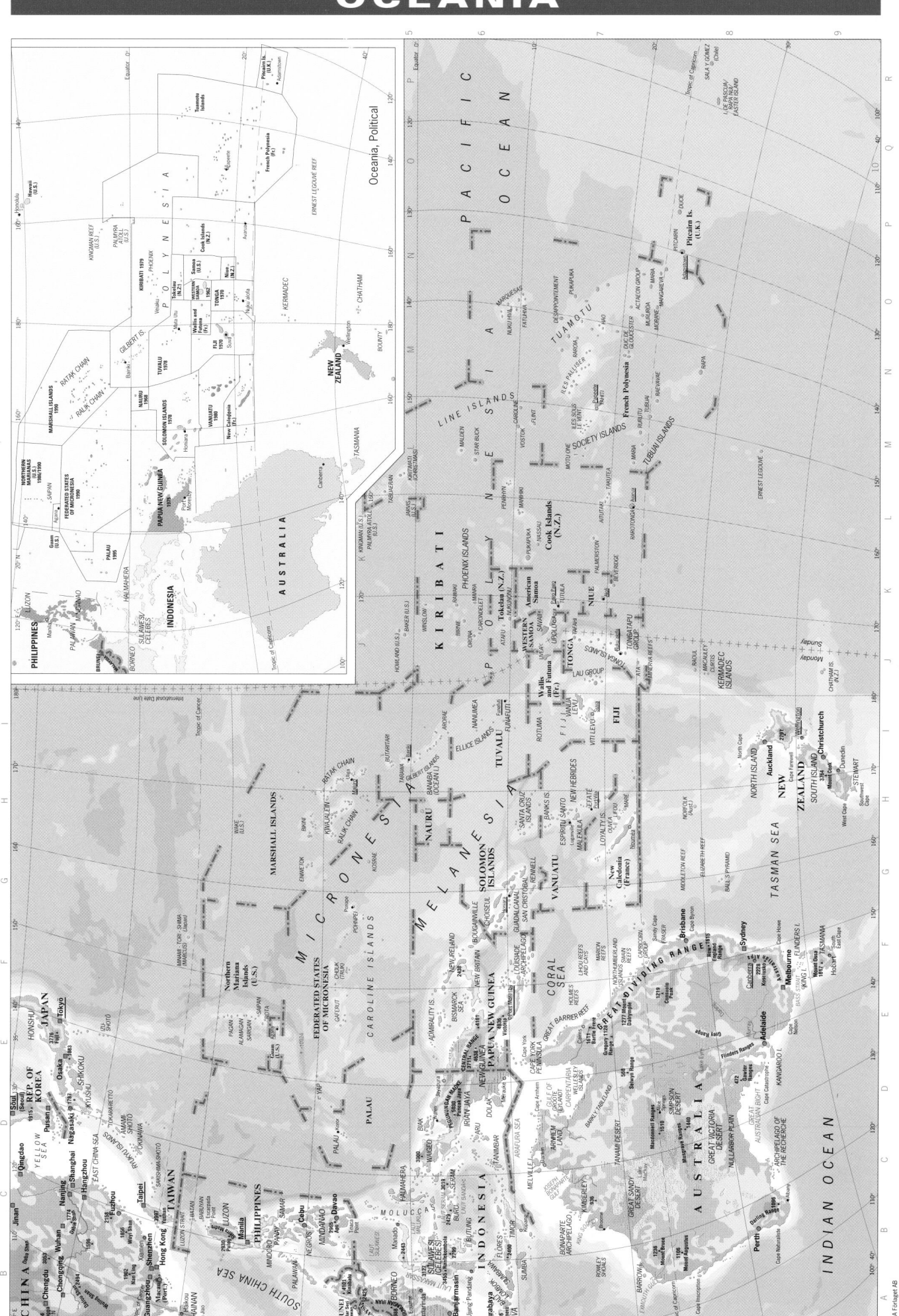

Oceania, Political

Scale 1 : 56 000 000

© ICA Förlaget AB

AUSTRALIA

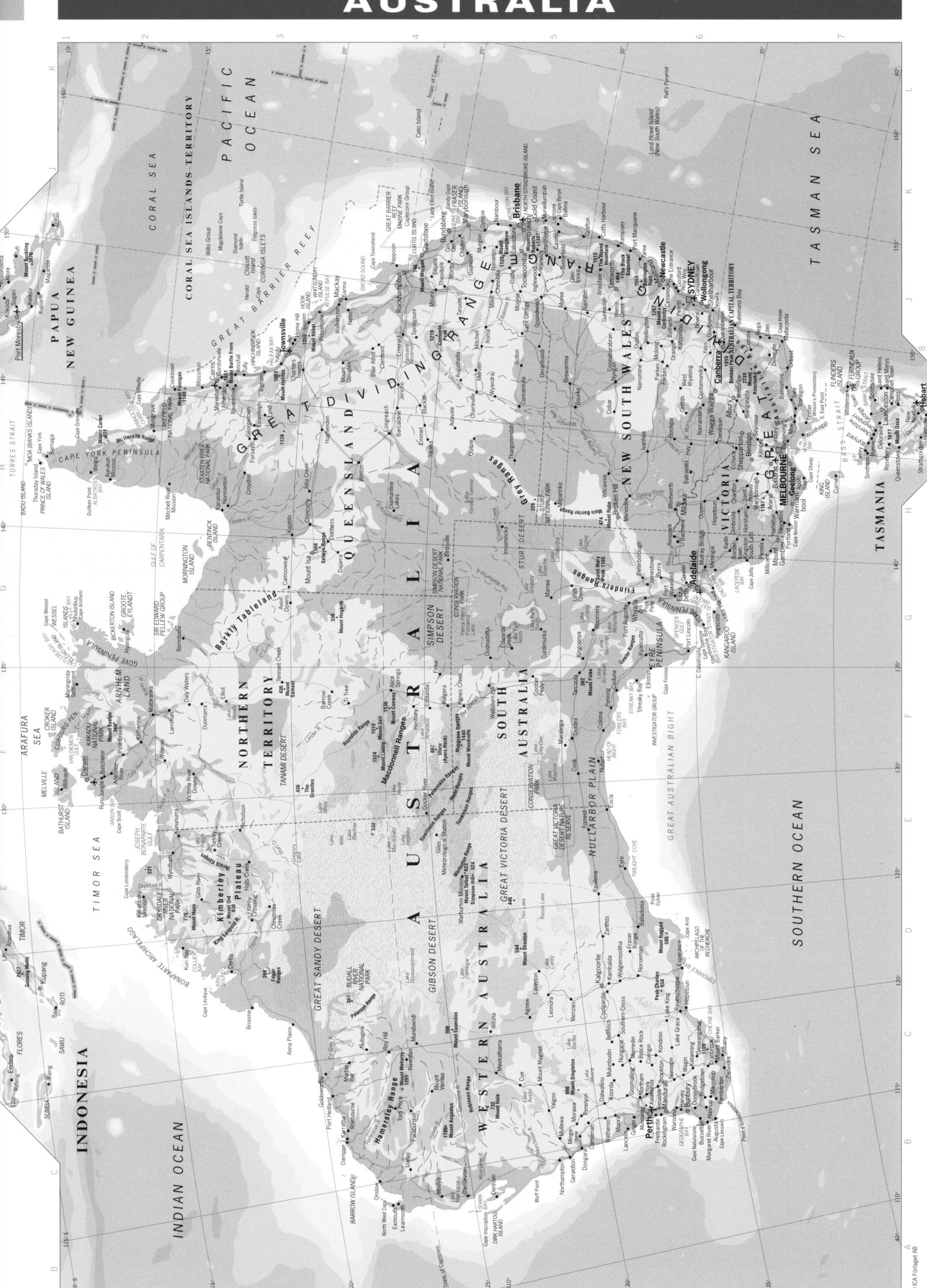

INDONESIA
INDIAN OCEAN
TIMOR SEA
ARAFURA SEA
PAPUA NEW GUINEA
CORAL SEA
CORAL SEA ISLANDS TERRITORY
PACIFIC OCEAN
TASMAN SEA
SOUTHERN OCEAN
GREAT AUSTRALIAN BIGHT
BASS STRAIT
TORRES STRAIT
GULF OF CARPENTARIA
GREAT BARRIER REEF
A U S T R A L I A
WESTERN AUSTRALIA
NORTHERN TERRITORY
SOUTH AUSTRALIA
QUEENSLAND
NEW SOUTH WALES
VICTORIA
TASMANIA
AUSTRALIAN CAPITAL TERRITORY
GREAT DIVIDING RANGE
GREAT SANDY DESERT
GIBSON DESERT
GREAT VICTORIA DESERT
SIMPSON DESERT
TANAMI DESERT
STURT DESERT
NULLARBOR PLAIN
CAPE YORK PENINSULA
ARNHEM LAND
Barkly Tableland
Kimberley Plateau
Hamersley Range
Macdonnell Ranges
Flinders Ranges
Grey Ranges
Perth
Adelaide
MELBOURNE
Canberra
SYDNEY
Newcastle
Wollongong
Brisbane
Gold Coast
Townsville
Cairns
Darwin
Hobart
Alice Springs
Tropic of Capricorn
© ICA Förlaget AB
Scale 1 : 19 150 000
0 200 400 600 km

NEW ZEALAND AND NEW GUINEA

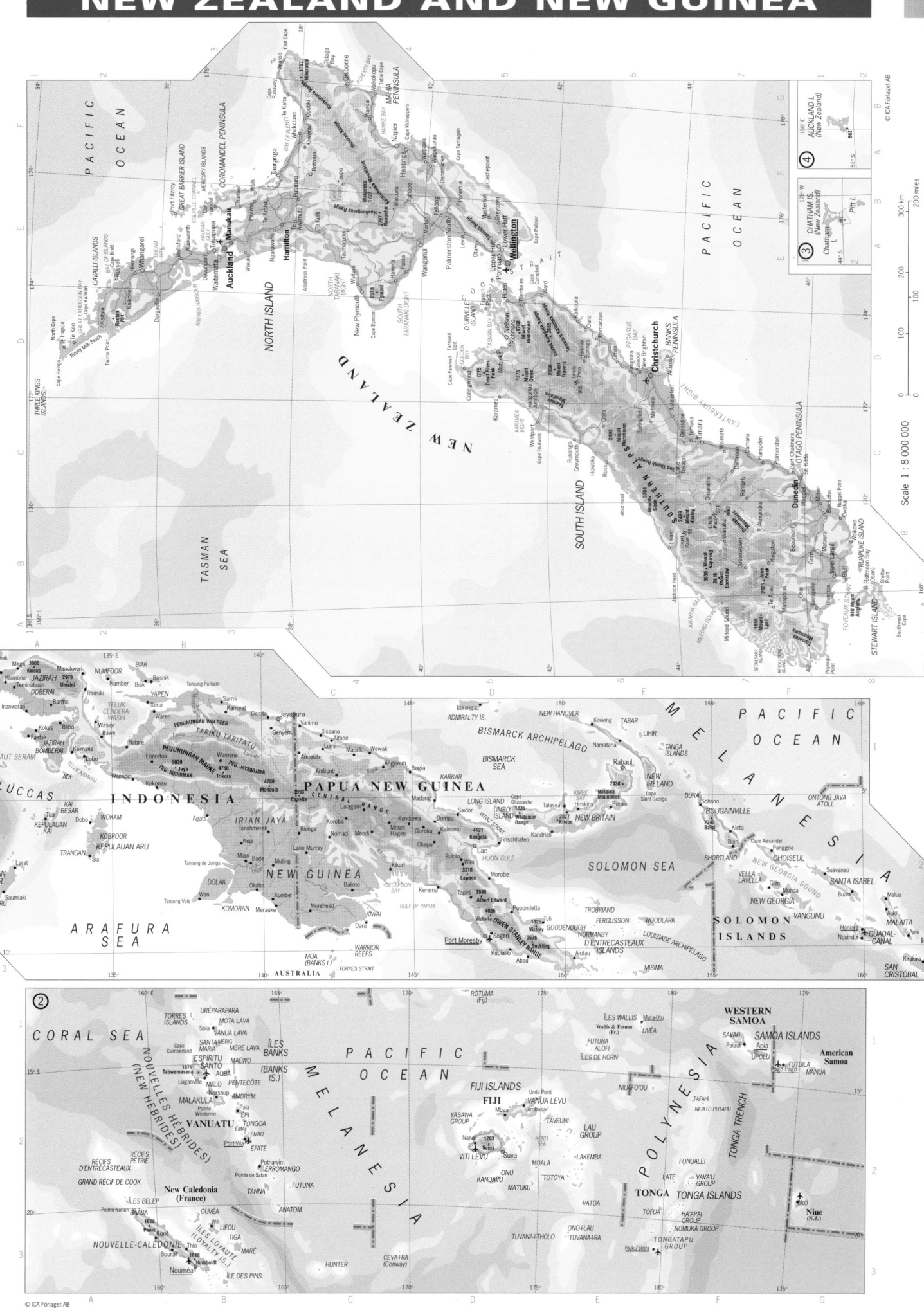

Scale 1 : 8 000 000

Scale 1 : 16 000 000

© ICA Förlaget AB

NORTH AMERICA

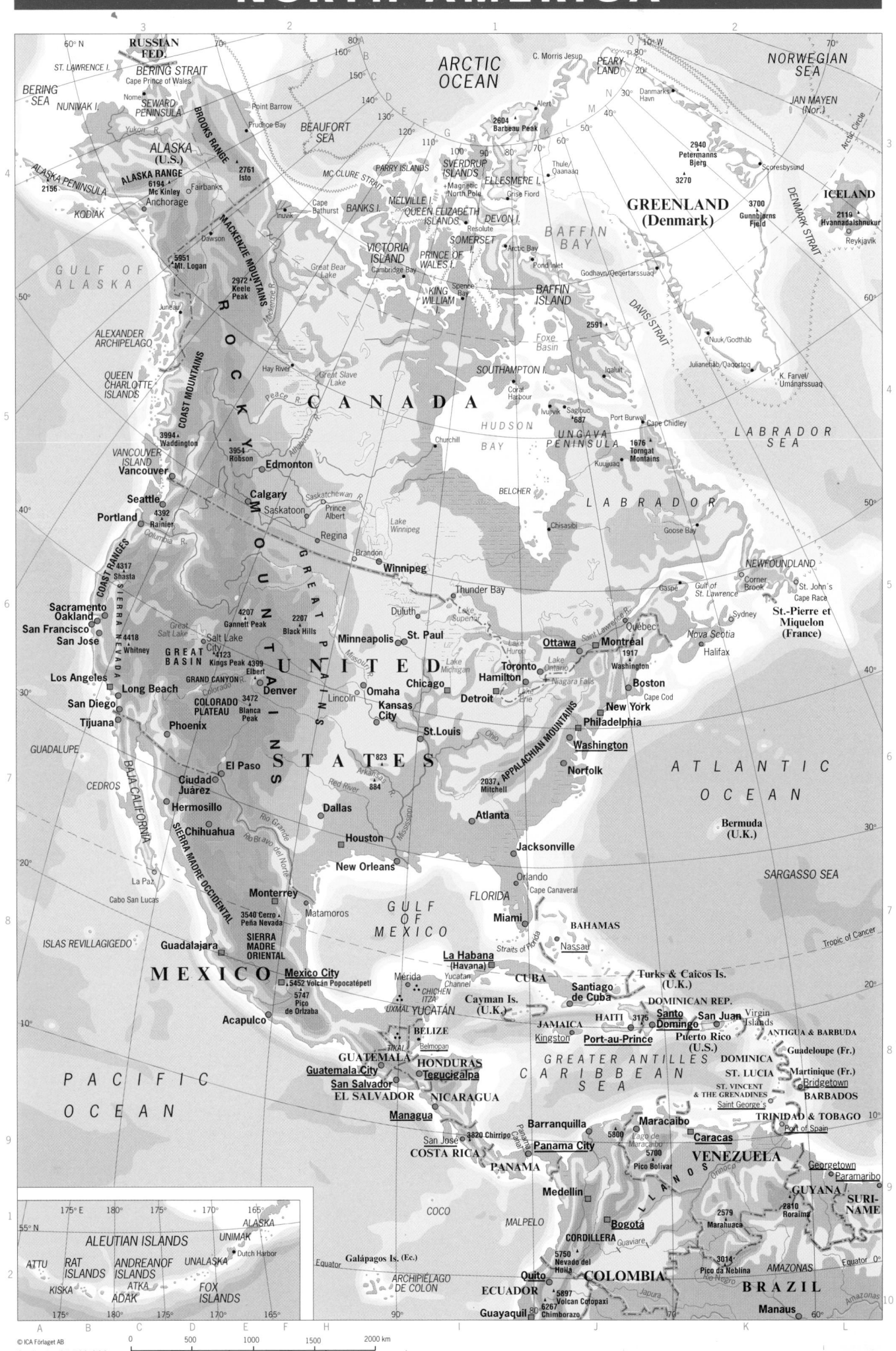
ARCTIC OCEAN
BEAUFORT SEA
BERING SEA
BERING STRAIT
GULF OF ALASKA
ALASKA (U.S.)
CANADA
HUDSON BAY
BAFFIN BAY
BAFFIN ISLAND
GREENLAND (Denmark)
ICELAND
NORWEGIAN SEA
LABRADOR SEA
LABRADOR
DAVIS STRAIT
DENMARK STRAIT
ROCKY MOUNTAINS
COAST MOUNTAINS
GREAT PLAINS
UNITED STATES
APPALACHIAN MOUNTAINS
ATLANTIC OCEAN
SARGASSO SEA
Bermuda (U.K.)
GULF OF MEXICO
MEXICO
SIERRA MADRE OCCIDENTAL
SIERRA MADRE ORIENTAL
PACIFIC OCEAN
CARIBBEAN SEA
GREATER ANTILLES
CUBA
BAHAMAS
JAMAICA
HAITI
DOMINICAN REP.
GUATEMALA
BELIZE
HONDURAS
EL SALVADOR
NICARAGUA
COSTA RICA
PANAMA
COLOMBIA
VENEZUELA
ECUADOR
BRAZIL
GUYANA
SURINAME
ALEUTIAN ISLANDS
Tropic of Cancer
Arctic Circle
Equator
Anchorage
Vancouver
Seattle
Portland
San Francisco
Los Angeles
San Diego
Edmonton
Calgary
Winnipeg
Minneapolis
Chicago
Detroit
Toronto
Ottawa
Montreal
Boston
New York
Philadelphia
Washington
Atlanta
Dallas
Houston
New Orleans
Miami
Denver
Phoenix
Mexico City
Guadalajara
Monterrey
La Habana (Havana)
Panama City
Caracas
Bogotá
Quito
© ICA Förlaget AB
Scale 1 : 36 000 000
0 500 1000 1500 2000 km
0 500 1000 miles

CENTRAL AMERICA

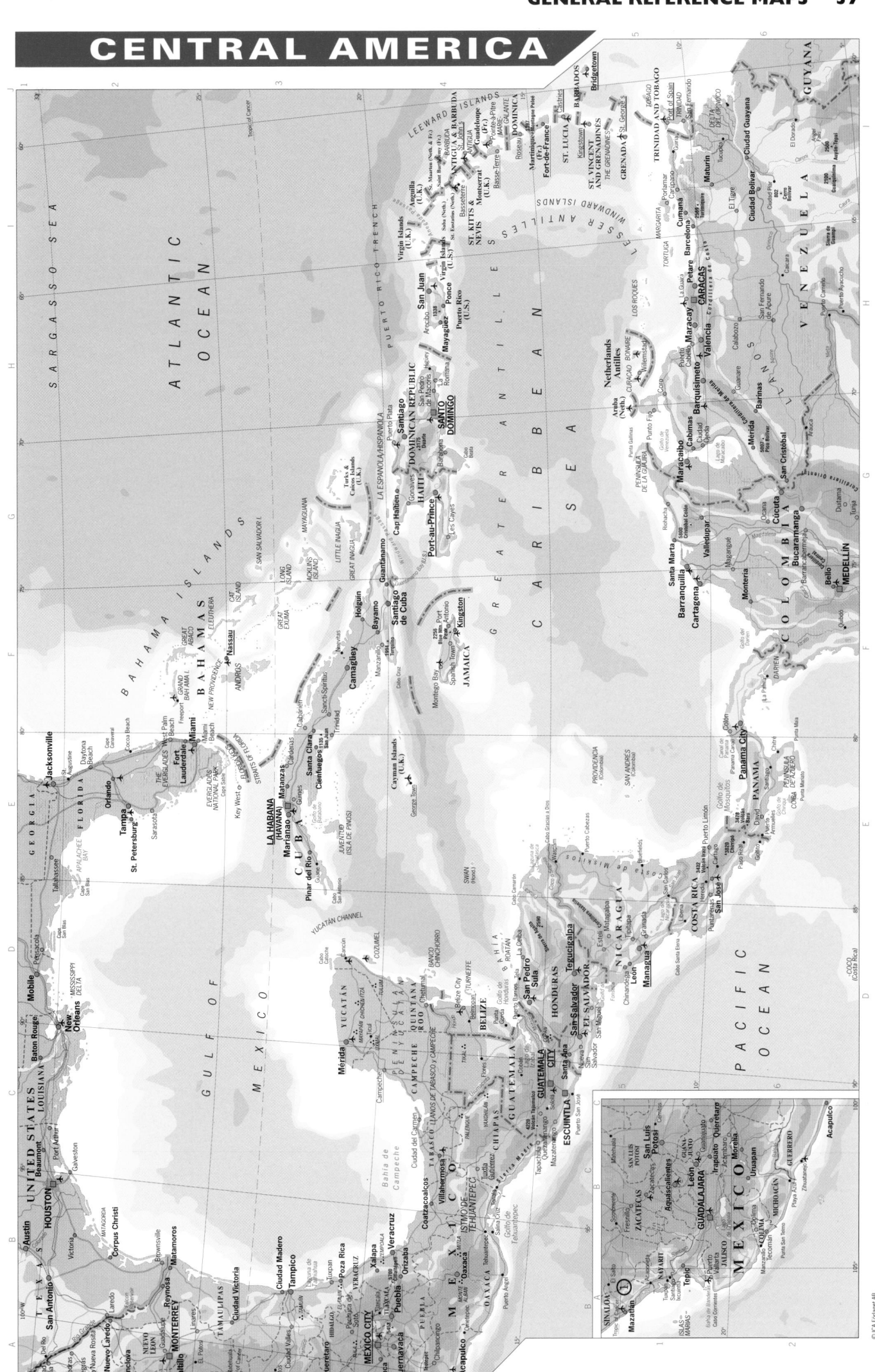

Scale 1 : 16 000 000

© ICA Förlaget AB

CANADA

© ICA Förlaget AB

Scale 1 : 12 000 000

0   200   400   600 km

0   200   200 miles

CANADA

BAFFIN BAY
BAFFIN ISLAND
KALAALLIT NUNAAT
GREENLAND
(Denmark)
DAVIS STRAIT
DENMARK STRAIT
LABRADOR SEA
NEWFOUNDLAND & LABRADOR
HUDSON STRAIT
HUDSON BAY
FOXE BASIN
LABRADOR
QUÉBEC
PLATEAU LAURENTIDES
ONTARIO
NEWFOUNDLAND
NOVA SCOTIA
NEW BRUNSWICK
PRINCE EDWARD ISLAND
GULF OF ST. LAWRENCE
GULF OF MAINE
ATLANTIC OCEAN
MAINE
NEW YORK
NEW HAMPSHIRE
VERMONT
NEW ENGLAND
PENNSYLVANIA
OHIO
MICHIGAN
INDIANA
Upernavik
Pond Inlet
Igloolik
Iqaluit (Frobisher Bay)
Pangnirtung
Nuuk/Godthåb
Kangiqsualujjuaq
Kuujjuaq
Nain
Schefferville
Labrador City
Goose Bay
Sept-Îles
Gaspé
Chicoutimi
Jonquière
Québec
Trois-Rivières
Sherbrooke
MONTRÉAL
Ottawa
Kingston
Toronto
Hamilton
Buffalo
Rochester
Syracuse
Albany
Boston
Hartford
Providence
New Haven
NEW YORK
Jersey City
Newark
Trenton
PHILADELPHIA
Pittsburgh
Cleveland
Toledo
DETROIT
Windsor
CHICAGO
Milwaukee
Madison
Thunder Bay
Sault Sainte Marie
Sudbury
Timmins
Moosonee
Fredericton
Moncton
Saint John
Halifax
Dartmouth
Sydney
Charlottetown
Corner Brook
Gander
St. John's
Saint-Pierre et Miquelon (Fr.)
Portland
Augusta
Bangor

UNITED STATES

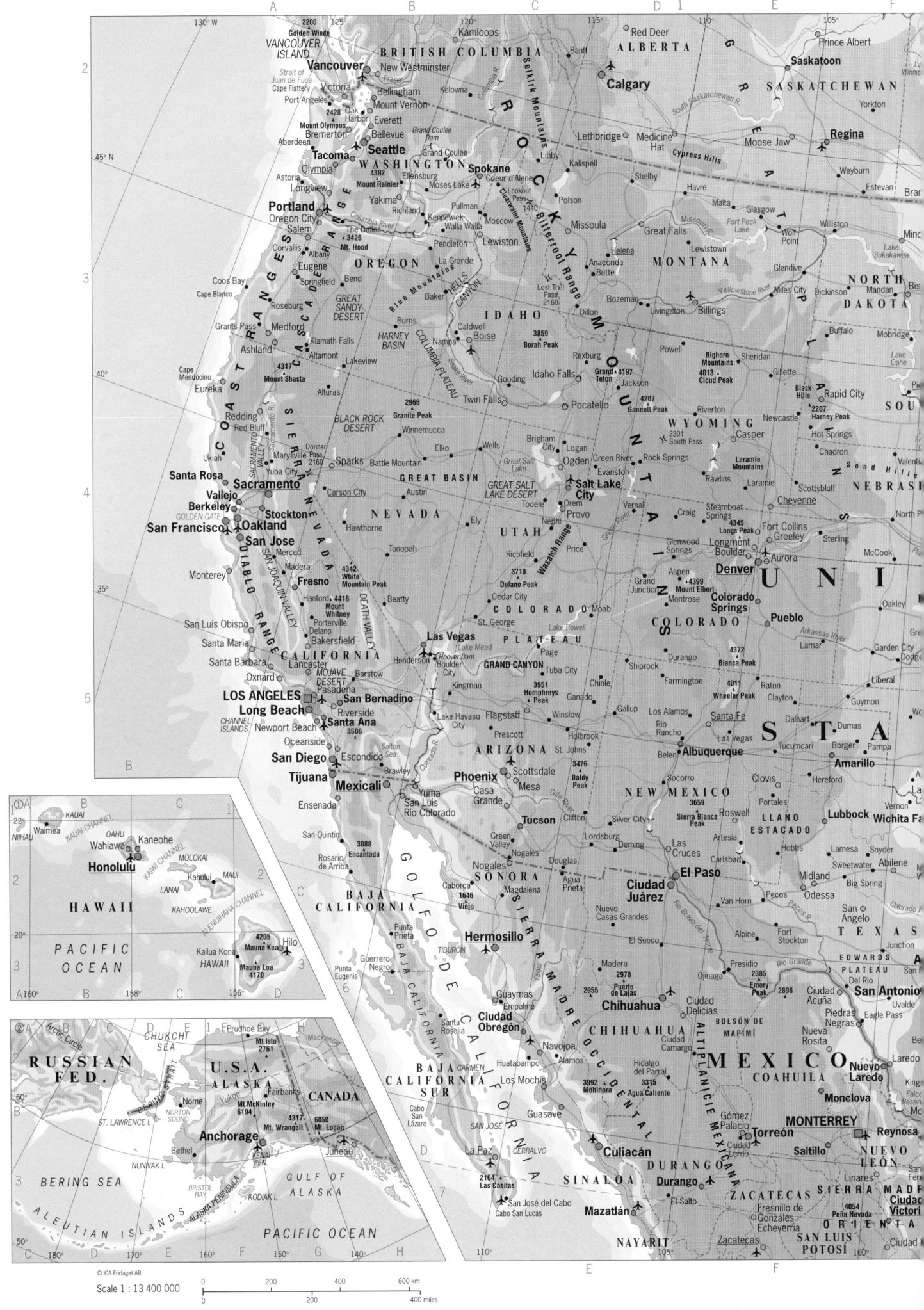

BRITISH COLUMBIA
ALBERTA
SASKATCHEWAN
WASHINGTON
OREGON
IDAHO
MONTANA
WYOMING
NEVADA
UTAH
CALIFORNIA
COLORADO
ARIZONA
NEW MEXICO
NORTH DAKOTA
BAJA CALIFORNIA
SONORA
CHIHUAHUA
COAHUILA
MEXICO
SINALOA
DURANGO
ZACATECAS
TEXAS
Seattle
Portland
San Francisco
Sacramento
LOS ANGELES
San Diego
Las Vegas
Salt Lake City
Denver
Phoenix
Albuquerque
El Paso
Vancouver
Calgary
HAWAII
PACIFIC OCEAN
Honolulu
RUSSIAN FED.
U.S.A. ALASKA
CANADA
Anchorage
BERING SEA
GULF OF ALASKA
© ICA Förlaget AB
Scale 1 : 13 400 000

UNITED STATES

ONTARIO
CANADA
QUÉBEC
PLATEAU LAURENTIDES
Winnipeg
Thunder Bay
Lake Superior
MONTRÉAL
Ottawa
MINNESOTA
Duluth
Saint Paul
Minneapolis
WISCONSIN
MICHIGAN
Lake Michigan
Lake Huron
Toronto
Hamilton
St. Catherines
Rochester
Buffalo
NEW YORK
Syracuse
Albany
Boston
Providence
Hartford
RHODE ISLAND
CONNECTICUT
NEW HAMPSHIRE
VERMONT
MAINE
NEW BRUNSWICK
Québec
Bangor
Portland
New Haven
Bridgeport
NEW YORK
Jersey City
Newark
Trenton
PHILADELPHIA
Baltimore
Washington D.C.
NEW JERSEY
DELAWARE
MARYLAND
PENNSYLVANIA
Pittsburgh
Erie
Cleveland
Akron
Toledo
DETROIT
Windsor
London
Milwaukee
Madison
Racine
Grand Rapids
CHICAGO
Rockford
Gary
South Bend
Fort Wayne
OHIO
Columbus
Dayton
Cincinnati
Indianapolis
INDIANA
ILLINOIS
Peoria
Springfield
Davenport
IOWA
Des Moines
Omaha
Kansas City
St. Louis
MISSOURI
Springfield
Topeka
Wichita
Tulsa
Oklahoma City
Louisville
KENTUCKY
Lexington
Evansville
Nashville
TENNESSEE
Knoxville
Memphis
Chattanooga
WEST VIRGINIA
Charleston
VIRGINIA
Richmond
Norfolk
Virginia Beach
APPALACHIANS
NORTH CAROLINA
Greensboro
Winston-Salem
Raleigh
Charlotte
SOUTH CAROLINA
Columbia
Charleston
GEORGIA
Atlanta
Savannah
Macon
ALABAMA
Birmingham
Huntsville
Montgomery
Mobile
MISSISSIPPI
Jackson
ARKANSAS
Little Rock
LOUISIANA
Shreveport
Baton Rouge
New Orleans
Dallas
HOUSTON
Beaumont
FLORIDA
Jacksonville
Tallahassee
Orlando
Tampa
St. Petersburg
Miami
Fort Lauderdale
ATLANTIC OCEAN
GULF OF MEXICO
BAHAMAS
Nassau
CUBA
LA HABANA (HAVANA)
Santa Clara
Key West
STRAITS OF FLORIDA
Tropic of Cancer

SOUTH AMERICA

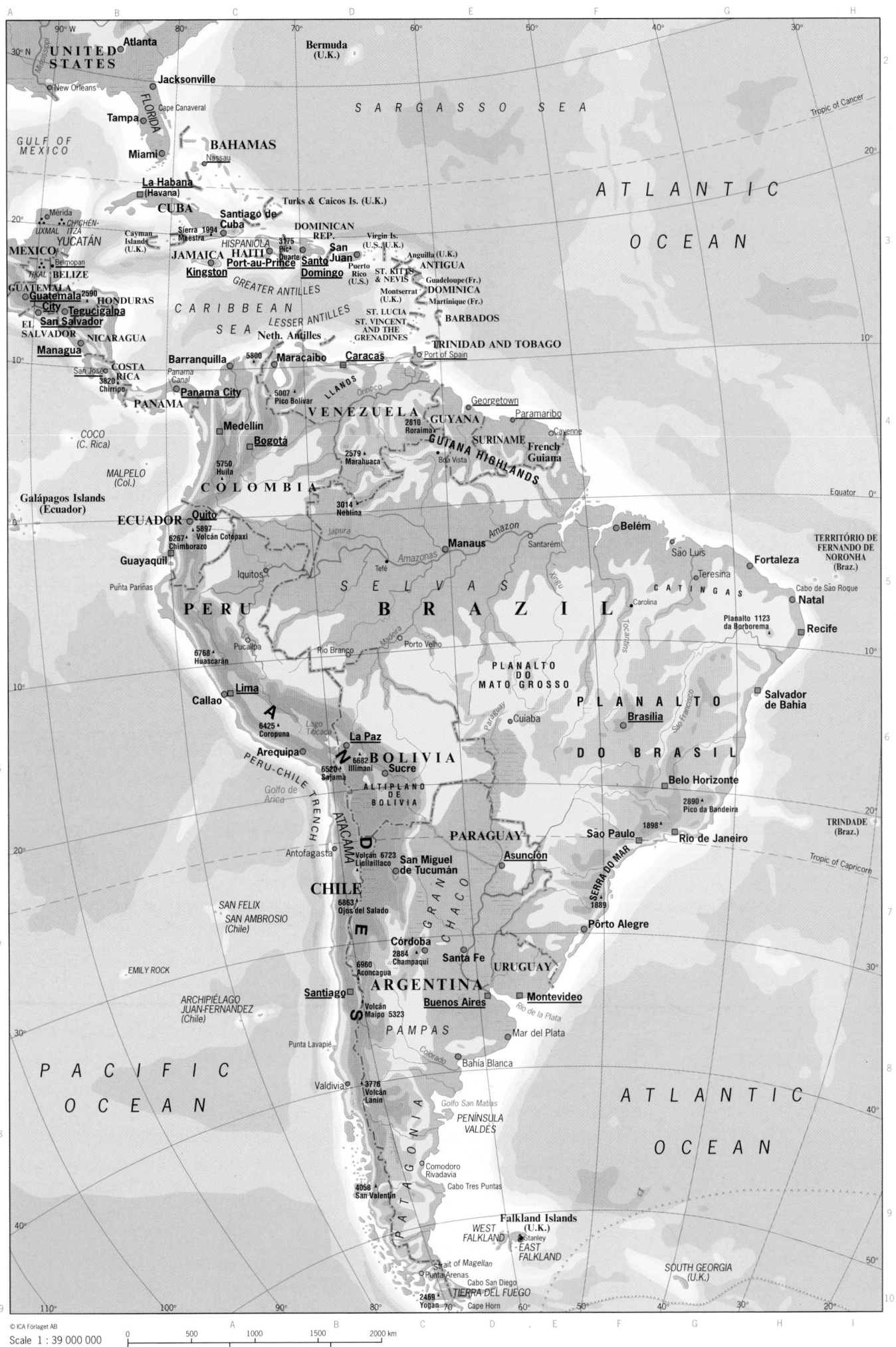

Atlanta
UNITED STATES
New Orleans
Jacksonville
Cape Canaveral
BERMUDA (U.K.)
Tampa
GULF OF MEXICO
BAHAMAS
Miami
Nassau
SARGASSO SEA
La Habana (Havana)
CUBA
Turks & Caicos Is. (U.K.)
Santiago de Cuba
Mérida
CHICHÉN-ITZÁ
UXMAL
YUCATÁN
Cayman Islands (U.K.)
Sierra 1994 Maestra
DOMINICAN REP.
HISPANIOLA
3175 Pico Duarte
Virgin Is. (U.S./U.K.)
ATLANTIC OCEAN
MEXICO
JAMAICA
HAITI
San Juan
Anguilla (U.K.)
ANTIGUA
Tikal
BELIZE
Kingston
Port-au-Prince
Santo Domingo
Puerto Rico (U.S.)
ST. KITTS & NEVIS
Guadeloupe(Fr.)
DOMINICA
Belmopan
GREATER ANTILLES
Montserrat (U.K.)
Martinique (Fr.)
GUATEMALA 2590
HONDURAS
CARIBBEAN SEA
LESSER ANTILLES
ST. LUCIA
ST. VINCENT AND THE GRENADINES
BARBADOS
Guatemala City
Tegucigalpa
San Salvador
EL SALVADOR
NICARAGUA
Neth. Antilles
TRINIDAD AND TOBAGO
Managua
Barranquilla
5800
Maracaibo
Caracas
Port of Spain
COSTA RICA
San José
3820 Chirripó
PANAMA
Panama Canal
Panama City
5007 Pico Bolívar
LLANOS
Orinoco
Georgetown
COCO (C. Rica)
VENEZUELA
GUYANA
Paramaribo
Medellín
2810 Roraima
SURINAME
French Guiana
Cayenne
MALPELO (Col.)
Bogotá
5750 Huila
2579 Marahuaca
Boa Vista
GUIANA HIGHLANDS
Galápagos Islands (Ecuador)
COLOMBIA
3014 Neblina
Equator
TERRITÓRIO DE FERNANDO DE NORONHA (Braz.)
ECUADOR
Quito
5897 Volcán Cotopaxi
6267 Chimborazo
Japurá
Belém
São Luis
Fortaleza
Guayaquil
Manaus
Santarém
Teresina
Puñta Parinas
Iquitos
Amazonas
Tefé
Amazon
CATINGAS
Cabo de São Roque
PERU
SELVAS
BRAZIL
Carolina
Natal
6768 Huascarán
Pucallpa
Rio Branco
Madeira
Porto Velho
Planalto 1123 da Borborema
Recife
Lima
PLANALTO DO MATO GROSSO
Callao
6425 Coropuna
Lago Titicaca
PLANALTO
Salvador de Bahia
Arequipa
La Paz
PERU-CHILE TRENCH
6682 Illimani
BOLIVIA
Sucre
Cuiabá
Brasília
São Francisco
DO BRASIL
Golfo de Arica
6520 Sajama
ALTIPLANO DE BOLIVIA
Belo Horizonte
ATACAMA
2890 Pico da Bandeira
Paraguay
TRINDADE (Braz.)
PARAGUAY
1898
São Paulo
Rio de Janeiro
Antofagasta
Volcán 6723 Llullaillaco
San Miguel de Tucumán
Asunción
SERRA DO MAR
Tropic of Capricorn
SAN FELIX
SAN AMBROSIO (Chile)
CHILE
6863 Ojos del Salado
GRAN CHACO
1889
Pôrto Alegre
Córdoba
2884 Champaquí
Santa Fe
URUGUAY
EMILY ROCK
6960 Aconcagua
ARGENTINA
ARCHIPIÉLAGO JUAN-FERNÁNDEZ (Chile)
Santiago
Volcán Maipo 5323
Buenos Aires
Montevideo
PAMPAS
Mar del Plata
PACIFIC OCEAN
3775 Volcán Lanín
Colorado
Bahía Blanca
Valdivia
Punta Lavapié
PENÍNSULA VALDÉS
Golfo San Matías
ATLANTIC OCEAN
PATAGONIA
Comodoro Rivadavia
Cabo Tres Puntas
4058 San Valentín
Falkland Islands (U.K.)
WEST FALKLAND
Stanley
EAST FALKLAND
Strait of Magellan
Punta Arenas
Cabo San Diego
SOUTH GEORGIA (U.K.)
2469 Yogan
TIERRA DEL FUEGO
Cape Horn

© ICA Förlaget AB
Scale 1 : 39 000 000

0   500   1000   1500   2000 km
0   500   1000 miles

NORTHERN SOUTH AMERICA

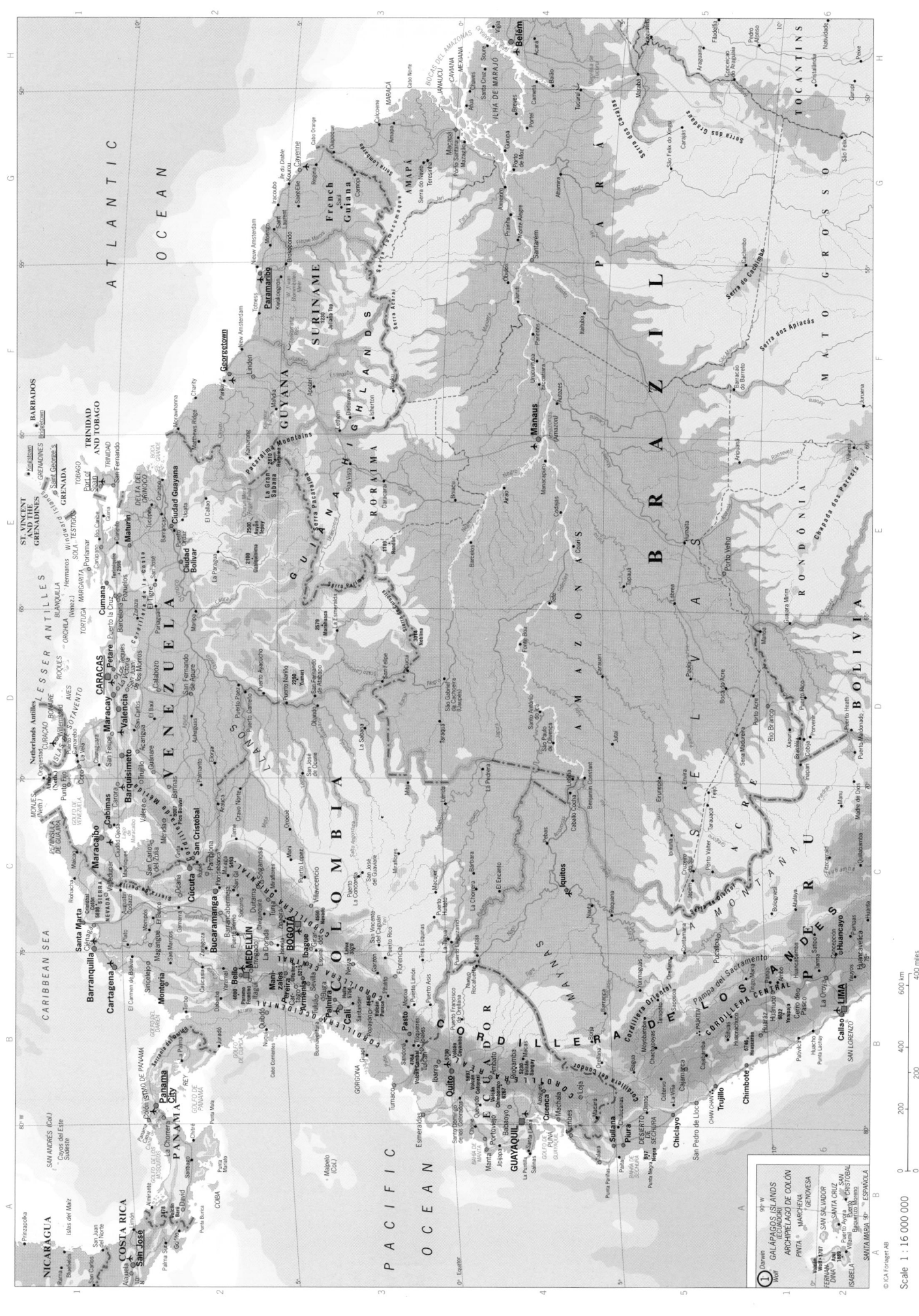

Scale 1 : 16 000 000

© ICA Forlaget AB

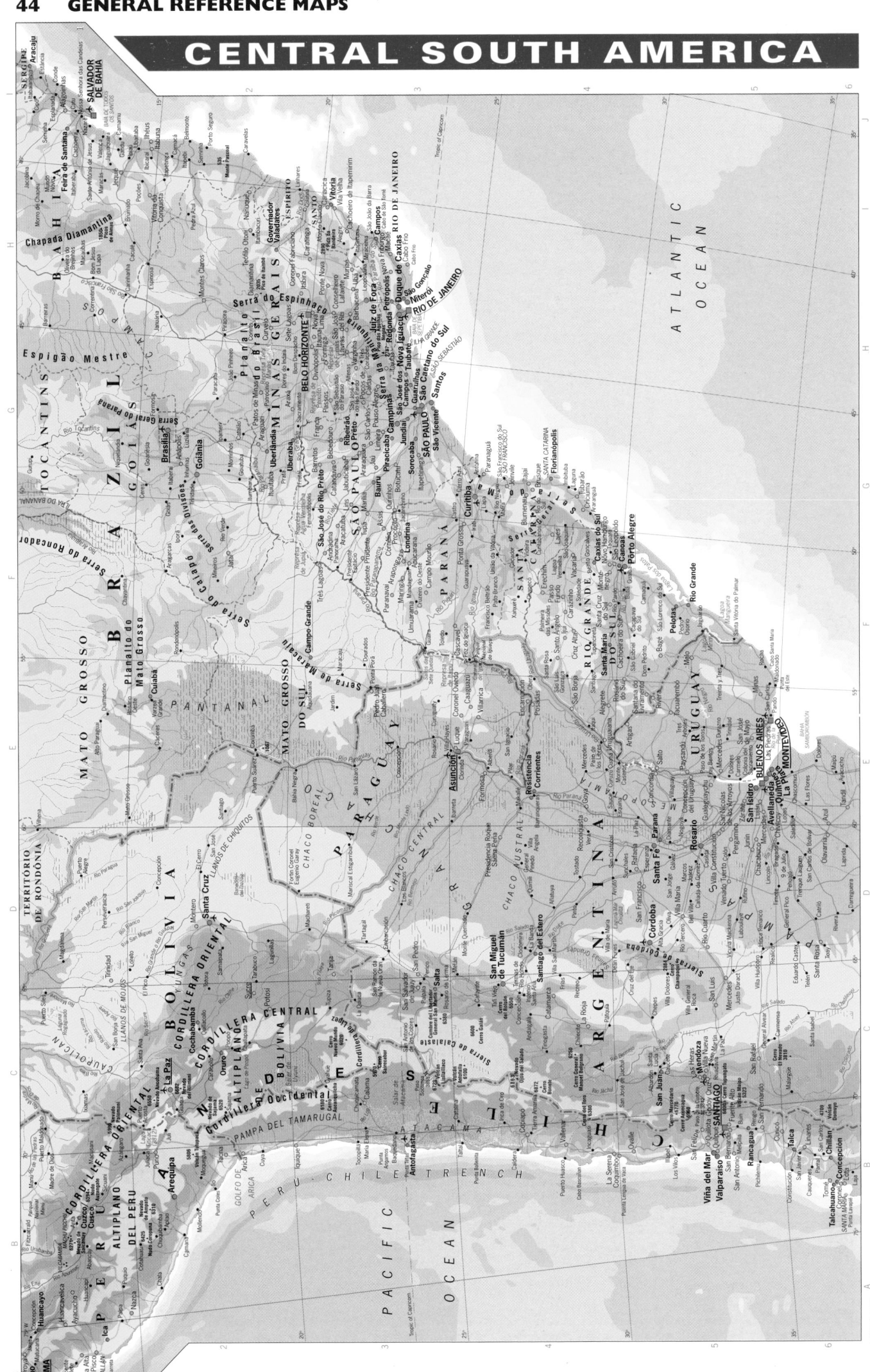
CENTRAL SOUTH AMERICA
ATLANTIC OCEAN
PACIFIC OCEAN
PERU-CHILE TRENCH
BRAZIL
BOLIVIA
PARAGUAY
ARGENTINA
URUGUAY
CHILE
PERU
MATO GROSSO
MINAS GERAIS
SÃO PAULO
BUENOS AIRES
MONTEVIDEO
RIO DE JANEIRO
SANTIAGO
Asunción
La Paz
LIMA
© ICA Forlaget AB
0 200 400 600 km

EAST BRAZIL AND SOUTHERN SOUTH AMERICA

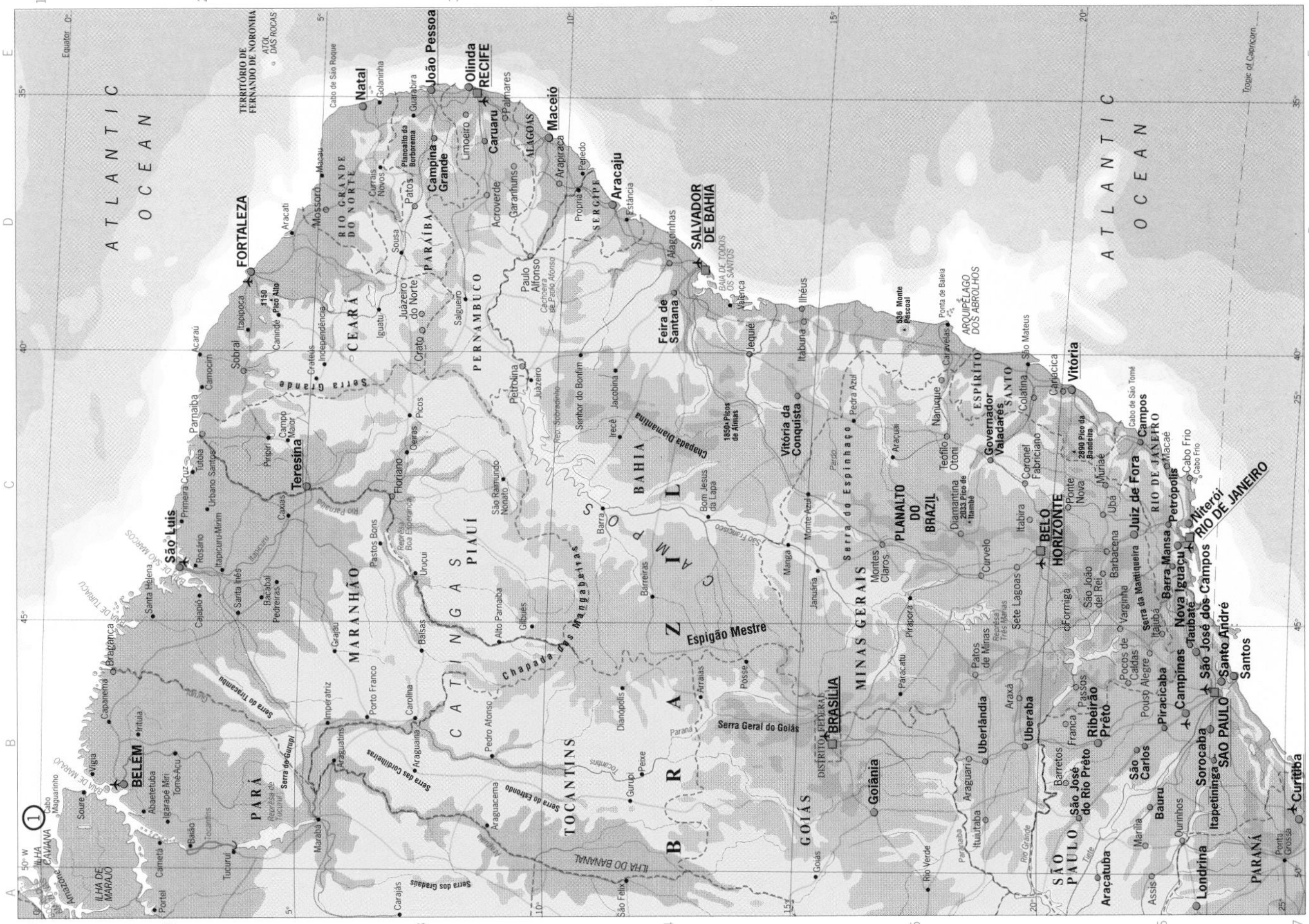

Upper map

ATLANTIC OCEAN

FORTALEZA · **São Luís** · **BELÉM** · **Teresina** · **Natal** · **João Pessoa** · **Olinda** · **RECIFE** · **Maceió** · **Aracaju** · **Caruaru** · **Campina Grande** · **SALVADOR DE BAHIA** · **Feira de Santana** · **Vitória da Conquista** · **Vitória** · **Governador Valadares** · **BELO HORIZONTE** · **BRASÍLIA** · **Goiânia** · **Uberlândia** · **Uberaba** · **Juiz de Fora** · **RIO DE JANEIRO** · **Niterói** · **Petrópolis** · **Campos** · **Barra Mansa** · **Volta Redonda** · **Nova Iguaçu** · **Campinas** · **Piracicaba** · **São José dos Campos** · **SÃO PAULO** · **Santo André** · **Santos** · **Sorocaba** · **Ribeirão Prêto** · **São José do Rio Prêto** · **Bauru** · **Londrina** · **CURITIBA**

TERRITÓRIO DE FERNANDO DE NORONHA · ATOL DAS ROCAS

RIO GRANDE DO NORTE · PARAÍBA · PERNAMBUCO · ALAGOAS · SERGIPE · CEARÁ · PIAUÍ · MARANHÃO · PARÁ · TOCANTINS · GOIÁS · BAHIA · MINAS GERAIS · ESPÍRITO SANTO · SÃO PAULO · PARANÁ

B R A Z I L · CAATINGAS · PLANALTO DO BRAZIL · DISTRITO FEDERAL

Serra da Espinhaço · Serra Geral do Goiás · Espigão Mestre · Chapada das Mangabeiras · Chapada Diamantina

ILHA DE MARAJÓ · ARQUIPÉLAGO DOS ABROLHOS · Cabo Frio · São Monte Pascoal

Scale 1 : 16 000 000
600 miles · 400 · 200 · 0
600 km · 400 · 200 · 0

© ICA Förlaget AB

Equator · Trópico of Capricorn

Lower map

ATLANTIC OCEAN · PACIFIC OCEAN

MONTEVIDEO · **BUENOS AIRES** · **La Plata** · **Mar del Plata** · **Rosario** · **Santa Fe** · **Paraná** · **Córdoba** · **San Juan** · **Mendoza** · **SANTIAGO** · **Valparaíso** · **Viña del Mar** · **Rancagua** · **Talca** · **Chillán** · **Concepción** · **Talcahuano** · **Temuco** · **Valdivia** · **Osorno** · **Puerto Montt** · **Bahía Blanca** · **Neuquén** · **General Roca** · **Comodoro Rivadavia** · **Río Gallegos** · **Punta Arenas**

U R U G U A Y · A R G E N T I N A · C H I L E · PAMPA · PATAGONIA

Santana do Livramento · Bagé · Melo · Minas · Treinta y Tres · Artigas · Salto · Paysandú · Mercedes · Durazno · Colonia · San José de Mayo · Las Piedras

PENÍNSULA VALDÉS · GOLFO SAN MATÍAS · GOLFO DE SAN JORGE · BAHÍA GRANDE · ESTRECHO DE MAGALLANES · TIERRA DEL FUEGO · ISLA GRANDE DE TIERRA DEL FUEGO · Drake Passage

Falkland Islands (U.K.) (ISLAS MALVINAS)
JASON ISLANDS · WEST FALKLAND · EAST FALKLAND · Stanley · Cape Dolphin

Cerro Aconcagua 6960 · Volcán Maipo 5323 · El Revetado 3810 · Nevado Tres Cruces

Sierra de Córdoba · RÍO DE LA PLATA

ARCHIPIÉLAGO DE LOS CHONOS · ARCHIPIÉLAGO GUAYANECO · ARCHIPIÉLAGO REINA ADELAIDA · ISLA WELLINGTON · ISLAS WOLLASTON · ISLA NAVARINO · ISLA DE CHILOÉ · Cabo de Hornos

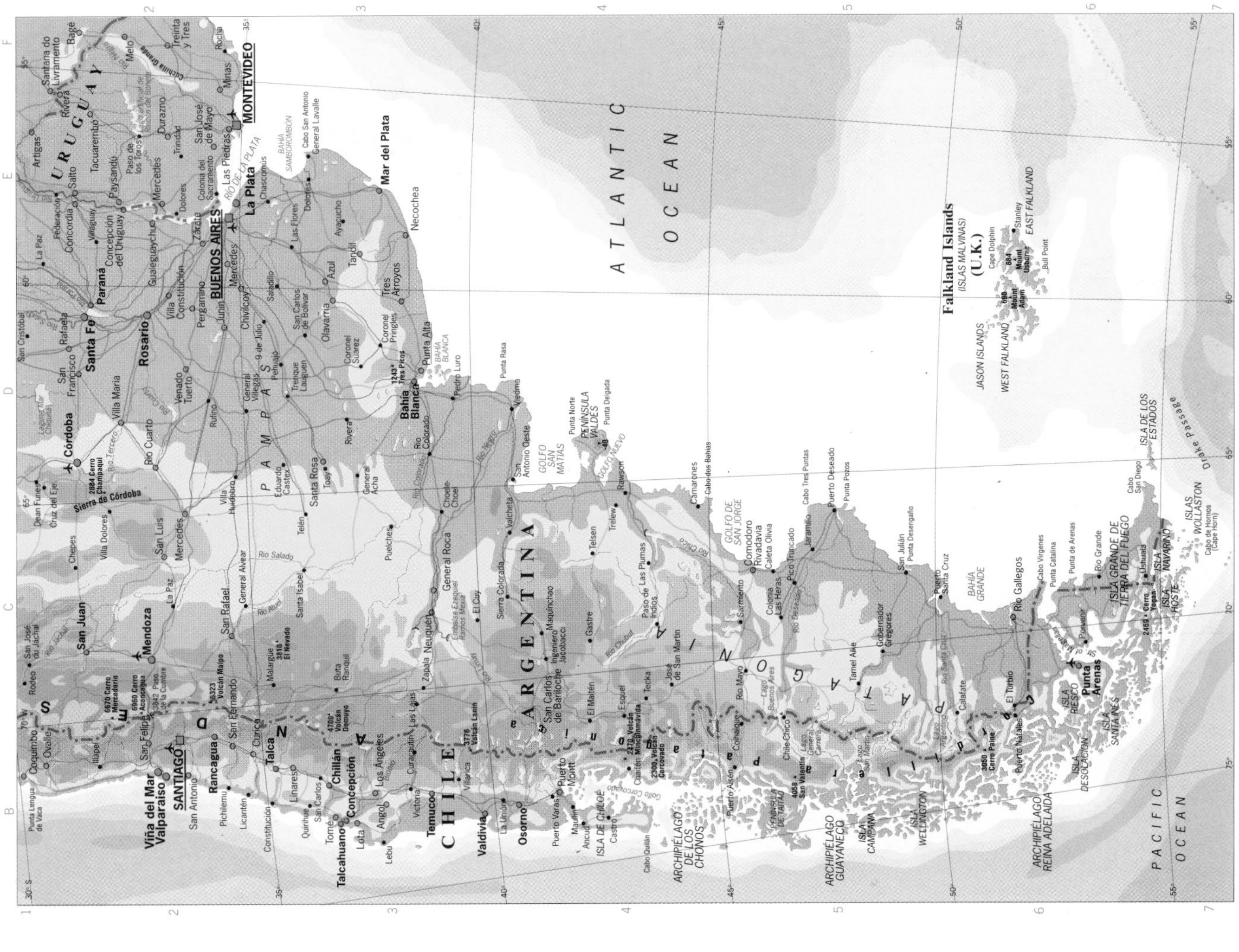

Scale 1 : 16 000 000
600 km · 400 · 200 · 0
400 miles · 200 · 0

© ICA Förlaget AB

POLAR REGIONS

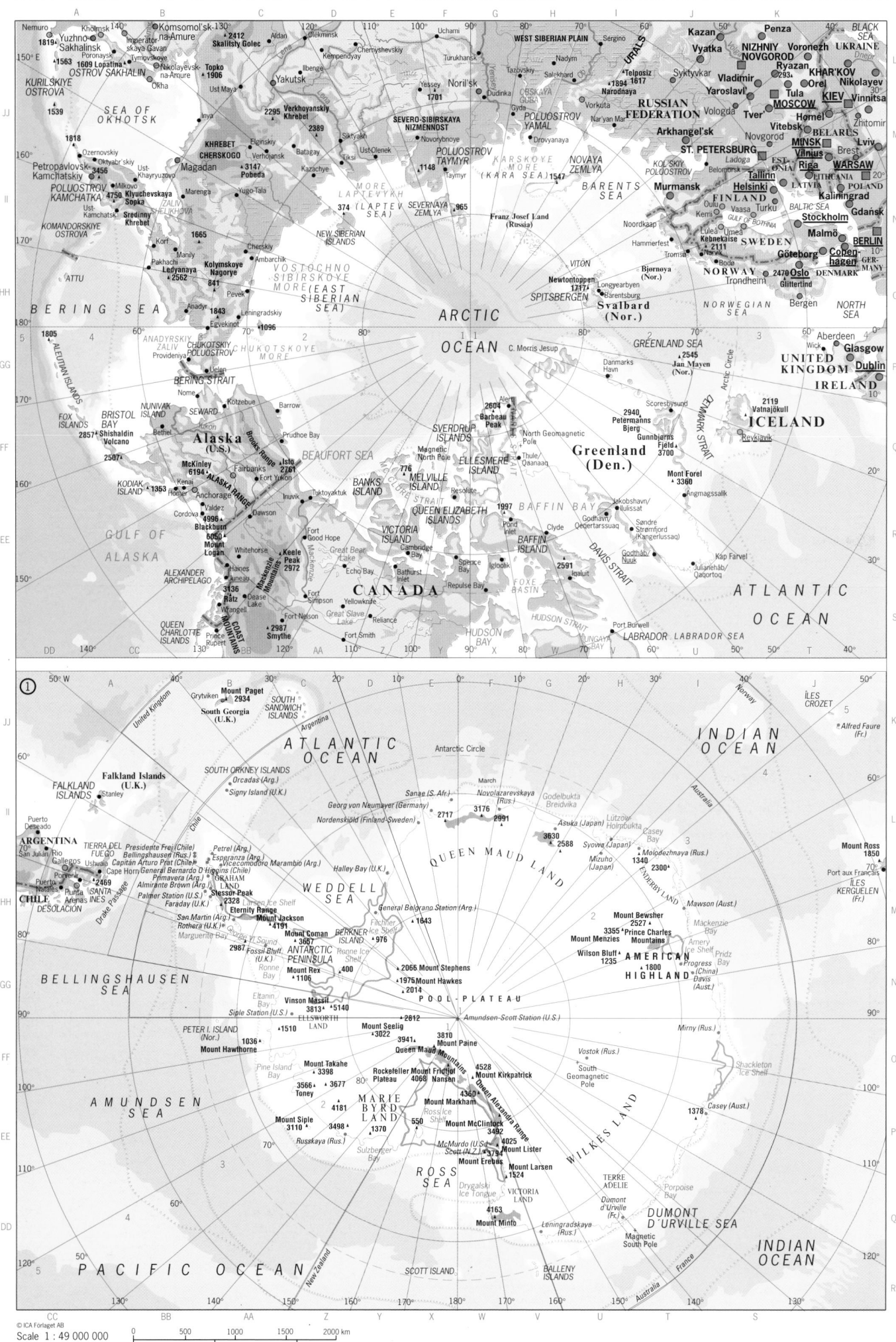

Scale 1 : 49 000 000

SPECIALIST MAP SECTION

North America
Climate	113
Railways and airports	114-115
Skiing	116

United States	117-121
Canada	112-123
Mexico	123
The Caribbean	124-125

South America
Climate	126
Languages	127
South America	127

Europe
Climate	65
Railways and ferries	66-67
Blue Flag beaches	68-69
Skiing	70
Historical	71
National parks	72
Leisure parks	73

United Kingdom	74-78
Ireland	79
Benelux	80
Germany	81-83
France	84-85
Spain	86-87
Portugal	88

Switzerland and Austria	89
Italy	90-91
Greece and Turkey	92-93
Malta and Cyprus	93
Scandinavia	94-95
Central Europe	96
Former Soviet Union	**96-97**

World
Climate	48
Time	49
Health	50
National income	51
Tourist income	51
Sport	52
Driving	53
Airports	54-56
Flight times	57
Cruising	58-59
Heritage sites	60-64
Relief maps	128-136
Appendices	137-140
Index	141-184
Outline maps	X1-X16

Africa
Climate	99
Languages	100
South Africa	100
Egypt	101
Kenya	101
Morocco	101

Tunisia	101
Tanzania	102
Zimbabwe	102
National parks and game reserves	102-103

Rest of Asia
Holy Land	98
Trade routes	98
Climate	104
India	105-106
Sri Lanka	106
Indian Ocean	106
China	107
South-East Asia	108-109
Indonesia	110

Australasia
Australia	111-112
New Zealand	112

Europe and the Former Soviet Union

North America

Rest of Asia

Africa

South America

Australasia

KEY TO MAP SYMBOLS

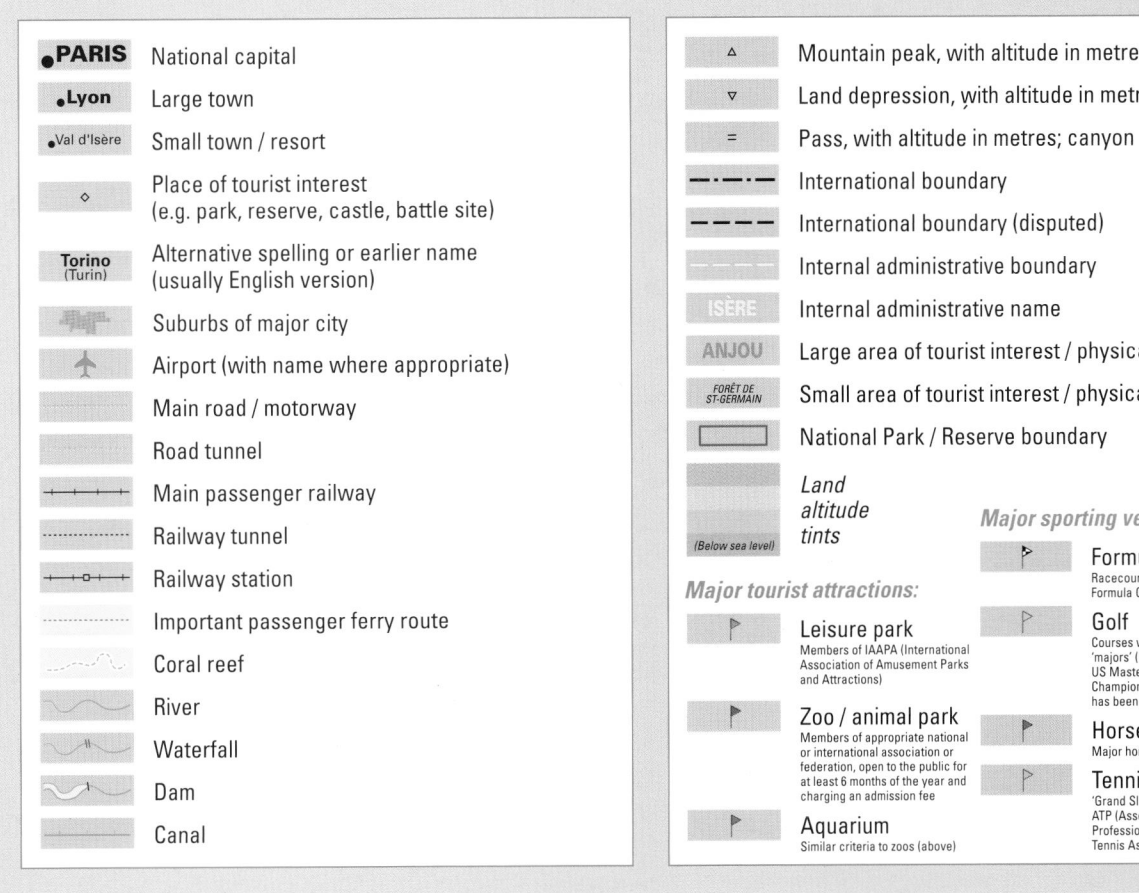

●**PARIS**	National capital
●**Lyon**	Large town
●Val d'Isère	Small town / resort
◇	Place of tourist interest (e.g. park, reserve, castle, battle site)
Torino (Turin)	Alternative spelling or earlier name (usually English version)
	Suburbs of major city
✈	Airport (with name where appropriate)
	Main road / motorway
	Road tunnel
	Main passenger railway
	Railway tunnel
	Railway station
	Important passenger ferry route
	Coral reef
	River
	Waterfall
	Dam
	Canal

△	Mountain peak, with altitude in metres
▽	Land depression, with altitude in metres
=	Pass, with altitude in metres; canyon
	International boundary
	International boundary (disputed)
	Internal administrative boundary
ISÈRE	Internal administrative name
ANJOU	Large area of tourist interest / physical region
FORÊT DE ST-GERMAIN	Small area of tourist interest / physical region
	National Park / Reserve boundary
	Land altitude tints (Below sea level)

Major tourist attractions:

⚐ **Leisure park**
Members of IAAPA (International Association of Amusement Parks and Attractions)

⚐ **Zoo / animal park**
Members of appropriate national or international association or federation, open to the public for at least 6 months of the year and charging an admission fee

⚐ **Aquarium**
Similar criteria to zoos (above)

Major sporting venues:

⚐ **Formula One**
Racecourses which have held a Formula One race since 1990

⚐ **Golf**
Courses where one of the four 'majors' (British Open, US Open, US Masters and US PGA Championship) or the Ryder Cup has been held since 1980

⚐ **Horse racing**
Major horse racecourses

⚐ **Tennis**
'Grand Slam' venues ATP (Association of Tennis Professionals) and WTA (Women's Tennis Association) tour venues

CLIMATE

Legend

Polar: no warm season (warmest month below 10°C)
Ice cap (perpetual frost: all months below 0°C) and tundra (warmest month between 0°C and 10°C)

Cooler humid: rainy climates with severe winters (coldest month below 0°C, warmest month above 10°C)
Subarctic (less than four months over 10°C), continental cool summer (warmest month below 22°C) and continental warm summer (warmest month above 22°C)

Warmer humid: rainy climates with mild winters (coolest month between 0°C and 18°C, warmest month above 10°C)
Marine west coast (warmest month below 22°C), humid subtropical (warmest month above 22°C) and mediterranean (dry season in summer)

Dry Steppe/semi-arid and desert/arid

Tropical humid: rainy climates with no winter (coolest month above 18°C)
Savanna (dry season in either summer or winter) and rainforest (constantly moist or monsoon rain with only a short dry season)

HOURS OF DAYLIGHT AND THE SEASONS

Northern hemisphere

	Northern hemisphere	Southern hemisphere
① Vernal equinox	21 Mar	23 Sep
② Summer solstice (longest day)	21 Jun	21 Dec
③ Autumnal equinox	23 Sep	21 Mar
④ Winter solstice (shortest day)	21 Dec	21 Jun

Dates are approximate

Latitude:
Equator
20°
40°
60°
80°

Excludes twilight, which lasts approximately 20 minutes before sunrise and 20 minutes after sunset at the Equator. This time increases to 30 minutes at 30° N or S and 40 minutes at 50° N or S.

Hours of daylight

WINTER SPRING SUMMER AUTUMN (FALL)

Jan Feb Mar Apr May Jun Jul Aug Sep Oct Nov Dec

Southern hemisphere

SUMMER AUTUMN (FALL) WINTER SPRING

Hours of daylight

Jan Feb Mar Apr May Jun Jul Aug Sep Oct Nov Dec

TEMPERATURE CONVERSION

Celsius	-10	0	10	20	30	40
Fahrenheit	14	32	50	68	86	104

RAINFALL CONVERSION

Millimetres	102	203	305	406	508	610
Inches	4	8	12	16	20	24

The Arctic Circle marks the northernmost point at which the sun can be seen during the winter solstice. Positioned at 66° 30' N.

The Tropics of Cancer and Capricorn are lines of latitude, 23° 28' N and S, where the sun appears directly overhead during the summer solstice in the respective northern and southern hemispheres.

The Antarctic Circle marks the southernmost point at which the sun can be seen during the winter solstice. Positioned at 66° 30' S.

Map labels

ARCTIC OCEAN
PACIFIC OCEAN
INDIAN OCEAN
SOUTHERN OCEAN
NORTH ATLANTIC OCEAN
SOUTH ATLANTIC OCEAN

SUNDAY / MONDAY — INTERNATIONAL DATE LINE

Wrangel I.
EAST SIBERIAN SEA
New Siberian Is.
LAPTEV SEA
KARA SEA
BARENTS SEA
Severnaya Zemlya
Franz Josef Land
Novaya Zemlya
Svalbard
GREENLAND SEA
NORWEGIAN SEA
ARCTIC CIRCLE
LINCOLN SEA
Greenland
Iceland
British Isles
Scandinavia
Lappland
NORTH SEA
North European Plain
Iberia
Atlas Mountains
MED. SEA
Carpathians
Alps
Caucasus
Black Sea
Anatolia
Ural Mountains
WEST SIBERIAN PLAIN
CENTRAL SIBERIAN PLATEAU
L. Ladoga
L. Baikal
Altay
GOBI
Manchurian Plain
STEPPE
Aral Sea
Caspian Sea
L. Balkhash
Tian Shan
Taklimakan
Plateau of Tibet
HIMALAYA
Thar Desert
Deccan
Red Basin
Indochina
Malay Peninsula
Hainan
SOUTH CHINA SEA
PHILIPPINE SEA
Philippine Is.
Formosa
EAST CHINA SEA
Ryukyu Is.
Kyushu
Shikoku
Honshū
Hokkaidō
SEA OF JAPAN
Sakhalin
Kuril Is.
SEA OF OKHOTSK
Kamchatka
Borneo
Celebes
Sumatra
Java
East Indies
New Guinea
Caroline Is.
Mariana (Ladrone) Is.
Micronesia
Melanesia
New Caledonia
Fiji Is.
New Zealand
Tasmania
TASMAN SEA
CORAL SEA
Great Dividing Range
Australia
Nullarbor Plain
Gibson Desert

BAY OF BENGAL
Ceylon
Maldive Is.
ARABIAN SEA
Arabian Peninsula
Red Sea
The Gulf
Chagos Archipelago
Seychelles
Maldive Is.
Mascarene Is.
Madagascar
Cape of Good Hope
Kalahari Desert
Congo Basin
Victoria
Ethiopian Highlands
SAHEL
SAHARA
Libyan Desert
GULF OF GUINEA

Azores
Madeira
Canary Is.
Cape Verde Is.
SOUTH ATLANTIC OCEAN
SCOTIA SEA
South Georgia
Falkland Is.
DRAKE PASSAGE
Cape Horn
Tierra del Fuego
Patagonia
Pampas
Gran Chaco
Mato Grosso
Brazilian Highlands
Selvas
Amazon Basin
Llanos
ANDES / CORDILLERA
Galapagos Is.
Easter I.
Trinidad
West Indies
CARIBBEAN SEA
Cuba
Hispaniola
Bahamas
GULF OF MEXICO
Sierra Madre
Baja California
Appalachians
Great Plains
ROCKY MOUNTAINS
L. Superior
L. Michigan
L. Huron
L. Erie
L. Ontario
Winnipeg
HUDSON BAY
Southampton I.
Baffin I.
BAFFIN BAY
Devon I.
Ellesmere I.
Axel Heiberg I.
Parry Is.
Victoria I.
Banks I.
Great Bear Lake
Great Slave Lake
Labrador
LABRADOR SEA
Long I.
Newfoundland
BEAUFORT SEA
ALASKA
GULF OF ALASKA
Queen Charlotte Is.
Vancouver I.
Aleutian Is.
BERING SEA
Hawaiian Is.
Polynesia

TROPIC OF CANCER
EQUATOR
TROPIC OF CAPRICORN
80° N, 60° N, 40° N, 20° N, 20° S, 40° S

TIME

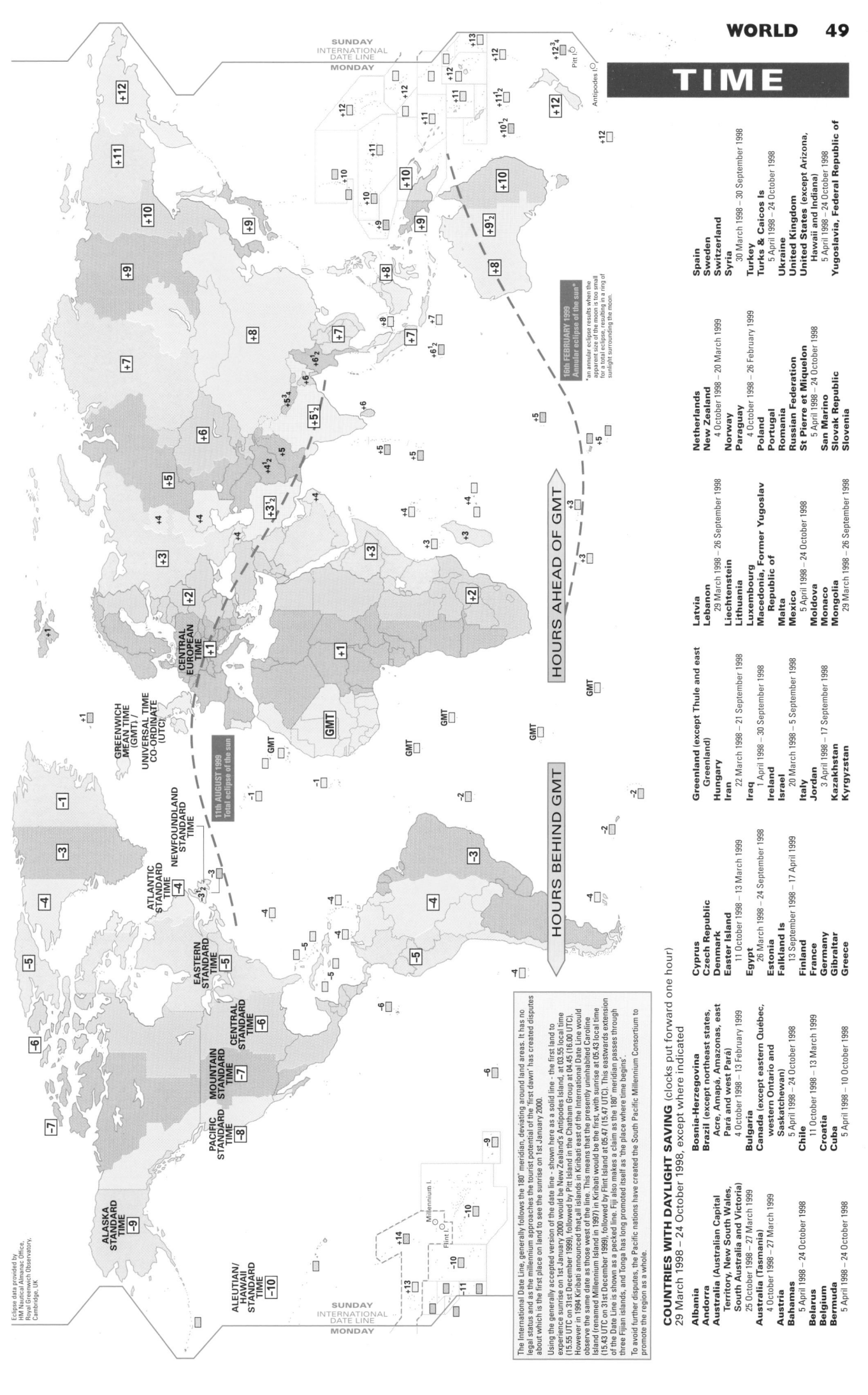

SUNDAY
INTERNATIONAL DATE LINE
MONDAY

+13

+12
+12 +12³₄
Pitt I.
Antipodes I.

+12
+12
+11
+11½
+12

+12
+11
+11
+10½

+11
+10
+10½

+10
+10
+9

+9
+9
+9½

+8
+8

16th FEBRUARY 1999
Annular eclipse of the sun*

*an annular eclipse results when the apparent size of the moon is too small for a total eclipse, resulting in a ring of sunlight surrounding the moon.

+12
+11
+10
+12
+10
+9
+9½

+8
+7
+8
+7
+7
+6½
+6
+5¾
+5½
+5
+5
+5
+5
+5

HOURS AHEAD OF GMT

+6
+6
+4½
+5
+4
+4
+4

+4
+3½
+4
+3
+3
+3

+3
+2
+2
+3

CENTRAL EUROPEAN TIME

+1
+1
+1
+1

GMT

GMT
GMT
GMT
GMT
GMT
GMT

GREENWICH MEAN TIME (GMT) / UNIVERSAL TIME CO-ORDINATE (UTC)

+1

−1

−2
−2
−2

−1

11th AUGUST 1999
Total eclipse of the sun

HOURS BEHIND GMT

NEWFOUNDLAND STANDARD TIME

−1
−3
−4

−3½
−3
−3½

ATLANTIC STANDARD TIME

−3
−4
−4

−4
−4
−4

−5

EASTERN STANDARD TIME

−5
−5

−6

CENTRAL STANDARD TIME

−6
−6

MOUNTAIN STANDARD TIME

−7

PACIFIC STANDARD TIME

−8

−7

−9

−9
−10

+14
Millennium I.
Flint I.

−10

+13

−10
−11

ALASKA STANDARD TIME
−9

ALEUTIAN/ HAWAII STANDARD TIME
−10

SUNDAY
INTERNATIONAL DATE LINE
MONDAY

Eclipse data provided by
HM Nautical Almanac Office,
Royal Greenwich Observatory,
Cambridge, UK

The International Date Line, generally follows the 180° meridian, deviating around land areas. It has no legal status and as the millennium approaches the tourist potential of the 'first dawn' has created disputes about which is the first place on land to see the sunrise on 1st January 2000.

Using the generally accepted version of the date line - shown here as a solid line - the first land to experience sunrise on 1st January 2000 would be New Zealand's Antipodes Island, at 03.55 local time (15.55 UTC on 31st December 1999), followed by Pitt Island in the Chatham Group at 04.45 (16.00 UTC). However in 1994 Kiribati announced that all islands in Kiribati east of the International Date Line would observe the same date as those west of the line. This means that the presently uninhabited Caroline Island (renamed Millennium Island in 1997) in Kiribati would be the first, with sunrise at 05.43 local time (15.43 UTC on 31st December 1999), followed by Flint Island at 05.47 (15.47 UTC). This eastwards extension of the of the Date Line is shown as a pecked line. Fiji also makes a claim as the 180° meridian passes through three Fijian islands, and Tonga has long promoted itself as 'the place where time begins'.

To avoid further disputes, the Pacific nations have created the South Pacific Millennium Consortium to promote the region as a whole.

COUNTRIES WITH DAYLIGHT SAVING (clocks put forward one hour)
29 March 1998 – 24 October 1998, except where indicated

Albania
Andorra
Australia (Australian Capital Territory, New South Wales, South Australia and Victoria)
25 October 1998 – 27 March 1999
Australia (Tasmania)
4 October 1998 – 27 March 1999
Austria
Bahamas
5 April 1998 – 24 October 1998
Belarus
Belgium
Bermuda
5 April 1998 – 24 October 1998

Bosnia-Herzegovina
Brazil (except northeast states, Acre, Amapá, Amazonas, east Pará and west Pará)
4 October 1998 – 13 February 1999
Bulgaria
Canada (except eastern Québec, western Ontario and Saskatchewan)
5 April 1998 – 24 October 1998
Chile
11 October 1998 – 13 March 1999
Croatia
Cuba
5 April 1998 – 10 October 1998

Cyprus
Czech Republic
Denmark
Easter Island
11 October 1998 – 13 March 1999
Egypt
26 March 1998 – 24 September 1998
Estonia
Falkland Is
13 September 1998 – 17 April 1999
Finland
France
Germany
Gibraltar
Greece

Greenland (except Thule and east Greenland)
Hungary
29 March 1998 – 26 September 1998
Iran
22 March 1998 – 21 September 1998
Iraq
1 April 1998 – 30 September 1998
Ireland
Israel
20 March 1998 – 5 September 1998
Italy
Jordan
3 April 1998 – 17 September 1998
Kazakhstan
Kyrgyzstan

Latvia
Lebanon
29 March 1998 – 26 September 1998
Liechtenstein
Lithuania
Luxembourg
Macedonia, Former Yugoslav Republic of
Malta
Mexico
5 April 1998 – 24 October 1998
Moldova
Monaco
Mongolia
29 March 1998 – 26 September 1998

Netherlands
New Zealand
4 October 1998 – 20 March 1999
Norway
Paraguay
4 October 1998 – 26 February 1999
Poland
Portugal
Romania
Russian Federation
St Pierre et Miquelon
5 April 1998 – 24 October 1998
San Marino
Slovak Republic
Slovenia

Spain
Sweden
Switzerland
Syria
30 March 1998 – 30 September 1998
Turkey
Turks & Caicos Is
5 April 1998 – 24 October 1998
Ukraine
United Kingdom
United States (except Arizona, Hawaii and Indiana)
5 April 1998 – 24 October 1998
Yugoslavia, Federal Republic of

HEALTH

MALARIA

The main antimalarial drugs and their side-effects

Chloroquine (CHL). Usually well tolerated. The few people who may experience uncomfortable side-effects, such as gastrointestinal disturbance, may tolerate it better by taking the drug with meals and in divided twice-weekly doses (see above).

Chloroquine + proguanil (C+P). Often causes gastrointestinal upsets (see above).

Mefloquine (MEF). Usually well tolerated. Mild side-effects such as dizziness or gastrointestinal effects may occur for a while during early prophylaxis, but spontaneously resolve. If these side-effects are unacceptable, C+P or DOX can be used instead. Major neurological and psychiatric disorders occur in about one in 10,000 users.

Doxycycline (DOX). Side-effects common. Tablets should always be taken with plenty of fluid, and never taken just prior to lying down.

All prophylactic regimens should begin at least one week before travel, in order to deal with possible side-effects before departure, which can occasionally be severe. Special caution should be exercised by pregnant women. All drugs should be continued for four weeks after the last possible exposure to infection.

In many countries of the Americas and South-East Asia (for example, China, Indonesia, Malaysia, Mexico, Myanmar and Philippines), malaria is largely confined to rural areas not visited by most travellers. Any travel to these areas is most often during day-time when there is minimal risk of exposure. Chemoprophylaxis is recommended only for those travellers who will be exposed outdoors during the evening or night-time in rural areas. Although chemoprophylaxis is not recommended in areas with very limited risk, travellers should be advised to use insect repellents and other personal protection measures.

Travellers are reminded that protection from biting mosquitoes is the first line of defence against malaria, and no antimalarial prophylactic regimen gives complete protection.

Malaria zones:

A Risk generally low and seasonal, no risk in many areas (for example urban areas). *Plasmodium falciparum* absent or sensitive to chloroquine.

Recommended prophylaxis:
Chloroquine, or (in case of very low risk), no prophylaxis, with chloroquine as a stand-by when prompt medical attention unavailable.

B Low risk in most areas. Chloroquine alone will protect against *P. vivax*. Chloroquine with proguanil will give some protection against *P. falciparum* and may alleviate the disease if it occurs despite prophylaxis.

Recommended prophylaxis:
Chloroquine + proguanil *or* chloroquine alone (if proguanil unavailable) *or* in the case of very low risk), no prophylaxis.

C In Africa, risk high except in some high-altitude areas. In Asia and America, risk low in most areas except in the Amazon basin (colonisation and mining areas), where the risk is high. Resistance to sulfadoxine-pyrimethamine is common in Asia, but variable in America. It is effective in most of Africa.

Recommended prophylaxis:
Mefloquine *or* chloroquine + proguanil, except in the border areas Cambodia/Myanmar/Thailand, where doxycycline is recommended.

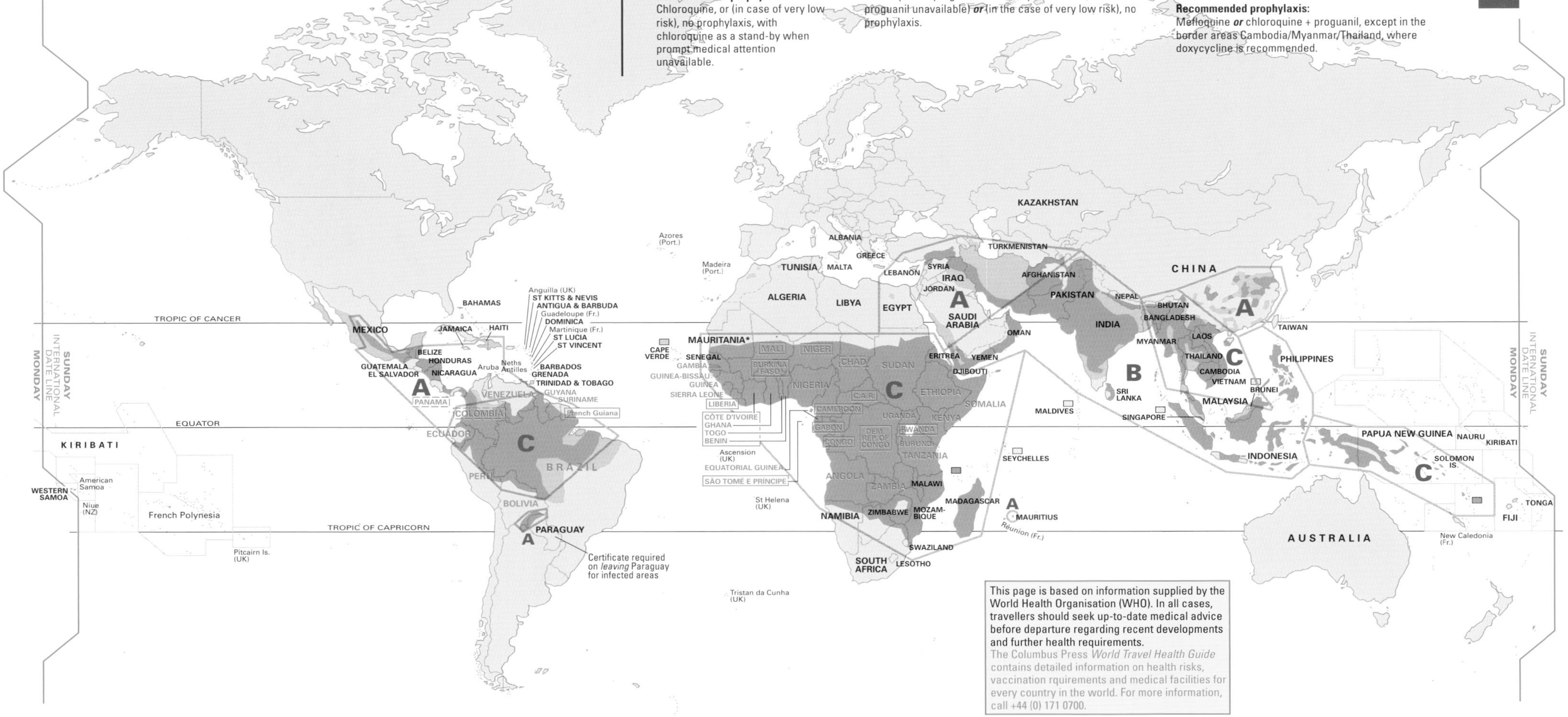

This page is based on information supplied by the World Health Organisation (WHO). In all cases, travellers should seek up-to-date medical advice before departure regarding recent developments and further health requirements.

The Columbus Press World Travel Health Guide contains detailed information on health risks, vaccination requirements and medical facilities for every country in the world. For more information, call +44 (0) 171 171 0700.

Legend

- Areas where malaria transmission occurs
- Areas with limited risk
- Areas in which malaria has disappeared, been eradicated or never existed

YELLOW FEVER

SUDAN

The yellow fever endemic zones cover areas of Africa and South America. Countries named in red type are either fully within a zone or have part of their area affected by it. Countries only partially within the yellow fever zones are:

Africa: southern parts of Mali, Niger, Chad and Sudan; all of Somalia except the northwest; far west of Zambia; all of Democratic Republic of Congo except the far south are regarded as endemic zones.

South America: all of Colombia except the southwest; eastern parts of Ecuador, Peru, Bolivia except the west; all of Brazil except the eastern coastal states are regarded as endemic zones.

EGYPT

Countries named in **black type** on the map require an *international certificate of vaccination against yellow fever* from travellers arriving from a yellow fever endemic zone.

All countries where yellow fever is endemic (marked in red type: see left) also require the certificate if travelling from an endemic area, with the exception of Colombia, Panama, Venezuela and Zambia, where no certificate is required.

Countries marked with an asterisk (*) require yellow fever certificates from those arriving from non-infected countries if they are staying for more than two weeks. Travellers should seek advice as above before entering the country by contacting the relevant embassies or telephoning the Travellers Healthline on 0891 224100 (in UK only).

NIGER

Countries marked with a box require a yellow fever vaccination certificate from *all* travellers, whether they are arriving from an infected area or not. Due to the risks involved, pregnant women and children under one year of age (or in some cases six to nine months of age) usually do not require a yellow fever certificate. However, those travelling with children should seek advice before entering the country by contacting the relevant embassies or telephoning the Travellers Healthline on 0891 224100 (in UK only).

CHAD

A dashed box indicates the country recommends yellow fever vaccinations for all travellers, but this is not a condition of entry.

Certificate required on *leaving* Paraguay for infected areas

NATIONAL INCOME

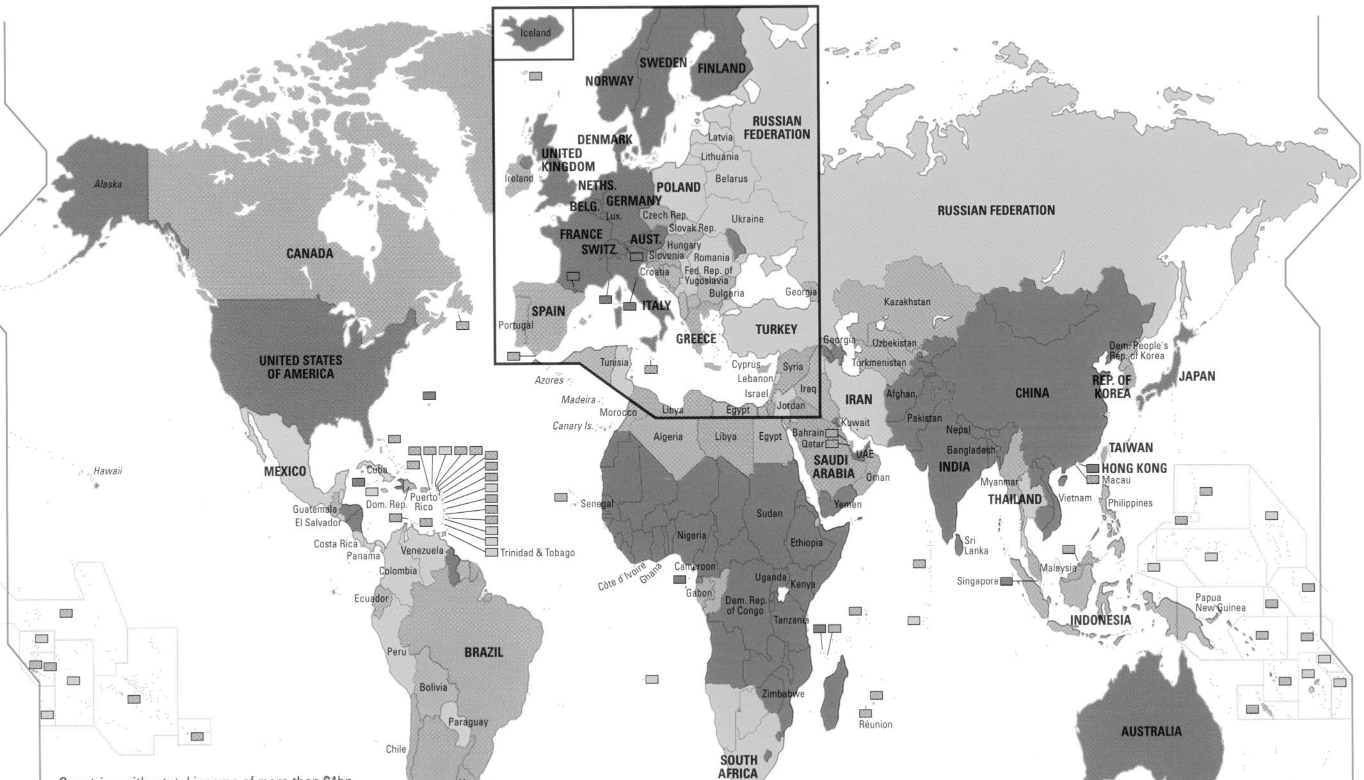

Iceland
SWEDEN FINLAND
NORWAY
RUSSIAN FEDERATION
Latvia
DENMARK Lithuania
UNITED POLAND Belarus
KINGDOM
Ireland NETHS. GERMANY
BELG. Czech Rep. Ukraine
Lux. Slovak Rep.
FRANCE AUST. Hungary
SWITZ. Slovenia Romania
Croatia Fed. Rep. of
SPAIN Yugoslavia
Portugal ITALY Bulgaria Georgia
GREECE TURKEY

Alaska

CANADA

RUSSIAN FEDERATION

Kazakhstan

Dem People's
Rep. of Korea
Uzbekistan JAPAN
Turkmenistan CHINA REP. OF
Georgia KOREA
Cyprus Syria
Tunisia Lebanon Iraq IRAN Afghan.
Azores Israel Jordan Pakistan TAIWAN
Madeira Libya Egypt Kuwait Nepal HONG KONG
Morocco Bahrain Bangladesh Macau
Canary Is. Qatar INDIA
Algeria Libya Egypt SAUDI UAE THAILAND Myanmar Vietnam
ARABIA Oman Philippines
Senegal Yemen Sri
Nigeria Sudan Lanka Singapore Malaysia
Ethiopia Papua
Côte d'Ivoire Cameroon New Guinea
Ghana Uganda Kenya
Gabon Dem. Rep. INDONESIA
of Congo Tanzania

Hawaii

MEXICO

Cuba
Guatemala Puerto
El Salvador Dom. Rep. Rico
Costa Rica Trinidad & Tobago
Panama Venezuela
Colombia
Ecuador

Peru BRAZIL

Bolivia

Paraguay AUSTRALIA

Chile

Zimbabwe Réunion

SOUTH
AFRICA

ARGENTINA New
Uruguay Zealand

Countries with a total income of more than $4bn
in 1995 are named on the map.
Those with an income of over $100bn are shown
in **BOLD CAPITALS**.

Statistics for Portugal include Azores and
Madeira, statistics for Spain include Canary Is.
and statistics for US include Alaska and Hawaii.

Source: The Economist.

Income per capita, 1996

■ US$17,000 and over	■ US$1,500 – $3,499
■ US$9,000 – $16,999	■ US$700 – $1,499
■ US$3,500 – $8,999	■ Less than US$700	□ No data available

INCOME FROM TOURISM

Iceland

Sweden
Norway Finland
Estonia
Denmark RUSSIAN
UNITED Lithuania FEDERATION
KINGDOM
IRELAND NETHS. GERMANY POLAND
BELG. CZECH REP
Lux.
FRANCE AUST. Slovak Rep.
SWITZ. HUNGARY
Slovenia Romania
Monaco Croatia
SPAIN San ITALY Bulgaria
PORT. Marino GREECE TURKEY
Tunisia
Malta Cyprus Syria
Lebanon Iraq

Alaska

CANADA

RUSSIAN FEDERATION

Bermuda
Azores
Madeira
Morocco Israel Iran
Canary Is. Egypt Jordan
Bahrain Rep. of
Algeria Egypt Qatar Pakistan Korea Japan
Saudi UAE
Bahamas Arabia Oman Nepal
US Virgin Is. British Virgin Is. CHINA
Cayman Is. St Maarten Taiwan
Cuba Antigua & Barbuda India HONG KONG
Jamaica Guadeloupe MACAU
Guatemala Hond. Puerto Martinique THAILAND Northern
El Salvador Dom. Rep. Rico St Lucia Eritrea Vietnam Mariana Is.
Nicaragua Aruba Barbados Cambodia Philippines
Costa Rica Curaçao Senegal Guam
Panama Venezuela Trinidad & Tobago Nigeria Sri Brunei
Colombia Lanka
Ecuador Côte d'Ivoire MALAYSIA
Ghana Maldives SINGAPORE
Uganda Kenya
Peru INDONESIA

Hawaii

MEXICO

Bolivia

Brazil Tanzania Fiji

Paraguay Zambia Mauritius AUSTRALIA

Zimbabwe Réunion
Chile Namibia Botswana
Swaziland
Uruguay South
ARGENTINA Africa New
Zealand

Countries with arrivals of more than 200,000 tourists
from abroad in 1996 are named on the map.
Those with over 4 million arrivals are shown
in **BOLD CAPITALS**.

Statistics for Portugal include Azores and Madeira,
statistics for Spain include Canary Is. and statistics
for US include Alaska and Hawaii.

*Excluding international transport.

Source: World Tourism Organisation.

International tourism receipts*, 1996

■ US$6,000 million and over	■ US$100m – $499m
■ US$2,000m – $5,999m	■ US$10m – $99m
■ US$500m – $1,999m	■ Less than US$10m	□ No data available

SPORT

SUMMER OLYMPICS

Shown on map: dates and venues of all Olympic Games

The first modern Olympic Games, founded by Frenchman Baron de Coubertin, were held at Athens in 1896. They are held every four years. An extra Olympics were held in 1906 to celebrate the tenth anniversary of the 1896 games. The next Summer Olympics are due to be held at Sydney in the year 2000 and at Athens in 2004.

WINTER OLYMPICS

Shown on map: dates and venues of all Winter Olympics

The first separate Winter Games took place in 1924 at Chamonix, France. The games originally took place in the same year as the Summer Olympics, but beginning in 1994, are now held in between the Summer Games. The next Winter Olympics are due to be held at Salt Lake City, Utah in 2002.

COMMONWEALTH GAMES

Shown on map: dates and venues of all Games

Originally the British Empire Games and first held in 1930 at Hamilton, Ontario. Renamed the British Empire and Commonwealth Games in 1954, the British Commonwealth Games in 1970 and the Commonwealth Games in 1978. Held every four years, the next games are due to be held at Kuala Lumpur, Malaysia in 1998.

WORLD ATHLETICS CHAMPIONSHIPS

Shown on map: dates and venues of all Championships

The World Athletics Championships were first held in Helsinki in 1983, and at four-year intervals until 1991. They are now held every two years. The next championships are due to be held at Valencia, Spain in 1999.

FOOTBALL WORLD CUP

Shown on map: all World Cups, indicating date and country, and venue for the final

Association Football's premier event. Brazil kept the Jules Rimet Trophy after winning it for the third time in 1970. The teams now compete for the FIFA World Cup. Held every four years, the next competition is in France in 1998. Japan and the Republic of Korea are due to co-host the event in 2002.

RUGBY UNION WORLD CUP

Shown on map: all World Cups, indicating date and country, and venue for the final

The first Rugby Union World Cup was held in 1987 and is now held every four years, with the next competition in Wales in 1999.

CRICKET WORLD CUP

Shown on map: all World Cups, indicating date and country, and venue for the final

The venue of the first Cricket World Cup in 1975 was England. Played every 4-5 years, it was not until 1987 that the competition was held outside England, but the next World Cup in 1999 will again see England as host.

WORLD CUP FINALS: RESULTS

FOOTBALL

1930	Uruguay 4	Argentina 2
1934	Italy 2	Czechoslovakia 1
1938	Italy 4	Hungary 2
1950	Uruguay 2	Brazil 1
1954	F.R. of Germany 3	Hungary 2
1958	Brazil 5	Sweden 2
1962	Brazil 3	Czechoslovakia 1
1966	England 4	F.R. of Germany 2
1970	Brazil 4	Italy 1
1974	F.R. of Germany 2	Netherlands 1
1978	Argentina 3	Netherlands 1
1982	Italy 3	F.R. of Germany 1
1986	Argentina 3	F.R. of Germany 2
1990	F.R. of Germany 1	Argentina 0
1994	Brazil 0	Italy 0
	(Brazil won 3-2 on penalties)	
1998	France 3	Brazil 0

RUGBY UNION

1987	New Zealand 29	France 9
1991	Australia 12	England 6
1995	South Africa 15	New Zealand 12

CRICKET

1975	West Indies (291-8) beat	Australia (274) by 17 runs
1979	West Indies (286-9) beat	England (194) by 92 runs
1983	India (183) beat	West Indies (140) by 43 runs
1987	Australia (253-5) beat	England (246-8) by 7 runs
1992	Pakistan (249-6) beat	England (227) by 22 runs
1996	Sri Lanka (245-3) beat	Australia (241) by 7 wickets

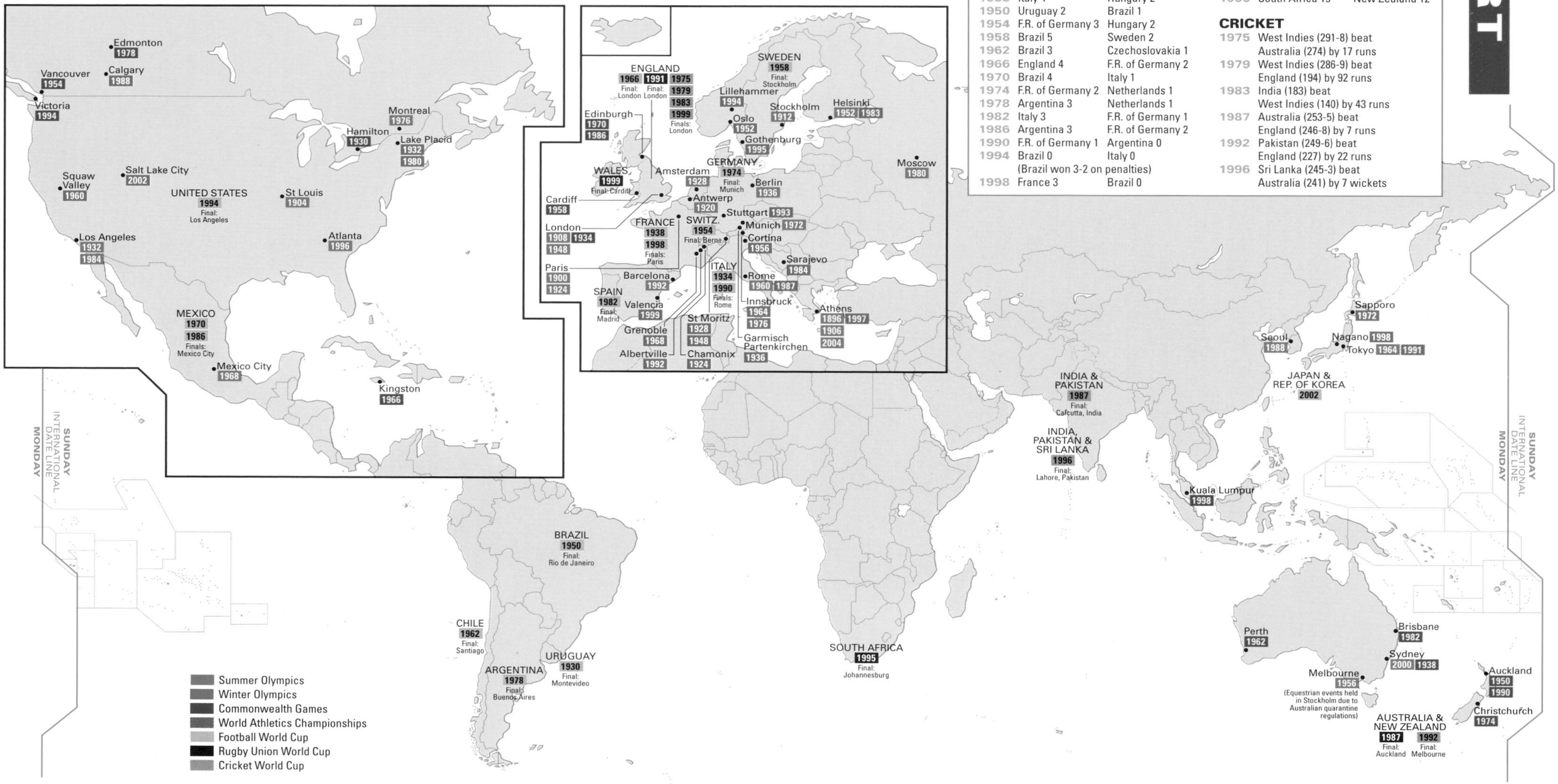

SUNDAY INTERNATIONAL DATE LINE MONDAY

SUNDAY INTERNATIONAL DATE LINE MONDAY

Map labels

Auckland 1950 1990
Christchurch 1974
Brisbane 1982
Sydney 2000 1938
AUSTRALIA & NEW ZEALAND
Final: Auckland 1987 / Final: Melbourne 1992
Melbourne 1956
(Equestrian events held in Stockholm due to Australian quarantine regulations)
Perth 1962

Sapporo 1972
Nagano 1998
Tokyo 1964 1991
Seoul 1988
JAPAN & REP. OF KOREA 2002
Kuala Lumpur 1998

INDIA & PAKISTAN 1987
Final: Calcutta, India
INDIA, PAKISTAN & SRI LANKA 1996
Final: Lahore, Pakistan

SOUTH AFRICA 1995
Final: Johannesburg

Moscow 1980
Helsinki 1952 1983
Final: Stockholm
SWEDEN 1958
Stockholm 1912
Gothenburg 1995
Lillehammer 1994
Oslo 1952
GERMANY 1974
Final: Munich
Berlin 1936
Antwerp 1920
Stuttgart 1993
Munich 1972
Cortina 1956
Sarajevo 1984
Athens 1896 1997 1906 2004
Innsbruck 1964 1976
Rome 1960 1987
Final: Rome
Garmisch Partenkirchen 1936
St Moritz 1928 1948
Chamonix 1924
SWITZ. 1954
Final: Berne
ITALY 1934 1990
Finals: Rome
Amsterdam 1928
Edinburgh 1970 1986
ENGLAND 1966 1991 1975 1979
Final: London 1983 1999
Finals: London
WALES 1999
Final: Cardiff
FRANCE 1938 1998
Finals: Paris
Barcelona 1992
Valencia 1999
Grenoble 1968
Albertville 1992
SPAIN 1982
Final: Madrid
Cardiff 1958
London 1908 1934 1948
Paris 1900 1924

Edmonton 1978
Calgary 1988
Vancouver 1954
Victoria 1994
Squaw Valley 1960
Los Angeles 1932 1984
Salt Lake City 2002
St Louis 1904
UNITED STATES 1994 1986
Final: Los Angeles
Atlanta 1996
Montreal 1976
Lake Placid 1932 1980
Hamilton 1930
Kingston 1966
MEXICO 1970 1986
Final: Mexico City
Mexico City 1968

BRAZIL 1950
Final: Rio de Janeiro
URUGUAY 1930
Final: Montevideo
ARGENTINA 1978
Final: Buenos Aires
CHILE 1962
Final: Santiago

Legend
- Summer Olympics
- Winter Olympics
- Commonwealth Games
- World Athletics Championships
- Football World Cup
- Rugby Union World Cup
- Cricket World Cup

DRIVING

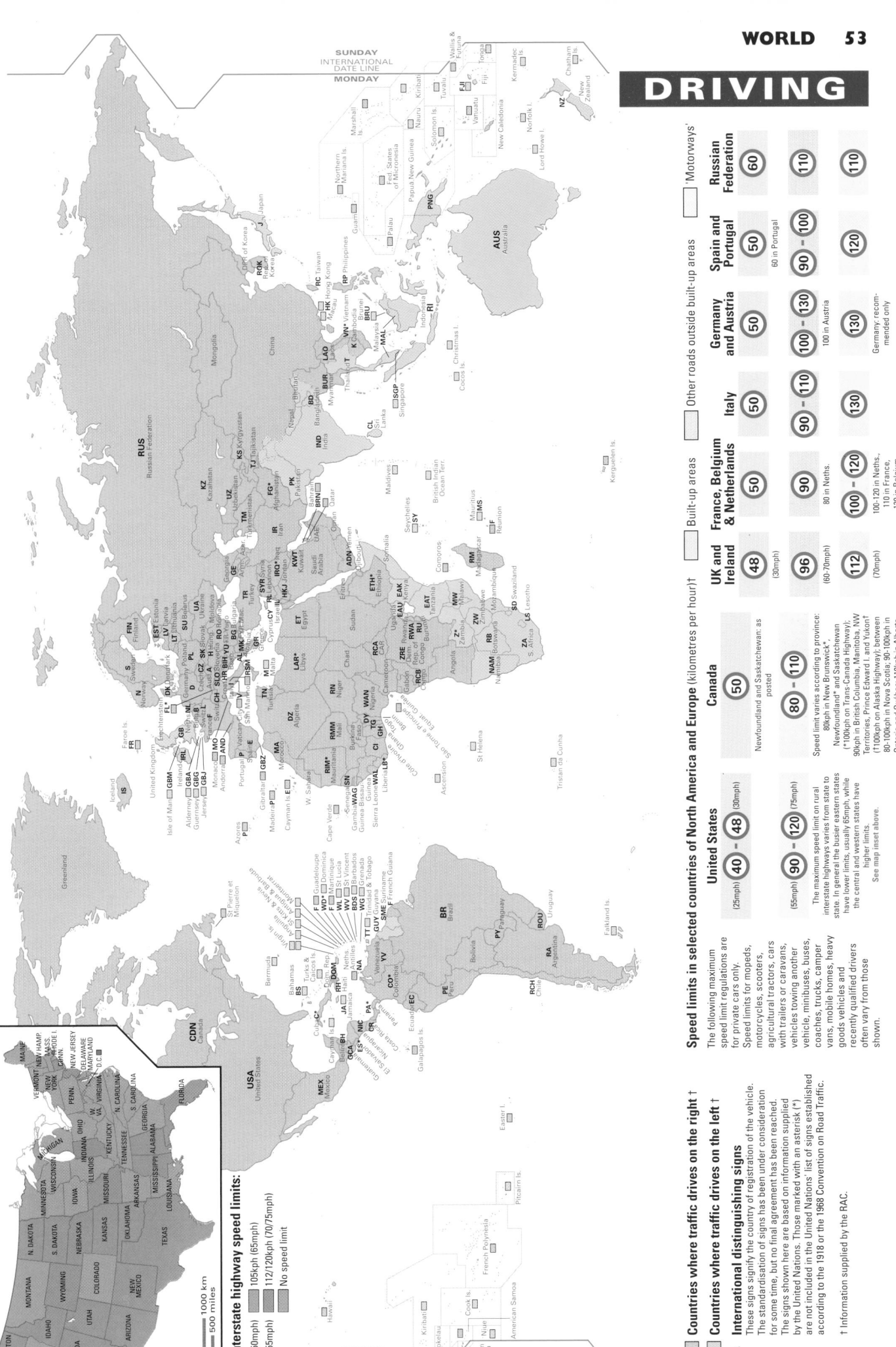

Speed limits in selected countries of North America and Europe (kilometres per hour)†

	Motorways¹	'Motorways'	Other roads outside built-up areas	Built-up areas
Russian Federation			110	60
Spain and Portugal	110	100 - 100	90 - 100	50 (60 in Portugal)
Germany and Austria	120	130 (Germany: recommended only)	100 - 130 (100 in Austria)	50
Italy	130		90 - 110	50
France, Belgium & Netherlands	100 - 120 (100-120 in Neths, 110 in France, 120 in Belgium)		90 (80 in Neths.)	50
UK and Ireland	112 (70mph)		96 (60-70mph)	48 (30mph)

Canada 50

Newfoundland and Saskatchewan: as posted

80 - 110

Speed limit varies according to province: 80kph in New Brunswick*, Newfoundland* and Saskatchewan (*100kph on Trans-Canada Highway); 90kph in British Columbia, Manitoba, NW Territories, Prince Edward I. and Yukon† (†100kph on Alaska Highway); between 80-100kph in Nova Scotia; 90-100kph in Ontario and Québec; 110kph in Alberta.

United States

(25mph) 40 - 48 (30mph)

(55mph) 90 - 120 (75mph)

The maximum speed limit on rural interstate highways varies from state to state. In general the busier eastern states have lower limits, usually 65mph, while the central and western states have higher limits.

See map inset above.

The following maximum speed limit regulations are for private cars only. Speed limits for mopeds, motorcycles, scooters, agricultural tractors, cars with trailers or caravans, vehicles towing another vehicle, minibuses, buses, coaches, trucks, camper vans, mobile homes, heavy goods vehicles and recently qualified drivers often vary from those shown.

Countries where traffic drives on the right †

Countries where traffic drives on the left †

International distinguishing signs

USA These signs signify the country of registration of the vehicle. The standardisation of signs has been under consideration for some time, but no final agreement has been reached. The signs shown here are based on information supplied by the United Nations. Those marked with an asterisk (*) are not included in the United Nations' list of signs established according to the 1918 or the 1968 Convention on Road Traffic.

† Information supplied by the RAC.

US rural interstate highway speed limits:

- 80kph (50mph)
- 90kph (55mph)
- 105kph (65mph)
- 112/120kph (70/75mph)
- No speed limit

ALASKA
HAWAII

1000 km
500 miles

AIRPORTS

MAP A

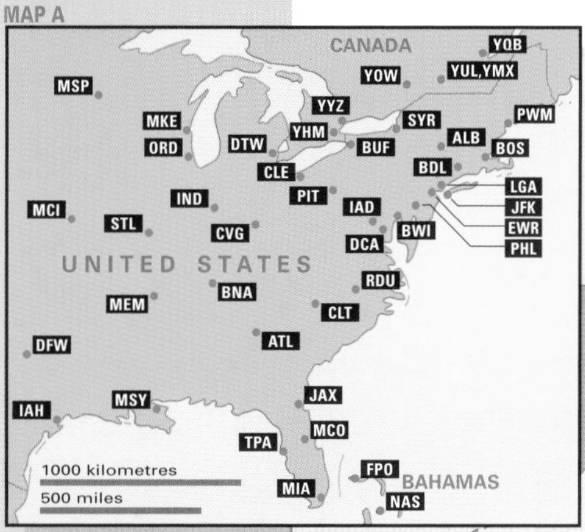

The world's main airports are shown here, together with their international three-letter code.

Where cities have more than one airport, the individual airport codes are used. For example, New York City code is NYC, but the airport codes are:

John F. Kennedy	JFK
LaGuardia	LGA
Newark International	EWR

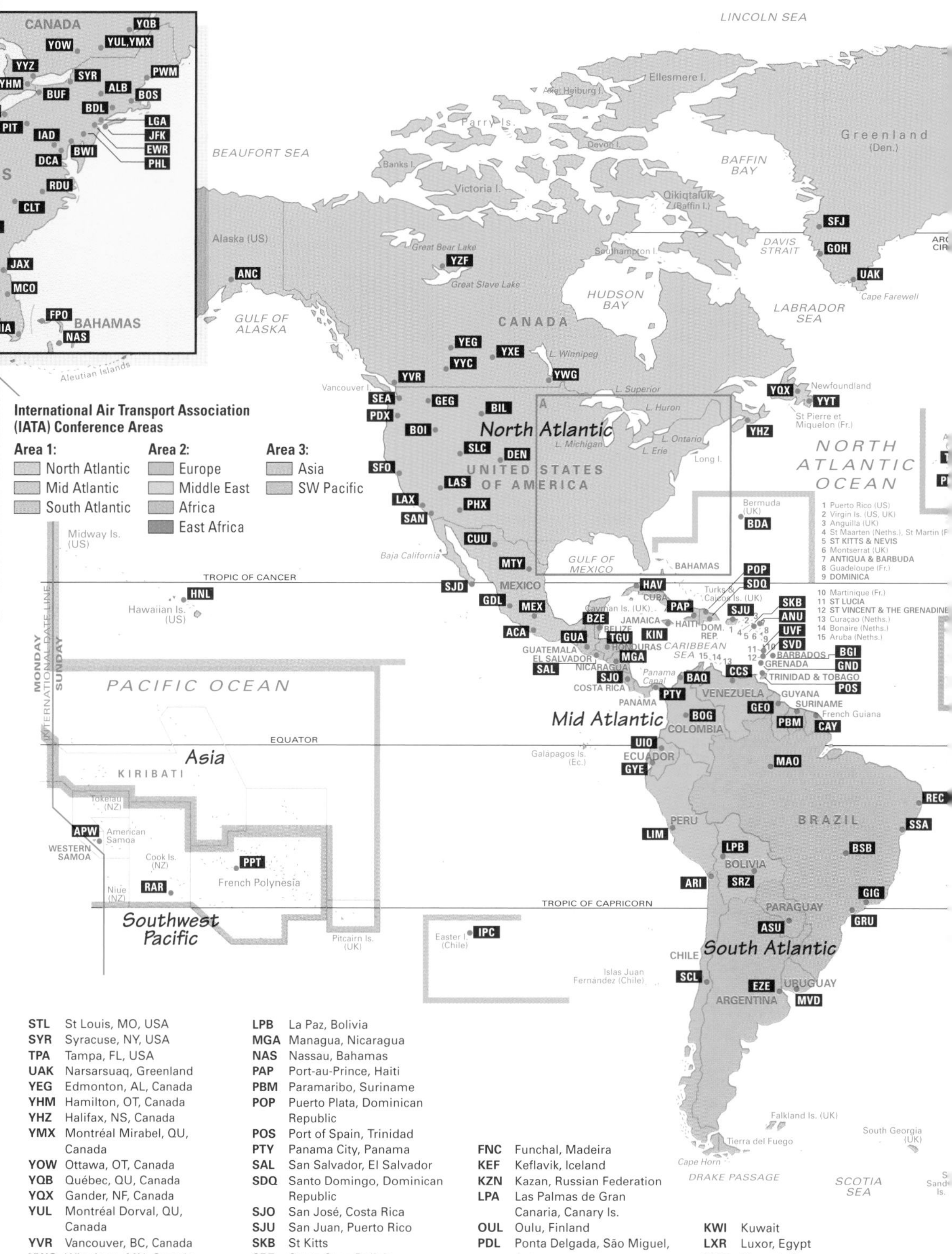

International Air Transport Association (IATA) Conference Areas

Area 1:
- North Atlantic
- Mid Atlantic
- South Atlantic

Area 2:
- Europe
- Middle East
- Africa
- East Africa

Area 3:
- Asia
- SW Pacific

AREA 1, NORTH ATLANTIC

For more information on airports in Canada and the United States, see pages 114–115.

ACA	Acapulco, Mexico
ALB	Albany, NY, USA
ANC	Anchorage, AK, USA
ATL	Atlanta, GA, USA
BDL	Hartford, CT, USA
BIL	Billings, MT, USA
BNA	Nashville, TN, USA
BOI	Boise, ID, USA
BOS	Boston, MA, USA
BUF	Buffalo, NY, USA
BWI	Baltimore / Washington International, MD, USA
CLE	Cleveland, OH, USA
CLT	Charlotte, NC, USA
CVG	Cincinnati, OH, USA
CUU	Chihuahua, Mexico
DCA	Washington National, VA, USA
DEN	Denver, CO, USA
DFW	Dallas-Fort Worth, TX, USA
DTW	Detroit, MI, USA
EWR	New York Newark, NJ, USA
GDL	Guadalajara, Mexico
GEG	Spokane, WA, USA
GOH	Nuuk (Godthåb), Greenland
HNL	Honolulu, HI, USA
IAD	Washington Dulles, VA, USA
IAH	Houston, TX, USA
IND	Indianapolis, IN, USA
JAX	Jacksonville, FL, USA
JFK	New York John F. Kennedy, NY, USA
LAS	Las Vegas, NV, USA
LAX	Los Angeles, CA, USA
LGA	New York LaGuardia, NY, USA
MCI	Kansas City, MO, USA
MCO	Orlando, FL, USA
MEM	Memphis, TN, USA
MEX	Mexico City, Mexico
MIA	Miami, FL, USA
MKE	Milwaukee, WI, USA
MSP	Minneapolis-St Paul, MN, USA
MSY	New Orleans, LA, USA
MTY	Monterrey, Mexico
ORD	Chicago, IL, USA
PDX	Portland, OR, USA
PHL	Philadelphia, PA, USA
PHX	Phoenix, AZ, USA
PIT	Pittsburgh, PA, USA
PWM	Portland, ME, USA
RDU	Raleigh-Durham, NC, USA
SAN	San Diego, CA, USA
SEA	Seattle, WA, USA
SFJ	Søndre Strømfjord, Greenland
SFO	San Francisco, CA, USA
SJD	San José del Cabo, Mexico
SLC	Salt Lake City, UT, USA
STL	St Louis, MO, USA
SYR	Syracuse, NY, USA
TPA	Tampa, FL, USA
UAK	Narsarsuaq, Greenland
YEG	Edmonton, AL, Canada
YHM	Hamilton, OT, Canada
YHZ	Halifax, NS, Canada
YMX	Montréal Mirabel, QU, Canada
YOW	Ottawa, OT, Canada
YQB	Québec, QU, Canada
YQX	Gander, NF, Canada
YUL	Montréal Dorval, QU, Canada
YVR	Vancouver, BC, Canada
YWG	Winnipeg, MN, Canada
YXE	Saskatoon, SA, Canada
YYC	Calgary, AL, Canada
YYT	St John's, NF, Canada
YYZ	Toronto, OT, Canada
YZF	Yellowknife, NT, Canada

AREA 1, MID ATLANTIC

ANU	Antigua
BAQ	Barranquilla, Colombia
BDA	Bermuda
BGI	Barbados
BOG	Bogotá, Colombia
BZE	Belize City, Belize
CAY	Cayenne, French Guiana
CCS	Caracas, Venezuela
FPO	Freeport, Bahamas
GEO	Georgetown, Guyana
GND	Grenada
GUA	Guatemala City, Guatemala
GYE	Guayaquil, Ecuador
HAV	La Habana (Havana), Cuba
KIN	Kingston, Jamaica
LIM	Lima, Peru
LPB	La Paz, Bolivia
MGA	Managua, Nicaragua
NAS	Nassau, Bahamas
PAP	Port-au-Prince, Haiti
PBM	Paramaribo, Suriname
POP	Puerto Plata, Dominican Republic
POS	Port of Spain, Trinidad
PTY	Panama City, Panama
SAL	San Salvador, El Salvador
SDQ	Santo Domingo, Dominican Republic
SJO	San José, Costa Rica
SJU	San Juan, Puerto Rico
SKB	St Kitts
SRZ	Santa Cruz, Bolivia
SVD	St Vincent
TGU	Tegucigalpa, Honduras
UIO	Quito, Ecuador
UVF	Hewanorra, St Lucia

AREA 1, SOUTH ATLANTIC

ARI	Arica, Chile
ASU	Asunción, Paraguay
BSB	Brasília, Brazil
EZE	Buenos Aires, Argentina
GIG	Rio de Janeiro, Brazil
GRU	São Paulo, Brazil
IPC	Easter Island
MAO	Manaus, Brazil
MVD	Montevideo, Uruguay
REC	Recife, Brazil
SCL	Santiago, Chile
SSA	Salvador, Brazil

AREA 2, EUROPE*

BAK	Baki (Baku), Azerbaijan
EVN	Yerevan, Armenia

AREA 2, MIDDLE EAST*

ADE	Adan (Aden), Yemen
AUH	Abu Dhabi, UAE
BAH	Bahrain
BGW	Baghdad, Iraq
DHA	Dhahran, Saudi Arabia
DOH	Doha, Qatar
DXB	Dubai, UAE
JED	Jiddah (Jeddah), Saudi Arabia
KRT	Al Khurtum (Khartoum), Sudan

FNC	Funchal, Madeira
KEF	Keflavik, Iceland
KZN	Kazan, Russian Federation
LPA	Las Palmas de Gran Canaria, Canary Is.
OUL	Oulu, Finland
PDL	Ponta Delgada, São Miguel, Azores
PXO	Porto Santo, Madeira
SMA	Vila do Porto, Santa Maria, Azores
TBS	Tbilisi, Georgia
TCI	Tenerife North, Canary Is.
TER	Terceira, Azores
TFS	Tenerife South, Canary Is.
TOS	Tromsø, Norway
VOG	Volgograd, Russian Federation

KWI	Kuwait
LXR	Luxor, Egypt
MCT	Muscat, Oman
RUH	Ar Riyad (Riyadh), Saudi Arabia
SAH	San'a, Yemen
THR	Tehran, Iran

AREA 2, AFRICA*

ABJ	Abidjan, Côte d'Ivoire
ABV	Abuja, Nigeria
ACC	Accra, Ghana
ADD	Addis Ababa, Ethiopia
ASM	Asmara, Eritrea
BEW	Beira, Mozambique
BGF	Bangui, Central African Rep.
BJL	Banjul, The Gambia
BJM	Bujumbura, Burundi
BKO	Bamako, Mali
BZV	Brazzaville, Congo
CKY	Conakry, Guinea
COO	Cotonou, Benin
CPT	Cape Town, South Africa
DKR	Dakar, Senegal
DLA	Douala, Cameroon
DUR	Durban, South Africa

AIRPORTS

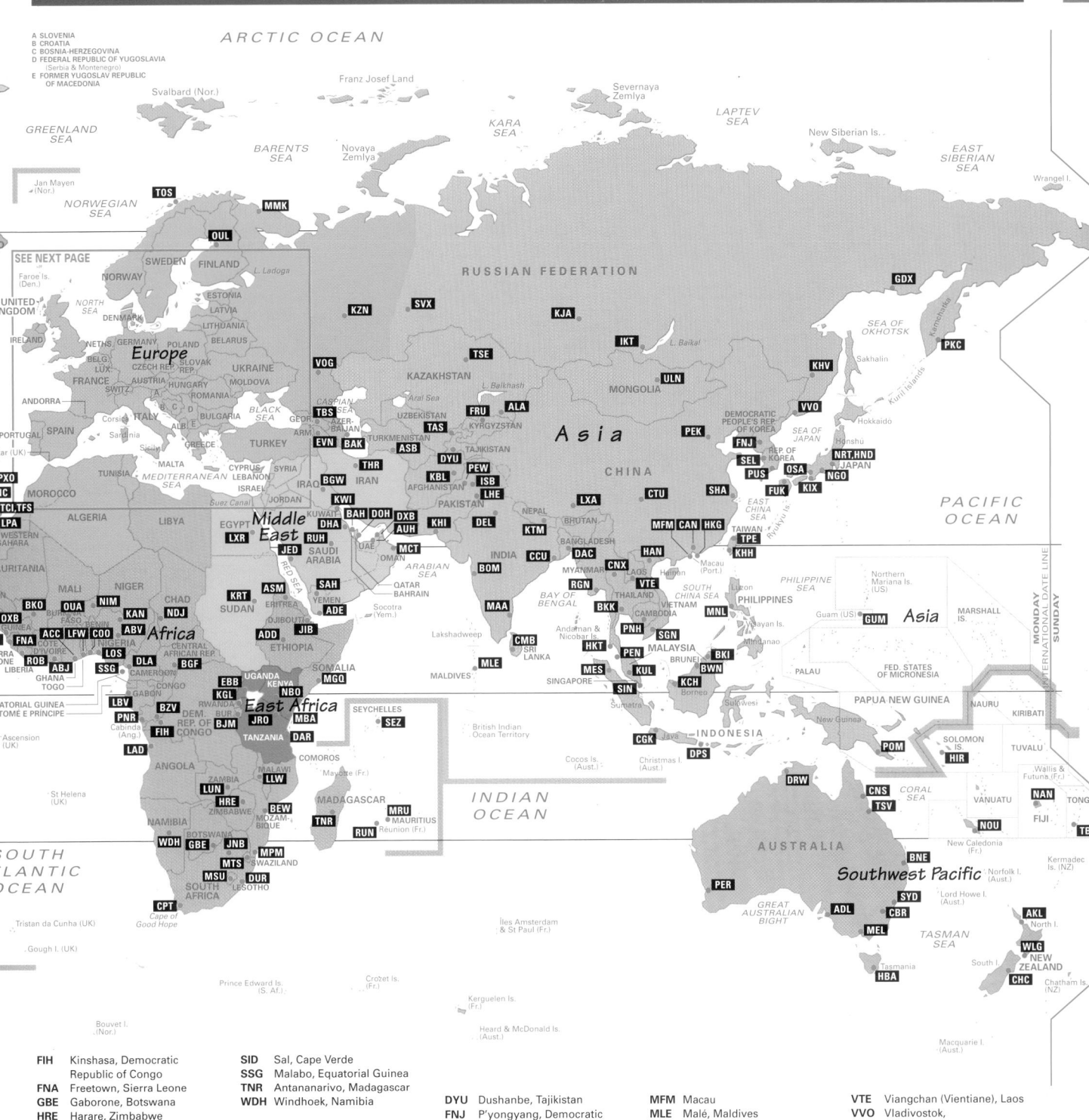

A SLOVENIA
B CROATIA
C BOSNIA-HERZEGOVINA
D FEDERAL REPUBLIC OF YUGOSLAVIA
    (Serbia & Montenegro)
E FORMER YUGOSLAV REPUBLIC
    OF MACEDONIA

FIH	Kinshasa, Democratic Republic of Congo	**SID**	Sal, Cape Verde
FNA	Freetown, Sierra Leone	**SSG**	Malabo, Equatorial Guinea
GBE	Gaborone, Botswana	**TNR**	Antananarivo, Madagascar
HRE	Harare, Zimbabwe	**WDH**	Windhoek, Namibia
JIB	Djibouti		
JNB	Johannesburg, South Africa	**AREA 2, EAST AFRICA**	
KAN	Kano, Nigeria	**DAR**	Dar es Salaam, Tanzania
KGL	Kigali, Rwanda	**EBB**	Entebbe, Uganda
LAD	Luanda, Angola	**JRO**	Kilimanjaro, Tanzania
LBV	Libreville, Gabon	**MBA**	Mombasa, Kenya
LFW	Lomé, Togo	**NBO**	Nairobi, Kenya
LLW	Lilongwe, Malawi		
LOS	Lagos, Nigeria	**AREA 3, ASIA**	
LUN	Lusaka, Zambia	**ALA**	Almaty, Kazakhstan
MGQ	Muqdisho (Mogadishu), Somalia	**ASB**	Ashgabat, Turkmenistan
MPM	Maputo, Mozambique	**BKI**	Kota Kinabalu, Malaysia
MRU	Mauritius	**BKK**	Krung Thep (Bangkok), Thailand
MSU	Maseru, Lesotho	**BOM**	Bombay, India
MTS	Manzini, Swaziland	**BWN**	Bandar Seri Begawan, Brunei
NDB	Nouadhibou, Mauritania	**CAN**	Guangzhou (Canton), China
NDJ	N'Djamena, Chad	**CCU**	Calcutta, India
NIM	Niamey, Niger	**CGK**	Jakarta, Indonesia
NKC	Nouakchott, Mauritania	**CMB**	Colombo, Sri Lanka
OUA	Ouagadougou, Burkina Faso	**CNX**	Chiang Mai, Thailand
OXB	Bissau, Guinea-Bissau	**CTU**	Chengdu, China
PNR	Pointe-Noire, Congo	**DAC**	Dhaka, Bangladesh
ROB	Monrovia, Liberia	**DEL**	Delhi, India
RUN	Réunion	**DPS**	Denpasar, Bali, Indonesia
SEZ	Mahé, Seychelles		

DYU	Dushanbe, Tajikistan	**MFM**	Macau	**VTE**	Viangchan (Vientiane), Laos
FNJ	P'yongyang, Democratic People's Republic of Korea	**MLE**	Malé, Maldives	**VVO**	Vladivostok, Russian Federation
FRU	Bishkek, Kyrgyzstan	**MMK**	Murmansk, Russian Federation		
FUK	Fukuoka, Japan	**MNL**	Manila, the Philippines		
GDX	Magadan, Russian Federation	**NGO**	Nagoya, Japan	**AREA 3, SOUTHWEST PACIFIC**	
GUM	Guam	**NRT**	Tokyo Narita, Japan	**ADL**	Adelaide, Australia
HAN	Hanoi, Vietnam	**OSA**	Osaka, Japan	**AKL**	Auckland, New Zealand
HKG	Hong Kong, China	**PEK**	Beijing (Peking), China	**APW**	Apia, Western Samoa
HKT	Phuket, Thailand	**PEN**	Pinang (Penang), Malaysia	**BNE**	Brisbane, Australia
HND	Tokyo Haneda, Japan	**PEW**	Peshawar, Pakistan	**CBR**	Canberra, Australia
IKT	Irkutsk, Russian Federation	**PKC**	Petropavlovsk Kamchatskiy, Russian Federation	**CHC**	Christchurch, New Zealand
ISB	Islamabad, Pakistan	**PNH**	Phnom Penh, Cambodia	**CNS**	Cairns, Australia
KBL	Kabul, Afghanistan	**POM**	Port Moresby, Papua New Guinea	**DRW**	Darwin, Australia
KCH	Kuching, Malaysia	**PUS**	Pusan, Rep. of Korea	**HBA**	Hobart, Tasmania, Australia
KHH	Kaohsiung, Taiwan	**RGN**	Yangon (Rangoon), Myanmar	**HIR**	Honiara, Solomon Is.
KHI	Karachi, Pakistan	**SEL**	Soul (Seoul), Rep. of Korea	**MEL**	Melbourne, Australia
KHV	Khabarovsk, Russian Federation	**SGN**	Ho Chi Minh City, Vietnam	**NAN**	Nadi, Fiji
KIX	Kansai, Japan	**SHA**	Shanghai, China	**NOU**	Nouméa, New Caledonia
KJA	Krasnoyarsk, Russian Federation	**SIN**	Singapore	**PER**	Perth, Australia
KTM	Kathmandu, Nepal	**SVX**	Yekaterinburg, Russian Federation	**PPT**	Papeete, Tahiti, French Polynesia
KUL	Kuala Lumpur, Malaysia	**TAS**	Tashkent, Uzbekistan	**RAR**	Rarotonga, Cook Is.
LHE	Lahore, Pakistan	**TPE**	Taipei, Taiwan	**SYD**	Sydney, Australia
LXA	Lhasa, China	**TSE**	Akmola, Kazakhstan	**TBU**	Tongatapu, Tonga
MAA	Madras, India	**ULN**	Ulaanbaatar (Ulan Bator), Mongolia	**TSV**	Townsville, Australia
MES	Medan, Indonesia			**WLG**	Wellington, New Zealand
				*	See next page for other airports in these areas

AIRPORTS

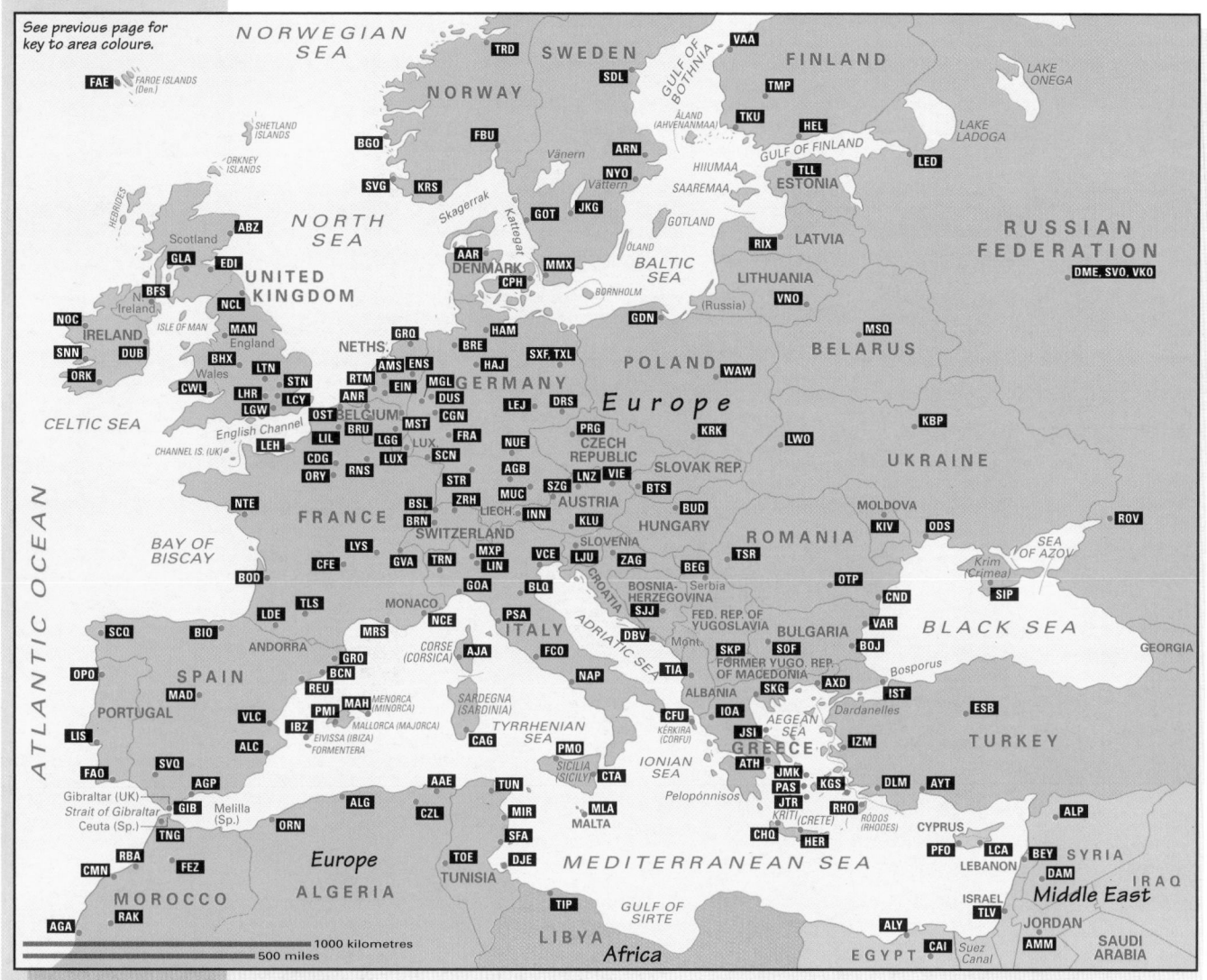

See previous page for key to area colours.

Where cities have more than one airport, the individual airport codes are used. For example, Berlin city code is BER, but the airport codes are:

Schönefeld   SXF
Tegel   TXL

AREA 2, EUROPE

For more information on airports in the UK, see pages 76–77

AAE   Annaba, Algeria
AAR   Århus, Denmark
ABZ   Aberdeen, Scotland
AGA   Agadir, Morocco
AGB   Augsburg, Germany
AGP   Málaga, Spain
AJA   Ajaccio, France
ALC   Alicante, Spain
ALG   Alger (Algiers), Algeria
AMS   Amsterdam, The Netherlands
ANR   Antwerpen (Antwerp), Belgium
ARN   Stockholm, Sweden
ATH   Athína (Athens), Greece
AXD   Alexandroúpoli, Greece
AYT   Antalya, Turkey
BCN   Barcelona, Spain
BEG   Beograd (Belgrade), Federal Republic of Yugoslavia
BFS   Belfast, Northern Ireland
BGO   Bergen, Norway
BHX   Birmingham, England
BIO   Bilbao, Spain
BLQ   Bologna, Italy
BOD   Bordeaux, France
BOJ   Burgas, Bulgaria
BRE   Bremen, Germany
BRN   Bern (Berne), Switzerland
BRU   Bruxelles (Brussel/Brussels), Belgium
BSL   Basel (Basle), Switzerland
BTS   Bratislava, Slovak Republic

BUD   Budapest, Hungary
CAG   Cágliari, Italy
CDG   Paris Charles de Gaulle, France
CFE   Clermont-Ferrand, France
CFU   Kérkira (Corfu), Greece
CGN   Köln (Cologne) / Bonn, Germany
CHQ   Hania (Canea), Greece
CMN   Deir el Beida (Casablanca), Morocco
CND   Constanta, Romania
CPH   København (Copenhagen), Denmark
CTA   Catánia, Italy
CWL   Cardiff, Wales
CZL   Constantine, Algeria
DBV   Dubrovnik, Croatia
DJE   Jerba, Tunisia
DLM   Dalaman, Turkey
DME   Moskva (Moscow) Domodedovo, Russian Fed.
DRS   Dresden, Germany
DUB   Dublin, Ireland
DUS   Düsseldorf, Germany
EDI   Edinburgh, Scotland
EIN   Eindhoven, The Netherlands
ENS   Enschede, The Netherlands
ESB   Ankara, Turkey
FAE   Vágar, Faroe Islands
FAO   Faro, Portugal
FBU   Oslo, Norway
FCO   Roma (Rome), Italy
FEZ   Fès, Morocco
FRA   Frankfurt am Main, Germany
GDN   Gdansk, Poland
GIB   Gibraltar
GLA   Glasgow, Scotland
GOA   Génova (Genoa), Italy
GOT   Göteborg (Gothenburg), Sweden
GRO   Girona, Spain
GRQ   Groningen, The Netherlands
GVA   Genève (Geneva), Switz.
HAJ   Hannover, Germany
HAM   Hamburg, Germany

HEL   Helsinki (Helsingfors), Finland
HER   Iráklio (Herakleion), Greece
IBZ   Eivissa (Ibiza), Spain
INN   Innsbruck, Austria
IOA   Ioánina, Greece
IST   Istanbul, Turkey
IZM   Izmir (Smyrna), Turkey
JKG   Jönköping, Sweden
JMK   Míkonos, Greece
JSI   Skiathos, Greece
JTR   Thíra, Greece
KBP   Kyyiv (Kiev), Ukraine
KGS   Kos (Cos), Greece
KIV   Chisinau (Kishinev), Moldova
KLU   Klagenfurt, Austria
KRK   Kraków (Cracow), Poland
KRS   Kristiansand, Norway
LCY   London City, England
LDE   Lourdes, France
LED   Sankt-Peterburg (St Petersburg), Russian Fed.
LEH   Le Havre, France
LEJ   Leipzig/Halle, Germany
LGG   Liège, Belgium
LGW   London Gatwick, England
LHR   London Heathrow, England
LIL   Lille, France
LIN   Milano (Milan) Linate, Italy
LIS   Lisboa (Lisbon), Portugal
LJU   Ljubljana, Slovenia
LNZ   Linz, Austria
LTN   London Luton, England
LUX   Luxembourg
LWO   Lviv (Lvov), Ukraine
LYS   Lyon, France
MAD   Madrid, Spain
MAH   Maó (Mahón), Spain
MAN   Manchester, England
MGL   Mönchengladbach, Germany
MIR   Monastir, Tunisia
MLA   Malta
MMX   Malmö, Sweden
MRS   Marseille, France
MSQ   Mensk (Minsk), Belarus
MST   Maastricht, The Netherlands

MUC   München (Munich), Germany
MXP   Milano (Milan) Malpensa, Italy
NAP   Nápoli (Naples), Italy
NCE   Nice, France
NCL   Newcastle, England
NOC   Knock, Ireland
NTE   Nantes, France
NUE   Nürnberg (Nuremberg), Germany
NYO   Nyköping, Sweden
ODS   Odesa (Odessa), Ukraine
OPO   Porto (Oporto), Portugal
ORK   Cork, Ireland
ORN   Oran, Algeria
ORY   Paris Orly, France
OST   Oostende (Ostend), Belgium
OTP   Bucuresti (Bucharest), Romania
PAS   Páros, Greece
PMI   Palma de Mallorca, Spain
PMO   Palermo, Italy
PRG   Praha (Prague), Czech Rep.
PSA   Pisa, Italy
RAK   Marrakech, Morocco
RBA   Rabat, Morocco
REU   Reus, Spain
RHO   Ródos (Rhodes), Greece
RIX   Riga, Latvia
RNS   Reims, France
ROV   Rostov-na-Donu, Russian Fed.
RTM   Rotterdam, The Netherlands
SCN   Saarbrücken, Germany
SCQ   Santiago de Compostela, Spain
SDL   Sundsvall, Sweden
SFA   Sfax, Tunisia
SIP   Simferopol, Ukraine
SJJ   Sarajevo, Bosnia-Herz.
SKG   Thessaloníki (Salonika), Greece
SKP   Skopje, FYR of Macedonia
SNN   Shannon, Ireland
SOF   Sofiya (Sofia), Bulgaria
STN   London Stansted, England
STR   Stuttgart, Germany

SVG   Stavanger, Norway
SVO   Moskva (Moscow) Sheremetyevo, Russian Fed.
SVQ   Sevilla (Seville), Spain
SXF   Berlin Schönefeld, Germany
SZG   Salzburg, Austria
TIA   Tiranë (Tirana), Albania
TKU   Turku (Åbo), Finland
TLL   Tallinn, Estonia
TLS   Toulouse, France
TMP   Tampere, Finland
TNG   Tanger (Tangier), Morocco
TOE   Tozeur, Tunisia
TRD   Trondheim, Norway
TRN   Torino (Turin), Italy
TSR   Timisoara, Romania
TUN   Tunis, Tunisia
TXL   Berlin Tegel, Germany
VAA   Vaasa (Vasa), Finland
VAR   Varna, Bulgaria
VCE   Venézia (Venice), Italy
VIE   Wien (Vienna), Austria
VKO   Moskva (Moscow) Vnukovo, Russian Fed.
VLC   Valencia, Spain
VNO   Vilnius, Lithuania
WAW   Warszawa (Warsaw), Poland
ZAG   Zagreb, Croatia
ZRH   Zürich, Switzerland

AREA 2, MIDDLE EAST

ALP   Halab (Aleppo), Syria
ALY   El Iskandarîya (Alexandria), Egypt
AMM   Amman, Jordan
BEY   Bayrut (Beirut), Lebanon
CAI   El Qâhira (Cairo), Egypt
DAM   Dimashq (Damascus), Syria
LCA   Larnaca, Cyprus
PFO   Paphos, Cyprus
TLV   Tel Aviv-Yafo, Israel

AREA 2, AFRICA

TIP   Tarabulus (Tripoli), Libya

FLIGHT TIMES

Average flight times from London, New York and Singapore to other major destinations. Hours do not include stopover time, when necessary, from one destination to another.

- Less than 2 hours
- 2 hours – 4 hours 59 mins
- 5 hours – 8 hours 59 mins
- 9 hours – 14 hours 59 mins
- 15 hours – 24 hours 59 mins
- 25 hours and over

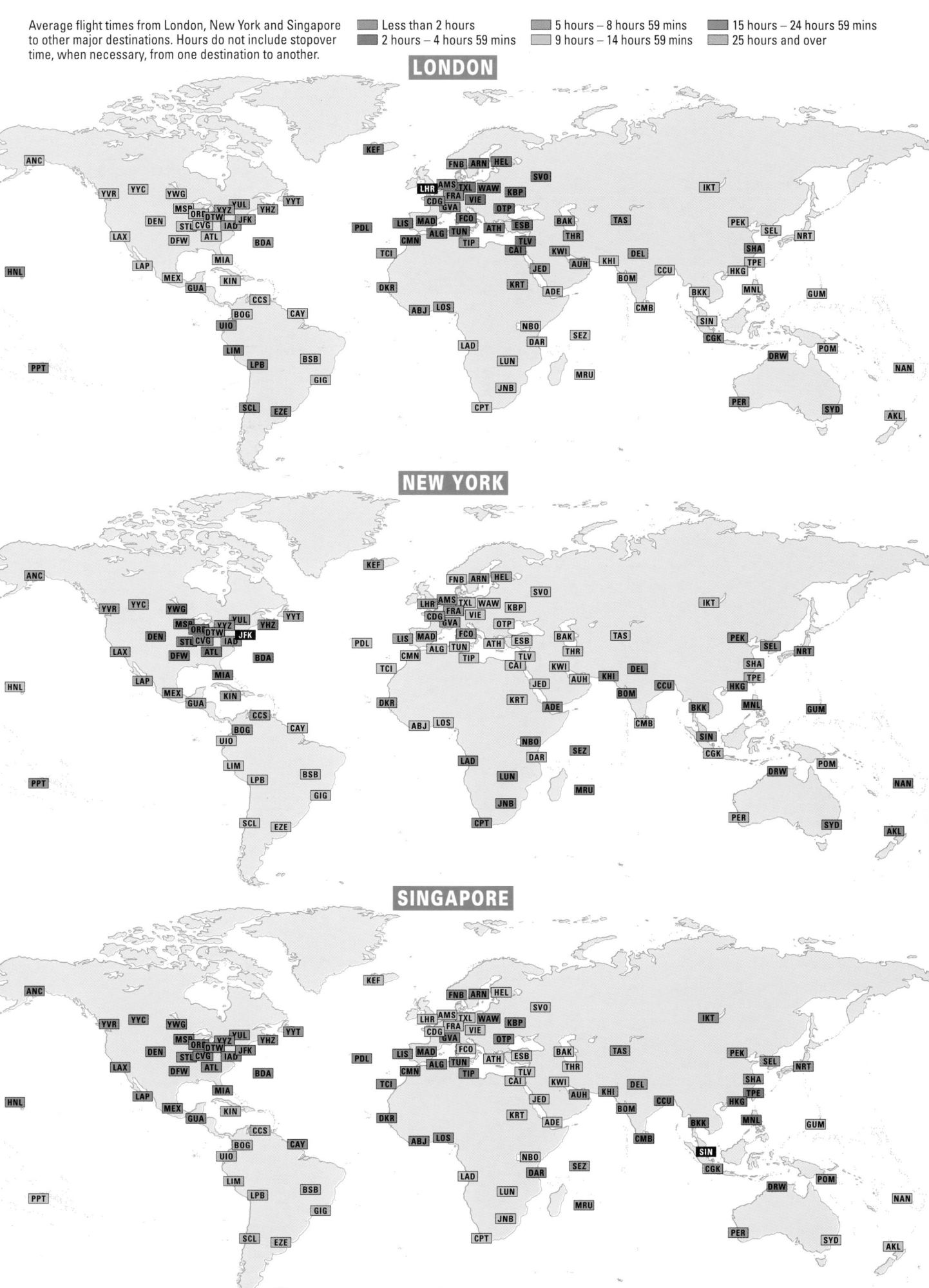

CRUISING

Cruising is one of the fastest-growing holiday choices in the world and, as new ships are built and new lines created, there is a continuing search for new ports of call. This map includes ports that are now beginning to be visited for the first time along with those which have featured in cruise brochures for decades. Key ports on the most popular river itineraries are also shown.

The main cruising areas are shown, as well as ports outside these areas that appear only on the schedules of world cruises.

Some of the places marked are accessible only by tender or, in some cases (notably Antarctica) by zodiac or other powered inflatable boat from the ship which will be anchored offshore.

The 'Round-the-World' cruise routes shown on the map are examples used by some passenger shipping companies. There are considerable variations, but cruise programmes offering 'Round-the-World' trips will call at many of the ports marked. Route variations might be caused due to size of ship, port-berthing facilities, weather conditions at particular times of year or marketing considerations.

Areas where the risk of bad weather is greatest are shaded different tints of purple. Those areas experiencing bad weather throughout the year are shown in the darkest tint. Areas with shorter seasons of bad weather are in lighter tints.

Period of bad weather risk

J F M **A M J J A S** O N D

Maximum frequency of bad weather

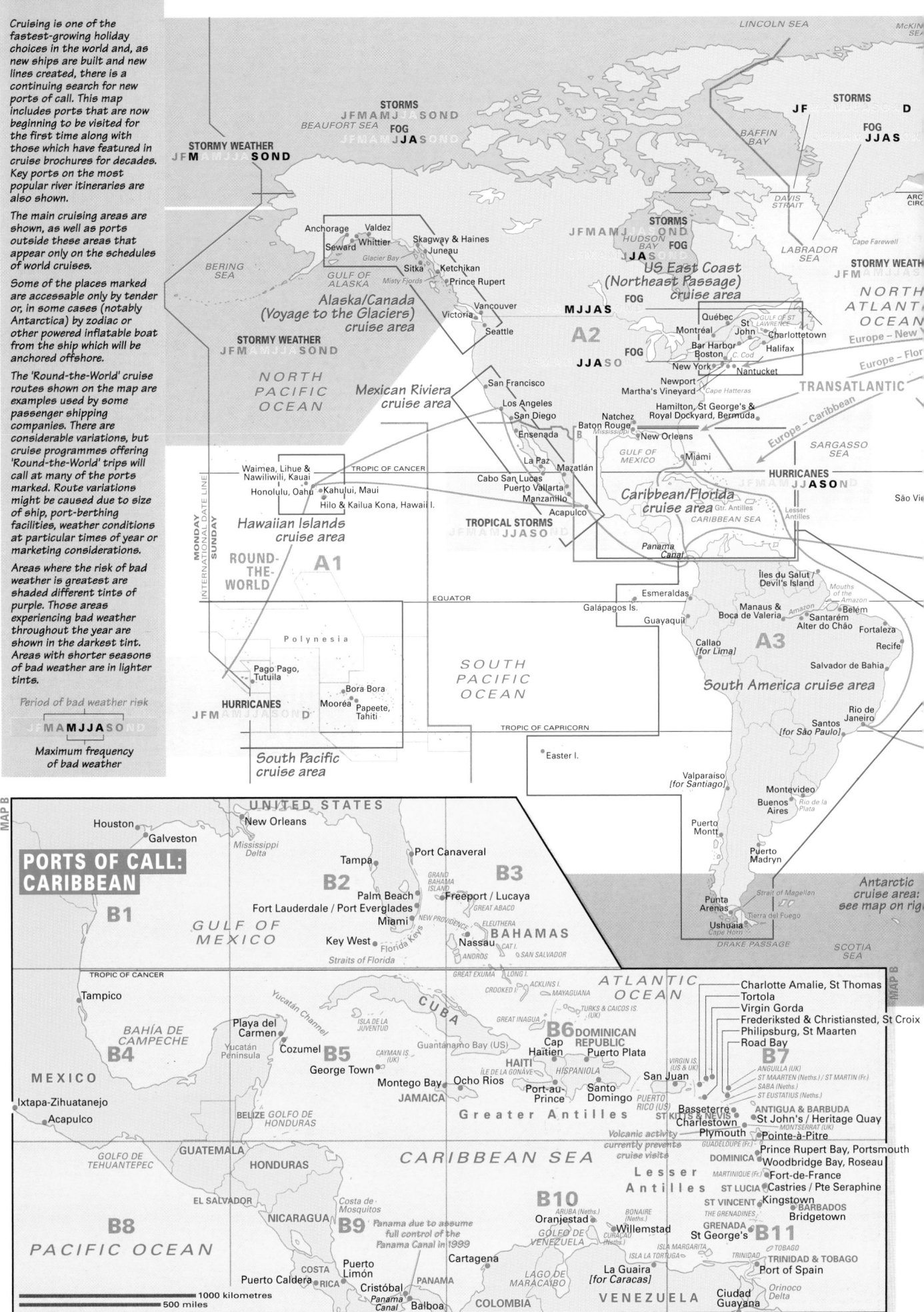

PORTS OF CALL: CARIBBEAN

CRUISING

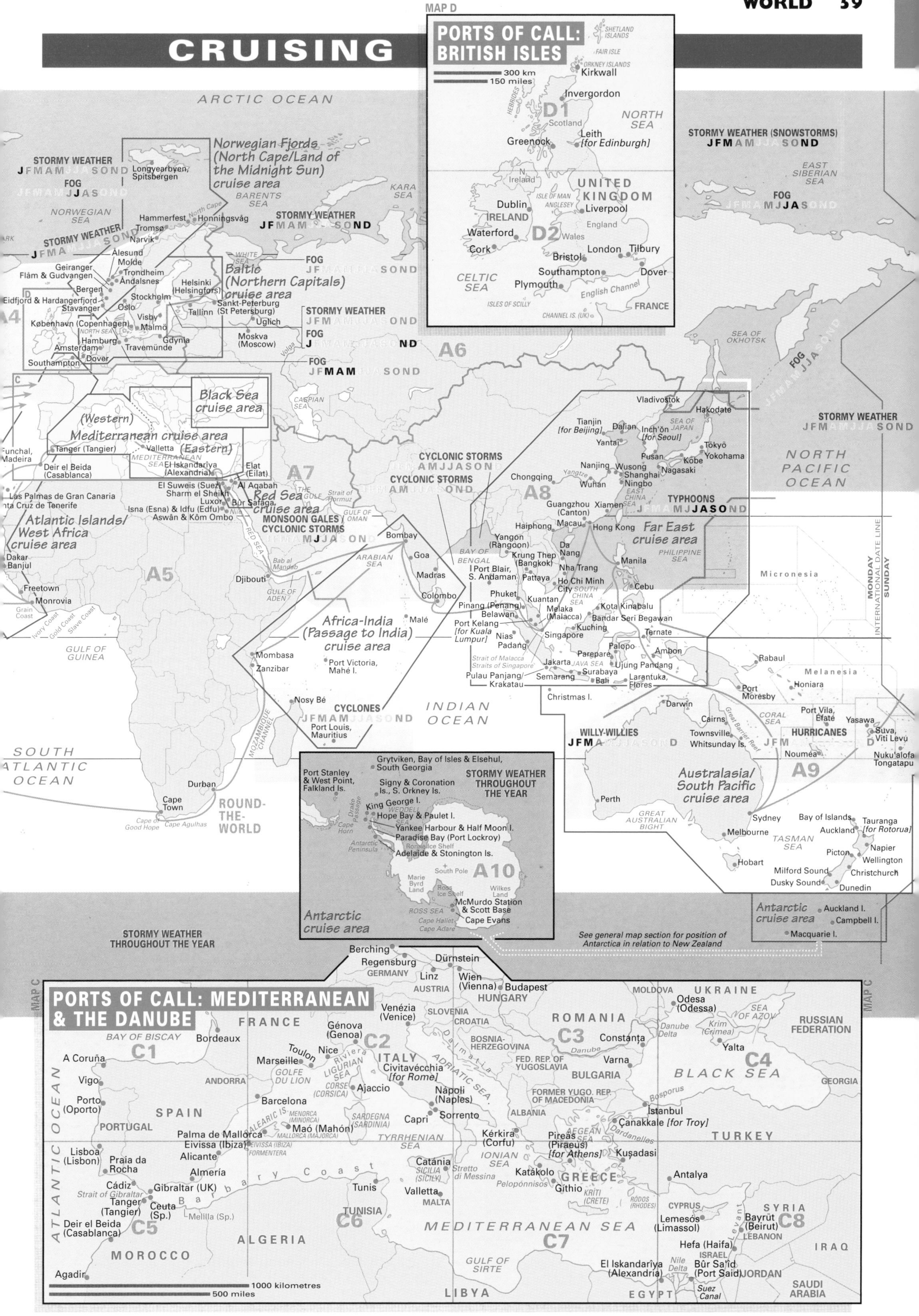

MAP D

PORTS OF CALL: BRITISH ISLES

300 km
150 miles

SHETLAND ISLANDS
FAIR ISLE
ORKNEY ISLANDS
Kirkwall
HEBRIDES
D1
Scotland
Invergordon
NORTH SEA
Greenock
Leith [for Edinburgh]
N. Ireland
Isle of Man
ANGLESEY
UNITED KINGDOM
Dublin
IRELAND
Liverpool
Wales
England
Waterford
D2
Cork
London
Tilbury
Bristol
Southampton
Dover
CELTIC SEA
Plymouth
English Channel
ISLES OF SCILLY
FRANCE
CHANNEL IS. (UK)

ARCTIC OCEAN

STORMY WEATHER
JFMAMJJASOND

FOG
JFMAMJJASOND

Longyearbyen, Spitsbergen

Norwegian Fjords (North Cape/Land of the Midnight Sun) cruise area

BARENTS SEA

KARA SEA

STORMY WEATHER (SNOWSTORMS)
JFMAMJJASOND

EAST SIBERIAN SEA

FOG
JFMAMJJASOND

NORWEGIAN SEA

STORMY WEATHER
JFMAMJJASOND

Hammerfest Honningsvåg
North Cape
Tromsø
Narvik

WHITE SEA

FOG
JFMAMJJASOND

Ålesund
Molde
Trondheim
Andalsnes
Geiranger
Flåm & Gudvangen
Bergen
Eidfjord & Hardangerfjord
Stavanger
København (Copenhagen)
Hamburg
Amsterdam
Southampton
Dover

Baltic (Northern Capitals) cruise area

Helsinki (Helsingfors)
Stockholm
Oslo
Visby
Malmö
Gdynia
Travemünde

Tallinn
Sankt-Peterburg (St Petersburg)
Uglich

STORMY WEATHER
JFMAMJJASOND

Moskva (Moscow)
Volga

FOG
JFMAMJJASOND

CASPIAN SEA

A6

SEA OF OKHOTSK

FOG
JFMAMJJASOND

Black Sea cruise area

(Western)

Mediterranean cruise area (Eastern)

MEDITERRANEAN SEA

Funchal, Madeira
Tanger (Tangier)
Valletta
Deir el Beida (Casablanca)
El Iskandarîya (Alexandria)
Elat (Eilat)

A7

Vladivostok
Hakodate
Tianjin [for Beijing]
Dalian
Yantai
Inch'ŏn [for Seoul]
Pusan
SEA OF JAPAN
Tōkyō
Yokohama
Kōbe
Nagasaki

STORMY WEATHER
JFMAMJJASOND

NORTH PACIFIC OCEAN

Las Palmas de Gran Canaria
Santa Cruz de Tenerife

Atlantic Islands/ West Africa cruise area

Dakar
Banjul

A5

Freetown
Monrovia

Grain Coast
Ivory Coast
Gold Coast
Slave Coast

GULF OF GUINEA

El Suweis (Suez)
Sharm el Sheikh
Luxor [Esna] & Idfu (Edfu)
Aswân & Kôm Ombo
Al Aqabah
Bûr Safâga

Red Sea cruise area

MONSOON GALES
CYCLONIC STORMS

Isna (Esna)

RED SEA

Strait of Hormuz

GULF OF OMAN

Djibouti

Bab al Mandab

GULF OF ADEN

ARABIAN SEA

Bombay

Goa
Madras
Colombo

Malé

Africa-India (Passage to India) cruise area

Mombasa
Zanzibar

Nosy Bé

MOZAMBIQUE CHANNEL

CYCLONES
JFMAMJJASOND

Port Louis, Mauritius

INDIAN OCEAN

Port Victoria, Mahé I.

CYCLONIC STORMS
AMJJASOND

CYCLONIC STORMS
AMJJASOND

Chongqing

Nanjing
Wuhan
Wusong
Shanghai
Ningbo
EAST CHINA SEA

TYPHOONS
JFMAMJJASOND

Guangzhou (Canton)
Xiamen
Hong Kong
Macau

Haiphong
Yangon (Rangoon)
Da Nang
Krung Thep (Bangkok)
Nha Trang
Ho Chi Minh City
Pattaya
Manila

Far East cruise area

PHILIPPINE SEA

Micronesia

MONDAY
SUNDAY
INTERNATIONAL DATE LINE

Port Blair, S. Andaman
Phuket
Kuantan
Melaka (Malacca)
Cebu
Kota Kinabalu
Pinang (Penang)
Belawan
Port Kelang [for Kuala Lumpur]
Nias
Padang
Bandar Seri Begawan
Kuching
Singapore
Ternate
Parepare
Palopo
Ambon

Jakarta
Ujung Pandang
Pulau Panjang
Semarang
Surabaya
Larantuka, Flores
Krakatau
Bali

Christmas I.

Darwin

WILLY-WILLIES
JFMAMJJASOND

Rabaul

Melanesia

Port Moresby
Honiara

CORAL SEA

Cairns
Townsville
Whitsunday Is.

HURRICANES
JFMAMJJASOND

Port Vila, Éfaté

Yasawa
Suva, Viti Levu
Nouméa

Nuku'alofa
Tongatapu

A9

Australasia/ South Pacific cruise area

GREAT AUSTRALIAN BIGHT

Perth

Sydney
Melbourne
TASMAN SEA

Bay of Islands
Auckland
Tauranga [for Rotorua]
Napier
Wellington

Picton
Christchurch

Hobart

Milford Sound
Dusky Sound
Dunedin

Antarctic cruise area

Auckland I.
Campbell I.
Macquarie I.

SOUTH ATLANTIC OCEAN

Durban
Cape Town
Cape of Good Hope
Cape Agulhas

ROUND-THE-WORLD

Port Stanley & West Point, Falkland Is.
Grytviken, Bay of Isles & Elsehul, South Georgia
Signy & Coronation Is., S. Orkney Is.
King George I.
Hope Bay & Paulet I.
Yankee Harbour & Half Moon I.
Paradise Bay (Port Lockroy)
Adelaide & Stonington Is.

DRAKE PASSAGE
WEDDELL SEA
Cape Horn
Antarctic Peninsula
Ronne Ice Shelf

STORMY WEATHER THROUGHOUT THE YEAR

Marie Byrd Land
South Pole
ROSS SEA
Ross Ice Shelf
Wilkes Land

A10

McMurdo Station & Scott Base
Cape Evans
Cape Hallett
Cape Adare

Antarctic cruise area

STORMY WEATHER THROUGHOUT THE YEAR

See general map section for position of Antarctica in relation to New Zealand

PORTS OF CALL: MEDITERRANEAN & THE DANUBE

Berching
Regensburg
GERMANY
Dürnstein
Linz
Wien (Vienna)
Budapest
AUSTRIA
HUNGARY

MOLDOVA
UKRAINE
Odesa (Odessa)
SEA OF AZOV
Krim (Crimea)
RUSSIAN FEDERATION

FRANCE
SLOVENIA
CROATIA
Venézia (Venice)
Génova (Genoa)
ROMANIA
Constanţa
Danube Delta

C3

BAY OF BISCAY
Bordeaux

C1

BOSNIA-HERZEGOVINA
FED. REP. OF YUGOSLAVIA
Danube
Varna
BULGARIA
Yalta

C4

A Coruña
Vigo
Porto (Oporto)
Toulon
Nice
Marseille
Riviera
LIGURIAN SEA
ITALY
Civitavécchia [for Rome]
Ajaccio
GOLFE DU LION
CORSE (Corsica)

C2

ADRIATIC SEA
Dalmatia
FORMER YUGO. REP. OF MACEDONIA
Istanbul
Bosporus
BLACK SEA
GEORGIA

SPAIN
ANDORRA
Barcelona
Napoli (Naples)
ALBANIA
Çanakkale [for Troy]
Dardanelles

PORTUGAL
Capri
Sorrento
Kérkira (Corfu)
Pireás (Piraeus) [for Athens]
TURKEY
Kuşadası

Lisboa (Lisbon)
Praia da Rocha
Palma de Mallorca
Maó (Mahón)
BALEARIC IS.
MENORCA (MINORCA)
MALLORCA (MAJORCA)
SARDEGNA (SARDINIA)
Catánia
SICILIA (SICILY)
Stretto di Messina
TYRRHENIAN SEA
IONIAN SEA
Peloponnisos
Katákolo
GREECE
Githio
KRITI (CRETE)
Antalya

Eivissa (Ibiza)
FORMENTERA
Alicante
Almería
AEGEAN SEA
RODOS (RHODES)

Cádiz
Gibraltar (UK)
Ceuta (Sp.)
Melilla (Sp.)
Tunis
Valletta
MALTA
CYPRUS
Lemesós (Limassol)
SYRIA
Bayrût (Beirut)
LEBANON

C8

Tanger (Tangier)
Strait of Gibraltar
Barbary Coast

C5

Deir el Beida (Casablanca)
ALGERIA
TUNISIA

C6

MEDITERRANEAN SEA

C7

Hefa (Haifa)
ISRAEL
El Iskandarîya (Alexandria)
Nile Delta
Bûr Sa'îd (Port Said)
JORDAN
IRAQ

Agadir
MOROCCO
GULF OF SIRTE
LIBYA
EGYPT
Suez Canal
SAUDI ARABIA

1000 kilometres
500 miles

UNESCO NATURAL HERITAGE SITES

All properties which belong to the UNESCO World Heritage List are considered to be of world importance either because of their natural features or their significant man-made contribution to world culture. Sites for consideration of heritage status are submitted by the appropriate government ministry. UNESCO then considers each proposal under strict criteria and designates sites where appropriate.

Some countries are not signatories to the convention, and so the UNESCO list is not fully comprehensive worldwide.

There are two main categories of property: natural and cultural.

NATURAL SITES.
(i) Natural features: physical and biological formations of scientific importance;
(ii) Geological and physiographical formations: delineated areas which constitute the habitat of threatened species of animals or plants;
(iii) Natural sites: areas of universal value in terms of natural beauty and conservation.

Properties named in red are included on the list of World Heritage in Danger.

For further information, contact:

The World Heritage Centre, UNESCO, 7 place de Fontenoy, 75352 Paris 07, France.

Tel: +33 1 45 68 10 00.

CANADA & UNITED STATES
1 Kluane National Park, Glacier Bay National Park & Preserve, Wrangell-St Elias National Park & Preserve and Tatshenshini-Alsek Provincial Wilderness Park, Alaska/Yukon
2 Nahanni National Park, Northwest Territories
3 Wood Buffalo National Park, Northwest Territories/ Alberta
4 Canadian Rocky Mountains Parks, British Columbia/Alberta
5 Waterton-Glacier International Peace Park, Alberta/ Montana
6 Dinosaur Provincial Park, Alberta
7 Gros Morne National Park, Newfoundland
8 Hawaii Volcanoes National Park, Hawaii
9 Olympic National Park, Washington
10 Redwood National Park, California
11 Yosemite National Park, California
12 Grand Canyon National Park, Arizona
13 Carlsbad Caverns National Park, New Mexico
14 Yellowstone National Park, Wyoming
15 Mammoth Cave National Park, Kentucky
16 Great Smoky Mountains National Park, Tennessee/ North Carolina
17 Everglades National Park, Florida

MEXICO, CENTRAL AMERICA & CARIBBEAN
18 El Vizcaíno whale sanctuary, Mexico
19 Reserva de la Biósfera Sian Ka'an, Mexico
20 Parque Nacional Tikal, Guatemala
21 Barrier Reef Reserve System, Belize
22 Reserva de la Biósfera Rio Platano, Honduras
23 Parque Nacional Isla del Coco, Costa Rica
24 Cordillera de Talamanca and Parque Internacional La Amistad, Costa Rica/Panama
25 Parque Nacional del Darién, Panama
26 Morne Trois Pitons National Park, Dominica

SOUTH AMERICA
27 Parque Nacional Canaima, Venezuela
28 Parque Nacional Los Katios, Colombia
29 Parque Nacional Sangay, Ecuador
30 Parque Nacional Galápagos
31 Parque Nacional Rio Abiseo, Peru
32 Parque Nacional Huascarán, Peru
33 Santuario histórico Machu Picchu, Peru
34 Parque Nacional Manú, Peru
35 Parque Nacional Serra da Capivara, Brazil
36 Parque Nacional do Iguaçu, Brazil
37 Parque Nacional de Iguazu, Argentina
38 Parque Nacional Los Glaciares, Argentina

EUROPE (including Atlantic islands and Turkey)
39 Lapponian area, Sweden
40 St Kilda, Scotland
41 Giant's Causeway and its coast, Northern Ireland
42 Messel Pit fossil site, Germany
43 Mont-St Michel and its bay, France
44 Paris: banks of the Seine, France
45 Golfe de Girolata, Golfe de Porto, les Calanche and Réserve Naturelle Scandola, Corsica, France
46 Monte Perdido, France/Spain
47 Parque Nacional Coto de Doñana, Spain
48 Parque Nacional de Garajonay, Gomera, Canary Is.
49 Bialowieza National Park & Beloveshskaya Pushcha, Poland/Belarus
50 Aggtelek Caves and the Slovak karst, Hungary/ Slovak Republic
51 Skocjan Caves, Slovenia
52 Plitvice Lakes National Park, Croatia
53 Durmitor National Park, Federal Republic of Yugoslavia
54 Kotor and its gulf, Federal Republic of Yugoslavia
55 Ohrid Lake and its region, Former Yugoslav Republic of Macedonia
56 Danube Delta, Romania

57 Srebarna Nature Reserve, Bulgaria
58 Pirin National Park, Bulgaria
59 Metéora, Greece
60 Olimbía (Olympía): archaeological site, Greece
61 Áthos, Greece
62 Hierapolis-Pamukkale, Turkey
63 Göreme National Park and Cappadocia rock sites, Turkey

FORMER SOVIET UNION
64 Komi virgin forests, Russian Federation
65 Lake Baikal, Russian Federation
66 Kamchatka volcanoes, Russian Federation

AFRICA
67 Ichkeul National Park, Tunisia
68 Tassili n'Ajjer, Algeria
69 Bandiagara Cliffs: Land of the Dogon, Mali
70 Banc d'Arguin National Park, Mauritania
71 Parc National des Oiseaux du Djoudj (Djoudj National Bird Sanctuary), Senegal
72 Parc National du Niokolo Koba, Senegal
73 Réserve du Monts Nimba, Guinea/Côte d'Ivoire
74 Parc National de la Comoé, Côte d'Ivoire
75 Parc National de Taï, Côte d'Ivoire
76 Parc National du "W", Niger
77 Réserve du Aïr and Réserve du Ténéré, Niger

UNESCO NATURAL HERITAGE SITES

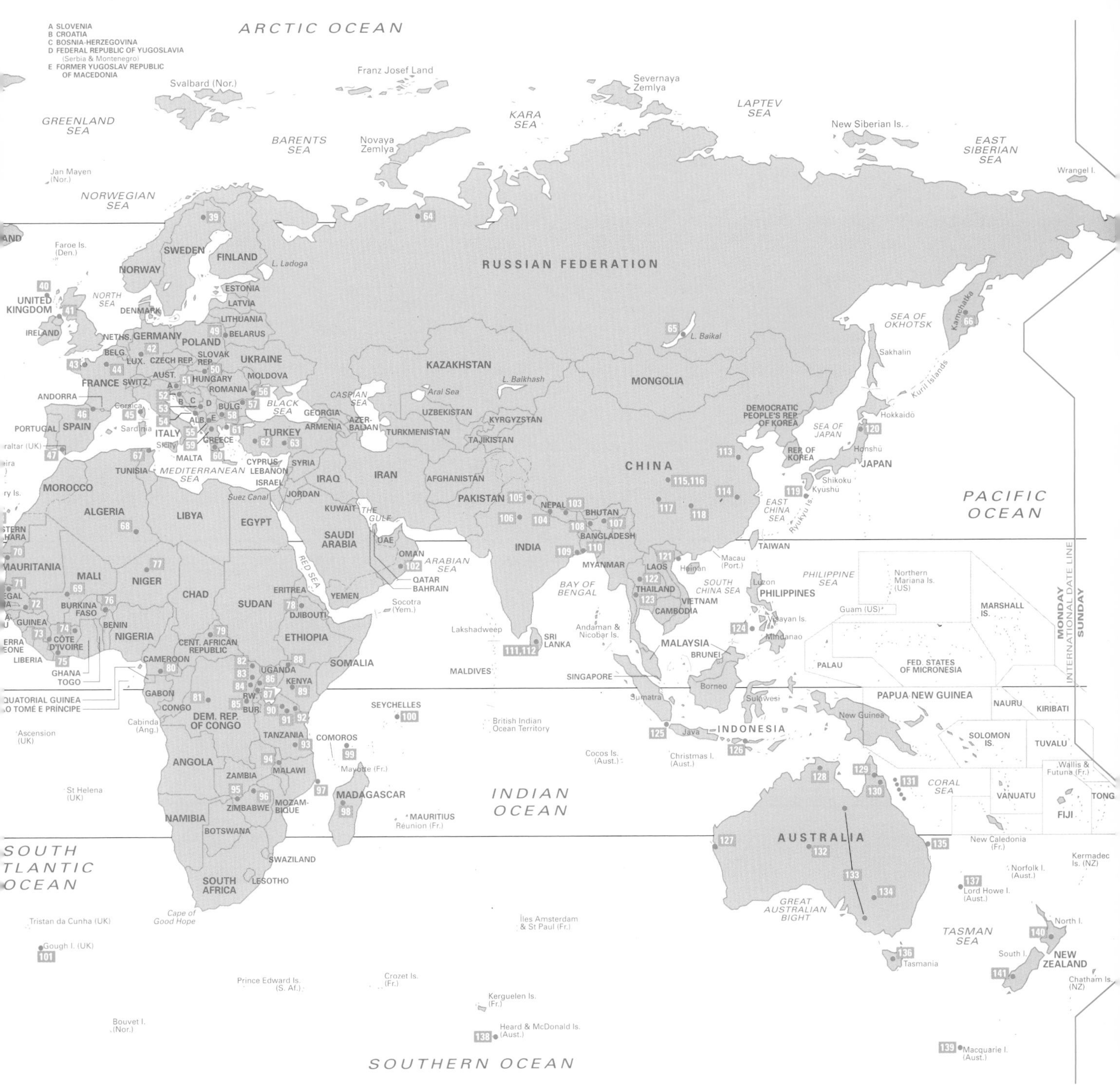

A SLOVENIA
B CROATIA
C BOSNIA-HERZEGOVINA
D FEDERAL REPUBLIC OF YUGOSLAVIA
  (Serbia & Montenegro)
E FORMER YUGOSLAV REPUBLIC
  OF MACEDONIA

ARCTIC OCEAN

GREENLAND SEA

NORWEGIAN SEA

SVALBARD (Nor.)

Franz Josef Land

Severnaya Zemlya

KARA SEA

New Siberian Is.

LAPTEV SEA

EAST SIBERIAN SEA

Novaya Zemlya

BARENTS SEA

Jan Mayen (Nor.)

Wrangel I.

Faroe Is. (Den.)

SWEDEN

FINLAND

L. Ladoga

RUSSIAN FEDERATION

Sakhalin

Kamchatka

SEA OF OKHOTSK

Kuril Islands

UNITED KINGDOM

NORWAY

NORTH SEA

DENMARK

ESTONIA
LATVIA
LITHUANIA

BELARUS

L. Baikal

MONGOLIA

Hokkaidō

IRELAND

NETHS. GERMANY POLAND

BELG. CZECH REP.
LUX. SLOVAK REP.

UKRAINE

MOLDOVA

KAZAKHSTAN

L. Balkhash

Aral Sea

DEMOCRATIC PEOPLE'S REP. OF KOREA

SEA OF JAPAN

JAPAN

Honshū

Shikoku

Kyūshū

REP. OF KOREA

FRANCE SWITZ.

AUST. HUNGARY
ROMANIA

CASPIAN SEA

UZBEKISTAN

KYRGYZSTAN

CHINA

PACIFIC OCEAN

Ryūkyū Is.

EAST CHINA SEA

ANDORRA

PORTUGAL SPAIN

ITALY

BLACK SEA

GEORGIA
ARMENIA AZER-
BAIJAN

TURKMENISTAN

TAJIKISTAN

TAIWAN

Macau (Port.)

PHILIPPINE SEA

Northern Mariana Is. (US)

MONDAY INTERNATIONAL DATE LINE SUNDAY

MALTA

GREECE

TURKEY

CYPRUS SYRIA
LEBANON

ISRAEL

IRAQ

IRAN

AFGHANISTAN

PAKISTAN

NEPAL

BHUTAN

BANGLADESH

Guam (US)

MARSHALL IS.

TUNISIA

MOROCCO

ALGERIA

LIBYA

EGYPT

JORDAN

KUWAIT

SAUDI ARABIA

THE GULF
QATAR
BAHRAIN

UAE

OMAN

ARABIAN SEA

INDIA

MYANMAR

LAOS

THAILAND

VIETNAM

CAMBODIA

SOUTH CHINA SEA

Luzon

PHILIPPINES

Visayan Is.

Mindanao

PALAU

FED. STATES OF MICRONESIA

MAURITANIA

MALI

NIGER

CHAD

ERITREA

SUDAN

YEMEN

Socotra (Yem.)

RED SEA

DJIBOUTI

Lakshadweep

BAY OF BENGAL

SRI LANKA

Andaman & Nicobar Is.

MALAYSIA

BRUNEI

SINGAPORE

MALDIVES

PAPUA NEW GUINEA

NAURU

KIRIBATI

BURKINA FASO

BENIN

NIGERIA

CENT. AFRICAN REPUBLIC

ETHIOPIA

SOMALIA

British Indian Ocean Territory

Sumatra

INDONESIA

Sulawesi

Borneo

New Guinea

SOLOMON IS.

TUVALU

Wallis & Futuna (Fr.)

GUINEA

CÔTE D'IVOIRE

LIBERIA

GHANA
TOGO

CAMEROON

UGANDA

KENYA

SEYCHELLES

Java

Christmas I. (Aust.)

Cocos Is. (Aust.)

VANUATU

FIJI

TONG.

New Caledonia (Fr.)

EQUATORIAL GUINEA
SÃO TOMÉ E PRÍNCIPE

GABON

CONGO

DEM. REP. OF CONGO

TANZANIA

COMOROS

Mayotte (Fr.)

INDIAN OCEAN

CORAL SEA

Ascension (UK)

Cabinda (Ang.)

ANGOLA

ZAMBIA

MALAWI

MADAGASCAR

MAURITIUS
Réunion (Fr.)

AUSTRALIA

Norfolk I. (Aust.)

Lord Howe I. (Aust.)

Kermadec Is. (NZ)

St Helena (UK)

NAMIBIA

ZIMBABWE

MOZAM-
BIQUE

GREAT AUSTRALIAN BIGHT

New Caledonia (Fr.)

North I.

NEW ZEALAND

SOUTH ATLANTIC OCEAN

Tristan da Cunha (UK)

Gough I. (UK)

BOTSWANA

SOUTH AFRICA

LESOTHO

SWAZILAND

Cape of Good Hope

Prince Edward Is. (S. Af.)

Îles Amsterdam & St Paul (Fr.)

Crozet Is. (Fr.)

TASMAN SEA

Tasmania

South I.

Chatham Is. (NZ)

Bouvet I. (Nor.)

Kerguelen Is. (Fr.)

Heard & McDonald Is. (Aust.)

Macquarie I. (Aust.)

SOUTHERN OCEAN

78 Simien National Park, Ethiopia
79 Parc National de Manovo-Gounda St Floris, Central African Republic
80 Réserve du Dja, Cameroon
81 Parc National de la Salonga, Dem. Rep. of Congo
82 Parc National de la Garamba, Dem. Rep. of Congo
83 Réserve du Okapi, Dem. Rep. of Congo
84 Parc National des Virunga, Dem. Rep. of Congo
85 Parc National du Kahuzi-Biega, Dem. Rep. of Congo
86 Ruwenzori Mountains National Park, Uganda
87 Bwindi Impenetrable National Park, Uganda
88 Sibiloi and Central Island National Parks, Kenya
89 Mount Kenya National Park and forest, Kenya
90 Serengeti National Park, Tanzania
91 Ngorongoro Conservation Area, Tanzania
92 Kilimanjaro National Park, Tanzania
93 Selous Game Reserve, Tanzania
94 Lake Malawi National Park, Malawi
95 Victoria Falls (Mosi-oa-Tunya), Zambia/Zimbabwe
96 Mana Pools National Park and Sapi & Chewore safari areas, Zimbabwe
97 Ilha da Moçambique, Mozambique
98 Réserve du Tsingy Bemaraha, Madagascar
99 Aldabra Atoll, Seychelles
100 Vallée de Mai Nature Reserve, Seychelles
101 Gough Island Wildlife Reserve

MIDDLE EAST
102 Arabian Oryx Sanctuary, Oman

SOUTH, EAST & SE ASIA
103 Sagarmatha National Park, Nepal
104 Royal Chitwan National Park, Nepal
105 Nanda Devi National Park, India
106 Keoladeo National Park, India
107 Manas Wildlife Sanctuary, India
108 Kaziranga National Park, India
109 Sundarbans National Park, India
110 Sundarbans, Bangladesh
111 Dambulla Golden Rock Temple, Sri Lanka
112 Sinharaja Forest Reserve, Sri Lanka
113 Tai Shan, Shandong, China
114 Huang Shan, Anhui, China
115 Jiuzhaigou Valley Scenic and Historic Interest Area, Sichuan, China
116 Huanglong Scenic and Historic Interest Area, Sichuan, China
117 Emei Shan and Leshan Giant Buddha, Sichuan, China
118 Wulingyuan Scenic and Historic Interest Area, Hunan, China
119 Yakushima, Japan
120 Shirakami-Sanchi, Japan
121 Ha Long Bay, Vietnam

122 Sukhothai and its region: historic towns, Thailand
123 Thung Yai-Huai Kha Khaeng Wildlife Sanctuaries, Thailand
124 Tubbataha Reef Marine Park, Philippines
125 Ujung Kulon National Park and Krakatau Nature Reserve, Indonesia
126 Komodo National Park, Indonesia

AUSTRALASIA & PACIFIC
127 Shark Bay, Australia
128 Kakadu National Park, Australia
129 Queensland wet tropics, Australia
130 Central eastern rainforest reserves, Australia
131 Great Barrier Reef, Australia
132 Uluru-Kata Tjuta National Park, Australia
133 Naracoorte & Riversleigh: fossil mammal sites, Australia
134 Willandra Lakes region, Australia
135 Fraser Island, Australia
136 Tasmanian wilderness, Australia
137 Lord Howe island group, Australia
138 Heard and McDonald Islands
139 Macquarie Island
140 Tongariro National Park, New Zealand
141 Te Wahipounamu-Southwest New Zealand
142 Fiordland National Park, New Zealand
143 Henderson Island

UNESCO CULTURAL HERITAGE SITES

All properties which belong to the UNESCO World Heritage List are considered to be of world importance either because of their natural features or their significant man-made contribution to world culture. Sites for consideration of heritage status are submitted by the appropriate government ministry. UNESCO then considers each proposal under strict criteria and designates sites where appropriate.

Some countries are not signatories to the convention, and so the UNESCO list is not fully comprehensive worldwide.

There are two main categories of property: natural and cultural.

CULTURAL SITES.
(i) Monuments: including sculptures, memorial stones, obelisks, cave paintings and inscriptions;
(ii) Groups of buildings: these can be separated or connected but are usually set in a unique landscape;
(iii) Sites of anthropological or archaeological importance.

Properties named in red are included on the list of World Heritage in Danger.

The Organization of World Heritage Cities (OWHC) was established in 1993, based on the idea that cultural or historic sites within cities experience particular pressures and require a more dynamic style of management than other sites. Most of these cities contain one or more UNESCO Cultural Heritage Sites, but this is not an essential requirement for membership of the OWHC.

World Heritage Cities are named on the map.

For further information, contact:

The World Heritage Centre, UNESCO,
7 place de Fontenoy,
75352 Paris 07,
France.

Tel: +33 1 45 68 10 00.

CANADA & UNITED STATES
1 Anthony Island, British Columbia
2 Head-Smashed-In Buffalo Jump, Alberta
3 Québec: historic area
4 Lunenburg: old city, Nova Scotia
5 L'Anse aux Meadows Historic Park, Newfoundland
6 Mesa Verde National Park, Colorado
7 Chaco Culture National Historical Park, New Mexico
8 Pueblo de Taos, New Mexico
9 Cahokia Mounds State Historic Site, Illinois
10 Charlottesville: Monticello and University of Virginia, Virginia
11 Philadelphia: Independence Hall, Pennsylvania
12 Statue of Liberty, New Jersey

MEXICO, CENTRAL AMERICA & CARIBBEAN
13 Sierra de la San Francisco: rock paintings, Mexico
14 Zacatecas: historic centre, Mexico
15 Guanajuato: historic town and adjacent mines, Mexico
16 Querétaro: historic monuments, Mexico
17 Teotihuacan: pre-Hispanic city, Mexico
18 El Tajin: pre-Hispanic city, Mexico
19 Guadalajara: Hospicio Cabañas, Mexico
20 Morelia: historic centre, Mexico
21 Mexico City: historic centre and Xochimilco, Mexico

22 Popocatépetl: monasteries, Mexico
23 Puebla: historic centre, Mexico
24 Oaxaca: historic centre and Monte Albán: archaeological site, Mexico
25 Palenque: pre-Hispanic city and National Park, Mexico
26 Uxmal: pre-Hispanic city, Mexico
27 Chichén Itzá: pre-Hispanic city, Mexico
28 Antigua, Guatemala
29 Quiriguá: archaeological park and ruins, Guatemala
30 Copán: Maya site, Honduras
31 Joya de Cerén: archaeological site, El Salvador
32 Portobelo and San Lorenzo: fortifications, Panama
33 Panama City: historic district and the Salón Bolívar, Panama
34 La Habana (Havana): old town and its fortifications, Cuba
35 Trinidad and Valley de los Ingenios, Cuba
36 Santiago de Cuba: San Pedro de la Roca Castle, Cuba
37 Citadel, Sans-Souci and Ramiers Historic Park, Haiti
38 Santo Domingo: colonial city, Dominican Republic
39 La Fortaleza and San Juan: historic sites, Puerto Rico
40 Willemstad: historic area, inner city and harbour, Curaçao

SOUTH AMERICA
41 Coro: town and its port, Venezuela
42 Cartagena: port, fortress and monuments, Colombia
43 Mompós: historic centre, Colombia
44 Parque Arqueológico Nacional Tierradentro, Colombia
45 Parque Arqueológico San Agustín, Colombia
46 Quito: old city, Ecuador
47 Chan Chan: archaeological area Peru

48 Chavin: archaeological site, Peru
49 Lima: historic centre, Peru
50 Santuario histórico Machu Picchu, Peru
51 Cuzco: old city, Peru
52 Nazca: geoglyphs and Pampas de Juma, Peru
53 Potosí, Bolivia
54 Sucre: historic city, Bolivia
55 Chiquitos Jesuit missions, Bolivia
56 Jesús and Trinidad: Jesuit missions, Paraguay
57 Brasília, Brazil
58 Parque Nacional Serra da Capivara, Brazil
59 São Luís: historic centre, Brazil
60 Olinda: historic centre, Brazil
61 Salvador de Bahia: historic centre, Brazil
62 Ouro Prêto: historic town, Brazil
63 Congonhas: Sanctuary of Bom Jesus, Brazil
64 São Miguel: Jesuit mission ruins, Brazil; Loreto, San Ignacio Miní, Santa Ana & Santa Maria Mayor: Guaraní Jesuit missions, Argentina
65 Colonia del Sacramento: historic quarter, Uruguay
66 Parque Nacional Rapa Nui, Easter Island

EUROPE* (including Atlantic islands)
67 Angra do Heroismo: central area, Azores
68 Urnes: stave church, Norway
69 Røros: mining town, Norway
70 Alta: rock drawings, Norway
71 Lapponian area, Sweden
72 Luleå: Gammelstad church town, Sweden
73 Rauma: old town, Finland
74 Petäjävesi: old church, Finland
75 Verla: groundwood and board mill, Finland

FORMER SOVIET UNION*
76 Solovetskiye Ostrova: cultural and historic ensemble, Russian Federation
77 Khizi Pogost, Russian Federation

78 Mtskheta: historic church, Georgia
79 Haghpat: monastery, Armenia
80 Itchan Kala, Uzbekistan
81 Bukhara: historic centre, Uzbekistan

AFRICA*
82 Thebes: ancient city and necropolis, Egypt
83 Abu Simbel to Philae: Nubian monuments, Egypt
84 Aksum: archaeological site, Ethiopia
85 Fasil Ghebbi & Gonder monuments, Ethiopia
86 Lalibela: rock-hewn churches, Ethiopia
87 Awash Lower Valley, Ethiopia
88 Tiya: carved steles, Ethiopia
89 Omo Lower Valley, Ethiopia
90 Tadrart Acacus: rock-art sites, Libya
91 Tassili n'Ajjer, Algeria
92 Chinguetti, Ouadane, Oualata and Tichitt: trading and religious centres, Mauritania
93 Timbuktu, Mali
94 Djenne: old towns, Mali
95 Île de Gorée, Senegal
96 Ashante traditional buildings, Ghana
97 Accra and Volta areas: forts and castles, Ghana
98 Abomey: royal palaces, Benin

MAP LABELS:

LINCOLN SEA
BEAUFORT SEA
Ellesmere I.
Axel Heiburg I.
Devon I.
Parry Is.
Greenland (Den.)
Banks I.
Victoria I.
Southampton I.
BAFFIN BAY
Qikiqtaluk (Baffin I.)
DAVIS STRAIT
Alaska (US)
Great Bear Lake
Great Slave Lake
HUDSON BAY
LABRADOR SEA
Cape Farewell
BERING SEA
CANADA
L. Winnipeg
L. Superior
Vancouver I.
Québec
Newfoundland
St Pierre et Miquelon (Fr.)
NORTH ATLANTIC OCEAN
Lunenburg
L. Huron
L. Michigan
L. Erie
L. Ontario
Long I.
UNITED STATES OF AMERICA
Bermuda (UK)
Angra do Heroismo
Azores (Po.)
Aleutian Islands
Hawaiian Is. (US)
TROPIC OF CANCER
Baja California
GULF OF ALASKA
GULF OF MEXICO
MEXICO
Zacatecas
La Habana (Havana)
CUBA
BAHAMAS
HAITI
Turks & Caicos Is. (UK)
Cayman Is. (UK)
JAMAICA
Santo Domingo
San Juan
Trinidad
BELIZE
GUATEMALA HONDURAS
EL SALVADOR NICARAGUA
COSTA RICA
Panama Canal
PANAMA
BARBADOS
GRENADA
TRINIDAD & TOBAGO
Coro
Vela
Cartagena
Mompós
VENEZUELA
COLOMBIA
GUYANA
SURINAME
French Guiana
Quito
ECUADOR
Galapagos Is. (Ec.)
PACIFIC OCEAN
KIRIBATI
Tokelau (NZ)
American Samoa
WESTERN SAMOA
Cook Is. (NZ)
Niue (NZ)
French Polynesia
PERU
Lima
Cuzco
BOLIVIA
Sucre
Potosí
BRAZIL
Brasília
Ouro Prêto
Salvador de Bahia
Olinda
PARAGUAY
URUGUAY
Colonia del Sacramento
ARGENTINA
CHILE
Pitcairn Is. (UK)
Easter I. (Chile)
Islas Juan Fernandez (Chile)
TROPIC OF CAPRICORN
Falkland Is. (UK)
Tierra del Fuego
Cape Horn
DRAKE PASSAGE
South Georgia (UK)
SCOTIA SEA
MONDAY INTERNATIONAL DATE LINE SUNDAY
EQUATOR

MAP A
BAHÍA DE CAMPECHE
Guanajuato
Querétaro
Morelia
Mexico City
Puebla
Oaxaca
MEXICO
Yucatán Peninsula
BELIZE
GUATEMALA
Antigua
EL SALVADOR
HONDURAS
NICARAG.
PACIFIC OCEAN
1000 km
500 miles

UNESCO CULTURAL HERITAGE SITES

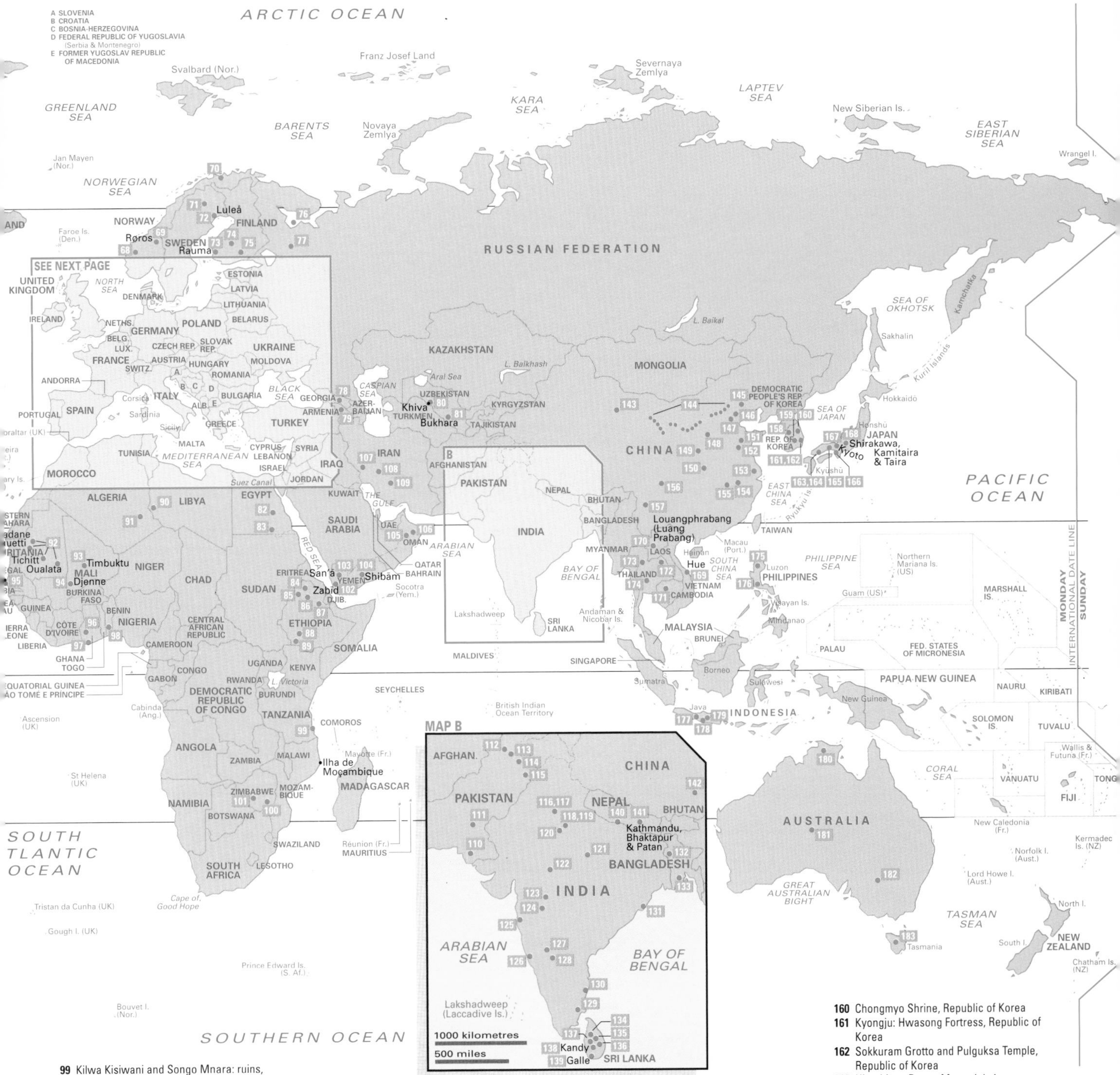

A SLOVENIA
B CROATIA
C BOSNIA-HERZEGOVINA
D FEDERAL REPUBLIC OF YUGOSLAVIA
  (Serbia & Montenegro)
E FORMER YUGOSLAV REPUBLIC
  OF MACEDONIA

Map labels (oceans, seas, countries and site numbers shown on the map)

ARCTIC OCEAN · NORWEGIAN SEA · GREENLAND SEA · BARENTS SEA · KARA SEA · LAPTEV SEA · EAST SIBERIAN SEA · SEA OF OKHOTSK · PACIFIC OCEAN · NORTH SEA · BLACK SEA · CASPIAN SEA · MEDITERRANEAN SEA · RED SEA · ARABIAN SEA · BAY OF BENGAL · SOUTH CHINA SEA · PHILIPPINE SEA · SOUTHERN OCEAN · SOUTH ATLANTIC OCEAN · CORAL SEA · TASMAN SEA

RUSSIAN FEDERATION · CHINA · INDIA · AUSTRALIA · JAPAN · MONGOLIA · KAZAKHSTAN

MAP B

1000 kilometres
500 miles

---

99 Kilwa Kisiwani and Songo Mnara: ruins, Tanzania
100 Great Zimbabwe National Monument, Zimbabwe
101 Khami Ruins National Monument, Zimbabwe

MIDDLE EAST*

102 Zabid: historic town, Yemen
103 San'a: old city, Yemen
104 Shibam: old walled city, Yemen
105 Bahla: fort, Oman
106 Bat, Al-Khutm and Al-Ayn: archaeolgical sites, Oman
107 Tchogha Zanbil: ziggurat and complex, Iran
108 Esfahan (Isfahan): Meidam Emam, Iran
109 Persepolis: ancient city, Iran

SOUTH, EAST & SE ASIA

110 Thatta: historical monuments, Pakistan
111 Mohenjodaro: archaeological site, Pakistan
112 Takht-i-Bakhi: Buddhist ruins; Sahr-i-Bahlol: remains of city, Pakistan
113 Taxila: archaeological site, Pakistan
114 Rohtas: fort, Pakistan
115 Lahore: fort and Shalimar Gardens, Pakistan
116 Delhi: Humayun's Tomb, India

117 Delhi: Qutb Minar and its monuments, India
118 Agra Fort, India
119 Taj Mahal, Agra, India
120 Fatehpur Sikri: Mongol city, India
121 Khajuraho: group of monuments, India
122 Sanchi: Buddhist monastery, India
123 Ajanta Caves, India
124 Ellora Caves, India
125 Elephanta Caves, India
126 Goa: churches and convents, India
127 Pattadakal: group of monuments, India
128 Hampi: group of monuments, India
129 Thanjavur: Brihadisvara Temple, India
130 Mahabalipuram: group of monuments, India
131 Konarak: Sun Temple, India
132 Paharpur: ruins of the Buddhist Vihara, Bangladesh
133 Bagerhat: historic city, Bangladesh
134 Anuradhapura: sacred city, Sri Lanka
135 Sigiriya: ancient city, Sri Lanka
136 Polonnaruwa: ancient city, Sri Lanka
137 Dambulla Golden Rock Temple, Sri Lanka
138 Kandy: sacred city, Sri Lanka
139 Galle: old town and its fortifications, Sri Lanka

140 Lumbini: birthplace of Lord Buddha, Nepal
141 Kathmandu Valley, Nepal
142 Lhasa: Potala Palace, Tibet, China
143 Mogao Caves, Gansu, China
144 Great Wall, China
145 Chengde: mountain resort and outlying temples, Hebei, China
146 Beijing (Peking): Imperial Palace of the Ming and Qing Dynasties, China
147 Zhoukoudian: Peking Man site, China
148 Pingyao: ancient city, Shanxi, China
149 Xi'an area: Mausoleum of the first Qin Emperor, Shaanxi, China
150 Wudangshan: ancient building complex, Hubei, China
151 Tai Shan, Shandong, China
152 Qufu: temple & cemetery of Confucius and Kong family monuments, Shandong, China
153 Suzhou: classical gardens, Jiangsu, China
154 Huang Shan, Anhui, China
155 Lu Shan, Jiangxi, China
156 Emei Shan and Leshan Giant Buddha, Sichuan, China
157 Lijiang: old town, Yunnan, China
158 Seoul: Ch'angdokkung Palace Complex, Republic of Korea
159 Haeinsa Temple, Republic of Korea

160 Chongmyo Shrine, Republic of Korea
161 Kyongju: Hwasong Fortress, Republic of Korea
162 Sokkuram Grotto and Pulguksa Temple, Republic of Korea
163 Hiroshima: Peace Memorial, Japan
164 Itsukushima Shrine, Japan
165 Himeji, Japan
166 Horyuji: Buddhist monuments, Japan
167 Kyoto: ancient city monuments, Japan
168 Shirakawa-Go and Gokayama: historic villages, Japan
169 Hue: monuments complex, Vietnam
170 Louangphrabang (Luang Prabang), Laos
171 Angkor, Cambodia
172 Ban Chiang: archaeological site, Thailand
173 Sukhothai and its region: historic towns, Thailand
174 Ayutthaya and its region: historic towns, Thailand
175 Cordillera Central: rice terraces, the Philippines
176 Manila: Baroque churches, the Philippines
177 Borobudur: temple compound, Indonesia
178 Prambanan: temple compound, Indonesia
179 Sangiran: early man site, Indonesia

AUSTRALASIA & PACIFIC

180 Kakadu National Park, Australia
181 Uluru-Kata Tjuta National Park, Australia
182 Willandra Lakes region, Australia
183 Tasmanian wilderness, Australia

* See next page for other sites in these areas

UNESCO CULTURAL HERITAGE SITES

Cities named on the map are members of the Organization of World Heritage Cities (OWHC). See previous page for explanation.
THE SEVEN WONDERS OF THE ANCIENT WORLD
A Statue of Zeus, Olympia 9-metre statue of the Greek god covered in gold and ivory
B Temple of Artemis, Ephesus Marble temple in honour of goddess of hunting and the moon
C Mausoleum, Halikarnassos Tomb of Mausolus built by his widow
D Colossus of Rhodes 32-metre high bronze statue of the sun god Helios
E Pharos of Alexandria World's first known lighthouse, 122 metres high
F Egyptian Pyramids Oldest of the ancient wonders and the only one surviving today
G Hanging Gardens of Babylon Series of terraces of trees and flowers along the banks of the Euphrates
SHETLAND ISLANDS
ORKNEY ISLANDS
HEBRIDES
NORTH SEA
Bergen
NORWAY
Vänern
Vättern
Skagerrak
Kattegat
SWEDEN
FIN.
ÅLAND (AHVENANMAA)
HIIUMAA
SAAREMAA
GULF OF FINLAND
ESTONIA
LAKE LADOGA
St Petersburg
Novgorod
RUSSIAN FEDERATION
Moskva (Moscow)
Visby
GOTLAND
ÖLAND
BALTIC SEA
BORNHOLM
LATVIA
LITHUANIA
(Russia)
Vilnius
BELARUS
Scotland
Edinburgh
UNITED KINGDOM
N. Ireland
IRELAND
ISLE OF MAN
England
Wales
Bath
DENMARK
Lübeck
Potsdam
NETHERLANDS
Goslar
Quedlinburg
GERMANY
BELGIUM
Luxembourg-Ville
Bamberg
CZECH REP.
Praha (Prague)
Kutná Hora
Český Krumlov
Telč
Warszawa (Warsaw)
POLAND
Kraków (Cracow)
Zamość
UKRAINE
CELTIC SEA
English Channel
CHANNEL IS. (UK)
Mont-St Michel
Paris
Nancy
Strasbourg
Bern (Berne)
SWITZ.
LIECH.
Salzburg
AUSTRIA
SLOVAK REP.
Banská Štiavnica
Budapest
HUNGARY
MOLDOVA
Biertan
ROMANIA
Krim (Crimea)
BAY OF BISCAY
FRANCE
Capriate San Gervasio
Vicenza
Ferrara
Venézia (Venice)
SLOVENIA
CROATIA
Serbia
BOSNIA-HERZEGOVINA
Split
Dubrovnik
Monte.
Kotor
FED. REP. OF YUGO.
BULGARIA
Nesebŭr (Nessebar)
BLACK SEA
GEORGIA
ATLANTIC OCEAN
Santiago de Compostela
ANDORRA
MONACO
Firenze (Florence)
San Gimignano
Siena
Pienza
ITALY
CORSE (CORSICA)
ADRIATIC SEA
Porto (Oporto)
Salamanca
Segovia
PORTUGAL
Ávila
Toledo
Cuenca
Cáceres
Mérida
SPAIN
Sintra
Évora
Córdoba
Granada
BALEARIC IS.
MENORCA (MINORCA)
MALLORCA (MAJORCA)
EIVISSA (IBIZA)
FORMENTERA
SARDEGNA (SARDINIA)
TYRRHENIAN SEA
Roma (Rome) & Vatican City
Nápoli (Naples)
Matera
ALBANIA
Ohrid
FORMER YUGO. REP. OF MACEDONIA
Bosporus
Istanbul
Safranbolu
KÉRKIRA (CORFU)
AEGEAN SEA
GREECE
Dardanelles
TURKEY
IONIAN SEA
SICILIA (SICILY)
Alger (Algiers)
Tunis
Gibraltar (UK)
Strait of Gibraltar
Ceuta (Sp.)
Melilla (Sp.)
MALTA
Valletta
Pelopónnisos
Ródos (Rhodes)
Halab (Aleppo)
SYRIA
CYPRUS
Sousse
Qairouan (Kairouan)
TUNISIA
KRÍTI (CRETE)
MEDITERRANEAN SEA
LEBANON
Bosra
Dimashq (Damascus)
IRAQ
ISRAEL
Jerusalem
JORDAN
Fès
Meknès
MOROCCO
ALGERIA
Ghardaya
Marrakech
GULF OF SIRTE
1000 kilometres
500 miles
Ghadāmis
LIBYA
EGYPT
El Qâhira (Cairo)
SAUDI ARABIA

Properties named in red are included on the list of World Heritage in Danger.

EUROPE (including Turkey)
1 Bergen: Bryggen area, Norway
2 Tanum: rock carvings, Sweden
3 Engelsberg: ironworks, Sweden
4 Birka and Hovgården: archaeological sites, Sweden
5 Drottningholm Palace, Sweden
6 Stockholm: Skogskyrkogarden, Sweden
7 Visby: Hanseatic town and former Viking site, Sweden
8 Helsinki (Helsingfors): Suomenlinna Fortress, Finland
9 Jelling: mounds, runic stones and church, Denmark
10 Roskilde: cathedral, Denmark
11 Skellig Michael: monastic complex, Ireland
12 Brú Na Bóinne: archaeological ensemble at the bend of the Boyne, Ireland
13 Edinburgh: old and new towns, Scotland
14 Castles and town walls of King Edward, northwest Wales
15 Hadrian's Wall, England
16 Durham: castle and cathedral, England
17 Studley Royal Park and Fountains Abbey ruins, England
18 Ironbridge Gorge, England
19 Bath, England
20 Stonehenge, Avebury and associated megalithic sites, England
21 Blenheim Palace, England
22 London: Tower of London, England
23 London: Westminster Palace, Abbey of Westminster and St Margaret's Church, England
24 London: Maritime Greenwich, England
25 Canterbury: cathedral, St Augustine's Abbey and St Martin's Church, England
26 Schokland: prehistoric settlements, The Netherlands
27 Amsterdam: defence line, The Netherlands
28 Kinderdijk-Elshout: mill network, The Netherlands
29 Luxembourg-Ville: old quarters and fortifications
30 Lübeck: Hanseatic city, Germany
31 Berlin and Potsdam: palaces and parks, Germany
32 Eisleben and Wittenberg: Luther memorials, Germany
33 Dessau and Weimar: Bauhaus buildings, Germany
34 Quedlinburg: Collegiate church, castle and old town, Germany
35 Goslar: historic town and Rammelsberg mines, Germany
36 Hildesheim: St Mary's Cathedral and St Michael's Church, Germany
37 Aachen (Aix-la-Chapelle): cathedral, Germany
38 Köln (Cologne): cathedral, Germany
39 Brühl: Augustusburg and Falkenlust Castles, Germany
40 Trier: Roman monuments, cathedral and Liebfrauen Church, Germany
41 Völklingen: ironworks, Germany
42 Maulbronn: Cistercian monastery complex, Germany
43 Speyer: cathedral, Germany
44 Lorsch: abbey and Altenmünster, Germany
45 Würzburg: Residence with the Court Gardens and Residence Square, Germany
46 Bamberg, Germany
47 Wies: pilgrimage church, Germany
48 Mont-St Michel and its bay, France
49 Amiens: cathedral, France
50 Reims: Notre-Dame Cathedral, former Abbey of St Remi and Tau Palace, France
51 Nancy: Place Stanislas, Place de la Carrière and Place d'Alliance, France
52 Strasbourg: Grand Île, France
53 Arc-et-Senans: royal saltworks, France
54 Fontenay: Cistercian abbey, France
55 Vézelay: basilica and hill, France
56 Bourges: cathedral, France
57 Fontainebleau: palace and park, France
58 Paris: banks of the Seine, France
59 Versailles: palace and park, France
60 Chartres: cathedral, France
61 Chambord: château and estate, France
62 St Savin-sur-Gartempe: church, France
63 Vallée du Vézère: Lascaux and other decorated grottoes, France
64 Canal du Midi, France
65 Remoulins: Pont du Gard Roman aqueduct, France
66 Orange: Roman theatre and its surroundings and the triumphal arch, France
67 Avignon: historic centre, France
68 Arles: Roman and Romanesque monuments, France
69 Carcassonne: historic fortified city, France
70 Monte Perdido, France/Spain
71 Barcelona: Parque & Palacio Güell and Casa Milá, Spain
72 Barcelona: Palau de la Música Catalaña and the Hospital de Sant Pau, Spain
73 Poblet: monastery, Spain
74 Valencia: La Lonja de la Sada, Spain
75 Teruel: Mujedar architecture, Spain
76 Cuenca: historic walled town, Spain
77 San Millán and Suso: monasteries, Spain
78 Burgos: cathedral, Spain
79 Las Médulas, Spain
80 Camino de Santiago: The Way of St James pilgrimage route, Spain
81 Altamira Cave, Spain
82 Asturias: churches of the Asturias Kingdom, Spain
83 Santiago de Compostela: old town, Spain
84 Salamanca: old city, Spain
85 Ávila: old town with extra-muros churches, Spain
86 Segovia: old town and aqueduct, Spain
87 El Escorial: monastery, Spain
88 Toledo: historic city, Spain
89 Guadalupe: Royal Monastery of Santa Maria, Spain
90 Cáceres: old town, Spain
91 Mérida: archaeological ensemble, Spain
92 Sevilla (Seville): cathedral, Alcazar and Archivo de Indias, Spain
93 Córdoba: mosque and historic centre, Spain
94 Granada: Alhambra, Generalife & Albaicín quarter, Spain
95 Porto (Oporto): historic centre, Portugal
96 Tomar: Convent of Christ, Portugal
97 Batalha: monastery, Portugal
98 Alcobaça: monastery, Portugal
99 Sintra: historic city, Portugal
100 Lisboa (Lisbon): Monastery of the Hieronymites and Tower of Belém, Portugal
101 Évora: historic centre, Portugal
102 Bern (Berne): old city, Switzerland
103 St Gallen: convent, Switzerland
104 Müstair: Benedictine Convent of St John, Switzerland
105 Salzburg: historic centre, Austria
106 Hallstadt-Dachstein-Salzkammergut: cultural landscape, Austria
107 Wien (Vienna): Schönbrunn Palace and Gardens, Austria
108 Torino (Turin): Residences of the Royal House of Savoy, Italy
109 Milano (Milan): Church and Dominican Convent of Santa Maria delle Grazie with "The Last Supper" by Leonardo da Vinci, Italy
110 Crespi d'Adda, Italy
111 Val Camónica: rock drawings, Italy
112 Vicenza: city and the Palladian Villas of the Veneto, Italy
113 Pádova (Padua): botanical garden, Italy
114 Venézia (Venice) and its lagoon, Italy
115 Ferrara, Renaissance city, Italy
116 Ravenna: early Christian monuments and mosaics, Italy
117 Modena: cathedral, Torre Civica and Piazza Grande, Italy
118 Firenze (Florence): historic centre, Italy
119 Portovénere, Cinque Terre, Ísola Palmária, Ísola del Tino and Ísola del Tinetto, Italy
120 Pisa: Piazza del Duomo, Italy
121 San Gimignano: historic centre, Italy
122 Siena: historic centre, Italy
123 Pienza: historic centre, Italy
124 Vatican City
125 Roma (Rome): historic centre, incl. extraterritorial properties of the Holy See & San Paolo fuori le Mura, Italy
126 Caserta: Royal Palace with park, Vanvitelli Aqueduct and San Leucio complex, Italy
127 Nápoli (Naples): historic centre, Italy
128 Herculaneum, Pompei and Torre Annunziata: archaeological areas, Italy
129 Costiera Amalfitana, Italy
130 Castel del Monte: medieval castle, Italy
131 Matera: I Sassi di Matera, Italy
132 Alberobello: Trulli houses, Italy
133 Villa Romana del Casale, Italy
134 Agrigento: archaeological area, Sicily, Italy
135 Su Nuraxi di Barúmini, Sardinia, Italy
136 Malbork: Teutonic castle, Poland
137 Torun: medieval town, Poland
138 Warszawa (Warsaw): historic centre, Poland
139 Zamosc: old city, Poland
140 Wieliczka: salt mines, Poland
141 Kraków (Cracow): historic centre, Poland
142 Oswiecim (Auschwitz): concentration camp, Poland
143 Praha (Prague): historic centre, Czech Republic
144 Kutná Hora: historical centre, Church of Santa Barbara and Cathedral of Our Lady at Sedlec, Czech Republic
145 Zelená Hora: St John of Nepomuk, Czech Republic
146 Cesky Krumlov: historic centre, Czech Republic
147 Telc: historic centre, Czech Republic
148 Lednice-Valtice: cultural landscape, Czech Republic
149 Banská Stiavnica, Slovak Republic
150 Vlkolínec, Slovak Republic
151 Spisské Pohradie: Spissky Hrad and associated monuments, Slovak Republic
152 Hollokö: traditional village, Hungary
153 Budapest: including the banks of the Danube and Buda Castle area, Hungary
154 Pannonhalma: Millenary Benedictine Abbey and its natural environment, Hungary
155 Porec: Episcopal complex, Croatia
156 Trogir: historic city, Croatia
157 Split: historic centre with Diocletian Palace, Croatia
158 Dubrovnik: old city, Croatia
159 Kotor and its gulf, Fed. Rep. of Yugoslavia
160 Stari Ras and Sopocani Monastery, Fed. Rep. of Yugoslavia
161 Studenica: monastery, Fed. Rep. of Yugoslavia
162 Ohrid Lake and its region, F.Y.R. of Macedonia
163 Butrinti (Buthrotum): archaeological site, Albania
164 Horezu: monastery, Romania
165 Biertan: town and fortified church, Romania
166 Moldavia churches, Romania
167 Boyana: church, Bulgaria
168 Sveshtari: Thracian tomb, Bulgaria
169 Ivanovo: rock-hewn churches, Bulgaria
170 Madara: horseman stone relief, Bulgaria
171 Nesebur (Nessebar): ancient city, Bulgaria
172 Kazanluk: Thracian tomb, Bulgaria
173 Rila: monastery, Bulgaria
174 Áthos, Greece
175 Thessaloníki (Salonika): Palaeochristian and Byzantine monuments, Greece
176 Vergina: archaeological site, Greece
177 Metéora, Greece
178 Delfí (Delphi): archaeological site, Greece
179 Olimbía (Olympía): archaeological site, Greece
180 Bassae: Temple of Apollo Epicurius, Greece
181 Místrás, Greece
182 Epídavros (Epidaurus): archaeological site, Greece
183 Athína (Athens): Acropolis, Greece
184 Híos (Chios): Daphni, Hossios, Luckas and Néa Moni monasteries, Greece
185 Sámos: Pythagoreion and Heraion, Greece
186 Dílos, Greece
187 Ródos (Rhodes): medieval city, Greece
188 Xanthos-Letoon, Turkey
189 Hierapolis-Pamukkale, Turkey
190 Istanbul: historic areas, Turkey
191 Safranbolu, Turkey
192 Hattusha: Hittite city, Turkey
193 Göreme National Park and Cappadocia rock sites, Turkey
194 Divrigi: Great Mosque and hospital, Turkey
195 Nemrut Dag: archaeological site, Turkey
196 Ggantija: megalithic temples, Malta
197 Hal Saflieni Hypogeum, Malta
198 Valletta: old city, Malta
199 Paphos: archaeological site, Cyprus
200 Troödos region: painted churches, Cyprus

FORMER SOVIET UNION
201 Tallinn: historic centre, Estonia
202 Riga: historic centre, Latvia
203 Vilnius: old city, Lithuania
204 Kyyiv (Kiev): St Sophia Cathedral, related monastic buildings and Lavra of Kyyiv-Pechersk, Ukraine
205 Sankt-Peterburg (St Petersburg): historic centre and related monuments, Russian Fed.
206 Novgorod: historic monuments and surroundings, Russian Fed.
208 Moskva (Moscow): Kremlin & Red Square, Russian Fed.
209 Moskva (Moscow): Church of the Ascension at Kolomenskoye, Russian Fed.
209 Sergiyev Posad: architectural ensemble of the Trinity Sergius Lavra, Russian Fed.
210 Vladimir and Suzdal: White Monuments, Russian Fed.
211 Upper Svaneti area, Georgia
212 Kutaisi: Bagrati Cathedral and Gelati Monastery, Georgia

AFRICA
213 Tétouan: medina, Morocco
214 Fès: medina, Morocco
215 Volubilis: archaeological site, Morocco
216 Meknès: historic city, Morocco
217 Marrakech: medina, Morocco
218 Aït Benhaddou: fortified village, Morocco
219 Tipasa: archaeological site, Algeria
220 Alger (Algiers): Kasbah, Algeria
221 Benî Hammâd: Al Qal'a, Algeria
222 Djemila: Roman ruins, Algeria
223 Timgad: Roman ruins, Algeria
224 M'Zab Valley, Algeria
225 Dougga, Tunisia
226 Tunis: medina, Tunisia
227 Carthage: archaeological site, Tunisia
228 Kerkouane: Punic town and its necropolis, Tunisia
229 Sousse: medina, Tunisia
230 El Jem: amphitheatre, Tunisia
231 Qairouan (Kairouan), Tunisia
232 Ghadamis: old town, Libya
233 Sabratha: archaeological site, Libya
234 Leptis Magna: archaeological site, Libya
235 Cyrene: archaeological site, Libya
236 Abu Mena: Christian ruins, Egypt
237 El Qâhira (Cairo): Islamic city, Egypt
238 Memphis: Pyramid fields from Giza to Dahshur and its necropolis, Egypt

MIDDLE EAST
239 Halab: ancient city of Aleppo, Syria
240 Tadmur: archaeological site of Palmyra, Syria
241 Dimashq (Damascus): ancient city, Syria
242 Bosra: ancient city, Syria
243 Anjar: archaeological site, Lebanon
244 Baalbek, Lebanon
245 Byblos, Lebanon
246 Soûr: archaeological site of Tyre, Lebanon
247 Jerusalem: old city and its walls (proposed by Jordan)
248 Qasr Amra, Jordan
249 Petra, Jordan
250 Hatra, Iraq

CLIMATE

TEMPERATURE CONVERSION

°Celsius	−10	0	10	20	30	40
°Fahrenheit	14	32	50	68	86	104

RAINFALL CONVERSION

Millimetres	102	203	305	406	508	610
Inches	4	8	12	16	20	24

WINTER

TEMPERATURE (January average, degrees Celsius)
- 10° – 19°
- 0° – 9°
- Minus 10° – minus 1°
- Below minus 10°

RAINFALL (November to April total)
- 500mm and over
- 250 – 499mm
- Less than 250mm

PREVAILING WIND shown as white arrows

NORWEGIAN SEA · NORTH SEA · BALTIC SEA · CELTIC SEA · ATLANTIC OCEAN · GULF OF BOTHNIA · GULF OF FINLAND · WHITE SEA · LAKE ONEGA · LAKE LADOGA · BLACK SEA · SEA OF AZOV · AEGEAN SEA · IONIAN SEA · TYRRHENIAN SEA · ADRIATIC SEA · MEDITERRANEAN SEA

SCANDINAVIA · BRITISH ISLES · IBERIAN PENINSULA · NORTH EUROPEAN PLAIN · CENTRAL RUSSIAN UPLANDS · ANATOLIA · ALPS · PYRENEES · APPENNINES · DINARIC ALPS · CARPATHIANS · CAUCASUS · TAURUS MOUNTAINS · ATLAS

Oban · Grampians · Belmullet · Dublin · ISLE OF MAN · HEBRIDES · Tynemouth · Pennines · Cambrian Mtns. · Birmingham · London · Plymouth · Brest · Nantes · Bordeaux · Tours · Paris · Paris Basin · Nancy · Brussels · Ardennes · Utrecht · Emden · Lübeck · Berlin · Erfurt · Frankfurt · Prague · Bohemian Forest · Black Forest · Munich · Zürich · Lugano · Tirol · Nice · Riviera · Genoa · Bastia · Corsica · Rome · Bari · Cágliari · SARDINIA · Palermo · SICILY · Valletta · MALTA · Tunis · Algiers · Almería · Cádiz · Sierra Nevada · Lisbon · Madrid · Bragança · Barcelona · Valencia · Palma de Mallorca · MINORCA · MAJORCA · IBIZA · FORMENTERA · BALEARIC IS. · A Coruña · Santander · Cantabrian Mountains · Andorra · Perpignan · Lyon · Massif Central · Jura · Venice · Zagreb · Graz · Budapest · Hungarian Plain · Bratislava · Tatra · Cluj-Napoca · Transylvanian Alps · Belgrade · Dubrovnik · Dalmatia · Tirana · Thessaloniki · Sofia · Rhodope · Balkan Mountains · Pindus · CORFU · Athens · Peloponnese · Náxos · RHODES · CRETE · Herakleion · CYPRUS · Nicosia · İzmir · Antalya · Şanlı Urfa · Erzurum · Ankara · Bursa · Bosporus · Dardanelles · Pontine Mountains · Sochi · Sevastopol · Crimea · Varna · Bucharest · Chişinău · Odessa · Khar'kov · Donets Basin · Kiev · Pripyat Marshes · Minsk · Warsaw · Wroclaw · Sudety · Kaunas · Gdynia · Riga · Tallinn · St Petersburg · L. Peipus · Valdai Hills · Vologda · Moscow · Helsinki · HIIUMAA · SAAREMAA · GOTLAND · ÖLAND · Stockholm · Vänern · Vättern · Gothenburg · Kalmar · Copenhagen · ZEALAND · BORNHOLM · JUTLAND · Vestervig · Kattegat · Skagerrak · Oslo · Bergen · Jotunheimen · Trondheim · Norwegian fjords · Östersund · Vaasa · Umeå · Kuopio · Oulu · Kem · Arkhangel'sk

1000 kilometres · 500 miles

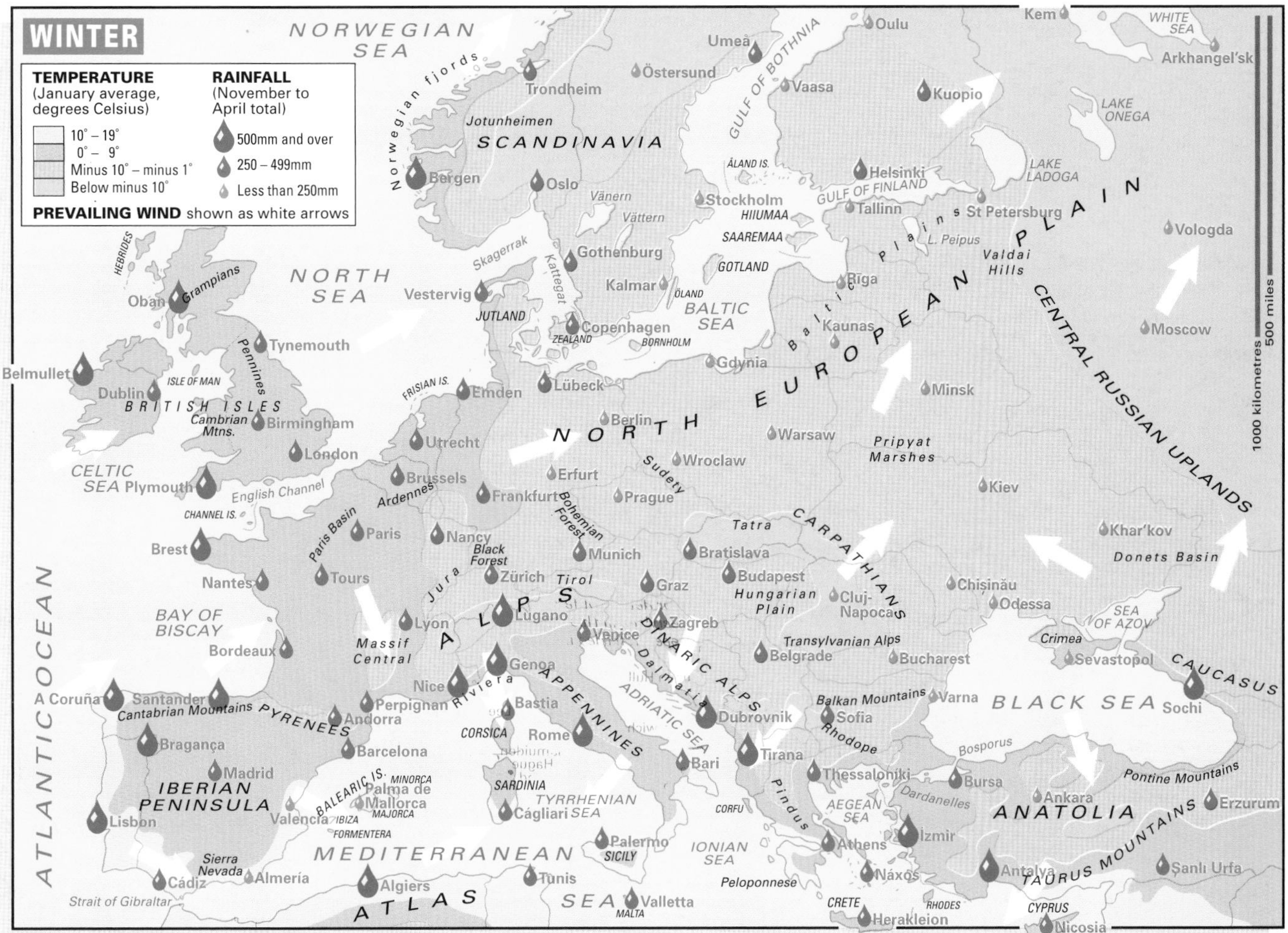

The Columbus Press World Travel Guide *contains detailed climate charts for every country in the world, including temperature, rainfall, sunshine and humidity. For more information, call +44 (0) 171 417 0700.*

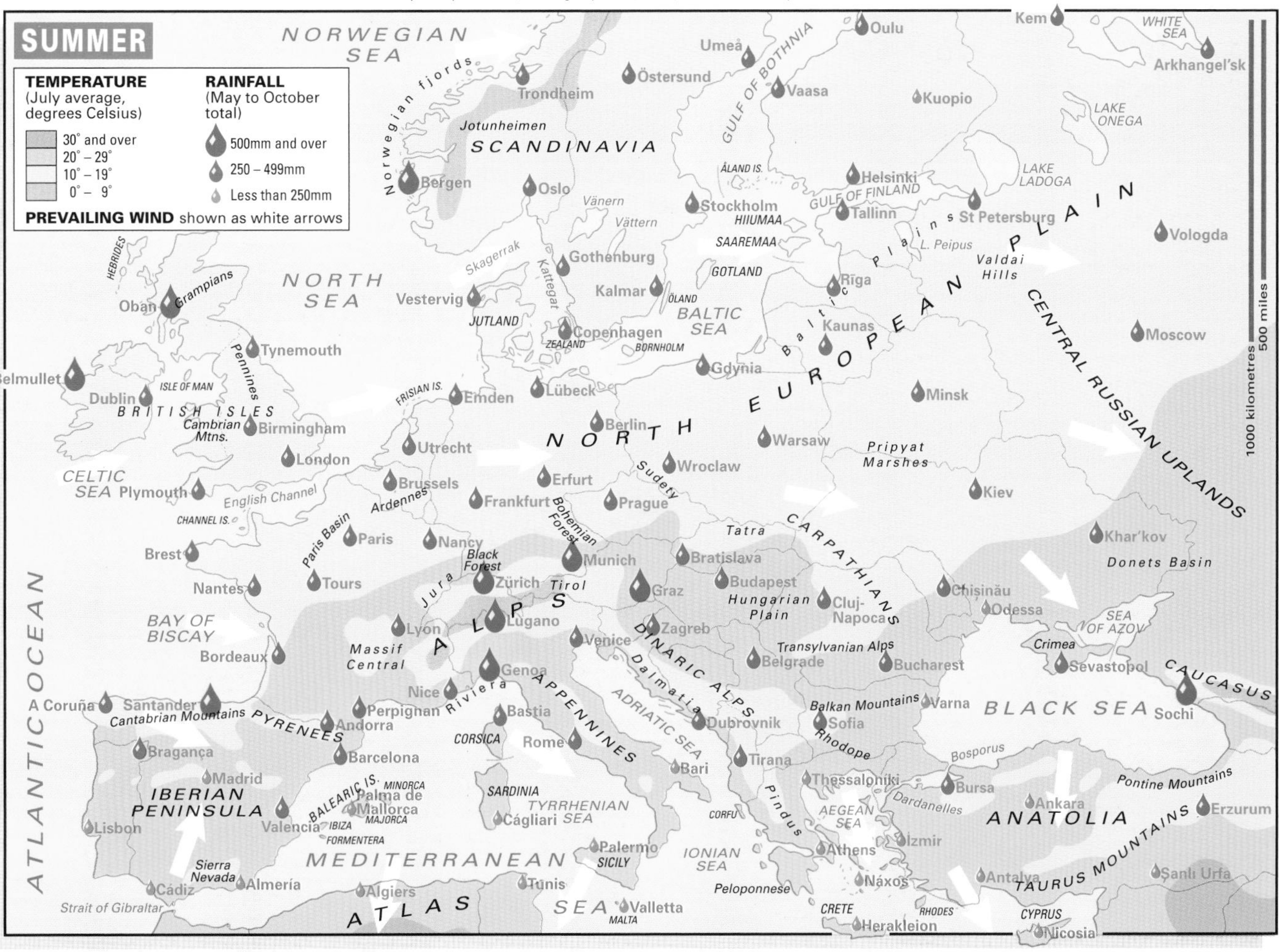

SUMMER

TEMPERATURE (July average, degrees Celsius)
- 30° and over
- 20° – 29°
- 10° – 19°
- 0° – 9°

RAINFALL (May to October total)
- 500mm and over
- 250 – 499mm
- Less than 250mm

PREVAILING WIND shown as white arrows

NORWEGIAN SEA · NORTH SEA · BALTIC SEA · CELTIC SEA · ATLANTIC OCEAN · GULF OF BOTHNIA · GULF OF FINLAND · WHITE SEA · LAKE ONEGA · LAKE LADOGA · BLACK SEA · SEA OF AZOV · AEGEAN SEA · IONIAN SEA · TYRRHENIAN SEA · ADRIATIC SEA · MEDITERRANEAN SEA

SCANDINAVIA · BRITISH ISLES · IBERIAN PENINSULA · NORTH EUROPEAN PLAIN · CENTRAL RUSSIAN UPLANDS · ANATOLIA · ALPS · PYRENEES · APPENNINES · DINARIC ALPS · CARPATHIANS · CAUCASUS · TAURUS MOUNTAINS · ATLAS

1000 kilometres · 500 miles

RAILWAYS AND FERRIES

This map shows principal rail and shipping routes in Europe. Some of the railways marked have limited services but are included because of their significance (such as connection to resort or international crossing).

A number of European rail passes are available, offering free travel on many rail and ferry services.

The Eurailpass is valid for first-class rail travel in the countries shown on the map. For those under 26, the Eurail Youthpass is valid in the same countries for second-class rail travel. The pass is not available to European residents or to visitors from Algeria, Morocco, Tunisia, Turkey or the former Soviet Union.

European residents are eligible for the Inter-Rail pass, offering train travel in the area shown on the map, excluding the country of issue. Passes are available for one or more zones within the validity area.

RAILWAYS:
- ——— Dedicated high-speed rail line
- ——— Other railway
- ·········· Direct Eurostar services (excluding seasonal services)

SHIPPING SERVICES (with average shortest journey times):
Times may vary depending on the operator, vessel and weather conditions. Night sailings usually take longer.
- ——— 3 hours or less
- ——— 3 hours 1 min – 10 hours
- ——— 10 hours 1 min – 20 hours
- ——— Over 20 hours

Pecked lines are used to identify individual routes and do not represent a different type of service.

EURAILPASS AND INTER-RAIL PASS:
- Inter-Rail pass *and* Eurailpass valid in these countries
- Inter-Rail pass valid, Eurailpass not valid

CHANNEL TUNNEL
Eurostar: Direct railway services between London (Waterloo International) and Paris (Gare du Nord), Disneyland Paris and Brussels (Gare du Midi / Zuidstation) via Ashford International, Calais-Fréthun and Lille-Europe. Services from Scotland and the north of England are planned.
Le Shuttle: Cars, coaches and motorcycles, together with their passengers, are carried on shuttles operating 24 hours a day throughout the year. Loading/unloading takes place at the Folkestone and Calais terminals.

For details of ferry services in this area, see UK ferries map

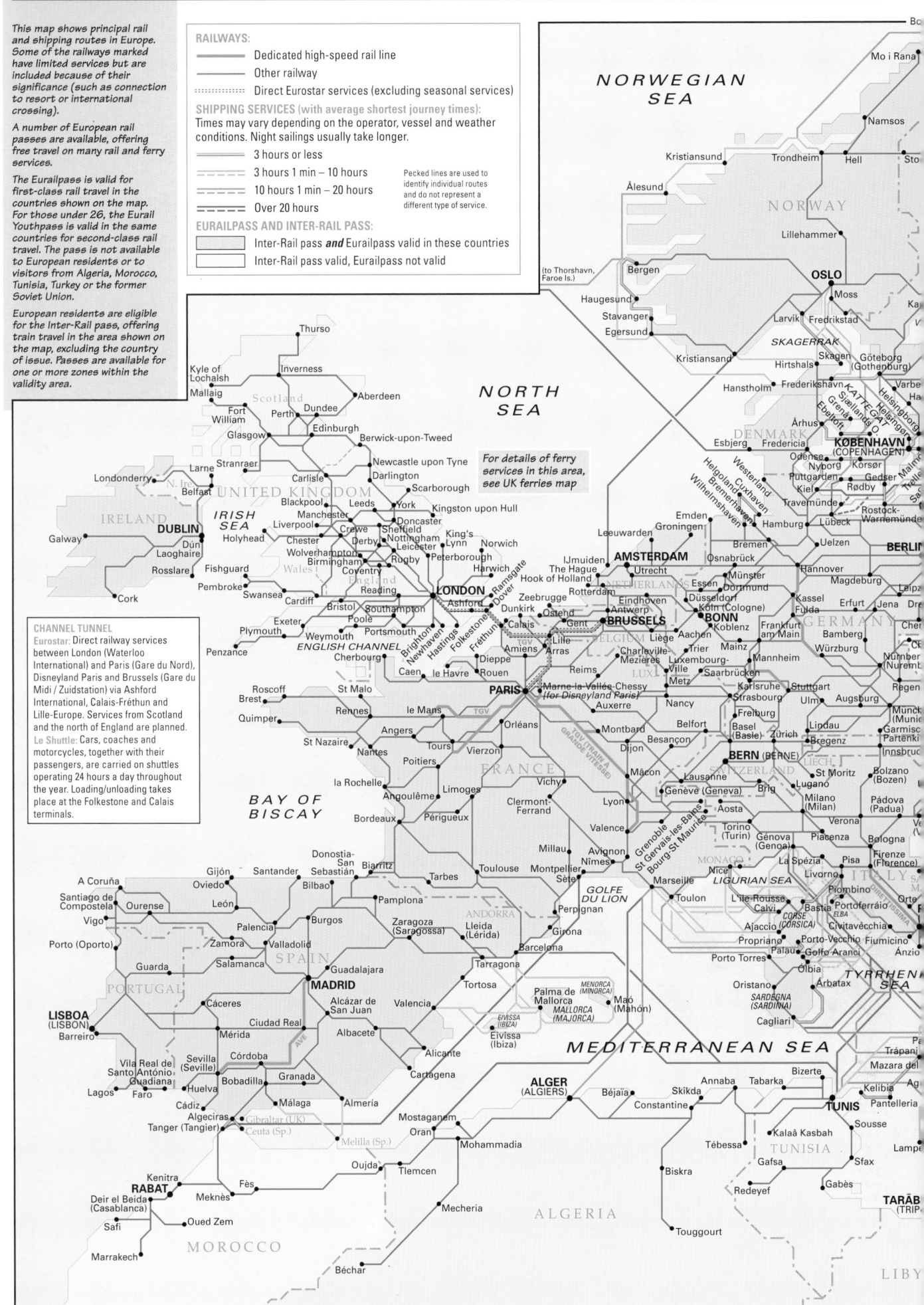

RAILWAYS AND FERRIES

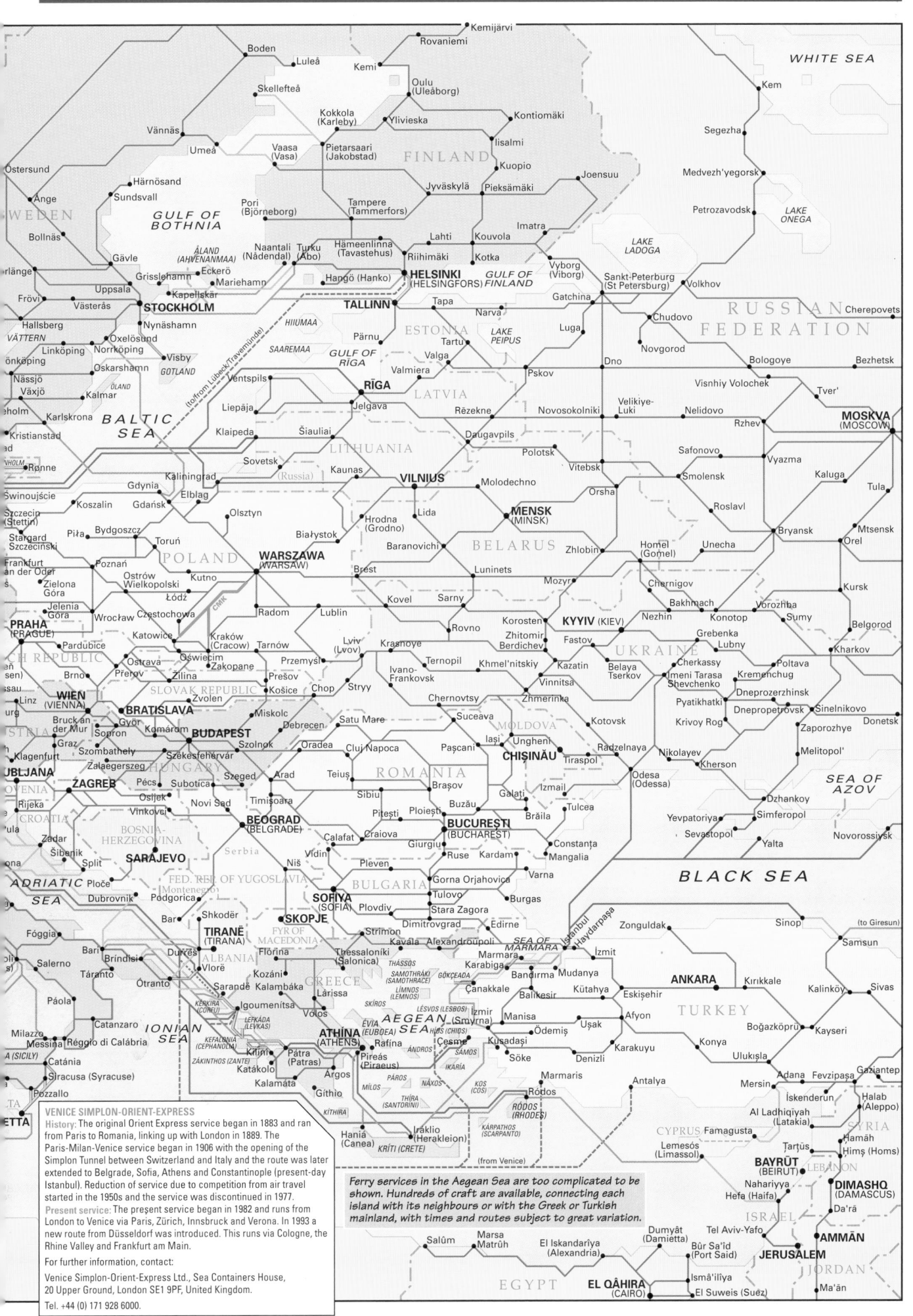

VENICE SIMPLON-ORIENT-EXPRESS

History: The original Orient Express service began in 1883 and ran from Paris to Romania, linking up with London in 1889. The Paris-Milan-Venice service began in 1906 with the opening of the Simplon Tunnel between Switzerland and Italy and the route was later extended to Belgrade, Sofia, Athens and Constantinople (present-day Istanbul). Reduction of service due to competition from air travel started in the 1950s and the service was discontinued in 1977.

Present service: The present service began in 1982 and runs from London to Venice via Paris, Zürich, Innsbruck and Verona. In 1993 a new route from Düsseldorf was introduced. This runs via Cologne, the Rhine Valley and Frankfurt am Main.

For further information, contact:

Venice Simplon-Orient-Express Ltd., Sea Containers House, 20 Upper Ground, London SE1 9PF, United Kingdom. Tel. +44 (0) 171 928 6000.

Ferry services in the Aegean Sea are too complicated to be shown. Hundreds of craft are available, connecting each island with its neighbours or with the Greek or Turkish mainland, with times and routes subject to great variation.

BLUE FLAG BEACHES

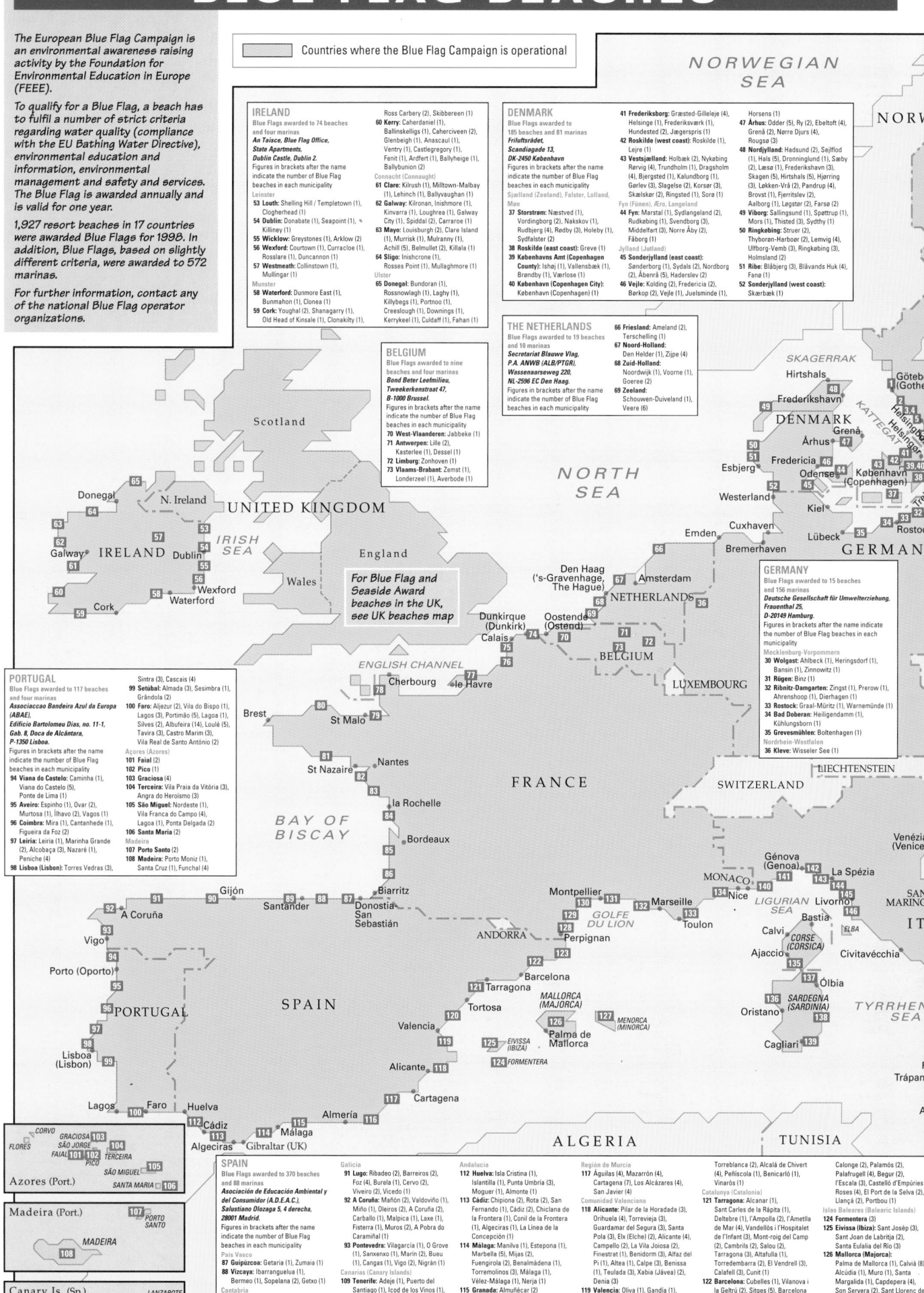

The European Blue Flag Campaign is an environmental awareness raising activity by the Foundation for Environmental Education in Europe (FEEE).

To qualify for a Blue Flag, a beach has to fulfil a number of strict criteria regarding water quality (compliance with the EU Bathing Water Directive), environmental education and information, environmental management and safety and services. The Blue Flag is awarded annually and is valid for one year.

1,927 resort beaches in 17 countries were awarded Blue Flags for 1998. In addition, Blue Flags, based on slightly different criteria, were awarded to 572 marinas.

For further information, contact any of the national Blue Flag operator organizations.

Countries where the Blue Flag Campaign is operational

IRELAND
Blue Flags awarded to 74 beaches and four marinas
An Taisce, Blue Flag Office, State Apartments, Dublin Castle, Dublin 2.
Figures in brackets after the name indicate the number of Blue Flag beaches in each municipality

Leinster
53 **Louth:** Shelling Hill / Templetown (1), Clogherhead (1)
54 **Dublin:** Donabate (1), Seapoint (1), Killiney (1)
55 **Wicklow:** Greystones (1), Arklow (2)
56 **Wexford:** Courtown (1), Curracloe (1), Rosslare (1), Duncannon (1)
57 **Westmeath:** Collinstown (1), Mullingar (1)

Munster
58 **Waterford:** Dunmore East (1), Bunmahon (1), Clonea (1)
59 **Cork:** Youghal (2), Shanagarry (1), Old Head of Kinsale (1), Clonakilty (1)
60 **Kerry:** Caherdaniel (1), Ballinskelligs (1), Cahercriveen (1), Glenbeigh (1), Anascaul (1), Ventry (1), Castlegregory (1), Fenit (1), Ardfert (1), Ballyheige (1), Ballybunion (2)

Connacht (Connaught)
61 **Clare:** Kilrush (1), Milltown-Malbay (1), Lehinch (1), Ballyvaughan (1)
62 **Galway:** Kilronan, Inishmore (1), Kinvarra (1), Loughrea (1), Galway City (1), Spiddal (2), Carraroe (1)
63 **Mayo:** Louisburgh (1), Clare Island (1), Murrisk (1), Mulranny (1), Achill (5), Belmullet (2), Killala (1)
64 **Sligo:** Inishcrone (1), Rosses Point (1), Mullaghmore (1)

Ulster
65 **Donegal:** Bundoran (1), Rossnowlagh (1), Laghy (1), Killybegs (1), Portnoo (1), Creeslough (1), Downings (1), Kerrykeel (1), Culdaff (1), Fahan (1)
Ross Carbery (2), Skibbereen (1)

DENMARK
Blue Flags awarded to 185 beaches and 81 marinas
Friluftsrådet, Scandiagade 13, DK-2450 København
Figures in brackets after the name indicate the number of Blue Flag beaches in each municipality

Sjælland (Zeeland), Falster, Lolland, Møn
37 **Storstrøm:** Næstved (1), Vordingborg (2), Nakskov (1), Rudbjerg (4), Rødby (4), Holeby (1), Sydfalster (2)
38 **Roskilde (east coast):** Greve (1)
39 **Københavns Amt (Copenhagen County):** Ishøj (1), Vallensbæk (1), Brøndby (1), Værløse (1)
40 **København (Copenhagen City):** København (Copenhagen) (1)

Fyn (Fünen), Ærø, Langeland
44 **Fyn:** Marstal (1), Sydlangeland (2), Rudkøbing (1), Svendborg (3), Middelfart (3), Norre Åby (2), Fåborg (1)
45 **Sønderjylland (east coast):** Sønderborg (1), Sydals (2), Nordborg (2), Åbenrå (5), Haderslev (2)
46 **Vejle:** Kolding (1), Fredericia (2), Børkop (2), Vejle (1), Juelsminde (1),

41 **Frederiksborg:** Græsted-Gilleleje (4), Helsinge (1), Frederiksværk (1), Hundested (2), Jægerspris (1)
42 **Roskilde (west coast):** Roskilde (1), Lejre (1)
43 **Vestsjælland:** Holbæk (2), Nykøbing Rørvig (4), Trundholm (1), Dragsholm (4), Bjergsted (1), Kalundborg (2), Gørlev (3), Slagelse (2), Korsør (3), Skælskør (2), Ringsted (1), Sorø (1)

Horsens (1)
47 **Århus:** Odder (5), Ry (2), Ebeltoft (4), Grenå (1), Nørre Djurs (4), Rougsø (3)
48 **Nordjylland:** Hadsund (2), Sejlflod (1), Hals (5), Dronninglund (1), Sæby (2), Læsø (1), Frederikshavn (3), Skagen (5), Hirtshals (5), Hjørring (3), Løkken-Vrå (2), Pandrup (4), Brovst (1), Fjerritslev (2), Aalborg (1), Løgstør (2), Farsø (2)
49 **Viborg:** Sallingsund (1), Spøttrup (1), Mors (1), Thisted (3), Sydthy (1)
50 **Ringkøbing:** Struer (2), Thyborøn-Harboør (2), Lemvig (4), Ulfborg-Vemb (1), Ringkøbing (3), Holmsland (2)
51 **Ribe:** Blåbjerg (3), Blåvands Huk (4), Fanø (1)
52 **Sønderjylland (west coast):** Skærbæk (1)

THE NETHERLANDS
Blue Flags awarded to 19 beaches and 10 marinas
Secretariat Blauwe Vlag, P.A. ANWB (ALB/PTGR), Wassenaarseweg 220, NL-2596 EC Den Haag.
Figures in brackets after the name indicate the number of Blue Flag beaches in each municipality

66 **Friesland:** Ameland (2), Terschelling (1)
67 **Noord-Holland:** Den Helder (1), Zijpe (4)
68 **Zuid-Holland:** Noordwijk (1), Voorne (1), Goeree (2)
69 **Zeeland:** Schouwen-Duiveland (1), Veere (6)

BELGIUM
Blue Flags awarded to nine beaches and four marinas
Bond Beter Leefmilieu, Tweekerkenstraat 47, B-1000 Brussel.
Figures in brackets after the name indicate the number of Blue Flag beaches in each municipality
70 **West-Vlaanderen:** Jabbeke (1)
71 **Antwerpen:** Lille (1), Kasterlee (1), Dessel (1)
72 **Limburg:** Zonhoven (1)
73 **Vlaams-Brabant:** Zemst (1), Londerzeel (1), Averbode (1)

GERMANY
Blue Flags awarded to 15 beaches and 156 marinas
Deutsche Gesellschaft für Umwelterziehung, Frauenthal 25, D-20149 Hamburg.
Figures in brackets after the name indicate the number of Blue Flag beaches in each municipality

Mecklenburg-Vorpommern
30 **Wolgast:** Ahlbeck (1), Heringsdorf (1), Bansin (1), Zinnowitz (1)
31 **Rügen:** Binz (1)
32 **Ribnitz-Damgarten:** Zingst (1), Prerow (1), Ahrenshoop (1), Dierhagen (1)
33 **Rostock:** Graal-Müritz (1), Warnemünde (1)
34 **Bad Doberan:** Heiligendamm (1), Kühlungsborn (1)
35 **Grevesmühlen:** Boltenhagen (1)
Nordrhein-Westfalen
36 **Kleve:** Wisseler See (1)

PORTUGAL
Blue Flags awarded to 117 beaches and four marinas
Associacao Bandeira Azul da Europa (ABAE), Edifício Bartolomeu Dias, no. 11-1, Gab. 8, Doca de Alcántara, P-1350 Lisboa.
Figures in brackets after the name indicate the number of Blue Flag beaches in each municipality

94 **Viana do Castelo:** Caminha (1), Viana do Castelo (5), Ponte de Lima (1)
95 **Aveiro:** Espinho (3), Ovar (2), Murtosa (1), Ílhavo (2), Vagos (3)
96 **Coimbra:** Mira (1), Cantanhede (1), Figueira da Foz (2)
97 **Leiria:** Leiria (1), Marinha Grande (2), Alcobaça (3), Nazaré (1), Peniche (4)
98 **Lisboa (Lisbon):** Torres Vedras (3),

Sintra (3), Cascais (4)
99 **Setúbal:** Almada (3), Sesimbra (1), Grândola (2)
100 **Faro:** Aljezur (2), Vila do Bispo (1), Lagos (3), Portimão (5), Lagoa (2), Silves (2), Albufeira (14), Loulé (5), Tavira (3), Castro Marim (3), Vila Real de Santo António (3)

Açores (Azores)
101 **Faial** (2)
102 **Pico** (1)
103 **Graciosa** (4)
104 **Terceira:** Vila Praia da Vitória (3), Angra do Heroísmo (3)
105 **São Miguel:** Nordeste (1), Vila Franca do Campo (4), Lagoa (1), Ponta Delgada (2)
106 **Santa Maria** (1)
Madeira
107 **Porto Santo** (2)
108 **Madeira:** Porto Moniz (1), Santa Cruz (1), Funchal (4)

SPAIN
Blue Flags awarded to 370 beaches and 88 marinas
Asociación de Educación Ambiental y del Consumidor (A.D.E.A.C.), Salustiano Olozaga 5, 4 derecha, 28001 Madrid.
Figures in brackets after the name indicate the number of Blue Flag beaches in each municipality

País Vasco
87 **Guipúzcoa:** Getaria (1), Zumaia (1)
88 **Vizcaya:** Ibarranguelua (1), Bermeo (1), Sopelana (2), Getxo (2)
Cantabria
89 **Castro-Urdiales (1), Laredo (1), Santoña (1), Noja (2), Arnuero (2), Santander (5), Comillas (1), San Vicente de la Barquera (1)
Principado de Asturias
90 **Llanes** (2)

Galicia
91 **Lugo:** Ribadeo (2), Barreiros (2), Foz (2), Burela (1), Cervo (2), Viveiro (2), Vicedo (1)
92 **A Coruña:** Mañón (2), Valdoviño (1), Miño (1), Oleiros (2), A Coruña (2), Carballo (1), Malpica (1), Laxe (1), Fisterra (1), Muros (2), A Pobra do Caramiñal (1)
93 **Pontevedra:** Vilagarcía (1), O Grove (1), Sanxenxo (1), Marín (2), Bueu (1), Cangas (1), Vigo (2), Nigrán (1)
Canarias (Canary Islands)
109 **Tenerife:** Adeje (1), Puerto de Santiago (1), Icod de los Vinos (1), Puerto de la Cruz (1), Tacoronte (1)
110 **Gran Canaria:** Las Palmas de Gran Canaria (1), San Bartolomé de Tirajana (3), Mogán (1)
111 **Lanzarote:** Haria (1), Teguise (3), Arrecife (1), Tías (1), Yaiza (2)

Andalucia
112 **Huelva:** Isla Cristina (1), Islantilla (1), Punta Umbría (1), Moguer (1), Almonte (1)
113 **Cádiz:** Chipiona (2), Rota (2), San Fernando (1), Cádiz (2), Chiclana de la Frontera (1), Conil de la Frontera (1), Algeciras (1), La Línea de la Concepción (1)
114 **Málaga:** Manilva (1), Estepona (1), Marbella (5), Mijas (2), Fuengirola (4), Benalmádena (1), Torremolinos (4), Málaga (1), Vélez-Málaga (1), Nerja (1)
115 **Granada:** Almuñécar (2)
116 **Almería:** Adra (1), El Ejido (3), Roquetas de Mar (3), Almería (5), Níjar (2), Carboneras (1), Mojácar (2), Vera (2), Cuevas de Almanzora (1), Pulpí (1)

Región de Murcia
117 **Águilas (1), Mazarrón (4), Cartagena (7), Los Alcázares (4), San Javier (4)
Comunidad Valenciana
118 **Alicante:** Pilar de la Horadada (3), Orihuela (4), Torrevieja (3), Guardamar del Segura (3), Santa Pola (3), Elx (Elche) (2), Alicante (4), Campello (1), La Vila Joiosa (2), Finestrat (1), Benidorm (3), Alfaz del Pi (1), Altea (1), Calpe (3), Benissa (1), Teulada (1), Xabia (Jávea) (2), Denia (3)
119 **Valencia:** Oliva (1), Gandia (1), Xeraco (1), Tavernes de la Valldigna (2), Cullera (4), Sueca (1), Valencia (1), Sagunto (2), Canet d'En Berenguer (1)
120 **Castellón:** Xilxes (1), Moncófar (1), Benicàsim (5), Oropesa (2),

Catalunya (Cataloña)
121 **Tarragona:** Alcanar (1), Sant Carles de la Ràpita (1), Deltebre (1), L'Ampolla (2), L'Ametlla de Mar (4), Vandellòs i l'Hospitalet de l'Infant (3), Mont-roig del Camp (2), Cambrils (2), Salou (2), Tarragona (3), Altafulla (1), Torredembarra (2), El Vendrell (3), Calafell (3), Cunit (1)
122 **Barcelona:** Cubelles (1), Vilanova i la Geltrú (2), Sitges (5), Barcelona (4), El Masnou (1), Canet de Mar (1), Calella (1), Pineda de Mar (1), Malgrat de Mar (1)
123 **Girona:** Blanes (3), Lloret de Mar (3), Tossa de Mar (1), Sant Feliu de Guíxols (1), Castell-Platja d'Aro (2),

Torreblanca (2), Alcalá de Chivert (4), Peñíscola (1), Benicarló (1), Vinaròs (1)
Calonge (2), Palamós (2), Palafrugell (4), Begur (2), l'Escala (3), Castelló d'Empúries (1), Roses (4), El Port de la Selva (2), Llançà (2), Portbou (1)
Islas Baleares (Balearic Islands)
124 **Formentera** (3)
125 **Eivissa (Ibiza):** Sant Josep (3), Sant Joan de Labritja (2), Santa Eulalia del Río (2)
126 **Mallorca (Majorca):** Palma de Mallorca (1), Calvià (8), Alcúdia (1), Muro (1), Santa Margalida (2), Capdepera (4), Son Servera (2), Sant Llorenç des Cardassar (2), Manacor (6), Felanitx (2), Santanyí (4), Ses Salines (1)
127 **Menorca (Minorca):** Es Mercadal (3), Maó (Mahón) (2), Alaior (1), Ferreries (1)

PORTUGAL
Azores (Port.)
Madeira (Port.)
Canary Is. (Sp.)
Not to scale

BLUE FLAG BEACHES

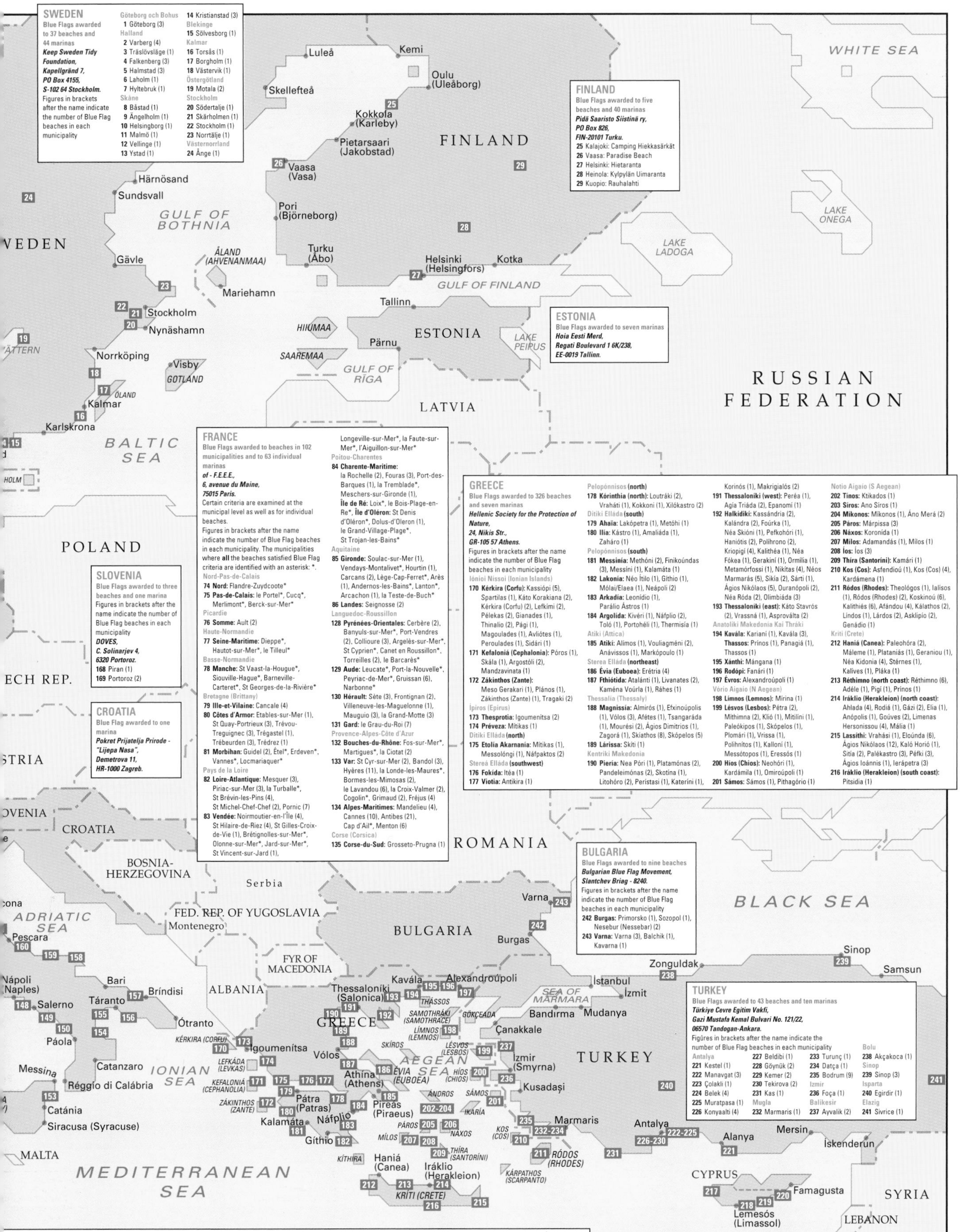

SWEDEN
Blue Flags awarded to 37 beaches and 44 marinas
Keep Sweden Tidy Foundation, Kapellgränd 7, PO Box 4155, S-102 64 Stockholm.
Figures in brackets after the name indicate the number of Blue Flag beaches in each municipality

Göteborg och Bohus
1 Göteborg (3)
Halland
2 Varberg (4)
3 Träslövsläge (1)
4 Falkenberg (1)
5 Halmstad (3)
6 Laholm (1)
7 Hyltebruk (1)
Skåne
8 Båstad (1)
9 Ängelholm (1)
10 Helsingborg (1)
11 Malmö (1)
12 Vellinge (1)
13 Ystad (1)
14 Kristianstad (3)
Blekinge
15 Sölvesborg (1)
Kalmar
16 Torsås (1)
17 Borgholm (1)
18 Västervik (1)
Östergötland
19 Motala (1)
Stockholm
20 Södertälje (1)
21 Skärholmen (1)
22 Stockholm (1)
23 Norrtälje (1)
Västernorrland
24 Ånge (1)

FINLAND
Blue Flags awarded to five beaches and 40 marinas
Pidä Saaristo Siistinä ry, PO Box 826, FIN-20101 Turku.
25 Kalajoki: Camping Hiekkasärkät
26 Vaasa: Paradise Beach
27 Helsinki: Hietaranta
28 Heinola: Kylpylän Uimaranta
29 Kuopio: Rauhalahti

ESTONIA
Blue Flags awarded to seven marinas
Hoia Eesti Merd, Regati Boulevard 1 6K/238, EE-0019 Tallinn.

SLOVENIA
Blue Flags awarded to three beaches and one marina
Figures in brackets after the name indicate the number of Blue Flag beaches in each municipality
DOVES, C. Solinarjev 4, 6320 Portoroz.
168 Piran (1)
169 Portoroz (2)

CROATIA
Blue Flag awarded to one marina
Pokret Prijatelja Prirode - "Lijepa Nasa", Demetrova 11, HR-1000 Zagreb.

FRANCE
Blue Flags awarded to beaches in 102 municipalities and to 63 individual marinas
ef - F.E.E.E, 6, avenue du Maine, 75015 Paris.
Certain criteria are examined at the municipal level as well as for individual beaches.
Figures in brackets after the name indicate the number of Blue Flag beaches in each municipality. The municipalities where all the beaches satisfied Blue Flag criteria are identified with an asterisk: *.

Nord-Pas-de-Calais
74 Nord: Flandre-Zuydcoote*
75 Pas-de-Calais: le Portel*, Cucq*, Merlimont*, Berck-sur-Mer*
Picardie
76 Somme: Ault (2)
Haute-Normandie
77 Seine-Maritime: Dieppe*, Hautot-sur-Mer*, le Tilleul*
Basse-Normandie
78 Manche: St Vaast-la-Hougue*, Siouville-Hague*, Barneville-Carteret*, St Georges-de-la-Rivière*
Bretagne (Brittany)
79 Ille-et-Vilaine: Cancale (4)
80 Côtes d'Armor: Etables-sur-Mer (1), St Quay-Portrieux (3), Trévou-Treguignec (3), Trégastel (1), Trébeurden (3), Trédrez (1)
81 Morbihan: Guidel (2), Étel*, Erdeven*, Vannes*, Locmariaquer*
Pays de la Loire
82 Loire-Atlantique: Mesquer (3), Piriac-sur-Mer (3), la Turballe*, St Brévin-les-Pins (4), St Michel-Chef-Chef (2), Pornic (7)
83 Vendée: Noirmoutier-en-l'Île (4), St Hilaire-de-Riez (4), St Gilles-Croix-de-Vie (1), Brétignolles-sur-Mer*, Olonne-sur-Mer*, Jard-sur-Mer*, St Vincent-sur-Jard (1)

Longeville-sur-Mer*, la Faute-sur-Mer*, l'Aiguillon-sur-Mer*
Poitou-Charentes
84 Charente-Maritime: la Rochelle (2), Fouras (3), Port-des-Barques (1), la Tremblade*, Meschers-sur-Gironde (1), Île de Ré: Loix*, le Bois-Plage-en-Re*, Île d'Oléron: St Denis d'Oléron*, Dolus-d'Oleron (1), le Grand-Village-Plage*, St Trojan-les-Bains*
Aquitaine
85 Gironde: Soulac-sur-Mer (1), Vendays-Montalivet*, Hourtin (1), Carcans (2), Lège-Cap-Ferret*, Arès (1), Andernos-les-Bains*, Lanton*, Arcachon (1), la Teste-de-Buch*
86 Landes: Seignosse (2)
Languedoc-Roussillon
128 Pyrénées-Orientales: Cerbère (2), Banyuls-sur-Mer*, Port-Vendres (2), Collioure (3), Argelès-sur-Mer*, St Cyprien*, Canet en Roussillon*, Torreilles (2), le Barcarès*
129 Aude: Leucate*, Port-la-Nouvelle*, Peyriac-de-Mer*, Gruissan (6), Narbonne*
130 Hérault: Sète (3), Frontignan (2), Villeneuve-les-Maguelonne (1), Mauguio (3), la Grand-Motte (1)
131 Gard: le Grau-du-Roi (7)
Provence-Alpes-Côte d'Azur
132 Bouches-du-Rhône: Fos-sur-Mer*, Martigues*, la Ciotat (2)
133 Var: St Cyr-sur-Mer (2), Bandol (3), Hyères (11), la Londe-les-Maures*, Bormes-les-Mimosas (2), le Lavandou (6), la Croix-Valmer (2), Cogolin*, Grimaud (2), Fréjus (4)
134 Alpes-Maritimes: Mandelieu (4), Cannes (10), Antibes (21), Cap d'Ail*, Menton (6)
Corse (Corsica)
135 Corse-du-Sud: Grosseto-Prugna (1)

GREECE
Blue Flags awarded to 326 beaches and seven marinas
Hellenic Society for the Protection of Nature, 24, Nikis Str., GR-105 57 Athens.
Figures in brackets after the name indicate the number of Blue Flag beaches in each municipality

Iónioi Nissoí (Ionian Islands)
170 Kérkira (Corfu): Kassiópi (5), Spartilas (1), Káto Korakiana (2), Kérkira (Corfu) (1), Lefkími (2), Pélekas (2), Gianades (1), Thinalio (2), Pági (1), Magoulades (1), Avliótes (1), Peroulades (1), Sidári (1)
171 Kefaloniá (Cephalonia): Póros (1), Skála (1), Argostóli (2), Mandzavinata (1)
172 Zákinthos (Zante): Meso Gerakari (1), Plános (1), Zákinthos (Zante) (1), Tragaki (2)
Ípiros (Epirus)
173 Thesprotia: Igoumenitsa (2)
174 Préveza: Mitikas (1)
Ditikí Elláda (north)
175 Etolía Akarnania: Mitikas (1), Messolóngi (1), Náfpaktos (2)
Stereá Elláda (southwest)
176 Fokida: Itéa (1)
177 Viotia: Antikira (1)

Pelopónnisos (north)
178 Kórinthia (north): Loutráki (2), Vraháti (1), Kokkoni (1), Xilókastro (2)
Ditikí Elláda (south)
179 Ahaïa: Lakópetra (1), Metóhi (1)
180 Ilia: Kástro (1), Amaliáda (1), Zaháro (1)
Pelopónnisos (south)
181 Messinía: Methóni (2), Finikoúndas (3), Messini (1), Kalamáta (1)
182 Lakonía: Néo Ítilo (1), Githio (1), Mólai/Elaea (1), Neápoli (2)
183 Arkadía: Leonídio (1), Parálio Ástros (1)
184 Argolída: Kivéri (1), Náfplio (2), Toló (1), Portohéli (1), Thermisia (1)
Atikí (Attica)
185 Atikí: Alimos (1), Vouliagméni (2), Anávissos (1), Markópoulo (1)
Stereá Elláda (northeast)
186 Évia (Euboea): Erétria (4)
187 Fthiótida: Atalánti (1), Livanates (2), Kaména Voúrla (1), Ráhes (1)
Thessalía (Thessaly)
188 Magnissía: Almirós (1), Efxinoúpolis (1), Vólos (3), Afétes (1), Tsangaráda (1), Mourési (2), Agios Dimitrios (1), Zagorá (1), Skiathos (8), Skópelos (1)
189 Lárissa: Skíti (1)
Kentrikí Makedonía
190 Pieria: Nea Póri (1), Platamónas (2), Pandeleimónas (2), Skotina (1), Litohóro (2), Perístasi (1), Kateríni (1)

Korinós (1), Makrigialós (2)
191 Thessaloníki (west): Peréa (1), Agia Triáda (2), Epanomí (1)
192 Halkidikí: Kassándria (2), Kalándra (2), Foúrka (1), Néa Skióni (1), Pefkohóri (1), Haniótis (2), Polihrono (2), Kriopigí (4), Kalithéa (1), Néa Fókea (1), Gerakiní (1), Ormília (1), Metamórfossi (1), Nikitas (4), Néos Marmarás (5), Sikiá (2), Sárti (1), Ágios Nikólaos (5), Ouranópoli (2), Néa Róda (2), Olimbiáda (3)
193 Thessaloníki (east): Káto Stavrós (1), Ierissós (1)
Anatolikí Makedonía Kai Thráki
194 Kavála: Kariani (1), Kavála (3), Thassós: Prínos (1), Panagiá (1), Thassos (1)
195 Xánthi: Mángana (1)
196 Rodópi: Fanári (1)
197 Évros: Alexandroúpoli (1)
Vório Aigaío (N Aegean)
198 Límnos (Lemnos): Mirina (1)
199 Lésvos (Lesbos): Pétra (2), Míthimna (2), Klió (1), Mitilíni (1), Paleókipos (1), Skópelos (1), Plomári (1), Vrissa (1), Polihnitos (1), Kalloní (1), Messótopos (1), Eressós (1)
200 Híos (Chios): Neohóri (1), Kardámila (1), Omiroúpoli (1)
201 Sámos: Sámos (1), Pithagório (1)

Notío Aigaío (S Aegean)
202 Tínos: Ktikados (1)
203 Síros: Ano Síros (1)
204 Míkonos: Míkonos (1), Áno Merá (2)
205 Páros: Márpissa (3)
206 Náxos: Koronída (1)
207 Mílos: Adamandás (1), Milos (1)
208 Íos: Íos (3)
209 Thíra (Santorini): Kamári (1)
210 Kos (Cos): Asfendioú (1), Kos (Cos) (4), Kardámena (1)
211 Ródos (Rhodes): Theológos (1), Ialísos (1), Ródos (Rhodes) (2), Koskinoú (6), Kalithiés (6), Afándou (4), Kálathos (2), Líndos (1), Lárdos (2), Asklipío (2), Genádio (1)
Kriti (Crete)
212 Haniá (Canea): Paleohóra (2), Máleme (1), Plataniás (1), Geraniou (1), Néa Kidonia (4), Stérnes (1), Kalives (1), Pláka (1)
213 Réthimno (north coast): Réthimno (6), Adéle (1), Pigí (1), Prínos (1)
214 Iráklio (Heracleion) (north coast): Ahláda (4), Rodiá (1), Gázi (2), Elía (1), Anópolis (1), Goúves (2), Limenas Hersonissou (4), Mália (1)
215 Lassíthi: Vrahási (1), Eloúnda (5), Ágios Nikólaos (12), Kaló Horió (1), Sitía (2), Palékastro (3), Péfki (3), Ágios Ioánnis (1), Ierápetra (3)
216 Iráklio (Heracleion) (south coast): Pitsidia (1)

BULGARIA
Blue Flags awarded to nine beaches
Bulgarian Blue Flag Movement, Slantchev Briag - 8240.
Figures in brackets after the name indicate the number of Blue Flag beaches in each municipality
242 Burgas: Primorsko (1), Sozopol (1), Nesebur (Nessebar) (2)
243 Varna: Varna (3), Balchik (1), Kavarna (1)

TURKEY
Blue Flags awarded to 43 beaches and ten marinas
Türkiye Cevre Egitim Vakfi, Gazi Mustafa Kemal Bulvari No. 121/22, 06570 Tandogan-Ankara.
Figures in brackets after the name indicate the number of Blue Flag beaches in each municipality

Antalya
221 Kestel (1)
222 Colakli (1)
224 Belek (4)
225 Muratpasa (1)
226 Konyaalti (4)
227 Beldibi (1)
229 Göynük (2)
229 Kemer (2)
230 Tekirova (2)
231 Kas (1)
232 Marmaris (1)
Mugla
232 Marmaris (1)
Turunç (2)
233 Datça (1)
235 Bodrum (3)
236 Foça (1)
Balikesir
237 Ayvalik (2)
Bolu
238 Akçakoca (1)
Sinop
239 Sinop (3)
Izmir
236 Foça (1)
Elazig
241 Sivrice (1)
Isparta
240 Egirdir (1)

CYPRUS
Blue Flags awarded to 25 beaches
CYMEPA, Irinis Square & Navarinou Str., P.O. Box 6671, 3309 Limassol.
Figures in brackets after the name indicate the number of Blue Flag beaches in each municipality
217 Paphos: Pólis (2), Péyia (2), Paphos (5), Geroskipou (1)
218 Lemesós (Limassol): Pissoúri (1), Yermasóyia (1), Áyios Tychon (5), Pyrgos (1)
219 Larnaca: Larnaca (2)
220 Famagusta: Ayia Nápa (4), Paralimni (1)

ITALY
Blue Flags awarded to beaches in 58 municipalities and to 44 marinas
FEE-Italia, ... della Guglia, 69b, ...186 Roma.
The Blue Flag is awarded, in most cases, to the local administrations and ... to individual beaches. The ... municipal authority is then responsible ... ensuring that the Blue Flag flies only ... those beaches which fulfil the ... criteria relating to beach management ... provision of environmental information. The following municipalities have been awarded Blue Flags or contain individual Blue Flag beaches.

Sardegna (Sardinia)
136 Nuoro (west coast): Bosa
137 Sassari: Castelsardo, Santa Teresa di Gallura, La Maddalena, Golfo Aranci
138 Nuoro (east coast): Siniscola
139 Cágliari: Quartu San'Elena
Liguria
140 Imperia: Bordighera, Taggia, Diano Marina, San

Bartolomeo al Mare, Cervo
141 Savona: Andora, Laigueglia, Finale Ligure, Noli, Bergeggi, Albisola Marina, Celle Ligure
142 Génova (Genoa): Portofino, Lavagna, Sestri Levante
143 La Spézia: Déiva Marina, Framura, Monterosso
Toscana (Tuscany)
144 Lucca: Forte dei Marmi, Camaiore, Viaréggio
145 Pisa: Tirrénia
146 Livorno: Rosignano

Marittimo, Castagneto Carducci
Lazio
147 Latina: Sperlonga
Campania
148 Nápoli (Naples): Anacapri
149 Salerno: Positano, Agrópoli, Póllica, Centola
Basilicata (west coast)
150 Potenza: Maratea
Sicilia (Sicily)
151 Palermo: Ustica

152 Agrigento: Menfi
153 Messina: Taormina
Calábria (east coast)
154 Cosenza: Roseto Capo
Basilicata (east coast)
155 Matera: Policoro
Puglia
156 Taranto: Ginosa
157 Brindisi: Ostuni
158 Fóggia: Vieste, Rodi Gargánico, Chiéuti
Molise
159 Campobasso: Térmoli

Abruzzo
160 Chieti: Vasto
161 Téramo: Tortoreto
Marche
162 Ascoli Piceno: Cupra Marittima
163 Ancona: Sirolo, Senigállia
Veneto
164 Venézia (Venice): Bibione
Friuli-Venézia Giulia
165 Udine: Lignano Sabbiadoro
166 Gorizia: Grado
167 Trieste: Trieste

SKIING

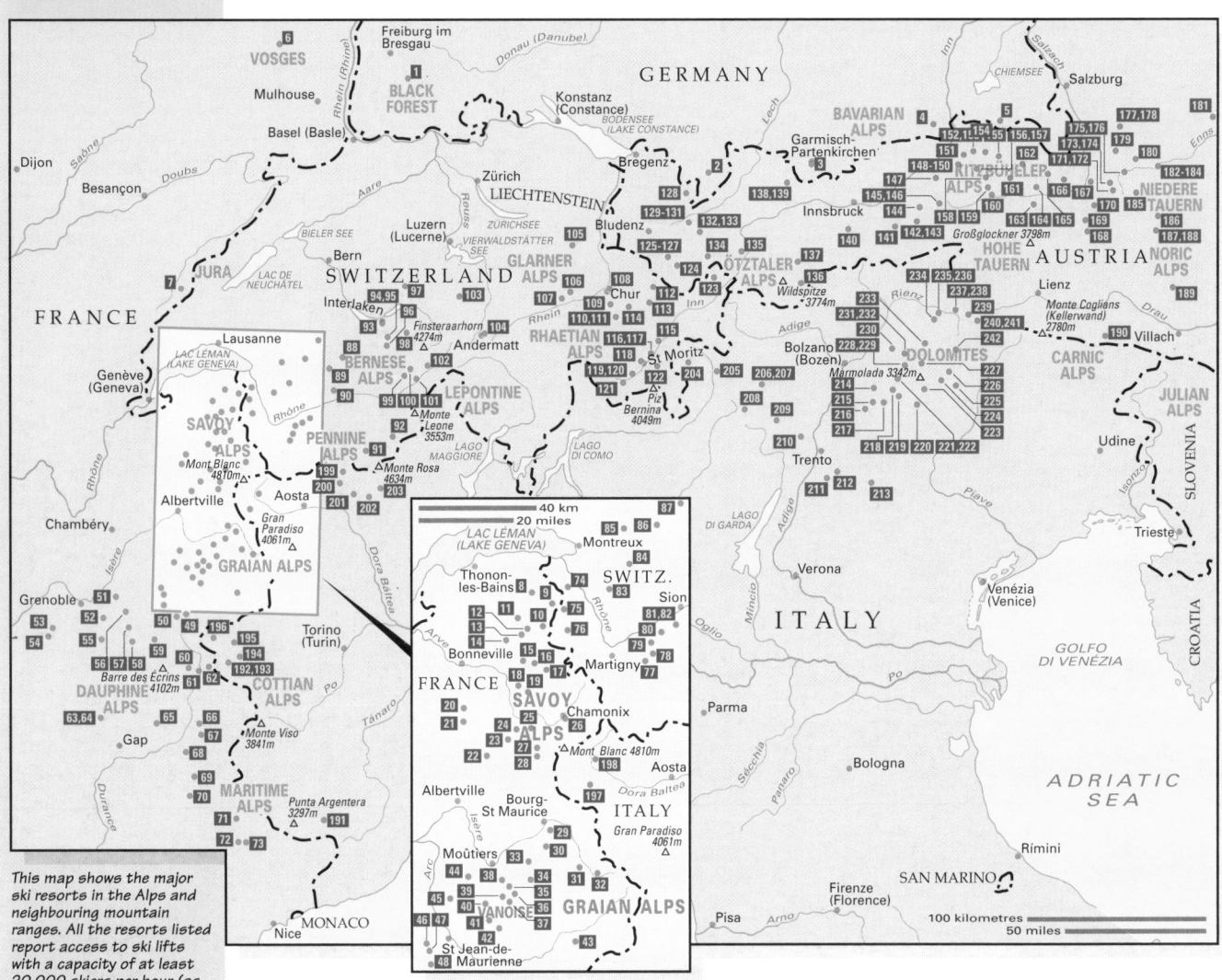

This map shows the major ski resorts in the Alps and neighbouring mountain ranges. All the resorts listed report access to ski lifts with a capacity of at least 20,000 skiers per hour (as at September 1997), with the exception of those marked with an asterisk (*), which are included because of their significance.

Resorts based on traditional villages are shown in normal type, modern-style purpose-built resorts in bold italics.

The classifications reflect skiing accessible from resorts which may also include terrain accessed from neighbouring resorts.

Data compiled by Snow-Hunter Ltd, all rights reserved.
Fax: +44 (0) 1463 741273.
email: patrick@snowhunt. demon.co.uk

Resort altitude:

□ 1,500 metres or above
□ 1,000 – 1,499 metres
No black square: under 1,000 metres

Skier uplift:

■ 100,000 skiers per hour or more
■ 50,000 – 99,999 skiers per hour
■ 30,000 – 49,999 skiers per hour
No colour: Less than 30,000

Altitude at top of highest ski run:

○ 3,000 metres or above
○ 2,000 – 2,999 metres
No black circle: under 2,000 metres

Maximum vertical drop:

● 2,000 metres or more
● 1,500 – 1,999 metres
● 1,000 – 1,499 metres
No colour: Less than 1,000 metres

Germany
1 Feldberg
2 Oberstdorf
3 Garmisch-Partenkirchen
4 Bayrischzell
5 Reit im Winkl

France
6 la Bresse-Hohneck
7 Métabief / le Mont d'Or
8 Abondance
9 Châtel
10 *Avoriaz*
11 St Jean-d'Aulps
12 Morzine
13 les Gets
14 *le Praz de Lys*
15 Morillon les Essert
16 Samoëns
17 Sixt
18 les Carroz
19 *Flaine*
20 le Grand-Bornand
21 la Clusaz
22 Notre-Dame-de-Bellecombe
23 Megève
24 Combloux
25 St Gervais / *le Bettex*
26 Chamonix-Mont Blanc
27 St Nicolas-de-Véroce
28 les Contamines-Montjoie*
29 *les Arcs*
30 Peisey-Nancroix-Vallandry
31 *Tignes*
32 Val d'Isère
33 *la Plagne / les Coches* / Montchavin / Plagne Montalbert
34 Champagny-en-Vanoise
35 *la Tania*
36 Courchevel
37 *la Rosière*
38 Brides-les-Bains
39 Méribel
40 St Martin-de-Belleville
41 *les Menuires*
42 *Val Thorens*
43 Val Cenis
44 *Valmorel*
45 *St François-Longchamp*
46 la Toussuire
47 le Corbier
48 St Jean d'Arves
49 Valmeinier
50 Valloire
51 *les Sept Laux*

(*le Pleiney / Prapoutel*)
52 Chamrousse
53 Villard-de-Lans / *Cote 2000*
54 Corrençon-en-Vercors
55 *Alpe du Grand Serre*
56 Vaujany / Oz-en-Oisans
57 *Alpe d'Huez* / Auris-en-Oisans / Villard-Reculas
58 *les Deux Alpes*
59 la Grave*
60 Serre-Chevalier
61 Briançon
62 Montgenèvre
63 la Joue du Loup
64 *Superdévoluy*
65 *Orcières-Merlette*
66 *Risoul*
67 Vars
68 *les Orres*
69 *Pra-Loup*
70 *la Foux-d'Allos*
71 Auron / St Étienne-de-Tinée
72 Valberg
73 Beuil-les-Launes

Switzerland
74 Torgon
75 Morgins
76 Champéry-Planachaux / Val-d'Illiez / Les Crosets
77 Le Châble / Bruson
78 Verbier
79 La Tzoumas (Mayens-de-Riddes)
80 Nendaz
81 Mayens-de-l'Ours
82 Veysonnaz / Les Collons
83 Villars-sur-Ollon / Gryon
84 Les Diablerets
85 Gstaad-Saanenland
86 Gstaad-Saanenland
87 Zweisimmen
88 Adelboden
89 Lenk
90 Crans-Montana
91 Zermatt
92 Saas Fee
93 Interlaken / Wilderswil bei Interlaken
94 Lauterbrunnen
95 Wengen
96 Mürren* / Stechelberg*
97 Grindelwald
98 Adelboden
99 Bettmeralp
100 Mörel-Breiten

101 Fiesch
102 Sörenberg
103 Engelberg
104 Andermatt*
105 Flumserberg
106 Flims
107 Laax
108 Chur*
109 Churwalden
110 Lenzerheide-Valbella
111 Parpan
112 Klosters / Fideris
113 Davos
114 La-Punt-Chaumes-ch.
115 La-Punt-Chaumes-ch.
116 Celerina
117 Samedan
118 St Moritz
119 Sils-Maria*
120 Silvaplana-Surlej*
121 Maloja
122 Pontresina*
123 Samnaun

Austria
124 Partenen
125 Gaschurn
126 Gortipohl
127 St Gallenkirch
128 Kleinwalsertal (Hirschegg / Mittelberg / Riezlern)
129 Lech / Oberlech
130 Zug
131 Zürs
132 St Anton am Arlberg / St Jakob am Arlberg
133 St Christoph am Arlberg
134 Ischgl / Silvretta
135 Serfaus
136 Obergurgl / Hochgurgl
137 Sölden
138 Lermoos*
139 Ehrwald
140 Neustift im Stubaital
141 Hintertux
142 Finkenberg
143 Mayrhofen
144 Zell am Ziller
145 Gerlos
146 Königsleiten
147 Wildschönau [Auffach / Mühltal / Niederau / Oberau / Thierbach]
148 Brixen im Thale
149 Hopfgarten im Brixental

150 Westendorf*
151 Söll
152 Scheffau
153 Ellmau / Going
154 St Johann in Tirol
155 Fieberbrunn*
156 Kirchberg in Tirol / Aschau in Tirol
157 Kitzbühel
158 Aurach
159 Jochberg / Pass Thurn
160 Mittersill / Pass Thurn
161 Saalbach Hinterglemm
162 Leogang
163 Kaprun
164 Zell am See
165 Maria Alm
166 Dienten am Hochkönig
167 St Johann im Pongau
168 Badgastein
169 Bad Hofgastein
170 Großarl
171 Flachauwinkel
172 Kleinarl
173 Flachau
174 Wagrain
175 Altenmarkt-Zauchensee
176 Radstadt
177 Gosau
178 Rußbach
179 Annaberg
180 Filzmoos
181 Tauplitz
182 Haus in Ennstal*
183 Ramsau am Dachstein*
184 Schladming
185 Obertauern
186 Mauterndorf / Mariapfarr
187 St Margarethen im Lungau
188 St Michael im Lungau
189 Bad Kleinkirchheim
190 Karnische Skiregion

Italy
191 Limone Piemonte
192 *San Sicário* / Cesana
193 Clavière
194 *Sestriere*
195 Sauze d'Oulx
196 Bardonécchia
197 la Thuile
198 Courmayeur*
199 *Breuil-Cervinia*
200 Valtournenche
201 Champoluc / Antagnod
202 Gressoney-la-Trinité /

Gressoney-St Jean
203 Alagna-Valsésia
204 Livigno
205 Bormio*
206 *Folgárida*
207 *Marilléva*
208 Passo Tonale
209 Madonna di Campiglio
210 Andalo
211 Folgaria
212 Lavarone / Luserna
213 Asiago / Canove
214 *Obereggen*
215 Alpe di Pampeago / Tésero
216 Cavalese*
217 Predazzo
218 Moena di Fassa
219 Bellamonte
220 San Martino di Castrozza / *Passo Rolle*
221 Pozza di Fassa*
222 Vigo di Fassa*
223 Falcade
224 Alleghe
226 Zoldo Alto / Valzoldana
227 Arabba
228 Campitello di Fassa*
229 Canazei*
230 Ortisei (St Ulrich)
231 Santa Cristina / Pranauron
232 Selva Gardena (Wolkenstein)
233 Alta Badia [Colfosco / Corvara / la Villa (Stern) / San Cassiano (St Kassian) / Pedráces / San Leonardo (St Leonhard)]
234 San Vigilio di Marebbe
235 Riscone (Reischach)
236 Valdáora (Olang)
237 Dobiacco (Toblach)
238 Villabassa (Niederdorf)
239 San Cándido (Innichen)
240 Sesto (Sexten)
241 Versciaco (Vierschach)
242 Cortina

The *World Ski and Snowboarding Guide*, published by Columbus Press, is a comprehensive guide to the world's ski resorts. For more information, call +44 (0) 171 417 0700.

HISTORICAL

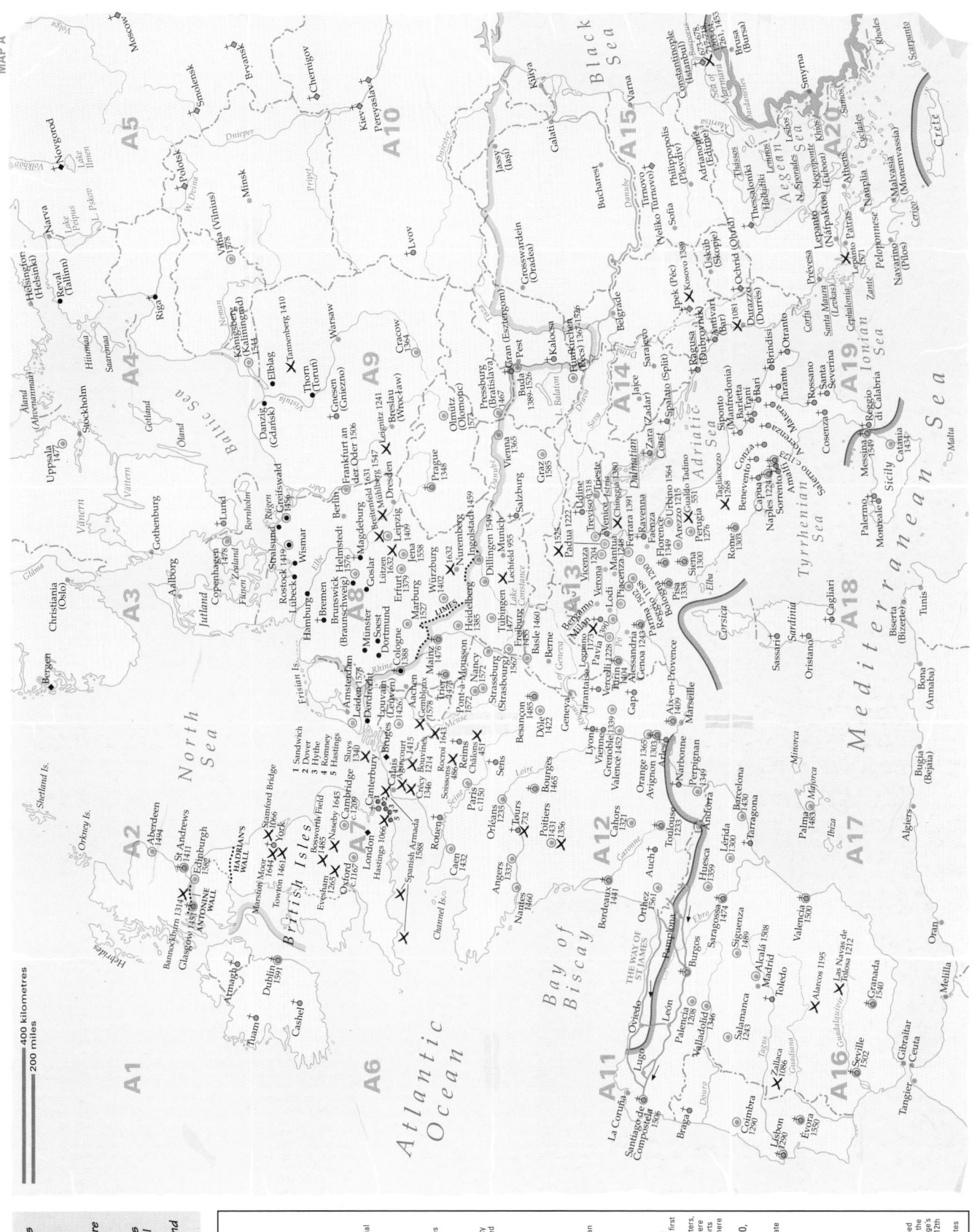

This map shows selected aspects of European history between the end of the Roman Empire in the 5th century and the Peace of Westphalia in 1648. Modern equivalents of important cities are included in parentheses. Current international boundaries are shown in grey but no attempt has been made to show any historical boundaries apart from the maximum extent of the Roman and Islamic conquests.

Northern limit of the Roman Empire at its greatest extent

Northern limit of Islamic conquests in Europe between the 7th and 11th centuries

Trieste Cities and regions which came under Venetian influence in any period prior to 1648
Venice acquired many trading posts at various times during this period of commercial expansion in the late Middle Ages

✕ Sites of major battles in the period 476–1648, with date
In general, battles have only been marked which had important political consequences

The Hanseatic League
A commercial union of northern European cities, designed to create economic security in an age of political chaos, which flourished in the 14th and 15th centuries

● Principal cities

◆ Principal foreign trading posts (kontore)

● Principal cities of the Lombard League
A shifting political alliance of northern Italian cities designed to combat the territorial ambitions of the Holy Roman Emperors (principally Frederick I and Frederick II) between 1153 and 1268

● The Cinque Ports
A loose confederation of towns in southern England whose defensive obligations were first established in the 11th century and subsequently redefined by many royal charters, principally that of 1278. At one time there were over 30 towns and villages in the Cinque Ports Confederation; the original five are shown here

○ Universities founded prior to 1600, with year of foundation
In some cases, particularly for the oldest universities, precise dates are open to debate

Major ecclesiastical centres, 16th century:

✠ ✠ Roman Catholic
(Patriarchal and Archiepiscopal Sees)

✠ ✠ Orthodox
(Patriarchal Sees and other major centres)

— Camino de Santiago (The Way of St James)
A medieval pilgrimage route which developed after the discovery of the tomb of St James the Apostle in Galicia in about 812; the pilgrimage's popularity was at its height in the 11th and 12th centuries, resulting in the legacy of many churches and chapels along its various routes

NATIONAL PARKS

Europe has a large variety of scenery, habitats and fauna, and most countries have set aside areas of natural beauty in order to preserve the landscape and wildlife. This map shows the most important areas designated as National Parks throughout Europe except for the former Soviet Union, but including the Baltic states. The best period for visiting each park is shown in blue (no date: all year / information not available).

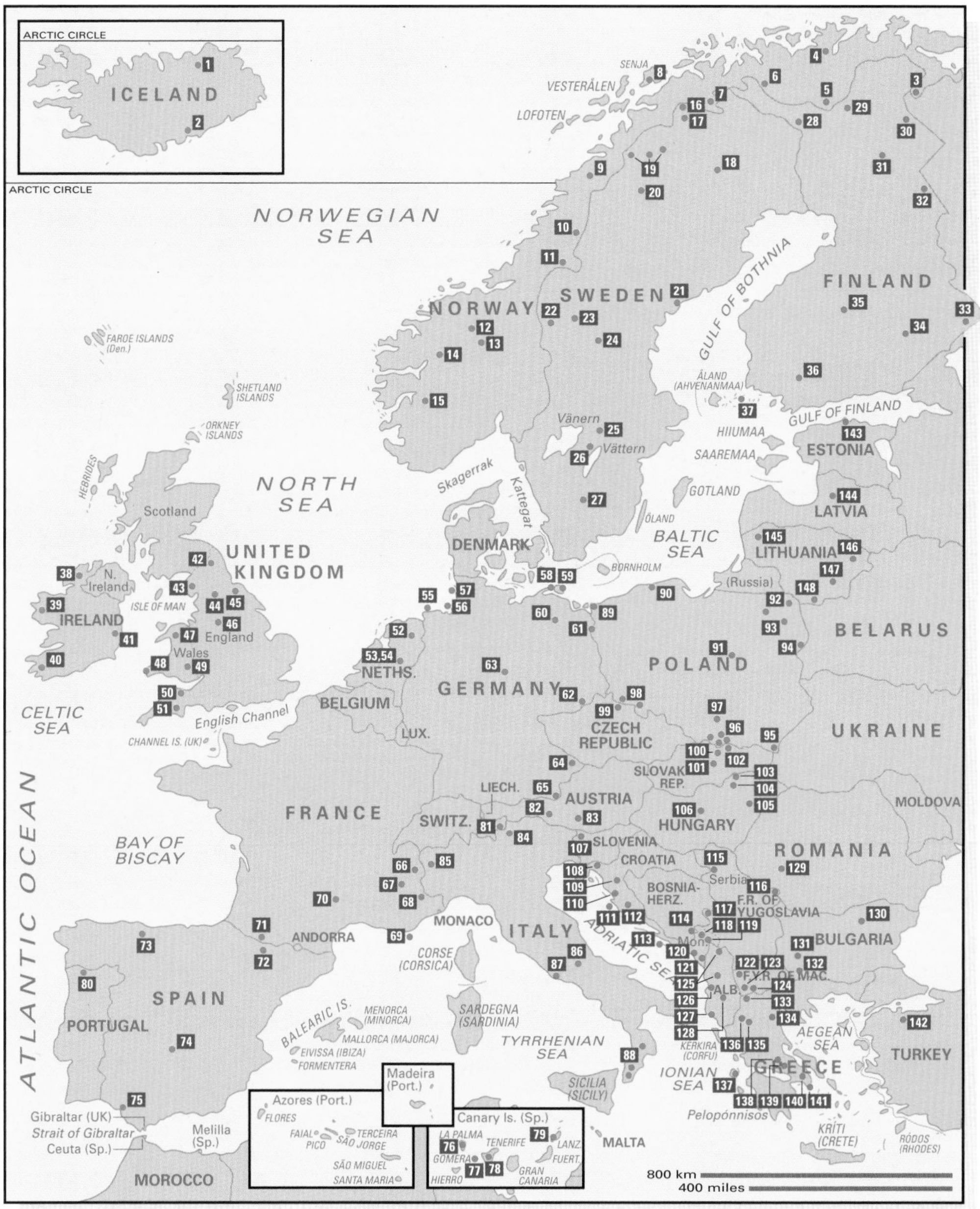

ARCTIC CIRCLE
ICELAND
NORWEGIAN SEA
SENJA
VESTERÅLEN
LOFOTEN
NORWAY
SWEDEN
FINLAND
GULF OF BOTHNIA
ÅLAND (AHVENANMAA)
GULF OF FINLAND
FAROE ISLANDS (Den.)
SHETLAND ISLANDS
ORKNEY ISLANDS
HEBRIDES
Vänern
Vättern
HIIUMAA
SAAREMAA
ESTONIA
Skagerrak
Kattegat
GOTLAND
ÖLAND
LATVIA
NORTH SEA
Scotland
UNITED KINGDOM
N. Ireland
IRELAND
ISLE OF MAN
England
Wales
DENMARK
BORNHOLM
BALTIC SEA
LITHUANIA
(Russia)
BELARUS
NETHS.
POLAND
GERMANY
BELGIUM
LUX.
CZECH REPUBLIC
UKRAINE
CELTIC SEA
English Channel
CHANNEL IS. (UK)
SLOVAK REP.
LIECH.
AUSTRIA
MOLDOVA
FRANCE
SWITZ.
HUNGARY
BAY OF BISCAY
SLOVENIA
CROATIA
ROMANIA
Serbia
BOSNIA-HERZ.
F.R. OF YUGOSLAVIA
MONACO
ANDORRA
ITALY
ADRIATIC SEA
BULGARIA
CORSE (CORSICA)
Mon.
F.Y.R. OF MAC.
ALB.
ATLANTIC OCEAN
SPAIN
PORTUGAL
BALEARIC IS.
MENORCA (MINORCA)
MALLORCA (MAJORCA)
EIVISSA (IBIZA)
FORMENTERA
SARDEGNA (SARDINIA)
TYRRHENIAN SEA
AEGEAN SEA
TURKEY
KERKIRA (CORFU)
IONIAN SEA
GREECE
Madeira (Port.)
Azores (Port.)
FLORES
FAIAL
PICO
TERCEIRA
SÃO JORGE
SÃO MIGUEL
SANTA MARIA
Canary Is. (Sp.)
LA PALMA
TENERIFE
LANZ.
FUERT.
GOMERA
HIERRO
GRAN CANARIA
SICILIA (SICILY)
MALTA
Pelopónnisos
KRÍTI (CRETE)
RÓDOS (RHODES)
Gibraltar (UK)
Strait of Gibraltar
Ceuta (Sp.)
Melilla (Sp.)
MOROCCO
800 km
400 miles

Iceland
1 Jokulsargljufur
Spectacular gorges
2 Skaftafell
Glacial country with icecap & sand plain

Norway
3 Øvre Pasvik May-Sep
Forest & tundra
4 Stabbursdalen May-Oct
Arctic landscape with tundra, lakes, gravel plains & forest
5 Øvre Anarjokka May-Sep
Undulating tundra with woodland & lakes
6 Reisa May-Oct
Mixed mountain country
7 Øvre Dividal May-Sep
Mountainous country with tundra & woodland
8 Ånderdalen May-Oct
Mixed mountain country
9 Saltfjellet-Svartisen May-Sep
Varied landscape; fjords, mountains & glacier
10 Børgefjell May-Oct
Remote mountain area with varied habitats
11 Gressåmoen May-Oct
Mountainous country & spruce forest
12 Dovrefjell May-Aug
Mountainous tundra & permanent snowfields; famous for its flora
13 Rondane May-Sep
Mountain country with varied landscapes
14 Jotunheimen May-Sep
Mountainous area with tundra, bogs & forest
15 Hardangervidda May-Oct
Large mountain plateau, a popular walking area

Sweden
16 Vadvetjåkka May-Sep
Mountainous country
17 Abisko May-Sep
Mountain & forest with tundra, lakes & rivers
18 Muddus May-Sep
Forest, tundra & bog
19 Padjelanta, Sarek and Stora Sjöfallet May-Sep
3 parks protect Europe's largest wilderness area; mixed landscape
20 Pieljekaise May-Sep
Wooded mountainous country with tundra, open water & bogs
21 Skuleskogen Apr-Oct
Forested hill country
22 Töfsingdalen May-Oct
Woodland, tundra & bog
23 Sånfjället May-Oct
Woodland, tundra & bog
24 Hamra May-Oct
Woodland, tundra & bog, noted for its insects
25 Garphyttan Apr-Oct
Forest & meadows
26 Tiveden May-Oct
Hilly forest, lakes & bogs
27 Store Mosse Apr-Jul
Predominantly boggy, with lakes & forest

Finland
28 Pallas-Ounastunturi May-Sep
Upland plateau & taiga, with lakes, tundra, gorges & forest
29 Lemmenjoki May-Sep
Wilderness mountain area; gold rush in 1940's
30 Urho Kekkonen May-Sep
Large wilderness area; fells and pine moors
31 Pyhätunturi May-Sep
Mountainous area with tundra, bogs & forest
32 Oulanka May-Sep
Varied tundra landscape
33 Petkeljärvi May-Oct
Typical Finnish lakeland scenery, with lakes, bogs, forest & moorland
34 Linnansaari May-Oct
Mainly lake with some islands
35 Pyhä-Häkki May-Sep
Mainly forest & bog
36 Liesjärvi May-Sep
Lakes, previously cultivated land & forest
37 Saaristomeri May-Sep
Extensive island group with mixed habitats

Ireland
38 Glenveagh Apr-Jul
Mixed upland area
39 Connemara Apr-Sep
Typical western Ireland mountain area
40 Killarney May-Oct
Ancient woodland with moorland, lakes, bogs, wetland & mountains
41 Wicklow Mountains May-Aug
Partly wooded mountains with upland moorland & grassland

United Kingdom
42 Northumberland Apr-Oct
Mainly upland grassy moorland; Hadrian's Wall in the south
43 Lake District Apr-Nov
Mountain & lakeland; very popular all year
44 Yorkshire Dales May-Jul
Varied upland country
45 North York Moors Apr-Sep
Hilly uplands with heather moorland
46 Peak District May-Jul
Limestone in the south, with many caves; high peat moors in the north
47 Snowdonia May-Aug
Mountain country with lakes, moorland, grassland & woodland
48 Pembrokeshire Coast Apr-Jul
Scenic coastline; varied seabird habitats
49 Brecon Beacons May-Oct
Mainly grass-covered mountain area
50 Exmoor May-Jul
High heather moorland & wooded valleys, with dramatic coastline
51 Dartmoor May-Sep
Granite uplands with heather & grassland

Netherlands
52 Dwingelderveld May-Sep
Heathland, fen & woodland with lakes
53 De Hoge Veluwe Apr-Oct
Variety of habitats: heathland, dunes, fens, wet heath & woodland
54 Veluwezoom Apr-Oct
Heath & mixed woodland

Germany
55 Niedersächsisches Wattenmeer
East Frisan Islands; mudflats & saltmarsh
56 Hamburgisches W'meer
Mudflats & saltmarsh
57 Schleswig-Holsteinisches W'meer
Mudflats & saltmarsh
58 Vorpommersche Boddenlandschaft
Mudflats & saltmarsh with dunes, lagoons, lakes & woodland
59 Jasmund May-Nov
Varied landscape with cliffs, lakes & woodland
60 Müritz Apr-Nov
Woodland & lakes with heath, marsh & pasture
61 Unteres Odertal Apr-Jun, Sep-Nov
Floodplain of the Oder; park shared with Poland
62 Sächsische Schweiz Apr-Oct
Numerous rock towers; lower slopes wooded; deep valleys
63 Hoch Harz May-Oct
Wooded mountains with moorland, bogs & lakes; affected by acid rain
64 Bayerischer Wald May-Aug
Wooded mountain area
65 Berchtesgaden May-Sep
Mountain landscape with Alpine pastures, small glaciers, cliffs, lakes & varied woodland

France
66 Vanoise Jun-Sep
High mountain scenery
67 Écrins Apr-Sep
High mountain scenery with many glaciers
68 Mercantour Apr-Sep
Some of the best parts of the Maritime Alps
69 Port-Cros Mar-Sep
Small wooded island
70 Cévennes May-Sep
Varied mountain & forest with bogs & moors
71 Pyrénées Occidentales May-Sep, Oct
Diverse mountain landscape; snowfields, pastures & woodland

Spain
72 Ordesa May-Jul
Spectacular mountain & gorge scenery; forests & Alpine pastures
73 Covadonga May-Sep
Mountain area with mixed woodlands, pasture & glacial lakes
74 Tablas de Daimiel Apr-Jul
Small wetland
75 Coto de Doñana Feb-Jun
Guadalquivir delta; important wildlife site
76 Caldera de Taburiente
Volcanic landscape
77 Garajonay
Heavily wooded area
78 Cañadas del Teide
Volcanic landscapes
79 Timanfaya
Volcanic landscapes

Portugal
80 Peneda-Gerês Apr-Oct
Mountain & forest area; cliffs & rock formations

Switzerland
81 The Swiss National Park May-Oct
Strictly controlled mountainous area; forests, pastures, lakes, cliffs & snowfields

Austria
82 Hohe Tauern May-Sep
High Alpine scenery; forests in lower areas
83 Nockberge Apr-Oct
Forested mountain area with bogs & moors

Italy
84 Stelvio Apr-Oct
Typical Alpine scenery & Italy's largest glacier
85 Gran Paradiso Apr-Oct
High Alpine country; famous for the Ibex
86 Abruzzo Apr-Oct
Wooded mountainous area
87 Circeo Mar-Jun
Coastal marsh & rocky promontory near Rome
88 Calàbria Apr-Jul
Three areas of wooded mountainous landscape

Poland
89 Wolinski Apr-Oct
Woodland, lakes and sea cliffs; white-tailed sea eagle the main attraction
90 Slowinski Apr-Jul
Coastal landscape with shifting sand dunes
91 Kampinoski May-Oct
Varied landscape close to Warsaw
92 Mazurski and Wigierski
Numerous lakes and extensive forests
93 Biebrzanski Apr-Jul
Central Europe's largest area of natural peat bogs
94 Bialowieski Apr-Jul
Europe's largest original lowland forest; European bison the main attraction
95 Bieszczadzki May-Sep
Remote wooded mtn area in E. Carpathians
96 Babiogórski, Tatrzanski, Gorczanski & Pieninski May-Oct
Four parks in the spectacular High Tatra mountains
97 Ojcowski May-Sep
Hilly landscape with many rock pinnacles
98 Gory Stolowe and Karkonoski May-Sep
Dramatic mountain scenery of the Sudeten Mountains

Czech Republic
99 Krkonose May-Oct
Wooded mountain area with Alpine pastures, meadows, bogs & lakes

Slovak Republic
100 Vysoké Tatry May-Oct
Spectacular mountain area with forests, lakes, grassland & bogs
101 Nizke Tatry Apr-Jul
Mountainous country with varied woodland, pastures, bogs & lakes
102 Pieninsky May-Oct
Limestone mountains with mixed forests

Hungary
103 Aggtelek Apr-Oct
Important karst scenery
104 Bukk Apr-Jul
Hilly forested region
105 Hortobágyi
Varied steppe landscape good for birdwatching
106 Kiskunság Apr-Jul
Wide range of lowland habitats

Slovenia
107 Triglav
Limestone mountain scenery & mixed forest

Croatia
108 Risnjak
Limestone mountain scenery & mixed forest
109 Plitvice Lakes
Scenic lakes linked by waterfalls ·
110 Paklenica
Limestone peaks, gorges & mixed forest
111 Kornati
Limestone islands with karst scenery
112 Krka
Follows the Krka river; lakes, dams, gorges, falls & woodland
113 Mljet
Western part of island

Bosnia-Herzegovina
114 Sutjeska
Wooded mountainous area; mixed landscape & reserve of virgin forest

Federal Republic of Yugoslavia
115 Fruska Gora
Wooded hilly valley
116 Djerdap
Gorge of the Danube; dam has created a long thin lake
117 Tara
Mixed upland scenery
118 Durmitor
Mountain area in the west, Tara Gorge in east; mixed landscape & karst
119 Biogradska Gora
Mountain area with high grasslands & five lakes
120 Lovcen
Wooded limestone mountains
121 Skadarsko jezero
Yugoslav part of Lake Scutari

Former Yugoslav Rep. of Macedonia
122 Mavrovo
Mountain area, partly wooded
123 Galicica
S. end of Dinaric Alps; mostly natural forest
124 Pelister
Wooded mountain area with Alpine pastures

Albania
125 Dajtit, Lura and Thethi
Three separate parks; forested mountain areas
126 Divjaka
Dunes & coastal woodland
127 Llogara
Woodland & pastures
128 Tomorri
Mountainous landscape with forests & pastures

Romania
129 Retezat May-Sep
Mountain country with extensive forests

Bulgaria
130 Rusenski Lom May-Oct
Deciduous woodland
131 Vitosa May-Oct
Varied mountain area
132 Pirin Apr-Oct
High mountains; forest & mixed landscape

Greece
133 Préspa Apr-Jul
Shallow lakes with reed- & sedge-beds
134 Olimbos (Olympus) Apr-Oct
Mountain area with maquis & forest
135 Píndos May-Oct
Wooded mountain area
136 Víkos-Aóos May-Jun
Wooded mountain area; Víkos & Aóos gorges
137 Aínos Mar-Jul
Area around Mt Aínos
138 Iti Óros May-Oct
Wooded mountain area
139 Parnassós Apr-Nov
Wilderness mountain area; mixed habitats
140 Párnitha Apr-Jul
Limestone area; maquis
141 Soúnion Mar-May
Typical Greek coast

Turkey
142 Manyas-Kuscenneti
Part of large lake

Estonia
143 Lahemaa
Wooded area & scenic coast

Latvia
144 Gauja
River & gorge scenery

Lithuania
145 Zemaitija
Lakeland area
146 Aukstaitija (Ignalina)
Forest & lakes; great diversity of wildlife
147 Trakai
Five lakes with Trakai Castle as centrepiece
148 Dzukija
Confluence of Nemunas & Merkys rivers

LEISURE PARKS

This map shows major theme parks and amusement parks in Europe. Most of those shown are members of either the International Association of Amusement Parks and Attractions (IAAPA) or the European Federation of Amusement and Leisure Parks ('Europark'). Many parks which primarily attract visitors from the local area are excluded for reasons of space. A number of zoos, waterparks and museums are also members of IAAPA or Europark.

For more information, contact:

IAAPA,
1448 Duke Street,
Alexandria,
Virginia 22314,
USA.

Tel. +1 703 836 4800.

Europark,
Floralaan West 143,
NL-5644 BH Eindhoven,
The Netherlands.

Tel. +31 40 212 8526.

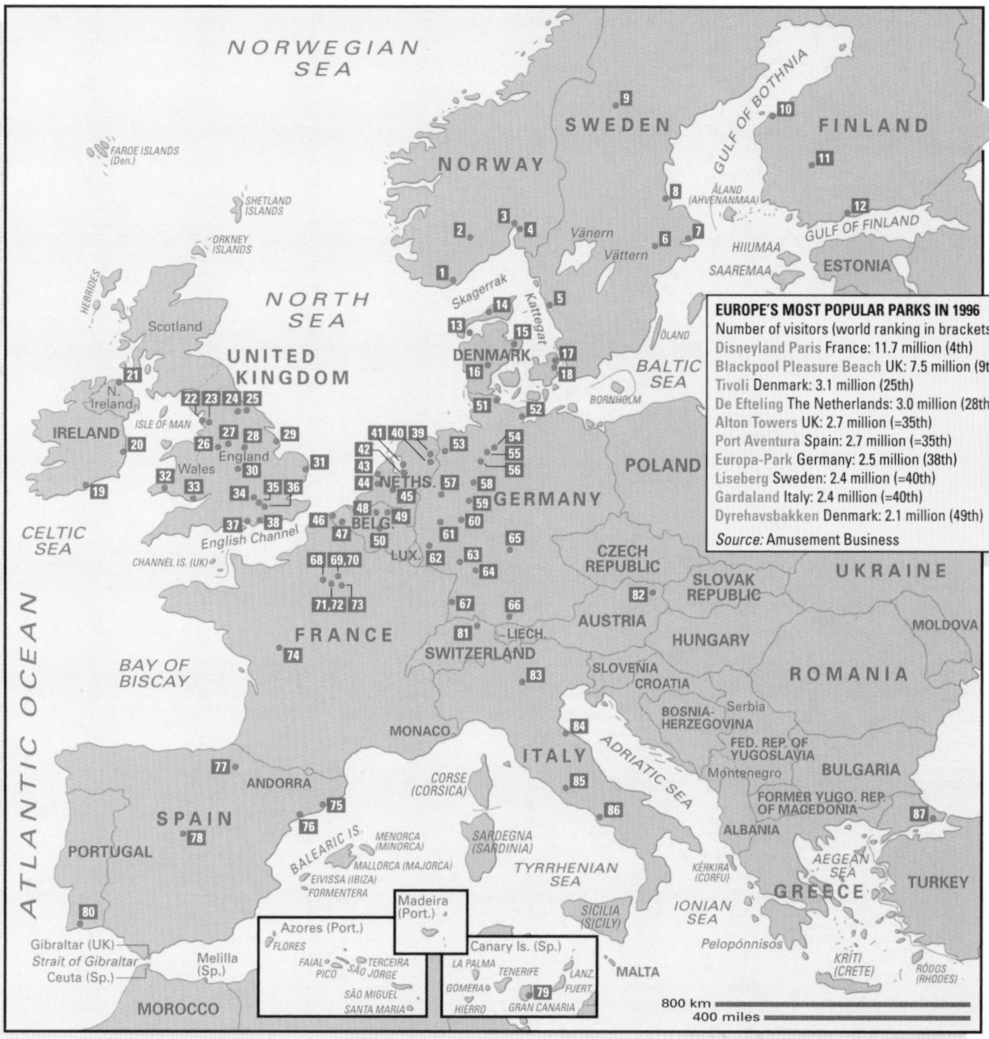

EUROPE'S MOST POPULAR PARKS IN 1996
Number of visitors (world ranking in brackets)
Disneyland Paris France: 11.7 million (4th)
Blackpool Pleasure Beach UK: 7.5 million (9th)
Tivoli Denmark: 3.1 million (25th)
De Efteling The Netherlands: 3.0 million (28th)
Alton Towers UK: 2.7 million (=35th)
Port Aventura Spain: 2.7 million (=35th)
Europa-Park Germany: 2.5 million (38th)
Liseberg Sweden: 2.4 million (=40th)
Gardaland Italy: 2.4 million (=40th)
Dyrehavsbakken Denmark: 2.1 million (49th)
Source: Amusement Business

Norway
1 Kristiansand Dyrepark
Combined animal park and entertainment park
2 Telemark Sommarland, Bø
Combined theme park and waterpark
3 Lunds Tivoli, Oslo
Amusement park
4 TusenFryd & VikingLandet, Vinterbru
Theme park with many rides and large Viking Land

Sweden
5 Liseberg, Gothenburg
Large theme park with convention facilities, exhibition hall and sports stadium
6 Parken Zoo i Eskilstuna
Theme park, waterpark and zoo
7 Gröna Lunds Tivoli, Stockholm
Amusement park in the centre of Stockholm
8 Furuviksparken, Gavle
Amusement park and zoo
9 Jamtli Historieland, Östersund
Historical theme park

Finland
10 Wasalandia, Vaasa
Amusement park; Tropical Bath Tropiclandia nearby
11 Tampereen Sarkanniemi Oy, Tampere
City-centre amusement park and entertainment centre; also includes an art museum
12 Linnanmaki, Helsinki
Finland's most popular amusement park

Denmark
13 Jesperhus Blomsterpark, Nykøbing, Mors
Amusement park, family entertainment centre and zoo
14 Fårup Aquapark & Sommerland, Saltum
Amusement park with 30 activities and Scandinavia's largest waterpark
15 Djurs Sommerland, Nimtofte
Amusement park with more than 50 activities in six attractions: Summerland, Waterland, Africa Land, Mexico Land, Cowboy Village and Lillensland
16 Legoland, Billund
Theme park based on Lego toy products; 22 family rides plus 75,000 square metres of Lego brick replicas of world monuments
17 Dyrehavsbakken ('Bakken'), Klampenborg
The world's oldest amusement park, with 24 rides
18 Tivoli, Copenhagen
Large amusement park

Ireland
19 Perks Pleasure Park, Youghal
Major rides include Vampire Ghost Train, Trabant and a giant big wheel supported by Perkie Bear
20 Clara Lara Fun Park, Wicklow
Park and amusement centre including Aqua Shuttle and Pirate Galleon plus a junior playground

United Kingdom
21 Barry's Amusement Park, Portrush
Star rides include Looping Dipper and Music Express
22 Blackpool Pleasure Beach
150 attractions including The Avalanche, Blackhole, Tagada, Nicky's Circus Ride, Beaver Creek, Believe It Or Not, Haunted Crypt, five wooden rollercoasters and a bobsleigh run
23 Camelot Theme Park, Chorley, Lancashire
A medieval world with over 100 attractions and rides including Excalibur, a 360° rotation swing ride
24 Lightwater Valley, Ripon
Theme park with unique attractions including the world's first suspended hang-glider ride and the world's longest rollercoaster
25 Flamingo Land, Malton
Popular holiday village and zoo with many rides in 150 hectares
26 Alton Towers, near Stoke-on-Trent
One of the UK's most popular theme parks with 125 rides and attractions including Nemesis and Storybook Land theme area
27 Gullivers Kingdom, Matlock Bath
Family theme park with over 40 rides, hot-air balloon flights and chair lift
28 American Adventure, Ilkeston
Theme park with Nightmare Niagara log flume
29 Magical World of Fantasy Island, Ingoldmells
Themed indoor family resort; based on Jules Verne
30 Drayton Manor Park, Tamworth
Theme park and zoo; 50 rides and attractions including Paratower, Jungle Cruise, Pirate's Adventure, Splash Canyon and The Haunting
31 Pleasurewood Hills, Lowestoft
East Anglia's no. 1 theme park with 50 rides including

Cannonball Express rollercoaster and the Log Flume
32 Oakwood Adventure, Narberth
Amusement park with over 40 attractions including Megafobia rollercoaster, Snake River Falls flume and a bobsleigh run
33 Barry Island Pleasure Beach, Barry
50 rides and attractions including Cyclone rollercoaster and African Experience ride
34 Legoland, Windsor
Children's theme park divided into five areas: The Beginning, The Imaginative Centre, Miniland, Duplo Gardens & Lego Traffic, My Town & The Wild Woods
35 Thorpe Park, Chertsey
Theme park with many rides including Canada Creek, Carousel Kingdom, A Drive in the Country, Flying Fish, Depth Charge and No Way Out, a backwards dark ride
36 Chessington World of Adventures
Zoo and amusement park with rides including Dragon River and Rameses Revenge
37 Fun Acres, Southsea
Seaside park with boat trips and 10 major rides
38 Harbour Park, Littlehampton
Seaside amusement park

The Netherlands
39 Ponypark, Slagharen
Theme park with over 40 rides
40 Avonturenpark Hellendoorn
Amusement park with many rides and animal attractions
41 Walibi Flevo, Dronten
Family amusement park with El Condor rollercoaster and Crazy River water flume
42 Zeedierenpark Harderwijk
Europe's largest marine park, with a research dept.
43 Duinrell, Wassenaar
Theme park close to the beach with over 50 rides and attractions, including Splash and Waterspin
44 Familiepark Drievliet, Rijswijk
More than 20 major attractions, including The Coppermine rollercoaster
45 De Efteling, Kaatsheuvel
Family leisure park with a full range of attractions including a golf course, Dreamflight dark ride, Fata Morgana, Inca City and two rollercoasters

Belgium
46 Meli Park, De Panne
Attractions and rides plus a bird and animal park
47 Bellewaerde Park, Ypres
Exotic animals on display and over 30 rides in four theme areas: Jungle, Western, Mexico and Orient
48 Action Planet, Antwerp
Indoor adventure sports park
49 Bobbejaanland, Lichtaart
Amusement and theme park with 45 major rides, including The Revolution and Arcade 2000; also includes Kinderland, a covered children's play area with 20 rides

50 Walibi, Wavre
Amusement park and waterpark with 40 rides including Rapid River, Shuttle Loop, Corkscrew and Jumbo Jet

Germany
51 Familien-Freizeitpark Tolk-Schau, Tolk
Amusement park situated in a scenic landscape
52 Hansapark, Neustadt in Holstein
Theme park with rides and attractions including an Aqua Stadium, a water circus and Adventureland
53 Ferienzentrum Schloß Dankern, Haren
Family entertainment centre with many water facilities
54 Heide-Park, Soltau
Amusement park with 36 major rides including a rapids ride, two monorails, a looping rollercoaster with four 360° turns and a bobsleigh ride
55 Serengeti Safaripark, Hodenhagen
Animal park with leisure attractions
56 Dinosaurier Park Münchehagen, Rehburg-Loccum
Dinosaur park
57 Warner Brothers Movie World, Bottrop
A unique movie theme park
58 Hollywood-Park, Stukenbrock
Combined safari park and amusement park, with attractions including Hollywood Theatre, a circus and a western show, a monkey area, Disco Round, Flying Carpet, a steam carousel and rollercoasters
59 Fort Fun Abenteuerland, Bestwig
Amusement park with a Western town
60 Panoramapark Sauerland, Kirchhundem
Wild animal park and amusement park with its own 500-kilowatt windpower station
61 Phantasialand, Brühl
Theme park divided into five areas: China Town, Old Berlin, Mexico, Petite Paris and Future World; many rides including Colorado Adventure and Michael Jackson Thrill Ride
62 Eifelpark, Gondorf bei Bitburg
Wild animal and amusement park, includes the Eifel Express
63 Holiday-Park, Haßloch
Theme park with many attractions including Thunder River, The Barrels of the Devil, Lilliput-Express, Aquascope, Stormship, a 180° cinema, Falkenstein Castle, Pfalz village and a looping rollercoaster
64 Erlebnispark Tripsdrill, Cleebronn
Germany's oldest amusement park
65 Freizeit-Land, Geiselwind
Theme park with many attractions including Cinema 2000, a Viking ship, a space adventure area, prehistoric world, Enterprise ride, Shuttle ride and a rollercoaster
66 Freizeit- und Miniaturpark Allgäu, Weitnau
Adventure park with many miniature buildings and trains; includes a large children's park with Nautic Jet, Luna Loop and Butterfly
67 Europa-Park, Rust
Large theme park with many rides

France
68 Mirapolis, Cergy-Pontoise
Large amusement park with activities related to legends and epics, includes Gargantua statue
69 La Mer de Sable, Ermenonville
Amusement park developed into themed areas: China, Wild West and Morocco; includes Babagattau Village
70 Parc Astérix, Plailly
Theme park based on comic strip hero Asterix with star rides Descent of the Styx, Big Splash and Goudume
71 Jardin d'Acclimation, Paris
Amusement park with family rides and a zoo
72 Parc Floral, Paris
Amusement park set within a large garden area
73 Disneyland Paris, Marne-la-Vallée
Divided into five 'lands': Main Street USA, Frontierland, Adventureland, Fantasyland and Discoveryland; rides include Space Mountain and Raiders of The Lost Ark
74 Futuroscope, Poitiers
Advanced visual-image technology in cinemas and leisure complexes; Showscan has a double-3D screen

Spain
75 Parque de Atracciones Tibidabo, Barcelona
Urban amusement park, founded 1899, renovated 1988
76 Port Aventura, Salou
Spain's largest theme park with five areas: Mediterrania, Polynesia, China, Mexico and Far West
77 Txiki Park, Pamplona
Family entertainment centre designed for children
78 Parque de Atracciones Casa de Campo, Madrid
Urban amusement park, Madrid's principal entertainment centre
79 Sioux City, San Agustín
Theme park with stage shows and concerts

Portugal
80 Zoomarine, Albufeira
Zoo and marine theme park

Switzerland
81 Conny-Land, Lipperswil
Amusement park with underwater and animal shows

Austria
82 Safari- und Abenteuerpark, Gänserndorf
Adventure park and drive-through safari park

Italy
83 Gardaland, Castelnuovo del Garda
Large amusement park with 25 different attractions, eleven entertainments and four themed villages
84 Fiabilandia, Rimini
Amusement park and funfair
85 Luneur, Rome
Amusement park and funfair
86 Edenlandia, Naples
Amusement/theme park

Turkey
87 Tatilya Turizm, Avcilar, Istanbul
World's fourth largest indoor entertainment centre

UNITED KINGDOM

See pages 6-7 for general map

SCOTTISH LOWLANDS

LAKE DISTRICT

HEART OF ENGLAND

SOUTHEAST ENGLAND

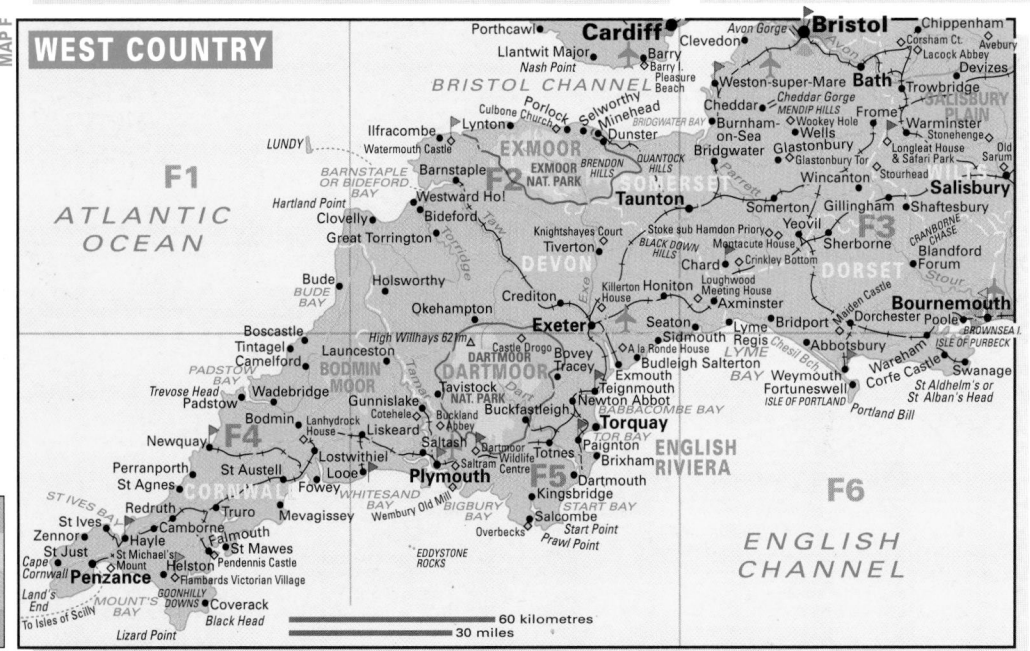

WEST COUNTRY

Geographical counties of the UK

These maps show the traditional geographical counties, not the local government divisions which are used for administrative purposes. Many of these geographical counties date back to Saxon times and have changed little for centuries. Each has distinct traditions and local loyalties.

In 1888 and 1889 administrative counties were created by Acts of Parliament in order to govern Britain's geographical counties, in most cases taking the same name and following the same boundaries. Although subsequent local government reorganisation has altered these administrative areas the geographical counties remain unchanged.

Major reviews of local government took place in the 1960s, the 1970s and the early 1990s; recently many familiar names have been replaced by numerous smaller unitary authorities throughout Great Britain and Northern Ireland, while some names abolished in the 1970s such as Rutland and Flintshire have been reinstated.

To further confuse the situation, the 'Post Counties' used by the Royal Mail are sometimes based on the geographical county and sometimes on the administrative county.

The heritage of each county has developed over hundreds of years and within the traditional geographical boundaries are places with common traditions and a similar cultural identity.

For further information, contact:

The Association of British Counties (ABC), c/o PO Box 5757, Royal Lytham St Anne's, Lancashire, FY8 2TE.

▸ Leisure park ▸ Zoo / animal park ▸ Aquarium ▸ Major tournament golf course ▸ Horse racing ▸ Major tennis venue

UK BEACHES AND NATIONAL PARKS

The European Blue Flag Campaign is an environmental awareness raising activity by the Foundation for Environmental Education in Europe (FEEE).

To qualify for a Blue Flag, a beach has to fulfil a number of strict criteria regarding water quality (compliance with the EU Bathing Water Directive), environment, education and information, beach area management and safety. The Blue Flag is awarded annually and is valid for one year.

45 beaches in the UK were awarded Blue Flags for 1998.

For further information, contact:

Tidy Britain Group, Seymour House, Muspole Street, Norwich, NR3 1DJ.

Tel. +44 (0) 1603 766076.

Ten of the most beautiful expanses of country in England and Wales have been awarded National Park status by Parliament in recognition of their scenic importance and use for open-air recreation.

For further information, contact:

The Countryside Commission, John Dower House, Crescent Place, Cheltenham, GL50 3RA.

Tel. +44 (0) 1242 521381.

The Seaside Award is awarded annually by the Tidy Britain Group to resort and rural beaches in the UK and Channel Is.

Resort beaches: busy beaches in or close to towns are assessed on 29 criteria including general cleanliness, water quality, safety provisions, beach facilities and provision for the disabled.

Rural beaches: usually in more remote locations, they are assessed on 13 similar key issues but are not expected to maintain the same standard of supervision or facilities as resort beaches.

247 beaches qualified for the Award for 1998.

Legend

1998 European Blue Flag:
○ Blue Flag beach

1998 Seaside Award:
● Resort beach
● Rural beach

Water quality results for the current season are updated weekly and are displayed at all Seaside Award beaches. All Award beaches have reached the 'Mandatory' standard of the EU bathing water directive the previous year. Beaches shown in **bold** type have achieved the higher 'Guideline' standard for the past five years (1993-97).

Beach character:
s Sandy
h Shingle
r Rocky
m Mud flats

Scotland
- s 1 Troon South
- s 2 Dornoch
- shr 3 Nairn Central
- s 4 St Andrews: West Sands
- s 5 Kingsbarns
- s 6 Aberdour: Silver Sands
- sr 7 Gullane Bents
- sr 8 Belhaven Bay

Northumbria
- s 9 Bamburgh
- s 10 Seahouses North: St Aidans
- s 11 Beadnell Bay
- s 12 **Low Newton**
- s 13 **Warkworth**
- sr 14 Amble Links
- s 15 Tynemouth: Cullercoats
- s 16 Tynemouth: Longsands South
- s 17 Whitburn North: Seaburn
- sh 18 Whitburn South: Roker
- s 19 Seaton Carew: Foreshore

Yorkshire
- sr 20 Runswick Bay
- sr 21 Whitby: West Cliff
- s 22 Robin Hood's Bay
- s 23 Scarborough: North Bay
- s 24 Scarborough: South Bay
- s 25 Filey
- shr 26 Flamborough: South Landing
- s 27 Bridlington North

East of England
- s 28 Mablethorpe Central
- s 29 Sutton on Sea Central
- sr 30 Skegness: Tower Esplanade
- shm 31 Snettisham
- s 32 Heacham North
- s 33 Heacham South
- s 34 Hunstanton
- s 35 **Sheringham**
- s 36 Cromer
- s 37 Mundesley
- s 38 Sea Palling
- s 39 Great Yarmouth Central
- s 40 Great Yarmouth: Gorleston
- sh 41 Lowestoft: Gunton
- s 42 Lowestoft: South
- s 43 Lowestoft: Victoria
- sh 44 Kessingland
- s 45 Southwold
- s 46 Southwold: Denes
- s 47 Sizewell
- sh 48 Thorpeness
- s 49 Aldeburgh
- s 50 Dovercourt
- s 51 Clacton-on-Sea West
- s 52 Brightlingsea
- sm 53 Shoeburyness East
- shm 54 Shoeburyness Common
- sm 55 Southend-on-Sea: Three Shells
- sm 56 Leigh-on-Sea: Bell Wharf

South East England
- shm 57 **Sheerness: Beach Street**
- hm 58 Sheerness: Minster Leas
- sh 59 Leysdown-on-Sea: Grove Avenue
- s 60 Herne Bay West
- s 61 Herne Bay East
- sr 62 Birchington: Minnis Bay
- s 63 **Broadstairs: Joss Bay**
- sr 64 Broadstairs: Viking Bay
- s 65 Dymchurch
- sh 66 Greatstone-on-Sea: Romney Sands
- s 67 Camber
- h 68 Winchelsea
- h 69 Bexhill
- h 70 Eastbourne: Pier to Wish Tower
- shr 71 Birling Gap
- h 72 Cuckmere Haven
- h 73 Seaford
- sh 74 Worthing Town
- s 75 Littlehampton
- s 76 West Wittering

Southern England
- s 77 Hayling Island: Beachlands Central
- sh 78 **Hayling Island: Beachlands West**
- h 79 Hill Head: Monks Hill/Salterns Beach
- h 80 Hill Head: Meon Shore
- shm 81 Lepe Country Park
- s 82 **Bournemouth: Fisherman's Walk**
- s 83 Bournemouth: Durley
- s 84 Poole: Sandbanks
- s 85 Swanage Central

Isle of Wight
- sh 86 Colwell Bay
- h 87 Cowes West
- sh 88 Cowes East
- s 89 Ryde East
- s 90 Springvale
- s 91 St Helens: Duver
- s 92 Sandown
- s 93 Shanklin
- h 94 Ventnor

West Country
- sh 95 Weymouth Central
- s 96 Dawlish Warren
- sr 97 Dawlish: Coryton Cove
- s 98 Teignmouth Town
- s 99 **Shaldon: Ness Cove**
- h 100 Torquay: Oddicombe
- s 101 Torquay: Meadfoot
- s 102 Torquay: Corbyn's Head
- s 103 Paignton South
- s 104 Broadsands
- s 105 Brixham: Shoalstone Breakwater
- sh 106 **Blackpool Sands**
- sh 107 Strete Gate
- h 108 Torcross: Slapton Sands
- h 109 Beesands
- s 110 Salcombe: North Sands
- s 111 Salcombe: South Sands
- s 112 Inner Hope: Hope Cove
- h 113 Outer Hope: Mouthwell
- s 114 **Thurlestone: South Milton Sands**
- s 115 Bantham
- s 116 Challaborough
- h 117 Par
- s 118 **St Austell: Porthpean**
- s 119 Gorran Haven: Little Perhaver
- s 120 Kennack Sands
- s 121 Sennen Cove
- s 122 St Ives: Porthmeor
- s 123 St Ives: Porthminster
- s 124 **Newquay: Fistral**
- s 125 Newquay: Porth
- s 126 Mawgan Porth
- shr 127 St Merryn: Treyarnon Bay
- s 128 **St Merryn: Constantine Bay**
- s 129 St Merryn: Harlyn Bay
- s 130 Polzeath

Wales
- sr 142 Porthcawl: Rest Bay
- s 143 Caswell Bay
- s 144 **Port-Eynon**
- s 145 **Rhossili/Llangennith**
- s 146 Pembrey Country Park: Cefn Sidan
- s 147 Saundersfoot: Coppet Hall
- s 148 Tenby North
- s 149 Tenby Castle
- s 150 Tenby South
- s 151 Lydstep
- s 152 Skrinkle
- sh 153 Manorbier
- s 154 Freshwater East
- s 155 **Barafundle Bay**
- s 156 Bosherton: Broadhaven
- s 157 Angle Bay West
- s 158 Dale
- s 159 Marloes
- s 160 Martin's Haven
- sr 161 St Brides Haven
- sr 162 Broad Haven South
- s 163 Newgale
- s 164 St David's: Caerfai
- s 165 St David's: Whitesands
- s 166 **Abereiddy**
- s 167 Dinas Cross: Cwm-yr-Eglwys
- s 168 Newport Sands
- s 169 St Dogmaels: Poppit Sands
- s 170 Mwnt
- s 171 Aberporth
- s 172 Tresaith
- s 173 Llangrannog
- s 174 Llangrannog: Cilborth
- hr 175 Cwmtydu
- s 176 New Quay: Traethgwyn
- s 177 New Quay: Traeth yr Harbwr
- s 178 New Quay: Traeth y Dolau
- s 179 Aberaeron South: Traeth y De
- s 180 Llanrhystud
- s 181 Aberystwyth South: Traeth y De
- s 182 Aberystwyth North: Traeth y Gogledd
- h 183 Clarach
- h 184 Borth
- s 185 Aberdyfi (Aberdovey)
- s 186 Tywyn
- sh 187 Fairbourne: Ffriog
- s 188 Barmouth: Abermaw
- sh 189 Llanenddwyn: Bennar-Morfa Dyffryn
- s 190 Llandanwg
- s 191 Harlech
- sh 192 Criccieth
- s 193 Pwllheli: Marian y De
- s 194 Abersoch
- s 195 Aberdaron
- s 196 **Dinas Dinlle**
- sh 197 Llanfairfechan
- s 198 Penmaenmawr
- s 199 Llandudno: North Shore
- s 200 Rhos-on-Sea
- s 201 Abergele: Pensarn
- s 202 Rhyl
- s 203 Prestatyn Central
- s 204 Talacre/Gronant

Anglesey
- s 205 Newborough: Llanddwyn
- s 206 Aberffraw: Traeth Mawr
- s 207 Llanfaelog: Porth Trecastell
- s 208 Llanfaelog: Porth Nobla
- s 209 Llanfaelog: Porth Tyn Tywyn
- s 210 **Rhosneigr: Traeth Llydan**
- s 211 **Rhosneigr: Traeth Crigyll**
- s 212 Holy Island: Traeth Llydan (Silver Bay)
- s 213 Holy Island: Borth Wen
- s 214 Holy Island: Trearddur Bay
- s 215 Holy Island: Porth Dafarch
- s 216 Llanfwrog: Porth Twyn Mawr
- s 217 Llanfaethlu: Porth Trefadog
- s 218 Llanfaethlu: Porth Trwyn
- s 219 Church Bay: Porth Swtan
- s 220 Cemlyn
- s 221 Cemaes Bay: Traeth Bach
- s 222 Cemaes Bay: Traeth Mawr
- s 223 Llaneilian: Porth Eilian
- s 224 Dulas: Traeth Lligwy
- s 225 Moelfre
- s 226 Benllech
- s 227 Pentraeth
- s 228 Llanddona
- s 229 Penmon
- s 230 Beaumaris

North West
- s 231 Formby: Lifeboat Road

Cumbria
- h 232 Silecroft
- sh 233 Allonby

Northern Ireland
- s 234 **Benone Strand**
- s 235 Portstewart Strand
- s 236 **Portrush West Strand**
- s 237 **Portrush East Strand**
- s 238 Ballycastle
- s 239 Cushendall
- s 240 Crawfordsburn
- shr 241 **Tyrella**
- s 242 Cranfield West

Channel Islands

Guernsey
- s 243 L'Erée Bay
- shr 244 Vazon Bay
- sh 245 Port Soif Bay
- s 246 **Pembroke/L'Ancresse Bay**
- s 247 Portelet Bay

Map boundaries legend
— English Tourist Board boundary
— geographical county boundary*
▨ National Park

100 kilometres
50 miles

*see note on the opposite page regarding the geographical counties and present-day administrative divisions

UK MOTORWAYS AND AIRPORTS

During the last few years regional UK airports have developed an international route network which supplements the London hub and this map aims to highlight the wide choice of destinations available.

All scheduled passenger flights to international destinations, licensed as at June 1998, are listed. Periods of operation or service are not indicated. Commercial or other considerations may result in services being suspended or withdrawn at short notice. Please check with the appropriate airport and/or airline to confirm details of flights. During the winter period additional services to winter resort destinations are scheduled.

Domestic routes within the UK (England, Wales, Scotland and Northern Ireland) have not been included, but flights to the Isle of Man and the Channel Islands are shown.

Where cities have more than one airport, the individual airport codes are used. For example, London city code is LON, but the airport codes are:

Biggin Hill	BQH
City	LCY
Gatwick	LGW
Heathrow	LHR
Luton	LTN
Stansted	STN

ABZ Aberdeen
Flights to nine destinations

Belgium: Brussels	BRU
Denmark: Esbjerg	EBJ
France: Nice	NCE
France: Paris Ch. de Gaulle	CDG
Netherlands: Amsterdam	AMS
Norway: Bergen	BGO
Norway: Haugesund	HAU
Norway: Skien	SKE
Norway: Stavanger	SVG

BHX Birmingham
Flights to 33 destinations

Belgium: Brussels	BRU
Canada: Toronto	YYZ
Channel Islands: Guernsey	GCI
Channel Islands: Jersey	JER
Cyprus: Larnaca	LCA
Cyprus: Paphos	PFO
Denmark: Copenhagen	CPH
France: Lyon	LYS
France: Paris Ch. de Gaulle	CDG
Germany: Berlin Tegel	TXL
Germany: Düsseldorf	DUS
Germany: Frankfurt a. Main	FRA
Germany: Hamburg	HAM
Germany: Hannover	HAJ
Germany: Munich	MUC
Germany: Stuttgart	STR
Ireland: Cork	ORK
Ireland: Dublin	DUB
Ireland: Knock	NOC
Ireland: Shannon	SNN
Isle of Man	IOM
Italy: Milan Linate	LIN
Malta	MLA
Netherlands: Amsterdam	AMS
Netherlands: Eindhoven	EIN
Netherlands: Rotterdam	RTM
Spain: Barcelona	BCN
Switzerland: Basle	BSL
Switzerland: Zürich	ZRH
Turkmenistan: Ashgabat	ASB
USA: Chicago	ORD
USA: New York JF Kennedy	JFK
USA: New York Newark	EWR

BLK Blackpool
Flights to two destinations

Channel Islands: Jersey	JER
Isle of Man	IOM

BOH Bournemouth
Flights to one destination

Ireland: Dublin	DUB

BRS Bristol
Flights to eight destinations

Belgium: Brussels	BRU
Channel Islands: Guernsey	GCI
Channel Islands: Jersey	JER
France: Paris Ch. de Gaulle	CDG
Ireland: Cork	ORK
Ireland: Dublin	DUB
Isle of Man	IOM
Netherlands: Amsterdam	AMS

BZZ Brize Norton
Flights to one destination

Falkland Islands	MPN

CBG Cambridge
Flights to one destination

Netherlands: Amsterdam	AMS

CWL Cardiff
Flights to seven destinations

Belgium: Brussels	BRU
Channel Islands: Guernsey	GCI
Channel Islands: Jersey	JER
France: Paris Ch. de Gaulle	CDG
Ireland: Dublin	DUB
Isle of Man	IOM
Netherlands: Amsterdam	AMS

EDI Edinburgh
Flights to 13 destinations

Belgium: Brussels	BRU
Channel Islands: Guernsey	GCI
Channel Islands: Jersey	JER

BFS Belfast International
Flights to four destinations

Belgium: Brussels	BRU
Channel Islands: Jersey	JER
France: Nice	NCE
France: Paris Ch. de Gaulle	CDG

BHD Belfast City
Flights to four destinations

Channel Islands: Jersey	JER
France: Paris Ch. de Gaulle	CDG
Germany: Düsseldorf	DUS
Isle of Man	IOM

LDY Londonderry
Flights to one destination

Isle of Man	IOM

Denmark: Copenhagen (EDI cont.)

Denmark: Copenhagen	CPH
France: Nice	NCE
France: Paris Ch. de Gaulle	CDG
Germany: Düsseldorf	DUS
Germany: Munich	MUC
Ireland: Dublin	DUB
Netherlands: Amsterdam	AMS
Portugal: Faro	FAO
Spain: Palma de Mallorca	PMI
Switzerland: Zürich	ZRH

EMA East Midlands
Flights to ten destinations

Belgium: Brussels	BRU
Channel Islands: Guernsey	GCI
Channel Islands: Jersey	JER
France: Nice	NCE
France: Paris Ch. de Gaulle	CDG
Ireland: Dublin	DUB
Netherlands: Amsterdam	AMS
Portugal: Faro	FAO
Spain: Málaga	AGP
Spain: Palma de Mallorca	PMI

EXT Exeter
Flights to four destinations

Channel Islands: Guernsey	GCI
Channel Islands: Jersey	JER
Ireland: Cork	ORK
Ireland: Dublin	DUB

GLA Glasgow
Flights to 23 destinations

Belgium: Brussels	BRU
Canada: Toronto	YYZ
Channel Islands: Guernsey	GCI
Channel Islands: Jersey	JER
Denmark: Copenhagen	CPH
Faroe Islands	FAE
France: Nice	NCE
France: Paris Ch. de Gaulle	CDG
Germany: Frankfurt a. Main	FRA
Germany: Hamburg	HAM
Germany: Hannover	HAJ
Iceland: Reykjavik	KEF
Ireland: Donegal	CFN
Ireland: Dublin	DUB
Isle of Man	IOM
Malta	MLA
Netherlands: Amsterdam	AMS
Norway: Stavanger	SVG
Spain: Palma de Mallorca	PMI
Sweden: Gothenburg	GOT
USA: Chicago	ORD
USA: New York JF Kennedy	JFK
USA: New York Newark	EWR

HUY Humberside
Flights to two destinations

Channel Islands: Jersey	JER
Netherlands: Amsterdam	AMS

LBA Leeds / Bradford
Flights to seven destinations

Belgium: Brussels	BRU
Channel Islands: Guernsey	GCI
France: Paris Ch. de Gaulle	CDG
Ireland: Dublin	DUB
Isle of Man	IOM
Netherlands: Amsterdam	AMS
Spain: Palma de Mallorca	PMI

LPL Liverpool
Flights to four destinations

Channel Islands: Jersey	JER
Ireland: Dublin	DUB
Isle of Man	IOM
Netherlands: Amsterdam	AMS

MAN Manchester
Flights to 68 destinations

Austria: Vienna	VIE
Belgium: Brussels	BRU
Canada: Toronto	YYZ
Channel Islands: Guernsey	GCI
Channel Islands: Jersey	JER
China: Hong Kong	HKG
Croatia: Dubrovnik	DBV
Croatia: Pula	PUY
Croatia: Split	SPU
Cuba: Havana	HAV
Cyprus: Larnaca	LCA
Cyprus: Paphos	PFO
Czech Republic: Prague	PRG
Denmark: Billund	BLL
Denmark: Copenhagen	CPH
Egypt: Cairo	CAI
Finland: Helsinki	HEL
France: Mulhouse	BSL
France: Paris Ch. de Gaulle	CDG
Germany: Berlin Tegel	TXL
Germany: Düsseldorf	DUS
Germany: Frankfurt a. Main	FRA
Germany: Hamburg	HAM
Germany: Hannover	HAJ
Germany: Munich	MUC
Germany: Stuttgart	STR
Gibraltar	GIB
India: Bombay	BOM
India: Delhi	DEL
Ireland: Cork	ORK
Ireland: Dublin	DUB
Ireland: Galway	GWY
Ireland: Knock	NOC
Ireland: Shannon	SNN
Ireland: Waterford	WAT
Isle of Man	IOM
Israel: Tel Aviv-Yafo	TLV
Italy: Milan Linate	LIN
Italy: Rome Fiumicino	FCO
Luxembourg	LUX
Malta	MLA
Mauritius	MRU
Netherlands: Amsterdam	AMS
Netherlands: Eindhoven	EIN
Netherlands: Rotterdam	RTM
Norway: Oslo	FBU
Pakistan: Islamabad	ISB
Pakistan: Karachi	KHI
Pakistan: Lahore	LHE
Poland: Warsaw	WAW
Portugal: Lisbon	LIS
Portugal: Oporto	OPO
Singapore	SIN
Slovenia: Ljubljana	LJU
Spain: Barcelona	BCN
Spain: Madrid	MAD
Sweden: Stockholm	ARN
Switzerland: Basle	BSL
Switzerland: Geneva	GVA
Switzerland: Zürich	ZRH
Turkey: Istanbul	IST
UAE: Dubai	DXB
USA: Atlanta	ATL
USA: Dallas-Fort Worth	DFW
USA: Chicago	ORD
USA: New York JF Kennedy	JFK
USA: New York Newark	EWR
USA: Orlando	MCO

MME Teesside
Flights to four destinations

Channel Islands: Jersey	JER
Ireland: Dublin	DUB
Ireland: Galway	GWY
Netherlands: Amsterdam	AMS

NCL Newcastle
Flights to 11 destinations

Belgium: Brussels	BRU
Denmark: Copenhagen	CPH
France: Paris Ch. de Gaulle	CDG
Germany: Düsseldorf	DUS
Ireland: Dublin	DUB
Isle of Man	IOM
Netherlands: Amsterdam	AMS
Norway: Bergen	BGO
Norway: Oslo	FBU
Norway: Stavanger	SVG
Switzerland: Zürich	ZRH

NWI Norwich
Flights to two destinations

France: Paris Ch. de Gaulle	CDG
Netherlands: Amsterdam	AMS

PLH Plymouth
Flights to three destinations

Channel Islands: Guernsey	GCI
Channel Islands: Jersey	JER
France: Paris Ch. de Gaulle	CDG

SOU Southampton
Flights to ten destinations

Belgium: Brussels	BRU
Channel Islands: Alderney	ACI
Channel Islands: Guernsey	GCI
Channel Islands: Jersey	JER
France: Paris Ch. de Gaulle	CDG
Germany: Düsseldorf	DUS
Ireland: Dublin	DUB
Isle of Man	IOM
Netherlands: Amsterdam	AMS
Switzerland: Zürich	ZRH

SZD Sheffield
Flights to one destination

Netherlands: Amsterdam	AMS

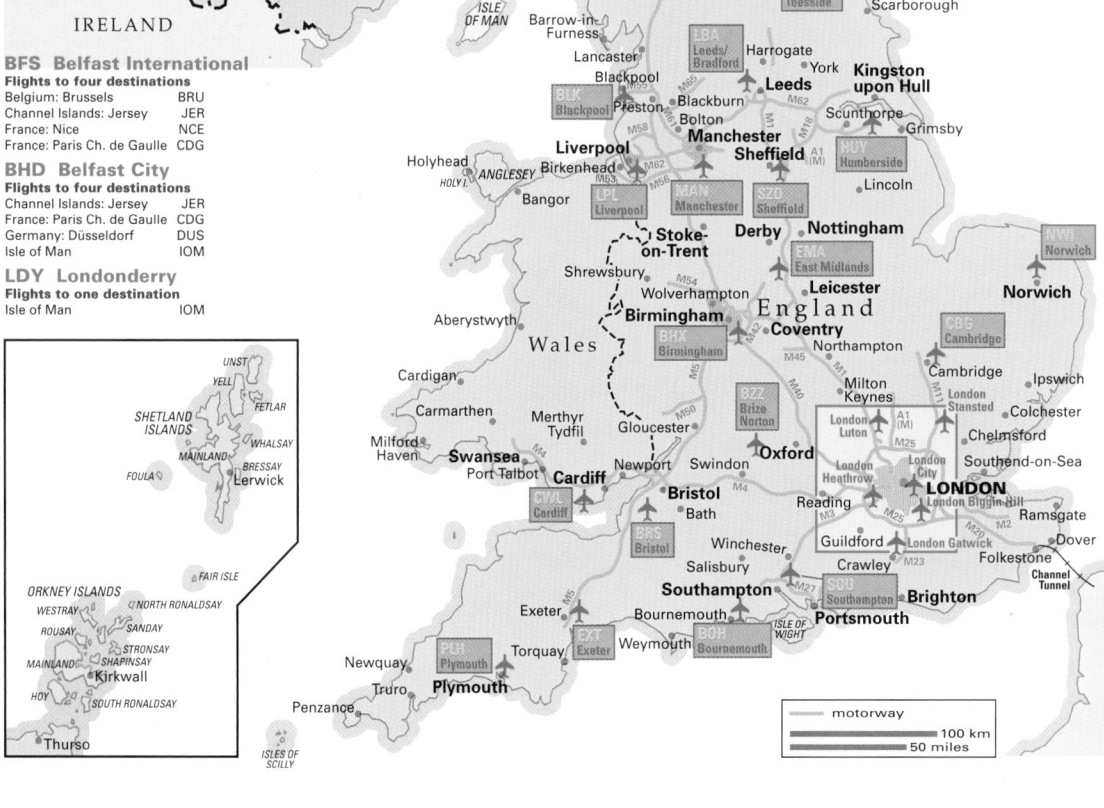

motorway

100 km
50 miles

LONDON AIRPORTS AND CONNECTIONS

This diagram shows principal public transport connections to London's airports from central London and links between airports.

It is not drawn to scale. Connections are shown as simple lines to improve legibility.

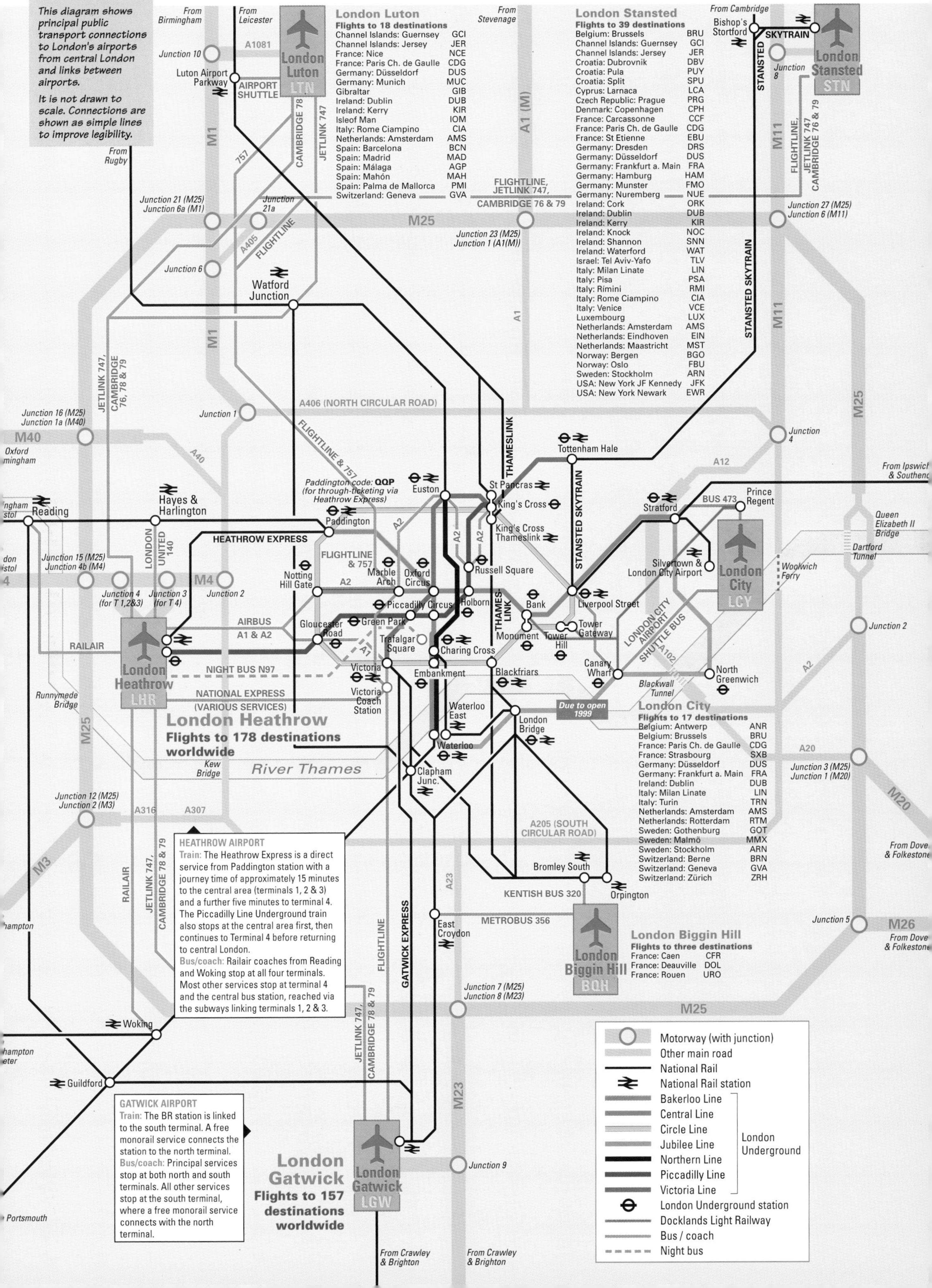

London Luton
Flights to 18 destinations

Channel Islands: Guernsey	GCI
Channel Islands: Jersey	JER
France: Nice	NCE
France: Paris Ch. de Gaulle	CDG
Germany: Düsseldorf	DUS
Germany: Munich	MUC
Gibraltar	GIB
Ireland: Dublin	DUB
Ireland: Kerry	KIR
Isle of Man	IOM
Italy: Rome Ciampino	CIA
Netherlands: Amsterdam	AMS
Spain: Barcelona	BCN
Spain: Madrid	MAD
Spain: Málaga	AGP
Spain: Mahón	MAH
Spain: Palma de Mallorca	PMI
Switzerland: Geneva	GVA

London Stansted
Flights to 39 destinations

Belgium: Brussels	BRU
Channel Islands: Guernsey	GCI
Channel Islands: Jersey	JER
Croatia: Dubrovnik	DBV
Croatia: Pula	PUY
Croatia: Split	SPU
Cyprus: Larnaca	LCA
Czech Republic: Prague	PRG
Denmark: Copenhagen	CPH
France: Carcassonne	CCF
France: Paris Ch. de Gaulle	CDG
France: St Etienne	EBU
Germany: Dresden	DRS
Germany: Düsseldorf	DUS
Germany: Frankfurt a. Main	FRA
Germany: Hamburg	HAM
Germany: Munster	FMO
Germany: Nuremberg	NUE
Ireland: Cork	ORK
Ireland: Dublin	DUB
Ireland: Kerry	KIR
Ireland: Knock	NOC
Ireland: Shannon	SNN
Ireland: Waterford	WAT
Israel: Tel Aviv-Yafo	TLV
Italy: Milan Linate	LIN
Italy: Pisa	PSA
Italy: Rimini	RMI
Italy: Rome Ciampino	CIA
Italy: Venice	VCE
Luxembourg	LUX
Netherlands: Amsterdam	AMS
Netherlands: Eindhoven	EIN
Netherlands: Maastricht	MST
Norway: Bergen	BGO
Norway: Oslo	FBU
Sweden: Stockholm	ARN
USA: New York JF Kennedy	JFK
USA: New York Newark	EWR

London Heathrow
Flights to 178 destinations worldwide

Paddington code: **QQP** (for through-ticketing via Heathrow Express)

HEATHROW AIRPORT
Train: The Heathrow Express is a direct service from Paddington station with a journey time of approximately 15 minutes to the central area (terminals 1, 2 & 3) and a further five minutes to terminal 4. The Piccadilly Line Underground train also stops at the central area first, then continues to Terminal 4 before returning to central London.
Bus/coach: Railair coaches from Reading and Woking stop at all four terminals. Most other services stop at terminal 4 and the central bus station, reached via the subways linking terminals 1, 2 & 3.

London City
Flights to 17 destinations

Belgium: Antwerp	ANR
Belgium: Brussels	BRU
France: Paris Ch. de Gaulle	CDG
France: Strasbourg	SXB
Germany: Düsseldorf	DUS
Germany: Frankfurt a. Main	FRA
Ireland: Dublin	DUB
Italy: Milan Linate	LIN
Italy: Turin	TRN
Netherlands: Amsterdam	AMS
Netherlands: Rotterdam	RTM
Sweden: Gothenburg	GOT
Sweden: Malmö	MMX
Sweden: Stockholm	ARN
Switzerland: Berne	BRN
Switzerland: Geneva	GVA
Switzerland: Zürich	ZRH

London Biggin Hill
Flights to three destinations

France: Caen	CFR
France: Deauville	DOL
France: Rouen	URO

London Gatwick
Flights to 157 destinations worldwide

GATWICK AIRPORT
Train: The BR station is linked to the south terminal. A free monorail service connects the station to the north terminal.
Bus/coach: Principal services stop at both north and south terminals. All other services stop at the south terminal, where a free monorail service connects with the north terminal.

Due to open 1999

Legend
- Motorway (with junction)
- Other main road
- National Rail
- National Rail station
- Bakerloo Line ⎫
- Central Line ⎪
- Circle Line ⎪
- Jubilee Line ⎬ London Underground
- Northern Line ⎪
- Piccadilly Line ⎪
- Victoria Line ⎭
- London Underground station
- Docklands Light Railway
- Bus / coach
- Night bus

Map labels
From Birmingham, From Leicester, From Stevenage, From Cambridge, A1081, A1 (M), Junction 10, Luton Airport Parkway, AIRPORT SHUTTLE, London Luton LTN, CAMBRIDGE 78, JETLINK 747, M1, 757, From Rugby, Junction 21 (M25) / Junction 6a (M1), Junction 21a, A405, FLIGHTLINE, Junction 6, Watford Junction, M25, Junction 23 (M25) / Junction 1 (A1(M)), FLIGHTLINE, JETLINK 747, CAMBRIDGE 76 & 79, JETLINK 747 / CAMBRIDGE 76, 78 & 79, Bishop's Stortford, SKYTRAIN, STANSTED, Junction 8, London Stansted STN, M11, FLIGHTLINE, JETLINK 747 / CAMBRIDGE 76 & 79, STANSTED SKYTRAIN, Junction 27 (M25) / Junction 6 (M11), M25, Junction 16 (M25) / Junction 1a (M40), M40, Oxford / Birmingham, A40, Junction 1, A406 (NORTH CIRCULAR ROAD), FLIGHTLINE & 757, Euston, St Pancras, King's Cross, King's Cross Thameslink, Tottenham Hale, THAMESLINK, STANSTED SKYTRAIN, A12, A1, Junction 4, From Ipswich & Southend, Reading, Hayes & Harlington, Paddington, HEATHROW EXPRESS, FLIGHTLINE & 757, Notting Hill Gate, Marble Arch, Oxford Circus, Russell Square, Stratford, BUS 473, Prince Regent, Queen Elizabeth II Bridge, Dartford Tunnel, Woolwich Ferry, Junction 15 (M25) / Junction 4b (M4), LONDON UNITED 140, M4, Junction 2, A2, Piccadilly Circus, Holborn, Bank, Silvertown & London City Airport, London City LCY, Junction 2, Junction 4 (for T 1,2&3), Junction 3 (for T 4), AIRBUS A1 & A2, Gloucester Road, Green Park, Trafalgar Square, Charing Cross, Monument, Tower Hill, Tower Gateway, Liverpool Street, LONDON CITY AIRPORT SHUTTLE BUS, North Greenwich, RAILAIR, London Heathrow LHR, NIGHT BUS N97, NATIONAL EXPRESS (VARIOUS SERVICES), Victoria, Victoria Coach Station, Embankment, Blackfriars, Canary Wharf, Blackwall Tunnel, Runnymede Bridge, M25, Kew Bridge, River Thames, Waterloo East, Waterloo, London Bridge, Clapham Junc., A20, Junction 3 (M25) / Junction 1 (M20), M20, Junction 12 (M25) / Junction 2 (M3), A316, A307, M3, JETLINK 747 / CAMBRIDGE 78 & 79, RAILAIR, A205 (SOUTH CIRCULAR ROAD), Bromley South, KENTISH BUS 320, Orpington, London Biggin Hill BQH, From Dover & Folkestone, Southampton / Exeter, Woking, METROBUS 356, East Croydon, GATWICK EXPRESS, FLIGHTLINE, London Biggin Hill, Junction 7 (M25) / Junction 8 (M23), M23, Junction 5, M26, From Dover & Folkestone, Portsmouth, Guildford, London Gatwick LGW, From Crawley & Brighton, Junction 9

UK FERRIES

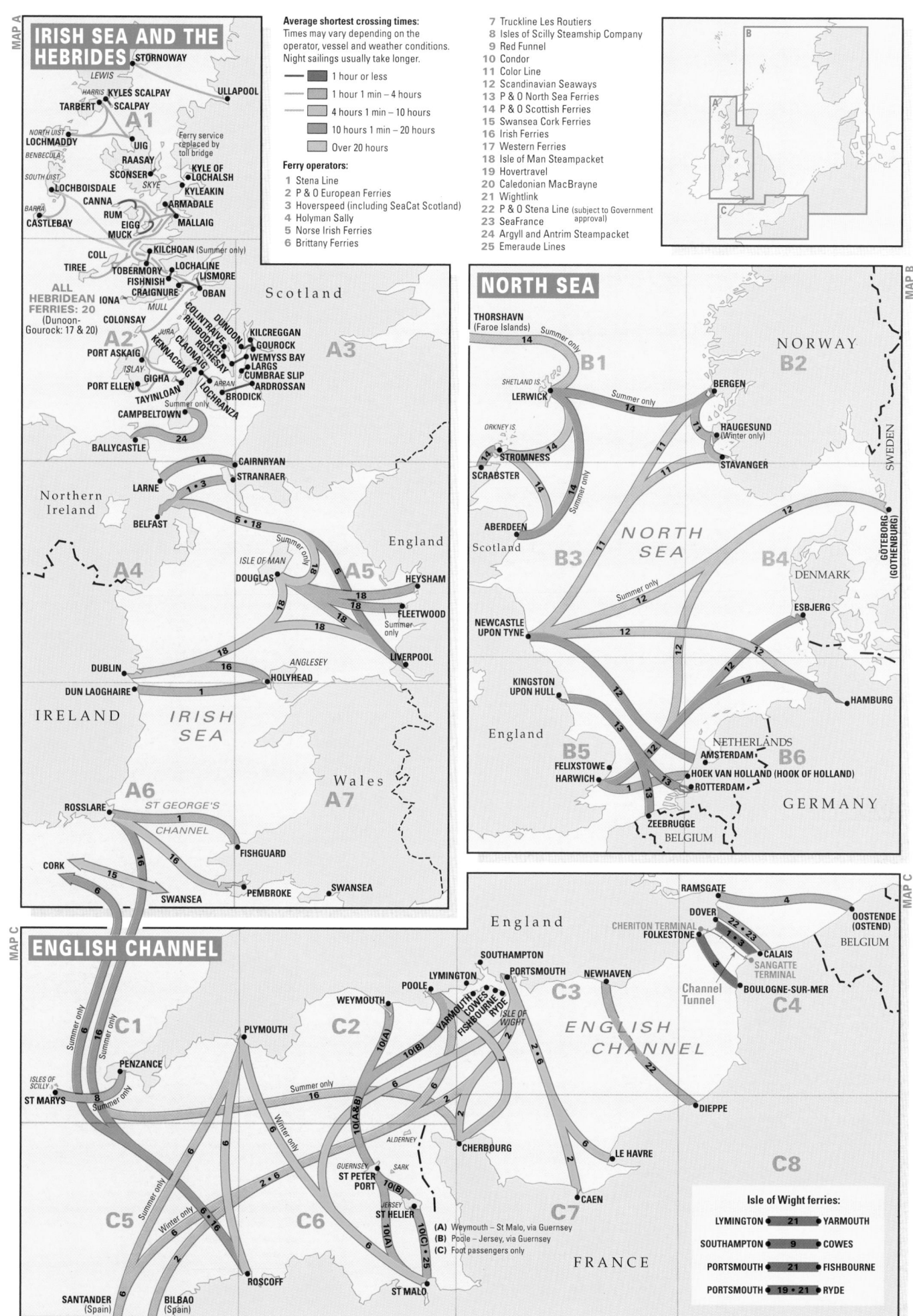
MAP A
IRISH SEA AND THE HEBRIDES
Average shortest crossing times:
Times may vary depending on the operator, vessel and weather conditions. Night sailings usually take longer.
1 hour or less
1 hour 1 min – 4 hours
4 hours 1 min – 10 hours
10 hours 1 min – 20 hours
Over 20 hours
Ferry operators:
1 Stena Line
2 P & O European Ferries
3 Hoverspeed (including SeaCat Scotland)
4 Holyman Sally
5 Norse Irish Ferries
6 Brittany Ferries
7 Truckline Les Routiers
8 Isles of Scilly Steamship Company
9 Red Funnel
10 Condor
11 Color Line
12 Scandinavian Seaways
13 P & O North Sea Ferries
14 P & O Scottish Ferries
15 Swansea Cork Ferries
16 Irish Ferries
17 Western Ferries
18 Isle of Man Steampacket
19 Hovertravel
20 Caledonian MacBrayne
21 Wightlink
22 P & O Stena Line (subject to Government approval)
23 SeaFrance
24 Argyll and Antrim Steampacket
25 Emeraude Lines
STORNOWAY
LEWIS
HARRIS
KYLES SCALPAY
TARBERT
SCALPAY
ULLAPOOL
A1
NORTH UIST
LOCHMADDY
UIG
Ferry service replaced by toll bridge
BENBECULA
RAASAY
SOUTH UIST
SCONSER
KYLE OF LOCHALSH
SKYE
LOCHBOISDALE
KYLEAKIN
CANNA
ARMADALE
BARRA
RUM
CASTLEBAY
EIGG
MALLAIG
MUCK
KILCHOAN (Summer only)
COLL
TIREE
TOBERMORY
LOCHALINE
FISHNISH
LISMORE
ALL HEBRIDEAN FERRIES: 20
(Dunoon-Gourock: 17 & 20)
IONA
CRAIGNURE
OBAN
MULL
Scotland
COLONSAY
DUNOON
COLINTRAIVE
RHUBODACH
ROTHESAY
KILCREGGAN
GOUROCK
JURA
A2
KENNACRAIG
CLAONAIG
WEMYSS BAY
LARGS
CUMBRAE SLIP
A3
PORT ASKAIG
ISLAY
GIGHA
ARRAN
ARDROSSAN
PORT ELLEN
TAYINLOAN
LOCHRANZA
BRODICK
Summer only
CAMPBELTOWN
24
BALLYCASTLE
CAIRNRYAN
STRANRAER
LARNE
Northern Ireland
BELFAST
England
Summer only
ISLE OF MAN
A4
A5
DOUGLAS
HEYSHAM
FLEETWOOD
Summer only
LIVERPOOL
ANGLESEY
DUBLIN
HOLYHEAD
DUN LAOGHAIRE
IRELAND
IRISH SEA
Wales
A6
A7
ROSSLARE
ST GEORGE'S CHANNEL
FISHGUARD
CORK
SWANSEA
PEMBROKE
SWANSEA
MAP B
NORTH SEA
THORSHAVN (Faroe Islands)
Summer only
B1
NORWAY
B2
SHETLAND IS.
LERWICK
Summer only
BERGEN
ORKNEY IS.
HAUGESUND (Winter only)
STROMNESS
SCRABSTER
STAVANGER
SWEDEN
Summer only
ABERDEEN
Scotland
NORTH SEA
B3
B4
GÖTEBORG (GOTHENBURG)
DENMARK
Summer only
ESBJERG
NEWCASTLE UPON TYNE
KINGSTON UPON HULL
HAMBURG
England
NETHERLANDS
B5
AMSTERDAM
B6
FELIXSTOWE
HARWICH
HOEK VAN HOLLAND (HOOK OF HOLLAND)
ROTTERDAM
GERMANY
ZEEBRUGGE
BELGIUM
MAP C
ENGLISH CHANNEL
RAMSGATE
England
DOVER
OOSTENDE (OSTEND)
CHERITON TERMINAL
FOLKESTONE
BELGIUM
CALAIS
SANGATTE TERMINAL
Channel Tunnel
BOULOGNE-SUR-MER
SOUTHAMPTON
LYMINGTON
PORTSMOUTH
NEWHAVEN
POOLE
C3
C4
WEYMOUTH
YARMOUTH
COWES
FISHBOURNE
RYDE
ISLE OF WIGHT
C1
C2
PLYMOUTH
ENGLISH CHANNEL
PENZANCE
ISLES OF SCILLY
ST MARYS
Summer only
DIEPPE
Winter only
ALDERNEY
CHERBOURG
LE HAVRE
C8
GUERNSEY
SARK
ST PETER PORT
JERSEY
ST HELIER
CAEN
C7
C5
C6
(A) Weymouth – St Malo, via Guernsey
(B) Poole – Jersey, via Guernsey
(C) Foot passengers only
FRANCE
ROSCOFF
ST MALO
SANTANDER (Spain)
BILBAO (Spain)
Isle of Wight ferries:
LYMINGTON 21 YARMOUTH
SOUTHAMPTON 9 COWES
PORTSMOUTH 21 FISHBOURNE
PORTSMOUTH 19 • 21 RYDE

IRELAND

See page 7 for general map

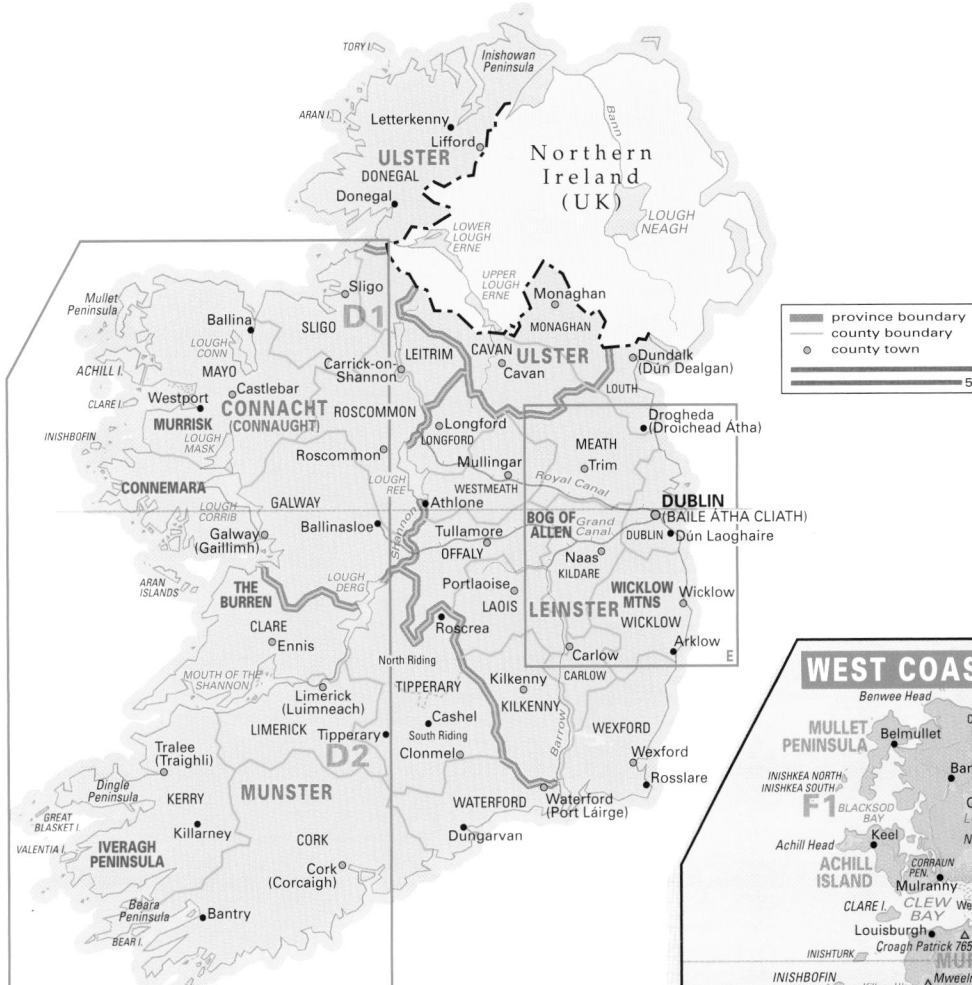

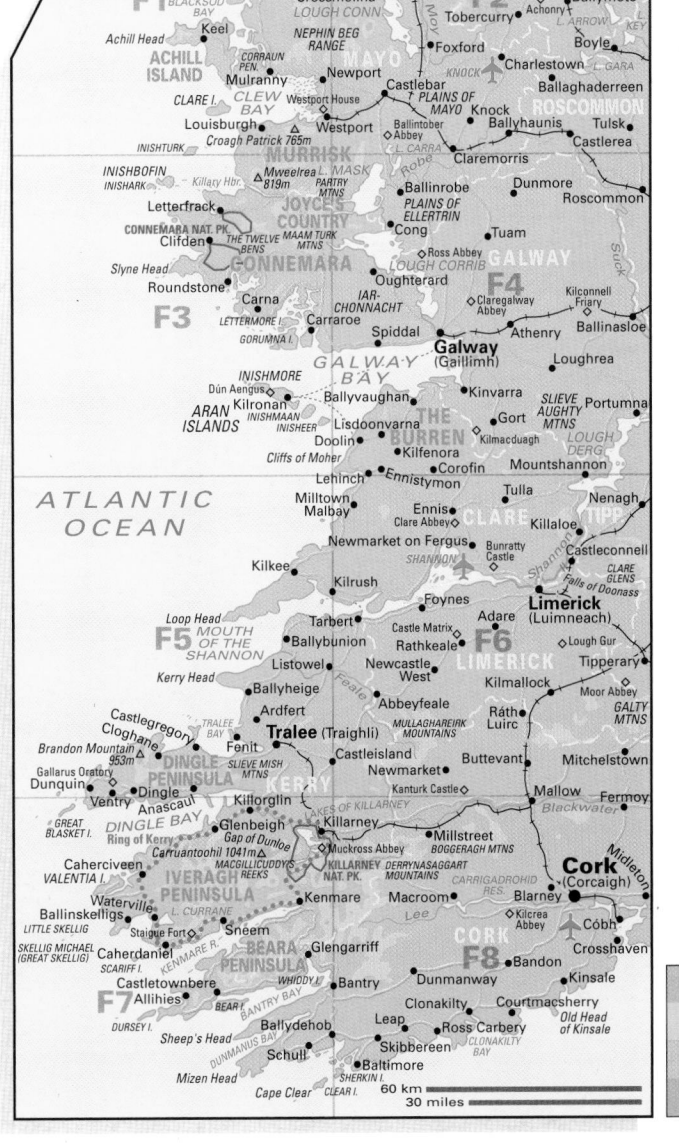

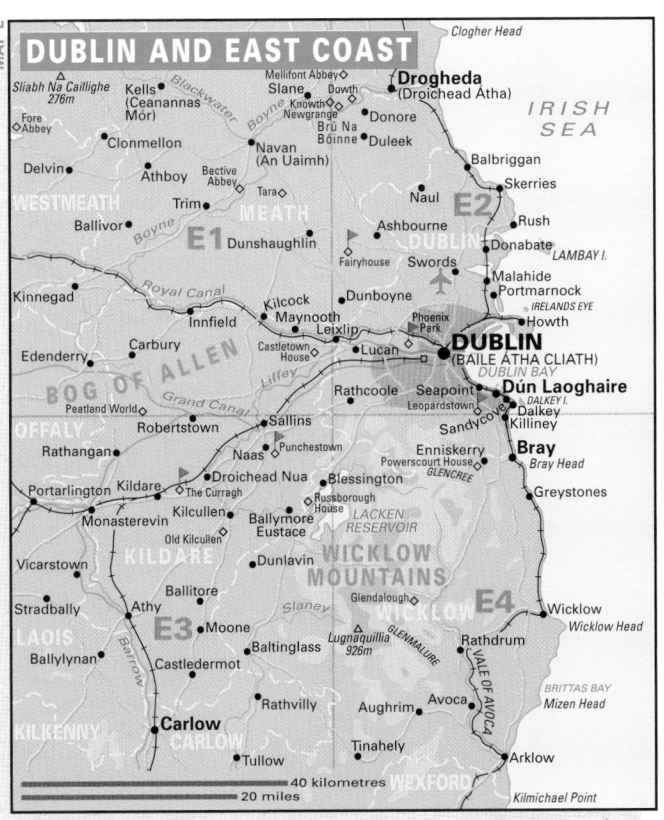

▲ Zoo / animal park   ▶ Horse racing

BELGIUM   NETHERLANDS   LUXEMBOURG

BENELUX

See page 5 for general map

BELGIAN COAST

Knokke-Heist
Zeebrugge
Blankenberge
Wenduine
De Haan
Bredene-aan-Zee
Oostende (Ostend)
Brugge
(Bruges)

NETHS.

Kanaal van Gent naar Oostende

Westende-Bad
Middelkirke-Bad
Jabbeke
Loppem
Lombardsijde-Bad
Nieuwpoort
Oostduinkerke-Bad
Koksijde-Bad
Sint-Idesbald
De Panne
Mefi Park
Veurne
Torhout

WEST-VLAANDEREN

Gistel

Diksmuide
Tielt

FR.

20 kilometres
10 miles

B1
B2

MAP B

NETHS.

MAP A

SCHIERMONNIKOOG
AMELAND
TERSCHELLING
Eemshaven
Uithuizen
Delfzijl
Emden
Dokkum
GRONINGEN
Marssum
Harlingen
Leeuwarden
Groningen
Hoogezand
VLIELAND
Bolsward
FRIESLAND
WADDENZEE
Sneek
Heerenveen
Assen
TEXEL
Den Helder
Stavoren
EELDE
DRENTHE
NATIONAAL PARK DWINGELDERVELD
Havelte
Hoogeveen
Emmen
Coevorden
DE ZIJPE
WIERINGER-MEER
IJSSELMEER
Giethoorn
Meppel
Wanneperveen
Ponypark
Broek op Langedijk
Enkhuizen
Emmeloord
Schokland prehistoric settlements
Alkmaar
Hoorn
NOORDOOST-POLDER
Zwolle
Ommen
Nordhorn
FLEVOLAND
Kampen
OVERIJSSEL
MARKER-MEER
Lelystad
Walibi Flevo
IJmuiden
Volendam
Haarlem
Zaanstad
Marken
FLEVOLAND
Deventer
Almelo
TWENTE
Zandvoort
AMSTERDAM
Almere
Zeedierenpark
Harderwijk
Apeldoorn
Hengelo
Enschede
Katwijk
Amstelveen
Naarden
Hilversum
Harderwijk
GELDERLAND
Zutphen
A8
Aalsmeer
Amersfoort
NATIONAAL PARK DE HOGE VELUWE
A7
Scheveningen
Leiden
ZUID-HOLLAND
Utrecht
UTRECHT
Ede
NATIONAAL PARK VELUWEZOOM
Wintersijk
Den Haag ('s-Gravenhage, The Hague)
Delft
Gouda
Lek
Oosterbeek battlefield
Arnhem
Rhenen
Hoek van Holland (Hook of Holland)
ZESTIENHOVEN
NETHERLANDS
Bocholt
Europoort
Rotterdam
Waal
Nijmegen
VOORNE
Zwijndrecht
Gorinchem
Dorsten
PUTTEN
Dordrecht
Grave battlefield
Xanten
HOEKSE WAARD
Kaatsheuvel
's-Hertogenbosch
Overloon
SCHOUWEN
DUIVELAND
OVERFLAKKEE
NOORD-BRABANT
Rhein (Rhine)
Bottrop
Gelsenkirchen
ZEELAND
Veere
NOORD-BEVELAND
Breda
De Efteling
Beekse Bergen
Essen
Oberhausen
A10
Roosendaal
Tilburg
Hilvarenbeek
Helmond
A12
Middelburg
ZUID-BEVELAND
Bergen op Zoom
Eindhoven
Venlo
Krefeld
Duisburg
Vlissingen (Flushing)
A9
A11
WELSCHAP
LIMBURG
Düsseldorf
Neuss
Solingen
Breskens
IJzendijke
Biervliet
Turnhout
Roermond
Mönchengladbach
Zeebrugge
Brugge (Bruges)
Terneuzen
Kasterlee
Bree
Oostende (Ostend)
St-Niklaas
Antwerpen (Antwerp)
Lille
Bobbejaanland
LIMBURG
Sittard
Köln (Cologne)
Nieuwpoort
DEURNE
Herentals
Geleen
Heerlen
Düren
WEST-VLAANDEREN
OOST-VLAANDEREN
Mechelen
Laarne
Aarschot
Scherpenheuvel-Zichem
Zonhoven
Valkenburg
Maastricht
Dunkerque (Dunkirk)
Veurne
ANTWERPEN
Genk
Aachen (Aix-la-Chapelle)
BONN
Gent (Gand, Ghent)
Londerzeel
Zemst
Diest
Hasselt
VLAAMS-BRABANT
ZAVENTEM
Leuven
BEEK
FLANDERS
Oudenaarde
Aalst
BRUSSELS
Tienen
GERMANY
Passchendaele battlefield
Poperinge
Zonnebeke battlefield
BRUXELLES (BRUSSEL, BRUSSELS)
Rixensart
Wavre
BRABANT WALLONIE
A15
Liège
Verviers
A16
Bellewaerde Park
Kortrijk
TGV
A14
Waterloo battlefield
Walibi
BIERSET
Spa
Ieper (Ypres)
Ath
Nivelles
A13
Tourcoing
HAINAUT
Huy
Modave
Spa-Francorchamps
Armentières
Roubaix
Tournai
Beloeil
Attre
Meuse
Château de Reinhardstein
FRANCE
Lille
Le Rœulx
Namur
Godinne
LIÈGE
St Vith
St Omer
Béthune
Mons
Charleroi
Profondeville
Annevoie
Yvoir
Spontin
Hotton
Gerolstein
Lens
Sambre
Escaut
Ourthe
Amblève
Douai
MEUSE VALLEY
80 km
40 miles
NAMUR
Dinant
Marche-en-Famenne
La Roche-en-Ardenne
Clervaux
RANDSTAD
Beverwijk
NOORD-HOLLAND
Edam
Volendam
Lelystad
Rochefort
Bastogne
Wiltz
Bitburg
Zaanse Schans
Purmerend
MARKERMEER
Han-sur-Lesse
Vianden
A20
Wormerveer
Monnickendam
MARKEN
Bohan
A19
Bourscheid
IJmuiden
Zaanstad
Broek in Waterland
OOSTVAARDERS PLASSEN
Rochehaut
Esch-sur-Sûre
Diekirch
Beaufort
Echternach
NATIONAAL PARK DE KENNEMER DUINEN
Santpoort
Spaarndam
FLEVOLAND
Charleville-Mézières
Neufchâteau
Mersch
Larochette
Auto Circuit Zandvoort
Haarlem
AMSTERDAM
Almere-Stad
FLEVOLAND
LUXEMBOURG
Trier
Zandvoort
Heemstede
Almere-Haven
Sedan
Bouillon
Florenville
Arlon
LUXEMBOURG
NORTH SEA
Hoofddorp
Weesp
Muiden
Huizen
Steinsel
FINDEL
C1
Hillegom
Polder
Aalsmeer
Amstelveen
Naarden
Hilversum
Bussum
Abbaye-d'Orval
Remich
Amsterdamse Waterleiding Duinen
Muiderslot
Baarn
Virton
LUXEMBOURG-VILLE
Noordwijk
Lisse
Keukenhof
Uithoorn
Mijdrecht
Amersfoort
Esch-sur-Alzette
Katwijk
Rijnsburg
LOODRECHTSE PLASSEN
Soest
Mondorf-les-Bains
Den Haag ('s-Gravenhage, The Hague)
Leiden
Alphen aan de Rijn
Maarssen
De Haar
Bilthoven
Longuyon
Stenay
Katwijkse Duinen
Boswachterij Wassenaar
Voorschoten
Utrecht
Zeist
Scheveningen
Duinrell
Wassenaar
Bodegraven
Madurodam
Voorburg
Boskoop
Woerden
ZUID-HOLLAND
Oudewater
UTRECHT
Ter Heijde
Monster
Zoetermeer
Gouda
Doorn
Rijswijk
Delft
Westland
Schieland
Hollandse IJssel
Lopikerwaard
GELDERLAND
Hoek van Holland (Hook of Holland)
Delfland
Krimpenerwaard
Schoonhoven
Culemborg
Maasvlakte
Maassluis
Schiedam
Vijfherenlanden
Tielerwaard
Geldermalsen
Tiel
Europoort
Brielle
Vlaardingen
Euromast
Pernis
Kinderdijk
Leerdam
Rotterdam
Hoogvliet
Ridderkerk
Alblasserwaard
C4
Haringvliet Dam
Spijkenisse
Botlek
Oud-Beijerland
Sliedrecht
Gorinchem
Hellevoetsluis
PUTTEN
Zwijndrecht
Land van Maas en Waal
VOORNE
Dordrecht
Biesbosch
OVERFLAKKEE
HOEKSE WAARD
Bommelerwaard
Spui
Maas
Land van Altena
40 kilometres
Middelharnis
20 miles
NOORD-BRABANT
MAP C

© Province capital

WEST-VLAANDEREN
OOST-VLAANDEREN
ANTWERPEN
LIMBURG
BRUSSELS
VLAAMS-BRABANT
HAINAUT
BRABANT WALLONIE
LIÈGE
BELGIUM
NAMUR
LUXEMBOURG

Flemish language region
French language region
German language region
Bilingual district (Flemish-French)

◆ Leisure park   ▶ Zoo / animal park   ◆ Aquarium   ▶ Formula One   ▶ Major tennis venue

400 metres
200 metres
Sea level

A1 A2 A3 A4 A5 A6

GERMANY

See pages 8-9 for general map

SYLT
NORDFRIESISCHE INSELN (NORTH FRISIAN ISLANDS)
Flensburg
HELGOLAND
Puttgarden — FEHMARN
ZINGST — RÜGEN — Saßnitz
Kiel
SCHLESWIG-HOLSTEIN
Warnemünde — Stralsund — Greifswald — USEDOM
OSTFRIESISCHE INSELN (EAST FRISIAN ISLANDS)
Travemünde — Rostock
Cuxhaven
D1
Lübeck
MECKLENBURG-VORPOMMERN
Wilhelmshaven — Bremerhaven — HAMBURG — Hamburg — Schwerin — Neubrandenburg
Emden — OST-FRIESLAND — BREMEN — Oldenburg — BREMEN
Lüneburg
UCKERMARK — Schwedt an der Oder
LÜNEBURGER HEIDE — PRIGNITZ
Uelzen — Wittenberge
EMSLAND — NIEDERSACHSEN (LOWER SAXONY) — ALTMARK — HAVELLAND
BERLIN — Frankfurt an der Oder
Celle — Wolfsburg — Hannover — Potsdam
Osnabrück — Hildesheim — Braunschweig — Salzgitter — Magdeburg — BRANDENBURG
MÜNSTERLAND — Bielefeld — SACHSEN-ANHALT — Cottbus
Münster — NORDRHEIN-WESTFALEN — Hamm — Paderborn
D2 — HARZ — NIEDERLAUSITZ
Gelsenkirchen — Dortmund — Lippe — Göttingen — Dessau
Essen — Bochum — Halle — Leipzig — OBERLAUSITZ
Duisburg — Hagen — Ruhr — Kassel — SACHSEN (SAXONY)
Düsseldorf — Wuppertal
Mönchengladbach — SAUERLAND — Dresden
Köln (Cologne) — Siegen — Erfurt — Jena — Gera — Chemnitz
Aachen (Aix-la-Chapelle) — HESSEN (HESSE) — Werra — THÜRINGEN (THURINGIA) — Zwickau — ERZGEBIRGE
BONN
WESTERWALD — Gießen — THÜRINGER WALD
Koblenz — Fulda — RHÖN
EIFEL — RHINE GORGE — Frankfurt am Main — Lahn — FICHTELGEBIRGE — BÖHMERWALD
TAUNUS — Wiesbaden — SPESSART — Bamberg — Bayreuth
Mosel — Mainz — Main — OBERPFÄLZER WALD
HUNSRÜCK — RHEINLAND-PFALZ (RHINELAND-PALATINATE) — Darmstadt — Würzburg — Main-Donau-Kanal — Erlangen
Trier — Nürnberg (Nuremberg) — Naab
SAARLAND — Ludwigshafen — Mannheim — Rothenburg ob der Tauber — Ansbach — FRÄNKISCHE ALB
Saarbrücken — PFÄLZER WALD — Heidelberg — Regensburg
BAYERISCHER WALD
Heilbronn — BADEN-WÜRTTEMBERG — Altmühl
Karlsruhe — Ingolstadt — NIEDERBAYERN
Stuttgart — SCHWÄBISCHE ALB — BAYERN (BAVARIA) — Donau (Danube) — Landshut — Passau
Tübingen — Neckar — Isar — Inn
D4 — Ulm — Augsburg — München (Munich)
SCHWARZWALD (BLACK FOREST) — SCHWABEN (SWABIA) — Lech — OBERBAYERN
Freiburg im Breisgau — Donau (Danube) — Berchtesgaden
Konstanz (Constance) — Iller
BODENSEE (LAKE CONSTANCE) — ALLGÄU — BAYERISCHE ALPEN (BAVARIAN ALPS) — Garmisch-Partenkirchen
Rhein (Rhine)

Legend
— Land boundary
⦿ Land capital
100 km
50 miles

RUHRGEBIET

BERLIN

1000 metres
500 metres
Sea level

▶ Leisure park   ▶ Zoo / animal park   ▶ Aquarium   ▶ Major tennis venue

GERMANY

See pages 8-9 for general map

Germany has a well-developed network of tourist routes passing through areas of scenic or historic interest. Some of the most well-known are:

Romantische Straße (Romantic Road). Established in 1950, it runs for 350 kilometres from northern Bavaria to the Bavarian Alps. See panel for the route.

Straße der Kaiser und Könige (Route of Emperors and Kings). One of Germany's oldest transit routes, running from Frankfurt am Main in the west, following the Main and Danube rivers, to Passau on the Austrian border and continuing to Vienna.

Weinstraße (Wine Road). Germany's oldest designated tourist route, passing through vineyards of the Pfalz.

Mosel Weinstraße (Mosel Wine Road). Follows the Mosel from Trier to Koblenz. Boat cruises are popular along this stretch of river.

Deutsche Märchenstraße (German Fairy-Tale Road). This route runs from Bremen to the River Main through many places connected with fairy tales.

Burgenstraße (Castle Road). Passes many fortifications in the Neckar valley between Mannheim and Heilbronn, then continues east to Nuremburg.

Schwarzwald-Hochstraße (Black Forest Highway). One of Germany's most famous roads, linking Baden-Baden with Freudenstadt.

ROMANTIC ROAD

- **Würzburg**
- Tauberbischofsheim
- Bad Mergentheim
- Weikersheim
- Röttingen
- Creglingen
- **Rothenburg ob der Tauber**
- Schillingsfürst
- Feuchtwangen
- Dinkelsbühl
- Wallerstein
- **Nördlingen im Ries**
- Harburg
- **Donauwörth**
- **Augsburg**
- Friedberg
- **Landsberg am Lech**
- Hohenfurch
- Schongau
- Peiting
- Rottenbuch
- Wildsteig
- Wieskirche
- Steingaden
- Schwangau
- **Füssen**

Diagrammatic only: not to scale

RHINE AND BLACK FOREST

RHINE GORGE AND MOSEL

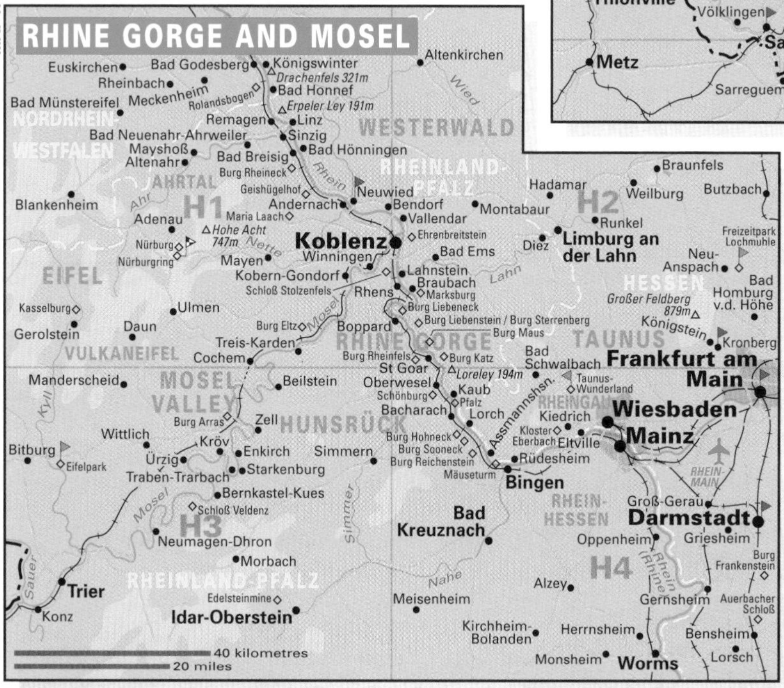

SOUTHERN BAVARIA

▶ Leisure park   ▶ Zoo / animal park   ◆ Aquarium   ▶ Formula One   ● Major tennis venue

GERMAN SPAS

Spa holidays are first and foremost to improve or restore one's health, but patients also have a chance to meet people and get to know a different culture. There are nearly 400 recognised spa institutions in Germany which are grouped according to the requirements shown on this page.

For further information, contact:

Deutscher Bäderverband e.V.,
Schumannstraße 111, D-53113 Bonn.

Tel. +49 (0) 228 262010

All registered spas satisfy a number of basic criteria regarding the treatment facilities (including facilities for treating specific conditions); scientific assessment of the main treatment areas and contraindications (with the exception of seaside spas); suitability of climate and good air quality.

The spas are categorised as follows, depending on the following points. Some spas of the same type have been grouped together.

- Spa
- Seaside spa (located within 2 kilometres of the seashore)
- Seaside health spa (located within 2 km of the seashore and scientific proof of a therapeutically suitable climate)
- Kneipp health spa (scientific proof of a therapeutically suitable climate)
- Kneipp spa (ten years of establishment as a Kneipp health spa with no complaints during that period)
- Climatic spa (scientific proof of a therapeutically suitable climate which is constantly monitored by meteorological stations and scientific proof of a specific air quality)
- Town with spa facilities

Schleswig-Holstein
1 Helgoland
2 Sylt: Hörnum / Kampen / Keitum (Sylt-Ost) / List / Rantum
2 Sylt: Wenningstedt / Westerland
3 Amrum: Nebel / Norddorf / Wittdün
4 Föhr: Nieblum / Utersum / Wyk
5 Pellworm
6 Nordstrand
7 St Peter Ording
8 Büsum
9 Friedrichskoog
10 Glücksburg
11 Gelting
12 Schönhagen
13 Damp
14 Eckernförde
15 Strande
16 Heikendorf
17 Laboe
18 Schönberg
19 Hohwacht
20 Weißenhaus
21 Heiligenhafen
22 Burg
23 Großenbrode
24 Dahme / Kellenhusen
25 Grömitz
26 Neustadt / Sierksdorf
27 Scharbeutz-Haffkrug
28 Timmendorf-Niendorf
29 Travemünde
30 Bad Schwartau
31 Bad Malente-Gremsmühlen
32 Eutin
33 Bad Bramstedt
34 Bad Segeberg
35 Mölln

Niedersachsen
36 Borkum
37 Juist
38 Norderney
39 Baltrum
40 Langeoog
41 Spiekeroog
42 Wangerooge
43 Norden
44 Dornum: Dornumersiel / Neßmersiel
45 Esens-Bensersiel
46 Neuharlingersiel
47 Carolinensiel
48 Horumersiel
49 Wilhelmshaven
50 Dangast
51 Bad Zwischenahn
52 Butjadingen: Burhave / Eckwarden / Tossens
53 Wursten: Dorum / Wremen
54 Cuxhaven
55 Neuhaus
56 Bad Bederkesa
57 Lüneburg
58 Bad Bevensen
59 Bodenteich
60 Soltau
61 Fallingbostel
62 Blenhorst
63 Bad Bentheim
64 Bad Iburg
65 Bad Laer / Bad Rothenfelde
66 Melle
67 Bad Essen
68 Bad Eilsen
69 Bad Nenndorf
70 Bad Münder
71 Bad Pyrmont
72 Salzhemmendorf
73 Bad Salzdetfurth
74 Bad Gandersheim
75 Bad Grund
76 Salzgitter-Bad

77 Hahnenklee
78 Bad Harzburg
79 Oberharz: Altenau / Buntenbock / Clausthal-Zellerfeld / Schulenberg / Wildemann
80 St Andreasberg / Braunlage
81 Hohegeiß / Wieda
82 Bad Lauterberg
83 Bad Sachsa

Nordrhein-Westfalen
84 Steinbeck
85 Randringhausen / Hüllhorst
86 Preußisch-Oldendorf
87 Levern
88 Rothenuffeln
89 Hopfenberg
90 Minden
91 Porta Westfalica
92 Vlotho: Bad Seebruch / Bad Senkelteich
93 Bad Salzuflen
94 Bad Oeynhausen / Wulferdingsen
95 Hiddesen
96 Bad Lippspringe
97 Bad Meinberg
98 Schieder
99 Bad Driburg / Bad Hermannsborn
100 Bruchhausen
101 Germete
102 Wünnenberg
103 Westernkotten
104 Bad Sassendorf
105 Bad Waldliesborn
106 Hamm
107 Ennepetal
108 Olsberg
109 Winterberg
110 Bad Fredeburg
111 Bad Berleburg
112 Bad Laasphe
113 Eckenhagen
114 Nümbrecht
115 Bad Honnef
116 Bad Münstereifel
117 Gemünd
118 Aachen

Hessen
119 Bad Karlshafen
120 Willingen: Usseln / Schwalefeld
121 Arolsen
122 Naumburg
123 Kassel-Wilhelmshöhe
124 Bad Emstal
125 Bad Wildungen
126 Bad Zwesten
127 Gladenbach
128 Bad Endbach
129 Weinhausen
130 Bad Sooden
131 Bad Hersfeld
132 Neukirchen
133 Gersfeld
134 Bad Salzschlirf
135 Herbstein
136 Bad Soden-Salmünster
137 Bad Orb
138 Bad Salzhausen
139 Bad Nauheim
140 Bad Camberg
141 Schlangenbad / Bad Schwalbach
142 Wiesbaden
143 Königstein
144 Bad Soden
145 Bad Homburg
146 Bad Vilbel
147 Bad König
148 Lindenfels
149 Grasellenbach

Rheinland-Pfalz
150 Bodendorf / Bad Breisig / Bad Neuenahr
151 Bad Hönningen
152 Rengsdorf / Ehlscheid
153 Bad Marienberg
154 Vallendar
155 Bad Ems / Lahnstein
156 Boppard
157 Bad Bertrich
158 Daun
159 Kyllburg
160 Manderscheid
161 Traben-Trarbach
162 Bad Sobernheim
163 Bad Münster am Stein
164 Bad Kreuznach
165 Bad Dürkheim
166 Bad Bergzabern

Saarland
167 Weiskirchen
168 Nonnweiler
169 Blieskastel

Baden-Württemberg
170 Eberbach
171 Bad Mergentheim
172 Bad Schönborn
173 Bad Rappenau / Bad Wimpfen
174 Schwäbisch Hall
175 Hoheneck
176 Stuttgart: St Berg / St Bad Cannstadt / Leutze
177 Bad Liebenzell
178 Schömberg
179 Waldbronn
180 Dobel / Bad Herrenalb
181 Baden-Baden / Gaggenau
182 Bad Teinach
183 Bad Wildbad
184 Sasbachwalden
185 Baiersbronn
186 Freudenstadt
187 Bad Peterstal
188 Bad Rippoldsau
189 Bad Imnau
190 Bad Niedernau
191 Sebastiansweiler
192 Beuren / Bad Urach
193 Bad Boll
194 Bad Ditzenbach / Bad Überkingen
195 Freiburg im Breisgau
196 Waldkirch
197 Schönwald / Triberg
198 Königsfeld
199 Villingen
200 Bad Dürrheim
201 Bad Krozingen
202 Badenweiler
203 Bad Bellingen
204 Bad Säckingen
205 Todtmoos
206 St Blasien
207 Höchenschwand
208 Schluchsee
209 Hinterzarten / Lenzkirch / Titisee
210 Friedenweiler
211 Radolfzell
212 Überlingen
213 Aulendorf
214 Bad Buchau / Saulgau
215 Biberach-Jordanbad
216 Bad Schussenried / Bad Waldsee
217 Bad Wurzach
218 Isny

Bayern
219 Bad Brückenau
220 Bad Bocklet / Bad Kissingen
221 Bad Neustadt
222 Bad Königshofen
223 Rodach

224 Staffelstein
225 Bad Steben
226 Bad Berneck
227 Bischofsgrün
228 Bad Alexandersbad
229 Bad Windsheim
230 Bad Gögging
231 Bad Abbach
232 Kötzting
233 Bodenmais
234 Krumbad
235 Bad Wörishofen
236 Ottobeuren
237 Grönenbach
238 Weiler-Simmerberg
239 Scheidegg
240 Oberstaufen
241 Fischen
242 Oberstdorf
243 Hindelang
244 Füssen: Bad Faulenberg / Hopfen am See / Weißensee
245 Schwangau
246 Garmisch-Partenkirchen
247 Oy-Mittelberg
248 Bad Bayersoien
249 Bad Kohlgrub
250 Murnau
251 Bad Heilbrunn
252 Bad Tölz
253 Bad Wiessee
254 Bad Aibling
255 Bad Endorf
256 Prien
257 Wildbad
258 Rottach-Egern / Tegernsee
259 Bayrischzell
260 Bad Feilnbach
261 Bad Reichenhall: Bayerisch Gmain / Karlstein-Nonn
262 Berchtesgaden: Bischofswiesen / Königssee / Markschellenberg / Oberau / Ramsau / Schönau
263 Bad Birnbach / Bad Griesbach
264 Bad Füssing
265 Kellberg

Mecklenburg-Vorpommern
266 Boltenhagen
267 Rerik
268 Kühlungsborn
269 Heiligendamm
270 Nienhagen / Warnemünde
271 Bad Doberan
272 Bad Sülze
273 Graal-Müritz
274 Dierhagen
275 Ahrenshoop / Wustrow
276 Prerow
277 Zingst
278 Hiddensee: Grieben / Neuendorf / Plogshagen / Vitte
279 Rügen: Binz
280 Rügen: Baabe / Göhren / Sellin
281 Rügen: Thießow
282 Lubmin
283 Usedom: Zempin / Zinnowitz
284 Usedom: Kölpinsee / Koserow / Ückeritz
285 Usedom: Ahlbeck / Bansin / Heringsdorf
286 Kurort Krakow am See

Brandenburg
287 Bad Wilsnack
288 Bad Freienwalde
289 Buckow
290 Bad Saarow
291 Bad Liebenwerda

Sachsen-Anhalt
292 Bad Schmiedeberg
293 Salzelmen
294 Blankenburg
295 Bad Suderode
296 Bad Kösen

Thüringen
297 Heilbad Heiligenstadt
298 Bad Frankenhausen
299 Bad Tennstedt
300 Bad Langensalza
301 Tabarz
302 Friedrichroda
303 Bad Liebenstein
304 Bad Salzungen
305 Bad Colberg
306 Stützerbach
307 Masserberg
308 Moorbad Lobenstein
309 Bad Berka
310 Bad Sulza
311 Bad Klosterlausnitz

Sachsen
312 Bad Düben
313 Bad Lausick
314 Schlema
315 Bad Elster
316 Bad Brambach
317 Kurort Oberwiesenthal
318 Bad Gottleuba
319 Berggießhübel
320 Bad Schandau
321 Bad Muskau

FRANCE

See page 10 for general map

WINE REGIONS

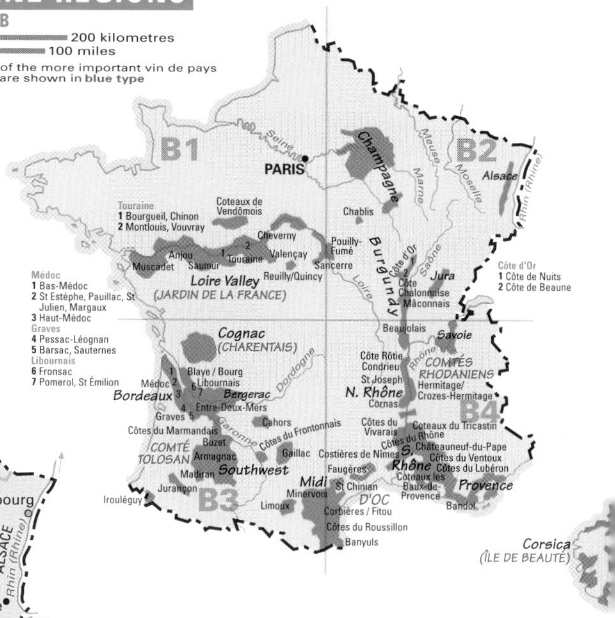

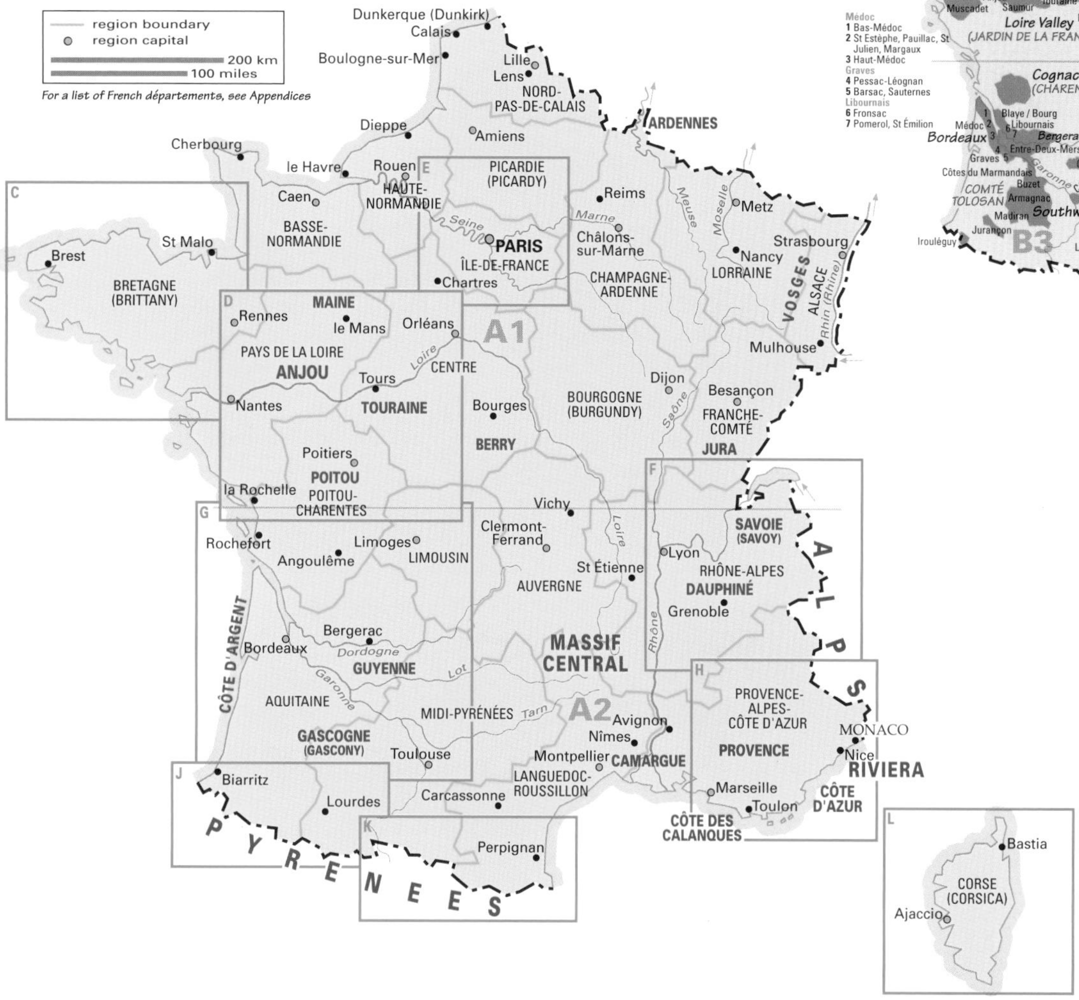

MAP B

200 kilometres
100 miles

some of the more important vin de pays
areas are shown in blue type

B1   B2

PARIS   Champagne   Alsace

Touraine
1 Bourgueil, Chinon
2 Montlouis, Vouvray

Coteaux de Vendômois   Chablis

Cheverny   Pouilly-Fumé   Jura   Côte d'Or

Anjou   Valençay   Reuilly/Quincy   1 Côte de Nuits
Muscadet   Saumur   1   2   Touraine   Sancerre   2 Côte de Beaune

Loire Valley
(JARDIN DE LA FRANCE)   Burgundy   Savoie

Médoc
1 Bas-Médoc
2 St Estèphe, Pauillac, St
  Julien, Margaux
3 Haut-Médoc

Graves
4 Pessac-Léognan
5 Barsac, Sauternes

Libournais
6 Fronsac
7 Pomerol, St Émilion

Cognac
(CHARENTAIS)   Beaujolais   Chalonnaise   Mâconnais

Côte Rôtie   COMTÉS
Condrieu   RHODANIENS
St Joseph   Hermitage/
Cornas   Crozes-Hermitage

Blaye / Bourg   N. Rhône
Médoc   1   Libournais   Châteauneuf-du-Pape
Bordeaux   4   7   Bergerac   Côtes du Tricastin
Graves   5   Entre-Deux-Mers   Côtes du
Côtes du Marmandais   Cahors   Côtes du Vivarais   Rhône
COMTÉ   Armagnac   Gaillac   Costières de Nîmes   Côtes du Ventoux
TOLOSAN   Buzet   Coteaux les   Côtes du Lubéron
Madiran   Southwest   Midi   Faugères   Baux-de-   Provence
Irouléguy   Jurançon   D'OC   St Chinian   Provence
Minervois   Bandol

Banyuls   Limoux   Corbières / Fitou
Côtes du Roussillon

Corsica
(ÎLE DE BEAUTÉ)

B3   B4

---

region boundary
region capital

200 km
100 miles

For a list of French départements, see Appendices

Dunkerque (Dunkirk)
Calais
Boulogne-sur-Mer
Lille
Lens
NORD-
PAS-DE-CALAIS
ARDENNES
Dieppe   Amiens
Cherbourg   le Havre   Rouen   PICARDIE   Reims
Caen   HAUTE-   (PICARDY)   Metz
St Malo   NORMANDIE   Châlons-   Nancy   Strasbourg
BASSE-   sur-Marne   LORRAINE
Brest   NORMANDIE   PARIS   CHAMPAGNE-   Mulhouse
BRETAGNE   MAINE   ÎLE-DE-FRANCE   ARDENNE
(BRITTANY)   Chartres   A1
Rennes   le Mans   Orléans   VOSGES
PAYS DE LA LOIRE   ALSACE
ANJOU   Tours   CENTRE   Dijon   Besançon
Nantes   TOURAINE   Bourges   BOURGOGNE   FRANCHE-
(BURGUNDY)   COMTÉ
Poitiers   BERRY   JURA
POITOU
la Rochelle   POITOU-   Vichy   F
CHARENTES   Clermont-   SAVOIE
Rochefort   Ferrand   Lyon   (SAVOY)
Limoges   RHÔNE-ALPES
Angoulême   LIMOUSIN   St Étienne   DAUPHINÉ
CÔTE D'ARGENT   AUVERGNE   Grenoble
Bergerac   A   L   P   S
Bordeaux   Dordogne   MASSIF
GUYENNE   CENTRAL   H
Garonne   PROVENCE-
AQUITAINE   MIDI-PYRÉNÉES   Tarn   A2   ALPES-
Avignon   CÔTE D'AZUR
GASCOGNE   Nîmes   PROVENCE   MONACO
(GASCONY)   Toulouse   Montpellier   CAMARGUE   Nice
Biarritz   Marseille   RIVIERA
Lourdes   Carcassonne   Toulon   CÔTE
LANGUEDOC-   D'AZUR
P   Y   R   E   N   E   E   S   ROUSSILLON   CÔTE DES
Perpignan   CALANQUES
J   K   L

CORSE
(CORSICA)

Bastia

Ajaccio

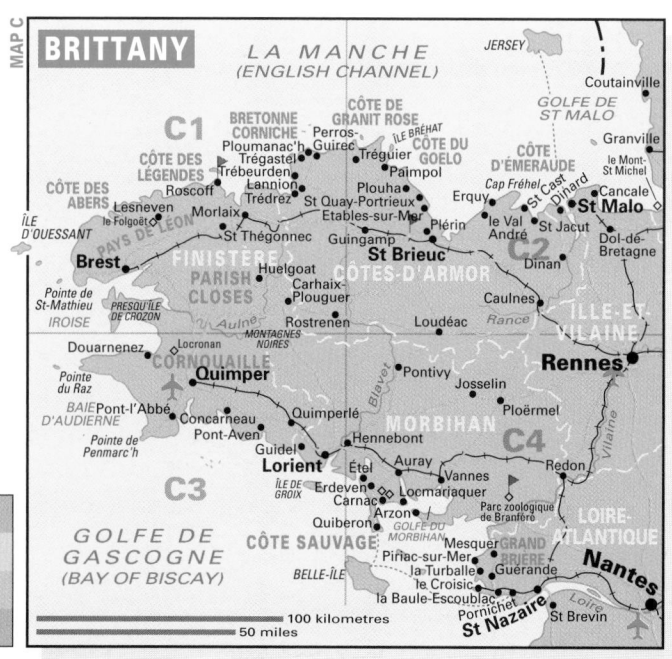

BRITTANY

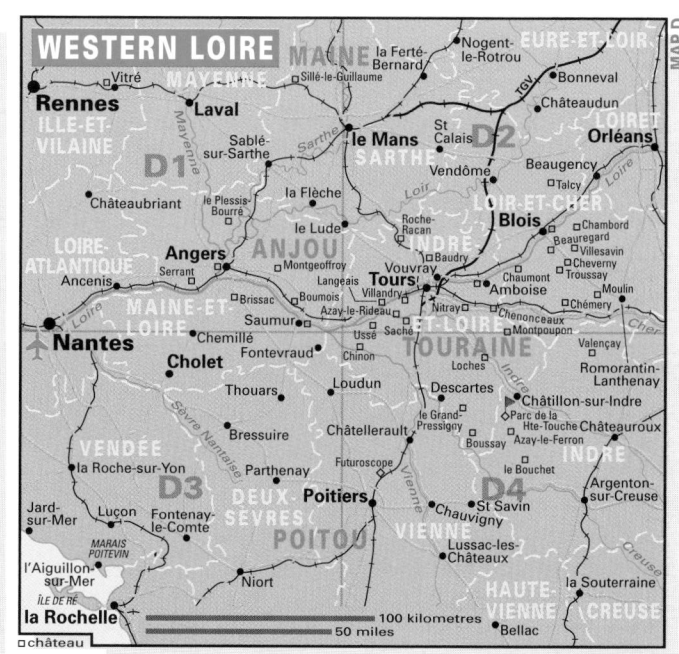

WESTERN LOIRE

Leisure park   Zoo / animal park   Aquarium   Formula One   Horse racing   Major tennis venue

FRANCE

See page 10 for general map

PARIS

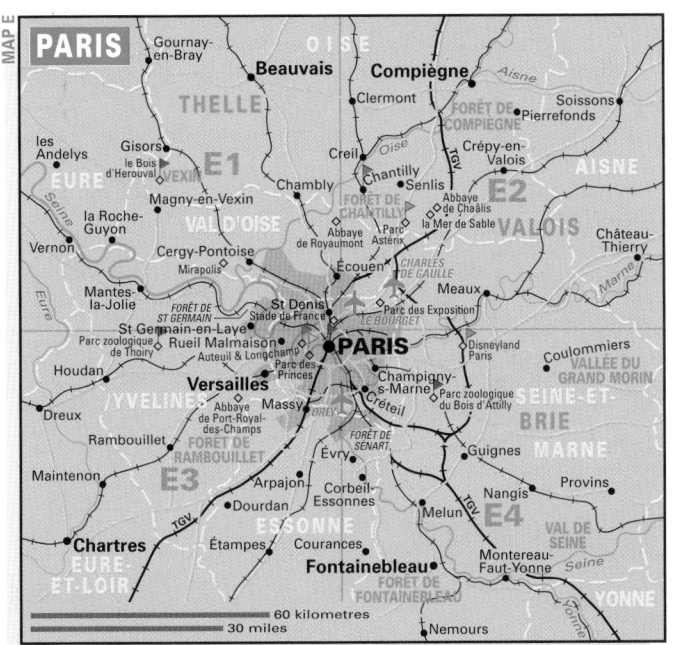

Gournay-en-Bray · Beauvais · Compiègne · Soissons · Pierrefonds · Clermont · les Andelys · Gisors · le Bois d'Herouval · Chantilly · Crépy-en-Valois · Senlis · Abbaye de Chaâlis · la Mer de Sable · Château-Thierry · Chambly · Creil · Abbaye de Royaumont · Parc Astérix · Meaux · Mantes-la-Jolie · la Roche-Guyon · Vernon · Cergy-Pontoise · Mirapolis · Écouen · Charles de Gaulle · Disneyland Paris · Coulommiers · St Germain-en-Laye · St Denis · Stade de France · PARIS · Champigny-s-Marne · Créteil · Parc zoologique du Bois d'Attilly · Houdan · Rueil Malmaison · Auteuil & Longchamp · Parc des Princes · Versailles · Massy · Orly · Dreux · Rambouillet · Abbaye de Port-Royal-des-Champs · FORÊT DE RAMBOUILLET · Arpajon · Corbeil-Essonnes · Évry · Maintenon · Dourdan · Melun · Nangis · Provins · Chartres · Étampes · Courances · Montereau-Faut-Yonne · Fontainebleau · FORÊT DE FONTAINEBLEAU · Nemours

60 kilometres / 30 miles

FRENCH ALPS

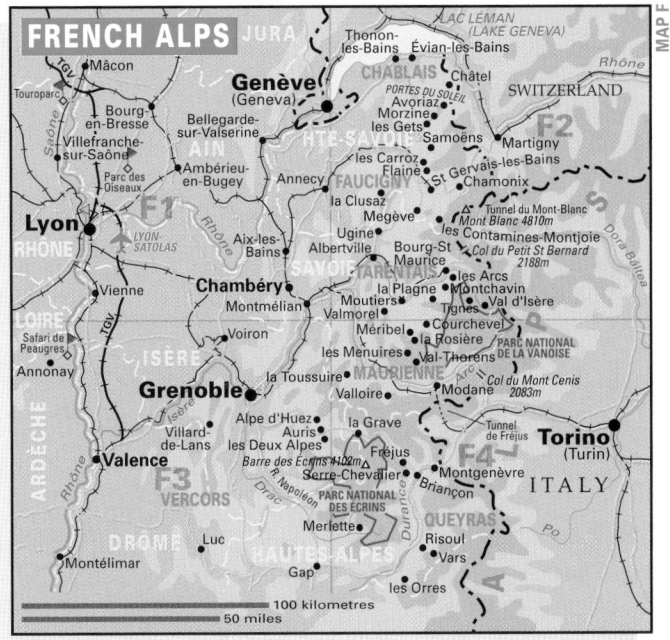

Thonon-les-Bains · Évian-les-Bains · Mâcon · Genève (Geneva) · Châtel · SWITZERLAND · Bourg-en-Bresse · Avoriaz · Morzine · les Gets · Samoëns · Martigny · Villefranche-sur-Saône · Annecy · les Carroz · Flaine · St Gervais-les-Bains · Chamonix · Lyon · Aix-les-Bains · la Clusaz · Megève · Mont Blanc 4810m · les Contamines-Montjoie · Vienne · Chambéry · Montmélian · Albertville · Bourg-St Maurice · les Arcs · Montchavin · Val d'Isère · la Plagne · Moutiers · Valmorel · Méribel · Courchevel · la Rosière · Col du Petit St Bernard 2188m · Grenoble · Villard-de-Lans · Auris · les Deux Alpes · la Toussuire · les Menuires · Val-Thorens · PARC NATIONAL DE LA VANOISE · Valence · Alpe d'Huez · la Grave · Valloire · Modane · Col du Mont Cenis 2083m · Torino (Turin) · Barre des Écrins 4102m · Fréjus · Montgenèvre · Briançon · Tunnel de Fréjus · ITALY · PARC NATIONAL DES ÉCRINS · Montélimar · Luc · Merlette · Risoul · Vars · Gap · les Orres

100 kilometres / 50 miles

SOUTHWEST FRANCE

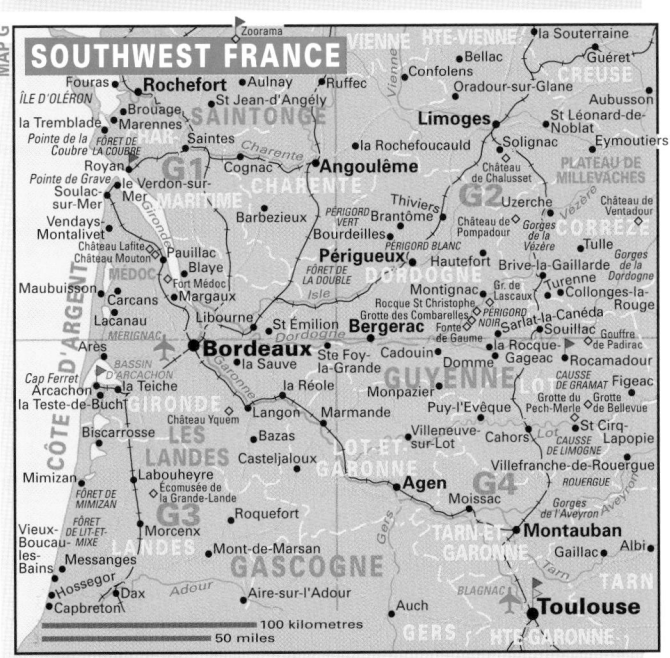

Zoorama · la Souterraine · Bellac · Confolens · Guéret · Fouras · Rochefort · Aulnay · Ruffec · Oradour-sur-Glane · Aubusson · Brouage · St Jean-d'Angély · Limoges · St Léonard-de-Noblat · Eymoutiers · Marennes · Saintes · la Rochefoucauld · Solignac · la Tremblade · Cognac · Angoulême · Royan · Barbezieux · Thiviers · Uzerche · Château de Ventadour · Soulac-sur-Mer · Brantôme · Bourdeilles · Château de Pompadour · Tulle · Château Lafite · Pauillac · Périgueux · Hautefort · Brive-la-Gaillarde · Collonges-la-Rouge · Château Mouton · Blaye · Fort Médoc · Montignac · Gr. de Lascaux · Turenne · Maubuisson · Carcans · Margaux · Libourne · Rocque St Christophe · Sarlat-la-Canéda · Souillac · Gouffre de Padirac · Lacanau · Ares · St Émilion · la Rocque · Gageac · Rocamadour · Bordeaux · la Sauve · Ste Foy-la-Grande · Domme · Cap Ferret · Arcachon · la Teiche · la Réole · Monpazier · Puy-l'Évêque · Figeac · Biscarrosse · Langon · Gazost · Villeneuve-sur-Lot · Cahors · St Cirq-Lapopie · Mimizan · Bazas · Casteljaloux · Marmande · Villefranche-de-Rouergue · Labouheyre · Écomusée de la Grande-Lande · Roquefort · Agen · Moissac · Vieux-Boucau-les-Bains · Morcenx · Montauban · Gaillac · Albi · Messanges · Mont-de-Marsan · Hossegor · Dax · Aire-sur-l'Adour · Auch · Capbreton · Toulouse · Blagnac

100 kilometres / 50 miles

CÔTE D'AZUR

les Orres · Barcelonnette · Super-Sauze · Pra-Loup · PARC NATIONAL DU MERCANTOUR · ITALY · Cúneo · Mont Pelat 3051m · Auron · Isola 2000 · Sisteron · Digne · Gorges de Daluis · le Boréon · Castellane · Gréolières-les-Neiges · Madone d'Utelle · Apt · Manosque · Pertuis · Grand Canyon du Verdon · Pas de la Faye · Gorges du Loup · Grasse · Vence · St Paul · Nice · Èze · Peillon · Menton · MONACO · Monte-Carlo · Aix-en-Provence · St Maximin la Ste Baume · Draguignan · Antibes · Cannes · Napoule-Plage · Juan-les-Pins · le Thoronet · le Luc · Fréjus · St Raphaël · ÎLES de LÉRINS · Marseille · Brignoles · Port-Grimaud · Ste Maxime · CÔTE D'AZUR · Circuit Paul Ricard · Cogolin · St Tropez · Aubagne · Ramatuelle · la Croix-Valmer · Cavalaire-sur-Mer · St Cyr-sur-Mer · la Ciotat · Toulon · Hyères · le Lavandou · MEDITERRANEAN SEA · Bandol · Sanary-sur-Mer · Hyères-Plage · CÔTE DES CALANQUES · Cap Sicié · Giens · ÎLES D'HYÈRES · ÎLE DU LEVANT · ÎLE DE PORT-CROS · PARC NATIONAL DE PORT-CROS · ÎLE DE PORQUEROLLES

100 kilometres / 50 miles

PYRENEES (WEST)

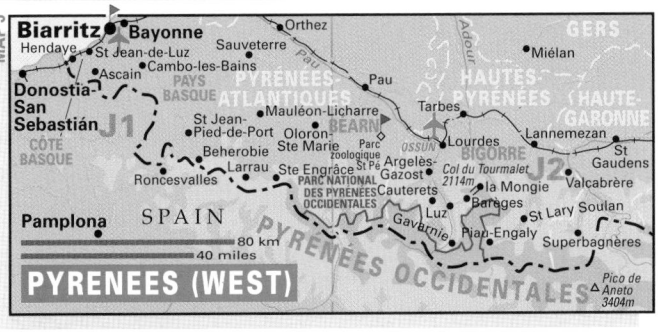

Biarritz · Bayonne · Orthez · Hendaye · St Jean-de-Luz · Sauveterre · Miélan · Ascain · Cambo-les-Bains · Pau · Donostia-San Sebastián · St Jean-Pied-de-Port · Mauléon-Licharre · Oloron Ste Marie · Tarbes · Lourdes · Lannemezan · CÔTE BASQUE · Beherobie · Larrau · Ste Engrâce · St Pé · Argelès-Gazost · St Gaudens · Pamplona · SPAIN · Roncesvalles · Cauterets · Col du Tourmalet 2114m · la Mongie · Valcabrère · Gavarnie · Luz · St Lary Soulan · Pian-Engaly · Superbagnères · Pico de Aneto 3404m

80 km / 40 miles

PYRENEES (EAST)

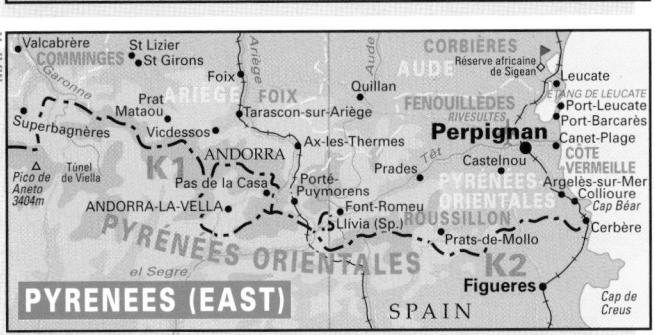

Valcabrère · St Lizier · St Girons · Quillan · CORBIÈRES · Réserve africaine de Sigean · Leucate · Superbagnères · Prat Mataou · Foix · Tarascon-sur-Ariège · Ax-les-Thermes · Port-Leucate · Port-Barcarès · Vicdessos · Castelnou · Canet-Plage · Túnel de Viella · ANDORRA · Porté-Puymorens · Prades · Perpignan · Argelès-sur-Mer · Collioure · Pico de Aneto 3404m · ANDORRA-LA-VELLA · Pas de la Casa · Font-Romeu · Llívia (Sp.) · Cap Béar · el Segre · Prats-de-Mollo · Cerbère · Figueres · SPAIN · Cap de Creus

CORSICA

ÎLE DE LA GIRAGLIA · Cap Corse · Rogliano · Macinaggio · Pino · Erbalunga · St-Florent · San-Martino-di-Lota · Bastia · Monticello · L'île Rousse · DÉSERT DES AGRIATES · NEBBIO · ÉTANG DE BIGUGLIA · Algajola · Belgodère · Oletta · PORETTA · la Canonica · Calvi · Calénzana · Feliceto · Borgo · Ponte-Leccia · Folelli · Réserve Naturelle Scandola · Monte Cinto 2706m · Corte · la Porta · GOLFE DE GIROLATA · Calacuccia · Moïta · GOLFE DE PORTO · Porto · les Calanche · Piana · Gorges de la Restonica · Venaco · Aléria · Cargèse · Vico · Monte Redonda 2622m · Vezzani · Sagone · Bocognano · Ghisoni · GOLFE DE SAGONE · Sari-d'Orcino · Bastelica · Ghisonaccia · Calcatoggio · Zicavo · Travo · Ajaccio · CAMPO DEL ORO · ÎLES SANGUINAIRES · Grosseto-Prugna · Petreto-Bicchisano · Col de Bavella · Solenzara · GOLFE D'AJACCIO · Quenza · Olmeto · Propriano · Pinarellu · GOLFE DE VALINCO · Zicavo · Sartène · Porto-Vecchio · Portigliolo · Figari · ÎLES CERBICALE · Bonifacio · Capo Pertusato · ÎLE CAVALLO · ÎLE LAVEZZI · STRAIT OF BONIFACIO · MEDITERRANEAN SEA · TYRRHENIAN SEA

80 km / 40 miles

2000 metres / 1000 metres / Sea level

▶ Leisure park   ▶ Zoo / animal park   ▶ Aquarium   ▶ Formula One   ▶ Horse racing   ▶ Major tennis venue

SPAIN

See page 11 for general map

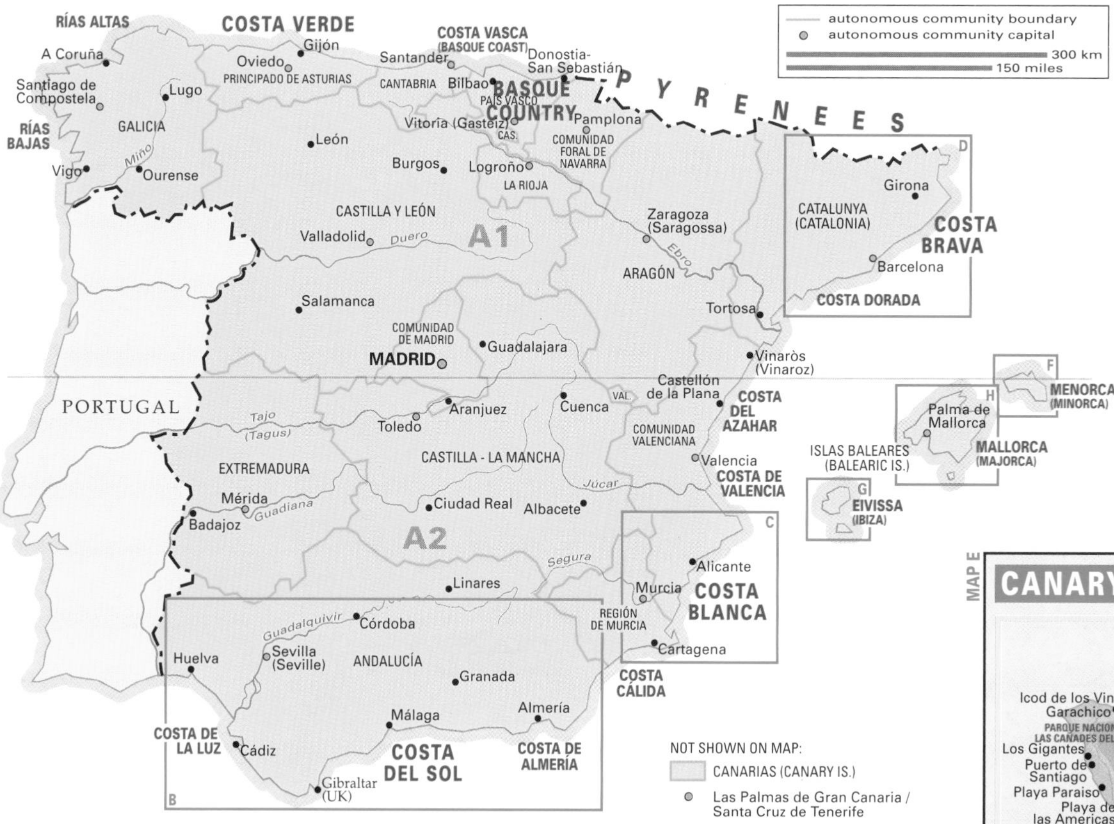

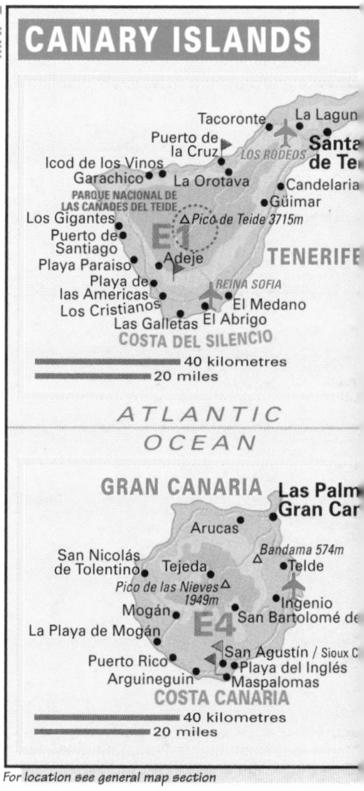

THE WAY OF ST JAMES

The 'Camino de Santiago' or 'Way of St James' leads to the tomb of St James the Apostle in Santiago de Compostela. From the four traditional gathering places in France (Paris, Vézelay, Le Puy and Arles), pilgrims would travel over the Pyrenees and continue through northern Spain on two routes. The 'French Route' is shown here. The northern or coastal route, used less by travellers, passes Hondarribia, Santillana (and Altamira Cave), Avilés and Mondoñedo.

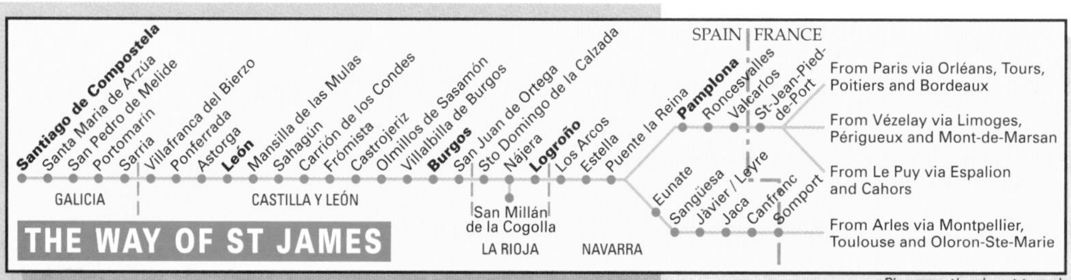

Diagrammatic only: not to scale

From Paris via Orléans, Tours, Poitiers and Bordeaux

From Vézelay via Limoges, Périgueux and Mont-de-Marsan

From Le Puy via Espalion and Cahors

From Arles via Montpellier, Toulouse and Oloron-Ste-Marie

CANARY ISLANDS

COSTA DEL SOL

SPAIN

See page 11 for general map

COSTA BLANCA

MAP C

Denia
Jávea
Cabo de la Nao
Benissa
Teulada
Moraira
Alcoy
Guadaleste
Calpe
Peñon de Ifach
Villena
Altea
Elda
Finestrat
Alfaz del Pi
Yecla
Benidorm
C1
Villajoyosa
C2
Jumilla
Novelda
Campello
Crevillente
Elx (Elche)
Alicante
COSTA BLANCA
Los Arenales del Sol
Cieza
Santa Pola
ISLOTE DE LA CANTERA
Orihuela
Guardamar del Segura
Segura
MEDITERRANEAN SEA
Murcia
Torrevieja
Pilar de la Horadada
Campoamor
Santiago de la Ribera
San Pedro del Pinatar
MURCIA
San Javier
C3
Los Alcázares
MAR MENOR
La Manga del Mar Menor
Mazarrón
La Unión
Cabo de Palos
C4
Cartagena
Puerto de Mazarrón
COSTA CÁLIDA

100 kilometres
50 miles

COSTA BRAVA

MAP D

Llívia (Sp.)
FRANCE
ANDORRA
Puigcerdà
la Jonquera
Portbou
Llança
Sant Pere de Rodes
la Seu d'Urgell
D1
Berga
Olot
EMPORDÀ
Figueres
Roses
Cap de Creus
Cadaqués
Sant Pere Pescador
Empúries
l'Escala
D2
l'Estartit
COSTA DE LA MORT
Vic
Girona
Begur
Palafrugell
Maçanet
COSTA DE LEVANT
Palamós
Manresa
Blanes
Platja d'Aro
Igualada
Granollers
Pineda de Mar
Tossa de Mar
S.Feliu d.Guíxols
Monestir de Montserrat
Terrassa
Calella
Lloret de Mar
Sabadell
Arenys de Mar
Malgrat de Mar
Reial Monestir de Poblet
Martorell
El Masnou
COSTA BRAVA
Montblanc
Vilafranca del Penedès
Badalona
Monestir de Santes Creus
D3
Barcelona
Valls
El Vendrell
Calafell
Castelldefels
D4
Reus
Comaruga
Sitges
Vilanova i la Geltrú
MEDITERRANEAN SEA
Torredembarra
Tarragona
COSTA DORADA
la Pineda
Salou / Port Aventura
Cambrils de Mar

100 kilometres
50 miles

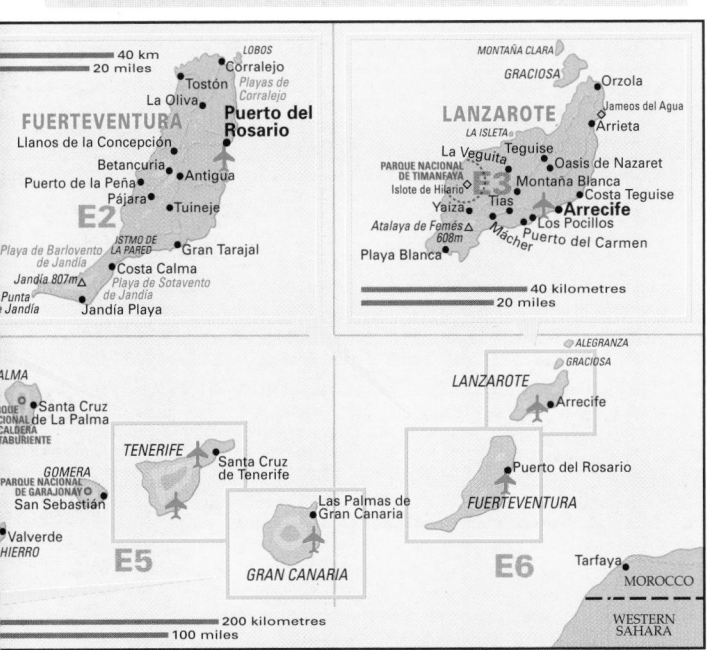

40 km
20 miles
LOBOS
Corralejo
Tostón
Plays de Corralejo
MONTAÑA CLARA
GRACIOSA
Orzola
La Oliva
Jameos del Agua
FUERTEVENTURA
LANZAROTE
Arrieta
Llanos de la Concepción
LA ISLETA
Teguise
Betancuria
Oasis de Nazaret
La Veguita
Antigua
PARQUE NACIONAL DE TIMANFAYA
Montaña Blanca
Puerto de la Peña
Islote de Hilario
Costa Teguise
Pájara
E2
Tuineje
Tias
Yaiza
Mácher
Arrecife
Atalaya de Femés 608m
Los Pocillos
Puerto del Carmen
ISTMO DE LA PARED
Gran Tarajal
Playa Blanca
Playa de Barlovento de Jandía
40 kilometres
20 miles
Jandía 807m
Costa Calma
Playa de Sotavento de Jandía
Punta de Jandía
Jandía Playa
ALEGRANZA
GRACIOSA
...LMA
LANZAROTE
Santa Cruz de La Palma
Arrecife
...NAL DE LA CALDERA TABURIENTE
TENERIFE
Santa Cruz de Tenerife
Puerto del Rosario
GOMERA
PARQUE NACIONAL DE GARAJONAY
Las Palmas de Gran Canaria
FUERTEVENTURA
San Sebastián
E5
E6
Valverde
HIERRO
GRAN CANARIA
Tarfaya
MOROCCO
200 kilometres
100 miles
WESTERN SAHARA

MINORCA

MAP F
MEDITERRANEAN SEA
Cap de Cavalleria
F1
Cala Morell
F2
Cala Tirant
Fornells
Es Delfins
Cala Forcat
S'Albufeira
Son Parc
Cala Blanes
Arenal d'en Castell
Ciutadella
Port d'Addaia
Cala de Santandria
Naveta d'Es Tudóns
Es Mercadal
Cap de Favàritx
Cala Blanca
Ferreries
ILLA D'EN COLOM
Es Migjorn Redones
Cala Santa Galdana
Gran Sant Cristóbal
Es Grau
Tamarinda
Alaior
Shangri-La
Cap d'Artrutx
Cala En Bosc
Sant Tomàs
Platja de Son Bou
Maó (Mahón)
Cala Llonga
Sant Jaume Mediterrani
Sant Climent
Son Bou de Baix
Villa Carlos
Cala En Porter
Trebaluger
Cales Coves
F4
Es Canutells
Sant Lluis
Binissafúller
S'Algar
Binibequer Vell
Cala Torret
Punta Prima
Biniancolla
ILLA DE L'AIRE
20 kilometres
10 miles

IBIZA

MAP G
Portinatx
Port de Sant Miquel
Sant Joan de Labritja
Sant Miquel de Balansat
Cala de Sant Vicenç
G1
Sant Carles de Peralta
G2
ILLA DE TAGOMAGO
Salada
Cala Llenya
Cala Gració
Sant Antoni de Portmany
Es Canyar
SA CONILLERA
Port d'es Torrent
Sant Rafael de Forca
Santa Eulalia del Río
ILLES BLEDES
Cala Bassa
Fantasylandia
Cala Llonga
Cala Conta
Sant Josep
Cala Tarida
Platja Talamanca
Cala Vadella
Sa Talaiassa de Sant Josep 475m
Eivissa (Ibiza)
Cubells
Ses Figueretes
ILLA ES VEDRA
Platja d'En Bossa
La Canal
Punta de ses Portes
ILLA DES PENJAT
MEDITERRANEAN SEA
ILLA ESPARDELL
G3
ILLA ESPALMADOR
G4
Es Savina
ESTANY PUDENT
Es Pujols
FORMENTERA
Cala Sahona
Sant Fransesc de Formentera
El Pilar
Platja de Migjorn
20 km
10 miles

MAJORCA

MAP H
Cap de Formentor
Cala de Sant Vicenç
Formentor
MEDITERRANEAN SEA
S'Horta
Port de Pollença
Pollença
Cap d'es Pinar
Sa Calobra
Alcúdia
Monestir de Lluc
Port d'Alcúdia
BADIA D'ALCUDIA
Sa Mesquida de Baix
Puig Major 1445m
Platja de Muro
Can Picafort
Cala Ratjada
Port de Sóller
S'ALBUFERA
Lluc Alcari
Sóller
Sa Pobla
Capdepera
Deià
Muro
Coves d'Artà
Santa Margalida
Cala Bona
Banyalbufar
Orient
Inca
Artà
Mirador de Ses Animas
Valldemossa
H2
Cala Millor
Estellencs
Sinéu
Sant Llorenç des Cardassar
COSTA DE LOS PINOS
Sant Telm
Calvià
ES PLA
Reserva Africana
Andratx
Castell de Bendinat
Palma de Mallorca
Manacor
Porto Cristo
ILLA DRAGONERA
SON SANT JOAN
Randa
S'Illot
Coves del Drac
13
Playa de Palma
Llucmajor
Santuari de Nostra Senyora de Cura
Cala Estany
COSTA DE LA CALMA
16
12
18
Felanitx
Cales de Mallorca
17
11 10
15
Cala Antena
Bahía Grande
BADIA DE PALMA
Cas Concos
Cala Murada
Cap de Cala Figuera
Campos
Alqueria Blanca
Porto Colom
H3
Cala Pi
Cala Marçal
La Rapita
Santanyí
Cala d'Or
Ses Salines
Cala Llonga
Porto Petro
Colònia de Sant Jordi
Platja dels Dols
Cala Mondragó
Cala Figuera
Cala Santanyí
ILLA CONILLERA
H4
Cala Llombarts
ILLA DE CABRERA

1 Cala Blava
2 Cala d'Egos
3 Cala Fornells
4 Cala Major / Sant Agusti
5 Cala Vinyes
6 Camp de Mar
7 Can Pastilla
8 Costa d'en Blanes
9 El Molinar
10 Illetes
11 Magalluf
12 Palma Nova
13 Peguera
14 Portals Nous / Puerto Portals
15 Portals Vells
16 Port de Andratx
17 Santa Ponça
18 S'Arenal

40 kilometres
20 miles

1000 metres
500 metres
Sea level

▶ Leisure park   ▶ Zoo / animal park   ▲ Aquarium   ■ Formula One   ● Major tournament golf course   ▼ Major tennis venue

PORTUGAL

See page 11 for general map

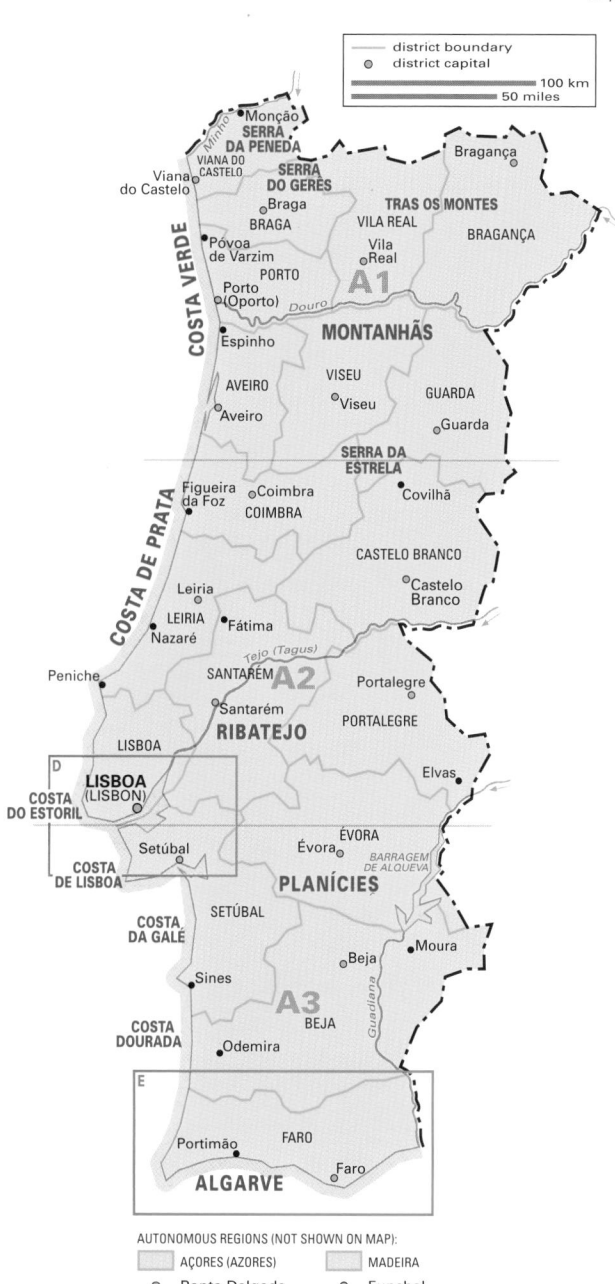

— district boundary
● district capital
100 km
50 miles

SERRA DA PENEDA
SERRA DO GERÊS
Monção
VIANA DO CASTELO
Viana do Castelo
Braga
BRAGA
Póvoa de Varzim
PORTO
Porto (Oporto)
Espinho
Douro
COSTA VERDE
Bragança
TRAS OS MONTES
VILA REAL
Vila Real
BRAGANÇA
A1
MONTANHÃS
AVEIRO
Aveiro
VISEU
Viseu
GUARDA
Guarda
SERRA DA ESTRELA
Figueira da Foz
Coimbra
COIMBRA
Covilhã
CASTELO BRANCO
Castelo Branco
COSTA DE PRATA
Leiria
LEIRIA
Fátima
Nazaré
Tejo (Tagus)
Peniche
SANTARÉM
A2
Santarém
RIBATEJO
Portalegre
PORTALEGRE
LISBOA
COSTA DO ESTORIL
LISBOA (LISBON)
Elvas
Setúbal
COSTA DE LISBOA
ÉVORA
Évora
BARRAGEM DE ALQUEVA
PLANÍCIES
SETÚBAL
COSTA DA GALÉ
Beja
Moura
Sines
BEJA
A3
COSTA DOURADA
Odemira
Guadiana
E
FARO
Portimão
Faro
ALGARVE

AUTONOMOUS REGIONS (NOT SHOWN ON MAP):
☐ AÇORES (AZORES) ☐ MADEIRA
● Ponta Delgada ● Funchal

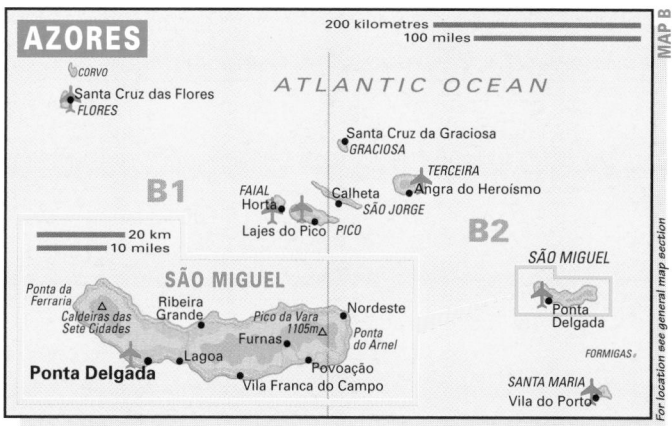

AZORES ATLANTIC OCEAN
200 kilometres
100 miles
CORVO
Santa Cruz das Flores
FLORES
Santa Cruz da Graciosa
GRACIOSA
B1
TERCEIRA
FAIAL
Horta
Calheta
Angra do Heroísmo
SÃO JORGE
Lajes do Pico
PICO
B2
20 km
10 miles
Ponta da Ferraria
SÃO MIGUEL
Caldeiras das Sete Cidades
Ribeira Grande
Pico da Vara 1105m
Nordeste
Ponta do Arnel
Lagoa
Furnas
Povoação
Ponta Delgada
Vila Franca do Campo
SÃO MIGUEL
Ponta Delgada
FORMIGAS
SANTA MARIA
Vila do Porto

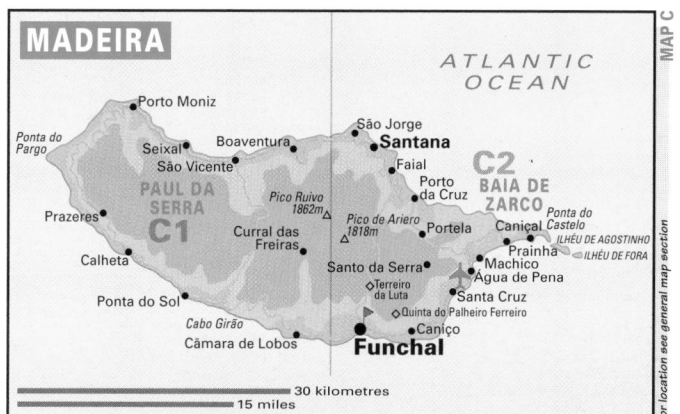

MADEIRA ATLANTIC OCEAN
Porto Moniz
São Jorge
Santana
C2
Ponta do Pargo
Seixal
Boaventura
Faial
BAIA DE ZARCO
São Vicente
Porto da Cruz
Prazeres
PAUL DA SERRA
C1
Pico Ruivo 1862m
Pico do Arieiro 1818m
Portela
Ponta do Caniçal Castelo
ILHÉU DE AGOSTINHO
Calheta
Curral das Freiras
Prainha
ILHÉU DE FORA
Santo da Serra
Machico
Santa Cruz
Ponta do Sol
Terreiro da Luta
Agua de Pena
Cabo Girão
Quinta do Palheiro Ferreiro
Caniço
Câmara de Lobos
Funchal
30 kilometres
15 miles

LISBON
Alenquer
Benavente
Ericeira
Mafra
Vila Franca de Xira
Coruche
LISBOA
SANTARÉM
ATLANTIC OCEAN
PORTELA DE SACAVÉM
RESERVA NATURAL DO ESTUARIO DO TEJO
Infantado
Praia das Maçãs
Praia Grande
Colares
SERRA Sintra
Amadora
Alcochete
Cabo da Roca
Malveira da Serra
SERRA DE SINTRA
Queluz
LISBOA (LISBON)
D2
Guincho
D1
Estoril
Belém
Montijo
SETÚBAL
Cabo Raso
Cascais
Carcavelos
Almada
Barreiro
Aguas de Moura
COSTA DO ESTORIL
Praia Parede
Costa da Caparica
Seixal
Palmela
COSTA AZUL (COSTA DO SOL)
Vila Nogueira de Azeitão
Setúbal
LAGOA DE ALBUFEIRA
Outão
Tróia
SERRA DA ARRÁBIDA
Sesimbra
Portinho da Arrábida
Sado
COSTA BELA
Cabo Espichel
30 kilometres
15 miles

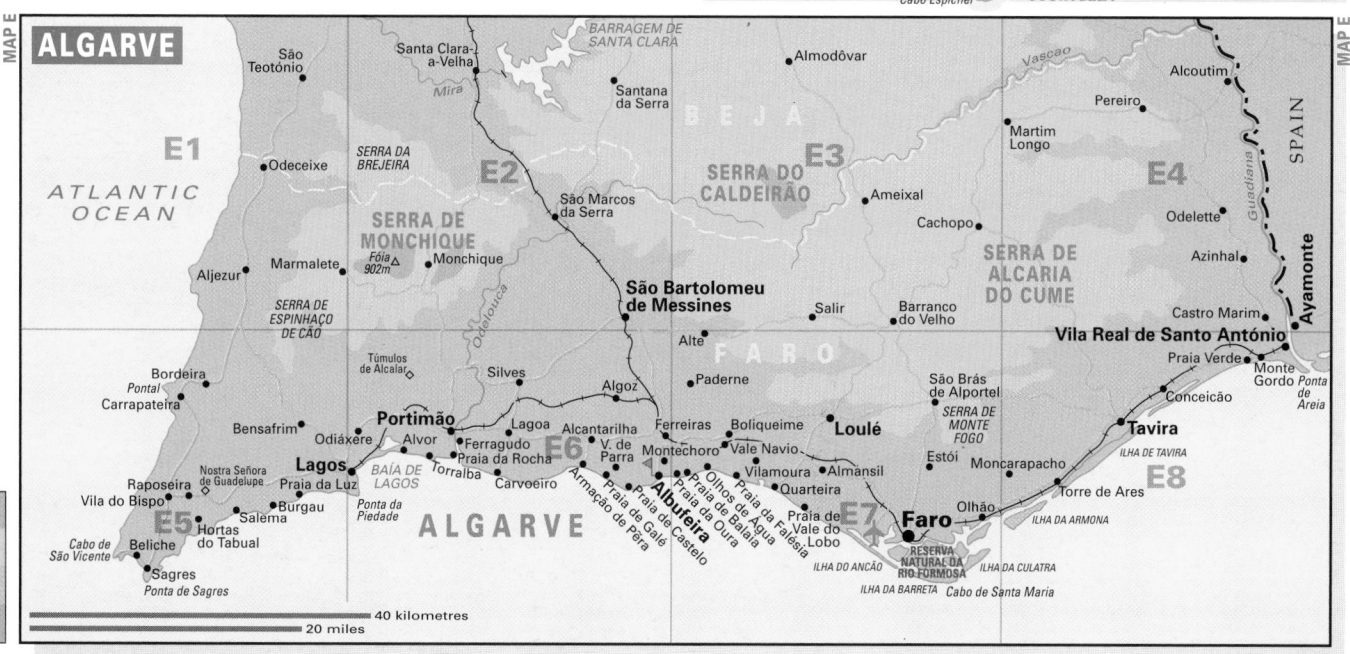

ALGARVE
São Teotónio
Santa Clara-a-Velha
BARRAGEM DE SANTA CLARA
Almodôvar
Alcoutim
E1
Odeceixe
SERRA DA BREJEIRA
E2
Santana da Serra
BEJA
Pereiro
E3
Mira
São Marcos da Serra
SERRA DO CALDEIRÃO
Martim Longo
E4
ATLANTIC OCEAN
SERRA DE MONCHIQUE
Fóia 902m
Monchique
Ameixal
SPAIN
Aljezur
Marmelete
SERRA DE ESPINHAÇO DE CÃO
São Bartolomeu de Messines
Salir
Cachopo
Odelette
Odelouca
Barranco do Velho
SERRA DE ALCARIA DO CUME
Azinhal
Bordeira
Pontal Carrapateira
Túmulos de Alcalar
Silves
Alte
FARO
São Brás de Alportel
Guadiana
Castro Marim
Ayamonte
Bensafrim
Odiáxere
Algoz
Paderne
SERRA DE MONTE FOGO
Vila Real de Santo António
Raposeira
Nostra Señora de Guadalupe
Alvor
Ferragudo
Lagoa
Alcantarilha
Ferreiras
Boliqueime
Estói
Praia Verde
Vila do Bispo
Lagos
Portimão
Praia da Rocha
V. de Parra
Montechoro
Vale Navio
Loulé
Moncarapacho
Conceição
Monte Gordo
E5
Praia da Luz
Torralba
Carvoeiro
Olhos de Agua
Vilamoura
Almansil
Tavira
Ponta de Areia
Beliche
Burgau
BAÍA DE LAGOS
Armação de Pera
Albufeira
Quarteira
ILHA DE TAVIRA
E8
Hortas do Tabual
Salema
Ponta da Piedade
ALGARVE
Praia da Falésia
Praia de Vale do Lobo
E7
Faro
Torre de Ares
Cabo de São Vicente
Sagres
Ponta de Sagres
Olhão
ILHA DA ARMONA
ILHA DO ANCÃO
RESERVA NATURAL DA RIO FORMOSA
ILHA DA CULATRA
ILHA DA BARRETA
Cabo de Santa Maria
40 kilometres
20 miles
500 metres
200 metres
Sea level

▶ Leisure park ▶ Zoo / animal park ▲ Aquarium ▶ Formula One ▶ Major tennis venue

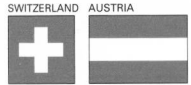

SWITZERLAND AND AUSTRIA

See pages 9, 10, 12 & 13 for general maps

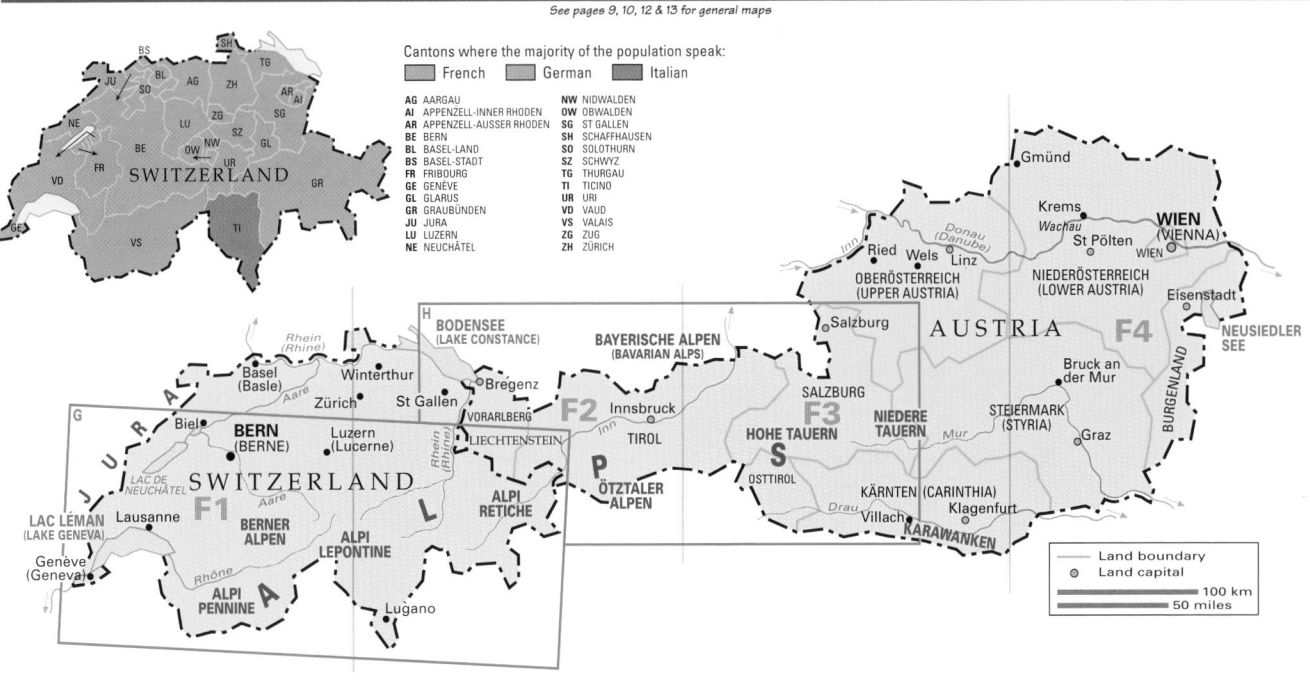

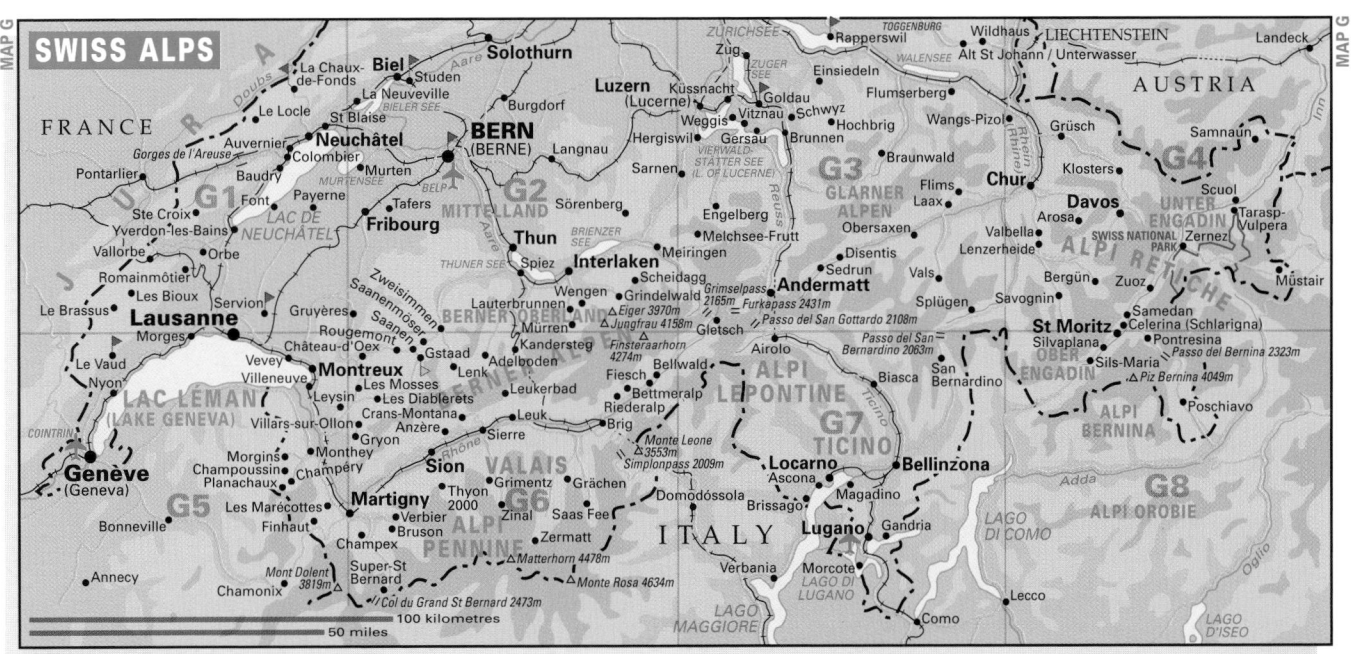

▶ Zoo / animal park   ▶ Major tennis venue

ITALY

See page 12 for general map

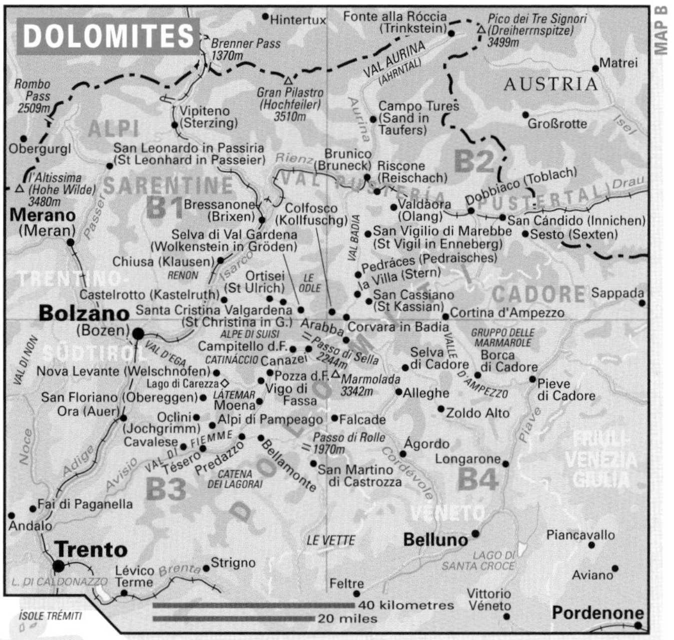

DOLOMITES

— Hintertux, Fonte alla Róccia (Trinkstein), Pico dei Tre Signori (Dreiherrnspitze) 3499m, MAP B

Brenner Pass 1370m, VAL AURINA (AHRNTAL), AUSTRIA, Matrei

Rombo Pass 2509m, Vipiteno (Sterzing), Gran Pilastro (Hochfeiler) 3510m, Campo Tures (Sand in Taufers), Großrotte

ALPI, Obergurgl, San Leonardo in Passiria (St Leonhard in Passeier), Brunico (Bruneck), Riscone (Reischach), B2

SARENTINE, l'Altissima (Hohe Wilde) 3480m, Bressanone (Brixen), Colfosco (Kolfuschg), Valdáora (Olang), Dobbiaco (Toblach), USTERTAL, Drau

Merano (Meran), B1, Chiusa (Klausen), Selva di Val Gardena (Wolkenstein in Gröden), San Vigilio di Marebbe (St Vigil in Enneberg), San Cándido (Innichen), Sesto (Sexten), Sappada

TRENTINO, RENON, Castelrotto (Kastelruth), Ortisei (St Ulrich), LE ODLE, Pedráces (Pedraisches) la Villa (Stern), CADORE

SÜDTIROL, Santa Cristina Valgardena (St Christina in G.), Arabba, San Cassiano (St Kassian), Cortina d'Ampezzo, GRUPPO DELLE MARMAROLE

Bolzano (Bozen), ALPE DI SUISI, Passo di Sella 2244m, Corvara in Badia, Selva di Cadore, Borca di Cadore, Pieve di Cadore

VAL DI NON, Nova Levante (Welschnofen), Campitello d.F., CATINACCIO, Canazei, LATEMAR, Pozza d.F., Marmolada 3342m, Alleghe, Zoldo Alto

San Floriano (Obereggen), Lago di Carezza, Moena, Vigo di Fassa, Ágordo, Longarone, FRIULI VENEZIA GIULIA

Ora (Auer), Oclini (Jochgrimm), Alpi di Pampeago, Falcade

Cavalese, FIEMME, Tésero, Predazzo, Passo di Rolle 1970m, San Martino di Castrozza, B4

Fai di Paganella, CATENA DEI LAGORAI, Bellamonte, VENETO

Andalo, DOLOMITI, B3, **Belluno**, Piancavallo

Trento, L. DI CALDONAZZO, Lévico Terme, Strigno, LE VETTE, Feltre, Lago di SANTA CROCE, Aviano

Brenta, Vittorio Véneto, **Pordenone**

40 kilometres / 20 miles

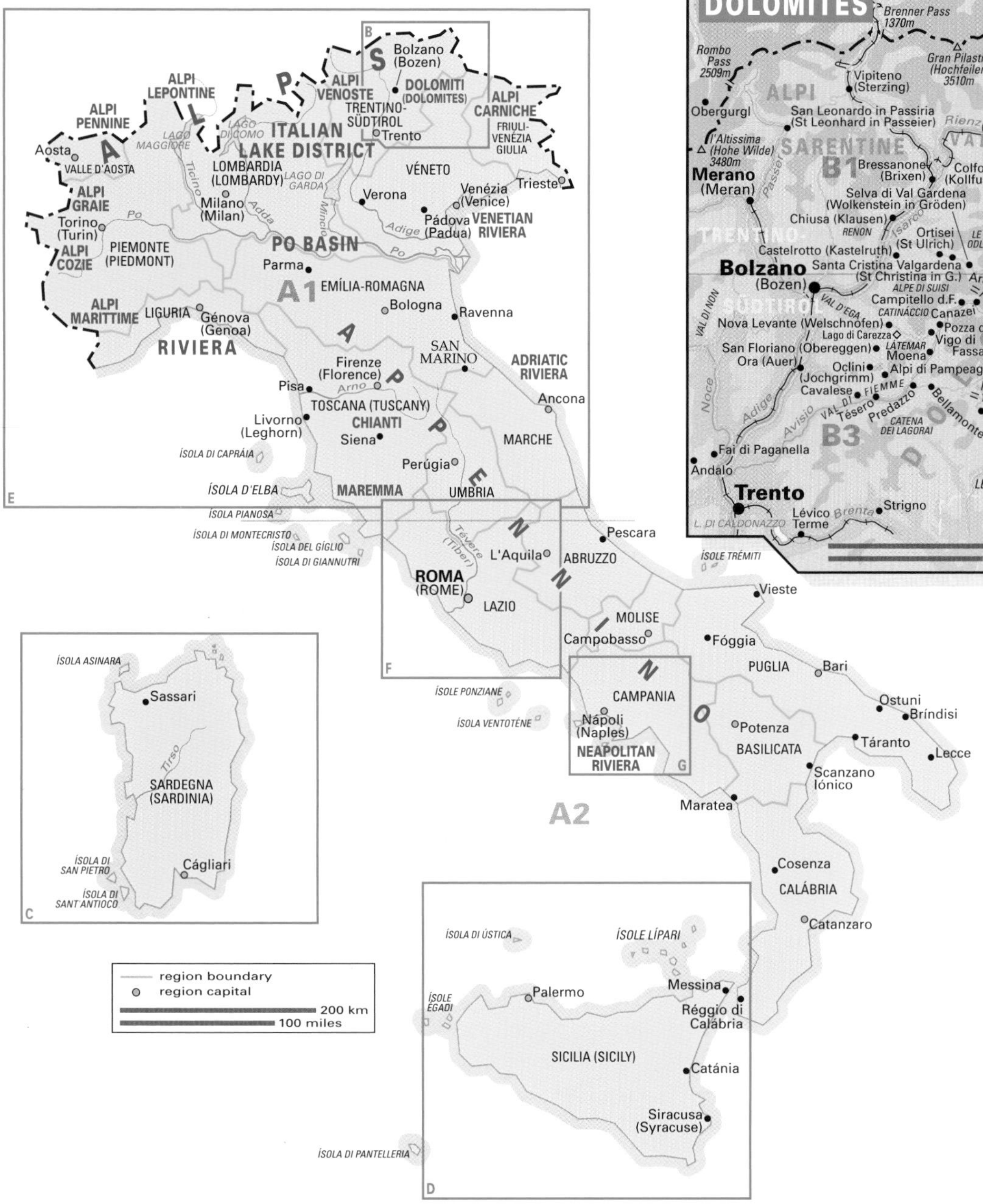

Main Italy map

ALPI LEPONTINE, ALPI VENOSTE (St Leonhard in Passeier), DOLOMITI (DOLOMITES), ALPI CARNICHE

ALPI PENNINE, ALPI GRAIE, VALLE D'AOSTA, Aosta, Torino (Turin), ALPI COZIE, ALPI MARITTIME

Bolzano (Bozen), TRENTINO-SÜDTIROL, FRIULI-VENEZIA GIULIA, Trento

ITALIAN LAKE DISTRICT, LOMBARDIA (LOMBARDY), Lago di GARDA, VÉNETO, Venézia (Venice), Trieste

Lago MAGGIORE, Lago di COMO, Milano (Milan), Adda, Verona, Pádova (Padua), VENETIAN RIVIERA

PIEMONTE (PIEDMONT), Ticino, Po, Mincio, Adige, PO BASIN

LIGURIA, Génova (Genoa), Parma, Bologna, EMÍLIA-ROMAGNA, Ravenna, ADRIATIC RIVIERA

RIVIERA, A1, Firenze (Florence), SAN MARINO, Ancona, MARCHE

Pisa, Arno, TOSCANA (TUSCANY), CHIANTI, Siena, Perúgia, UMBRIA

Livorno (Leghorn), ÍSOLA DI CAPRÁIA, ÍSOLA D'ELBA, MAREMMA

ÍSOLA PIANOSA, ÍSOLA DI MONTECRISTO, ÍSOLA DEL GIGLIO, ÍSOLA DI GIANNUTRI

ROMA (ROME), L'Aquila, ABRUZZO, Pescara, Vieste

LAZIO, Tévere, MOLISE, Campobasso, Fóggia, PUGLIA, Bari

ÍSOLE PONZIANE, ÍSOLE VENTOTÉNE, CAMPANIA, Potenza, Ostuni, Brindisi

Nápoli (Naples), NEAPOLITAN RIVIERA, BASILICATA, Táranto, Lecce

A2, Scanzano Iónico, Maratea, Cosenza, CALÁBRIA, Catanzaro

APPENNINO

ÍSOLA ASINARA, Sassari, SARDEGNA (SARDINIA), Cágliari, ÍSOLA DI SAN PIETRO, ÍSOLA DI SANT'ANTIOCO, C

— region boundary
○ region capital
200 km / 100 miles

ÍSOLA DI ÚSTICA, ÍSOLE LÍPARI, ÍSOLE EGADI, Palermo, Messina, Réggio di Calábria

SICILIA (SICILY), Catánia, Siracusa (Syracuse)

ÍSOLA DI PANTELLERIA, D

SARDINIA

MAP C, STRAIT OF BONIFACIO, ÍSOLA MADDALENA, ÍSOLA CAPRERA

Capo Testa, Santa Teresa di Gallura, Porto Rafael, Palau, GOLFO DI MARINELLA

ÍSOLA ASINARA, GOLFO DELL' ASINARA, Báia Sardinia, Porto Rotondo, COSTA SMERALDA, Ólbia, C2

Capo del Falcone, Castelsardo, Santíssima Trinità di Saccargia, ÍSOLA TAVOLARA, ÍSOLA MOLARA

Porto Torres, LA NURRA, **Sassari**, Posada, la Caletta, BARONIA

Porto Conte, Grotta di Nettuno, Alghero, Necrópoli di S Andria Priu, Orosei, Cala Liberotto

RIVIERA DEL CORALLO, Bosa, Nuoro, Villaggio nuragico di Serra Orrios, GOLFO DI OROSEI

Monte Ferru 1050m, Macomér, Olíena, MONTI DEL GENNARGENTU

Santa Caterina di Pittinuri, SINIS, SARDEGNA, Punta La Mármora 1834m, Árbatax

Thárros, Oristano, Su Nuraxi di Barúmini, Ulássai, Flumendosa

GOLFO DI ORISTANO, Barúmini, COSTA VERDE, C3, C4, COSTA REI

Iglesias, **Cágliari**

Portoscuso, Sant'Antíoco, ÍSOLA DI SAN PIETRO, Capo Boi, Villasímius, Capo Carbonara

ÍSOLA DI SANT'ANTIOCO, Pula, Santa Margherita di Pula, Nora, GOLFO DI CÁGLIARI

Chia, Bithia, Capo Spartivento, COSTA DEL SUD

MEDITERRANEAN SEA, TYRRHENIAN SEA

2000 metres / 1000 metres / Sea level

100 km / 50 miles

SICILY

MAP D, TYRRHENIAN SEA, Í. STRÓMBOLI, from Naples

Í. PANAREA, ÍSOLE LÍPARI, Í. FILICUDI, Í. SALINA, Í. ALICUDI, Í. LÍPARI, Strétto di Messina

ÍSOLA DI ÚSTICA, GOLFO DI CASTELLAMMARE, PUNTA RAISI, Mondello, Í. VULCANO, Milazzo, D2

D1, San Vito lo Capo, **Palermo**, GOLFO DI TERMINI IMERESE, Tindari

ÍSOLE EGADI, Í. FAVIGNANA, Erice, Monreale, Cefalù, Mazzarò, Taormina, **Messina**

Í. MARÉTTIMO, Í. LEVANZO, **Trápani**, VAL DEMONE, Giardini-Naxos, **Réggio di Calábria**

Í. DELLA STAGNONE, Marsala, VAL DI MAZARA, MADONIE, SICILIA, Monte Etna 3323m, Acireale, Aci Trezza

Segesta, Selinunte, Belice, Enna, FONTANA ROSSA, **Catánia**

Eraclea Minoa, Plátani, Caltanissetta, Piazza Armerina, Villa Romana del Casale, GOLFO DI CATÁNIA, Augusta

Agrigento, Porteo Empédocle, Naro, Salso, VAL DI NOTO, **Siracusa (Syracuse)**

Valle dei Templi, Gela, Cómiso, Ragusa, Ávola, GOLFO DI NOTO

D3, GOLFO DI GELA, Cava d'Ispico, D4

MEDITERRANEAN SEA, Pozzallo, Capo Pássero

100 kilometres / 50 miles

▶ Leisure park   ▶ Zoo / animal park   ▲ Aquarium   ■ Formula One   ■ Major tennis venue

ITALY

See page 12 for general map

NORTH ITALY

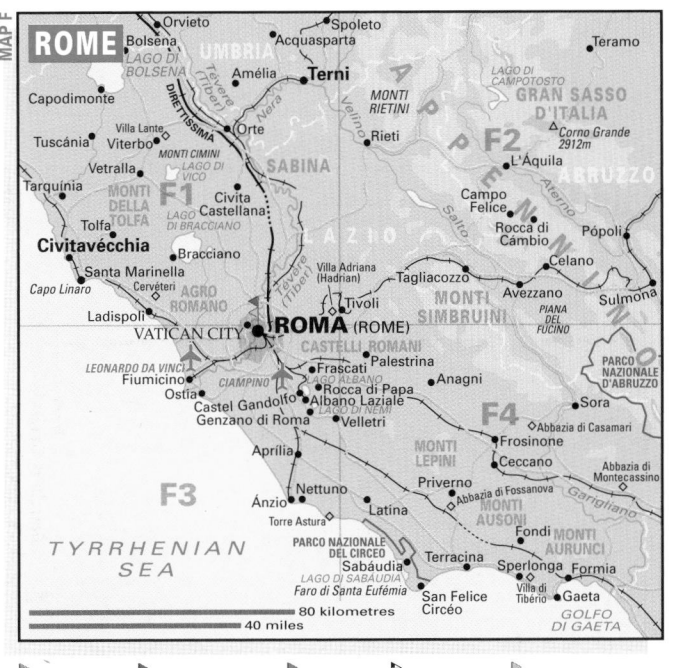

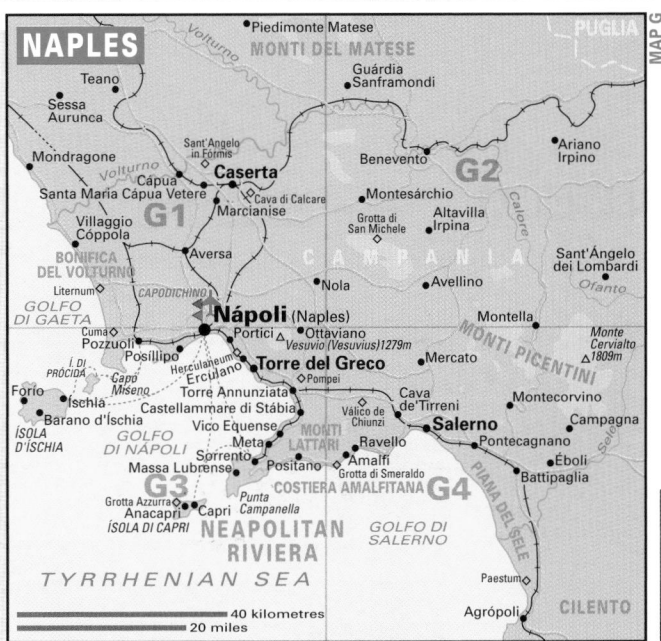

ROME

NAPLES

GREECE · TURKEY

GREECE AND TURKEY

See page 15 for general map

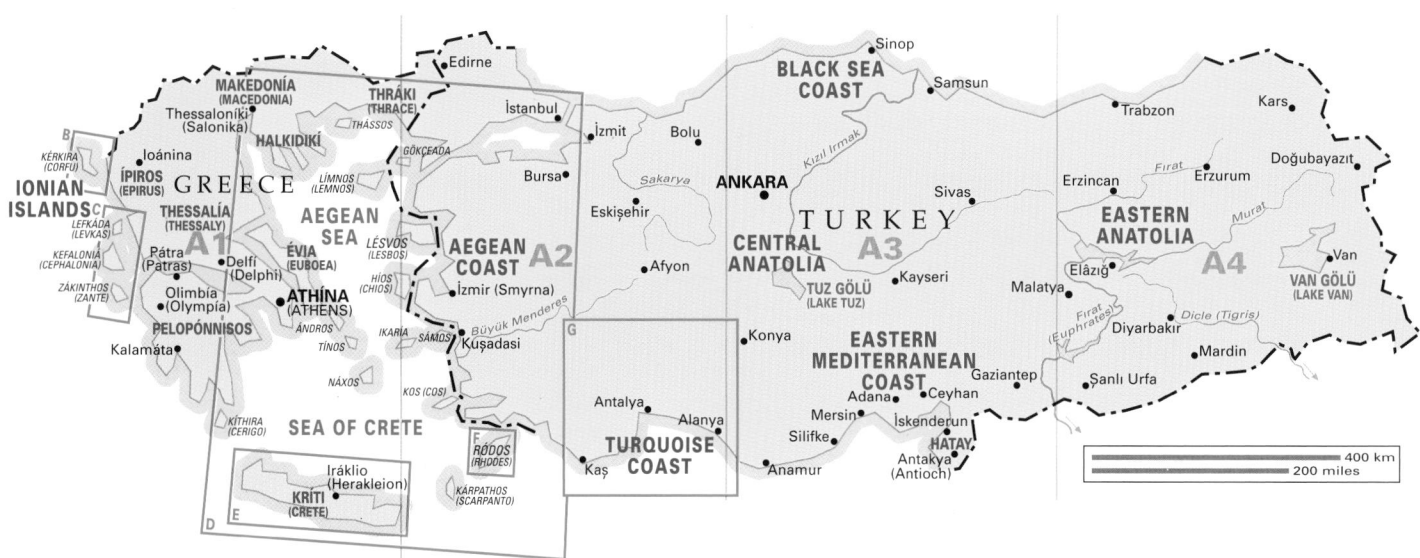

AEGEAN, CRETE & TURKISH COAST

▶ Leisure park   ▶ Major tennis venue

GREECE | TURKEY | MALTA | CYPRUS

GREECE AND TURKEY

See page 15 for general map

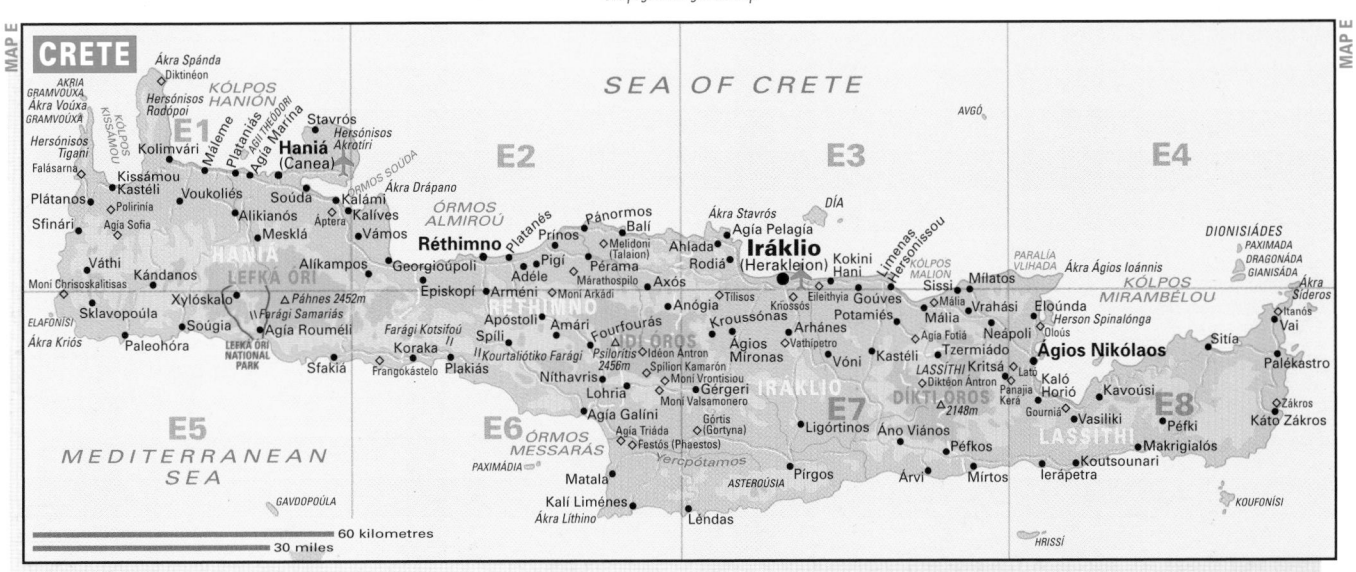

CRETE

SEA OF CRETE

MEDITERRANEAN SEA

60 kilometres
30 miles

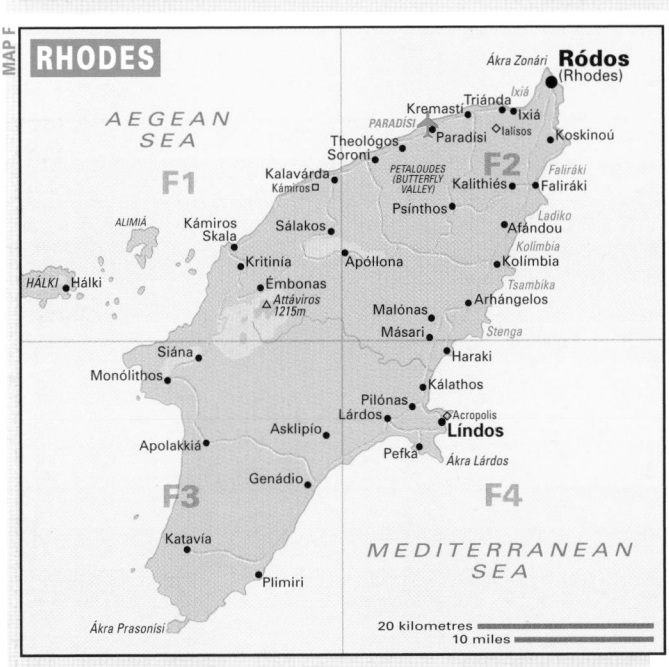

RHODES

AEGEAN SEA

MEDITERRANEAN SEA

20 kilometres
10 miles

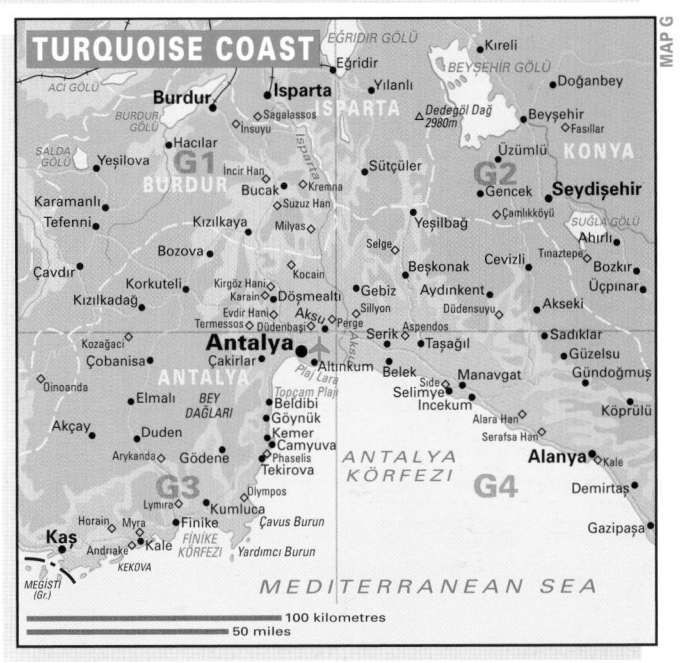

TURQUOISE COAST

MEDITERRANEAN SEA

100 kilometres
50 miles

MALTA

See page 12 for general map

CYPRUS

See page 15 for general map

MEDITERRANEAN SEA

10 kilometres
5 miles

MEDITERRANEAN SEA

MEDITERRANEAN SEA

80 kilometres
40 miles

1000 metres
500 metres
Sea level

NORWAY

SCANDINAVIA

See page 16 for general map

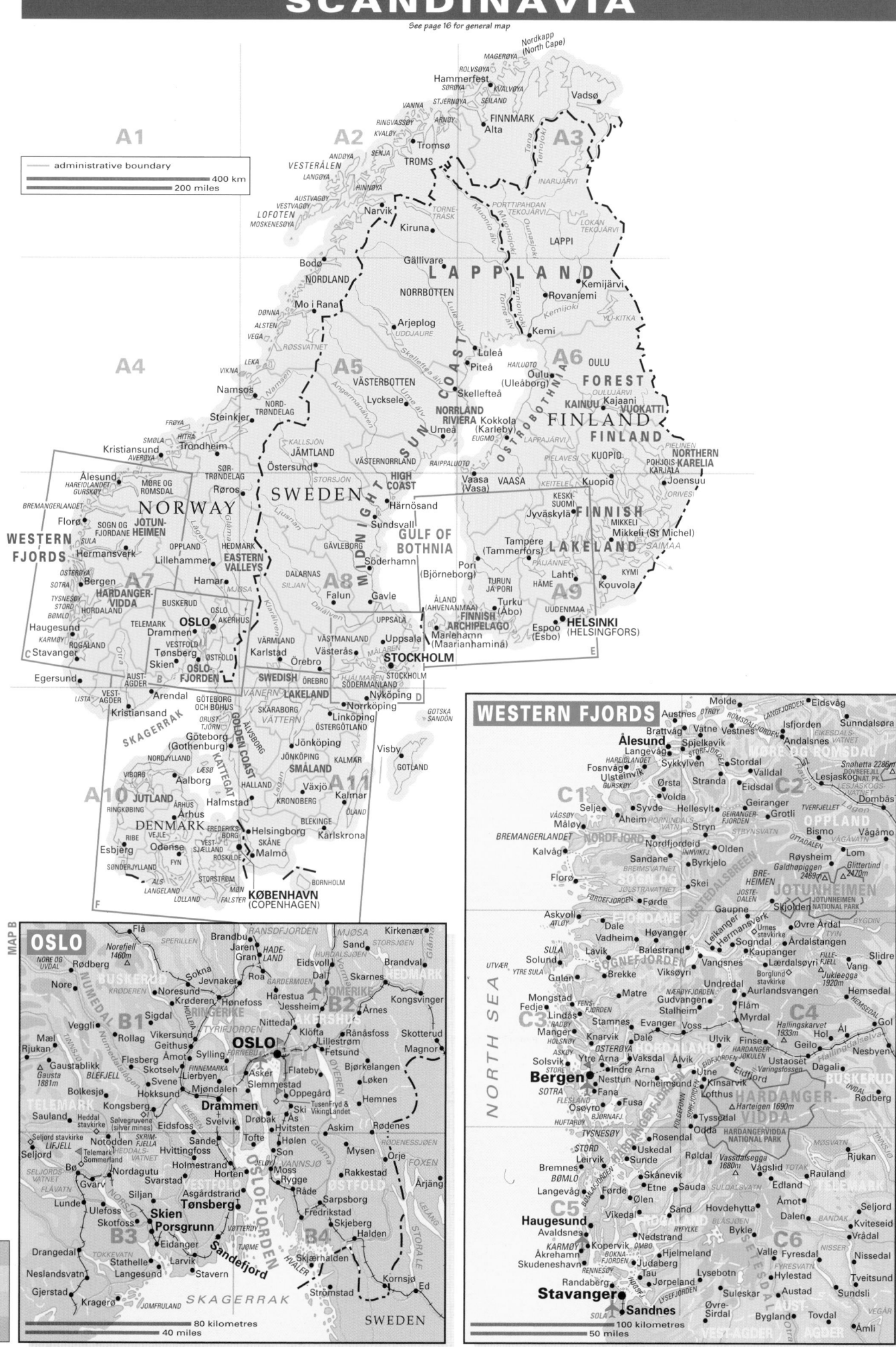

administrative boundary
400 km
200 miles
A1
A2
A3
A4
A5
A6
A7
A8
A9
A10
A11
Nordkapp (North Cape)
Hammerfest
Vadsø
FINNMARK
Alta
Tromsø
TROMS
VESTERÅLEN
LOFOTEN
Narvik
Kiruna
LAPPI
Bodø
NORDLAND
Gällivare
L A P P L A N D
Kemijärvi
NORRBOTTEN
Rovaniemi
Mo i Rana
Arjeplog
Kemi
Luleå
Piteå
OULU
Oulu (Uleåborg)
FOREST
VÄSTERBOTTEN
Namsos
Lycksele
Skellefteå
NORD-TRØNDELAG
NORRLAND RIVIERA
Kokkola (Karleby)
KAINUU
Kajaani
VUOKATTI
Steinkjer
Umeå
FINLAND
FINLAND
Kristiansund
Trondheim
JÄMTLAND
NORTHERN KARELIA
KUOPIO
Östersund
VÄSTERNORRLAND
Ålesund
MØRE OG ROMSDAL
SØR-TRØNDELAG
Røros
HIGH COAST
Vaasa (Vasa)
VAASA
Kuopio
Joensuu
NORWAY
SWEDEN
Härnösand
Jyväskylä
FINNISH
Florø
SOGN OG FJORDANE
JOTUN-HEIMEN
Sundsvall
GULF OF BOTHNIA
Mikkeli (St Michel)
WESTERN FJORDS
Hermansverk
OPPLAND
Lillehammer
HEDMARK
EASTERN VALLEYS
GÄVLEBORG
Söderhamn
Tampere (Tammerfors)
LAKELAND
Pori (Björneborg)
Bergen
HARDANGER-VIDDA
Hamar
DALARNAS
Falun
Gavle
Lahti
Kouvola
Haugesund
OSLO
Drammen
Turku (Åbo)
FINNISH ARCHIPELAGO
HELSINKI (HELSINGFORS)
Espoo (Esbo)
Stavanger
Tønsberg
Skien
OSLO-FJORDEN
VÄRMLAND
Karlstad
Uppsala
Västerås
Mariehamn (Maarianhamina)
STOCKHOLM
Egersund
Örebro
SWEDISH LAKELAND
Arendal
Kristiansand
Nyköping
Norrköping
SKAGERRAK
Göteborg (Gothenburg)
GOLDEN COAST
Linköping
Jönköping
Visby
SMÅLAND
Aalborg
KATTEGAT
JUTLAND
Halmstad
Växjö
Kalmar
Århus
DENMARK
Helsingborg
Karlskrona
Esbjerg
Odense
Malmö
KØBENHAVN (COPENHAGEN)
BORNHOLM
MAP B
OSLO
Flå
Norefjell 1460m
Brandbu
Jaren
HADELAND
Gran
Kirkenær
Sand
Rødberg
Eidsvoll
Brandval
BUSKERUD
Sokna
Jevnaker
Roa
Dal
Skarnes
HEDMARK
Nore
Noresund
Krøderen
Hønefoss
Harestua
Jessheim
Kongsvinger
B1
B2
Sigdal
Veggli
Nittedal
Arnes
Mæl
Vikersund
Rollag
Kløfta
Rånåsfoss
Skotterud
Rjukan
Geithus
Sylling
OSLO
Lillestrøm
Fetsund
Magnor
Gaustablikk
Gausta 1881m
Flesberg
Skotselv
Lierbyen
Asker
Flateby
Bjørkelangen
Svene
Slemmestad
Løken
Bolkesjø
Hokksund
Mjøndalen
Drammen
Oppegård
TELEMARK
Kongsberg
Hemnes
Sauland
Svelvik
Drøbak
Ski
Ås
Eidsfoss
Sande
Tofte
Hvitsten
Askim
Rødenes
Notodden
Seljord
Hvittingfoss
Hølen
Son
Mysen
Holmestrand
Horten
Moss
Rygge
Rakkestad
Bø
Nordagutu
Svarstad
Gvarv
Siljan
Åsgårdstrand
Råde
Årjäng
Lunde
Skien
Tønsberg
Sarpsborg
Ulefoss
Fredrikstad
Skotfoss
Porsgrunn
Skjeberg
B3
B4
Eidanger
Halden
Drangedal
Stathelle
Larvik
Sandefjord
Skjærhalden
Neslandsvatn
Langesund
Stavern
Kornsjø
Gjerstad
Strömstad
Ed
Kragerø
SKAGERRAK
SWEDEN
80 kilometres
40 miles
1000 metres
500 metres
Sea level
MAP C
WESTERN FJORDS
Molde
Eidsvåg
Austnes
Brattvåg
Vatne
Vestnes
Isfjorden
Sunndalsøra
Ålesund
Langevåg
Spjelkavik
Andalsnes
Fosnvåg
Sykkylven
Stordal
MØRE OG ROMSDAL
Ulsteinvik
Snøhetta 2286m
Valldal
Lesjaskog
Ørsta
Stranda
Eidsdal
C2
Volda
C1
Dombås
Selje
Syvde
Hellesylt
Geiranger
Grotli
Måløy
Åheim
Stryn
OPPLAND
Bismo
Vågåmo
Nordfjordeid
Olden
Kalvåg
Lom
Sandane
Byrkjelo
Røysheim
Florø
Skei
JOTUNHEIMEN
Førde
Gaupne
Askvoll
Dale
Øvre Årdal
Vadheim
Høyanger
Sogndal
Ardalstangen
Lavik
Balestrand
Kaupanger
Slidre
Solund
Vangsnes
Lærdalsøyri
Vang
Brekke
Viksøyri
Undredal
Gulen
Aurlandsvangen
Hemsedal
Mongstad
Matre
Gudvangen
Fedje
Stalheim
Flåm
C4
C3
Lindås
Myrdal
Manger
Stamnes
Evanger
Voss
Gol
Knarvik
Dale
Ulvik
Finse
Ål
Hol
Geilo
Nesbyen
Solsvik
Ytre Arna
Indre Arna
Ålvik
Ustaoset
Dagali
Bergen
Nesttun
Norheimsund
Utne
Kinsarvik
Eidfjord
Fana
Lofthus
HARDANGER-VIDDA
Rødberg
Fusa
Os
Tyssedal
Odda
Rosendal
Uskedal
Sunde
Røldal
Vågslid
Rjukan
Leirvik
Bremnes
Skånevik
Rauland
Langevåg
Førde
Etne
Sauda
Edland
Ølen
Åmot
C5
Haugesund
Sand
Hovdehytta
Seljord
Vikedal
Dalen
Kviteseid
Avaldsnes
Nedstrand
Bykle
Vrådal
C6
Kopervik
Åkrehamn
Hjelmeland
Valle
Fyresdal
Nissedal
Skudeneshavn
Judaberg
Tau
Hylestad
Randaberg
Jørpeland
Lysebotn
Tveitsund
Stavanger
Suleskar
Austad
Sundsli
Øvre Sirdal
Sandnes
Bygland
Tovdal
100 kilometres
50 miles
Åmli
NORTH SEA
Leisure park
Aquarium

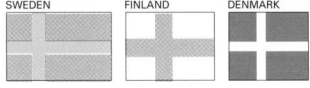

SCANDINAVIA

See page 16 for general map

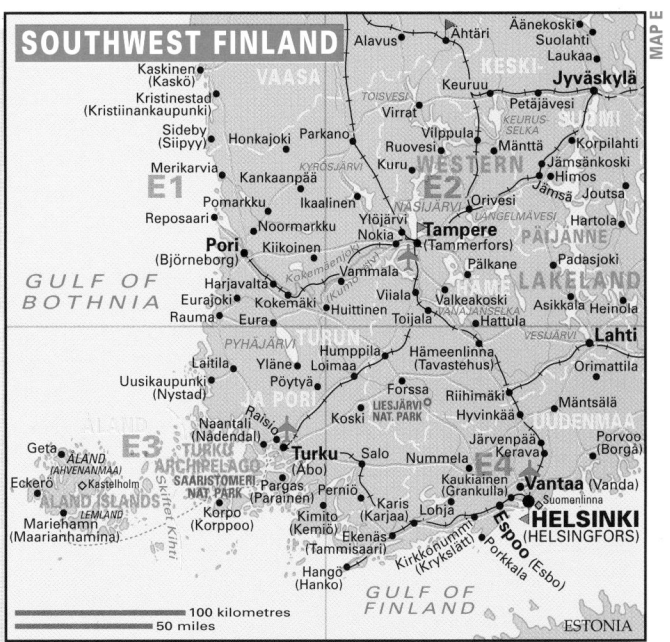

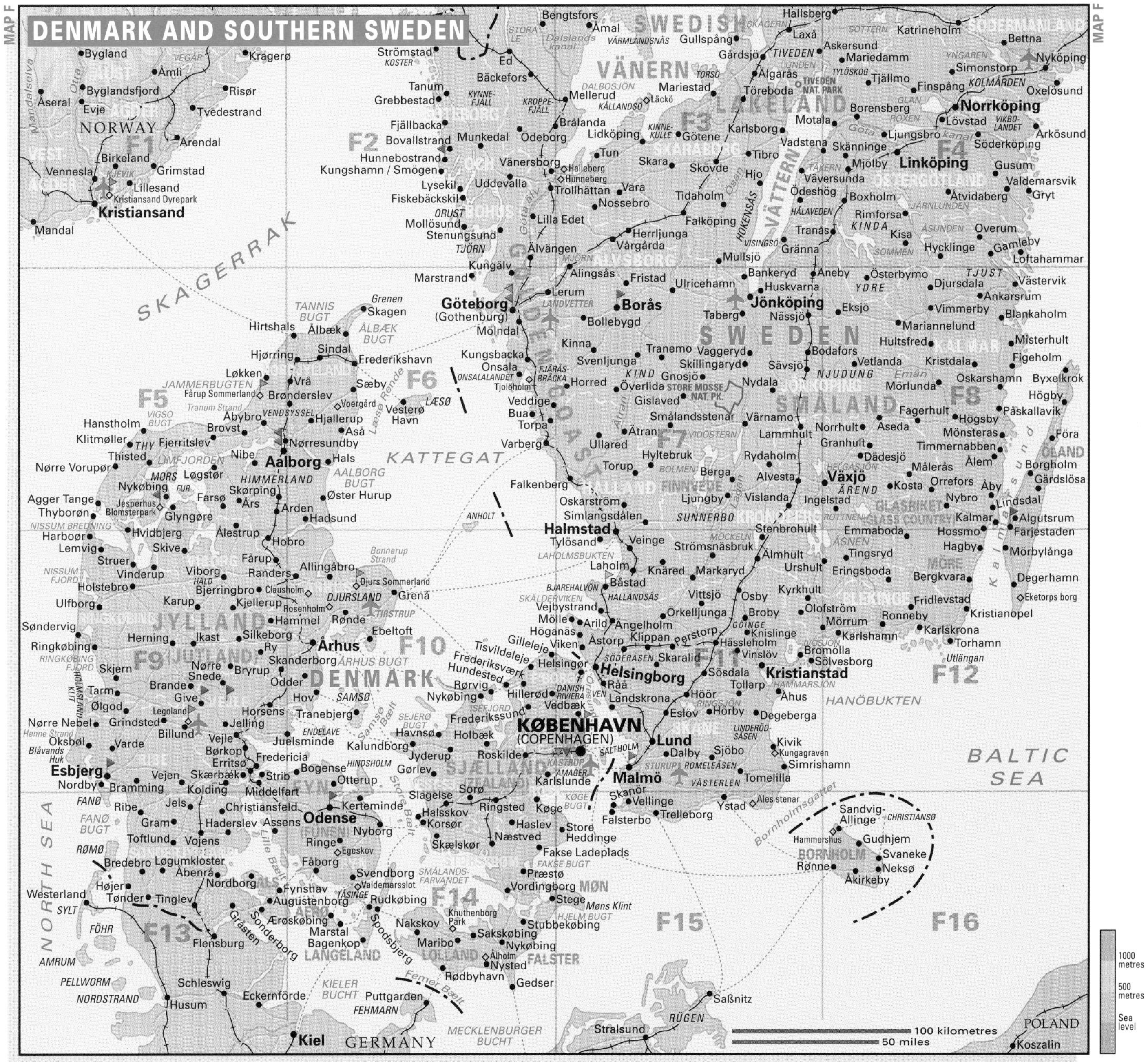

Leisure park   Zoo / animal park   Aquarium   Major tennis venue

CZECH REPUBLIC

CENTRAL EUROPE AND...

See pages 13 & 14 for general maps

OSTROV GREEM BELL

ZEMLYA GEORGA

ZEMLYA VILCHEKA

OSTROV USHAKOVA

OSTROV KOMSOMOLETS

OSTROV PIONER

OSTROV OKTYABR REVOLYU

ZEMLYA FRANTSA-IOSIFA
(FRANZ JOSEF LAND)

N O V A Y A   Z E M L Y A

OSTROV BELYY

POLUOSTROV YAMAL
(YAMAL PENINSULA)

GYDANSKIY POLUOSTROV
(GYDAN PENINSULA)

OSTROV VAYGACH

OSTROV KOLGUYEV

Murmansk

KOLSKIY POLUOSTROV
(KOLA PENINSULA)

WHITE SEA

KARELIA

Vorkuta

OBSKAYA GUBA
(OB ESTUARY)

Noril'sk

T Y U M E N

ZAPADNO SIBIRSKOYE RAVNINA
(WEST SIBERIAN PLAIN)

A4

R U S S I A N

Arkhangel'sk

K O M I

Pechora

Surgut

Kotlas

Syktyvkar

Ob

U R A L   M O U N T A I N S

Nizhnyaya Tunguska

Legend:
- — · — · boundary of the Former Soviet Union
- Russian Federation
- Republic within the Russian Federation
- ○ Capital of Republic within the Russian Federation

LAKE ONEGA

● Khizi Pogost

Petrozavodsk

VALAAM

LAKE LADOGA

Yenisey

TALLINN

HIIUMAA SAAREMAA

ESTONIA

Sankt-Peterburg
(St Petersburg)

Novgorod

A2

Yaroslavl'

Tver'

Perm

Yekaterinburg

Chelyabinsk

A3

Irtysh

Trans-Siberian Railway

Omsk

Novosibirsk

Krasnoyarsk

Tayshe

An

RIGA

BALTIC REPUBLICS

LATVIA

Polotsk

GOLDEN RING

Nizhniy Novgorod

MARI-EL Yoshkar-Ola

UDMURTIA Izhevsk

MOSKVA (MOSCOW)

Cheboksary CHUVASHIA

Kazan TATARSTAN

Ufa BASHKORTOSTAN

LITHUANIA

Kaliningrad
(Russian Fed.)

A1

VILNIUS

Smolensk

Saransk MORDOVIA

Simbirsk

Samara

Pavlodar

Gorno-Altaysk

KHAKASSIA

Abakan

ALTAY

TUVA

MENSK (MINSK)

Brest BELARUS

Bryansk

CITIES OF THE VOLGA

AKMOLA

Karaganda

Semey

Uskemen

Kyzyl

KYYIV (KIEV)

Lviv (Lvov)

UKRAINE

Voronezh

Saratov

Orenburg

TURGAY BASIN

TIEN SHAN

CHIȘINĂU

MOLDOVA

MAP B

DONETS BASIN

Rostov-na-Donu

Volgograd

VOLGA DELTA

Atyraū

KIRGIZ STEPPE

K A Z A K H S T A N

Baikonur Cosmodrome

LAKE BALKHASH

Don

Volga

Ural

Elista KALMYKIA

Astrakhan

ARAL SEA

Kzyl-Orda

Taldy-Kurgan

Odesa (Odessa)

SEA OF AZOV

CRIMEA

Sevastopol

Yalta

RUSSIAN BLACK SEA COAST

USTYURT PLATEAU

Syr Darya

FERGANA BASIN

Aulie-Ata

Almaty

Dagomys Sochi

CAUCASUS MTNS 1 2 3 4 5 6 7

CASPIAN SEA

U Z B E K I S T A N

Nukus

Chimkent

BISHKEK

TASHKENT

KYRGYZSTAN

BLACK SEA COAST

Sukhumi

GEORGIA

TBILISI

Khiva

Bukhara

Samarkand

BOSPORUS

ARMENIA

YEREVAN

BAKI (BAKU)

Türkmenbashi

T U R K M E N I S T A N

TAJIKISTAN

PAMIR

DUSHANBE

AZERBAIJAN

ASHGABAT

Mary

Amu Darya

Russian Republics in the Caucasus
1 Adygeya (capital: Maykop)   5 Ingushetia (Nazran)
2 Karachay-Cherkessia (Cherkessk) 6 Chechnya (Groznyy)
3 Kabardino-Balkaria (Nalchik)   7 Dagestan (Makhachkala)
4 North Ossetia (Vladikavkaz)

CENTRAL EUROPE

MAP B

BALTIC COAST

Gdynia

POMERANIA

Gdańsk

Kętrzyn

MASURIA

Szczecin (Stettin)

Poznań

Wisła (Vistula)

WARSZAWA (WARSAW)

POLAND

B1

● Łódź

Lublin

Odra (Oder)

Wrocław

SILESIA

Częstochowa

PRAHA (PRAGUE)

SUDETY

C

Plzeň (Pilsen)

CZECH REPUBLIC

BOHEMIA

MORAVIA

Ostrava

Kraków (Cracow)

Oświęcim (Auschwitz)

Zakopane

TATRY

Brno

Levoča

Košice

Nitra

SLOVAK REPUBLIC

CARPATHIANS

BRATISLAVA

Miskolc

Tokaj

BUDAPEST

Debrecen

BUKOVINA

JULIAN ALPS

Bled

Lake Balaton

HUNGARY

HUNGARIAN PLAIN

Pécs

Szeged

ROMANIA

Sibiu

MOLDAVIA

LJUBLJANA

SLOVENIA

Portorož

ZAGREB

CROATIA

Brasov

Sinaia

TRANSYLVANIAN ALPS

BUCUREȘTI (BUCHAREST)

DANUBE DELTA

D

ISTRA (ISTRIA)

Rijeka

Zadar

DINARIC ALPS

DALMATIA

BOSNIA-HERZEGOVINA

SARAJEVO

B2

WALACHIA

Danube

Constanța

BLACK SEA COAST

Split

Makarska

FEDERAL REPUBLIC OF YUGOSLAVIA

BEOGRAD (BELGRADE)

SOFIYA (SOFIA)

Varna

Burgas

DALMATIAN COAST

Dubrovnik

Kotor

Podgorica

Priština

BULGARIA

Borovets

Plovdiv

TIRANË (TIRANA)

SKOPJE

Pamporovo

RILA

RHODOPE

ALBANIA

Ohrid

FORMER YUGOSLAV REPUBLIC OF MACEDONIA

Vlorë

Gjirokastër

400 km
200 miles

BOHEMIA

MAP C

Dresden

Elbe

Rumburk

POLAND

Jelenia Gora

Freiburg

Zittau

Liberec

Frýdlant

ČESKÉ ŠVÝCARSKO (BOHEMIAN SWITZERLAND)

Děčín

Benešov

Jablonné v Podještědí

Harrachov

Chemnitz

Greiz

Zwickau

Aue

Teplice

Ústí nad Labem

Česká Lípa

Sněžka 1602m

Janske

KRKONOŠE NAT. PARK

Plauen

KRUŠNÉ HORY

C1

Litvínov

Litoměřice

Mnichovo Hradiště

Lázně

Jáchymov

Most

Terezín

Mladá Boleslav

Jičín

Ratibořice

Trutnov

Klingenthal

Klínovec 1244m

Chomutov

Louny

Lovosice

Libčchov

Mělník

Sobotka

Aš

Kadaň

Žatec

Loket

Ostrov

Karlovy Vary (Karlsbad)

Sokolov

SLAVKOVSKÝ LES

Kladno

Přerov nad Labem

Poděbrady

C2

Jaroměř

Frantiskovy Lázně

Cheb

ZÁHRADA ČECH (GARDEN OF BOHEMIA)

PRAHA (PRAGUE)

Kolín

Hradec Králové

Marktredwitz

Křivoklát

RUZYNĚ

Kouřim

Kutná Hora

Čáslav

Mariánské Lázně (Marienbad)

KŘIVOKLÁTSKO VRCHOVINA

Karlštejn

Vyšehrad

Sázava

Český Šternberk

Žleby

Bor

Kladruby

Hořovice

Benešov

Pardubice

Lichnice

Weiden

Plzeň (Pilsen)

Rokycany

Příbram

Jemniště

Havlíčkův Brod

Pribyslav

Mže

Plasy

Orlík

Konopiště

R E P U B L I C

Lipnice nad Sázavou

Klenčí pod Čerchovem

CZECH

Berounka

Švihov

Blatná

Zvíkov

Milevsko

Kaliště

Jihlava

GERMANY

Cham

Domažlice

Klatovy

Radbuza

Úhlava

Chýnovská jeskyně

Kámen

Pelhřimov

Červená Lhota

Telč

Třebíč

Regensburg

Železná Ruda

Sušice

Rabí

Strakonice

Písek

Bechyně

Tábor

Kratochvíle

Hluboká

Telč

Jindřichův Hradec

Slavonice

ŠUMAVA

Vimperk

Prachatice

České Budějovice

Třeboň

Raabs

Znojmo

C3

Plechy 1378m

Vltava

Holašovice

Zlatá Koruna

LIPENSKÁ PŘEHRADNÍ NÁDRŽ

C4

Deggendorf

Volary

Český Krumlov

Rožmberk

Gmünd

Straubing

Danube

Vyšší Brod

Isar

Landshut

Passau

Freistadt

AUSTRIA

Krems

100 kilometres
50 miles

▶ Zoo / animal park   ▶ Major tennis venue

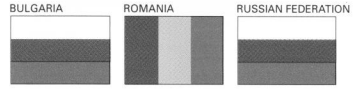

...THE FORMER SOVIET UNION

See pages 16, 17, 26 & 27 for general maps

Map labels

RNAYA ZEMLYA
(ORTH LAND)

ROV BOLSHEVIK

POLUOSTROV TAYMYR
(TAYMYR PENINSULA)

OSTROV BOLSHOY
BEGICHEV

LENA DELTA

NOVOSIBIRSKIYE OSTROVA
(NEW SIBERIAN ISLANDS)

OSTROV KOTELNYY

LYAKHOVSKIY
OSTROVA

OSTROV
NOVAYA SIBIR

SEVERO SIBIRSKOYE NIZMENNOST
(NORTH SIBERIAN LOWLANDS)

KOLYMSKAYA NIZMENNOST
(KOLYMA LOWLANDS)

NE SIBIRSKOYE PLOSKOGORYE
(CENTRAL SIBERIAN PLATEAU)

A5

SAKHA
(YAKUTIA)

A6

FEDERATION

Vilyuysk

Yakutsk

CHUKCHI

A7

A8

Okhotsk

Magadan

OSTROV
KARAGINSKIY

POLUOSTROV
KAMCHATKA
(KAMCHATKA
PENINSULA)

KOMANDORSKIYE
OSTROVA

BAM Railway
(Baikal-Amur Railway)

Ayam Line
Berkakit
Tynda

Okha

LAKE
BAIKAL

OSTROVA
USHKANIY

Severobaikalsk

Trans-Siberian
Railway

Bamovskoye

Komsomol'sk-
na-Amure

Petropavlovsk-
Kamchatskiy

OSTROV
OLKHON

BURYATIA

Ulan-Ude Chita Kuenga

Karimskoye

Sretensk

SAKHALIN

Imperatorskaya Gavan

KURIL ISLANDS

nga

To Ulan Bator, Mongolia
& Beijing, China

To Harbin, China

Khabarovsk

Vladivostok
Sailings to
Niigata, Japan

Nakhodka

See pages 16, 17, 26 & 27 for general maps

TRANS-SIBERIAN RAILWAY

	Distance from Moscow	
	Kilometres	Miles
Moscow	0	0
Alexandrov	112	70
Yaroslavl'	282	175
Danilov	357	222
Buy	450	280
Kotelnich	870	541
Kirov	957	595
Perm	1437	893
Yekaterinburg	1818	1130
Tyumen	2144	1332
Ishim	2433	1512
Omsk	2716	1688
Tatarsk	2585	1606
Novosibirsk	3343	2077
Yurga	3498	2174
Tayga	3571	2219
Achinsk	3920	2436
Krasnoyarsk	4104	2550
Uyar	4235	2632
Kansk	4351	2704
Tayshet	4522	2810
Irkutsk	5191	3226
Slyudyanka	5317	3304
Ulan-Ude	5647	3509
Ulan Bator	6304	3917
Beijing	7865	4887
Khilok	5940	3691
Chita	6204	3855
Karimskoye	6300	3915
Harbin	7610	4729
Bamovskoye	7281	4524
Skovorodino	7313	4544
Belogorsk	7873	4892
Izvestkovyy	8242	5121
Khabarovsk	8531	5301
Bikin	8764	5446
Spassk Dalny	9057	5628
Ussuriysk	9185	5707
Nakhodka	9446	5869
Ugolnaya	9264	5756
Vladivostok	9297	5777

In 1891, approval was given to begin construction of a railway across Siberia, linking Moscow to the Pacific. The route was divided into six sections for construction:

West Siberian Line (Yekaterinburg to Novosibirsk, completed 1896); Mid-Siberian Line (Novosibirsk to Irkutsk, 1899); Circum-Baikal Loop (1904); Trans-Baikal Line (Lake Baikal to Sretensk, 1900); Amur Line (Kuenga to Khabarovsk, 1916); Ussuri Line (Khabarovsk to Vladivostok, 1897).

Prior to the completion of the Circum-Baikal Loop, a ferry service was introduced to cross Lake Baikal. The ferry 'Baikal' was able to carry the complete train on its deck. The original rail link from Chita to Vladivostok, the Chinese Eastern Railway, ran through Manchuria, with steamer services on the Amur linking Sretensk with Khabarovsk. The Amur Line was only constructed when the Manchurian connection became vulnerable after the Russo-Japanese war.

Three long-distance services currently run from Moscow: Trans-Siberian (Moscow to Vladivostok); Trans-Manchurian (Moscow to Beijing via Chita and Harbin); Trans-Mongolian (Moscow to Beijing via Ulan-Ude and Ulan Bator).

ROMANIAN AND BULGARIAN COAST

MAP D

Galați MOL. UKRAINE
Izmail Kiliya

Moreni Brăila Crișan Sulina
Ploiești ROMANIA Făurei Tulcea DANUBE
Pitești Tîrgoviște Stîntu Gheorghe DELTA
Titu Buftea D1 MUNTENIA Urziceni Giurgeni Dăeni Babadag
Găești Hîrșova LACUL RAZELM
Slobozia Slobozia Fetești D2 LACUL SINOE
Videle Cernavodă MIHAIL KOGALNICEANU
BUCUREȘTI Techirghiol Mamaia-Sat
(BUCHAREST) Oltenița Ion Mamaia-Băi
Roșiori de Vede Silistra Corvin Constanța
Alexandria Srebarna Negru Eforie Nord / Eforie Sud
Giurgiu Dunav Alfatar Vodă Costinești
Zimnicea Ruse Tervel Kardam Neptun-Olimp / Jupiter
RUSENSKI LOM Venus-Aurora / Saturn
Svishtov NATIONAL PARK Dobrich Mangalia
Levski Razgrad Shabla Durankulak
Popovo Türgovishte Pliska Kavarna Tyulenovo
Gorna Shumen Novi Rusalka
Oryahovica Preslav Madara Pazar Tuzlata
Sevlievo Provadiya Zlatni Pyasütsi (Golden Sands) Balchik
Gabrovo Veliko Türnovo Ivanovo Kamchiya Albena
Tryavna BULGARIA Smyadovo Varna Druzhba
Sipčenski prohod (Shipka Pass) 1185m Novo Orjahovo Galata
VALLEY Kazanlük Byala
OF ROSES Obzor
Tulovo Nova Yambol Aytos Slünchev Bryag (Sunny Beach)
Stara Zagora Sliven Pomorie
Dimitrovgrad Grudovo Burgas Nesebür (Nessebar)
Topolovgrad Chernomorets
Khaskovo Primorsko Sozopol
TURKEY Lozenets Michurin
Akhtopol
Rezovo

D3 D4

BLACK SEA

200 kilometres
100 miles

MOSCOW AND ST PETERSBURG

MAP E

OZERO LADOZHSKOYE (LAKE LADOGA)
OSTROV KOTLIN
Kronstadt Sankt-Peterburg
PULKOVO (St Petersburg)
Kolpino Volkhov Tikhvin Babayevo Sokol
Pavlovsk
Gatchina Tsarskoye Selo Kirishi Kaduy Vologda
Vyritsa SHEKSNA Cherepovets
Chudovo Tesovo-Netyl'skiy E1 Gryazovets
Torkovichi Malaya Vishera E2
Novgorod Borovichi Pestovo RYBINSKOYE VODOKHRANILISHCHE
Okulovka Danilov
OZERO ILMEN Staraya Valday Bologoye Bezhetsk Rybinsk Kostroma
Russa Yaroslavl'
OZERO SELIGER Vishniy Uglich
Kholm Ostashkov Volochek Torzhok Kimry Rostov Ivanovo
OZERO VOLGA Kashin Kalyazin Teykovo
GOLDEN
Velikiye- Toropets Tver' Dubna RING
Luki Konakovo Sergiyev Suzdal
VALDAYSKAYA VOZVYSHENNOST Dmitrov Posad Bogolyubovo
Nelidovo Rzhev Klin Aleksandrov
BELARUS Demidov Lyubertsy Vladimir
Gagarin MOSKVA SHEREMETYEVO Orekhovo-Zuyevo
(MOSCOW) Mytishchi
Noginsk
Demidov Podolsk Vnukovo DOMODEDOVO Kolomna
Vyazma Obninsk Serpukhov

E3 E4

1000 metres
500 metres
Sea level

200 kilometres
100 miles

▶ Zoo / animal park   ▶ Aquarium   ▶ Major tennis venue

THE HOLY LAND AND CENTRAL ASIA

See pages 18, 26 & 29 for general maps

Crucible of ancient civilizations, harsh landscape of the Prophets of the Old Testament revered by Jew, Muslim and Christian alike, and dramatic setting for the story of Christ from his birth in Bethlehem to his crucifixion outside Jerusalem, the Holy Land is a region of monumental and complex significance - as Promised Land, place of pilgrimage and miracles and the setting for the rise and fall of empires and kingdoms.

No city symbolises this rich heritage more than Jerusalem. As the site of the ancient Temples of Judaism, so central to the ancient Jewish state, Jerusalem is the region's spiritual heart. For Christians, Jerusalem is the site of the Crucifixion, the culmination of the life of Christ. The city is also an integral part of the sacred geography of Islam, which also reveres the Old Testament Patriarchs, and is the third most sacred site in Islam after Mecca and Medina. In addition to sites of great spiritual significance, the Holy Land contains archaeological and architectural sites of immense importance.

Since the proclamation of the state of Israel in 1948, the politics of the area have been dominated by conflict between Israel and surrounding Arab states. Recent developments have offered some hope of future peace, which should herald a significant rise in the number of visitors to the region.

Legend:
- ✡ Site significant in Judaism
- † Site significant in Christianity
- ☾ Site significant in Islam
- ◉ Important location relating to the life of Jesus
- 🏰 Crusader castle or fortifications
- ⚜ Other important historical site
- • City of the Decapolis
- The Twelve Tribes of Israel

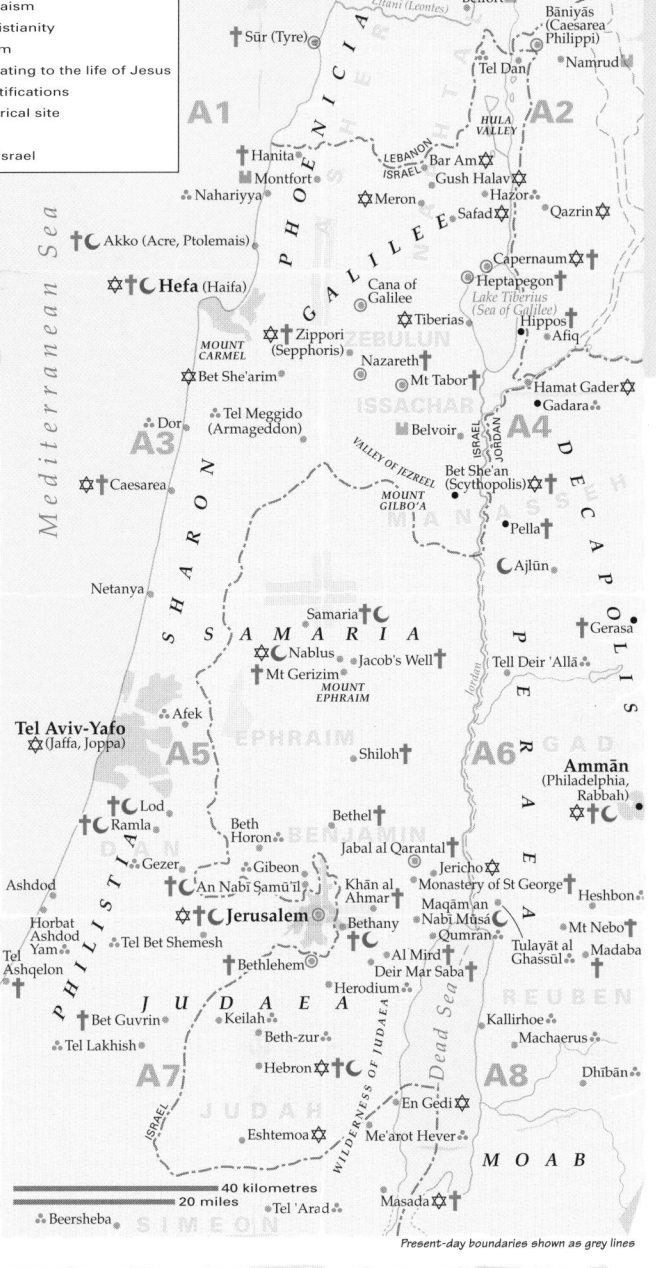

THE HOLY LAND

Present-day boundaries shown as grey lines

PRINCIPAL DATES IN THE HISTORY OF THE HOLY LAND

1600	Abraham, the first of the Patriarchs, migrates from Ur in Mesopotamia to Palestine.
1250	Jews released from captivity in Egypt by Moses.
1006-966	Under the reign of David, Jerusalem becomes the religious and political capital of the ancient Jewish state.
966-926	Reign of Solomon: the golden age for the ancient Jewish state, which was divided after his death into the Kingdoms of Israel and Judah.
587	Conquest and destruction of Jerusalem by Babylon.
332	Capture of Palestine by Alexander the Great.
63	Palestine becomes part of the Roman Empire.
39-4	Reign of Herod the Great.
6*	Birth of Jesus Christ.
29*	Crucifixion of Christ outside Jerusalem.
66-70	Jewish revolt against Roman rule, culminating in the razing of the Temple in AD70.
133	Jewish revolt suppressed, leading to the forced emigration of Jews to locations throughout the Roman Empire (diaspora).
570	Birth of Mohammed in Mecca.

622	Hegira: flight of Mohammed to Medina; the beginning of the Islamic calendar.
633	Death of Mohammed.
638	Jerusalem is conquered by the Caliph Omar, after which the Dome of the Rock Mosque is constructed in the city.
1100	Conquest of Jerusalem by the armies of the First Crusade and establishment of several Christian states in the region.
1187	Capture of Jerusalem by Saladin after the Battle of Hattin.
1260	Defeat of the Mongol army by the Mamaluks at the Battle of Goliath's Well (Ain Jalut), thus preserving Islamic control in the region.
1291	Overthrow of the last Christian state at Acre.
1517	Capture of Jerusalem by the Ottoman Turks.
1920	After the First World War, the Ottoman Empire is dismembered and Palestine and Trans-Jordan become British Protectorates.
1948	State of Israel proclaimed.
1990s	Ongoing peace talks between Israelis and Palestinians over the political future of the region.

* The exact dates of Christ's birth and death are not known with certainty

The ancient trade routes between Europe and the Far East have been used for many centuries, but the Central Asian region has been virtually closed to travellers for the last 70 years. With the recent independence of the former Soviet republics and the opening up of tourism in China, fabled cities like Bukhara, Kashgar and Samarkand are now once again accessible to travellers and tourists.

The famous Silk Road, once linking China with Europe, is in fact not one road, but a number of different routes depending on the season and local conditions. With the opening of the borders between China and the Central Asian republics, together with improved road and rail links, it is possible to visit many ancient sites associated with the Silk Road and package tours are available linking many of these places.

The modern Karakoram Highway crosses the Khunjerab Pass, one of the chief routes over the Himalayas between Jammu and Kashmir and China. The road is still vulnerable to closure along its 1200 km length.

ANCIENT TRADE ROUTES

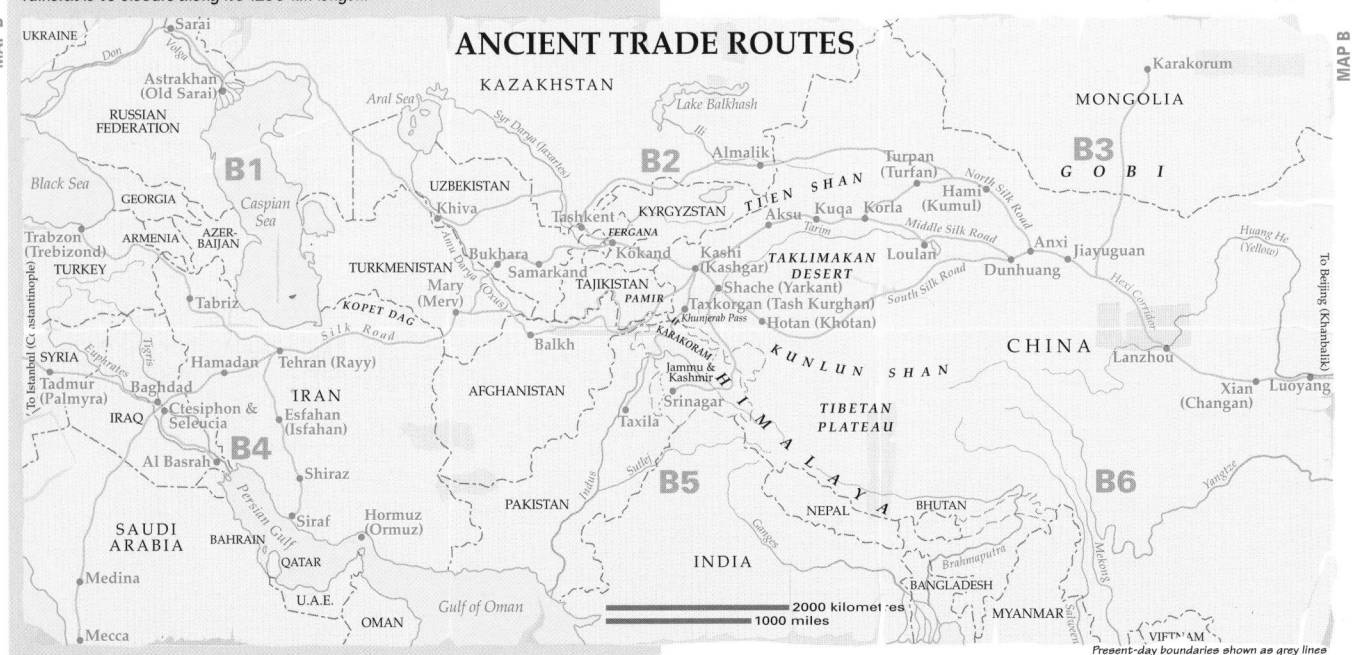

Present-day boundaries shown as grey lines

CLIMATE

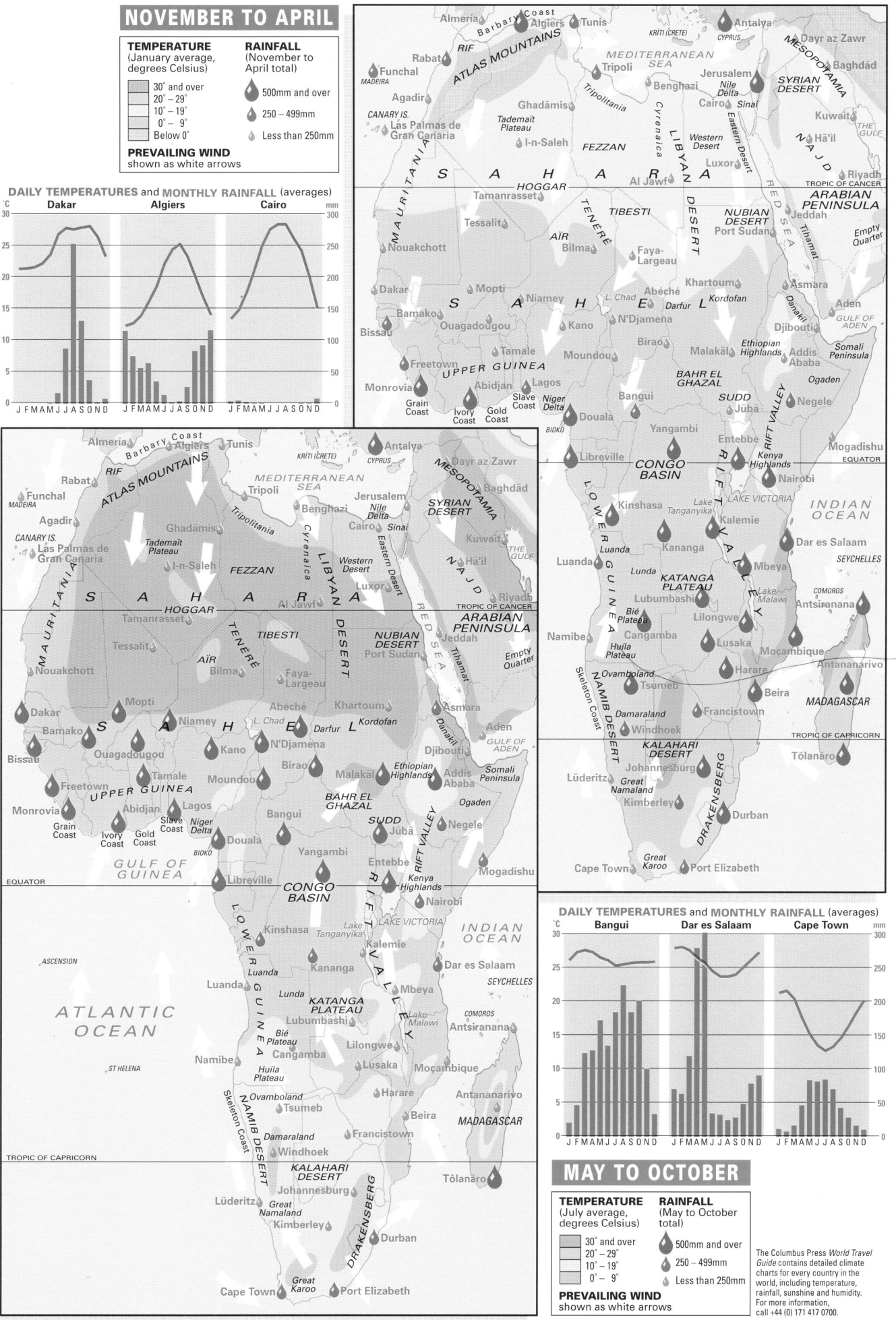

SOUTH AFRICA

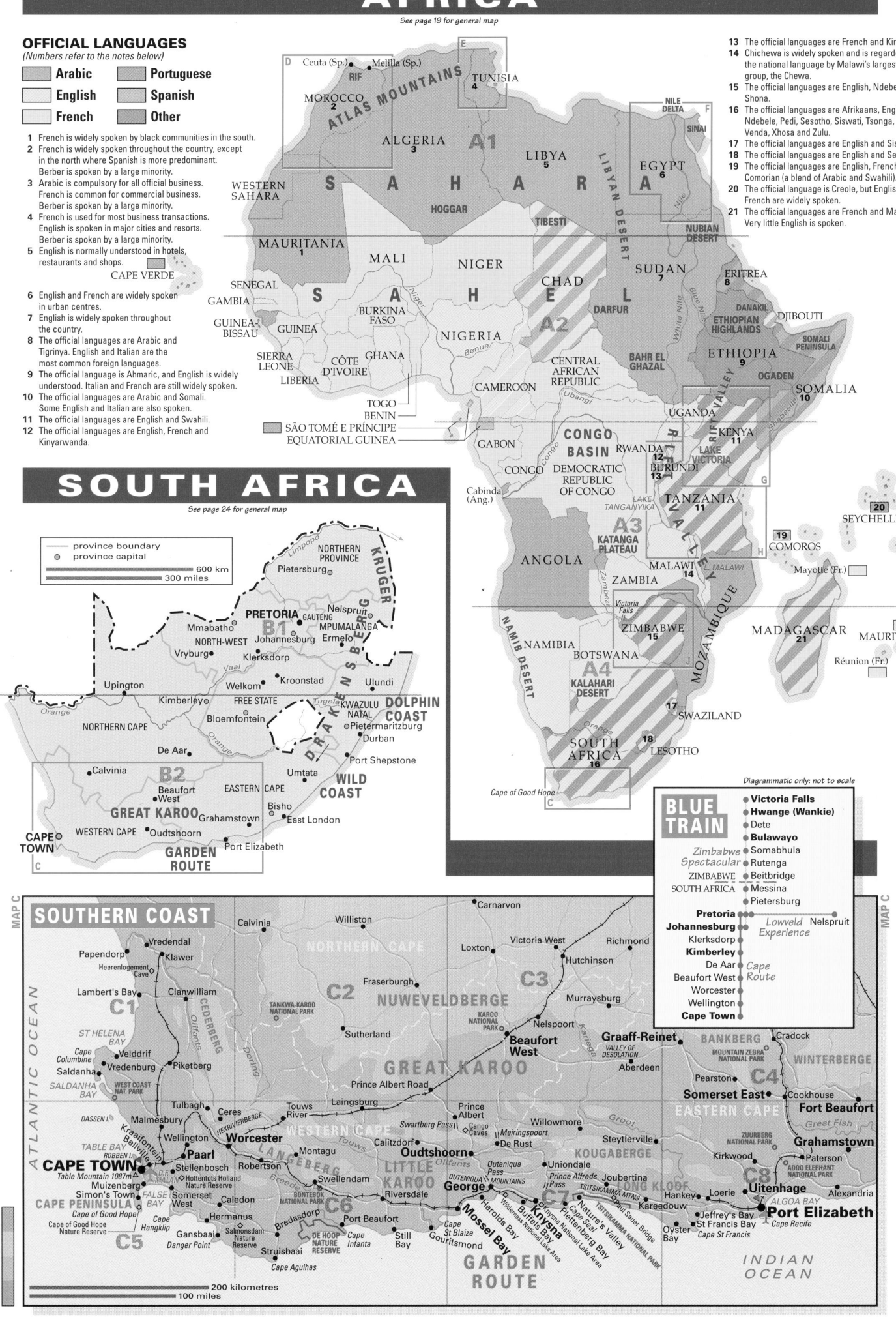
AFRICA
See page 19 for general map
OFFICIAL LANGUAGES
(Numbers refer to the notes below)
Arabic
Portuguese
English
Spanish
French
Other
1 French is widely spoken by black communities in the south.
2 French is widely spoken throughout the country, except in the north where Spanish is more predominant. Berber is spoken by a large minority.
3 Arabic is compulsory for all official business. French is common for commercial business. Berber is spoken by a large minority.
4 French is used for most business transactions. English is spoken in major cities and resorts. Berber is spoken by a large minority.
5 English is normally understood in hotels, restaurants and shops.
6 English and French are widely spoken in urban centres.
7 English is widely spoken throughout the country.
8 The official languages are Arabic and Tigrinya. English and Italian are the most common foreign languages.
9 The official language is Ahmaric, and English is widely understood. Italian and French are still widely spoken.
10 The official languages are Arabic and Somali. Some English and Italian are also spoken.
11 The official languages are English and Swahili.
12 The official languages are English, French and Kinyarwanda.
13 The official languages are French and Kirund
14 Chichewa is widely spoken and is regarded a the national language by Malawi's largest eth group, the Chewa.
15 The official languages are English, Ndebele a Shona.
16 The official languages are Afrikaans, English, Ndebele, Pedi, Sesotho, Siswati, Tsonga, Tsw Venda, Xhosa and Zulu.
17 The official languages are English and Siswa
18 The official languages are English and Sesot
19 The official languages are English, French an Comorian (a blend of Arabic and Swahili).
20 The official language is Creole, but English ar French are widely spoken.
21 The official languages are French and Malag Very little English is spoken.
Ceuta (Sp.)
Melilla (Sp.)
RIF
MOROCCO 2
ATLAS MOUNTAINS
TUNISIA 4
ALGERIA 3
A1
LIBYA 5
EGYPT 6
NILE DELTA
SINAI
WESTERN SAHARA
SAHARA
HOGGAR
TIBESTI
LIBYAN DESERT
NUBIAN DESERT
MAURITANIA 1
MALI
NIGER
CHAD
SUDAN 7
ERITREA 8
CAPE VERDE
SENEGAL
GAMBIA
GUINEA-BISSAU
GUINEA
SAHEL
BURKINA FASO
NIGERIA
A2
DARFUR
DANAKIL
DJIBOUTI
ETHIOPIAN HIGHLANDS
SOMALI PENINSULA
SIERRA LEONE
LIBERIA
CÔTE D'IVOIRE
GHANA
CENTRAL AFRICAN REPUBLIC
BAHR EL GHAZAL
ETHIOPIA 9
OGADEN
SOMALIA 10
CAMEROON
TOGO
BENIN
SÃO TOMÉ E PRÍNCIPE
EQUATORIAL GUINEA
UGANDA
KENYA 11
GABON
CONGO BASIN
RWANDA 12
BURUNDI 13
LAKE VICTORIA
CONGO
DEMOCRATIC REPUBLIC OF CONGO
RIFT VALLEY
Cabinda (Ang.)
LAKE TANGANYIKA
TANZANIA 11
SEYCHELLES 20
A3
KATANGA PLATEAU
COMOROS 19
ANGOLA
MALAWI 14
L. MALAWI
Mayotte (Fr.)
ZAMBIA
Victoria Falls
ZIMBABWE 15
MOZAMBIQUE
MADAGASCAR 21
MAURITIUS
Réunion (Fr.)
NAMIB DESERT
NAMIBIA
BOTSWANA
A4
KALAHARI DESERT
SWAZILAND 17
SOUTH AFRICA 16
LESOTHO 18
Cape of Good Hope
SOUTH AFRICA
See page 24 for general map
province boundary
province capital
600 km
300 miles
NORTHERN PROVINCE
Pietersburg
KRUGER
PRETORIA
GAUTENG
Nelspruit
Mmabatho
NORTH-WEST
Johannesburg
MPUMALANGA
Ermelo
Vryburg
Klerksdorp
DRAKENSBERG
Upington
Welkom
Kroonstad
Ulundi
Kimberley
FREE STATE
KWAZULU NATAL
DOLPHIN COAST
NORTHERN CAPE
Bloemfontein
Pietermaritzburg
Durban
De Aar
Port Shepstone
Calvinia
B2
Umtata
Beaufort West
EASTERN CAPE
WILD COAST
GREAT KAROO
Bisho
Grahamstown
East London
CAPE TOWN
WESTERN CAPE
Oudtshoorn
Port Elizabeth
GARDEN ROUTE
Diagrammatic only: not to scale
BLUE TRAIN
Victoria Falls
Hwange (Wankie)
Dete
Bulawayo
Zimbabwe Spectacular
Somabhula
Rutenga
ZIMBABWE
Beitbridge
SOUTH AFRICA
Messina
Pietersburg
Pretoria
Johannesburg
Lowveld Experience
Nelspruit
Klerksdorp
Kimberley
De Aar
Cape Route
Beaufort West
Worcester
Wellington
Cape Town
MAP C
SOUTHERN COAST
ATLANTIC OCEAN
INDIAN OCEAN
GREAT KAROO
GARDEN ROUTE
200 kilometres
100 miles
2000 metres
1000 metres
Sea level

Zoo / animal park
Aquarium

 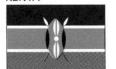
AFRICA

See pages 20-23 for general maps

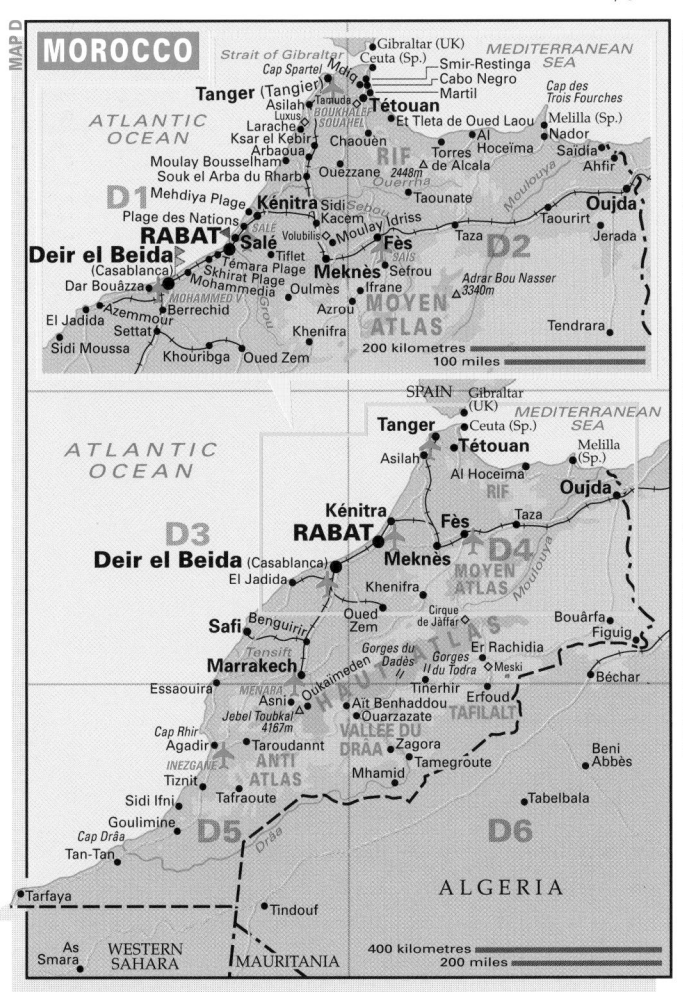

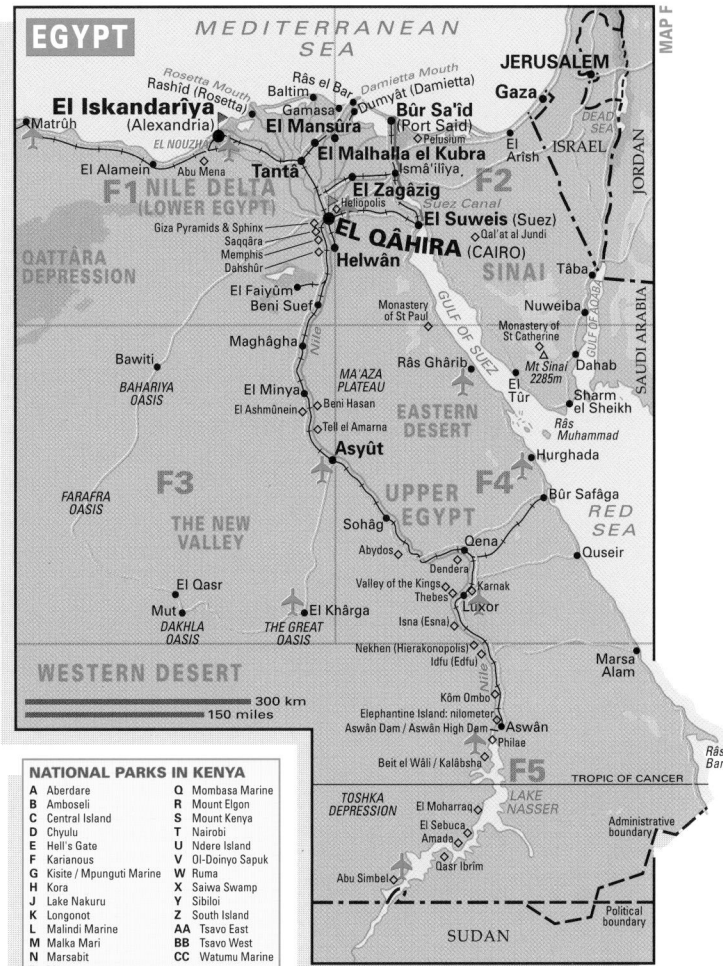

NATIONAL PARKS IN KENYA

A	Aberdare	Q	Mombasa Marine
B	Amboseli	R	Mount Elgon
C	Central Island	S	Mount Kenya
D	Chyulu	T	Nairobi
E	Hell's Gate	U	Ndere Island
F	Karianous	V	Ol-Doinyo Sapuk
G	Kisite / Mpunguti Marine	W	Ruma
H	Kora	X	Saiwa Swamp
J	Lake Nakuru	Y	Sibiloi
K	Longonot	Z	South Island
L	Malindi Marine	AA	Tsavo East
M	Malka Mari	BB	Tsavo West
N	Marsabit	CC	Watamu Marine
P	Meru		

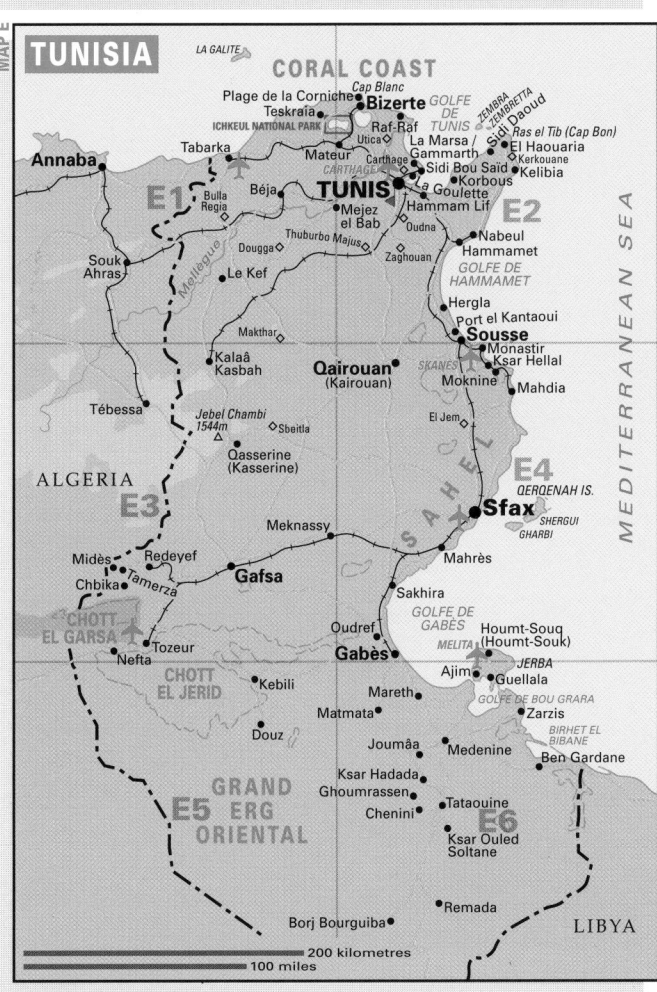

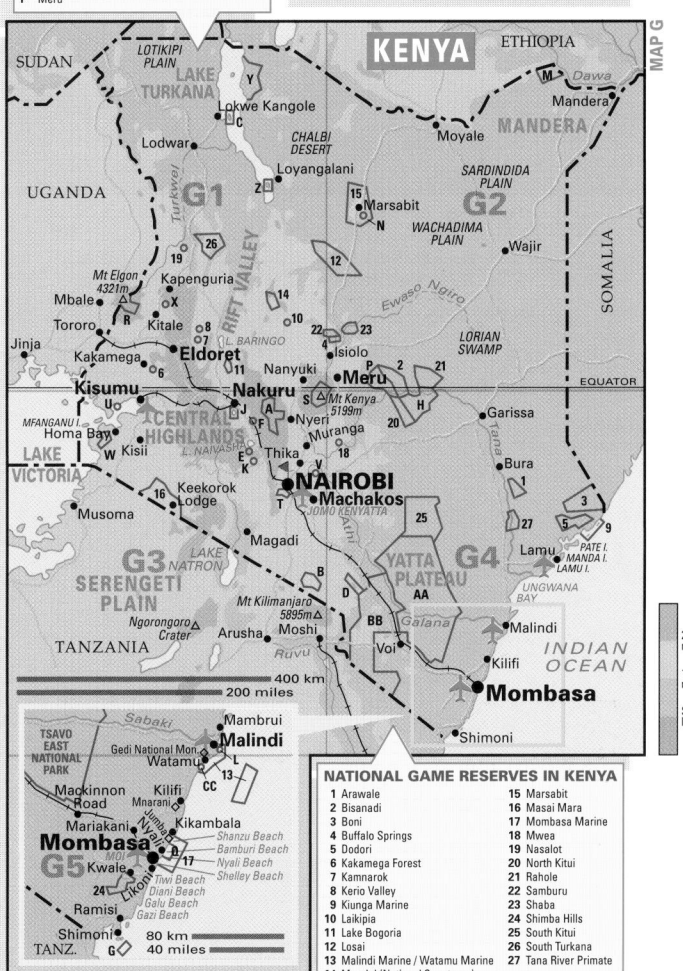

NATIONAL GAME RESERVES IN KENYA

1	Arawale	15	Marsabit
2	Bisanadi	16	Masai Mara
3	Boni	17	Mombasa Marine
4	Buffalo Springs	18	Mwea
5	Dodori	19	Nasalot
6	Kakamega Forest	20	North Kitui
7	Kamnarok	21	Rahole
8	Kerio Valley	22	Samburu
9	Kiunga Marine	23	Shaba
10	Laikipia	24	Shimba Hills
11	Lake Bogoria	25	South Kitui
12	Losai	26	South Turkana
13	Malindi Marine / Watamu Marine	27	Tana River Primate
14	Maralal (National Sanctuary)		

2000 metres
1000 metres
Sea level

▌ Leisure park ▶ Zoo / animal park ▲ Aquarium ▶ Major tennis venue

AFRICA

See pages 20-23 for general maps

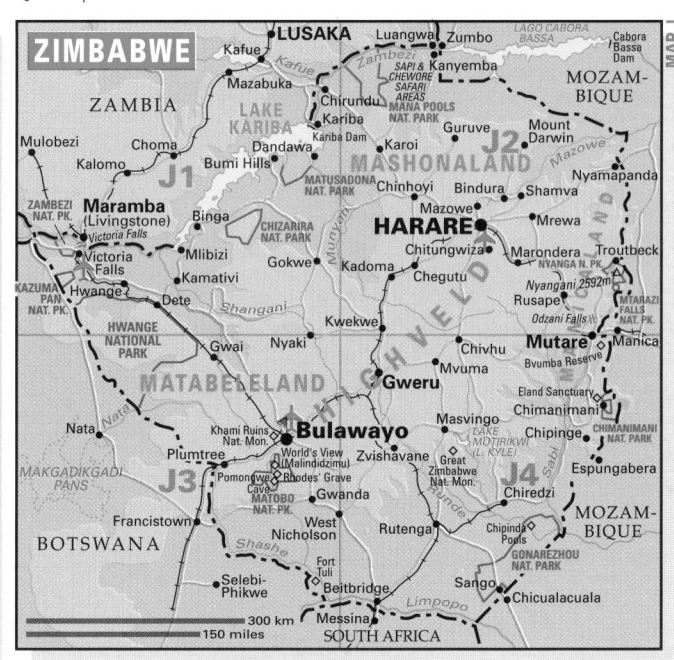

▶ Zoo / animal park

Africa is a prime destination for wildlife holidays: its national parks, game reserves and wildlife sanctuaries feature prominently in package holidays and tourist itineraries to the continent. Many parks, such as the Masai Mara, Serengeti and Kruger, are well-known throughout the world and some have been recognised by both UNESCO and the WWF for their unique and important character (UNESCO's World Heritage list is featured elsewhere in this atlas).

The area of Africa south of the Sahara is featured here. Although there are areas of wildlife interest in northern Africa, particularly on the Mediterranean coast, these are generally on a much smaller scale and do not usually provide the primary motivation for travel to these countries.

The map and table features the major parks and reserves used by tour operators and visited by overseas tourists. Some lesser-known parks are also included to give a broader geographical spread; access to many of these may be difficult due to poor infrastructure or political problems.

The table lists the major species most likely to be seen while visiting each park or those animals for which the park is famous, according to independent reports and government literature. Quality of information varies considerably from country to country and the following table should be regarded as a rough guide only; in some cases no species information is currently available. Poaching is a serious problem in some countries, particularly where wildlife tourism is less developed.

	COUNTRY	PARK/RESERVE	Notes
1	Mauritania	Banc d'Arguin National Park	MIGRATING BIRDS
2	Mali	Lac Faguibine	MIGRATING BIRDS
3	Niger	Parc National du "W"	
4	Niger	Réserve du Aïr	
5	Niger	Réserve du Ténéré	
6	Senegal	Parc National des Oiseaux du Djoudj	MIGRATING BIRDS
7	Senegal	Parc National de la Langue de Barbarie	WATERFOWL (FLAMINGOS ETC)
8	Senegal	Parc National du Delta du Saloum	SMALL MAMMALS & MIGRATING BIRDS
9	Senegal	Parc National de Basse-Casamance	
10	Senegal	Parc National de Niokolo Koba	
11	The Gambia	Abuko Nature Reserve	BUDGERIGARS
12	The Gambia	Kiang West National Park	
13	Sierra Leone	Outamba-Kilimi National Park	
14	Sierra Leone	Mount Bintumani	
15	Sierra Leone	Mamunta-Mayoso Wildlife Sanctuary	BIRDS & SMALL MAMMALS
16	Sierra Leone	Gola Forest Reserve	BUDGERIGARS
17	Sierra Leone	Tiwai Island Wildlife Sanctuary	BUTTERFLIES & BUDGERIGARS
18	Liberia	Sapo National Park	
19	Côte d'Ivoire	Parc National de Taï	
20	Côte d'Ivoire	Parc National de la Marahoué	
21	Côte d'Ivoire	Parc National de la Comoé	
22	Ghana	Mole National Park	
23	Ghana	Bui National Park	
24	Ghana	Kujani Game Reserve	
25	Ghana	Owabi Wildlife Sanctuary	BIRDS & SMALL MAMMALS
26	Ghana	Bia National Park	
27	Ghana	Kakum Nature Park	
28	Burkina Faso	Parc National d'Arly	
29	Togo	Parc National de la Kéran	
30	Togo	Parc National de Fazao-Malfakassa	
31	Benin	Parc National de la Pendjari	
32	Nigeria	Kamuku Wildlife Reserve	BUDGERIGARS
33	Nigeria	Hadejia-Nguru Wetlands	WETLAND BIRDS
34	Nigeria	Yankari National Park	
35	Nigeria	Gashaka Game Reserve	
36	Nigeria	Okomo Sanctuary	
37	Nigeria	Cross River National Park	
38	Cameroon	Parc National du Korup	BUDGERIGARS & RAINFOREST BIRDS
39	Cameroon	Réserve du Dja	
40	Cameroon	Parc National de la Bénoué	
41	Cameroon	Parc National de Bouba Ndjida	
42	Cameroon	Parc National de Waza	
43	Chad	Parc National de Zakouma	(Widespread poaching; greatly depleted stocks)
44	Central African Rep.	Parc National Manovo-Gounda-St Floris	
45	Central African Rep.	Parc National du Bamingui-Bangoran	
46	Central African Rep.	Réserve du Dzanga-Sangha	
47	Gabon	Réserve de Lopé	
48	Gabon	Parc National de l'Okanda	OKAPI
49	Gabon	Réserve d'Iguéla	

	COUNTRY	PARK/RESERVE	Notes
50	Gabon	Réserve de Petit-Loango	LEATHERBACK SEA TURTLE
51	Gabon	Réserve de la Moukalaba	LEATHERBACK SEA TURTLE
52	Gabon	Réserve de Ndendé	
53	Congo, Dem. Rep.	Parc National de la Salonga	
54	Congo, Dem. Rep.	Parc National de la Garamba	
55	Congo, Dem. Rep.	Réserve du Okapi	OKAPI
56	Congo, Dem. Rep.	Parc National des Virunga	
57	Congo, Dem. Rep.	Parc National de la Maiko	
58	Congo, Dem. Rep.	Parc National du Kahuzi-Biega	
59	Congo, Dem. Rep.	Parc National de l'Upemba	
60	Congo, Dem. Rep.	Parc National de Kundelungu	
61	Sudan	Dinder National Park	(Data unavailable)
62	Ethiopia	Simien National Park	(Data unavailable)
63	Ethiopia	Awash National Park	(Data unavailable)
64	Ethiopia	Langano & Shala-Abiyata Lakes Nat. Pk.	(Data unavailable)
65	Ethiopia	Bale Mountains National Park	(Data unavailable)
66	Ethiopia	Omo and Mago National Parks	(Data unavailable)
67	Somalia	Hargeysa National Park	(Data unavailable)
68	Somalia	Kismayo National Park	(Data unavailable)
69	Uganda	Ruwenzori National Park	
70	Uganda	Queen Elizabeth National Park	
71	Uganda	Bwindi Impenetrable National Park	
72	Rwanda	Parc des Volcans	
73	Rwanda	Parc National de l'Akagera	BIRDLIFE
74	Kenya	Sibiloi National Park	
75	Kenya	Marsabit National Park	
76	Kenya	Mount Elgon National Park	
77	Kenya	Samburu National Reserve	
78	Kenya	Meru National Park	
79	Kenya	Mount Kenya National Park	
80	Kenya	Aberdare National Park	
81	Kenya	Lake Nakuru National Park	FLAMINGOS
82	Kenya	Masai Mara National Reserve	
83	Kenya	Nairobi National Park	
84	Kenya	Amboseli National Park	
85	Kenya	Tsavo National Park	
86	Kenya	Shimba Hills National Reserve	SABLE ANTELOPE
87	Tanzania	Rubondo Island National Park	WETLAND BIRDS
88	Tanzania	Serengeti National Park	
89	Tanzania	Ngorongoro Conservation Area	
90	Tanzania	Kilimanjaro National Park	
91	Tanzania	Arusha National Park	
92	Tanzania	Tarangire National Park	
93	Tanzania	Gombe National Park	
94	Tanzania	Ruaha National Park	
95	Tanzania	Selous Game Reserve	
96	Malawi	Nyika National Park	BUTTERFLIES & BIRDS
97	Malawi	Kasungu National Park	
98	Malawi	Lake Malawi National Park	

Species column headers (both tables): ELEPHANT · RHINOCEROS · HIPPOPOTAMUS · BUFFALO · ZEBRA · GIRAFFE · ANTELOPE · LION · LEOPARD · CHEETAH · HYENA · WARTHOG · GORILLA · CHIMPANZEE · MONKEY

WILDLIFE PARKS AND RESERVES

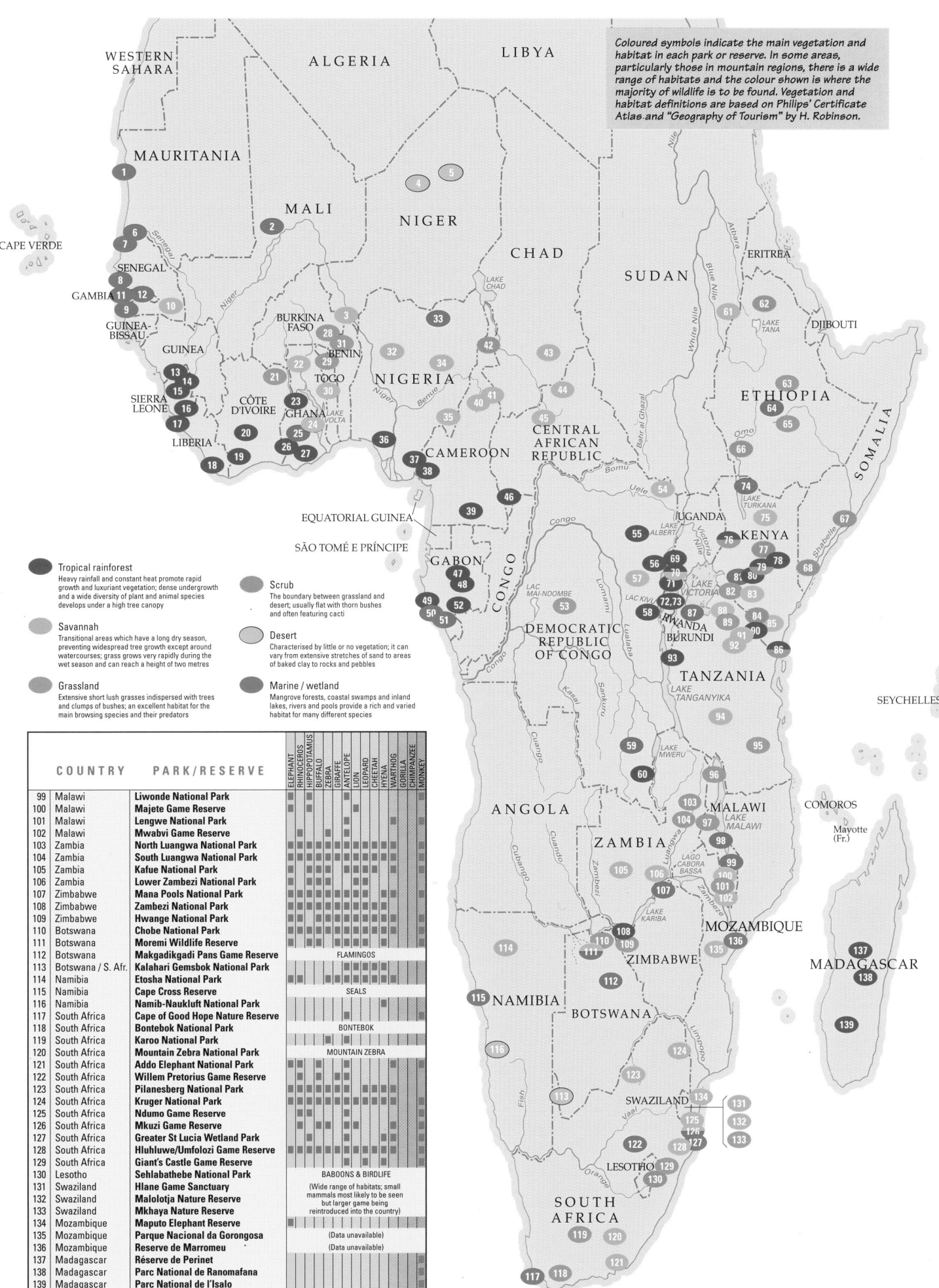

Coloured symbols indicate the main vegetation and habitat in each park or reserve. In some areas, particularly those in mountain regions, there is a wide range of habitats and the colour shown is where the majority of wildlife is to be found. Vegetation and habitat definitions are based on Philips' Certificate Atlas and "Geography of Tourism" by H. Robinson.

Tropical rainforest
Heavy rainfall and constant heat promote rapid growth and luxuriant vegetation; dense undergrowth and a wide diversity of plant and animal species develops under a high tree canopy

Savannah
Transitional areas which have a long dry season, preventing widespread tree growth except around watercourses; grass grows very rapidly during the wet season and can reach a height of two metres

Grassland
Extensive short lush grasses indispersed with trees and clumps of bushes; an excellent habitat for the main browsing species and their predators

Scrub
The boundary between grassland and desert; usually flat with thorn bushes and often featuring cacti

Desert
Characterised by little or no vegetation; it can vary from extensive stretches of sand to areas of baked clay to rocks and pebbles

Marine / wetland
Mangrove forests, coastal swamps and inland lakes, rivers and pools provide a rich and varied habitat for many different species

	COUNTRY	PARK/RESERVE	ELEPHANT	RHINOCEROS	HIPPOPOTAMUS	BUFFALO	ZEBRA	GIRAFFE	ANTELOPE	LION	LEOPARD	CHEETAH	HYENA	WARTHOG	GORILLA	CHIMPANZEE	MONKEY
99	Malawi	Liwonde National Park															
100	Malawi	Majete Game Reserve															
101	Malawi	Lengwe National Park															
102	Malawi	Mwabvi Game Reserve															
103	Zambia	North Luangwa National Park															
104	Zambia	South Luangwa National Park															
105	Zambia	Kafue National Park															
106	Zambia	Lower Zambezi National Park															
107	Zimbabwe	Mana Pools National Park															
108	Zimbabwe	Zambezi National Park															
109	Zimbabwe	Hwange National Park															
110	Botswana	Chobe National Park															
111	Botswana	Moremi Wildlife Reserve															
112	Botswana	Makgadikgadi Pans Game Reserve	FLAMINGOS														
113	Botswana / S. Afr.	Kalahari Gemsbok National Park															
114	Namibia	Etosha National Park															
115	Namibia	Cape Cross Reserve	SEALS														
116	Namibia	Namib-Naukluft National Park															
117	South Africa	Cape of Good Hope Nature Reserve															
118	South Africa	Bontebok National Park	BONTEBOK														
119	South Africa	Karoo National Park															
120	South Africa	Mountain Zebra National Park	MOUNTAIN ZEBRA														
121	South Africa	Addo Elephant National Park															
122	South Africa	Willem Pretorius Game Reserve															
123	South Africa	Pilanesberg National Park															
124	South Africa	Kruger National Park															
125	South Africa	Ndumo Game Reserve															
126	South Africa	Mkuzi Game Reserve															
127	South Africa	Greater St Lucia Wetland Park															
128	South Africa	Hluhluwe/Umfolozi Game Reserve															
129	South Africa	Giant's Castle Game Reserve															
130	Lesotho	Sehlabathebe National Park	BABOONS & BIRDLIFE														
131	Swaziland	Hlane Game Sanctuary	(Wide range of habitats; small mammals most likely to be seen but larger game being reintroduced into the country)														
132	Swaziland	Malolotja Nature Reserve															
133	Swaziland	Mkhaya Nature Reserve															
134	Mozambique	Maputo Elephant Reserve															
135	Mozambique	Parque Nacional da Gorongosa	(Data unavailable)														
136	Mozambique	Reserve de Marromeu	(Data unavailable)														
137	Madagascar	Réserve de Perinet															
138	Madagascar	Parc National de Ranomafana															
139	Madagascar	Parc National de l'Isalo															

CLIMATE

TEMPERATURE CONVERSION

°Celsius	−10	0	10	20	30	40
°Fahrenheit	14	32	50	68	86	104

RAINFALL CONVERSION

Millimetres	102	203	305	406	508	610
Inches	4	8	12	16	20	24

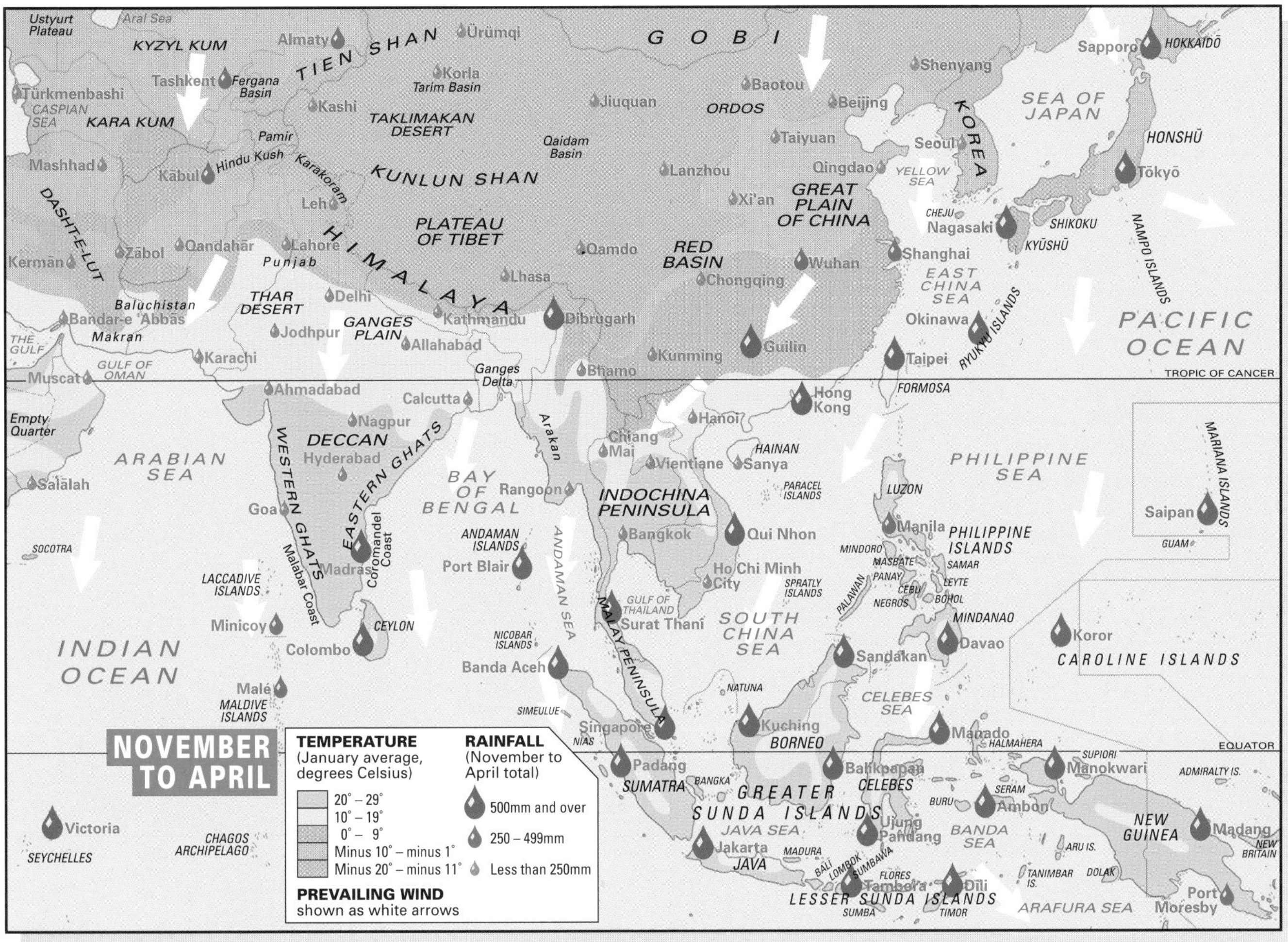

NOVEMBER TO APRIL

TEMPERATURE (January average, degrees Celsius)
- 20° – 29°
- 10° – 19°
- 0° – 9°
- Minus 10° – minus 1°
- Minus 20° – minus 11°

RAINFALL (November to April total)
- 500mm and over
- 250 – 499mm
- Less than 250mm

PREVAILING WIND shown as white arrows

The Columbus Press World Travel Guide contains detailed climate charts for every country in the world, including temperature, rainfall, sunshine and humidity. For more information, call +44 (0) 171 417 0700.

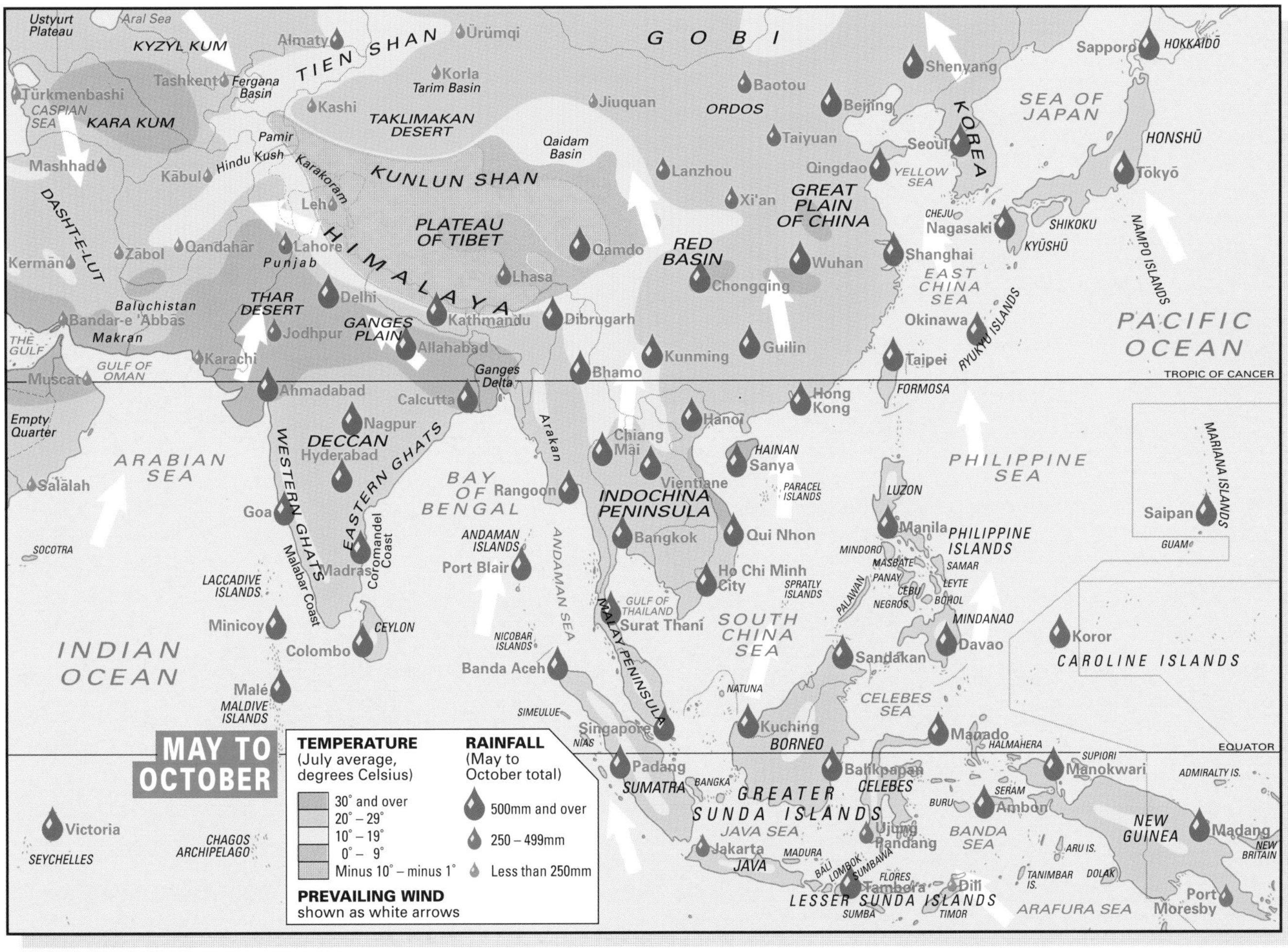

MAY TO OCTOBER

TEMPERATURE (July average, degrees Celsius)
- 30° and over
- 20° – 29°
- 10° – 19°
- 0° – 9°
- Minus 10° – minus 1°

RAINFALL (May to October total)
- 500mm and over
- 250 – 499mm
- Less than 250mm

PREVAILING WIND shown as white arrows

INDIA

See page 28 for general map

PALACE ON WHEELS

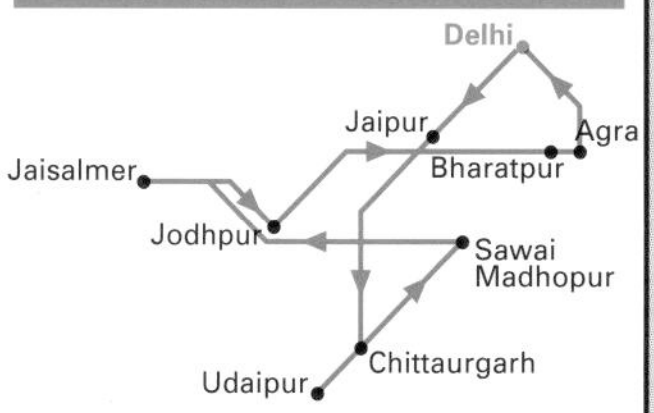

The Palace on Wheels is a luxury train service linking Delhi and Agra with a number of historic cities in Rajasthan. Following its success, a number of other similar services are now in preparation. The first of these, the Royal Orient, entered service in 1995.

ROYAL ORIENT

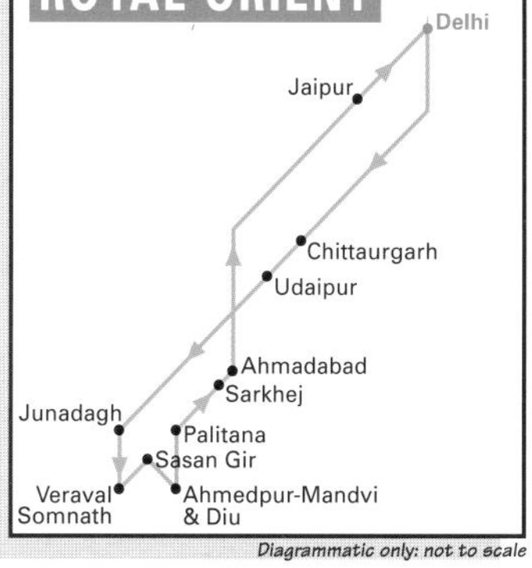

Diagrammatic only: not to scale

GOA BEACHES

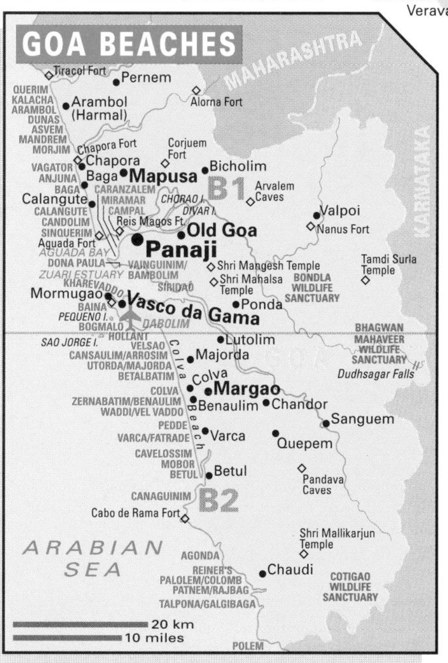

CENTRAL NORTH INDIA

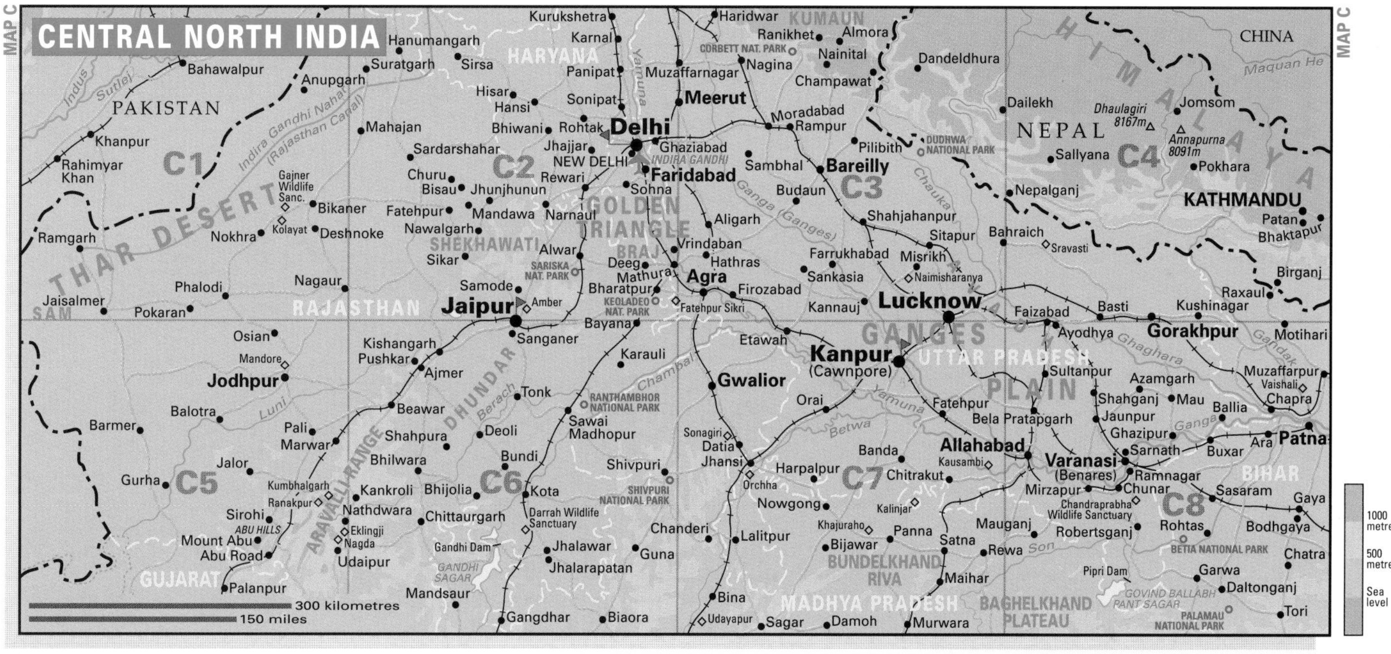

tourist region boundary
state/union territory boundary*
state/union territory capital

600 km
300 miles

*union territories in **bold** type
Chandigarh is the capital of Haryana State and of Punjab State, as well as Chandigarh Union Territory

▶ Zoo / animal park

  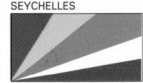

INDIA SRI LANKA MALDIVES SEYCHELLES

INDIA AND SRI LANKA

See page 28 for general map

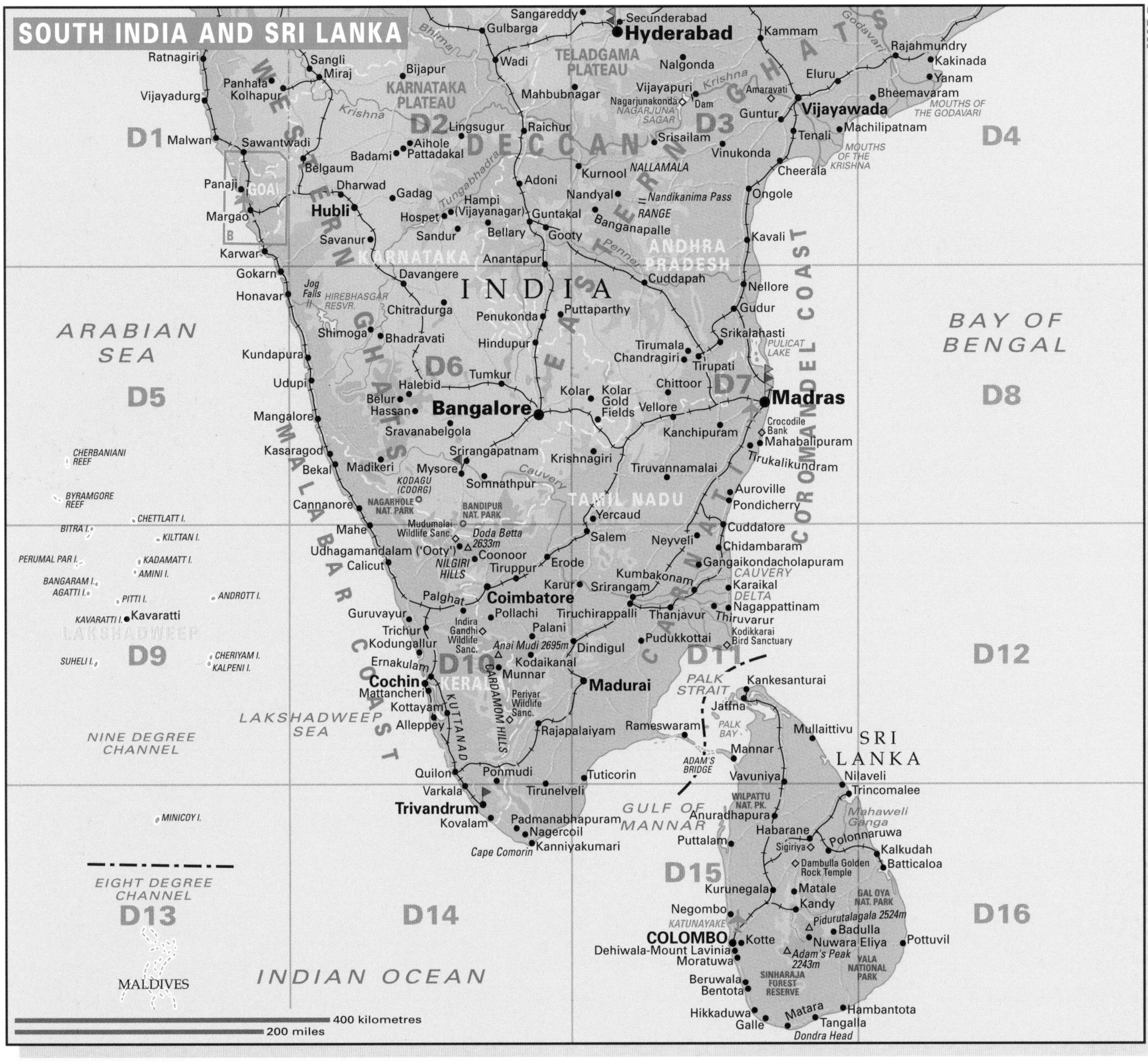

SOUTH INDIA AND SRI LANKA

MAP D

ARABIAN SEA

Ratnagiri, Panhala, Sangli, Miraj, Bijapur, Wadi, Gulbarga, Sangareddy, Secunderabad, Hyderabad, Kammam, Rajahmundry, Kakinada, Yanam
Vijayadurg, Kolhapur, Karnataka Plateau, Mahbubnagar, Nalgonda, Eluru, Bheemavaram, Mouths of the Godavari
Malwan, Sawantwadi, Badami, Lingsugur, Raichur, Nagarjunakonda, Nagarjuna Sagar Dam, Vijayapuri, Amaravati, Guntur, Vijayawada, Machilipatnam, Mouths of the Krishna
D1, Belgaum, Aihole, Pattadakal, Srisailam, Nandyal, Kurnool, Nallamala, Vinukonda, Cheerala, Tenali
Panaji, GOA, Dharwad, Gadag, Hampi (Vijayanagar), Guntakal, Adoni, Nandikanima Pass, Range, Ongole
Margao, Hubli, Hospet, Sandur, Bellary, Gooty, Banganapalle, Kavali
Karwar, Savanur, Anantapur, Andhra Pradesh, Nellore, D4
Gokarn, Davangere, INDIA, Cuddapah, Gudur
Honavar, Jog Falls, Chitradurga, Penukonda, Puttaparthy, Srikalahasti, BAY OF BENGAL
Shimoga, Bhadravati, Hindupur, Tumkur, Kolar, Tirumala, Chandragiri, Tirupati, D8
Kundapura, Halebid, Kolar Gold Fields, Chittoor
Udupi, Belur, Hassan, Bangalore, Kanchipuram, Vellore, Krishnagiri, Madras, Crocodile Bank, Mahabalipuram
Mangalore, Sravanabelgola, Mysore, Somnathpur, Yercaud, Tiruvannamalai, Tirukalikundram
Kasaragod, Madikeri, Kodagu (Coorg), Bandipur Nat. Park, Tamil Nadu, Auroville, Pondicherry
Bekal, Cannanore, Nagarhole Nat. Park, Mudumalai Wildlife Sanc., Doda Betta 2633m, Salem, Neyveli, Cuddalore
Mahe, Udhagamandalam ('Ooty'), Coonoor, Nilgiri Hills, Erode, Kumbakonam, Chidambaram, Gangaikondacholapuram, Cauvery Delta
Calicut, Tiruppur, Karur, Srirangam, Karaikal, Nagappattinam
Guruvayur, Palghat, Pollachi, Tiruchirappalli, Thanjavur, Thiruvarur, Kodikkarai Bird Sanctuary
Trichur, Palani, Indira Gandhi Wildlife Sanc., Anai Mudi 2695m, Dindigul, Pudukkottai
Kodungallur, Coimbatore, Kodaikanal, Kankesanturai
Ernakulam, Kerala, Munnar, Madurai, Jaffna, Palk Strait
Cochin, Mattancheri, Kottayam, Alleppey, Periyar Wildlife Sanc., Rajapalaiyam, Rameswaram, Palk Bay, Mullaittivu, SRI LANKA, Nilaveli, Trincomalee
Lakshadweep Sea, Kuttanad, Cardamom Hills, Adam's Bridge, Mannar, Vavuniya, Mahaweli Ganga
Quilon, Ponmudi, Tuticorin, Wilpattu Nat. Pk., Anuradhapura, Polonnaruwa, Kalkudah, Batticaloa
Varkala, Tirunelveli, Gulf of Mannar, Habarane, Sigiriya, Dambulla Golden Rock Temple
Trivandrum, Kovalam, Padmanabhapuram, Nagercoil, Kanniyakumari, Puttalam, D15, Kurunegala, Matale, Gal Oya Nat. Park, Pidurutalagala 2524m
Cape Comorin, Negombo, Kandy, Badulla, Pottuvil
Katunayake, Colombo, Kotte, Nuwara Eliya, Adam's Peak 2243m, Yala National Park
Dehiwala-Mount Lavinia, Moratuwa, Sinharaja Forest Reserve
Beruwala, Bentota, Hikkaduwa, Matara, Hambantota, Tangalla, Galle, Dondra Head

INDIAN OCEAN

CHERBANIANI REEF, BYRAMGORE REEF, CHETLLATT I., BITRA I., KILTTAN I., PERUMAL PAR I., KADAMATT I., AMINI I., BANGARAM I., AGATTI I., PITTI I., ANDROTT I., KAVARATTI I., Kavaratti, LAKSHADWEEP, CHERIYAM I., SUHELI I., KALPENI I., D9
NINE DEGREE CHANNEL
MINICOY I.
EIGHT DEGREE CHANNEL, D13
MALDIVES
D14

400 kilometres / 200 miles

MALDIVES

See page 28 for general map

MAP E

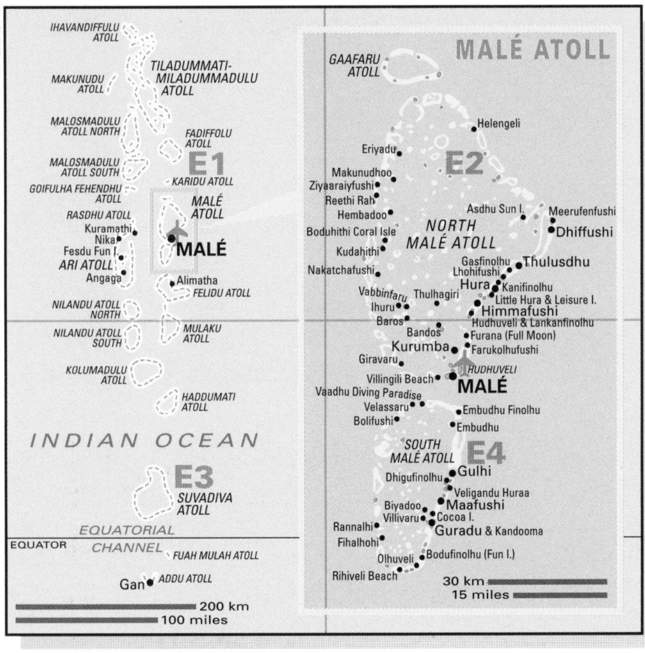

IHAVANDIFFULU ATOLL, TILADUMMATI-MILADUMMADULU ATOLL, MALÉ ATOLL
MAKUNUDU ATOLL, FADIFFOLU ATOLL, GAAFARU ATOLL
MALOSMADULU ATOLL NORTH, KARIDU ATOLL, Helengeli, Eriyadu, Makunudhoo, Ziyaraiyfushi, Reethi Rah, Hembadoo, Boduhithi Coral Isle, Kudahithi, Asdhu Sun I., Meerufenfushi, Dhiffushi
MALOSMADULU ATOLL SOUTH, E1, E2, NORTH MALÉ ATOLL, Gasfinolhu, Lhohifushi, Thulusdhu
GOIFULHA FEHENDHU ATOLL, RASDHU ATOLL, Kuramathi, Nika, Fesdu Fun I., MALÉ ATOLL, MALÉ, Vabbinfaru, Thulhagiri, Hura, Kanifinolhu, Little Hura & Leisure I.
ARI ATOLL, Alimatha, Ihuru, Himmafushi, Hudhuveli & Lankanfinolhu, Furana (Full Moon)
NILANDU ATOLL NORTH, FELIDU ATOLL, Baros, Bandos, Kurumba, Farukolhufushi
NILANDU ATOLL SOUTH, MULAKU ATOLL, Giravaru, MALÉ, Vaadhu Diving Paradise, Velassaru, Embudhu Finolhu
KOLUMADULU ATOLL, Villingili Beach, Bolifushi, Embudhu, SOUTH MALÉ ATOLL, E4
HADDUMATI ATOLL, Dhigufinolhu, Gulhi, Veligandu Huraa, Maafushi
INDIAN OCEAN, Rannalhi, Biyadoo, Villivaru, Cocoa I., Guradu & Kandooma
E3, SUVADIVA ATOLL, Fihalhohi, Olhuveli, Bodufinolhu (Fun I.), Rihiveli Beach
EQUATORIAL CHANNEL, FUAH MULAH ATOLL
Gan, ADDU ATOLL

EQUATOR

1000 metres / 500 metres / Sea level

200 km / 100 miles
30 km / 15 miles

SEYCHELLES

See page 24 for general map

MAP F

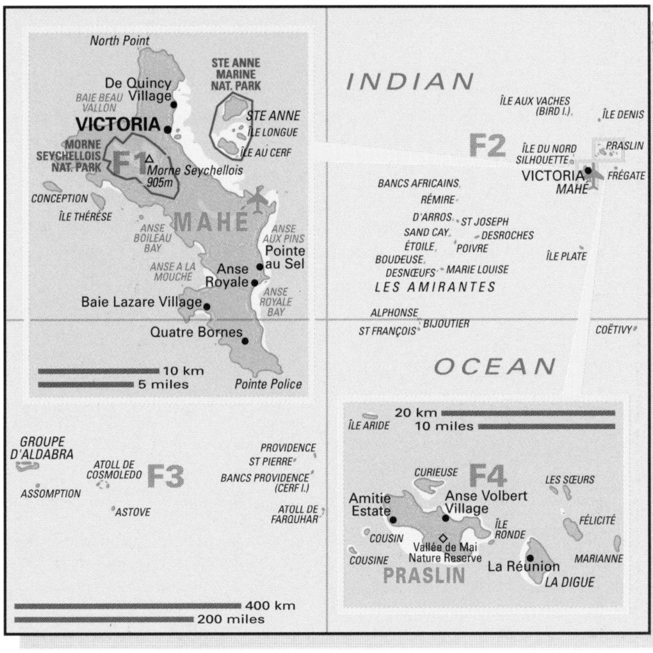

North Point, De Quincy Village, STE ANNE MARINE NAT. PARK, INDIAN
BAIE BEAU VALLON, VICTORIA, STE ANNE, ÎLE LONGUE, ÎLE AUX VACHES (BIRD I.), ÎLE DENIS
MORNE SEYCHELLOIS NAT. PARK, ÎLE AU CERF, F2, ÎLE DU NORD, SILHOUETTE, PRASLIN
CONCEPTION, ÎLE THÉRÈSE, Morne Seychellois 905m, MAHÉ, VICTORIA, MAHÉ, FRÉGATE
F1, ANSE BOILEAU BAY, ANSE A LA MOUCHE, Pointe au Sel, BANCS AFRICAINS, RÉMIRE, D'ARROS, ST JOSEPH, SAND CAY, DESROCHES
Baie Lazare Village, Anse Royale, ANSE ROYALE BAY, ÉTOILE, POIVRE, BOUDEUSE, DESNŒUFS, MARIE LOUISE, ÎLE PLATE
Quatre Bornes, Pointe Police, LES AMIRANTES, ALPHONSE, ST FRANÇOIS, BIJOUTIER, COËTIVY
GROUPE D'ALDABRA, ATOLL DE COSMOLEDO, F3, PROVIDENCE, ST PIERRE, BANCS PROVIDENCE (CERF I.), OCEAN
ASSOMPTION, ASTOVE, ATOLL DE FARQUHAR, ÎLE ARIDE, CURIEUSE, LES SŒURS
AMITIÉ ESTATE, Anse Volbert Village, ÎLE RONDE, FÉLICITÉ, COUSIN, Vallée de Mai Nature Reserve, MARIANNE
COUSINE, La Réunion, LA DIGUE, PRASLIN, F4

10 km / 5 miles
20 km / 10 miles
400 km / 200 miles

▶ Leisure park   ▶ Zoo / animal park   ▶ Major tennis venue

CHINA

See pages 28, 29 & 31 for general maps
China takes over administration of Macau in December 1999

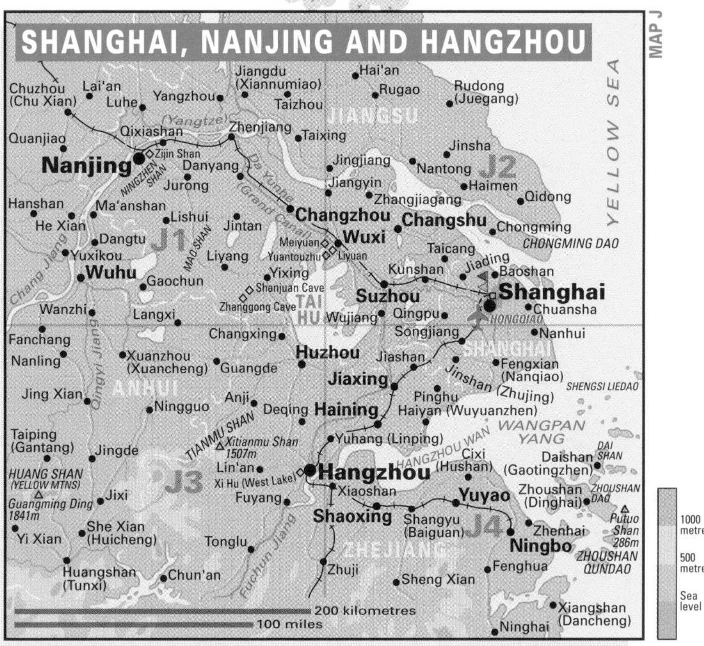

MALAYSIA   SINGAPORE   VIETNAM

INDOCHINA

See page 31 for general map

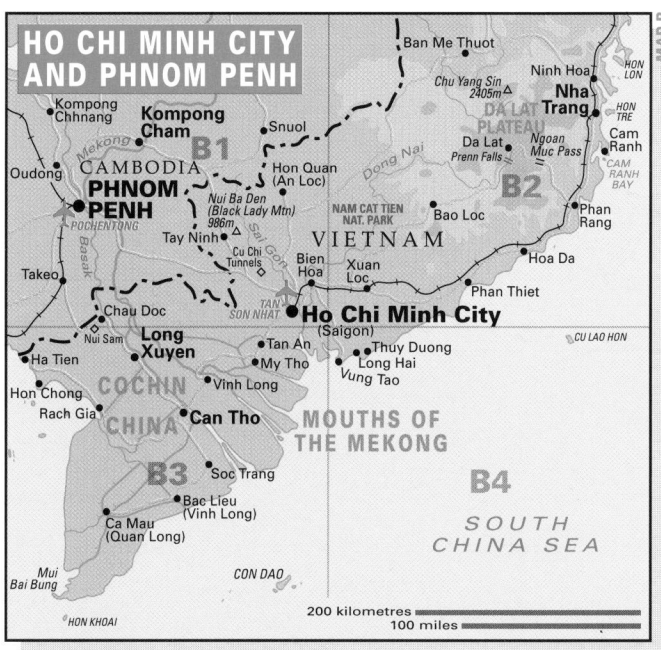

HO CHI MINH CITY AND PHNOM PENH

PENANG

KUALA LUMPUR

SINGAPORE

▶ Leisure park   ▶ Zoo / animal park   ▶ Aquarium   ▶ Major tennis venue

THAILAND

See page 31 for general map

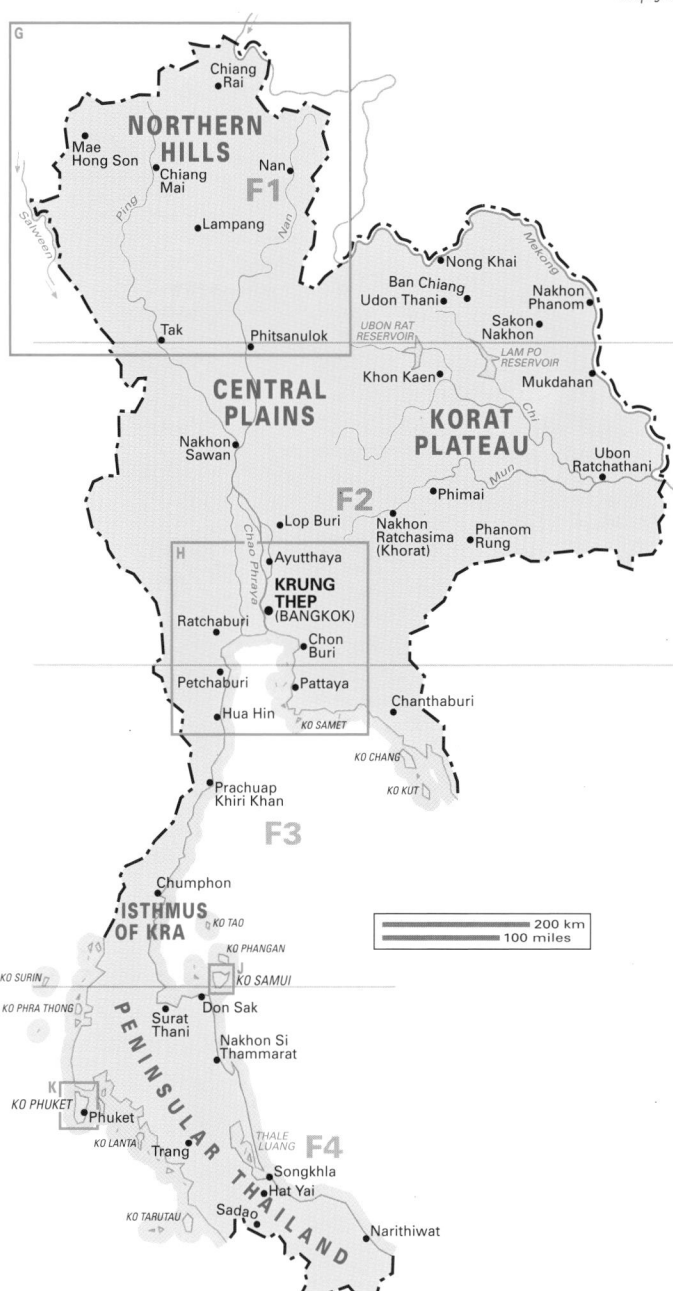

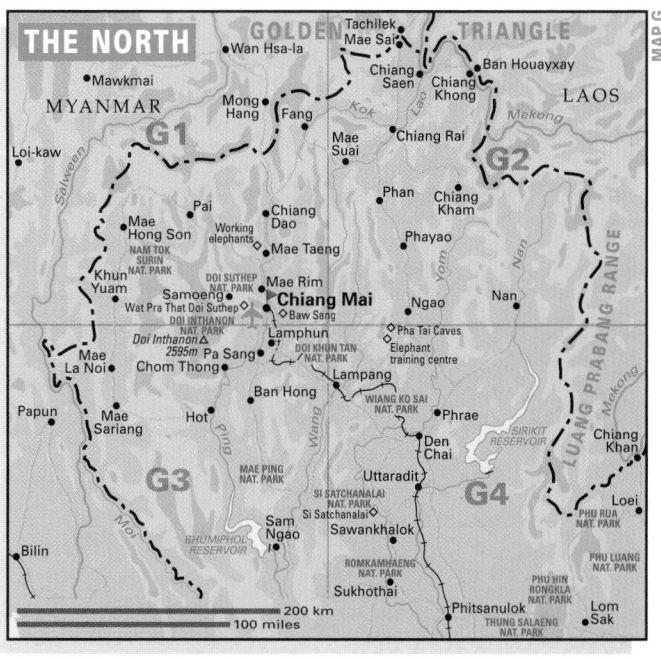

THE NORTH

BANGKOK

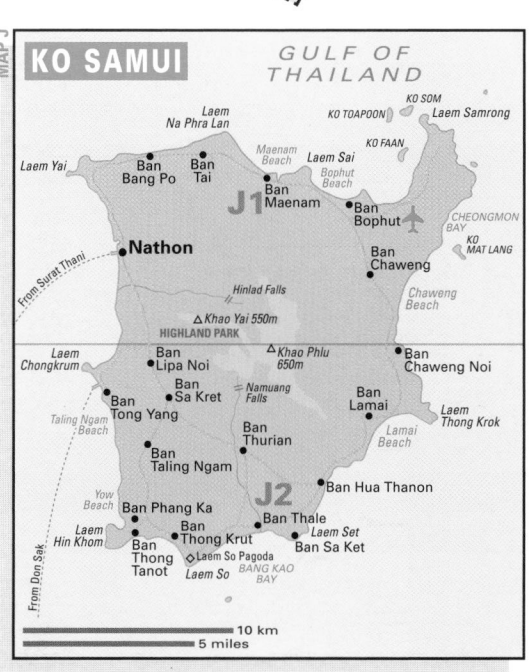

KO SAMUI

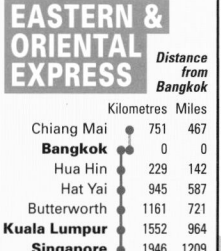

EASTERN & ORIENTAL EXPRESS

	Distance from Bangkok	
	Kilometres	Miles
Chiang Mai	751	467
Bangkok	0	0
Hua Hin	229	142
Hat Yai	945	587
Butterworth	1161	721
Kuala Lumpur	1552	964
Singapore	1946	1209

The Eastern & Oriental Express is a luxury train service connecting Thailand, Malaysia and Singapore. The journey takes two days. An overnight service to Chiang Mai is also available.

For further information, contact:

Venice-Simplon-Orient-Express Ltd., Sea Containers House, 20 Upper Ground, London SE1 9PF, United Kingdom. Tel. +44 (0) 171 928 6000.

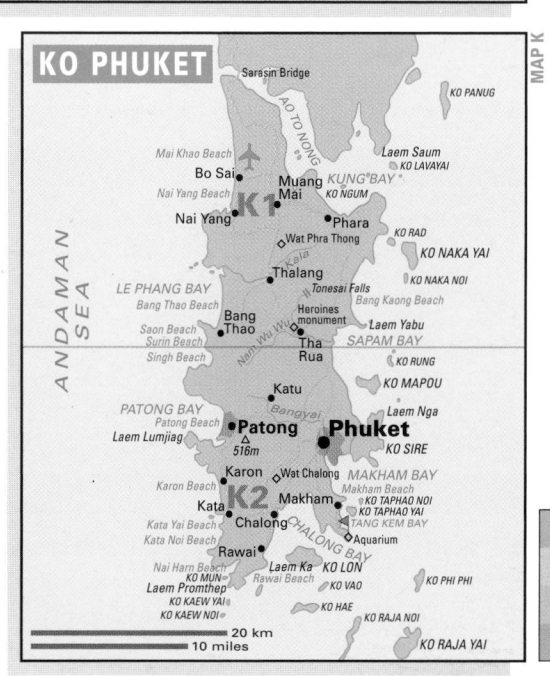

KO PHUKET

▸ Leisure park   ▸ Zoo / animal park   ▸ Aquarium   ▸ Major tennis venue

INDONESIA

See page 32 for general maps

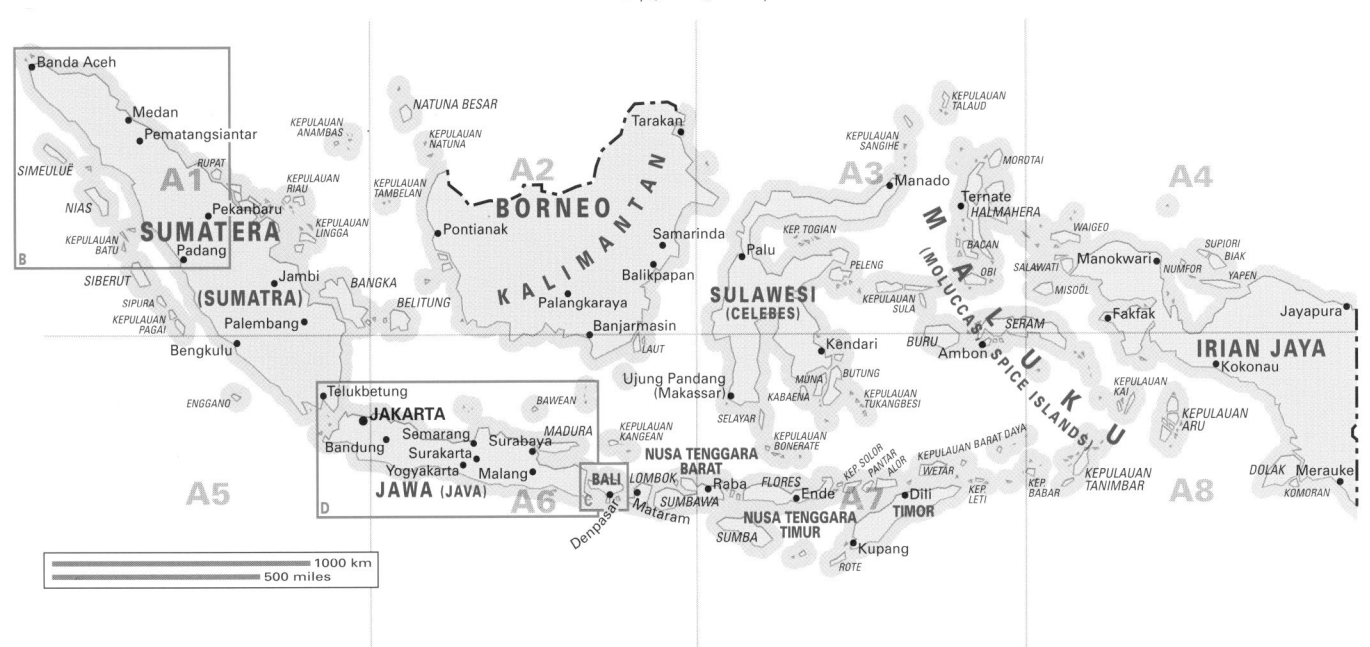

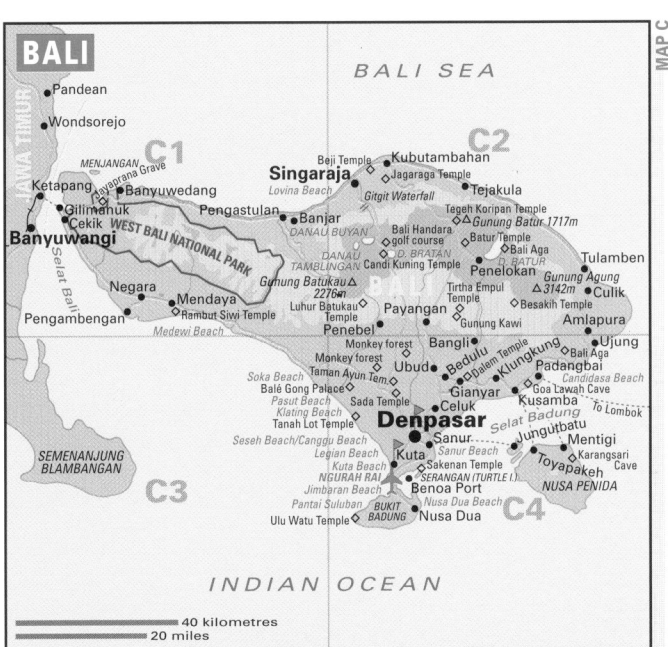

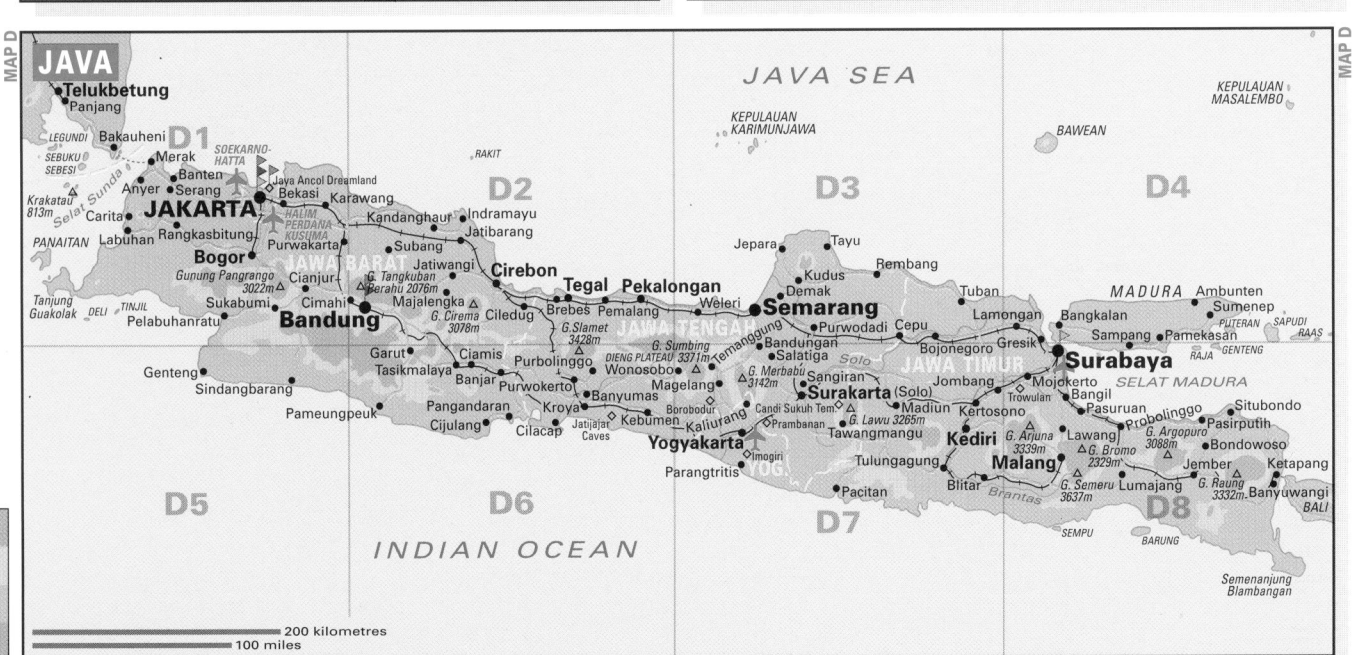

AUSTRALIA

See page 34 for general map

state/territory boundary
○ state/territory capital

1000 km
500 miles

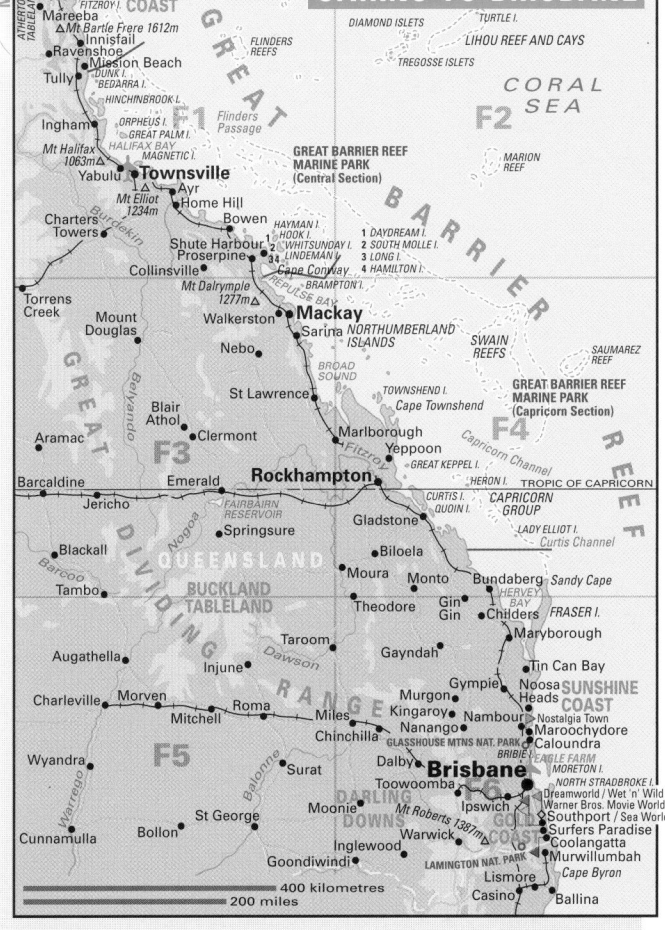

CAIRNS TO BRISBANE

400 kilometres
200 miles

SYDNEY TO MELBOURNE

300 kilometres
150 miles

1000 metres
500 metres
Sea level

▶ Leisure park   ▶ Zoo / animal park   ▶ Aquarium   ▶ Formula One   ▶ Horse racing   ▶ Major tennis venue

AUSTRALIA
See page 34 for general map

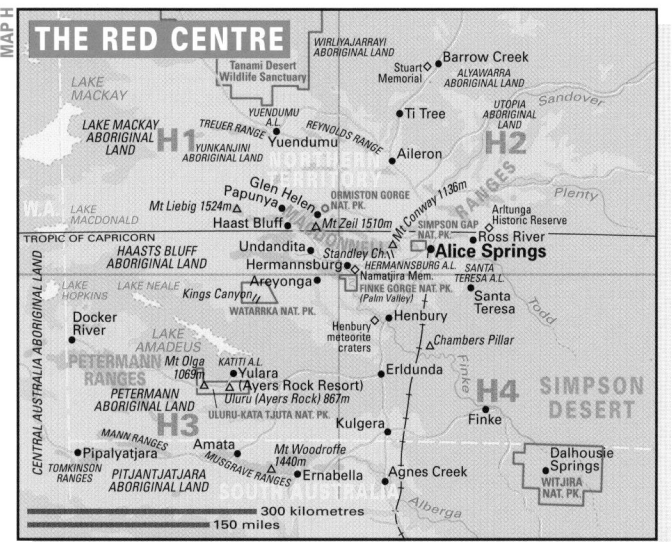

THE RED CENTRE

MAP H

LAKE MACKAY
LAKE MACKAY ABORIGINAL LAND
H1
W.A.
LAKE MACDONALD
TREUER RANGE
Tanami Desert Wildlife Sanctuary
WIRLIYAJARRAYI ABORIGINAL LAND
Stuart Memorial
Barrow Creek
ALYAWARRA ABORIGINAL LAND
YUENDUMU A.L.
Yuendumu
REYNOLDS RANGE
Ti Tree
UTOPIA ABORIGINAL LAND
Sandover
YUNKANJINI ABORIGINAL LAND
Aileron
H2
Plenty
Glen Helen
Papunya
Mt Liebig 1524m△
Haast Bluff
ORMISTON GORGE NAT. PK.
Mt Zeil 1510m△
Mt Conway 1136m
Arltunga Historic Reserve
SIMPSON GAP NAT. PK.
Ross River
TROPIC OF CAPRICORN
HAASTS BLUFF ABORIGINAL LAND
Undandita
Standley Ch.
Hermannsburg
HERMANNSBURG A.L.
Alice Springs
Namatjira Mem.
SANTA TERESA A.L.
LAKE HOPKINS
LAKE NEALE
Areyonga
Kings Canyon
FINKE GORGE NAT. PK. (Palm Valley)
Henbury
Santa Teresa
Todd
Docker River
LAKE AMADEUS
WATARRKA NAT. PK.
Henbury meteorite craters
Erldunda
SIMPSON DESERT
PETERMANN RANGES
Mt Olga 1069m△
KATITI A.L.
△ (Ayers Rock Resort)
Uluru-Kata Tjuta NAT. PK.
Uluru (Ayers Rock) 867m
Kulgera
Chambers Pillar
H4
CENTRAL AUSTRALIA ABORIGINAL LAND
MANN RANGES
Pipalyatjara
PETERMANN ABORIGINAL LAND
H3
Amata
Mt Woodroffe 1440m△
MUSGRAVE RANGES
Finke
Finke
TOMKINSON RANGES
PITJANTJATJARA ABORIGINAL LAND
Ernabella
Agnes Creek
Dalhousie Springs
WITJIRA NAT. PK.
SOUTH AUSTRALIA
Alberga
300 kilometres
150 miles

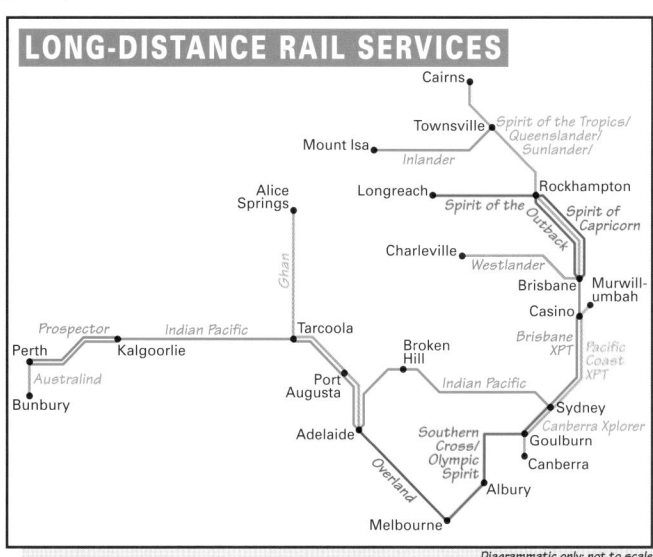

LONG-DISTANCE RAIL SERVICES

Cairns
Townsville
Spirit of the Tropics/ Queenslander/ Sunlander/
Mount Isa
Inlander
Alice Springs
Longreach
Rockhampton
Spirit of the Outback
Spirit of Capricorn
Ghan
Charleville
Westlander
Brisbane
Murwill-umbah
Casino
Brisbane XPT
Pacific Coast XPT
Prospector
Indian Pacific
Tarcoola
Broken Hill
Perth
Kalgoorlie
Australind
Port Augusta
Indian Pacific
Sydney
Canberra Xplorer
Bunbury
Adelaide
Goulburn
Canberra
Southern Cross/ Olympic Spirit
Albury
Overland
Melbourne

Diagrammatic only: not to scale

NEW ZEALAND
See page 35 for general map

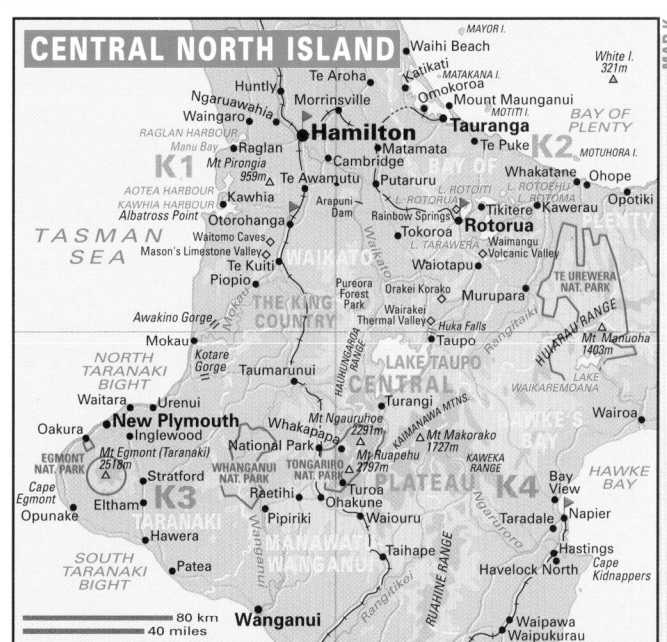

CENTRAL NORTH ISLAND

MAP K

MAYOR I.
Waihi Beach
Te Aroha
Katikati
MATAKANA I.
White I. 321m
Huntly
Ngaruawahia
Morrinsville
Omokoroa
Mount Maunganui
MOTITI I.
Waingaro
RAGLAN HARBOUR
Hamilton
Tauranga
BAY OF PLENTY
Manu Bay
Raglan
Mt Pirongia 959m
Matamata
Te Puke
K2
MOTUHORA I.
K1
Cambridge
Whakatane
Te Awamutu
Putaruru
Ohope
AOTEA HARBOUR
Kawhia
Arapuni Dam
L. ROTOITI
L. ROTOEHU
Opotiki
KAWHIA HARBOUR
Rainbow Springs
L. ROTORUA
Tikitere
Kawerau
Albatross Point
Otorohanga
Tokoroa
Rotorua
L. ROTOMA
TASMAN SEA
Waitomo Caves
Mason's Limestone Valley
Waimangu Volcanic Valley
TE UREWERA NAT. PARK
Te Kuiti
Pureora Forest Park
Orakei Korako
Waiotapu
Piopio
Wairakei Thermal Valley
Murupara
THE KING COUNTRY
Huka Falls
Mt Manuoha 1403m
Awakino Gorge
Mokau
Kotare Gorge
Taupo
HUIARAU RANGE
NORTH TARANAKI BIGHT
Waitara
Urenui
Taumarunui
LAKE TAUPO
LAKE WAIKAREMOANA
Oakura
New Plymouth
Inglewood
National Park
Mt Ngauruhoe 2291m
Turangi
CENTRAL
KAIMANAWA MTNS.
HAWKE'S
Whakapapa
Mt Makorako 1727m
Wairoa
EGMONT NAT. PARK
Mt Egmont (Taranaki) 2518m
Stratford
TONGARIRO NAT. PARK
Mt Ruapehu 2797m
KAWEKA RANGE
Cape Egmont
Raetihi
Turoa
Ohakune
Waiouru
Bay View
Napier
Opunake
Eltham
Pipiriki
Taihape
Havelock North
Hastings
Hawera
PLATEAU
K4
Cape Kidnappers
Patea
RUAHINE RANGE
SOUTH TARANAKI BIGHT
MANAWATU WANGANUI
Waipawa
Waipukurau
Wanganui
Rangitikei
80 km
40 miles

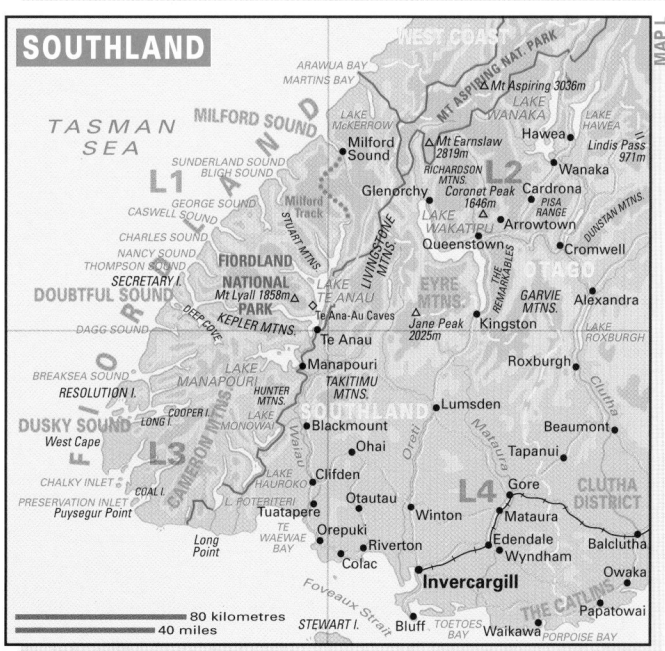

SOUTHLAND

WEST COAST
MT ASPIRING NAT. PARK
ARAWUA BAY
MARTINS BAY
Mt Aspiring 3036m
LAKE WANAKA
TASMAN SEA
MILFORD SOUND
LAKE McKERROW
Hawea
LAKE HAWEA
Milford Sound
Mt Earnslaw 2819m
RICHARDSON MTNS.
Lindis Pass 971m
SUNDERLAND SOUND
BLIGH SOUND
Glenorchy
Coronet Peak 1646m
Cardrona
Wanaka
GEORGE SOUND
STUART MTNS.
PISA RANGE
CASWELL SOUND
LIVINGSTONE MTNS.
LAKE WAKATIPU
L2
Arrowtown
DUNSTAN MTNS.
CHARLES SOUND
NANCY SOUND
THOMPSON SOUND
FIORDLAND NATIONAL PARK
Mt Lyall 1858m
THE REMARKABLES
EYRE MTNS.
OTAGO
Queenstown
Cromwell
SECRETARY I.
Te Ana-Au Caves
Jane Peak 2025m
Kingston
Alexandra
DOUBTFUL SOUND
DEEP COVE
KEPLER MTNS.
LAKE TE ANAU
GARVIE MTNS.
DAGG SOUND
Te Anau
Roxburgh
LAKE ROXBURGH
BREAKSEA SOUND
LAKE MANAPOURI
Manapouri
HUNTER MTNS.
TAKITIMU MTNS.
Lumsden
Beaumont
RESOLUTION I.
Blackmount
Tapanui
DUSKY SOUND
LONG I.
LAKE MONOWAI
SOUTHLAND
Gore
West Cape
Ohai
CLUTHA DISTRICT
COOPER I.
Clifden
Otautau
Winton
Mataura
CHALKY INLET
COAL I.
LAKE HAUROKO
L. POTERITERI
Tuatapere
Orepuki
Clinton
Edendale
Wyndham
Balclutha
PRESERVATION INLET
Puysegur Point
Riverton
Colac
Invercargill
Owaka
Long Point
TE WAEWAE BAY
Foveaux Strait
Bluff
THE CATLINS
Waikawa
Papatowai
1000 metres
500 metres
Sea level
STEWART I.
TOETOES BAY
PORPOISE BAY
80 kilometres
40 miles

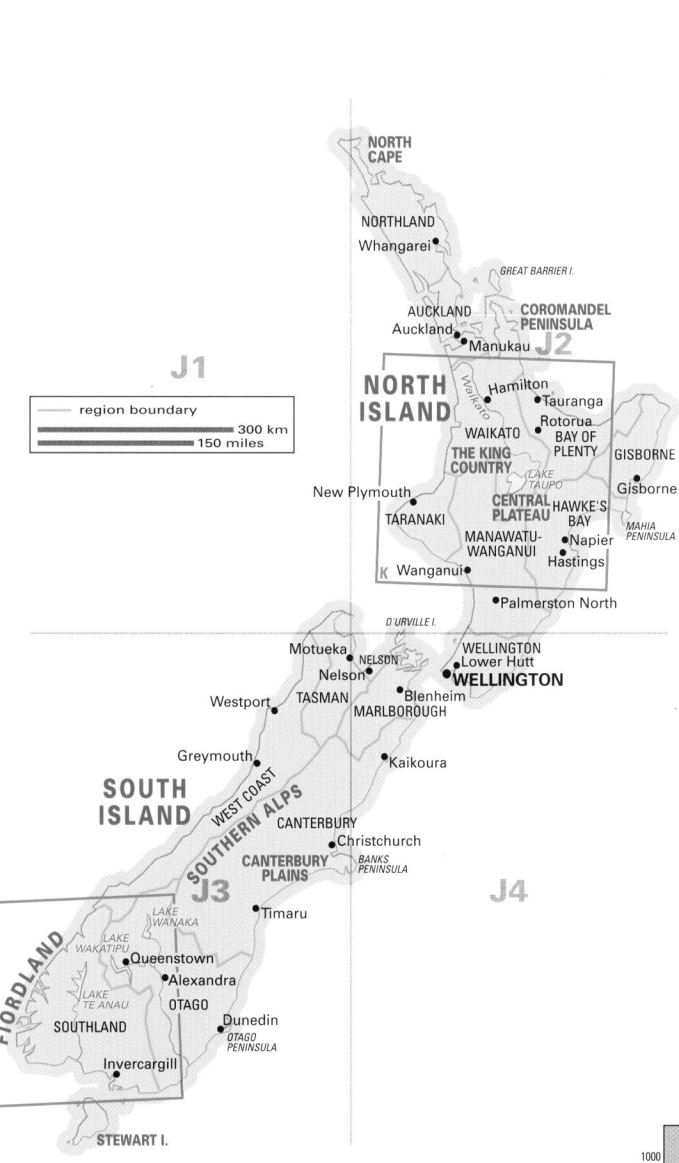

J1

region boundary
300 km
150 miles

NORTH CAPE
NORTHLAND
Whangarei
GREAT BARRIER I.
AUCKLAND
Auckland
Manukau
COROMANDEL PENINSULA
J2
NORTH ISLAND
Waikato
Hamilton
Tauranga
Rotorua
BAY OF PLENTY
WAIKATO
THE KING COUNTRY
GISBORNE
LAKE TAUPO
New Plymouth
Gisborne
CENTRAL PLATEAU
HAWKE'S BAY
TARANAKI
MAHIA PENINSULA
MANAWATU-WANGANUI
Napier
Wanganui
Hastings
Palmerston North
D'URVILLE I.
Motueka
WELLINGTON
NELSON
Lower Hutt
Nelson
WELLINGTON
Westport
TASMAN
Blenheim
MARLBOROUGH
Greymouth
Kaikoura
SOUTH ISLAND
WEST COAST
SOUTHERN ALPS
CANTERBURY
CANTERBURY PLAINS
Christchurch
BANKS PENINSULA
J3
J4
FIORDLAND
LAKE WANAKA
Timaru
Queenstown
LAKE TE ANAU
Alexandra
SOUTHLAND
OTAGO
Dunedin
OTAGO PENINSULA
Invercargill
STEWART I.

▶ Zoo / animal park   ▶ Aquarium

TEMPERATURE CONVERSION

°Celsius	−10	0	10	20	30	40
°Fahrenheit	14	32	50	68	86	104

RAINFALL CONVERSION

Millimetres	102	203	305	406	508	610
Inches	4	8	12	16	20	24

CLIMATE

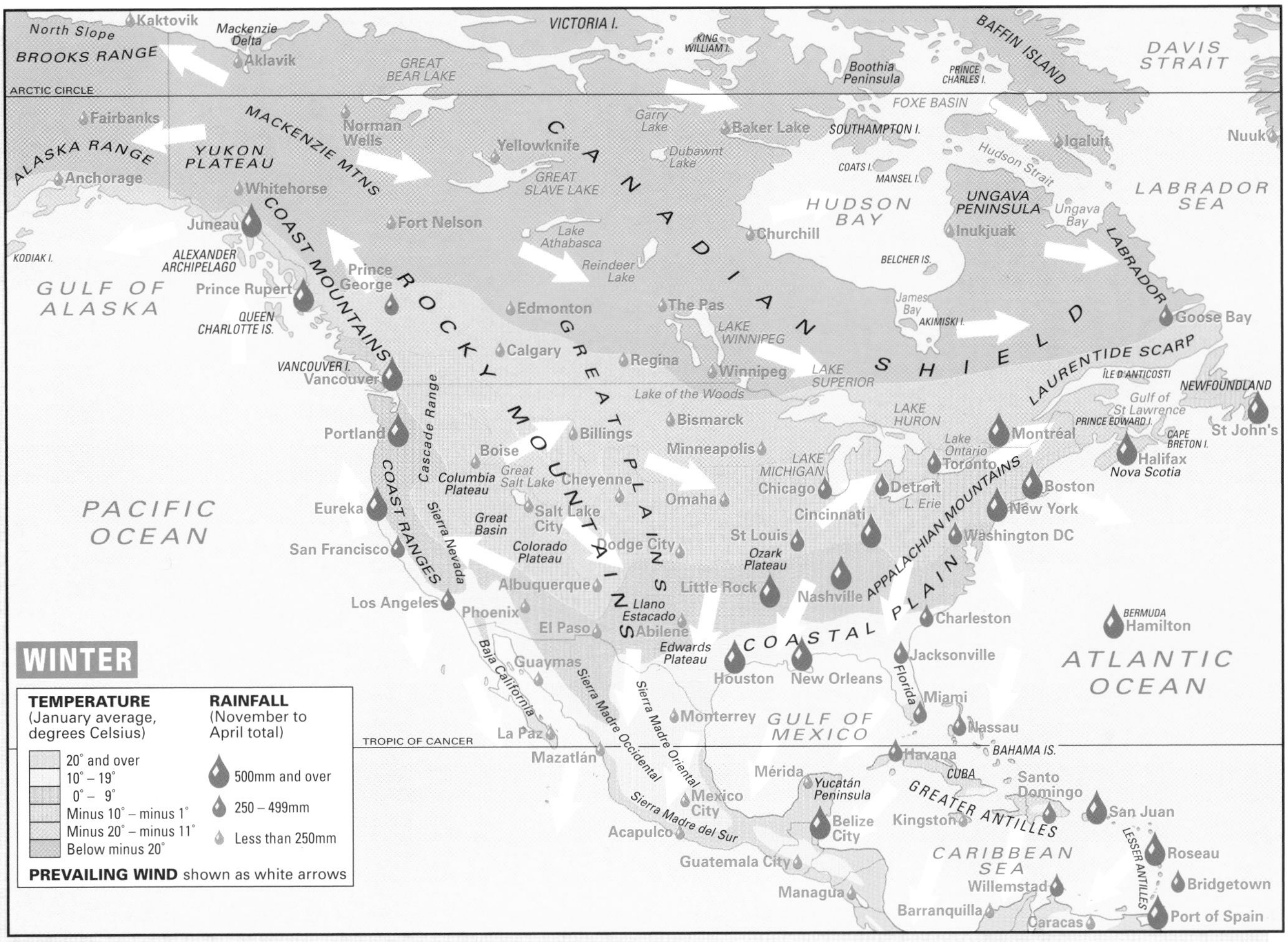

WINTER

TEMPERATURE
(January average, degrees Celsius)

- 20° and over
- 10° – 19°
- 0° – 9°
- Minus 10° – minus 1°
- Minus 20° – minus 11°
- Below minus 20°

RAINFALL
(November to April total)

- 500mm and over
- 250 – 499mm
- Less than 250mm

PREVAILING WIND shown as white arrows

The Columbus Press *World Travel Guide* contains detailed climate charts for every country in the world, including temperature, rainfall, sunshine and humidity. For more information, call +44 (0) 171 417 0700.

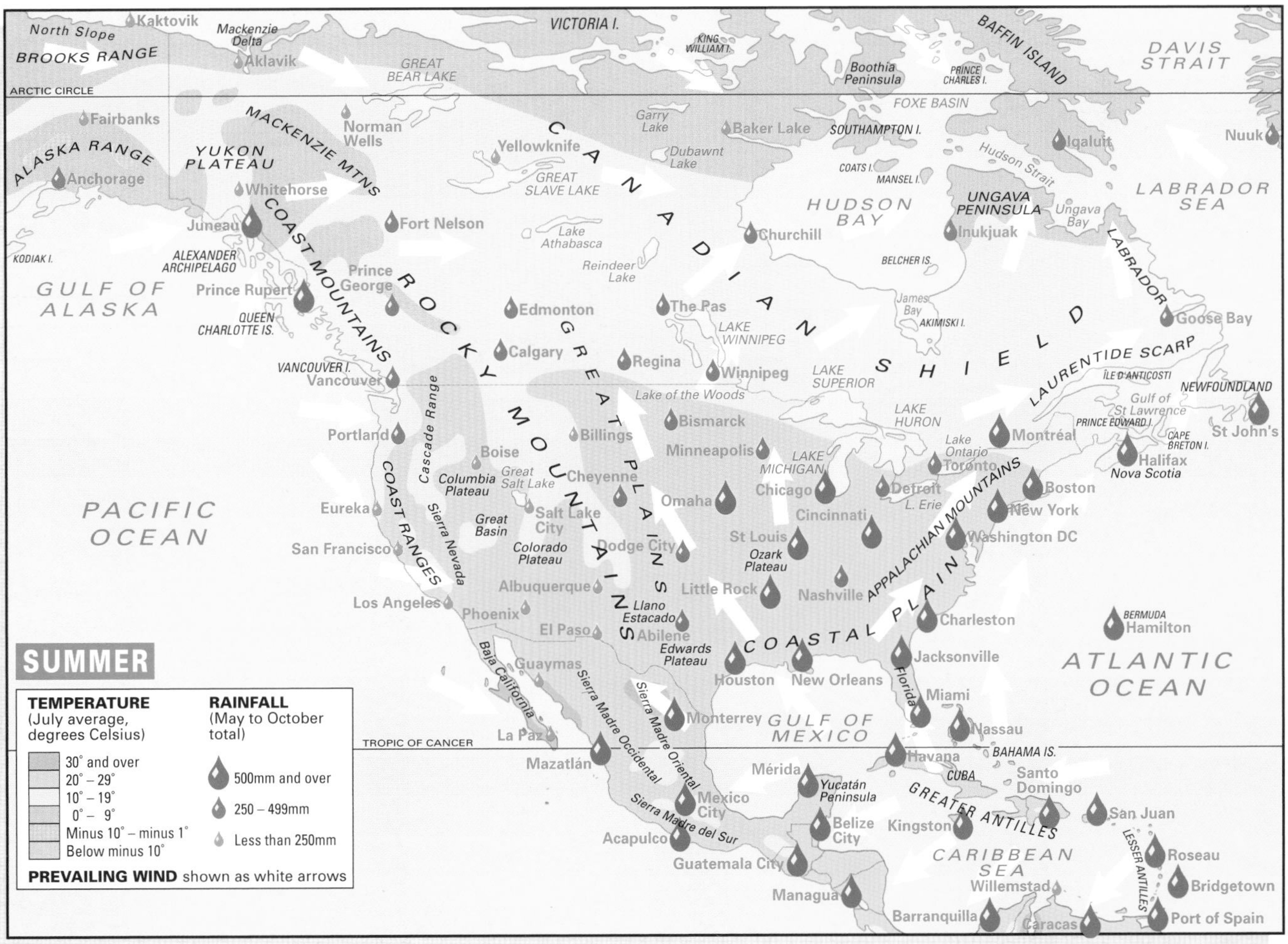

SUMMER

TEMPERATURE
(July average, degrees Celsius)

- 30° and over
- 20° – 29°
- 10° – 19°
- 0° – 9°
- Minus 10° – minus 1°
- Below minus 10°

RAINFALL
(May to October total)

- 500mm and over
- 250 – 499mm
- Less than 250mm

PREVAILING WIND shown as white arrows

CANADA   UNITED STATES

RAILWAYS AND AIRPORTS

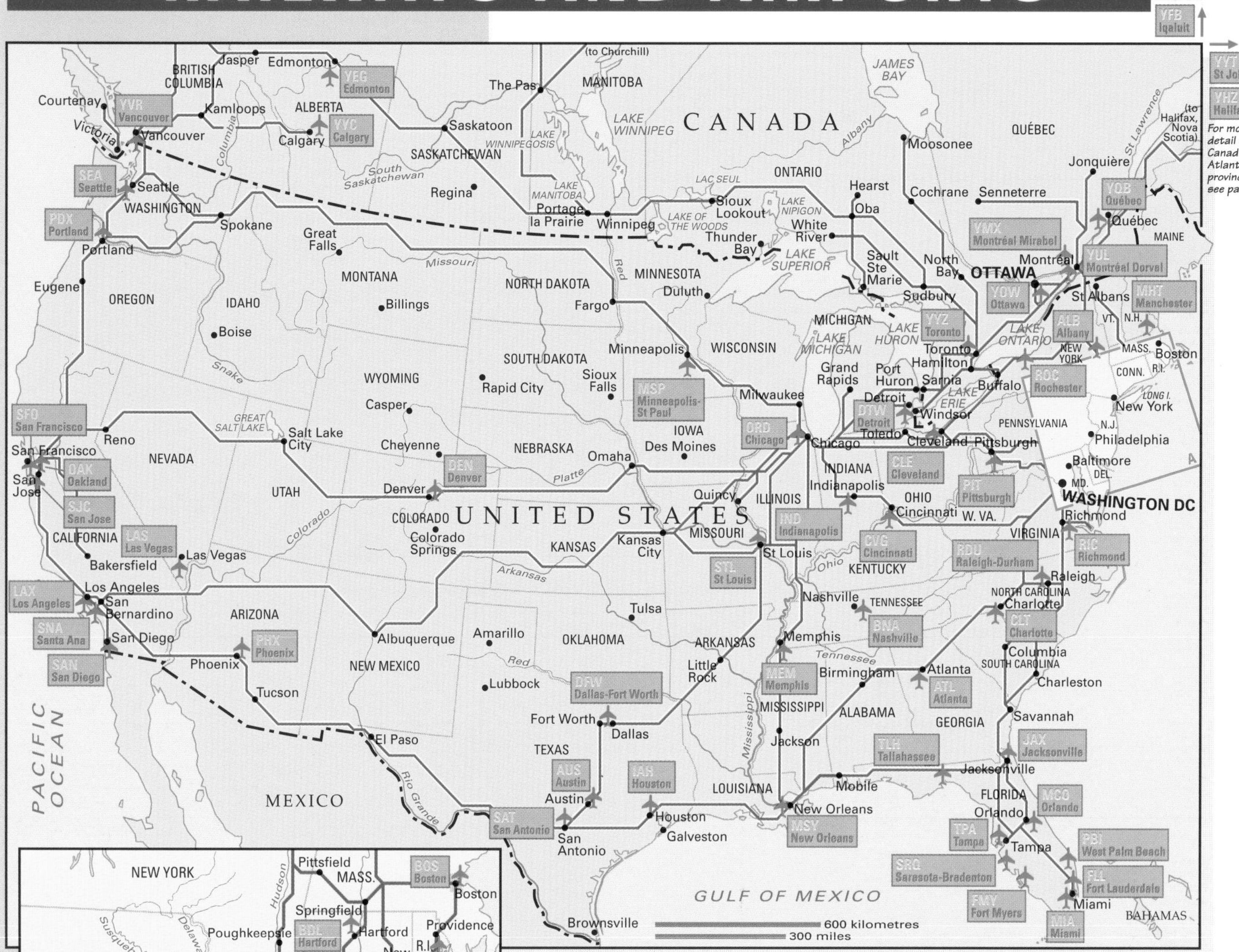

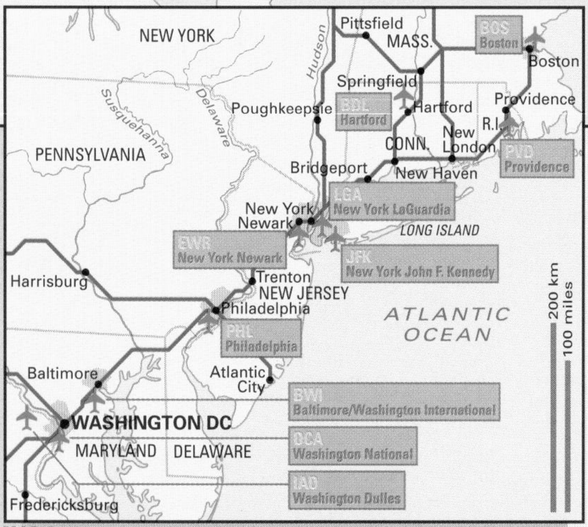

(map of North America showing railways and airports, with inset maps: MAP A – northeastern US; Hawaii; Alaska)

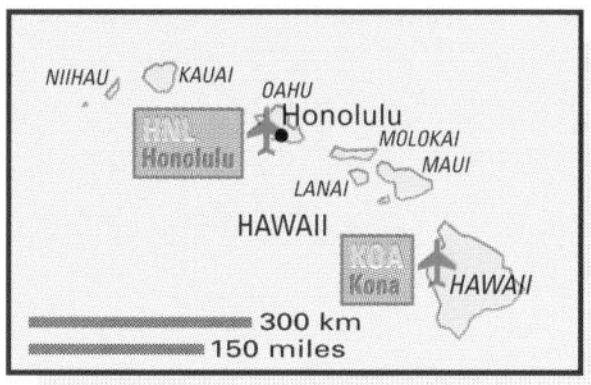

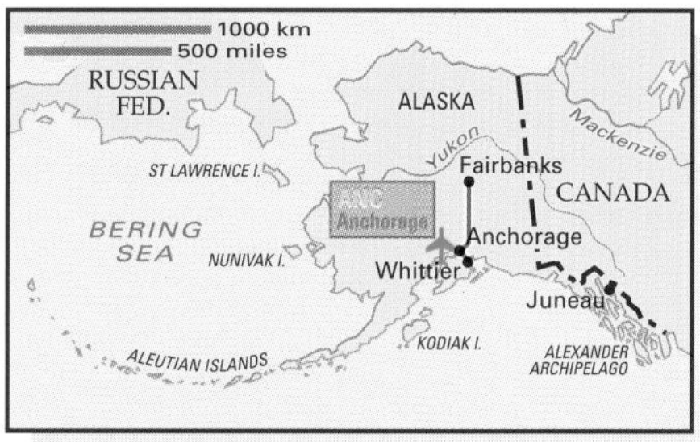

AIR: This map shows the major US and Canadian airports with international direct flights. Deregulation of the route licencing system has seen the rapid growth of these routes, avoiding the traditional gateways of New York and Toronto. North American airlines have developed, for marketing and economic reasons, regional hubs where passengers can make convenient inter-flight connections. The table opposite provides a comprehensive guide to the countries which these airports offer direct flights to or from.

All scheduled passenger flights to international destinations, licensed as at June 1998, are included. Periods of operation or service are not indicated. Commercial or other considerations may result in services being suspended or withdrawn at short notice. Please check with the appropriate airport and/or airline to confirm details of flights. During the winter period additional services to winter resort destinations are scheduled.

Flights between the US and Canada have not been included in the list. Airports operating flights solely between Canada, the United States and Mexico (for example Tucson airport) are also not shown.

Where cities have more than one airport, the individual airport code is used. For example, New York City code is NYC, but the airport codes are:

John F. Kennedy   JFK
LaGuardia   LGA
Newark International   EWR

RAIL: The map also shows the main passenger routes in the US and Canada. The transcontinental services are provided by Amtrak in the US and by VIA Rail in Canada. Services on these routes vary considerably in terms of times and days of operation so details should be obtained from the appropriate rail companies. The principal long-distance services are shown on the right.

These routes are supplemented by interurban and suburban rail services and in addition there is a comprehensive network of long-distance buses.

LONG-DISTANCE RAIL SERVICES

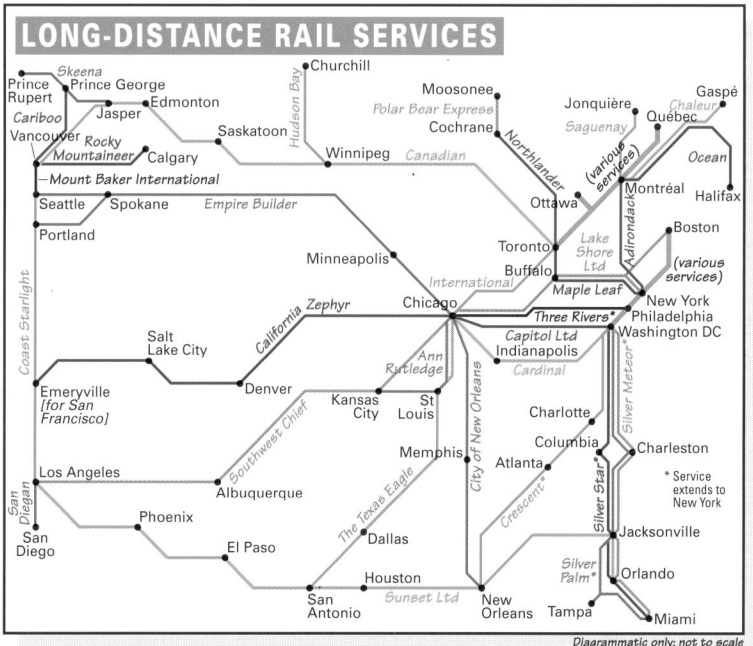

Diagrammatic only: not to scale

CANADA UNITED STATES

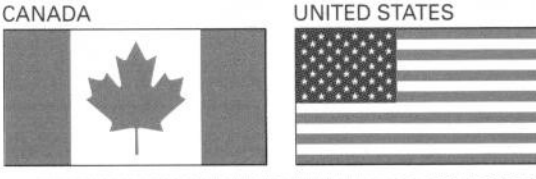

AIRPORTS

This table shows the number of airports in each country with direct connections from individual US or Canadian airports, licensed as of June 1998. Code-sharing routes (where passengers need to change aircraft) are not included. In general, at least one route is to the international airport/s serving the country's capital (see page viii). Figures are in red where this is NOT the case.

Column headers

CANADA: YEG Edmonton · YFB Iqaluit · YHZ Halifax · YMX Montréal Mirabel · YOW Ottawa · YQB Québec · YUL Montréal Dorval · YVR Vancouver · YYC Calgary · YYT St John's · YYZ Toronto

UNITED STATES: ALB Albany · ANC Anchorage · ATL Atlanta · AUS Austin · BDL Hartford · BNA Nashville · BOS Boston · BWI Baltimore / Washington Int. · CLE Cleveland · CLT Charlotte · CVG Cincinnati · DCA Washington National · DEN Denver · DFW Dallas-Fort Worth · DTW Detroit · EWR New York Newark · FLL Fort Lauderdale · FMY Fort Myers · HNL Honolulu · IAD Washington Dulles · IAH Houston · IND Indianapolis · JAX Jacksonville · JFK New York John F. Kennedy · KOA Kona, Hawaii · LAS Las Vegas · LAX Los Angeles · LGA New York LaGuardia · MCO Orlando · MEM Memphis · MHT Manchester · MIA Miami · MSP Minneapolis-St Paul · MSY New Orleans · OAK Oakland · ORD Chicago · PBI West Palm Beach · PDX Portland · PHL Philadelphia · PHX Phoenix · PIT Pittsburgh · PVD Providence · RDU Raleigh-Durham · RIC Richmond · ROC Rochester · SAN San Diego · SAT San Antonio · SEA Seattle · SFO San Francisco · SJC San Jose · SNA Santa Ana · SRQ Sarasota-Bradenton · STL St Louis · TLH Tallahassee · TPA Tampa

IATA AREAS

AREA 1, NORTH ATLANTIC
- Greenland
- Mexico

AREA 1, MID ATLANTIC
- Antigua & Barbuda
- Aruba
- Bahamas
- Barbados
- Belize
- Bermuda
- Bolivia
- Bonaire
- Cayman Is.
- Colombia
- Costa Rica
- Cuba
- Curaçao
- Dominican Republic
- Ecuador
- El Salvador
- French Guiana
- Grenada
- Guadeloupe
- Guatemala
- Guyana
- Haiti
- Honduras
- Jamaica
- Martinique
- Nicaragua
- Panama
- Peru
- Puerto Rico
- St Lucia
- St Maarten
- Trinidad & Tobago
- Turks & Caicos Is.
- Venezuela

AREA 1, SOUTH ATLANTIC
- Argentina
- Brazil
- Chile
- Paraguay
- Uruguay

AREA 2, EUROPE
- Austria
- Azores
- Belgium
- Bulgaria
- Czech Republic
- Denmark
- Finland
- France
- Germany*
- Greece
- Hungary
- Iceland
- Ireland
- Italy
- Luxembourg
- Morocco
- Netherlands
- Norway
- Poland
- Portugal
- Romania
- Russian Fed. (Europe)
- Spain
- Sweden
- Switzerland
- Turkey
- Ukraine
- United Kingdom

AREA 2, MIDDLE EAST
- Israel
- Jordan
- Kuwait
- Saudi Arabia
- United Arab Emirates

AREA 2, AFRICA
- Côte d'Ivoire
- Egypt
- Ghana
- Senegal
- South Africa†

AREA 3, ASIA
- Bangladesh
- China
- Guam
- India
- Indonesia
- Japan
- Kiribati (E)
- Korea, Republic of
- Malaysia
- Marshall Is.
- Micronesia, Fed. States
- Pakistan
- Philippines
- Russian Fed. (Asia)
- Singapore
- Taiwan
- Thailand
- Uzbekistan

AREA 3, SOUTHWEST PACIFIC
- American Samoa
- Australia
- Cook Is.
- Fiji
- French Polynesia (SW)
- Kiribati (W)
- New Zealand
- Tonga
- Western Samoa

For the purposes of this table: *Bonn is regarded as Germany's sole capital. † Pretoria is regarded as South Africa's sole capital.

CANADA UNITED STATES

SKIING

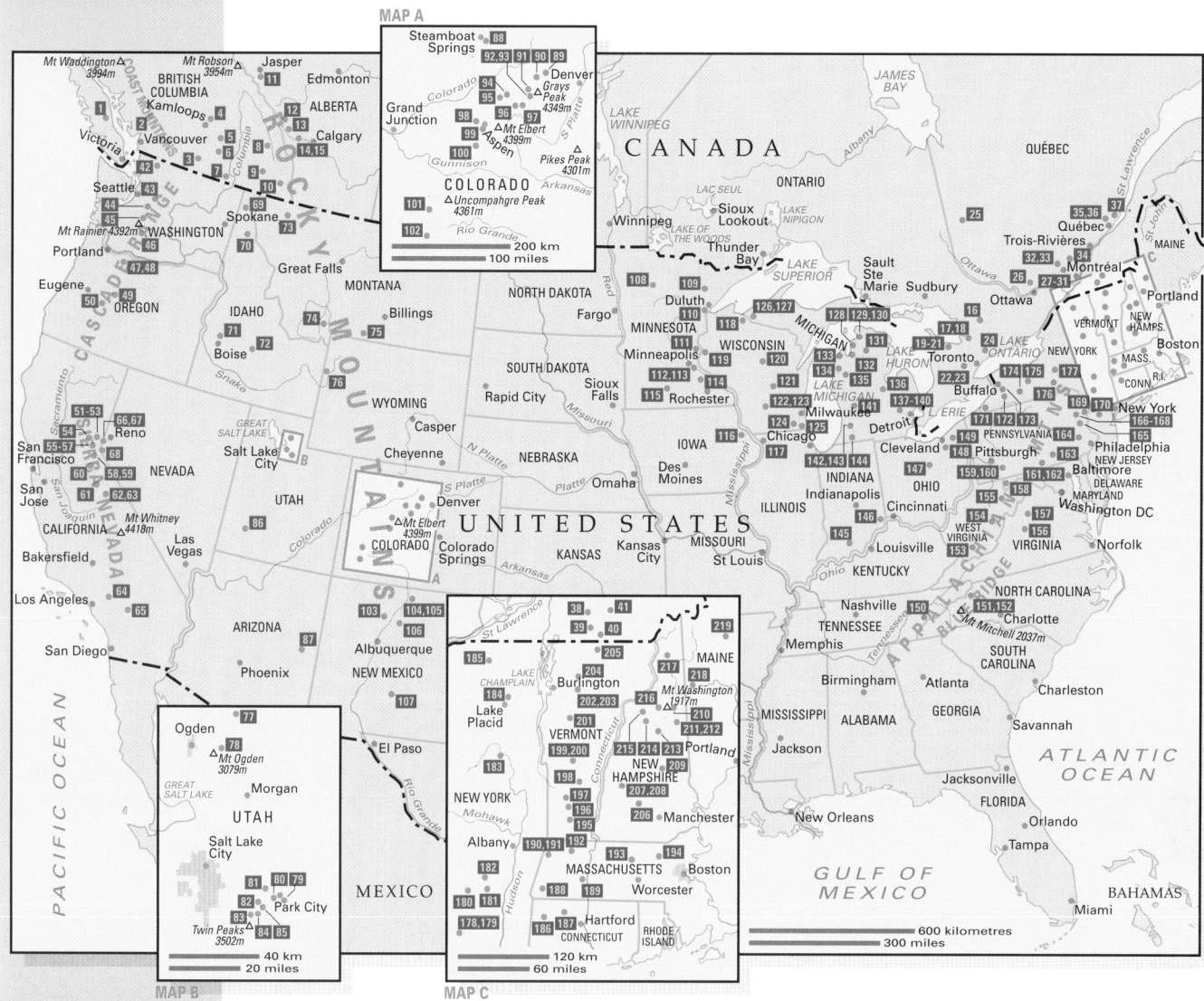

This map shows the major US and Canadian ski resorts (excluding Alaska). All the resorts listed report access to ski lifts with a capacity of at least 6,000 skiers per hour (as at September 1997), with the exception of those marked with an asterisk (*), which are included because of their significance.

Resorts without slopeside accommodation are shown in italics.

Data compiled by Snow-Hunter Ltd., all rights reserved.
Fax: +44 (0) 1463 741273.
email: patrick@snowhunt.
demon.co.uk

Resort altitude:
□ 2,500 metres or above
□ 500 – 2,499 metres
No black square: under 500 metres

Skier uplift:
■ 40,000 skiers per hour or more
■ 25,000 – 39,999 skiers per hour
■ 10,000 – 24,999 skiers per hour
No colour: Less than 10,000

Altitude at top of highest ski run:
● 3,000 metres or above
○ 1,000 – 2,999 metres
No black circle: under 1,000 metres

Maximum vertical drop:
● 1,000 metres or more
● 750 – 999 metres
● 500 – 749 metres
No colour: Less than 500 metres

Canada

British Columbia
1 Mount Washington
2 Whistler & Blackcomb
3 Apex
4 Sun Peaks (formerly Tod Mountain)
5 Silver Star
6 Big White
7 *Red Mountain*
8 Panorama
9 Kimberley
10 Fernie Snow Valley

Alberta
11 *Marmot Basin (Jasper)*
12 *Lake Louise (Banff)*
13 Sunshine Village (Banff)
14 *Fortress Mountain*
15 Nakiska

Ontario
16 *Sir Sam's*
17 *Mount St Louis / Moonstone*
18 *Ski Snow Valley*
19 *Beaver Valley*
20 Blue Mountain
21 *Talisman*
22 *Caledon*
23 *Glen Eden*
24 *Ski Dagmar*

Québec
25 *Mont Video*
26 *Edelweiss Valley*
27 *Mont Gabriel*
28 *Mont Olympia*
29 *Mont Ste Sauveur*
30 *Ski le Chantecler*
31 *Ski Morin Heights*
32 *Mont Blanc*
33 Tremblant
34 *Val St Come*
35 Mont Ste Anne
36 *Le Relais*
37 Stoneham
38 *Bromont*
39 *Mont Sutton*
40 *Owl's Head*
41 Mont Orford

United States

Washington
42 *Mount Baker*
43 *Stevens Pass*
44 **The Pass** [Alpental / Hyak / Ski Acres / Snoqualmie]
45 Crystal Mountain

Oregon
46 *White Pass Village*
47 *Mount Hood Meadows*
48 *Timberline*
49 *Mount Bachelor*
50 *Willamette Pass*

California
51 *Donner Ski Ranch*
52 *Northstar-at-Tahoe*
53 *Sugar Bowl*
54 *Boreal*
55 *Alpine Meadows*
56 *Homewood*
57 Squaw Valley (Squaw Creek)
58 Sierra-at-Tahoe
59 *Kirkwood*
60 *Bear Valley*
61 *Dodge Ridge*
62 *June Mountain*
63 Mammoth Mountain
64 *Mountain High*
65 *Snow Summit*

Nevada
66 Diamond Peak
67 *Mount Rose*
68 Heavenly

Idaho
69 *Schweitzer Mountain*
70 *Silver Mountain*
71 *Bogus Basin*
72 Sun Valley

Montana
73 *Big Mountain*
74 Big Sky
75 *Red Lodge Mountain*

Wyoming
76 Jackson Hole, Teton

Utah
77 *Powder Mountain*
78 *Snowbasin*
79 Deer Valley
80 Park City
81 The Canyons (formerly Wolf Mountain and Park West)
82 Solitude
83 Snowbird
84 Alta
85 Brighton
86 *Brian Head*

Arizona
87 Sunrise Park

Colorado
88 Steamboat
89 *Eldora Mountain*

90 Winter Park (Mary Jane)
91 Loveland
92 Arapahoe Basin
93 Keystone
94 Vail
95 Beaver Creek
96 Copper Mountain
97 Breckenridge
98 Snowmass
99 Aspen
100 Crested Butte
101 Telluride
102 Purgatory

New Mexico
103 *Pajarito Mountain*
104 *Red River*
105 Taos
106 *Santa Fe*
107 *Ski Apache*

Minnesota
108 Buena Vista
109 Giants Ridge
110 Spirit Mountain
111 Wild Mountain
112 Afton Alps
113 Buck Hill
114 Welch Village
115 Mount Kato

Iowa
116 Sundown Mountain

Illinois
117 Chestnut Mountain

Wisconsin
118 *Whitecap Mountains*
119 *Trollhaugen*
120 Rib Mountain
121 Nordic Mountain
122 Cascade Mountain
123 Devils Head
124 Alpine Valley
125 Wilmot Mountain

Michigan
126 Big Powderhorn Mountain
127 Indianhead Mountain & Bear Creek
128 Boyne Mountain
129 Boyne Highlands
130 *Nub's Nob*
131 *Treetops / Sylvan*
132 Shanty Creek / Schuss Mountain
133 Caberfae Peaks
134 Sugar Loaf
135 Crystal Mountain

136 *Brintz Apple Mountain*
137 Alpine Valley
138 *Mount Brighton*
139 *Mount Holly*
140 Pine Knob
141 Cannonsburg
142 Bittersweet
143 Timber Ridge
144 Swiss Valley

Indiana
145 Paoli Peaks
146 Perfect North Slopes

Ohio
147 Snow Trails
148 Boston Mills / Brandywine
149 Alpine Valley

Tennessee
150 Ober Gatlinburg

North Carolina
151 Ski Beech Mountain
152 Sugar Mountain

West Virginia
153 Winterplace
154 Snowshoe
155 Canaan Valley

Virginia
156 Wintergreen
157 Massanutten

Maryland
158 Wisp

Pennsylvania
159 Hidden Valley
160 Seven Springs
161 Ski Liberty
162 *Whitetail*
163 Ski Roundtop
164 Doe Mountain
165 Blue Mountain
166 Big Boulder
167 Camelback
168 Jack Frost
169 Shawnee Mountain

New Jersey
170 Vernon Valley

New York
171 Peek'n Peak
172 Holiday Valley
173 Kissing Bridge
174 Swain
175 Bristol Mountain
176 Greek Peak
177 Labrador Mountain
178 Big Vanilla at Davos
179 Holiday Mountain

180 Belleayre
181 Hunter Mountain
182 Ski Windham
183 Gore Mountain
184 Whiteface Mountain
185 Titus Mountain

Connecticut
186 Mohawk Mountain
187 Ski Sundown

Massachusetts
188 Butternut Basin
189 Mount Tom
190 Brodie
191 Jiminy Peak
192 Berkshire East
193 Wachusett Mountain
194 Nashoba Valley

Vermont
195 Mount Snow (Haystack / Carinthia)
196 Stratton
197 Bromley Mountain
198 Okemo Mountain
199 Killington
200 Pico
201 Sugarbush
202 Bolton Valley
203 Stowe (Mount Mansfield)
204 Smugglers' Notch
205 Jay Peak

New Hampshire
206 Pats Peak
207 King Ridge
208 Mount Sunapee
209 Gunstock
210 Wildcat
211 Attitash-Bear Peak
212 Cranmore
213 Waterville Valley
214 Loon
215 Cannon
216 Bretton Woods
217 *The Balsams**

Maine
218 Sunday River
219 Sugarloaf USA

The World Ski and Snowboarding Guide, published by Columbus Press, is a comprehensive guide to the world's ski resorts. For more information, call +44 (0) 171 417 0700.

UNITED STATES

See pages 40–41 for general map

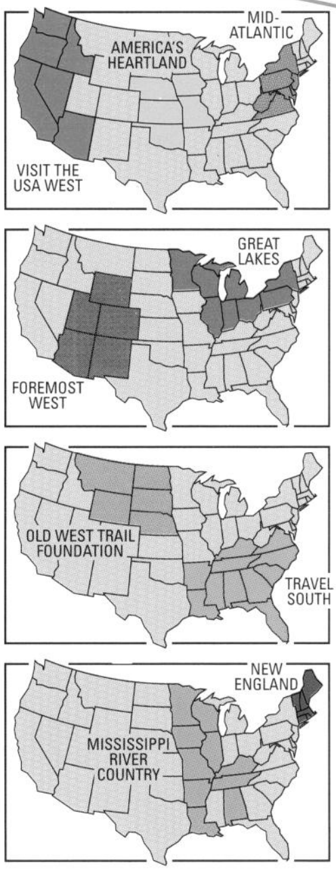

Tourist regions in the USA are organised on a voluntary basis and dependent on each state's allocated budget. Therefore a state may be represented in more than one region, and participation is subject to variation.

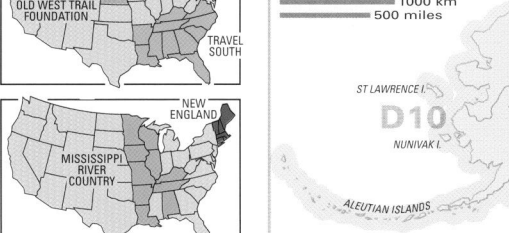

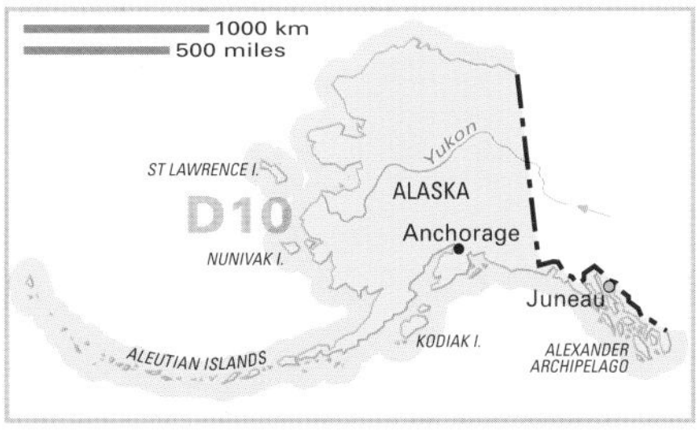

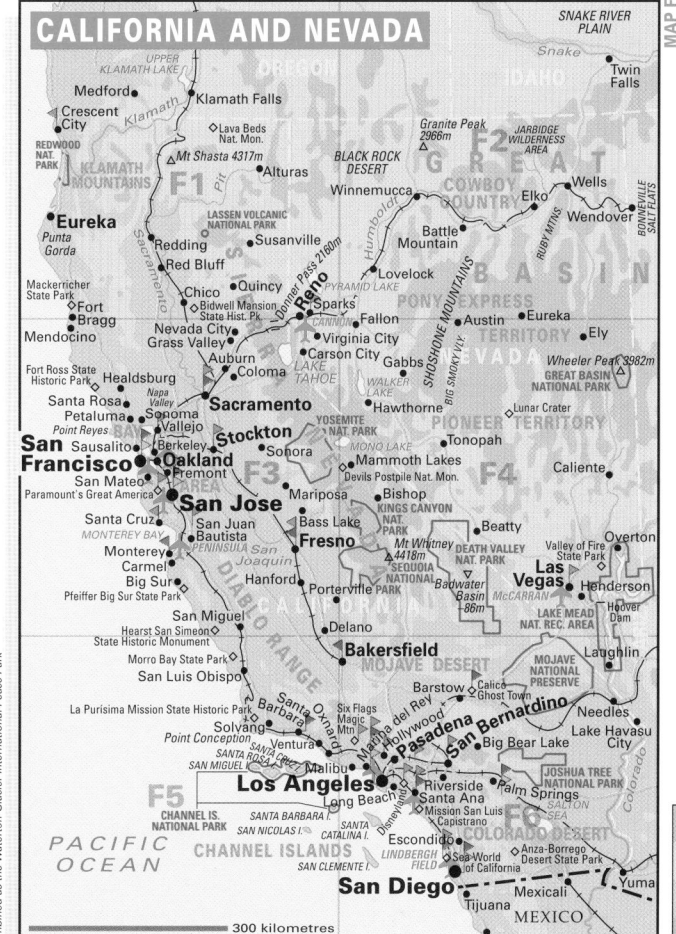

CALIFORNIA AND NEVADA

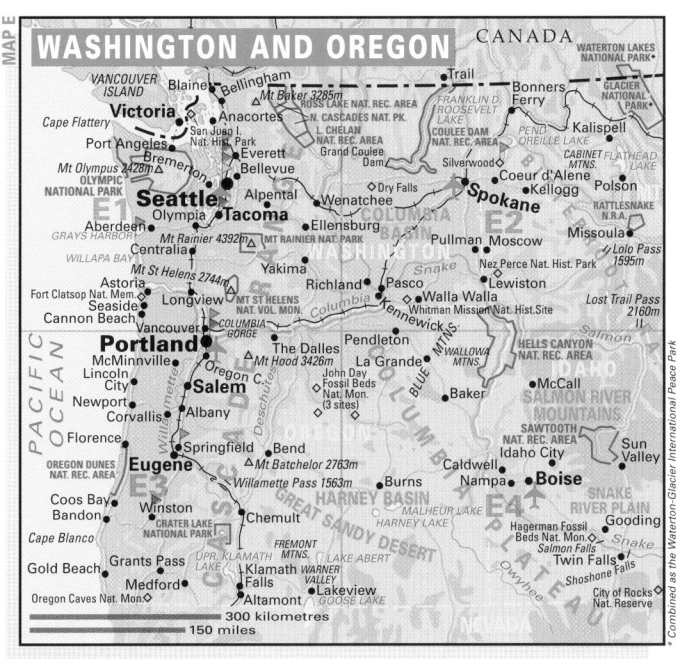

WASHINGTON AND OREGON

Leisure park Zoo / animal park Aquarium Major tournament golf course Major tennis venue

UNITED STATES

See pages 40-41 for general map

MAINE, NEW HAMPSHIRE AND VERMONT

1 Lebanon
2 St Gaudens National Historic Site
3 Claremont
4 Sunapee

CENTRAL EASTERN SEABOARD

1 Brooklyn
2 Bronx
3 Manhattan
4 Queens
5 Staten Island
6 Six Flags Great Adventure & Six Flags Wild Safari Animal Park
7 Washington Crossing State Historical Site
8 Valley Forge National Historical Park
9 Brandywine Battlefield State Historic Site

WEST OF THE RIO GRANDE

LOUISIANA

INCOME FROM TOURISM

Total spent in each state by domestic and foreign tourists and travellers, 1994

$20,000 million and over*
$10,000m – $19,999m
$5,000m – $9,999m
$2,000m – $4,999m
Less than $2,000m
*Actual figure on map

CALIFORNIA 43,982
TEXAS 21,157
FLORIDA 29,050
NEW YORK 20,713

EMPLOYMENT IN TOURISM

Employment generated by travel and tourism as a percentage of total state employment, 1994

7.0% and over*
5.0% – 6.9%
3.0% – 4.9%
Less than 3.0%
*Actual figure on map

NEVADA 37.2
WYOMING 10.1
ALASKA 8.6
HAWAII 16.0
FLORIDA 7.9

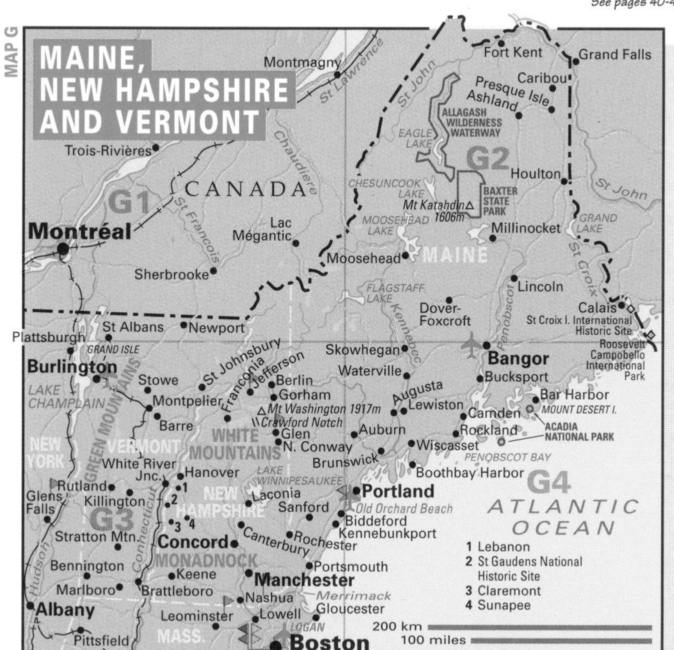

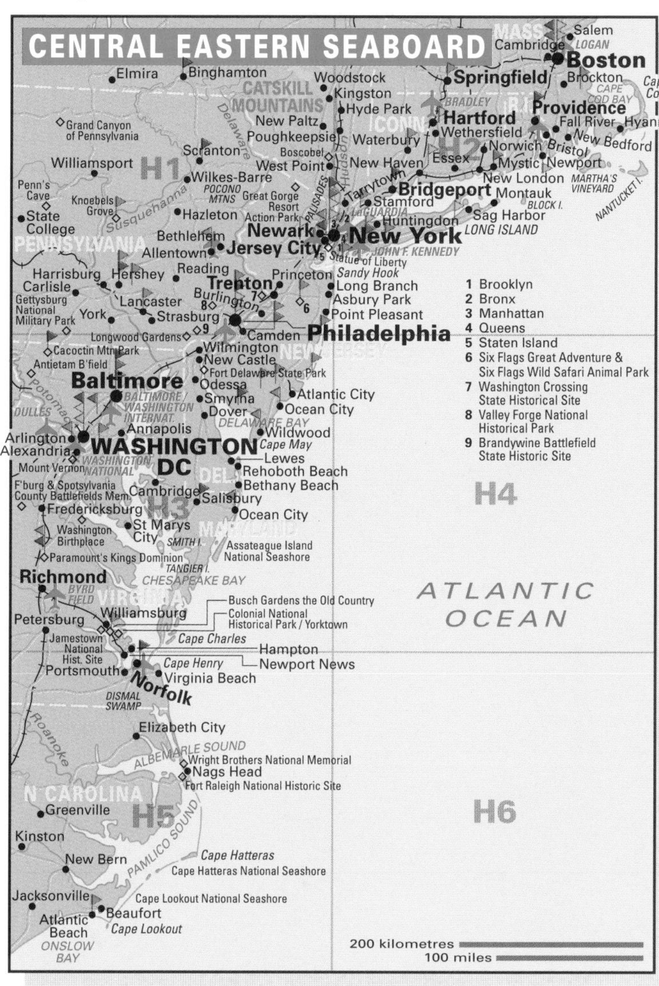

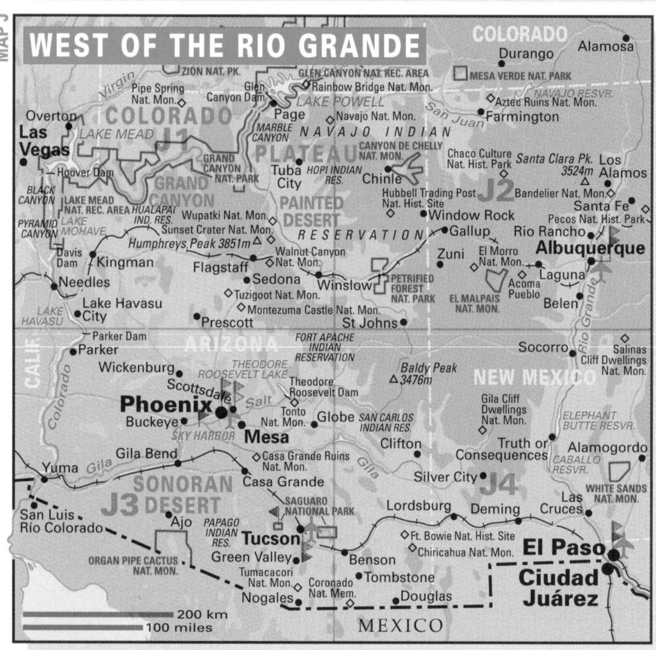

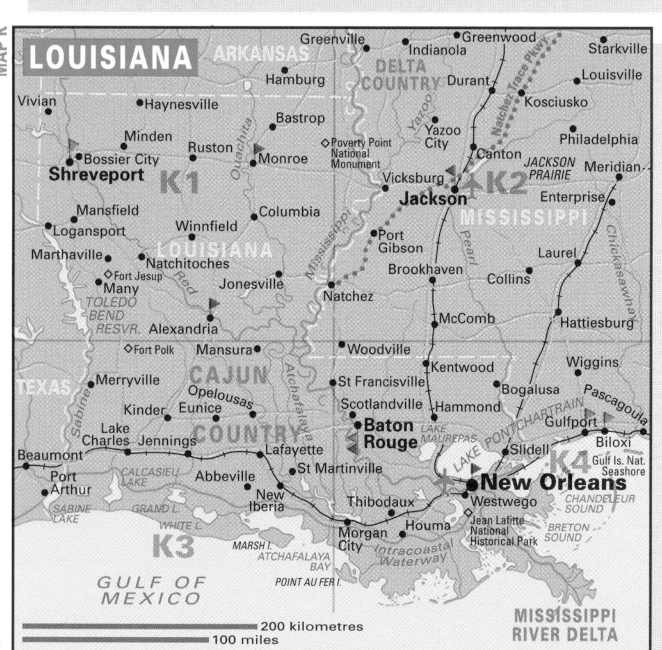

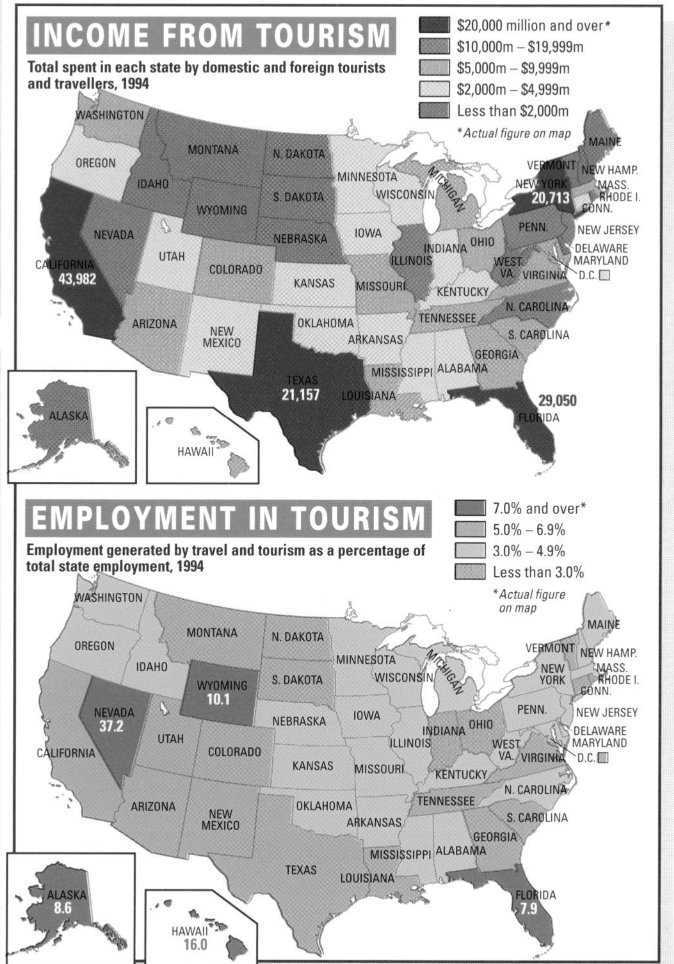

Source: Travel Industry Association of America

▶ Leisure park   ▶ Zoo / animal park   ▲ Aquarium   ▶ Major tournament golf course   ▶ Horse racing   ▶ Major tennis venue

UNITED STATES

See pages 40-41 for general map

HAWAII

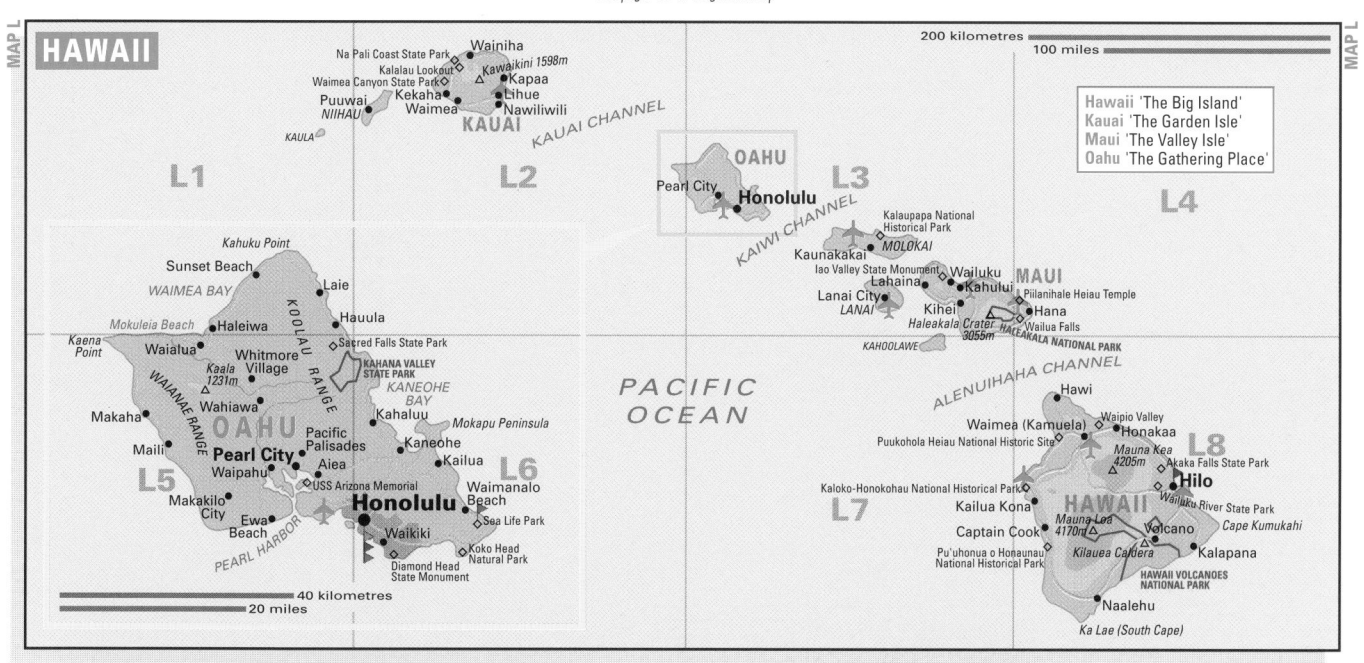

Hawaii 'The Big Island'
Kauai 'The Garden Isle'
Maui 'The Valley Isle'
Oahu 'The Gathering Place'

FLORIDA

EAST TEXAS

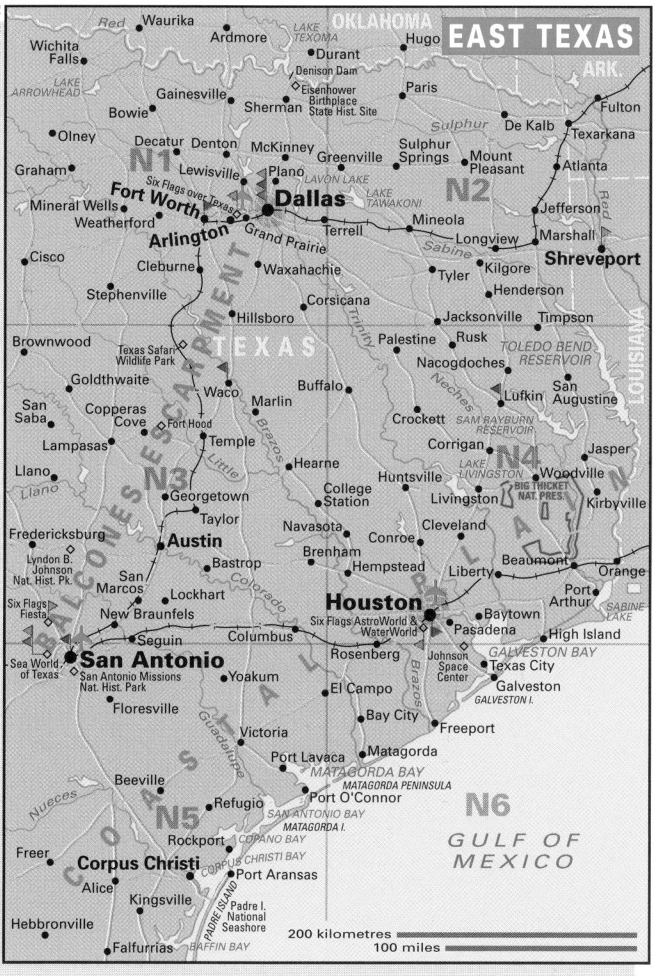

Leisure park   Zoo / animal park   Aquarium   Major tournament golf course

Horse racing   Major tennis venue

2000 metres
1000 metres
Sea level

US NATIONAL PARKS...

National Park Service:
- National Park / Preserve
- National Memorial
- National Monument
- National Recreation Area / Seashore / Lakeshore
- National Battlefield / Battlefield Park / Battlefield Site / Military Park
- National Historic Site / Historical Park
- Theme park

The National Park Service is responsible for over 360 sites set aside to preserve the natural, historical and cultural heritage of the United States. For further information, contact:

National Park Service, 1849 C Street Northwest, Washington DC, 20240.

Tel. +1 202 208 4747.

The map also shows some of the more well-known theme parks, from Disneyland in California to Sea World of Florida. For further information, contact:

International Association of Amusement Parks and Attractions (IAAPA), 1448 Duke Street, Alexandria, Virginia 22314.

Tel. +1 703 836 4800.

TOP US THEME PARKS IN 1996
Number of visitors in millions (world ranking in brackets)

Disneyland CA: 15.0 (2nd)
Magic Kingdom FL: 13.8 (3rd)
EPCOT Center FL: 11.2 (5th)
Disney-MGM Studios FL: 10.0 (6th)
Universal Studios FL: 8.4 (7th)
Universal Studios CA: 5.4 (11th)
Sea World FL: 5.1 (13th)
Busch Gardens FL: 4.2 (14th)
Six Flags NJ: 4.0 (16th)
Sea World CA: 3.9 (17th)
Kings Island OH: 3.6 (19th)
Berry Farm CA: 3.6 (20th)
Cedar Point OH: 3.5 (21st)
Santa Cruz Beach CA: 3.2 (=23rd)
Six Flags TX: 3.1 (=25th)
Six Flags IL: 3.0 (28th)
Camp Snoopy MN: 2.6 (37th)
Great America CA: 2.5 (=38th)
Kings Dominion VA: 2.4 (=40th)
AstroWorld TX: 2.4 (=40th)
Circus Circus NV: 2.3 (45th)
Six Flags GA: 2.2 (=46th)
Busch Gardens VA: 2.2 (=46th)
Six Flags Fiesta TX: 2.1 (=49th)
Dollywood TN: 2.1 (=49th)
Hersheypark PA: 2.1 (=49th)

Source: Amusement Business

Alaska
1. Cape Krusenstern National Monument
2. Noatak National Preserve
3. Gates of the Arctic National Park and Preserve
4. Kobuk Valley National Park
5. Bering Land Bridge National Preserve
6. Yukon-Charley Rivers National Preserve
7. Denali National Park and Preserve
8. Lake Clark National Park and Preserve
9. Katmai National Park and Preserve
10. Aniachak National Monument and Preserve
11. Kenai Fjords National Park
12. Wrangell-St Elias National Park and Preserve
13. Glacier Bay National Park and Preserve
14. Sitka National Historical Park
15. Klondike Gold Rush National Historical Park

Hawaii
16. USS Arizona Memorial
17. Kalaupapa National Historical Park
18. Haleakala National Park
19. Puukohola Heiau National Historic Site
20. Kaloko-Honokohau National Historical Park
21. Pu'uhonua o Honaunau National Historical Park
22. Hawaii Volcanoes National Park

Washington
23. San Juan Island National Historical Park
24. Olympic National Park
25. Ebey's Landing National Historical Reserve
26. North Cascades National Park
27. Ross Lake National Recreation Area
28. Lake Chelan National Recreation Area
29. Coulee Dam National Recreation Area
30. Whitman Mission National Historic Site
31. Mount Rainier National Park
32. Fort Vancouver National Historic Site

Oregon
33. Fort Clatsop National Memorial
34. McLoughlin House National Historic Site
35. John Day Fossil Beds National Monument
36. Crater Lake National Park
37. Oregon Caves National Monument

California
38. Redwood National Park
39. Lava Beds National Monument
40. Whiskeytown-Shasta-Trinity National Recreation Area
41. Lassen Volcanic National Park
42. Point Reyes National Seashore
43. Muir Woods National Monument
44. Fort Point National Historic Site
45. Golden Gate National Recreation Area
46. San Francisco Maritime National Historical Park
47. Port Chicago Naval Magazine National Memorial
48. John Muir National Historic Site
49. Eugene O'Neill National Historic Site
50. Pinnacles National Monument
51. Yosemite National Park
52. Devils Postpile National Monument
53. Sequoia and Kings Canyon National Parks
54. Manzanar National Historic Site
55. Death Valley National Park
56. Channel Islands National Park
57. Santa Monica Mountains National Recreation Area
58. Cabrillo National Monument
59. Joshua Tree National Park
60. Mojave National Preserve

Nevada
61. Lake Mead National Recreation Area
62. Great Basin National Park

Idaho
63. City of Rocks National Reserve
64. Hagerman Fossil Beds National Monument
65. Craters of the Moon National Monument
66. Nez Perce National Historical Park

Montana
67. Glacier National Park
68. Grant-Kohrs Ranch National Historic Site
69. Big Hole National Battlefield
70. Bighorn Canyon National Recreation Area
71. Little Bighorn Battlefield National Monument

Wyoming
72. Devils Tower National Monument
73. Fort Laramie National Historic Site
74. Yellowstone National Park
75. John D. Rockefeller, Jr. Memorial Parkway
76. Grand Teton National Park
77. Fossil Butte National Monument

Utah
78. Golden Spike National Historic Site
79. Timpanogos Cave National Monument
80. Zion National Park
81. Cedar Breaks National Monument
82. Bryce Canyon National Park
83. Capitol Reef National Park
84. Rainbow Bridge National Monument
85. Natural Bridges National Monument
86. Canyonlands National Park
87. Arches National Park

Colorado
88. Dinosaur National Monument
89. Rocky Mountain National Park
90. Colorado National Monument
91. Black Canyon of the Gunnison National Monument
92. Curecanti National Recreation Area

93. Florissant Fossil Beds National Monument
94. Hovenweep National Monument
95. Yucca House National Monument
96. Mesa Verde National Park
97. Great Sand Dunes National Monument
98. Bent's Old Fort National Historic Site

Arizona
99. Pipe Spring National Monument
100. Grand Canyon National Park
101. Glen Canyon National Recreation Area (also in Utah)
102. Navajo National Monument
103. Canyon de Chelly National Monument
104. Hubbell Trading Post National Historic Site
105. Wupatki National Monument
106. Sunset Crater National Monument
107. Walnut Canyon National Monument
108. Tuzigoot National Monument
109. Montezuma Castle National Monument
110. Petrified Forest National Park
111. Tonto National Monument
112. Hohokam Pima National Monument
113. Casa Grande Ruins National Monument
114. Organ Pipe Cactus National Monument
115. Tumacacori National Historical Park
116. Coronado National Memorial
117. Saguaro National Park
118. Fort Bowie National Historic Site
119. Chiricahua National Monument

New Mexico
120. Gila Cliff Dwellings National Monument
121. White Sands National Monument
122. Carlsbad Caverns National Park
123. Salinas Pueblo Missions National Monument
124. Aztec Ruins National Monument
125. Chaco Culture National Historical Park
126. El Morro National Monument
127. El Malpais National Monument
128. Petroglyph National Monument
129. Bandelier National Monument
130. Pecos National Historical Park
131. Fort Union National Monument
132. Capulin Volcano National Monument

Texas
133. Lake Meredith National Recreation Area
134. Alibates Flint Quarries National Monument
135. Chamizal National Memorial
136. Guadalupe Mountains National Park
137. Fort Davis National Historic Site
138. Big Bend National Park
139. Amistad National Recreation Area
140. Lyndon B. Johnson National Historical Park
141. San Antonio Missions National Historical Park
142. Palo Alto Battlefield National Historic Site
143. Padre Island National Seashore
144. Big Thicket National Preserve

Oklahoma
145. Chickasaw National Recreation Area

North Dakota
146. International Peace Garden
147. Fort Union Trading Post National Historic Site
148. Theodore Roosevelt National Park (North and South Units)
149. Knife River Indian Villages National Historic Site

South Dakota
150. Jewel Cave National Monument
151. Mount Rushmore National Memorial
152. Wind Cave National Park
153. Badlands National Park

Minnesota
154. Pipestone National Monument
155. Voyageurs National Park
156. Grand Portage National Monument

Wisconsin
157. Apostle Islands National Lakeshore
158. Ice Age National Scientific Reserve

Michigan
159. Isle Royale National Park
160. Keweenaw National Historical Park
161. Pictured Rocks National Lakeshore
162. Father Marquette National Memorial and Museum
163. Sleeping Bear Dunes National Lakeshore

Nebraska
164. Agate Fossil Beds National Monument
165. Scotts Bluff National Monument
166. Chimney Rock National Historic Site
167. Homestead National Monument of America

Iowa
168. Effigy Mounds National Monument
169. Herbert Hoover National Historic Site

Kansas
170. Fort Larned National Historic Site

171. Brown v. Board of Education National Historic Site
172. Fort Scott National Historic Site

Missouri
173. Harry S. Truman National Historic Site
174. George Washington Carver National Monument
175. Wilson's Creek National Battlefield
176. Ulysses S. Grant National Historic Site
177. Jefferson National Expansion Memorial

Illinois
178. Lincoln Home National Historic Site
179. Illinois and Michigan Canal National Heritage Corridor
180. Chicago Portage National Historic Site

Indiana
181. Indiana Dunes National Lakeshore
182. George Rogers Clark National Historical Park
183. Lincoln Boyhood National Memorial

Ohio
184. William Howard Taft National Historic Site
185. Dayton Aviation National Historical Park
186. Hopewell Culture National Historical Park
187. Perry's Victory and International Peace Memorial
188. James A. Garfield National Historic Site
189. David Berger National Memorial
190. Cuyahoga Valley National Recreation Area

Arkansas
191. Pea Ridge National Military Park
192. Fort Smith National Historic Site
193. Hot Springs National Park
194. Arkansas Post National Memorial

Louisiana
195. Poverty Point National Monument
196. Cane River Creole National Historical Park and National Heritage Area
197. New Orleans Jazz National Historical Park
198. Jean Lafitte National Historical Park

Mississippi
199. Natchez National Historical Park
200. Vicksburg National Military Park
201. Natchez Trace Parkway (also in Alabama and Tennessee)
202. Tupelo National Battlefield
203. Brices Cross Roads National Battlefield Site

Alabama
204. Tuskegee Institute National Historic Site
205. Horseshoe Bend National Military Park

Seattle, WASHINGTON, Spokane, Portland, Eugene, OREGON, Columbia, Great Falls, Missouri, MONTANA, Billings, IDAHO, Boise, Snake, WYOMING, Casper, Rapid City, SOU DAK, N Platte, Cheyenne, NEBR, Sacramento, Reno, NEVADA, GREAT SALT LAKE, Salt Lake City, UTAH, Colorado, COLORADO, Denver, Colorado Springs, S Platte, Platte, KAN, San Francisco, San Jose, San Joaquin, CALIFORNIA, Bakersfield, Las Vegas, Arkansas, Los Angeles, San Bernardino, ARIZONA, Phoenix, Albuquerque, NEW MEXICO, Amarillo, Lubbock, San Diego, Tucson, El Paso, Rio Grande, TEX, San Anto

ST LAWRENCE I., Yukon, ALASKA, Anchorage, Juneau, NUNIVAK I., KODIAK I., ALEXANDER ARCHIPELAGO, ALEUTIAN ISLANDS, 1000 km, 500 miles

NIIHAU, KAUAI, OAHU, Honolulu, MOLOKAI, LANAI, MAUI, HAWAII, 300 km, 150 miles

...AND THEME PARKS

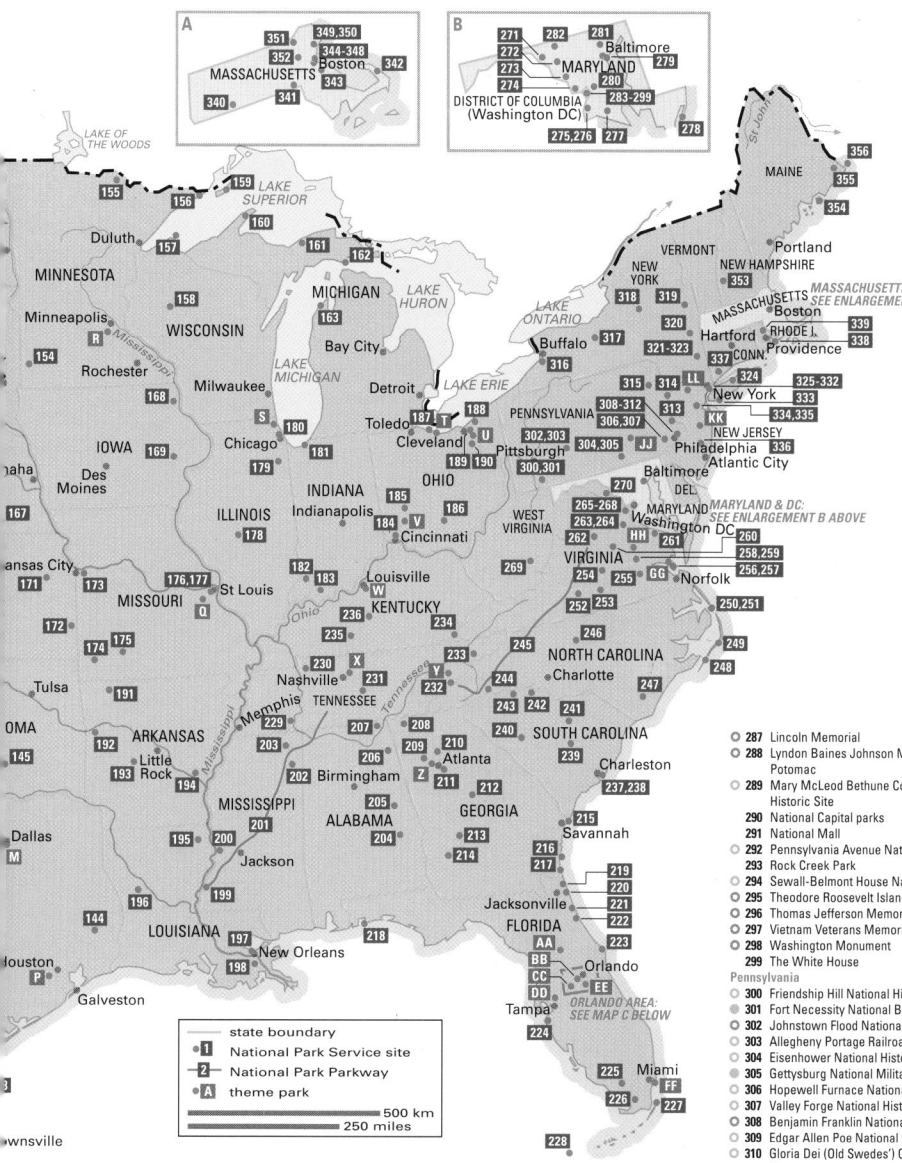

330 St Paul's Church National Historic Site
331 Statue of Liberty National Monument
332 Theodore Roosevelt Birthplace National Historic Site
333 Fire Island National Seashore
New Jersey
334 Edison National Historical Site
335 Morristown National Historical Park
336 Pinelands National Reserve
Connecticut
337 Weir Farm National Historic Site
Rhode Island
338 Touro Synagogue National Historic Site
339 Roger Williams National Memorial
Massachusetts
340 Springfield Armory National Historic Site
341 Blackstone River Valley National Heritage Corridor
342 Cape Cod National Seashore
343 Adams National Historical Park
344 Boston African American National Historical Site
345 Boston National Historical Park
346 Frederick Law Olmsted National Historic Site
347 John F. Kennedy National Historic Site
348 Longfellow National Historic Site
349 Saugus Iron Works National Historic Site
350 Salem Maritime National Historic Site
351 Lowell National Historical Park
352 Minute Man National Historical Park
New Hampshire
353 St-Gaudens National Historic Site
Maine
354 Acadia National Park
355 St Croix Island International Historic Site
Canada
New Brunswick
356 Roosevelt Campobello International Park
(Not shown on map):
Puerto Rico
San Juan National Historic Site
US Virgin Islands
Buck Island Reef National Monument
Christiansted National Historic Site
Salt River Bay National Historical Park and Ecological Preserve
Virgin Islands National Park
American Samoa
The National Park of American Samoa
Northern Mariana Islands
American Memorial Park
War in the Pacific National Historical Park

THEME PARKS
A Marine World Africa USA, Vallejo, California
B Paramount's Great America, Santa Clara, California
C Santa Cruz Beach Boardwalk, Santa Cruz, California
D Six Flags Magic Mountain, Valencia, California
E Universal Studios Hollywood, Universal City, Los Angeles, California
F Raging Waters, San Dimas, Los Angeles, California
G Knott's Berry Farm, Buena Park, Los Angeles, California
H Disneyland, Anaheim, Los Angeles, California
J Sea World of California, San Diego, California
K Circus Circus, Las Vegas, Nevada
L Six Flags over Texas, Arlington, Texas
M Fair Park, Dallas, Texas
N Six Flags Fiesta, San Antonio, Texas
O Sea World of Texas, San Antonio, Texas
P Six Flags AstroWorld / Six Flags WaterWorld, Houston, Texas
Q Six Flags over Mid-America, Eureka, Missouri
R Knott's Camp Snoopy, Bloomington, Minnesota
S Six Flags Great America, Gurnee, Illinois
T Cedar Point, Sandusky, Ohio
U Sea World of Ohio, Aurora, Ohio
V Paramount's Kings Island, Kings Mills, Ohio
W Kentucky Kingdom – The Thrill Park, Louisville, Kentucky
X Opryland USA, Nashville, Tennessee
Y Dollywood, Pigeon Forge, Tennessee
Z Six Flags over Georgia, Atlanta, Georgia
AA Florida's Silver Springs, Silver Springs, Florida
BB Universal Studios Florida, Orlando, Florida
CC Walt Disney World Resort Complex (including the Magic Kingdom theme park, EPCOT Center, Disney-MGM Studios theme park, Fort Wilderness recreation area), Lake Buena Vista, Florida
DD Busch Gardens Tampa Bay, Florida
EE Sea World of Florida, Orlando, Florida
FF Miami Seaquarium, Miami, Florida
HH Paramount's Kings Dominion, Doswell, Virginia
GG Busch Gardens the Old Country, Williamsburg, Virginia
JJ Hersheypark, Hershey, Pennsylvania
KK Six Flags Great Adventure, Jackson, New Jersey
LL Great Gorge Resort Action Park, McAfee, New Jersey

287 Lincoln Memorial
288 Lyndon Baines Johnson Memorial Grove on the Potomac
289 Mary McLeod Bethune Council House National Historic Site
290 National Capital parks
291 National Mall
292 Pennsylvania Avenue National Historic Site
293 Rock Creek Park
294 Sewall-Belmont House National Historic Site
295 Theodore Roosevelt Island
296 Thomas Jefferson Memorial
297 Vietnam Veterans Memorial
298 Washington Monument
299 The White House
Pennsylvania
300 Friendship Hill National Historic Site
301 Fort Necessity National Battlefield
302 Johnstown Flood National Memorial
303 Allegheny Portage Railroad National Historic Site
304 Eisenhower National Historic Site
305 Gettysburg National Military Park
306 Hopewell Furnace National Historic Site
307 Valley Forge National Historical Park
308 Benjamin Franklin National Memorial
309 Edgar Allen Poe National Historic Site
310 Gloria Dei (Old Swedes') Church National Historic Site
311 Independence National Historical Park
312 Thaddeus Kosciuszko National Memorial
313 Delaware and Lehigh Navigation Canal National Heritage Corridor
314 Delaware Water Gap National Recreation Area
315 Steamtown National Historic Site
New York
316 Theodore Roosevelt Inaugural National Historic Site
317 Women's Rights National Historical Park
318 Fort Stanwix National Monument
319 Saratoga National Historical Park
320 Martin Van Buren National Historic Site
321 Eleanor Roosevelt National Historic Site
322 Vanderbilt Mansion National Historic Site
323 Home of Franklin Delano Roosevelt National Historic Site
324 Sagamore Hill National Historic Site
325 Castle Clinton National Monument
326 Federal Hall National Memorial
327 Gateway National Recreation Area (also in New Jersey)
328 General Grant National Memorial
329 Hamilton Grange National Memorial

206 Little River Canyon National Preserve
207 Russell Cave National Monument
Georgia
208 Chickamauga and Chattanooga National Military Park
209 Kennesaw Mountain National Battlefield Park
210 Chattahoochee River National Recreation Area
211 Martin Luther King Jr. National Historic Site
212 Ocmulgee National Monument
213 Andersonville National Historic Site
214 Jimmy Carter National Historic Site
215 Fort Pulaski National Monument
216 Fort Frederica National Monument
217 Cumberland Island National Seashore
Florida
218 Gulf Islands National Seashore (also in Mississippi)
219 Timucuan Ecological and Historic Preserve
220 Fort Caroline National Memorial
221 Castillo de San Marcos National Monument
222 Fort Matanzas National Monument
223 Canaveral National Seashore
224 De Soto National Memorial
225 Big Cypress National Preserve
226 Everglades National Park
227 Biscayne National Park
228 Dry Tortugas National Park
Tennessee
229 Shiloh National Military Park
230 Fort Donelson National Battlefield
231 Stones River National Battlefield and Cemetery
232 Great Smoky Mountains National Park (also in North Carolina)
233 Andrew Johnson National Historic Site
Kentucky
234 Cumberland Gap National Historical Park
235 Mammoth Cave National Park
236 Abraham Lincoln Birthplace National Historic Site
South Carolina
237 Fort Sumter National Monument
238 Charles Pinckney National Historic Site
239 Congaree Swamp National Monument
240 Ninety Six National Historic Site
241 Historic Camden
242 Kings Mountain National Military Park
243 Cowpens National Battlefield
North Carolina
244 Carl Sandburg Home National Historic Site
245 Blue Ridge Parkway (also in Virginia)

246 Guilford Courthouse National Military Park
247 Moores Creek National Battlefield
248 Cape Lookout National Seashore
249 Cape Hatteras National Seashore
250 Fort Raleigh National Historic Site
251 Wright Brothers National Memorial
Virginia
252 Booker T. Washington National Monument
253 Red Hill Patrick Henry National Memorial
254 Appomattox Court House National Historical Park
255 Petersburg National Battlefield
256 Jamestown National Historic Site
257 Colonial National Historical Park
258 Maggie L. Walker National Historic Site
259 Richmond National Battlefield Park
260 Green Springs Historic District
261 George Washington Birthplace National Monument
262 Shenandoah National Park
263 Fredericksburg and Spotsylvania County Battlefields Memorial
264 Prince William Forest Park
265 Manassas National Battlefield Park
266 Wolf Trap Farm Park for the Performing Arts
267 George Washington Memorial Parkway
268 Arlington House, The Robert E. Lee Memorial
West Virginia
269 Gauley River National Recreation Area
270 Harpers Ferry National Historical Park
Maryland
271 Antietam National Battlefield
272 Monocacy National Battlefield
273 Chesapeake and Ohio Canal National Historical Park
274 Clara Barton National Historic Site
275 Fort Washington Park
276 Piscataway Park
277 Thomas Stone National Historic Site
278 Assateague Island National Seashore
279 Fort McHenry National Monument and Historic Shrine
280 Greenbelt Park
281 Hampton National Historic Site
282 Catoctin Mountain Park
District of Columbia
283 Constitution Gardens
284 Ford's Theatre National Historic Site
285 Frederick Douglass National Historic Site
286 Korea War Veterans Memorial

Legend:
state boundary
1 National Park Service site
2 National Park Parkway
A theme park
500 km
250 miles

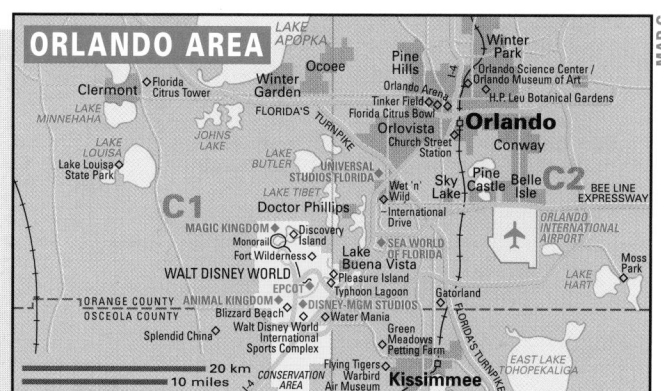

CANADA

See pages 38-39 for general map

Yukon
Alaska (US)
MACKENZIE DELTA
Tuktoyaktuk
Inuvik
BANKS I.
STEFANSSON I.
SOMERSET I.
PRINCE OF WALES I.
VICTORIA ISLAND
Boothia Peninsula
GULF OF BOOTHIA
KING WILLIAM I.
QIKIQTALUK (BAFFIN ISLAND)
A1
Dawson
YUKON TERRITORY
Mackenzie
Norman Wells
GREAT BEAR LAKE
A2
Melville Peninsula
FOXE BASIN
PRINCE CHARLES I.
A3
Iqaluit (Frobisher Bay)
MACKENZIE MOUNTAINS
Upper Yukon
Pelly
Whitehorse
NORTHWEST TERRITORIES
NUNAVUT (1999)
SOUTHAMPTON I.
HUDSON STRAIT
BARREN GROUNDS
Yellowknife
DUBAWNT LAKE
COATS I.
MANSEL I.
PÉNINSULE D'UNGAVA
BAIE D'UNGAVA
A4
ROCKY MOUNTAINS
COAST MOUNTAINS
Hay River
GREAT SLAVE LAKE
Slave
Nain
NEWFOUNDLAND AND LABRADOR
LABRADOR
Fort Nelson
Peace
Uranium City
LAKE ATHABASCA
HUDSON BAY
Inukjuak
SMALLWOOD RESERVOIR
Churchill
Goose Bay
WILLISTON LAKE
Churchill
Churchill Falls
Gander
Prince Rupert
QUEEN CHARLOTTE IS.
Dawson Creek
BELCHER IS.
St John's
BRITISH COLUMBIA
ALBERTA
REINDEER LAKE
Nelson
La Grande Rivière
NEWFOUNDLAND
Prince George
Athabasca
La Ronge
MANITOBA
Chisasibi (Fort George)
RÉSERVOIR LA GRANDE 2
ÎLE D'ANTICOSTI
GULF OF ST LAWRENCE
St Pierre et Miquelon (Fr.)
A5
Jasper
Edmonton
SASKATCHEWAN
North Saskatchewan
A6
Flin Flon
AKIMISKI I.
JAMES BAY
QUÉBEC
Péninsule de Gaspésie
A8
ÎLES DE LA MADELEINE
CAPE BRETON I.
VANCOUVER ISLAND
Kamloops
Fraser
Columbia
Calgary
South Saskatchewan
Saskatoon
WINNIPEGOSIS LAKE
LAKE WINNIPEG
Albany
A7
Moosonee
St Lawrence
NEW BRUNSWICK
PRINCE EDWARD ISLAND
Charlottetown
Victoria
Vancouver
Regina
LAKE MANITOBA
ONTARIO
Fredericton
NOVA SCOTIA
Halifax
Saint John
Sioux Lookout
LAKE NIPIGON
Québec
Trois-Rivières
Winnipeg
Portage la Prairie
Red
LAKE OF THE WOODS
Thunder Bay
LAKE SUPERIOR
Sault Ste Marie
Montréal
Ottawa
B
Sudbury
OTTAWA
D
MANITOULIN I.
LAKE ONTARIO
LAKE HURON
Toronto
C
GREAT LAKES
Hamilton
LAKE MICHIGAN
London
LAKE ERIE

province/territory boundary
province/territory capital
1000 km
500 miles

For an alphabetical list of Canadian provinces and territories, see Appendices

Leisure park
Zoo / animal park
Aquarium
Formula One
Major tennis venue

GUADA

MAP C

SW CANADA

400 kilometres
200 miles
Alaska Highway
WILLISTON LAKE
Fort St John
Peace River
Skeena
W.A.C. Bennett Dam
Peace
LESSER SLAVE LAKE
Hazelton
Dawson Creek
ROCKY MOUNTAINS
Slave Lake
Crooked
C1
Grande Prairie
C2
Houston
Athabasca
Nechako
Mt Robson 3954m
MT ROBSON PROV. PARK
ELK ISLAND NATIONAL PARK
Vanderhoof
Fraser
Edson
Edmonton
TWEEDSMUIR PROV. PARK
Prince George
BOWRON LAKE PROV. PARK
ALBERTA
Quesnel
JASPER NATIONAL PARK
North Saskatchewan
COAST MOUNTAINS
Barkerville
Jasper
BRITISH COLUMBIA
Yellowhead Pass 1133m
COLUMBIA ICEFIELD
HAMBER PROV. PARK
Red Deer
WELLS GRAY PROV. PARK & RECREATION AREA
Mt Columbia 3747m
Drumheller
Williams Lake
KINBASKET LAKE
BANFF NAT. PARK
Kicking Horse Pass 1627m
Mt Waddington 3994m
YOHO NAT. PARK
Lake Louise
GLACIER NAT. PARK
Calgary
MT REVELSTOKE NAT. PARK
Banff
Calaway Park
Bear Cove
Revelstoke
MT ASSINIBOINE PROV. PK.
Lillooet
Thompson
Radium Hot Springs
VANCOUVER ISLAND
C3
Kamloops
KOOTENAY NAT. PARK
Fairmount Hot Springs
C4
Fort Macleod
Whistler
STRATHCONA PROV. PARK
Courtenay
GARIBALDI PROV. PARK
Kelowna
Okanagan
Columbia
Fort Steele
WATERTON LAKES NATIONAL PARK*
Paradise Sea-Side Resort
Vancouver
Hope
Kootenay
Cranbrooke
Port Alberni
Dinotown
Penticton
Trail
PACIFIC RIM NATIONAL PARK RESERVE
Nanaimo
Duncan
CASCADE MTNS.
Bonners Ferry
PACIFIC OCEAN
Victoria
Fort Rod Hill
Anacortes
UNITED STATES
GLACIER NATIONAL PARK*
Str. of Juan de Fuca
From Seattle

* Combined as the Waterton-Glacier International Peace Park

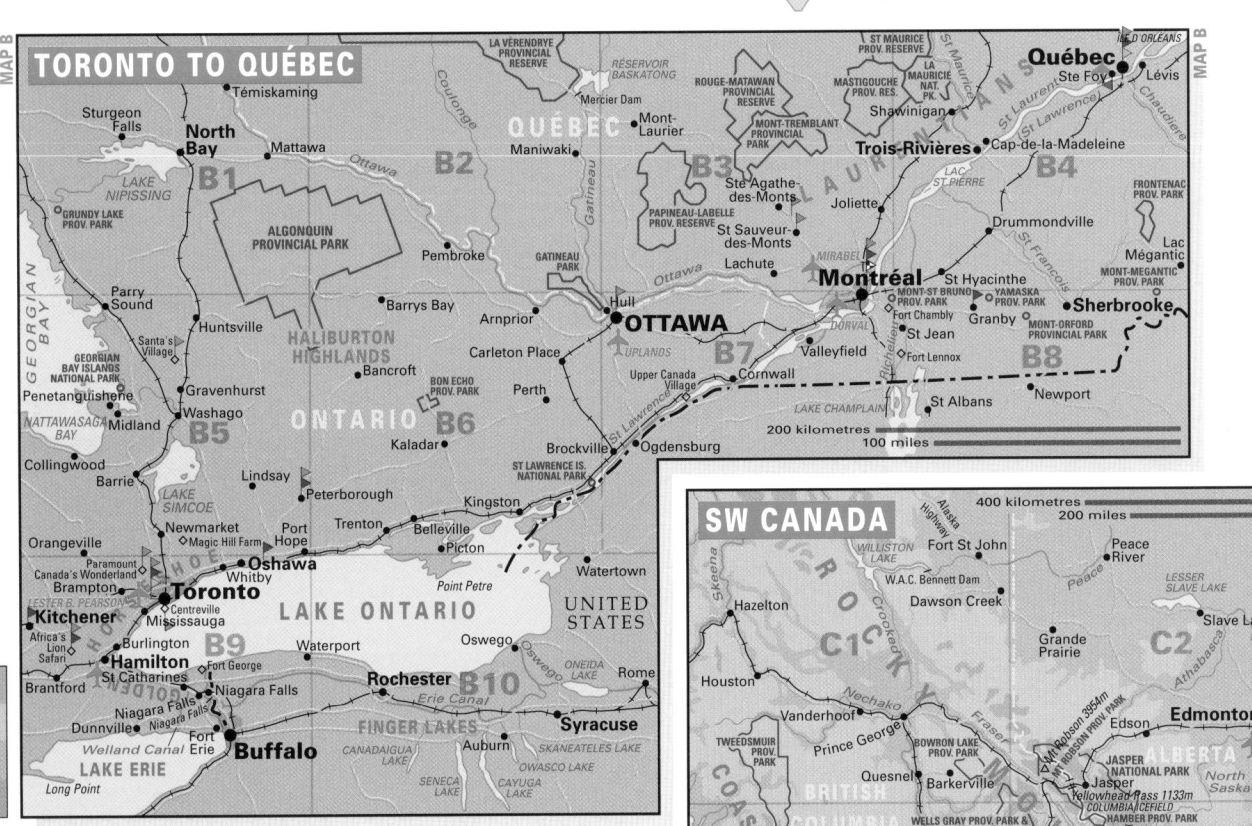

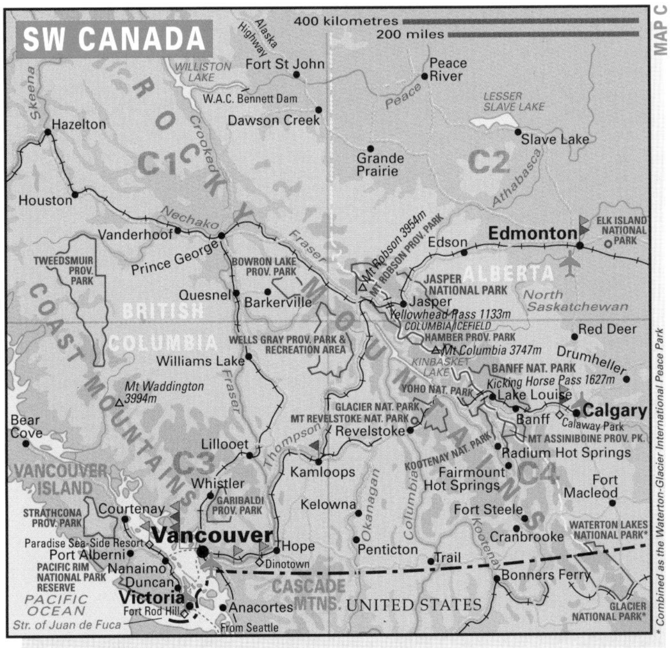

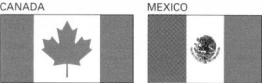

CANADA

See pages 38-39 for general map

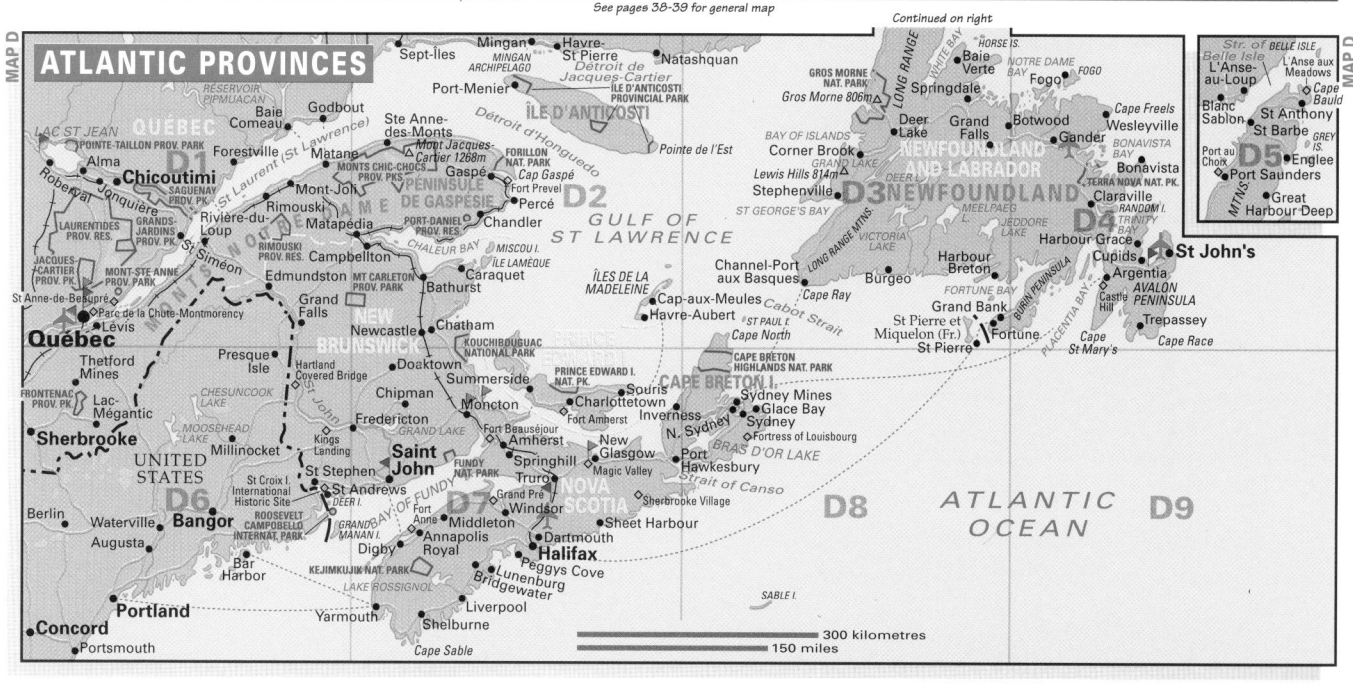

MEXICO

See page 37 for general map

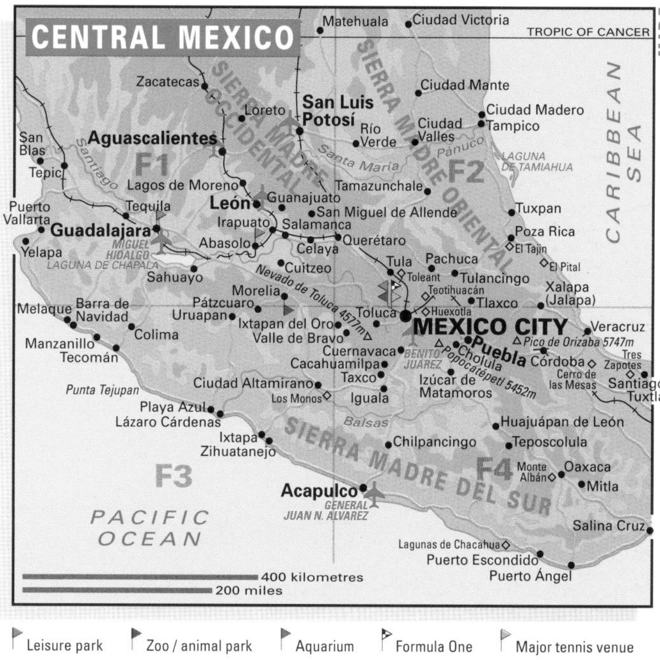

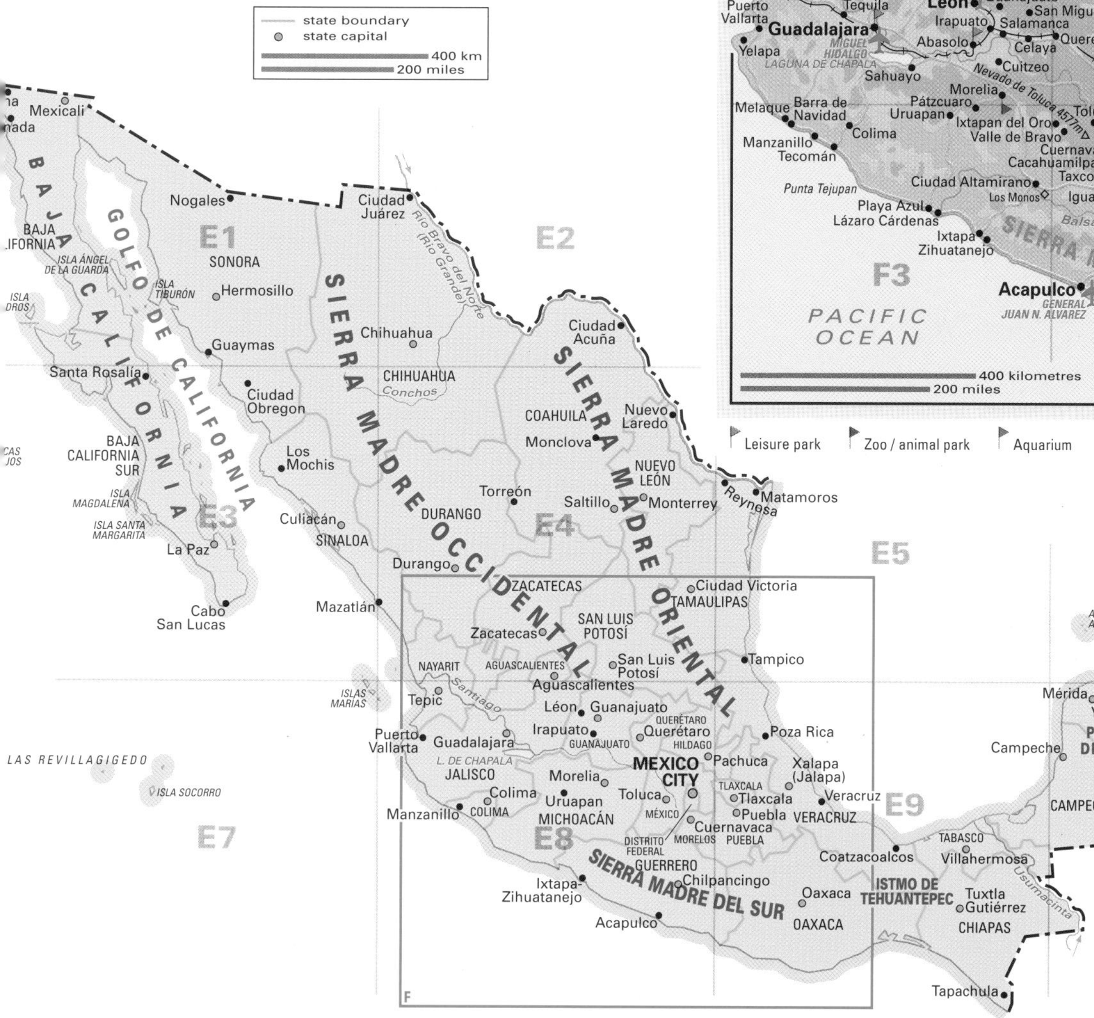

THE CARIBBEAN

See page 37 for general map

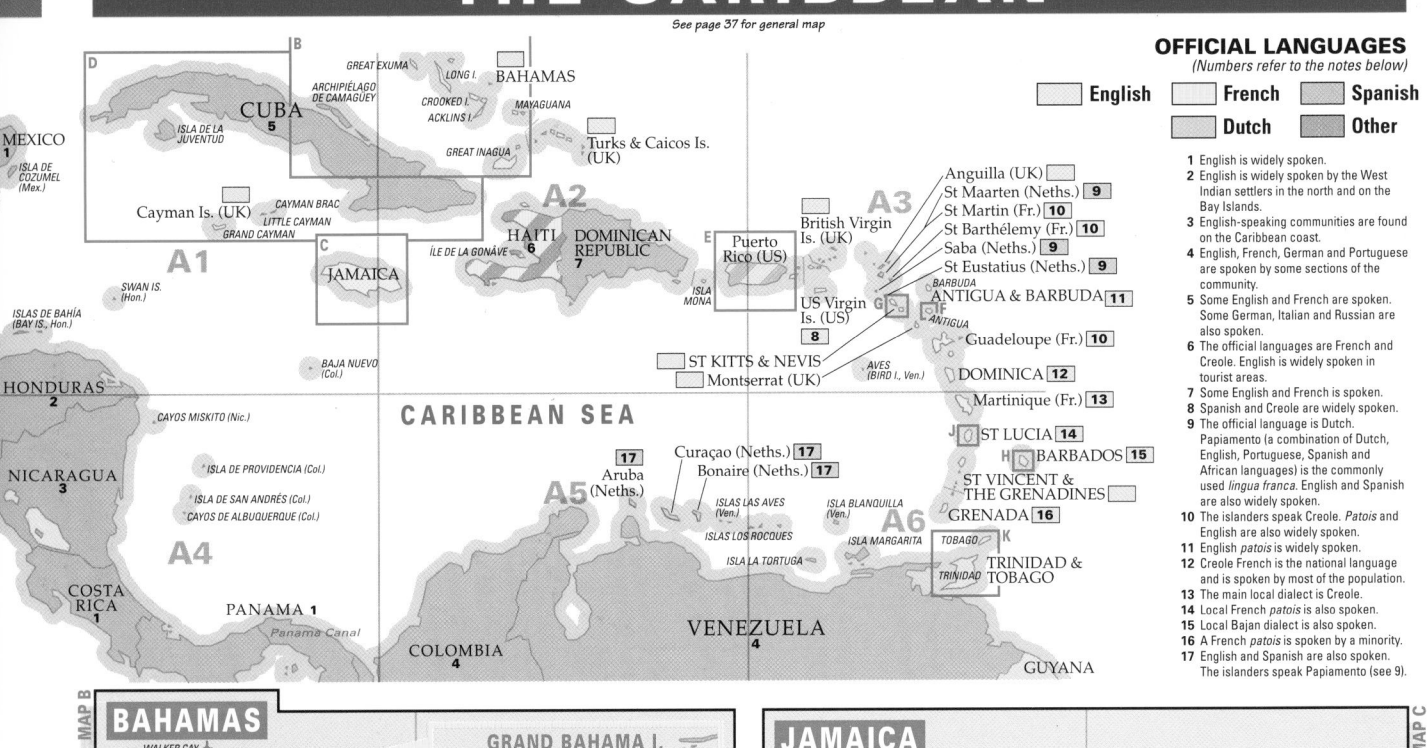

OFFICIAL LANGUAGES
(Numbers refer to the notes below)

English French Spanish
Dutch Other

1 English is widely spoken.
2 English is widely spoken by the West Indian settlers in the north and on the Bay Islands.
3 English-speaking communities are found on the Caribbean coast.
4 English, French, German and Portuguese are spoken by some sections of the community.
5 Some English and French are spoken. Some German, Italian and Russian are also spoken.
6 The official languages are French and Creole. English is widely spoken in tourist areas.
7 Some English and French is spoken.
8 Spanish and Creole are widely spoken.
9 The official language is Dutch. Papiamento (a combination of Dutch, English, Portuguese, Spanish and African languages) is the commonly used *lingua franca*. English and Spanish are also widely spoken.
10 The islanders speak Creole. *Patois* and English are also widely spoken.
11 English *patois* is widely spoken.
12 Creole French is the national language and is spoken by most of the population.
13 The main local dialect is Creole.
14 Local French *patois* is also spoken.
15 Local Bajan dialect is also spoken.
16 A French *patois* is spoken by a minority.
17 English and Spanish are also spoken. The islanders speak Papiamento (see 9).

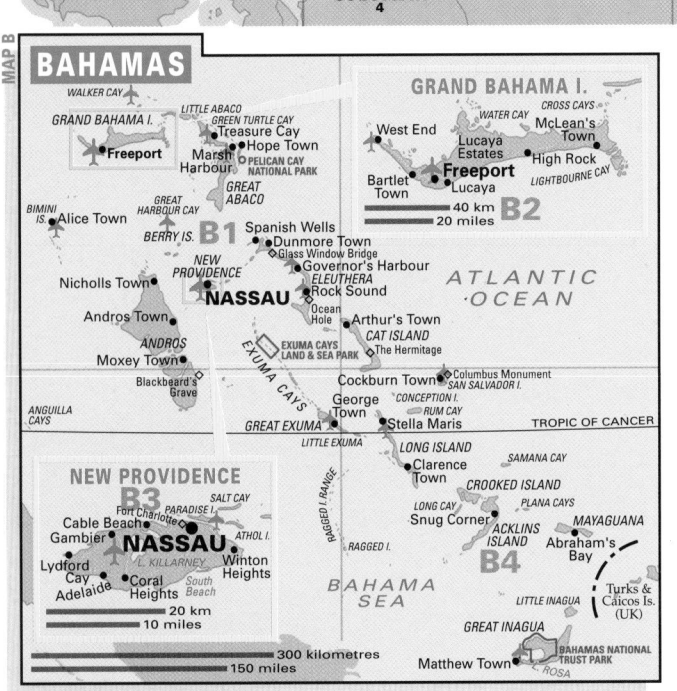

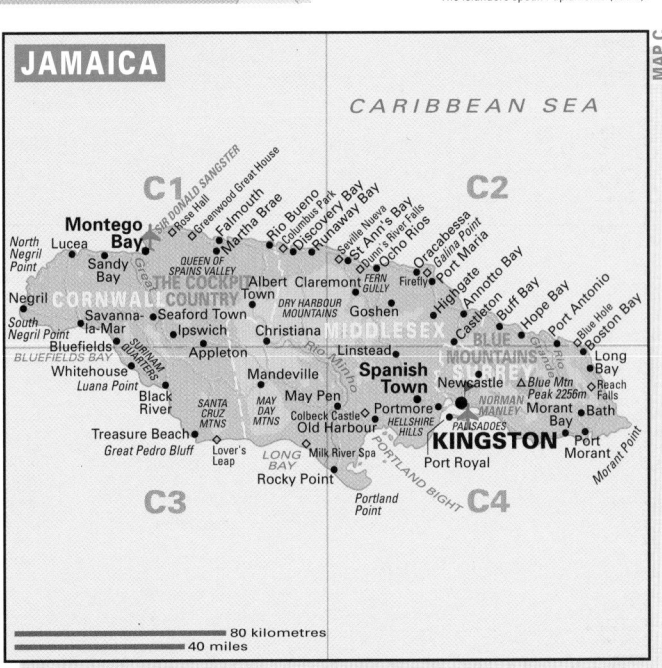

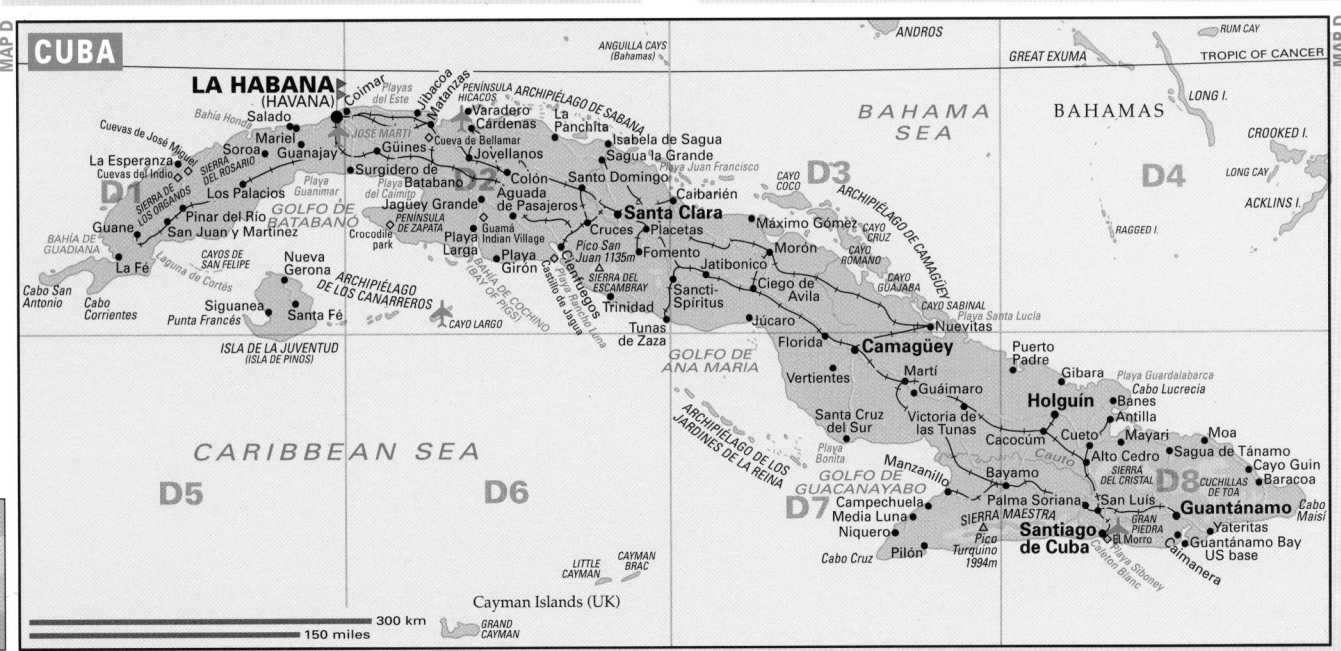

▶ Zoo / animal park   ▲ Aquarium

THE CARIBBEAN

See page 37 for general map

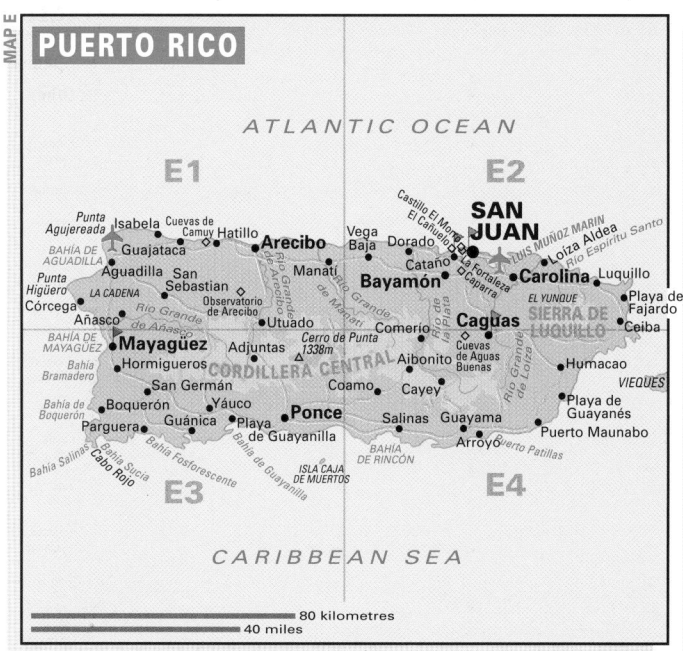

PUERTO RICO

ATLANTIC OCEAN

E1   E2

Punta Aguijereada · Isabela · Cuevas de Camuy · Hatillo
Punta Higüero · Guajataca · Arecibo
BAHÍA DE AGUADILLA · Aguadilla · San Sebastián · Manatí · Vega Baja · Dorado
Córcega · LA CADENA · Observatorio de Arecibo · Cataño
Bahía Bramadero · Mayagüez · Hormigueros · Utuado · Comerío
Bahía de Mayagüez · San Germán · Adjuntas · Cerro de Punta 1338m · Aibonito · Cuevas de Aguas Buenas
Boquerón · Yáuco · Coamo · Cayey
Bahía de Boquerón · Parguera · Guánica · Playa · Ponce · Salinas · Guayama
Bahía Salinas · Cabo Rojo · ISLA CAJA DE MUERTOS · Playa de Guayanilla · BAHÍA DE RINCÓN · Arroyo · Puerto Patillas
Bahía Fosforescente

SAN JUAN
Castillo El Morro · El Cañuelo · La Fortaleza · Caparra · Bayamón · Carolina · Luquillo
Rio Espíritu Santo · Loíza Aldea
Caguas · EL YUNQUE · SIERRA DE LUQUILLO · Playa de Fajardo · Ceiba
Humacao · Playa de Guayanés · Puerto Maunabo
VIEQUES

CARIBBEAN SEA

E3   E4

80 kilometres
40 miles

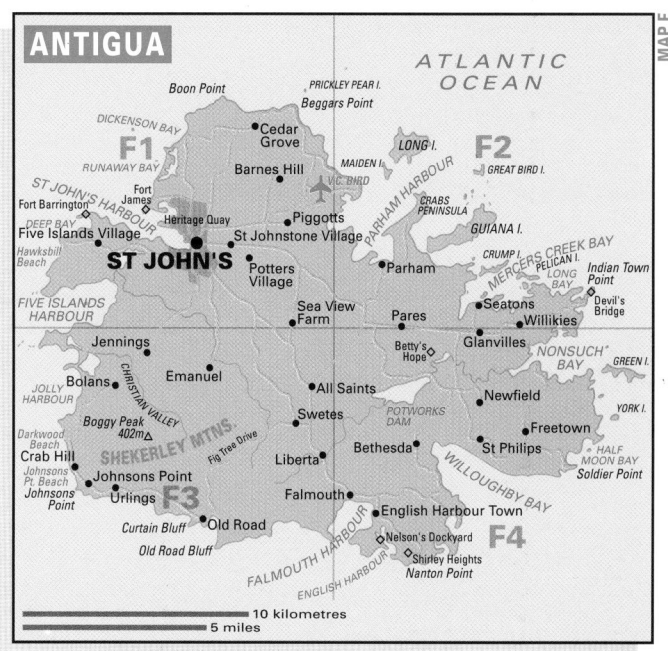

ANTIGUA

ATLANTIC OCEAN

Boon Point · PRICKLY PEAR I. · Beggars Point
DICKENSON BAY · Cedar Grove · LONG I. · F2 · GREAT BIRD I.
F1 · RUNAWAY BAY · Barnes Hill · MAIDEN I. · VIC BIRD
ST JOHN'S HARBOUR · Fort Barrington · Fort James · Heritage Quay · Piggotts · PARHAM HARBOUR · CRABS PENINSULA · GUIANA I.
DEEP BAY · Five Islands Village · St Johnstone Village · Parham · CRUMP I. · MERCERS CREEK BAY · Indian Town Point
Hawksbill Beach · ST JOHN'S · Potters Village · LONG BAY · PELICAN I. · Devil's Bridge
FIVE ISLANDS HARBOUR · Sea View Farm · Pares · Seatons · Willikies
Jennings · Betty's Hope · Glanvilles · NONSUCH BAY · GREEN I.
JOLLY HARBOUR · Bolans · Emanuel · All Saints · Newfield · YORK I.
Boggy Peak 402m · Swetes · POTWORKS DAM · HALF MOON BAY
Darkwood Beach · CHRISTIAN VALLEY · SHEKERLEY MTNS · Liberta · Bethesda · St Philips · Freetown
Crab Hill · Johnsons Pt. Beach · Johnsons Point · Johnsons Point · Fig Tree Drive · Falmouth · English Harbour Town · WILLOUGHBY BAY · Soldier Point
Urlings · F3 · Old Road · Nelson's Dockyard · F4
Curtain Bluff · Old Road Bluff · FALMOUTH HARBOUR · Shirley Heights · Nanton Point · ENGLISH HARBOUR

10 kilometres
5 miles

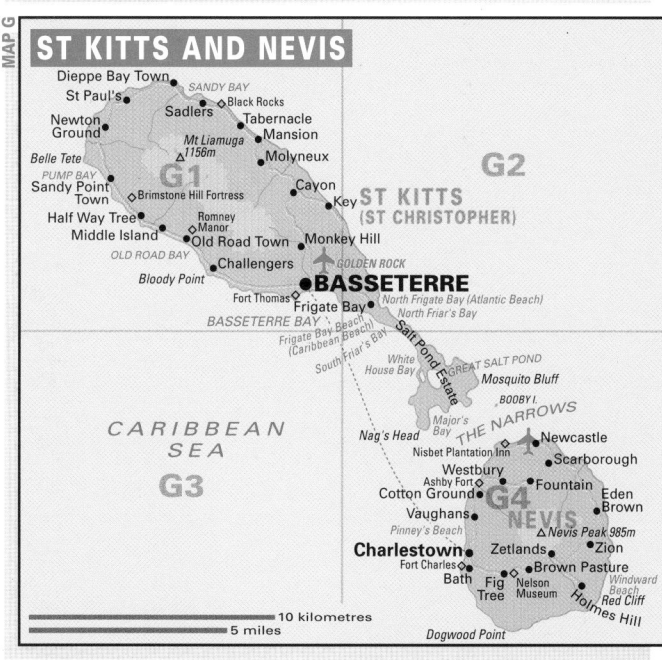

ST KITTS AND NEVIS

Dieppe Bay Town · SANDY BAY
St Paul's · Black Rocks
Newton Ground · Sadlers · Tabernacle · Mansion
Belle Tête · Mt Liamuga 1156m · Molyneux · G2
PUMP BAY · Sandy Point Town · Brimstone Hill Fortress · Cayon · ST KITTS (ST CHRISTOPHER)
Half Way Tree · Romney Manor · Key
Middle Island · Old Road Town · Monkey Hill
OLD ROAD BAY · Challengers · GOLDEN ROCK
Bloody Point · Fort Thomas · BASSETERRE
Frigate Bay · North Frigate Bay (Atlantic Beach)
BASSETERRE BAY · North Friar's Bay
Frigate Bay Beach (Caribbean Beach) · Salt Pond Estate
South Friar's Bay · White House Bay · GREAT SALT POND
CARIBBEAN SEA · Mosquito Bluff · BOOBY I.
Major's Bay · THE NARROWS
Nag's Head · Newcastle
G3 · Nisbet Plantation Inn · Scarborough
Westbury · Fountain · Eden Brown
Ashby Fort · G4
Cotton Ground · Vaughans · NEVIS
Pinney's Beach · Nevis Peak 985m
Charlestown · Zetlands · Zion
Fort Charles · Brown Pasture
Bath · Fig Tree · Nelson Museum · Windward Beach · Red Cliff
Dogwood Point · Holmes Hill

10 kilometres
5 miles

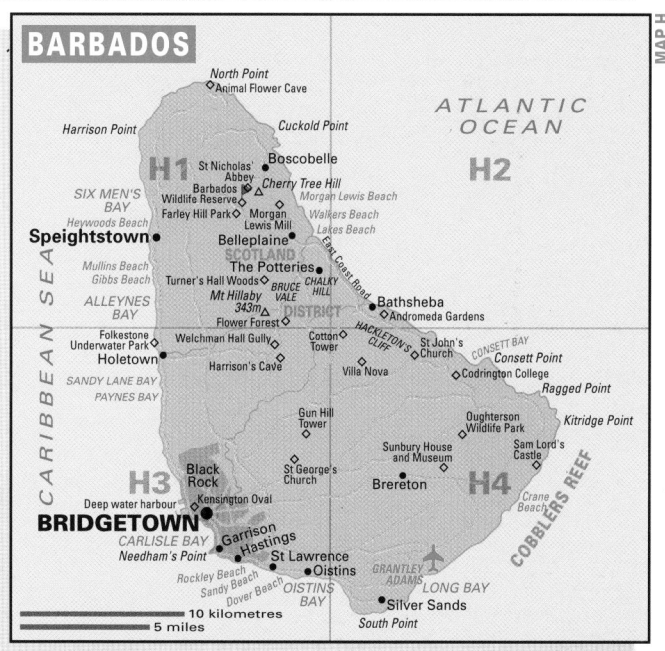

BARBADOS

North Point · Animal Flower Cave
Harrison Point · Cuckold Point · ATLANTIC OCEAN
H1 · St Nicholas' Abbey · Boscobelle · H2
SIX MEN'S BAY · Barbados Wildlife Reserve · Cherry Tree Hill
Farley Hill Park · Morgan Lewis Mill · Morgan Lewis Beach
Heywoods Beach · Belleplaine · Walkers Beach
Speightstown · The Potteries · SCOTLAND · Lakes Beach
Mullins Beach · Turner's Hall Woods · BRUCE VALE · CHALKY HILL
Gibbs Beach · Mt Hillaby 343m · DISTRICT · Bathsheba
ALLEYNES BAY · Flower Forest · Andromeda Gardens
Folkestone Underwater Park · Welchman Hall Gully · Cotton Tower · St John's Church · Consett Bay
Holetown · Harrison's Cave · Villa Nova · Codrington College · Consett Point
SANDY LANE BAY · HACKLETON'S CLIFF · Ragged Point
PAYNES BAY · Gun Hill Tower · Oughterson Wildlife Park · Kitridge Point
H3 · Black Rock · Sunbury House and Museum · Sam Lord's Castle
Deep water harbour · Kensington Oval · St George's Church · Brereton · H4
BRIDGETOWN · Garrison · Crane Beaches · COBBLERS REEF
CARLISLE BAY · Hastings · GRANTLEY ADAMS
Needham's Point · St Lawrence · Oistins · LONG BAY
Rockley Beach · Sandy Beach · Dover Beach · OISTINS BAY · Silver Sands
South Point

10 kilometres
5 miles

CARIBBEAN SEA

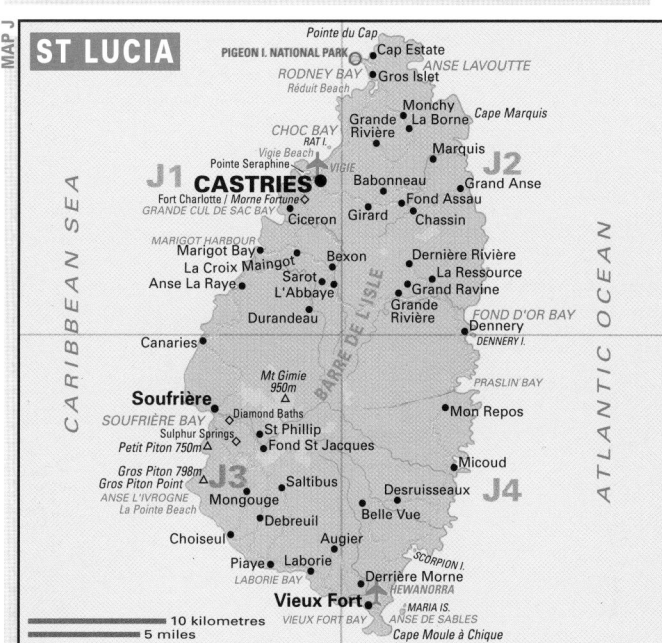

ST LUCIA

Pointe du Cap
PIGEON I. NATIONAL PARK · Cap Estate · ANSE LAVOUTTE
RODNEY BAY · Gros Islet
Réduit Beach
CHOC BAY · RAT I. · Monchy · La Borne · Cape Marquis
Vigie Beach · Grande Rivière
Pointe Seraphine · VIGIE · Marquis
J1 · CASTRIES · Babonneau · Grand Anse · J2
Fort Charlotte / Morne Fortune · Fond Assau
GRANDE CUL DE SAC BAY · Ciceron · Girard · Chassin
MARIGOT HARBOUR · Bexon · Dernière Rivière
Marigot Bay · Sarot · La Ressource
La Croix Maingot · L'Abbaye · Grand Ravine
Anse La Raye · Durandeau · Grande Rivière · FOND D'OR BAY
Canaries · Dennery · DENNERY I.
Mt Gimie 950m · PRASLIN BAY
Soufrière · St Phillip · Mon Repos
SOUFRIÈRE BAY · Diamond Baths · Fond St Jacques
Sulphur Springs · Micoud
Petit Piton 750m
Gros Piton 798m · Saltibus · Desruisseaux
Gros Piton Point · J3 · Mongouge · Belle Vue · J4
ANSE L'IVROGNE · La Pointe Beach · Debreuil · Augier
Choiseul · Piaye · Laborie · SCORPION I.
LABORIE BAY · Derrière Morne · HEWANORRA
Vieux Fort · MARIA IS. · ANSE DE SABLES
VIEUX FORT BAY · Cape Moule à Chique

CARIBBEAN SEA   *ATLANTIC OCEAN*

10 kilometres
5 miles

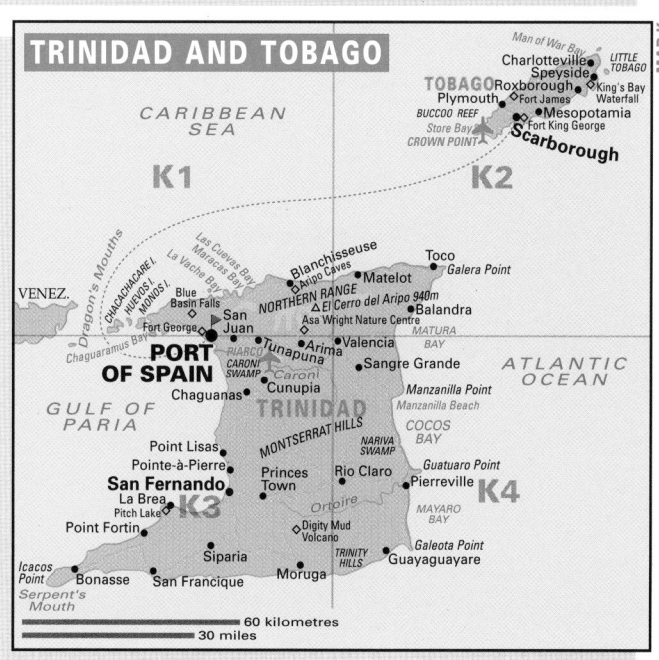

TRINIDAD AND TOBAGO

Man of War Bay
Charlotteville · LITTLE TOBAGO
Speyside
TOBAGO · Roxborough · King's Bay
Plymouth · Fort James · Mesopotamia
BUCCOO REEF · Waterfall
Store Bay · Fort King George
CROWN POINT · Scarborough
K1 · K2
CARIBBEAN SEA
Blanchisseuse · Toco
VENEZ. · Las Cuevas Bay · Maracas Bay · Aripo Caves · Matelot · Galera Point
Dragon's Mouths · La Vache Bay · NORTHERN RANGE · El Cerro del Aripo 940m · Balandra
CHACACHACARE I. · HUEVOS I. · MONOS I. · Blue Basin Falls · Asa Wright Nature Centre · MATURA BAY
Fort George · San Juan · Arima · Valencia
Chaguaramas Bay · PORT OF SPAIN · Tunapuna · Sangre Grande
CARONI SWAMP · Chaguanas · Cunupia · ATLANTIC OCEAN
GULF OF PARIA · Caroni · TRINIDAD · Manzanilla Point
Manzanilla Beach
Point Lisas · MONTSERRAT HILLS · NARIVA SWAMP · COCOS BAY
Pointe-à-Pierre · Princes Town · Rio Claro · Guataro Point
San Fernando · Pierreville
La Brea · K3 · Ortoire · MAYARO BAY · K4
Pitch Lake · Digity Mud Volcano · Galeota Point
Point Fortin · Siparia · Guatuaro Point · Guayaguayare
Icacos Point · Bonasse · San Francique · Moruga · TRINITY HILLS
Serpent's Mouth

60 kilometres
30 miles

1000 metres
500 metres
Sea level

▲ Leisure park   ▶ Zoo / animal park

CLIMATE

TEMPERATURE CONVERSION						
°Celsius	−10	0	10	20	30	40
°Fahrenheit	14	32	50	68	86	104

RAINFALL CONVERSION						
Millimetres	102	203	305	406	508	610
Inches	4	8	12	16	20	24

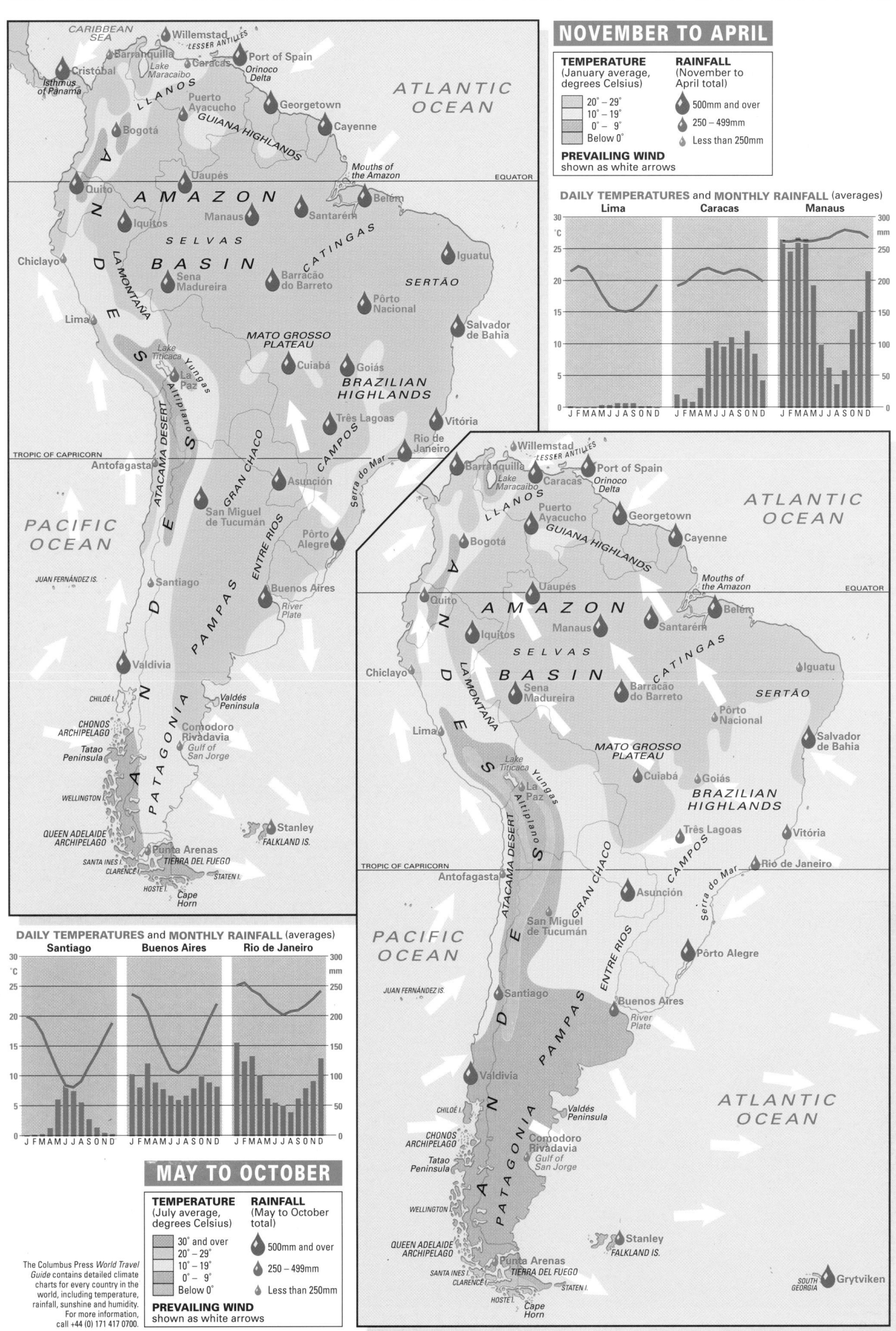

NOVEMBER TO APRIL

TEMPERATURE (January average, degrees Celsius)
- 20° – 29°
- 10° – 19°
- 0° – 9°
- Below 0°

RAINFALL (November to April total)
- 500mm and over
- 250 – 499mm
- Less than 250mm

PREVAILING WIND shown as white arrows

DAILY TEMPERATURES and MONTHLY RAINFALL (averages)
Lima   Caracas   Manaus

DAILY TEMPERATURES and MONTHLY RAINFALL (averages)
Santiago   Buenos Aires   Rio de Janeiro

MAY TO OCTOBER

TEMPERATURE (July average, degrees Celsius)
- 30° and over
- 20° – 29°
- 10° – 19°
- 0° – 9°
- Below 0°

RAINFALL (May to October total)
- 500mm and over
- 250 – 499mm
- Less than 250mm

PREVAILING WIND shown as white arrows

The Columbus Press *World Travel Guide* contains detailed climate charts for every country in the world, including temperature, rainfall, sunshine and humidity. For more information, call +44 (0) 171 417 0700.

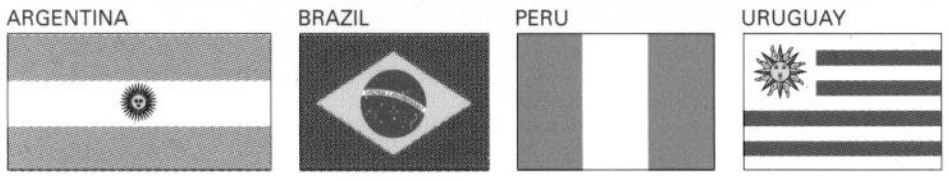

ARGENTINA BRAZIL PERU URUGUAY

SOUTH AMERICA

See pages 43-45 for general maps

OFFICIAL LANGUAGES
(Numbers refer to the notes below)

- ▨ Spanish
- ▨ Portuguese
- ☐ English
- ▨ French
- ▨ Dutch

1. Spanish, English, Italian, French and German are widely spoken, especially in tourist areas.
2. Most of the population speak a Creole *patois*.
3. *Sranan Tongo*, originating in Creole, is the popular language. The other main languages are Hindi and Javanese. English, Chinese, French and Spanish are also spoken.
4. Creole, Hindi, Urdu and Amerindian are also spoken.
5. English, French, German and Portuguese are spoken by some sections of the community.
6. Local Indian dialects and some English, French, German and Italian are spoken.
7. Quechua, the Inca tongue, and other indigenous languages are common. Some English is spoken.
8. Quechua is the most important native language and is spoken in the majority of the Andean cities. Aymará is spoken in some areas of Puno Department. Many other dialects exist in the jungle regions. English is spoken in major tourist areas.
9. The Indians of the Altiplano speak Aymará and elsewhere Quechua is spoken. English is also spoken by a small number of officials and businessmen in commercial centres.
10. Guaraní is widely spoken. Most Paraguayans are bilingual, but prefer to speak Guaraní outside Asunción.
11. English is widely spoken.
12. English, German, French and Italian are sometimes spoken.
13. Some English is spoken in tourist resorts.

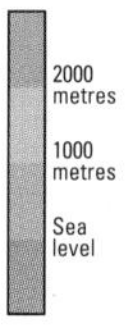

Main map labels

PEN. DE GUAJIRA · PEN. DE PARAGUANÁ · I. MARGARITA · PEN. DE PARIA · ORINOCO DELTA · LLANOS · VENEZUELA · GUYANA · SURINAME · French Guiana · GUIANA HIGHLANDS · Angel Falls · MOUTHS OF THE AMAZON · COLOMBIA · ECUADOR · A1 · PENEDOS SÃO PEDRO É SÃO PAULO · ATOL DAS ROCAS · FERNANDO DE NORONHA · AMAZON · SELVAS · CATINGAS · BASIN · BRAZIL · PERU · MATO GROSSO PLATEAU · A2 · BRAZILIAN HIGHLANDS · LAGO DE TITICACA · BOLIVIA · I. DA TRINIDADE · IS. MARTIN VAZ · SAN FÉLIX · SAN AMBROSIO · GRAN CHACO · CAMPOS · ENTRE RÍOS · PARAGUAY · ARCHIÉPELAGO JUAN FERNÁNDEZ · CHILE · A3 · PAMPAS · URUGUAY · ARGENTINA · I. DE CHILOÉ · PENÍNSULA VALDÉS · ARCHIÉPELAGO DE LOS CHONOS · PENÍNSULA DE TAITAO · A4 · PATAGONIA · Falkland Is. (UK) · I. WELLINGTON · ARCHIÉPELAGO REINA ADELAIDA · I. DESOLACIÓN · I. SANTA INÉS · I. CLARENCE · I. HOSTE · TIERRA DEL FUEGO · I. DE LOS ESTADOS · I. NAVARINO · Cape Horn

ANDES · CORDILLERA · ATACAMA DESERT

RIO DE JANEIRO REGION

MAP C · ESPÍRITO SANTO

C1 · C2 · C3 · C4 · MINAS GERAIS · RIO DE JANEIRO · SP

Governador Valadares · São Gotardo · Dores do Indaiá · Sete Lagoas · Coronel Fabriciano · Ipatinga · Aimorés · Belo Horizonte · Itabira · Sabará · Caratinga · Colatina · Bom Despacho · Bambuí · Itaúna · Nova Lima · Manhuaçu · Afonso Cláudio · Vitória · Vila Velha · Divinópolis · Mariana · Formiga · Congonhas · Ouro Prêto · Ponte Nova · Iúna · Pico da Bandeira 2890m · Furnas Dam · REPRÊSA DE FURNAS · Conselheiro Lafaiete · Alegre · Guarapari · Passos · São João del Rei · Tiradentes · Ubá · Muriaé · Itaperuna · Cachoeiro de Itapemirim · Guaxupé · Lavras · Barbacena · Miracema · Itabapoana · Alfenas · Varginha · Santos Dumont · Leopoldina · Santo Antônio de Pádua · São João da Barra · Três Corações · Andrelândia · Juiz de Fora · Além Paraíba · Campos · Poços de Caldas · Lambari · Caxambu · Três Rios · RIO DE JANEIRO · Cabo de São Tomé · Pouso Alegre · São Lourenço · Pico das Agulhas Negras (Itatiaia) 2787m · Nova Friburgo · Macaé · LAGO FEIA · Itajubá · Volta Redonda · Teresópolis · Rio das Ostras · SERRA DA MANTIQUEIRA · Campos do Jordão · Cruzeiro · Barra Mansa · Nova Iguaçu · Petrópolis · Reserva biológica Poço das Antas · Bragança Paulista · Aparecida do Norte · Duque de Caxias · Búzios · LAGO DE ARARUAMA · Cabo Frio · Atibaia · S. José d. Campos · Taubaté · Parati · Mangaratiba · Niterói · Guarulhos · Ubatuba · ILHA GRANDE · Rio de Janeiro · São Paulo · Caraguatatuba · Santo André · Bertioga · ILHA DE SÃO SEBASTIÃO (ILHABELA) · Guarujá · Santos · TROPIC OF CAPRICORN · ATLANTIC OCEAN · 1 Barra de Tijuca · 2 Leblon · 3 Ipanema · 4 Copacabana · 300 kilometres · 150 miles

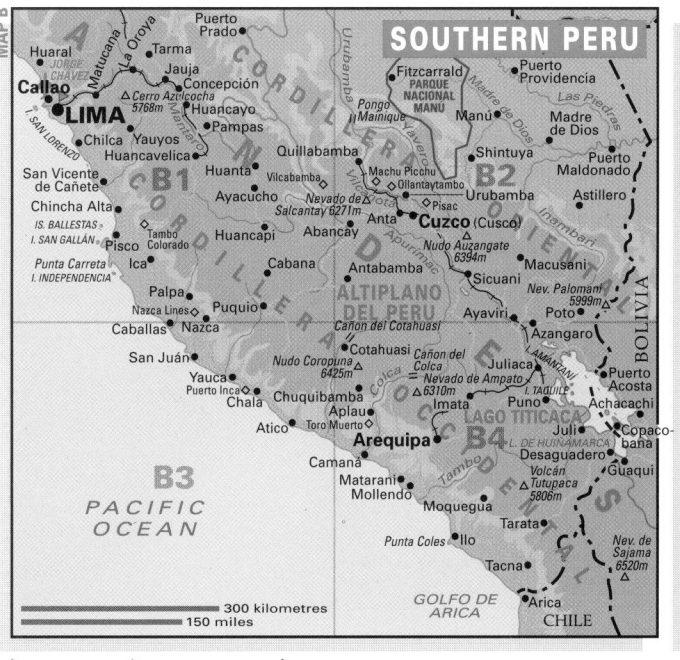

SOUTHERN PERU

MAP B · B1 · B2 · B3 · B4

Huaral · Puerto Prado · La Oroya · Tarma · CORDILLERA · Fitzcarrald · Puerto Providencia · Callao · JORGE CHÁVEZ · Jauja · Concepción · PARQUE NACIONAL MANU · Las Piedras · LIMA · Cerro Azulcocha 5768m · Huancayo · Pongo Mainique · Manú · Madre de Dios · Chilca · Yauyos · Pampas · Quillabamba · Shintuya · Puerto Maldonado · SAN LORENZO · Huancavelica · Huanta · Machu Picchu · Urubamba · Astillero · San Vicente de Cañete · Ayacucho · Vilcabamba · Ollantaytambo · Pisac · Chincha Alta · Huancapi · Nevado de Salcantay 6271m · Anta · Cuzco (Cusco) · IS. BALLESTAS · I. SAN GALLÁN · Pisco · Tambo Colorado · Abancay · Pampa Carreta · Ica · Cabana · Antabamba · Nudo Auzangate 6394m · Macusani · I. INDEPENDENCIA · Palpa · Puquio · Sicuani · Caballas · Nazca · ALTIPLANO DEL PERU · Nev. Palomani 5999m · Nazca Lines · Cotahuasi · Ayaviri · Azángaro · San Juan · Cañón del Cotahuasi · Nudo Coropuna 6425m · Juliaca · Puerto Acosta · Yauca · Cañón del Colca · Nevado de Ampato 6310m · AMANTANÍ · Achacachi · Puerto Inca · Chuquibamba · Imata · Juli · TAQUILE · LAGO TITICACA · Chala · Aplau · Copacabana · Atico · Toro Muerto · Arequipa · I. DE HUINAMARCA · Camaná · Desaguadero · Guaqui · Matarani · Volcán Tutupaca 5806m · Mollendo · Moquegua · Tarata · Punta Coles · Nev. de Sajama 6520m · Ilo · Tacna · PACIFIC OCEAN · GOLFO DE ARICA · Arica · CHILE · 300 kilometres · 150 miles

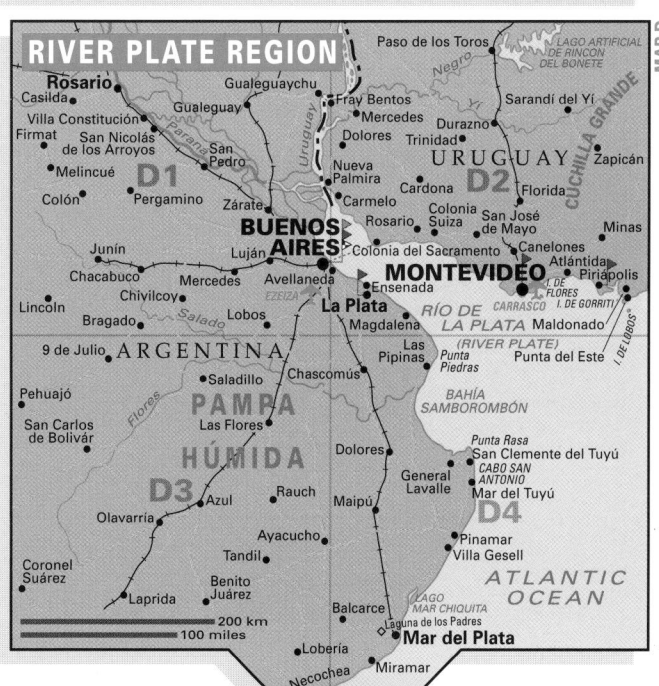

RIVER PLATE REGION

MAP D · D1 · D2 · D3 · D4

Paso de los Toros · LAGO ARTIFICIAL DEL RINCON DEL BONETE · Rosario · Casilda · Gualeguaychu · Fray Bentos · Sarandí del Yí · Villa Constitución · Gualeguay · Mercedes · Durazno · Zapicán · Firmat · San Nicolás de los Arroyos · Dolores · Trinidad · URUGUAY · San Pedro · Nueva Palmira · Cardona · Florida · Minas · Melincué · Colón · Pergamino · Zárate · Carmelo · Colonia Suiza · San José de Mayo · Junín · Rosario · Colonia del Sacramento · Canelones · Atlántida · BUENOS AIRES · Chacabuco · Luján · Avellaneda · MONTEVIDEO · Piriápolis · Lincoln · Mercedes · Chivilcoy · Ensenada · CARRASCO · I. DE FLORES · I. DE GORRITI · Bragado · Lobos · La Plata · Magdalena · Maldonado · 9 de Julio · ARGENTINA · Las Pipinas · Punta del Este · Chascomús · Punta Piedras · I. DE LOBOS · Pehuajó · BAHÍA SAMBOROMBÓN · PAMPA · Saladillo · Punta Rasa · San Clemente del Tuyú · San Carlos de Bolívar · Las Flores · Dolores · CABO SAN ANTONIO · HÚMIDA · General Lavalle · Mar del Tuyú · D3 · Olavarría · Azul · Rauch · Maipú · D4 · Pinamar · Villa Gesell · Ayacucho · ATLANTIC OCEAN · Coronel Suárez · Tandil · LAGO MAR CHIQUITA · Laguna de los Padres · Benito Juárez · Balcarce · Laprida · Loberia · Mar del Plata · Necochea · Miramar · Quequén · 200 km · 100 miles · 2000 metres · 1000 metres · Sea level

▼ Leisure park   ▼ Zoo / animal park   ▼ Formula One

WORLD

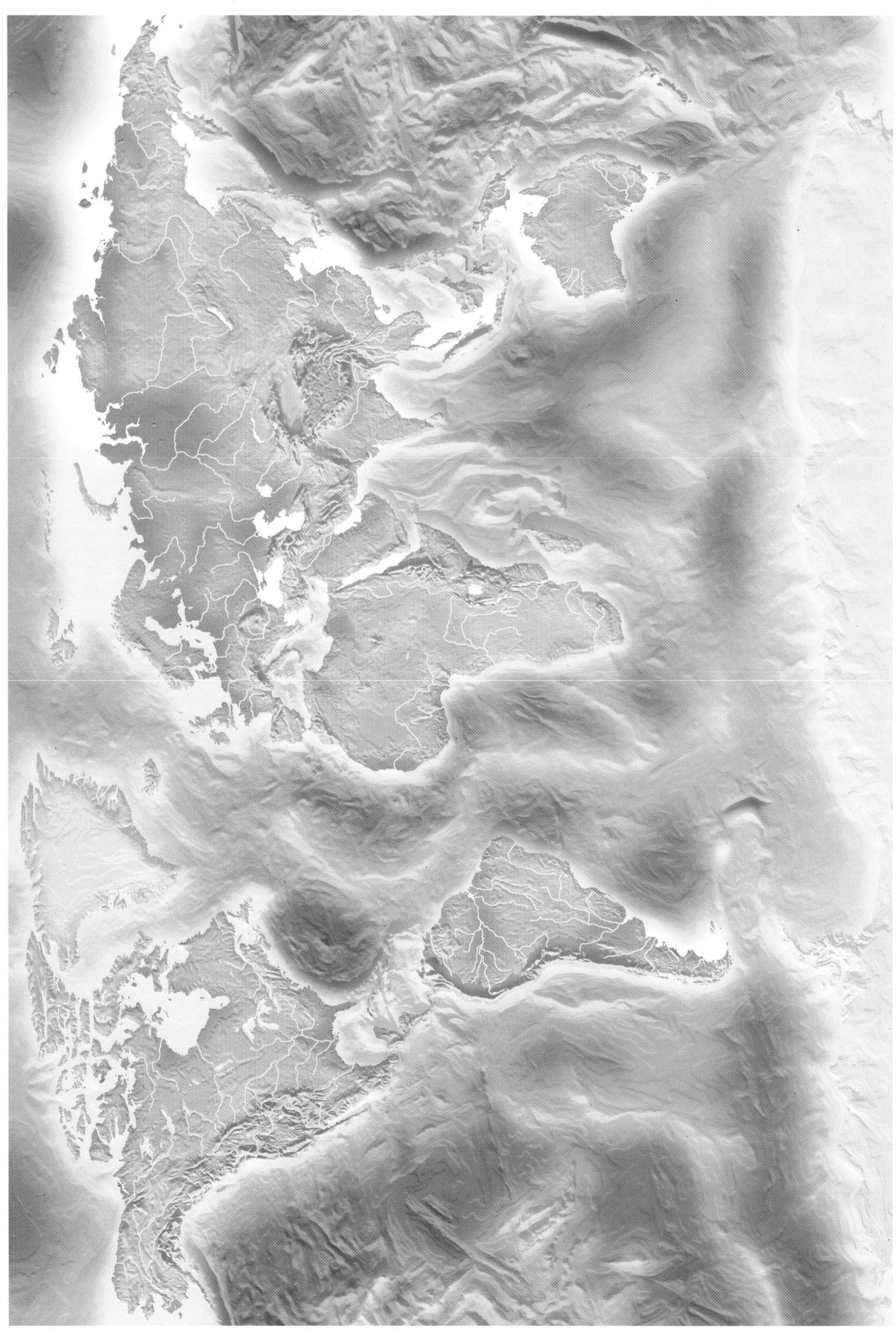

EUROPE

The British Isles

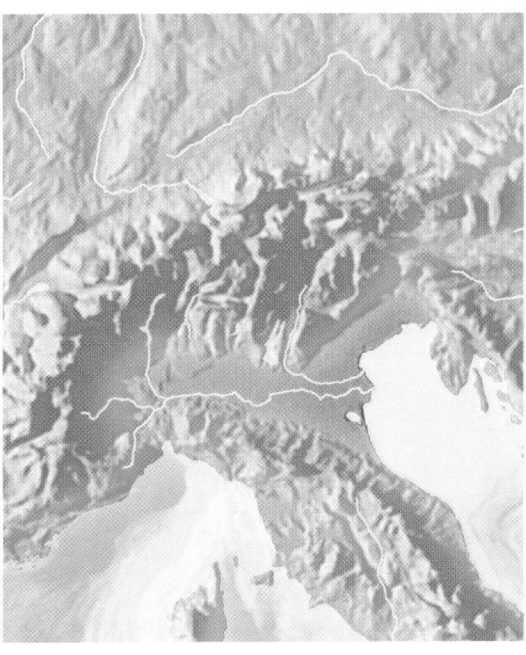

The Alps

AFRICA

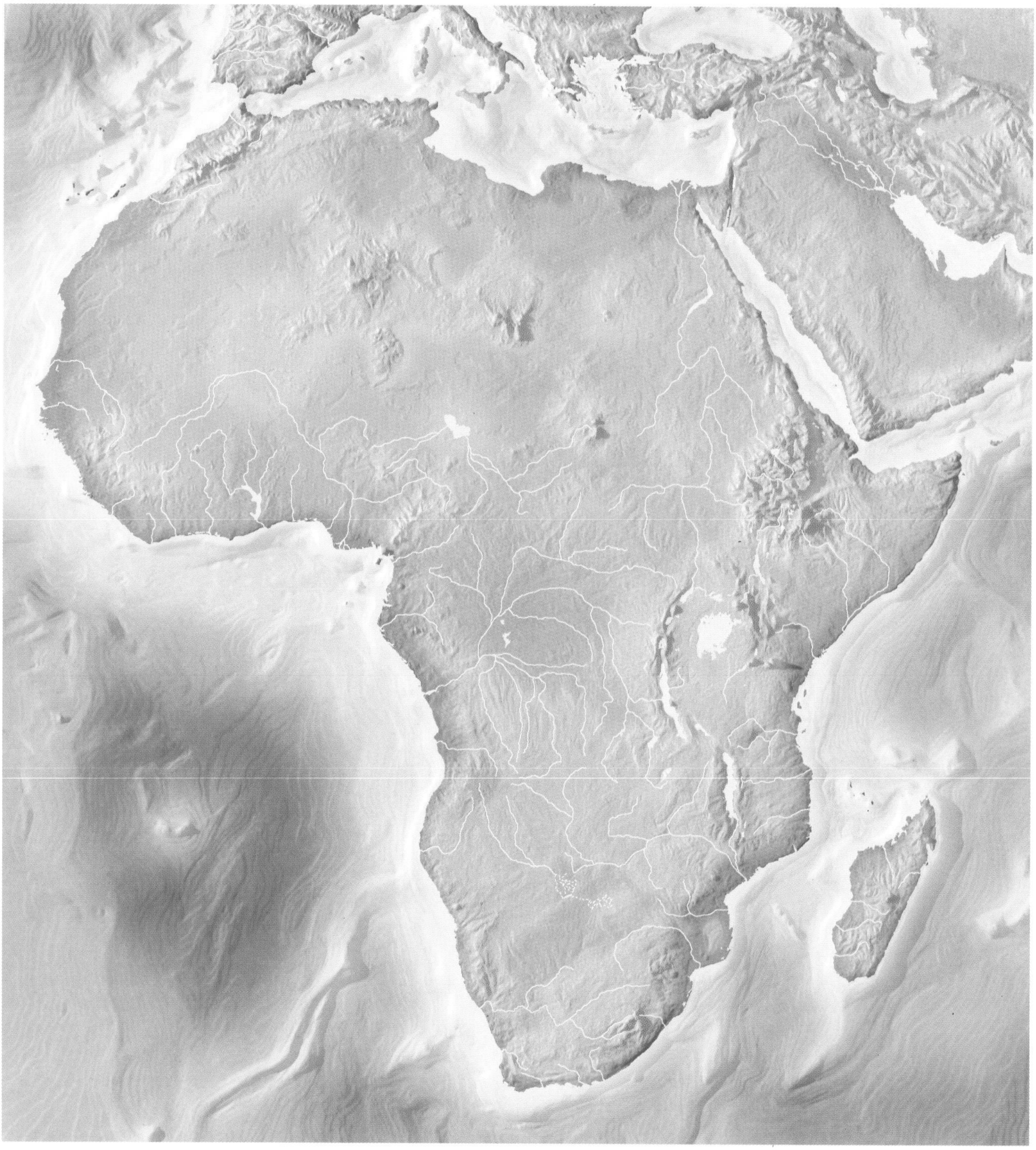

Nile Delta, Sinai
and the Suez Canal

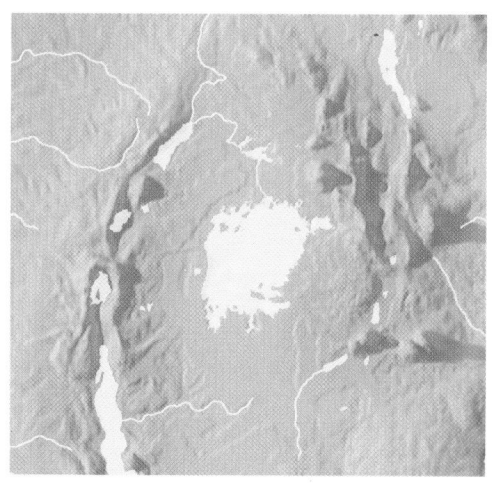

Lake Victoria region

ASIA

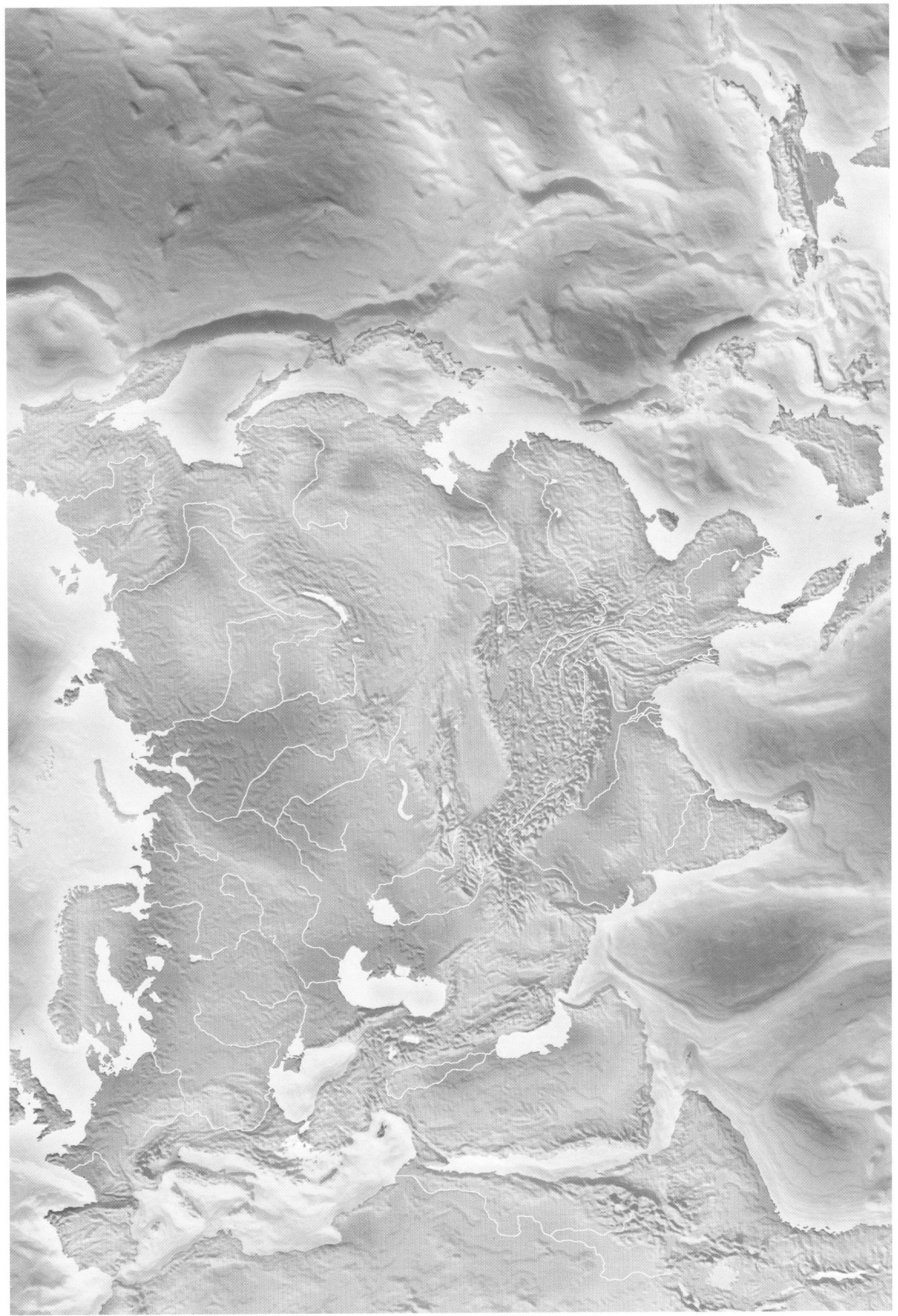

NORTH AMERICA

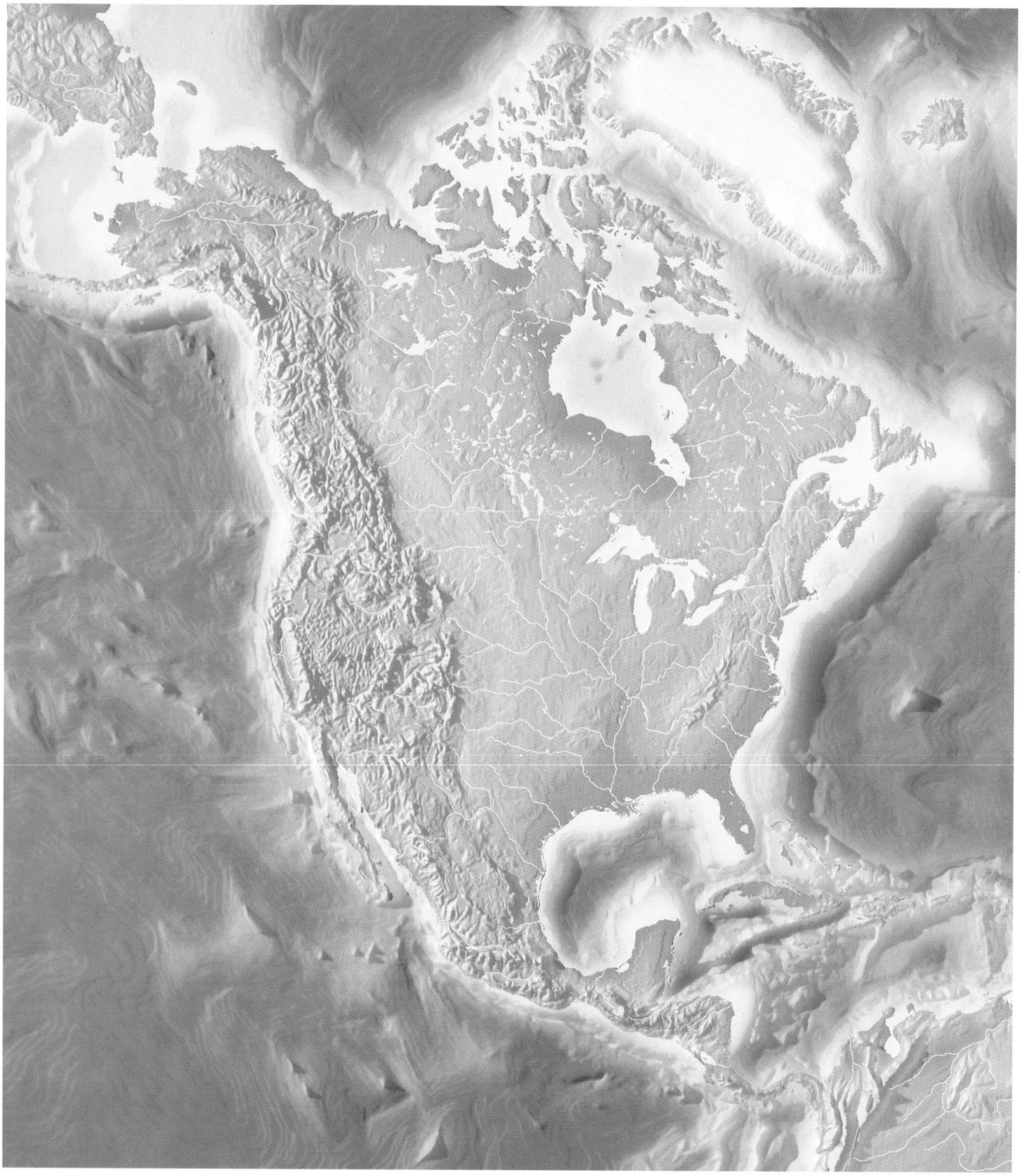

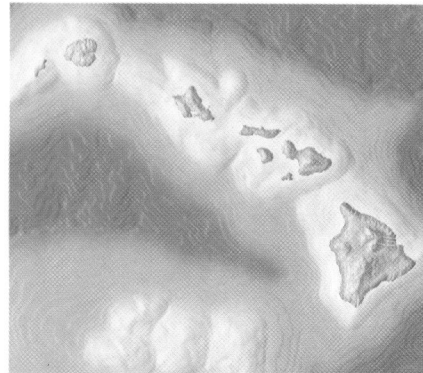

Hawaii

Panama and the Panama Canal

Northern Caribbean

SOUTH AMERICA

AUSTRALIA AND NEW ZEALAND

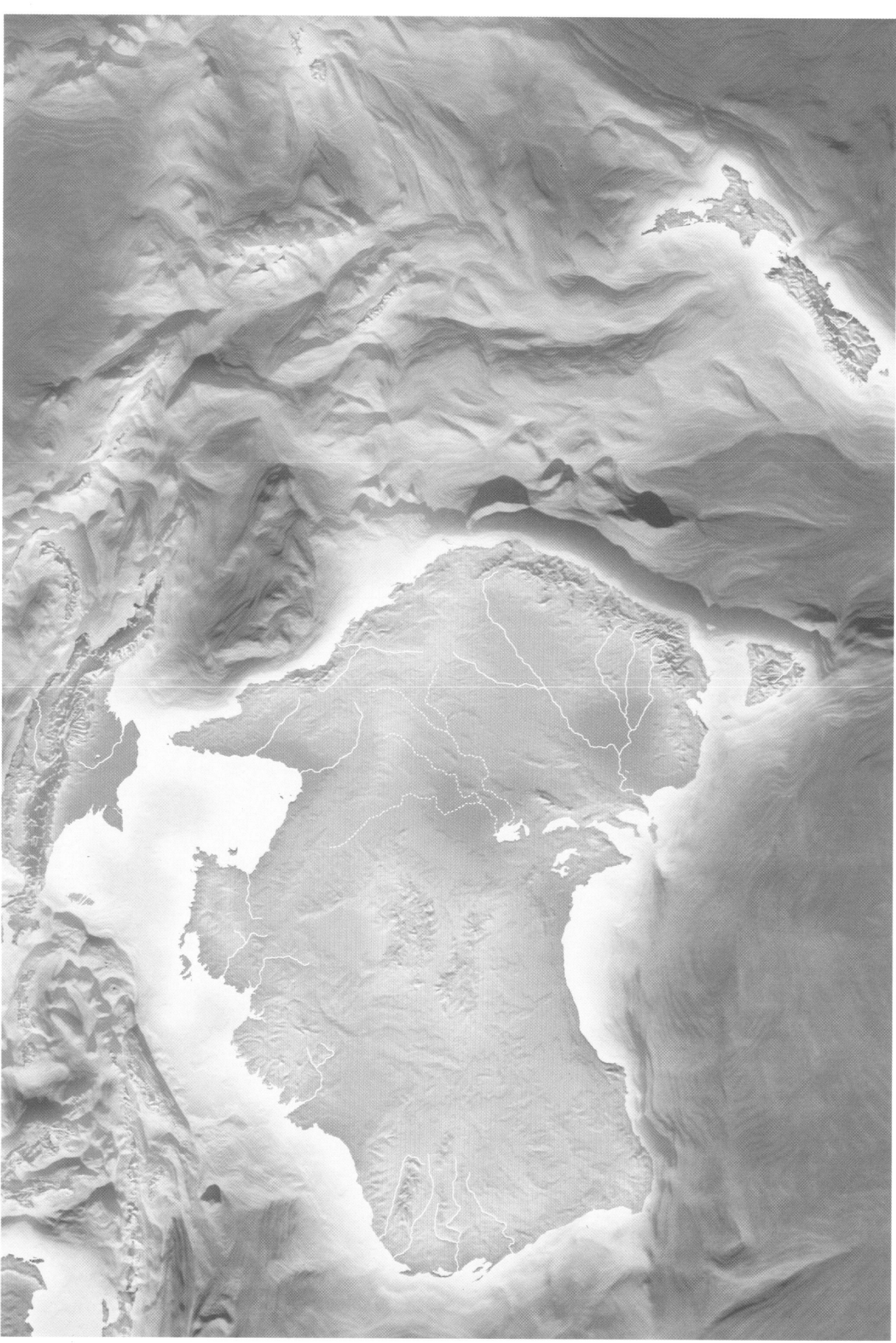

POLAR REGIONS

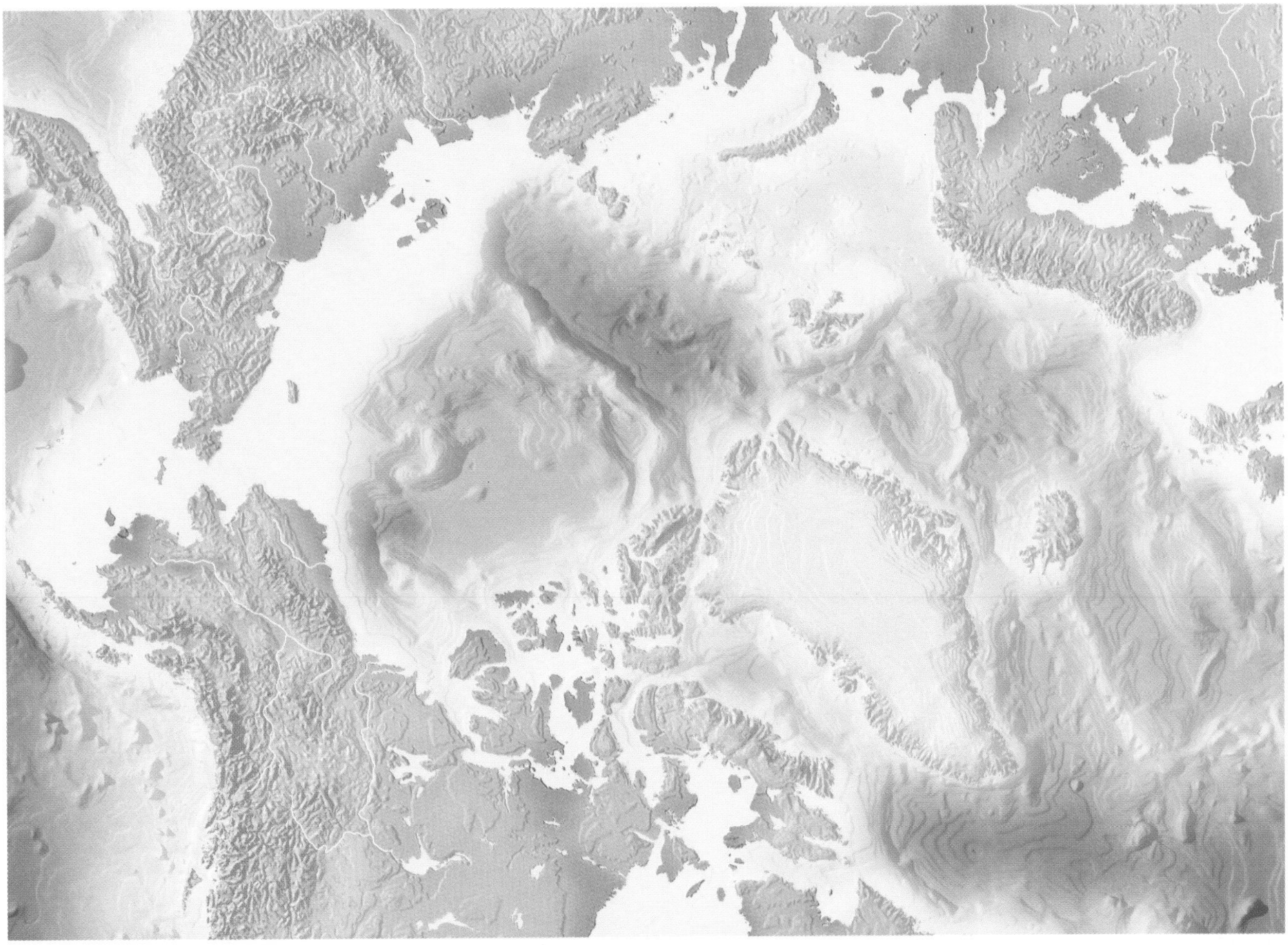

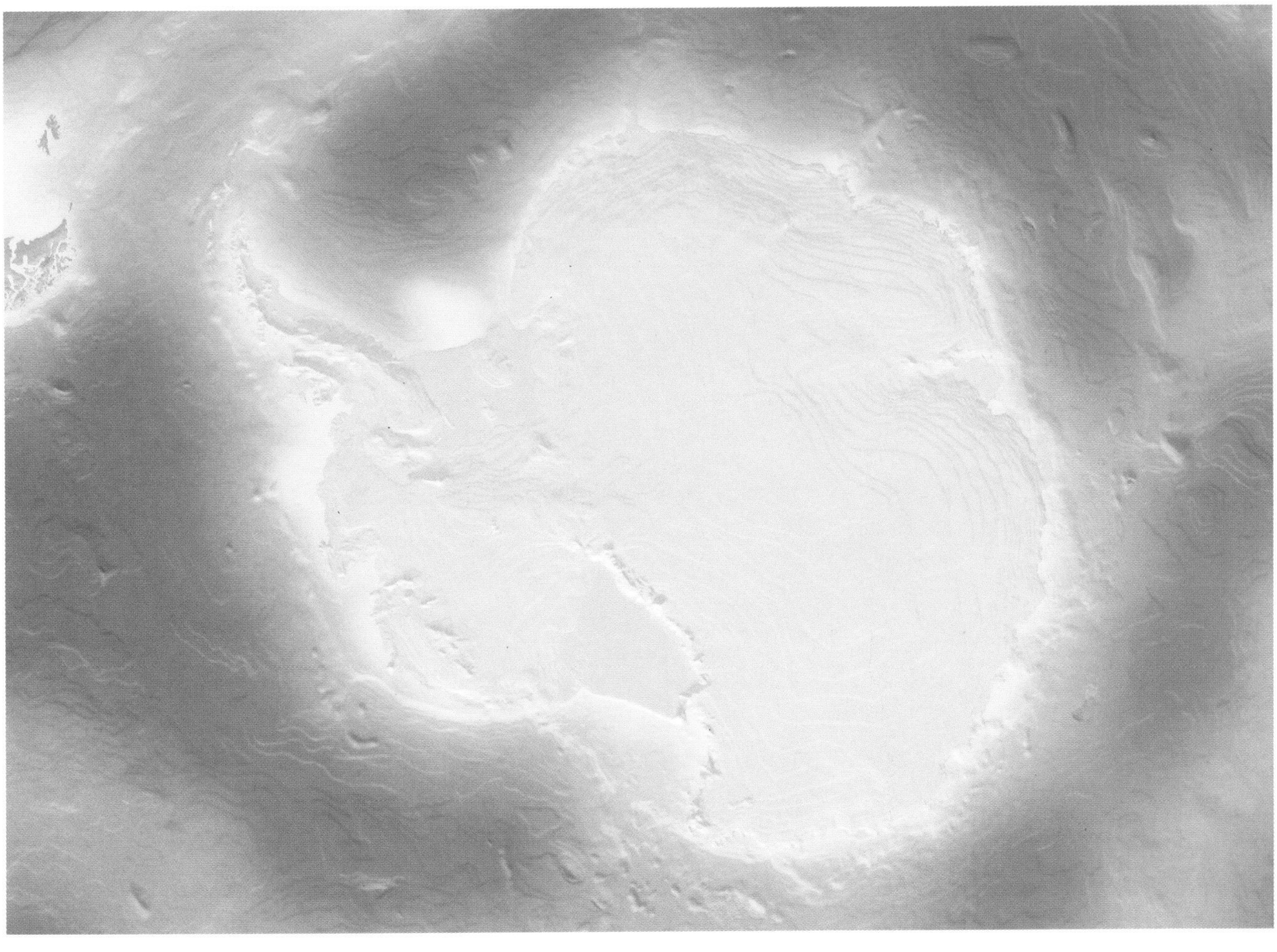

EARTH FROM SPACE

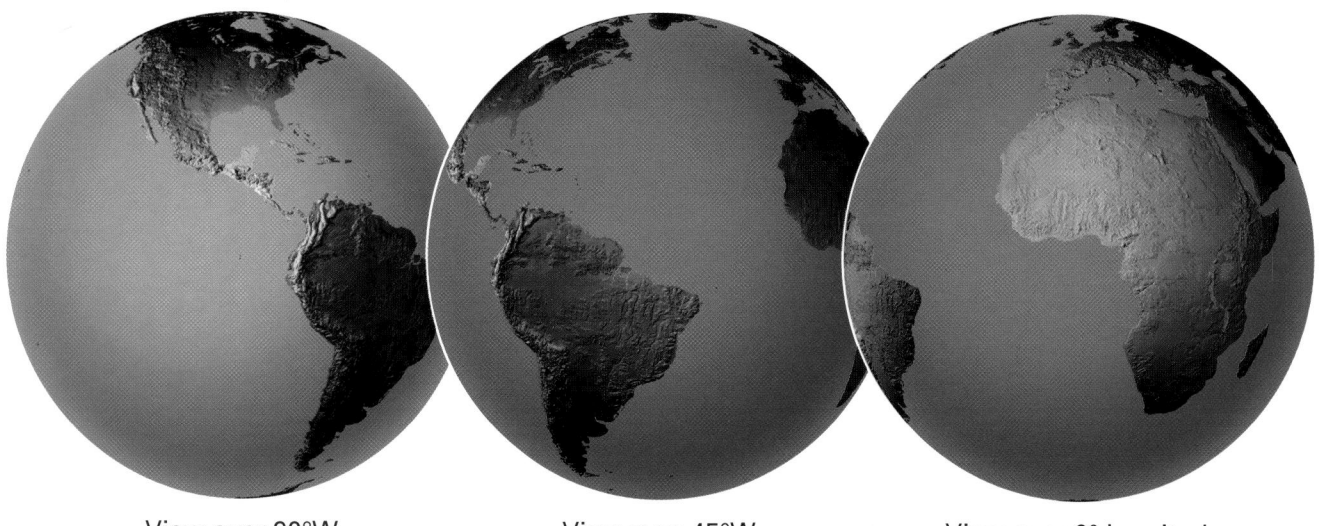

View over 90°W   View over 45°W   View over 0° longitude

PACIFIC OCEAN   ## ATLANTIC OCEAN

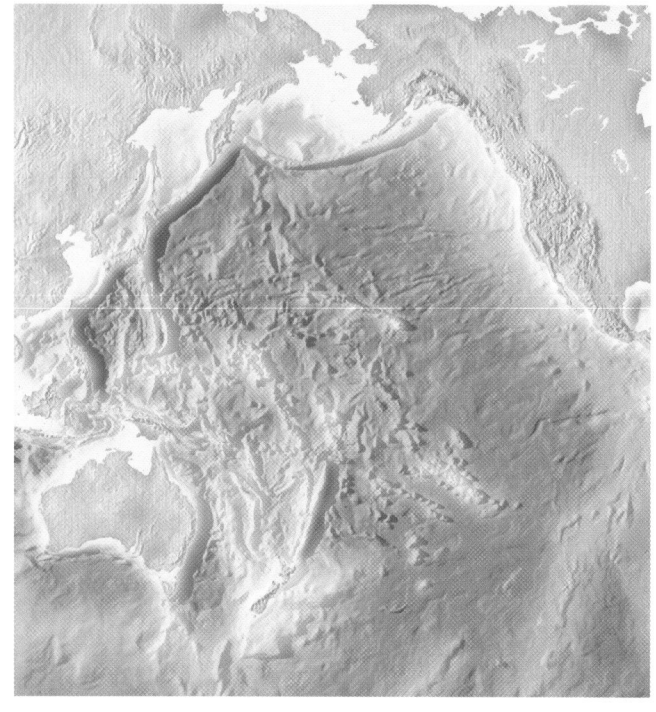   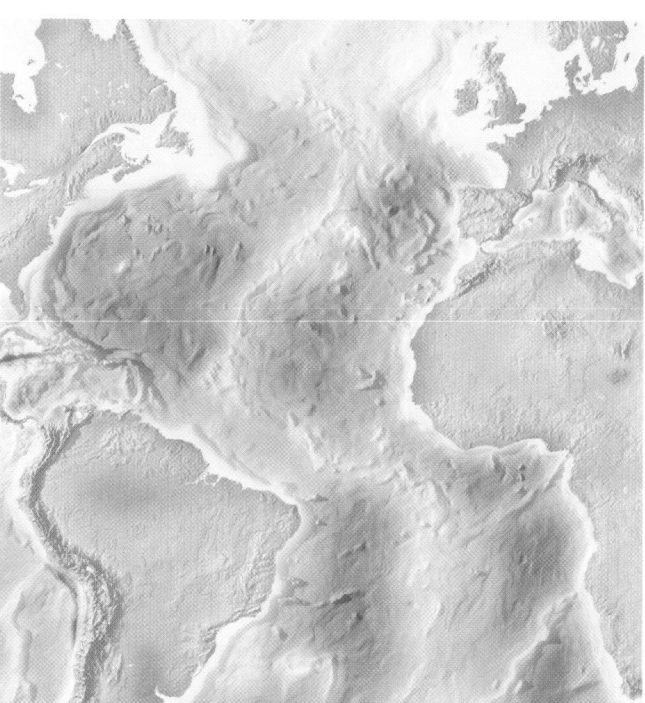

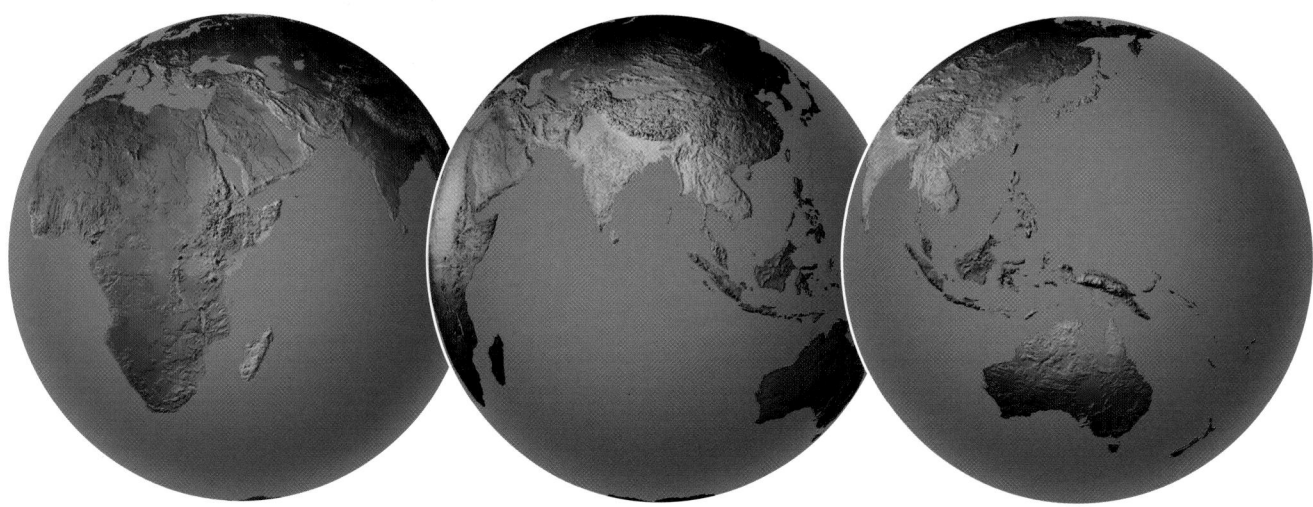

View over 45°E   View over 90°E   View over 135°E

BRITISH ISLES

Public surface transport in Europe is dominated by the train. The extensive rail network is seen in the maps on pages 137 to 143 which are taken from the *Thomas Cook European Timetable*. The Timetable shows, as it has done for the last 125 years, the routes and timings of the major railway lines of Europe. Also covered are the many ferry services in Europe,

shown on the maps by dotted lines. Originally just an internal document for Thomas Cook staff use, the timetable is now sold to customers in Thomas Cook Travel shops and by mail order throughout the world. Place names given are as used by the transport authorities concerned and may differ from those employed in the rest of this atlas.

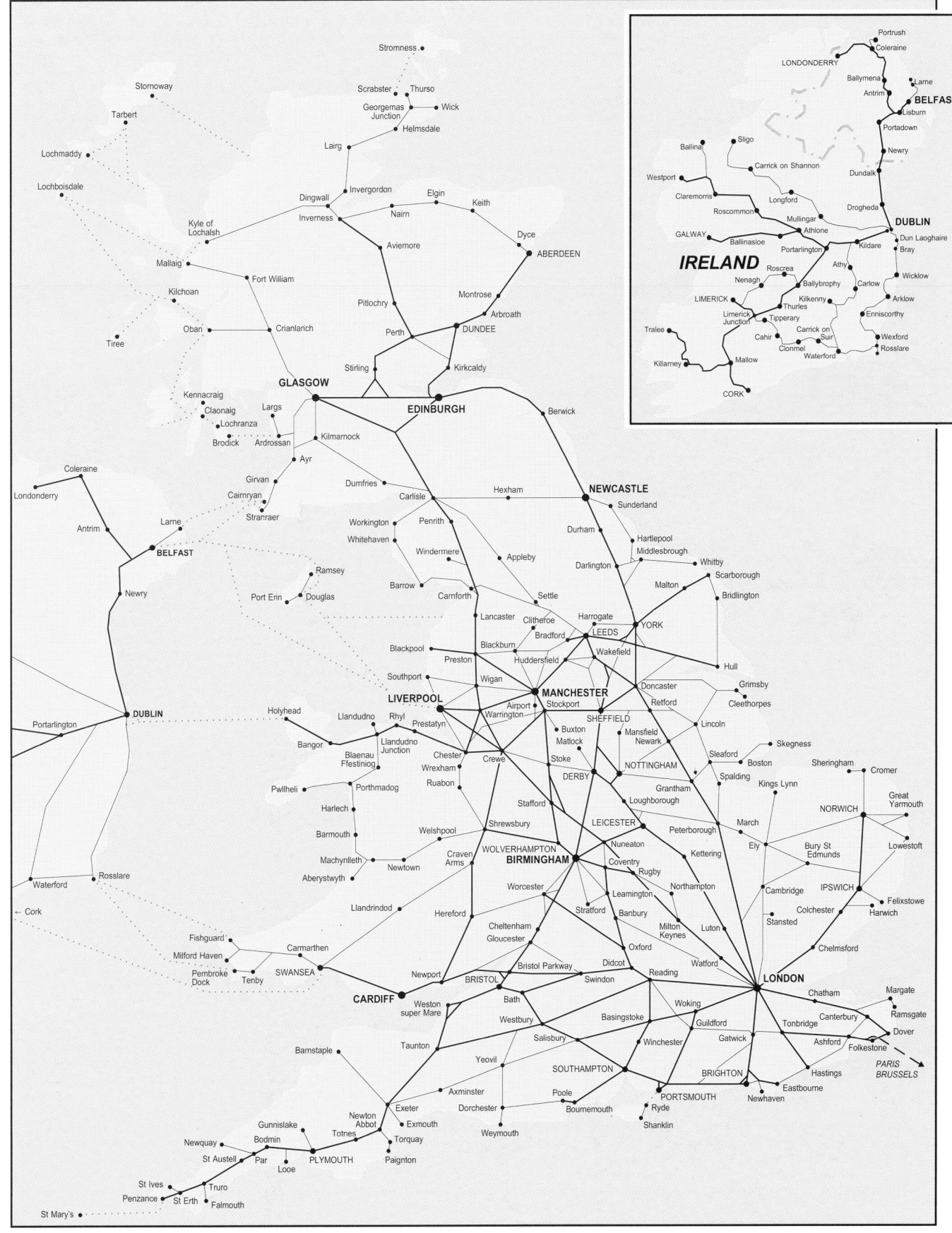

FRANCE

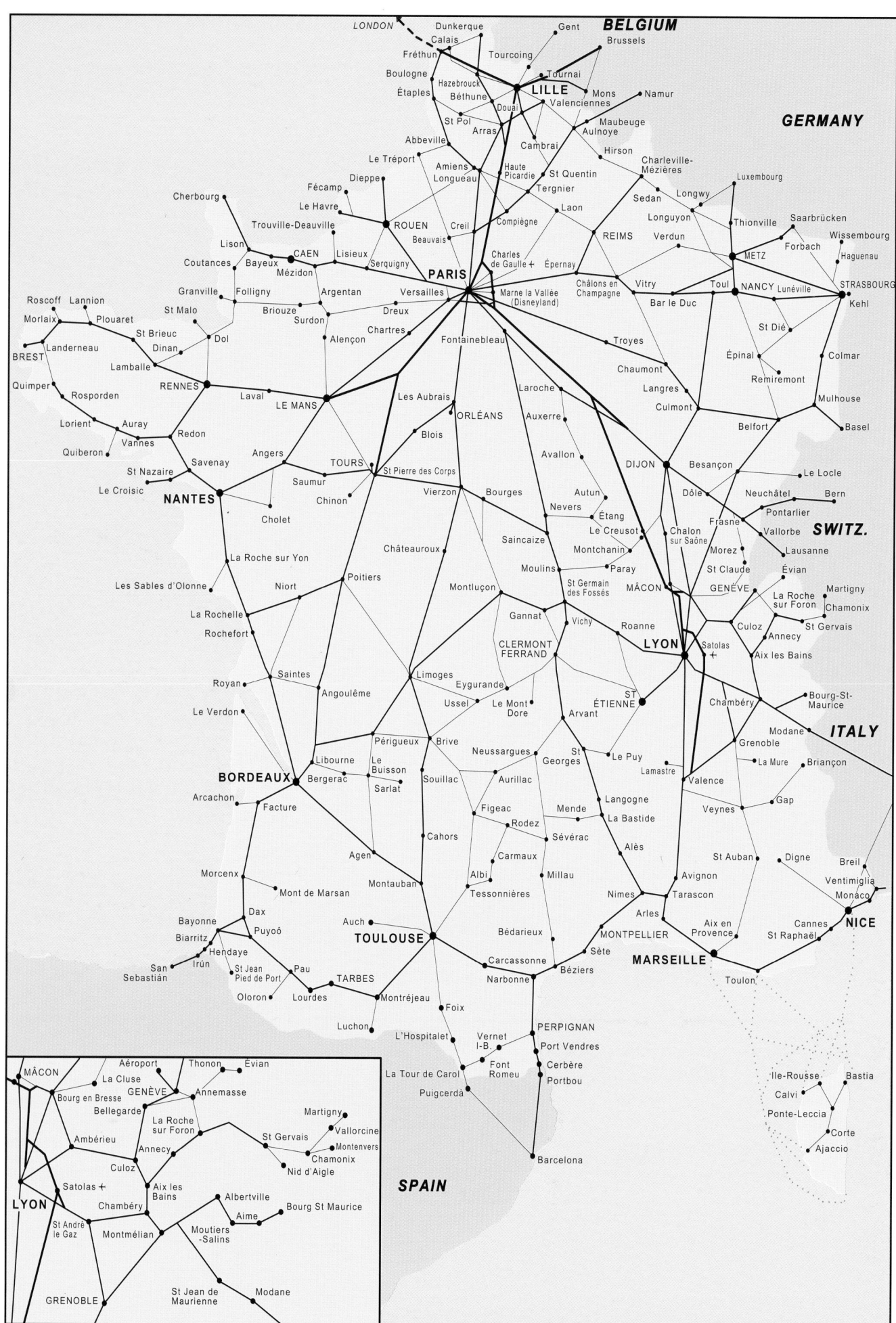
LONDON
Dunkerque
Calais
Gent
BELGIUM
Brussels
Fréthun
Tourcoing
Boulogne
Tournai
Hazebrouck
LILLE
Étaples
Béthune
Mons
Douai
Valenciennes
Namur
St Pol
Arras
Maubeuge
Aulnoye
GERMANY
Abbeville
Cambrai
Hirson
Le Tréport
Amiens
Longueau
Haute Picardie
St Quentin
Charleville-Mézières
Luxembourg
Dieppe
Fécamp
Tergnier
Sedan
Longwy
Cherbourg
Le Havre
Laon
Longuyon
Thionville
Saarbrücken
Trouville-Deauville
ROUEN
Creil
Compiègne
Beauvais
REIMS
Verdun
Wissembourg
Lison
Forbach
CAEN
Lisieux
Charles de Gaulle
Épernay
METZ
Haguenau
Coutances
Bayeux
Mézidon
Serquigny
PARIS
STRASBOURG
Kehl
Granville
Folligny
Argentan
Versailles
Marne la Vallée (Disneyland)
Châlons en Champagne
Vitry
Toul
NANCY
Lunéville
Roscoff
Lannion
St Malo
Briouze
Surdon
Dreux
Bar le Duc
Morlaix
Plouaret
Dol
Chartres
St Dié
St Brieuc
Alençon
Fontainebleau
Troyes
Dinan
Landerneau
Colmar
BREST
Lamballe
Épinal
Chaumont
Remiremont
Quimper
RENNES
Laval
Laroche
Langres
Rosporden
LE MANS
Les Aubrais
Mulhouse
Culmont
ORLÉANS
Auxerre
Lorient
Auray
Belfort
Basel
Vannes
Redon
Blois
Quiberon
Avallon
Angers
Savenay
TOURS
St Pierre des Corps
DIJON
Besançon
St Nazaire
Le Locle
Saumur
Le Croisic
NANTES
Chinon
Vierzon
Bourges
Autun
Dôle
Neuchâtel
Bern
Nevers
Cholet
Étang
Pontarlier
Frasne
Le Creusot
Chalon sur Saône
Vallorbe
SWITZ.
Saincaize
Montchanin
Châteauroux
Morez
Lausanne
La Roche sur Yon
Moulins
Paray
St Claude
Évian
Poitiers
Niort
Les Sables d'Olonne
Montluçon
St Germain des Fossés
MÂCON
GENÈVE
Martigny
La Roche sur Foron
Chamonix
La Rochelle
Gannat
Vichy
Roanne
Culoz
St Gervais
Rochefort
CLERMONT FERRAND
Annecy
LYON
Satolas
Aix les Bains
Saintes
Limoges
Royan
Angoulême
Eygurande
Bourg-St-Maurice
Ussel
Le Mont Dore
ST ÉTIENNE
Chambéry
Le Verdon
Arvant
Modane
ITALY
Périgueux
Brive
Grenoble
Neussargues
St Georges
Le Puy
Libourne
Le Buisson
La Mure
Briançon
BORDEAUX
Lamastre
Bergerac
Souillac
Aurillac
Valence
Sarlat
Arcachon
Facture
Langogne
Figeac
Mende
Veynes
Gap
Rodez
La Bastide
Cahors
Sévérac
Alès
Agen
Carmaux
St Auban
Digne
Breil
Morcenx
Millau
Albi
Avignon
Ventimiglia
Montauban
Mont de Marsan
Tessonnières
Nimes
Tarascon
Monaco
Dax
Arles
Bayonne
Auch
Aix en Provence
Cannes
NICE
Puyoô
Bédarieux
MONTPELLIER
St Raphaël
Biarritz
TOULOUSE
Hendaye
Sète
MARSEILLE
Carcassonne
San Sebastián
Irún
St Jean Pied de Port
Pau
Béziers
Narbonne
Toulon
TARBES
Oloron
Lourdes
Montréjeau
Foix
Luchon
PERPIGNAN
L'Hospitalet
Vernet I-B.
Port Vendres
Font Romeu
Cerbère
La Tour de Carol
Portbou
Ile-Rousse
Bastia
Puigcerdà
Calvi
Ponte-Leccia
Corte
Ajaccio
Barcelona
SPAIN
MÂCON
Aéroport
Thonon
Évian
La Cluse
Bourg en Bresse
GENÈVE
Annemasse
Bellegarde
Martigny
La Roche sur Foron
Vallorcine
Ambérieu
St Gervais
Montenvers
Annecy
Chamonix
Culoz
Nid d'Aigle
Satolas
Aix les Bains
LYON
Albertville
Chambéry
Bourg St Maurice
Aime
St André le Gaz
Montmélian
Moutiers -Salins
GRENOBLE
St Jean de Maurienne
Modane

GERMANY

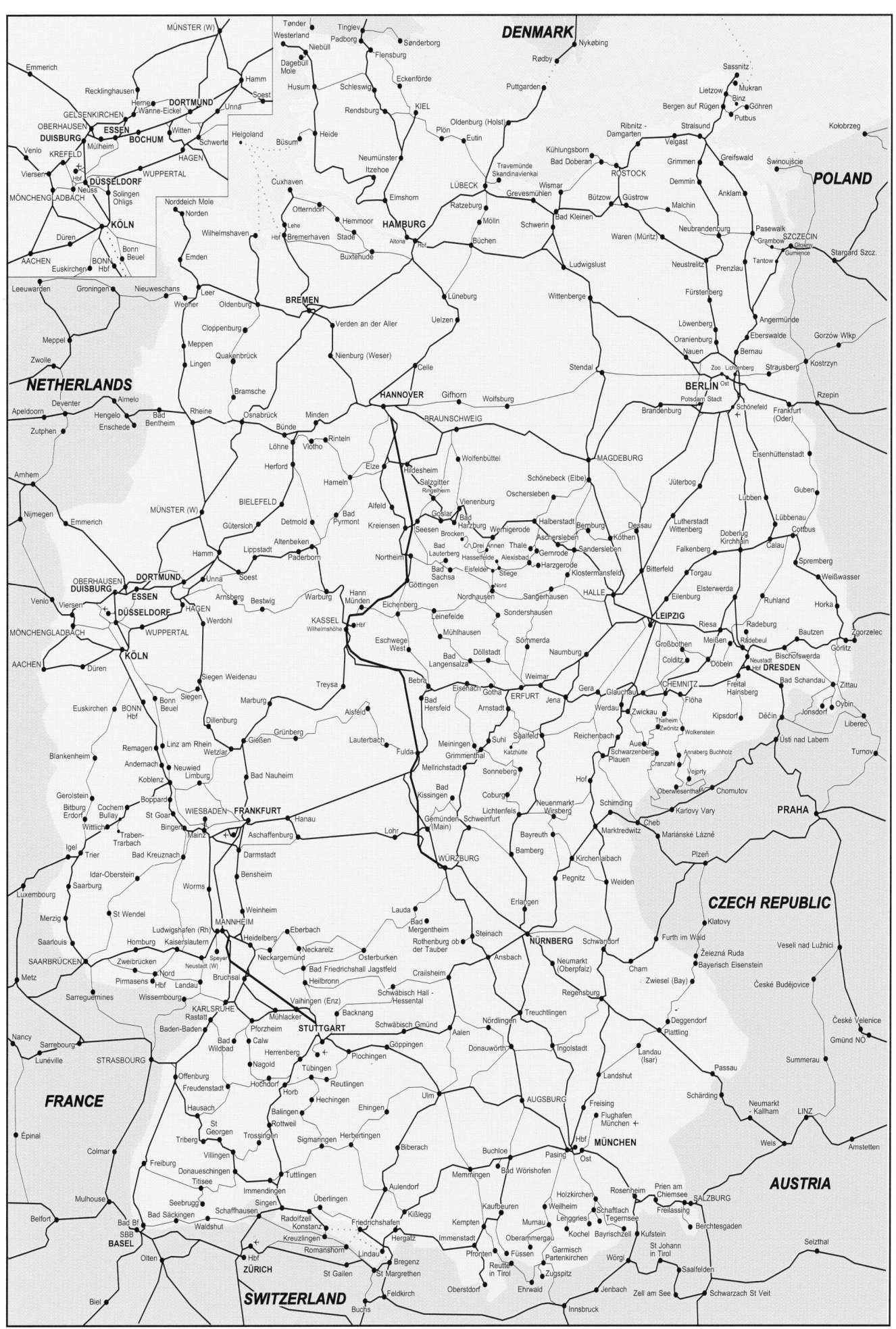
DENMARK
POLAND
NETHERLANDS
CZECH REPUBLIC
FRANCE
SWITZERLAND
AUSTRIA
MÜNSTER (W)
Emmerich
Recklinghausen
Hamm
Soest
Herne
DORTMUND
Wanne-Eickel
Unna
GELSENKIRCHEN
OBERHAUSEN
ESSEN
DUISBURG
BOCHUM
Witten
Mülheim
Schwerte
Venlo
KREFELD
HAGEN
Viersen
Hbf
DÜSSELDORF
WUPPERTAL
MÖNCHENGLADBACH
Neuss
Solingen Ohligs
KÖLN
Düren
Bonn Beuel
AACHEN
BONN Hbf
Euskirchen
Tønder
Tinglev
Westerland
Padborg
Sønderborg
Niebüll
Flensburg
Dagebüll Mole
Husum
Schleswig
Eckenförde
Rendsburg
KIEL
Helgoland
Büsum
Heide
Plön
Eutin
Oldenburg (Holst)
Neumünster
Itzehoe
Cuxhaven
Elmshorn
Norddeich Mole
Norden
Otterndorf
Lehe
Hemmoor
Wilhelmshaven
Bremerhaven
Stade
HAMBURG
Altona
Buxtehude
Emden
Leer
Weener
Oldenburg
BREMEN
Leeuwarden
Groningen
Nieuweschans
Meppel
Zwolle
Cloppenburg
Meppen
Lingen
Quakenbrück
Verden an der Aller
Nienburg (Weser)
Bramsche
Deventer
Apeldoorn
Almelo
Hengelo
Enschede
Bad Bentheim
Zutphen
Rheine
Osnabrück
Bünde
Minden
Rinteln
Löhne
Vlotho
Herford
Hameln
Arnhem
Nijmegen
Emmerich
BIELEFELD
MÜNSTER (W)
Gütersloh
Detmold
Bad Pyrmont
Lippstadt
Altenbeken
Paderborn
Hamm
OBERHAUSEN
DORTMUND
DUISBURG
Unna
Soest
ESSEN
Venlo
Viersen
DÜSSELDORF
HAGEN
Arnsberg
Bestwig
Warburg
Hann Münden
Werdohl
MÖNCHENGLADBACH
WUPPERTAL
KASSEL
Wilhelmshöhe
Hbf
KÖLN
AACHEN
Düren
Siegen Weidenau
Siegen
Euskirchen
BONN Hbf
Bonn Beuel
Marburg
Treysa
Dillenburg
Alsfeld
Remagen
Linz am Rhein
Wetzlar
Gießen
Grünberg
Lauterbach
Blankenheim
Andernach
Neuwied
Limburg
Koblenz
Bad Nauheim
Gerolstein
Boppard
Bitburg Erdorf
Cochem Bullay
St Goar
WIESBADEN
FRANKFURT
Hanau
Wittlich
Traben-Trarbach
Bingen
Mainz
Aschaffenburg
Igel
Trier
Bad Kreuznach
Darmstadt
Idar-Oberstein
Saarburg
Bensheim
Luxembourg
Worms
Weinheim
Merzig
St Wendel
MANNHEIM
Ludwigshafen (Rh)
Saarlouis
Homburg
Kaiserslautern
Heidelberg
Eberbach
SAARBRÜCKEN
Zweibrücken
Speyer
Neckarelz
Neckargemünd
Metz
Neustadt (W)
Nord
Pirmasens
Hbf
Landau
Bruchsal
Sarreguemines
Wissembourg
KARLSRUHE
Rastatt
Baden-Baden
Nancy
Sarrebourg
Lunéville
STRASBOURG
Bad Wildbad
Pforzheim
Calw
Herrenberg
Nagold
Offenburg
Freudenstadt
Hochdorf
Horb
Hausach
St Georgen
Triberg
Épinal
Colmar
Freiburg
Villingen
Donaueschingen
Titisee
Mulhouse
Seebrugg
Bad Säckingen
Waldshut
Belfort
Bad Bf
SBB
BASEL
Olten
Biel
Hbf
ZÜRICH
Schaffhausen
Singen
Radolfzell
Konstanz
Kreuzlingen
Romanshorn
St Gallen
St Margrethen
Buchs
Feldkirch
Bregenz
Lindau
Friedrichshafen
Überlingen
Immendingen
Tuttlingen
Trossingen
Rottweil
Balingen
Hechingen
Sigmaringen
Herbertingen
Tübingen
Reutlingen
Plochingen
Göppingen
STUTTGART
Mühlacker
Vaihingen (Enz)
Backnang
Schwäbisch Gmünd
Aalen
Schwäbisch Hall - Hessental
Heilbronn
Bad Friedrichshall Jagstfeld
Osterburken
Crailsheim
Lauda
Bad Mergentheim
Rothenburg ob der Tauber
Ansbach
Ehingen
Ulm
Biberach
Aulendorf
Kißlegg
Hergatz
Immenstadt
Kempten
Memmingen
Buchloe
Bad Wörishofen
Kaufbeuren
Pfronten
Reutte in Tirol
Füssen
Oberstdorf
Oberammergau
Murnau
Ehrwald
Garmisch Partenkirchen
Zugspitz
Weilheim
Holzkirchen
Lenggries
Kochel
Bayrischzell
Schaftlach
Tegernsee
Rosenheim
Prien am Chiemsee
Freilassing
SALZBURG
Berchtesgaden
Kufstein
Wörgl
St Johann in Tirol
Saalfelden
Jenbach
Zell am See
Schwarzach St Veit
Innsbruck
Selzthal
Pasing
Hbf
MÜNCHEN
Ost
Flughafen München
Freising
Landshut
AUGSBURG
Donauwörth
Nördlingen
Ingolstadt
Treuchtlingen
Landau (Isar)
Plattling
Deggendorf
Passau
Schärding
Neumarkt - Kallham
LINZ
Wels
Amstetten
Summerau
Gmünd NÖ
České Velenice
České Budějovice
Veseli nad Lužnici
Zwiesel (Bay)
Bayerisch Eisenstein
Železná Ruda
Klatovy
Furth im Wald
Cham
Regensburg
Neumarkt (Oberpfalz)
Schwandorf
NÜRNBERG
Steinach
Erlangen
Bamberg
Bayreuth
Pegnitz
Weiden
Kirchenlaibach
Marktredwitz
Cheb
Mariánské Lázně
Plzeň
Karlovy Vary
PRAHA
Chomutov
Oberwiesenthal
Vejprty
Cranzahl
Annaberg Buchholz
Schirnding
Hof
Neuenmarkt Wirsberg
Lichtenfels
Coburg
Sonneberg
Schweinfurt
Gemünden (Main)
WÜRZBURG
Lohr
Bad Kissingen
Mellrichstadt
Grimmenthal
Meiningen
Suhl
Katzhütte
Saalfeld
Fulda
Bebra
Bad Hersfeld
Eisenach
Gotha
Arnstadt
ERFURT
Weimar
Jena
Gera
Glauchau
Werdau
Zwickau
Reichenbach
Plauen
Schwarzenberg
Aue
Thalheim
Zwönitz
Wolkenstein
CHEMNITZ
Flöha
Kipsdorf
Děčín
Ústí nad Labem
Liberec
Turnov
Jonsdorf
Oybin
Zittau
Bad Schandau
Neustadt
Hbf
DRESDEN
Freital Hainsberg
Colditz
Döbeln
Großbothen
Meißen
Radebeul
Riesa
Radeburg
Bischofswerda
Bautzen
Görlitz
Zgorzelec
Horka
Ruhland
Elsterwerda
Eilenburg
LEIPZIG
HALLE
Bitterfeld
Torgau
Falkenberg
Lutherstadt Wittenberg
Doberlug Kirchhain
Calau
Cottbus
Spremberg
Weißwasser
Lübbenau
Lübben
Guben
Eisenhüttenstadt
Jüterbog
Dessau
Köthen
Bernburg
Sandersleben
Aschersleben
Halberstadt
Klostermansfeld
Sangerhausen
Sondershausen
Sömmerda
Naumburg
Döllstadt
Bad Langensalza
Mühlhausen
Leinefelde
Eschwege West
Eichenberg
Nordhausen
Göttingen
Northeim
Bad Sachsa
Eisfelder
Stiege
Nord
Hasselfelde
Alexisbad
Harzgerode
Gernrode
Thale
Drei Annen
Wernigerode
Bad Lauterberg
Brocken
Bad Harzburg
Goslar
Vienenburg
Seesen
Kreiensen
Alfeld
Elze
Hildesheim
Salzgitter Ringelheim
Wolfenbüttel
Oschersleben
Schönebeck (Elbe)
MAGDEBURG
BRAUNSCHWEIG
HANNOVER
Gifhorn
Wolfsburg
Celle
Uelzen
Lüneburg
Stendal
Brandenburg
BERLIN
Zoo
Lichtenberg
Ost
Potsdam Stadt
Schönefeld
Frankfurt (Oder)
Rzepin
Kostrzyn
Strausberg
Gorzów Wlkp
Bernau
Eberswalde
Angermünde
Nauen
Oranienburg
Löwenberg
Fürstenberg
Wittenberge
Ludwigslust
Büchen
Mölln
Ratzeburg
LÜBECK
Travemünde Skandinavienkai
Grevesmühlen
Wismar
Schwerin
Bad Kleinen
Bützow
Güstrow
Waren (Müritz)
Neustrelitz
Prenzlau
Malchin
Neubrandenburg
Pasewalk
Grambow
SZCZECIN
Głowny
Gumience
Tantow
Stargard Szcz.
Demmin
Anklam
Greifswald
Grimmen
Stralsund
Velgast
Ribnitz - Damgarten
ROSTOCK
Bad Doberan
Kühlungsborn
Puttgarden
Rødby
Nykøbing
Sassnitz
Lietzow
Mukran
Binz
Göhren
Bergen auf Rügen
Putbus
Świnoujście
Kołobrzeg

SCANDANAVIA, BENELUX, IBERIA...

FINLAND
NORWAY
SWEDEN
DENMARK
GERMANY
KØBENHAVN
Århus
Ebeltoft
Helsingborg
Sj. Odde
Helsingør
Samsø
Lund
Vejle
Kalundborg
Malmö
Fredericia
Odense
Ringsted
Trelleborg
Korsør
Nyborg
Bøjden
Svendborg
Vordingborg
Nakskov
Fynshav
Nykøbing
Rødby
Sønderborg
Gedser
Narvik
Kiruna
Bodö
Fauske
Gällivare
Boden
Luleå
Mo i Rana
Arvidsjaur
Sandnessjøen
Mosjøen
Brønnøysund
Bastuträsk
Storuman
Rørvik
Vännäs
Umeå
Steinkjer
Mellansel
TRONDHEIM
Åre
Östersund
Kristiansund
Hell
Storlien
Långsele
Støren
Härnösand
Molde
Ånge
Sundsvall
Røros
Sveg
Ålesund
Oppdal
Hudiksvall
Åndalsnes
Dombås
Orsa
Bollnäs
Söderhamn
Eckerö
Mora
Måløy
Rättvik
Mariehamn
Sogndal
Falun
Gävle
Balestrand
Lærdal
Lillehammer
Elverum
Borlänge
Grisslehamn
Flåm
Gjøvik
Hamar
Myrdal
Gol
Eidsvoll
Avesta
Ludvika
Kapellskär
Voss
Roa
Kongsvinger
Uppsala
Geilo
Fagersta
Norrtälje
BERGEN
Hønefoss
Charlottenberg
Västerås
Lillestrøm
Frövi
STOCKHOLM
Drammen
OSLO
Kil
Eskilstuna
Södertälje
Notodden
Örebro
Nynäshamn
Karlstad
Katrineholm
Haugesund
Nordagutu
Skien
Fredrikstad
Laxå
Hallsberg
Larvik
Kornsjø
Mariestad
Motala
Norrköping
Strömstad
Linköping
Stavanger
Nelaug
Uddevalla
Öxnered
Mjölby
Trollhättan
Falköping
Västervik
Arendal
Herrljunga
Visby
Egersund
Moi
Kristiansand
Jönköping
Nässjö
Hirtshals
Borås
Hjørring
GÖTEBORG
Oskarshamn
Frederikshavn
Ålborg
Varberg
Alvesta
Växjö
Kalmar
Thisted
Emmaboda
Randers
Halmstad
Karlskrona
Grenaa
Struer
Langå
Holstebro
Kristianstad
see inset above
Århus
Helsingborg
Hässleholm
Skjern
Herning
Helsingør
KØBENHAVN
Lund
Fredericia
Esbjerg
Malmö
Ystad
Korsør
Fanø
Ribe
Odense
Nyborg
Trelleborg
Rønne
Tønder
Sønderborg
Nykøbing
Padborg
Rødby
Gedser
Niebüll
Puttgarden
Sassnitz
Flensburg
Kiel
Rostock

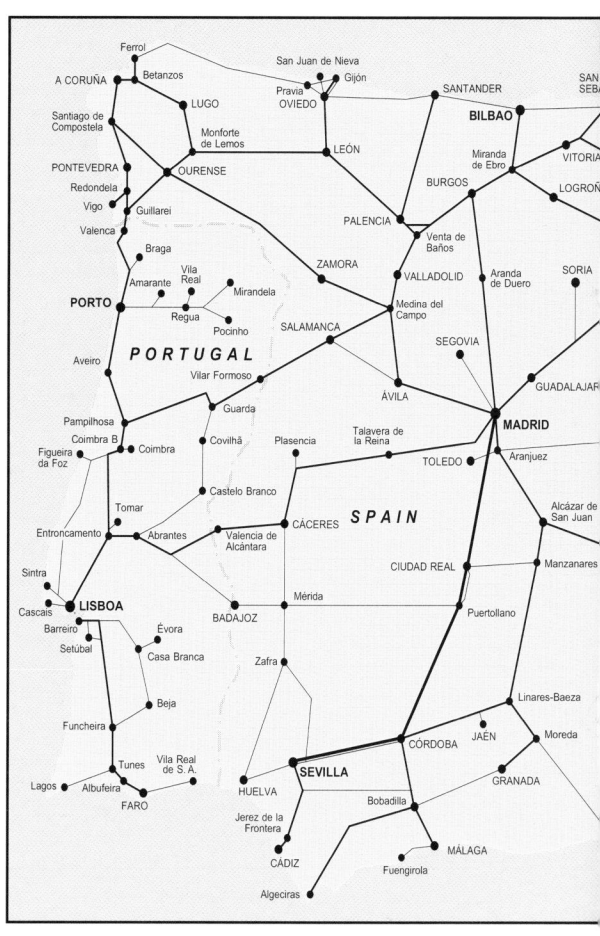
Ferrol
San Juan de Nieva
Betanzos
A CORUÑA
Gijón
Pravia
SAN SEB
SANTANDER
OVIEDO
LUGO
Santiago de Compostela
BILBAO
Monforte de Lemos
Miranda de Ebro
VITORIA
LEÓN
PONTEVEDRA
OURENSE
BURGOS
LOGROÑ
Redondela
Vigo
Guillarei
PALENCIA
Valenca
Venta de Baños
Braga
ZAMORA
Vila Real
SORIA
Aranda de Duero
Amarante
VALLADOLID
Mirandela
PORTO
Regua
Medina del Campo
Pocinho
SALAMANCA
SEGOVIA
Aveiro
PORTUGAL
Vilar Formoso
GUADALAJAR
ÁVILA
Guarda
Pampilhosa
MADRID
Coimbra B
Talavera de la Reina
Figueira da Foz
Coimbra
Covilhã
Plasencia
TOLEDO
Aranjuez
Castelo Branco
Tomar
Alcázar de San Juan
SPAIN
CÁCERES
Entroncamento
Abrantes
Valencia de Alcántara
Manzanares
CIUDAD REAL
Sintra
LISBOA
Mérida
Cascais
BADAJOZ
Puertollano
Barreiro
Évora
Setúbal
Casa Branca
Zafra
Beja
Linares-Baeza
Funcheira
JAÉN
Moreda
CÓRDOBA
Tunes
Vila Real de S. A.
SEVILLA
Lagos
Albufeira
HUELVA
GRANADA
FARO
Bobadilla
Jerez de la Frontera
MÁLAGA
CÁDIZ
Fuengirola
Algeciras

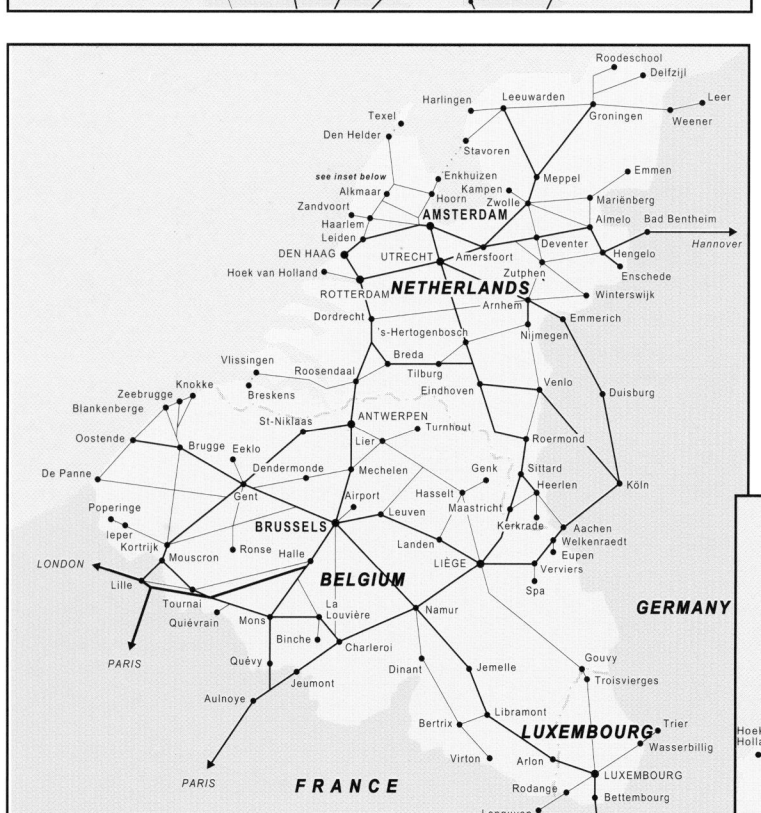
Roodeschool
Delfzijl
Harlingen
Leeuwarden
Leer
Texel
Groningen
Weener
Den Helder
Stavoren
see inset below
Enkhuizen
Meppel
Emmen
Alkmaar
Kampen
Zandvoort
Hoorn
Zwolle
Mariënberg
Haarlem
AMSTERDAM
Almelo
Bad Bentheim
Leiden
Hannover
DEN HAAG
UTRECHT
Amersfoort
Deventer
Hengelo
Hoek van Holland
Enschede
ROTTERDAM
NETHERLANDS
Zutphen
Winterswijk
Dordrecht
Arnhem
Emmerich
's-Hertogenbosch
Nijmegen
Vlissingen
Breda
Roosendaal
Tilburg
Knokke
Zeebrugge
Breskens
Eindhoven
Venlo
Duisburg
Blankenberge
St-Niklaas
ANTWERPEN
Turnhout
Oostende
Lier
Roermond
Brugge
Eeklo
De Panne
Dendermonde
Mechelen
Genk
Sittard
Gent
Airport
Heerlen
Köln
Poperinge
Hasselt
BRUSSELS
Leuven
Maastricht
Ieper
Kerkrade
Aachen
Kortrijk
Ronse
Landen
Welkenraedt
Mouscron
Halle
Eupen
LONDON
LIÈGE
Verviers
BELGIUM
Lille
Tournai
La Louvière
Spa
GERMANY
Namur
Quiévrain
Mons
PARIS
Binche
Charleroi
Gouvy
Quévy
Dinant
Jemelle
Troisvierges
Jeumont
Aulnoye
Libramont
Trier
Bertrix
LUXEMBOURG
Wasserbillig
Virton
Arlon
PARIS
FRANCE
LUXEMBOURG
Rodange
Bettembourg
Longuyon
Enkhuizen
Alkmaar
Hoorn
Lelystad
IJmuiden
Haarlem
Zandvoort aan Zee
Sloterdijk
AMSTERDAM
Almere
Schiphol
Weesp
Hilversum
Duivendrecht
Amersfoort
Leiden
Alphen
DEN HAAG
UTRECHT
Delft
Gouda
Hoek van Holland
ROTTERDAM
Tiel
Geldermalsen
Dordrecht

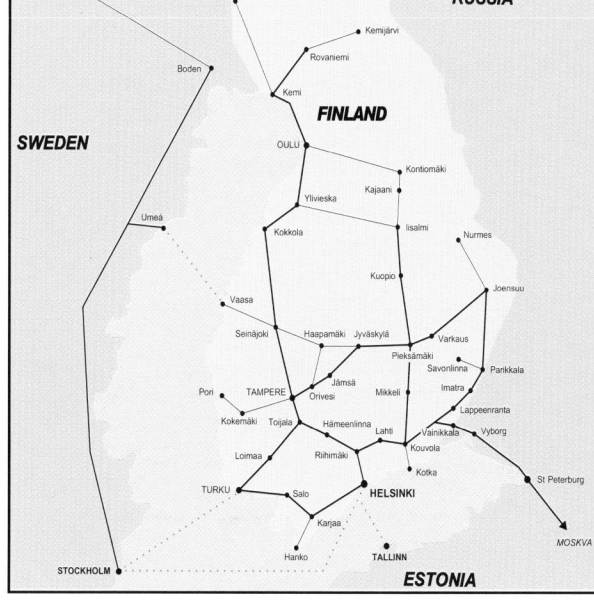
Kolari
RUSSIA
Kemijärvi
Rovaniemi
Boden
Kemi
FINLAND
SWEDEN
OULU
Kontiomäki
Kajaani
Ylivieska
Umeå
Iisalmi
Kokkola
Nurmes
Kuopio
Joensuu
Vaasa
Seinäjoki
Haapamäki
Jyväskylä
Varkaus
Pieksämäki
Savonlinna
Parikkala
Jämsä
Pori
TAMPERE
Orivesi
Mikkeli
Imatra
Kokemäki
Toijala
Hämeenlinna
Lappeenranta
Lahti
Vainikkala
Vyborg
Kouvola
Loimaa
Riihimäki
St Peterburg
Kotka
TURKU
Salo
HELSINKI
Karjaa
MOSKVA
Hanko
TALLINN
STOCKHOLM
ESTONIA

...THE BALKANS & ITALY

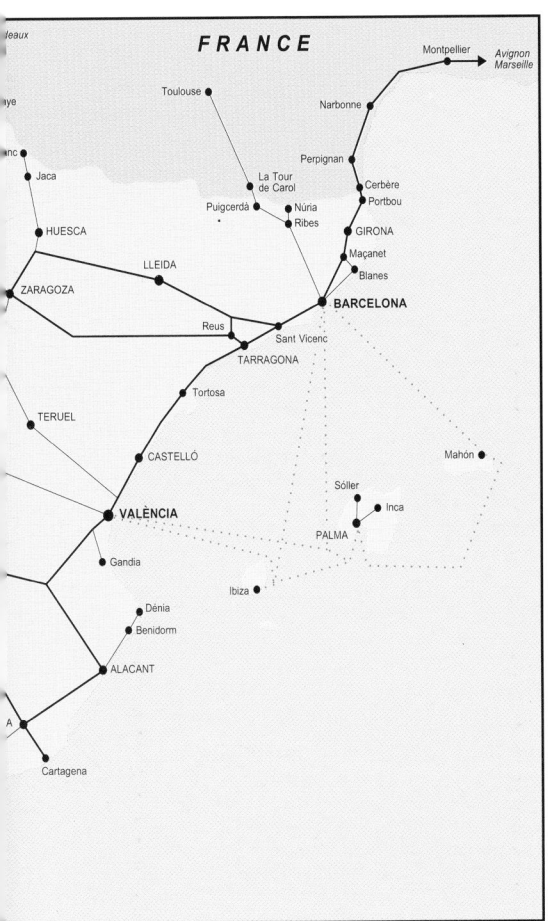

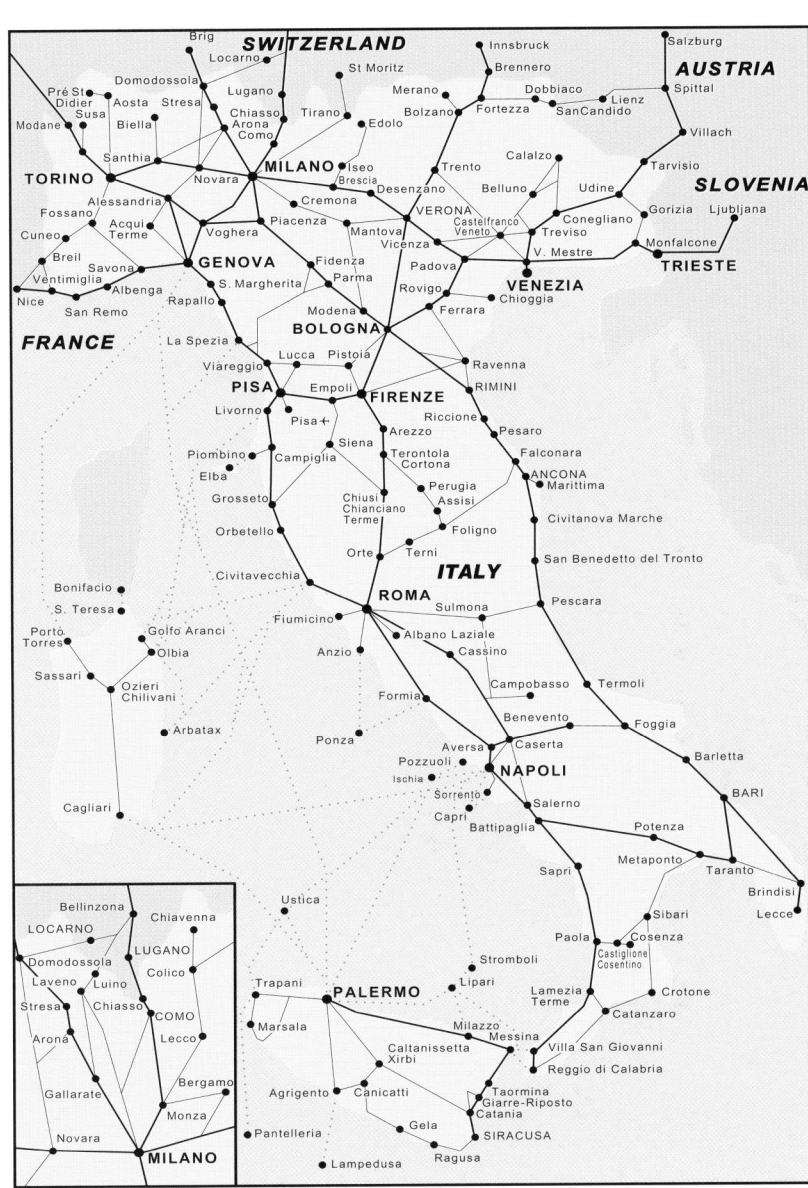

Remember...

Maps in this atlas have been grouped into four sections: General, Specialist, Relief and Transport. For more information, consult the Contents on pages ii and iii.

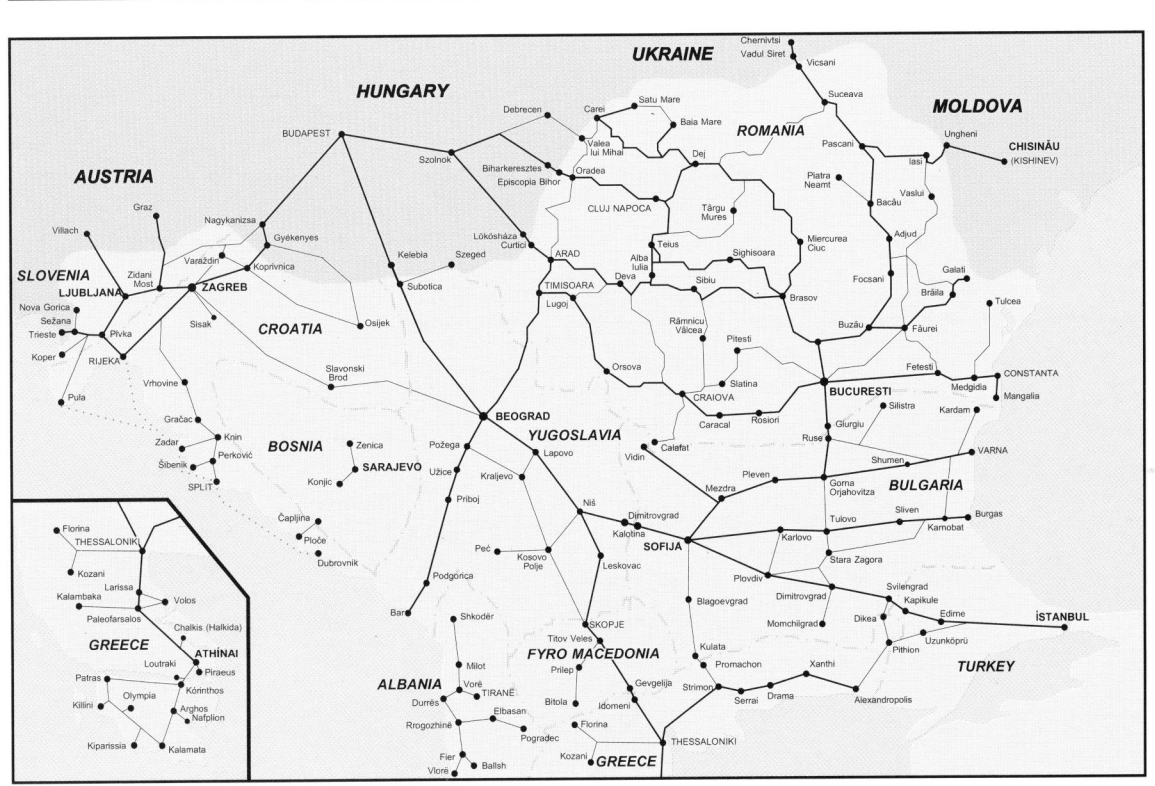

AUSTRIA & SWITZERLAND

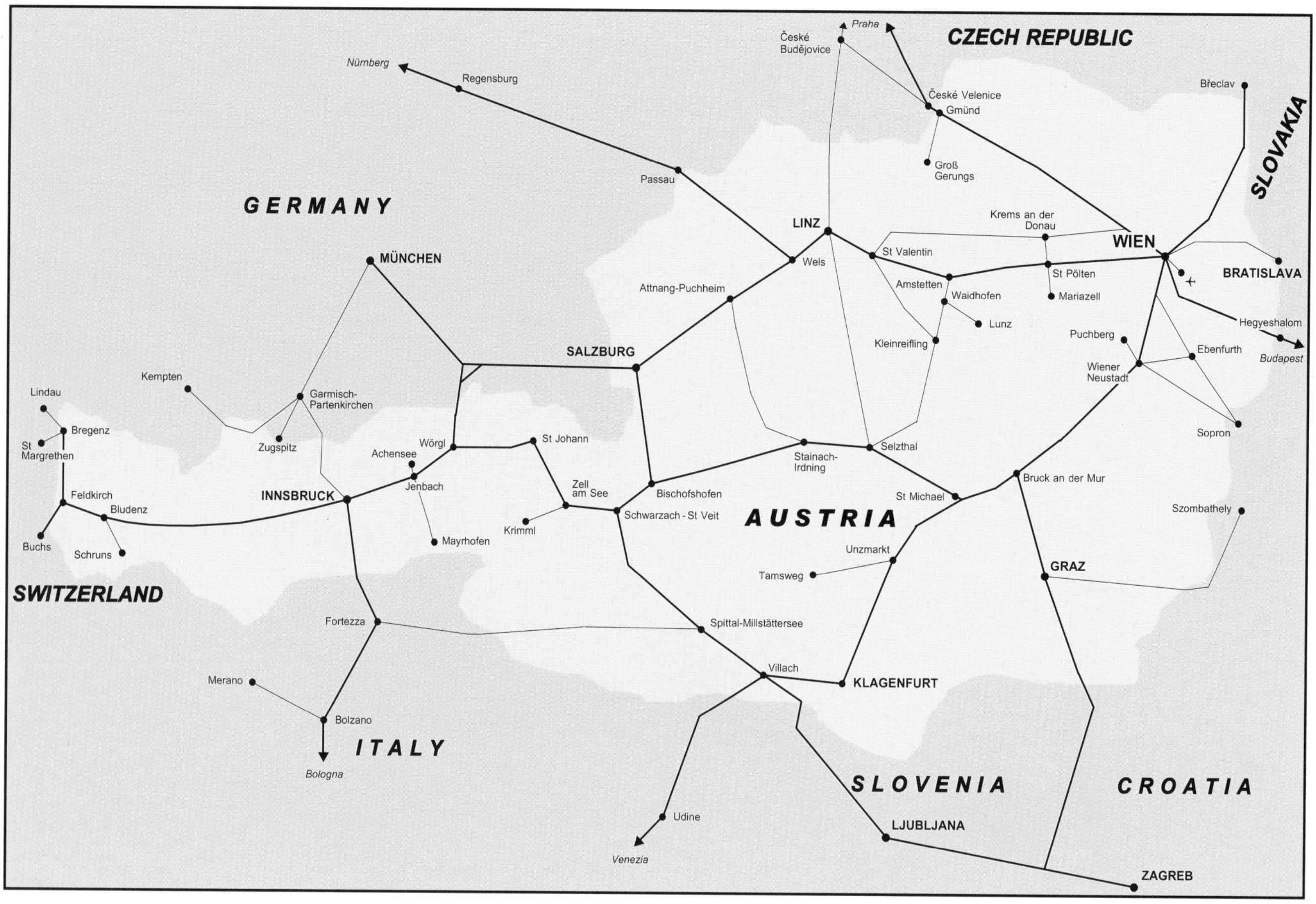

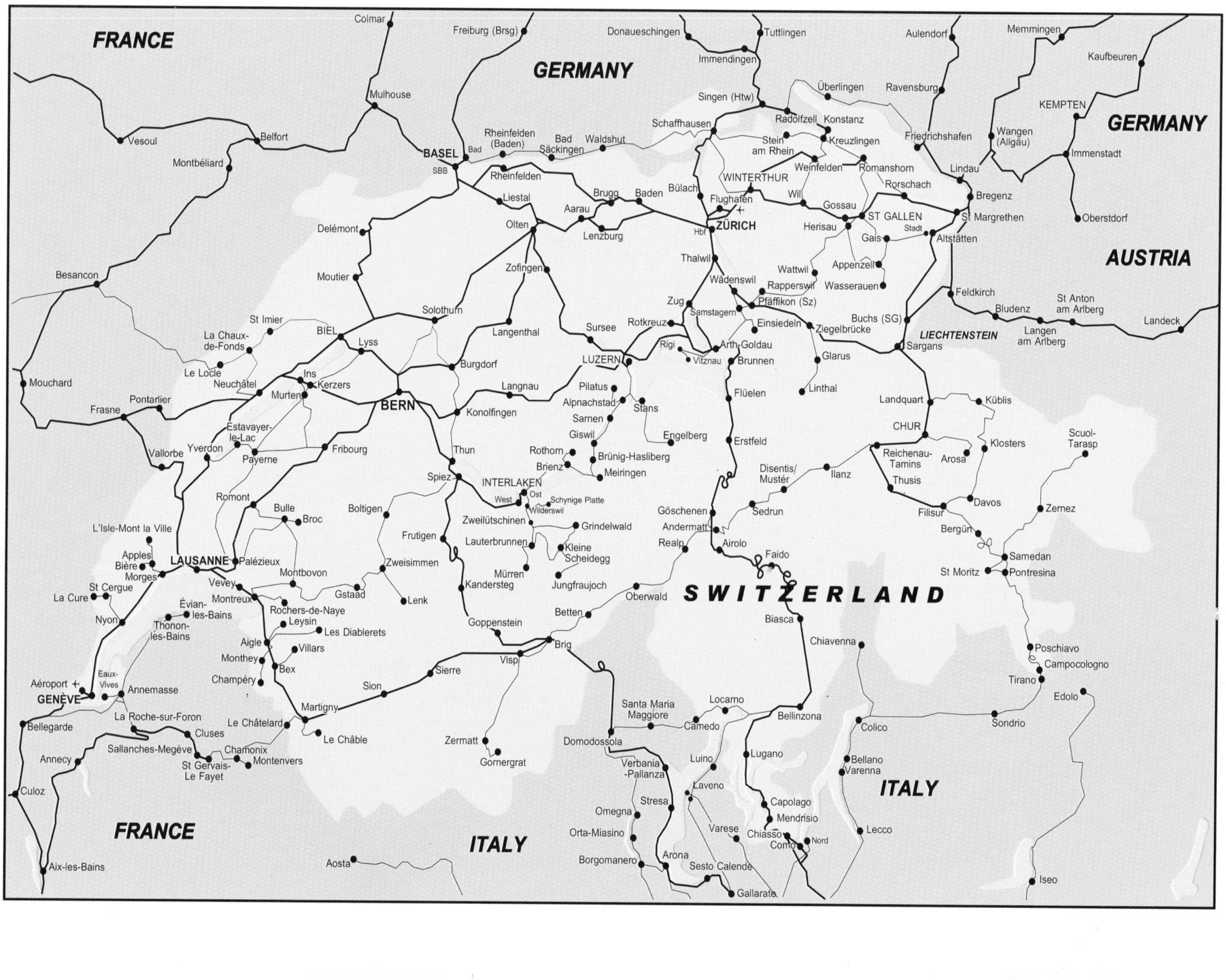

Nürnberg
Regensburg
Passau

České Budějovice
Praha
CZECH REPUBLIC
České Velenice
Gmünd
Břeclav
SLOVAKIA

GERMANY

Groß Gerungs

LINZ
Krems an der Donau
WIEN

MÜNCHEN

St Valentin
Wels
Attnang-Puchheim
Amstetten
Waidhofen
St Pölten
Mariazell
BRATISLAVA

Kempten
Lindau
Bregenz
St Margrethen
Feldkirch
Bludenz
Buchs
Schruns

SALZBURG

Garmisch-Partenkirchen
Zugspitz
Achensee
Wörgl
St Johann
Jenbach
INNSBRUCK
Zell am See
Krimml
Mayrhofen

Kleinreifling
Lunz
Puchberg
Wiener Neustadt
Ebenfurth
Hegyeshalom
Budapest
Sopron

Selzthal
Stainach-Irdning
Bischofshofen
Schwarzach - St Veit
AUSTRIA
St Michael
Bruck an der Mur
Szombathely

Unzmarkt
GRAZ

SWITZERLAND

Tamsweg

Fortezza
Spittal-Millstättersee

Merano
Villach
KLAGENFURT

Bolzano
Bologna
ITALY

SLOVENIA
CROATIA

Udine
LJUBLJANA

Venezia
ZAGREB

FRANCE
Colmar
Freiburg (Brsg)
Donaueschingen
Tuttlingen
Aulendorf
Memmingen
GERMANY
Kaufbeuren

Vesoul
Belfort
Mulhouse
Immendingen
Überlingen
Ravensburg
KEMPTEN
GERMANY

Montbéliard
Rheinfelden (Baden)
Bad Säckingen
Waldshut
Schaffhausen
Singen (Htw)
Radolfzell
Konstanz
Friedrichshafen
Wangen (Allgäu)
Immenstadt

BASEL
Bad
SBB
Rheinfelden
Brugg
Baden
Bülach
Stein am Rhein
Weinfelden
Kreuzlingen
Romanshorn
Lindau
Bregenz
Oberstdorf

Besancon
Delémont
Liestal
Aarau
Olten
Lenzburg
WINTERTHUR
Flughafen
Wil
Gossau
ST GALLEN
Stadt
St Margrethen
AUSTRIA

Moutier
Zofingen
Hbf
ZÜRICH
Herisau
Gais
Altstätten
Feldkirch
St Anton am Arlberg
Landeck

La Chaux-de-Fonds
St Imier
Solothurn
Langenthal
Sursee
Thalwil
Wädenswil
Wattwil
Appenzell
Wasserauen
Buchs (SG)
Bludenz
Langen am Arlberg

Mouchard
Le Locle
BIEL
Lyss
Burgdorf
Rotkreuz
Zug
Samstagern
Rapperswil
Pfäffikon (Sz)
Einsiedeln
Ziegelbrücke
LIECHTENSTEIN
Sargans

Frasne
Pontarlier
Neuchâtel
Ins
Kerzers
Murten
Langnau
LUZERN
Rigi
Arth-Goldau
Vitznau
Brunnen
Glarus
Landquart
Küblis
Scuol-Tarasp

Vallorbe
Yverdon
Estavayer-le-Lac
Payerne
BERN
Konolfingen
Pilatus
Alpnachstad
Stans
Flüelen
Linthal
CHUR
Klosters

Fribourg
Thun
Sarnen
Giswil
Engelberg
Erstfeld
Reichenau-Tamins
Arosa

Romont
Spiez
Rothorn
Brünig-Hasliberg
Meiringen
Disentis/Müstér
Ilanz
Thusis
Filisur
Davos
Zernez

L'Isle-Mont la Ville
Bulle
Broc
Boltigen
INTERLAKEN
West
Ost
Schynige Platte
Wilderswil
Grindelwald
Göschenen
Sedrun
Bergün
Samedan

Apples
Bière
Morges
LAUSANNE
Palézieux
Montbovon
Frutigen
Zweilütschinen
Lauterbrunnen
Kleine Scheidegg
Andermatt
Realp
Airolo
Faido
St Moritz
Pontresina

St Cergue
Vevey
Montreux
Rochers-de-Naye
Gstaad
Zweisimmen
Mürren
Jungfraujoch
Oberwald

La Cure
Nyon
Évian-les-Bains
Leysin
Les Diablerets
Kandersteg
Betten
Biasca

Thonon-les-Bains
Aigle
Villars
Goppenstein
Chiavenna
Poschiavo
Campocologno

Aéroport
GENÈVE
Monthey
Champéry
Bex
Sion
Sierre
Visp
Brig
Tirano
Edolo

Eaux-Vives
Annemasse
La Roche-sur-Foron
Le Châtelard
Martigny
Zermatt
Gornergrat
Santa Maria Maggiore
Locarno
SWITZERLAND
Colico
Sondrio

Bellegarde
Cluses
Sallanches-Megève
Chamonix
Montenvers
St Gervais-Le Fayet
Domodossola
Camedo
Luino
Bellinzona
Lugano
Bellano
Varenna
Lecco
ITALY

Annecy
Culoz
Verbania-Pallanza
Laveno
Capolago
Mendrisio
Iseo

Omegna
Stresa
Varese
Chiasso
Nord
Como

Orta-Miasino
Arona
Sesto Calende

Aix-les-Bains
FRANCE
Aosta
ITALY
Borgomanero
Gallarate

CENTRAL & EASTERN EUROPE

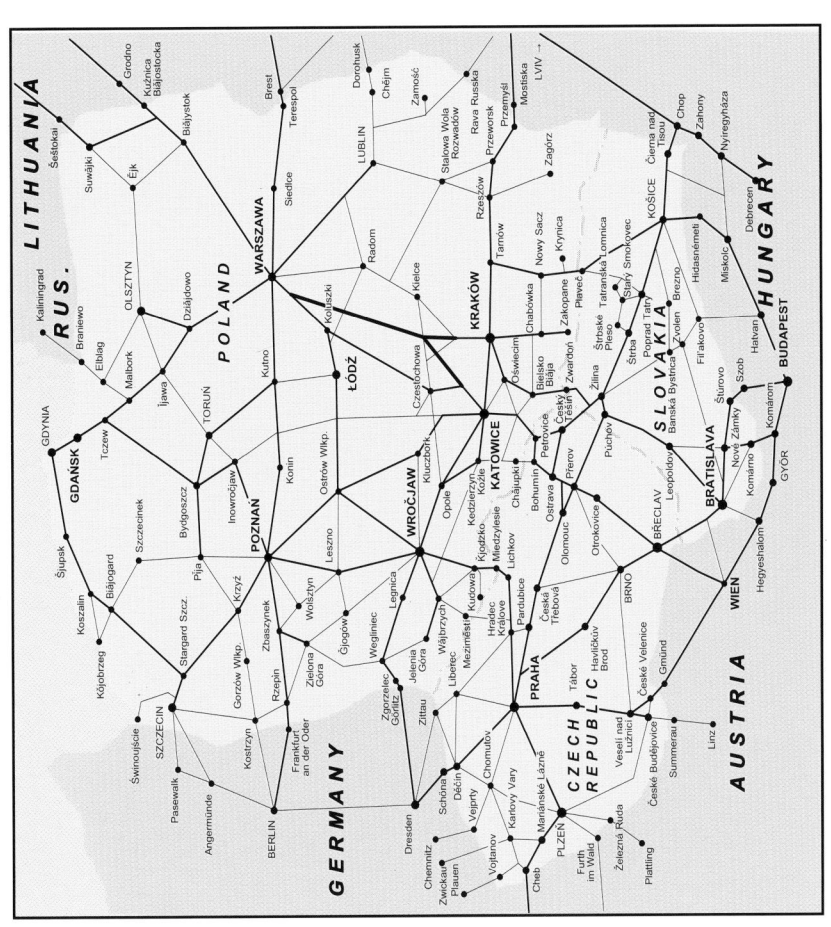

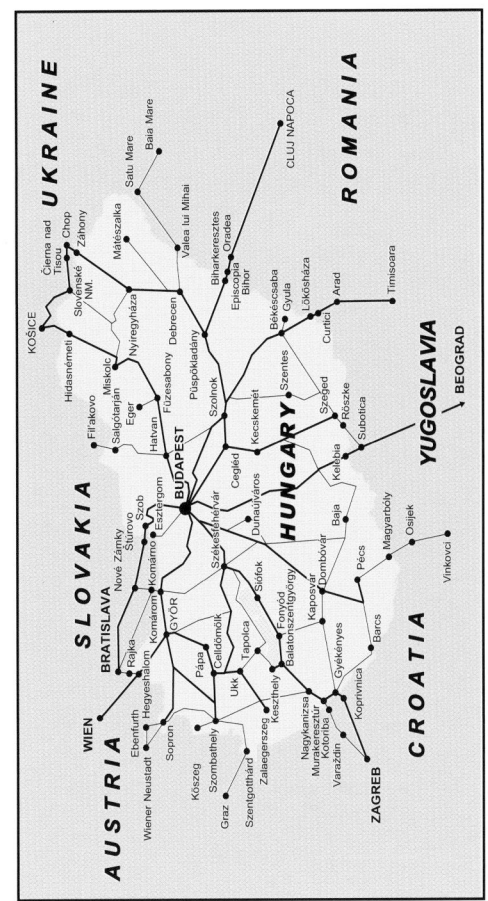

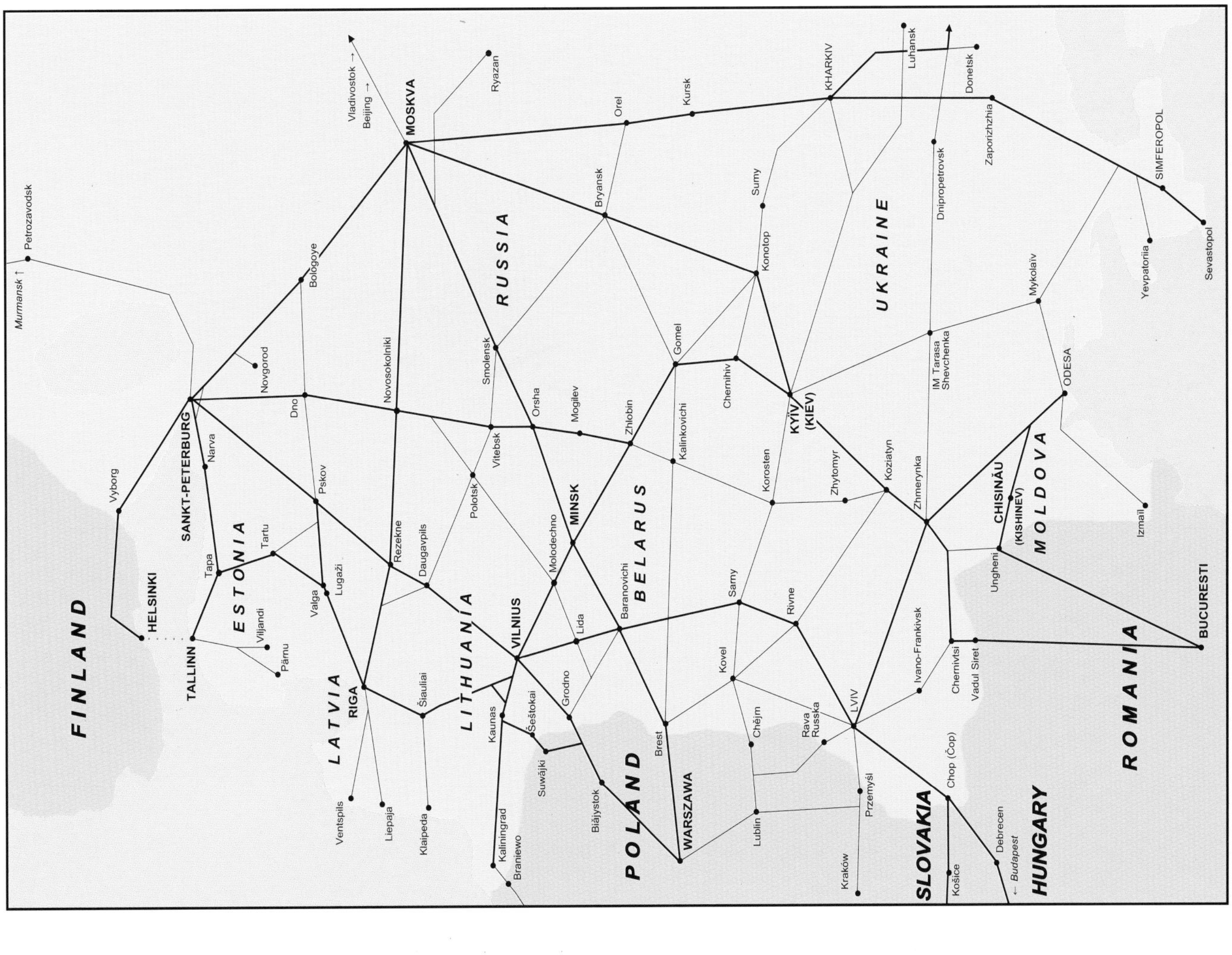

ISRAEL & THE MIDDLE EAST

Outside of Europe the railway system is not so extensive, although some countries such as Russia, Japan, India and China still rely heavily on it for public transport. The flexibility and economy of the bus makes it ideal for remoter areas. The maps on pages 144 to 168 are taken from the *Thomas Cook Overseas Timetable*. This Timetable is a sister publication to the *European Timetable* and includes details of major rail, ferry and bus services throughout the rest of the world. Rail services are shown as **black** lines, ferries as **blue** dotted lines and bus services as **red** lines. Place names given are as used by the transport authorities concerned and may differ from those employed in the rest of this atlas.

Remember...

Maps in this atlas have been grouped into four sections:

General
Specialist
Relief
Transport

There are also several statistical tables at the front of the book and several appendices at the back.

For more information, consult the Contents on pages ii and iii.

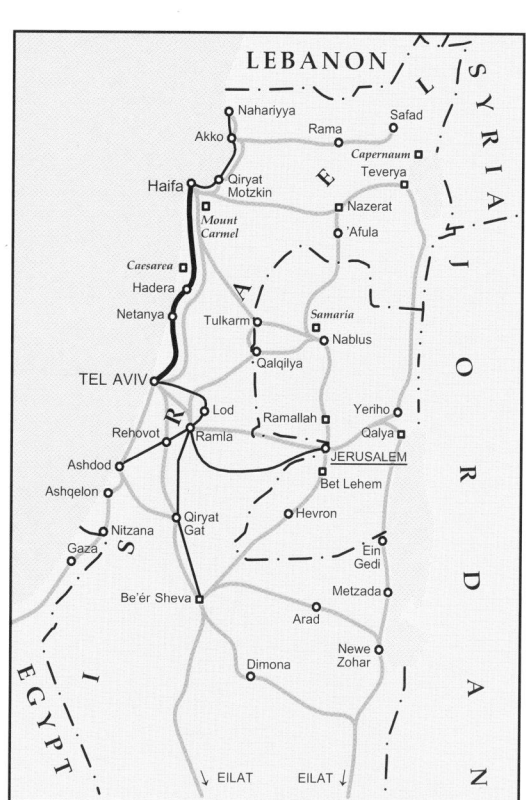

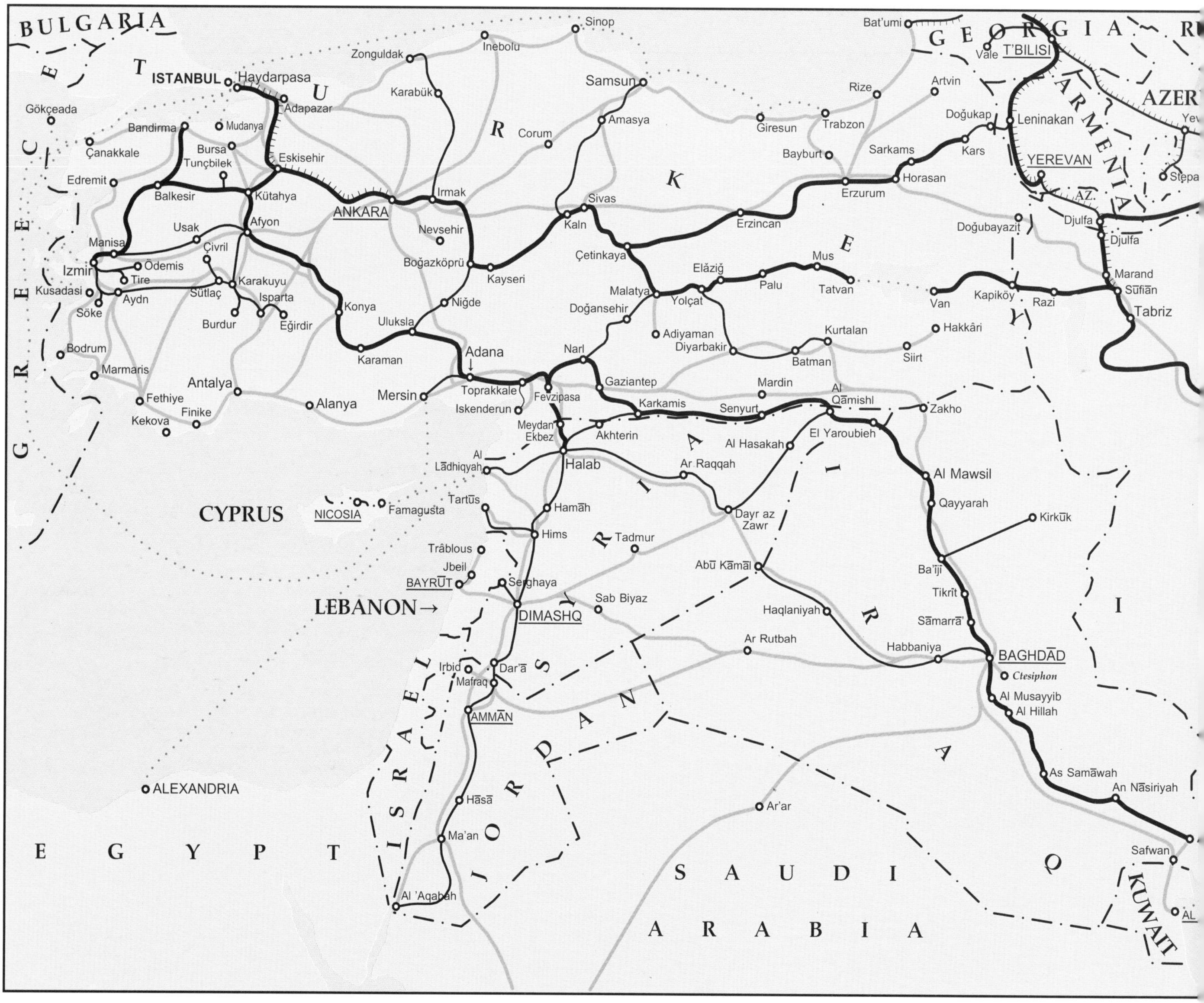

ARABIA & NORTHEAST AFRICA

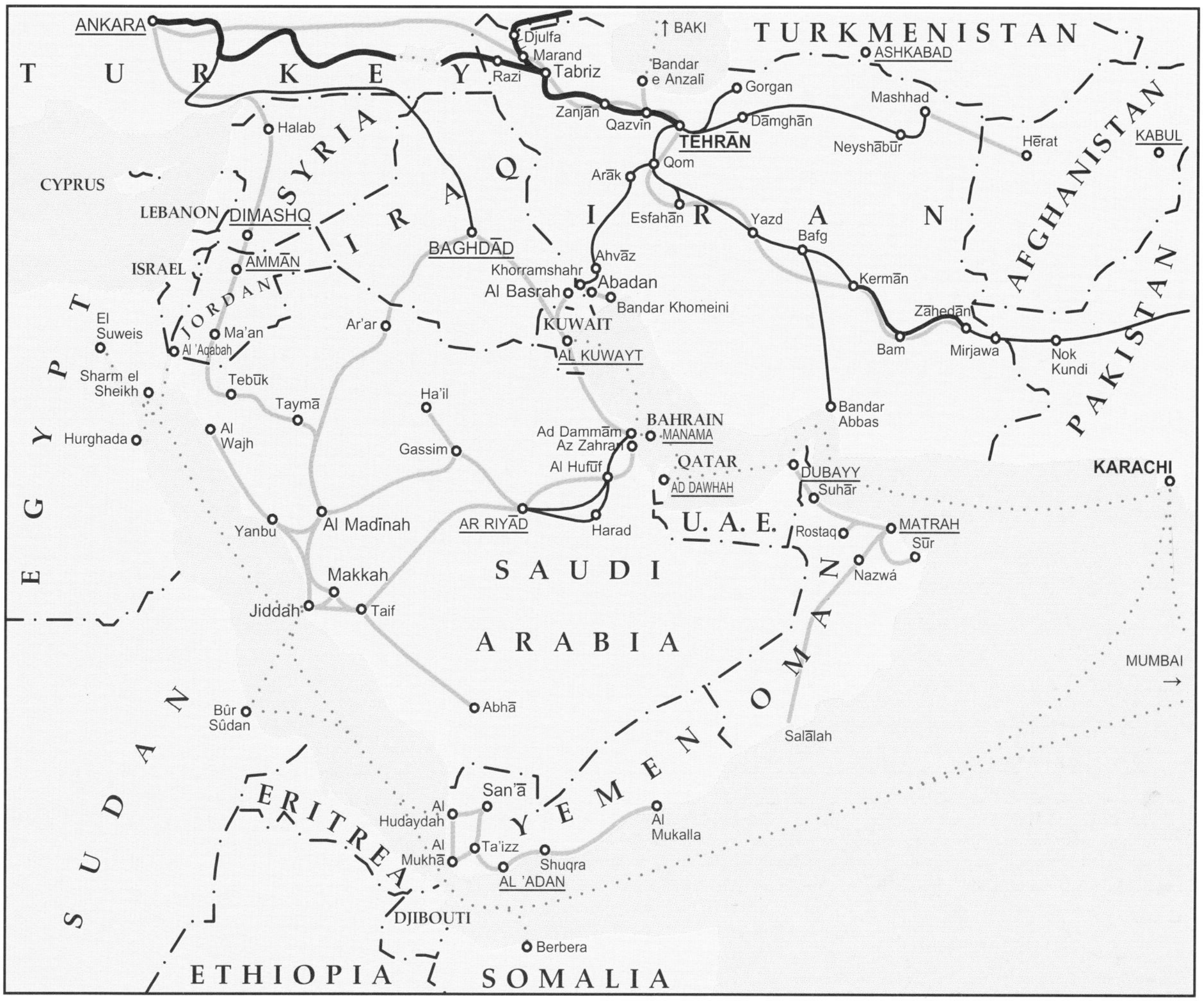

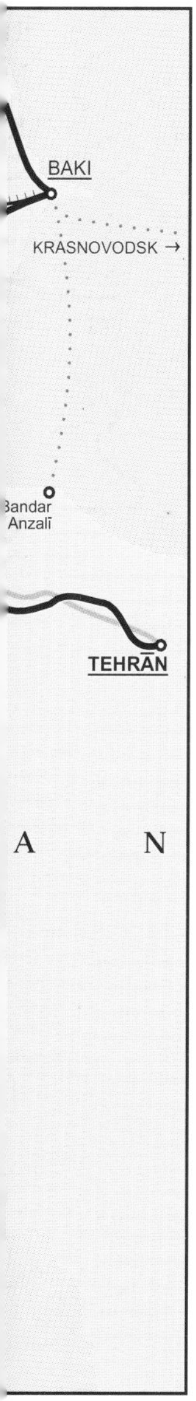

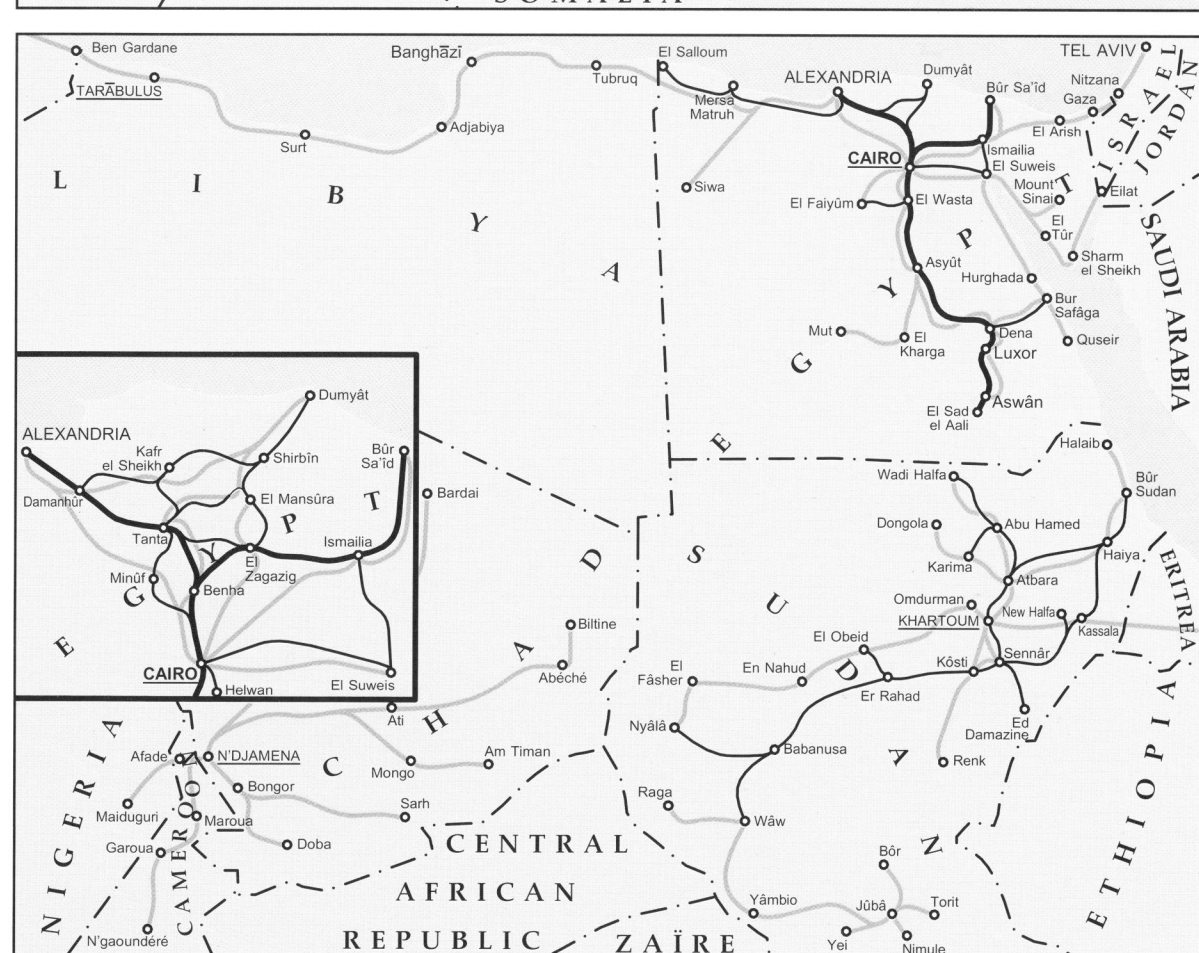

NORTHWEST AFRICA

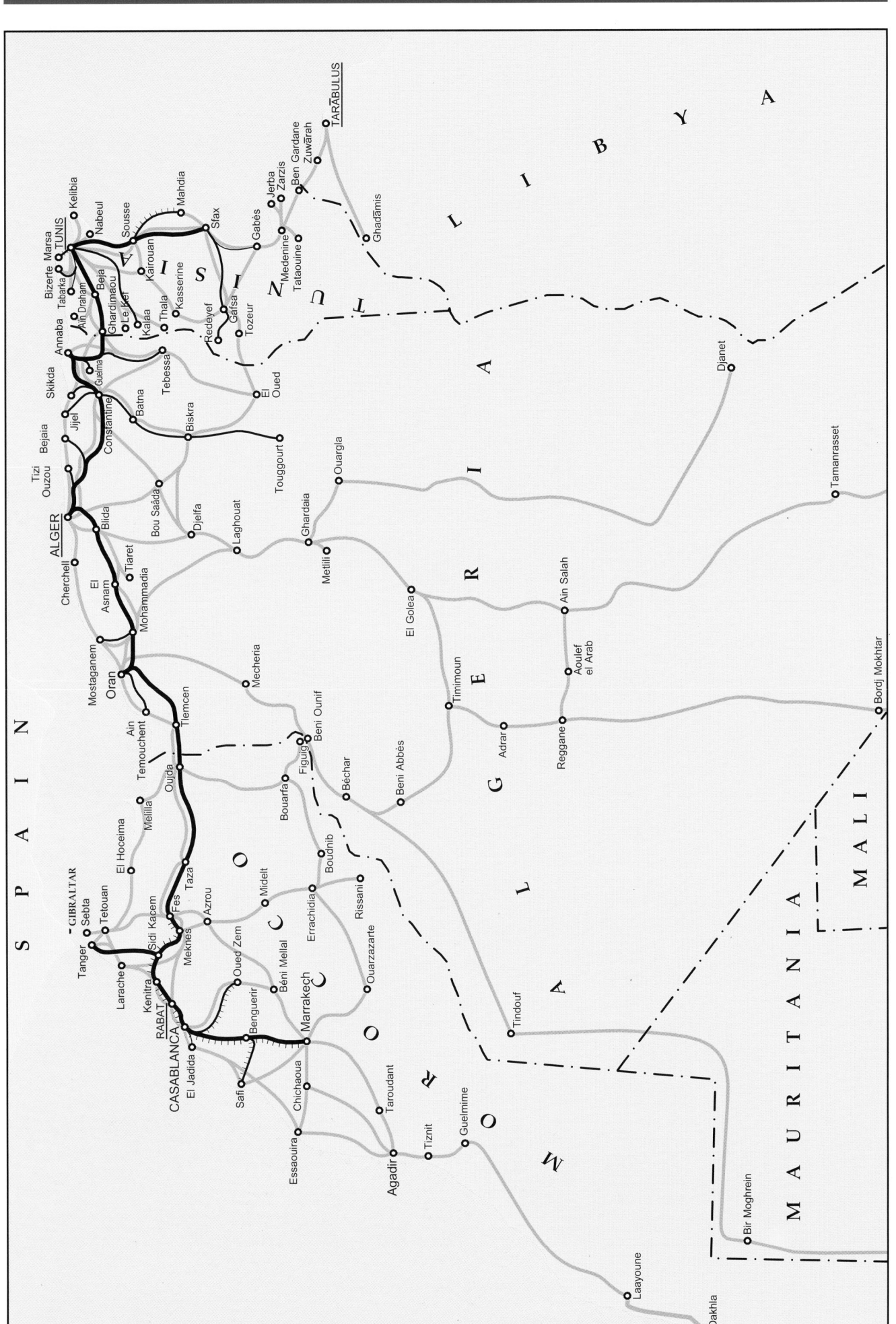
SPAIN
GIBRALTAR
MOROCCO
ALGERIA
TUNISIA
LIBYA
MAURITANIA
MALI
TUNIS
ALGER
RABAT
TARĀBULUS
Bizerte
Marsa
Kelibia
Nabeul
Sousse
Mahdia
Sfax
Kairouan
Tabarka
Beja
Ain Draham
Ghardimaou
Le Kef
Kalaa
Thala
Kasserine
Gafsa
Redeyef
Tozeur
Gabès
Jerba
Zarzis
Medenine
Tataouine
Ben Gardane
Zuwārah
Ghadāmis
Annaba
Guelma
Skikda
Jijel
Bejaia
Tizi Ouzou
Constantine
Batna
Tebessa
Biskra
El Oued
Touggourt
Ouargla
Djanet
Tamanrasset
Bou Saâda
Djelfa
Laghouat
Ghardaia
Metlili
Blida
Cherchell
El Asnam
Tiaret
Mohammadia
Mostaganem
Oran
Ain Temouchent
Tlemcen
Mecheria
Oujda
Melilla
El Hoceima
Beni Ounif
Figuig
Bouarfa
Béchar
Beni Abbès
El Golea
Ain Salah
Aoulef el Arab
Timimoun
Adrar
Reggane
Bordj Mokhtar
Boudnib
Rissani
Errachidia
Midelt
Taza
Fes
Azrou
Meknes
Sidi Kacem
Tetouan
Sebta
Tanger
Larache
Kenitra
CASABLANCA
El Jadida
Oued Zem
Béni Mellal
Benguerir
Marrakech
Ouarzazarte
Safi
Chichaoua
Essaouira
Taroudant
Agadir
Tiznit
Guelmime
Tindouf
Laayoune
Dakhla
Bir Moghrein

WEST AFRICA

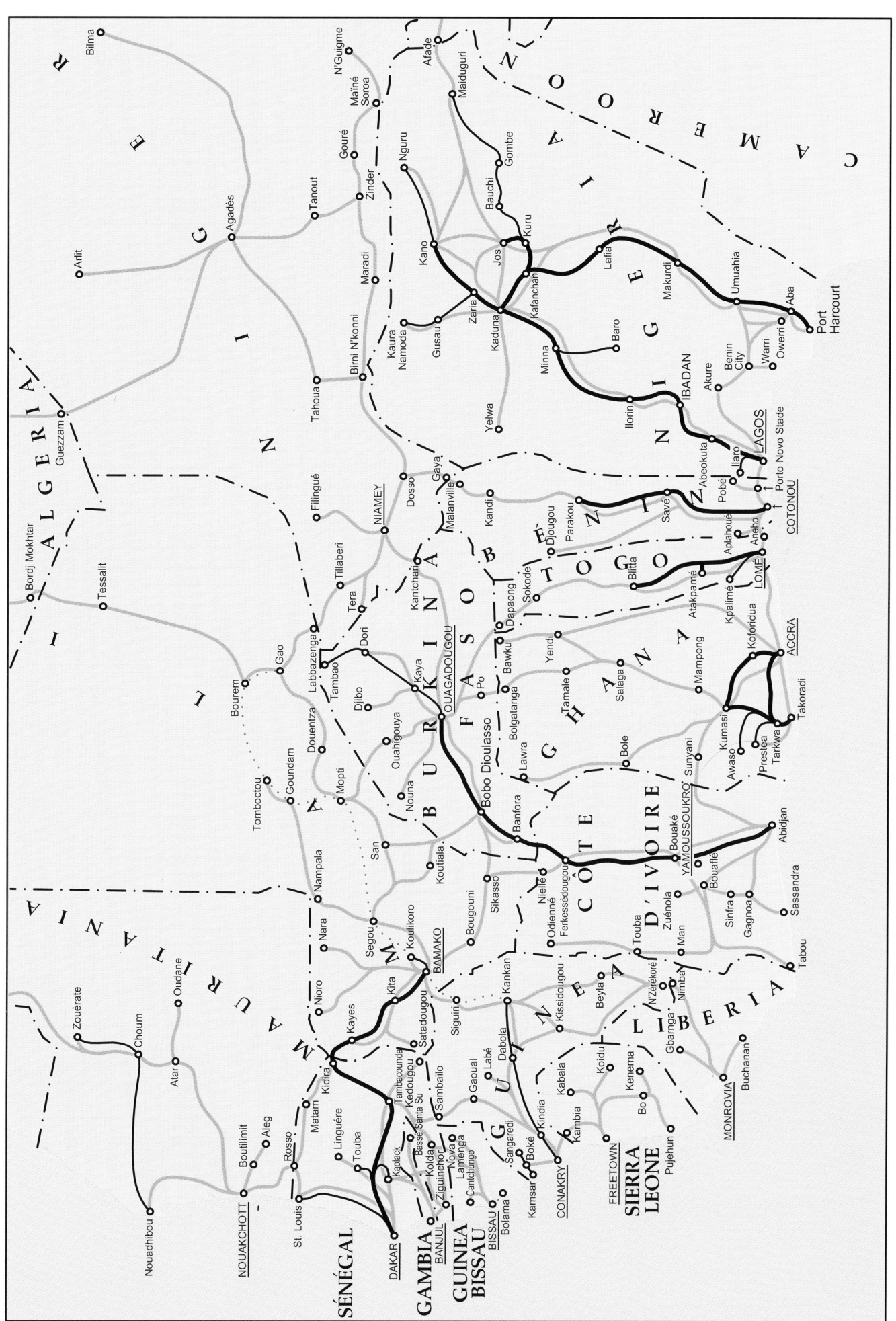
ALGERIA
NIGER
MALI
MAURITANIA
SÉNÉGAL
GAMBIA
GUINEA BISSAU
GUINEA
SIERRA LEONE
LIBERIA
CÔTE D'IVOIRE
BURKINA FASO
GHANA
TOGO
BÉNIN
NIGERIA
CAMEROON
Bilma
N'Guigme
Mainé Soroa
Gouré
Zinder
Tanout
Agadès
Arlit
Maradi
Birni N'Konni
Tahoua
Guezzam
Bordj Mokhtar
Tessalit
Filingué
NIAMEY
Dosso
Gaya
Malanville
Kandi
Tillaberi
Tera
Gao
Bourem
Labbazenga
Tambao
Dori
Djibo
Kaya
Kantchari
OUAGADOUGOU
Po
Ouahigouya
Douentza
Tombouctou
Goundam
Mopti
Nouna
Bobo Dioulasso
Banfora
San
Koutiala
Nampala
Nara
Segou
Koulikoro
BAMAKO
Bougouni
Sikasso
Kita
Kayes
Nioro
Kidira
Satadougou
Siguiri
Kankan
Dabola
Labé
Gaoual
Sambaïlo
Tambacounda
Kedougou
Santa Su
Basse
Kolda
Ziguinchor
Nova Lamenga
Cantchungo
Sangaredi
Boké
Kamsar
Kindia
CONAKRY
Kambia
Kabala
Koidu
Kenema
Bo
Pujehun
FREETOWN
Kissidougou
Beyla
N'Zérékoré
Nimba
Gbarnga
MONROVIA
Buchanan
Zouérate
Choum
Oudane
Atar
Nouadhibou
NOUAKCHOTT
Boutilimit
Aleg
Rosso
St. Louis
Matam
Linguère
Touba
Kaolack
DAKAR
BANJUL
BISSAU
Bolama
Odienné
Ferkessédougou
Nielle
Touba
Man
Zuénola
Bouaké
YAMOUSSOUKRO
Bouaflé
Sinfra
Gagnoa
Sassandra
Tabou
Abidjan
Bole
Lawra
Bolgatanga
Bawku
Dapaong
Tamale
Salaga
Yendi
Sokode
Djougou
Parakou
Savé
Bitta
Atakpamé
Kpalimé
LOMÉ
Aného
Aplahoué
Pobé
COTONOU
Porto Novo Stade
Ilaro
LAGOS
Abeokuta
IBADAN
Ilorin
Akure
Benin City
Warri
Owerri
Aba
Port Harcourt
Umuahia
Makurdi
Lafia
Kafanchan
Kuru
Jos
Bauchi
Gombe
Maiduguri
Afade
Nguru
Kano
Zaria
Kaduna
Gusau
Kaura Namoda
Minna
Baro
Yelwa
Kumasi
Mampong
Koforidua
ACCRA
Takoradi
Tarkwa
Prestea
Awaso
Sunyani

CENTRAL & EAST AFRICA

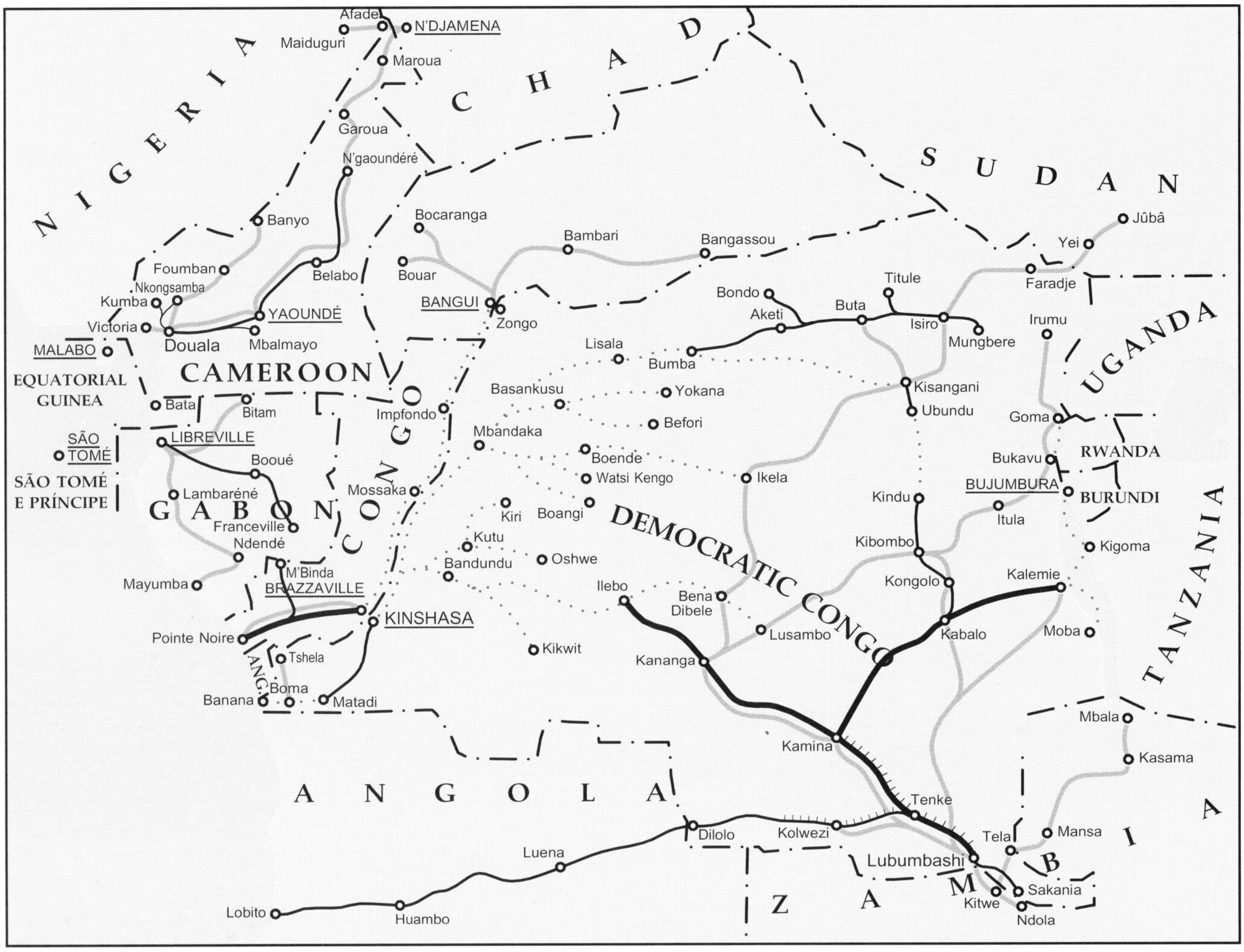

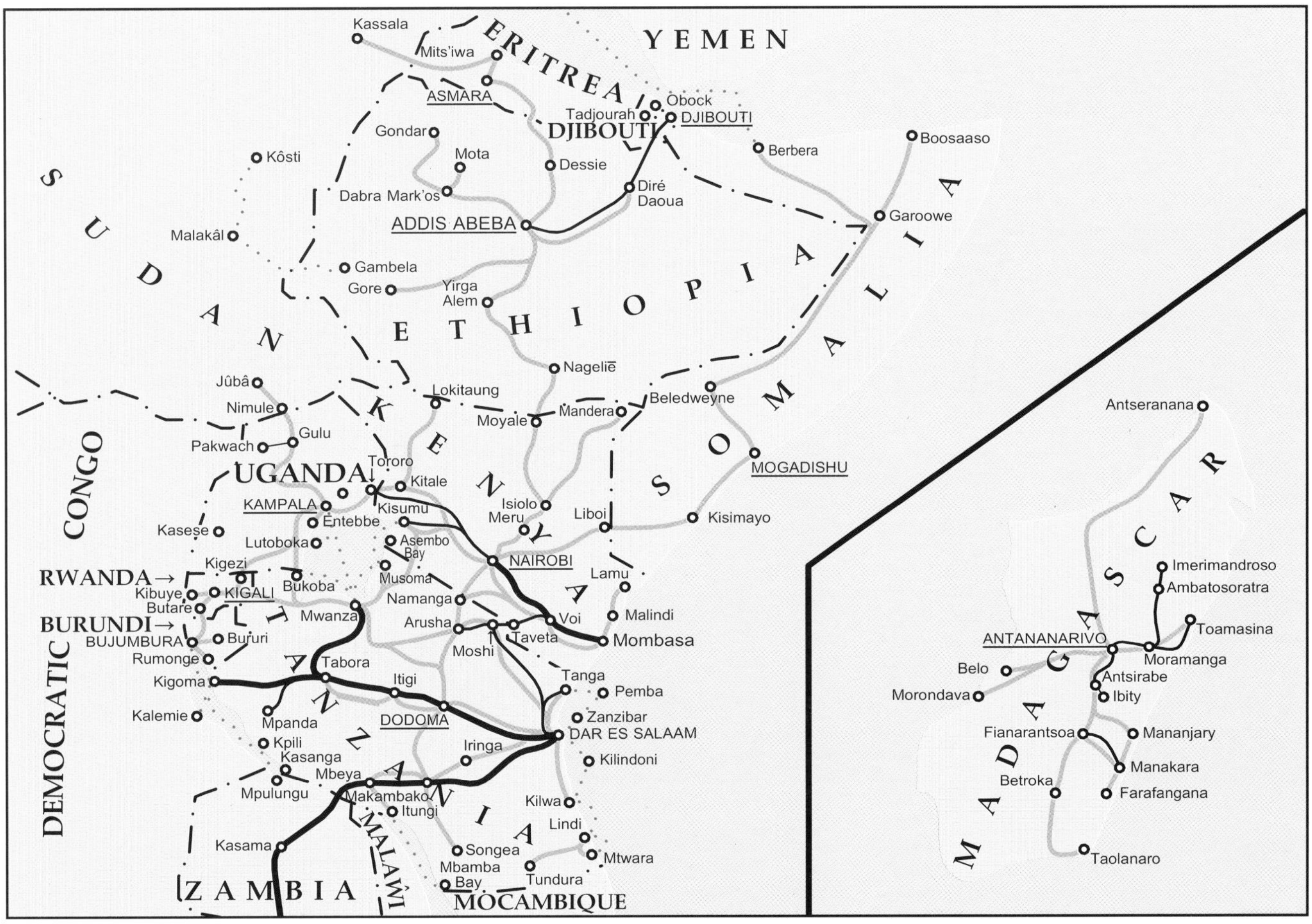

Map 1 (top):

NIGERIA

Afade
Maiduguri
N'DJAMENA
Maroua
CHAD
Garoua
N'gaoundéré
Banyo
Bocaranga
Bambari
Bangassou
Júbâ
Yei
SUDAN
Foumban
Belabo
Bouar
Bondo
Titule
Faradje
Nkongsamba
Buta
Isiro
Irumu
Kumba
YAOUNDÉ
BANGUI
Aketi
Mungbere
UGANDA
Victoria
Douala
Zongo
Lisala
Bumba
Kisangani
Goma
MALABO
Mbalmayo
Basankusu
Yokana
Ubundu
RWANDA
EQUATORIAL GUINEA
CAMEROON
Impfondo
Befori
Bukavu
BUJUMBURA
Bata
Bitam
Mbandaka
Boende
Watsi Kengo
Ikela
BURUNDI
SÃO TOMÉ
LIBREVILLE
Booué
Kiri
Boangi
DEMOCRATIC CONGO
Kindu
Itula
Kigoma
SÃO TOMÉ E PRÍNCIPE
Lambaréné
Mossaka
Kutu
Oshwe
Kibombo
GABON
Franceville
Bandundu
Ilebo
Bena Dibele
Kongolo
Kalemie
Ndendé
Mayumba
M'Binda
BRAZZAVILLE
Lusambo
Kabalo
Moba
TANZANIA
Pointe Noire
KINSHASA
Kikwit
Kananga
Tshela
Banana
Boma
Matadi
Kamina
Mbala
Kasama
ANGOLA
Tenke
Luena
Dilolo
Kolwezi
Tela
Mansa
Lobito
Huambo
Lubumbashi
Kitwe
Sakania
Ndola
ZAMBIA

Map 2 (bottom left):

Kassala
ERITREA
YEMEN
Mits'iwa
ASMARA
Obock
Kôsti
Gondar
Tadjourah
DJIBOUTI
Berbera
Boosaaso
Mota
DJIBOUTI
Dessie
SUDAN
Dabra Mark'os
Diré Daoua
Garoowe
Malakâl
ADDIS ABEBA
Gambela
Gore
Yirga Alem
ETHIOPIA
Nagelie
SOMALIA
Júbâ
Lokitaung
Nimule
Moyale
Mandera
Beledweyne
Pakwach
Gulu
Tororo
Kitale
Isiolo
Meru
Liboi
MOGADISHU
UGANDA
KAMPALA
Kisumu
CONGO
Kasese
Entebbe
Asembo Bay
NAIROBI
Kisimayo
Lutoboka
Kigezi
Musoma
Namanga
Lamu
RWANDA
Kibuye
KIGALI
Bukoba
Arusha
Voi
Malindi
Butare
Mwanza
Moshi
Taveta
Mombasa
BURUNDI
Bururi
KENYA
BUJUMBURA
Rumonge
Tabora
Tanga
Pemba
Kigoma
Itigi
Zanzibar
Kalemie
Mpanda
DODOMA
DAR ES SALAAM
Kpili
Iringa
Kasanga
Mbeya
Kilindoni
TANZANIA
Mpulungu
Makambako
Kilwa
Kasama
Itungu
Lindi
Songea
Mtwara
MALAWI
Mbamba Bay
Tundura
ZAMBIA
MOÇAMBIQUE

Inset (Madagascar):

Antseranana
MADAGASCAR
Imerimandroso
Ambatosoratra
ANTANANARIVO
Toamasina
Belo
Moramanga
Antsirabe
Morondava
Ibity
Fianarantsoa
Mananjary
Betroka
Manakara
Farafangana
Taolanaro

SOUTHERN AFRICA

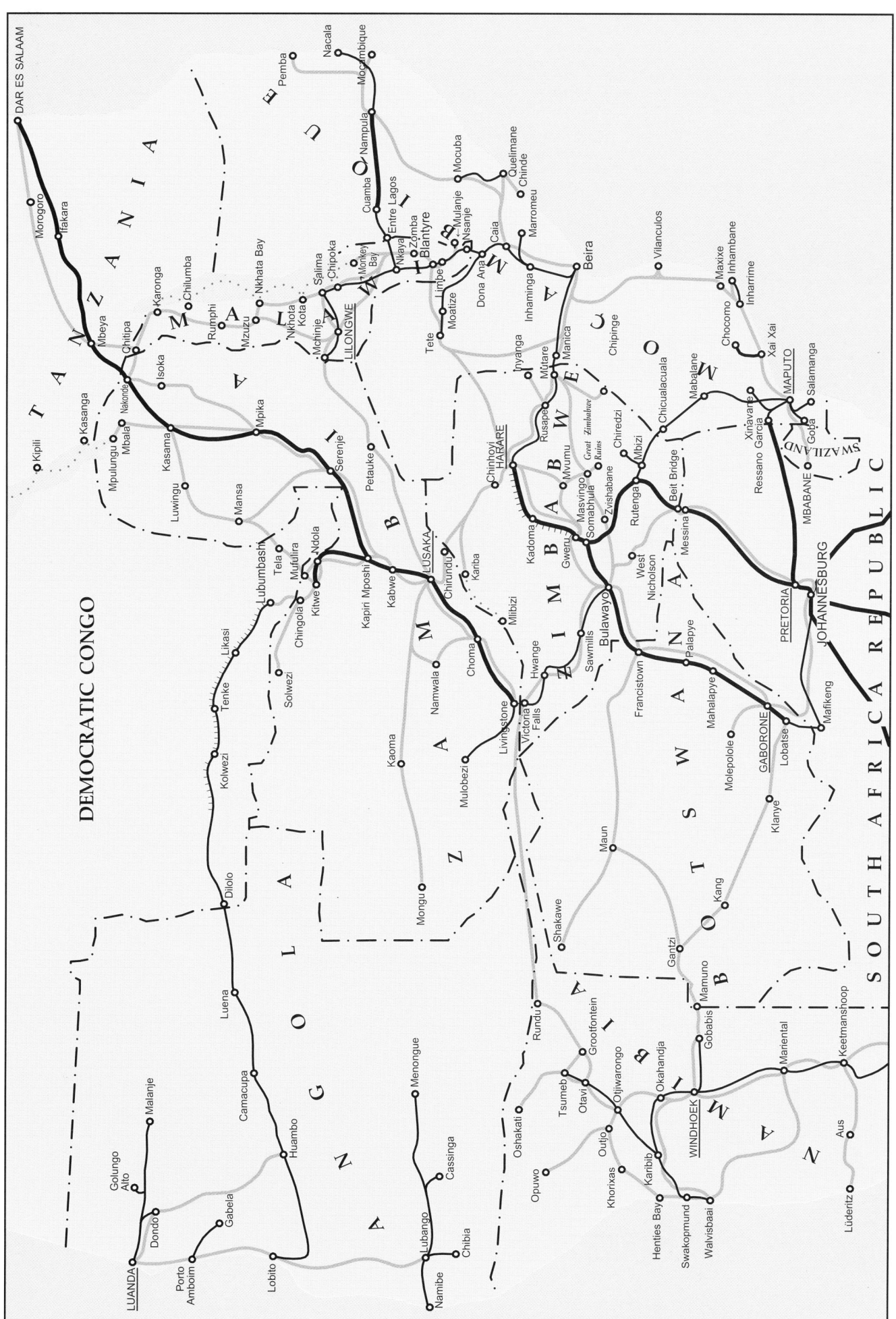
DEMOCRATIC CONGO
TANZANIA
MOZAMBIQUE
MALAWI
ZAMBIA
ZIMBABWE
ANGOLA
BOTSWANA
NAMIBIA
SOUTH AFRICA REPUBLIC
SWAZILAND
DAR ES SALAAM
Morogoro
Ifakara
Kipili
Kasanga
Mbeya
Mpulungu
Mbala
Nakonde
Chitipa
Karonga
Isoka
Kasama
Luwingu
Chilumba
Rumphi
Mzuzu
Nkhata Bay
Mansa
Mpika
Pemba
Nkhota Kota
Salima
Chipoka
Mchinje
LILONGWE
Monkey Bay
Nacala
Mocambique
Cuamba
Nampula
Entre Lagos
Nkaya
Zomba
Blantyre
Limbe
Mulanje
Nsanje
Mocuba
Tete
Moatize
Dona Ana
Caia
Quelimane
Chinde
Marromeu
Inhaminga
Inyanga
Mutare
Manica
Rusape
Beira
Chipinge
Vilanculos
Maxixe
Inhambane
Inharrime
Chocomo
Xai Xai
Xinavane
Ressano Garcia
MAPUTO
Salamanga
Goba
MBABANE
Mabalane
Chicualacuala
Chiredzi
Mbizi
Rutenga
Beit Bridge
Messina
West Nicholson
Zvishabane
Masvingo
Great Zimbabwe Ruins
Mvumu
Somabhula
Gweru
Kadoma
Chinhoyi
HARARE
Bulawayo
Sawmills
Hwange
Victoria Falls
Livingstone
Mlibizi
Kariba
Chirundu
LUSAKA
Choma
Namwala
Mulobezi
Kabwe
Kapiri Mposhi
Petauke
Serenje
Ndola
Kitwe
Mufulira
Chingola
Tela
Lubumbashi
Solwezi
Likasi
Tenke
Kolwezi
Dilolo
Luena
Camacupa
Huambo
Lobito
Porto Amboim
Gabela
LUANDA
Dondo
Golungo Alto
Malanje
Kaoma
Mongu
Lubango
Namibe
Chibia
Cassinga
Menongue
Oshakati
Opuwo
Rundu
Tsumeb
Otavi
Grootfontein
Outjo
Khorixas
Otjiwarongo
Karibib
Okahandja
Henties Bay
Swakopmund
Walvisbaai
WINDHOEK
Gobabis
Mamuno
Gantzi
Kang
Shakawe
Maun
Francistown
Palapye
Mahalapye
Molepolole
GABORONE
Lobatse
Klanye
Mafikeng
PRETORIA
JOHANNESBURG
Mariental
Keetmanshoop
Aus
Lüderitz

SOUTH AFRICA

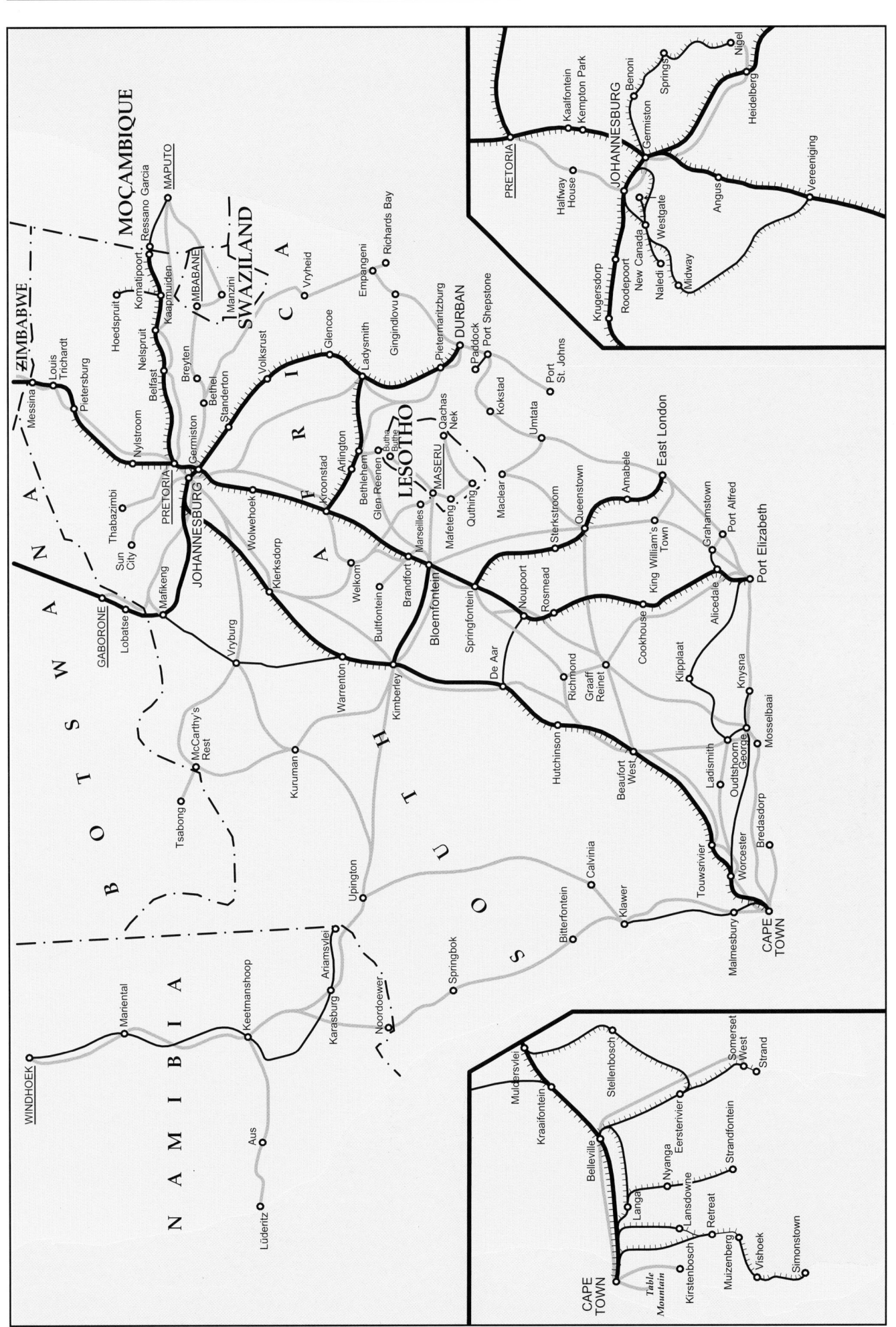

ZIMBABWE

MOÇAMBIQUE

MAPUTO

Ressano Garcia

SWAZILAND

MBABANE

Manzini

Komatipoort

Kaapmuiden

Hoedspruit

Nelspruit

Belfast

Breyten

Bethal

Standerton

Volksrust

Vryheid

Glencoe

Ladysmith

Gingindlovu

Empangeni

Richards Bay

Pietermaritzburg

DURBAN

Paddock

Port Shepstone

Messina

Louis Trichardt

Pietersburg

Nylstroom

Germiston

PRETORIA

JOHANNESBURG

Wolwehoek

Kroonstad

Arlington

Bethlehem

Glen-Reenen

Marseilles

Mafeteng

Quthing

LESOTHO

MASERU

Buthe-Buthe

Qachas Nek

Maclear

Kokstad

Umtata

Port St. Johns

AFRICA

Thabazimbi

Sun City

Mafikeng

GABORONE

Lobatse

Klerksdorp

Welkom

Bultfontein

Brandfort

Bloemfontein

Springfontein

De Aar

Noupoort

Rosmead

Sterkstroom

Queenstown

Amabele

King William's Town

East London

BOTSWANA

McCarthy's Rest

Vryburg

Warrenton

Kimberley

Richmond

Graaff Reinet

Cookhouse

Klipplaat

Alicedale

Grahamstown

Port Alfred

Port Elizabeth

Knysna

Mosselbaai

Tsabong

Kuruman

Hutchinson

Beaufort West

Ladismith

Oudtshoorn

George

Bredasdorp

NAMIBIA

Mariental

Keetmanshoop

Upington

Springbok

Calvinia

Bitterfontein

Klawer

Touwsrivier

Worcester

Malmesbury

CAPE TOWN

Ariamsvlei

Noordoewer

WINDHOEK

Karasburg

Lüderitz

Aus

PRETORIA

JOHANNESBURG

Kaalfontein

Kempton Park

Benoni

Springs

Nigel

Germiston

Heidelberg

Halfway House

Westgate

Angus

Vereeniging

Krugersdorp

Roodepoort

New Canada

Naledi

Midway

CAPE TOWN

Muldersvlei

Kraaifontein

Stellenbosch

Somerset West

Strand

Belleville

Nyanga

Eersterivier

Strandfontein

Langa

Lansdowne

Retreat

Vishoek

Simonstown

Kirstenbosch

Muizenberg

Table Mountain

NORTHERN ASIA

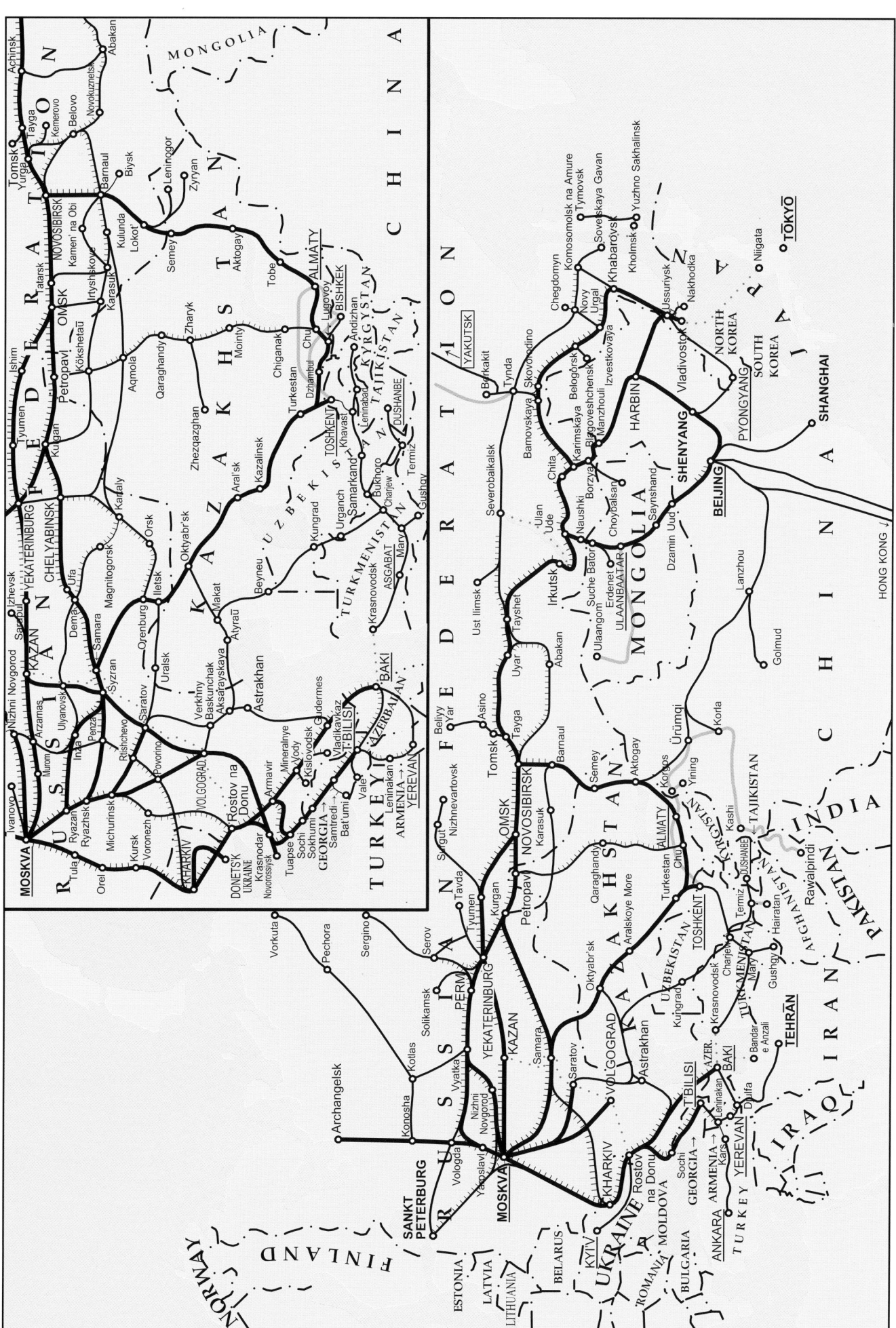
RUSSIAN FEDERATION
KAZAKHSTAN
CHINA
MONGOLIA
UZBEKISTAN
TURKMENISTAN
KYRGYSTAN
TAJIKISTAN
TURKEY
AZERBAIJAN
MOSKVA
Ivanovo
Nizhni Novgorod
Sarapul
Izhevsk
YEKATERINBURG
Tyumen
Ishim
Tomsk
Yurga
Tayga
Achinsk
Tula
Ryazan
Ryazhsk
Murom
Arzamas
KAZAN
Ulyanovsk
Inza
Penza
Dema
Ufa
CHELYABINSK
Kurgan
Petropavl
OMSK
Tatarsk
NOVOSIBIRSK
Kemerovo
Belovo
Novokuznetsk
Abakan
Orel
Michurinsk
Rtishchevo
Syzran
Samara
Magnitogorsk
Kartaly
Kökshetaū
Irtyshskoye
Karasuk
Kamen' na Obi
Barnaul
Biysk
Kulunda
Lokot'
Kursk
Voronezh
Povorino
Saratov
Orenburg
Orsk
Iletsk
Uralsk
Aqmola
Qaraghandy
Semey
Leninogor
Zyryan
KHARKIV
VOLGOGRAD
Verkhny Baskunchak
Aksarayskaya
Makat
Oktyabr'sk
Zhezqazghan
Zharyk
DONETS'K
UKRAINE
Rostov na Donu
Atyraū
Aral'sk
Mointy
Aktogay
Krasnodar
Novorossiysk
Astrakhan
Beyneu
Kazalinsk
Chiganak
Tobe
Armavir
Mineralnye Vody
Tuapse
Sochi
Sokhumi
Kislovodsk
Gudermes
Turkestan
Dzhambul
Chu
ALMATY
GEORGIA →
Samtredi →
Bat'umi
Vladikavkaz
T'BILISI
Kungrad
TOSHKENT
Lugovoy
BISHKEK
Urganch
Samarkand
Khavast
Leninabad
Andizhan
Vale
Krasnovodsk
Bukhoro
Charjew
DUSHANBE
Leninakan
ARMENIA →
YEREVAN
BAKI
ASGABAT
Mary
Termiz
Gushgy
Vorkuta
Pechora
Archangelsk
Sergino
NORWAY
FINLAND
SANKT PETERBURG
Konosha
Kotlas
Solikamsk
Serov
Surgut
Nizhnevartovsk
Beliyy Yar
ESTONIA
Vologda
Vyatka
PERM
Tavda
LATVIA
Yaroslavl
Nizhni Novgorod
YEKATERINBURG
Asino
Ust Ilimsk
Severobaikalsk
YAKUTSK
Berkakit
LITHUANIA
Tynda
Uyar
Tayshet
Bamovskaya
Skovorodino
Ulan Ude
Irkutsk
Chita
BELARUS
Chegdomyn
Komosomolsk na Amure
Tymovsk
Naushki
Karimskaya
Belogorsk
Blagoveshchensk
Novy Urgal
KYI'V
UKRAINE
Ulaangom
Suche Bator
Borzya
Manzhouli
Sovetskaya Gavan
Erdenet
ULAANBAATAR
Choybalsan
Izvestkovaya
Khabarovsk
Aralskoye More
Kholmsk
Yuzhno Sakhalinsk
ROMANIA
MOLDOVA
Saynshand
HARBIN
Dzamin Uud
Ussuriysk
BULGARIA
Korgos
Ürümqi
Yining
SHENYANG
Vladivostok
Nakhodka
ANKARA
Kars
AZER.
Korla
BEIJING
NORTH KOREA
Kashi
Julfa
Bandar e Anzali
Hairatan
←TAJIKISTAN
Lanzhou
PYONGYANG
SOUTH KOREA
Niigata
JAPAN
Golmud
TEHRĀN
AFGHANISTAN
Rawalpindi
TŌKYŌ
IRAQ
IRAN
PAKISTAN
INDIA
SHANGHAI
HONG KONG ↓

CHINA

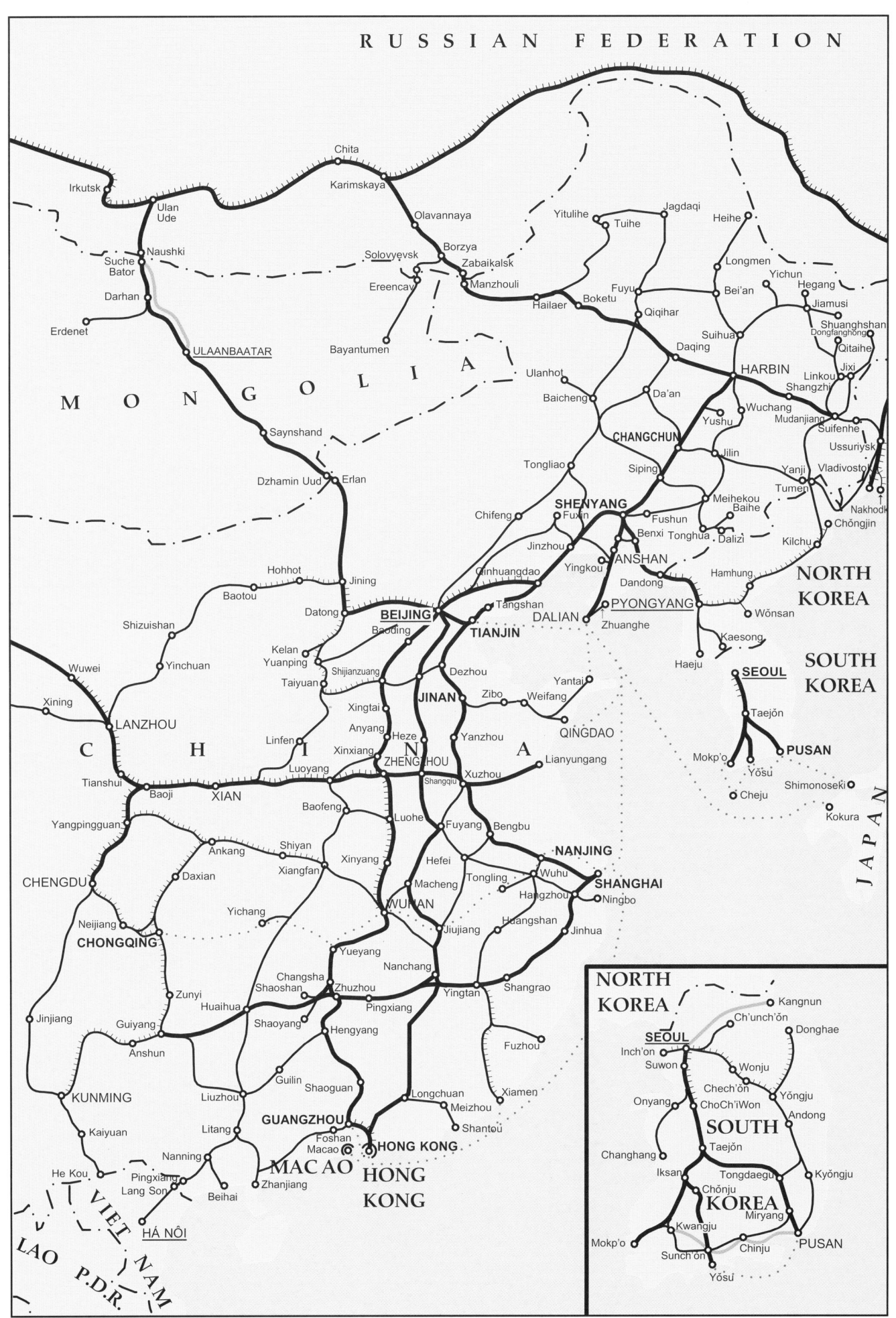

RUSSIAN FEDERATION

Irkutsk
Chita
Karimskaya
Ulan Ude
Olavannaya
Yitulihe
Tuihe
Jagdaqi
Heihe
Naushki
Solovyevsk
Borzya
Longmen
Yichun
Hegang
Suche Bator
Zabaikalsk
Fuyu
Bei'an
Jiamusi
Darhan
Ereencav
Manzhouli
Boketu
Qiqihar
Suihua
Shuanghshan
Dongfanghong
Erdenet
Hailaer
Daqing
HARBIN
Qitaihe
Linkou
Jixi
ULAANBAATAR
Bayantumen
Ulanhot
Da'an
Shangzhi
Wuchang
Mudanjiang
Suifenhe
Ussuriysk
M O N G O L I A
Saynshand
Baicheng
CHANGCHUN
Yushu
Jilin
Yanji
Vladivostok
Tumen
Dzhamin Uud
Erlan
Tongliao
Siping
Meihekou
Baihe
Nakhodk
Chŏngjin
Chifeng
SHENYANG
Fuxin
Fushun
Dalizi
Kilchu
Hohhot
Jining
Jinzhou
Benxi Tonghua
Baotou
Qinhuangdao
Yingkou
ANSHAN
Hamhung
NORTH KOREA
Shizuishan
Datong
Tangshan
Dandong
PYONGYANG
Wŏnsan
BEIJING
DALIAN
Zhuanghe
Wuwei
Yinchuan
Kelan
Yuanping
Baoding
TIANJIN
Kaesong
SOUTH KOREA
Xining
Taiyuan
Shijianzuang
Dezhou
Yantai
Haeju
SEOUL
Lanzhou
JINAN
Zibo
Weifang
Taejŏn
Xingtai
Anyang
Yanzhou
QINGDAO
Mokp'o
Pusan
C H I N A
Linfen
Heze
Yŏsu
Shimonoseki
Tianshui
Xinxiang
ZHENGZHOU
Xuzhou
Lianyungang
Cheju
Baoji
XIAN
Shangqiu
Luoyang
Kokura
Yangpingguan
Baofeng
Luohe
Fuyang
Bengbu
Ankang
Shiyan
Xinyang
Hefei
NANJING
CHENGDU
Daxian
Xiangfan
Macheng
Tongling
Wuhu
SHANGHAI
Yichang
WUHAN
Hangzhou
Ningbo
Neijiang
Jiujiang
Huangshan
Jinhua
CHONGQING
Yueyang
Nanchang
Zunyi
Changsha
Shaoshan
Zhuzhou
Yingtan
Shangrao
Jinjiang
Guiyang
Huaihua
Pingxiang
Anshun
Shaoyang
Hengyang
Fuzhou
Guilin
Shaoguan
Longchuan
Xiamen
KUNMING
Liuzhou
Meizhou
Kaiyuan
Litang
GUANGZHOU
Shantou
Nanning
Foshan
Macao
HONG KONG
He Kou
Pingxiang
Lang Son
Zhanjiang
MACAO
HONG KONG
Beihai
HÁ NÔI
V I E T N A M
LAO P.D.R.

NORTH KOREA
Kangnun
Ch'unch'ŏn
Donghae
SEOUL
Inch'on
Wonju
Suwon
Chech'ŏn
Yŏngju
Onyang
ChoCh'iWon
Andong
Changhang
Taejŏn
SOUTH KOREA
Iksan
Tongdaegu
Kyŏngju
Chŏnju
Miryang
Kwangju
KOREA
Mokp'o
Chinju
PUSAN
Sunch'ŏn
Yŏsu

J A P A N

PAKISTAN

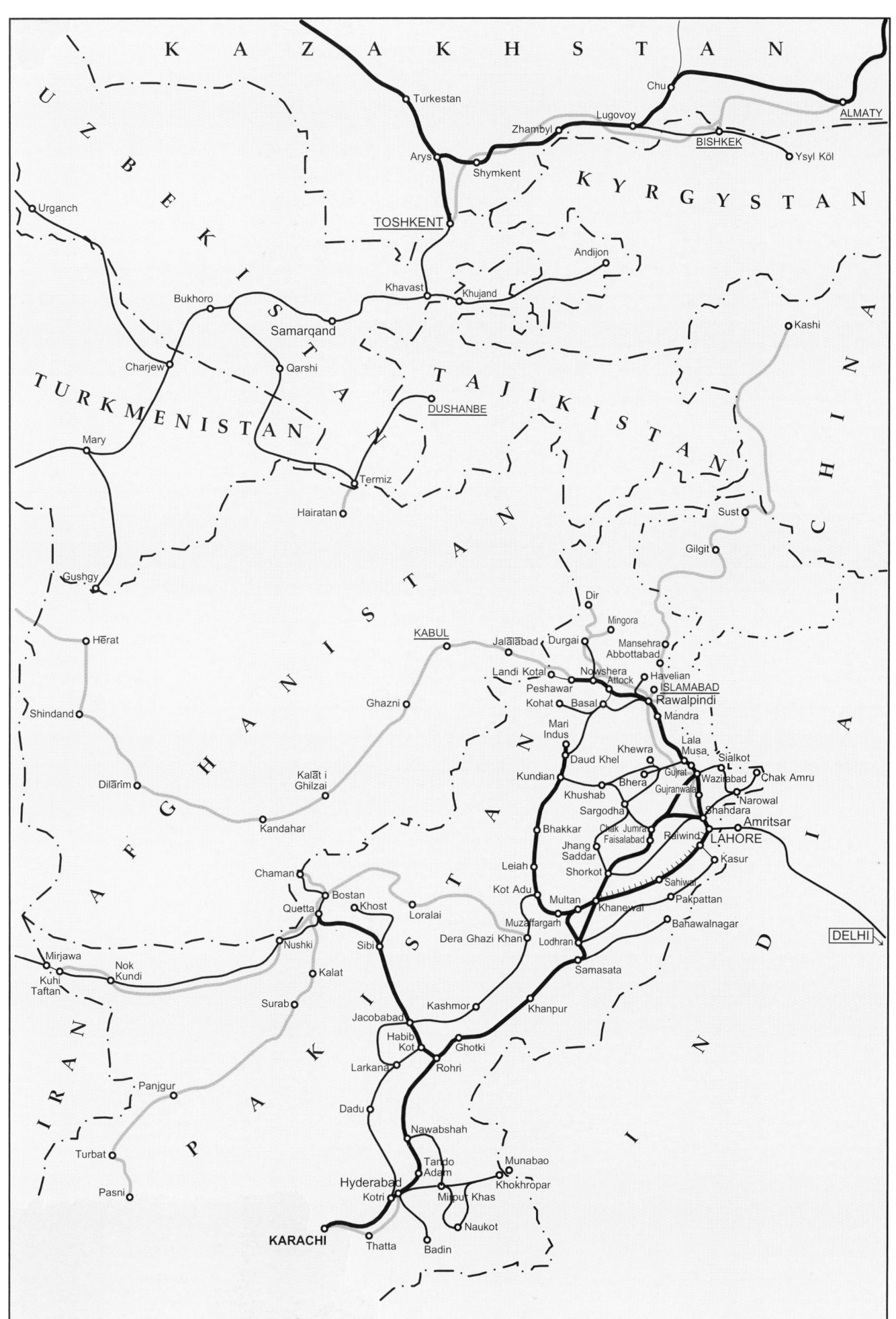

KAZAKHSTAN

UZBEKISTAN

TURKMENISTAN

TAJIKISTAN

KYRGYSTAN

CHINA

AFGHANISTAN

PAKISTAN

IRAN

INDIA

Turkestan

Chu

ALMATY

Lugovoy

Zhambyl

BISHKEK

Ysyl Köl

Arys

Shymkent

Andijon

Urganch

Khavast

Khujand

Kashi

Bukhoro

Samarqand

TOSHKENT

Charjew

Qarshi

DUSHANBE

Mary

Termiz

Sust

Hairatan

Gilgit

Gushgy

Dir

Mingora

Hērat

KABUL

Jalalabad

Durgai

Mansehra

Abbottabad

Havelian

Landi Kotal

Nowshera

Attock

ISLAMABAD

Shindand

Ghazni

Peshawar

Kohat

Basal

Rawalpindi

Mandra

Mari
Indus

Khewra

Lala
Musa

Sialkot

Dilārim

Kalāt i
Ghilzai

Daud Khel

Kundian

Bhera

Gujrat

Wazirabad

Chak Amru

Khushab

Gujranwala

Narowal

Kandahar

Sargodha

Shahdara

Amritsar

Bhakkar

Chak Jumra

Faisalabad

Raiwind

LAHORE

Chaman

Jhang
Saddar

Shorkot

Kasur

Leiah

Sahiwal

Bostan

Khost

Loralai

Kot Adu

Multan

Khanewal

Pakpattan

Quetta

Muzaffargarh

Lodhran

Bahawalnagar

Dera Ghazi Khan

Samasata

DELHI

Mirjawa

Nok
Kundi

Nushki

Sibi

Kuhi
Taftan

Kalat

Kashmor

Khanpur

Surab

Jacobabad

Habib
Kot

Ghotki

Panjgur

Larkana

Rohri

Dadu

Turbat

Nawabshah

Pasni

Munabao

Tando
Adam

Khokhropar

Hyderabad

Kotri

Mirpur Khas

Naukot

KARACHI

Thatta

Badin

NORTHERN INDIA

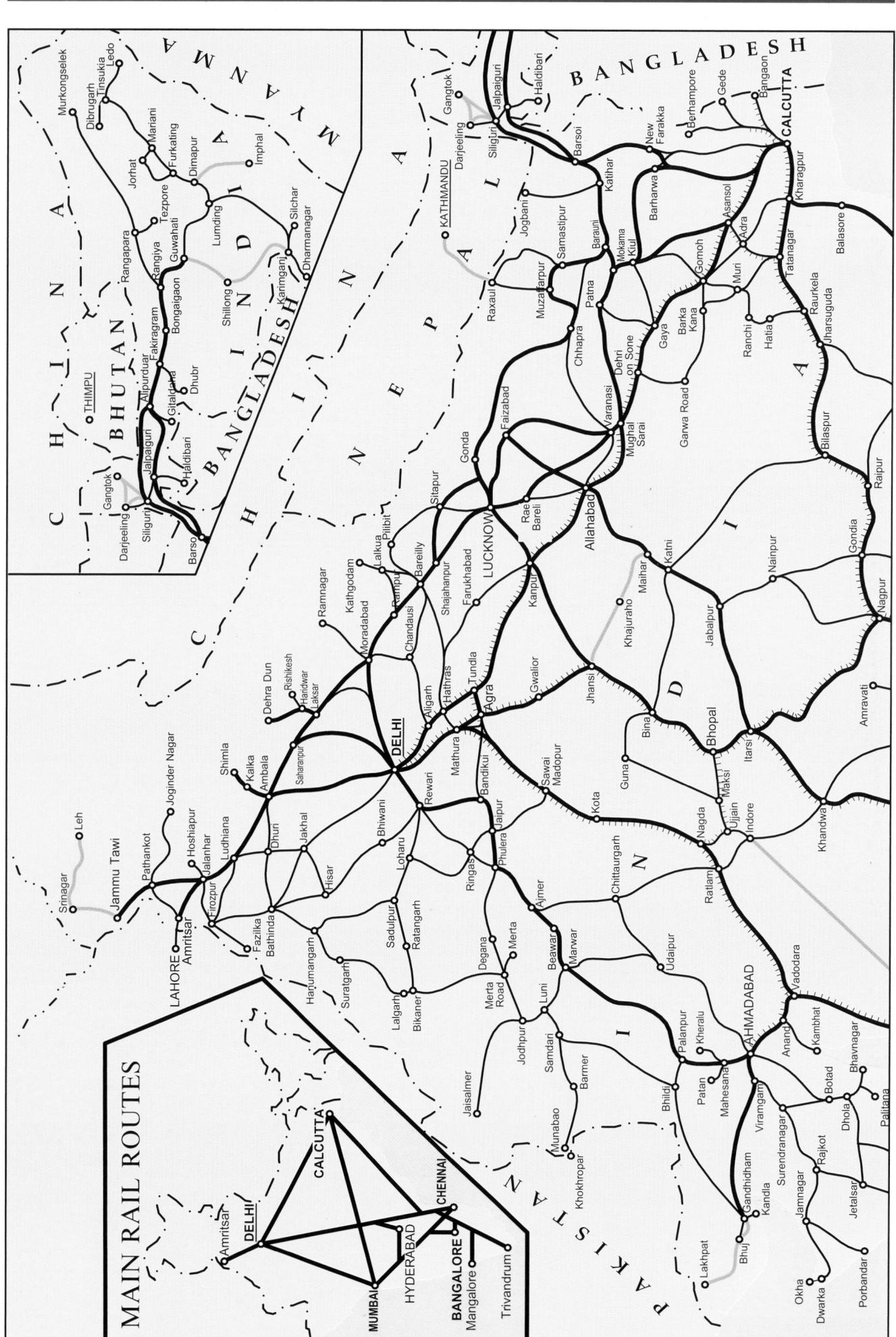
MAIN RAIL ROUTES
DELHI
CALCUTTA
Amritsar
MUMBAI
HYDERABAD
CHENNAI
BANGALORE
Mangalore
Trivandrum
CHINA
BHUTAN
MYANMAR
INDIA
BANGLADESH
NEPAL
PAKISTAN
THIMPU
KATHMANDU
LAHORE
Murkongselek
Dibrugarh
Tinsukia
Ledo
Mariani
Jorhat
Furkating
Dimapur
Imphal
Tezpore
Rangapara
Guwahati
Lumding
Silchar
Dharmanagar
Karimganj
Shillong
Rangiya
Bongaigaon
Fakiragram
Alipurduar
Gitaldaha
Dhubr
Jalpaiguri
Haldibari
Gangtok
Darjeeling
Siliguri
Barso
Barsoi
Katihar
New Farakka
Berhampore
Gede
Bangaon
Barharwa
Jogbani
Samastipur
Barauni
Mokama
Kiul
Asansol
Gomoh
Adra
Kharagpur
Balasore
Tatanagar
Muri
Raxaul
Muzaffarpur
Patna
Chhapra
Gaya
Barka Kana
Ranchi
Hatia
Raurkela
Jharsuguda
Dehri on Sone
Garwa Road
Varanasi
Mughal Sarai
Faizabad
Gonda
Bilaspur
Raipur
Sitapur
Rae Bareli
Allahabad
Lucknow
Pilibit
Lalkua
Bareilly
Shajahanpur
Farukhabad
Kanpur
Maihar
Katni
Khajuraho
Nainpur
Gondia
Jabalpur
Nagpur
Kathgodam
Ramnagar
Rampur
Moradabad
Chandausi
Aligarh
Hathras
Tundla
Agra
Gwalior
Jhansi
Bina
Bhopal
Itarsi
Amravati
Dehra Dun
Rishikesh
Haridwar
Laksar
Saharanpur
Mathura
Sawai Madopur
Guna
Maksi
Ujjain
Indore
Nagda
Kota
Khandwa
Shimla
Kalka
Ambala
Rewari
Bandikui
Jaipur
Phulera
Ringas
Joginder Nagar
Hoshiapur
Leh
Srinagar
Jammu Tawi
Pathankot
Jalanhar
Ludhiana
Dhuri
Jakhal
Bhiwani
Loharu
Hisar
Amritsar
Firozpur
Fazilka
Bathinda
Hanumangarh
Suratgarh
Sadulpur
Ratangarh
Lalgarh
Bikaner
Degana
Merta
Merta Road
Ajmer
Beawar
Marwar
Chittaurgarh
Udaipur
Ratlam
Luni
Jodhpur
Samdari
Barmer
Jaisalmer
Munabao
Khokhropar
Palanpur
Kheralu
AHMADABAD
Vadodara
Anand
Kambhat
Bhildi
Patan
Mahesana
Viramgam
Surendranagar
Botad
Bhavnagar
Dhola
Palitana
Rajkot
Jetalsar
Jamnagar
Gandhidham
Kandla
Bhuj
Lakhpat
Okha
Dwarka
Porbandar

SOUTHERN INDIA

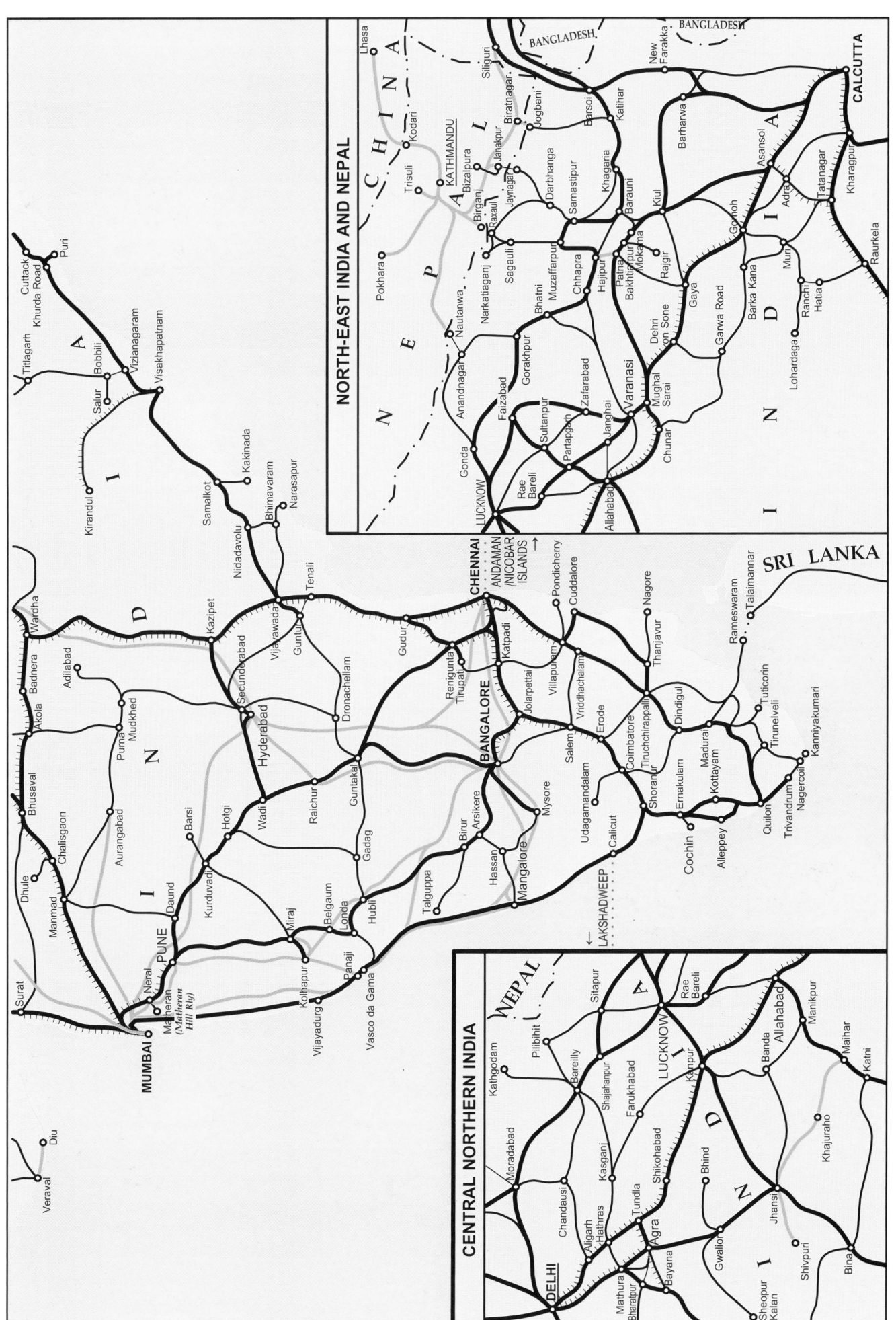

NORTH-EAST INDIA AND NEPAL

CHINA

Lhasa

NEPAL

BANGLADESH
BANGLADESH

Siliguri
Kodari
Trisuli
KATHMANDU
Biratnagar
Jogbani
Jahakpur
Bizalpura
Birganj
Raxaul
Jaynagar
Barsoi
Kathar
Barharwa
New Farakka
CALCUTTA
Asansol
Adra
Tatanagar
Kharagpur
Raurkela

Pokhara
Nautanwa
Anandnagar
Narkatiaganj
Sagauli
Muzaffarpur
Darbhanga
Samastipur
Khagaria
Barauni
Kiul
Gomoh
Ranchi
Hatia
Lohardaga
Barka Kana
Muri

Gonda
Faizabad
Gorakhpur
Bhatni
Chhapra
Hajipur
Patna
Bakhtiarpur
Mokama
Rajgir
Gaya
Ganwa Road

LUCKNOW
Rae Bareli
Sultanpur
Partapgarh
Janghai
Zafarabad
Varanasi
Mughal Sarai
Dehri on Sone
Chunar
Allahabad

CENTRAL NORTHERN INDIA

NEPAL

Kathgodam
Pilibhit
Sitapur
Rae Bareli
Bareilly
Shajahanpur
Farukhabad
LUCKNOW
Kanpur
Banda
Allahabad
Manikpur
Maihar
Katni

Moradabad
Kasganj
Shikohabad
Bhind
Khajuraho

Chandausi
Aligarh
Hathras
Tundla
Agra
Jhansi
Shivpuri
Bina

DELHI
Mathura
Bharatpur
Bayana
Gwalior
Sheopur Kalan

SRI LANKA

Puri
Cuttack
Khurda Road
Titlagarh
Salur
Bobbili
Vizianagaram
Visakhapatnam
Kirandul
Samalkot
Kakinada
Bhimavaram
Narasapur
Nidadavolu

Wardha
Badnera
Akola
Adilabad
Mudkhed
Purna
Kazipet
Tenali
Vijayawada
Guntur
Secunderabad
Dronachellam
Gudur
Renigunta
Tirupati
CHENNAI
ANDAMAN NICOBAR ISLANDS
Pondicherry
Cuddalore

Bhusaval
Chalisgaon
Aurangabad
Mudkhed
Hyderabad
Raichur
Wadi
Guntakal
Birur
Arsikere
BANGALORE
Katpadi
Villupuram
Vriddhachalam
Jolarpettai
Nagore
Thanjavur
Rameswaram
Talaimannar

Surat
Dhule
Manmad
Daund
PUNE
Neral
Matheran
(Matheran Hill Rly.)
MUMBAI
Barsi
Hotgi
Kurduvadi
Miraj
Kolhapur
Panaji
Vijayadurg
Vasco da Gama
Belgaum
Londa
Hubli
Gadag
Talguppa
Hassan
Mangalore
Mysore
Udagamandalam
Calicut
Salem
Erode
Coimbatore
Shoranur
Ernakulam
Cochin
Alleppey
Quilon
Trivandrum
Nagercoil
Dindigul
Madurai
Kottayam
Tiruchirappalli
Tirunelveli
Tuticorin
Kanniyakumari

Veraval
Diu

LAKSHADWEEP

ASIAN ISLANDS & BANGLADESH

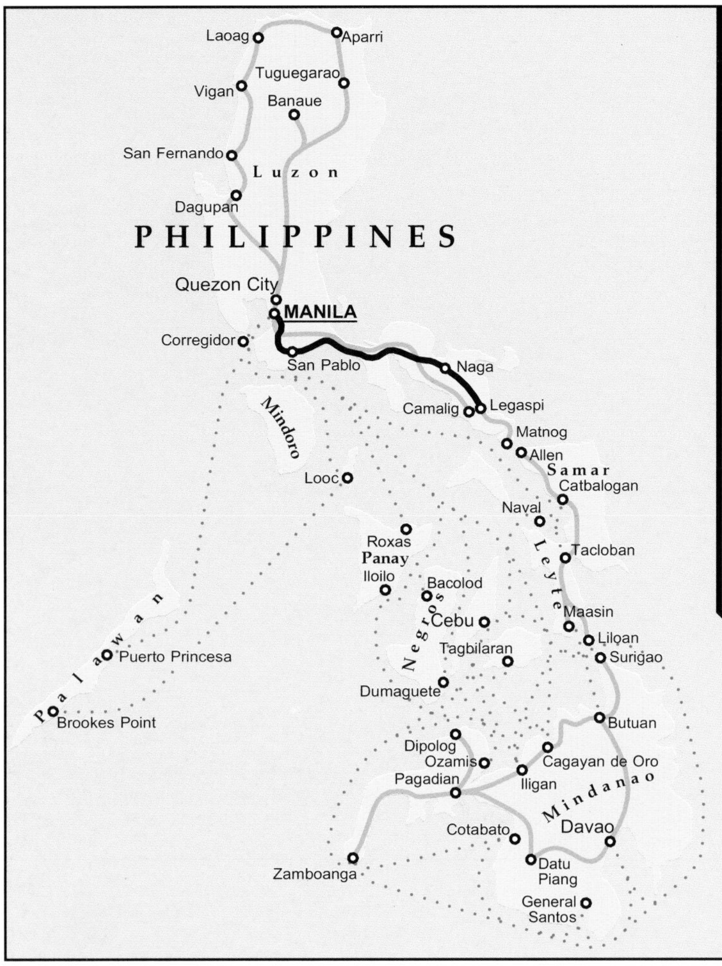

Philippines (Luzon, Samar, Leyte, Panay, Negros, Cebu, Mindanao, Palawan, Mindoro)

Laoag, Aparri, Tuguegarao, Vigan, Banaue, San Fernando, Dagupan, Luzon, PHILIPPINES, Quezon City, Corregidor, MANILA, San Pablo, Naga, Camalig, Legaspi, Matnog, Allen, Samar, Catbalogan, Naval, Tacloban, Roxas, Panay, Iloilo, Bacolod, Maasin, Negros, Cebu, Liloan, Tagbilaran, Surigao, Dumaguete, Butuan, Puerto Princesa, Palawan, Brookes Point, Dipolog, Ozamis, Cagayan de Oro, Pagadian, Iligan, Mindanao, Cotabato, Davao, Zamboanga, Datu Piang, General Santos

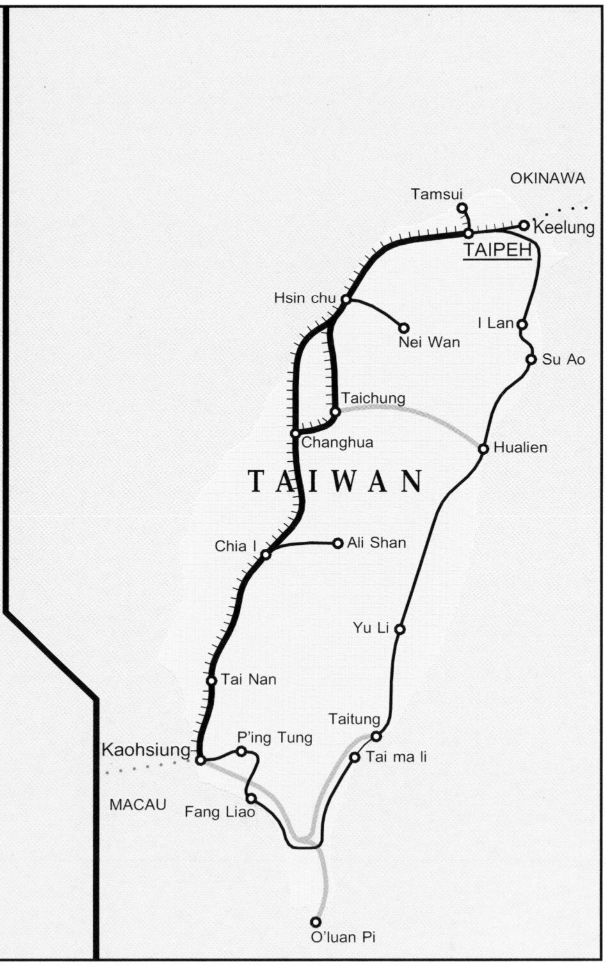

Taiwan

OKINAWA, Tamsui, Keelung, TAIPEH, Hsin chu, Nei Wan, I Lan, Su Ao, Taichung, Changhua, Hualien, TAIWAN, Chia I, Ali Shan, Yu Li, Tai Nan, Taitung, Kaohsiung, P'ing Tung, Tai ma li, MACAU, Fang Liao, O'luan Pi

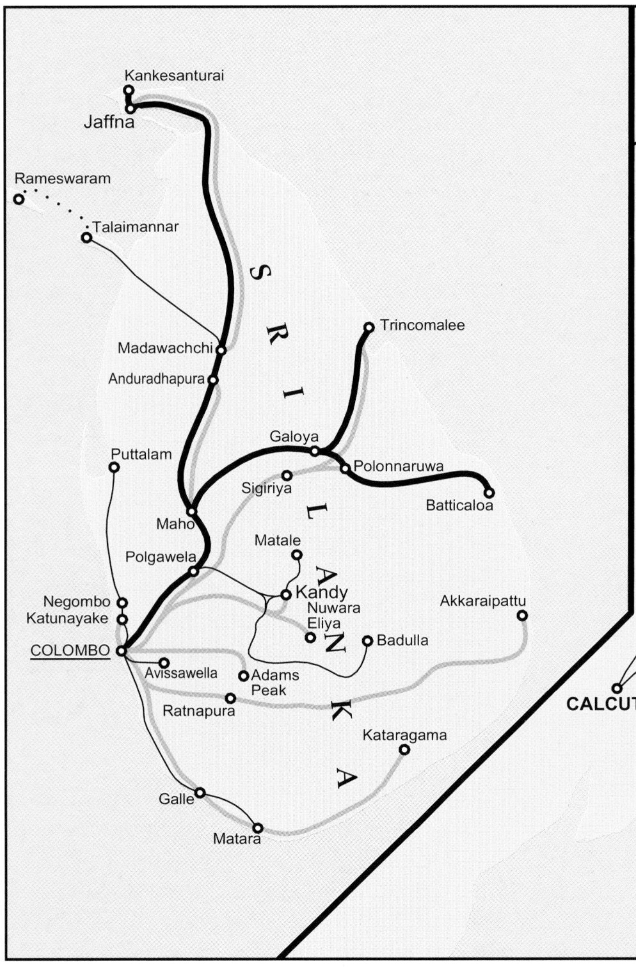

Sri Lanka

Kankesanturai, Jaffna, Rameswaram, Talaimannar, Trincomalee, SRI LANKA, Madawachchi, Anuradhapura, Galoya, Puttalam, Sigiriya, Polonnaruwa, Maho, Batticaloa, Matale, Polgawela, Kandy, Nuwara Eliya, Akkaraipattu, Negombo, Katunayake, COLOMBO, Badulla, Avissawella, Adams Peak, Ratnapura, Kataragama, Galle, Matara

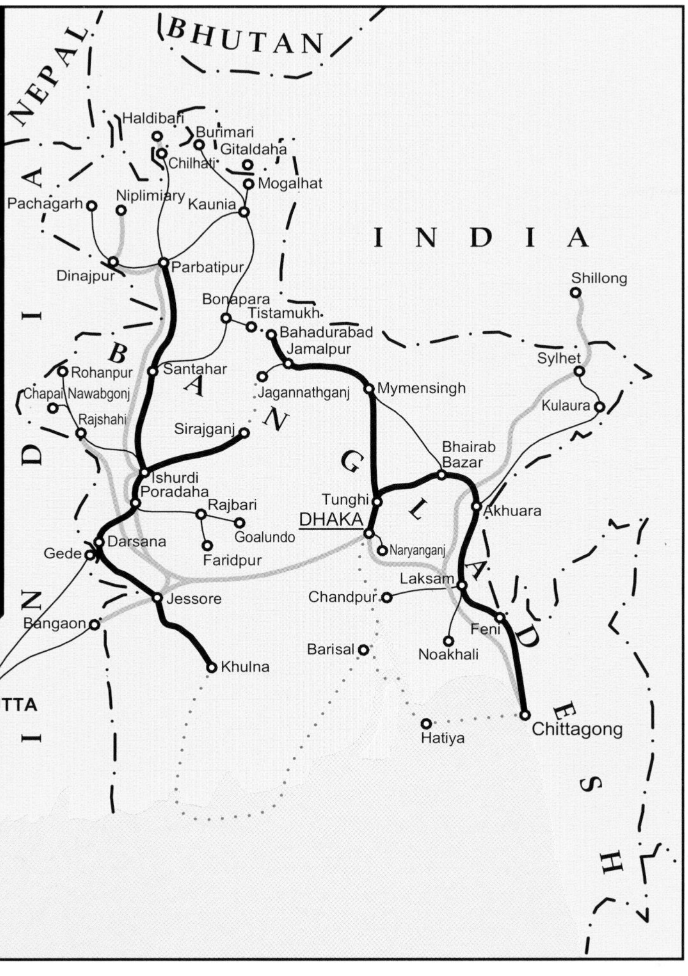

India & Bangladesh

BHUTAN, NEPAL, INDIA, Haldibari, Burimari, Gitaldaha, Chilhati, Mogalhat, Pachagarh, Niplimiary, Kaunia, Parbatipur, Dinajpur, Bonapara, Tistamukh, Shillong, Bahadurabad, Jamalpur, BANGLA, Rohanpur, Santahar, Jagannathganj, Mymensingh, Sylhet, Chapai Nawabgonj, Rajshahi, Sirajganj, Kulaura, Ishurdi, Poradaha, Rajbari, Bhairab Bazar, Akhuara, Tunghi, DHAKA, Darsana, Goalundo, Naryanganj, Gede, Faridpur, Laksam, Chandpur, Jessore, Feni, Bangaon, Barisal, Noakhali, CALCUTTA, Khulna, Hatiya, Chittagong

SOUTHEAST ASIA

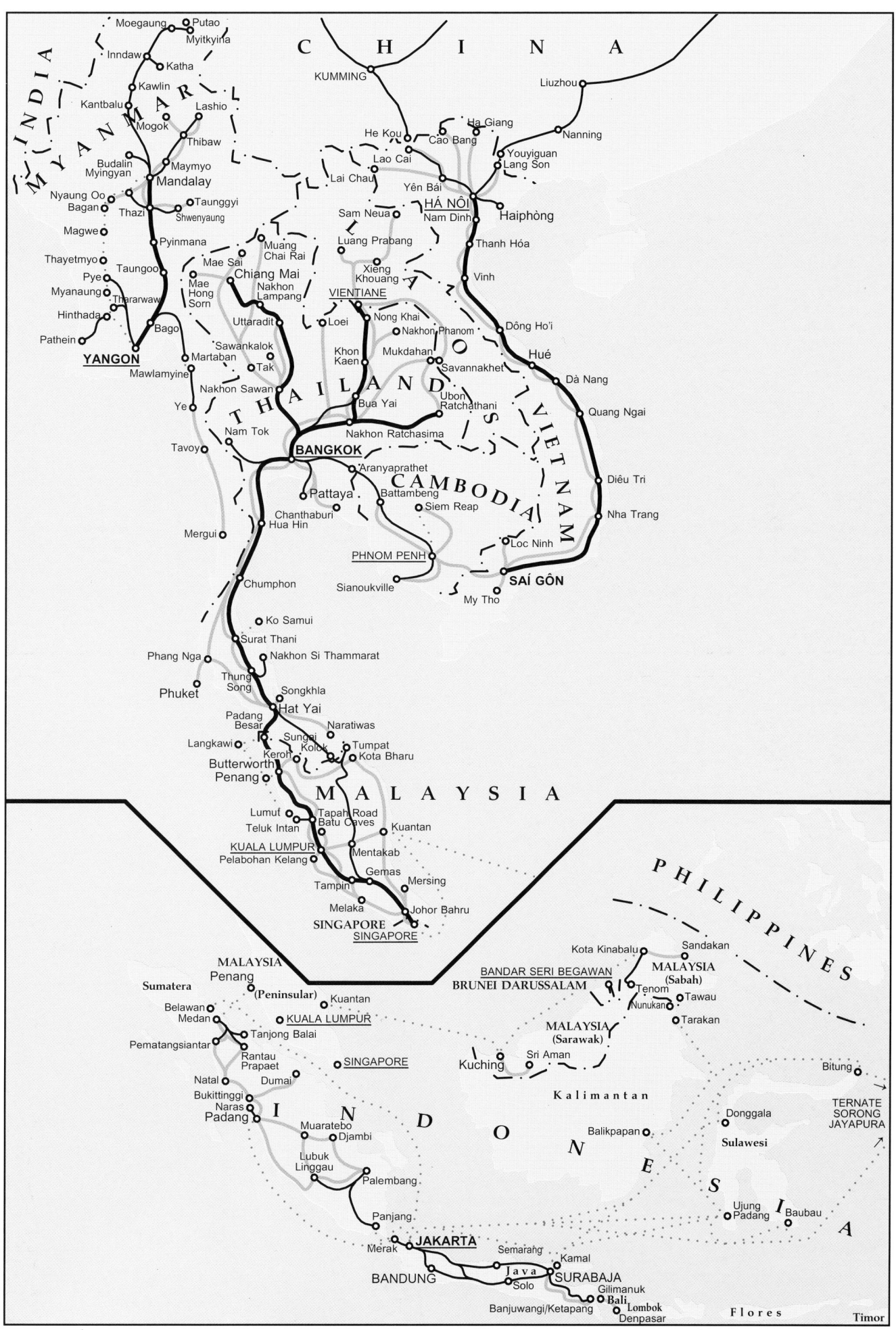

C H I N A
I N D I A
M Y A N M A R
L A O S
T H A I L A N D
C A M B O D I A
V I E T N A M
M A L A Y S I A
P H I L I P P I N E S
I N D O N E S I A
Moegaung
Putao
Myitkyina
Inndaw
Katha
Kawlin
Kantbalu
Lashio
Mogok
Thibaw
Budalin
Myingyan
Maymyo
Mandalay
Nyaung Oo
Bagan
Thazi
Taunggyi
Shwenyaung
Magwe
Pyinmana
Thayetmyo
Taungoo
Pye
Myanaung
Thararwaw
Hinthada
Pathein
Bago
YANGON
Mawlamyine
Martaban
Ye
Tavoy
Mergui
Mae Sai
Muang
Chai Rai
Chiang Mai
Mae
Hong
Sorn
Nakhon
Lampang
Uttaradit
Sawankalok
Tak
Nakhon Sawan
Nam Tok
BANGKOK
Pattaya
Chanthaburi
Hua Hin
Chumphon
Ko Samui
Surat Thani
Nakhon Si Thammarat
Phang Nga
Phuket
Thung
Song
Songkhla
Hat Yai
Padang
Besar
Naratiwas
Langkawi
Sungai
Kolok
Tumpat
Kota Bharu
Keroh
Butterworth
Penang
Lumut
Teluk Intan
Tapah Road
Batu Caves
Kuantan
KUALA LUMPUR
Pelabohan Kelang
Mentakab
Gemas
Mersing
Tampin
Melaka
Johor Bahru
SINGAPORE
SINGAPORE
KUMMING
Liuzhou
Nanning
He Kou
Ha Giang
Cao Bang
Youyiguan
Lang Son
Lao Cai
Lai Chau
Yên Bái
HÀ NÔI
Nam Dinh
Haiphòng
Sam Neua
Luang Prabang
Thanh Hóa
Xieng
Khouang
Vinh
VIENTIANE
Loei
Nong Khai
Nakhon Phanom
Dông Ho'i
Khon
Kaen
Mukdahan
Savannakhet
Hué
Dà Nang
Ubon
Ratchathani
Bua Yai
Quang Ngai
Nakhon Ratchasima
Aranyaprathet
Battambeng
Siem Reap
Diêu Tri
Nha Trang
Loc Ninh
PHNOM PENH
Sianoukville
SAÍ GÔN
My Tho
Kota Kinabalu
Sandakan
MALAYSIA
(Sabah)
BANDAR SERI BEGAWAN
BRUNEI DARUSSALAM
Tenom
Tawau
Nunukan
Tarakan
MALAYSIA
Penang
(Peninsular)
Sumatera
Kuantan
Belawan
Medan
KUALA LUMPUR
Tanjong Balai
Pematangsiantar
Rantau
Prapaet
SINGAPORE
MALAYSIA
(Sarawak)
Kuching
Sri Aman
Natal
Dumai
Bitung
Kalimantan
Bukittinggi
Naras
Padang
TERNATE
SORONG
JAYAPURA
Donggala
Muaratebo
Djambi
Balikpapan
Sulawesi
Lubuk
Linggau
Palembang
Ujung
Padang
Baubau
Panjang
Merak
JAKARTA
Semarang
Kamal
Java
SURABAJA
BANDUNG
Solo
Gilimanuk
Bali
Banjuwangi/Ketapang
Lombok
Denpasar
Flores
Timor

JAPAN

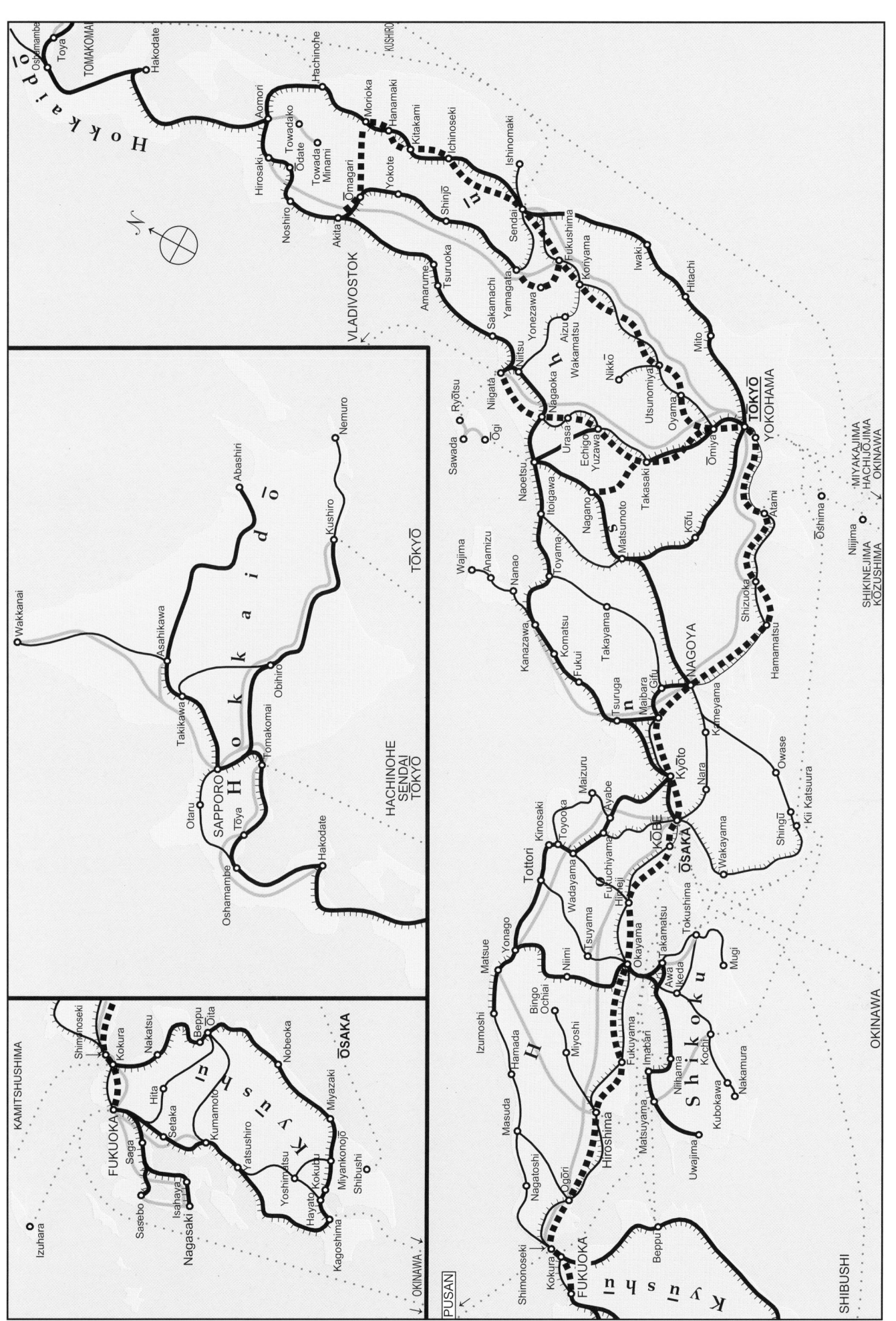
Hokkaidō
Oshamambe
Toya
TOMAKOMAI
Hakodate
Hachinohe
KUSHIRO
Aomori
Hirosaki
Towadako
Ōdate
Towada Minami
Morioka
Hanamaki
Kitakami
Ichinoseki
Ishinomaki
Noshiro
Akita
Ōmagari
Yokote
Shinjō
Sendai
Fukushima
Kōriyama
Iwaki
Hitachi
Mito
VLADIVOSTOK
Amarume
Tsuruoka
Sakamachi
Yamagata
Yonezawa
Niitsu
Niigata
Aizu Wakamatsu
Nikkō
Utsunomiya
Oyama
TŌKYŌ
YOKOHAMA
Ryōtsu
Sawada
Ogi
Nagaoka
Urasa
Echigo Yuzawa
Naoetsu
Itoigawa
Nagano
Takasaki
Ōmiya
Matsumoto
Kōfu
Atami
Ōshima
Niijima
SHIKINEJIMA
KŌZUSHIMA
MIYAKAJIMA
HACHIJŌJIMA
OKINAWA
Wajima
Anamizu
Nanao
Toyama
Kanazawa
Komatsu
Fukui
Takayama
Shizuoka
Hamamatsu
NAGOYA
Gifu
Maibara
Tsuruga
Kameyama
Kyōto
Nara
Owase
Shingū
Kii Katsuura
Wakayama
ŌSAKA
KŌBE
Maizuru
Ayabe
Kinosaki
Toyooka
Fukuchiyama
Himeji
Tottori
Wadayama
Tsuyama
Tokushima
Mugi
Takamatsu
Okayama
Yonago
Matsue
Niimi
Izumoshi
Bingo Ochiai
Miyoshi
Fukuyama
Imabari
Awa Ikeda
Kōchi
Nakamura
Kubokawa
Niihama
Matsuyama
Uwajima
Shikoku
Hamada
Masuda
Hiroshima
Nagatoshi
Ogōri
Shimonoseki
Kokura
FUKUOKA
Beppu
PUSAN
SHIBUSHI
OKINAWA
Kyūshū
Wakkanai
Abashiri
Nemuro
Asahikawa
Takikawa
Kushiro
Obihiro
Tomakomai
SAPPORO
Otaru
Tōya
Oshamambe
Hakodate
HACHINOHE
SENDAI
TŌKYŌ
KAMITSHUSHIMA
Shimonoseki
Kokura
Nakatsu
Beppu
Ōita
Nobeoka
ŌSAKA
Hita
Setaka
Kumamoto
Yatsushiro
Miyazaki
Miyankonojō
Shibushi
Yoshimatsu
Kokubu
Hayato
Kagoshima
FUKUOKA
Saga
Sasebo
Isahaya
Nagasaki
Izuhara
OKINAWA

CENTRAL JAPAN

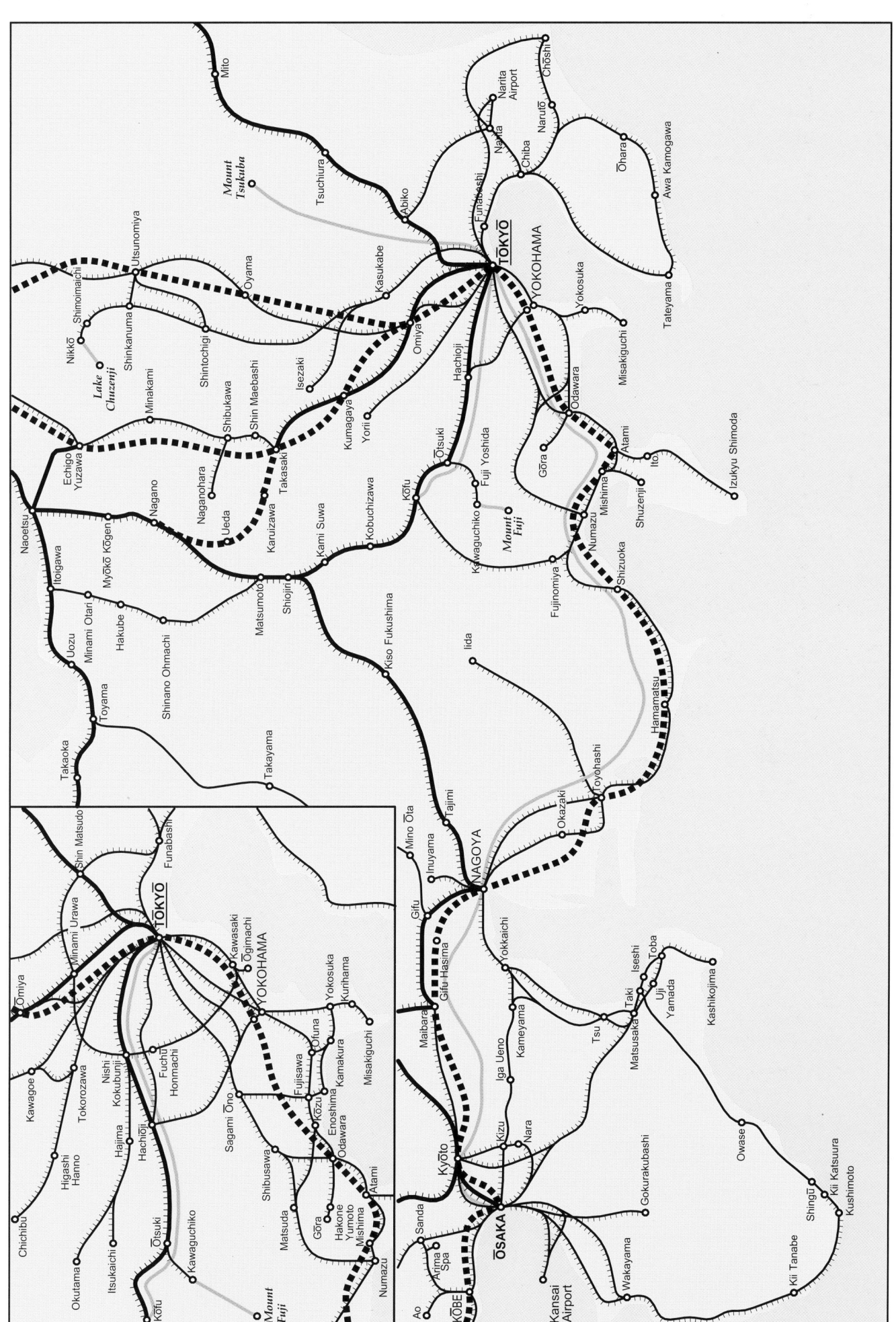

Mito
Chōshi
Narita Airport
Narita
Naka
Chiba
Funabashi
Ōhara
Tsuchiura
Awa Kamogawa
Mount Tsukuba
TŌKYŌ
YOKOHAMA
Utsunomiya
Oyama
Kasukabe
Yokosuka
Shimoimaichi
Omiya
Hachioji
Misakiguchi
Odawara
Tateyama
Nikkō
Shinkanuma
Shintochigi
Isezaki
Ōtsuki
Gōra
Atami
Lake Chuzenji
Minakami
Shibukawa
Shin Maebashi
Kumagaya
Yorii
Fuji Yoshida
Mishima
Ito
Izukyu Shimoda
Echigo Yuzawa
Naganohara
Takasaki
Kami Suwa
Kōfu
Kawaguchiko
Numazu
Shuzenji
Nagano
Ueda
Karuizawa
Kobuchizawa
Mount Fuji
Shizuoka
Naoetsu
Myōkō Kōgen
Matsumoto
Shiojiri
Fujinomiya
Itoigawa
Minami Otari
Hakube
Shinano Ohmachi
Kiso Fukushima
Iida
Hamamatsu
Uozu
Toyama
Toyohashi
Takaoka
Takayama
Okazaki
Mino Ōta
Tajimi
Toyohashi
Inuyama
NAGOYA
Gifu
Yokkaichi
Gifu Hasima
Tsu
Toba
Maibara
Iga Ueno
Kameyama
Taki
Iseshi
Uji
Yamada
Kashikojima
Matsusaka
Kizu
Nara
Owase
Kyōto
Gokurakubashi
Shingū
Kii Katsuura
Kushimoto
Sanda
Arima Spa
Kii Tanabe
ŌSAKA
Wakayama
Ao
KŌBE
Kansai Airport

Shin Matsudo
Funabashi
Minami Urawa
TŌKYŌ
Kawasaki
Ōgimachi
YOKOHAMA
Omiya
Yokosuka
Kawagoe
Nishi Kokubunji
Fuchū Honmachi
Kurihama
Higashi Hanno
Tokorozawa
Hajima
Hachioji
Sagami Ōno
Ōfuna
Kamakura
Misakiguchi
Kōzu
Fujisawa
Enoshima
Chichibu
Shibusawa
Odawara
Atami
Okutama
Itsukaichi
Ōtsuki
Matsuda
Gōra
Kawaguchiko
Hakone Yumoto
Mishima
Numazu
Kōfu
Mount Fuji

AUSTRALIA

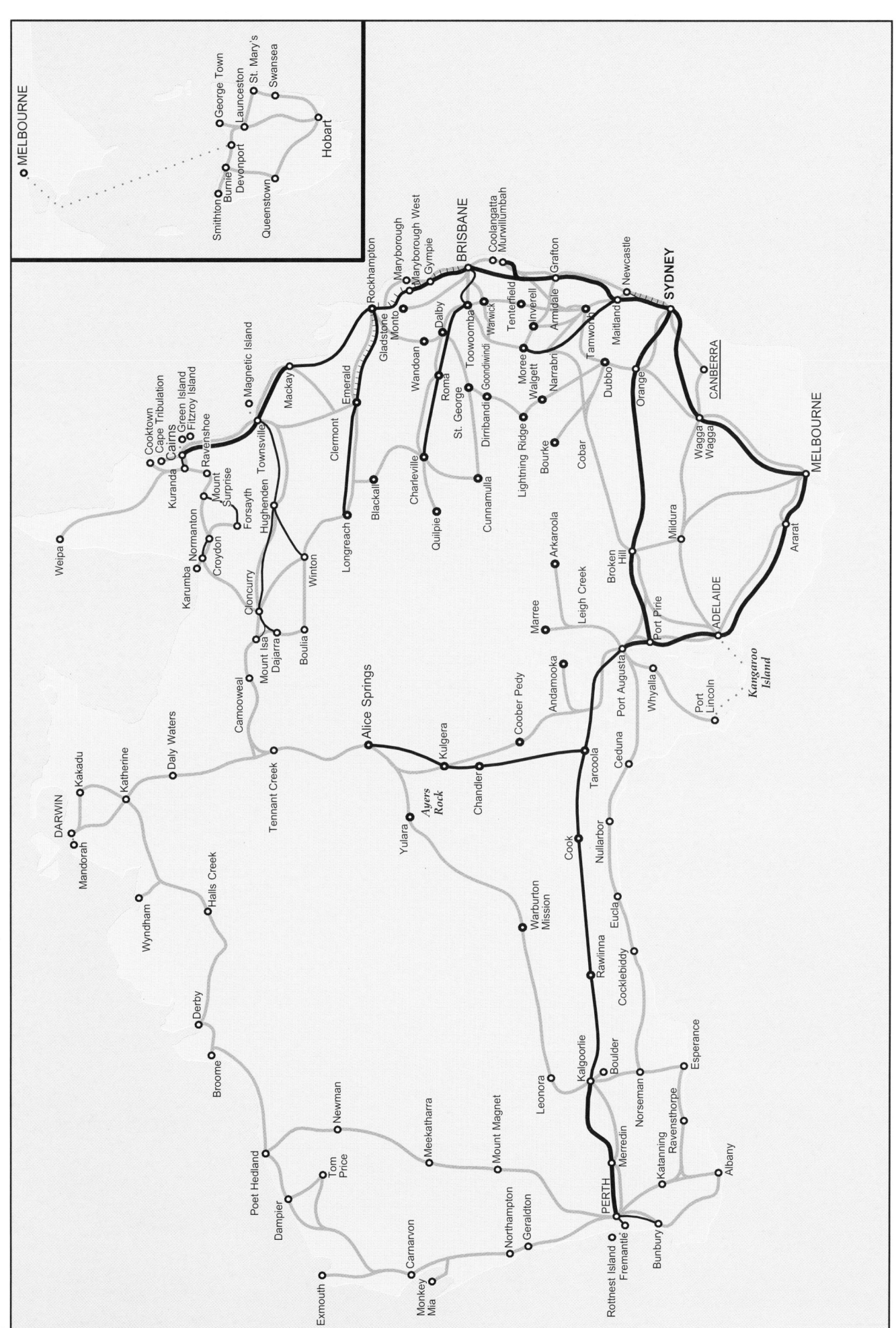

MELBOURNE

George Town
St. Mary's
Launceston
Swansea
Smithton
Burnie
Devonport
Queenstown
Hobart

Coolangatta
Murwillumbah
Maryborough
Maryborough West
Gympie
BRISBANE
Grafton
Rockhampton
Newcastle
SYDNEY
Gladstone
Monto
Dalby
Toowoomba
Warwick
Tenterfield
Inverell
Armidale
Maitland
Wandoan
Goondiwindi
Moree
Narrabri
Tamworth
CANBERRA
Magnetic Island
Mackay
Emerald
Roma
Walgett
Dubbo
Orange
St. George
Lightning Ridge
Bourke
Cobar
Wagga Wagga
Clermont
Charleville
MELBOURNE
Cooktown
Cape Tribulation
Green Island
Fitzroy Island
Cairns
Ravenshoe
Townsville
Dirranbandi
Kuranda
Mount Surprise
Hughenden
Blackall
Cunnamulla
Mildura
Ararat
Forsayth
Longreach
Quilpie
Arkaroola
Broken Hill
Karumba
Normanton
Croydon
Winton
Port Pirie
ADELAIDE
Weipa
Cloncurry
Leigh Creek
Mount Isa
Dajarra
Boulia
Marree
Port Augusta
Whyalla
Port Lincoln
Kangaroo Island
Camooweal
Andamooka
Coober Pedy
Alice Springs
Kulgera
Tarcoola
Ceduna
Daly Waters
Tennant Creek
Chandler
Ayers Rock
Cook
Nullarbor
Kakadu
Katherine
Yulara
DARWIN
Mandorah
Warburton Mission
Eucla
Halls Creek
Rawlinna
Wyndham
Cocklebiddy
Esperance
Derby
Leonora
Boulder
Norseman
Ravensthorpe
Broome
Kalgoorlie
Poet Hedland
Newman
Merredin
Albany
Dampier
Tom Price
Meekatharra
Mount Magnet
Katanning
Carnarvon
Northampton
Geraldton
PERTH
Fremantle
Rottnest Island
Bunbury
Exmouth
Monkey Mia

SE AUSTRALIA & NEW ZEALAND

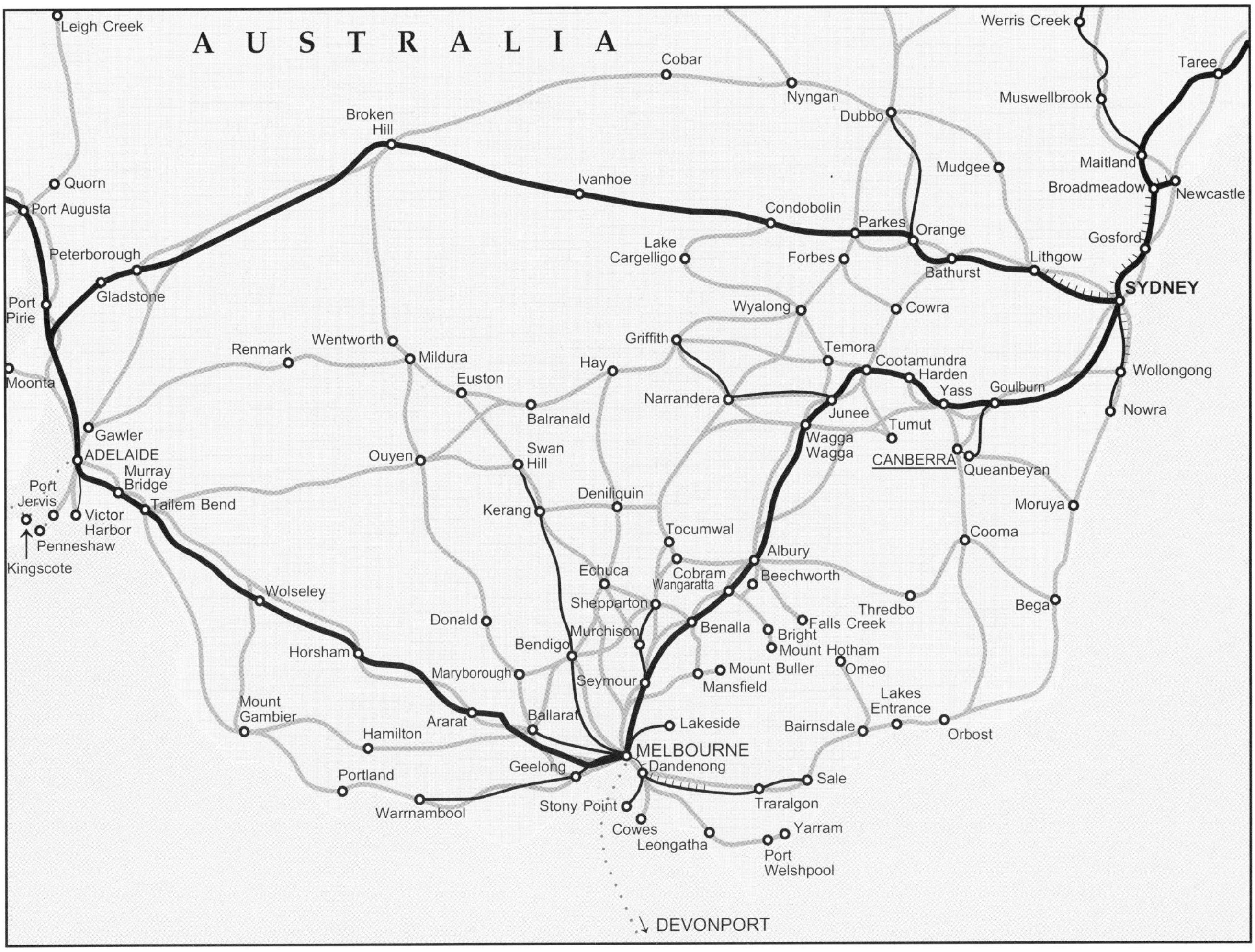

AUSTRALIA

Leigh Creek
Cobar
Werris Creek
Taree
Nyngan
Muswellbrook
Broken Hill
Dubbo
Quorn
Ivanhoe
Mudgee
Maitland
Port Augusta
Condobolin
Broadmeadow
Newcastle
Peterborough
Parkes
Orange
Gosford
Forbes
Bathurst
Lithgow
Port Pirie
Gladstone
Wyalong
Cowra
SYDNEY
Moonta
Renmark
Wentworth
Mildura
Griffith
Temora
Cootamundra
Wollongong
Harden
Euston
Hay
Narrandera
Yass
Goulburn
Nowra
Gawler
ADELAIDE
Balranald
Junee
CANBERRA
Moruya
Murray Bridge
Ouyen
Swan Hill
Wagga Wagga
Tumut
Queanbeyan
Port Jervis
Victor Harbor
Tailem Bend
Deniliquin
Cooma
Penneshaw
Kerang
Tocumwal
Albury
Kingscote
Wolseley
Echuca
Cobram
Beechworth
Thredbo
Bega
Donald
Shepparton
Wangaratta
Falls Creek
Horsham
Bendigo
Murchison
Benalla
Bright
Mount Hotham
Omeo
Maryborough
Seymour
Mount Buller
Mansfield
Lakes Entrance
Mount Gambier
Ararat
Ballarat
Lakeside
Bairnsdale
Orbost
Hamilton
MELBOURNE
Dandenong
Portland
Geelong
Sale
Warrnambool
Stony Point
Traralgon
Cowes
Yarram
Leongatha
Port Welshpool

DEVONPORT

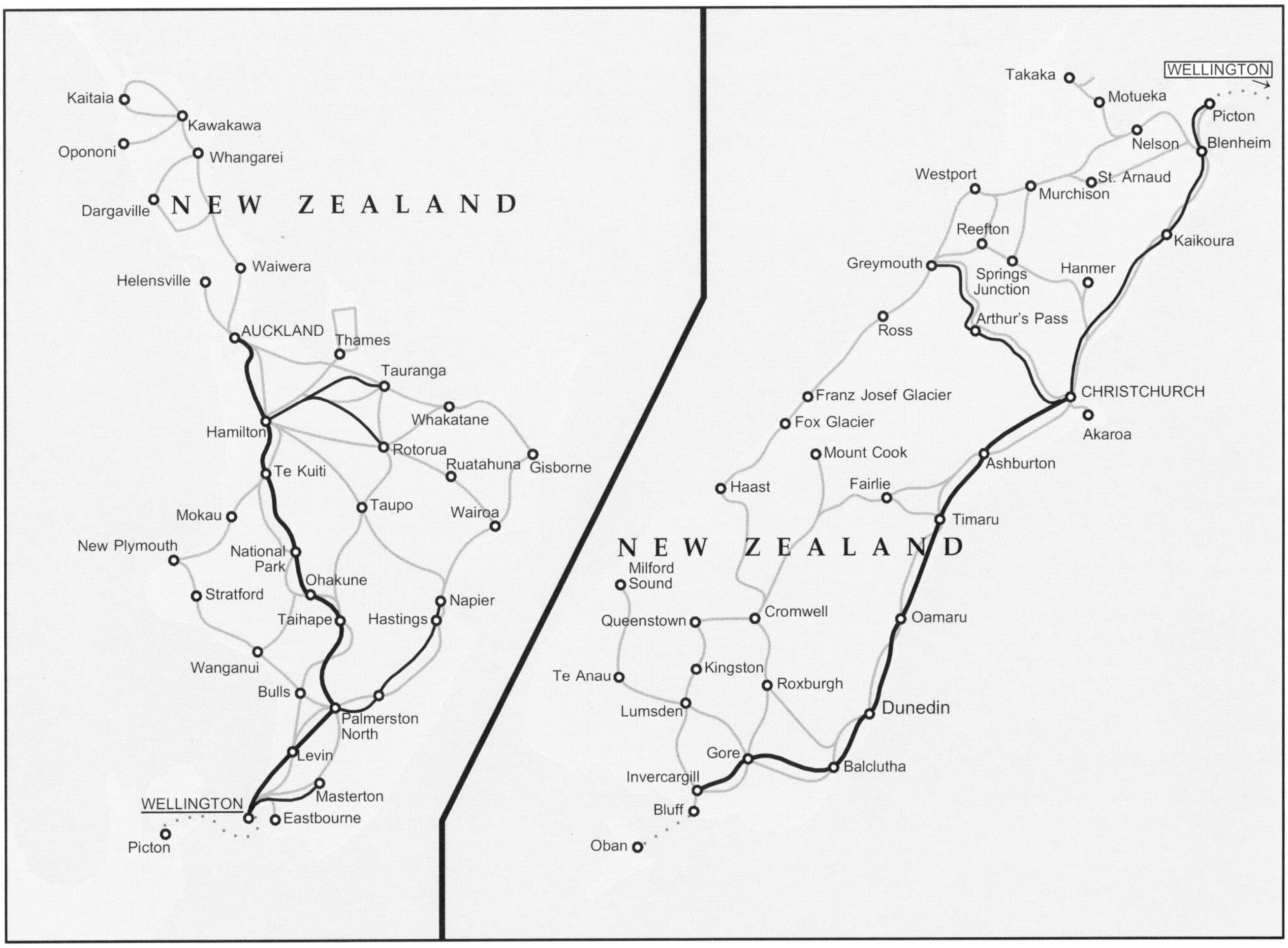

NEW ZEALAND

Kaitaia
Kawakawa
Opononi
Whangarei
Dargaville
NEW ZEALAND
Helensville
Waiwera
AUCKLAND
Thames
Tauranga
Whakatane
Hamilton
Rotorua
Mokau
Te Kuiti
Ruatahuna
Gisborne
Taupo
Wairoa
New Plymouth
National Park
Ohakune
Napier
Stratford
Taihape
Hastings
Wanganui
Bulls
Palmerston North
Levin
WELLINGTON
Masterton
Eastbourne
Picton

Takaka
WELLINGTON
Motueka
Picton
Nelson
Blenheim
Westport
Murchison
St. Arnaud
Reefton
Kaikoura
Greymouth
Springs Junction
Hanmer
Ross
Arthur's Pass
Franz Josef Glacier
CHRISTCHURCH
Fox Glacier
Akaroa
Mount Cook
Ashburton
Haast
Fairlie
Timaru
NEW ZEALAND
Milford Sound
Cromwell
Oamaru
Queenstown
Te Anau
Kingston
Roxburgh
Dunedin
Lumsden
Gore
Balclutha
Invercargill
Bluff
Oban

WESTERN CANADA

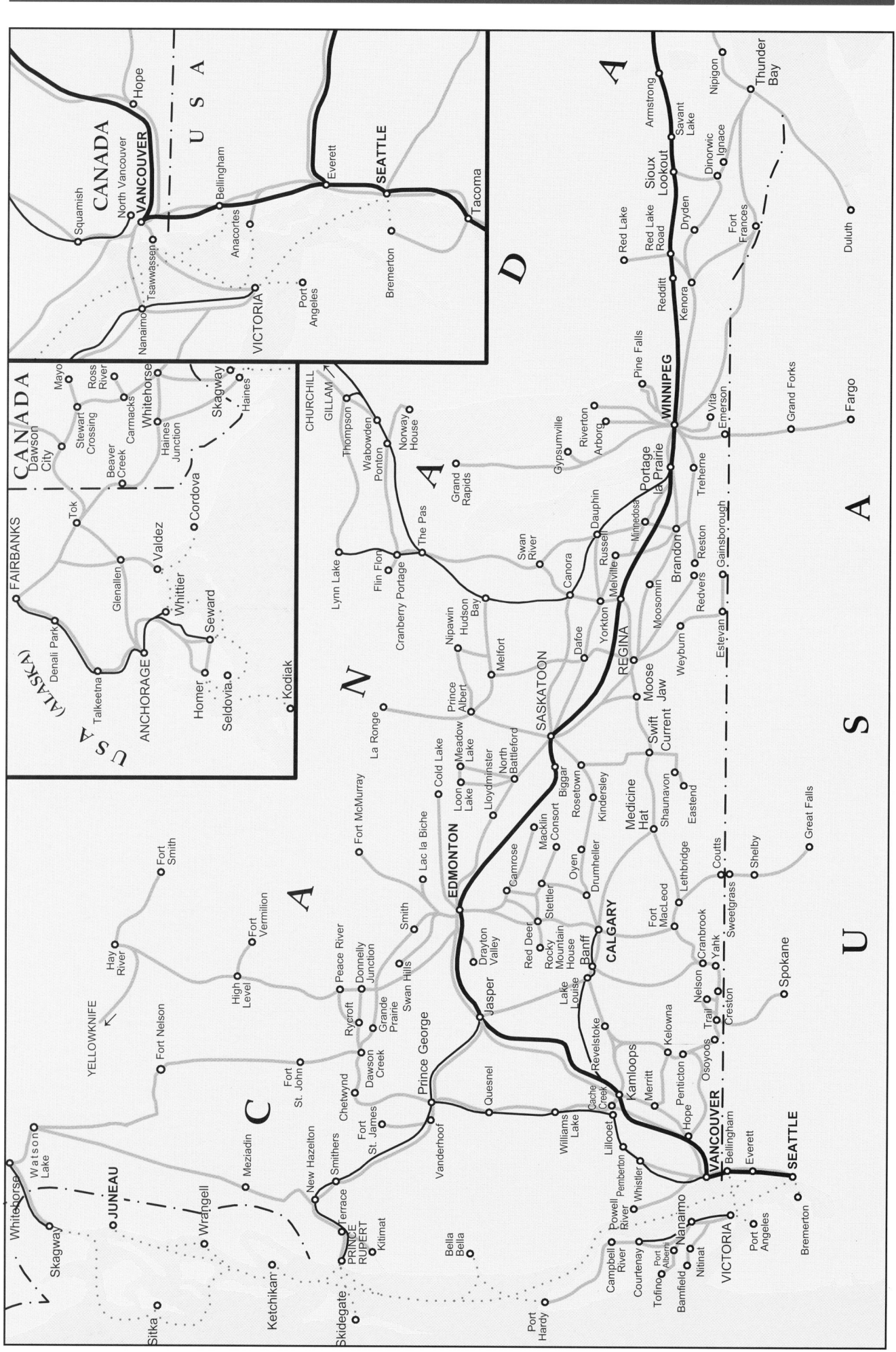
CANADA
USA
VANCOUVER
North Vancouver
Squamish
Hope
Bellingham
Anacortes
Everett
SEATTLE
Tacoma
Bremerton
Tsawwassen
Nanaimo
VICTORIA
Port Angeles
USA (ALASKA)
FAIRBANKS
Denali Park
Talkeetna
ANCHORAGE
Glenallen
Tok
Valdez
Whittier
Seward
Homer
Seldovia
Kodiak
Cordova
Dawson City
Stewart Crossing
Mayo
Ross River
Carmacks
Beaver Creek
Haines Junction
Whitehorse
Skagway
Haines
CHURCHILL
GILLAM
Thompson
Wabowden
Ponton
Norway House
The Pas
Flin Flon
Cranberry Portage
Lynn Lake
Grand Rapids
Gypsumville
Riverton
Arborg
Pine Falls
WINNIPEG
Portage la Prairie
Treherne
Vita
Emerson
Grand Forks
Fargo
Swan River
Dauphin
Minnedosa
Russell
Canora
Melville
Brandon
Reston
Gainsborough
Redvers
Moosomin
Yorkton
Dafoe
Hudson Bay
Nipawin
Melfort
REGINA
Weyburn
Estevan
Moose Jaw
SASKATOON
Prince Albert
La Ronge
Swift Current
Shaunavon
Eastend
Biggar
Rosetown
Kindersley
North Battleford
Lloydminster
Meadow Lake
Loon Lake
Cold Lake
Macklin
Consort
Oyen
Medicine Hat
Lethbridge
Coutts
Sweetgrass
Shelby
Great Falls
Fort MacLeod
Cranbrook
Yahk
Creston
Spokane
Nelson
Trail
Osoyoos
Penticton
Kelowna
Merritt
Kamloops
Revelstoke
Lake Louise
Banff
CALGARY
Drumheller
Stettler
Camrose
Red Deer
Rocky Mountain House
EDMONTON
Drayton Valley
Lac la Biche
Fort McMurray
Smith
Swan Hills
Jasper
Hope
Cache Creek
Lillooet
Pemberton
Whistler
Williams Lake
Quesnel
Prince George
Vanderhoof
Fort St. James
Chetwynd
Dawson Creek
Grande Prairie
Rycroft
Peace River
Donnelly Junction
High Level
Fort Vermilion
Hay River
Fort Smith
YELLOWKNIFE
Fort Nelson
Fort St. John
Smithers
New Hazelton
Terrace
PRINCE RUPERT
Kitimat
Meziadin
Watson Lake
JUNEAU
Wrangell
Ketchikan
Sitka
Skidegate
Bella Bella
Port Hardy
Campbell River
Powell River
Courtenay
Port Alberni
Tofino
Bamfield
Nitinat
Armstrong
Savant Lake
Sioux Lookout
Nipigon
Thunder Bay
Dinorwic
Ignace
Dryden
Red Lake
Red Lake Road
Redditt
Kenora
Fort Frances
Duluth
C
A
N
A
D
A
U
S
A

EASTERN CANADA

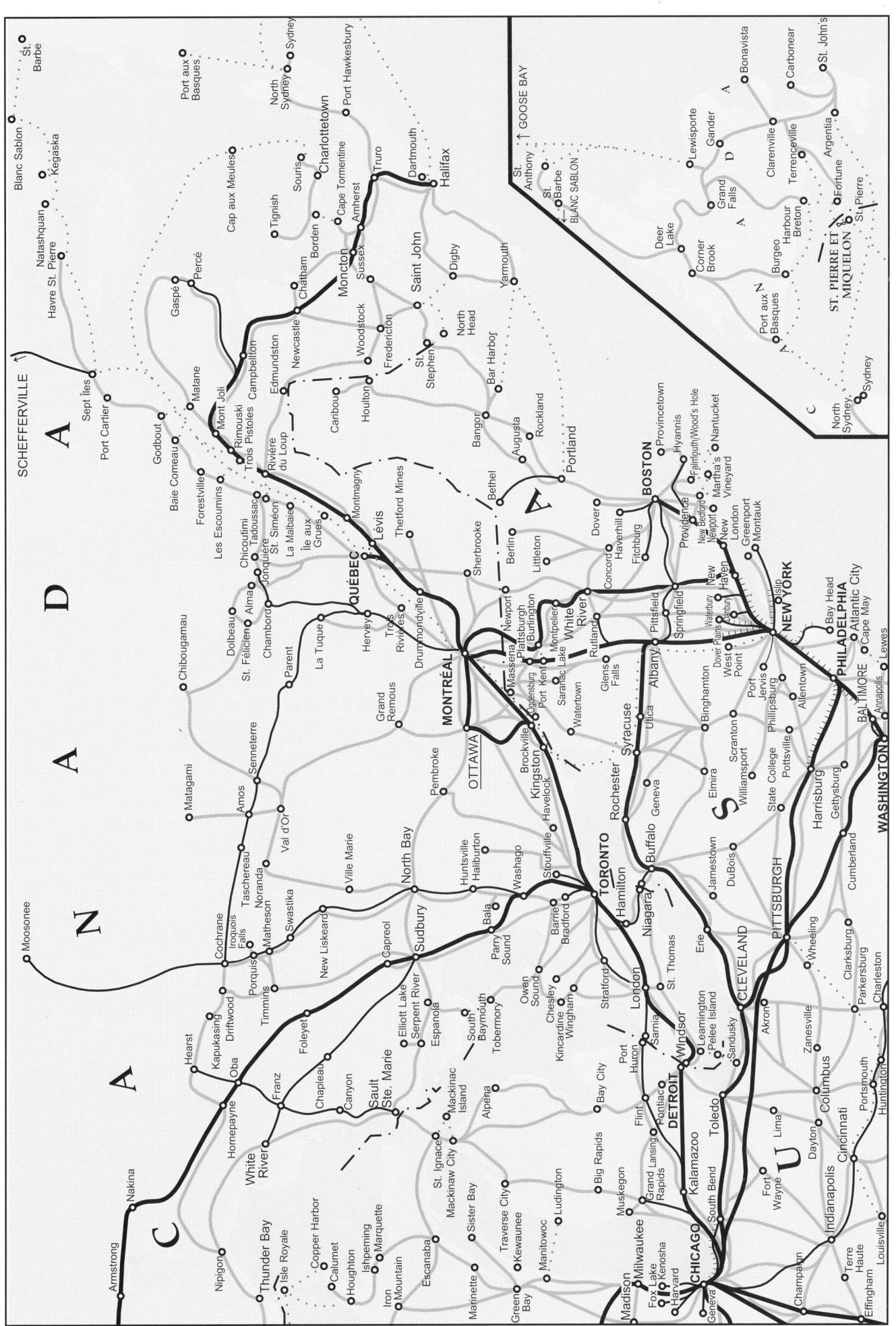
CANADA
USA
SCHEFFERVILLE
GOOSE BAY
BLANC SABLON
ST. PIERRE ET MIQUELON
Blanc Sablon
St. Barbe
Natashquan
Kegaska
Havre St. Pierre
Sept Îles
Port Cartier
Port aux Basques
North Sydney
Sydney
Port Hawkesbury
Charlottetown
Cap aux Meules
Souris
Tignish
Borden
Cape Tormentine
Amherst
Truro
Dartmouth
Halifax
Digby
Yarmouth
Saint John
Sussex
Moncton
Chatham
Newcastle
Fredericton
Woodstock
Houlton
Caribou
St. Stephen
North Head
Bar Harbor
Bangor
Augusta
Rockland
Portland
Bethel
Gaspé
Percé
Matane
Godbout
Baie Comeau
Mont Joli
Rimouski
Trois Pistoles
Campbellton
Edmundston
Rivière du Loup
Forestville
Les Escoumins
Tadoussac
St. Siméon
La Malbaie
Île aux Grues
Montmagny
Lévis
QUÉBEC
Chicoutimi
Jonquière
Alma
Dolbeau
St. Félicien
Chambord
Chibougamau
La Tuque
Parent
Hervey
Trois Rivières
Drummondville
Thetford Mines
Sherbrooke
MONTRÉAL
OTTAWA
Grand Remous
Pembroke
Newport
Plattsburgh
Burlington
Montpelier
White River
Rutland
Massena
Ogdensburg
Port Kent
Saranac Lake
Watertown
Brockville
Kingston
Havelock
Matagami
Senneterre
Amos
Val d'Or
Taschereau
Noranda
Moosonee
Cochrane
Iroquois Falls
Matheson
Swastika
Porquis
Timmins
Kapuskasing
Driftwood
Hearst
Oba
Hornepayne
Franz
White River
Nakina
Armstrong
Nipigon
Thunder Bay
Isle Royale
Copper Harbor
Calumet
Houghton
Ishpeming
Marquette
Iron Mountain
Escanaba
Foleyet
Chapleau
Canyon
Sault Ste. Marie
Elliott Lake
Serpent River
Espanola
Sudbury
Capreol
New Liskeard
Ville Marie
North Bay
Huntsville
Haliburton
Washago
Bala
Parry Sound
South Baymouth
Tobermory
Owen Sound
Chesley
Kincardine
Wingham
Barrie
Bradford
Stouffville
TORONTO
Hamilton
Niagara
Stratford
London
St. Thomas
Port Huron
Sarnia
Windsor
DETROIT
Leamington
Pelee Island
Sandusky
Mackinac Island
St. Ignace
Mackinaw City
Alpena
Bay City
Flint
Pontiac
Big Rapids
Sister Bay
Traverse City
Ludington
Muskegon
Grand Rapids
Lansing
Kalamazoo
Kewaunee
Manitowoc
Green Bay
Marinette
Milwaukee
Madison
Kenosha
Fox Lake
Harvard
CHICAGO
Geneva
South Bend
Toledo
Fort Wayne
Lima
Dayton
Columbus
Cincinnati
Indianapolis
Terre Haute
Champaign
Effingham
Louisville
Portsmouth
Huntington
Charleston
Parkersburg
Clarksburg
Zanesville
Akron
CLEVELAND
Erie
Wheeling
PITTSBURGH
Cumberland
Jamestown
DuBois
Buffalo
Rochester
Geneva
Syracuse
Utica
Albany
Glens Falls
Pittsfield
Springfield
Binghamton
Elmira
Williamsport
State College
Scranton
Pottsville
Harrisburg
Gettysburg
Allentown
Phillipsburg
Port Jervis
West Point
Dover Plains
Waterbury
Danbury
New Haven
NEW YORK
Islip
Greenport
Montauk
New London
Newport
New Bedford
Providence
Martha's Vineyard
Falmouth/Wood's Hole
Nantucket
Hyannis
Provincetown
BOSTON
Fitchburg
Haverhill
Concord
Dover
Littleton
Berlin
PHILADELPHIA
Atlantic City
Cape May
Bay Head
Lewes
BALTIMORE
Annapolis
WASHINGTON
St. Anthony
St. Barbe
Deer Lake
Corner Brook
Lewisporte
Gander
Grand Falls
Bonavista
Clarenville
Carbonear
St. John's
Terrenceville
Argentia
Harbour Breton
Fortune
St. Pierre
Burgeo
Port aux Basques
North Sydney
Sydney

WESTERN USA

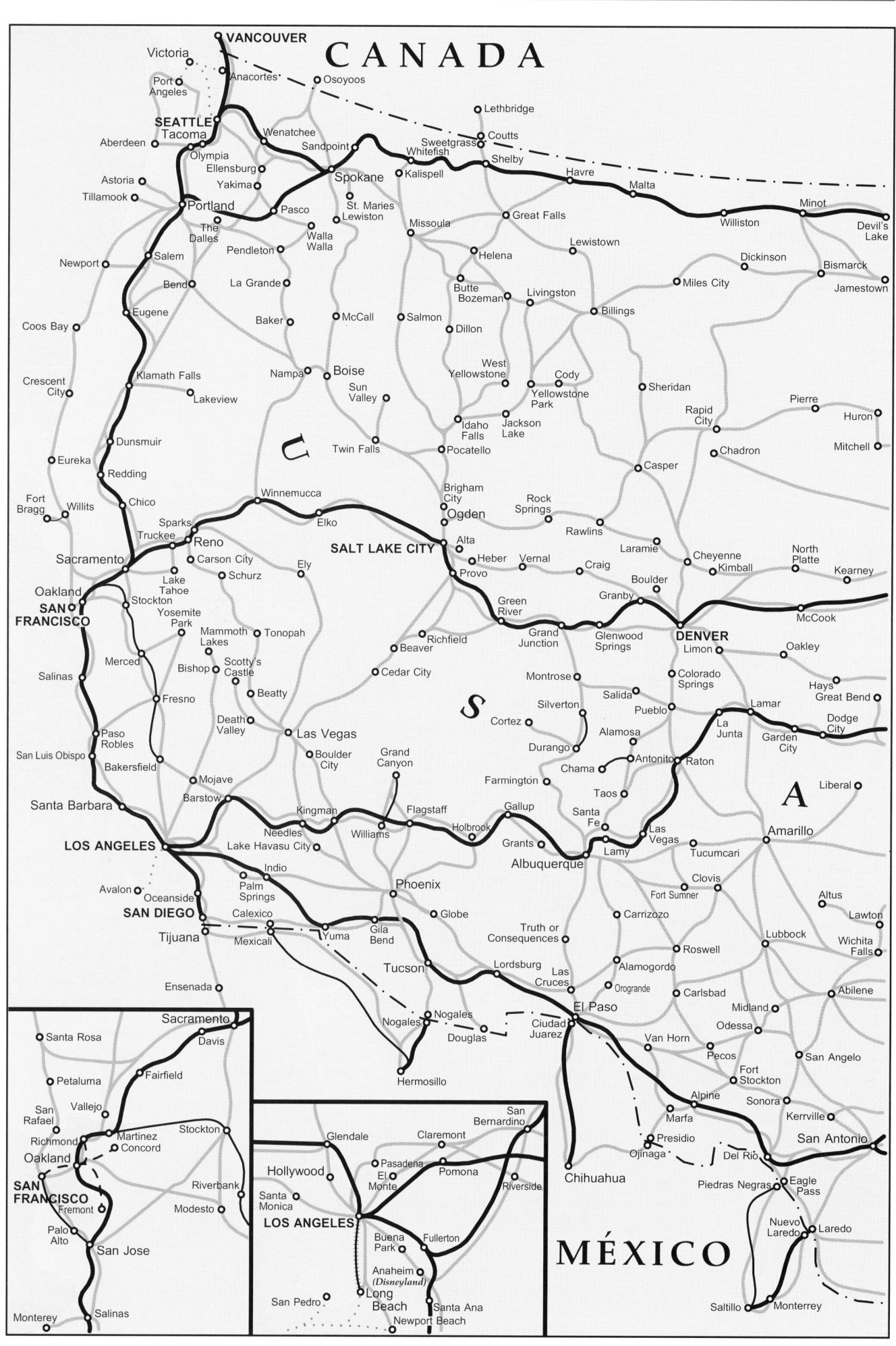

CANADA

VANCOUVER
Victoria
Port Angeles
Anacortes
Osoyoos
Lethbridge
SEATTLE
Tacoma
Wenatchee
Coutts
Sweetgrass
Aberdeen
Olympia
Sandpoint
Whitefish
Shelby
Ellensburg
Spokane
Kalispell
Havre
Malta
Astoria
Yakima
Minot
Tillamook
Portland
Pasco
St. Maries
Lewiston
Missoula
Great Falls
Williston
Devil's Lake
The Dalles
Walla Walla
Pendleton
Helena
Lewistown
Dickinson
Bismarck
Newport
Salem
Butte
Bozeman
Livingston
Miles City
Jamestown
Bend
La Grande
Billings
Coos Bay
Eugene
Baker
McCall
Salmon
Dillon
Sheridan
Crescent City
Klamath Falls
Nampa
Boise
West Yellowstone
Cody
Yellowstone Park
Rapid City
Pierre
Huron
Lakeview
Sun Valley
Mitchell
Dunsmuir
Twin Falls
Idaho Falls
Jackson Lake
Pocatello
Casper
Chadron
Eureka
Redding
Brigham City
Rock Springs
North Platte
Fort Bragg
Willits
Chico
Winnemucca
Elko
Ogden
Rawlins
Kearney
Sparks
Truckee
Reno
Alta
Heber
Vernal
Laramie
Cheyenne
Kimball
Sacramento
Carson City
Schurz
Ely
SALT LAKE CITY
Provo
Craig
Boulder
Granby
McCook
Oakland
Lake Tahoe
Stockton
Green River
Glenwood Springs
DENVER
Oakley
SAN FRANCISCO
Yosemite Park
Grand Junction
Limon
Mammoth Lakes
Tonopah
Richfield
Beaver
Montrose
Salida
Colorado Springs
Hays
Great Bend
Merced
Bishop
Scotty's Castle
Cedar City
Silverton
Pueblo
Lamar
Dodge City
Salinas
Fresno
Beatty
Cortez
Durango
Alamosa
La Junta
Garden City
Death Valley
Las Vegas
Farmington
Chama
Antonito
Raton
Liberal
Paso Robles
San Luis Obispo
Bakersfield
Boulder City
Grand Canyon
Taos
Mojave
Santa Fe
Las Vegas
Amarillo
Santa Barbara
Barstow
Kingman
Flagstaff
Gallup
Tucumcari
LOS ANGELES
Needles
Williams
Holbrook
Grants
Lamy
Albuquerque
Clovis
Altus
Lake Havasu City
Indio
Fort Sumner
Lawton
Avalon
Palm Springs
Phoenix
Carrizozo
Lubbock
Oceanside
Calexico
Globe
Truth or Consequences
Roswell
Wichita Falls
SAN DIEGO
Yuma
Gila Bend
Alamogordo
Tijuana
Mexicali
Tucson
Lordsburg
Las Cruces
Orogrande
Carlsbad
Midland
Abilene
Ensenada
Nogales
El Paso
Van Horn
Pecos
San Angelo
Nogales
Douglas
Ciudad Juarez
Fort Stockton
Odessa
Hermosillo
Alpine
Sonora
Marfa
Kerrville
Presidio
San Antonio
Ojinaga
Chihuahua
Del Rio
Piedras Negras
Eagle Pass
MÉXICO
Nuevo Laredo
Laredo
Saltillo
Monterrey

Sacramento
Santa Rosa
Davis
Petaluma
Fairfield
San Rafael
Vallejo
Stockton
Richmond
Martinez
Concord
Oakland
Riverbank
SAN FRANCISCO
Fremont
Palo Alto
Modesto
San Jose
Monterey
Salinas

San Bernardino
Glendale
Claremont
Hollywood
Pasadena
Pomona
El Monte
Santa Monica
Riverside
LOS ANGELES
Buena Park
Fullerton
Anaheim (Disneyland)
San Pedro
Long Beach
Santa Ana
Newport Beach

EASTERN USA

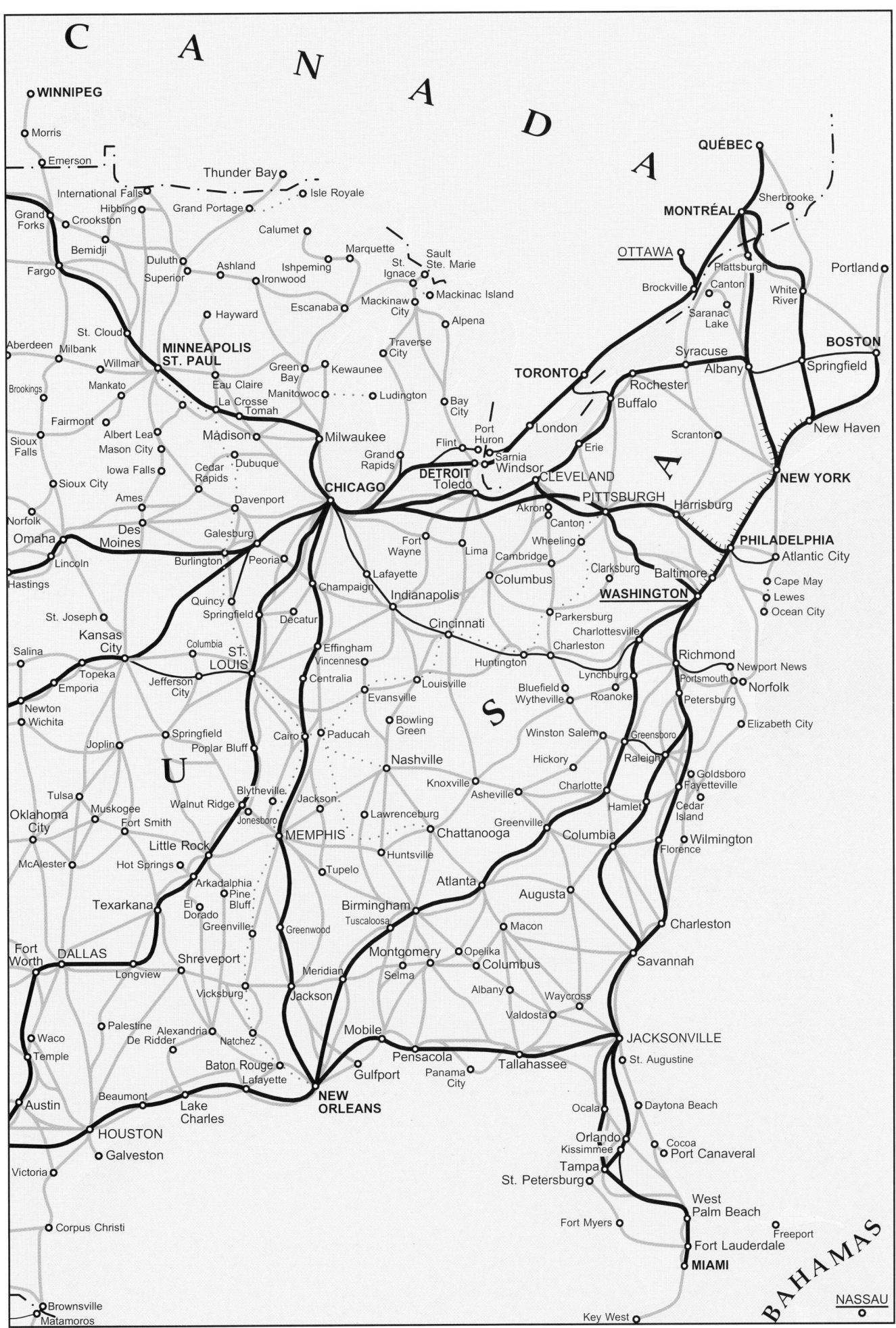
CANADA
WINNIPEG
Morris
Emerson
Thunder Bay
International Falls
Isle Royale
Grand Forks
Hibbing
Crookston
Grand Portage
Calumet
Bemidji
Marquette
Sault Ste. Marie
Fargo
Duluth
Superior
Ashland
Ishpeming
Ironwood
St. Ignace
Mackinac Island
Escanaba
Mackinaw City
Hayward
Alpena
St. Cloud
Aberdeen
Milbank
MINNEAPOLIS ST. PAUL
Traverse City
Willmar
Green Bay
Kewaunee
Brookings
Mankato
Eau Claire
Manitowoc
Ludington
La Crosse
Tomah
Bay City
Fairmont
Albert Lea
Madison
Milwaukee
Flint
Port Huron
Sioux Falls
Mason City
Dubuque
Grand Rapids
Sarnia
Iowa Falls
Cedar Rapids
DETROIT
Windsor
Sioux City
Toledo
CHICAGO
Ames
Davenport
Norfolk
Des Moines
Galesburg
Omaha
Fort Wayne
Lima
Lincoln
Burlington
Peoria
Hastings
Lafayette
Champaign
Quincy
Indianapolis
St. Joseph
Springfield
Decatur
Kansas City
Cincinnati
Salina
Columbia
ST. LOUIS
Effingham
Topeka
Vincennes
Jefferson City
Centralia
Louisville
Emporia
Evansville
Newton
Wichita
Springfield
Bowling Green
Joplin
Poplar Bluff
Cairo
Paducah
U
Nashville
Tulsa
Blytheville
Jackson
Muskogee
Walnut Ridge
Oklahoma City
Jonesboro
Lawrenceburg
Fort Smith
MEMPHIS
Little Rock
Huntsville
McAlester
Hot Springs
Tupelo
Arkadalphia
Pine Bluff
Texarkana
El Dorado
Greenville
Greenwood
Tuscaloosa
Birmingham
Fort Worth
DALLAS
Shreveport
Longview
Meridian
Vicksburg
Jackson
Palestine
Alexandria
Natchez
De Ridder
Waco
Temple
Baton Rouge
Lafayette
Austin
Beaumont
Lake Charles
NEW ORLEANS
HOUSTON
Galveston
Victoria
Corpus Christi
Brownsville
Matamoros
QUÉBEC
Sherbrooke
MONTRÉAL
OTTAWA
Plattsburgh
Portland
Brockville
Canton
White River
Saranac Lake
Syracuse
BOSTON
TORONTO
Albany
Springfield
Rochester
Buffalo
London
New Haven
Scranton
Erie
NEW YORK
CLEVELAND
PITTSBURGH
Harrisburg
Akron
Canton
Wheeling
PHILADELPHIA
Cambridge
Atlantic City
Clarksburg
Baltimore
Columbus
Cape May
WASHINGTON
Lewes
Ocean City
Parkersburg
Charlottesville
Charleston
Huntington
Richmond
Newport News
Lynchburg
Portsmouth
Norfolk
Bluefield
Wytheville
Roanoke
Petersburg
S
Elizabeth City
Winston Salem
Greensboro
Raleigh
Hickory
Goldsboro
Knoxville
Fayetteville
Asheville
Charlotte
Hamlet
Cedar Island
Chattanooga
Greenville
Columbia
Wilmington
Florence
Atlanta
Augusta
Macon
Charleston
Montgomery
Opelika
Selma
Columbus
Savannah
Albany
Waycross
Valdosta
Mobile
JACKSONVILLE
Pensacola
St. Augustine
Gulfport
Panama City
Tallahassee
Daytona Beach
Ocala
Orlando
Kissimmee
Cocoa
Port Canaveral
Tampa
St. Petersburg
West Palm Beach
Fort Myers
Freeport
Fort Lauderdale
MIAMI
BAHAMAS
NASSAU
Key West

MEXICO & CENTRAL AMERICA

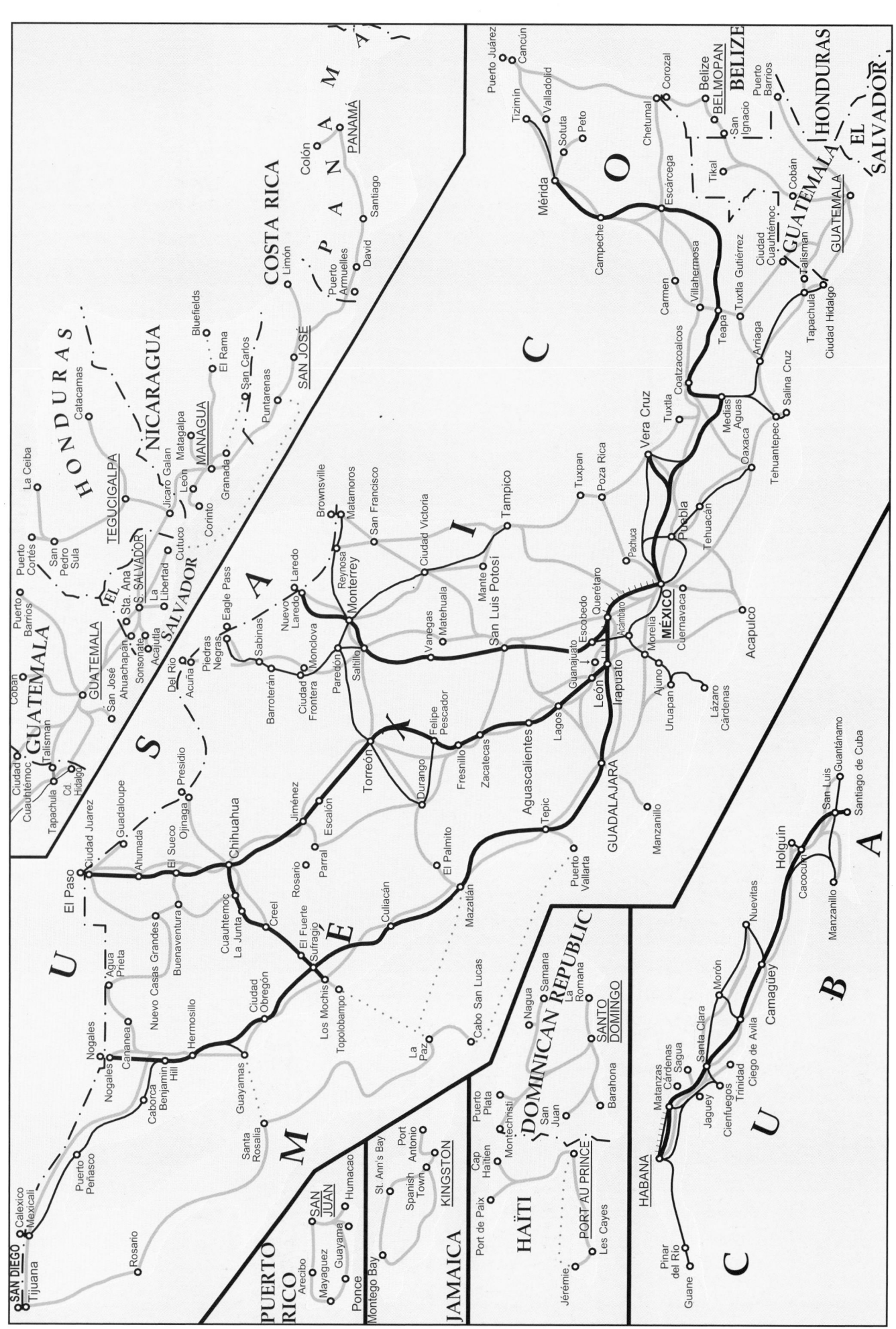

MÉXICO
GUATEMALA
HONDURAS
NICARAGUA
EL SALVADOR
COSTA RICA
PANAMÁ
BELIZE
CUBA
JAMAICA
PUERTO RICO
HAÏTI
DOMINICAN REPUBLIC
SAN DIEGO
Tijuana
Calexico
Mexicali
Rosario
Puerto Peñasco
Caborca
Nogales
Cananea
Agua Prieta
Benjamin Hill
Hermosillo
Guayamas
Santa Rosalia
Ciudad Obregón
Los Mochis
Topolobampo
El Fuerte
Suffragio
Culiacán
Mazatlán
La Paz
Cabo San Lucas
Nuevo Casas Grandes
Buenaventura
El Paso
Ciudad Juarez
Ahumada
Guadaloupe
El Sueco
Ojinaga
Presidio
Chihuahua
Cuauhtemoc
La Junta
Creel
Rosario
Parral
Jiménez
Escalón
Torreón
Durango
El Palmito
Felipe Pescador
Fresnillo
Zacatecas
Aguascalientes
Tepic
Puerto Vallarta
GUADALAJARA
Manzanillo
Lagos
León
Irapuato
Guanajuato
Escobedo
Querétaro
Acámbaro
Morelia
Uruapan
Lázaro Cárdenas
MÉXICO
Cuernavaca
Acapulco
Pachuca
Puebla
Tehuacán
Oaxaca
Vera Cruz
Tuxpan
Poza Rica
Tampico
San Luis Potosí
Mante
Vanegas
Matehuala
Ciudad Victoria
San Francisco
Saltillo
Paredón
Monterrey
Reynosa
Matamoros
Brownsville
Monclova
Ciudad Frontera
Barroterán
Sabinas
Piedras Negras
Eagle Pass
Nuevo Laredo
Laredo
Del Rio
Acuña
Medias Aguas
Coatzacoalcos
Tuxtla
Tehuantepec
Salina Cruz
Arriaga
Tuxtla Gutiérrez
Tapachula
Ciudad Hidalgo
Talisman
Teapa
Villahermosa
Carmen
Campeche
Escárcega
Mérida
Tizimin
Valladolid
Sotuta
Peto
Puerto Juárez
Cancún
Chetumal
Corozal
Belize
BELMOPAN
San Ignacio
Tikal
Cobán
Puerto Barrios
Ciudad Cuauhtémoc
Cd. Hidalgo
San José
Ahuachapán
Sonsonate
Acajutla
Sta. Ana
S. SALVADOR
La Libertad
Cutuco
Puerto Cortés
San Pedro Sula
La Ceiba
TEGUCIGALPA
Catacamas
Jicaro Galan
León
Corinto
MANAGUA
Matagalpa
Granada
Bluefields
El Rama
San Carlos
Puntarenas
SAN JOSÉ
Limón
Puerto Armuelles
David
Santiago
Colón
PANAMÁ
Guane
Pinar del Rio
HABANA
Matanzas
Cárdenas
Sagua
Santa Clara
Jaguey
Cienfuegos
Trinidad
Ciego de Avila
Morón
Camagüey
Nuevitas
Holguín
Cacocum
Manzanillo
San Luis
Guantánamo
Santiago de Cuba
Montego Bay
St. Ann's Bay
Spanish Town
Port Antonio
KINGSTON
Arecibo
Mayaguez
Ponce
Guayama
SAN JUAN
Humacao
Port de Paix
Cap Haïtien
Jérémie
Les Cayes
PORT AU PRINCE
Montechristi
Puerto Plata
San Juan
Nagua
Samana
La Romana
SANTO DOMINGO
Barahona

NORTHERN SOUTH AMERICA

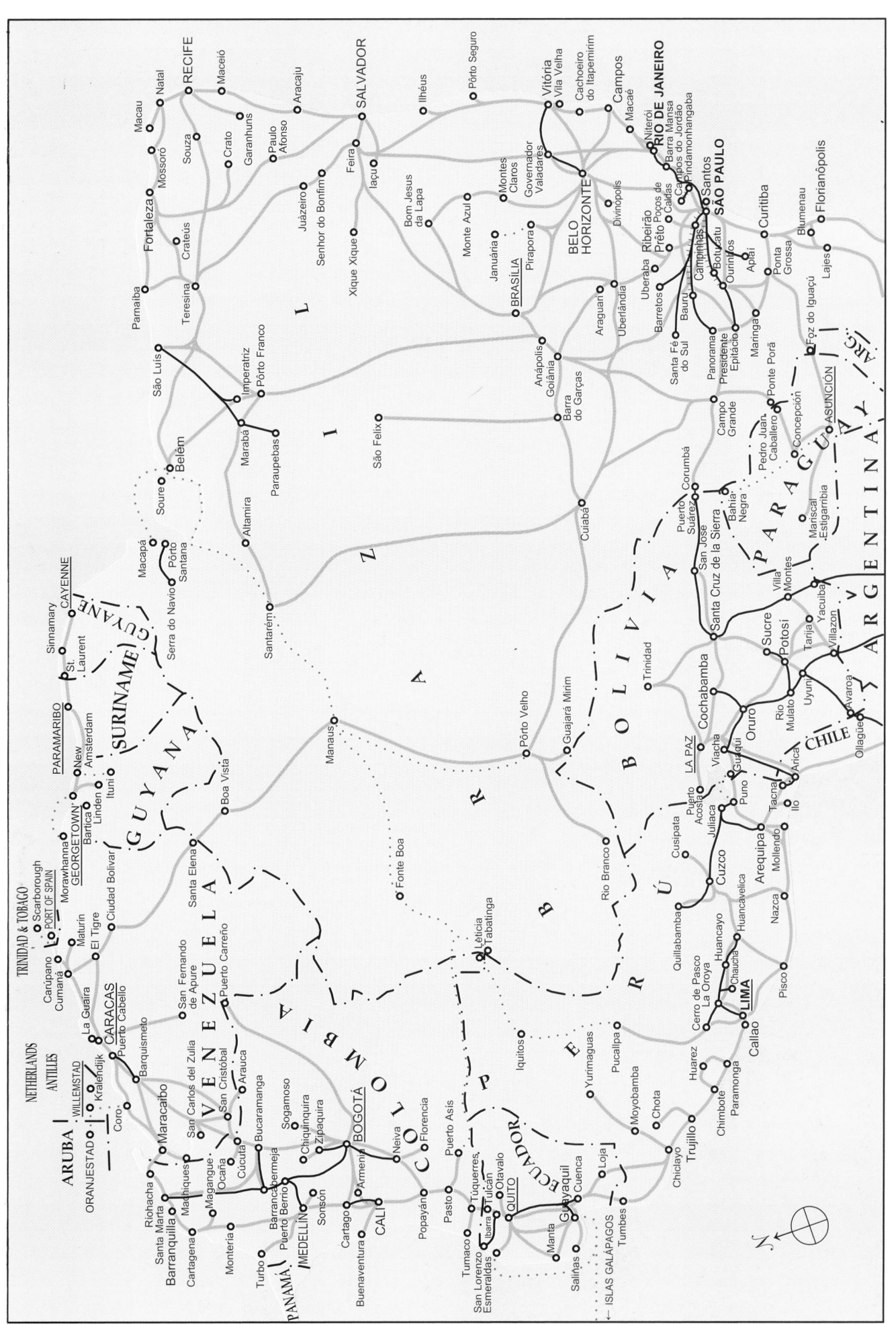

ARUBA
ORANJESTAD
NETHERLANDS ANTILLES
WILLEMSTAD
Kralendijk
Coro
TRINIDAD & TOBAGO
Scarborough
PORT OF SPAIN
Carúpano
Cumaná
Maturín
El Tigre
Ciudad Bolivar
La Guaira
CARACAS
Puerto Cabello
Barquisimeto
Maracaibo
San Carlos del Zulia
San Cristóbal
San Fernando de Apure
Puerto Carreño
Arauca
Bucaramanga
Sogamoso
Chiquinquira
Zipaquira
BOGOTÁ
Riohacha
Santa Marta
Barranquilla
Cartagena
Machiques
Magangue
Ocaña
Cúcuta
Montería
Barrancabermeja
Puerto Berrio
MEDELLÍN
Sonson
Turbo
PANAMÁ
Cartago
Armenia
CALI
Buenaventura
Neiva
Florencia
Popayán
Pasto
Puerto Asís
Tumaco
Túquerres
Tulcán
Ibarra
Otavalo
QUITO
San Lorenzo
Esmeraldas
Manta
Guayaquil
Cuenca
Salinas
Loja
Tumbes
ISLAS GALÁPAGOS
VENEZUELA
COLOMBIA
ECUADOR
GUYANA
SURINAME
GUYANE
Morawhanna
GEORGETOWN
Bartica
Linden
New Amsterdam
Ituni
PARAMARIBO
St. Laurent
Sinnamary
CAYENNE
Santa Elena
Boa Vista
Macapá
Pôrto Santana
Serra do Navio
Soure
Belém
Santarém
Manaus
Fonte Boa
Leticia
Tabatinga
Iquitos
Yurimaguas
Pucallpa
Moyobamba
Chota
Chiclayo
Trujillo
Chimbote
Huarez
Paramonga
Callao
LIMA
Cerro de Pasco
La Oroya
Chaucha
Huancayo
Huancavelica
Quillabamba
Cuzco
Cusipata
Juliaca
Puno
Puerto Acosta
Arequipa
Mollendo
Nazca
Pisco
Ilo
Tacna
Arica
LA PAZ
Viacha
Guaqui
Oruro
Cochabamba
Rio Mulato
Uyuni
Potosí
Sucre
Tarija
Villazon
Yacuiba
Avaroa
Ollagüe
CHILE
ARGENTINA
ARG.
Trinidad
Santa Cruz de la Sierra
San José
Puerto Suárez
Corumbá
Bahia Negra
Villa Montes
Mariscal Estigarribia
Pedro Juan Caballero
Concepción
ASUNCIÓN
PARAGUAY
Ponte Porã
Foz do Iguaçú
BOLIVIA
PERÚ
BRAZIL
Rio Branco
Guajará Mirim
Pôrto Velho
Cuiabá
Altamira
Marabá
Parauapebas
Imperatriz
Pôrto Franco
São Luís
São Félix
Barra do Garças
Goiânia
Anápolis
BRASÍLIA
Januária
Pirapora
Campo Grande
Panorama
Presidente Epitácio
Santa Fé do Sul
Barretos
Bauru
Uberaba
Uberlândia
Araguari
Maringá
Ponta Grossa
Curitiba
Lajes
Blumenau
Florianópolis
Apiaí
Ourinhos
Botucatu
Campinas
Santos
SÃO PAULO
Ribeirão Prêto
Poços de Caldas
Campos do Jordão
Pindamonhangaba
Barra Mansa
RIO DE JANEIRO
Niterói
Macaé
Campos
Cachoeiro do Itapemirim
Vila Velha
Vitória
Divinópolis
BELO HORIZONTE
Governador Valadares
Montes Claros
Monte Azul
Bom Jesus da Lapa
Pôrto Seguro
Ilhéus
Iaçu
Feira
SALVADOR
Aracaju
Paulo Afonso
Garanhuns
Maceió
RECIFE
Natal
Macau
Mossoró
Souza
Crato
Juàzeiro
Senhor do Bonfim
Xique Xique
Fortaleza
Crateús
Teresina
Parnaíba

SOUTHERN SOUTH AMERICA

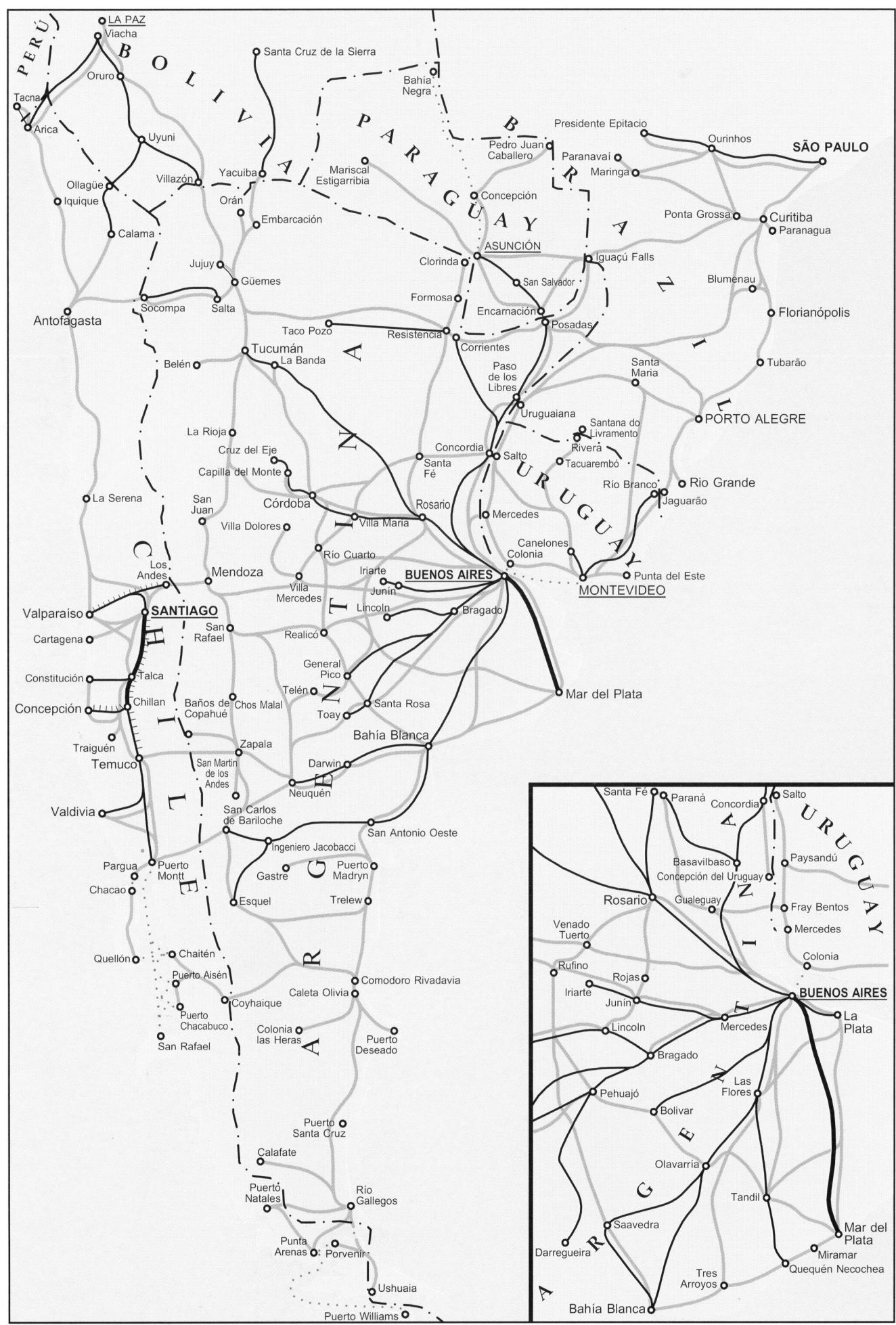
PERÚ
BOLIVIA
PARAGUAY
BRAZIL
ARGENTINA
CHILE
URUGUAY
LA PAZ
Viacha
Oruro
Tacna
Arica
Uyuni
Ollagüe
Iquique
Calama
Villazón
Yacuiba
Orán
Embarcación
Santa Cruz de la Sierra
Bahía Negra
Mariscal Estigarribia
Pedro Juan Caballero
Presidente Epitacio
Ourinhos
SÃO PAULO
Paranavaí
Maringa
Concepción
ASUNCIÓN
Clorinda
Formosa
San Salvador
Iguaçú Falls
Ponta Grossa
Curitiba
Paranagua
Blumenau
Florianópolis
Tubarão
Encarnación
Posadas
Resistencia
Corrientes
Taco Pozo
Jujuy
Güemes
Salta
Socompa
Antofagasta
Tucumán
La Banda
Belén
Paso de los Libres
Uruguaiana
Santa Maria
PORTO ALEGRE
Santana do Livramento
Rivera
Tacuarembó
Río Branco
Jaguarão
Rio Grande
La Rioja
Cruz del Eje
Capilla del Monte
Concordia
Santa Fé
Salto
Córdoba
Rosario
Villa Maria
Mercedes
La Serena
San Juan
Villa Dolores
Río Cuarto
Canelones
Colonia
MONTEVIDEO
Punta del Este
Los Andes
Mendoza
Villa Mercedes
Iriarte
Junín
BUENOS AIRES
Lincoln
Bragado
Valparaiso
SANTIAGO
Cartagena
San Rafael
Realicó
General Pico
Constitución
Talca
Telén
Santa Rosa
Mar del Plata
Concepción
Chillan
Baños de Copahué
Chos Malal
Toay
Bahía Blanca
Traiguén
Zapala
Temuco
San Martin de los Andes
Darwin
Neuquén
Valdivia
San Carlos de Bariloche
San Antonio Oeste
Ingeniero Jacobacci
Pargua
Puerto Montt
Chacao
Gastre
Puerto Madryn
Esquel
Trelew
Quellón
Chaitén
Puerto Aisén
Coyhaique
Puerto Chacabuco
San Rafael
Caleta Olivia
Comodoro Rivadavia
Colonia las Heras
Puerto Deseado
Puerto Santa Cruz
Calafate
Puerto Natales
Río Gallegos
Punta Arenas
Porvenir
Ushuaia
Puerto Williams
Santa Fé
Paraná
Concordia
Salto
Basavilbaso
Concepción del Uruguay
Paysandú
Rosario
Gualeguay
Fray Bentos
Venado Tuerto
Mercedes
Rufino
Colonia
Rojas
Iriarte
Junín
BUENOS AIRES
La Plata
Lincoln
Mercedes
Bragado
Las Flores
Pehuajó
Bolivar
Olavarría
Tandil
Saavedra
Darregueira
Mar del Plata
Miramar
Quequén Necochea
Tres Arroyos
Bahía Blanca

APPENDICES

1: GEOGRAPHICAL DEFINITIONS

The following list includes names and abbreviations which appear in this atlas, together with other terms that are commonly used in the travel industry. Various authorities differ on the exact definitions of some of these entries; the definitions given here are those which are generally understood within the travel trade.

Arabian Peninsula
Geographical region comprising: Bahrain, Kuwait, Oman, Qatar, Saudi Arabia, United Arab Emirates, Yemen.

ASEAN (Association of South-East Asian Nations)
Regional organisation comprising the following member countries: Brunei, Indonesia, Laos, Malaysia, Myanmar, the Philippines, Singapore, Thailand, Vietnam.

Australasia
Geographical region comprising: Australia, New Caledonia, New Zealand, Solomon Islands, Vanuatu and the island of New Guinea including all of Papua New Guinea. Often described as equivalent to all of Oceania between the Equator and 47°S. The term is not commonly used, especially in Australia and New Zealand because of confusion with Australia.

Bahama Islands
Group of islands in the Atlantic Ocean comprising the Commonwealth of the Bahamas and the Turks and Caicos Islands.

Balkans, The
The Balkan Peninsula, which is bordered by the Adriatic and Ionian Seas to the west, the Aegean and Black Seas to the east and the Mediterranean Sea to the south. The countries occupying this peninsula are described as Balkan states: Albania, Bosnia-Herzegovina, Bulgaria, Croatia, Greece, Former Yugoslav Republic of Macedonia, Romania, Slovenia, Federal Republic of Yugoslavia and the European part of Turkey.

Borneo
Island in the Malay Archipelago divided between Brunei, Indonesia (the provinces of Central, East, South and West Kalimantan) and Malaysia (the states of Sabah and Sarawak).

British Isles
Geographical region comprising: United Kingdom, Republic of Ireland, Isle of Man, Channel Islands.

Caribbean
General tourist destination term used to describe the West Indies.

Caroline Islands
Archipelago in the west Pacific Ocean. Islands comprise the Federated States of Micronesia and Palau.

Celebes
Island in the Malay Archipelago called Sulawesi in Indonesian.

Central America
Geographical region comprising: Belize, Costa Rica, El Salvador, Guatemala, Honduras, Nicaragua, Panama. Usually considered part of the North American continent.

Ceylon
Island off the southeast coast of India, officially Sri Lanka.

Channel Islands
Group of islands comprising Jersey, Guernsey, Alderney, Sark and Herm, situated off the northwest coast of France. They are possessions of the British Crown and not officially part of the United Kingdom.

CIS (Commonwealth of Independent States)
Countries of the former Soviet Union with the exception of Estonia, Latvia and Lithuania.

Commonwealth, The
Free association of sovereign independent states comprising the following countries: Antigua and Barbuda, Australia, Bahamas, Bangladesh, Barbados, Belize, Botswana, Brunei, Cameroon, Canada, Cyprus, Dominica, Fiji, The Gambia, Ghana, Grenada, Guyana, India, Jamaica, Kenya, Kiribati, Lesotho, Malawi, Malaysia, Maldives, Malta, Mauritius, Mozambique, Namibia, Nauru, New Zealand, Pakistan, Papua New Guinea, St Kitts and Nevis, St Lucia, St Vincent and the Grenadines, Seychelles, Sierra Leone, Singapore, Solomon Islands, South Africa, Sri Lanka, Swaziland, Tanzania, Tonga, Trinidad and Tobago, Tuvalu, Uganda, United Kingdom, Vanuatu, Western Samoa, Zambia, Zimbabwe. Dependencies and associated states of Australia, New Zealand and the UK are also members. Nigeria's membership was suspended in November 1995. Fiji was re-admitted in October 1997 after a period of suspension.

East Indies
General geographical term sometimes applied loosely to India, Indochina and the Malay Archipelago. Often used as alternative to the Malay Archipelago or the Republic of Indonesia itself. The term is rarely used.

EU (European Union)
Regional organisation comprising the following member countries: Austria, Belgium, Denmark, Finland, France, Germany, Greece, Ireland, Italy, Luxembourg, The Netherlands, Portugal, Spain, Sweden, United Kingdom.

Europe
Continent. Northern boundary formed by Arctic Ocean. Eastern boundary formed by Ural Mountains, Ural river and Caspian Sea. Southern boundary formed by Caucasus Mountains, Black Sea, Bosporus, Aegean Sea and Mediterranean Sea. Western boundary formed by Atlantic Ocean. Includes Iceland, Svalbard and area of Turkey west of the Bosporus.

Far East
General geographical term describing east and South-East Asia: Brunei, Cambodia, China, Indonesia, Japan, Democratic People's Republic of Korea (North Korea), Republic of Korea (South Korea), Laos, Malaysia, Myanmar, the Philippines, Singapore, Taiwan, Thailand, Vietnam. Sometimes extended to include Mongolia and the eastern Siberian region of the Russian Federation.

FEEE (Foundation for Environmental Education in Europe)
A network of organisations working to promote environmental education in Europe. The FEEE's Blue Flag Campaign for beaches and marinas is presently operating in the following countries: Belgium, Bulgaria, Cyprus, Denmark, Estonia, Finland, France, Germany, Greece, Ireland, Italy, The Netherlands, Portugal, Slovenia, Spain, Sweden, Turkey, United Kingdom.

Formosa
Island off the southeast coast of the People's Republic of China, known variously as the Republic of China or Taiwan.

Franc Zone
Countries whose currencies are linked with the French franc at a fixed exchange rate. Each country has its own central issuing bank and its currency is freely covertible into French francs. Members are Benin, Burkina Faso, Cameroon, Central African Republic, Chad, Comoros, Congo, Côte d'Ivoire, Equatorial Guinea, Gabon, Guinea-Bissau, Mali, Niger, Senegal, Togo.

FSU (Former Soviet Union)
Armenia, Azerbaijan, Belarus, Estonia, Georgia, Kazakhstan, Kyrgyzstan, Latvia, Lithuania, Moldova, Russian Federation, Tajikistan, Turkmenistan, Ukraine, Uzbekistan.

Great Britain
Geographical region comprising: England, Scotland, Wales.

Greater Antilles
Group of Caribbean islands comprising: Cayman Islands, Cuba, Hispaniola, Jamaica, Puerto Rico.

Hispaniola
Island in the Greater Antilles divided between the Dominican Republic and Haiti.

IATA (International Air Transport Association)
An association which acts as a governing body of the major airlines, responsible for establishing fare levels and for rules and regulations concerning international passenger and cargo services. It has over 100 tariff members and a further 100 trade associate airlines.

Iberia
Peninsula in southwest Europe occupied by Spain, Portugal, Andorra and Gibraltar.

Indochina
Geographical region comprising: Cambodia, Laos, Malaysia (Peninsular), Myanmar, Singapore, Thailand, Vietnam.

Lesser Antilles
Group of Caribbean islands comprising: Virgin Islands, Leeward Islands, Windward Islands, Aruba, Barbados, Bonaire, Curaçao, Trinidad and Tobago. Also includes the chain of small Venezuelan islands east of Bonaire.

Leeward Islands
Group of Caribbean islands comprising: Anguilla, Antigua and Barbuda, Dominica, Guadeloupe, Montserrat, Saba, St Eustatius, St Kitts and Nevis, St Maarten/St Martin.

Low Countries
Geographical region comprising: Belgium, Luxembourg, The Netherlands.

Maghreb
Arabic name for northwest Africa and, during the Moorish period, Spain. Algeria, Morocco and Tunisia are described as Maghreb countries.

Malay Archipelago
The largest island group in the world, off the southeast coast of Asia and between the Indian and Pacific Oceans. Major islands include Borneo, Sulawesi (Celebes), Jawa (Java), New Guinea and Sumatera (Sumatra). Countries within this archipelago: Brunei, Indonesia, Malaysia (East), Papua New Guinea, the Philippines.

Mediterranean
General tourist destination term used to describe the islands of the Mediterranean Sea and the countries bordering it.

Melanesia
Collective name for the islands in the southwest Pacific Ocean, south of the Equator and northeast of Australia. Includes: Fiji, Nauru, New Caledonia, Papua New Guinea (excluding New Guinea mainland), Solomon Islands, Vanuatu.

Micronesia
Collective name for the islands in the west Pacific Ocean, north of the Equator and east of the Philippines. Includes: Guam, Kiribati (west), Marshall Islands, Federated States of Micronesia, Northern Mariana Islands, Palau.

Middle East
General geographical term describing a loosely defined area comprising: countries of the Arabian Peninsula, Egypt, Iran, Iraq, Israel, Jordan, Lebanon, Syria. Usually extended to include Algeria, Cyprus, Libya, Morocco, Sudan, Tunisia and Turkey.

NAFTA (North American Free Trade Agreement)
Regional organisation comprising: Canada, Mexico, USA.

Near East
Rarely used general geographical term describing an area of SW Asia: the Arabian Peninsula, Cyprus, Israel, Jordan, Lebanon, Syria, Turkey. Usually extended to Egypt and Sudan.

Netherlands Antilles
Islands of the West Indies administered by The Netherlands, comprising: Bonaire, Curaçao, Saba, St Eustatius, St Maarten. Aruba, formerly part of the Netherlands Antilles is now administered from The Netherlands separately.

New Guinea
Island in the Malay Archipelago divided between Papua New Guinea and the Indonesian province of Irian Jaya.

North America
Continent comprising: Bermuda, Canada, Mexico, USA, West Indies. Generally considered to include Central America and Greenland.

Oceania
General geographical term describing the islands of the central and south Pacific Ocean, including Melanesia, Micronesia and Polynesia. Sometimes extended to include Australia, New Zealand and the Malay Archipelago.

OECD (Organisation for Economic Cooperation and Development)
International organisation comprising the following member countries: Australia, Austria, Belgium, Canada, Czech Republic, Denmark, Finland, France, Germany, Greece, Hungary, Iceland, Ireland, Italy, Japan, Republic of Korea, Luxembourg, Mexico, The Netherlands, New Zealand, Norway, Poland, Portugal, Spain, Sweden, Switzerland, Turkey, United Kingdom, USA.

OPEC (Organisation of the Petroleum Exporting Countries)
International organisation comprising the following member countries: Algeria, Indonesia, Iran, Iraq, Kuwait, Libya, Nigeria, Qatar, Saudi Arabia, United Arab Emirates, Venezuela.

Polynesia
Collective name for the islands of the central and south Pacific Ocean. Includes: American Samoa, Cook Islands, Easter Island, French Polynesia, Hawaii, Kiribati (east), New Zealand, Niue, Pitcairn Islands, Tokelau, Tonga, Tuvalu, Wallis and Futuna, Western Samoa.

Scandinavia
Geographical region comprising: Denmark, Norway, Sweden. Often extended to include Finland and Iceland.

Schengen Agreement
Agreement of European Union states with the intention of facilitating movement between member countries. Established in March 1995, all EU countries except for Ireland and the UK are members. The agreement is implemented in Austria, Belgium, France, Germany, Italy, Luxembourg, The Netherlands, Portugal, Spain. For further details, please refer to the Columbus Press *World Travel Guide*.

South America
Continent comprising: countries on mainland south of Panama, Falkland Islands, Galapagos Islands.

Ulster
Geographical region comprising Northern Ireland plus the counties of Cavan, Donegal and Monaghan in the Republic of Ireland. It is often used (incorrectly) as an unofficial term to describe Northern Ireland.

UNESCO (United Nations Educational, Scientific and Cultural Organisation)
Specialized agency of the United Nations. Its purpose is to contribute to peace and security by promoting collaboration among the nations through education, science and culture.

United Kingdom
Country comprising Great Britain and Northern Ireland (the Isle of Man and the Channel Islands are Crown dependencies and not officially part of the UK).

United Nations
International organisation. Every state in the world is a member with the exception of Kiribati, Nauru, Switzerland, Taiwan, Tonga, Tuvalu and the Vatican City.

West Indies
Islands enclosing the Caribbean Sea, divided into the following groups: Bahama Islands, Greater Antilles, Lesser Antilles.

Windward Islands
Group of Caribbean islands comprising: Grenada, Martinique, St Lucia, St Vincent and the Grenadines.

WWF (World-Wide Fund For Nature / World Wildlife Fund)
One of the world's largest private international nature conservation organisations. Its aim is to conserve nature by preserving genetic, species and ecosystem diversity.

APPENDICES

2: US STATES

ISO abbreviation*	Name	Nickname	Date of admission to the Union	State capital
AK	Alaska	Last Frontier	3rd Jan 1959	Juneau
AL	Alabama	Yellowhammer State	14th Dec 1819	Montgomery
AR	Arkansas	The Natural State	15th June 1836	Little Rock
AZ	Arizona	Grand Canyon State	14th Feb 1912	Phoenix
CA	California	Golden State	9th Sept 1850	Sacramento
CO	Colorado	Centennial State	1st Aug 1876	Denver
CT	Connecticut	Constitution State	9th Jan 1788 †	Hartford
DC	District of Columbia	(Federal District, coextensive with the city of Washington)		
DE	Delaware	Diamond State	7th Dec 1787 †	Dover
FL	Florida	Sunshine State	3rd Mar 1845	Tallahassee
GA	Georgia	Peach State	2nd Jan 1788 †	Atlanta
HI	Hawaii	Aloha State	21st Aug 1959	Honolulu
IA	Iowa	Hawkeye State	28th Dec 1846	Des Moines
ID	Idaho	Gem State	3rd July 1890	Boise
IL	Illinois	Land of Lincoln	3rd Dec 1818	Springfield
IN	Indiana	Hoosier State	11th Dec 1816	Indianapolis
KS	Kansas	Sunflower State	29th Jan 1861	Topeka
KY	Kentucky	Bluegrass State	1st June 1792	Frankfort
LA	Louisiana	Pelican State	30th Apr 1812	Baton Rouge
MA	Massachusetts	Bay State	6th Feb 1788 †	Boston
MD	Maryland	Old Line State	28th Apr 1788 †	Annapolis
ME	Maine	Pine Tree State	15th Mar 1820	Augusta
MI	Michigan	Great Lakes State	26th Jan 1837	Lansing
MN	Minnesota	North Star State	11th May 1858	St Paul
MO	Missouri	Show Me State	10th Aug 1821	Jefferson City
MS	Mississippi	Magnolia State	10th Dec 1817	Jackson
MT	Montana	Treasure State	8th Nov 1889	Helena
NC	North Carolina	Tar Heel State	21st Nov 1789 †	Raleigh
ND	North Dakota	Peace Garden State	2nd Nov 1889	Bismarck
NE	Nebraska	Cornhusker State	1st Mar 1867	Lincoln
NH	New Hampshire	Granite State	21st June 1788 †	Concord
NJ	New Jersey	Garden State	18th Dec 1787 †	Trenton
NM	New Mexico	Land of Enchantment	6th Jan 1912	Santa Fe
NV	Nevada	Silver State	31st Oct 1864	Carson City
NY	New York	Empire State	26th July 1788 †	Albany
OH	Ohio	Buckeye State	1st Mar 1803	Columbus
OK	Oklahoma	Sooner State	16th Nov 1907	Oklahoma City
OR	Oregon	Beaver State	14th Feb 1859	Salem
PA	Pennsylvania	Keystone State	12th Dec 1787 †	Harrisburg
RI	Rhode Island	The Ocean State	29th May 1790 †	Providence
SC	South Carolina	Palmetto State	23rd May 1788 †	Columbia
SD	South Dakota	Mount Rushmore State	2nd Nov 1889	Pierre
TN	Tennessee	Volunteer State	1st June 1796	Nashville
TX	Texas	Lone Star State	29th Dec 1845	Austin
UT	Utah	Beehive State	4th Jan 1896	Salt Lake City
VA	Virginia	The Old Dominion State	25th June 1788 †	Richmond
VT	Vermont	Green Mountain State	4th Mar 1791	Montpelier
WA	Washington	Evergreen State	11th Nov 1889	Olympia
WI	Wisconsin	Badger State	29th May 1848	Madison
WV	West Virginia	Mountain State	20th June 1863	Charleston
WY	Wyoming	Equality State / Cowboy State	10th July 1890	Cheyenne

International Standards Organisation. † Original thirteen states: date of ratification of the Constitution.

3: CANADIAN PROVINCES AND TERRITORIES

ISO abbrev.	Name	Language*	Date of entry to the Dominion	Province/ territory capital
AL	Alberta	English	1st Sept 1905	Edmonton
BC	British Columbia	English	20th July 1871	Victoria
MN	Manitoba	English	15th July 1870	Winnipeg
NB	New Brunswick	English †	1st July 1867	Fredericton
NF	Newfoundland and Labrador	English	31st March 1949	St John's
NS	Nova Scotia	English	1st July 1867	Halifax
NT	Northwest Territories	English	1870	Yellowknife
NU	Nunavut (territory)	Inuktitut **	(to be established on 1st April 1999)	Iqaluit
OT	Ontario	English	1st July 1867	Toronto
PE	Prince Edward Island	English	1st July 1873	Charlottetown
QU	Québec	French	1st July 1867	Québec
SA	Saskatchewan	English	1st Sept 1905	Regina
YT	Yukon Territory	English	13th June 1898	Whitehorse

*Although Canada is officially bilingual (English & French), this column indicates the most commonly-spoken language in each region. † Approx. 35% of the population are French-speaking. ** The language of the Inuit.*

4: AUSTRALIAN STATES AND TERRITORIES

ISO abbrev.	Name	Nickname	Date of granting of responsible gov't	State/territory capital
AC	Australian Capital Territory	Nation's Capital	1911 *	Canberra
CL	Coral Sea Territory	(External Territory bordering the Queensland coast and Gt. Barrier Reef)		
NS	New South Wales	Premier State	1788 †	Sydney
NT	Northern Territory	Outback Australia	1911 **	Darwin
QL	Queensland	Sunshine State	1859	Brisbane
SA	South Australia	Festival State	1856	Adelaide
TS	Tasmania	Holiday Isle	1856	Hobart
VI	Victoria	Garden State	1855	Melbourne
WA	Western Australia	State of Excitement	1890	Perth

*Canberra became the seat of the Australian government on 9th May 1927. † Date of first settlement: New South Wales originally covered the whole island with the exception of Western Australia. ** Transferred to Commonwealth from South Australia in 1911, self-government within the Commonwealth granted 1978.*

5: FRENCH DÉPARTEMENTS

Dept. no.	Name	Département capital	Region
01	Ain	Bourg-en-Bresse	Rhône-Alpes
02	Aisne	Laon	Picardie
03	Allier	Moulins	Auvergne
04	Alpes-de-Haute-Provence	Digne	Provence-Alpes-Côte d'Azur
05	Hautes-Alpes	Gap	Provence-Alpes-Côte d'Azur
06	Alpes-Maritimes	Nice	Provence-Alpes-Côte d'Azur
07	Ardèche	Privas	Rhône-Alpes
08	Ardennes	Charleville-Mézières	Champagne-Ardenne
09	Ariège	Foix	Midi-Pyrénées
10	Aube	Troyes	Champagne-Ardenne
11	Aude	Carcassonne	Languedoc-Roussillon
12	Aveyron	Rodez	Midi-Pyrénées
13	Bouches-du-Rhône	Marseille	Provence-Alpes-Côte d'Azur
14	Calvados	Caen	Basse-Normandie
15	Cantal	Aurillac	Auvergne
16	Charente	Angoulême	Poitou-Charentes
17	Charente-Maritime	La Rochelle	Poitou-Charentes
18	Cher	Bourges	Centre
19	Corrèze	Tulle	Limousin
20 2A	Corse-du-Sud	Ajaccio	Corse
20 2B	Haute-Corse	Bastia	Corse
21	Côte-d'Or	Dijon	Bourgogne
22	Côtes-d'Armor	St Brieuc	Bretagne
23	Creuse	Guéret	Limousin
24	Dordogne	Périgueux	Aquitaine
25	Doubs	Besançon	Franche-Comté
26	Drôme	Valence	Rhône-Alpes
27	Eure	Évreux	Haute-Normandie
28	Eure-et-Loir	Chartres	Centre
29	Finistère	Quimper	Bretagne
30	Gard	Nîmes	Languedoc-Roussillon
31	Haute-Garonne	Toulouse	Midi-Pyrénées
32	Gers	Auch	Midi-Pyrénées
33	Gironde	Bordeaux	Aquitaine
34	Hérault	Montpellier	Languedoc-Roussillon
35	Ille-et-Vilaine	Rennes	Bretagne
36	Indre	Châteauroux	Centre
37	Indre-et-Loire	Tours	Centre
38	Isère	Grenoble	Rhône-Alpes
39	Jura	Lons-le-Saunier	Franche-Comté
40	Landes	Mont-de-Marsan	Aquitaine
41	Loir-et-Cher	Blois	Centre
42	Loire	St Étienne	Rhône-Alpes
43	Haute-Loire	Le Puy	Auvergne
44	Loire-Atlantique	Nantes	Pays de la Loire
45	Loiret	Orléans	Centre
46	Lot	Cahors	Midi-Pyrénées
47	Lot-et-Garonne	Agen	Aquitaine
48	Lozère	Mende	Languedoc-Roussillon
49	Maine-et-Loire	Angers	Pays de la Loire
50	Manche	St Lô	Basse-Normandie
51	Marne	Châlons-sur-Marne	Champagne-Ardenne
52	Haute-Marne	Chaumont	Champagne-Ardenne
53	Mayenne	Laval	Pays de la Loire
54	Meurthe-et-Moselle	Nancy	Lorraine
55	Meuse	Bar-le-Duc	Lorraine
56	Morbihan	Vannes	Bretagne
57	Moselle	Metz	Lorraine
58	Nièvre	Nevers	Bourgogne
59	Nord	Lille	Nord-Pas-de-Calais
60	Oise	Beauvais	Picardie
61	Orne	Alençon	Basse-Normandie
62	Pas-de-Calais	Arras	Nord-Pas-de-Calais
63	Puy-de-Dôme	Clermont-Ferrand	Auvergne
64	Pyrénées-Atlantiques	Pau	Aquitaine
65	Hautes-Pyrénées	Tarbes	Midi-Pyrénées
66	Pyrénées-Orientales	Perpignan	Languedoc-Roussillon
67	Bas-Rhin	Strasbourg	Alsace
68	Haut-Rhin	Colmar	Alsace
69	Rhône	Lyon	Rhône-Alpes
70	Haute-Sâone	Vesoul	Franche-Comté
71	Saône-et-Loire	Mâcon	Bourgogne
72	Sarthe	Le Mans	Pays de la Loire
73	Savoie	Chambéry	Rhône-Alpes
74	Haute-Savoie	Annecy	Rhône-Alpes
75	Paris	Paris	Île-de-France
76	Seine-Maritime	Rouen	Haute-Normandie
77	Seine-et-Marne	Melun	Île-de-France
78	Yvelines (canton)	Versailles	Île-de-France
79	Deux-Sèvres	Niort	Poitou-Charentes
80	Somme	Amiens	Picardie
81	Tarn	Albi	Midi-Pyrénées
82	Tarn-et-Garonne	Montauban	Midi-Pyrénées
83	Var	Toulon	Provence-Alpes-Côte d'Azur
84	Vaucluse	Avignon	Provence-Alpes-Côte d'Azur
85	Vendée	La Roche-sur-Yon	Pays de la Loire
86	Vienne	Poitiers	Poitou-Charentes
87	Haute-Vienne	Limoges	Limousin
88	Vosges	Épinal	Lorraine
89	Yonne	Auxerre	Bourgogne
90	Territoire-de-Belfort	Belfort	Franche-Comté
91	Essonne (canton)	Évry	Île-de-France
92	Hauts-de-Seine (canton)	Nanterre	Île-de-France
93	Seine-St-Denis (canton)	Bobigny	Île-de-France
94	Val-de-Marne (canton)	Créteil	Île-de-France
95	Val-d'Oise (canton)	Cergy	Île-de-France

APPENDICES

6: THE WORLD'S MAJOR URBAN AREAS

This list shows the world's fifty largest urban agglomerations in 1995, according to the UN, with estimates of their population in 1995 and forecasts for the year 2000.

Urban agglomeration and country	Population ('000) 1995	2000
Tokyo-Yokohama-Kawasaki-Chiba, Japan	26,836	27,856
São Paulo, Brazil	16,417	17,803
New York-Jersey City-Newark, USA	16,329	16,640
Mexico City-Fed. Dist., Mexico	15,643	16,354
Bombay, India	15,093	18,121
Shanghai, China	15,082	17,213
Los Angeles-Long Beach, USA	12,410	13,148
Beijing, China	12,362	14,206
Calcutta, India	11,673	12,660
Seoul, Rep. of Korea	11,641	12,278
Jakarta, Indonesia	11,500	14,091
Buenos Aires, Argentina	10,990	11,378
Tianjin, China	10,687	12,369
Osaka-Kobe, Japan	10,601	10,601
Lagos, Nigeria	10,287	13,455
Rio de Janeiro, Brazil	9,888	10,213
Delhi, India	9,882	11,678
Karachi, Pakistan	9,863	12,079
Cairo, Egypt	9,656	10,731
Paris, France	9,469	9,551
Metro Manila, Philippines	9,280	10,801
Moscow, Russian Fed.	9,233	9,282
Dhaka, Bangladesh	7,832	10,193
Istanbul-Usküdar, Turkey	7,817	9,316
Lima-Callao, Peru	7,452	8,381

Urban agglomeration and country	Population ('000) 1995	2000
Greater London, United Kingdom	7,335	7,335
Chicago-Gary-Hammond, USA	6,846	6,962
Tehran, Iran	6,830	7,347
Bangkok, Thailand	6,566	7,320
Essen-Dortmund-Duisburg, Germany	6,481	6,518
Madras, India	5,906	6,561
Bogotá, Colombia	5,614	6,323
Hong Kong, China	5,574	5,712
Hyderabad, India	5,343	6,678
Shenyang, China	5,310	6,134
St Petersburg, Russian Fed.	5,111	5,111
Lahore, Pakistan	5,085	6,201
Santiago, Chile	5,065	5,439
Bangalore, India	4,749	5,527
Toronto, Canada	4,483	4,930
Baghdad, Iraq	4,478	5,068
Wuhan, China	4,399	5,101
Philadelphia-Camden, USA	4,304	4,413
Milan, Italy	4,251	4,251
Kinshasa, Dem. Rep. of Congo	4,214	5,121
Washington DC-Alexandria-Arlington, USA	4,111	4,474
Pusan, Rep. of Korea	4,082	4,244
Madrid, Spain	4,072	4,072
Guangzhou, China	4,056	4,676
Belo Horizonte, Brazil	3,899	4,429

7: THE WORLD'S LONGEST RIVERS

Lengths include the river plus the tributaries comprising the longest watercourse, shown to the nearest 10 km/miles. Local names are shown in square brackets: [ ].

River	Length: (km)	(miles)	Source(s) and outflow
Nile-Kagera-Ruvuvu-Luvironza	6,690	4,160	Lake Victoria region – Mediterranean Sea
Amazon-Ucayali-Tambo-Ene-Apurimac	6,570	4,080	Peruvian Andes – Atlantic Ocean
Mississippi-Missouri-Beaverhead-Red Rock	6,020	3,740	SW Montana – Gulf of Mexico
Chang Jiang (Yangtze)-[Jinsha-Tongtian-Tuotuo]	5,980	3,720	Tanggula Shan, China – East China Sea
Yenisey-Angara-Selenga-Ider	5,870	3,650	Western Mongolia – Kara Sea
Amur-Argun-Kerulen	5,780	3,590	Eastern Mongolia – Sea of Japan
Ob-Irtysh-[Ertix]	5,410	3,360	Altay Mountains, China – Kara Sea
Paraná-Rio Grande	4,880	3,030	Sa. da Mantiquera, Brazil – Atlantic Ocean
Huang He (Yellow)	4,840	3,010	Bayan Har Shan, China – Yellow Sea
Congo-Lualaba	4,630	2,880	Katanga Plat., Congo D.R. – Atlantic Ocean
Lena	4,400	2,730	Baikal Mtns, Russian Fed., – Laptev Sea
Mackenzie-Slave-Peace-Finlay	4,240	2,630	Omineca Mtns, BC, Canada– Beaufort Sea
Mekong-[Lancang-Za]	4,180	2,600	Tanggula Shan, China – South China Sea
Niger-[Joliba/Kworra]	4,100	2,550	Guinea/Sierra Leone bdr. – Gulf of Guinea

8: HIGHEST AND LOWEST

Name	Metres	Feet	Country
AFRICA			
Kilimanjaro (Kibo)	5,895	19,340	Tanzania
Lake Assal	–155	–509	Djibouti
ANTARCTICA			
Vinson Massif	5,140	16,860	Antarctica
(ice covered)	–2,538	–8,327	Antarctica
ASIA			
Everest (Qomolangma Feng/ Sagarmatha)	8,848	29,028	China-Nepal
Dead Sea	–395	–1,296	Israel-Jordan
AUSTRALASIA			
Cook	3,764	12,349	New Zealand
Lake Eyre	–16	–52	Australia
EUROPE			
Elbrus	5,642	18,510	Russian Fed.
Caspian Sea	–28	–92	
NORTH AMERICA			
McKinley (Denali)	6,194	20,320	Alaska, USA
Death Valley	–86	–282	California, USA
SOUTH AMERICA			
Aconcagua	6,960	22,834	Argentina
Valdés Peninsula	–40	–131	Argentina

Name	Metres	Feet	Country
SOME OTHER SIGNIFICANT MOUNTAINS			
K2 (Godwin Austin/ Qogir Feng)	8,611	28,250	China-Kashmir
Kangchenjunga	8,586	28,170	India-Nepal
Makalu	8,463	27,766	China-Nepal
Dhaulagiri	8,167	26,795	Nepal
Nanga Parbat	8,126	26,660	Kashmir
Annapurna	8,091	26,545	Nepal
Xixabangma Feng (Gosainthan)	8,012	26,286	China
Qullai Kommunizm	7,495	24,590	Tajikistan
Ojos del Salado	6,863	22,516	Argentina-Chile
Huascarán	6,768	22,205	Peru
Logan	5,951	19,524	Yukon, Canada
Citlaltépetl (Orizaba)	5,700	18,701	Mexico
Damavand	5,670	18,602	Iran
Kenya (Kirinyaga)	5,199	17,057	Kenya
Ararat	5,165	16,946	Turkey
Mont Blanc	4,810	15,781	France-Italy
Ras Dashen	4,620	15,158	Ethiopia
Whitney	4,418	14,495	California, USA
Kinabalu	4,101	13,455	Malaysia
Fuji	3,776	12,388	Japan

9: CONVERSIONS

Kilometres 0 10 20 30 40 50 60 70 80 90 100
Miles 0 10 20 30 40 50 60

Metres 0 100 200 300 400 500 600 700 800 900 1,000
Feet 0 500 1,000 1,500 2,000 2,500 3,000

Millimetres 0 10 20 30 40 50 60 70 80 90 100
Inches 0 0.5 1.0 1.5 2.0 2.5 3.0 3.5 4.0

°Centigrade -10 -5 0 5 10 15 20 25 30 35 40
°Fahrenheit 20 30 32 40 50 60 70 80 90 100

Freezing point

10: INTERNATIONAL GLOSSARY

The following list provides the English equivalents for some of the most common words used in this atlas and other international atlases.

Term	Language	English
Å, -å	Danish, Norwegian	Stream
Abar, Abyar	Arabic	Wells
Açude	Portuguese	Reservoir
Adalar	Turkish	Islands
Adasi	Turkish	Island
Agía, Ágios	Greek	Saint
Aiguille(s)	French	Peak(s)
Ain, Aïn	Arabic	Spring, well
-air	Indonesian	Stream
Ákra, Akrotírion	Greek	Cape, point
Ala-	Finnish	Lower
A'lá	Arabic	Upper
Alt-	German	Old
Alta, Alto	Italian, Portug., Spanish	Upper
Altiplanicie	Spain	High plain, mesa
Älv, -älven	Swedish	River
am, an	German	On, upon
Áno	Greek	Upper
Anse	French	Bay
Ao	Chinese, Thai	Bay
'Aqabat	Arabic	Pass
Arrecife	Spanish	Reef
Arroio / Arroyo	Portuguese / Spanish	Watercourse
Archipiélago	Spanish	Archipelago
Aust-	Norwegian	East, eastern
Austral	Spanish	Southern
'Ayn	Arabic	Spring, well
Baai	Afrikaans	Bay
Bab	Arabic	Strait
Bach	German	Stream
Bad	German	Spa
Badiyat	Arabic	Desert
Bælt	Danish	Strait
Baharu	Malay	New
Bahía	Spanish	Bay
Bahiret	Arabic	Lagoon
Bahr	Arabic	Bay, canal, lake
Bahra / Bahrat	Arabic	Lagoon / Lake
Baía / Baie	Portuguese / French	Bay
Baixo	Portuguese	Lower
Baja, Bajo	Spanish	Lower
Bala	Persian	Upper
Ban	Cambodian, Laotian, Thai	Village
-bana	Japanese	Cape, point
Bañado	Spanish	Marshy land
Banc / Banco	French / Spanish	Sandbank
Bandao	Chinese	Peninsula
Bandar	Arabian, Malay, Persian	Inlet, port
-bando	Korean	Peninsula
Baraj, Baraji	Turkish	Dam
Barat	Indonesian, Malay	West, western
Barqa	Arabic	Hill
Barra	Portuguese	Sandbank
Barracão	Portuguese	Dam, weir
Barragem	Portuguese	Reservoir
Baruun	Mongolian	Western
Bas, Basse	French	Lower
Bassin	French	Basin
Batin, Batn	Arabic	Depression
Becken	German	Basin
Beek	Flemish	Stream
bei	German	At, near
Bei	Chinese	North, northern
Beinn, Ben	Gaelic	Mountain
Belogor'ye	Russian	Mountain
Bereg	Russian	Bank, shore
-berg	Norwegian, Swedish	Mountain
Berg(e)	German	Mountain(s)
Besar	Indonesian, Malay	Big, great
Bir, Bîr / Bi'ar	Arabic	Well / Wells
Birkat, Birket	Arabic	Pool, well
-bjerg	Danish	Hill
Boca	Portuguese, Spanish	Mouth
Bocche	Italian	Estuary, mouths
Bodden	German	Bay, gulf
Bogazi	Turkish	Strait
Bogen	Norwegian	Bay
Bois	French	Woods
Boloto	Russian	Bog, marsh
Bol'sh-aya, -iye, -oy, -oye	Russian	Big
-bong	Korean	Mountain
Boquerón	Spanish	Pass
Bor	Polish	Forest
-botn / -botten	Norwegian / Swedish	Valley floor
Bouche	French	Estuary, mouth
-bre, -breen	Norwegian	Glacier
Bredning	Danish	Bay
Bron	Afrikaans	Spring, well
-brønn	Norwegian	Spring, well
Bucht / Bugt	German / Danish	Bay
Buhayrat, Buheirat	Arabic	Lake
Bukhta	Russian	Bay
Bukit	Malay	Hill
Bukt, Bukten	Norwegian, Swedish	Bay
Bulag	Mongolian	Spring
Bulak	Russian, Uighur	Spring
Burg	German	Castle
Burun, Burnu	Turkish	Cape, point
Büyük	Turkish	Big
Cabeço	Portuguese	Summit
Cabeza	Spanish	Summit
Cabo	Portuguese, Spanish	Cape, headland
Cachoeira	Portuguese	Waterfall
Cala / Caleta	Catalan / Spanish	Inlet
Cañada	Spanish	Ravine
Cañadón	Spanish	Gorge
Canal	Portuguese, Spanish	Channel
Cañe	Spanish	Stream
Cañon	Spanish	Canyon
Cap / Capo	Catalan, French / Italian	Cape, headland
Catarata	Spanish	Waterfall
Cayo(s)	Spanish	Islet(s), rock(s)
Cerro	Spanish	Hill, peak
Chaco	Spanish	Plain
Chaîne	French	Mountain chain
Chalb	Arabic	Watercourse
Chapada	Portuguese	Hills, uplands
Chebka	Arabic	Hill
-chedo	Korean	Archipelago
Chenal	French	Channel
Chiang	Thai	Town
-ch'on	Korean	River
Chong	Thai	Bay
Chott	Arabic	Marsh, salt lake
Chuluu	Mongolian	Mountain
Chute	French	Waterfall
Ci	Indonesian	Stream
Ciénaga	Spanish	Marshy lake
Cima / Cime	Italian / French	Summit
Città / Ciudad	Italian / Spanish	City, town
Co	Tibetan	Lake
Col	French	High pass
Collado	Spanish	Hill, saddle
Colle	Italian	Pass
Collina	Italian	Hill
Colline(s)	French	Hill(s)
Combe	French	Valley
Conca	Italian	Hollow
Cordillera	Spanish	Mountain chain
Corne / Corno	French / Italian	Peak
Costa	Italian, Portug., Spanish	Coast, shore
Côte	French	Coast, slope
Coteau(x)	French	Hill(s)
Cove	Catalan	Cave
Cuchilla	Spanish	Mountain chain
Cuenca	Spanish	River basin
Cueva	Spanish	Cave
Cun	Chinese	Village
Da	Chinese	Big
Dag / Dagh	Turkish / Persian	Mountain
Daglar	Turkish	Mountain
-dake	Japanese	Peak
-dal	Afrikaans, Danish, Norwegian, Swedish	Valley
Danau	Indonesian	Lake
Dao	Chinese	Island
Darreh	Persian	Valley
Daryacheh	Persian	Lake
Dasht	Persian, Urdu	Desert
Davaa	Mongolian	Pass
Denizi	Turkish	Sea
Dhar	Arabic	Hills, mountain
-diep	Flemish	Channel
Djebel / Djibâl	Arabic	Mountain / Mtns
-do	Korean	Island
Dolina	Russian	Valley
Dolna / Dolní	Bulgarian / Czech	Lower
Dolny	Polish	Lower
Dong	Chinese	East, eastern
Dong	Thai	Mountain
-dong	Korean	Village
Donja, Donji	Serbo-Croat	Lower
Dorf	German	Village
-dorp	Afrikaans	Village
Dûr	Arabic	Mountains
Dzüün	Mongolian	East, eastern
Eiland(en)	Afrikaans, Flemish	Island(s)
-elv, -elva	Norwegian	River
Embalse	Spanish	Reservoir
Embouchure	French	Estuary
Ensenada	Spanish	Bay
Erg	Arabian	Desert & dunes
Eski	Turkish	Old
Estero	Spanish	Inlet, estuary, swamp
Estrecho	Spanish	Strait
Estreito	Portuguese	Strait
Étang	French	Lake, lagoon
Fajj	Arabic	Watercourse
Fels	German	Rock
Feng	Chinese	Peak
Fiume	Italian	River
-fjäll, -fjället	Swedish	Mountain
-fjärden	Swedish	Fjord
-fjell, -fjellet	Norwegian	Mountain
-fjord, -fjorden	Danish, Norwegian	Fjord, lagoon
Fleuve	French	River
Foce	Italian	River-mouth
-fonn	Norwegian	Glacier
Förde	German	Inlet
Forêt / Forst	French / German	Forest
-foss	Norwegian	Waterfall
Fuente	Spanish	Source, well
-gan	Japanese	Rock
Gang	Chinese	Harbour
Garet	Arabic	Hill
Gardaneh	Persian	Pass
Gat	Flemish	Channel
-gata	Japanese	Inlet, lagoon
Gau	German	District
Gave	French	Torrent
-gawa	Japanese	River
Gebel	Arabic	Mountain
Gebergte	Afrikaans	Mountain range
Gebiet	German	District, region
Gebirge	German	Mountains
Gedigi	Turkish	Pass
Gezîret / Gezâir	Arabic	Island / Islands
Ghadfat	Arabic	Watercourse
Ghadir	Arabic	Well
Ghard	Arabic	Sand dunes
Ghubbat	Arabic	Bay
Gipfel	German	Peak
Gletscher	German	Glacier
Gobi	Mongolian	Desert
Gol	Mongolian	River
Göl, Gölü	Turkish	Lake
Golfe	French	Bay, gulf
Golfete	Spanish	Bay
Golfo	Italian, Spanish	Bay, gulf
Gora	Bulgarian	Forest
Gora / Góra	Russian, Serbo-Croat / Polish	Mountain
Górka	Polish	Hill
Gornja, Gornji	Serbo-Croat	Upper
Gory / Góry	Russian / Polish	Mountains
Goulet	French	Narrow entrance
Grabean	German	Ditch, trench
-grad	Bulgarian, Russian, Serbo-Croat	Town, castle
Grand, Grands	French	Big
Grat	German	Crest, ridge
Greben'	Russian	Ridge
-gród	Polish	Town, castle
Groot	Afrikaans	Big
Groß, -e, -en, -er	German	Big
Grotta / Grotte	Italian / French	Cave, grotto
Grund	German	Ground, valley
Gryada	Russian	Ridge
Guan	Chinese	Pass
Guba	Russian	Bay
Guelta	Arabic	Well
-gunto	Japanese	Island group
Gunung	Indonesian, Malay	Mountain
Hadabat	Arabic	Plain
Hadh, Hadhat	Arabic	Sand dunes
-haehyop	Korean	Strait
Hafar	Arabic	Wells
Hafen	German	Harbour, port
Haff	German	Bay
Hai	Chinese	Sea
Halbinsel	German	Peninsula
-halvøya	Norwegian	Peninsula
Hamad-a, -et	Arabic	Plateau
Hammad-ah, -at	Arabic	Plain, rocky plat.
-hamn	Norwegian, Swedish	Harbour
Hamun	Persian	Marsh
-hanto	Japanese	Peninsula
Hardt	German	Wooded hills
Harrat	Arabic	Lava fields
Hassi / Hasy	Arabic	Well
-haug	Norwegian	Hill
Haut, -e	French	Upper
Hawr	Arabic	Lake
-havn	Danish, Norwegian	Harbour
Hazm	Arabic	Plateau
He	Chinese	River
-hede	Danish, Norwegian	Heath
-hegység	Hungarian	Mountains
-hei / Heide	Norwegian / German	Heath, moor
Hersónisos	Greek	Peninsula
Higashi-	Japanese	East, eastern
-hisar	Turkish	Castle
Hisn	Arabic	Fort
-hø	Norwegian	Peak
Hoch / Hoë	German / Afrikaans	High
Hoek	Flemish	Cape, point
Hög / -høg(d)	Swedish / Norwegian	High, height
Höhe, Hohen-	German	Height
Hoog	Flemish	High

APPENDICES

10: INTERNATIONAL GLOSSARY

Continued from previous page

Term	Language	Meaning
-høj	Danish	Hill
Hora / Hory	Czech	Mountain / Mtns.
Horn	German	Peak, summit
Horní	Czech	Upper
Hot	Mongolian	Town
-høy	Norwegian	Height
-hrad	Czech	Castle
Hu	Chinese	Lake
Hügel	German	Hill

I

Term	Language	Meaning
Idd	Arabic	Well
Idhan	Arabic	Sand dunes
'Idwet	Arabic	Mountain
Île(s) / Ilha(s)	French / Portuguese	Island(s)
Illa, Illes	Catalan	Island, islands
im, in	German	In
Inférieur, -e	French	Lower
Insel(n)	German	Island(s)
Irmak	Turkish	Large river
'Irq	Arabic	Sand dunes
Isla(s) / Isle	Spanish / French	Island(s)
Islote	Spanish	Small island
Iso	Finnish	Big
Ísola, Isole	Italian	Island, islands
Istmo	Spanish	Isthmus

J

Term	Language	Meaning
Jabal	Arabic	Mountain
-järvi	Finnish	Lake
-jaure, -javrre	Lappish	Lake
Jazirat / Jaza'ir	Arabic	Island / Islands
Jbel, Jebel	Arabic	Mountain
Jezero / Jezioro	Serbo-Croat / Polish	Lake
Jiang	Chinese	River
Jiao	Chinese	Point, reef
Jibal	Arabic	Mountains
-jima	Japanese	Island
-joki / -jokka	Finnish / Lappish	River
-jøkulen	Norwegian	Glacier
-jökull	Icelandic	Glacier
Jun	Arabic	Bay

K

Term	Language	Meaning
Kaap	Afrikaans	Cape
-kai	Japanese	Sea, bay, inlet
Kali	Indonesian	River
Kamm	German	Crest, ridge
Kampung	Indonesian, Malay	Village
Kanaal / Kanal	Flemish / German, Russian	Canal
-kapp	Norwegian	Cape
Karif	Arabic	Well
Kathib	Arabic	Sand dunes
Káto	Greek	Lower
-kawa	Japanese	River
Kecil	Indonesian, Malay	Small
Kepulauan	Indonesian	Archipelago
Kereb	Arabic	Hill, ridge
Keski-	Finnish	Central, middle
Khalīg, Khalij	Arabic	Bay, gulf
Khao	Thai	Peak
Khashm	Arabic	Mountain
Khawr, Khor / Khowr	Arabic / Persian	Inlet
Khrebet	Russian	Mountain range
Kis-	Hungarian	Small
Kita-	Japanese	North, northern
Klamm	German	Ravine
Klein	Afrikaans, German	Small
Klint / Klit	Danish	Cliff / Dunes
Klong	Thai	Canal, creek
Kloof	Afrikaans	Gorge
Ko / Koh	Thai / Cambodian	Island
-ko	Japanese	Lake, inlet
Kólpos	Greek	Gulf
Koog	German	Polder
Kop / Kopf	Afrikaans / German	Hill
Körfezi	Turkish	Bay, gulf
Kotlina	Czech, Polish	Basin, depression
Kotlovina	Russian	Depression
-köy	Turkish	Village
Kraj	Czech, Polish, Serbo-Croat	Region
Kray	Russian	Region
Kreis	German	District
Kryazh	Russian	Ridge
Kuala	Malay	Estuary
Küçük	Turkish	Small
Kuduk	Russian	Spring, well
Kuh	Persian	Mountain
Kul'	Russian	Lake
Kület	Arabic	Hill
Kum	Russian	Sandy desert
-kundo	Korean	Island group
-kylä	Finnish	Village

L

Term	Language	Meaning
Lac	French	Lake
Laem	Thai	Point
Lago	Italian, Portug., Spanish	Lake
Lagoa	Portuguese	Lagoon
Laguna	Spanish	Lagoon, lake
Lam	Thai	Stream
Län	Swedish	Province
Land	German	Province, area
Lande	French	Heath, sandy moor
Las / Les	Polish / Czech, Russian	Forest, wood
Laut	Indonesia	Sea
Lednik	Russian	Glacier
lès, lez	French	Beside, near
Liedao	Chinese	Island group
Lille	Danish, Norwegian	Small
Liman	Russian	Bay, gulf
Liman, Limani	Turkish	Harbour, port
Límni	Greek	Lake, lagoon
Ling	Chinese	Mountain range
Llano	Spanish	Plain, prairie
Loma	Spanish	Hill
-luoto	Finnish	Rocky island
-lyng	Danish	Heath

M

Term	Language	Meaning
Macizo	Spanish	Massif
Madinat	Arabic	City, town
Mae Nam	Thai	River
Mala / Malé	Serbo-Croat / Czech	Small
Malaya, -oye, -yy	Russian	Small
-man	Korean	Bay
Manâqir	Arabic	Hills
Mar	Portuguese, Spanish	Sea
Marais	French	Marsh, swamp
Mare	Italian / Romanian	Sea / Big
Marsá	Arabic	Anchorage, inlet
Marsch	German	Fen, marsh
Masabb	Arabic	Estuary
Mashâsh	Arabic	Well
Massif	French	Mountains, upland
Mayor	Spanish	Higher, larger
Meer	Afrikaans, Flemish, German	Lake, sea
Méga, Megál-a, -i, -o	Greek	Big
Menor	Portuguese, Spanish	Lesser, smaller
Mer	French	Sea
Mersa	Arabic	Anchorage, inlet
Mesa, Meseta	Spanish	Tableland
Mesto	Czech, Serbo-Croat	Town
Mezzo	Italian	Middle, mid-
Miasto	Polish	Town
Mic / Mikr-i, ön	Romanian / Greek	Small
Mina'	Arabic	Harbour, port
Minami-	Japanese	South, southern
Minqār	Arabic	Hill
-misaki	Japanese	Cape, point
Mishāsh / Mushāsh	Arabic	Well
Miti	Greek	Cape
Mittel-, Mitten-	German	Central, middle
Mjesto	Serbo-Croat	Town
Monasterio / Moni	Spanish / Greek	Monastery
Mont / Monte	French / Italian, Portuguese, Spanish	Mountain
Montagne(s)	French	Mountain(s)
Monti	Italian	Mountains
Moor	German	Bog, moor, swamp
Moos	German	Bog, moss
More	Russian	Sea
Mörön	Mongolian	River
Morro	Portuguese	Hill, mountain
-mose	Danish	Bog, moor
Moyen, -ne	French	Middle, mid-
Muara	Indonesian	Estuary
Mudiriyat	Arabic	Province
Muntii	Romanian	Mountains
-myr	Norwegian, Swedish	Moor, swamp
Mys	Russian	Cape

N

Term	Language	Meaning
na	Bulgarian, Russian, Serbo-Croat	On
nad	Czech, Polish, Russian	Above, over
-nada	Japanese	Gulf, sea
Nádrž	Czech	Reservoir
-naes	Danish	Cape, point
Nafud	Arabic	Desert, dune
Nagor'ye	Russian	Highland, uplands
Nagy-	Hungarian	Big, great
Nahr	Arabic	River
Nakhon	Thai	Town
Nam	Korean, Vietnamese	South, southern
Nam	Burmese, Thai, Vietnamese	River
Nan	Chinese	South, southern
Naqb	Arabic	Pass
Nasb	Arabic	Hill, mountain
Né-a, -on, -os	Greek	New
Neder-	Flemish	Lower
Nehri	Turkish	River
Nei	Chinese	Inner
-nes	Icelandic, Norwegian	Cape, point
Neu- / Neuf, Neuve	German / French	New
Nevado	Spanish	Peak
-ni	Korean	Village
Nieder-	German	Lower
Nieu	Afrikaans	New
Nieuw, -e, -en, -er	Flemish	New
Nishi	Japanese	West, western
-nisi	Greek	Island
Nizhn-eye, -iy, -iye, -yaya	Russian	Lower
Nízina / Nizni	Czech	Lowland / Lower
Nizmennost'	Russian	Lowland
Noord-	Flemish	North, northern
Nord	Danish, French, German	North, northern
Nordre, Nørre	Danish	Northern
Norra	Swedish	Northern
Norte	Portuguese, Spanish	North
Nos	Bulgarian, Russian	Point, spit
Nótios	Greek	Southern
Nou	Romanian	New
Nouv-eau, -elle	French	New
Nova	Italian	New
Nova, Novi	Bulgarian, Serbo-Croat	New
Nova, Novo	Portuguese	New
Nová, Nové, Nový	Czech	New
Nov-aya, -o, -oye, -yy, -yye	Russian	New
Nowa, Nowe, Nowy	Polish	New
Nudo	Spanish	Mountain
Nueva, Nuevo	Spanish	New
Nuruu	Mongolian	Mountains
Nusa	Indonesian	Island
Nuur	Mongolian	Lake
Ny-	Danish, Norweg., Swedish	New

O

Term	Language	Meaning
-ö, -ön / -ø	Swedish / Danish	Island
-oaivi, -oaivve	Lappish	Hill, mountain
Ober-	German	Upper
Oblast'	Russian	Province
Occidental	Spanish	Western
-odde	Danish, Norwegian	Cape, point
Ogla, Oglet	Arabic	Well
Okrug	Russian	District
Ömnö-	Mongolian	South, southern
Onder	Flemish	Lower
Öndör-	Mongolian	Upper
-oog	German	Island
Oost, -er, -elijk	Flemish	East, eastern
Orasu	Romanian	Town
Oriental, -e	French, Romanian, Spanish	Eastern
Ormani	Turkish	Forest
Órmos	Greek	Bay
Óros / Óri	Greek	Mountain / Mtns.
Ost- / Øster-	German / Danish, Norweg.	East, eastern
Ostan	Persian	Province
Östra-	Swedish	East, eastern
Ostrov(a)	Russian	Island(s)
Otok / Otoci	Serbo-Croat	Island / Islands
Oud, -e, -en, -er	Flemish	Old
Oued	Arabic	Dry river-bed
Ovasi	Turkish	Plain
Over-	Danish, Flemish	Upper
Över-, Övre-	Norwegian, Swedish	Upper
-øy, -a	Norwegian	Island
Ozero, Ozera	Russian	Lake, lakes

P

Term	Language	Meaning
-pää	Finnish	Hill
Palai-á, -ó, Palió	Greek	Old
Parbat	Urdu	Mountain
Parc	French	Park
Pas	French	Low pass, strait
Paso	Spanish	Pass, strait
Pass / Passo	Spanish / Italian	Pass
Pays	French	Region
Pegunungan	Indonesian	Mountain range
Peña(s)	Spanish	Cliff(s), rocks(s)
Pendi	Chinese	Basin
Penisola	Italian	Peninsula
Peñon	Spanish	Cliff
Pereval	Russian	Pass
Perv-o, -yy	Russian	First
Peski	Russian	Sands, desert
Petit, -e, -es	French	Little
Pic	French, Spanish	Peak, summit
Pico / Picacho	Portuguese, Spanish	Peak, summit
Pik	Russian	Peak, summit
Pingyuan	Chinese	Plain
Pizzo	Italian	Peak, summit
-plaat	Dutch	Sandbank, shoal
Plage	French	Beach
Plaine / Planicie	French / Spanish	Plain
Plaj(i)	Turkish	Beach(es)
Planalto	Portuguese	Plateau
Planina	Bulgarian, Serbo-Croat	Mountains
Platja / Playa	Catalan / Spanish	Beach
Plato	Afrikaans, Bulg., Russian	Plateau
Platte	German	Plateau, plain
Plosina	Czech	Tableland
Ploskogor'ye	Russian	Plateau
pod	Czech, Russian	Under
Pohor-i, -ie	Czech	Mountain range
Pointe	French	Cape, point
Poluostrov	Russian	Peninsula
Pólwysep	Polish	Peninsula
Pongo	Spanish	Water gap
Ponta, Pontal	Portuguese	Point
Portile	Romanian	Gate
Portillo	Spanish	Gap, pass
Porto	Catalan, Italian, Portug.	Harbour, port
Pradesh	Hindi	State
Praia	Portuguese	Beach, shore
près	French	Near
Presqu'île	French	Peninsula
Pri-	Russian	Near
Proliv	Russian	Strait
Protoka	Russian	Channel
Prusmyk	Czech	Pass
Przelecz	Polish	Pass
Pubu	Chinese	Waterfall
Pueblo	Spanish	Village
Puente	Spanish	Bridge
Puerta	Spanish	Narrow pass
Puerto	Spanish	Harbour, port
Puk-	Korean	North, northern
Pulau	Indonesian, Malay	Island
Puna	Spanish	Desert plateau
Punta	Catalan, Italian, Spanish	Cape, point
Puntjak	Indonesian	Mountain
Puy	French	Peak

Q

Term	Language	Meaning
Qa	Arabic	Depression
Qalamat, Qalib	Arabic	Well
Qanat	Arabic, Persian	U'ground conduit
Qararat	Arabic	Depression
Qāret	Arabic	Hill
Qiao	Chinese	Bridge
Qiuling	Chinese	Hills
Qoz	Arabic	Hill
Qu	Tibetan	Stream
Quan	Chinese	Spring
Quedas	Portuguese	Rapids
Qulban	Arabic	Wells
Qum	Persian	Sand
Qundao	Chinese	Archipelago
Qūr, Qurayyat	Arabic	Hills
Qurnat	Arabic	Peak
Quwayrat / Qurūn	Arabic	Hill / Hills

R

Term	Language	Meaning
Ramlat	Arabic	Sands
Râs / Ra's	Arabic / Arabic, Persian	Cape, point
Raso	Portuguese	Upland
Ravnina / Razlivy	Russian	Plain
Região	Portuguese	Region
Reprêsa	Portuguese	Dam
Reshteh	Persian	Mountain range
-retto	Japanese	Island chain
-rev	Norwegian	Cliff, reef
Ri	Tibetan	Mountain
-ri	Korean	Village
Ria / Ria	Portuguese / Spanish	River-mouth
Ribeirão	Portuguese	River
Ribeiro	Portuguese	Stream
Rio / Río	Portuguese / Spanish	River
Rivier / Rivière	Afrikaans / French	River
Rocher	French	Cliff, rock
Rocque	French	Rock
Rt	Serbo-Croat	Cape, point
Rücken	German	Ridge
Rud / Rudkhaneh	Persian	River
Rudohorie	Czech	Mountains

S

Term	Language	Meaning
-saari	Finnish	Island
Sabkhat	Arabic	Salt-flat
Sagar, Sagara	Hindi	Lake
Sahl	Arabic	Plain
Sahra	Arabic	Desert
-saki	Japanese	Cape, point
Salada / Salar, Salina	Spanish	Salt lake / Salt pan
Salto	Portuguese, Spanish	Waterfall
-san	Japanese, Korean	Mountain
-sanchi	Japanese	Mountainous area
Saniyat	Arabic	Well
Sanmaek	Korean	Mountain range
-sanmyaku	Japanese	Mountain range
San	Italian, Portug., Spanish	Saint
Sankt / Sant	German / Catalan	Saint
Santa, Santo	Italian, Portug., Spanish	Saint
São	Portuguese	Saint
Satu	Romanian	Village
Schloß	German	Castle, mansion
Schutzgebeit	German	Reserve
Sebkra	Arabic	Salt-flat
See	German	Lake
-sehir	Turkish	Town
Selat	Indonesian	Channel, strait
Selatan	Indonesian, Malay	South, southern
-selkä	Finnish	Open water, ridge
Selo	Russian, Serbo-Croat	Village
Selva	Spanish	Forest, wood
-sen	Japanese	Mountain
Serra / Serrania	Catalan, Portug. / Span.	Mountain range
-seto	Japanese	Channel, strait
Sever-naya, -noye, -nyy, -o	Russian	North, northern
Sfintu	Romanian	Saint
Shahr	Persian	Town
Sha'ib, -an	Arabic	Watercourse
Shamo	Chinese	Desert
Shan	Chinese	Mountain(s)
Shandi	Chinese	Mountainous area
Shang	Chinese	Upper
Shankou	Chinese	Pass
Shanmai	Chinese	Mountain range
Sharm	Arabic	Cove, inlet
Shatt	Arabic	River, river-mouth
-shima / -shoto	Japanese	Island / Island group
Shuiku	Chinese	Reservoir
Sierra	Spanish	Mountain range
Silsilesi	Turkish	Mountain range
Sint	Afrikaans, Flemish	Saint
-sjø / sjön	Norwegian / Swedish	Lake
Skala, Skaly	Czech	Cliff, rock
-skog	Norwegian	Woods
-slette	Norwegian	Plain
Sliabh, Slieve	Gaelic	Mountain, upland
Sloboda	Russian	Suburb, large village
Sø	Danish, Norwegian	Lake
Söder-, Södra	Swedish	Southern
Solonchak	Russian	Salt lake
Sommet	French	Peak, summit
Sønder-	Danish	Southern
Søndre	Danish, Norwegian	Southern
Sopka	Russian	Hill
Sør	Norwegian	Southern
sous	French	Under
Spitze	German	Peak
Sredn-a, -i	Bulgarian	Central, middle
Sredn-e, -eye, -iy, -yaya	Russian	Central, middle
-stad	Afrikaans, Norwegian, Swedish	Town
-stadt	German	Town
Stara, Stari	Serbo-Croat	Old
Stará, Staré	Czech	Old
Star-aya, oye, -yy, -yye	Russian	Old
Stausee	German	Reservoir
Stenó	Greek	Pass, strait
Step'	Russian	Steppe
Stít	Czech	Peak
Stor-, Stora / Store	Swedish / Danish	Big
Strand	Gaelic, German	Beach
-strand	Danish, Norweg., Swedish	Beach
Straße	German	Road
-strede	Norwegian	Passage, strait
Strelka	Russian	Spit
Stretto	Italian	Strait
Sud	French	South
Süd(er)	German	South (southern)
Suhul	Arabic	Plain
Suid	Afrikaans	South
-suido	Japanese	Channel, strait
Sul	Portuguese	South
sul, sull'	Italian	On
Sund	Swedish	Sound, strait
Sungai	Indonesian, Malay	River
-suo	Finnish	Marsh, swamp
Supérieur / Superior	French / Spanish	Upper
Sur	Spanish	South
sur	French	On
Sveti	Serbo-Croat	Saint
Szent-	Hungarian	Saint

T

Term	Language	Meaning
-take	Japanese	Peak
Tal	German	Valley
Tall(āt)	Arabic	Hill(s)
Tang	Persian	Pass, strait
Tanjung	Indonesian, Malay	Cape, point
Taraq	Arabic	Hills
Tasek	Malay	Lake
Tau	Russian	Mountain(s)
Tekojärvi	Finnish	Reservoir
Tell	Arabic	Hill
Teluk	Indonesian	Bay
Tengah	Indonesian	Middle
Teniet	Arabic	Pass
Tepe, Tepesi	Turkish	Hill, peak
Tepeler, Tepeleri	Turkish	Hills, peaks
Terre / Tierra	French / Spanish	Land
Thale	Thai	Lake
Tilat	Arabic	Hill
Timur	Indonesian	East, eastern
-tind, -tinderne	Norwegain	Peak, peaks
Tir'at	Arabic	Canal
-tji	Indonesian	Stream
-to	Japanese	Island
-toge	Japanese	Pass
-tong	Korean	Village
Tonle	Cambodian	Lake
-topp	Norwegian	Peak
Torrente	Spanish	Rapids
Travesia	Spanish	Desert
Tulul	Arabic	Hills
Túnel	Spanish	Tunnel

U

Term	Language	Meaning
über	German	Above
-udden	Swedish	Cape, point
Új-	Hungarian	New
Ujung	Indonesian	Cape, point
-umi	Japanese	Inlet
Unter-	German	Lower
'Uqlat	Arabic	Well
-ura	Japanese	Inlet
'Urayq	Arabic	Sand ridge
'Uruq	Arabic	Area of dunes
Ust'ye	Russian	Estuary
Utara	Indonesian	North, northern
Uttar	Hindi	Northern
Uul	Mongolian	Mountains
Uval	Russian	Hill
'Uyun	Arabic	Springs

V

Term	Language	Meaning
-vaara(t)	Finnish	Hill(s)
-vaart	Flemish	Canal
-våg	Norwegian	Bay
Val, Vall	Italian, Spanish	Valley
Vale	Portuguese, Romanian	Valley
Valle / Vallée	Italian, Spanish / French	Valley
Vallon	French	Small valley
-vann	Norwegian	Lake
-város	Hungarian	Town
-varre	Norwegian	Mountain
Väster, Västra	Swedish	Western
-vatn	Icelandic, Norwegian	Lake
-vatnet	Norwegian	Lake
-vatten, vattnet	Swedish	Lake
Vaux	French	Valleys
Vecchio	Italian	Old
Vechi	Romanian	Old
Velha, Velho	Portuguese	Old
Velik-a, -i	Serbo-Croat	Big
Velik-aya, -iy, -iye	Russian	Big
Vel'k-á, -é, -ý	Czech	Big
Verkhn-e, -eye, -iy, -yaya	Russian	Upper
-vesi	Finnish	Lake, water
Vester	Danish	Western
Vest, Vestre	Norwegian	West, western
-vidda	Norwegian	Plateau
Vieja, Viejo / Vieux	Spanish / French	Old
Vig / -vik	Danish / Norwegian	Bay
Vila	Portuguese	Small town
Ville	French	Town
Víztároló	Hungarian	Reservoir
Vodokhranilishche	Russian	Reservoir
Volcán	Spanish	Volcano
Vorota	Russian	Channel, strait
Vostochn-aya, -oye, -yy	Russian	Eastern
Vozvyshennost'	Russian	Uplands
Vpadina	Russian	Depression
Vrch(y)	Czech	Mountain(s)
Vrchovina	Czech	Mountainous area
Vysocina	Czech	Upland
Vysok-aya, -oye	Russian	Upper

W

Term	Language	Meaning
Wad	Flemish	Sand-flat
Wādi, Wadi	Arabic	Watercourse
Wahat	Arabic	Oasis
Wai	Chinese	Outer
Wald	German	Forest
Wan / -wan	Chinese / Japanese	Bay
Wand	German	Cliff
Wasser	German	Lake, water
Wes-	Afrikaans	West
West, Wester	Flemish, German	West
Wielk-a, -i, -ie, -o	Polish	Big
Wysok-a, -i, -ie	Polish	Upper

X

Term	Language	Meaning
Xi	Chinese	Stream, west
Xia	Chinese	Gorge, lower
Xian	Chinese	County
Xiao	Chinese	Small
Xu	Chinese	Islet

Y

Term	Language	Meaning
-yama	Japanese	Mountain(s)
Yang	Chinese	Ocean
Yarimadasi	Turkish	Peninsula
Yeni	Turkish	New
Yli-	Finnish	Upper
Ytre-	Norwegian	Outer
Ytter-	Norwegian, Swedish	Outer
Yuan	Chinese	Spring
Yugo-	Russian	Southern
Yunhe	Chinese	Canal
Yuzhn-aya, -o, -oye, -yy	Russian	South, southern

Z

Term	Language	Meaning
-zaki	Japanese	Cape, point
Zalew	Polish	Bay, inlet, lagoon
Zaliv	Russian	Bay
-zan	Japanese	Mountain
Zapadn-aya, -o, -oye, -yy	Russian	West, western
Zatoka	Polish	Gulf
-zee	Flemish	Sea
Zemlya	Russian	Land
-zhen	Chinese	Town
Zhong	Chinese	Middle
Zhou	Chinese	Islet
Zui	Chinese	Point, spit
Zuid	Flemish	South
Zuid-elijk, er	Flemish	Southern

INDEX

A - Alexandria

COMPREHENSIVE INDEX TO THE COMPLETE ATLAS

This index lists all locations and features which appear throughout this atlas, with the exception of the following special-subject map pages:

- World climate
- World time
- World health
- World income
- World sport
- World driving
- World airports*
- World flight times
- Europe climate
- Europe rail and ferries
- UK airports*
- Africa climate
- Asia climate
- North America climate
- US and Canada rail and air*
- South America climate
- The transport maps between pages 137 and 168

Maps marked * include a list of locations on the page itself

GENERAL ABBREVIATIONS

(for Australian, Canadian and US state/province abbreviations, see previous page)

Arch.	Archaeological
Hist.	Historic/Historical
I.	Island, Ile and equivalents
Int.	International
Is.	Islands, Iles and equivalents
Mem.	Memorial
Mon.	Monument
Mt	Mount/Mont
Mtn	Mountain/Montagne
Mtns	Mountains/Monts
Nac.	Nacional
Nat.	National
Naz.	Nazionale
Prov.	Provincial
St	Saint/Sankt/Sint

(All 'St' entries are treated as if spelt 'Saint' and are located in the index accordingly)

Ste	Sainte
Vdkhr.	Vodokhranilishche

Hyphens have been removed in certain cases for consistency and ease of viewing. The correct form appears on the map pages.

The following names, which appear in bold, indicate the entry is featured in one of the special subject maps:

Beach	Beach map
Park	National Park or leisure park map
Ski	Ski map
Spa	Spa map
Heritage C	UNESCO cultural heritage map
Heritage N	UNESCO natural heritage map

The following abbreviations appear occasionally, particularly to distinguish features with the same name:

[Adm]	Administrative region
[Apt]	Airport
[Riv]	River

A

A • Norway **16** G3
A Coruña • Spain **11** C1
A Coruña **Beach** • Spain **68** [92]
A la Ronde House • United Kingdom **74** F5
A Pobra do Caramiñal **Beach** • Spain **68** [92]
A'ali an Nil • Sudan **23** E2
A'nyêmaqên Shan • China **29** B4
Aachen **Heritage C** • Germany **64** [37]
Aachen • Germany **82** G1
Aachen **Spa** • Germany **83** [118]
Aaiún, El • Western Sahara **20** C3
Aalborg **Beach** • Denmark **68** [48]
Aalborg • Denmark **95** F5
Aalborg Bugt • Denmark **95** F6
Aalen • Germany **9** F8
Aalsmeer • Netherlands **80** C2
Aalst • Belgium **80** A14
Äänekoski • Finland **95** E2
Aarau • Switzerland **9** D9
Aare • Switzerland **89** G2
Aargub, El • Western Sahara **20** B4
Aarschot • Belgium **80** A15
Aazanèn • Morocco **11** H9
Aba • Nigeria **22** F3
Aba • Dem. Rep. of Congo **23** E3
Abadan • Iran **18** E3
Abadeh • Iran **18** F3
Abadia, El • Algeria **11** M8
Abaetetuba • Brazil **45** (1) B2
Abagnar Qi • China **29** F2
Abakan • Russian Fed. **26** P7
Abakan [Riv] • Russian Fed. **26** P7
Abala • Niger **20** F6
Abalak • Niger **20** G5
Abancay • Peru **127** B2
Abano • Italy **91** E7
Abashiri • Japan **30** M2
Abasolo • Mexico **123** E1
Abau • Papua New Guinea **35** (1) D3
Abay • Ethiopia **21** G5
Abay • Kazakhstan **26** L8
Abaya, Lake • Ethiopia **23** F2
Abbeville • France **10** G3
Abbeville • LA, United States **118** K3
Abbeyfeale • Ireland **79** F6
Abbot, Mt • QL, Australia **34** I4
Abbotsbury • United Kingdom **74** F6
Abbotsinch [Apt] • United Kingdom **74** B3
Abd al Kuri • Yemen **18** F7
Abdul Ghadir • Somalia **23** G1
Abdulino • Russian Fed. **17** I4
Abe, Lake • Ethiopia **21** H5
Abéché • Chad **21** D5
Abengourou • Côte d'Ivoire **22** D3
Abenrå **Beach** • Denmark **68** [45]
Abenrå • Denmark **95** F13
Abensberg • Germany **9** G8
Abeokuta • Nigeria **22** E3
Aberaeron • United Kingdom **7** H9
Aberaeron **Beach** • United Kingdom **75** [179]
Aberdare Nat. Park • Kenya **101** G3
Aberdare Nat. Park **Park** • Kenya **103** [80]
Aberdare Range • Kenya **23** F4
Aberdaron **Beach** • United Kingdom **75** [195]
Aberdeen • United Kingdom **6** J4
Aberdeen • SD, United States **41** G2
Aberdeen • South Africa **100** C3
Aberdeen • Hong Kong, China **107** H5
Aberdeen • WA, United States **117** E1
Aberdeen Lake • NU, Canada **38** L4
Aberdeenshire • United Kingdom **75** A1
Aberdour • United Kingdom **74** B4
Aberdour **Beach** • United Kingdom **75** [6]
Aberdovey **Beach** • United Kingdom **75** [185]
Aberdyfi **Beach** • United Kingdom **75** [185]
Abereiddy **Beach** • United Kingdom **75** [166]
Aberfeldy • United Kingdom **74** B1
Aberffraw **Beach** • United Kingdom **75** [206]
Aberfoyle • United Kingdom **74** B1
Abergavenny • United Kingdom **74** D3
Abergele **Beach** • United Kingdom **75** [201]
Aberporth **Beach** • United Kingdom **75** [171]
Abers, Côte des • France **84** C1
Abersoch **Beach** • United Kingdom **75** [194]
Abert, Lake • OR, United States **117** E3
Aberystwyth • United Kingdom **7** H9
Aberystwyth **Beach** • United Kingdom **75** [181-182]
Abez • Russian Fed. **26** J4
Abha • Saudi Arabia **18** D6
Abidjan • Côte d'Ivoire **22** D3
Abilene • TX, United States **40** G5
Abingdon • United Kingdom **74** D4
Abisko • Sweden **16** J2
Abisko Nat. Park **Park** • Sweden **72** [17]
Abitibi • OT, Canada **39** O6
Abo • Finland **95** E3
Abo, Massif d' • Chad **21** C3
Abomey • Benin **22** E3
Abomey **Heritage C** • Benin **63** [98]
Abondance **Ski** • France **70** [8]
Abong Mbang • Cameroon **22** G4
Abony • Hungary **13** I10
Aborigen, pik • Russian Fed. **27** O4
Abraham's Bay • Bahamas **124** B4
Abrántes • Portugal **11** C5
Abri • Sudan **21** F3
Abrolhos, Arquipelago dos • Brazil **45** (1) D5
Abruzzo • Italy **12** H6
Abruzzo, Parco Naz. d' **Park** • Italy **72** [86]
Abruzzo, Parco Naz. d' • Italy **91** F4
Absaroka Range • MT/WY, United States **38** I7
Abu Dhabi • United Arab Emirates **18** F5
Abu Hamad • Sudan **21** F4
Abu Hills • India **105** C5
Abu Libdah, Khashm • Saudi Arabia **21** I3
Abu Madd, Ra's • Saudi Arabia **18** C5
Abu Matariq • Sudan **23** D1
Abu Mena **Heritage C** • Egypt **64** [236]
Abu Mena • Egypt **101** F1
Abu Road • India **105** C5
Abu Shajarah, Ra's • Sudan **21** G3
Abu Simbel **Heritage C** • Egypt **63** [83]
Abu Simbel • Egypt **101** F5
Abuja • Nigeria **22** F3
Abuko Nature Reserve **Park** • Gambia **103** [11]
Abut Head • New Zealand **35** C6
Abuyemeda • Ethiopia **23** F1
Aby • Ostergötland, Sweden **95** D3
Aby • Kalmar, Sweden **95** F8
Abyad, Ar Ra's al • Saudi Arabia **18** C5
Abyar ash Shuwayrif • Libya **21** B2
Abybro • Denmark **95** F5
Abydos • Egypt **101** F4
Açaba, El • Mauritania **20** C5
Acadia Nat. Park • ME, United States **118** G4
Acadia Nat. Park **Park** • ME, United States **121** [354]
Acámbaro • Mexico **37** (1) B1
Acaponeta • Mexico **37** (1) A1
Acapulco • Mexico **123** E4
Acará • Brazil **43** H4
Acarai, Serra • Brazil **43** F3
Acaraú • Brazil **45** (1) C2
Acarigua • Venezuela **43** D2
Accra • Ghana **22** D3
Accra area **Heritage C** • Ghana **63** [97]
Aceh • Indonesia **110** B1
Acerenza • Italy **71** A19
Achacachi • Bolivia **127** B4
Achaguas • Venezuela **43** D2
Achegour • Niger **20** H5
Achern • Germany **9** D8
Achill **Beach** • Ireland **68** [63]
Achill Head • Ireland **79** F1
Achill I. • Ireland **79** F1
Achim • Germany **8** E3
Achinsk • Russian Fed. **26** P6
Achonry • Ireland **79** F2
Aci Gölü • Turkey **93** G1
Aci Trezza • Sicily, Italy **90** D4
Acireale • Sicily, Italy **90** D4
Acklins I. • Bahamas **124** B4
Acoma Pueblo • NM, United States **118** J2
Aconcagua, Cerro • Argentina/Chile **44** C5
Açores • Atlantic Ocean **20** (1) B2
Acquasanta • Italy **91** E12
Acquasparta • Italy **91** F1
Acqui Terme • Italy **91** E6
Acraman, Lake • SA, Australia **34** G6
Acre • Brazil **43** C5
Acre • Israel **98** A1
Acre [Riv] • Bolivia/Brazil **43** D6
Acropolis • Rhodes, Greece **93** F4
Acroverde • Brazil **45** (1) D3
Actaeon Group • French Polynesia **33** N8
Action Planet **Park** • Belgium **73** [48]
Ada • OK, United States **41** G5
Adair, Cape • NU, Canada **39** Q2
Adak • AK, United States **36** (1) C2
Adale • Somalia **23** H3
Adam, Mt • Falkland Is. **45** D6
Adam's Bridge • India/Sri Lanka **106** D11
Adam's Peak • Sri Lanka **106** D15
Adamandás **Beach** • Greece **69** [207]
Adamaoua • Cameroon **22** G3
Adámas • Greece **92** D7
Adams, Grantley [Apt] • Barbados **125** H4
Adams, Mt • WA, United States **38** G7
Adams Nat. Hist. Site **Park** • MA, United States **121** [343]
Adamstown • Pitcairn Is. **33** O8
Adan • Yemen **18** E7
Adana • Turkey **18** B2
Adapazari • Turkey **15** L3
Adarama • Sudan **18** B6
Adare • Ireland **79** F6
Adare, Cape • Antarctica **59** A10
Adavale • QL, Australia **34** H5
Adda • Italy **91** E2
Addis Ababa • Ethiopia **23** F2
Addis Zemen • Ethiopia **23** F1
Addo Elephant Nat. Park • South Africa **100** C8
Addo Elephant Nat. Park **Park** • South Africa **103** [121]
Addu Atoll • Maldives **106** E3
Adeje **Beach** • Tenerife, Canary Is. **68** [109]
Adeje • Tenerife, Canary Is. **86** E1
Adelaide • SA, Australia **34** G6
Adelaide • Bahamas **124** B3
Adelaide I. • Antarctica **59** A10
Adelaide Peninsula • NU, Canada **38** L3
Adelaide [Riv] • NT, Australia **34** F2
Adelaide River • NT, Australia **34** F2
Adelboden **Ski** • Switzerland **70** [88]
Adelboden • Switzerland **89** G6
Adéle **Beach** • Crete, Greece **69** [213]
Adéle • Crete, Greece **93** E2
Ademuz • Spain **11** J4
Aden • Yemen **18** E7
Aden, Gulf of • Africa/Asia **19** I4
Adenau • Germany **82** H1
Aderbissinat • Niger **20** G5
Adi • Indonesia **32** (1) D3
Adige • Italy **91** E7
Adigrat • Eritrea **21** G5
Adilabad • India **28** C5
Adiri • Libya **21** B2
Adirondack Mtns • NY, United States **41** L3
Adjuntas • Puerto Rico **125** E3
Admiralty I. • AK, United States **38** E5
Admiralty Inlet • NU, Canada **39** N2
Admiralty Is. • Papua New Guinea **35** (1) D1
Adok • Sudan **23** E2
Adoni • India **106** D2
Adour • France **85** J2
Adra **Beach** • Spain **68** [116]
Adra • Spain **86** B8
Adrano • Sicily, Italy **12** I11
Adrar • Algeria **20** E3
Adrar Bou Nasser • Morocco **101** D2
Adrar des Iforas • Mali **20** F5
Adriana, Villa • Italy **91** F1
Adrianople • Turkey **71** A15
Adriatic Coast • Croatia **96** B2
Adriatic Riviera • Italy **91** E12
Adriatic Sea • Europe **12** I5
Adula • Switzerland **12** D2
Adulis • Eritrea **21** G4
Adwa • Ethiopia **21** G5
Adygalakh • Russian Fed. **27** O4
Adygeya • Russian Fed. **17** G6
Adzopé • Côte d'Ivoire **22** D3
Aegean Coast • Turkey **92** A2
Aegean Sea • Greece/Turkey **92** D
Ærø • Denmark **95** F14
Æroskōbing • Denmark **95** F14
Afafi, Massif d' • Chad **21** C3
Afándou **Beach** • Rhodes, Greece **69** [211]
Afándou • Rhodes, Greece **93** F2
Afek • Israel **98** A5
Afétes **Beach** • Greece **69** [188]
Affollé • Mauritania **20** C5
Affroun • Algeria **11** N8
Afghanistan • Asia **18** I3
Afif • Saudi Arabia **18** D5
Afikpo • Nigeria **22** F3
Afiq • Syria **98** A4
Afitos • Greece **92** D1
Aflou • Algeria **20** F2
Afmadow • Somalia **23** G3
Afonso Cláudio • Brazil **127** C2
Afore • Papua New Guinea **34** I1
Afragola • Italy **12** I8
Africa's Lion Safari • OT, Canada **122** B9
Africa-India cruise area • Indian Ocean **59** A5/8
Africains, Bancs • Seychelles **106** F2
Africana, Reserva • Majorca, Spain **87** H2
Afsluitdijk • Netherlands **80** A3
Afton Alps **Ski** • MN, United States **116** [112]
Afuá • Brazil **43** G4
Afyon • Turkey **15** L5
Afyonkarahisar • Turkey **18** B2
Agadem • Niger **20** H5
Agadez • Niger **20** G5
Agadir • Morocco **101** D5
Agadyr • Kazakhstan **26** L8
Agalega • Mauritius **24** (2) C3
Agalta, Sierra de • Honduras **37** D4
Agana • Guam **33** F4
Agano • Japan **30** J6
Agartala • India **28** F4
Agate Fossil Beds Nat. Mon. **Park** • NE, United States **120** [164]
Agathonissi • Greece **92** D8
Agats • Indonesia **32** (1) E4
Agatti I. • India **106** D9
Agboville • Côte d'Ivoire **22** D3
Agde • France **11** O1
Agdz • Morocco **20** D2
Agen • France **85** G4
Agger • Germany **81** E4
Agger Tange • Denmark **95** F5
Aggtelek Caves **Heritage N** • Hungary **61** [50]
Aggtelek Nat. Park **Park** • Hungary **72** [103]
Agía Fotiá • Crete, Greece **93** E7
Agía Galíni • Crete, Greece **93** E6
Agía Marína • Léros, Greece **15** H6
Agía Marína • Attica, Greece **92** D4
Agía Marína • Crete, Greece **93** E1
Agía Pelagía • Kíthira, Greece **92** D7
Agía Pelagía • Crete, Greece **93** E3
Agía Rouméli • Crete, Greece **93** E5
Agía Sofia • Crete, Greece **93** E1
Agía Triáda **Beach** • Greece **69** [191]
Agía Triáda • Crete, Greece **93** E6
Agiássos • Greece **15** H4
Agincourt • France **71** A7
Agio Oros • Greece **92** D1
Agios Apóstoli • Greece **92** D4
Agios Dimitrios **Beach** • Greece **69** [188]
Agios Dimitrios • Greece **92** D4
Agios Efstratios • Greece **92** D4
Agios Górdis • Corfu, Greece **92** B1
Agios Ioánnis **Beach** • Crete, Greece **69** [215]
Agios Ioánnis, Akra • Crete, Greece **93** E4
Agios Kírikos • Greece **92** D8
Agios Míronas • Crete, Greece **93** E7
Agios Nikitas • Greece **92** C1
Agios Nikólaos **Beach** • Halkidikí, Greece **69** [192]
Agios Nikólaos **Beach** • Crete, Greece **69** [215]
Agios Nikólaos • Crete, Greece **93** E8
Agios Stefanos • Corfu, Greece **92** B1
Agiou Orous, Kólpos • Greece **15** E3
Agnes Creek • SA, Australia **112** H4
Agnew • WA, Australia **34** D5
Agnita • Romania **14** L4
Agonda Beach • Goa, India **105** B2
Agordat • Eritrea **21** G4
Agordo • Italy **90** B4
Agostinho, I. de • Madeira **88** C2
Agostóli • Greece **92** C2
Agra **Heritage C** • India **63** [118-119]
Agra • India **105** C3
Agreda • Spain **11** J3
Agriá • Greece **92** D4
Agriates, Désert des • Corsica, France **85** L2
Agrigento **Heritage C** • Sicily, Italy **64** [134]
Agrigento • Sicily, Italy **90** D3
Agrínio • Greece **15** C5
Agro Romano • Italy **91** F1
Agropoli **Beach** • Italy **69** [149]
Agrópoli • Italy **91** G4
Agua • Brazil **44** F2
Agua Caliente • Mexico **40** E6
Agua de Pena • Madeira **88** C2
Agua Prieta • Mexico **40** E5
Agua Vermelha, Represa • Brazil **44** F2
Aguada Bay • Goa, India **105** B1
Aguada de Pasajeros • Cuba **124** D2
Aguada Fort • Goa, India **105** B1
Aguadilla • Puerto Rico **125** E1
Aguadilla, Bahía de • Puerto Rico **125** E1
Aguadulce • Spain **86** B8
Aguas Buenas, Cuevas de • Puerto Rico **125** E4
Aguas de Moura • Portugal **88** D2
Aguascalientes • Mexico **123** E1
Agudo • Spain **11** G6
Agueda • Spain **11** E4
Aguelhok • Mali **20** F5
Agüenit • Western Sahara **20** C4
Aguilar de Campóo • Spain **11** G2
Aguilas • Spain **11** J7
Aguilas **Beach** • Spain **68** [117]
Agujereada, Punta • Puerto Rico **125** E1
Agulhas, Cape • South Africa **100** C6
Agulhas Negras, Pico das • Brazil **127** C3
Agung, Gunung • Bali, Indonesia **110** C2
Agva • Turkey **15** K2
Ahaggar • Algeria **20** G4
Aharnés • Greece **15** E5
Ahaus • Germany **8** B4
Aheim • Norway **94** C1
Ahelóos • Greece **15** C4
Ahfir • Morocco **101** D2
Ahirli • Turkey **93** G2
Ahlada **Beach** • Crete, Greece **69** [214]
Ahlada • Crete, Greece **93** E3
Ahlbeck **Beach** • Germany **69** [30]
Ahlbeck **Spa** • Germany **83** [285]
Ahlen • Germany **8** C5
Ahmadabad • India **28** B4
Ahmadnagar • India **28** B5
Ahmar • Ethiopia **23** G2
Ahon, Tarso • Chad **20** I4
Ahr • Germany **82** H1
Ahrensburg • Germany **8** F3
Ahrenshoop **Beach** • Germany **68** [32]
Ahrenshoop **Spa** • Germany **83** [275]
Ahrntal • Italy **90** B2
Ahrtal • Germany **82** H1
Ahtäri • Finland **95** E2
Ahus • Sweden **95** F11
Ahvaz • Iran **18** E3
Ahvenanmaa • Finland **95** E3
Ahwar • Yemen **18** E7
Aibonito • Puerto Rico **125** E4
Aichach • Germany **9** G8
Aiea • HI, United States **119** L5
Aierbach • Germany **9** H6
Aigle, l' • France **5** D6
Aigóual, Mt • France **10** I9
Aigues • France **10** K9
Aiguillon-sur-Mer, l' **Beach** • France **68** [83]
Aiguillon-sur-Mer, l' • France **84** D3
Aihole • India **106** D2
Aihui • China **27** K6
Ailao Shan • China **31** C2
Aileron • NT, Australia **112** H2
Aim • Russian Fed. **27** L5
Aimorés • Brazil **127** C2
Ain [Adm] • France **85** F1
Aïn Beïda • Algeria **20** G1
Aïn Defla • Algeria **11** M8
Aïn el Hadjel • Algeria **11** O9
Aïn Galakka • Chad **20** I5
Aïn Ouessera • Algeria **20** F1
Ain [Riv] • France **10** K7
Aïn Sefra • Algeria **20** E2
Aïn Taya • Algeria **11** O8
Ainazi • Latvia **16** M8
Aínos Nat. Park **Park** • Greece **72** [137]
Aínsa • Spain **11** L2
Aïr • Niger **20** G5
Air Force I. • NU, Canada **39** Q3
Air Hitam • Penang, Malaysia **108** C1
Air Hitam Dam • Penang, Malaysia **108** C1
Aïr, Réserve du **Heritage N** • Niger **61** [77]
Aïr, Réserve du **Park** • Niger **103** [4]
Airão • Brazil **43** E4
Aire • France **5** I5
Aire • United Kingdom **7** K8
Aire, Canal d' • France **5** F4
Aire, I. de l' • Minorca, Spain **87** F4
Aire-sur-l'Adour • France **85** G3
Aire-sur-la-Lys • France **5** F4
Airolo • Switzerland **89** G7
Aisawan Tippaya Asna • Thailand **109** H1
Aisch • Germany **9** F7
Aisne • France **10** I4
Aïssa, Djebel • Algeria **20** E2
Aït Benhaddou **Heritage C** • Morocco **64** [218]
Aït Benhaddou • Morocco **101** D5
Aitape • Papua New Guinea **35** (1) C1
Aitutaki • Cook Is. **33** K7
Aiud • Romania **14** K3
Aix-en-Provence • France **85** H3
Aix-la-Chapelle **Heritage C** • Germany **64** [37]
Aix-la-Chapelle • Germany **82** G1
Aix-les-Bains • France **85** F1
Aizawl • India **28** F4
Aizuwakamatsu • Japan **30** J6
Ajaccio • Corsica, France **85** L3
Ajaccio, Golfe d' • Corsica, France **85** L3
Ajanta Caves **Heritage C** • India **63** [123]
Ajdabiya • Libya **21** D1
Ajigasawa • Japan **30** K4
Ajim • Tunisia **101** E6
Ajka • Hungary **13** G10
Ajlun • Jordan **98** A4
Ajmer • India **105** C6
Ajo • AZ, United States **118** J3
Ajo, Cabo de • Spain **11** H1
Aju, Kepulauan • Indonesia **32** (1) D2
Ak Dag • Turkey **15** K7
Akagera, Parc nat. de l' **Park** • Rwanda **103** [73]
Akaishi-Sanmayaky • Japan **30** I7
Akaka Falls State Park • HI, United States **119** L8
Akaki • Ethiopia **23** F2
Akanthoú • Cyprus **93** J2
Akaroa • New Zealand **35** D6
Akayzi • Turkey **15** L3
Akbaytal • Tajikistan **26** L10
Akçakoca • Turkey **15** M2
Akçakoca **Beach** • Turkey **69** [238]
Akçay • Turkey **93** G3
Akçay [Riv] • Turkey **15** J6
Akdag • Izmir, Turkey **15** H5
Akdag • Kütahya, Turkey **15** J4
Akdag • Denizli, Turkey **15** K5
Aker • Sweden **95** D3
Akersberga • Sweden **95** D4
Akershus • Norway **94** B2
Aketi • Dem. Rep. of Congo **23** C3
Akhdar, Al Jabal al • Oman **18** G5
Akhdar, Al Jabal al • Libya **21** D1
Akhisar • Turkey **92** D6
Akhtopol • Bulgaria **97** D4
Akhtubinsk • Russian Fed. **17** H5
Akimiski • NU, Canada **39** O6
Akirkeby • Denmark **95** F16
Akita • Japan **30** K5
Akjoujt • Mauritania **20** C5
Akka • Morocco **20** D3
Akkajaure • Sweden **16** J3
Akko • Israel **98** A1
Akköy • Turkey **15** I6
Akmeqit • China **26** M10
Akmola • Kazakhstan **26** L7
Akobo • Sudan **23** E2
Akobo [Riv] • Ethiopia/Sudan **23** E2
Akola • India **28** C4
Akören • Turkey **15** N6
Akosombo Dam • Ghana **22** E3
Akpatok I. • NU, Canada **39** R4
Akranes • Iceland **16** (1) B2
Akrehamn • Norway **94** C5
Akritas, Akra • Greece **15** C7
Akron • OH, United States **41** J3
Akrotíri • Greece **92** D8
Akrotíri • Cyprus **93** J3
Akrotíri Bay • Cyprus **93** J3
Akrotíri, Hersónisos • Crete, Greece **93** E1
Aksai Chin • China **28** C1
Aksakal • Turkey **15** J3
Aksaray • Cyprus **15** O8
Aksay • Kazakhstan **17** I6
Aksayqin Hu • China **28** C1
Aksehir • Turkey **15** M5
Aksehir Gölü • Turkey **15** M5
Akseki • Turkey **93** G2
Aksha • Russian Fed. **27** H6
Aksoran • Kazakhstan **26** M8
Aksu • China **26** N9
Aksu • Turkey **93** G1
Aksu [Riv] • Turkey **93** G4
Aksum • Ethiopia **21** G5
Aksum **Heritage C** • Ethiopia **63** [84]
Aktau • Uzbekistan **26** J9
Aktion • Greece **92** C1
Aktöbe • Kazakhstan **26** I7
Aktogay • Kazakhstan **26** M8
Akune • Japan **30** F9
Akure • Nigeria **22** F3
Akureyri • Iceland **16** (1) D2
Al • Norway **94** C4
Al Ayn **Heritage C** • Oman **63** [106]
Al Hoceïma • Morocco **101** D2
Al Jaghbub • Libya **21** D2
Al Jahrah • Kuwait **21** I2
Al Khums • Libya **21** B1
Al Khutm **Heritage C** • Oman **63** [106]
Al Mird • Jordan **98** A8
Al Qaryah ash Sharqiyah • Libya **21** B1
Al Qatrun • Libya **21** B3
Al Uwaynat • Libya **21** B2
Ala Dag • Turkey **15** N6
Alabama • United States **41** I5
Alabama [Riv] • AL, United States **41** I5
Alaçam Daglari • Turkey **15** J4
Alaçati • Turkey **15** H5
Alacranes, Arrecife • Mexico **123** E6
Aladzha Manastir • Bulgaria **97** D4
Alagna-Valsésia **Ski** • Italy **70** [203]
Alagnon • France **10** I8
Alagoas • Brazil **45** (1) D3
Alagoinhas • Brazil **44** I1
Alaior **Beach** • Minorca, Spain **68** [127]
Alaior • Minorca, Spain **87** F4
Alajuela • Costa Rica **43** A1
Alaköl • Kazakhstan **26** N8
Alakurtti • Russian Fed. **16** P3
Alam • QU, Canada **123** D1
Alamagan • Northern Mariana Is. **33** F4
Alamein, El • Egypt **101** F1
Alamo • Somalia **23** G3
Alamogordo • NM, United States **118** J4
Alamos • Mexico **40** E6
Alamosa • CO, United States **118** J2
Aland • Finland **95** E3
Aland [Adm] • Finland **95** E3
Alands Hav • Finland/Sweden **95** D2
Alantika, Mts • Cameroon **22** G3
Alanya • Turkey **93** G4
Alaotra, Lac • Madagascar **24** H3
Alapayevsk • Russian Fed. **26** J6
Alapli • Turkey **15** M2
Alara Han • Turkey **93** G4
Alarcon, Embalse de • Spain **11** I5
Alarcos • Spain **71** A16
Alas • Indonesia **110** B1
Alasasua • Spain **11** I2
Alasehir • Turkey **92** D6
Alaska • United States **40** (2) F2
Alaska, Gulf of • AK, United States **36** B4
Alaska Highway • BC, Canada **122** C1
Alaska Peninsula • AK, United States **40** (2) F2
Alaska Range • AK, United States **36** B3
Alaska/Canada cruise area • N. America **58** A2
Alássio • Italy **91** E9
Alatri • Italy **12** H7
Alatyr • Russian Fed. **17** H3
Alavus • Finland **95** E2
Alayskiy • Kyrgyzstan **26** L10
Alazeya • Russian Fed. **27** P2
Alba • Italy **91** E5
Alba Iulia • Romania **14** K3
Albacete • Spain **11** J5
Albæk • Denmark **95** F6
Albæk Bugt • Denmark **95** F6
Albanel, Lac • QU, Canada **39** Q6
Albania • Europe **17** A2
Albano, Lago • Italy **91** F3
Albano Laziale • Italy **91** F3
Albany • WA, Australia **34** C6
Albany • OT, Canada **39** O6
Albany • GA, United States **41** J5
Albany • OR, United States **117** E3
Albany • NY, United States **118** G3
Albardón • Argentina **44** C5
Albatross Bay • QL, Australia **34** H2
Albatross Point • New Zealand **112** K1
Albéces, Chaine des • France **11** N2
Albemarle Sound • NC, United States **118** H5
Albena • Bulgaria **97** D4
Albenga • Italy **91** E9
Alberche • Spain **11** G4
Alberdi • Paraguay **44** E4
Alberga • SA, Australia **112** H4
Alberobello **Heritage C** • Italy **64** [132]
Albert • France **5** F4
Albert Edward • Papua New Guinea **35** (1) D2
Albert Kanaal • Belgium **5** H3
Albert, Lake • Uganda/Dem. Rep. of Congo **23** E3
Albert Lea • MN, United States **41** H3
Albert Nile • Uganda **23** E3
Albert Town • Jamaica **124** C1
Alberta • Canada **38** H5
Albertville • France **85** F2
Albi • France **85** G4
Albina, Ponta • Angola **24** A3
Albisola Marina **Beach** • Italy **68** [141]
Alblasserwaard • Netherlands **80** C4
Alborán, I. de • Spain **11** H9
Alborz, Reshteh-ye Kuhha-ye • Iran **18** F2
Alboux • Spain **11** I7
Albufeira **Beach** • Portugal **68** [100]
Albufeira • Portugal **88** E6
Albufeira, Lagoa de • Portugal **88** D1
Albuquerque • NM, United States **118** J2
Albury • NS, Australia **111** G3
Alcácer do Sal • Portugal **11** C6
Alcalá de Chivert **Beach** • Spain **68** [120]
Alcalá de Guadaira • Spain **11** F7
Alcalá de Henares • Spain **11** H4
Alcalá del Júcar • Spain **11** J5
Alcalá la Real • Spain **86** B3
Alcalar, Túmulos de • Portugal **88** E6
Alcamo • Sicily, Italy **12** G11
Alcanar **Beach** • Spain **68** [121]
Alcañiz • Spain **11** K3
Alcántara, Embalse de • Spain **11** E5
Alcantarilha • Portugal **88** E6
Alcantarilla • Spain **11** J6
Alcaraz • Spain **11** I6
Alcaraz, Sierra de • Spain **11** I6
Alcaria do Cume, Serra de • Portugal **88** E4
Alcaudete • Spain **11** G7
Alcázar de San Juan • Spain **11** H5
Alcira • Spain **11** K5
Alcobaça • Portugal **11** C5
Alcobaça **Beach** • Portugal **68** [97]
Alcobaça **Heritage C** • Portugal **64** [98]
Alcobendas • Spain **11** H4
Alcochete • Portugal **88** D2
Alcolea del Pinar • Spain **11** I3
Alcoutim • Portugal **88** E4
Alcoy • Spain **87** C1
Alcúdia **Beach** • Majorca, Spain **68** [126]
Alcúdia • Majorca, Spain **87** H2
Alcúdia, Badia d' • Majorca, Spain **87** H2
Aldabra Atoll **Heritage N** • Seychelles **61** [99]
Aldabra, Groupe d' • Seychelles **106** F3
Aldan • Russian Fed. **27** K5
Aldan [Riv] • Russian Fed. **27** L4
Aldanskoye Nagorye • Russian Fed. **27** K5
Aldeburgh • United Kingdom **5** E2
Aldeburgh **Beach** • United Kingdom **75** [49]
Alderney • Channel Is. **7** J12
Aldershot • United Kingdom **5** C3
Aleg • Mauritania **20** C5
Alegranza • Canary Is. **87** E6
Alegre • Brazil **127** C2
Alegrete • Brazil **44** E4
Aleksandrov • Russian Fed. **97** E4
Aleksandrovsk-Sakhalinskiy • Russian Fed. **27** N6
Aleksandrów Lodzki • Poland **13** I6
Alem • Sweden **95** F8
Além Paraíba • Brazil **127** C4
Alençon • France **10** F5
Alenhuihaha Channel • HI, United States **119** L8
Alenquer • Portugal **88** D2
Aleppo • Syria **18** C2
Aléria • Corsica, France **85** L4
Alert • NU, Canada **36** J1
Alès • France **10** J9
Ales stenar • Sweden **95** F15
Alessándra • Italy **91** E6
Alestrup • Denmark **95** F5
Alesund • Norway **94** C1
Aleutian Is. • AK, United States **36** (1) C2
Aleutian Trench • AK, United States **25** T5
Alexander Archipelago • AK, United States **38** D5
Alexander, Cape • Solomon Is. **35** (1) F2
Alexanderbaai • South Africa **24** B5
Alexandra • New Zealand **112** L2
Alexandria • Romania **97** D1
Alexandria • South Africa **100** C8
Alexandria • Egypt **101** F1
Alexandria • VA, United States **118** H3
Alexandria • LA, United States **118** K1

Alexandroúpoli **Beach** • Greece **69** [197]
Alexandroúpoli • Greece **92** D2
Alexandrów Kujawski • Poland **13** H5
Aleysk • Russian Fed. **26** N7
Alf • Germany **5** K4
Alfambra • Spain **11** J4
Alfatar • Bulgaria **97** D1
Alfaz del Pi **Beach** • Spain **68** [118]
Alfaz del Pi • Spain **87** C2
Alfenas • Brazil **127** C1
Alfiós • Greece **15** C6
Alföld • Hungary **13** J11
Alfred Faure [Base] • Pacific Ocean **46** (1) K5
Algajola • Corsica, France **85** L1
Algarås • Sweden **95** F3
Algarve • Portugal **88** E
Algeciras **Beach** • Spain **68** [113]
Algeciras • Spain **86** B6
Algeciras, Bahía de • Spain **11** F8
Alger • Algeria **20** F1
Alger **Heritage C** • Algeria **64** [220]
Algeria • Africa **20** F3
Alghero • Sardinia, Italy **90** C1
Algiers • Algeria **20** F1
Algiers **Heritage C** • Algeria **64** [220]
Algoa Bay • South Africa **100** C8
Algodonales • Spain **86** B6
Algonquin Prov. Park • OT, Canada **122** B1
Algoz • Portugal **88** E6
Algutsrum • Sweden **95** F8
Alholm • Denmark **95** F14
Aliabad • Iran **18** G4
Aliaga • Spain **11** K4
Aliaga • Turkey **15** I5
Alibates Flint Quarries Nat. Mon. **Park** • TX, United States **120** [134]
Alibey • Turkey **92** D5
Alicante **Beach** • Spain **68** [118]
Alicante • Spain **87** C1
Alice • TX, United States **119** N5
Alice, Punta • Italy **12** L9
Alice Springs • NT, Australia **112** H2
Alice Town • Bahamas **124** B1
Alicudi, I. • Italy **90** D2
Aligarh • India **105** C3
Alijos, Rocas • Mexico **123** E3
Alíkampos • Crete, Greece **93** E2
Alikés • Greece **92** C3
Alikianós • Crete, Greece **93** E1
Alima • Congo **22** H5
Alimatha • Maldives **106** E1
Alimiá • Greece **93** F1
Alimnía • Greece **92** D9
Alímos **Beach** • Greece **69** [185]
Alímos • Greece **92** D7
Alingsås • Sweden **95** F3
Alivéri • Greece **15** F5
Aljezur **Beach** • Portugal **68** [100]
Aljezur • Portugal **88** E1
Alkmaar • Netherlands **80** A7
All Saints • Antigua & Barbuda **125** F3
Allagash Wilderness Waterway • ME, United States **118** G2
Allahabad • India **105** C8
Allakh-Yun • Russian Fed. **27** M4
Allanmyo • Myanmar **28** G5
Alleghe **Ski** • Italy **70** [224]
Alleghe • Italy **90** B4
Allegheny Mtns • VA/WV United States **41** J4
Allegheny Portage Railroad Nat. Hist. Site **Park** • PA, United States **121** [303]
Allen • Philippines **31** G4
Allen, Bog of • Ireland **79** E1
Allen, Lough • Ireland **7** D7
Allentown • PA, United States **118** H1
Alleppey • India **106** D10
Aller • Germany **8** E4
Allerheiligen • Germany **82** G6
Alleynes Bay • Barbados **125** H1
Allgäu • Germany **82** J6
Allgäuer Alpen • Germany **82** J6
Allier • France **10** I7
Allihies • Ireland **79** F7
Allingåbro • Denmark **95** F10
Alloa • United Kingdom **74** B3
Allonby **Beach** • United Kingdom **75** [233]
Alma-Ata • Kazakhstan **26** M9
Almada **Beach** • Portugal **68** [99]
Almada • Portugal **88** D1
Almadén • Spain **11** G6
Almalik • Kazakhstan **98** B2
Almansa • Spain **11** J6
Almansil • Portugal **88** E7
Almanzor, Pico de • Spain **11** F4
Almanzora • Spain **11** I7
Almas, Picos de • Brazil **44** H1
Almaty • Kazakhstan **26** M9
Almazán • Spain **11** I3
Almeirim • Brazil **43** G4
Almelo • Netherlands **80** A9
Almenar de Soria • Spain **11** I3
Almendra, Embalse de • Spain **11** E3
Almendralejo • Spain **11** E6
Almere-Haven • Netherlands **80** C2
Almere-Stad • Netherlands **80** C2
Almería **Beach** • Spain **68** [116]
Almería • Spain **86** B8
Almería, Costa de • Spain **86** B8
Almería, Golfo de • Spain **86** B8
Almerimar • Spain **86** B8
Almhult • Sweden **95** F11
Almijara, Sierra da • Spain **86** B7
Almirante • Panama **43** A2
Almirante Brown [Base] • Antarctica **46** (1) II3
Almirós **Beach** • Greece **69** [188]
Almiroú, Ormos • Crete, Greece **93** E2
Almodôvar • Portugal **88** E3
Almodóvar del Pinar • Spain **11** J5
Almodóvar del Rio • Spain **86** B2
Almonte **Beach** • Spain **68** [112]
Almonte • Spain **86** B1
Almora • India **105** C3
Almsta • Sweden **95** D2
Almuñécar **Beach** • Spain **68** [115]
Almuñécar • Spain **86** B7
Alofi • Wallis & Futuna **35** (2) E1
Alofi • Niue **35** (2) G2
Alónissos • Greece **92** D4
Alor, Kepulauan • Indonesia **32** (1) B4
Alorna Fort • Goa, India **105** B1
Alotau • Papua New Guinea **35** (1) E3
Alpbach • Austria **89** H3
Alpe d'Huez **Ski** • France **70** [57]
Alpe d'Huez • France **85** F3
Alpe di Pampeago **Ski** • Italy **70** [215]
Alpe di Suisi • Italy **90** B3
Alpe du Grand Serre **Ski** • France **70** [55]
Alpen • Germany **81** E1
Alpena • MI, United States **41** J3
Alpental **Ski** • WA, United States **116** [44]
Alpental • WA, United States **117** E1
Alpes Cottiennnes • France/Italy **10** L8
Alpes de Haute-Provence • France **85** H1
Alpes Graies • France/Italy **10** M8
Alpes Maritimes • France/Italy **10** L9
Alpes Maritimes [Adm] • France **85** H2
Alpes Pennines • France/Switzerland **10** M7
Alphen aan de Rijn • Netherlands **80** C1
Alphonse • Seychelles **106** F2
Alpi Bernina • Italy **89** G8
Alpi Carniche • Italy **91** E4
Alpi Cozie • France/Italy **91** E5
Alpi di Pampeago • Italy **90** B3
Alpi Graie • France/Italy **12** A3
Alpi Lepontine • Italy/Switzerland **89** G7
Alpi Marittime • France/Italy **12** B4
Alpi Orobie • Italy **89** G8
Alpi Pennine • Italy/Switzerland **89** G6
Alpi Retiche • Italy/Switzerland **89** G4
Alpi Sarentine • Italy **90** B1
Alpi Venoste • Italy **91** E3
Alpine • TX, United States **40** F5
Alpine Meadows **Ski** • CA, United States **116** [55]
Alpine Valley **Ski** • WI, United States **116** [124]
Alpine Valley **Ski** • MI, United States **116** [137]
Alpine Valley **Ski** • OH, United States **116** [149]
Alpirsbach • Germany **82** G6
Alps • Europe **4** L7
Alqueria Blanca • Majorca, Spain **87** H4
Alqueva, Barragem de • Portugal **88** A3
Als • Denmark **95** F13
Alsace • France **10** M5
Alsandak • Cyprus **15** O8
Alsfeld • Germany **82** G2
Alslev • Denmark **8** G2
Alsten • Norway **94** A5
Alt St Johann • Switzerland **89** G3
Alta • Norway **16** L1
Alta **Heritage C** • Norway **63** [70]
Alta **Ski** • UT, United States **116** [84]
Alta Badia **Ski** • Italy **70** [233]
Alta Gracia • Argentina **44** D5
Altaelva • Norway **16** L2
Altafulla **Beach** • Spain **68** [121]
Altamira • Brazil **43** G4
Altamira Cave **Heritage C** • Spain **64** [81]
Altamont • OR, United States **117** E3
Altamura • Italy **12** K8
Altas, Rías • Spain **11** C1
Altavilla Irpina • Italy **91** G2
Altay • Russian Fed. **26** O7
Altay • Mongolia **29** B1
Altayn Nuruu • Mongolia **29** A1
Altdorf bei Nürnberg • Germany **9** G7
Alte • Portugal **88** E7
Altea **Beach** • Spain **68** [118]
Altea • Spain **87** C2
Altena • Germany **81** E4
Altenahr • Germany **82** H1
Altenau **Spa** • Germany **83** [79]
Altenburg • Germany **9** H6
Altenkirchen • Germany **82** H2
Altenmarkt • Austria **89** H4
Altenmarkt-Zauchensee **Ski** • Austria **70** [175]
Alter do Chão • Brazil **58** A3
Altet [Apt] • Spain **87** C1
Altevatnet • Norway **16** J2
Altinkum • Aydin, Turkey **92** D8
Altinkum • Antalya, Turkey **93** G3
Altinoluk • Turkey **15** H4
Altissima, l' • Austria/Italy **90** B1
Altlandsberg • Germany **81** F2
Altmark • Germany **8** G4
Altmühl • Germany **9** G8
Alto Alentejo • Portugal **11** D6
Alto Cedro • Cuba **124** D8
Alto Douro • Portugal **11** D3
Alto Paraguai • Brazil **44** E1
Alto Parnaiba • Brazil **45** (1) B3
Alto, Pico • Brazil **45** (1) D2
Altomünster • Germany **82** J3
Alton Towers **Park** • United Kingdom **73** [25]
Altoona • PA, United States **41** K3
Altötting • Germany **82** J4
Altun-Shan • China **26** O10
Alturas • CA, United States **117** F1
Altus • OK, United States **40** G5
Alur Setar • Malaysia **32** C1
Alvängen • Sweden **95** F2
Alvarez, General Juan N. [Apt] • Mexico **123** E4
Alvdalen • Sweden **16** H6
Alvesta • Sweden **95** F7
Alvik • Norway **94** C3
Alvkarleby • Sweden **16** I6
Alvor • Portugal **88** E6
Alvsborg • Sweden **95** F7
Alwar • India **105** C2
Alyangula • NT, Australia **34** G2
Alyawarra Aboriginal Land • NT, Australia **112** H2
Alysbyn • Sweden **16** K4
Alytus • Lithuania **13** N3
Alz • Germany **82** J4
Alzamay • Russian Fed. **26** Q6
Alzey • Germany **82** H4
Am Dam • Chad **22** I2
Am Géréda • Chad **23** C1
Am Timan • Chad **21** D5
Amacon • France **10** J6
Amada • Egypt **101** F5
Amadeus, Lake • NT, Australia **112** H3
Amadjuak Lake • NU, Canada **39** Q3
Amadora • Portugal **88** D1
Amadror • Algeria **20** G3
Amager • Denmark **95** F11
Amahai • Indonesia **32** (1) C3
Amakusa • Japan **30** E8
Amal • Sweden **95** F3
Amalfi • Italy **91** G4
Amaliáda • Greece **15** C6
Amaliáda **Beach** • Greece **69** [180]
Amami • Japan **29** H5
Amami-Shoto • Japan **31** H1
Aman • Malaysia **108** C4
Amanab • Papua New Guinea **35** (1) C1
Amänningen • Sweden **95** D1
Amantaní, I. • Peru **127** B4
Amantea • Italy **12** K9
Amapá • Brazil **43** G3
Amapá [Adm] • Brazil **43** G3
Amara • Ethiopia **21** G5
Amarah, Al • Iraq **18** E3
Amaravati • India **106** D3
Amári • Crete, Greece **93** E6
Amarillo • TX, United States **40** F4
Amasra • Turkey **15** N2
Amata • SA, Australia **112** H3
Amathus • Cyprus **93** J3
Amazon • S. America **42** E5
Amazon Basin • S. America **127** A1
Amazon, Mouths of the • Brazil **127** A1
Amazonas • Brazil **43** F4
Amazonas [Adm] • Brazil **43** D4
Ambala • India **28** C2
Ambam • Cameroon **22** G4
Ambanja • Madagascar **24** H2
Ambarchik • Russian Fed. **27** R3
Ambato • Ecuador **43** B4
Amber • India **105** C2
Amberg • Germany **9** G7
Ambérieu-en-Bugey • France **85** F1
Ambilobe • Madagascar **24** H2
Amble Links **Beach** • United Kingdom **75** [14]
Ambleside • United Kingdom **74** C4
Amblève • Belgium **80** A15
Ambo • Peru **43** B6
Amboise • France **84** D2
Amboise [Château] • France **84** D2
Ambon • Indonesia **32** (1) C3
Ambon [I.] • Indonesia **32** (1) C3
Ambongo • Madagascar **24** H3
Amboseli Nat. Park • Kenya **101** G3
Amboseli Nat. Park **Park** • Kenya **103** [84]
Ambositra • Madagascar **24** H4
Ambre, Mt d' • Madagascar **24** H2
Ambriz • Angola **23** A5
Ambrym • Vanuatu **35** (2) B2
Ambunten • Indonesia **110** D4
Ambunti • Papua New Guinea **35** (1) C1
Amded • Algeria **20** F4
Amderma • Russian Fed. **26** J4
Amdo • China **28** F2
Ameixal • Portugal **88** E3
Ameland **Beach** • Netherlands **68** [66]
Ameland • Netherlands **80** A3
Amélia • Italy **91** F1
Amendolara • Italy **12** K9
American Adventure **Park** • United Kingdom **73** [27]
American Highland • Antarctica **46** (1) M2
American Samoa • Pacific Ocean **35** (2) F1
Amersfoort • Netherlands **80** C2
Amery Ice Shelf • Antarctica **46** (1) M3
Ames • IA, United States **41** H3
Ametlla de Mar, l' **Beach** • Spain **68** [121]
Amfilohía • Greece **15** C5
Amga • Russian Fed. **27** L4
Amga [Riv] • Russian Fed. **27** L4
Amguema • Russian Fed. **27** U3
Amguid • Algeria **20** G3
Amguid [Adm] • Algeria **20** G3
Amgun • Russian Fed. **27** M6
Amherst • NS, Canada **123** D7
Amherst, Fort • PE, Canada **123** D7
Amiens • France **10** H4
Amiens **Heritage C** • France **64** [49]
Amini I. • India **106** D9
Amistad Nat. Recreation Area **Park** • TX, United States **120** [139]
Amitie Estate • Seychelles **106** F4
Amlapura • Bali, Indonesia **110** C2
Amli • Norway **94** C6
Amlwch • United Kingdom **7** H8
Amman • Jordan **18** B3
Ammarnäs • Sweden **16** I4
Ammassalik • Greenland **4** C3
Ammersee • Germany **82** J2
Amnok-kang • China/D.P.R. of Korea **29** H2
Amok • China/D.P.R. of Korea **30** D4
Amol • Iran **18** F2
Amolianí • Greece **92** D1
Amorbach • Germany **82** G4
Amorgós • Greece **92** D8
Amorosa, Fontana • Cyprus **93** J3
Amot • Buskerud, Norway **94** B1
Amot • Telemark, Norway **94** C6
Amoy • China **107** G8
Ampato, Nevado de • Peru **127** B4
Amper • Germany **82** J3
Ampezzo, Valle d' • Italy **90** B4
Ampolla, l' **Beach** • Spain **68** [121]
Amposta • Spain **11** L4
Amravati • India **28** C4
Amritsar • India **28** B2
Amrum • Germany **8** D2
Amrum **Spa** • Germany **83** [3]
Amsittene, Jebel • Morocco **20** D2
Amstelveen • Netherlands **80** C2
Amsterdam **Heritage C** • Netherlands **64** [27]
Amsterdam • Netherlands **80** C2
Amsterdam-Rijnkanaal • Netherlands **80** C2
Amsterdamse Waterleiding Duinen • Netherlands **80** C1
Amstetten • Austria **13** D9
Amu Darya • Turkmenistan **18** H2
Amundsen Gulf • NT, Canada **38** G2
Amundsen Sea • Pacific Ocean **46** (1) EE4
Amundsen-Scott Station [Base] • Antarctica **46** (1) A1
Amuntai • Indonesia **32** F3
Amur • Russian Fed. **27** K6
Amurang • Indonesia **32** (1) B2
Amursk • Russian Fed. **27** M6
Amvrakikós Kólpos • Greece **15** B4
An Loc • Vietnam **108** B1
An Nabi Samu'il • Jordan **98** A5
An Tan • Vietnam **31** D3
An Uaimh • Ireland **79** E1
Ana Maria, Golfo de • Cuba **124** D7
Anabar • Russian Fed. **27** H2
Anabarskoye Ploskogorye • Russian Fed. **26** S3
Anacapri **Beach** • Italy **69** [148]
Anacapri • Italy **91** G3
Anaconda • MT, United States **40** D2
Anacortes • WA, United States **117** E1
Anadyr • Russian Fed. **27** U4
Anadyrskiy Zaliv • Russian Fed. **27** V4
Anadyrskiye Ploskogorye • Russian Fed. **27** T3
Anáfi • Greece **92** D8
Anafonítria • Greece **92** C3
Anagni • Italy **91** F4
Anai Mudi • India **106** D10
Analalava • Madagascar **24** H2
Anambas, Kepulauan • Indonesia **32** D2
Anambra • Nigeria **22** F3
Anamur • Turkey **15** N7
Anamur Burun • Turkey **15** N7
Anan • Japan **30** H8
Anantapur • India **106** D2
Anantnag • Pakistan **18** K3
Anapa • Russian Fed. **17** F6
Anápolis • Brazil **44** G2
Anarak • Iran **18** F3
Anascaul **Beach** • Ireland **68** [60]
Anascaul • Ireland **79** F5
Añasco • Puerto Rico **125** E1
Añasco, Río Grande de • Puerto Rico **125** E1
Anatolia • Turkey **15** L5
Anatolia, Central • Turkey **92** A3
Anatolia, Eastern • Turkey **92** A4
Anatolikí Rodópi • Greece **15** G2
Anatom • Vanuatu **35** (2) B3
Añatuya • Argentina **44** D4
Anávissos **Beach** • Greece **69** [185]
Anávissos • Greece **92** D7
Anazah, Jabal • Saudi Arabia **21** G1
Anbyon • D.P.R. of Korea **30** D5
Ancão, I. do • Portugal **88** E7
Ancenis • France **84** D1
Anchorage • AK, United States **40** (2) G2
Anclote Keys • FL, United States **119** M5
Ancohuma, Nevado • Bolivia **44** C2
Ancona • Italy **91** E12
Ancud • Chile **45** B4
Anda • China **27** K7
Andalgalá • Argentina **44** C4
Andalo **Ski** • Italy **70** [210]
Andalo • Italy **90** B3
Andalsnes • Norway **94** C2
Andalucía • Spain **11** G7
Andaman Is. • India **28** F6
Andaman Sea • India/Myanmar **31** B4
Andara • Namibia **24** C3
Andelys, les • France **85** E1
Andenes • Norway **16** I2
Andenne • Belgium **5** I4
Andéranboukane • Mali **20** F5
Anderdalen Nat. Park **Park** • Norway **72** [8]
Andermatt **Ski** • Switzerland **70** [104]
Andermatt • Switzerland **89** G3
Andernach • Germany **82** H1
Andernos-les-Bains **Beach** • France **68** [85]
Anderson • NT, Canada **38** F3
Anderson • IN, United States **41** I3
Anderson • SC, United States **41** J5
Andersonville Nat. Hist. Site **Park** • GA, United States **121** [213]
Andes • S. America **42** D7
Andhra Pradesh • India **106** D3
Andikíthira • Greece **92** D10
Andipáros • Greece **92** D7
Andirlangar • China **28** D1
Andizhan • Uzbekistan **18** J1
Andkhvoy • Afghanistan **18** I2
Andong • Rep. of Korea **30** E6
Andora **Beach** • Italy **68** [141]
Andorra • Europe **85** K1
Andorra la Vella • Andorra **85** K1
Andover • United Kingdom **7** K10
Andøya • Norway **16** H2
Andradina • Brazil **44** F3
Andratx • Majorca, Spain **87** H1
Andreanov Is. • AK, United States **36** (1) C2
Andréas, Cape • Cyprus **93** J2
Andrelândia • Brazil **127** C3
Andrespol • Poland **13** I6
Andria • Italy **12** K7
Andriake • Turkey **93** G3
Androka • Madagascar **24** G5
Andromeda Gardens • Barbados **125** H2
Andros • Greece **92** D7
Andros • Bahamas **124** B1
Andros [I.] • Greece **92** D7
Andros Town • Bahamas **124** B1
Andrott I. • India **106** D9
Andselv • Norway **16** J2
Andújar • Spain **11** G6
Andulo • Angola **23** B6
Andutan • South China Sea **31** E5
Aneby • Sweden **95** F7
Anéfis • Mali **20** F5
Anegada Passage • West Indies **37** I4
Aneto, Pico de • Spain **85** K1
Aney • Niger **20** H5
Angaga • Maldives **106** E1
Angamos, Punta • Chile **44** B3
Angara • Russian Fed. **27** E5
Angarsk • Russian Fed. **27** F6
Ange • Sweden **16** H5
Ange **Beach** • Sweden **69** [24]
Angel de la Guarda, I. • Mexico **123** E1
Angel Falls • Venezuela **43** E2
Angeles • Philippines **31** G3
Angelholm **Beach** • Sweden **68** [9]
Angelholm • Sweden **95** F11
Angermanälven • Sweden **16** I5
Angermünde • Germany **8** J3
Angers • France **84** D1
Angers [Château] • France **84** D1
Angkor • Cambodia **31** C4
Angkor **Heritage C** • Cambodia **63** [171]
Angle Bay **Beach** • United Kingdom **75** [157]
Anglem, Mt • New Zealand **35** A8
Anglesberg • Sweden **95** D1
Anglesey • United Kingdom **7** H8
Angmagssalik • Greenland **39** X3
Angoche • Mozambique **24** F3
Angol • Chile **45** B3
Angola • Africa **24** B2
Angoram • Papua New Guinea **35** (1) C1
Angoulême • France **85** G1
Angra do Heroísmo **Beach** • Terceira, Azores **68** [104]
Angra do Heroísmo **Heritage C** • Azores **62** [67]
Angra do Heroísmo • Azores **88** B2
Angren • Uzbekistan **18** J1
Anguilla • West Indies **37** I4
Anguilla Cays • Bahamas **124** B3
Angus • United Kingdom **75** A2
Anholt • Denmark **95** F6
Anhui • China **107** G8
Aniachak Nat. Mon. & Preserve **Park** • AK, United States **120** [10]
Anie, Pic d' • France/Spain **11** K2
Animal Flower Cave • Barbados **125** H1
Animal Kingdom • FL, United States **121** C1
Aniva, mys • Russian Fed. **27** N7
Aniva, Zaliv • Russian Fed. **27** N7
Anjar **Heritage C** • Lebanon **64** [243]
Anji • China **107** J3
Anjou • France **84** D1
Anjouan • Comoros **24** G2
Anju • D.P.R. of Korea **30** C5
Anjuna Beach • Goa, India **105** B1
Ankang • China **29** D4
Ankara • Turkey **15** N4
Ankara [Riv] • Turkey **15** N4
Ankara-Altindag • Turkey **15** N4
Ankara-Çankaya • Turkey **15** N4
Ankara-Yenimahalle • Turkey **15** O4
Ankaratra • Madagascar **24** H3
Ankarsrum • Sweden **95** F8
Ankhor • Somalia **23** H1
Anklam • Germany **8** I3
Anlong • China **31** D2
Ann Arbor • MI, United States **41** J3
Anna Plains • WA, Australia **34** D3
Annaba • Algeria **101** E1
Annaberg **Ski** • Austria **70** [179]
Annaberg-Buchholz • Germany **9** I6
Annam • Vietnam **31** C3
Annapolis • MD, United States **118** H3
Annapolis Royal • NS, Canada **123** D7
Annapurna • Nepal **28** D3
Anne, Fort • NS, Canada **123** D7
Annecy • France **85** F1
Annevoie • Belgium **80** A15
Anniston • AL, United States **41** I5
Annobón • Gabon **22** F5
Annonay • France **85** F3
Annotto Bay • Jamaica **124** C2
Annweiler • Germany **82** G6
Ano Merá **Beach** • Greece **69** [204]
Ano Síros **Beach** • Greece **69** [203]
Ano Viános • Crete, Greece **93** E7
Anógia • Crete, Greece **93** E6
Anópolis **Beach** • Crete, Greece **69** [214]
Anqing • China **29** F4
Ansbach • Germany **9** F7
Anse Boileau Bay • Seychelles **106** F1
Anse l'Ivrogne • St Lucia **125** J3
Anse la Raye • St Lucia **125** J1
Anse la Sables • St Lucia **125** J4
Anse Lavoutte • St Lucia **125** J2
Anse Royale • Seychelles **106** F1
Anse Royale Bay • Seychelles **106** F1
Anse Volbert Village • Seychelles **106** F4
Anshan • China **29** G2
Anshun • China **29** D5
Anson Bay • NT, Australia **34** F2
Ansongo • Mali **20** F5
Anta • Peru **127** B2
Antabamba • Peru **127** B2
Antagnod **Ski** • Italy **70** [201]
Antalaha • Madagascar **24** I2
Antalya • Turkey **93** G3
Antalya [Adm] • Turkey **93** G3
Antalya Körfezi • Turkey **93** G4
Antananarivo • Madagascar **24** H3
Antarctic cruise area • Antarctica **59** A10
Antarctic Peninsula • Antarctica **46** (1) II2
Antelao • Italy **13** B11
Antequera • Spain **86** B3
Anthony I. **Heritage C** • BC, Canada **62** [1]
Anti Atlas • Morocco **101** D5
Antibes **Beach** • France **68** [134]
Antibes • France **85** H4
Antibes, Cap d' • France **85** H4
Anticosti, I. d' • QU, Canada **123** D2
Anticosti, I. d', Prov. Park • QU, Canada **123** D2
Antietam Nat. Battlefield • MD, United States **118** H3
Antietam Nat. Battlefield **Park** • MD, United States **121** [271]
Antifer, Cap d' • France **5** D5
Antigua **Heritage C** • Guatemala **62** [28]
Antigua • Fuerteventura, Canary Is. **87** E2
Antigua • Antigua & Barbuda **125** F
Antigua & Barbuda • West Indies **37** I4
Antikira **Beach** • Greece **69** [177]
Antilla • Cuba **124** D8
Antioch • Turkey **92** A3
Antioche, Pertuis d' • France **10** D7
Antiphonitis Monastery • Cyprus **93** J2
Antivari • Fed. Rep. of Yugoslavia **71** A14
Antofagasta • Chile **44** B3
Antofalla, Volcán • Argentina **44** C4
Antongil, Baie d' • Madagascar **24** H3
Antonina • Brazil **44** G4
Antonine Wall • United Kingdom **71** A2
Antrim • United Kingdom **7** F7
Antrim Mtns • United Kingdom **7** F6
Antrodoco • Italy **12** H6
Antsalova • Madagascar **24** G3
Antsirabe • Madagascar **24** H4
Antsiranana • Madagascar **24** H2
Antu • China **30** E3
Antwerp • Belgium **80** A10
Antwerpen • Belgium **80** A10
Antwerpen [Adm] • Belgium **80** A15
Anupgarh • India **105** C1
Anuradhapura **Heritage C** • Sri Lanka **63** [134]
Anuradhapura • Sri Lanka **106** D15
Anxi • China **29** B2
Anyang • China **29** E3
Anyer • Java, Indonesia **110** D1
Anza-Borrego Desert • CA, United States **117** F6
Anzanigo • Spain **11** K2
Anzère • Switzerland **89** G6
Anzhero-Sudzhensk • Russian Fed. **26** O6
Anzhou, Ostrova • Russian Fed. **27** N1
Anzio • Italy **91** F3
Ao To Nong • Phuket, Thailand **109** K1
Aoba • Vanuatu **35** (2) B2
Aomori • Japan **30** K4
Aosta • Italy **91** E1
Aotea Harbour • New Zealand **112** K1
Aotou • China **107** H2
Aouk, Bahr • Central African Rep./Chad **21** C6
Aoukale • Central African Rep./Chad **23** C1
Aoukâr • Mauritania **20** D5
Aoulef • Algeria **20** F3
Aozou • Chad **21** C3
Ap Lei Chau • Hong Kong, China **107** H5
Apacha • Russian Fed. **27** Q6
Apalachee Bay • FL, United States **37** E2
Apalachicola • FL, United States **119** M2
Apalachicola [Riv] • FL, United States **119** M2
Apaporis • Colombia **43** C4
Aparecida do Norte • Brazil **127** C3
Aparri • Philippines **31** G3
Apatity • Russian Fed. **17** E1
Apeldoorn • Netherlands **80** A8
Apere • Bolivia **44** C1
Apex **Ski** • BC, Canada **116** [3]
Api • Nepal **28** D2
Apia • Western Samoa **35** (2) F1
Apiacás, Serra dos • Brazil **43** F6
Apio • Solomon Is. **35** (1) G2
Aplau • Peru **127** B4
Apo, Mt • Philippines **31** H5
Apolakkiá • Rhodes, Greece **93** F3
Apolda • Germany **9** G5
Apollo Bay • VI, Australia **111** G3
Apollo Beach • Greece **92** D7
Apóllona • Rhodes, Greece **93** F2
Apollonia • Albania **15** A3
Apollonia • Libya **21** D1
Apopka, Lake • FL, United States **119** M5
Apostle Is. Nat. Lakeshore **Park** • WI, United States **121** [157]
Apóstoli • Crete, Greece **93** E6
Apoteri • Guyana **43** F3
Appalachians • United States **41** J4
Appennines • Italy **12** G5
Appennino • Italy **12** E4
Appennino Calabro • Italy **12** K10
Appennino Campano • Italy **12** J8
Appennino Ligure • Italy **12** C4
Appennino Lucano • Italy **12** K8
Appennino Tosco-Emiliano • Italy **12** E4
Appenweier • Germany **5** K6
Appenzell • Switzerland **82** J5
Appleby • United Kingdom **7** J7
Appleton • WI, United States **41** I3
Appleton • Jamaica **124** C1
Appomattox Court House Nat. Hist. Park **Park** • VA, United States **121** [254]
Aprica • Italy **91** E2
Aprília • Italy **91** F3
Apt • France **85** H1
Aptera • Crete, Greece **93** E1
Apucarana • Brazil **44** F3
Apurímac • Peru **127** B2
Aqaba, Gulf of • Egypt/Saudi Arabia **101** F2
Aqabah, Al • Jordan **18** B4
Aqitag • China **26** P9
Aqqikkol Hu • China **28** E1
Aqtau • Kazakhstan **17** I6
Aquidauana • Brazil **44** E3
Aquileia • Italy **91** E4
Aquitaine • France **10** F9
Ar Horqin Qi • China **27** J8
Ar Raqqah • Syria **18** C2
Ar Riyad • Saudi Arabia **18** E5
Ar Ruways • United Arab Emirates **18** F5
Ara • India **105** C8
Arab, Bahr al • Sudan **23** D2
Arabba **Ski** • Italy **70** [227]
Arabba • Italy **90** B4
Arabian Oryx Sanctuary **Heritage N** • Oman **61** [102]
Arabian Sea • Asia **18** H6
Araç • Turkey **15** O2
Aracaju • Brazil **44** I1
Aracati • Brazil **45** (1) D2
Araçatuba • Brazil **44** F3
Aracena • Spain **86** B1
Aracena, Sierra de • Spain **11** E7
Araçuai • Brazil **45** (1) C5
Arad • Romania **14** I3
Arafali • Eritrea **21** G4
Arafura Sea • Australia/Indonesia **33** E7
Aragarças • Brazil **44** F2
Aragón [Adm] • Spain **11** K3
Aragón [Riv] • Spain **11** J2
Aragona • Sicily, Italy **12** H11
Araguacema • Brazil **45** (1) B3
Araguaia • Brazil **44** F1
Araguaina • Brazil **45** (1) B3
Araguari • Brazil **44** G2
Araguatins • Brazil **45** (1) B3
Arak • Iran **18** E3
Arak • Algeria **20** F3
Arakan Yoma • Myanmar **31** A2
Araks • Azerbaijan **18** E2
Aral Sea • Kazakhstan/Uzbekistan **26** J8
Aral'sk • Kazakhstan **26** J8
Aral'skoye More • Kazakhstan/Uzbekistan **26** I8
Aramac • QL, Australia **111** F3
Arambol • Goa, India **105** B1
Arambol Beach • Goa, India **105** B1
Aran I. • Ireland **7** D7
Aran Is. • Ireland **79** F3
Aranda de Duero • Spain **11** H3
Aranjuez • Spain **11** H4
Araouane • Mali **20** E5
Arapahoe Basin **Ski** • CO, United States **116** [92]
Arapiraca • Brazil **45** (1) D3
Arápis, Akra • Greece **15** F3
Arapongas • Brazil **44** F3
Arapuni Dam • New Zealand **112** K2
Araranguá • Brazil **44** G4
Araraquara • Brazil **44** G3
Ararat • Turkey **18** D2
Ararat • VI, Australia **111** G3
Araruama, Lago de • Brazil **127** C4
Aras • Asia **18** E2
Arauca • Colombia **43** C2
Aravalli Range • India **105** C5
Arawale Game Reserve • Kenya **101** G4
Arawua Bay • New Zealand **112** L2
Araxá • Brazil **44** G2
Araxos, Akra • Greece **15** C5
Arba • Spain **10** D11
Arba Minch • Ethiopia **23** F2
Arbanasi • Bulgaria **97** D3
Arbaoua • Morocco **101** D1
Arbatax • Sardinia, Italy **90** C4
Arbil • Iraq **18** D2
Arboga • Sweden **95** D3
Arbon • Switzerland **9** E9
Arbroath • United Kingdom **74** B2
Arc • France **85** F4
Arc-et-Senans **Heritage C** • France **64** [53]
Arcachon **Beach** • France **68** [85]
Arcachon • France **85** G3
Arcachon, Bassin de • France **85** G3
Arcadia • Greece **15** D6
Arches Nat. Park **Park** • UT, United States **120** [87]
Archidona • Spain **11** G7
Arcidosso • Italy **12** F6
Arcos de Valdevez • Portugal **11** C3
Arcs, les **Ski** • France **70** [29]
Arcs, les • France **85** F2

Arctic Bay • NU, Canada 36 J2
Arctic Red River • NT, Canada 38 E3
Arctic Red River [Riv] • NT, Canada 38 E3
Arctic Village • AK, United States 38 B3
Arda • Bulgaria 15 G2
Ardabil • Iran 18 E2
Ardakan • Iran 18 F3
Ardalstangen • Norway 94 C4
Ardee • Ireland 7 F8
Arden • Denmark 95 F5
Ardennes • Belgium 80 A19
Ardennes, Canal des • France 5 H5
Ardfert **Beach** • Ireland 68 [60]
Ardfert • Ireland 79 F5
Ardila • Portugal 11 D6
Ardmore • OK, United States 119 N1
Ardrossan • United Kingdom 6 H6
Are • Sweden 16 G5
Arecibo • Puerto Rico 125 E1
Arecibo, Observatorio de • Puerto Rico 125 E1
Arecibo, Río Grande de • Puerto Rico 125 E1
Arée, Monts d' • France 10 B5
Areia, Ponta de • Portugal 88 E8
Areiro, Pico de • Madeira 88 C2
Arena d'en Castell • Minorca, Spain 87 F2
Arenas, Punta de • Argentina 45 C6
Arend • Sweden 95 F8
Arendal • Norway 95 F1
Arenys de Mar • Spain 87 D4
Aréopoli • Greece 15 D7
Arequipa • Peru 127 B4
Arès **Beach** • France 68 [85]
Arès • France 85 G3
Areuse, Gorges de l' • Switzerland 89 G1
Areyonga • NT, Australia 112 H3
Arezzo • Italy 91 E11
Arga • Spain 10 D11
Arganda • Spain 11 H4
Argássi • Greece 92 C3
Argelès-Gazost • France 85 J2
Argelès-sur-Mer **Beach** • France 68 [128]
Argen • Germany 82 J5
Argent, Côte d' • France 85 G
Argentan • France 10 E5
Argentera, Punta • Italy 91 E5
Argenteuil • France 10 G5
Argentia • NF, Canada 123 D4
Argentina • S. America 42 D8
Argentino, Lago • Argentina 45 B6
Argenton-sur-Creuse • France 84 D4
Arges • Romania 14 M5
Arghandab • Afghanistan 28 A2
Argonne • France 5 I5
Argopuro, Gunung • Java, Indonesia 110 D8
Argos • Greece 15 D6
Argostóli **Beach** • Greece 69 [171]
Arguineguin • Gran Canaria, Canary Is. 86 E4
Argun • Russian Fed. 27 J6
Argyle, Lake • WA, Australia 34 E3
Argyllshire • United Kingdom 75 A2
Arhánes • Crete, Greece 93 E7
Arhángelos • Rhodes, Greece 93 F2
Arhus • Denmark 95 F10
Arhus [Adm] • Denmark 95 F10
Arhus Bugt • Denmark 95 F10
Ari Atoll • Maldives 106 E1
Ariano Irpino • Italy 91 G2
Aribinda • Burkina Faso 20 E6
Arica • Chile 44 B2
Arica, Golfo de • Chile/Peru 127 B4
Aricha, El • Algeria 20 E2
Arid, Cape • WA, Australia 34 D6
Aride, I. • Seychelles 106 F4
Aridéa • Greece 14 J9
Ariège • France 10 G10
Aries • Romania 14 K3
Arild • Sweden 95 F11
Arima • Trinidad & Tobago 125 K3
Aripo Caves • Trinidad & Tobago 125 K1
Aripuanã • Brazil 43 E5
Arisa • Ethiopia 23 G1
Arîsh, El • Egypt 101 F2
Ariza • Spain 11 I3
Arizona • United States 118 J
Arjang • Sweden 94 B4
Arjeplog • Sweden 16 I3
Arjuna, Gunung • Java, Indonesia 110 D8
Arkadelphia • AR, United States 41 H5
Arkádi, Moní • Crete, Greece 93 E6
Arkalyk • Kazakhstan 26 K7
Arkansas • United States 41 H4
Arkansas City • KS, United States 41 G4
Arkansas Post Nat. Mem. **Park** • AR, United States 121 [194]
Arkansas [Riv] • United States 40 F4
Arkanu • Libya 21 D3
Arkatag • China 26 O10
Arkhangel'sk • Russian Fed. 17 G2
Arkí • Greece 92 D8
Arklow **Beach** • Ireland 68 [55]
Arklow • Ireland 79 E4
Arkona, Kap • Germany 8 I2
Arkösund • Sweden 95 F4
Arkoúdi • Greece 92 C1
Arkticheskogo Instituta, Ostrov • Russian Fed. 26 N2
Arla • Sweden 95 D3
Arlanda [Apt] • Sweden 95 D2
Arlanza • Spain 10 B11
Arles • France 10 J10
Arles **Heritage C** • France 64 [68]
Arlington • VA, United States 118 H3
Arlington • TX, United States 119 N1
Arlington House **Park** • VA, United States 121 [267]
Arlit • Niger 20 G5
Arlon • Belgium 80 A20
Arltunga Hist. Reserve • NT, Australia 112 H2
Arly, Parc nat. d' **Park** • Burkina Faso 103 [28]
Armação de Pera • Portugal 88 E6
Armadale • WA, Australia 34 C6
Armadale • United Kingdom 78 A1
Armageddon • Israel 98 A3
Armagh • United Kingdom 7 F7
Armagnac • France 84 B3
Armant • Egypt 21 F2
Armavir • Russian Fed. 17 G5
Arméni • Crete, Greece 93 E2
Armenia • Asia 18 D1
Armenia • Colombia 43 B3
Armentières • France 10 H3
Armidale • NS, Australia 34 J6
Armier Bay • Malta 93 H1
Armona, I. da • Portugal 88 E8
Armutcuk Dag • Turkey 15 I3
Armutlu • Turkey 15 J3
Arnaud • QU, Canada 39 Q4
Arnaúti, Cape • Cyprus 93 J3
Arnéa • Greece 15 E3
Arnel, Ponta de • Azores 88 B2
Arnes • Norway 94 B2
Arnhem • Netherlands 80 A8
Arnhem, Cape • NT, Australia 34 G2
Arnhem Land • NT, Australia 34 F2
Arno • Italy 91 E11
Arnøy • Norway 16 K1
Arnprior • OT, Canada 122 B6
Arnsberg • Germany 8 D5
Arnstadt • Germany 9 G6
Arnuero **Beach** • Spain 68 [89]
Aroab • Namibia 24 B5
Aroche, Pico de • Spain 11 E6
Arolsen • Germany 5 L3
Arolsen **Spa** • Germany 83 [121]
Arona • Italy 91 E2
Arorae • Kiribati 33 I6
Arosa **Ski** • Switzerland 70 [114]
Arosa • Switzerland 89 G4
Arosa, Ria de • Spain 11 C2
Arpajon • France 85 E3
Arrábida, Serra da • Portugal 88 D2
Arraias • Brazil 45 (1) B4
Arran • United Kingdom 6 G6
Arras • France 10 H3
Arras, Burg • Germany 82 H3
Arrecife **Beach** • Lanzarote, Canary Is. 68 [111]
Arrecife • Lanzarote, Canary Is. 87 E3
Arrieta • Lanzarote, Canary Is. 87 E3
Arrochar • United Kingdom 74 B1
Arrosim Beach • Goa, India 105 B2
Arrow Lake • BC, Canada 38 H6
Arrow, Lough • Ireland 79 F2
Arrowhead, Lake • TX, United States 119 N1
Arrowtown • New Zealand 112 L2
Arroyo • Puerto Rico 125 E4
Arroyo de la Luz • Spain 11 E5
Arrufó • Argentina 44 D5
Ars • Denmark 95 F5
Arsenyev • Russian Fed. 30 G2
Arta • Greece 15 B4
Artà • Majorca, Spain 87 H2
Artà, Coves d' • Majorca, Spain 87 H2
Artem • Russian Fed. 30 G3
Artemovsk • Russian Fed. 26 P7
Artesia • NM, United States 40 F5
Arthur's Town • Bahamas 124 B2
Artigas • Uruguay 44 E5
Artillery Lake • NT, Canada 38 J4
Artois • France 10 G3
Artrutx, Cap d' • Minorca, Spain 87 F3
Artyk • Russian Fed. 27 O4
Aru, Kepulauan • Indonesia 32 (1) D4
Arua • Uganda 23 E3
Aruba • West Indies 37 G5
Arucas • Gran Canaria, Canary Is. 86 E4
Arunachal Pradesh • India 28 F3
Arundel • United Kingdom 74 E3
Arungu • Nigeria 22 E2
Arusha • Tanzania 102 H2
Arusha Nat. Park • Tanzania 102 H2
Arusha Nat. Park **Park** • Tanzania 103 [91]
Aruwimi • Dem. Rep. of Congo 23 D3
Arvalem Caves • Goa, India 105 B1
Arvayheer • Mongolia 29 C1
Arvi • Crete, Greece 93 E7
Arviat • NU, Canada 38 M4
Arvidsjaur • Sweden 16 J4
Arvika • Sweden 16 G7
Arviksand • Norway 16 K1
Arykanda • Turkey 93 G3
Arys • Kazakhstan 26 K9
Arzamas • Russian Fed. 17 G3
Arzew • Algeria 20 E1
Arzew, Gulf of • Algeria 11 K9
Arzgir • Russian Fed. 17 G5
As • Norway 94 B2
As • Czech Rep. 96 C1
As Sidr • Libya 21 C1
As Sidrah • Libya 21 C1
As Smara • Western Sahara 101 D5
Aså • Denmark 95 F6
Asa Wright Nature Centre • Trinidad & Tobago 125 K1
Asab • Namibia 24 B5
Asahan • Indonesia 110 B2
Asahikawa • Japan 30 L3
Asan-man • Rep. of Korea 30 D6
Asansol • India 28 E4
Asbury Park • NJ, United States 118 H1
Ascain • France 85 J1
Ascension • Atlantic Ocean 19 C6
Aschaffenburg • Germany 82 G4
Aschau in Tirol **Ski** • Austria 70 [156]
Aschersleben • Germany 8 G5
Asco, Gorges de l' • Corsica, France 85 L2
Ascoli Piceno • Italy 91 E12
Ascona • Switzerland 89 G7
Ascot • United Kingdom 74 E1
Asdhu Sun I. • Maldives 106 E2
Aseda • Sweden 95 F8
Asela • Ethiopia 23 F2
Asele • Sweden 16 I4
Asenovgrad • Bulgaria 14 L7
Aseral • Norway 95 F1
Aseri • Estonia 16 N7
Asfendioú **Beach** • Greece 69 [210]
Asgårdstrand • Norway 94 B4
Ash Shariqah • United Arab Emirates 18 G4
Ashante **Heritage C** • Ghana 63 [96]
Ashbourne • Ireland 79 E2
Ashburton • New Zealand 35 C6
Ashby Fort • St Kitts & Nevis 125 G4
Ashdod • Israel 98 A5
Ashdown Forest • United Kingdom 74 E3
Asher • Israel/Lebanon 98 A2
Asheville • NC, United States 41 J4
Ashford • United Kingdom 74 E4
Ashgabat • Turkmenistan 18 G2
Ashington • United Kingdom 7 K6
Ashizuri-Misaki • Japan 30 G8
Ashkharah, Al • Oman 18 G5
Ashland • OR, United States 40 B3
Ashland • ME, United States 118 G2
Ashmûnein, El • Egypt 101 F3
Ashuanipi Lake • QU, Canada 39 R6
Asia, Kepulauan • Indonesia 32 (1) D2
Asiago **Ski** • Italy 70 [213]
Asikkala • Finland 95 E2
Asilah • Morocco 101 D1
Asinara, Golfo del' • Sardinia, Italy 90 C1
Asinara, I. • Sardinia, Italy 90 C1
Asinou Church • Cyprus 93 J3
Asir • Saudi Arabia 18 D6
Asker • Norway 94 B2
Askersund • Sweden 95 F3
Askham • United Kingdom 74 C2
Askim • Norway 94 B4
Asklipío **Beach** • Rhodes, Greece 69 [211]
Asklipío • Rhodes, Greece 93 F3
Askøy • Norway 94 C3
Askvoll • Norway 94 C3
Asmara • Eritrea 21 G4
Asnen • Sweden 95 F11
Asni • Morocco 101 D5
Asola • Italy 91 E7
Aspen • CO, United States 40 E4
Aspen **Ski** • CO, United States 116 [99]
Aspendos • Turkey 93 G4
Aspiring, Mt • New Zealand 112 L2
Asprókavos, Akra • Corfu, Greece 92 B1
Asproválta **Beach** • Greece 69 [193]
Assab • Eritrea 21 H5
Assal, Lake • Ethiopia 21 H5
Assam • India 28 F3
Assamakka • Niger 20 G5
Assateague I. Nat. Seashore • MD, United States 118 H3
Assateague I. Nat. Seashore **Park** • MD, United States 121 [278]
Assen • Netherlands 80 A4
Assens • Denmark 95 F13
Assiniboine • MN, Canada 38 L7
Assiniboine, Mt • BC, Canada 38 I6
Assiniboine, Mt, Prov. Park • BC, Canada 122 C4
Assis • Brazil 44 F3
Assisi • Italy 91 E12
Assmannshausen • Germany 82 H4
Assomption • Seychelles 106 F3
Assos • Greece 92 C2
Astakós • Greece 15 C5
Astérix, Parc • France 85 E2
Asteroúsia • Crete, Greece 93 E7
Asti • Italy 91 E5
Astillero • Peru 127 B2
Astipálea • Greece 92 D8
Astorga • Spain 11 E2
Astoria • OR, United States 117 E1
Astove • Seychelles 106 F3
Astrakhan • Russian Fed. 17 H5
Astura, Torre • Italy 91 F3
Asturias **Heritage C** • Spain 64 [82]
Asturias, Principado de • Spain 11 E1
Asuka [Base] • Antarctica 46 (1) H2
Asunción • Paraguay 44 E4
Asunden • Sweden 95 F4
Asvem Beach • Goa, India 105 B1
Aswa • Uganda 23 E3
Aswân • Egypt 101 F5
Aswân Dam • Egypt 101 F5
Aswân High Dam • Egypt 101 F5
Asyût • Egypt 101 F3
Ata • Tonga 33 J8
Atacama • Chile 44 C3
Atafu • Tokelau 33 J6
Atálanti • Greece 15 D5
Atalánti **Beach** • Greece 69 [187]
Atalaya • Peru 43 C6
Atalaya de Femés • Lanzarote, Canary Is. 87 E3
Atambua • Indonesia 32 (1) B4
Atâr • Mauritania 20 C4
Atasu • Kazakhstan 26 L8
Ataturk [Apt] • Turkey 92 D3
Atauri • Spain 11 I2
Atbarah • Sudan 21 F4
Atbarah [Riv] • Sudan 21 G4
Atbasar • Kazakhstan 26 K7
Atchafalaya • LA, United States 118 K3
Atchafalaya Bay • LA, United States 118 K3
Atchinson • KS, United States 41 G4
Aterno • Italy 91 F2
Ath • Belgium 80 A14
Athabasca • AL, Canada 38 H6
Athabasca Lake • AL/SA, Canada 38 J5
Athboy • Ireland 79 E1
Athenry • Ireland 79 F4
Athens **Heritage C** • Greece 64 [183]
Athens • Greece 92 D4
Atherton • QL, Australia 34 I3
Atherton Tableland • QL, Australia 111 F1
Athi • Kenya 101 G4
Athína **Heritage C** • Greece 64 [183]
Athína • Greece 92 D4
Athlone • Ireland 7 E8
Athol I. • Bahamas 124 B3
Athos **Heritage N** • Greece 61 [61]
Athos **Heritage C** • Greece 64 [174]
Athos • Greece 92 D1
Athy • Ireland 79 E3
Ati • Chad 21 C5
Atibaia • Brazil 127 C3
Atico • Peru 127 B3
Atka • Russian Fed. 27 P4
Atka • AK, United States 36 (1) C2
Atlanta • GA, United States 41 J5
Atlanta • TX, United States 119 N2
Atlantic Beach • NC, United States 118 H5
Atlantic Beach • St Kitts & Nevis 125 G2
Atlantic City • NJ, United States 118 H3
Atlantic Islands cruise area • Atlantic Ocean 59 A5
Atlantic Ocean • 2 K5
Atlántida • Uruguay 127 D2
Atlas Bogdo-Ula • Mongolia 29 B2
Atlas Mtns • Algeria/Morocco 19 D2
Atlas Saharien • Algeria 20 F2
Atlin • BC, Canada 38 E5
Atlin Lake • YT, Canada 38 E4
Atløy • Norway 94 C3
Atokos • Greece 92 C2
Atol das Rocas • Brazil 45 (1) E2
Atrak • Iran 18 G2
Atran • Sweden 95 F7
Atran [Riv] • Sweden 95 F7
Atraro • Colombia 43 B2
Atrek • Turkmenistan 18 G2
Atri • Italy 12 H6
Atrun, Al • Sudan 21 E4
Atsumi • Japan 30 J5
Attaf, El • Algeria 11 M8
Attapu • Laos 31 D4
Attáviros • Rhodes, Greece 93 F1
Attawapiskat • OT, Canada 39 O6
Attawapiskat [Riv] • OT, Canada 39 O6
Attersee • Austria 89 H4
Attila Line • Cyprus 93 J4
Attitash-Bear Peak **Ski** • NH, United States 116 [211]
Attre • Belgium 80 A14
Attu • AK, United States 36 (1) A2
Atuel • Argentina 44 C6
Atvidaberg • Sweden 95 F4
Atyrau • Kazakhstan 17 I5
Au • Austria 89 H1
Auas Mtns • Namibia 24 B4
Aubagne • France 85 H3
Aube • France 10 J5
Aubry Lake • NT, Canada 38 F3
Auburn • CA, United States 117 F3
Auburn • ME, United States 118 G4
Aubusson • France 85 G2
Aucanquílcha, Cerro • Chile 44 C3
Auch • France 85 G4
Auckland • New Zealand 35 E3
Auckland [Adm] • New Zealand 112 J2
Auckland I. • New Zealand 35 (4)
Aude • France 85 K2
Audierne • France 10 A5
Audierne, Baie d' • France 84 C3
Audincourt • France 9 B9
Audo • Ethiopia 23 G2
Aue • Germany 9 H6
Aue [Riv] • Germany 5 M2
Auer • Italy 90 B3
Auerbacher Schloß • Germany 82 H4
Auffach **Ski** • Austria 70 [147]
Auffach • Austria 89 H3
Augathella • QL, Australia 111 F5
Aughrim • Ireland 79 E4
Aughty, Slieve • Ireland 79 F4
Augier • St Lucia 125 J3
Augrabies Falls • South Africa 24 C5
Augsburg • Germany 82 J2
Augusta • WA, Australia 34 C6
Augusta • GA, United States 41 J5
Augusta • Sicily, Italy 90 D4
Augusta • ME, United States 118 G4
Augustenborg • Denmark 95 F13
Augustin Codazzi • Colombia 43 C2
Augustów • Poland 13 M4
Augustus, Mt • WA, Australia 34 C4
Auki • Solomon Is. 35 (1) G2
Aukstaitija Nat. Park **Park** • Lithuania 72 [146]
Aulendorf • Germany 82 J1
Aulendorf **Spa** • Germany 83 [213]
Aulie-Ata • Kazakhstan 26 L9
Aulla • Italy 12 E4
Aulnay • France 85 G1
Aulne • France 84 C1
Ault **Beach** • France 68 [76]
Aumale • France 5 E5
Auob • Africa 24 C5
Aurach **Ski** • Austria 70 [158]
Aurangabad • India 28 C5
Auray • France 84 C4
Aurdal • Norway 16 E6
Aurich • Germany 8 C3
Aurillac • France 10 H9
Aurina • Italy 90 B2
Aurina, Val • Italy 90 B2
Auris • France 85 F3
Auris-en-Oisans **Ski** • France 70 [57]
Aurlandsvangen • Norway 94 C4
Auron **Ski** • France 70 [71]
Auron • France 85 H2
Aurora • CO, United States 40 F4
Aurora • IL, United States 41 I3
Auroville • India 106 D7
Aurukun Mission • QL, Australia 34 H2
Aurunci, Monti • Italy 91 F4
Auschwitz • Poland 13 I7
Auschwitz **Heritage C** • Poland 64 [142]
Ausoni, Monti • Italy 91 F4
Aust Agder • Norway 16 E7
Austad • Norway 94 C6
Austin • NV, United States 117 F4
Austin • TX, United States 119 N3
Austin, Lake • WA, Australia 34 C5
Austnes • Norway 94 C1
Australasia cruise area • Oceania 59 A9
Australia • Oceania 34
Australia's Wonderland • NS, Australia 111 G2
Australian Alps • NS/VI, Australia 111 G4
Australian Capital Territory • Australia 111 G2
Australian rainforest reserves **Heritage N** • QL, Australia 61 [130]
Austria • Europe 4 M7
Austvågøy • Norway 16 H2
Autazes • Brazil 43 F4
Authie • France 10 G3
Autieul • France 85 E3
Autun • France 10 J7
Auvergne • France 10 I8
Auvernier • Switzerland 89 G1
Aux Sources, Mont • South Africa 24 D5
Auxerre • France 10 I6
Auxi-le-Château • France 5 F4
Auyan Tepuy • Venezuela 43 E2
Auzangate, Nudo • Peru 127 B2
Avadh • India 105 C3
Avaldsnes • Norway 94 C5
Avalon Peninsula • NF, Canada 123 D4
Avarua • Cook Is. 33 L8
Avebury **Heritage C** • United Kingdom 64 [20]
Avebury • United Kingdom 74 F3
Aveiro • Portugal 11 C4
Aveiro [Adm] • Portugal 88 A1
Avellaneda • Argentina 127 D2
Avellino • Italy 91 G2
Averbode **Beach** • Belgium 68 [73]
Averøya • Norway 16 D5
Aversa • Italy 91 G1
Aves • Venezuela 43 D1
Aves • West Indies 124 A3
Avesnes-sur-Helpe • France 5 G4
Avesta • Sweden 95 D1
Aveyron • France 85 G4
Aveyron, Gorges de l' • France 85 G4
Avezzano • Italy 91 F2
Avgó • Greece 93 E3
Aviano • Italy 90 B4
Aviés • Spain 11 F1
Avigliano • Italy 14 C9
Avignon • France 10 J10
Avignon **Heritage C** • France 64 [67]
Avila • Spain 11 G4
Avila **Heritage C** • Spain 64 [85]
Avisio • Italy 90 B3
Avliótes **Beach** • Corfu, Greece 69 [170]
Avoca • Ireland 79 E4
Avoca, Vale of • Ireland 79 E4
Avola • Sicily, Italy 90 D4
Avon • United Kingdom 5 B4
Avon • United Kingdom 74 D2
Avon • United Kingdom 74 F3
Avon Downs • NT, Australia 34 G4
Avon Gorge • United Kingdom 74 F3
Avonturenpark Hellendoorn **Park** • Netherlands 73 [40]
Avoriaz **Ski** • France 70 [10]
Avoriaz • France 85 F2
Avranches • France 10 D5
Avre • France 5 E6
Avre • France 10 H4
Awa • Japan 30 J5
Awaji • Japan 30 H7
Awakino Gorge • New Zealand 112 K1
Awash • Ethiopia 23 G2
Awash Lower Valley **Heritage C** • Ethiopia 63 [87]
Awash Nat. Park **Park** • Ethiopia 103 [63]
Awash [Riv] • Ethiopia 23 G1
Awaso • Ghana 22 D3
Awbari • Libya 21 B2
Awbari' Sahra' • Libya 21 B2
Awe, Loch • United Kingdom 6 G5
Awjilah • Libya 21 D2
Ax-les-Thermes • France 85 K1
Axamer Lizum • Austria 89 H6
Axarfjördur • Iceland 16 (1) E1
Axiós • Greece 15 D3
Axminster • United Kingdom 74 F3
Axós • Crete, Greece 93 E2
Ayabe • Japan 30 H7
Ayacucho • Peru 127 B1
Ayacucho • Argentina 127 D3
Ayaguz • Kazakhstan 26 N8
Ayakkum Hu • China 28 E1
Ayam Line • Russian Fed. 97 A6
Ayamonte • Spain 11 D7
Ayan • Russian Fed. 27 G5
Ayan • Russian Fed. 27 M5
Ayanka • Russian Fed. 27 S4
Ayas • Turkey 15 N3
Ayaviri • Peru 127 B2
Aybak • Afghanistan 28 A1
Aydin • Turkey 92 D9
Aydin Daglari • Turkey 15 I5
Aydingkol Hu • China 26 O9
Aydinkent • Turkey 93 G2
Ayer Chawan • Singapore 108 E3
Ayer Hitam • Malaysia 108 D4
Ayer Merbau • Singapore 108 E3
Ayers Rock • NT, Australia 112 H3
Ayers Rock Resort • NT, Australia 112 H3
Ayía Nápa **Beach** • Cyprus 69 [220]
Ayía Nápa • Cyprus 93 J4
Ayios Séryios • Cyprus 93 J2
Ayios Tychon **Beach** • Cyprus 69 [218]
Aykhal • Russian Fed. 27 H3
Ayn al Ghazal • Libya 21 D3
Aynunah • Saudi Arabia 18 B4
Ayod • Sudan 23 E2
Ayodhya • India 105 C8
Ayorou • Niger 20 F6
Ayoun el Atroûs • Mauritania 20 D5
Ayr • United Kingdom 6 H6
Ayr • QL, Australia 111 F1
Ayr [Riv] • United Kingdom 6 H6
Ayrshire • United Kingdom 75 A3
Aysha • Ethiopia 23 G1
Aytos • Bulgaria 97 D3
Ayutthaya **Heritage C** • Thailand 63 [174]
Ayutthaya • Thailand 109 H1
Ayvacik • Turkey 15 H4
Ayvalik • Turkey 15 H4
Ayvalik **Beach** • Turkey 69 [237]
Az Zahran • Saudi Arabia 18 E4
Az Zawiyah • Libya 21 B1
Azahar, Costa del • Spain 11 K5
Azaila • Spain 11 K3
Azamgarh • India 105 C8
Azangaro • Peru 127 B4
Azaouâd • Mali 20 E5
Azaouak, Vallée de l' • Mali/Niger 20 F5
Azare • Nigeria 22 G2
Azay-le-Ferron [Château] • France 84 D4
Azay-le-Rideau [Château] • France 84 D2
Azbine • Niger 20 G5
Azdavay • Turkey 15 O2
Azemmour • Morocco 101 D1
Azerbaijan • Asia 18 E1
Azinhal • Portugal 88 E4
Azogues • Ecuador 43 B4
Azores • Atlantic Ocean 88 B
Azov, Sea of • Russian Fed./Ukraine 17 F5
Azpeitia • Spain 11 I1
Azrou • Morocco 101 D2
Aztec Ruins Nat. Mon. • NM, United States 118 J2
Aztec Ruins Nat. Mon. **Park** • NM, United States 120 [124]
Azuaga • Spain 11 F6
Azuero, Península de • Panama 37 E6
Azul • Galapagos Is. 43 (1) A2
Azul • Argentina 127 D3
Azul, Costa • Portugal 88 D1
Azulcocha, Cerro • Peru 127 B1
Azur, Côte d' • France 85 H
Azure Window • Malta 93 H1
Azzel Matti, Sebkha • Algeria 20 F3
Azzurra, Grotta • Italy 91 G3

B

Ba'qubah • Iraq 18 D3
Baa • Indonesia 32 (1) B5
Baâba • New Caledonia 35 (2) A3
Baabe **Spa** • Germany 83 [280]
Baalbek **Heritage C** • Lebanon 64 [244]
Baarn • Netherlands 80 C2
Baba Burun • Çanakkale, Turkey 15 H4
Baba Burun • Zonguldak, Turkey 15 M2
Baba Dagi • Turkey 15 K7
Babadag • Romania 97 D2
Babaeski • Turkey 15 I2
Babanusah • Sudan 23 D1
Babaoyo • Ecuador 43 B4
Babar • Indonesia 32 (1) C4
Babayevo • Russian Fed. 97 E2
Babbacombe Bay • United Kingdom 74 F5
Babenhausen • Germany 82 J2
Baberton • South Africa 24 E5
Babian Jiang • China 29 C6
Babine Lake • BC, Canada 38 F6
Babiogórski Nat. Park **Park** • Poland 72 [96]
Babo • Indonesia 32 (1) D3
Babol • Iran 18 F2
Babonneau • St Lucia 125 J2
Babr • Poland 13 E6
Babruysk • Belarus 17 D4
Babuna • F.Y.R. of Macedonia 14 I8
Babuyan • Philippines 31 F4
Babuyan Is. • Philippines 31 G3
Babylon • Iraq 18 D3
Bac Lieu • Vietnam 108 B3
Bac Phan • Vietnam 31 D2
Bacabal • Brazil 45 (1) C2
Bacan • Indonesia 32 (1) C3
Bacau • Romania 14 N3
Baccarat • France 9 B8
Bacharach • Germany 82 H4
Back • NU, Canada 38 L3
Backa • F.R. of Yugoslavia 14 G4
Backa Topola • F.R. of Yugoslavia 14 G4
Bäckefors • Sweden 95 F2
Backnang • Germany 9 E8
Bacolod • Philippines 31 G4
Bad • Iran 18 F3
Bad Abbach **Spa** • Germany 83 [231]
Bad Aibling • Germany 82 J3
Bad Aibling **Spa** • Germany 83 [254]
Bad Alexandersbad **Spa** • Germany 83 [228]
Bad Aussee • Austria 89 H4
Bad Bayersoien • Germany 82 J6
Bad Bayersoien **Spa** • Germany 83 [248]
Bad Bederkesa **Spa** • Germany 83 [56]
Bad Bellingen **Spa** • Germany 83 [203]
Bad Bentheim **Spa** • Germany 83 [63]
Bad Bergzabern • Germany 82 G6
Bad Bergzabern **Spa** • Germany 83 [166]
Bad Berka **Spa** • Germany 83 [309]
Bad Berleburg • Germany 5 L3
Bad Berleburg **Spa** • Germany 83 [111]
Bad Berneck **Spa** • Germany 83 [226]
Bad Bertrich **Spa** • Germany 83 [157]
Bad Bevensen **Spa** • Germany 83 [58]
Bad Birnbach • Germany 82 J4
Bad Birnbach **Spa** • Germany 83 [263]
Bad Bocklet **Spa** • Germany 83 [220]
Bad Boll **Spa** • Germany 83 [193]
Bad Brambach **Spa** • Germany 83 [316]
Bad Bramstedt **Spa** • Germany 83 [33]
Bad Breisig • Germany 82 H1
Bad Breisig **Spa** • Germany 83 [150]
Bad Brückenau **Spa** • Germany 83 [219]
Bad Buchau • Germany 82 J1
Bad Buchau **Spa** • Germany 83 [214]
Bad Camberg **Spa** • Germany 83 [140]
Bad Colberg **Spa** • Germany 83 [305]
Bad Ditzenbach **Spa** • Germany 83 [194]
Bad Doberan • Germany 8 G2
Bad Doberan • Germany 13 A3
Bad Doberan **Spa** • Germany 83 [271]
Bad Driburg **Spa** • Germany 83 [99]
Bad Düben **Spa** • Germany 83 [312]
Bad Dürkheim • Germany 82 G4
Bad Dürkheim **Spa** • Germany 83 [165]
Bad Dürrheim **Spa** • Germany 83 [200]
Bad Eilsen **Spa** • Germany 83 [68]
Bad Elster **Spa** • Germany 83 [315]
Bad Ems • Germany 82 H2
Bad Ems **Spa** • Germany 83 [155]
Bad Emstal **Spa** • Germany 83 [124]
Bad Endbach **Spa** • Germany 83 [128]
Bad Endorf • Germany 82 J4
Bad Endorf **Spa** • Germany 83 [255]
Bad Essen **Spa** • Germany 83 [67]
Bad Faulenberg **Spa** • Germany 83 [244]
Bad Feilnbach • Germany 82 J7
Bad Feilnbach **Spa** • Germany 83 [260]
Bad Frankenhausen **Spa** • Germany 83 [298]
Bad Fredeburg **Spa** • Germany 83 [110]
Bad Freienwalde • Germany 8 J4
Bad Freienwalde **Spa** • Germany 83 [288]
Bad Füssing **Spa** • Germany 83 [264]
Bad Gandersheim **Spa** • Germany 83 [74]
Bad Godesberg • Germany 82 H1
Bad Gögging **Spa** • Germany 83 [230]
Bad Goisem • Austria 89 H4
Bad Gottleuba **Spa** • Germany 83 [318]
Bad Griesbach **Spa** • Germany 83 [263]
Bad Grund **Spa** • Germany 83 [75]
Bad Harzburg • Germany 8 F5
Bad Harzburg **Spa** • Germany 83 [78]
Bad Heilbrunn • Germany 82 J7
Bad Heilbrunn **Spa** • Germany 83 [251]
Bad Hermannsborn **Spa** • Germany 83 [99]
Bad Herrenalb **Spa** • Germany 83 [180]
Bad Hersfeld • Germany 9 E6
Bad Hersfeld **Spa** • Germany 83 [131]
Bad Hofgastein **Ski** • Austria 70 [169]
Bad Hofgastein • Austria 89 H8
Bad Homburg **Spa** • Germany 83 [145]
Bad Homburg vor der Höhe • Germany 82 H2
Bad Honnef • Germany 82 H1
Bad Honnef **Spa** • Germany 83 [115]
Bad Hönningen • Germany 82 H1
Bad Hönningen **Spa** • Germany 83 [151]
Bad Iburg **Spa** • Germany 83 [64]
Bad Imnau **Spa** • Germany 83 [189]
Bad Ischl • Austria 89 H4
Bad Karlshafen **Spa** • Germany 83 [119]
Bad Kissingen • Germany 9 F6
Bad Kissingen **Spa** • Germany 83 [220]
Bad Kleinkirchheim **Ski** • Austria 70 [189]
Bad Klosterlausnitz **Spa** • Germany 83 [311]
Bad Kohlgrub • Germany 82 J6
Bad Kohlgrub **Spa** • Germany 83 [249]
Bad König **Spa** • Germany 83 [147]
Bad Königshofen **Spa** • Germany 83 [222]
Bad Kösen **Spa** • Germany 83 [296]
Bad Kreuznach • Germany 82 H4
Bad Kreuznach **Spa** • Germany 83 [164]
Bad Krozingen • Germany 9 C9
Bad Krozingen **Spa** • Germany 83 [201]
Bad Laasphe **Spa** • Germany 83 [112]
Bad Laer **Spa** • Germany 83 [65]
Bad Langensalza • Germany 9 F5
Bad Langensalza **Spa** • Germany 83 [300]
Bad Lausick **Spa** • Germany 83 [313]
Bad Lauterberg • Germany 8 F5
Bad Lauterberg **Spa** • Germany 83 [82]
Bad Liebenstein **Spa** • Germany 83 [303]
Bad Liebenwerda **Spa** • Germany 83 [291]
Bad Liebenzell **Spa** • Germany 83 [177]
Bad Lippspringe **Spa** • Germany 83 [96]
Bad Malente-Gremsmühlen **Spa** • Germany 83 [31]
Bad Marienberg **Spa** • Germany 83 [153]
Bad Meinberg **Spa** • Germany 83 [97]
Bad Mergentheim • Germany 9 E7
Bad Mergentheim **Spa** • Germany 83 [171]
Bad Münder **Spa** • Germany 83 [70]
Bad Münster am Stein **Spa** • Germany 83 [163]
Bad Münstereifel • Germany 82 H1
Bad Münstereifel **Spa** • Germany 83 [116]
Bad Muskau **Spa** • Germany 83 [321]

Bad Nauheim • Germany 5 L4
Bad Nauheim • Germany 9 D6
Bad Nauheim **Spa** • Germany 83 [139]
Bad Nenndorf **Spa** • Germany 83 [69]
Bad Neuenahr **Spa** • Germany 83 [150]
Bad Neuenahr-Ahrweiler • Germany 82 H1
Bad Neustadt **Spa** • Germany 83 [221]
Bad Neustadt an der Saale • Germany 9 F6
Bad Niedernau **Spa** • Germany 83 [190]
Bad Oeynhausen **Spa** • Germany 83 [94]
Bad Oldesloe • Germany 16 F10
Bad Orb • Germany 5 M4
Bad Orb **Spa** • Germany 83 [137]
Bad Peterstal **Spa** • Germany 83 [187]
Bad Pyrmont • Germany 8 E5
Bad Pyrmont **Spa** • Germany 83 [71]
Bad Rappenau **Spa** • Germany 83 [173]
Bad Reichenhall • Germany 82 J8
Bad Reichenhall **Spa** • Germany 83 [261]
Bad Rippoldsau **Spa** • Germany 83 [188]
Bad Rothenfelde **Spa** • Germany 83 [65]
Bad Saarow **Spa** • Germany 83 [290]
Bad Sachsa **Spa** • Germany 83 [83]
Bad Säckingen **Spa** • Germany 83 [204]
Bad Salzdetfurth **Spa** • Germany 83 [73]
Bad Salzhausen **Spa** • Germany 83 [138]
Bad Salzschlirf **Spa** • Germany 83 [134]
Bad Salzuflen • Germany 8 D4
Bad Salzuflen **Spa** • Germany 83 [93]
Bad Salzungen • Germany 9 F6
Bad Salzungen **Spa** • Germany 83 [304]
Bad Sassendorf **Spa** • Germany 83 [104]
Bad Schandau **Spa** • Germany 83 [320]
Bad Schmiedeberg **Spa** • Germany 83 [292]
Bad Schönborn **Spa** • Germany 83 [172]
Bad Schussenried • Germany 82 J1
Bad Schussenried **Spa** • Germany 83 [216]
Bad Schwalbach • Germany 82 H4
Bad Schwalbach **Spa** • Germany 83 [141]
Bad Schwartau • Germany 8 F3
Bad Schwartau **Spa** • Germany 83 [30]
Bad Seebruch **Spa** • Germany 83 [92]
Bad Segeberg • Germany 8 F3
Bad Segeberg **Spa** • Germany 83 [34]
Bad Senkelteich **Spa** • Germany 83 [92]
Bad Sobernheim **Spa** • Germany 83 [162]
Bad Soden **Spa** • Germany 83 [144]
Bad Soden-Salmünster **Spa** • Germany 83 [136]
Bad Sooden **Spa** • Germany 83 [130]
Bad Steben **Spa** • Germany 83 [225]
Bad Suderode **Spa** • Germany 83 [295]
Bad Sulza **Spa** • Germany 83 [310]
Bad Sülze **Spa** • Germany 83 [272]
Bad Teinach **Spa** • Germany 83 [182]
Bad Tennstedt **Spa** • Germany 83 [299]
Bad Tölz • Germany 82 J7
Bad Tölz **Spa** • Germany 83 [252]
Bad Überkingen **Spa** • Germany 83 [194]
Bad Urach • Germany 82 G6
Bad Urach **Spa** • Germany 83 [192]
Bad Vilbel **Spa** • Germany 83 [146]
Bad Waldliesborn **Spa** • Germany 83 [105]
Bad Waldsee • Germany 82 J1
Bad Waldsee **Spa** • Germany 83 [216]
Bad Wiessee • Germany 82 J7
Bad Wiessee **Spa** • Germany 83 [253]
Bad Wildbad • Germany 82 G6
Bad Wildbad **Spa** • Germany 83 [183]
Bad Wildungen • Germany 5 M3
Bad Wildungen • Germany 9 E5
Bad Wildungen **Spa** • Germany 83 [125]
Bad Wilsnack **Spa** • Germany 83 [287]
Bad Wimpfen • Germany 82 G4
Bad Wimpfen **Spa** • Germany 83 [173]
Bad Windsheim • Germany 9 F7
Bad Windsheim **Spa** • Germany 83 [229]
Bad Wörishofen • Germany 82 J2
Bad Wörishofen **Spa** • Germany 83 [235]
Bad Wurzach • Germany 82 J1
Bad Wurzach **Spa** • Germany 83 [217]
Bad Zwesten **Spa** • Germany 83 [126]
Bad Zwischenahn • Germany 8 D3
Bad Zwischenahn **Spa** • Germany 83 [51]
Badain Jaran Shamo • Mongolia 29 C2
Badajoz • Spain 11 E6
Badalona • Spain 87 D4
Badami • India 106 D2
Badanah • Saudi Arabia 18 D3
Badda • Ethiopia 23 F2
Bade • Indonesia 32 (1) E4
Baden • Switzerland 9 D9
Baden • Austria 13 F9
Baden-Baden • Germany 82 G6
Baden-Baden **Spa** • Germany 83 [181]
Baden-Württemberg • Germany 9 E8
Badenweiler • Germany 82 G7
Badenweiler **Spa** • Germany 83 [202]
Badgastein **Ski** • Austria 70 [168]
Badgastein • Austria 89 H8
Badia, Val • Italy 90 B2
Badiyat ash Sham • Iraq/Jordan 18 C3
Badlands • United States 117 D2
Badlands Nat. Park **Park** • SD, United States 120 [153]
Badr Hunayn • Saudi Arabia 18 C5
Badu I. • QL, Australia 34 H2
Badulla • Sri Lanka 106 D15
Badung, Bukit • Bali, Indonesia 110 C4
Badung, Selat • Indonesia 110 C4
Badwater Basin • CA, United States 117 F4
Baena • Spain 86 B3
Bafang • Cameroon 22 G3
Bafatá • Guinea-Bissau 22 B2
Baffin Bay • Canada/Greenland 36 K2
Baffin Bay • TX, United States 119 N5
Baffin I. • NU, Canada 39 P2
Baffing • Guinea/Mali 22 B2
Bafia • Cameroon 22 G4
Bafoulabé • Mali 20 C6
Bafoussam • Cameroon 22 G3
Bafq • Iran 18 G3
Baga • Goa, India 105 B1
Baga Beach • Goa, India 105 B1
Bagamoyo • Tanzania 102 H2
Bagan Datuk • Malaysia 108 D1
Bagansiapiapi • Indonesia 110 B4
Bagata • Dem. Rep. of Congo 23 B4
Bagdarin • Russian Fed. 27 H6
Bagé • Brazil 44 F5
Bagenkop • Denmark 95 F14
Bagerhat **Heritage C** • Bangladesh 63 [133]
Baggs, Bill, Cape Florida State Recreation Area • FL, United States 119 M8
Baghdad • Iraq 18 D3
Baghelkhand Plateau • India 105 C8
Bagheria • Sicily, Italy 12 H10
Baghlan • Afghanistan 18 I2
Baghwan Mahaveer Wildlife Sanctuary • Goa, India 105 B2
Baginton [Apt] • United Kingdom 74 D2
Bagnères-de-Bigorre • France 11 L1
Bagnères-de-Luchon • France 11 L2
Bagno di Romagna • Italy 12 F5
Bagoe • Mali 22 C2
Bagua • Peru 43 B5
Baguio • Philippines 31 G3
Bagzane, Mts • Niger 20 G5
Bahama Is. • West Indies 37 F2
Bahama Sea • West Indies 124 D3
Bahamas • West Indies 124 B
Bahamas Nat. Trust Park • Bahamas 124 B4
Bahariya Oasis • Egypt 101 F3
Bahau • Malaysia 108 D4
Bahawalnagar • Pakistan 28 B3
Bahawalpur • Pakistan 28 B3
Bahía • Honduras 37 D4
Bahia • Brazil 44 H1
Bahía Blanca • Argentina 45 D3
Bahía Grande • Majorca, Spain 87 H3
Bahía Honda • Cuba 124 D1
Bahia Honda State Recreation Area • FL, United States 119 M8
Bahía Negra • Paraguay 44 E3
Bahías, Camarones Cabo dos • Argentina 45 C4
Bahla **Heritage C** • Oman 63 [105]
Bahr • Chad/Sudan 21 D5
Bahr al Abyad, Al • Sudan 21 F5
Bahr al Azraq, Al • Sudan 21 F5
Bahr al Ghazal • Sudan 23 D2
Bahr Dar • Ethiopia 21 G5
Bahr el Arab • Sudan 19 G4
Bahraich • India 105 C3
Bahrain • Asia 18 F4
Bai Bung, Mui • Vietnam 108 B3
Baia Mare • Romania 14 K2
Baia Sardinia • Sardinia, Italy 90 C2
Baião • Brazil 45 (1) B2
Baibokoum • Chad 21 C6
Baicheng • China 29 G1
Baie Comeau • QU, Canada 123 D1
Baie Lazare Village • Seychelles 106 F1
Baie Verte • NF, Canada 123 D3
Baiersbronn • Germany 82 G6
Baiersbronn **Spa** • Germany 83 [185]
Baiguan • China 107 J4
Baijiahohu • China 107 H3
Baikal, Lake • Russian Fed. 27 G6
Baikal, Lake **Heritage N** • Russian Fed. 61 [65]
Baikal-Amur Railway • Russian Fed. 97 A5
Baikonur Cosmodrome • Kazakhstan 96 A2
Baile Atha Cliath • Ireland 79 E2
Bailén • Spain 11 H6
Bailundo • Angola 23 B6
Baina Beach • Goa, India 105 B1
Bainbridge • FL, United States 119 M2
Baing • Indonesia 32 (1) B5
Baingoin • China 28 E2
Baio Grande • Spain 11 C1
Baird Peninsula • NU, Canada 39 P3
Bairiki • Kiribati 33 I5
Bairnsdale • VI, Australia 111 G3
Baise • France 10 F10
Baitenghu Resort • Zhuhai, China 107 H3
Baitou • D.P.R. of Korea 30 E4
Baixo Longa • Angola 24 B3
Baixo-Alentejo • Portugal 11 C6
Baiyun [Apt] • China 107 H1
Baja • Hungary 13 H11
Baja California • Mexico 40 D6
Baja California [Adm] • Mexico 40 C6
Baja California Sur • Mexico 40 D6
Baja Nuevo • West Indies 124 A1
Bajas, Rías • Spain 11 B2
Baka • Sudan 23 E3
Bakadzicito • Bulgaria 15 H1
Bakal • Russian Fed. 26 I7
Bakala • Central African Rep. 22 I3
Bakanas • Kazakhstan 26 M9
Bakauheni • Indonesia 110 D1
Bakchar • Russian Fed. 26 N6
Bake • Indonesia 32 C3
Bakel • Senegal 22 B2
Baker • Pacific Ocean 33 J5
Baker • OR, United States 117 E4
Baker Lake • NU, Canada 38 L4
Baker Lake [Lake] • NU, Canada 38 L4
Baker, Mt • WA, United States 117 E1
Bakersfield • CA, United States 117 F6
Bakhta • Russian Fed. 26 O5
Bakhtaran • Iran 18 E3
Bakhuhn, Kuh-e • Iran 18 G4
Baki • Azerbaijan 18 E1
Bakir • Turkey 15 I4
Bakken **Park** • Denmark 73 [17]
Bakony • Hungary 13 G10
Bakoye • Mali 20 D6
Baku • Azerbaijan 18 E1
Bakungan • Indonesia 110 B1
Bala • Turkey 15 O4
Bala Morghab • Afghanistan 26 J10
Balabac • Philippines 31 F5
Balabac [I.] • Philippines 31 F5
Balabac, Selat • Malaysia/Philippines 31 F5
Balaban • Turkey 15 O4
Balaghat • India 28 C4
Balagne • Corsica, France 85 L1
Balaguer • Spain 11 L3
Balakovo • Russian Fed. 17 H4
Balan Dagi • Turkey 15 J7
Balandra • Trinidad & Tobago 125 K2
Balashov • Russian Fed. 17 G4
Balassagyarmat • Hungary 13 I9
Balaton • Hungary 13 G11
Balatonfüred • Hungary 13 G11
Balaurin • Indonesia 32 (1) B4
Balazote • Spain 11 I6
Balbi • Papua New Guinea 35 (1) E2
Balboa • Panama 58 B9
Balbriggan • Ireland 79 E2
Balcarce • Argentina 127 D4
Balchik Beach • Bulgaria 69 [243]
Balchik • Bulgaria 97 D4
Balclutha • New Zealand 112 L4
Balcones Escarpment • TX, United States 119 N3
Balderschwang • Germany 82 J5
Baldeneysee • Germany 81 E2
Baldy Peak • AZ, United States 118 J4
Balé Gong Palace • Bali, Indonesia 110 C4
Bale Mts Nat. Park **Park** • Ethiopia 103 [65]
Baleares, Is. • Spain 11 N5
Balearic Is. • Spain 11 N5
Balease, Gunung • Indonesia 32 (1) B3
Baleia, Ponta de • Brazil 45 (1) D5
Baleine, Grande Rivière de la • QU, Canada 39 P5
Baleine, Rivière à la • QU, Canada 39 R5
Baler • Philippines 31 G3
Baleshwar • India 28 E4
Balestrand • Norway 94 C4
Baley • Russian Fed. 27 I6
Balhaf • Yemen 18 E7
Bali • Crete, Greece 93 E2
Bali • Indonesia 110 C
Bali Aga • Bali, Indonesia 110 C2
Bali Handara • Bali, Indonesia 110 C2
Bali Sea • Indonesia 110 C2
Bali, Selat • Indonesia 110 C1
Balik Pulau Forest Reserve • Penang, Malaysia 108 C3
Balikesir • Turkey 92 D3
Balikpapan • Indonesia 32 F3
Balimbing • Indonesia 32 C4
Balimo • Papua New Guinea 35 (1) C2
Balingen • Germany 82 G6
Balkash Köli • Kazakhstan 26 M8
Balkhash • Kazakhstan 26 L8
Balkhash, Lake • Kazakhstan 26 M8
Ball's Pyramid • NS, Australia 34 K6
Balladonia • WA, Australia 34 D6
Ballaghaderreen • Ireland 79 F2
Ballangen • Norway 16 I2
Ballantrae • United Kingdom 7 H6
Ballarat • VI, Australia 111 G3
Ballâs • Egypt 21 F3
Ballenita, Punta • Chile 44 B4
Balleny Is. • Antarctica 46 (1) V3
Ballestas, Is. • Peru 127 B1
Ballia • India 105 C8
Ballina • NS, Australia 111 F6
Ballinasloe • Ireland 79 F4
Ballinrobe • Ireland 79 F4
Ballinskelligs **Beach** • Ireland 68 [60]
Ballinskelligs • Ireland 79 F7
Ballintober Abbey • Ireland 79 F2
Ballivor • Ireland 79 E1
Ballranald • NS, Australia 111 G1
Ballybunion **Beach** • Ireland 68 [60]
Ballybunion • Ireland 79 F5
Ballycastle **Beach** • United Kingdom 75 [238]
Ballycastle • United Kingdom 78 A2
Ballycastle • Ireland 79 F2
Ballydehob • Ireland 79 E4
Ballyhaunis • Ireland 79 F2
Ballyheige **Beach** • Ireland 68 [60]
Ballyheige • Ireland 79 F5
Ballylynan • Ireland 79 E3
Ballymena • United Kingdom 7 F7
Ballymore Eustace • Ireland 79 E3
Ballymote • Ireland 79 F2
Ballyshannon • Ireland 7 D7
Ballytore • Ireland 79 E3
Ballyvaughan **Beach** • Ireland 68 [61]
Ballyvaughan • Ireland 79 F4
Balmoral • United Kingdom 6 I4
Balochistan • Pakistan 18 H4
Balonne • QL, Australia 111 F5
Balotra • India 105 C5
Balranald • NS, Australia 34 H6
Bals • Romania 14 L5
Balsams, The **Ski** • NH, United States 116 [217]
Balsas • Brazil 45 (1) B3
Balsas • Mexico 123 E4
Bålsta • Sweden 95 D2
Balti • Moldova 14 O2
Baltic Coast • Poland 96 B1
Baltic cruise area • Europe 59 A4
Baltic Republics • Europe 96 A1
Baltic Sea • Europe 16 J8
Baltim • Egypt 101 F1
Baltimore • Ireland 79 F8
Baltimore • MD, United States 118 H3
Baltimore Washington Int. Airport • MD, United States 118 H3
Baltinglass • Ireland 79 E3
Baltiysk • Russian Fed. 13 I3
Baltrum • Germany 8 C3
Baltrum **Spa** • Germany 83 [39]
Balve • Germany 9 C5
Balya • Turkey 15 I4
Bam • Iran 18 G4
Bam Co • China 28 F2
BAM Railway • Russian Fed. 97 A5
Bama • Nigeria 22 G2
Bamaga • QL, Australia 34 H2
Bamako • Mali 22 C2
Bambari • Central African Rep. 23 C2
Bamberg • Germany 9 F7
Bamberg **Heritage C** • Germany 64 [46]
Bambili • Dem. Rep. of Congo 23 D3
Bambio • Central African Rep. 22 H4
Bambolim Beach • Goa, India 105 B1
Bamboutos, Mts • Cameroon 22 G3
Bambui • Brazil 127 C1
Bamburgh **Beach** • United Kingdom 75 [9]
Bamburi Beach • Kenya 101 G5
Bamenda • Cameroon 22 G3
Bamian • Afghanistan 18 I3
Bamingui-Bangoran, Parc nat. du **Park** • Central African Rep. 103 [45]
Bamovskoye • Russian Fed. 97 A6
Bampur • Iran 18 H4
Bampur [Riv] • Iran 18 G4
Ban Bang Po • Ko Samui, Thailand 109 J1
Ban Bophut • Ko Samui, Thailand 109 J1
Ban Chaweng • Ko Samui, Thailand 109 J1
Ban Chaweng Noi • Ko Samui, Thailand 109 J2
Ban Chiang **Heritage C** • Thailand 63 [172]
Ban Chiang • Thailand 109 F1
Ban Hong • Thailand 109 G3
Ban Houayxay • Laos 31 C2
Ban Hua Thanon • Ko Samui, Thailand 109 J2
Ban Klaeng • Thailand 109 H4
Ban Laem • Thailand 109 H3
Ban Lamai • Ko Samui, Thailand 109 J2
Ban Lipa Noi • Ko Samui, Thailand 109 J2
Ban Maenam • Ko Samui, Thailand 109 J1
Ban Me Thuot • Vietnam 108 B2
Ban Pae • Thailand 109 H4
Ban Phang Ka • Ko Samui, Thailand 109 J2
Ban Pong • Thailand 109 H1
Ban Sa Ket • Ko Samui, Thailand 109 J2
Ban Sa Kret • Ko Samui, Thailand 109 J2
Ban Tah • Thailand 109 H3
Ban Tai • Ko Samui, Thailand 109 J1
Ban Taling Ngam • Ko Samui, Thailand 109 J2
Ban Thale • Ko Samui, Thailand 109 J2
Ban Thong Krut • Ko Samui, Thailand 109 J2
Ban Thong Tanot • Ko Samui, Thailand 109 J2
Ban Thurian • Ko Samui, Thailand 109 J2
Ban Tong Yang • Ko Samui, Thailand 109 J2
Banaadir • Somalia 23 G3
Banaba • Kiribati 33 I6
Banados del Izozog • Bolivia 44 D2
Banalia • Dem. Rep. of Congo 23 D3
Banamba • Mali 22 C2
Bananga • India 28 F7
Banâs, Râs • Egypt 101 F5
Banat • Romania 14 I4
Banaz • Turkey 15 K5
Banaz [Riv] • Turkey 15 K5
Banbury • United Kingdom 74 D4
Banc d'Arguin Nat. Park **Heritage N** • Mauritania 61 [70]
Banc d'Arguin Nat. Park **Park** • Mauritania 103 [1]
Banco Chinchorro • Mexico 37 D4
Bancroft • OT, Canada 122 B6
Banda • India 105 C7
Banda Aceh • Indonesia 110 B1
Banda, Kepulauan • Indonesia 32 (1) C3
Banda Sea • Indonesia 32 (1) C4
Bandak • Norway 94 C6
Bandama • Côte d'Ivoire 22 D3
Bandama • Gran Canaria, Canary Is. 86 E4
Bandar Seri Begawan • Brunei 32 E2
Bandar-e 'Abbas • Iran 18 G4
Bandar-e Anzali • Iran 18 E2
Bandar-e Khomeyni • Iran 18 E3
Bandar-e Langeh • Iran 18 F4
Bandar-e Maqam • Iran 18 F4
Bandar-e Torkeman • Iran 18 F2
Bandeira, Pico da • Brazil 127 C2
Bandelier Nat. Mon. • NM, United States 118 J2
Bandelier Nat. Mon. **Park** • NM, United States 120 [129]
Banderas, Bahía de • Mexico 37 (1) A1
Bandiagara Cliffs **Heritage N** • Mali 61 [69]
Bandipur Nat. Park • India 106 D6
Bandirma • Turkey 92 D3
Bandirma Körfezi • Turkey 15 J3
Bandol **Beach** • France 68 [133]
Bandol • France 85 H3
Bandon • Ireland 79 F8
Bandon • OR, United States 117 E3
Bandos • Maldives 106 E4
Bandundu • Dem. Rep. of Congo 23 B4
Bandundu [Adm] • Dem. Rep. of Congo 23 B4
Bandung • Java, Indonesia 110 D2
Bandungan • Java, Indonesia 110 D7
Baneasa [Apt] • Romania 97 D1
Banes • Cuba 124 D8
Banff • AL, Canada 122 C4
Banff Nat. Park • AL, Canada 122 C4
Banffshire • United Kingdom 75 A1
Bang Kaong Beach • Phuket, Thailand 109 K1
Bang Pa-In • Thailand 109 H1
Bang Saen • Thailand 109 H4
Bang Thao • Phuket, Thailand 109 K1
Bang Thao Beach • Phuket, Thailand 109 K1
Bangalore • India 106 D6
Banganapalle • India 106 D3
Bangang Co • China 28 C2
Bangaram I. • India 106 D9
Bangassou • Central African Rep. 23 C3
Bangeta • Papua New Guinea 35 (1) D2
Banggai • Indonesia 32 (1) B3
Banggi • Malaysia 31 F5
Banghazi • Libya 21 C1
Bangil • Java, Indonesia 110 D8
Bangka • Indonesia 32 D3
Bangkalan • Indonesia 110 D4
Bangkao Bay • Ko Samui, Thailand 109 J2
Bangkok • Thailand 109 H1
Bangkok, Bight of • Thailand 109 H3
Bangladesh • Asia 28 E4
Bangli • Bali, Indonesia 110 C4
Bangor • N. Ireland, UK 7 G7
Bangor • Wales, UK 7 H8
Bangor • Ireland 79 F1
Bangor • ME, United States 118 G4
Bangui • Central African Rep. 23 B3
Bangweulu, Lake • Zambia 24 D2
Bangyai • Phuket, Thailand 109 K2
Bani • Mali 22 C2
Bani Walid • Libya 21 B1
Baniyas • Syria 98 A2
Banja Luka • Bosnia-Herz. 14 E5
Banjar • Bali, Indonesia 110 C1
Banjar • Java, Indonesia 110 D6
Banjarmasin • Indonesia 32 E3
Banjul • Gambia 22 A2
Bank I. • BC, Canada 38 E6
Bankas • Mali 20 E6
Bankberg • South Africa 100 C4
Bankeryd • Sweden 95 F7
Banks I. • QL, Australia 34 H2
Banks I. • NT, Canada 38 G2
Banks Is. • Vanuatu 35 (2) B1
Banks Peninsula • New Zealand 35 D6
Banks Strait • TS, Australia 34 I8
Bann • United Kingdom 7 F7
Bannockburn • United Kingdom 74 B3
Bannu • Pakistan 28 B2
Bansin **Beach** • Germany 69 [30]
Bansin **Spa** • Germany 83 [285]
Banská Bystrica • Slovak Rep 13 I9
Banská Stiavnica • Slovak Rep. 13 H9
Banská Stiavnica **Heritage C** • Slovak Rep. 64 [149]
Banten • Java, Indonesia 110 D1
Bantham **Beach** • United Kingdom 75 [115]
Bantry • Ireland 79 F7
Bantry Bay • Ireland 79 F7
Bañuelo • Spain 11 G6
Banyak, Kepulauan • Indonesia 110 B3
Banyalbufar • Majorca, Spain 87 H1
Banyo • Cameroon 22 G3
Banyoles • Spain 11 N2
Banyuls • France 84 B4
Banyuls-sur-Mer **Beach** • France 68 [128]
Banyumas • Java, Indonesia 110 D6
Banyuwangi • Java, Indonesia 110 D8
Banyuwedang • Bali, Indonesia 110 C1
Bao Loc • Vietnam 108 B2
Bao'an • China 107 H3
Baoding • China 29 F3
Baoji • China 29 D4
Baoqing • China 27 L7
Baoshan • Yunnan, China 29 B5
Baoshan • Shanghai, China 107 J2
Baotou • China 29 E2
Baoulé • Côte d'Ivoire/Mali 22 C2
Bapulé • Mali 22 C2
Baquedano • Chile 44 C3
Bar • France 5 H5
Bar • F.R. of Yugoslavia 14 G7
Bar Am • Israel 98 A2
Bar Harbor • ME, United States 118 G4
Bar-le-Duc • France 10 K5
Barabinsk • Russian Fed. 26 M6
Barabinskaya Step • Russian Fed. 26 M6
Baracaldo • Spain 11 H1
Baracoa • Cuba 124 D8
Barafundle Bay **Beach** • United Kingdom 75 [155]
Baraganului, Cimpia • Romania 14 O5
Barahona • Dominican Rep. 37 G4
Baraki Barak • Afghanistan 18 I3
Baranja • Hungary 14 F4
Barano d'Ischia • Italy 91 G3
Baranov I. • AK, United States 38 D5
Baranovichi • Belarus 16 N10
Barat Daya, Kepulauan • Indonesia 110 A7
Baratang • India 28 F6
Barawe • Somalia 23 G3
Barbacena • Brazil 127 C1
Barbados • West Indies 125 H
Barbar • Sudan 21 F4
Bárbara • Colombia 43 C4
Barbaresco • Italy 91 E5
Barbaros • Turkey 15 I3
Barbary Coast • Africa 59 C5-6
Barbastro • Spain 11 L2
Barbate de Franco • Spain 86 B5
Barbâti • Corfu, Greece 92 B1
Barbeau Peak • NU, Canada 36 J1
Barbezieux • France 85 G1
Barbuda • Antigua & Barbuda 37 I4
Barca de Alva • Portugal 11 E3
Barcaldine • QL, Australia 111 F3
Barcarès, le **Beach** • France 68 [128]
Barcarrota • Spain 11 E6
Barcellona Pozzo di Gotto • Sicily, Italy 12 J10
Barcelona • Venezuela 43 E2
Barcelona **Beach** • Spain 68 [122]
Barcelona **Heritage C** • Spain 64 [71-72]
Barcelona • Spain 87 D3
Barcelonette • France 85 H2
Barcelos • Brazil 43 E4
Barcoo • QL, Australia 111 E7
Barcs • Hungary 14 E4
Bardaï • Chad 21 C3
Bardejov • Slovak Rep. 13 K8
Bardere • Somalia 23 G3
Bardeskan • Iran 26 I10
Bardo • Tunisia 12 E12
Bardolino • Italy 91 E7
Bardonécchia **Ski** • Italy 70 [196]
Bardonécchia • Italy 91 E5
Bareda • Somalia 23 I1
Barèges • France 85 J2
Bareilly • India 105 C3
Barentin • France 10 F4
Barents Sea • Arctic Ocean 4 S2
Barentsburg • Svalbard 46 N2
Barfleur • France 5 B5
Barfleur, Point de • France 5 B5
Barga • China 28 D2
Bargal • Somalia 23 I1
Bargarh • India 28 D4
Barguzinskiy Khrebet • Russian Fed. 27 H6
Bari • Italy 12 K7
Barinas • Venezuela 43 C2
Baringo, Lake • Kenya 101 G1
Baripada • India 28 E4
Barisal • Bangladesh 28 E4
Barisov • Belarus 17 D4
Barito • Indonesia 32 E3
Barka • Oman 18 G5
Barkat Nasser • Egypt 18 B5
Barkerville • BC, Canada 122 C1
Barkly Tableland • NT, Australia 34 G3
Barlee, Lake • WA, Australia 34 C5
Barletta • Italy 12 K7
Barlinek • Poland 13 E4
Barlovento de Jandía, Playa de • Fuerteventura, Canary Is. 87 E2
Barma • Indonesia 32 (1) D3
Barmer • India 105 C5
Barmera • SA, Australia 34 H6
Barmouth • United Kingdom 7 H9
Barmouth **Beach** • United Kingdom 75 [188]
Barnaul • Russian Fed. 26 N7
Barnes Hill • Antigua & Barbuda 125 F1
Barneville-Carteret • France 10 D4
Barneville-Carteret **Beach** • France 68 [78]
Barnsley • United Kingdom 7 K8
Barnstaple • United Kingdom 74 F2
Barnstaple Bay • United Kingdom 74 F2
Barolo • Italy 91 E5
Baronia • Sardinia, Italy 90 C2
Baros • Maldives 106 E2
Barossa Valley • SA, Australia 111 E7
Barqah al Bahriyah • Egypt/Libya 21 E1
Barqu, Jabal • Tunisia 12 D12
Barquisimeto • Venezuela 43 D2
Barra • United Kingdom 6 E4
Barra • Brazil 45 (1) C4
Barra de Navidad • Mexico 123 E3
Barra de Tijuca • Brazil 127 C3
Barra do Cuanza • Angola 23 A5
Barra Falsa, Ponta da • Mozambique 24 F4
Barra Mansa • Brazil 127 C3
Barra, Ponta da • Mozambique 24 F4
Barracão do Barreto • Brazil 43 F5
Barranca • Peru 43 B4
Barrancabermeja • Colombia 43 C2
Barrancas • Venezuela 43 E2
Barranco do Velho • Portugal 88 E3
Barranqueras • Argentina 44 E4
Barranquilla • Colombia 43 C1
Barre • VT, United States 118 G3
Barre de l'Isle • St Lucia 125 J2
Barre des Ecrins • France 85 F4
Barreiras • Brazil 45 (1) C4
Barreiro • Portugal 88 D2
Barreiros **Beach** • Spain 68 [91]
Barren • Madagascar 24 G3
Barren Grounds • NU, Canada 122 A2
Barreta, I. da • Portugal 88 E7
Barretos • Brazil 44 G3
Barrie • OT, Canada 122 B5
Barrier Reef Reserve System **Heritage N** • Belize 60 [21]
Barrington, Fort • Antigua & Barbuda 125 F1
Barrington Tops • NS, Australia 34 J6
Barrow • Ireland 7 F9
Barrow • AK, United States 46 EE2
Barrow Creek • NT, Australia 112 H2
Barrow I. • WA, Australia 34 C4
Barrow, Point • AK, United States 36 B2
Barrow-in-Furness • United Kingdom 74 C3
Barry • United Kingdom 74 F2
Barry I. Pleasure Beach **Park** • United Kingdom 73 [33]
Barry I. Pleasure Beach • United Kingdom 74 F2
Barry's Amusement Park **Park** • United Kingdom 73 [21]
Barrys Bay • OT, Canada 122 B6
Barsac • France 84 B3
Barsinghausen • Germany 8 E4
Barstow • CA, United States 117 F6
Barth • Germany 8 H2
Bartin • Turkey 15 N2
Bartle Frere, Mt • QL, Australia 111 F1
Bartlet Town • Bahamas 124 B2
Bartoszyce • Poland 13 J3
Baru, Volcán • Panama 37 E6
Barùmini • Sardinia, Italy 90 C4
Barumun • Indonesia 110 B4
Barun Bagdo-Ula • Mongolia 29 C1
Barung • Indonesia 110 D8
Barwon • NS/QL, Australia 111 E8
Barycz • Poland 13 F6
Bas Médoc • France 84 B3
Basak • Cambodia 108 B1
Basankusu • Dem. Rep. of Congo 23 B3
Basauri • Spain 11 I1
Bascuñan, Cabo • Chile 44 B4
Basdorf • Germany 81 F2
Basel • Switzerland 9 C9
Basey • Philippines 31 H4
Bashi Haixia • Taiwan 31 G2
Bashkortostan • Russian Fed. 17 J3
Basilan • Philippines 31 G5
Basildon • United Kingdom 74 E2
Basilicata • Italy 12 K8
Basingstoke • United Kingdom 7 K10
Baskatong, Réservoir • QU, Canada 122 B3
Basle • Switzerland 82 G7
Basoko • Dem. Rep. of Congo 23 C3
Basque Coast • Spain 86 A1
Basque, Côte • France 85 J1
Basque Country • Spain 86 A1
Basque, Pays • France 85 J1
Basrah, Al • Iraq 18 E3
Bass Lake • CA, United States 117 F3
Bass Strait • TS/VI, Australia 34 I7
Bassae **Heritage C** • Greece 64 [180]
Bassar • Togo 22 E3
Basse da India • Reunion 24 F4
Basse Normandie • France 84 A1
Basse Terre • Guadeloupe 37 I4
Basse-Casamance, Parc nat. de **Park** • Senegal 103 [9]
Bassein • Myanmar 31 A3
Bassenthwaite • United Kingdom 74 C1
Bassenthwaite Lake • United Kingdom 74 C1
Basseterre • St Kitts & Nevis 125 G1
Basseterre Bay • St Kitts & Nevis 125 G1
Bassila • Benin 22 E3
Basso, Plateau de • Chad 21 D4
Bassum • Germany 5 L2
Båstad **Beach** • Sweden 68 [8]
Båstad • Sweden 95 F11
Bastelica • Corsica, France 85 L3
Basti • India 105 C4
Bastia • Italy 12 G5
Bastia • Corsica, France 85 L2
Bastogne • Belgium 80 A19
Bastrop • LA, United States 118 K1
Bastrop • TX, United States 119 N3
Bat **Heritage C** • Oman 63 [106]
Bata • Equatorial Guinea 22 F4
Batabanó, Golfo de • Cuba 124 D1
Batagay • Russian Fed. 27 L3
Batagay-Alyta • Russian Fed. 27 L3
Batak • Bulgaria 14 L8
Bataklik Gölü • Turkey 15 O6
Batalha **Heritage C** • Portugal 64 [97]
Batan Is. • Philippines 31 G2
Batang • China 29 B5
Batangafo • Central African Rep. 23 B2
Batanghari • Indonesia 32 C3
Batangos • Philippines 31 G4
Batchelor • NT, Australia 34 F2
Batchelor, Mt • OR, United States 117 E3
Batdâmbâng • Cambodia 31 C4
Batéké, Plateaux • Congo 22 G5
Batemans Bay • NS, Australia 111 G2
Bath **Heritage C** • United Kingdom 64 [19]
Bath • United Kingdom 74 F3
Bath • Jamaica 124 C4
Bath • St Kitts & Nevis 125 G4
Batha • Chad 21 C5
Bathgate • United Kingdom 74 B4
Bathsheba • Barbados 125 H2
Bathurst • NU, Canada 38 L1
Bathurst • NS, Australia 111 G2
Bathurst • NB, Canada 123 D2
Bathurst, Cape • NT, Canada 38 F2
Bathurst I. • NT, Australia 34 F2
Bathurst Inlet • NU, Canada 46 Z3
Batna • Algeria 20 G1
Bato-Bato • Philippines 31 F5
Baton Rouge • LA, United States 118 K4
Batouri • Cameroon 23 A3
Battenberg • Germany 9 D5
Batti Maly • India 28 F7
Batticaloa • Sri Lanka 106 D16
Battipaglia • Italy 91 G4
Battle • AL, Canada 38 I6
Battle • United Kingdom 74 E4
Battle Creek • MI, United States 41 I3
Battle Harbour • NF, Canada 39 T6
Battle Mountain • NV, United States 117 F2
Batu • Ethiopia 23 F2
Batu Berinchang, Gunung • Malaysia 108 D1
Batu Caves • Malaysia 108 D4
Batu Gajah • Malaysia 108 D1
Batu, Kepulauan • Indonesia 110 B4
Batu Pahat • Malaysia 32 C2
Batu Putih, Gunung • Malaysia 108 D1
Batuasa • Indonesia 32 (1) D3
Batukau, Gunung • Bali, Indonesia 110 C2
Batumi • Georgia 17 G6

Batur, Danau • Bali, Indonesia 110 C2
Batur, Gunung • Bali, Indonesia 110 C2
Batur Temple • Bali, Indonesia 110 C2
Baturaja • Indonesia 32 C3
Baturino • Russian Fed. 26 O6
Batusangkar • Indonesia 110 B4
Baubau • Indonesia 32 (1) B4
Baucau • East Indies 32 (1) C4
Bauchi • Nigeria 22 F2
Bauchi [Adm] • Nigeria 22 G3
Baudry • Switzerland 89 G1
Baudry [Château] • France 84 D2
Bauld, Cape • NF, Canada 123 D5
Baule-Escoublac, la • France 84 C4
Bauru • Brazil 44 G3
Bauska • Latvia 13 N1
Bautzen • Germany 9 J5
Bavaria • Germany 81 D4
Bavarian Alps • Germany 81 D4
Bavella, Col de • Corsica, France 85 L4
Båven • Sweden 95 D3
Baw Sang • Thailand 109 G1
Bawamataluo • Indonesia 110 B3
Bawe • Indonesia 32 (1) D3
Bawean • Indonesia 110 D4
Bawiti • Egypt 101 F3
Bawku • Ghana 22 D2
Baxoi • China 28 G2
Baxter State Park • ME, United States 118 G2
Bay Area • CA, United States 117 F3
Bay City • MI, United States 41 J3
Bay City • TX, United States 119 N6
Bay Is. • Honduras 124 A1
Bay of Islands • New Zealand 35 E2
Bay of Isles • South Georgia 59 A10
Bay of Plenty [Adm] • New Zealand 112 J2
Bay View • New Zealand 112 K4
Bayad, Al • Saudi Arabia 18 E5
Bayadh, El • Algeria 20 F2
Bayah Har Shan • China 28 G2
Bayamo • Cuba 124 D8
Bayamón • Puerto Rico 125 E2
Bayan • Mongolia 26 Q9
Bayan Har Shan • China 29 B4
Bayan Lepas • Penang, Malaysia 108 C3
Bayan Lepas [Apt] • Penang, Malaysia 108 C3
Bayan Obo • China 29 D2
Bayan Uul • Mongolia 27 H7
Bayana • India 105 C6
Bayanga • Central African Rep. 23 B3
Bayda, Al • Libya 21 D1
Baydaratskaya Guba • Russian Fed. 26 K4
Bayerisch Gmain Spa • Germany 83 [261]
Bayerische Alpen • Germany 82 J7
Bayerischer Wald • Germany 9 I8
Bayern • Germany 9 G8
Bayeux • France 10 E4
Baykal, Ozero • Russian Fed. 25 L4
Baykalskiy Khrebet • Russian Fed. 27 G6
Baykit • Russian Fed. 26 Q5
Baykonyr • Kazakhstan 26 K8
Bayona • Spain 11 C2
Bayonne • France 85 J1
Bayram-Ali • Turkmenistan 18 H2
Bayramiç • Turkey 15 H4
Bayreuth • Germany 9 G7
Bayrischer Wald, Nationalpark Park • Germany 72 [64]
Bayrischzell Ski • Germany 70 [4]
Bayrischzell • Germany 82 J7
Bayrischzell Spa • Germany 83 [259]
Bayrut • Lebanon 18 B3
Baytik Shan • China 26 O8
Baytown • TX, United States 119 N4
Bayy al Kabir • Libya 21 B1
Baza • Spain 86 B4
Bazardüzü • Azerbaijan 17 H6
Bazas • France 85 G3
Be'er Shiva • Israel 18 B3
Beachy Head • United Kingdom 74 E3
Beadnell Bay Beach • United Kingdom 75 [11]
Béalanana • Madagascar 24 H2
Bear, Cap • France 85 K2
Bear Cove • BC, Canada 122 C3
Bear Creek Ski • MI, United States 116 [127]
Bear I. • Ireland 79 F7
Bear Valley Ski • CA, United States 116 [60]
Beara Peninsula • Ireland 79 F7
Béarn • France 85 J2
Beata, Cabo • Dominican Rep. 37 G4
Beatrice • NE, United States 41 G3
Beatty • NV, United States 117 F4
Beau Vallon, Baie • Seychelles 106 F1
Beaufort • Malaysia 32 F1
Beaufort • Luxembourg 80 A20
Beaufort • NC, United States 118 H5
Beaufort I. • Hong Kong, China 107 H6
Beaufort Sea • Arctic Ocean 36 C2
Beaufort West • South Africa 100 C3
Beaugency • France 84 D2
Beaujolais • France 84 B4
Beaulieu-sur-Mer • France 85 H2
Beaumaris Beach • United Kingdom 75 [230]
Beaumont • France 5 B5
Beaumont • New Zealand 112 L4
Beaumont • TX, United States 119 N4
Beaune • France 10 J6
Beauregard [Château] • France 84 D2
Beauséjour, Fort • NB, Canada 123 D7
Beauté, I. de • France 84 B4
Beauvais • France 85 E1
Beauval • SA, Canada 38 J5
Beauvoir-sur-Mer • France 10 C7
Beaver Creek Ski • CO, United States 116 [95]
Beaver Valley Ski • OT, Canada 116 [19]
Beawar • India 105 C6
Bebedouro • Brazil 44 G3
Bebra • Germany 9 E6
Becej • F.R. of Yugoslavia 14 H4
Béchar • Algeria 20 E2
Bechet • Romania 14 K6
Bechyne • Czech Rep. 96 C4
Beckley • WV, United States 41 J4
Beckum • Germany 8 D5
Bective Abbey • Ireland 79 E1
Bedarieux • France 10 I10
Bedarra I. • QL, Australia 111 F1
Bedburg • Germany 81 E3
Bedford • United Kingdom 7 L9
Bedford Level • United Kingdom 5 C2
Bedfordshire • United Kingdom 75 A5
Bedulu • Bali, Indonesia 110 C4
Beek [Apt] • Netherlands 80 A15
Beekse Bergen • Netherlands 80 A11
Beersheba • Israel 98 A7
Beesands Beach • United Kingdom 75 [109]
Beeston • United Kingdom 7 K9
Beeville • TX, United States 119 N5
Bega • NS, Australia 111 G4
Begejski Kanal • F.R. of Yugoslavia/Romania 14 H4
Beggars Point • Antigua & Barbuda 125 F1
Begna • Norway 16 E6
Begur Beach • Spain 68 [123]
Begur • Spain 87 D2
Behérobie • France 85 J1
Behshahr • Iran 18 F2
Bei Jiang • China 31 E2
Bei'an • China 27 K7
Beida He • China 29 B3
Beihai • China 29 D6
Beijing • China 29 F3
Beijing Heritage C • China 63 [146]
Beijing [Adm] • China 107 G3
Beila • Mauritania 20 B5
Beilstein • Germany 82 H3
Beira • Mozambique 24 E3
Beira Alta • Portugal 11 D4
Beira Baixa • Portugal 11 D5
Beira Litoral • Portugal 11 C4
Beirut • Lebanon 18 B3
Beit el Wali • Egypt 101 F5
Beitbridge • Zimbabwe 102 J4
Beius • Romania 14 J3
Beja • Portugal 11 D6
Béja • Tunisia 101 E1
Beja [Adm] • Portugal 88 A3
Béjaïa • Algeria 20 G1
Béjar • Spain 11 F4
Beji Temple • Bali, Indonesia 110 C2
Bekal • India 106 D6
Bekasi • Java, Indonesia 110 D1
Bekdash • Turkmenistan 18 F1
Békés • Hungary 13 K11
Bekily • Madagascar 24 H4
Bela • Pakistan 28 A3
Bela, Costa • Portugal 88 D2
Bela Crkva • F.R. of Yugoslavia 14 I5
Bela Pratapgarh • India 105 C8
Bela Vista • Mozambique 24 E5
Belaga • Malaysia 32 E2
Belang • Indonesia 32 (1) B2
Belarus • Europe 15 D4
Belawan • Indonesia 110 B2
Belaya • Russian Fed. 4 V6
Belaya • Russian Fed. 27 T3
Belayan • Indonesia 32 F3
Belchatów • Poland 13 I6
Belchen • Germany 82 G8
Belcher Is. • NU, Canada 39 P5
Belchite • Spain 10 E12
Beldibi Beach • Turkey 69 [227]
Beldibi • Turkey 93 G3
Beled Weyne • Somalia 23 H3
Belek Beach • Turkey 69 [224]
Belek • Turkey 93 G4
Belém • Brazil 45 (1) B2
Belém • Portugal 88 D1
Belen • NM, United States 118 J2
Belep, Is. • New Caledonia 35 (2) A2
Beleye • Ethiopia 23 F1
Belfast • United Kingdom 7 G7
Belford • United Kingdom 6 K6
Belfort • France 10 L6
Belfort • Lebanon 98 A2
Belfry, The • United Kingdom 74 D2
Belgaum • India 106 D2
Belgium • Europe 5 H4
Belgodore • Corsica, France 85 L1
Belgorod • Russian Fed. 17 F4
Belgrade • F.R. of Yugoslavia 14 H5
Belhaven Bay Beach • United Kingdom 75 [8]
Bélice • Sicily, Italy 90 D1
Beliche • Portugal 88 E5
Bélinga • Gabon 22 G4
Belitung • Indonesia 32 D3
Belize • C. America 37 D4
Belize City • Belize 37 D4
Beljanica • F.R. of Yugoslavia 14 I5
Bell • QU, Canada 39 P7
Bell Peninsula • NU, Canada 39 O4
Bell Ville • Argentina 44 D5
Bella Coola • BC, Canada 38 F6
Bellac • France 84 D4
Bellágio • Italy 91 E2
Bellamonte Ski • Italy 70 [219]
Bellamonte • Italy 90 B3
Bellaria • Italy 12 G4
Bellary • India 106 D2
Belle Glade • FL, United States 119 M6
Belle Isle • FL, United States 121 C2
Belle Isle • NF, Canada 123 D5
Belle Isle, Strait of • NF, Canada 123 D5
Belle Tete • St Kitts & Nevis 125 G1
Belle Vue • St Lucia 125 J4
Belle-Ile • France 84 C4
Belleayre Ski • NY, United States 116 [180]
Bellegarde-sur-Valserine • France 85 F1
Bellépais Abbey • Cyprus 93 J1
Belleplaine • Barbados 125 H1
Belleville • OT, Canada 122 B6
Belleville • WA, United States 117 E1
Bellevue, Grotte de • France 85 G4
Bellewaerde Park Park • Belgium 73 [47]
Bellewaerde Park • Belgium 80 A13
Bellingham • WA, United States 117 E1
Bellingshausen [Base] • Antarctica 46 (1) JJ4
Bellingshausen Sea • Pacific Ocean 46 (1) GG4
Bellinzona • Switzerland 89 G7
Bello • Colombia 43 B2
Belluno • Italy 90 B4
Bellville • South Africa 100 C5
Bellwald • Switzerland 89 G6
Belm • Germany 8 D4
Belmonte • Brazil 44 I2
Belmopan • Belize 37 D4
Belmullet Beach • Ireland 68 [63]
Belmullet • Ireland 79 F1
Belo Horizonte • Brazil 127 C1
Belo-Tsiribihina • Madagascar 24 G3
Belœil • Belgium 80 A14
Belogorsk • Russian Fed. 27 K6
Belomorsk • Russian Fed. 17 E2
Beloretsk • Russian Fed. 26 I7
Belot, Lac • NT, Canada 38 F3
Belovezhskaya Pushcha Heritage N • Belarus 61 [49]
Belovo • Russian Fed. 26 O7
Beloye More • Russian Fed. 17 F1
Beloye Ozero • Russian Fed. 17 F2
Belozersk • Russian Fed. 17 F3
Belp [Apt] • Switzerland 89 G2
Belukha, gora • Kazakhstan/Russian Fed. 26 O8
Belur • India 106 D6
Belvoir • Israel 98 A4
Belyando • QL, Australia 111 F3
Belyy, Ostrov • Russian Fed. 26 L3
Bemaraha, Plateau du • Madagascar 24 G3
Bembe • Angola 22 G6
Ben Gardane • Tunisia 101 E6
Ben Mehidi • Algeria 12 B12
Bena Dibele • Dem. Rep. of Congo 23 C4
Benabarre • Spain 10 F11
Benalla • VI, Australia 111 G3
Benalmádena Beach • Spain 68 [114]
Benalmádena Costa • Spain 86 B7
Benares • India 105 C8
Benaulim • Goa, India 105 B2
Benaulim Beach • Goa, India 105 B2
Benavente • Spain 11 F3
Benavente • Portugal 88 D2
Benbecula • United Kingdom 75 A1
Benbulbin • Ireland 79 F2
Bend • OR, United States 117 E3
Bendara, Bukit • Penang, Malaysia 108 C1
Bendel • Nigeria 22 F3
Bender • Moldova 14 Q3
Bender Bayla • Somalia 23 I2
Bendigo • VI, Australia 111 G3
Bendinat, Castell de • Majorca, Spain 87 H3
Bendorf • Germany 82 H1
Bénéna • Mali 20 E6
Benesov • Severocesky, Czech Rep. 96 C2
Benesov • Stredocesky, Czech Rep. 96 C2
Benevento • Italy 91 G2
Bengal, Bay of • Indian Ocean 28 E5
Bengbu • China 29 F4
Benghazi • Libya 21 C1
Bengkalis • Indonesia 32 C2
Bengkulu • Indonesia 32 C3
Bengo, Baia do • Angola 22 G6
Bengtsfors • Sweden 95 F2
Benguela • Angola 23 A6
Benguirir • Morocco 101 D3
Bengut, Cap • Algeria 20 F1
Beni • Dem. Rep. of Congo 23 D3
Beni • Bolivia 44 C1
Beni Abbès • Algeria 20 E2
Beni Boufrah • Morocco 11 G9
Benï Hammâd Heritage C • Algeria 64 [221]
Beni Hasan • Egypt 101 F3
Beni Mellal • Morocco 20 D2
Beni Saf • Algeria 11 J9
Beni Suef • Egypt 101 F1
Benicarló • Spain 11 L4
Benicarló Beach • Spain 68 [120]
Benicássim Beach • Spain 68 [120]
Benidorm Beach • Spain 68 [118]
Benidorm • Spain 87 C2
Benin • Africa 22 E3
Benin, Bight of • Nigeria 22 E3
Benin City • Nigeria 22 F3
Benin Forcados • Nigeria 22 E3
Benissa Beach • Spain 68 [118]
Benissa • Spain 87 C2
Benito Juárez • Argentina 127 D3
Benitses • Corfu, Greece 92 B1
Benjamin • Jordan 98 A6
Benjamin Constant • Brazil 43 D4
Benkovac • Croatia 14 C5
Benllech Beach • United Kingdom 75 [226]
Bennett, W.A.C., Dam • BC, Canada 122 C1
Bennington • VT, United States 118 G3
Benoa Port • Bali, Indonesia 110 C4
Benom • Malaysia 108 D2
Benone Beach • United Kingdom 75 [234]
Benoni • South Africa 24 D5
Bénoue • Cameroon/Chad 22 G3
Bénoue, Parc nat. de la Park • Cameroon 103 [40]
Benrath, Schloß • Germany 81 E3
Bensafrim • Portugal 88 E5
Bensheim • Germany 82 H4
Benson • AZ, United States 118 J4
Bent's Old Fort Nat. Hist. Site Park • CO, United States 120 [98]
Benta Sebarang • Malaysia 108 D2
Benteng • Togian, Indonesia 32 (1) B3
Benteng • Selajar, Indonesia 32 (1) B4
Bentinck I. • QL, Australia 34 G3
Bentiu • Sudan 23 D2
Bento Gonçalves • Brazil 44 F4
Bentong • Malaysia 108 D2
Bentota • Sri Lanka 106 D15
Benue • Nigeria 22 G3
Benue [Adm] • Nigeria 22 G3
Benwee Head • Ireland 79 F1
Benxi • China 29 G2
Beo • Indonesia 32 (1) C2
Beograd • F.R. of Yugoslavia 14 H5
Beppu • Japan 30 F8
Ber-Chogur • Kazakhstan 26 I8
Berach • India 105 C6
Berat • Albania 15 A3
Beratus, Gunung • Indonesia 32 F3
Berbera • Somalia 23 G1
Berbérati • Central African Rep. 23 B3
Berchtesgaden • Germany 82 J8
Berchtesgaden Spa • Germany 83 [262]
Berchtesgaden, Nationalpark Park • Germany 72 [65]
Berchtesgaden, Nationalpark • Germany 82 J8
Berck • France 10 G3
Berck-sur-Mer Beach • France 68 [75]
Berdichev • Ukraine 17 D5
Berdyansk • Ukraine 17 F5
Berechid • Morocco 101 D1
Beregovo • Ukraine 13 L9
Berehove • Ukraine 14 J1
Berenice • Egypt 18 B5
Beresti • Romania 14 Q3
Berettyóújfalu • Hungary 13 K10
Bereznik • Russian Fed. 17 G2
Berezniki • Russian Fed. 26 I6
Berezovo • Russian Fed. 26 J5
Berg • Germany 82 J3
Berga • Spain 87 D1
Berga • Sweden 95 F7
Bergama • Turkey 15 I4
Bérgamo • Italy 91 E6
Bergara • Spain 11 I1
Bergby • Sweden 16 I6
Bergeggi Beach • Italy 68 [141]
Bergen • Germany 8 E4
Bergen • Germany 8 I2
Bergen Heritage C • Norway 64 [1]
Bergen • Norway 94 C3
Bergen op Zoom • Netherlands 80 A10
Berger, David, Nat. Mem. Park • OH, United States 121 [189]
Bergerac • France 85 G2
Berggießhübel Spa • Germany 83 [319]
Bergisch Gladbach • Germany 81 E4
Bergisch Gladbach: Bensberg • Germany 81 E4
Bergischer Dom • Germany 81 E4
Bergkamen • Germany 81 E2
Bergkvara • Sweden 95 F12
Bergnaustadt • Germany 81 E4
Bergshamra • Sweden 95 D2
Bergün • Switzerland 89 G4
Berhampur • India 28 D5
Bering Land Bridge Nat. Preserve Park • AK, United States 120 [5]
Bering Sea • Pacific Ocean 46 HH4
Bering Strait • Russian Fed./United States 40 (2) E2
Beringa, Ostrov • Russian Fed. 27 S5
Beringen • Belgium 5 I3
Beringov Proliv • Russian Fed. 27 X3
Berja • Spain 11 I8
Berkåk • Norway 16 F5
Berkakit • Russian Fed. 27 J5
Berkel • Netherlands 5 J2
Berkner I. • Antarctica 46 (1) JJ2
Berkshire • United Kingdom 75 A5
Berkshire Downs • United Kingdom 7 K10
Berkshire East Ski • MA, United States 116 [192]
Berlengas, Is. • Portugal 11 B5
Berlevåg • Norway 16 Q1
Berlin Heritage C • Germany 64 [31]
Berlin • Germany 81 F2
Berlin • NH, United States 118 G3
Berlin [Adm] • Germany 81 F2
Berlin: Buch • Germany 81 F2
Berlin: Buchow • Germany 81 F4
Berlin: Dahlem • Germany 81 F3
Berlin: Frohnau • Germany 81 F1
Berlin: Köpenik • Germany 81 F4
Berlin: Kreuzberg • Germany 81 F4
Berlin: Lichtenberg • Germany 81 F4
Berlin: Lichtenrade • Germany 81 F4
Berlin: Marzahn • Germany 81 F2
Berlin: Mitte • Germany 81 F2
Berlin: Neukölln • Germany 81 F4
Berlin: Pankow • Germany 81 F2
Berlin: Prenzlauer Berg • Germany 81 F2
Berlin: Reinickendorf • Germany 81 F2
Berlin: Schöneberg • Germany 81 F4
Berlin: Spandau • Germany 81 F1
Berlin: Steglitz • Germany 81 F4
Berlin: Tegel • Germany 81 F2
Berlin: Tiergarten • Germany 81 F2
Berlin: Treptow • Germany 81 F2
Berlin: Wannsee • Germany 81 F3
Berlin: Wedding • Germany 81 F2
Berlin: Wedding • Germany 81 F2
Berlin: Weissensee • Germany 81 F2
Berlin: Wilmersdorf • Germany 81 F3
Berlin: Zehlendorf • Germany 81 F3
Bermejo • Argentina 44 C5
Bermeo • Spain 10 C10
Bermeo Beach • Spain 68 [88]
Bermillo de Sayago • Spain 11 E3
Bermuda • Atlantic Ocean 36 K6
Bern Heritage C • Switzerland 64 [102]
Bern • Switzerland 89 G2
Bernalda • Italy 12 K8
Bernam • Malaysia 108 D1
Bernau bei Berlin • Germany 81 F2
Bernau-Hof • Germany 82 G8
Bernay • France 10 F4
Bernburg • Germany 8 G5
Berne Heritage C • Switzerland 64 [102]
Berne • Switzerland 89 G2
Berner Alpen • Switzerland 89 G6
Berner Oberland • Switzerland 89 G2
Bernina, Passo del • Switzerland 89 G8
Bernina, Piz • Italy/Switzerland 89 G8
Bernkastel-Kues • Germany 82 H3
Berntorffs Isfjord • Greenland 39 W4
Beroroha • Madagascar 24 H4
Beroun • Germany 13 D8
Berounka • Czech Rep. 96 C1
Berovo • F.Y.R. of Macedonia 15 D2
Berrow Beach • United Kingdom 75 [139]
Berry • France 10 H7
Berry Is. • Bahamas 124 B1
Bertioga • Brazil 127 C3
Bertoua • Cameroon 22 G4
Beruas • Malaysia 108 D1
Beruwala • Sri Lanka 106 D15
Berwick-upon-Tweed • United Kingdom 6 J6
Berwickshire • United Kingdom 75 A3
Besakih Temple • Bali, Indonesia 110 C2
Besalampy • Madagascar 24 G3
Besançon • France 10 L6
Besar, Gunung • Indonesia 32 F3
Beshwer, Mt • Antarctica 46 (1) L2
Besikama • Indonesia 32 (1) B4
Beskid Niski • Poland 13 K8
Beskidy Zachodnie • Poland 13 I8
Beskonak • Turkey 93 G2
Besna Kobila • F.R. of Yugoslavia 14 J7
Besparmak Dagi • Turkey 15 I6
Bessarabia • Moldova 14 P2
Bestensee • Germany 81 F4
Bestobe • Kazakhstan 26 L7
Bestyakh • Russian Fed. 27 J3
Bet Guvrin • Israel 98 A7
Bet She'an • Israel 98 A4
Bet She'arim • Israel 98 A3
Betalbatim Beach • Goa, India 105 B2
Betancuria • Fuerteventura, Canary Is. 87 E2
Betanzos, Ria de • Spain 11 C1
Beth Horon • Jordan 98 A5
Beth-zur • Jordan 98 A7
Bethany • Jordan 98 A8
Bethany Beach • DE, United States 118 H3
Bethel • AK, United States 40 (2) E2
Bethel • AK, United States 46 FF3
Bethel • Jordan 98 A6
Bethesda • Antigua & Barbuda 125 F4
Bethlehem • South Africa 24 D5
Bethlehem • Jordan 98 A7
Bethlehem • PA, United States 118 H1
Béthune • France 10 H3
Bethune, Mary McLeod, Council House Nat. Hist. Site Park • DC, United States 121 [289]
Béthune [Riv] • France 5 E5
Betla Nat. Park • India 105 C8
Béticos, Sistemas • Spain 11 G7
Betong • Malaysia 108 C3
Bétou • Congo 22 H4
Betpak-Dala • Russian Fed. 26 K8
Betroka • Madagascar 24 H4
Bette • Libya 21 C3
Bettex, le Ski • France 70 [25]
Bettmeralp Ski • Switzerland 70 [99]
Bettmeralp • Switzerland 89 G6
Bettna • Sweden 95 D3
Betty's Hope • Antigua & Barbuda 125 F4
Betul • Madhya Pradesh, India 28 C4
Betul • Goa, India 105 B2
Betul Beach • Goa, India 105 B2
Betwa • India 105 C7
Betzdorf • Germany 9 C6
Beuil-les-Launes Ski • France 70 [73]
Beuren Spa • Germany 83 [192]
Beuren, Kloster • Germany 82 G8
Beveridge • Cook Is. 33 K8
Beverley • United Kingdom 7 L8
Beverungen • Germany 8 E5
Beverwijk • Netherlands 80 C1
Bexhill Beach • United Kingdom 75 [69]
Bexhill-on-Sea • United Kingdom 74 E4
Bexon • St Lucia 125 J1
Bey Daglari • Turkey 93 G3
Beykoz • Turkey 15 K2
Beyla • Guinea 22 C3
Beyneu • Kazakhstan 26 I8
Beypazari • Turkey 15 M3
Beysehir • Turkey 93 G2
Beysehir Gölü • Turkey 93 G2
Bezhetsk • Russian Fed. 97 E2
Béziers • France 10 I10
Bhadravati • India 106 D6
Bhagalpur • India 28 E3
Bhaktapur • Nepal 105 C4
Bhamo • Myanmar 31 B2
Bharatpur • India 105 C2
Bharuch • India 28 B4
Bhatinda • India 28 B2
Bhatpara • India 28 E4
Bhavnagar • India 28 B4
Bheemavaram • India 106 D4
Bheri • Nepal 28 D3
Bhijolia • India 105 C6
Bhilwara • India 105 C6
Bhima • India 106 D2
Bhiwani • India 105 C2
Bhopal • India 28 C4
Bhubaneswar • India 28 E4
Bhuj • India 28 A4
Bhumiphol Reservoir • Thailand 109 G3
Bhutan • Asia 28 E3
Bi'r al Hakim • Libya 21 D1
Bi'r al Wa'r • Libya 21 B3
Bi'r Allaq • Libya 21 B1
Bi'r Misahah • Egypt 21 E3
Bia Nat. Park Park • Ghana 103 [26]
Biafra, Bight of • Africa 22 F4
Biak • Indonesia 32 (1) D3
Biak • Indonesia 32 (1) E3
Biala Podlaska • Poland 13 M5
Biala Slatina • Bulgaria 14 K6
Bialogard • Poland 13 E3
Bialowieski Nat. Park Park • Poland 72 [94]
Bialowieza Nat. Park Heritage N • Poland 61 [49]
Bialystok • Poland 13 M4
Biaora • India 105 C6
Biarritz • France 85 J1
Biasca • Switzerland 89 G7
Bibai • Japan 30 K3
Biberach • Germany 82 J1
Biberach-Jordanbad Spa • Germany 83 [215]
Bibione Beach • Italy 68 [164]
Bibione • Italy 91 E8
Bicaz • Romania 14 M3
Bicholim • Goa, India 105 B1
Bickerton I. • NT, Australia 34 G2
Bida • Nigeria 22 F3
Bidar • India 28 C5
Biddeford • ME, United States 118 G3
Bideford • United Kingdom 74 F2
Bideford Bay • United Kingdom 74 F2
Bidur • Malaysia 108 D1
Bidwell Mansion State Hist. Park • CA, United States 117 F1
Bie, Planalto do • Angola 23 B6
Biebrza • Poland 13 L4
Biebrzanski Nat. Park Park • Poland 72 [93]
Biedenkopf • Germany 9 D6
Biel • Switzerland 89 G2
Bielefeld • Germany 8 D4
Bieler See • Switzerland 89 G2
Biella • Italy 91 E5
Bielsk Podlaski • Poland 13 M5
Bielsko-Biala • Poland 13 I8
Bien Hoa • Vietnam 108 B1
Bienville, Lac • QU, Canada 39 Q5
Bierset [Apt] • Belgium 80 A15
Biertan Heritage C • Romania 64 [165]
Biervliet • Netherlands 80 A10
Biesbosch • Netherlands 80 C4
Biesenthal • Germany 81 F2
Bieszczady • Poland 13 L8
Bieszczadzki Nat. Park Park • Poland 72 [95]
Bifuka • Japan 30 L2
Big Bear Lake • CA, United States 117 F6
Big Bend Nat. Park Park • TX, United States 120 [138]
Big Boulder Ski • PA, United States 116 [166]
Big Cypress Nat. Preserve • FL, United States 119 M8
Big Cypress Nat. Preserve Park • FL, United States 121 [225]
Big Cypress Swamp • FL, United States 119 M8
Big Hole Nat. Battlefield Park • MT, United States 120 [69]
Big Mtn Ski • MT, United States 116 [73]
Big Pine Key • FL, United States 119 M8
Big Powderhorn Mtn Ski • MI, United States 116 [126]
Big Sioux • IA/SD, United States 38 L8
Big Sky Ski • MT, United States 116 [74]
Big Smoky Valley • NV, United States 117 F4
Big Spring • TX, United States 40 F5
Big Sur • CA, United States 117 F3
Big Thicket Nat. Preserve • TX, United States 119 N4
Big Thicket Nat. Preserve Park • TX, United States 121 [144]
Big Trout Lake • OT, Canada 39 M6
Big Vanilla at Davos Ski • NY, United States 116 [178]
Big White Ski • BC, Canada 116 [6]
Biga • Turkey 15 I3
Bigadiç • Turkey 15 J4
Bigbury Bay • United Kingdom 74 F5
Biggar • United Kingdom 74 B4
Bighorn • MT/WY, United States 38 J8
Bighorn Canyon Nat. Recreation Area Park • MT, United States 120 [70]
Bighorn Mtns • WY, United States 40 E3
Bigorre • France 85 J2
Biguglia, Etang de • Corsica, France 85 L2
Bihac • Bosnia-Herz. 14 C5
Bihar • India 28 E3
Bihar [Adm] • India 28 E4
Biharamulo • Tanzania 102 H1
Bihoro • Japan 30 M3
Bijapur • India 106 D2
Bijawar • India 105 C7
Bijeljina • Bosnia-Herz. 14 G5
Bijoutier • Seychelles 106 F4
Bikaner • India 105 C1
Bikin • Russian Fed. 29 I1
Bikin [Riv] • Russian Fed. 27 M7
Bikini • Marshall Is. 33 H4
Bikoro • Dem. Rep. of Congo 22 H5
Bila Tserkov • Ukraine 17 E5
Bilaspur • India 28 D4
Bilauktaung Range • Myanmar/Thailand 31 B4
Bilbao • Spain 11 I1
Bilecik • Turkey 15 K3
Bilesha Plain • Kenya 23 G3
Bilibino • Russian Fed. 27 S3
Bilin • Myanmar 109 G3
Biliu • China 30 B5
Billings • MT, United States 40 E2
Billund • Denmark 95 F9
Bilma • Niger 20 H5
Bilma, Grand Erg de • Niger 20 H5
Biloela • QL, Australia 111 F4
Bilogora • Croatia 14 D4
Bilogoraj • Poland 13 L7
Biloku • Guyana 43 F3
Biloxi • MS, United States 118 K4
Bilthoven • Netherlands 80 C2
Biltine • Chad 21 D5
Bimberi Peak • AC/NS, Australia 34 I7
Bimbo • Central African Rep. 23 B3
Bimini Is. • Bahamas 124 B1
Bin Ghunayah, Jabal • Libya 21 C3
Bina • India 105 C7
Bindura • Zimbabwe 102 J2
Binga • Zimbabwe 102 J1
Bingen • Germany 82 H4
Binghampton • NY, United States 118 H1
Biniancolla • Minorca, Spain 87 F4
Binibequer Vell • Minorca, Spain 87 F4
Binissafúller • Minorca, Spain 87 F4
Binjai • Indonesia 110 B2
Bintan • Indonesia 32 C2
Bintulu • Malaysia 32 E2
Bintumani, Mt Park • Sierra Leone 103 [14]
Binz • Germany 8 I2
Binz Beach • Germany 68 [31]
Binz Spa • Germany 83 [279]
Biobio • Chile 45 B3
Biograd na Moru • Croatia 12 J5
Biogradska Gora Nat. Park Park • Fed. Rep. of Yugoslavia 72 [119]
Bioko • Equatorial Guinea 22 F4
Biokovo • Croatia 14 E6
Bir • India 28 C5
Bir Gandus • Western Sahara 20 B4
Bir Lehlú • Western Sahara 20 D3
Bir Mogrein • Mauritania 20 C3
Bir Shalatein • Egypt 21 G3
Bira Racing Circuit • Thailand 109 H4
Birak • Libya 21 B2
Birao • Central African Rep. 23 C1
Biratnagar • Nepal 28 E3
Birchington Beach • United Kingdom 75 [61]
Bird • MN, Canada 38 M5
Bird I. • Seychelles 106 F2
Bird I. • West Indies 124 A3
Bird, V.C. [Apt] • Antigua & Barbuda 125 F1
Birdsville • QL, Australia 34 G5
Bireuen • Indonesia 110 B1
Birganj • Nepal 28 D3
Birhet el Bibane • Tunisia 101 E6
Birjand • Iran 18 G3
Birk, Al • Saudi Arabia 18 D6
Birka Heritage C • Sweden 64 [4]
Birkeland • Norway 95 F1
Birkenhead • United Kingdom 7 I8
Birkenwerder bei Berlin • Germany 81 F1
Bîrlad • Romania 14 Q3
Bîrlad [Riv] • Romania 14 Q3
Birling Gap Beach • United Kingdom 75 [71]
Birmingham • AL, United States 41 I5
Birmingham • United Kingdom 74 D2
Birni Nkonni • Niger 20 G6
Birnie • Kiribati 33 J6
Birnin Gwari • Nigeria 20 G6
Birnin Kebbi • Nigeria 22 E2
Birobidzhan • Russian Fed. 27 L7
Birr • Ireland 7 E8
Birsk • Russian Fed. 17 J3
Biru • China 28 F2
Biruni • Uzbekistan 26 J9
Biryusa • Russian Fed. 27 E5
Birzai • Lithuania 13 N1
Birzebbuga • Malta 93 H4
Bisanadi Game Reserve • Kenya 101 G2
Bisau • India 105 C2
Biscarosse • France 85 G3
Biscay, Bay of • France 4 J8
Biscayne Nat. Park • FL, United States 119 M8
Biscayne Nat. Park Park • FL, United States 121 [227]
Bisceglie • Italy 14 D8
Bischofsgrün Spa • Germany 83 [227]
Bischofshofen • Austria 9 I8
Bischofswerda • Germany 9 J5
Bischofswiesen Spa • Germany 83 [262]
Biserta • Tunisia 71 A18
Bisevo • Croatia 14 D7
Bisevski Kanal • Croatia 14 D6
Bishkek • Kyrgyzstan 26 L9
Bisho • South Africa 24 D6
Bishop • CA, United States 117 F4

Bishop Auckland

Bishop Auckland • United Kingdom 7 K7
Bishop's Stortford • United Kingdom 74 E1
Biskra • Algeria 20 G2
Biskupiec • Poland 13 J4
Bislig • Philippines 31 H5
Bismarck • ND, United States 40 F2
Bismarck Archipelago • Papua New Guinea 35 (1) D1
Bismarck Sea • Pacific Ocean 35 (1) D1
Bismo • Norway 94 C2
Bissau • Guinea-Bissau 22 A2
Bistcho Lake • AL, Canada 38 H5
Bistrita • Romania 14 L2
Bistrita [Riv] • Romania 14 M2
Bitam • Gabon 22 G4
Bitburg • Germany 82 H3
Bitche • France 5 K5
Bitea • Chad 21 D5
Bithia • Sardinia, Italy 90 C4
Bitkine • Chad 20 I6
Bitola • F.Y.R. of Macedonia 14 I8
Bitonto • Italy 12 K7
Bitra I. • India 106 D9
Bitterfeld • Germany 8 H5
Bitterfontein • South Africa 24 B6
Bitterroot Range • ID/MT, United States 117 E2
Bittersweet **Ski** • MI, United States 116 [142]
Bitti • Sardinia, Italy 12 D8
Bitumount • AL, Canada 38 I5
Biu • Nigeria 22 G2
Bivolari • Romania 14 O2
Biwako • Japan 30 I7
Biya • Russian Fed. 26 O7
Biyadoo • Maldives 106 E4
Biysk • Russian Fed. 26 O7
Bizerte • Tunisia 101 E2
Bjarehalvön • Sweden 95 F11
Bjelolasica • Croatia 14 B4
Bjelovar • Croatia 14 D4
Bjergsted **Beach** • Denmark 68 [43]
Bjerringbro • Denmark 95 F9
Bjeshkët e Nemuna • Albania/F.R. of Yugoslavia 14 G7
Bjørkelangen • Norway 94 B2
Björklinge • Sweden 95 D2
Björko • Sweden 95 D2
Björkvik • Sweden 95 D3
Björna • Sweden 16 J5
Bjørnafjorden • Norway 94 C3
Björneborg • Finland 95 E1
Björnlunda • Sweden 95 D3
Björnön • Arctic Ocean 4 O2
Bla • Mali 22 C2
Blåbjerg **Beach** • Denmark 68 [51]
Black Canyon • AZ/NV, United States 118 J1
Black Canyon of the Gunnison Nat. Mon. **Park** • CO, United States 120 [91]
Black Country • United Kingdom 74 D2
Black Forest • Germany 82 G8
Black Head • United Kingdom 74 F4
Black Hills • SD, United States 40 F3
Black Lady Mtn • Vietnam 108 B1
Black Mountains • United Kingdom 74 D3
Black [Riv] • China/Vietnam 108 A1
Black River • Jamaica 124 C3
Black Rock • Barbados 125 H3
Black Rock Desert • NV, United States 117 F2
Black Rocks • St Kitts & Nevis 125 G1
Black Sea • Europe 17 E6
Black Sea Coast • Turkey 92 A3
Black Sea Coast • Bulgaria/Romania 97 D
Black Sea cruise area • Asia/Europe 59 C
Black Sugarloaf, The • NS, Australia 34 J6
Blackall • QL, Australia 111 F3
Blackbeard's Grave • Bahamas 124 B3
Blackburn • United Kingdom 7 J8
Blackburn, Mt • AK, United States 38 C4
Blackcomb **Ski** • BC, Canada 116 [2]
Blackdown Hills • United Kingdom 74 F2
Blackmount • New Zealand 112 L3
Blackness Castle • United Kingdom 74 B4
Blackpool • United Kingdom 7 I8
Blackpool Pleasure Beach **Park** • United Kingdom 73 [22]
Blackpool Sands **Beach** • United Kingdom 75 [106]
Blacksburg • VA, United States 41 J4
Blacksod Bay • Ireland 79 F1
Blackstone River Valley Nat. Heritage Corridor **Park** • MA, United States 121 [341]
Blackwater • Neath, Ireland 79 E1
Blackwater • Cork, Ireland 79 F8
Blåfjellhatten • Norway 16 G4
Blagnac [Apt] • France 85 G4
Blagoevgrad • Bulgaria 14 K7
Blagoveshchensk • Russian Fed. 27 K6
Blaine • WA, United States 117 E1
Blair Athol • QL, Australia 111 F3
Blair Drummond Safari Park • United Kingdom 74 B3
Blairgowrie • United Kingdom 74 B2
Blaj • Romania 14 K3
Blambangan, Semenanjung • Java, Indonesia 110 D8
Blanc, Cap • Majorca, Spain 11 N5
Blanc, Cap • Tunisia 101 E2
Blanc, Mont • France/Italy 85 F2
Blanc Sablon • QU, Canada 123 D5
Blanca, Bahía • Argentina 45 D3
Blanca, Costa • Spain 87 C
Blanca Peak • CO, United States 40 E4
Blanche, Lake • SA, Australia 34 G5
Blanchisseuse • Trinidad & Tobago 125 K1
Blanco • Bolivia 44 D2
Blanco, Cape • OR, United States 117 E3
Blandford Forum • United Kingdom 74 F3
Blanes **Beach** • Spain 68 [123]
Blanes • Spain 87 D4
Blangkerejen • Indonesia 110 B1
Blangy-sur-Bresle • France 5 E5
Blankaholm • Sweden 95 F8
Blankenberge • Belgium 80 B2
Blankenburg **Spa** • Germany 83 [294]
Blankenfelde • Germany 81 F4
Blankenheim • Germany 82 H1
Blanquilla • Venezuela 43 E1
Blanquilla, I. • Venezuela 124 A6
Blansko • Czech Rep. 13 F8
Blantyre • Malawi 24 F3
Blantyre-Limbe • Malawi 24 E3
Blarney • Ireland 79 F8
Blåsjøen • Norway 94 C6
Blatna • Czech Rep. 96 C3
Blaubeuren • Germany 82 J1
Blåvands Huk **Beach** • Denmark 68 [51]
Blåvands Huk • Denmark 95 F9
Blavet • France 84 C4
Blaye • France 85 G1
Bledes, Is. • Ibiza, Spain 87 G1
Blefjell • Norway 94 B1
Blekinge • Sweden 95 F12
Blenheim • New Zealand 35 D5
Blenheim Palace **Heritage C** • United Kingdom 64 [21]
Blenheim Palace • United Kingdom 74 D4
Blenhorst **Spa** • Germany 83 [62]
Blessington • Ireland 79 E3
Bletchley • United Kingdom 7 L10
Blida • Algeria 11 N8
Blidö • Sweden 95 D2
Blies • Germany 5 K5
Blieskastel • Germany 82 G3
Blieskastel **Spa** • Germany 83 [169]
Bligh Sound • New Zealand 112 L1
Blind River • OT, Canada 39 O7
Blitar • Java, Indonesia 110 D7
Blitta • Togo 22 E3
Blizzard Beach • FL, United States 121 C1
Block I. • NY, United States 118 H2
Bloemfontein • South Africa 24 D5
Blois • France 84 D2
Blois [Château] • France 84 D2
Blommestein, W.J. van, Meer • Suriname 43 F3
Bloody Point • St Kitts & Nevis 125 G1
Bloomington • IL, United States 41 I3
Bloomington • IN, United States 41 I4
Bludenz • Austria 89 H5
Blue Basin Falls • Trinidad & Tobago 125 K1
Blue Grotto • Malta 93 H4
Blue Hole • Jamaica 124 C2
Blue Lagoon • Malta 93 H1
Blue Mtn **Ski** • OT, Canada 116 [20]
Blue Mtn **Ski** • PA, United States 116 [165]
Blue Mtn Peak • Jamaica 124 C4
Blue Mtns • NS, Australia 111 G2
Blue Mtns • OR, United States 117 E4
Blue Mtns • Jamaica 124 C4
Blue Nile • Sudan 21 F5
Blue Ridge • United States 117 D8
Blue Ridge Parkway **Park** • NC/VA, United States 121 [245]
Bluefields • Nicaragua 37 E5
Bluefields • Jamaica 124 C1
Bluefields Bay • Jamaica 124 C3
Bluenose Lake • NU, Canada 38 H3
Bluff • New Zealand 112 L4
Bluff Point • WA, Australia 34 B5
Blumberg • Germany 9 D9
Blumberg • Germany 81 F2
Blumenau • Brazil 44 G4
Blyth • United Kingdom 7 K6
Bo • Sierra Leone 22 B3
Bø • Norway 94 B3
Bo Hai • China 29 F3
Bo River • Sudan 23 D2
Bo Sai • Phuket, Thailand 109 K1
Boa Esperanca, Reprêsa • Brazil 45 (1) C3
Boa Vista • Cape Verde 22 (1) B1
Boa Vista • Brazil 43 E3
Boac • Philippines 31 G4
Boaventura • Madeira 88 C1
Bobadilla • Spain 86 B2
Bobbejaanland **Park** • Belgium 73 [49]
Bóbbio • Italy 12 D4
Bobingen • Germany 82 J2
Böblingen • Germany 82 G6
Bobo Dioulasso • Burkina Faso 22 D2
Bóbr • Poland 13 E6
Bobrov • Russian Fed. 17 G4
Boby, Pic • Madagascar 24 H4
Boca de Valeria • Brazil 58 A3
Boca do Acre • Brazil 43 D5
Boca Grande • Venezuela 43 E2
Boca Raton • FL, United States 119 M6
Bocaranga • Central African Rep. 22 H3
Bocas del Amazonas • Brazil 43 H3
Bochnia • Poland 13 J8
Bocholt • Germany 8 B5
Bochum • Germany 81 E2
Bochum: Wattenscheid • Germany 81 E2
Bocognano • Corsica, France 85 L4
Boda • Central African Rep. 22 H4
Bodafors • Sweden 95 F7
Bodaybo • Russian Fed. 27 H5
Bode • Germany 8 G5
Bodegraven • Netherlands 80 C3
Bodelé • Chad 21 C4
Boden • Sweden 16 K4
Bodendorf **Spa** • Germany 83 [150]
Bodenmais **Spa** • Germany 83 [233]
Bodensee • Germany 82 J5
Bodenteich **Spa** • Germany 83 [59]
Bodhgaya • India 105 C8
Bodmin • United Kingdom 74 F4
Bodmin Moor • United Kingdom 74 F4
Bodø • Norway 16 H3
Bodrum **Beach** • Turkey 69 [235]
Bodrum • Turkey 92 D9
Bodufinolhu • Maldives 106 E4
Boduhithi Coral Isle • Maldives 106 E2
Boende • Dem. Rep. of Congo 23 C4
Bogalusa • LA, United States 118 K4
Bogarra • Spain 11 I6
Bogbonga • Dem. Rep. of Congo 22 H4
Bogcang Zangbo • China 28 E2
Bogda Feng • China 26 O9
Bogda Shan • China 26 O9
Bogen • Norway 16 I2
Bogenfels • Namibia 24 B5
Bogense • Denmark 95 F10
Boggeragh Mtns • Ireland 79 F8
Boggy Peak • Antigua & Barbuda 125 F3
Bogia • Papua New Guinea 35 (1) C1
Bogmalo Beach • Goa, India 105 B1
Bognor Regis • United Kingdom 74 E3
Bogolyubovo • Russian Fed. 97 E4
Bogor • Java, Indonesia 110 D1
Bogotá • Colombia 43 C3
Bogotol • Russian Fed. 26 O6
Bogøy • Norway 16 H3
Boguchany • Russian Fed. 26 Q6
Bogué • Mauritania 20 C5
Bogue Forts Museum • China 107 H2
Bogus Basin **Ski** • ID, United States 116 [71]
Bohan • Belgium 80 A19
Bohemia • Czech Rep. 96 C1
Bohemia, Garden of • Czech Rep. 96 C2
Bohemian Switzerland • Czech Rep. 96 C1
Böhmen • Czech Rep. 13 D8
Böhmerwald • Germany 9 H7
Bohol • Philippines 31 G4
Bohol Sea • Philippines 31 G5
Boiaçu • Brazil 43 E4
Boina • Madagascar 24 H3
Bois d'Attilly, Parc zoologique du • France 85 E4
Bois, Lac des • NT, Canada 38 F3
Bois-Plage-en-Re, le **Beach** • France 68 [84]
Boise • ID, United States 117 E4
Boizenburg • Germany 8 F3
Bojador, Cabo • Morocco 20 C3
Bojano • Italy 12 I7
Bojnurd • Iran 18 G2
Bojonegoro • Java, Indonesia 110 D3
Bok Tower Gardens • FL, United States 119 M5
Boka Kotorska • F.R. of Yugoslavia 14 F7
Boké • Guinea 22 B2
Boknafjorden • Norway 94 C5
Boko • Congo 22 G5
Bokol Mayo • Ethiopia 23 G3
Bokoro • Chad 22 H2
Bokpyin • Myanmar 31 B4
Bol • Chad 21 B5
Bolama • Guinea-Bissau 20 B6
Bolans • Antigua & Barbuda 125 F3
Bolbec • France 10 F4
Bole • Ghana 22 D3
Bole • China 26 N9
Bolehov • Ukraine 13 M9
Boleslawiec • Poland 13 E6
Bolgatanga • Ghana 22 D2
Bolgrad • Ukraine 14 P4
Bolia • Dem. Rep. of Congo 23 B4
Boliden • Sweden 16 K4
Bolifushi • Maldives 106 E4
Boliqueime • Portugal 88 E7
Bolívar, Cerro • Venezuela 43 C2
Bolívar, Pico • Venezuela 37 I6
Bolivia • S. America 44 D2
Bolivia, Altiplano de • Bolivia 44 C2
Bolkesjø • Norway 94 B1
Bollebygd • Sweden 95 F7
Bollnäs • Sweden 16 I6
Bollon • QL, Australia 111 F5
Bolmen • Sweden 95 F7
Bolobo • Dem. Rep. of Congo 23 B4
Bologna • Italy 91 E7
Bolognesi • Peru 43 C6
Bologoye • Russian Fed. 97 E1
Bolomba • Dem. Rep. of Congo 23 B3
Bolombo • Dem. Rep. of Congo 23 C4
Bolovens Plateau • Laos 108 A2
Bolsena • Italy 91 F1
Bolsena, Lago di • Italy 91 F1
Bolshaya Murta • Russian Fed. 26 P6
Bolshevik, Ostrov • Russian Fed. 97 A5
Bolshezemelskaya Tundra • Russian Fed. 26 I4
Bolshoy Anyuy • Russian Fed. 27 R3
Bolshoy Begichev, Ostrov • Russian Fed. 27 H2
Bolshoy Kamen • Russian Fed. 30 G3
Bolshoy Lyakhovskiy, Ostrov • Russian Fed. 27 N2
Bolsón, Cerro del • Argentina 44 C4
Bolsón de Mapimí • Mexico 40 F6
Bolsward • Netherlands 80 A3
Boltenhagen • Germany 8 G2
Boltenhagen **Beach** • Germany 68 [35]
Boltenhagen **Spa** • Germany 83 [266]
Bolton • United Kingdom 7 J8
Bolton Valley **Ski** • VT, United States 116 [202]
Bolu • Turkey 15 M3
Bolu Daglari • Turkey 15 M3
Boluntay • China 28 F1
Bolvadin • Turkey 15 M5
Bolzano • Italy 90 B3
Bom Despacho • Brazil 127 C1
Bom Jesus da Lapa • Brazil 44 H1
Boma • Dem. Rep. of Congo 23 A5
Bomano, Cayo • Cuba 124 D3
Bomassa • Congo 22 H4
Bombay • India 28 B5
Bomberai, Jazirah • Indonesia 32 (1) D3
Bomboma • Dem. Rep. of Congo 22 H4
Bomi • China 28 F2
Bomi Hills • Liberia 22 B3
Bømlafjorden • Norway 94 C5
Bømlo • Norway 94 C5
Bommelerwaard • Netherlands 80 C4
Bomu • Central African Rep./Dem. Rep. of Congo 23 C3
Bon, Cap • Tunisia 101 E2
Bon Echo Prov. Park • OT, Canada 122 B6
Bona • Algeria 71 A18
Bonaire • West Indies 37 H5
Bonaparte Archipelago • WA, Australia 34 D3
Bonasse • Trinidad & Tobago 125 K3
Bonavista • NF, Canada 123 D4
Bonavista Bay • NF, Canada 123 D4
Bondeno • Italy 12 F4
Bondla Wildlife Sanctuary • Goa, India 105 B1
Bondo • Dem. Rep. of Congo 23 C3
Bondoukou • Côte d'Ivoire 22 D3
Bondowoso • Java, Indonesia 110 D8
Bonerate, Kepulauan • Indonesia 110 A7
Bonete, Cerro • Argentina 44 C4
Bongabong • Philippines 31 G4
Bongandanga • Dem. Rep. of Congo 23 C3
Bongo, Massif des • Central African Rep. 23 C2
Bongolava • Madagascar 24 H3
Bongor • Chad 21 C5
Boni Game Reserve • Kenya 101 G4
Bonifacio • Corsica, France 85 L4
Bonifacio, Strait of • France/Italy 12 D7
Bonifica del Volturno • Italy 91 G1
Bonita, Playa • Cuba 124 D7
Bonita Springs • FL, United States 119 M7
Bonn • Germany 82 G1
Bonners Ferry • ID, United States 117 E2
Bonnerup Strand • Denmark 95 F10
Bonneval • France 84 D2
Bonneville • France 89 G5
Bonneville Salt Flats • UT, United States 117 F2
Bonny • Nigeria 22 F4
Bonorva • Sardinia, Italy 12 C8
Bontebok Nat. Park • South Africa 100 C6
Bontebok Nat. Park **Park** • South Africa 103 [118]
Booby I. • St Kitts & Nevis 125 G4
Booligar • NS, Australia 111 G1
Boon Point • Antigua & Barbuda 125 F1
Böön Tsagaan Nuur • Mongolia 29 B1
Boot • United Kingdom 74 C3
Boothbay Harbor • ME, United States 118 G4
Boothia, Gulf of • NU, Canada 38 M2
Boothia Peninsula • NU, Canada 38 M2
Booué • Gabon 22 G4
Bopfingen • Germany 9 F8
Bophut Beach • Ko Samui, Thailand 109 J1
Boppard • Germany 82 H2
Boppard **Spa** • Germany 83 [156]
Boquerón • Puerto Rico 125 E3
Boquerón, Bahía de • Puerto Rico 125 E3
Bor • Russian Fed. 17 G3
Bor • Sudan 23 E2
Bor • Czech Rep. 96 C3
Bora Bora • French Polynesia 58 A1
Borah Peak • ID, United States 40 D3
Borås • Sweden 95 F7
Borborema, Planoalto da • Brazil 45 (1) D3
Borca di Cadore • Italy 90 B4
Borchen • Germany 8 D5
Bordeaux • France 85 G3
Bordeira • Portugal 88 E5
Borden Peninsula • NU, Canada 39 O2
Bordertown • SA, Australia 34 H7
Bordeyri • Iceland 16 (1) C2
Bordighera **Beach** • Italy 68 [140]
Bordighera • Italy 91 E9
Bordj Bou Arreridj • Algeria 20 F1
Bordj el Kiffan • Algeria 11 O8
Bordj Fly St Marie • Algeria 20 E3
Bordj Menaïel • Algeria 11 O8
Bordj Messouda • Algeria 20 G2
Bordj Moktar • Algeria 20 F4
Bordj Omar Driss • Algeria 20 G3
Boreal **Ski** • CA, United States 116 [54]
Borensberg • Sweden 95 F4
Boréon, le • France 85 H2
Borgå • Finland 95 E4
Borgafjällen • Sweden 16 H4
Borgarnes • Iceland 16 (1) C2
Børgefjell • Norway 16 G4
Børgefjell Nat. Park **Park** • Norway 72 [10]
Borger • TX, United States 40 F4
Borgholm **Beach** • Sweden 69 [17]
Borgholm • Sweden 95 F8
Borglund stavkirke • Norway 94 C4
Borgo • Corsica, France 85 L2
Borislav • Ukraine 13 M8
Borisoglebsk • Russian Fed. 17 G4
Borj Bourguiba • Tunisia 101 E6
Borja • Peru 43 B4
Borken • Germany 8 B5
Borken • Germany 9 E5
Børkop **Beach** • Denmark 68 [46]
Børkop • Denmark 95 F9
Borkou • Chad 21 C4
Borkum • Germany 8 B3
Borkum **Spa** • Germany 83 [36]
Borlänge • Sweden 16 H6
Borlu • Turkey 15 J5
Bormes-les-Mimosas **Beach** • France 68 [133]
Bormio **Ski** • Italy 70 [205]
Bormio • Italy 91 E3
Borna • Germany 9 H5
Borneo • East Indies 32 E3
Bornholm [Adm] • Denmark 94 A10
Bornholm [I.] • Denmark 95 F16
Bornholmsgattet • Denmark/Sweden 95 F15
Börnicke • Germany 81 F1
Borno • Nigeria 22 G2
Bornova • Turkey 15 I5
Borobodur **Heritage C** • Java, Indonesia 63 [177]
Borobodur • Java, Indonesia 110 D7
Borodino • Russian Fed. 27 E5
Borohoro Shan • China 25 J5
Boromo • Burkina Faso 20 E6
Borovets • Bulgaria 96 B2
Borovichi • Russian Fed. 97 E1
Borroloola • NT, Australia 34 G3
Borrowdale • United Kingdom 74 C2
Borsa • Romania 14 L2
Borth **Beach** • United Kingdom 75 [184]
Borzya • Russian Fed. 27 I6
Bosa **Beach** • Sardinia, Italy 68 [136]
Bosa • Sardinia, Italy 90 C1
Bosanska Dubica • Croatia 12 K3
Bosanska Gradiska • Bosnia-Herz. 12 L3
Bosanski Petrovac • Bosnia-Herz. 12 K4
Bosaso • Somalia 23 H1
Boscastle • United Kingdom 74 F4
Boscobel • NY, United States 118 H1
Boscobel House • United Kingdom 74 D1
Boscobelle • Barbados 125 H1
Bosherton **Beach** • United Kingdom 75 [156]
Boshnyakovo, gora • Russian Fed. 27 N7
Boskoop • Netherlands 80 C3
Bosna • Bosnia-Herz. 14 F5
Bosna • Bulgaria 15 I1
Bosnia-Herzegovina • Europe 14 F6
Bosnik • Indonesia 32 (1) D3
Boso • Japan 30 K7
Bosporus • Turkey 92 D3
Bosra **Heritage C** • Syria 64 [242]
Bossangoa • Central African Rep. 23 B2
Bossentélé • Central African Rep. 23 A2
Bossier City • LA, United States 118 K1
Bosso • Niger 20 H6
Bosten Hu • China 26 O9
Boston • United Kingdom 7 L8
Boston • MA, United States 118 G3
Boston African American Nat. Hist. Site **Park** • MA, United States 121 [344]
Boston Mills **Ski** • OH, United States 116 [148]
Boston Mtns • AR, United States 41 H4
Boston Nat. Hist. Park **Park** • MA, United States 121 [345]
Boswachterij Wassenaar • Netherlands 80 C1
Bosworth Field • United Kingdom 74 D2
Botany Bay • NS, Australia 111 G2
Botevgrad • Bulgaria 15 E1
Bothnia, Gulf of • Finland/Sweden 16 J6
Botlek • Netherlands 80 C3
Botosani • Romania 14 N2
Botrange • Belgium 5 J4
Botswana • Africa 24 C4
Botte Donato • Italy 12 K9
Bottrop • Germany 81 E1
Botucatu • Brazil 44 G3
Botwood • NF, Canada 123 D3
Bötzow • Germany 81 F1
Bou Djébéha • Mali 20 E5
Bou Grara, Golfe de • Tunisia 101 E6
Bou Izakarn • Morocco 20 D3
Bou Maad, Djebel • Algeria 11 N8
Bou Saâda • Algeria 20 F1
Bouaké • Côte d'Ivoire 22 C3
Bouar • Central African Rep. 23 A2
Bouârfa • Morocco 101 D4
Bouba Ndjida, Parc nat. de **Park** • Cameroon 103 [41]
Bouca • Central African Rep. 22 H3
Bouchet, le [Château] • France 84 D4
Boudenib • Morocco 20 E2
Boudeuse • Seychelles 106 F2
Boufarik • Algeria 11 N8
Bougainville • Papua New Guinea 35 (1) F2
Bougouni • Mali 22 C2
Bouguenais • France 10 D6
Bouillon • Belgium 80 A19
Bouira • Algeria 11 O8
Boulder • CO, United States 40 E4
Boulder City • NV, United States 40 D4
Boulogne-Billancourt • France 5 F6
Boulogne-sur-Mer • France 10 G3
Boultoum • Niger 20 H6
Boumois [Château] • France 84 D1
Bouna • Côte d'Ivoire 22 D3
Bourail • New Caledonia 35 (2) B3
Bourbonnais • France 10 I7
Bourdeilles • France 85 G2
Bourem • Mali 20 E5
Bourg • France 84 B3
Bourg-en-Bresse • France 85 F1
Bourg-St-Maurice • France 85 F2
Bourges • France 10 H6
Bourges **Heritage C** • France 64 [56]
Bourget, le [Apt] • France 85 E2
Bourgneuf, Baie de • France 10 C6
Bourgogne • France 10 J6
Bourgueil • France 84 B1
Bourke • NS, Australia 34 I6
Bournemouth • United Kingdom 74 F3
Bournemouth **Beach** • United Kingdom 75 [82-83]
Bourscheid • Luxembourg 80 A20
Bourton-on-the-Water • United Kingdom 74 D4
Boussay [Château] • France 84 D4
Boussens • France 11 L1
Bousso • Chad 23 B1
Boutilimit • Mauritania 20 C5
Boutonne • France 10 E7
Bouvines • France 71 A7
Bova Marina • Italy 12 J11
Bovallstrand • Sweden 95 F2
Bovey Tracey • United Kingdom 74 F5
Bow • AL, Canada 38 I6
Bowen • QL, Australia 111 F1
Bowie • TX, United States 119 N1
Bowie, Fort, Nat. Hist. Site • AZ, United States 118 J4
Bowie, Fort, Nat. Hist. Site **Park** • AZ, United States 120 [118]
Bowling Green • KY, United States 41 I4
Bowness-on-Windermere • United Kingdom 74 C4
Bowo • China 28 F2
Bowral • NS, Australia 111 G2
Bowron Lake Prov. Park • BC, Canada 122 C1
Boxholm • Sweden 95 F4
Boxmeer • Netherlands 5 I3
Boxtel • Netherlands 5 I3
Boyana **Heritage C** • Bulgaria 64 [167]
Boyle • Ireland 79 F2
Boyne • Ireland 79 E1
Boyne Highlands **Ski** • MI, United States 116 [129]
Boyne Mtn **Ski** • MI, United States 116 [128]
Boynton Beach • FL, United States 119 M6
Boz Burun • Turkey 15 J3
Boz Dagi • Turkey 15 K6
Boz Daglari • Turkey 15 I5
Bozanski Novi • Croatia 12 K3
Bozburun • Turkey 15 J7
Bozburun Dagi • Turkey 15 M6
Bozcaada • Turkey 15 H4
Bozcaada [I.] • Turkey 92 D2
Bozdogan • Turkey 15 J6
Bozeman • MT, United States 40 D2
Bozen • Italy 90 B3
Bozene • Dem. Rep. of Congo 22 H4
Bozkir • Turkey 93 G2
Bozouls • France 10 H9
Bozoum • Central African Rep. 23 B2
Bozova • Turkey 93 G1
Bozovici • Romania 14 I5
Bözüyük • Turkey 15 L4
Bra • Italy 12 B4
Brabant Wallonie • Belgium 80 A15
Brac • Croatia 14 D6
Bracciano • Italy 91 F1
Bracciano, Lago di • Italy 91 F1
Bräcke • Sweden 16 H5
Brackenheim • Germany 82 G6
Bracki kanal • Croatia 14 D6
Bracknell • United Kingdom 7 L10
Brad • Romania 14 J3
Bradano • Italy 12 K8
Bradenton • FL, United States 119 M5
Bradford • United Kingdom 7 K8
Bradley [Apt] • CT, United States 118 H2
Braemar • United Kingdom 6 I4
Braga [Adm] • Portugal 88 A1
Braga [Adm] • Portugal 88 A1
Bragado • Argentina 127 D1
Bragança • Portugal 11 E3
Bragança • Brazil 45 (1) B2
Bragança [Adm] • Portugal 88 A1
Bragança Paulista • Brazil 127 C3
Brahestad • Finland 16 M4
Brahmani • India 28 E4
Brahmaputra • Asia 28 E3
Braila • Romania 97 D2
Braithwaite • United Kingdom 74 C1
Braj • India 105 C2
Braja • Portugal 11 C3
Brake • Germany 8 D3
Brålanda • Sweden 95 F3
Bramadero, Bahía • Puerto Rico 125 E3
Bramming • Denmark 95 F9
Brampton • OT, Canada 122 B9
Brampton I. • QL, Australia 111 F3
Bramsche • Germany 8 C4
Branco • Brazil 43 E3
Brand • Austria 89 H5
Brandberg • Namibia 24 A4
Brandbu • Norway 94 B2
Brande • Denmark 95 F9
Brandenburg • Germany 8 H4
Brandenburg [Adm] • Germany 8 I4
Brandenburger Tor • Germany 81 F2
Brandon • MN, Canada 38 L7
Brandon Mtn • Ireland 79 F5
Brands Hatch • United Kingdom 74 E1
Brandval • Norway 94 B2
Brandywine **Ski** • OH, United States 116 [148]
Brandywine Battlefield State Hist. Site • PA, United States 118 H1
Branesti • Romania 97 D1
Branféré, Parc zoologique de • France 84 C4
Brani • Singapore 108 E4
Braniewo • Poland 13 I3
Brantas • Java, Indonesia 110 D8
Brantford • OT, Canada 122 B9
Brantôme • France 85 G2
Bras d'Or Lake • NS, Canada 123 D8
Brasil, Planalto do • Brazil 42 F6
Brasiléia • Brazil 43 D6
Brasília • Brazil 44 G2
Brasília **Heritage C** • Brazil 62 [57]
Braslav • Belarus 16 N9
Brasov • Romania 14 M4
Brass • Nigeria 22 F4
Brasschaat • Belgium 5 H3
Brastagi • Indonesia 110 B2
Brataj • Albania 15 A3
Bratan, Danau • Bali, Indonesia 110 C2
Bratislava • Slovak Rep. 13 G9
Bratsk • Russian Fed. 26 R6
Bratskoye Vdkhr. • Russian Fed. 27 F5
Brattleboro • VT, United States 118 G3
Brattvåg • Norway 94 C2
Braubach • Germany 82 H2
Braunau • Austria 13 C9
Braunfels • Germany 82 H2
Braunlage **Spa** • Germany 83 [80]
Braunschweig • Germany 8 F4
Braunwald • Switzerland 89 G3
Brauweiler • Germany 81 E3
Brava • Cape Verde 22 (1) B2
Brava, Costa • Spain 87 D
Bravo del Norte, Rio • Mexico/United States 40 E5
Brawley • CA, United States 40 C5
Bray • NU, Canada 39 P3
Bray • Ireland 79 E4
Bray Head • Ireland 79 E4
Brazil • S. America 42 E5
Brazilian Highlands • Brazil 127 A2
Brazo Casiquiare • Venezuela 43 D3
Brazos • TX, United States 119 N3
Brazzaville • Congo 22 H5
Brcko • Bosnia-Herz. 14 F5
Breadalbane • United Kingdom 74 B1
Breaksea Sound • New Zealand 112 L3
Bream Bay • New Zealand 35 E2
Brean **Beach** • United Kingdom 75 [140]
Brebes • Java, Indonesia 110 D2
Breckenridge **Ski** • CO, United States 116 [97]
Breckerfeld • Germany 81 E4
Breckland • United Kingdom 5 D2
Breclav • Czech Rep. 13 F9
Brecon • United Kingdom 7 I10
Brecon Beacons • United Kingdom 7 I10
Brecon Beacons Nat. Park **Park** • United Kingdom 72 [49]
Brecon Beacons Nat. Park • United Kingdom 75 A5
Breconshire • United Kingdom 75 A5
Breda • Netherlands 80 A11
Bredasdorp • South Africa 100 C6
Bredebro • Denmark 95 F13
Bredene-aan-Zee • Belgium 80 B1
Bredstedt • Germany 8 D2
Bree • Belgium 80 A11
Breede • South Africa 100 C6
Bregalnica • F.Y.R. of Macedonia 14 J8
Bregenz • Austria 89 H1
Bréhat, I. • France 84 C2
Breheimen • Norway 94 C2
Breidafjördur • Iceland 16 (1) B2
Breimsvatnet • Norway 94 C1
Breisach • Germany 82 G7
Breitachklamm • Germany 82 J6
Breitenfeld • Germany 71 A8
Brejeira, Serra da • Portugal 88 E2
Brekke • Norway 94 C3
Brekstad • Norway 16 E5
Bremangerlandet • Norway 94 C1
Bremen • Germany 8 D3
Bremen [Adm] • Germany 81 D1
Bremerhaven • Germany 8 D3
Bremerton • WA, United States 117 E1
Bremervörde • Germany 8 E3
Bremnes • Norway 94 C5
Brendon Hills • United Kingdom 74 F2
Brenham • TX, United States 119 N3
Brenner Pass • Austria/Italy 89 H7
Brenta • Italy 91 E3
Brenta [Riv] • Italy 12 F3
Brentwood • United Kingdom 7 M10
Brereton • Barbados 125 H4
Bréscia • Italy 91 E6
Breskens • Netherlands 80 A10
Breslau • Poland 71 A9
Bressanone • Italy 90 B1
Bressay • United Kingdom 75 A7
Bresse-Hohneck, la **Ski** • France 70 [6]
Bressuire • France 84 D3
Brest • Belarus 13 M5
Brest • France 84 C1
Bretagne • France 10 B5
Brétignolles-sur-Mer **Beach** • France 68 [83]
Breton, Pertuis • France 10 D7
Breton Sound • LA, United States 118 K4
Bretonne Corniche • France 84 C1
Brett, Cape • New Zealand 35 E2
Bretten • Germany 9 D7
Bretton Woods **Ski** • NH, United States 116 [216]
Breueh • Indonesia 110 B1
Breuil-Cervínia **Ski** • Italy 70 [199]
Breuil-Cervínia • Italy 91 E1
Breves • Brazil 43 G4
Brewarrina • NS, Australia 34 I5
Brezno • Slovak Rep. 13 I9

Bria • Central African Rep. 23 C2
Brian Head **Ski** • UT, United States 116 [86]
Briançon **Ski** • France 70 [61]
Briançon • France 85 F4
Bribie • QL, Australia 111 F6
Brices Cross Roads Nat. Battlefield Site **Park** • MS, United States 121 [203]
Brides-les-Bains **Ski** • France 70 [38]
Bridge of Orchy • United Kingdom 74 B1
Bridgend • United Kingdom 7 I10
Bridgeport • CT, United States 118 H2
Bridgetown • WA, Australia 34 C6
Bridgetown • Barbados 125 H3
Bridgewater • NS, Canada 123 D7
Bridgnorth • United Kingdom 74 D1
Bridgwater • United Kingdom 74 F3
Bridlington • United Kingdom 7 L7
Bridlington **Beach** • United Kingdom 75 [27]
Bridport • United Kingdom 74 F3
Brie • France 85 E4
Brielle • Netherlands 80 C3
Brienzer See • Switzerland 89 G2
Brieselang • Germany 81 F1
Briey • France 5 I5
Brig • Switzerland 89 G6
Brigham City • ID, United States 40 D3
Brightlingsea **Beach** • United Kingdom 75 [52]
Brighton • United Kingdom 74 E3
Brighton **Ski** • UT, United States 116 [85]
Brignoles • France 85 H3
Brimstone Hill Fortress • St Kitts & Nevis 125 G1
Brindisi • Italy 12 L8
Brintz Apple Mtn **Ski** • MI, United States 116 [136]
Brisbane • QL, Australia 111 F6
Brissac [Château] • France 84 D1
Brissago • Switzerland 89 G7
Bristol • United Kingdom 74 F3
Bristol • RI, United States 118 H2
Bristol Bay • AK, United States 40 (2) E3
Bristol Channel • United Kingdom 74 F2
Bristol Mtn **Ski** • NY, United States 116 [175]
British Columbia • Canada 38 F5
British Indian Ocean Territory • Indian Ocean 3 R7
British Mtns • Canada/United States 38 C3
British Virgin Is. • West Indies 37 I4
Brittstown • South Africa 24 C6
Brittany • France 84 C
Brittas Bay • Ireland 79 E4
Brive-la-Gaillarde • France 85 G2
Brixen • Italy 90 B1
Brixen im Thale **Ski** • Austria 70 [148]
Brixham • United Kingdom 74 F5
Brixham **Beach** • United Kingdom 75 [105]
Brno • Czech Rep. 13 F8
Broad Haven **Beach** • United Kingdom 75 [162]
Broad Sound • QL, Australia 111 F3
Broadback • QU, Canada 39 P6
Broadford • United Kingdom 6 G4
Broads, The • United Kingdom 5 E2
Broadsands **Beach** • United Kingdom 75 [104]
Broadstairs • United Kingdom 74 F4
Broadstairs **Beach** • United Kingdom 75 [63-64]
Broadway • United Kingdom 74 D4
Broby • Sweden 95 F11
Brocken • Germany 8 F5
Brockhole Visitor Centre • United Kingdom 74 C4
Brockton • MA, United States 118 H2
Brockville • OT, Canada 122 B7
Brod • F.Y.R. of Macedonia 15 C2
Brodeur Peninsula • NU, Canada 39 N2
Brodick • United Kingdom 119 N4
Brodie **Ski** • MA, United States 116 [190]
Brodnica • Poland 13 I4
Broek in Waterland • Netherlands 80 C2
Broek op Langedijk • Netherlands 80 A7
Broich, Schloß • Germany 81 E1
Broken Arrow • OK, United States 41 G4
Broken Hill • NS, Australia 34 H6
Brokopondo • Suriname 43 F3
Bromley Mtn **Ski** • VT, United States 116 [197]
Bromma [Apt] • Sweden 95 D4
Bromo, Gunung • Java, Indonesia 110 D8
Bromolla • Sweden 95 F11
Bromont **Ski** • QU, Canada 116 [38]
Brøndby **Beach** • Denmark 68 [39]
Brønderslev • Denmark 95 F6
Brønnøysund • Norway 16 G4
Bronte • Sicily, Italy 12 I11
Bronx • NY, United States 118 H2
Brook's Point • Philippines 31 F5
Brookhaven • MS, United States 118 K2
Brookings • SD, United States 41 G3
Brooklyn • NY, United States 118 H2
Brooks • AL, Canada 38 I6
Brooks Range • AK, United States 38 B3
Brookton • WA, Australia 34 C6
Broome • WA, Australia 34 D3
Brora • United Kingdom 6 I3
Brouage • France 85 G1
Brougham Castle • United Kingdom 74 C2
Broughton in Furness • United Kingdom 74 C3
Broughty Ferry • United Kingdom 74 B2
Brovst **Beach** • Denmark 68 [48]
Brovst • Denmark 95 F5
Brown Pasture • St Kitts & Nevis 125 G4
Brown v. Board of Education Nat. Hist. Site **Park** • KS, United States 121 [171]
Brownsea I. • United Kingdom 74 F3
Brownsville • TX, United States 41 G6
Brownwood • TX, United States 119 N3
Brú, Jökulsá á • Iceland 16 (1) F2
Brú Na Bóinne **Heritage C** • Ireland 64 [12]
Brú Na Bóinne • Ireland 79 E2
Bruay-en-Artois • France 10 H3
Bruce, Mt • WA, Australia 33 C8
Bruce Peninsula • OT, Canada 39 O7
Bruce Rock • WA, Australia 34 C6
Bruce Vale • Barbados 125 H1
Bruche • France 5 K6
Bruchhausen **Spa** • Germany 83 [100]
Bruchsal • Germany 82 G6
Bruck an der Mur • Austria 13 E10
Bruckmühl • Germany 82 J3
Bruges • Belgium 80 B2
Brugge • Belgium 80 B2
Brühl **Heritage C** • Germany 64 [39]
Brühl • Germany 82 G1
Brumado • Brazil 44 H1
Brumunddal • Norway 16 F6
Bruneck • Italy 90 B2
Brunei • Asia 31 E6
Brunico • Italy 90 B2
Brunnen • Switzerland 89 G3
Brunsbüttel • Germany 8 E3
Brunswick • GA, United States 41 J5
Brunswick • Germany 71 A8
Brunswick • ME, United States 118 G4
Brusa • Turkey 71 A20
Bruson **Ski** • Switzerland 70 [77]
Bruson • Switzerland 89 G6
Brusque • Brazil 44 G4
Brussel • Belgium 80 A14
Brussels • Belgium 80 A14
Bruxelles • Belgium 80 A14
Bryansk • Russian Fed. 17 E4
Bryce Canyon Nat. Park **Park** • UT, United States 120 [82]
Bryrup • Denmark 95 F9
Brzeg • Poland 13 G7
Bu Craa • Western Sahara 20 C3
Bu'ayrat al Hasun • Libya 21 C1
Bua • Sweden 95 F6
Bua Yai • Thailand 31 C3
Buala • Solomon Is. 35 (1) F2
Buapinang • Indonesia 32 (1) B3
Buatan • Indonesia 32 C2
Buca • Turkey 15 I5
Bucak • Turkey 93 G1
Bucaramanga • Colombia 43 C2
Buccoo Reef • Trinidad & Tobago 125 K2
Buchanan • Liberia 22 B3
Bucharest • Romania 97 D1
Buchen • Germany 9 E7
Buchholz in der Nordheide • Germany 8 E3
Buchloe • Germany 82 J2
Buck Hill **Ski** • MN, United States 116 [113]
Buckeye • AZ, United States 118 J3
Buckfastleigh • United Kingdom 74 F5
Buckinghamshire • United Kingdom 75 A5
Buckland Abbey • United Kingdom 74 F5
Buckland Tableland • QL, Australia 111 F3
Buckow **Spa** • Germany 83 [289]
Bucksport • ME, United States 118 G4
Buco Zau • Angola 22 G5
Bucuresti • Romania 97 D1
Bud • Norway 16 D5
Buda • Hungary 71 A14
Budapest • Hungary 13 I10
Budapest **Heritage C** • Hungary 64 [153]
Budardalur • Iceland 16 (1) C2
Budaun • India 105 C3
Bude • United Kingdom 74 F1
Bude **Beach** • United Kingdom 75 [131-134]
Bude Bay • United Kingdom 74 F1
Büdelsdorf • Germany 8 E2
Budennovsk • Russian Fed. 17 G6
Büdingen • Germany 82 G2
Budleigh Salterton • United Kingdom 74 F5
Budzjak • Moldova 14 P3
Buena Vista **Ski** • MN, United States 116 [108]
Buenaventura • Colombia 43 B3
Buenos Aires • Argentina 127 D1
Buenos Aires, Lago • Argentina/Chile 45 B5
Bueu **Beach** • Spain 68 [93]
Buff Bay • Jamaica 124 C2
Buffalo • SD, United States 40 F2
Buffalo • NY, United States 41 K3
Buffalo • TX, United States 119 N4
Buffalo Lake • NT, Canada 38 H4
Buffalo Narrows • SA, Canada 38 J5
Buffalo Springs Game Reserve • Kenya 101 G2
Buffavento Castle • Cyprus 93 J2
Buffels Bay • South Africa 100 C7
Buftea • Romania 97 D1
Buga • Colombia 43 B3
Bugia • Algeria 71 A17
Bugibba • Malta 93 H2
Bugojno • Bosnia-Herz. 12 L4
Bugulma • Russian Fed. 17 I4
Bühl • Germany 9 D8
Buhusi • Romania 14 N3
Bui Dam • Ghana 22 D3
Bui Nat. Park **Park** • Ghana 103 [23]
Builth Wells • United Kingdom 7 I9
Buin • Papua New Guinea 35 (1) F2
Buin • Chile 44 B5
Buinsk • Russian Fed. 17 H3
Buir Nur • Mongolia 29 F1
Bujanovac • F.R. of Yugoslavia 15 C1
Bujaraloz • Spain 11 K3
Bujumbura • Burundi 23 D4
Bük • Hungary 14 D2
Buka • Papua New Guinea 35 (1) E2
Bukama • Dem. Rep. of Congo 23 D5
Bukavu • Dem. Rep. of Congo 23 D4
Bukhara • Uzbekistan 18 H2
Bukhara **Heritage C** • Uzbekistan 63 [81]
Bukit Ferringhi • Penang, Malaysia 108 C1
Bukit Gemuruh Forest Reserve • Penang, Malaysia 108 C3
Bukit Genting Forest Reserve • Penang, Malaysia 108 C3
Bukit Juru Forest Reserve • Penang, Malaysia 108 C4
Bukit Kerajaan Forest Reserve • Penang, Malaysia 108 C1
Bukit Mertajam • Malaysia 31 C5
Bukit Pulau • Penang, Malaysia 108 C5
Bukit Relau Forest Reserve • Penang, Malaysia 108 C3
Bukit Tengah • Penang, Malaysia 108 C4
Bukit Timah Nature Reserve • Singapore 108 E1
Bukittinggi • Indonesia 110 B4
Bukk Nat. Park **Park** • Hungary 72 [104]
Bukoba • Tanzania 102 H1
Bukoma • Dem. Rep. of Congo 24 D1
Bukovina • Ukraine 14 M1
Bukum • Singapore 108 E3
Bula • Indonesia 32 (1) D3
Bulan • Philippines 31 G4
Bulawayo • Zimbabwe 102 J3
Buldan • Turkey 15 J5
Bulgan • Mongolia 29 B2
Bulgaria • Europe 14 L7
Bull Point • Falkland Is. 45 E6
Bulla Regia • Tunisia 101 E1
Bullfinch • WA, Australia 34 C6
Bullahar • Somalia 21 H5
Bulo Berde • Somalia 23 H3
Bulolo • Papua New Guinea 35 (1) D2
Bulukumba • Indonesia 32 (1) B4
Bulungu • Dem. Rep. of Congo 23 B4
Bumba • Dem. Rep. of Congo 23 C3
Bumi Hills • Zimbabwe 102 J1
Bunbury • WA, Australia 34 C6
Bundaberg • QL, Australia 111 F4
Bünde • Germany 8 D4
Bundelkhand Riva • India 105 C7
Bundi • India 105 C6
Bundoran **Beach** • Ireland 68 [65]
Bundoran • Ireland 79 F2
Bungku • Indonesia 32 (1) B3
Bungle Bungle • WA, Australia 111 E2
Bungo • Angola 22 H6
Bungo [Riv] • Angola/Zambia 24 C2
Bungo-Suido • Japan 30 G8
Bunja • Dem. Rep. of Congo 23 E3
Bunmahon **Beach** • Ireland 68 [58]
Bunratty Castle • Ireland 79 F6
Buntenbock **Spa** • Germany 83 [79]
Buntok • Indonesia 32 E3
Burkhaya, Guba • Russian Fed. 27 L2
Buqayq • Saudi Arabia 18 E4
Bur Gabo • Somalia 23 G4
Bur Hakkaba • Somalia 23 G3
Bûr Sa'îd • Egypt 101 F2
Bûr Safâga • Egypt 101 F4
Bur Sudan • Sudan 21 G4
Bur'o • Somalia 23 H2
Bura • Kenya 101 G4
Buran • Kazakhstan 26 O8
Buraydah • Saudi Arabia 18 D4
Burbach • Germany 9 D6
Burdekin • QL, Australia 111 F1
Burdur • Turkey 93 G1
Burdur [Adm] • Turkey 93 G1
Burdur Gölü • Turkey 93 G1
Burdwan • India 28 E4
Bure • United Kingdom 5 E2
Bure • Ethiopia 23 F1
Bureinskiy Khrebet • Russian Fed. 27 L6
Burela **Beach** • Spain 68 [91]
Büren • Germany 8 D5
Bürenhayrhan • Mongolia 26 P8
Burg • Germany 8 G2
Burg **Spa** • Germany 83 [22]
Burg bei Magdeburg • Germany 8 G4
Burg, Schloß • Germany 81 E4
Burgas • Bulgaria 97 D3
Burgaski Zaliv • Bulgaria 14 O7
Burgau • Germany 82 J2
Burgau • Portugal 88 E5
Burgdorf • Switzerland 89 G2
Burgenland • Austria 13 E10
Burgeo • NF, Canada 123 D3
Burghausen • Germany 82 J4
Burgkirchen • Germany 82 J4
Burglengenfeld • Germany 9 H7
Burgos • Spain 11 H2
Burgos **Heritage C** • Spain 64 [78]
Burgsvik • Sweden 16 J8
Burgundy • France 84 A1
Burhaniye • Turkey 15 I4
Burhanpur • India 28 C4
Burhave **Spa** • Germany 83 [52]
Burias • Philippines 31 G4
Burica, Punta • Costa Rica 43 A2
Burin Peninsula • NF, Canada 123 D4
Burjal Hattabah • Tunisia 21 A1
Burjasot • Spain 11 K5
Burkina Faso • Africa 20 E6
Burlington • IA, United States 41 H3
Burlington • VT, United States 118 G3
Burlington • NJ, United States 118 H1
Burlington • OT, Canada 122 B9
Burma • Asia 31 B2
Burma Road • China/Myanmar 29 B5
Burmah, Al • Tunisia 21 A1
Burnazului, Cimpia • Romania 14 M6
Burnham-on-Sea • United Kingdom 74 F3
Burnham-on-Sea **Beach** • United Kingdom 75 [138]
Burnie • TS, Australia 34 I8
Burnley • United Kingdom 7 J8
Burns • OR, United States 117 E4
Burnside • NU, Canada 38 I3
Burqin • China 26 O8
Burra • SA, Australia 34 G6
Burrelli • Albania 15 B2
Burren, The • Ireland 79 F4
Burriana • Spain 11 L5
Bursa • Turkey 92 D3
Burscheid • Germany 81 E4
Bürserberg • Austria 89 H5
Burton-upon-Trent • United Kingdom 7 K9
Buru • Indonesia 32 (1) C3
Burun Shibertuy, gora • Russian Fed. 27 G7
Burundi • Africa 23 D4
Burutu • Nigeria 22 F3
Buruun Urt • Mongolia 27 H7
Bury • United Kingdom 7 J8
Bury St Edmunds • United Kingdom 7 M9
Buryatia • Russian Fed. 27 H6
Busch Gardens Tampa Bay • FL, United States 119 M5
Busch Gardens Tampa Bay **Park** • FL, United States 121 [DD]
Busch Gardens the Old Country **Park** • VA, United States 121 [GG]
Busch Gardens Williamsburg • VA, United States 118 H3
Bushehr • Iran 18 F4
Busing • Singapore 108 E3
Businga • Dem. Rep. of Congo 23 C3
Buskerud • Norway 16 E6
Busko-Zdrój • Poland 13 J7
Bussana • Italy 91 E9
Busselton • WA, Australia 34 C6
Bussum • Netherlands 80 C2
Busto Arsizio • Italy 12 C3
Busuanga • Philippines 31 F4
Büsum • Germany 8 D2
Büsum **Spa** • Germany 83 [8]
Buta • Dem. Rep. of Congo 23 D3
Buta Ranquil • Argentina 45 C3
Butanah, Al • Sudan 18 B6
Butare • Rwanda 23 D4
Butaritari • Kiribati 33 I5
Bute • United Kingdom 6 G6
Butembo • Dem. Rep. of Congo 23 D3
Buteshire • United Kingdom 75 A3
Butha Qi • China 29 G1
Buthrotum **Heritage C** • Albania 64 [163]
Buthrotum • Albania 92 B1
Butiá • Brazil 44 F5
Butjadingen **Spa** • Germany 83 [52]
Butler, Lake • FL, United States 121 C1
Butrinti **Heritage C** • Albania 64 [163]
Butt of Lewis • United Kingdom 6 F3
Butte • MT, United States 40 D2
Butterfly Valley • Rhodes, Greece 93 F2
Buttermere • United Kingdom 74 C1
Buttermere [Lake] • United Kingdom 74 C1
Butternut Basin **Ski** • MA, United States 116 [188]
Butterworth • Penang, Malaysia 108 C2
Buttevant • Ireland 79 F6
Butuan • Philippines 31 H5
Butung • Indonesia 32 (1) B4
Butzbach • Germany 82 H2
Buxar • India 105 C8
Buxtehude • Germany 8 E3
Buxton • United Kingdom 7 K8
Buy • Russian Fed. 17 G3
Buyan, Danau • Bali, Indonesia 110 C2
Büyük Agri Dagi • Turkey 18 D2
Büyük Kemiki Burnu • Turkey 15 H3
Büyük Menderes • Turkey 15 K5
Büyükanafarta • Turkey 15 H3
Buyun • China 30 B4
Buzachi, Poluostrov • Kazakhstan 17 I6
Buzau • Romania 14 N4
Buzau [Riv] • Romania 97 D1
Buzet • France 84 B3
Búzios • Brazil 127 C4
Buzuluk • Russian Fed. 17 I4
Bvumba Reserve • Zimbabwe 102 J4
Bwindi Impenetrable Nat. Park **Heritage N** • Uganda 61 [87]
Bwindi Impenetrable Nat. Park **Park** • Uganda 103 [71]
Byala • Lovec, Bulgaria 14 M6
Byala • Burgas, Bulgaria 97 D4
Byam Martin, Cape • NU, Canada 39 P2
Byam Martin I. • NU, Canada 38 K1
Byblos **Heritage C** • Lebanon 64 [245]
Bydgoszcz • Poland 13 G4
Bygdin • Norway 94 C4
Bygland • Norway 94 C6
Byglandsfjord • Norway 95 F1
Bykle • Norway 94 C6
Bykovo [Apt] • Russian Fed. 97 E4
Bykovski • Russian Fed. 27 L2
Bylot I. • NU, Canada 39 P2
Byramgore Reef • India 106 D5
Byrd Field [Apt] • VA, United States 118 H3
Byrkjelo • Norway 94 C2
Byron, Cape • NS, Australia 111 F6
Byrranga, Gory • Russian Fed. 26 P3
Bystrzyca Klodzka • Poland 13 F7
Bytca • Slovak Rep. 13 H8
Bytom • Poland 13 H7
Bytów • Poland 13 G3
Byxelkrok • Sweden 95 F8
Bzura • Poland 13 I5

C

Ca Mau • Vietnam 108 B3
Caaguazú • Paraguay 44 E4
Caballas • Peru 127 B3
Caballo Cocha • Peru 43 C4
Caballo Reservoir • NM, United States 118 J4
Cabana • Peru 127 B1
Cabanatuan • Philippines 31 G3
Caberfae Peaks **Ski** • MI, United States 116 [133]
Cabimas • Venezuela 43 C1
Cabinda • Angola 22 G6
Cabinda [Adm] • Angola 22 G6
Cabinet Mtns • MT, United States 117 E2
Cable Beach • Bahamas 124 B3
Cabo Bojador • Western Sahara 20 C3
Cabo de Rama Fort • Goa, India 105 B2
Cabo Negro • Morocco 101 D2
Cabonga, Réservoir • QU, Canada 39 P7
Caborca • Mexico 40 D5
Caboro Bassa Dam • Mozambique 24 E3
Caboro Bassa, Lago • Mozambique 24 E3
Cabot Strait • NF/NS, Canada 123 D3
Cabra • Spain 11 G7
Cabrera, I. de • Spain 87 H4
Cabriel • Spain 11 J5
Cabrillo Nat. Mon. **Park** • CA, United States 120 [58]
Caçador • Brazil 44 F4
Cacahuamilpa • Mexico 123 E4
Cacak • F.R. of Yugoslavia 14 H6
Caçapava do Sul • Brazil 44 F5
Cáceres • Spain 11 E5
Cáceres • Brazil 44 E2
Cáceres **Heritage C** • Spain 64 [90]
Cachimbo • Brazil 43 G5
Cachimbo, Serra do • Brazil 43 F5
Cachoeira • Brazil 44 I1
Cachoeira de Paulo Afonso • Brazil 45 (1) D3
Cachoeira do Sul • Brazil 44 F5
Cachoeiro de Itapemirim • Brazil 127 C2
Cachopo • Portugal 88 E3
Cacoctin Mtn **Park** • MD, United States 118 H3
Cacocúm • Cuba 124 D8
Cacolo • Angola 23 B6
Caconda • Angola 24 B2
Caculé • Brazil 44 H1
Cadaqués • Spain 87 D2
Cadca • Slovak Rep. 13 H8
Cadena Costero Catalana • Spain 11 M3
Cadenábbia • Italy 91 E2
Cadillac • MI, United States 41 I3
Cadiz • Philippines 31 G4
Cádiz **Beach** • Spain 68 [113]
Cádiz • Spain 86 B5
Cádiz, Bahía de • Spain 86 B5
Cádiz, Golfo de • Spain 11 D8
Cadore • Italy 90 B2
Cadouin • France 85 G4
Caen • France 10 E4
Caernarfon • United Kingdom 7 H8
Caernarfon Bay • United Kingdom 7 H8
Caernarfonshire • United Kingdom 75 A4
Caerphilly • United Kingdom 7 I10
Caesarea • Israel 98 A3
Caesarea Philippi • Syria 98 A2
Cafayate • Argentina 44 C4
Cagayan • Philippines 31 G3
Cagayan de Oro • Philippines 31 G5
Cagayan Sulu • Philippines 31 F5
Çagis • Turkey 15 J4
Cágliari • Sardinia, Italy 90 C4
Cágliari, Golfo di • Sardinia, Italy 90 C4
Cagnes-sur-Mer • France 85 H4
Caguas • Puerto Rico 125 E4
Cagyl • Turkmenistan 18 G1
Caherciveen **Beach** • Ireland 68 [60]
Caherciveen • Ireland 79 F7
Caherdaniel **Beach** • Ireland 68 [60]
Caherdaniel • Ireland 79 F7
Cahir • Ireland 7 E9
Cahokia Mounds State Hist. Site **Heritage C** • IL, United States 62 [9]
Cahors • France 85 G4
Cahul • Moldova 14 P4
Caiapó, Serra do • Brazil 44 F2
Caibarién • Cuba 124 D3
Caicara • Venezuela 37 H6
Caimanera • Cuba 124 D8
Caimito, Playa del • Cuba 124 D2
Caine • Bolivia 44 C2
Cairngorm Mtns • United Kingdom 6 I4
Cairnryan • United Kingdom 78 A4
Cairns • QL, Australia 111 F1
Cairo • IL, United States 41 I4
Cairo **Heritage C** • Egypt 64 [237]
Cairo • Egypt 101 F1
Caithness • United Kingdom 75 A1
Caiundo • Angola 24 B3
Cajabamba • Peru 43 B5
Cajamarca • Peru 43 B5
Cajapió • Brazil 45 (1) C2
Cajun Country • LA, United States 118 K3
Çakirlar • Turkey 93 G3
Cakovec • Croatia 13 F11
Cala Antena • Majorca, Spain 87 H4
Cala Bassa • Ibiza, Spain 87 G1
Cala Blanca • Minorca, Spain 87 F1
Cala Blanes • Minorca, Spain 87 F1
Cala Blava • Majorca, Spain 87 H3
Cala Bona • Majorca, Spain 87 H2
Cala Conta • Ibiza, Spain 87 G1
Cala d'Egos • Majorca, Spain 87 H3
Cala d'Or • Majorca, Spain 87 H4
Cala de Sant Vicenç • Ibiza, Spain 87 G2
Cala de Sant Vicenç • Majorca, Spain 87 H2
Cala de Santandria • Minorca, Spain 87 F1
Cala En Bosc • Minorca, Spain 87 F3
Cala En Porter • Minorca, Spain 87 F4
Cala Estany • Majorca, Spain 87 H2
Cala Figuera • Majorca, Spain 87 H4
Cala Figuera, Cap de • Majorca, Spain 87 H3
Cala Forcat • Minorca, Spain 87 F1
Cala Fornells • Majorca, Spain 87 H3
Cala Gració • Ibiza, Spain 87 G1
Cala Liberotto • Sardinia, Italy 90 C2
Cala Llenya • Ibiza, Spain 87 G2
Cala Llombarts • Majorca, Spain 87 H4
Cala Llonga • Minorca, Spain 87 F4
Cala Llonga • Ibiza, Spain 87 G2
Cala Llonga • Majorca, Spain 87 H4
Cala Major • Majorca, Spain 87 H3
Cala Marçal • Majorca, Spain 87 H4
Cala Millor • Majorca, Spain 87 H2
Cala Mondragó • Majorca, Spain 87 H4
Cala Morell • Minorca, Spain 87 F1
Cala Murada • Majorca, Spain 87 H4
Cala Pi • Majorca, Spain 87 H3
Cala Ratjada • Majorca, Spain 87 H2
Cala Sahona • Formentera, Spain 87 G3
Cala Salada • Ibiza, Spain 87 G1
Cala Santa Galdana • Minorca, Spain 87 F3
Cala Santanyí • Majorca, Spain 87 H4
Cala Tarida • Ibiza, Spain 87 G1
Cala Tirant • Minorca, Spain 87 F2
Cala Torret • Minorca, Spain 87 F4
Cala Vadella • Ibiza, Spain 87 G1
Cala Vinyes • Majorca, Spain 87 H3
Calabar • Nigeria 22 F3
Calabozo • Venezuela 43 D2
Calábria • Italy 12 K9
Calábria, Parco Naz. della **Park** • Italy 72 [88]
Calacuccia • Corsica, France 85 L1
Calafat • Romania 14 J6
Calafate • Argentina 45 B6
Calafell **Beach** • Spain 68 [121]
Calafell • Spain 87 D3
Calahonda • Spain 86 B7
Calahorra • Spain 11 I2
Calais • France 10 G3
Calais • ME, United States 118 G2
Calalaste, Sierra de • Argentina 44 C4
Calama • Chile 44 C3
Calamian Group • Philippines 31 F4
Calamocha • Spain 11 J4
Calanche, les **Heritage N** • Corsica, France 61 [45]
Calanche, les • Corsica, France 85 L1
Calang • Indonesia 110 B1
Calangute • Goa, India 105 B1
Calangute Beach • Goa, India 105 B1
Calanques, Côte des • France 85 H3
Calapan • Philippines 31 G4
Calarasi • Moldova 14 P2
Calarasi • Romania 97 D1
Calatayud • Spain 11 J3
Calbayog • Philippines 31 G4
Calcare, Cava di • Italy 91 G1
Calcasieu Lake • LA, United States 118 K3
Calcatoggio • Corsica, France 85 L3
Calçoene • Brazil 43 G3
Calcutta • India 28 E4
Caldas da Rainha • Portugal 11 B5
Caldbeck • United Kingdom 74 C2
Caldeirão, Serra do • Portugal 88 E3
Calder Hall • United Kingdom 74 C3
Caldera • Chile 44 B4
Caldera de Taburiente, Parque Nac. de **Park** • La Palma, Canary Is. 72 [76]
Caldera de Taburiente, Parque Nac. de • La Palma, Canary Is. 87 E5
Caldonazzo, Lago di • Italy 90 B3
Caldwell • ID, United States 117 E4
Caledon • South Africa 100 C5
Caledon **Ski** • OT, Canada 116 [22]
Caledon [Riv] • South Africa 24 D6
Caledonian Canal • United Kingdom 6 H4
Calella **Beach** • Spain 68 [122]
Calella • Spain 87 D4
Calenzana • Corsica, France 85 L1
Cales Coves • Minorca, Spain 87 F4
Cales de Mallorca • Majorca, Spain 87 H4
Caleta Olivia • Argentina 45 C5
Caleton Blanc • Cuba 124 D8
Caletta, la • Sardinia, Italy 90 C2
Calgary • AL, Canada 122 C4
Calheta • Azores 88 B2
Calheta • Madeira 88 C1
Cali • Colombia 43 B3
Calico Ghost Town • CA, United States 117 F6
Calicut • India 106 D10
Cálida, Costa • Spain 87 C3
Caliente • NV, United States 117 F4
California • United States 117 F
California, Golfo de • Mexico 40 D6
Calitzdorf • South Africa 100 C6
Callabonna, Lake • SA, Australia 34 G5
Callao • Peru 127 B1
Callosa de Segura • Spain 11 K6
Calma, Costa • Fuerteventura, Canary Is. 87 E2
Calonge **Beach** • Spain 68 [123]
Calore • Italy 91 G2
Caloundra • QL, Australia 111 F6
Calpe **Beach** • Spain 68 [118]
Calpe • Spain 87 C2
Caltagirone • Sicily, Italy 12 I11
Caltanissetta • Sicily, Italy 90 D4
Caluango • Angola 22 H6
Calulo • Angola 22 G6
Calvados, Côte du • France 5 C5
Calvi • Corsica, France 85 L1
Calvià **Beach** • Majorca, Spain 68 [126]
Calvià • Majorca, Spain 87 H1
Calvinia • South Africa 100 C2
Calw • Germany 82 G6
Cam • United Kingdom 5 D2
Cam Ranh • Vietnam 108 B2
Cam Ranh Bay • Vietnam 108 B2
Camabatela • Angola 23 B5
Camacá • Brazil 44 I2
Camagüey • Cuba 124 D7
Camagüey, Archipiélago de • Cuba 124 D3
Camaiore **Beach** • Italy 68 [144]
Camamu • Brazil 44 I1
Camaná • Peru 127 B4
Camaquã • Brazil 44 F5
Câmara de Lobos • Madeira 88 C1
Camargo • Spain 11 H1
Camargue • France 10 J10
Camariñas • Spain 11 B1
Camarón, Cabo • Honduras 37 D4
Camarones • Argentina 45 C4
Camas • Spain 11 F7
Cambados • Spain 11 C2
Camber **Beach** • United Kingdom 75 [67]
Cambo-les-Bains • France 85 J1
Cambodia • Asia 31 C4
Camborne • United Kingdom 74 F4
Cambrai • France 10 I3
Cambrian Mtns • United Kingdom 7 I9
Cambridge • United Kingdom 7 M9
Cambridge • New Zealand 112 K1
Cambridge • MA, United States 118 H2
Cambridge • MD, United States 118 H3
Cambridge Bay • NU, Canada 38 J3
Cambridgeshire • United Kingdom 75 A5
Cambrils **Beach** • Spain 68 [121]
Cambrils de Mar • Spain 87 D3
Camden • ME, United States 118 G4
Camden • NJ, United States 118 H1
Camden **Park** • SC, United States 121 [241]
Camelback **Ski** • PA, United States 116 [167]
Camelford • United Kingdom 74 F4
Camelot Theme Park **Park** • United Kingdom 73 [23]
Camenca • Moldova 14 P1
Cameron Highlands • Malaysia 108 D1
Cameron Hills • NT, Canada 38 H4
Cameron Mtns • New Zealand 112 L3
Cameroon • Africa 22 G3
Cameroun, Mt • Cameroon 22 F4
Cametá • Brazil 43 H4
Caminha **Beach** • Portugal 68 [94]
Camino de Santiago **Heritage C** • Spain 64 [80]
Çamlikköyü • Turkey 93 G2
Camocim • Brazil 45 (1) C2
Camooweal • QL, Australia 34 G3
Camopi • French Guiana 43 G3
Camorta • India 28 F7
Camp de Mar • Majorca, Spain 87 H3
Campagna • Italy 91 G4
Campal Beach • Goa, India 105 B1
Campana, I. • Chile 45 A5
Campanella, Punta • Italy 91 G3
Campania • Italy 12 J8
Campbell, Cape • New Zealand 35 E5
Campbell Town • TS, Australia 34 I8
Campbelltown • NS, Australia 111 G2
Campbelltown • NB, Canada 123 D2
Campbeltown • United Kingdom 6 G6
Campeche • Mexico 37 C4
Campeche [Adm] • Mexico 37 C4
Campeche, Bahía de • Mexico 37 C4
Campechuela • Cuba 124 D7
Campello **Beach** • Spain 68 [118]
Campello • Spain 87 C2
Campi Dano • Sardinia, Italy 12 C9
Campiglia Marittime • Italy 12 E5
Campina Grande • Brazil 45 (1) D3
Campinas • Brazil 44 G3
Campitello di Fassa **Ski** • Italy 70 [228]
Campitello di Fassa • Italy 90 B3
Campo del Oro [Apt] • Corsica, France 85 L3
Campo Felice • Italy 91 F2
Campo Grande • Brazil 44 F3
Campo Maior • Brazil 45 (1) C2
Campo Mourão • Brazil 44 F3
Campo Tures • Italy 90 B2
Campoamor • Spain 87 C3
Campobasso • Italy 12 I7
Campos • Brazil 45 (1) C4
Campos • Majorca, Spain 87 H4
Campos • Brazil 127 C4
Campos do Jordão • Brazil 127 C3
Campotosto, Lago di • Italy 91 F2
Campsie Fells • United Kingdom 74 B3
Camrose • AL, Canada 38 I6
Camsell Portage • SA, Canada 38 J5

Camyuva • Turkey 93 G3
Can • Turkey 15 I3
Can Pastilla • Majorca, Spain 87 H3
Can Picafort • Majorca, Spain 87 H2
Can Tho • Vietnam 108 B3
Cana • United Kingdom 75 A2
Cana of Galilee • Israel 98 A4
Canaan Valley **Ski** • WV, United States 116 [155]
Canada • N. America 36
Cañada de Gomez • Argentina 44 D5
Canadaigua Lake • NY, United States 122 B10
Cañadas del Teide, Parque Nac. de las **Park** • Tenerife, Canary Is. 72 [78]
Cañades del Teide, Parque Nac. de las • Tenerife, Canary Is. 86 E1
Canadian Rocky Mtns parks **Heritage N** • AL/BC, Canada 60 [4]
Canadian Shield • Canada 38/39
Canaguinim Beach • Goa, India 105 B2
Canaima, Parque Nac. **Heritage N** • Venezuela 60 [27]
Çanakkale • Turkey 92 D2
Çanakkale Bogazi • Turkey 92 D2
Canal du Midi **Heritage C** • France 64 [64]
Canaria, Costa • Gran Canaria, Canary Is. 86 E4
Canarias • Atlantic Ocean 86 E
Canaries • St Lucia 125 J3
Canarreros, Archipiélago de los • Cuba 124 D2
Canary Is. • Atlantic Ocean 86 E
Canaveral, Cape • FL, United States 41 J6
Canaveral Nat. Seashore • FL, United States 119 M6
Canaveral Nat. Seashore **Park** • FL, United States 121 [223]
Canazei **Ski** • Italy 70 [229]
Canazei • Italy 90 B3
Canberra • AC, Australia 111 G2
Cancale **Beach** • France 68 [79]
Cancale • France 84 C2
Canche • France 5 E4
Cancún • Mexico 37 D3
Çandarli • Turkey 15 H5
Çandarli Körfezi • Turkey 15 H5
Candelaria • Tenerife, Canary Is. 86 E1
Candi Kuning Temple • Bali, Indonesia 110 C2
Candi Sukuh Temple • Java, Indonesia 110 D7
Candidasa Beach • Bali, Indonesia 110 C4
Candolim Beach • Goa, India 105 B1
Cane River Creole Nat. Hist. Park & Nat. Heritage Area **Park** • LA, United States 121 [196]
Canea • Crete, Greece 93 E1
Canelones • Uruguay 127 D2
Canet d'En Berenguer **Beach** • Spain 68 [119]
Canet de Mar **Beach** • Spain 68 [122]
Canet en Roussillon **Beach** • France 68 [128]
Canet-Plage • France 85 K2
Cañete • Spain 11 J4
Canfranc • Spain 11 K2
Cangamba • Angola 24 B2
Cangas • Spain 11 C2
Cangas **Beach** • Spain 68 [93]
Canggu Beach • Bali, Indonesia 110 C4
Cango Caves • South Africa 100 C7
Cangzhou • China 29 F3
Caniapiscau, Lac • QU, Canada 39 R6
Caniçal • Madeira 88 E2
Canicatti • Sicily, Italy 12 H11
Caniço • Madeira 88 C2
Canindé • Brazil 45 (1) D2
Cankiri • Turkey 15 O3
Canna • United Kingdom 78 A1
Cannanore • India 106 D6
Cannes **Beach** • France 68 [134]
Cannes • France 85 H4
Cannock • United Kingdom 5 A2
Cannock Chase • United Kingdom 74 D2
Cannon **Ski** • NH, United States 116 [215]
Cannon [Apt] • NV, United States 117 F3
Cannon Beach • OR, United States 117 E1
Cannonsburg **Ski** • MI, United States 116 [141]
Canoas • Brazil 44 F4
Canonica, la • Corsica, France 85 L2
Canosa di Puglia • Italy 14 D8
Canove **Ski** • Italy 70 [213]
Cansaulim Beach • Goa, India 105 B2
Canso, Strait of • NS, Canada 123 D8
Cantabria • Spain 11 G1
Cantábrica, Cordillera • Spain 11 F2
Cantábrico, Mar • Spain 11 E1
Cantanhede **Beach** • Portugal 68 [96]
Cantera, I. de la • Spain 87 C1
Canterbury **Heritage C** • United Kingdom 64 [25]
Canterbury • United Kingdom 74 E4
Canterbury • New Zealand 112 J3
Canterbury • NH, United States 118 G3
Canterbury Bight • New Zealand 35 C6
Canterbury Plains • New Zealand 112 J3
Canton • OH, United States 41 J3
Canton • China 107 H1
Canton • MS, United States 118 K2
Canumã • Brazil 43 F4
Canvey I. • United Kingdom 74 E2
Canyon de Chelly Nat. Mon. • AZ, United States 118 J2
Canyon de Chelly Nat. Mon. **Park** • AZ, United States 120 [103]
Canyonlands Nat. Park **Park** • UT, United States 120 [86]
Canyons, The **Ski** • UT, United States 116 [81]
Caombo • Angola 22 H6
Caorle • Italy 91 E8
Cap aux Meules • QU, Canada 123 D2
Cap d'Ail **Beach** • France 68 [134]
Cap d'Ambre • Madagascar 24 H2
Cap de la Madeleine • QU, Canada 122 B4
Cap Estate • St Lucia 125 J2
Cap Esterel • France 85 H4
Capanema • Brazil 45 (1) B2
Caparaó, Serra do • Brazil 127 C2
Caparra • Puerto Rico 125 E2
Capbreton • France 85 G3
Capdepera **Beach** • Majorca, Spain 68 [126]
Capdepera • Majorca, Spain 87 H2
Cape Breton Highlands Nat. Park • NS, Canada 123 D8
Cape Breton I. • NS, Canada 123 D8
Cape Canaveral • FL, United States 119 M6
Cape Coast • Ghana 22 D3
Cape Coral • FL, United States 119 M5
Cape Cross Reserve **Park** • Namibia 103 [115]
Cape Evans • Antarctica 59 A10
Cape Girardeau • MO, United States 41 I4
Cape Hatteras Nat. Seashore **Park** • NC, United States 121 [249]
Cape Krusenstern Nat. Mon. **Park** • AK, United States 120 [1]
Cape Lookout Nat. Seashore **Park** • NC, United States 121 [248]
Cape of Good Hope Nature Reserve **Park** • South Africa 103 [117]
Cape of Good Hope Nature Resrve • South Africa 100 C5
Cape Peninsula • South Africa 100 C5
Cape Soúnio • Greece 92 D7
Cape Town • South Africa 100 C5
Cape Verde • Atlantic Ocean 22 (1)
Capella Telefomin • Indonesia 32 (1) F3
Capelle, la • France 10 I4
Capernaum • Israel 98 A2
Capileira • Spain 86 B3
Capitán Arturo Prat [Base] • Antarctica 46 (1) JJ4
Capitol Reef Nat. Park **Park** • UT, United States 120 [83]
Capivara, Parque Nac. Serra da **Heritage N** • Brazil 60 [35]
Capivara, Parque Nac. Serra da **Heritage C** • Brazil 62 [58]
Capo Boi • Sardinia, Italy 90 C4
Capodichino [Apt] • Italy 91 G1
Capodimonte • Italy 91 F1
Cappadocia **Heritage N** • Turkey 61 [63]
Cappadocia **Heritage C** • Turkey 64 [193]
Cappenberg, Schloß • Germany 81 E2
Capráia, I. di • Italy 91 E10
Caprera, I. • Sardinia, Italy 90 C2
Capri • Italy 91 G3
Capri, I. di • Italy 91 G3
Capriate San Gervasio • Italy 91 E6
Capricorn Channel • QL, Australia 111 F4
Capricorn Group • QL, Australia 111 F4
Caprivi Strip • Namibia 24 C3
Captain Cook • HI, United States 119 L8
Captiva I. • FL, United States 119 M5
Càpua • Italy 91 G1
Capulin Volcano Nat. Mon. **Park** • NM, United States 120 [132]
Caputh • Germany 81 F3
Caqueta • Colombia 43 C4
Car Nicobar • India 28 F7
Caracal • Romania 14 L5
Caracarai • Brazil 43 E3
Caracas • Venezuela 43 D1
Caracollo • Bolivia 44 C2
Caraguatatuba • Brazil 127 C3
Carais, Serra dos • Brazil 43 G5
Carajás • Brazil 43 G5
Caransebes • Romania 14 J4
Caranzalem Beach • Goa, India 105 B1
Caraquet • NB, Canada 123 D2
Caratasca, Laguna de • Honduras 37 E4
Caratinga • Brazil 127 C2
Carauari • Brazil 43 D5
Caravaca de la Cruz • Spain 11 J6
Caravelas • Brazil 44 I2
Carázinho • Brazil 44 F4
Carballo • Spain 11 C1
Carballo **Beach** • Spain 68 [92]
Carbon, Cap • Algeria 11 K9
Carbonara, Capo • Sardinia, Italy 90 C4
Carbondale • IL, United States 41 I4
Carboneras **Beach** • Spain 68 [116]
Carboneras • Spain 86 B4
Carbonia • Sardinia, Italy 12 C9
Carbury • Ireland 79 E1
Carcans **Beach** • France 68 [85]
Carcans • France 85 G1
Carcassonne • France 10 H10
Carcassonne **Heritage C** • France 64 [69]
Carcavelos • Portugal 88 D1
Çardak • Çanakkale, Turkey 15 H3
Çardak • Denizli, Turkey 15 K6
Cardamom Hills • India 106 D10
Cárdenas • Cuba 124 D2
Cardiff • United Kingdom 74 F2
Cardigan • United Kingdom 7 H9
Cardigan Bay • United Kingdom 7 H9
Cardiganshire • United Kingdom 75 A5
Cardona • Uruguay 127 D2
Cardrona • New Zealand 112 L2
Carei • Romania 14 J2
Carentan • France 10 D4
Carey, Lake • WA, Australia 34 D5
Carezza, Lago di • Italy 90 B3
Cargados Carajos • Indian Ocean 19 J7
Cargèse • Corsica, France 85 L3
Carhaix-Plouguer • France 84 C1
Cariacica • Brazil 44 H3
Caribbean Beach • St Kitts & Nevis 125 G2
Caribbean Sea • America 37 G4
Caribbean/Florida cruise area • America 58 B
Cariboo Mtns • BC, Canada 38 G6
Caribou • MN, Canada 38 L5
Caribou • ME, United States 118 G2
Caribou Mtns • AL, Canada 38 H5
Cariè • Turkey 15 J6
Carignan • France 5 I5
Carinhanha • Brazil 44 H1
Carinthia • Austria 89 F3
Carinthia **Ski** • VT, United States 116 [195]
Caripito • Venezuela 43 E1
Carita • Java, Indonesia 110 D1
Carlet • Spain 11 K5
Carleton Place • OT, Canada 122 B6
Carlisle • PA, United States 118 H1
Carlisle Bay • Barbados 125 H3
Carlow • Ireland 79 E3
Carlow [Adm] • Ireland 79 D2
Carlsbad • NM, United States 40 F5
Carlsbad Caverns Nat. Park **Heritage N** • NM, United States 60 [13]
Carlsbad Caverns Nat. Park **Park** • NM, United States 120 [122]
Carmacks • YT, Canada 38 D4
Carmagnola • Italy 12 B4
Carmarthen • United Kingdom 7 H10
Carmarthen Bay • United Kingdom 7 H10
Carmarthenshire • United Kingdom 75 A5
Carmaux • France 10 H9
Carmel • CA, United States 117 F3
Carmel, Mount • Israel 98 A3
Carmelo • Uruguay 127 D2
Carmen • Mexico 40 D6
Carmensa • Argentina 44 C5
Carmona • Spain 86 B2
Carna • Ireland 79 F3
Carnac • France 84 C4
Carnamah • WA, Australia 34 C5
Carnarvon • WA, Australia 34 B4
Carnarvon • South Africa 100 C3
Carnati • India 106 D11
Carnegie, Lake • WA, Australia 34 D5
Carnot • Central African Rep. 23 B3
Carnoustie • United Kingdom 74 B2
Carnsore Point • Ireland 7 F9
Carolina • Brazil 45 (1) B3
Carolina • Puerto Rico 125 E2
Caroline • Kiribati 33 L7
Caroline, Fort, Nat. Mem. • FL, United States 119 M3
Caroline, Fort, Nat. Mem. **Park** • FL, United States 121 [220]
Caroline Is. • Fed. States of Micronesia 33 F5
Carolinensiel **Spa** • Germany 83 [47]
Carondelet • Kiribati 33 J6
Caroni • Venezuela 37 I6
Caroni • Trinidad & Tobago 125 K3
Caroni Swamp • Trinidad & Tobago 125 K3
Carora • Venezuela 43 C1
Carpathians • Europe 4 O7
Carpatii Meridionali • Romania 14 K4
Carpatii Occidentali • Romania 13 L11
Carpentaria, Gulf of • NT/QL, Australia 34 G3
Carpi • Italy 12 E4
Carra, Lough • Ireland 79 F4
Carrapateira • Portugal 88 E5
Carrara • Italy 91 E10
Carraroe **Beach** • Ireland 68 [62]
Carraroe • Ireland 79 F3
Carrasco • Uruguay 127 D2
Carreño • Spain 11 F1
Carreta, Punta • Peru 127 B1
Carrick-on-Shannon • Ireland 7 D8
Carrick-on-Suir • Ireland 7 E9
Carrickfergus • United Kingdom 7 G7
Carrigadrohid Reservoir • Ireland 79 F8
Carroz, les **Ski** • France 70 [18]
Carroz-d'Arâches, les • France 85 F2
Carruantoohil • Ireland 79 F7
Carson City • NV, United States 117 F3
Cartagena • Colombia 43 B1
Cartagena **Beach** • Spain 68 [117]
Cartagena **Heritage C** • Colombia 62 [42]
Cartagena • Spain 87 C3
Cartago • Costa Rica 37 E6
Cartago • Colombia 43 B3
Cartaya • Spain 86 B1
Carter, Jimmy, Nat. Hist. Site **Park** • GA, United States 121 [214]
Carter, Mt • QL, Australia 34 H2
Carthage • MO, United States 41 H4
Carthage **Heritage C** • Tunisia 64 [227]
Carthage • Tunisia 101 E2
Carthage [Apt] • Tunisia 101 E2
Caruaru • Brazil 45 (1) D3
Carúpano • Venezuela 43 E1
Carver, George Washington, Nat. Mon. **Park** • MO, United States 121 [174]
Carvoeiro • Portugal 88 E6
Carvoeiro, Cabo • Portugal 11 B5
Cas Concos • Majorca, Spain 87 H4
Casa de Campo, Parque de Atracciones **Park** • Spain 73 [78]
Casa Grande • AZ, United States 118 J3
Casa Grande Ruins Nat. Mon. • AZ, United States 118 J3
Casa Grande Ruins Nat. Mon. **Park** • AZ, United States 120 [113]
Casablanca • Morocco 101 D1
Casale Monferrato • Italy 91 E6
Casalmaggiore • Italy 12 E4
Casamari, Abbazia di • Italy 91 F4
Casares • Spain 86 B6
Cascade Mtn **Ski** • WI, United States 116 [122]
Cascade Range • OR/WA, United States 117 E
Cascais **Beach** • Portugal 68 [98]
Cascais • Portugal 88 D1
Cascavel • Brazil 44 F4
Cascina • Italy 12 E5
Caserta **Heritage C** • Italy 64 [126]
Caserta • Italy 91 G1
Casey [Base] • Antarctica 46 (1) Q3
Casey Bay • Antarctica 46 (1) J3
Caseyr, Râs • Somalia 23 I1
Cashel • Ireland 7 E9
Casilda • Argentina 127 D1
Casino • NS, Australia 111 F6
Cáslav • Czech Rep. 96 C2
Caspe • Spain 11 K3
Casper • WY, United States 40 E3
Caspian Sea • Asia 4 T8
Cassai • Angola 24 C2
Cassano allo Ionio • Italy 12 K9
Cassiar • BC, Canada 38 F5
Cassiar Mtns • BC, Canada 38 E5
Cassinga • Angola 24 B3
Cassino • Italy 12 H7
Castagneto Carducci **Beach** • Italy 68 [146]
Castagneto Carducci • Italy 91 E11
Castel del Monte **Heritage C** • Italy 64 [130]
Castel di Sangro • Italy 12 I7
Castel Gandolfo • Italy 91 F3
Castelfranco Véneto • Italy 12 F3
Casteljaloux • France 85 G3
Castell-Platja d'Aro **Beach** • Spain 68 [123]
Castellammare di Stábia • Italy 91 G3
Castellammare, Golfo di • Sicily, Italy 90 D1
Castellana Grotte • Italy 12 L8
Castellane • France 85 H2
Castelldefels • Spain 87 D3
Castelli Romani • Italy 91 F3
Castelló d'Empúries **Beach** • Spain 68 [123]
Castellón de la Plana • Spain 11 K4
Castellote • Spain 11 K4
Castelnaudary • France 11 M1
Castelnou • France 85 K2
Castelo Branco • Portugal 11 D5
Castelo Branco [Adm] • Portugal 88 A2
Castelo, Ponto do • Madeira 88 C2
Castelrotto • Italy 90 B1
Castelsardo **Beach** • Sardinia, Italy 68 [137]
Castelsardo • Sardinia, Italy 90 C1
Castelvetrano • Sicily, Italy 12 G11
Castiglioncello • Italy 91 E11
Castiglione del Lago • Italy 91 E11
Castiglione della Pescáia • Italy 91 E11
Castilla, Playa de • Spain 86 B1
Castilla-la Mancha • Spain 11 G5
Castilla-y-León • Spain 11 G3
Castillo de Jagua • Cuba 124 D2
Castillo de San Marcos Nat. Mon. • FL, United States 119 M4
Castillo de San Marcos Nat. Mon. **Park** • FL, United States 121 [221]
Castle Clinton Nat. Mon. **Park** • NY, United States 121 [325]
Castle Drogo • United Kingdom 74 F5
Castle Hill • NF, Canada 123 D4
Castle Matrix • Ireland 79 F6
Castle Peak • Hong Kong, China 107 H5
Castlebar • Ireland 79 F2
Castlebay • United Kingdom 78 A1
Castleconnell • Ireland 79 F6
Castledermot • Ireland 79 E3
Castledown House • Ireland 79 E1
Castlegregory **Beach** • Ireland 68 [60]
Castlegregory • Ireland 79 F5
Castleisland • Ireland 79 F5
Castlepoint • New Zealand 35 F5
Castlerea • Ireland 79 F2
Castlereagh Bay • NT, Australia 34 G2
Castlerigg Stone Circle • United Kingdom 74 C2
Castletown • Jamaica 124 C2
Castletownbere • Ireland 79 F7
Castres • France 10 H10
Castries • St Lucia 125 J1
Castro • Brazil 44 F3
Castro • Chile 45 B4
Castro Marim **Beach** • Portugal 68 [100]
Castro Marim • Portugal 88 E4
Castro-Urdiales **Beach** • Spain 68 [89]
Castrojeriz • Spain 11 G2
Castrop-Rauxel • Germany 81 E2
Castrovillari • Italy 12 K9
Caswell Bay **Beach** • United Kingdom 75 [143]
Caswell Sound • New Zealand 112 L1
Cat I. • Bahamas 124 B2
Cat Lake • OT, Canada 39 M6
Çatal Dag • Turkey 15 J4
Catalão • Brazil 44 G2
Çatalca • Turkey 15 J2
Catalina • Chile 44 C4
Catalina, Punta • Chile 45 C6
Catalonia • Spain 86 A1
Cataluña • Spain 11 M3
Catalunya • Spain 11 M3
Catamarca • Argentina 44 C4
Catanduanes • Philippines 31 G4
Catanduva • Brazil 44 G3
Catánia • Sicily, Italy 90 D4
Catánia, Golfo di • Sicily, Italy 90 D4
Cataño • Puerto Rico 125 E2
Catanzaro • Italy 12 K10
Catarata Ruancaná • Angola/Namibia 24 A3
Catarman • Philippines 31 G4
Catastrophe, Cape • SA, Australia 34 G6
Cataway Park • AL, Canada 122 C4
Catbalogan • Philippines 31 G4
Catena Costierra • Italy 12 K9
Catena dei Lagorai • Italy 90 B3
Catináccio • Italy 90 B3
Catingas • Brazil 45 (1) B3
Catió • Guinea-Bissau 22 A2
Catlins, The • New Zealand 112 L4
Cato I. • CL, Australia 34 K4
Catoche, Cabo • Mexico 37 D3
Catoctin Mtn Park **Park** • MD, United States 121 [282]
Catriló • Argentina 44 D6
Catskill Mtns • NY, United States 118 H1
Cattólica • Italy 91 E12
Catu • Brazil 44 I1
Cauca • Colombia 43 B2
Caucasia • Colombia 43 B2
Caucasus • Asia/Europe 17 G6
Caucete • Argentina 44 C5
Caudry • France 5 G4
Caulnes • France 84 C2
Caulonia • Italy 12 K10
Caungula • Angola 24 B1
Caupolican • Bolivia 44 C1
Cauquenes • Chile 44 B6
Caura • Venezuela 43 E2
Causani • Moldova 14 Q3
Causeway Bay • Hong Kong, China 107 H6
Cauterets • France 85 J2
Cauto • Cuba 124 D8
Cauvery • India 106 D6
Cauvery Delta • India 106 D11
Caux, Pays de • France 5 D5
Cava de' Tirreni • Italy 91 G4
Cavado • Portugal 11 C3
Cavalaire-sur-Mer • France 85 H4
Cavalese **Ski** • Italy 70 [216]
Cavalese • Italy 90 B3
Cavalleria, Cap de • Minorca, Spain 87 F2
Cavalli Is. • New Zealand 35 D2
Cavallo, I. • Corsica, France 85 L4
Cavally • Côte d'Ivoire/Liberia 22 C3
Cavan • Ireland 7 E8
Cavan [Adm] • Ireland 79 D1
Cavarzere • Italy 12 G3
Çavdir • Turkey 93 G1
Cavelossim Beach • Goa, India 105 B2
Caviana • Brazil 43 G3
Cavtat • Croatia 14 F7
Çavus Burun • Turkey 93 G3
Cawnpore • India 105 C7
Caxambu • Brazil 127 C3
Caxias • Brazil 45 (1) C2
Caxias do Sul • Brazil 44 F4
Caxito • Angola 23 A5
Çay • Turkey 15 M5
Cayambe, Volcán • Ecuador 43 B4
Cayenne • French Guiana 43 G3
Cayey • Puerto Rico 125 E4
Cayman Brac • Cayman Is. 124 D6
Cayman Is. • West Indies 37 E4
Cayo Guin • Cuba 124 D8
Cayon • St Kitts & Nevis 125 G1
Cayos del Este Sudeste • Colombia 43 A1
Cayuga Lake • NY, United States 122 B10
Cazombo • Angola 23 C6
Ceananna Mór • Ireland 79 D1
Ceará • Brazil 45 (1) D3
Cebollera, Sierra • Spain 10 C11
Cebreros • Spain 11 G4
Cebu • Philippines 31 G4
Cebu [I.] • Philippines 31 G4
Ceccano • Italy 91 F4
Cece • Hungary 14 F3
Cecina • Italy 12 E5
Cedar Breaks Nat. Mon. **Park** • UT, United States 120 [81]
Cedar City • UT, United States 40 D4
Cedar Falls • IA, United States 41 H3
Cedar Grove • Antigua & Barbuda 125 F1
Cedar Keys Nat. Wildlife Refuge • FL, United States 119 M3
Cedar Lake • MN, Canada 38 K6
Cedar Point **Park** • OH, United States 121 [T]
Cedar Rapids • IA, United States 41 H3
Cederberg • South Africa 100 C1
Cedros • Mexico 36 F7
Ceduna • SA, Australia 34 F6
Cefalù • Sicily, Italy 90 D2
Cegar Perah • Malaysia 108 D2
Cegléd • Hungary 13 I10
Cehegin • Spain 11 J6
Ceiba • Puerto Rico 125 E2
Céide Fields • Ireland 79 F2
Cekik • Bali, Indonesia 110 C1
Celano • Italy 91 F2
Celaya • Mexico 123 E1
Celebes • Indonesia 32 (1) A3
Celebes Sea • Indonesia 32 (1) B2
Celerina **Ski** • Switzerland 70 [116]
Celerina • Switzerland 89 G4
Celje • Slovenia 13 E11
Celldömölk • Hungary 13 G10
Celle • Germany 8 F4
Celle Ligure **Beach** • Italy 68 [141]
Celorico da Beira • Portugal 11 D4
Celtic Sea • Ireland/UK 7 E10
Celuk • Bali, Indonesia 110 C4
Cemaes Bay **Beach** • United Kingdom 75 [221-222]
Cemlyn **Beach** • United Kingdom 75 [220]
Cenajo, Embalse de • Spain 11 J6
Cenderawasih, Teluk • Indonesia 35 (1) A1
Cento • Italy 91 E7
Centola **Beach** • Italy 69 [149]
Central • Hong Kong, China 107 H5
Central African Rep. • Africa 23 C2
Central Australia Aboriginal Land • WA, Australia 112 H3
Central Highlands • Kenya 101 G3
Central I. Nat. Park **Heritage N** • Kenya 61 [88]
Central I. Nat. Park • Kenya 101 G1
Central Lowland • IL/MO, United States 41 H3
Central Makran Range • Pakistan 18 H4
Central Plains • Thailand 109 F2
Central Plateau • Russian Fed. 4 R6
Central Plateau • New Zealand 112 K4
Central Range • Papua New Guinea 35 (1) C2
Central Siberian Plateau • Russian Fed. 25 L3
Central Siberian Uplands • Russian Fed. 26 Q5
Central, Sistema • Spain 11 F4
Centralia • WA, United States 117 E1
Centre • France 84 A1
Centreville • OT, Canada 122 B9
Cephalonia • Greece 92 C2
Cepu • Java, Indonesia 110 D3
Ceram • Indonesia 32 (1) C3
Cerbère **Beach** • France 68 [128]
Cerbère • France 85 K2
Cerbicale, Is. • Corsica, France 85 L4
Ceres • Brazil 44 G2
Ceres • South Africa 100 C5
Cerf I. • Seychelles 106 F3
Cerf, I. au • Seychelles 106 F1
Cergy-Pontoise • France 85 E1
Cerignola • Italy 12 J7
Cerigo • Greece 92 D7
Çerkes • Turkey 15 N3
Çerkezköy • Turkey 15 I2
Cermei • Romania 13 K11
Cermenika • Albania 14 H8
Cerna Skala • Bulgaria/F.Y.R. of Macedonia 15 D1
Cernavoda • Romania 97 D2
Cerni vrah • Bulgaria 15 E1
Cernòbbio • Italy 91 E2
Cerralvo • Mexico 40 E7
Cerritos • Mexico 37 A3
Cerro Azul • Brazil 44 G3
Cerro de las Mesas • Mexico 123 E4
Cerro de Pasco • Peru 43 B6
Cervaro • Italy 12 J7
Cervená Lhota • Czech Rep. 96 C4
Cervéteri • Italy 91 F1
Cèrvia • Italy 91 E8
Cervialto, Monte • Italy 91 G4
Cervo **Beach** • Spain 68 [91]
Cervo **Beach** • Italy 68 [140]
Cervonograd • Ukraine 13 N7
Cesana **Ski** • Italy 70 [192]
Cesena • Italy 12 G4
Cesenático • Italy 91 E8
Cesis • Latvia 16 M8
Ceská Lipa • Czech Rep. 96 C2
Ceské Budejovice • Czech Rep. 96 C4
Ceské Svycarsko • Czech Rep. 96 C1
Ceské Zeme • Czech Rep. 13 D8
Ceskomoravská Vysocina • Czech Rep. 13 E8
Cesky Krumlov **Heritage C** • Czech Rep. 64 [146]
Cesky Krumlov • Czech Rep. 96 C4
Cesky Les • Czech Rep. 9 H7
Cesky Sternberk • Czech Rep. 96 C2
Çesme • Turkey 92 D5
Cessnock • NS, Australia 111 G2
Cestos • Côte d'Ivoire/Liberia 22 C3
Cetarro • Italy 12 J9
Cetinje • F.R. of Yugoslavia 14 F7
Ceuta • Africa 101 D2
Ceva-i-Ra • Fiji 35 (2) C3
Cévennes • France 10 I9
Cévennes, Parc nat. des **Park** • France 72 [70]
Cevizli • Turkey 93 G2
Ceylon • Asia 28 D7
Ch'onan • Rep. of Korea 30 D6
Ch'ongjin • D.P.R. of Korea 30 E4
Ch'ongju • Rep. of Korea 30 D6
Ch'orwon • Rep. of Korea 30 D5
Ch'unch'on • Rep. of Korea 30 D6
Ch'ungju • Rep. of Korea 30 D6
Cha-Am • Thailand 109 H3
Chaâlis, Abbaye de • France 85 E2
Chablais • France 85 F2
Chablis • France 84 B2
Chacabuco • Argentina 127 D1
Chacachacare I. • Trinidad & Tobago 125 K1
Chacahua, Lagunas de • Mexico 123 E4
Chachapoyas • Peru 43 B5
Chachoengsao • Thailand 109 H2
Chaco Austral • Argentina 44 D4
Chaco Boreal • Paraguay 44 D3
Chaco Central • Argentina 44 D3
Chaco Culture Nat. Hist. Park **Heritage C** • NM, United States 62 [7]
Chaco Culture Nat. Hist. Park • NM, United States 118 J2
Chaco Culture Nat. Hist. Park **Park** • NM, United States 120 [125]
Chad • Africa 21 C4
Chad, Lake • Africa 21 B5
Chadan • Russian Fed. 26 P7
Chadileuvu • Argentina 44 C6
Chadron • NE, United States 40 F3
Chafarinas, Is. • Spain 11 I9
Chagai Hills • Pakistan 18 H4
Chagcharan • Afghanistan 18 I3
Chagda • Russian Fed. 27 L5
Chaguanas • Trinidad & Tobago 125 K3
Chaguaramus Bay • Trinidad & Tobago 125 K3
Chah Bahar • Iran 18 H4
Chahar Borjak • Afghanistan 18 H3
Chaillu, Massif du • Gabon 22 G5
Chainat • Thailand 31 C3
Chaitén • Chile 45 B4
Chake Chake • Tanzania 102 H2
Chakhansur • Afghanistan 18 H3
Chala • Peru 127 B3
Chalbi Desert • Kenya 101 G1
Chaleur Bay • NB/QU, Canada 123 D2
Chalky Hill • Barbados 125 H1
Chalky Inlet • New Zealand 112 L3
Challaborough **Beach** • United Kingdom 75 [116]
Challapata • Bolivia 44 C2
Challenger Deep • Fed. States of Micronesia 25 P8
Challengers • St Kitts & Nevis 125 G1
Chalon-sur-Saône • France 10 J7
Chalong • Phuket, Thailand 109 K2
Chalong Bay • Phuket, Thailand 109 K2
Chalong, Wat • Phuket, Thailand 109 K2
Châlons-sur-Marne • France 10 J5
Chalusset, Château de • France 85 G2
Cham • Germany 9 H7
Châm • Mauritania 20 B4
Chaman • Pakistan 28 A2
Chamba • India 28 C2
Chamba • Tanzania 102 H4
Chambal • India 105 C6
Chambers Pillar • NT, Australia 112 H4
Chambéry • France 85 F1
Chambeshi • Zambia 24 E2
Chambi, Jebel • Tunisia 101 E3
Chambly • France 85 E1
Chambly, Fort • QU, Canada 122 B7
Chambord **Heritage C** • France 64 [61]
Chambord [Château] • France 84 D2
Chamizal Nat. Mem. **Park** • TX, United States 120 [135]
Chamois • Italy 91 E1
Chamonix • France 85 F2
Chamonix-Mont Blanc **Ski** • France 70 [26]
Champ du Feu • France 10 M5
Champagne-Ardennes • France 84 A1
Champagnole • France 10 K7
Champagny-en-Vanoise **Ski** • France 70 [34]
Champaign • IL, United States 41 I3
Champaqui, Cerro • Argentina 44 D5
Champasak • Laos 108 A2
Champawat • India 105 C3
Champéry • Switzerland 89 G5
Champéry-Planachaux **Ski** • Switzerland 70 [76]
Champex • Switzerland 89 G6
Champigny-sur-Marne • France 85 E4
Champlain, Lake • NY/VT, United States 118 G3
Champoluc **Ski** • Italy 70 [201]
Champoussin • Switzerland 89 G5
Chamrousse **Ski** • France 70 [52]
Chan Chan • Peru 43 B5
Chan Chan **Heritage C** • Peru 62 [47]
Chandalar • AK, United States 38 B3
Chandeleur Sound • LA, United States 118 K4
Chanderi • India 105 C7
Chandigarh • India 28 C2
Chandigarh [Adm] • India 105 A1
Chandler • QU, Canada 123 D2
Chandor • Goa, India 105 B2
Chandragiri • India 106 D7
Chandraprabha Wildlife Sanctuary • India 105 C8
Chandrapur • India 28 C5
Chang Jiang • China 29 F4
Chang, Ko • Thailand 31 C4
Chang Zhou • China 107 J1
Changajn Nuruu • Mongolia 25 K5
Changan • China 98 B6
Changane • Mozambique 24 E4
Changbai • China 30 E4
Changbai Shan • China 30 D4
Changcheng • China 29 D3
Changchun • China 29 H2
Changde • China 29 E5
Changhua • Taiwan 29 G6
Changi [Apt] • Singapore 108 E2
Changjiang Kou • China 29 G4
Changjin-Up • D.P.R. of Korea 30 D4
Changping • China 107 H2
Changsha • China 29 E5
Changshu • China 107 J2
Changxing • China 107 J3
Changyon • D.P.R. of Korea 30 C5
Channel Country • QL, Australia 111 E7
Channel Is. • Europe 7 J12
Channel Is. • CA, United States 117 F5
Channel Is. Nat. Park • CA, United States 117 F5
Channel Is. Nat. Park **Park** • CA, United States 120 [56]
Channel Port-aux-Basques • NF, Canada 123 D3
Channel Tunnel • France/UK 74 E4
Chantada • Spain 11 D2
Chantada, Faro de • Spain 11 D2
Chanthaburi • Thailand 31 C4
Chantilly • France 85 E2
Chantilly, Forêt de • France 85 E2
Chao Phraya • Thailand 109 H1
Chaouèn • Morocco 101 D2
Chaozhou • China 29 F6
Chapada das Mangabeiras • Brazil 45 (1) B3
Chapada Diamantina • Brazil 44 H1
Chapala, Laguna de • Mexico 123 E1
Chapayevo • Kazakhstan 17 I5
Chapecó • Brazil 44 F4
Chapleau • OT, Canada 39 O7
Chaplino, mys • Russian Fed. 27 W4
Chapora • Goa, India 105 B1
Chapora Fort • Goa, India 105 B1
Chappra • India 105 C8
Char • Mauritania 20 C4
Chara • Russian Fed. 27 I5
Chard • United Kingdom 74 F3
Chardzhou • Turkmenistan 18 H2
Charentais • France 84 B3
Charente [Adm] • France 85 G1
Charente [Riv] • France 85 G1
Charente-Maritime • France 85 G1
Chari • Chad 21 C5
Charity • Guyana 43 F2
Charleroi • Belgium 80 A14
Charles, Cape • NF, Canada 39 T6
Charles, Cape • VA, United States 118 H3
Charles, Fort • St Kitts & Nevis 125 G4
Charles I. • NU, Canada 39 Q4
Charles, Peak • WA, Australia 34 D6

Charles Sound • New Zealand 112 L1
Charleston • IL, United States 41 I4
Charleston • WV, United States 41 J4
Charleston • SC, United States 41 K5
Charlestown • Ireland 79 F2
Charlestown • St Kitts & Nevis 125 G4
Charleville • QL, Australia 111 F5
Charleville-Mézières • France 10 J4
Charlotte • NC, United States 41 J4
Charlotte Amalie • US Virgin Is. 58 B7
Charlotte, Fort • Bahamas 124 B3
Charlotte, Fort • St Lucia 125 J1
Charlotte Harbor • FL, United States 119 M5
Charlottenburg, Schloß • Germany 81 F1
Charlottesville • VA, United States 41 K4
Charlottesville **Heritage C** • VA, United States 62 [10]
Charlottetown • PE, Canada 123 D7
Charlotteville • Trinidad & Tobago 125 K2
Charlton • VI, Australia 111 G3
Charnwood Forest • United Kingdom 74 D2
Charters Towers • QL, Australia 111 F1
Chartres **Heritage C** • France 64 [60]
Chartres • France 85 E3
Chartwell • United Kingdom 74 E3
Chascomús • Argentina 127 D4
Chasong • D.P.R. of Korea 30 D4
Chassengue • Angola 23 B6
Chassin • St Lucia 125 J2
Château-Arnoux • France 10 L9
Château-d'Oex **Ski** • Switzerland 70 [85]
Château-d'Oex • Switzerland 89 G6
Château-du-Loir • France 10 F6
Château-Gontier • France 10 E6
Château-Salins • France 5 J6
Château-Thierry • France 85 E2
Châteaubriant • France 84 D1
Châteaudun • France 84 D2
Châteaulin • France 10 A5
Châteauneuf-du-Pape • France 84 B4
Châteauroux • France 84 D4
Châtel **Ski** • France 70 [9]
Châtel • France 85 F2
Châtelet • Belgium 5 H4
Châtellerault • France 84 D4
Chatham • United Kingdom 74 E2
Chatham • NB, Canada 123 D2
Chatham I. • New Zealand 35 (3) B1
Chatham Is. • New Zealand 33 J10
Chatham Is. • New Zealand 35 (3)
Châtillon-sur-Indre • France 84 D4
Chatkal-yau • Kyrgyzstan 26 L9
Chatra • India 105 C8
Châtre, la • France 10 H7
Chattahoochee River Nat. Recreation Area **Park** • GA, United States 121 [210]
Chattanooga • TN, United States 41 I4
Châttilon-sur-Seine • France 10 J6
Chau Doc • Vietnam 108 B1
Chaudi • Goa, India 105 B2
Chaudiere • QU, Canada 122 B4
Chauka • India 105 C3
Chaumont • France 10 K5
Chaumont [Château] • France 84 D2
Chaunskaya Guba • Russian Fed. 27 S3
Chauny • France 5 G5
Chauvigny • France 84 D4
Chavantina • Brazil 44 F1
Chaves • Portugal 11 D3
Chaves • Brazil 43 G4
Chávez, Jorge [Apt] • Peru 127 B1
Chavin **Heritage C** • Peru 62 [48]
Chavuma • Zambia 24 C2
Chaweng Beach • Ko Samui, Thailand 109 J1
Chayamangkalaram, Wat • Penang, Malaysia 108 C2
Chbika • Tunisia 101 E3
Cheb • Czech Rep. 96 C1
Cheboksary • Russian Fed. 17 H3
Chech, Erg • Algeria 20 E4
Chechnya • Russian Fed. 17 H6
Chechuysk • Russian Fed. 27 G5
Cheddar • United Kingdom 74 F3
Cheddar Gorge • United Kingdom 74 F3
Cheduba • Myanmar 31 A3
Chedworth Roman Villa • United Kingdom 74 D4
Cheerala • India 106 D3
Chegga • Mauritania 20 D3
Chegutu • Zimbabwe 102 J2
Cheju • Rep. of Korea 30 D8
Cheju [I.] • Rep. of Korea 30 D8
Cheju-Haehyop • Rep. of Korea 30 D8
Chek Lap Kok • Hong Kong, China 107 H5
Cheliff • Algeria 20 F1
Cheliff, Plaine du • Algeria 11 L8
Cheliff [Riv] • Algeria 20 F1
Chelkar • Kazakhstan 26 I8
Chelm • Poland 13 M6
Chelmno • Poland 13 H4
Chelmsford • United Kingdom 74 E2
Chelmza • Poland 13 H4
Chelsea • United Kingdom 74 E1
Cheltenham • United Kingdom 74 D4
Chelva • Spain 11 J5
Chelyabinsk • Russian Fed. 26 J6
Chelyuskin, mys • Russian Fed. 26 S2
Chembe • Zambia 23 D6
Chemdal'sk • Russian Fed. 26 R6
Chémery [Château] • France 84 D2
Chemillé • France 84 D3
Chemnitz • Germany 9 H6
Chemult • OR, United States 117 E3
Chenab • Pakistan 28 B2
Chenachane • Algeria 20 E3
Chenachane [Riv] • Algeria 20 E3
Chengde • China 29 F2
Chengde **Heritage C** • China 63 [145]
Chengdu • China 29 C4
Chengshan Jiao • China 29 G3
Chenini • Tunisia 101 E6
Chenonceaux [Château] • France 84 D2
Chentijn Nuruu • Mongolia/Russian Fed. 27 H7
Chenxian • China 29 E5
Cheongmon Bay • Ko Samui, Thailand 109 J1
Chepca • Russian Fed. 17 I3
Chepes • Argentina 44 C5
Chepstow • United Kingdom 74 D3
Cher • France 10 G6
Cherangany Hills • Kenya 23 F3
Cherating • Malaysia 108 A4
Cherbaniani Reef • India 106 D5
Cherbourg • France 10 D4
Cherchell • Algeria 11 N8
Cheremkhovo • Russian Fed. 27 F6
Cherepovets • Russian Fed. 97 E2
Cheriton Terminal • United Kingdom 78 C4
Cheriyam I. • India 106 D9
Cherkassy • Ukraine 17 E5
Cherkessk • Russian Fed. 17 G6
Cherlak • Russian Fed. 26 L7
Chernigov • Ukraine 17 E4
Chernobyl • Ukraine 17 E4
Chernomorets • Bulgaria 97 D3
Chernovtsy • Ukraine 14 M1
Chernyakhovsk • Russian Fed. 13 K3
Chernysevskiy • Russian Fed. 27 H4
Cherrapunji • India 28 F3
Cherry Tree Hill • Barbados 125 H1
Cherskiy • Russian Fed. 27 R3
Cherskogo, Khrebet • Russian Fed. 27 N3
Chesapeake • VA, United States 41 K4
Chesapeake Bay • VA, United States 118 H3
Chesapeake & Ohio Canal Nat. Hist. Park **Park** • MD, United States 121 [273]
Cheshire • United Kingdom 75 A4
Cheshkaya Guba • Russian Fed. 17 H1
Chesil Beach • United Kingdom 74 F6
Chesne, le • France 5 H5
Chessington World of Adventures **Park** • United Kingdom 73 [36]
Chessington World of Adventures • United Kingdom 74 E1
Chester • United Kingdom 7 J8
Chesterfield • United Kingdom 7 K8
Chesterfield Inlet • NU, Canada 39 M4
Chestnut Mtn **Ski** • IL, United States 116 [117]
Chesuncook Lake • ME, United States 118 G2
Chettlatt I. • India 106 D5
Chetumal • Mexico 37 D4
Cheung Chau • Hong Kong, China 107 H5
Cheverny • France 84 B1
Cheverny [Château] • France 84 D2
Cheviot Hills • United Kingdom 7 J6
Cheviot, The • United Kingdom 6 J6
Chew Bahir • Ethiopia/Kenya 23 F3
Chewore safari area **Heritage N** • Zimbabwe 61 [96]
Cheyenne • WY, United States 40 F3
Cheyenne [Riv] • United States 38 K8
Cheyne Bay • WA, Australia 34 C6
Chi • Thailand 109 F2
Chia • Sardinia, Italy 90 C4
Chiang Dao • Thailand 109 G1
Chiang Kham • Thailand 109 G2
Chiang Khan • Thailand 109 G4
Chiang Khong • Thailand 109 G2
Chiang Mai • Thailand 109 G1
Chiang Rai • Thailand 109 G2
Chiang Saen • Thailand 109 G2
Chianje • Angola 24 A3
Chianti • Italy 91 E11
Chiapas • Mexico 37 C4
Chiávari • Italy 91 E6
Chiayi • Taiwan 29 G6
Chiba • Japan 30 K7
Chibougamou • QU, Canada 39 Q6
Chicago • IL, United States 41 I3
Chicago Portage Nat. Hist. Site **Park** • IL, United States 121 [180]
Chichagof I. • AK, United States 38 D5
Chichaoua • Morocco 20 D2
Chichén Itzá • Mexico 37 D3
Chichén Itzá **Heritage C** • Mexico 62 [27]
Chichester • United Kingdom 74 E3
Chickamauga & Chattanooga Nat. Military Park **Park** • GA, United States 121 [208]
Chickasaw Nat. Recreation Area **Park** • OK, United States 121 [145]
Chickasawhay • MS, United States 118 K2
Chiclana de la Frontera **Beach** • Spain 68 [113]
Chiclana de la Frontera • Spain 86 B5
Chiclayo • Peru 43 B5
Chico • CA, United States 117 F1
Chicoutimi • QU, Canada 123 D1
Chicualacuala • Mozambique 102 J4
Chidambaram • India 106 D11
Chidley, Cape • NU, Canada 39 S4
Chiemsee • Germany 82 J4
Chiengi • Zambia 23 D5
Chiesa • Italy 91 E2
Chieti • Italy 12 I6
Chiéuti **Beach** • Italy 69 [158]
Chifeng • China 29 F2
Chigu Co • China 28 F3
Chigubo • Mozambique 24 E4
Chihuahua • Mexico 40 E6
Chihuahua [Adm] • Mexico 40 E6
Chikurachki, Vulkan • Russian Fed. 27 Q6
Chilca • Peru 127 B1
Chilcott I. • CL, Australia 34 J3
Childers • QL, Australia 111 F6
Chile • S. America 42 C7
Chile-Chico • Chile 45 B5
Chilecito • Argentina 44 C4
Chillán • Chile 44 B6
Chiloé, I. de • Chile 45 B4
Chilpancingo • Mexico 123 E4
Chiltern Hills • United Kingdom 74 E1
Chilumba • Malawi 24 E2
Chilung • Taiwan 29 G5
Chilwa, Lake • Malawi 24 F3
Chimanimani • Zimbabwe 102 J4
Chimanimani Nat. Park • Zimbabwe 102 J4
Chimbay • Uzbekistan 26 I9
Chimborazo, Volcán • Ecuador 43 B4
Chimbote • Peru 43 B5
Chimkent • Kazakhstan 26 K9
Chimney Rock Nat. Hist. Site **Park** • NE, United States 120 [166]
Chin • Rep. of Korea 30 D7
Chin • Myanmar 31 A2
China • Asia 25 K6
China Folk Culture Villages • Shenzhen, China 107 H3
Chinandega • Nicaragua 37 D5
Chincha Alta • Peru 127 B1
Chinchilla • QL, Australia 111 F6
Chindwin • Myanmar 31 A2
Chinese & Japanese Garden • Singapore 108 E1
Chingola • Zambia 24 D2
Chinguetti • Mauritania 20 C4
Chinguetti **Heritage C** • Mauritania 63 [92]
Chinhae • Rep. of Korea 30 E7
Chinhoyi • Zimbabwe 102 J2
Chinju • Rep. of Korea 30 D7
Chinko • Africa 23 C2
Chinle • AZ, United States 118 J2
Chinon • France 84 B1
Chinon [Château] • France 84 D4
Chióggia • Italy 91 E8
Chios **Heritage C** • Greece 64 [184]
Chios • Greece 92 D5
Chipata • Zambia 24 E2
Chiperone • Mozambique 24 F3
Chipinda Pools • Zimbabwe 102 J4
Chipinge • Zimbabwe 102 J4
Chipiona **Beach** • Spain 68 [113]
Chipiona • Spain 86 B5
Chipman • NB, Canada 123 D7
Chippenham • United Kingdom 74 F3
Chiquinquirá • Colombia 43 C2
Chiquitos, Llanos de • Bolivia 44 D2
Chiquitos missions **Heritage C** • Bolivia 62 [55]
Chirchik • Uzbekistan 26 K9
Chiredzi • Zimbabwe 102 J4
Chirfa • Niger 20 H4
Chiri • Rep. of Korea 30 D7
Chiricahua Nat. Mon. • AZ, United States 118 J4
Chiricahua Nat. Mon. **Park** • AZ, United States 120 [119]
Chirinda • Russian Fed. 26 R4
Chirip, Vulkan • Russian Fed. 27 O7
Chirpan • Bulgaria 97 D3
Chirripó • Costa Rica 37 E6
Chirundu • Zimbabwe 102 J1
Chisamba • Zambia 24 D2
Chisasibi • QU, Canada 39 P6
Chisinau • Moldova 14 P2
Chistopol • Russian Fed. 17 I3
Chita • Russian Fed. 27 H6
Chitina • AK, United States 38 C4
Chitradurga • India 106 D6
Chitrakut • India 105 C7
Chitral • Pakistan 28 B1
Chitré • Panama 37 E6
Chittagong • Bangladesh 28 F4
Chittaurgarh • India 105 C6
Chittoor • India 106 D7
Chitungwiza • Zimbabwe 102 J2
Chiumbe • Angola 24 C2
Chiume • Angola 24 C3
Chiunzi, Válico de • Italy 91 G4
Chiusa • Italy 90 B1
Chiusi • Italy 91 E11
Chivasso • Italy 91 E5
Chivhu • Zimbabwe 102 J4
Chivilcoy • Argentina 127 D1
Chiwan • Shenzhen, China 107 H5
Chizarira Nat. Park • Zimbabwe 102 J1
Chizha • Russian Fed. 17 G1
Chobe • Botswana/Namibia 24 C3
Chobe Nat. Park **Park** • Botswana 103 [110]
Choc Bay • St Lucia 125 J1
Chodov • Czech Rep. 13 B7
Chodziez • Poland 13 F5
Choele-Choel • Argentina 45 C3
Choiseul • Solomon Is. 35 (1) F2
Choiseul • St Lucia 125 J3
Chojnice • Poland 13 G4
Chojnów • Poland 13 E6
Chokai • Japan 30 K5
Choke • Ethiopia 23 F1
Cholet • France 84 D3
Cholula • Mexico 123 E4
Chom Thong • Thailand 109 G3
Choma • Zambia 24 D3
Chomutov • Czech Rep. 96 C1
Chon Buri • Thailand 109 H4
Chone • Ecuador 43 A4
Chongkrum, Laem • Ko Samui, Thailand 109 J2
Chongming • China 107 J2
Chongming Dao • China 107 J2
Chongmyo Shrine **Heritage C** • Rep. of Korea 63 [160]
Chongqing • China 29 D5
Chongup • Rep. of Korea 30 D7
Chonju • Rep. of Korea 30 D7
Chonos, Archipiélago de los • Chile 45 A5
Chorao I. • Goa, India 105 B1
Chorzów • Poland 13 H7
Choshi • Japan 30 K7
Choszczno • Poland 13 E4
Chota Nagpur • India 105 A2
Chott Ech Chergui • Algeria 20 F2
Choum • Mauritania 20 C4
Choybalsan • Mongolia 27 H7
Choyr • Mongolia 29 D1
Chrisoskalitisas, Moní • Crete, Greece 93 E5
Christchurch • New Zealand 35 D6
Christian, Cape • NU, Canada 39 R2
Christian Sound • AK, United States 38 D5
Christian Valley • Antigua & Barbuda 125 F3
Christiana • Norway 71 A3
Christiana • Jamaica 124 C1
Christiansfeld • Denmark 95 F13
Christiansø • Denmark 95 F16
Christiansted • US Virgin Is. 58 B7
Christie Bay • NT, Canada 38 I4
Christmas • Kiribati 33 L5
Christmas Creek • WA, Australia 34 E3
Christmas I. • Indian Ocean 32 D5
Chritstianshåb • Greenland 39 U3
Chrysorroyiatissa Monastery • Cyprus 93 J3
Chrzanów • Poland 13 I7
Chu • Kazakhstan 26 L9
Chu [Riv] • Kazakhstan 26 K9
Chu Xian • China 107 J1
Chu Yang Sin • Vietnam 108 B2
Chu Zhou • China 107 J1
Chuansha • China 107 J2
Chubokulakh, gora • Russian Fed. 27 P3
Chudjand • Tajikistan 18 I1
Chudovo • Russian Fed. 97 E1
Chudskoye Ozero • Estonia/Russia 16 N7
Chugoku-Sanchi • Japan 30 G7
Chukai • Malaysia 32 C2
Chukchi • Russian Fed. 97 A7
Chukchi Sea • Arctic Ocean 40 (2) D2
Chukotskiy Poluostrov • Russian Fed. 27 W3
Chukotskoye More • Russian Fed. 46 GG2
Chulman • Russian Fed. 27 J5
Chulucanas • Peru 43 A5
Chulym • Russian Fed. 26 N7
Chumikan • Russian Fed. 27 M6
Chumphon • Thailand 31 B4
Chun'an • China 107 J3
Chunar • India 105 C8
Chunski • Russian Fed. 26 Q6
Chuor Phnum Krâvanh • Cambodia/Thailand 31 C4
Chuquibamba • Peru 127 B4
Chuquicamata • Chile 44 C3
Chur **Ski** • Switzerland 70 [108]
Chur • Switzerland 89 G4
Churapcha • Russian Fed. 27 L4
Church Bay **Beach** • United Kingdom 75 [219]
Churchill • SA, Canada 38 K5
Churchill • MN, Canada 38 M5
Churchill • NF, Canada 39 S6
Churchill Falls • NF, Canada 122 A8
Churchill Falls [Falls] • NF, Canada 39 S6
Churchill Lake • SA, Canada 38 J5
Churchill Peak • BC, Canada 38 F5
Churu • India 105 C2
Churuguara • Venezuela 43 D1
Churún Merú • Venezuela 43 E2
Churwalden **Ski** • Switzerland 70 [109]
Chusovoy • Russian Fed. 26 I6
Chust • Ukraine 13 M9
Chute-Montmorency, Parc de la • QU, Canada 123 D1
Chuuk • Fed. States of Micronesia 33 G5
Chuvashia • Russian Fed. 17 H3
Chuxiong • China 31 C2
Chynovska jeskyne • Czech Rep. 96 C4
Chyulu Nat. Park • Kenya 101 G4
Ciamis • Java, Indonesia 110 D6
Ciampino [Apt] • Italy 91 F3
Cianjar • Java, Indonesia 110 D1
Cicarija • Croatia 14 B4
Ciceron • St Lucia 125 J1
Cide • Turkey 15 N2
Ciechanów • Poland 13 J5
Ciechanowiec • Poland 13 L5
Ciego de Avila • Cuba 124 D3
Ciénaga • Colombia 43 C1
Cienfuegos • Cuba 124 D2
Cieza • Spain 87 C1
Çifteler • Turkey 15 M4
Cihanbeyli Platosu • Turkey 15 N5
Cijara, Embalse de • Spain 11 G5
Cijulang • Java, Indonesia 110 D6
Cilacap • Java, Indonesia 110 D6
Ciledug • Java, Indonesia 110 D2
Cilento • Italy 91 G4
Cilo Dag • Turkey 18 D2
Cimahi • Java, Indonesia 110 D2
Cimini, Monti • Italy 91 F1
Cimone • Italy 12 E4
Cîmpina • Romania 14 M4
Cîmpulung • Romania 14 M4
Cina, Tanjung • Indonesia 32 C4
Çinarcik • Turkey 15 K3
Cinca • Spain 10 F11
Cincar • Bosnia-Herz. 14 E6
Cincinnati • OH, United States 41 J4
Cindrelu, Virful • Romania 14 K4
Çine • Turkey 15 J6
Ciney • Belgium 5 I4
Cinque Terre **Heritage C** • Italy 64 [119]
Cinque Terre • Italy 91 E10
Cinto, Monte • Corsica, France 85 L1
Cintra, Golfo de • Western Sahara 20 B4
Ciotat, la **Beach** • France 68 [132]
Ciotat, la • France 85 H3
Cipó • Brazil 44 I1
Circeo, Parco Naz. del **Park** • Italy 72 [87]
Circeo, Parco Naz. del • Italy 91 F4
Circle • AK, United States 38 C3
Circus Circus **Park** • NV, United States 120 [K]
Cirebon • Java, Indonesia 110 D2
Cirema, Gunung • Java, Indonesia 110 D2
Cirencester • United Kingdom 74 D4
Cirò Marina • Italy 12 L9
Cirque Mtn • NF, Canada 39 S5
Cisco • TX, United States 119 N1
Cisnadie • Romania 14 L4
Citlaltépetl • Mexico 37 B4
Città di Castello • Italy 91 E12
Cittadella • Italy 91 E7
City of Rocks Nat. Reserve • ID, United States 117 E4
City of Rocks Nat. Reserve **Park** • ID, United States 120 [63]
Ciucasu, Virful • Romania 14 M4
Ciudad Acuña • Mexico 37 A2
Ciudad Altamirano • Mexico 123 E3
Ciudad Bolívar • Venezuela 43 E2
Ciudad Camargo • Mexico 40 F6
Ciudad del Carmen • Mexico 37 C4
Ciudad Delicias • Mexico 40 E6
Ciudad Guayana • Venezuela 43 E2
Ciudad Juárez • Mexico 40 E5
Ciudad Lerdo • Mexico 40 F6
Ciudad Madero • Mexico 123 E2
Ciudad Mante • Mexico 123 E2
Ciudad Obregón • Mexico 40 E6
Ciudad Ojeda • Venezuela 43 C1
Ciudad Piar • Venezuela 37 I6
Ciudad Real • Spain 11 H6
Ciudad Rodrigo • Spain 11 E4
Ciudad Valles • Mexico 37 B3
Ciudad Valles • Mexico 123 E2
Ciudad Victoria • Mexico 123 E2
Ciutadella • Minorca, Spain 87 F1
Cividale del Friuli • Italy 13 C11
Civita Castellana • Italy 91 F1
Civitanova Marche • Italy 91 E12
Civitavécchia • Italy 91 F1
Çivril • Turkey 15 K5
Cixi • China 107 J4
Cizre • Turkey 18 D2
Clackmannanshire • United Kingdom 74 B2
Clacton-on-Sea • United Kingdom 74 E2
Clacton-on-Sea **Beach** • United Kingdom 75 [51]
Clamecy • France 10 I6
Clanwilliam • South Africa 100 C1
Claonaig • United Kingdom 78 A2
Clara Barton Nat. Hist. Site **Park** • MD, United States 121 [274]
Clara Lara Fun Park **Park** • Ireland 73 [20]
Clarach **Beach** • United Kingdom 75 [183]
Claraville • NF, Canada 123 D4
Clare • Ireland 79 F6
Clare Abbey • Ireland 79 F6
Clare Glens • Ireland 79 F6
Clare I. • Ireland 79 F1
Clare Island **Beach** • Ireland 68 [63]
Claregalway Abbey • Ireland 79 F4
Claremont • NH, United States 118 G3
Claremont • Jamaica 124 C2
Claremorris • Ireland 79 F2
Clarence, I. • Chile 127 A4
Clarence Town • Bahamas 124 B4
Clark Fork • ID, United States 38 H7
Clark, George Rogers, Nat. Hist. Park **Park** • IN, United States 121 [182]
Clarksville • TN, United States 41 I4
Clatsop, Fort, Nat. Mem. • OR, United States 117 E1
Clatsop, Fort, Nat. Mem. **Park** • OR, United States 120 [33]
Clausholm • Denmark 95 F10
Clausthal-Zellerfeld **Spa** • Germany 83 [79]
Clavière **Ski** • Italy 70 [193]
Clavière • Italy 91 E5
Clay Belt • OT/QU, Canada 39 O6
Clayton • NM, United States 40 F4
Clear, Cape • Ireland 79 F7
Clear I. • Ireland 79 F7
Clear Water Bay • Hong Kong, China 107 H6
Clearwater • AL/SA, Canada 38 I5
Clearwater • FL, United States 119 M5
Clearwater Mtns • ID, United States 38 H7
Cleator Moor • United Kingdom 74 C1
Cleburne • TX, United States 119 N1
Cleethorpes • United Kingdom 7 L8
Clermont • France 85 E2
Clermont • QL, Australia 111 F3
Clermont • FL, United States 121 C1
Clermont-Ferrand • France 10 I8
Clervaux • Luxembourg 80 A20
Clevedon • United Kingdom 74 F3
Cleveland • OH, United States 41 J3
Cleveland • TX, United States 119 N4
Clew Bay • Ireland 79 F1
Clifden • Ireland 79 F3
Clifden • New Zealand 112 L3
Clifton • AZ, United States 118 J4
Clinton • BC, Canada 38 G6
Clinton-Colden Lake • NT, Canada 38 J4
Clodomira • Argentina 44 D4
Cloghane • Ireland 79 F5
Clogher Head • Ireland 79 E2
Clogherhead **Beach** • Ireland 68 [53]
Clonakilty **Beach** • Ireland 68 [59]
Clonakilty • Ireland 79 F8
Clonakilty Bay • Ireland 79 F8
Cloncurry • QL, Australia 34 H4
Clonea **Beach** • Ireland 68 [58]
Clonmel • Ireland 7 E9
Clonmellon • Ireland 79 E1
Clorinda • Argentina 44 E4
Cloud Peak • WY, United States 40 E3
Clovelly • United Kingdom 74 F2
Clovis • NM, United States 40 F5
Cluane Lake • YT, Canada 38 D4
Cluj-Napoca • Romania 14 K3
Clun Forest • United Kingdom 74 D1
Clusaz, la **Ski** • France 70 [21]
Clusaz, la • France 85 F2
Clutha • New Zealand 112 L4
Clutha District • New Zealand 112 L4
Clyde • NU, Canada 46 V2
Clyde • United Kingdom 74 B3
Clyde, Firth of • United Kingdom 6 G6
Clydebank • United Kingdom 74 B3
Coahuila • Mexico 40 F6
Coal I. • New Zealand 112 L3
Coalville • United Kingdom 7 K9
Coamo • Puerto Rico 125 E4
Coari • Brazil 43 E4
Coast Mtns • BC, Canada 38 F6
Coast Ranges • CA/OR, United States 40 B3
Coastal Plain • United States 119 N
Coats I. • NU, Canada 39 O4
Coatzacoalcos • Mexico 37 C4
Cobán • Guatemala 37 C4
Çobanisa • Turkey 93 G3
Cobar • NS, Australia 34 I6
Cobblers Reef • Barbados 125 H4
Cóbh • Ireland 79 F8
Cobija • Bolivia 43 D6
Cobourg • OT, Canada 39 P8
Cobourg Peninsula • NT, Australia 34 F2
Cóbùe • Mozambique 23 E6
Coburg • Germany 9 F6
Cochabamba • Bolivia 44 C2
Cochem • Germany 82 H1
Coches, les **Ski** • France 70 [33]
Cochin • India 106 D10
Cochin China • Vietnam 108 B3
Cochino, Bahía de • Cuba 124 D2
Cochrane • OT, Canada 39 O7
Cockburn Town • Bahamas 124 B4
Cockermouth • United Kingdom 74 C1
Cockpit Country, The • Jamaica 124 C1
Coco • Pacific Ocean 42 A4
Coco, Cayo • Cuba 124 D3
Coco Channel • India 28 F6
Coco Is. • India 28 F6
Coco o Segovia • Honduras/Nicaragua 37 E5
Coco, Parque Nac. Isla del **Heritage N** • Costa Rica 60 [23]
Cocoa Beach • FL, United States 119 M6
Cocoa I. • Maldives 106 E4
Cocos Bay • Trinidad & Tobago 125 K4
Cod Bay, Cape • MA, United States 118 H2
Cod, Cape • MA, United States 118 H2
Cod, Cape, Nat. Seashore **Park** • MA, United States 121 [342]
Coda Cavallo, Capo • Sardinia, Italy 12 D8
Codajás • Brazil 43 E4
Codigoro • Italy 12 G4
Codrington College • Barbados 125 H4
Coesfeld • Germany 8 C5
Coëtivy • Seychelles 106 F4
Coeur d'Alene • ID, United States 117 E2
Coevorden • Netherlands 80 A8
Coffs Harbour • NS, Australia 34 J6
Cofrentes • Spain 11 K5
Cogalnic • Moldova 14 P3
Coglians, Monte • Austria/Italy 91 E4
Cognac • France 85 G1
Cogolin **Beach** • France 68 [133]
Cogolin • France 85 H4
Coiba • Panama 37 E6
Coihaique • Chile 45 B5
Coimar • Cuba 124 D2
Coimbatore • India 106 D10
Coimbra • Portugal 11 C4
Coimbra [Adm] • Portugal 88 A2
Coín • Spain 11 G8
Cointrin [Apt] • Switzerland/France 89 G5
Colac • VI, Australia 111 G3
Colac • New Zealand 112 L4
Çolakli **Beach** • Turkey 69 [223]
Colares • Portugal 88 D1
Colatina • Brazil 127 C2
Colbeck Castle • Jamaica 124 C4
Colca • Peru 127 B4
Colca, Cañon del • Peru 127 B4
Colchester • United Kingdom 74 E2
Coleraine • United Kingdom 7 F6
Coles, Punta • Peru 127 B4
Colfosco **Ski** • Italy 70 [233]
Colfosco • Italy 90 B2
Colima • Mexico 123 E3
Colima [Adm] • Mexico 37 (1) B2
Colintraive • United Kingdom 78 A2
Coll • United Kingdom 6 F5
College Station • TX, United States 119 N3
Collier Bay • WA, Australia 34 D3
Collingwood • New Zealand 35 D5
Collingwood • OT, Canada 122 B5
Collins • MS, United States 118 K2
Collinstown **Beach** • Ireland 68 [57]
Collinsville • QL, Australia 111 F1
Collioure **Beach** • France 68 [128]
Collioure • France 85 K2
Collonges-la-Rouge • France 85 G2
Collooney • Ireland 79 F2
Colmar • France 10 M5
Colmenar Viejo • Spain 11 H4
Colôane • Macau 107 H3
Colôane Village • Macau 107 H3
Cologne **Heritage C** • Germany 64 [38]
Cologne • Germany 81 E3
Coloma • CA, United States 117 F3
Colomb Beach • Goa, India 105 B2
Colombia • S. America 43 C3
Colombier • Switzerland 89 G1
Colombo • Sri Lanka 106 D15
Colombo, Cristofo [Apt] • Italy 91 E6
Colón • Panama 37 F6
Colón • Cuba 124 D2
Colón • Argentina 127 D1
Colón, Archipiélago de • Pacific Ocean 43 (1) A1
Colona • SA, Australia 34 F6
Colònia de Sant Jordi • Majorca, Spain 87 H4
Colonia del Sacramento **Heritage C** • Uruguay 62 [65]
Colonia del Sacramento • Uruguay 127 D2
Colonia Las Heras • Argentina 45 C5
Colonia Suiza • Uruguay 127 D2
Colonial Nat. Hist. Park • VA, United States 118 H3
Colonial Nat. Hist. Park **Park** • VA, United States 121 [257]
Colonna, Capo • Italy 12 L9
Colonsay • United Kingdom 6 F5
Colorado • Argentina 45 D3
Colorado [Adm] • United States 40 E4
Colorado Desert • CA, United States 117 F6
Colorado Nat. Mon. **Park** • CO, United States 120 [90]
Colorado Plateau • United States 118 J1
Colorado [Riv] • Mexico/United States 40 D5
Colorado [Riv] • TX, United States 40 G5
Colorado Springs • CO, United States 40 F4
Columbia • MO, United States 41 H4
Columbia • TN, United States 41 I4
Columbia • SC, United States 41 J5
Columbia • LA, United States 118 K1
Columbia Basin • WA, United States 117 E2
Columbia Gorge • OR/WA, United States 117 E1
Columbia Icefield • AL, Canada 122 C4
Columbia, Mt • AL/BC, Canada 122 C4
Columbia Mtns • BC, Canada 38 G6
Columbia Plateau • United States 117 E4
Columbia [Riv] • BC, Canada 38 H6
Columbine, Cape • South Africa 100 C1
Columbus • NE, United States 41 G3
Columbus • MS, United States 41 I5
Columbus • OH, United States 41 J4
Columbus • GA, United States 41 J5
Columbus • TX, United States 119 N3
Columbus Monument • Bahamas 124 B4
Columbus Park • Jamaica 124 C1
Colva • Goa, India 105 B2
Colva Beach • Goa, India 105 B2
Colville Channel • New Zealand 35 E3
Colville Lake • NT, Canada 38 F3
Colwell Bay **Beach** • United Kingdom 75 [86]
Colwyn Bay • United Kingdom 7 I8
Comácchio • Italy 12 G4
Comácchio, Lido di • Italy 91 E8
Coman, Mt • Antarctica 46 (1) II2
Comaruga • Spain 87 D3
Combarelles, Groote des • France 85 G2
Combermere Bay • Myanmar 31 A3
Combloux **Ski** • France 70 [24]
Comerío • Puerto Rico 125 E4
Comillas **Beach** • Spain 68 [89]
Comino • Malta 93 H1
Cominotto • Malta 93 H1
Cómiso • Sicily, Italy 90 D4
Commercy • France 5 I6
Comminges • France 85 K1
Como • Italy 91 E2
Como, Lago di • Italy 91 E2
Comodoro Rivadavia • Argentina 45 C5
Comoé, Parc nat. de la **Heritage N** • Côte d'Ivoire 61 [74]
Comoé, Parc nat. de la **Park** • Côte d'Ivoire 103 [21]
Comorin, Cape • India 106 D14
Comoros, Archipel des • Comoros 24 G2
Compiègne • France 85 E2
Compiègne, Forêt de • France 85 E2
Comrat • Moldova 14 P3
Comté Tolosan • France 84 B3
Comtés Rhodaniens • France 84 B4
Con Dao • Vietnam 108 B3
Conakry • Guinea 22 B3
Concarneau • France 84 C3
Conceicão • Portugal 88 E8
Conceiçao do Araguaia • Brazil 43 H5
Concepción • Chile 44 B6
Concepción • Argentina 44 C4
Concepción • Bolivia 44 D2
Concepción • Paraguay 44 E3
Concepción • Peru 127 B1
Concepción del Uruguay • Argentina 44 E5
Conception • Seychelles 106 F1
Conception I. • Bahamas 124 B4
Conception, Point • CA, United States 117 F5
Concord • NH, United States 118 G3
Concordia • Argentina 44 E5
Conde • Brazil 44 I1
Condobolin • NS, Australia 111 G1
Condor, Cordillera del • Ecuador/Peru 43 B4
Condrieu • France 84 B4
Condroz • Belgium 5 I4
Conegliano • Italy 12 G3
Conero, Costa • Italy 91 E12
Coney Beach **Park** • United Kingdom 73 [32]
Confolens • France 85 G2
Cong • Ireland 79 F4
Congaree Swamp Nat. Mon. **Park** • SC, United States 121 [239]
Congo • Africa 22 H4
Congo Basin • Africa 100 A3
Congo, Democratic Republic of • Africa 23 C4
Congo [Riv] • Congo/Dem. Rep. of Congo 23 D4

Congonhas

Congonhas **Heritage C** • Brazil ..... 62 [63]
Congonhas • Brazil 127 C1
Conil de la Frontera **Beach** • Spain ..... 68 [113]
Conil de la Frontera • Spain 86 B5
Conillera, I. • Spain 87 H4
Coniston • United Kingdom 74 C4
Coniston Water • United Kingdom 74 C4
Conn, Lough • Ireland 79 F2
Connacht • Ireland 7 D8
Connaught • Ireland 7 D8
Connecticut [Adm] • United States 118 H2
Connecticut [Riv] • United States 118 G3
Connemara • Ireland 79 F3
Connemara Nat. Park **Park** • Ireland ..... 72 [39]
Connemara Nat. Park • Ireland 79 F3
Conny-Land **Park** • Switzerland ..... 73 [81]
Conroe • TX, United States 119 N4
Conselheiro Lafaiete • Brazil 127 C1
Consett • United Kingdom 7 K7
Consett Bay • Barbados 125 H4
Consett Point • Barbados 125 H4
Constance • Germany 82 G8
Constance, Lake • Germany 82 J5
Constanta • Romania 97 D2
Constantina • Spain 86 B2
Constantine • Algeria 20 G1
Constantinople • Turkey 71 A15
Constitución • Chile 44 B6
Constitution Gardens **Park** • DC, United States ..... 121 [283]
Consuegra • Spain 11 H5
Consuelo Peak • QL, Australia 34 I4
Contamana • Peru 43 C5
Contamines-Montjoie, les **Ski** • France ..... 70 [28]
Contamines-Montjoie, les • France 85 F2
Contreras, • Spain 11 J5
Contwoyto Lake • NT/NU, Canada 38 I3
Conway • Fiji 35 (2) C3
Conway • FL, United States 121 C2
Conway, Cape • QL, Australia 111 F1
Conway, Mt • NT, Australia 112 H2
Conwy • United Kingdom 7 I8
Coober Pedy • SA, Australia 34 F5
Cook • SA, Australia 34 F6
Cook Is. • Pacific Ocean 33 K7
Cook, Mt • New Zealand 35 C6
Cook Strait • New Zealand 35 E5
Cookeville • TN, United States 41 I4
Cookhouse • South Africa 100 C4
Cooktown • QL, Australia 34 I3
Coolangatta • QL, Australia 111 F6
Coolgardie • WA, Australia 34 D6
Cooma • NS, Australia 111 G4
Coonabarabran • NS, Australia 34 I6
Coonoor • India 106 D10
Cooper • AK, United States 38 C4
Cooper Creek • QL/SA, Australia 34 H5
Cooper I. • New Zealand 112 L3
Coorg • India 106 D6
Coos Bay • OR, United States 117 E3
Cootamundra • NS, Australia 111 G1
Copacabana • Bolivia 127 B4
Copacabana • Brazil 127 C4
Copán • Honduras 37 D5
Copán **Heritage C** • Honduras ..... 62 [30]
Copano Bay • TX, United States 119 N5
Copeland Forest • United Kingdom 74 C1
Copenhagen **Beach** • Denmark ..... 68 [40]
Copenhagen • Denmark 95 F11
Copiapó • Chile 44 B4
Coporolo • Angola 24 A2
Copper Mtn **Ski** • CO, United States ..... 116 [96]
Copperas Cove • TX, United States 119 N3
Coppermine • NU, Canada 38 H3
Coppermine [Riv] • NT/NU, Canada 38 H3
Coqen • China 28 E2
Coquimbo • Chile 44 B5
Corabia • Romania 14 L6
Coral Bay • Cyprus 93 J3
Coral Coast • Tunisia 101 E2
Coral Gables • FL, United States 119 M8
Coral Harbour • NU, Canada 39 O4
Coral Heights • Bahamas 124 B3
Coral Sea • Australia 33 G7
Coral Sea Is. Territory • Australia 34 I3
Coral Springs • FL, United States 119 M8
Coralarium, Sentosa • Singapore 108 E4
Corallo, Riviera del • Sardinia, Italy 90 C1
Corantijn • Guyana/Suriname 43 F3
Corato • Italy 14 D8
Corbeil-Essonnes • France 85 E4
Corbett Nat. Park • India 105 C3
Corbier, le **Ski** • France ..... 70 [47]
Corbières • France 85 K2
Corby • United Kingdom 7 L9
Corcaigh • Ireland 79 F8
Córcega • Puerto Rico 125 E1
Corcovado, Golfo • Chile 45 B4
Corcovado, Volcán • Chile 45 B4
Cordele • GA, United States 41 J5
Cordévole • Italy 90 B4
Cordilheiras, Serra das • Brazil 45 (1) B3
Cordillera Central • Colombia 43 B3
Cordillera Central • Peru 43 B5
Cordillera Central • Bolivia 44 C2
Cordillera Central **Heritage C** • Philippines ..... 63 [175]
Cordillera Central • Puerto Rico 125 E3
Cordillera Occidental • Colombia 43 B3
Cordillera Occidental • Bolivia/Chile 44 C2
Cordillera Oriental • Peru 43 B5
Cordillera Oriental • Colombia 43 C2
Cordillera Oriental • Bolivia/Peru 44 C1
Cordillera Real • Ecuador 43 B4
Córdoba • Argentina 44 D5
Córdoba **Heritage C** • Spain ..... 64 [93]
Córdoba • Spain 86 B2
Córdoba • Mexico 123 E4
Córdoba, Sierras de • Argentina 44 D5
Cordova • AK, United States 46 DD3
Corfe Castle • United Kingdom 74 F6
Corfu **Beach** • Corfu, Greece ..... 69 [170]
Corfu • Corfu, Greece 92 B1
Corfu [I.] • Greece 92 B1
Coria • Spain 11 E5
Coria del Río • Spain 11 E7
Coricudgy, Mt • NS, Australia 34 J6
Corigliano Calabro • Italy 12 K9
Corinaldo • Italy 91 E12
Coringa Is. • CL, Australia 34 J3
Corinth • Greece 92 D4
Corinth Canal • Greece 15 D6
Corinto • Brazil 44 H2
Corjuem Fort • Goa, India 105 B1
Cork • Ireland 79 F8
Cork [Adm] • Ireland 79 F8
Çorlu • Turkey 15 I2
Çorlu [Riv] • Turkey 15 I2
Cornas • France 84 B4
Cornélio • Brazil 44 F3
Corner Brook • NF, Canada 123 D3
Cornesti • Moldova 14 P2
Corniche, la • France 85 H2
Corno Grande • Italy 91 F2
Cornouaille • France 84 C3
Cornwall • United Kingdom 74 F4
Cornwall • OT, Canada 122 B7
Cornwall • Jamaica 124 C1
Cornwall, Cape • United Kingdom 74 F4
Cornwallis I. • NU, Canada 38 L1
Coro • Venezuela 43 D1
Coro **Heritage C** • Venezuela ..... 62 [41]
Corofin • Ireland 79 F4
Coromandel • New Zealand 35 E3
Coromandel Coast • India 106 D7
Coromandel Peninsula • New Zealand 35 E3
Coron • Philippines 31 G4
Coronado Nat. Mem. • AZ, United States 118 J4
Coronado Nat. Mem. **Park** • AZ, United States ..... 120 [116]
Coronation Gulf • NU, Canada 38 I3
Coronation I. • Antarctica 59 A10
Coronel • Chile 44 B6
Coronel Fabriciano • Brazil 127 C2
Coronel Oviedo • Paraguay 44 E4
Coronel Pringles • Argentina 45 D3
Coronel Suárez • Argentina 127 D3
Coronet Peak • New Zealand 112 L2
Coropuna, Nudo • Peru 127 B4
Çorovodë • Albania 15 B3
Corpus Christi • TX, United States 119 N5
Corpus Christi Bay • TX, United States 119 N5
Corralejo • Fuerteventura, Canary Is. 87 E2
Corralejo, Playas de • Fuerteventura, Canary Is. 87 E2
Corraun Peninsula • Ireland 79 F1
Corrençon-en-Vercors **Ski** • France ..... 70 [54]
Correntina • Brazil 44 H1
Corrib, Lough • Ireland 79 F4
Corrientes • Argentina 44 E4
Corrientes, Cabo • Mexico 37 (1) A1
Corrientes, Cabo • Colombia 43 B2
Corrientes, Cabo • Cuba 124 D1
Corrigan • TX, United States 119 N4
Corrigin • WA, Australia 34 C6
Corse • France 12 D6
Corse, Cap • Corsica, France 85 L2
Corse-du-Sud • Corsica, France 85 L3
Corsham Court • United Kingdom 74 F3
Corsica • France ..... 85 L
Corsica, Canale di • France/Italy 12 D6
Corsicana • TX, United States 119 N1
Corte • Corsica, France 85 L2
Cortés, Laguna de • Cuba 124 D1
Cortina **Ski** • Italy ..... 70 [242]
Cortina d'Ampezzo • Italy 90 B2
Cortona • Italy 91 E11
Corubal • Guinea/Guinea-Bissau 22 B2
Coruche • Portugal 88 D2
Corumbá • Brazil 44 E2
Corvallis • OR, United States 117 E3
Corvara **Ski** • Italy ..... 70 [233]
Corvara in Badia • Italy 90 B2
Corvo • Azores 88 B1
Cos **Beach** • Greece ..... 69 [210]
Cos • Greece 92 D8
Cosenza • Italy 12 K9
Cosmoledo, Atoll de • Seychelles 106 F3
Cosne-sur-Loire • France 10 H6
Costa, Cordillera de la • Venezuela 43 E2
Costa d'en Blanes • Majorca, Spain 87 H3
Costa da Caparica • Portugal 88 D1
Costa Rica • C. America 37 D5
Costa Teguise • Lanzarote, Canary Is. 87 E3
Costiera Amalfitana **Heritage C** • Italy ..... 64 [129]
Costières de Nîmes • France 84 B4
Costinesti • Romania 97 D2
Coswig • Germany 13 C6
Cotabato • Philippines 31 G5
Cotahuasi • Peru 127 B4
Cotahuasi, Cañon del • Peru 127 B4
Cote 2000 **Ski** • France ..... 70 [53]
Côte Chalonnaise • France 84 B2
Côte d'Azur • France ..... 85 H
Côte d'Ivoire • Africa 22 C3
Côte d'Or • France 10 J6
Côte de Beaune • France 84 B2
Côte de Nuits • France 84 B2
Côte Rotie • France 84 B2
Coteaux de Vendômois • France 84 B1
Coteaux du Tricastin • France 84 B4
Coteaux les Baux-de-Provence • France 84 B4
Cotehele • United Kingdom 74 F5
Cotentin • France 10 D4
Côtes d'Armor • France 84 C2
Côtes du Frontonnais • France 84 B3
Côtes du Lubéron • France 84 B4
Côtes du Marmandais • France 84 B3
Côtes du Rhône • France 84 B4
Côtes du Roussillon • France 84 B4
Côtes du Ventoux • France 84 B4
Côtes du Vivarais • France 84 B4
Cotigao Wildlife Sanctuary • Goa, India 105 B2
Coto de Doñana, Parque Nac. **Heritage N** • Spain ..... 61 [47]
Coto de Doñana, Parque Nac. **Park** • Spain ..... 72 [75]
Coto de Doñana, Parque Nac. • Spain 86 B1
Cotonou • Benin 22 E3
Cotopaxi, Volcán • Ecuador 43 B4
Cotswold Hills • United Kingdom 74 D4
Cotswold Wildlife Park • United Kingdom 74 D4
Cottbus • Germany 8 J5
Cotton Ground • St Kitts & Nevis 125 G4
Cotton Tower • Barbados 125 H4
Coubre, Fôret de la • France 85 G1
Coubre, Pointe de la • France 85 G1
Coulee Dam Nat. Recreation Area • WA, United States 117 E2
Coulee Dam Nat. Recreation Area **Park** • WA, United States ..... 120 [29]
Coulogne • QU, Canada 122 B2
Coulommiers • France 85 E4
Council Bluffs • IA, United States 41 G3
Courances • France 85 E4
Courchevel **Ski** • France ..... 70 [36]
Courchevel • France 85 F4
Courmayeur **Ski** • Italy ..... 70 [198]
Courmayeur • Italy 91 E1
Courtenay • BC, Canada 122 C3
Courtmacsherry • Ireland 79 F8
Courtown **Beach** • Ireland ..... 68 [56]
Cousin • Seychelles 106 F4
Cousine • Seychelles 106 F4
Coutainville • France 84 C2
Coutances • France 10 D4
Couvin • Belgium 5 H4
Covadonga, Parque Nac. de la Montaña de **Park** • Spain ..... 72 [73]
Coventry • United Kingdom 74 D2
Coverack • United Kingdom 74 F4
Covilhã • Portugal 11 D4
Cowboy Country • NV, United States 117 F2
Cowdenbeath • United Kingdom 74 B4
Cowes • United Kingdom 5 B4
Cowes **Beach** • United Kingdom ..... 75 [87-88]
Cowpens Nat. Battlefield **Park** • SC, United States ..... 121 [243]
Cowra • NS, Australia 111 G2
Cox's Bazar • Bangladesh 28 F4
Crab Hill • Antigua & Barbuda 125 F3
Crabs Peninsula • Antigua & Barbuda 125 F2
Cracow **Heritage C** • Poland ..... 64 [141]
Cradock • South Africa 100 C4
Craig • CO, United States 40 E3
Craignure • United Kingdom 78 A2
Crailsheim • Germany 9 F7
Craiova • Romania 14 K5
Cranborne Chase • United Kingdom 74 F3
Cranbrook • WA, Australia 34 C6
Cranbrooke • BC, Canada 122 C4
Crane Beach • Barbados 125 H4
Cranfield **Beach** • United Kingdom ..... 75 [242]
Cranmore **Ski** • NH, United States ..... 116 [212]
Crans-Montana **Ski** • Switzerland ..... 70 [90]
Crans-Montana • Switzerland 89 G6
Crasna • Romania 14 J2
Crater Lake Nat. Park • OR, United States 117 E3
Crater Lake Nat. Park **Park** • OR, United States ..... 120 [36]
Craters of the Moon Nat. Mon. **Park** • ID, United States ..... 120 [65]
Crateús • Brazil 45 (1) C3
Crati • Italy 12 K9
Crato • Brazil 45 (1) D3
Crauford, Cape • NU, Canada 39 O2
Cravo Norte • Colombia 43 C2
Crawford Notch • NH, United States 118 G3
Crawfordsburn **Beach** • United Kingdom ..... 75 [240]
Crawley • United Kingdom 74 E3
Crécy • France 71 A7
Crediton • United Kingdom 74 F2
Cree Lake • SA, Canada 38 J5
Creerlea Abbey • Ireland 79 F2
Creeslough **Beach** • Ireland ..... 68 [65]
Creil • France 85 E2
Crema • Italy 91 E6
Cremona • Italy 91 E6
Crépy-en-Valois • France 85 E2
Cres • Croatia 14 B5
Cres [I.] • Croatia 14 B5
Crescent City • CA, United States 117 F1
Crescent I. • Hong Kong, China 107 H4
Crespi d'Adda **Heritage C** • Italy ..... 64 [110]
Crested Butte **Ski** • CO, United States ..... 116 [100]
Creswell Bay • NU, Canada 38 M2
Crete • Greece ..... 93 E
Crete, Sea of • Greece 92 D11
Créteil • France 85 E4
Creus, Cap de • Spain 87 D2
Creuse • France 84 D4
Creusot, le • France 10 J7
Crevillente • Spain 87 C1
Crewe • United Kingdom 7 J8
Crianlarich • United Kingdom 74 B1
Criccieth **Beach** • United Kingdom ..... 75 [192]
Crichton Castle • United Kingdom 74 B4
Criciúma • Brazil 44 G4
Crieff • United Kingdom 74 B1
Crikvenica • Croatia 12 I3
Crimea • Ukraine 17 E5
Crimmitschau • Germany 9 H6
Crinkley Bottom • United Kingdom 74 F3
Crisan • Romania 97 D2
Cristal, Sierra del • Cuba 124 D8
Cristalândia • Brazil 43 H6
Cristóbal • Panama 58 B9
Cristóbal Colón • Colombia 43 C1
Crisul Negru • Romania 13 L11
Crisul Repede • Romania 13 L10
Crna • F.Y.R. of Macedonia 15 C2
Crna Gora • F.R. of Yugoslavia 14 G7
Crni Drim • Albania 14 H8
Crni vrh • Slovenia 13 E11
Croagh Patrick • Ireland 79 F1
Croatia • Europe 14 D4
Crockett • TX, United States 119 N4
Crocodile Farm • Singapore 108 E2
Crocodile Farm • Bangkok, Thailand 109 H2
Crocodile Paradise • Singapore 108 E1
Croisic, le • France 84 C4
Croix-Valmer, la **Beach** • France ..... 68 [133]
Croix-Valmer, la • France 85 H4
Croker I. • NT, Australia 34 F2
Cromer • United Kingdom 7 N9
Cromer **Beach** • United Kingdom ..... 75 [36]
Cromwell • New Zealand 112 L2
Crooked • BC, Canada 122 C1
Crooked I. • Hong Kong, China 107 H4
Crooked I. • Bahamas 124 B4
Cross Cays • Bahamas 124 B2
Cross River • Nigeria 22 F3
Cross River Nat. Park **Park** • Nigeria ..... 103 [37]
Cross Sound • AK, United States 38 D5
Crosshaven • Ireland 79 F8
Crossmolina • Ireland 79 F2
Crotone • Italy 12 L9
Crown Point • Trinidad & Tobago 125 K2
Crown Prince Frederik • NU, Canada 39 N2
Crowsnest Pass • AL, Canada 38 I7
Croyde Bay **Beach** • United Kingdom ..... 75 [135]
Croydon • QL, Australia 34 H3
Croydon • United Kingdom 74 E1
Crozes-Hermitage • France 84 B4
Crozet, Is. • Indian Ocean 19 J10
Crozon, Presqu'île de • France 84 C1
Crudes • Cuba 124 D2
Cruese • France 10 G7
Crummock Water • United Kingdom 74 C1
Crump I. • Antigua & Barbuda 125 F2
Cruz Alta • Brazil 44 F4
Cruz, Cabo • Cuba 124 D7
Cruz, Cayo • Cuba 124 D3
Cruz del Eje • Argentina 44 D5
Cruzeiro • Brazil 127 C3
Cruzeiro do Oeste • Brazil 44 F3
Cruzeiro do Sul • Brazil 43 C5
Crystal Mtn **Ski** • WA, United States ..... 116 [45]
Crystal Mtn **Ski** • MI, United States ..... 116 [135]
Cserhát • Hungary 14 G2
Csurgó • Hungary 14 E3
Ctesiphon • Iraq 98 B4
Cu Chi Tunnels • Vietnam 108 B1
Cu Lao Hon • Vietnam 108 B4
Cuamba • Mozambique 24 F2
Cuangar • Angola 24 B3
Cuango • Angola 23 B5
Cuango [Riv] • Angola 23 B5
Cuanza • Angola 23 B6
Cuarto • Argentina 45 D2
Cuba • Portugal 11 D6
Cuba • West Indies ..... 124 D
Cubango • Angola/Namibia 24 B3
Cubelles **Beach** • Spain ..... 68 [122]
Cubells • Ibiza, Spain 87 G3
Çubuk • Turkey 15 O3
Cuchilla Grande • Uruguay 45 F2
Cuchilla Grande • Uruguay 127 D2
Cuchillas de Toa • Cuba 124 D8
Cuckmere Haven **Beach** • United Kingdom ..... 75 [72]
Cuckold Point • Barbados 125 H1
Cucq **Beach** • France ..... 68 [75]
Cucuí • Brazil 43 D3
Cúcuta • Colombia 43 C2
Cuddalore • India 106 D7
Cuddapah • India 106 D7
Cue • WA, Australia 34 C5
Cuéllar • Spain 11 G3
Cuenca • Spain 11 I4
Cuenca • Ecuador 43 B4
Cuenca **Heritage C** • Spain ..... 64 [76]
Cuenca, Serrania de • Spain 11 J4
Cuernavaca • Mexico 123 E4
Cueto • Cuba 124 D8
Cueva de Bellamar • Cuba 124 D2
Cuevas de Almanzora **Beach** • Spain ..... 68 [116]
Cuevas de Camuy • Puerto Rico 125 E1
Cuevas del Indio • Cuba 124 D1
Cui Heng • China 107 H2
Cuiabá • Brazil 44 E2
Cuilo • Angola 23 B5
Cuima • Angola 24 B2
Cuito • Angola 24 B3
Cuitzeo • Mexico 123 E1
Culatra, I. da • Portugal 88 E7
Culbone Church • United Kingdom 74 F2
Culcairn • NS, Australia 111 G1
Culdaff **Beach** • Ireland ..... 68 [65]
Culemborg • Netherlands 80 C4
Culgoa • QL, Australia 111 E8
Culiacán • Mexico 40 E7
Culik • Bali, Indonesia 110 C2
Culion • Philippines 31 F4
Culion [I.] • Philippines 31 F4
Cullera • Spain 11 K5
Cullera **Beach** • Spain ..... 68 [119]
Cullman • AL, United States 41 I5
Culver, Point • WA, Australia 34 D6
Cuma • Italy 91 G3
Cumana • Venezuela 43 E1
Cumbal, Volcán • Colombia 43 B3
Cumberland • MD, United States 41 K4
Cumberland • United Kingdom 75 A3
Cumberland, Cape • Vanuatu 35 (2) B1
Cumberland Gap Nat. Hist. Park **Park** • KY, United States ..... 121 [234]
Cumberland I. Nat. Seashore **Park** • GA, United States ..... 121 [217]
Cumberland Peninsula • NU, Canada 39 R3
Cumberland Sound • NU, Canada 39 R3
Cumbernauld • United Kingdom 74 B3
Cumbrae Slip • United Kingdom 78 A3
Cumbre del Libertador General San Martin • Argentina 44 C3
Cumbre, Paso de la • Argentina/Chile 44 B5
Cumbria • United Kingdom 75 A3
Cumbrian Mtns • United Kingdom 7 I7
Cumerna • Bulgaria 14 M7
Cumra • Turkey 15 N6
Cunene • Angola/Namibia 24 A3
Cúneo • Italy 91 E5
Cunit **Beach** • Spain ..... 68 [121]
Cunnamulla • QL, Australia 111 F5
Cunninghame • United Kingdom 74 B3
Cunupia • Trinidad & Tobago 125 K3
Cuokka rassa • Norway 16 M2
Cupar • United Kingdom 74 B2
Cupica, Golfo de • Colombia 43 B2
Cupids • NF, Canada 123 D4
Cupra Marittima **Beach** • Italy ..... 69 [162]
Cupra Marittima • Italy 91 E12
Curaçao • West Indies 37 H5
Curacautín • Chile 45 B3
Curdimurka • SA, Australia 34 G5
Cure • France 10 I6
Curecanti Nat. Recreation Area **Park** • CO, United States ..... 120 [92]
Curepipe • Mauritius 24 (1) B2
Curiapo • Venezuela 43 E2
Curicó • Chile 44 B5
Curieuse • Seychelles 106 F4
Curitabanos • Brazil 44 F4
Curitiba • Brazil 44 G4
Curium • Cyprus 93 J3
Curoca • Angola 24 A3
Curracloe **Beach** • Ireland ..... 68 [56]
Curragh, The • Ireland 79 E3
Currais Novos • Brazil 45 (1) D3
Curral das Freiras • Madeira 88 C1
Curral-Velho • Cape Verde 22 (1) B1
Currane, Lough • Ireland 79 F7
Currie • TS, Australia 34 H7
Curtain Bluff • Antigua & Barbuda 125 F3
Curtea de Arges • Romania 14 L4
Curtis • New Zealand 33 J9
Curtis Channel • QL, Australia 111 F4
Curtis I. • QL, Australia 111 F4
Curuguaty • Paraguay 44 E3
Curupira, Serra de • Brazil/Venezuela 43 D3
Curuzú Cuatiá • Argentina 44 E4
Curvelo • Brazil 44 H2
Cusco • Peru 127 B2
Cushendall **Beach** • United Kingdom ..... 75 [239]
Cutato • Angola 23 B6
Cutervo • Peru 43 B5
Cutro • Italy 12 L9
Cuttack • India 28 E4
Cuvo • Angola 23 A6
Cuxhaven • Germany 8 D3
Cuxhaven **Spa** • Germany ..... 83 [54]
Cuya • Chile 44 B2
Cuyahoga Valley Nat. Recreation Area **Park** • OH, United States ..... 121 [190]
Cuyuni • Guyana/Venezuela 43 E2
Cuzco **Heritage C** • Peru ..... 62 [51]
Cuzco • Peru 127 B2
Cwmtydu **Beach** • United Kingdom ..... 75 [175]
Cyclades • Greece 92 D8
Cypress Hills • AL/SA, Canada 38 I7
Cyprus • Europe ..... 93 J
Cyrenaica • Libya 21 D1
Cyrene • Libya 21 D1
Cyrene **Heritage C** • Libya ..... 64 [235]
Czech Republic • Europe 13 D8
Czechowice-Dziedzice • Poland 13 H8
Czersk • Poland 13 G4
Czestochówa • Poland 13 I7

D

D'Arros • Seychelles 106 F2
D'Entrecasteaux Is. • Papua New Guinea 35 (1) E2
D'Urville I. • New Zealand 35 D5
Da Hinggan Ling • China 27 I8
Da Lat • Vietnam 108 B2
Da Lat Plateau • Vietnam 108 B2
Da Nang • Vietnam 31 D3
Da Qaidam • China 29 B3
Da, Song • Vietnam 108 A1
Da Vinci, Leonardo [Apt] • Italy 91 F3
Da Xi • China 31 F1
Da Yunhe • China 29 F3
Daba Shan • China 29 D4
Dabakala • Côte d'Ivoire 22 D3
Dabas • Hungary 13 I10
Dabeiba • Colombia 43 B2
Dabie Shan • China 29 F4
Dabola • Guinea 22 B2
Dabolim [Apt] • Goa, India 105 B1
Dabsan Hu • China 28 F1
Dachau • Germany 82 J3
Dachstein • Austria 89 H4
Dadanawa • Guyana 43 F3
Daday • Turkey 15 O2
Dadès, Gorges du • Morocco 101 D4
Dädesjö • Sweden 95 F8
Dadra • India 28 B4
Dadu • Pakistan 28 A3
Dadu He • China 29 C4
Daeni • Romania 97 D2
Dafnoúdi, Akra • Greece 92 C2
Dafok, Am • Sudan 23 C1
Dagali • Norway 94 C4
Dagana • Senegal 20 B5
Dagestan • Russian Fed. 17 H6
Dagg Sound • New Zealand 112 L1
Dagomys • Russian Fed. 17 F6
Dagomys • Russian Fed. 96 A2
Dagupan • Philippines 31 G3
Dahab • Egypt 101 F4
Dahlak • Eritrea 21 H4
Dahme • Germany 8 I4
Dahme **Spa** • Germany ..... 83 [24]
Dahna, Ad • Saudi Arabia 18 E4
Dahongliutan • China 28 C1
Dahra • Algeria 11 L8
Dahra • Libya 21 C2
Dahra • Senegal 22 A1
Dahshur • Egypt 101 F1
Dai Shan • China 107 J4
Daiet el Kisria • Algeria 11 N9
Dailekh • Nepal 28 D3
Daimiel • Spain 11 H5
Daimiel, Parque Nac. de las Tablas de **Park** • Spain ..... 72 [74]
Daio-Zaki • Japan 30 I7
Daishan • China 107 J4
Daito-Shoto • Japan 29 I5
Dajarra • QL, Australia 34 G4
Dajtit Nat. Park **Park** • Albania ..... 72 [125]
Dakar • Senegal 22 A2
Dakhla • Western Sahara 20 B4
Dakhla Oasis • Egypt 101 F3
Dakoro • Niger 20 G6
Dakovica • F.R. of Yugoslavia 14 H7
Dakovo • Croatia 14 F4
Dal • Norway 94 B2
Dala • Angola 24 C2
Dalaas • Austria 89 H5
Dalaba • Guinea 22 B2
Dalälven • Sweden 16 I6
Dalaman • Turkey 92 D9
Dalaman [Riv] • Turkey 15 J7
Dalandzadgad • Mongolia 29 C2
Dalarnas • Sweden 16 G6
Dalarö • Sweden 95 D4
Dalbandin • Pakistan 18 H4
Dalbosjön • Sweden 95 F3
Dalby • Sweden 95 F11
Dalby • QL, Australia 111 F6
Dale **Beach** • United Kingdom ..... 75 [158]
Dale • Sogn og Fjordane, Norway 94 C3
Dale • Hordaland, Norway 94 C3
Dalem Temple • Bali, Indonesia 110 C4
Dalen • Norway 94 C6
Dalhart • TX, United States 40 F4
Dalhousie Springs • SA, Australia 112 H4
Dali • China 29 C5
Dalian • China 29 G3
Dalkey • Ireland 79 E2
Dalkey I. • Ireland 79 E2
Dall I. • AK, United States 38 E6
Dallas • TX, United States 119 N1
Dallgow • Germany 81 F1
Dallol Bosso • Niger 20 F6
Dalmatia • Croatia 14 C6
Dalmeny • United Kingdom 74 B4
Dalnegorsk • Russian Fed. 27 M8
Dalnyaya, gora • Russian Fed. 27 U3
Daloa • Côte d'Ivoire 22 C3
Dalou Shan • China 29 D5
Dalqu • Sudan 21 F3
Dalrymple, Mt • QL, Australia 111 F3
Dalslands kanal • Sweden 95 F2
Dalton • GA, United States 41 J5
Dalton-in-Furness • United Kingdom 74 C3
Daltonganj • India 105 C8
Daluis, Gorges de • France 85 H2
Dalwallinu • WA, Australia 34 C6
Daly • NT, Australia 34 F2
Daly Waters • NT, Australia 34 F3
Dalyan • Turkey 92 D9
Dam Qu • China 28 F2
Daman • India 28 B4
Daman [Adm] • India 28 B4
Damanhûr • Egypt 21 F1
Damar • Indonesia 32 (1) C4
Damascus • Syria 18 C3
Damascus **Heritage C** • Syria ..... 64 [241]
Damaturu • Nigeria 20 H6
Damazin, Ad • Sudan 23 E1
Damba • Angola 22 H6
Dambulla Golden Rock Temple **Heritage N** • Sri Lanka ..... 61 [111]
Dambulla Golden Rock Temple **Heritage C** • Sri Lanka ..... 63 [137]
Dambulla Golden Rock Temple • Sri Lanka 106 D15
Damietta • Egypt 101 F2
Damietta Mouth • Egypt 101 F2
Damir, Ad • Sudan 21 F4
Dammam, Ad • Saudi Arabia 18 E4
Damme • Germany 8 D4
Damoh • India 105 C7
Damp **Spa** • Germany ..... 83 [13]
Dampier • WA, Australia 34 C4
Damqalt • Yemen 18 F6
Damqog Kanbab • China 28 E3
Damüls • Austria 89 H1
Dan • Israel 98 A5
Danakil • Ethiopia 21 H5
Dancheng • China 107 J4
Dandawa • Zimbabwe 102 J1
Dandeldhura • Nepal 28 D3
Dandenong • VI, Australia 111 G3
Dangan Liedao • Zhuhai, China 107 H4
Dangast **Spa** • Germany ..... 83 [50]
Danger Point • South Africa 100 C5
Dangoura, Mt • Central African Rep. 23 D2
Dangtu • China 107 J1
Dania • FL, United States 119 M8
Danilov • Russian Fed. 97 E2
Danish Riviera • Denmark 95 F11
Danmarks Havn • Greenland 36 O2
Dannemora • Sweden 95 D2
Dannenberg • Germany 8 G3
Dannevirke • New Zealand 35 F5
Danshui • China 107 H2
Danube • Europe 4 P8
Danube Delta **Heritage N** • Romania ..... 61 [56]
Danube Delta • Romania 97 D2
Danville • VA, United States 41 K4
Danyang • China 107 J1
Dargio • Poland 13 H3
Dao Phu Quoc • Vietnam 31 C4
Dao Timni • Niger 20 H4
Dapaong • Togo 22 E2
Daqing • China 29 G1
Dar Bouâzza • Morocco 101 D1
Dar es Salaam • Tanzania 102 H4
Dar Rounga • Central African Rep./Sudan 23 C2
Dar Sila • Chad 23 C1
Dar'a • Syria 18 C3
Darabani • Romania 14 N1
Daracya Yarimadasi • Turkey 15 J7
Daravica • F.R. of Yugoslavia 14 H7
Darbhanga • India 28 E3
Dardanelles • Turkey 92 D2
Darfo Boario Terme • Italy 12 E3
Darfur • Chad/Sudan 100 A2
Darfur al Janubijah • Sudan 23 C1
Darganata • Uzbekistan 18 H1
Dargaville • New Zealand 35 D2
Darhan • Mongolia 27 G7
Darién • Panama 37 F6
Darién, Golfo del • Colombia/Panama 43 B2
Darién, Parque Nac. del **Heritage N** • Panama ..... 60 [25]
Darién, Serranía del • Colombia/Panama 43 B2
Darjeeling • India 28 E3
Darkwood Beach • Antigua & Barbuda 125 F3
Darling • NS, Australia 34 H6
Darling Downs • QL, Australia 111 F6
Darling, J.N. 'Ding', Nat. Wildlife Refuge • FL, United States 119 M5
Darling Range • WA, Australia 33 C9
Darlington • United Kingdom 7 K7
Darlowo • Poland 13 F3
Darmstadt • Germany 82 H4
Darnah • Libya 21 D1
Daroca • Spain 11 J3
Darrah Wildlife Sanctuary • India 105 C6
Darregueira • Argentina 44 D6
Darss • Germany 8 H2
Dart • United Kingdom 74 F5
Dartmoor • United Kingdom 74 F5
Dartmoor Nat. Park **Park** • United Kingdom ..... 72 [51]
Dartmoor Nat. Park • United Kingdom 74 F5
Dartmoor Wildlife Centre • United Kingdom 74 F5
Dartmouth • United Kingdom 74 F5
Dartmouth • NS, Canada 123 D7
Daru • Papua New Guinea 35 (1) C2
Daruvar • Croatia 14 E4
Darvaza • Turkmenistan 18 G1
Darvel, Teluk • Malaysia 31 F6
Darwin • NT, Australia 34 F2
Darwin • Galapagos Is. 43 (1) A1
Daryacheh-ye Hamun-e Hirmand • Afghanistan/Iran 18 H3
Dashen, Ras • Ethiopia 21 G5
Dassel • Germany 8 E5
Dassen I. • South Africa 100 C5
Dassiá • Corfu, Greece 92 B1
Datça **Beach** • Turkey ..... 69 [234]
Datça • Turkey 92 D9
Date • Japan 30 K3
Datia • India 105 C7
Datong • China 29 E2
Daugava • Latvia 16 N8
Daugavpils • Latvia 16 N9
Daun • Germany 82 H1
Daun **Spa** • Germany ..... 83 [158]
Daunia, Monti della • Italy 14 B8
Dauphin • MN, Canada 38 L6
Dauphine • France 10 K8
Davangere • India 106 D6
Davao • Philippines 31 H5
Davao Gulf • Philippines 31 H5
Davar Panah • Iran 18 H4
Davenport • IA, United States 41 H3
David • Panama 37 E6
Davis [Base] • Antarctica 46 (1) N3
Davis Dam • AZ/NV, United States 118 J1
Davis, Fort, Nat. Hist. Site **Park** • TX, United States ..... 120 [137]
Davis Strait • Canada/Greenland 39 T3
Davos **Ski** • Switzerland ..... 70 [113]
Davos • Switzerland 89 G4
Dawa • China 30 B4
Dawa • Ethiopia 101 G2
Dawlish **Beach** • United Kingdom ..... 75 [97]

Dawlish Warren **Beach** • United Kingdom 75 [96]
Dawson • YT, Canada 38 D4
Dawson • QL, Australia 111 F5
Dawson Creek • BC, Canada 122 C1
Dawu • China 29 C4
Dax • France 85 G3
Daxue Shan • China 29 C5
Daydream I. • QL, Australia 111 F1
Daylesford • VI, Australia 111 G3
Dayr • Sudan 21 F5
Dayr az Zawr • Syria 18 C2
Dayton • OH, United States 41 J4
Dayton Aviation Nat. Hist. Park **Park** • OH, United States 121 [185]
Daytona Beach • FL, United States 119 M4
De Aar • South Africa 24 C6
De Bay, Laguna • Philippines 31 G4
De Efteling **Park** • Netherlands 73 [45]
De Efteling • Netherlands 80 A11
De Funiak Springs • FL, United States 119 M2
De Gaulle, Charles [Apt] • France 85 E2
De Grey • WA, Australia 34 D4
De Haan • Belgium 80 B2
De Haar • Netherlands 80 C2
De Hoge Veluwe, Nat. Park **Park** • Netherlands 72 [53]
De Hoge Veluwe, Nat. Park • Netherlands 80 A7
De Hoop Nature Reserve • South Africa 100 C6
De Jongs, Tanjung • Indonesia 32 (1) E4
De Kalb • TX, United States 119 N2
De Land • FL, United States 119 M4
De Panne • Belgium 80 B1
De Quincy Village • Seychelles 106 F1
De Rust • South Africa 100 C7
De Soto Nat. Mem. • FL, United States 119 M5
De Soto Nat. Mem. **Park** • FL, United States 121 [224]
De Timimoun, Sebkha • Algeria 20 F3
De Zijpe • Netherlands 80 A3
Dead Sea • Israel/Jordan 98 A8
Deal • United Kingdom 74 E4
Dean, Forest of • United Kingdom 74 D3
Deán Funes • Argentina 44 D5
Dease • BC, Canada 38 F5
Dease Arm • NT/NU, Canada 38 G3
Dease Lake • BC, Canada 38 F5
Dease Strait • NU, Canada 38 J3
Death Valley Nat. Park • CA, United States 117 F4
Death Valley Nat. Park **Park** • CA, United States 120 [55]
Deauville • France 5 D5
Debica • Poland 13 K7
Debin • Russian Fed. 27 P4
Deblin • Poland 13 K6
Debno • Poland 13 D5
Débo, Lac • Mali 20 E5
Debre Berhan • Ethiopia 23 F2
Debre Markos • Ethiopia 21 G5
Debrecen • Hungary 13 K10
Debreuil • St Lucia 125 J3
Decapolis • Asia 98 A4
Decatur • IL, United States 41 I4
Decatur • AL, United States 41 I5
Decatur • TX, United States 119 N1
Deccan • India 106 D2
Deception Bay • Papua New Guinea 35 (1) C2
Decín • Czech Rep. 96 C2
Decize • France 10 I7
Dedegöl Dag • Turkey 93 G2
Dee • Scotland, UK 6 J4
Dee • England/Wales, UK 7 I9
Deeg • India 105 C2
Deep Bay • China 107 H3
Deep Bay • Antigua & Barbuda 125 F1
Deep Cove • New Zealand 112 L1
Deer I. • NB, Canada 123 D6
Deer Lake • NF, Canada 123 D3
Deer Lake [Lake] • NF, Canada 123 D3
Deer Valley **Ski** • UT, United States 116 [79]
Degeberga • Sweden 95 F11
Degeh Bur • Ethiopia 23 G2
Degerhamn • Sweden 95 F12
Deggendorf • Germany 9 H8
Degirmendere • Turkey 15 I5
Dehibat • Tunisia 20 H2
Dehiwala • Sri Lanka 106 D15
Dehra Dun • India 28 C2
Dehui • China 27 K8
Deià • Majorca, Spain 87 H1
Deinze • Belgium 5 G3
Deir el Beida • Morocco 101 D1
Deir Mar Saba • Jordan 98 A8
Déiva Marina **Beach** • Italy 68 [143]
Dej • Romania 14 K2
Dejës • Albania 15 B2
DeKalb • IL, United States 41 I3
Dekese • Dem. Rep. of Congo 23 C4
Dekoa • Central African Rep. 22 H3
Del Prat [Apt] • Spain 87 D3
Del Rio • TX, United States 40 F6
Delano • CA, United States 117 F3
Delano Peak • UT, United States 40 D4
Delaram • Afghanistan 18 H3
Delaware • United States 118 H1
Delaware Bay • DE/NJ, United States 118 H3
Delaware, Fort, State Park • DE, United States 118 H3
Delaware & Lehigh Navigation Canal Nat. Heritage Corridor **Park** • PA, United States 121 [313]
Delaware Water Gap Nat. Recreation Area **Park** • PA, United States 121 [314]
Delegate • NS, Australia 111 G4
Delémont • Switzerland 9 C9
Delfi • Greece 15 D5
Delfi **Heritage C** • Greece 64 [178]
Delfland • Netherlands 80 C3
Delft • Netherlands 80 C3
Delfzijl • Netherlands 80 A4
Delgada, Punta • Argentina 45 D4
Delgado, Cabo • Mozambique 24 G2
Delhi **Heritage C** • India 63 [116-117]
Delhi • India 105 C2
Deli • Indonesia 110 D1
Delimara Point • Malta 93 H4
Delingha • China 28 G1
Delitzsch • Germany 8 H5
Delmenhorst • Germany 8 D3
Delnice • Croatia 14 B4
Deloraine • TS, Australia 34 I8
Delphi • Greece 15 D5
Delphi **Heritage C** • Greece 64 [178]
Delray Beach • FL, United States 119 M6
Delta Country • MS, United States 118 K2
Delta du Saloum, Parc nat. du **Park** • Senegal 103 [8]
Delta Junction • AK, United States 38 B4
Deltebre **Beach** • Spain 68 [121]
Delvin • Ireland 79 E1
Delvináki • Greece 15 B4
Demak • Java, Indonesia 110 D3
Demba • Dem. Rep. of Congo 23 C5
Dembi Dolo • Ethiopia 23 E2
Demidov • Russian Fed. 97 E3
Deming • NM, United States 118 J4
Demirci • Turkey 15 J4
Demirköy • Turkey 15 I2
Demirtas • Turkey 93 G4
Demmin • Germany 8 I3
Demone, Val • Sicily, Italy 90 D2
Dempo, Gunung • Indonesia 32 C3
Dêmqog • China 28 C2
Demta • Indonesia 32 (1) F3
Demyanskoye • Russian Fed. 26 K6
Den Chai • Thailand 109 G4
Den Haag • Netherlands 80 C1
Den Helder **Beach** • Netherlands 68 [67]
Den Helder • Netherlands 80 A3
Denain • France 10 I3
Denali Nat. Park & Preserve **Park** • AK, United States 120 [7]
Denau • Uzbekistan 18 I2
Denbighshire • United Kingdom 75 A4
Dendang • Indonesia 32 D3
Dender • Belgium 5 G4
Dendera • Egypt 101 F4
Denezkin Kamen • Russian Fed. 26 I5
Dengkou • China 29 D2
Dêngqên • China 28 F2
Denham • WA, Australia 34 B5
Denia **Beach** • Spain 68 [118]
Denia • Spain 87 C2
Denilquin • NS, Australia 111 G1
Denis, I. • Seychelles 106 F2
Denison Dam • OK/TX, United States 119 N1
Denizli • Turkey 92 D9
Denmark • WA, Australia 34 C6
Denmark • Europe 95 F
Denmark Strait • Greenland/Iceland 4 E3
Dennery • St Lucia 125 J2
Dennery I. • St Lucia 125 J4
Denpasar • Bali, Indonesia 110 C4
Denton • TX, United States 119 N1
Denver • CO, United States 40 F4
Deoli • India 105 C6
Deqing • China 107 J3
Der, Lac du • France 5 H6
Dera Ghazi Khan • Pakistan 28 B2
Dera Ismail Khan • Pakistan 28 B2
Derbent • Russian Fed. 17 H6
Derby • United Kingdom 7 K9
Derby • WA, Australia 34 D3
Derbyshire • United Kingdom 75 A4
Dereköy • Turkey 15 G3
Derg, Lough • Ireland 79 F4
Dernière Rivière • St Lucia 125 J2
Déroute, Passage de la • France 5 B5
Derrière Morne • St Lucia 125 J4
Derrynasaggart Mtns • Ireland 79 F8
Derventa • Bosnia-Herz. 14 E5
Derwent • Derbyshire, UK 5 B1
Derwent • Cumbria, UK 74 C1
Derwent River • TS, Australia 34 I8
Derwent Water • United Kingdom 74 C2
Des Moines • IA, United States 41 H3
Desaguadero • Argentina 44 C5
Desaguadero • Peru 127 B4
Désappointement • French Polynesia 33 M7
Desaru • Malaysia 108 A4
Descartes • France 84 D4
Deschutes • OR, United States 117 E3
Dese • Ethiopia 21 G5
Deseado • Argentina 45 C5
Desengaño, Punta • Argentina 45 C5
Desenzano • Italy 91 E7
Deshnoke • India 105 C1
Deskáti • Greece 15 C4
Desna • Ukraine 17 E4
Desnœfs • Seychelles 106 F2
Desolacion, I. • Chile 45 B6
Desolation, Valley of • South Africa 100 C3
Despotikó • Greece 92 D7
Desroches • Seychelles 106 F2
Desruisseaux • St Lucia 125 J4
Dessau • Germany 8 H5
Dessau **Heritage C** • Germany 64 [33]
Dessel **Beach** • Belgium 68 [71]
Destin • FL, United States 119 M2
Deta • Romania 14 I4
Dete • Zimbabwe 102 J1
Detmold • Germany 8 D5
Detroit • MI, United States 41 J3
Detva • Slovak Rep. 13 I9
Deurne [Apt] • Belgium 80 A10
Deutsche Bucht • North Sea 8 C2
Deux Alpes, les **Ski** • France 70 [58]
Deux Alpes, les • France 85 F3
Deux Sèvres • France 84 D3
Deva • Romania 14 J4
Deventer • Netherlands 80 A8
Devil River Peak • New Zealand 35 D5
Devil's Bridge • Antigua & Barbuda 125 F2
Devil's I. • French Guiana 58 A3
Devils Head **Ski** • WI, United States 116 [123]
Devils Postpile Nat. Mon. • CA, United States 117 F4
Devils Postpile Nat. Mon. **Park** • CA, United States 120 [52]
Devils Tower Nat. Mon. **Park** • WY, United States 120 [72]
Devin • Bulgaria 14 L8
Devizes • United Kingdom 74 F3
Devolli • Albania 15 B3
Devon • United Kingdom 74 F2
Devon I. • NU, Canada 39 N1
Devonport • TS, Australia 34 I8
Devonport • New Zealand 35 E3
Devrek • Turkey 15 M2
Devrez • Turkey 15 O3
Dewa • Ethiopia/Kenya 23 G3
Dey-Dey, Lake • SA, Australia 34 F5
Dezful • Iran 18 E3
Dezhneva, mys • Russian Fed. 25 U3
Dezhou • China 29 F3
Dháfni • Greece 15 C6
Dhahran • Saudi Arabia 18 E4
Dhaka • Bangladesh 28 E4
Dháli • Cyprus 93 J4
Dhamar • Yemen 18 D7
Dhamtari • India 28 D4
Dharwad • India 106 D2
Dhaulagiri • Nepal 28 D3
Dhefterá • Cyprus 93 J3
Dhekélia • Cyprus 93 J4
Dhiban • Jordan 98 A8
Dhiffushi • Maldives 106 E2
Dhigufinolhu • Maldives 106 E4
Dhiórix Potidhaia • Greece 15 E3
Dhubri • India 28 E3
Dhule • India 28 B4
Dhundar • India 105 C6
Dia • Greece 93 E3
Diable, I. du • French Guiana 43 G2
Diablo Range • CA, United States 117 F3
Diamante • Italy 12 J9
Diamante • Argentina 44 D5
Diamantina • QL, Australia 34 H4
Diamantina • Brazil 44 H2
Diamantina Lakes • QL, Australia 34 H4
Diamantino • Brazil 44 E1
Diamond Baths • St Lucia 125 J3
Diamond Head State Mon. • HI, United States 119 L6
Diamond Is. • CL, Australia 111 F2
Diamond Jenness Peninsula • NT, Canada 38 H2
Diamond Peak **Ski** • NV, United States 116 [66]
Diani Beach • Kenya 101 G5
Diano Marina **Beach** • Italy 68 [140]
Diano Marina • Italy 91 E9
Dianópolis • Brazil 45 (1) B4
Diapaga • Burkina Faso 22 E2
Dibang • India 28 G3
Dibaya-Lubue • Dem. Rep. of Congo 23 B4
Dibella • Niger 20 H5
Dibrugarh • India 28 F3
Dickenson Bay • Antigua & Barbuda 125 F1
Dickinson • ND, United States 40 F2
Dicle • Turkey 18 D2
Didcot • United Kingdom 74 D4
Dideso • Ethiopia 23 F2
Didiéni • Mali 20 D6
Didim • Turkey 92 D8
Didyma • Turkey 92 D8
Die • France 10 K9
Dieburg • Germany 9 D7
Diego Suarez • Madagascar 24 H2
Diekirch • Luxembourg 80 A20
Diéma • Mali 22 C2
Diemel • Germany 8 D5
Dien Bien Phu • Vietnam 31 C2
Dieng Plateau • Java, Indonesia 110 D6
Dienten am Hochkönig **Ski** • Austria 70 [166]
Diepholz • Germany 8 D4
Dieppe • France 10 G4
Dieppe **Beach** • France 68 [77]
Dieppe Bay Town • St Kitts & Nevis 125 G1
Dierhagen **Beach** • Germany 68 [32]
Dierhagen **Spa** • Germany 83 [274]
Dießen-Rieden • Germany 82 J2
Diest • Belgium 80 A15
Dieuze • France 5 J6
Diez • Germany 82 H2
Diffa • Niger 20 H6
Differdange • Luxembourg 5 I5
Digby • NS, Canada 123 D7
Digity Mud Volcano • Trinidad & Tobago 125 K3
Digne • France 85 H1
Digoin • France 10 I7
Digue, la • Seychelles 106 F4
Digul • Indonesia 32 (1) E4
Dihang • India 28 F3
Dijlah • Iraq 18 D2
Dijon • France 10 K6
Dik • Chad 23 B2
Dikili • Turkey 15 H4
Diksmuide • Belgium 80 B1
Dikson • Russian Fed. 26 N3
Diktéon Antron • Crete, Greece 93 E7
Diktinéon • Crete, Greece 93 E1
Dikwa • Nigeria 22 G2
Dili • East Indies 32 (1) B4
Dillenburg • Germany 82 G2
Dillia • Niger 21 B4
Dilling • Sudan 23 D1
Dillingen • Germany 71 A8
Dillon • MT, United States 40 D2
Dilly • Mali 20 D6
Dilolo • Dem. Rep. of Congo 23 C6
Dilos **Heritage C** • Greece 64 [186]
Dilos • Greece 92 D8
Dimashq • Syria 18 C3
Dimashq **Heritage C** • Syria 64 [241]
Dimbokro • Côte d'Ivoire 22 D3
Dimboola • VI, Australia 34 H7
Dimbovita • Romania 97 D1
Dimitrovgrad • Russian Fed. 17 H4
Dimitrovgrad • Bulgaria 97 D3
Dinagat • Philippines 31 H4
Dinajpur • Bangladesh 28 E3
Dinan • France 84 C2
Dinant • Belgium 80 A19
Dinar • Turkey 15 L5
Dinara • Bosnia-Herz./Croatia 14 D5
Dinard • France 84 C2
Dinaric Alps • Bosnia-Herz./Croatia 96 B2
Dinas Cross **Beach** • United Kingdom 75 [167]
Dinas Dinlle **Beach** • United Kingdom 75 [196]
Dinder Nat. Park **Park** • Sudan 103 [61]
Dindigul • India 106 D11
Dinga • Dem. Rep. of Congo 22 H6
Dinghai • China 107 J4
Dingle • Ireland 79 F5
Dingle Bay • Ireland 79 F7
Dingle Peninsula • Ireland 79 F5
Dingli Cliffs • Malta 93 H4
Dingolfing • Germany 9 H8
Dingwall • United Kingdom 6 H4
Dingxian • China 29 F3
Dinkelsbühl • Germany 9 F7
Dinosaur Nat. Mon. **Park** • CO, United States 120 [88]
Dinosaur Prov. Park **Heritage N** • Canada 60 [6]
Dinosaurier Park Münchehagen **Park** • Germany 73 [56]
Dinotown • BC, Canada 122 C3
Dinslaken • Germany 81 E1
Dioila • Mali 22 C2
Dionisiádes • Greece 93 E4
Dioura • Mali 20 D6
Diourbel • Senegal 22 A2
Dipolog • Philippines 31 G5
Dire Dawa • Ethiopia 23 G1
Dirfis, Oros • Greece 15 E5
Dirj • Libya 21 A1
Dirk Hartog I. • WA, Australia 34 B5
Dirkou • Niger 20 H5
Dirranbandi • QL, Australia 34 I5
Disappointment, Lake • WA, Australia 34 D4
Discovery Bay • Jamaica 124 C1
Discovery I. • FL, United States 121 C1
Disentis • Switzerland 89 G3
Disko • Greenland 39 U3
Dismal Swamp • VA, United States 118 H5
Disney, Walt, World Int. Sports Complex • FL, United States 121 C1
Disney, Walt, World Resort Complex • FL, United States 121 C1
Disney-MGM Studios • FL, United States 121 C1
Disneyland • CA, United States 117 F6
Disneyland **Park** • CA, United States 120 [H]
Disneyland Paris **Park** • France 73 [73]
Disneyland Paris • France 85 E4
Dispur • India 28 F3
Distington • United Kingdom 74 C1
District of Columbia • United States 118 H3
Distrito Federal • Brazil 45 (1) B5
Ditikí Rodópi • Greece 15 F2
Diu • India 28 B4
Diu [Adm] • India 28 B4
Divar I. • Goa, India 105 B1
Dives • France 5 C5
Divinópolis • Brazil 127 C1
Divisoes, Serra das • Brazil 44 F2
Divisor, Serra de • Brazil/Peru 43 C5
Divjaka Nat. Park **Park** • Albania 72 [126]
Divo • Côte d'Ivoire 22 C3
Divrigi **Heritage C** • Turkey 64 [194]
Diwaniyah, Ad • Iraq 18 D3
Dixon Entrance • BC, Canada 38 E6
Diyala • Iraq 18 E3
Diyarbakir • Turkey 18 D2
Dja • Cameroon/Congo 22 G4
Dja, Réserve du **Heritage N** • Cameroon 61 [80]
Dja, Réserve du **Park** • Cameroon 103 [39]
Djado • Niger 20 H4
Djado, Plateau de • Niger 20 H4
Djambala • Congo 22 G5
Djanet • Algeria 20 G4
Djaret • Algeria 20 F3
Djavat • F.Y.R. of Macedonia 15 C2
Djedi • Algeria 20 F2
Djelfa • Algeria 20 F2
Djemila • Algeria 20 G1
Djemila **Heritage C** • Algeria 64 [222]
Djenne • Mali 20 E6
Djenne **Heritage C** • Mali 63 [94]
Djerdap Nat. Park **Park** • Fed. Rep. of Yugoslavia 72 [116]
Djerem • Cameroon 22 G3
Djibo • Burkina Faso 22 D2
Djibouti • Djibouti 21 H5
Djibouti • Africa 21 H5
Djoua • Congo/Gabon 22 G4
Djoudj Nat. Bird Sanctuary **Heritage N** • Senegal 61 [71]
Djoudj, Parc nat. des Oiseaux du **Heritage N** • Senegal 61 [71]
Djoudj, Parc nat. des Oiseaux du **Park** • Senegal 103 [6]
Djouf, El • Mali/Mauritania 20 D4
Djoum • Cameroon 22 G4
Djourab, Erg du • Chad 22 H1
Djúpivogur • Iceland 16 (1) F2
Djurs Sommerland **Park** • Denmark 73 [15]
Djurs Sommerland • Denmark 95 F10
Djursdala • Sweden 95 F8
Djursland • Denmark 95 F10
Dmitriya Lapteva, Proliv • Russian Fed. 27 N2
Dmitrov • Russian Fed. 97 E4
Dnepr • Ukraine 17 E5
Dneprodzerzhinsk • Ukraine 17 E5
Dnepropetrovsk • Ukraine 17 F5
Dnestr • Moldova/Ukraine 17 D5
Doaktown • NB, Canada 123 D7
Doba • Chad 23 B2
Dobbiaco • Italy 90 B2
Dobel **Spa** • Germany 83 [180]
Dobele • Latvia 16 L8
Döbeln • Germany 9 I5
Doberai, Jazirah • Indonesia 32 (1) D3
Dobiacco **Ski** • Italy 70 [237]
Dobo • Indonesia 32 (1) D4
Doboj • Bosnia-Herz. 14 F5
Dobreta-Turnu Severin • Romania 14 J5
Dobrich • Bulgaria 97 D4
Dobrodsja • Romania 97 D2
Dobrudzansko Plato • Bulgaria 14 O6
Doce • Brazil 127 C2
Docker River • NT, Australia 112 H3
Doctor Phillips • FL, United States 121 C2
Doda Betta • India 106 D10
Dodecanese • Greece 92 D8
Dodekánissa • Greece 15 I7
Dodge City • KS, United States 40 F4
Dodge Ridge **Ski** • CA, United States 116 [61]
Dodoma • Tanzania 102 H2
Dodóni • Greece 15 B4
Dodori Game Reserve • Kenya 101 G4
Doe Mtn **Ski** • PA, United States 116 [164]
Doetinchem • Netherlands 5 J3
Dofa • Indonesia 32 (1) C3
Dog I. • FL, United States 119 M2
Dogai Coring • China 28 E2
Doganbey • Turkey 93 G2
Dogger Bank • North Sea 7 N7
Dogo • Japan 30 G6
Dogu Karadeniz Daglari • Turkey 18 D1
Dogubayazit • Turkey 92 A4
Dogwood Point • St Kitts & Nevis 125 G4
Doha • Qatar 18 F4
Dohad • India 18 J5
Doi Inthanon • Thailand 109 G3
Doi Inthanon Nat. Park • Thailand 109 G3
Doi Khun Tan Nat. Park • Thailand 109 G3
Doi Suthep Nat. Park • Thailand 109 G1
Dokhara, Dunes de • Algeria 20 G2
Dokkum • Netherlands 80 A3
Dokós • Greece 92 D7
Dol-de-Bretagne • France 84 C2
Dolak • Indonesia 32 (1) E4
Dôle • France 10 K6
Dolent, Mt • France/Italy/Switzerland 89 G5
Dolgellau • United Kingdom 7 I9
Dolina • Ukraine 14 K1
Dollard • Germany/Netherlands 8 C3
Dollywood **Park** • TN, United States 121 [Y]
Dolny Kubin • Slovak Rep. 13 I8
Dolo • Ethiopia 23 G3
Dolomites • Italy 90 B
Dolomiti • Italy 90 B
Dolonnur • China 29 F2
Dolores • Uruguay 127 D2
Dolores • Argentina 127 D4
Dolphin, Cape • Falkland Is. 45 E6
Dolphin Coast • South Africa 100 B2
Dolus-d'Oleron **Beach** • France 68 [84]
Dom Pedrito • Brazil 44 F5
Domazlice • Czech Rep. 96 C3
Dombås • Norway 94 C2
Dombóvár • Hungary 13 H11
Domburg • Belgium 5 G3
Domfront • France 5 C6
Dominica • West Indies 37 I4
Dominican Republic • West Indies 37 G4
Domme • France 85 G4
Dommel • Netherlands 5 I3
Domo • Ethiopia 23 H2
Domodedovo [Apt] • Russian Fed. 97 E4
Domodóssola • Italy 91 E2
Domokós • Greece 15 D4
Domuyo, Volcán • Argentina 44 B6
Don • United Kingdom 6 J4
Don • Russian Fed. 17 F4
Don Benito • Spain 11 F6
Don Muang [Apt] • Thailand 109 H2
Don Sak • Thailand 109 F4
Dona Paula Beach • Goa, India 105 B1
Donabate **Beach** • Ireland 68 [54]
Donabate • Ireland 79 E2
Donau • Austria/Germany 9 G8
Donaueschingen • Germany 82 G8
Donauwörth • Germany 9 F8
Doncaster • United Kingdom 7 K8
Dondo • Angola 23 A5
Dondo • Mozambique 24 E3
Dondra Head • Sri Lanka 25 J9
Dondra Head • Sri Lanka 106 D15
Donegal • Ireland 7 D7
Donegal [Adm] • Ireland 79 D1
Donegal Bay • Ireland 7 D7
Donegal Mtns • Ireland 7 D7
Donelson, Fort, Nat. Battlefield **Park** • TN, United States 121 [230]
Donets Basin • Russian Fed./Ukraine 96 A2
Donetsk • Ukraine 17 F5
Dong Bai • China 29 G1
Dong Hai • Asia 29 H5
Dong Hoi • Vietnam 31 D3
Dong Jiang • China 31 F2
Dong Ujmqin Qi • China 27 I7
Dongara • WA, Australia 34 B5
Dongchuan • China 31 C1
Dongfang • China 31 D3
Donggou • China 30 C5
Dongguan • China 107 H2
Dongkala • Indonesia 32 (1) B4
Dongnan Qiuling • China 31 E2
Dongou • Congo 22 H4
Dongsha Qundao • China 31 F2
Dongting Hu • China 29 E5
Dønna • Norway 16 G3
Donner Pass • CA, United States 117 F3
Donner Ski Ranch **Ski** • CA, United States 116 [51]
Donnybrook • WA, Australia 34 C6
Donore • Ireland 79 E2
Donostia • Spain 11 J1
Donoússa • Greece 92 D8
Doolin • Ireland 79 F4
Doonass, Falls of • Ireland 79 F6
Doorn • Netherlands 80 C4
Dor • Israel 98 A3
Dora Baltea • Italy 91 E5
Dora Riparia • Italy 10 M8
Dorada, Costa • Spain 87 D3
Dorado • Puerto Rico 125 E2
Dorchester • United Kingdom 74 F3
Dordogne • France 85 G1
Dordogne [Adm] • France 85 G2
Dordogne, Gorges de la • France 85 G2
Dordrecht • Netherlands 80 C3
Dore • France 10 I8
Doré Lake • SA, Canada 38 J6
Dores do Indaiá • Brazil 127 C1
Dorfen • Germany 82 J3
Dorfgastein • Austria 89 H4
Dorgali • Sardinia, Italy 12 D8
Dori • Burkina Faso 22 D2
Doring • South Africa 100 C2
Dormagen • Germany 81 E3
Dornbirn • Austria 89 H1
Dornoch • United Kingdom 6 H4
Dornoch **Beach** • United Kingdom 75 [2]
Dornoch Firth • United Kingdom 6 I4
Dornum **Spa** • Germany 83 [44]
Dornumersiel **Spa** • Germany 83 [44]
Dorog • Hungary 13 H10
Dorohoi • Romania 14 N2
Dorotea • Sweden 16 H4
Dorset • United Kingdom 74 F3
Dorsten • Germany 81 E1
Dortmund • Germany 81 E2
Dortmund, Florianturm • Germany 81 E2
Dortmund: Syburg • Germany 81 E2
Dortmund, Tierpark • Germany 81 E2
Dortmund-Ems-Kanal • Germany 8 C4
Dorum **Spa** • Germany 83 [53]
Dorval [Apt] • QU, Canada 122 B7
Dos Hermanas • Spain 11 F7
Dösmealti • Turkey 93 G1
Dospat • Bulgaria 15 E2
Dosso • Niger 20 F6
Dothan • AL, United States 119 M2
Douai • France 10 I3
Douala • Cameroon 22 F4
Douarnenez • France 84 C3
Double, Fôret de la • France 85 G1
Double I. • Hong Kong, China 107 H4
Doubs • France 10 L6
Doubtful Sound • New Zealand 112 L1
Douentza • Mali 20 E6
Douera • Algeria 11 N8
Dougga **Heritage C** • Tunisia 64 [225]
Dougga • Tunisia 101 E1
Douglas • Isle of Man 7 H7
Douglas • South Africa 24 C5
Douglas • GA, United States 41 J5
Douglas • AZ, United States 118 J4
Douglas, Mt • QL, Australia 111 F3
Douglass, Frederick, Nat. Hist. Site **Park** • DC, United States 121 [285]
Doukáto, Akra • Greece 92 C1
Doullens • France 10 H3
Dounmen • Zhuhai, China 107 H1
Dourada, Costa da • Portugal 88 A3
Dourados • Brazil 44 F3
Dourdan • France 85 E3
Douro • Portugal 11 D3
Douz • Tunisia 101 E5
Dove Cottage • United Kingdom 74 C2
Dover • United Kingdom 74 E4
Dover • DE, United States 118 H3
Dover, Strait of • France/UK 74 E4
Dover-Foxcroft • ME, United States 118 G2
Dovercourt **Beach** • United Kingdom 75 [50]
Dovrefjell • Norway 16 E5
Dovrefjell Nat. Park **Park** • Norway 72 [12]
Dovrefjell Nat. Park • Norway 94 C2
Down • United Kingdom 75 A3
Downings **Beach** • Ireland 68 [65]
Downpatrick • United Kingdom 7 G7
Downunderland • NS, Australia 111 G2
Dowth • Ireland 79 E2
Drâa • Algeria/Morocco 101 D5
Drâa, Cap • Morocco 101 D5
Draa el Baguel • Algeria 20 G2
Drâa, Vallée du • Morocco 101 D6
Drac • France 85 F3
Drac, Coves del • Majorca, Spain 87 H2
Drachenfels • Germany 82 H1
Drachten • Netherlands 5 J1
Dragan • Sweden 16 H4
Dragasani • Romania 14 L5
Dragon's Mouths • Trinidad/Venezuela 125 K1
Dragonáda • Greece 93 E4
Dragonera, I. • Majorca, Spain 87 H1
Dragsholm **Beach** • Denmark 68 [43]
Draguignan • France 85 H4
Drake Passage • Antarctica 46 (1) HH4
Drakensberg • South Africa 24 D6
Dráma • Greece 92 D1
Drammen • Norway 94 B1
Drangajökull • Iceland 16 (1) B1
Drangedal • Norway 94 B3
Drápano, Akra • Crete, Greece 93 E2
Drau • Austria 13 D11
Drava • Croatia 14 E4
Drayton Manor Park **Park** • United Kingdom 73 [29]
Drayton Manor Park • United Kingdom 74 D2
Dreamworld • QL, Australia 111 F6
Dreihermspitze • Austria/Italy 90 B2
Drenthe • Netherlands 80 A4
Drépano, Akra • Greece 15 E4
Dresden • Germany 9 I5
Dreux • France 85 E3
Drievliet, Familiepark **Park** • Netherlands 73 [44]
Drina • F.R. of Yugoslavia 14 G5
Drinit, Gjiri i • Albania 14 G8
Driochead Atha • Ireland 79 E2
Drøbak • Norway 94 B2
Drochia • Moldova 14 O1
Drogheda • Ireland 79 E2
Drogobych • Ukraine 13 M8
Droichead Nua • Ireland 79 E3
Drôme • France 10 K9
Dronne • France 10 F8
Dronningslund **Beach** • Denmark 68 [48]
Drosia • Greece 92 D4
Drottningholm • Sweden 95 D4
Drottningholm Palace **Heritage C** • Sweden 64 [5]
Drovyanaya • Russian Fed. 46 H2
Drumcliff • Ireland 79 F2
Drumheller • AL, Canada 122 C4
Drummondville • QU, Canada 122 B4
Drusillas Park • United Kingdom 74 E3
Druzhba • Kazakhstan 26 N8
Druzhba • Bulgaria 97 D4
Drvar • Bosnia-Herz. 14 D5
Drweca • Poland 13 I4
Dry Falls • WA, United States 117 E2
Dry Harbour Mtns • Jamaica 124 C1
Dry Tortugas Nat. Park • FL, United States 119 M7
Dry Tortugas Nat. Park **Park** • FL, United States 121 [228]
Drygalski Ice Tongue • Antarctica 46 (1) W2
Drysdale • WA, Australia 34 E2
Drysdale River Nat. Park • WA, Australia 34 E3
Dschang • Cameroon 22 G3
Dsungar Alatau • China/Kazakhstan 26 N8
Du'ayn, Ad • Sudan 23 D1
Duarte • Dominican Rep. 37 G4
Dubai • United Arab Emirates 18 G4
Dubasari • Moldova 14 O2
Dubawnt • NT, Canada 38 K4
Dubawnt Lake • NT/NU, Canada 38 K4
Dubbo • NS, Australia 34 I6
Dublin • Ireland 79 E2
Dublin [Adm] • Ireland 79 E2
Dublin Bay • Ireland 79 E2
Dubna • Russian Fed. 97 E4
Dubrovnik • Croatia 14 F7
Dubrovnik **Heritage C** • Croatia 64 [158]
Dubuque • IA, United States 41 H3
Duc de Gloucester • French Polynesia 33 M8
Duchess • QL, Australia 34 G4
Ducie • Pitcairn Is. 33 O8
Duddon • United Kingdom 74 C3
Duden • Turkey 93 G3
Düdenbasi • Turkey 93 G1
Düdensuyu • Turkey 93 G2
Duderstadt • Germany 8 F5
Dudhsagar Falls • Goa, India 105 B2
Dudhwa Nat. Park • India 105 C3
Dudinka • Russian Fed. 26 O4
Duero • Spain 11 E3
Dugi Otok • Croatia 14 B5
Duino • Italy 91 E4
Duinrell **Park** • Netherlands 73 [43]
Duinrell • Netherlands 80 C1
Duisburg • Germany 81 E1
Duisburg: Hamborn • Germany 81 E1
Duisburg: Homberg • Germany 81 E1
Duisburg: Rheinhausen • Germany 81 E1
Duitama • Colombia 43 C2
Duiveland • Netherlands 80 A10
Dujuma • Somalia 23 G3
Dukagjini • Albania 14 G7
Dukhan • Qatar 18 F4
Dukou • China 29 C5
Dulan • China 29 B3
Dulas **Beach** • United Kingdom 75 [224]
Dulce • Argentina 44 D4
Duleek • Ireland 79 E2
Dulles [Apt] • VA, United States 118 H3
Dülmen • Germany 8 C5
Duluth • MN, United States 41 H2
Dumaguete • Philippines 31 G5
Dumai • Indonesia 110 B4
Dumas • TX, United States 40 F4
Dumbarton • United Kingdom 74 B3
Dumford, Punta • Western Sahara 20 B4
Dumfries • United Kingdom 7 I6
Dumfriesshire • United Kingdom 75 A3
Dümmersee • Germany 5 L2
Dumont d'Urville [Base] • Antarctica 46 (1) T3
Dumont d'Urville Sea • Antarctica 46 (1) S3
Dumpu • Papua New Guinea 35 (1) D2
Dümrek • Turkey 15 J5
Dumyât • Egypt 101 F2
Dún Aengus • Ireland 79 F3

Dún Dealgan • Ireland 7 F7
Dún Laoghaire • Ireland 79 E2
Duna • Hungary 13 H11
Duna-Tisza Köz • Hungary 14 G3
Dunaföldvár • Hungary 13 H11
Dunaj • Slovak Rep. 13 G9
Dunajská Sreda • Slovak Rep. 13 G9
Dunántúl • Hungary 13 G11
Dunarea • Romania 14 K6
Dunas Beach • Goa, India 105 B1
Dunaújváros • Hungary 13 H10
Dunav • Europe 14 L6
Dunay • Russian Fed. 30 G3
Dunbartonshire • United Kingdom 74 B3
Dunblane • United Kingdom 74 B1
Dunboyne • Ireland 79 E2
Duncan • BC, Canada 122 C3
Duncan Passage • India 28 F6
Duncannon **Beach** • Ireland 68 [56]
Dundalk • Ireland 7 F7
Dundalk Bay • Ireland 7 F8
Dundas Peninsula • NT, Canada 38 I2
Dundee • United Kingdom 74 B2
Dunedin • New Zealand 35 C7
Dunfanaghy • Ireland 7 E6
Dunfermline • United Kingdom 74 B4
Dungarvan • Ireland 7 E9
Dungeness • United Kingdom 74 E4
Dunhua • China 27 K8
Dunhuang • China 29 A2
Dunk I. • QL, Australia 111 F1
Dunkeld • United Kingdom 74 B2
Dunkerque • France 10 H2
Dunkery Beacon • United Kingdom 7 I10
Dunkirk • France 80 A13
Dunlavin • Ireland 79 E3
Dunloe, Gap of • Ireland 79 F7
Dunmanus Bay • Ireland 79 F7
Dunmanway • Ireland 79 F8
Dunmarra • NT, Australia 34 F3
Dunmore • Ireland 79 F4
Dunmore East **Beach** • Ireland 68 [58]
Dunmore Town • Bahamas 124 B1
Dunn's River Falls • Jamaica 124 C2
Dunnet Head • United Kingdom 6 I3
Dunnville • OT, Canada 122 B9
Dunoon • United Kingdom 78 A3
Dunquin • Ireland 79 F5
Dunqulah • Sudan 21 F4
Dunshaughlin • Ireland 79 E1
Dunstan Mtns • New Zealand 112 L2
Dunster • United Kingdom 74 F2
Duntroon • New Zealand 35 C7
Duolun • China 29 F2
Dupnitsa • Bulgaria 15 E1
Duqm • Oman 18 G6
Duque de Caxias • Brazil 127 C4
Durack Ranges • WA, Australia 34 E3
Durance • France 10 L9
Durandeau • St Lucia 125 J1
Durango • Spain 11 I1
Durango • Mexico 40 F7
Durango • CO, United States 118 J2
Durango [Adm] • Mexico 40 F7
Durankulak • Bulgaria 97 D2
Durant • MS, United States 118 K2
Durant • OK, United States 119 N1
Durazno • Uruguay 127 D2
Durazzo • Albania 71 A19
Durban • South Africa 24 E5
Düren • Germany 82 G1
Durgapur • India 28 E4
Durham • United Kingdom 7 K7
Durham • NC, United States 41 K4
Durham **Heritage C** • United Kingdom 64 [16]
Durmitor • F.R. of Yugoslavia 14 F6
Durmitor Nat. Park **Heritage N** • F.R. of Yugoslavia 61 [53]
Durmitor Nat. Park **Park** • Fed. Rep. of Yugoslavia 72 [118]
Durrës • Albania 14 G8
Durresit, Gjiri i • Albania 14 G8
Dursey I. • Ireland 79 F7
Dursunbey • Turkey 15 J4
Durusu Gölü • Turkey 15 J2
Duruz • Syria 21 G1
Dusa Mareb • Somalia 23 H2
Dushan • China 31 D1
Dushanbe • Tajikistan 18 I2
Dusky Sound • New Zealand 112 L3
Düsseldorf • Germany 81 E3
Düsseldorf: Kaiserswerth • Germany 81 E3
Dutch Harbor • AK, United States 36 (1) E2
Duvkh Tsirkov, gora • Russian Fed. 27 S3
Duvno • Bosnia-Herz. 14 E6
Duwayhin • United Arab Emirates 18 F5
Duwaym, Ad • Sudan 21 F5
Duyfken Point • QL, Australia 34 H2
Duyun • China 29 D5
Düzce • Turkey 15 M3
Dvinskaya Guba • Russian Fed. 17 F2
Dwingelderveld, Nat. Park **Park** • Netherlands 72 [52]
Dwingelderveld, Nat. Park • Netherlands 80 A4
Dyje • Czech Rep. 13 F9
Dylewska Góra • Poland 13 I4
Dymchurch • United Kingdom 74 E4
Dymchurch **Beach** • United Kingdom 75 [65]
Dyrehavsbakken **Park** • Denmark 73 [17]
Dzamin Üüd • Mongolia 29 E2
Dzanga-Sangha, Réserve du **Park** • Central African Rep. 103 [46]
Dzaoudzi • Comoros 24 H2
Dzerzhinsk • Belarus 16 N10
Dzerzhinsk • Russian Fed. 17 G3
Dzhagdy, Khrebet • Russian Fed. 27 L6
Dzhankoy • Ukraine 17 E5
Dzhardzhan • Russian Fed. 27 J3
Dzhebel • Bulgaria 15 G2
Dzhetygara • Kazakhstan 26 J7
Dzhezkazgan • Kazakhstan 26 K8
Dzhugdzhur, Khrebet • Russian Fed. 27 M5
Dzhusaly • Kazakhstan 26 J8
Dzialdowo • Poland 13 J4
Dzialoszyce • Poland 13 J7
Dzierzoniów • Poland 13 F7
Dzukija Nat. Park **Park** • Lithuania 72 [148]

Eagle Farm [Apt] • QL, Australia 111 F6
Eagle Lake • ME, United States 118 G2
Eagle Pass • TX, United States 40 F6
Earn • United Kingdom 74 B1
Earn, Loch • United Kingdom 74 B1
Earnslaw, Mt • New Zealand 112 L2
East Alligator • NT, Australia 34 F2
East Anglia • United Kingdom 75 A5
East Cape • New Zealand 35 G3
East China Sea • Asia 29 H5
East Coast Park • Singapore 108 E4
East Falkland • Falkland Is. 45 E6
East Grinstead • United Kingdom 5 C3
East Kilbride • United Kingdom 74 B3
East Lake Tohopekaliga • FL, United States 121 C2
East London • South Africa 24 D6
East Lothian • United Kingdom 75 A2
East Prussia • Poland 13 J3
East Retford • United Kingdom 5 C1
East Riding • United Kingdom 75 A4
East Siberian Sea • Arctic Ocean 46 II2
Eastbourne • United Kingdom 74 E3
Eastbourne **Beach** • United Kingdom 75 [70]
Easter I. • Pacific Ocean 33 Q8
Eastern Cape • South Africa 24 D6
Eastern Desert • Egypt 101 F4
Eastern Mediterranean Coast • Turkey 92 A3
Eastern Valleys • Norway 94 A7
Eastleigh • United Kingdom 7 K11
Eastmain • QU, Canada 39 P6
Eastmain [Riv] • QU, Canada 39 Q6
Eau Claire • WI, United States 41 H3
Ebbw Vale • United Kingdom 7 I10
Ebebiyin • Equatorial Guinea 22 G4
Ebeltoft **Beach** • Denmark 68 [47]
Ebeltoft • Denmark 95 F10
Eber Gölü • Turkey 15 M5
Eberbach • Germany 82 G4
Eberbach **Spa** • Germany 83 [170]
Eberbach, Kloster • Germany 82 H4
Ebersberg • Germany 82 J3
Eberswalde-Finow • Germany 8 I4
Ebey's Landing Nat. Hist. Reserve **Park** • WA, United States 120 [25]
Eboli • Italy 91 G4
Ebolowa • Cameroon 22 G4
Ebre, Delta de l' • Spain 11 L4
Ebro • Spain 11 K3
Ebro, Embalse del • Spain 11 H2
Ebschloh • Germany 5 L3
Echdeina • Western Sahara 20 C3
Echo Bay • NT, Canada 38 H3
Echternach • Luxembourg 80 A20
Echuca • VI, Australia 111 G3
Ecija • Spain 86 B2
Eckenhagen **Spa** • Germany 83 [113]
Eckental • Germany 9 G7
Eckernförde • Germany 8 E2
Eckernförde **Spa** • Germany 83 [14]
Eckerö • Finland 95 E3
Eckwarden **Spa** • Germany 83 [52]
Eclipse Sound • NU, Canada 39 P2
Ecouen • France 85 E1
Ecrins, Parc nat. des **Park** • France 72 [67]
Ecrins, Parc nat. des • France 85 F4
Ecuador • S. America 43 B4
Ed • Sweden 95 F2
Edam • Netherlands 80 C2
Eday • United Kingdom 6 J2
Edchera • Western Sahara 20 C3
Eddystone Rocks • United Kingdom 74 F5
Ede • Nigeria 22 E3
Ede • Netherlands 80 A7
Edea • Cameroon 22 G4
Edelsteinmine • Germany 82 H3
Edelweiss Valley **Ski** • QU, Canada 116 [26]
Edemissen • Germany 8 F4
Eden • United Kingdom 74 C2
Eden • NS, Australia 111 G4
Eden Brown • St Kitts & Nevis 125 G4
Edendale • New Zealand 112 L4
Edenderry • Ireland 79 E1
Edenlandia **Park** • Italy 73 [86]
Eder • Germany 9 D5
Eder-Stausee • Germany 5 M3
Edessa • Greece 15 D3
Edewecht • Germany 8 D3
Edfu • Egypt 101 F5
Edgar Ranges • WA, Australia 34 D3
Edgeleh • Algeria 20 G3
Edgell I. • NU, Canada 39 S4
Edinburgh **Heritage C** • United Kingdom 64 [13]
Edinburgh • United Kingdom 74 B4
Edincik • Turkey 15 I3
Edirne • Turkey 15 H2
Edison Nat. Hist. Site **Park** • NJ, United States 121 [334]
Edland • Norway 94 C6
Edmonton • AL, Canada 122 C2
Edmunston • NB, Canada 123 D1
Edremit • Turkey 92 D5
Edremit Körfezi • Turkey 15 H4
Edsbro • Sweden 95 D2
Edson • AL, Canada 122 C2
Eduardo Castex • Argentina 44 D6
Edward, Lake • Uganda/Dem. Rep. of Congo 23 D4
Edwards Creek • SA, Australia 34 G5
Edwards Plateau • TX, United States 40 F5
Edzo • NT, Canada 38 H4
Eeklo • Netherlands 5 G3
Eelde [Apt] • Netherlands 80 A4
Eemshaven • Netherlands 80 A4
Efaté • Vanuatu 35 (2) B2
Eferding • Austria 9 I8
Efes • Turkey 92 D9
Effigy Mounds Nat. Mon. **Park** • IA, United States 121 [168]
Eflani • Turkey 15 N2
Eforie Nord • Romania 97 D2
Eforie Sud • Romania 97 D2
Efxinoúpolis **Beach** • Greece 69 [188]
Ega • Spain 10 C11
Ega, Val d' • Italy 90 B3
Egadi, Is. • Italy 90 D1
Eger • Germany 9 H6
Eger • Hungary 13 J10
Egersund • Norway 16 D7
Egeskov • Denmark 95 F14
Eggenfelden • Germany 82 J4
Eghezée • Belgium 5 H4
Egina • Greece 92 D7
Egio • Greece 15 C2
Egirdir **Beach** • Turkey 69 [240]
Eglab Dersa • Algeria 20 E3
Eglab, El • Algeria 20 E3
Egmont, Cape • New Zealand 112 K3
Egmont, Mt • New Zealand 112 K3
Egmont Nat. Park • New Zealand 112 K3
Egnazia • Italy 14 E9
Egremont • United Kingdom 74 C1
Egridir • Turkey 93 G2
Egridir Gölü • Turkey 15 L5
Egrigöz Dagi • Turkey 15 K4
Egvekinot • Russian Fed. 27 V3
Egypt • Africa 21 E3
Ehingen • Germany 82 J1
Ehlscheid **Spa** • Germany 83 [152]
Ehrenbreitstein • Germany 82 H2
Ehrwald **Ski** • Austria 70 [139]
Ehrwald • Austria 89 H2
Eibar • Spain 11 I1
Eichstätt • Germany 9 G8
Eichwalde • Germany 81 F4
Eidanger • Norway 94 B3
Eider • Germany 8 E2
Eidfjord • Norway 94 C4
Eidfjorden • Norway 94 C4
Eidsdal • Norway 94 C2
Eidsfoss • Norway 94 B1
Eidsvåg • Norway 94 C2
Eidsvoll • Norway 94 B2
Eifel • Germany 82 G1
Eifelpark **Park** • Germany 73 [62]
Eifelpark • Germany 82 H3
Eigat • Egypt 21 G3
Eiger • Switzerland 89 G2
Eigg • United Kingdom 6 F5
Eight Degree Channel • Indian Ocean 106 D13
Eikeren • Norway 94 B1
Eikesdalsvatnet • Norway 94 C2
Eilat • Israel 18 B4
Eileithyia • Crete, Greece 93 E3
Einasleigh • QL, Australia 34 H3
Einbeck • Germany 8 E5
Eindhoven • Netherlands 80 A11
Einsiedeln • Switzerland 89 G3
Einslow • AZ, United States 118 J1
Eirunepé • Brazil 43 D5
Eisenach • Germany 9 F6
Eisenberg • Germany 9 G6
Eisenerz • Austria 13 D10
Eisenhower Birthplace State Hist. Site • TX, United States 119 N1
Eisenhower Nat. Hist. Site **Park** • PA, United States 121 [304]
Eisenhüttenstadt • Germany 8 J4
Eisenstadt • Austria 13 F10
Eisenwurzen • Austria 14 B2
Eisleben • Germany 8 G5
Eisleben **Heritage C** • Germany 64 [32]
Eitorf • Germany 5 K4
Eivissa • Ibiza, Spain 87 G2
Eivissa [I.] • Spain 87 G
Eje, Sierra del • Spain 11 E2
Ejea de los Caballeros • Spain 11 J2
Ekenäs • Finland 95 E4
Eketorpsborg • Sweden 95 F12
Ekibastuz • Kazakhstan 26 M7
Eklingji • India 105 C5
Ekoli • Dem. Rep. of Congo 23 C4
Ekoln • Sweden 95 D2
Ekonda • Russian Fed. 26 S3
Eksjö • Sweden 95 F8
Ekwan • OT, Canada 39 O6
El Abrigo • Tenerife, Canary Is. 86 E1
El Arahal • Spain 11 F7
El Banco • Colombia 43 C2
El Baúl • Venezuela 43 D2
El Cabo de Gata • Spain 86 B8
El Callao • Venezuela 43 E2
El Campo • TX, United States 119 N5
El Cañuelo • Puerto Rico 125 E2
El Carmen de Bolivar • Colombia 43 B2
El Cerro • Bolivia 44 D2
El Cerro de Aripo • Trinidad & Tobago 125 K1
El Cuy • Argentina 45 C3
El Dorado • Venezuela 37 I6
El Dorado • AR, United States 41 H5
El Ejido **Beach** • Spain 68 [116]
El Ejido • Spain 86 B8
El Encanto • Colombia 43 C4
El Escorial • Spain 11 G4
El Escorial **Heritage C** • Spain 64 [87]
El Ferrol • Spain 11 C1
El Jem **Heritage C** • Tunisia 64 [230]
El Maestrazgo • Spain 11 K4
El Maitén • Argentina 45 B4
El Malpais Nat. Mon. • NM, United States 118 J2
El Malpais Nat. Mon. **Park** • NM, United States 120 [127]
El Masnou **Beach** • Spain 68 [122]
El Masnou • Spain 87 D4
El Medano • Tenerife, Canary Is. 86 E1
El Molinar • Majorca, Spain 87 H1
El Morro • Cuba 124 D8
El Morro, Castillo • Puerto Rico 125 E2
El Morro Nat. Mon. • NM, United States 118 J2
El Morro Nat. Mon. **Park** • NM, United States 120 [126]
El Nevado, Cerro • Argentina 44 C6
El Palo • Spain 86 B7
El Paso • TX, United States 118 J4
El Pico • Bolivia 44 D2
El Pilar • Formentera, Spain 87 G4
El Pital • Mexico 123 E2
El Port de la Selva **Beach** • Spain 68 [123]
El Potosí • Mexico 37 A3
El Prat de Llobregat • Spain 11 N3
El Puerto de Santa Maria • Spain 86 B5
El Qâhira **Heritage C** • Egypt 64 [237]
El Rompido • Spain 86 B1
El Salto • Mexico 37 (1) A1
El Salvador • C. America 37 D5
El Sueco • Mexico 40 E6
El Tajín **Heritage C** • Mexico 62 [18]
El Tajín • Mexico 123 E2
El Tigre • Venezuela 43 E2
El Torro • Minorca, Spain 87 F2
El Turbio • Argentina 45 B6
El Vendrell **Beach** • Spain 68 [121]
El Vendrell • Spain 87 D3
El Vizcaíno whale sanctuary **Heritage N** • Mexico 60 [18]
El Yunque • Puerto Rico 125 E2
Elaea **Beach** • Greece 69 [182]
Elafonisi • Crete, Greece 93 E5
Eland Sanctuary • Zimbabwe 102 J4
Elassóna • Greece 15 D4
Elat • Israel 18 E12
Eláti • Greece 15 B5
Elâzig • Turkey 15 C2
Elba, I. d' • Italy 91 E10
Elbasan • Albania 14 H8
Elbe • Germany 8 F3
Elbert, Mt • CO, United States 40 E4
Elbeuf • France 10 F4
Elblag • Poland 13 I3
Elbrus • Georgia/Russian Fed. 17 G6
Elburz • Iran 18 E2
Elche **Beach** • Spain 68 [118]
Elche • Spain 87 C1
Elcho I. • NT, Australia 34 G2
Elda • Spain 87 C1
Eldab • Somalia 23 H2
Elde • Germany 8 G3
Eldikan • Russian Fed. 27 M4
Eldora Mtn **Ski** • CO, United States 116 [89]
Eldoret • Kenya 101 G1
Elephant Butte Reservoir • NM, United States 118 J4
Elephant Village • Pattaya, Thailand 109 H4
Elephanta Caves **Heritage C** • India 63 [125]
Elephantine I. • Egypt 101 F5
Eleuthera • Bahamas 124 B1
Elgin • United Kingdom 6 I4
Elgin • IL, United States 41 I3
Elginskiy • Russian Fed. 27 N4
Elgon, Mt • Kenya/Uganda 101 G1
Elgoran • Ethiopia 23 G2
Elgyay • Russian Fed. 27 I4
Elia **Beach** • Crete, Greece 69 [214]
Elila • Dem. Rep. of Congo 23 D4
Elin Pelin • Bulgaria 14 K7
Eliot • NT, Australia 34 F3
Elista • Russian Fed. 17 G5
Elizabeth • SA, Australia 34 G6
Elizabeth City • NC, United States 118 H5
Elizabeth Reef • Australia 33 H9
Elizabethtown • KY, United States 41 I4
Elk • Poland 13 L4
Elk I. Nat. Park • AL, Canada 122 C2
Elkhovo • Bulgaria 97 D3
Elko • NV, United States 117 F2
Ellensburg • WA, United States 117 E1
Ellertrin, Plains of • Ireland 79 F4
Ellesmere I. • NU, Canada 36 I2
Ellice Is. • Tuvalu 33 I6
Elliot Lake • OT, Canada 39 O7
Elliot, Mt • QL, Australia 111 F1
Elliston • SA, Australia 34 F6
Ellmau **Ski** • Austria 70 [153]
Ellmau • Austria 89 H3
Ellora Caves **Heritage C** • India 63 [124]
Ellsworth Land • Antarctica 46 (1) FF2
Ellwangen • Germany 9 F8
Elmali • Turkey 93 G3
Elmdon [Apt] • United Kingdom 74 D2
Elmira • NY, United States 118 H1
Elmshorn • Germany 8 E3
Elne • France 11 O2
Elorza • Venezuela 43 D2
Eloúnda **Beach** • Crete, Greece 69 [215]
Eloúnda • Crete, Greece 93 E8
Elsdorf • Germany 81 E3
Else • Germany 5 L2
Elsehul • South Georgia 59 A10
Elsen Nur • China 28 F1
Elstal • Germany 81 F1
Elsterwerda • Germany 8 I5
Eltanin Bay • Antarctica 46 (1) GG2
Eltham • New Zealand 112 K3
Eltville • Germany 82 H4
Eltz, Burg • Germany 82 H1
Elura • India 28 B5
Eluru • India 106 D3
Elvas • Portugal 11 D6
Elverum • Norway 16 F6
Elx **Beach** • Spain 68 [118]
Elx • Spain 87 C1
Ely • United Kingdom 7 M9
Ely • NV, United States 117 F4
Elzas • France 9 C8
Emal • Vanuatu 35 (2) B2
Emamshar • Iran 18 G2
Emån • Sweden 95 F8
Emanuel • Antigua & Barbuda 125 F3
Emao • Vanuatu 35 (2) B2
Emba • Kazakhstan 26 I8
Emba [Riv] • Kazakhstan 26 I8
Embarcación • Argentina 44 D3
Embarras Portage • AL, Canada 38 I5
Embonas • Rhodes, Greece 93 F1
Embrun • France 85 F4
Embudhu • Maldives 106 E4
Embudhu Finolhu • Maldives 106 E4
Emden • Germany 8 C3
Emei Shan **Heritage N** • China 61 [117]
Emei Shan **Heritage C** • China 63 [156]
Emei Shan • China 107 G7
Emerald • QL, Australia 111 F3
Emeraude, Côte d' • France 84 C2
Emet • Turkey 15 K4
Emi Koussi • Chad 21 C4
Emilia-Romagna • Italy 91 E7
Emily Rock • Pacific Ocean 42 B7
Emine, Nos • Bulgaria 14 O7
Emirdag • Turkey 15 M4
Emlichheim • Germany 8 B4
Emmaboda • Sweden 95 F12
Emmaste • Estonia 16 L7
Emmeloord • Netherlands 80 A7
Emmen • Netherlands 80 A8
Emmendingen • Germany 9 C8
Emmerich • Germany 5 J3
Emmet • QL, Australia 34 H4
Emory Peak • TX, United States 40 F6
Empalme • Mexico 40 D6
Empoli • Italy 12 E5
Emporda • Spain 87 D2
Emporia • KS, United States 41 G4
Empúries • Spain 87 D2
Ems • Germany 8 C4
Ems-Jade-Kanal • Germany 5 K1
Emsdetten • Germany 5 K2
Emsland • Germany 8 C4
En Colom, I. d' • Minorca, Spain 87 F4
En Gedi • Israel 98 A8
Enaratoli • Indonesia 32 (1) E3
Enare träsk • Finland 16 N2
Encantada • Mexico 40 C5
Encarnación • Paraguay 44 E4
Enchi • Ghana 22 D3
Encounter Bay • SA, Australia 34 G7
Ende • Indonesia 32 (1) B4
Endelave • Denmark 95 F10
Enderby Land • Antarctica 46 (1) K3
Ené • Peru 44 B1
Enez • Turkey 15 H3
Enez Körfezi • Turkey 15 G3
Enfidaville • Tunisia 12 E12
Engelberg **Ski** • Switzerland 70 [103]
Engelberg • Switzerland 89 G3
Engels • Russian Fed. 17 H4
Engelsberg **Heritage C** • Sweden 64 [3]
Engelskirchen • Germany 81 E4
Enggano • Indonesia 32 C4
England • United Kingdom 7
England, East • United Kingdom 75 A5
England, North West • United Kingdom 75 A4
England, Southeast • United Kingdom 74 E
England, Southern • United Kingdom 75 A6
Englee • NF, Canada 123 D5
English Channel • France/UK 10 D3
English Harbour • Antigua & Barbuda 125 F4
English Harbour Town • Antigua & Barbuda 125 F4
English Riviera • United Kingdom 74 F5
Enh-Gajvan • Mongolia 26 Q8
Enid • OK, United States 41 G4
Eniwetok • Marshall Is. 33 H4
Enkhuizen • Netherlands 80 A7
Enkirch • Germany 82 H3
Enköping • Sweden 95 D1
Enna • Sicily, Italy 90 D4
Ennadai Lake • NU, Canada 38 K4
Ennedi • Chad 21 D4
Ennepetal • Germany 81 E4
Ennepetal **Spa** • Germany 83 [107]
Ennerdale Water • United Kingdom 74 C1
Enneri Miski • Chad 21 C4
Ennis • Ireland 79 F6
Enniscorthy • Ireland 7 F9
Enniskerry • Ireland 79 E4
Enniskillen • United Kingdom 7 E7
Ennistymon • Ireland 79 F4
Enns • Austria 13 D10
Eno • Finland 16 P5
Enontekiö • Finland 16 L2
Enschede • Netherlands 80 A8
Ensenada • Mexico 40 C5
Ensenada • Argentina 127 D2
Enshi • China 29 D4
Entebbe • Uganda 23 E3
Entenbühl • Czech Rep./Germany 9 H7
Enterprise • NT, Canada 38 H4
Enterprise • MS, United States 118 K2
Enterprise • AL, United States 119 M2
Entrance, The • NS, Australia 111 G2
Entre Rios • Argentina 127 A3
Entre-Deux-Mers • France 84 B3
Entrecasteaux, Point d' • WA, Australia 34 C6
Entrecasteaux, Récifs d' • New Caledonia 35 (2) A2
Enugu • Nigeria 22 F3
Envigado • Colombia 43 B2
Envira • Brazil 43 C5
Enz • Germany 9 D8
Enzan • Japan 30 J7
Epanomi **Beach** • Greece 69 [191]
EPCOT Center • FL, United States 121 C1
Epernay • France 10 I4
Ephesus • Turkey 92 D9
Ephraim • Jordan 98 A5
Ephraim, Mount • Jordan 98 A6
Epi • Vanuatu 35 (2) B2
Epidamnus • Albania 14 G8
Epidaurus **Heritage C** • Greece 64 [182]
Epidaurus • Greece 92 D7
Epidavros **Heritage C** • Greece 64 [182]
Epidavros • Greece 92 D7
Epinal • France 10 L5
Epirus • Greece 92 A1
Episkopi • Crete, Greece 93 E2
Episkopi Bay • Cyprus 93 J3
Epping • United Kingdom 74 E1
Epsom • United Kingdom 7 L10
Epsom Downs • United Kingdom 74 E3
Epte • France 10 G4
Epupa Falls • Angola/Namibia 24 A3
Equateur • Dem. Rep. of Congo 23 C3
Equatorial Channel • Maldives 106 E3
Equatorial Guinea • Africa 22 F4
Er Rachidia • Morocco 101 D4
Eraclea Minoa • Sicily, Italy 90 D3
Eratini • Greece 15 D6
Erbach • Germany 5 M5
Erbach • Germany 82 J1
Erbalunga • Corsica, France 85 L2
Erbeskopf • Germany 9 C7
Erciyas Dagi • Turkey 18 C2
Erculano • Italy 91 G3
Erd • Hungary 13 H10
Erdao • China 30 D3
Erdek • Turkey 92 D3
Erdek Körfezi • Turkey 15 I3
Erdeven **Beach** • France 68 [81]
Erdeven • France 84 C4
Erdi • Chad 21 D4
Erdi Ma • Chad 21 D4
Erding • Germany 82 J3
Erdre • France 10 D6
Erebus, Mt • Antarctica 46 (1) W2
Erechim • Brazil 44 F4
Eregli • Turkey 15 M2
Ereke • Indonesia 32 (1) B3
Erenhot • China 29 E2
Eressós **Beach** • Greece 69 [199]
Eressós • Greece 92 D5
Erétria • Greece 15 E5
Erétria **Beach** • Greece 69 [186]
Erfoud • Morocco 101 D6
Erft • Germany 5 J4
Erft • Germany 81 E3
Erftstadt • Germany 82 G1
Erfurt • Germany 9 G6
Ergene • Turkey 15 H2
Ergig, Bahr • Chad 22 H2
Ergun He • China 27 J6
Ergun Zuoqi • China 27 J6
Erice • Sicily, Italy 90 D1
Ericeira • Portugal 88 D1
Ericht, Loch • United Kingdom 6 H5
Erie • PA, United States 41 K3
Erie Canal • NY, United States 122 B10
Erie, Lake • Canada/United States 39 O8
Erigabo • Somalia 23 H1
Erimanthos • Greece 15 C6
Erimo-Misaki • Japan 30 L4
Eringsboda • Sweden 95 F12
Eritrea • Africa 21 G4
Eriydu • Maldives 106 E2
Erken • Sweden 95 D2
Erkner • Germany 81 F4
Erkrath • Germany 81 E3
Erl • Austria 89 H3
Erlangen • Germany 9 G7
Erldunda • NT, Australia 112 H4
Erlebnispark Tripsdrill **Park** • Germany 73 [64]
Erlebnispark Tripsdrill • Germany 82 G6
Erlong Shan • China 27 K8
Ermelo • South Africa 24 E5
Ermenek • Turkey 15 N7
Ermesinde • Portugal 11 C3
Ermióni • Greece 92 D7
Ermones • Corfu, Greece 92 B1
Ernabella • SA, Australia 112 H3
Ernakulam • India 106 D10
Erne, Lough, Lower • United Kingdom 7 E7
Erne, Lough, Upper • United Kingdom 7 E7
Ernest Legouvé • Pacific Ocean 33 L9
Erode • India 106 D10
Erpeler Ley • Germany 82 H1
Erquy • France 84 C2
Errego • Mozambique 24 F3
Erritsø • Denmark 95 F9
Erromango • Vanuatu 35 (2) B2
Erstein • France 9 C8
Erzen • Albania 15 A2
Erzgebirge • Germany 9 I6
Erzin • Russian Fed. 26 Q7
Erzincan • Turkey 92 A4
Erzurum • Turkey 18 D2
Es Canutells • Minorca, Spain 87 F4
Es Canyar • Ibiza, Spain 87 G2
Es Delfins • Minorca, Spain 87 F1
Es Grau • Minorca, Spain 87 F4
Es Mercadal **Beach** • Minorca, Spain 68 [127]
Es Mercadal • Minorca, Spain 87 F2
Es Migjorn Redones Gran Sant Cristòbal • Minorca, Spain 87 F3
Es Pla • Majorca, Spain 87 H2
Es Pujols • Formentera, Spain 87 G4
Es Savina • Formentera, Spain 87 G4
Es Tudóns, Naveta d' • Minorca, Spain 87 F1
Esashi • Japan 30 L2
Esbjerg • Denmark 95 F9
Esbo • Finland 95 E4
Escala, L' **Beach** • Spain 68 [123]
Escala, l' • Spain 87 D2
Escambia • AL/FL, United States 119 M1
Escambray, Sierra del • Cuba 124 D2
Escanaba • MI, United States 41 I2
Escaut • France 80 A14
Esch-sur-Alzette • Luxembourg 80 A20
Esch-sur-Sûre • Luxembourg 80 A20
Eschwege • Germany 9 F5
Eschweiler • Germany 9 B6
Escondido • CA, United States 117 F6
Escuintla • Guatemala 37 C5
Esens-Bensersiel **Spa** • Germany 83 [45]
Esfahan • Iran 18 F3
Esfahan **Heritage C** • Iran 63 [108]
Eshtemoa • Jordan 98 A7
Esino • Italy 12 H5
Esk • United Kingdom 74 C3
Eskilstuna • Sweden 95 D3
Eskimo Lake • NT, Canada 38 E3
Eskisehir • Turkey 15 L4
Eslöv • Sweden 95 F11
Esme • Turkey 15 J5
Esmeraldas • Ecuador 43 B3
Esna • Egypt 101 F4
Espalmador, I. • Ibiza, Spain 87 G4
Española • Galapagos Is. 43 (1) B2
Espardell, I. • Ibiza, Spain 87 G4
Espelkamp • Germany 5 L2
Esperance • WA, Australia 34 D6
Esperance Bay • WA, Australia 34 D6
Esperanza • Argentina 44 D5
Esperanza [Base] • Antarctica 46 (1) JJ3
Espichel, Cabo • Portugal 88 D1
Espigão Mestre • Brazil 44 G1
Espinal • Colombia 43 C3
Espinhaço de Cão, Serra de • Portugal 88 E1
Espinhaço, Serra do • Brazil 44 H2
Espinho • Portugal 11 C3
Espinho **Beach** • Portugal 68 [95]
Espinosa • Brazil 44 H1
Espírito Santo • Brazil 44 H2
Espíritu Santo • Vanuatu 35 (2) B2
Espíritu Santo, Río • Puerto Rico 125 E2
Esplanada • Brazil 44 I1
Espoo • Finland 95 E4
Esposende • Portugal 11 C3
Espungabera • Mozambique 24 E4
Esquel • Argentina 45 B4
Esquina • Argentina 44 E5
Essaouira • Morocco 101 D3
Essen • Germany 81 E1
Essen: Werden • Germany 81 E1
Essendon, Mt • WA, Australia 34 D5
Essequibo • Guyana 43 F3
Essex • United Kingdom 74 E2
Essex • CT, United States 118 H2
Esslingen am Neckar • Germany 82 G6
Esso • Russian Fed. 27 Q5
Essonne • France 85 E3
Est, Pointe de l' • QU, Canada 123 D2
Estados, I. de los • Argentina 45 D6
Estância • Brazil 44 I1
Estarreja • Portugal 11 C4
Estartit, l' • Spain 87 D2
Este • Italy 12 F3
Este, Playas del • Cuba 124 D2
Esteli • Nicaragua 37 D5
Estella • Spain 11 I2
Estellencs • Majorca, Spain 87 H1
Estepa • Spain 86 B2
Estepona **Beach** • Spain 68 [114]
Estepona • Spain 86 B6
Esterel, l' • France 85 H4
Estevan • SA, Canada 38 K7
Estói • Portugal 88 E7
Estonia • Europe 16 M7
Estoril • Portugal 88 D1
Estoril, Costa do • Portugal 88 D1
Estrela, Serra da • Portugal 11 D4
Estremadura • Portugal 11 B5
Estremoz • Portugal 11 D6
Estrondo, Serra do • Brazil 45 (1) B4
Estuario do Tejo, Reserva Natural • Portugal 88 D2
Esztergom • Hungary 13 H10
Et Tleta de Oued Laou • Morocco 101 D2
Etables-sur-Mer **Beach** • France 68 [80]
Etables-sur-Mer • France 84 C2
Etain • France 5 I5
Etampes • France 85 E3
Etaples • France 10 G3
Etawah • India 105 C7
Etel **Beach** • France 68 [81]
Etel • France 84 C4
Eternity Range • Antarctica 46 (1) II3
Ethiopia • Africa 19 H5
Etna, Monte • Sicily, Italy 90 D2
Etne • Norway 94 C5
Etoile • Seychelles 106 F2
Etolin I. • AK, United States 38 E5
Eton • United Kingdom 74 E1
Etorofu To • Russian Fed. 27 O8
Etosha Nat. Park **Park** • Namibia 103 [114]
Etosha Pan • Namibia 24 B3
Etoumbi • Congo 23 B3
Etretat • France 5 D5
Ettal • Germany 82 J6
Ettelbruck • Luxembourg 5 J5
Ettlingen • Germany 5 L6
Eu • France 5 E4
Euboea • Greece 92 D4
Eucla • WA, Australia 34 E6
Eucumbene, Lake • NS, Australia 111 G4
Eugene • OR, United States 117 E3
Eugenia, Punta • Mexico 40 C6
Eugmo • Finland 16 L5
Eunice • LA, United States 118 K3
Eupen • Belgium 5 J4
Euphrates • Asia 18 D3
Eura • Finland 95 E1
Eurajoki • Finland 95 E1
Eure • France 10 G5
Eureka • CA, United States 117 F1
Eureka • NV, United States 117 F2

Euromast • Netherlands 80 C3
Europa Park **Park** • Germany 73 [67]
Europa Park • Germany 82 G7
Europa, Picos de • Spain 11 G1
Europa, Punta de • Gibraltar 86 B6
Europoort • Netherlands 80 C3
Euskirchen • Germany 82 H1
Eutin • Germany 8 F2
Eutin **Spa** • Germany 83 [32]
Evale • Angola 24 B3
Evanger • Norway 94 C3
Evans, Lac • QU, Canada 39 P6
Evans Strait • NU, Canada 39 O4
Evanston • WY, United States 40 D3
Evansville • IN, United States 41 I4
Evciler • Turkey 15 H4
Evdir Hani • Turkey 93 G1
Evelyn, Mt • NT, Australia 34 F2
Evensk • Russian Fed. 27 Q4
Everest, Mt • China/Nepal 28 E3
Everett • WA, United States 117 E1
Everglades • FL, United States 119 M8
Everglades Nat. Park **Heritage N** • FL, United States 60 [17]
Everglades Nat. Park • FL, United States 119 M8
Everglades Nat. Park **Park** • FL, United States 121 [226]
Evesham • United Kingdom 74 D4
Evesham, Vale of • United Kingdom 74 D4
Evia • Greece 92 D4
Evian-les-Bains • France 85 F2
Evinayong • Equatorial Guinea 22 G4
Evje • Norway 95 F1
Evora • Portugal 11 D6
Evora **Heritage C** • Portugal 64 [101]
Evora [Adm] • Portugal 88 A3
Evreux • France 10 G5
Evros • Greece 15 H2
Evry • France 85 E4
Ewa Beach • HI, United States 119 L5
Ewaso Ngiro • Kenya 101 G2
Ewo • Congo 22 G5
Exe • United Kingdom 74 F2
Exeter • United Kingdom 74 F2
Exmoor • United Kingdom 74 F2
Exmoor Nat. Park **Park** • United Kingdom 72 [50]
Exmoor Nat. Park • United Kingdom 74 F2
Exmouth • WA, Australia 34 B4
Exmouth • United Kingdom 74 F5
Exmouth Gulf • WA, Australia 33 C8
Exposition, Parc des • France 85 E2
Externsteine • Germany 5 L3
Extremadura • Spain 11 F5
Exuma Cays • Bahamas 124 B3
Exuma Cays Land & Sea Park • Bahamas 124 B1
Eyasi, Lake • Tanzania 102 H2
Eyl • Somalia 23 H2
Eymoutiers • France 85 G2
Eyre • WA, Australia 34 E6
Eyre, Lake, North • SA, Australia 34 G5
Eyre, Lake, South • SA, Australia 34 G5
Eyre Mtns • New Zealand 112 L2
Eyre Peninsula • SA, Australia 34 G6
Eze • France 85 H2
Ezeiza [Apt] • Argentina 127 D1
Ezequiel Ramos Mexia, Embalse • Argentina 45 C3

Faan, Ko • Thailand 109 J1
Faber Lake • NT, Canada 38 H4
Fåborg **Beach** • Denmark 68 [44]
Fåborg • Denmark 95 F14
Fabriano • Italy 12 G5
Fachi • Niger 20 H5
Fada • Chad 21 D4
Fada-Ngourma • Burkina Faso 22 E2
Faddeya, Zaliv • Russian Fed. 26 S2
Faddeyevskiy, Ostrov • Russian Fed. 27 N1
Fadiffolu Atoll • Maldives 106 E1
Faenza • Italy 91 E7
Fafen • Ethiopia 23 G2
Fagaras • Romania 14 L4
Fagerhult • Sweden 95 F8
Fagernes • Norway 16 E6
Fagersta • Sweden 95 D1
Fagita • Indonesia 32 (1) D3
Faguibine, Lac • Mali 20 E5
Faguibine, Lac **Park** • Mali 103 [2]
Fahan **Beach** • Ireland 68 [65]
Fahrland • Germany 81 F3
Fahrlander See • Germany 81 F3
Fahs, El • Tunisia 12 D12
Fai di Paganella • Italy 90 B3
Faial **Beach** • Azores 68 [101]
Faial • Azores 88 B1
Faial • Madeira 88 C2
Fair Isle • United Kingdom 6 K2
Fair Park **Park** • TX, United States 121 [M]
Fairbanks • AK, United States 38 B4
Fairbourne **Beach** • United Kingdom 75 [187]
Fairmont • MN, United States 41 H3
Fairmont • WV, United States 41 J4
Fairmount Hot Springs • BC, Canada 122 C4
Fairview Park • Hong Kong, China 107 H3
Fairweather, Mt • Canada/United States 38 D5
Fairyhouse • Ireland 79 E2
Faisalabad • Pakistan 28 B2
Faiyûm, El • Egypt 101 F1
Faizabad • India 105 C8
Fakfak • Indonesia 32 (1) D3
Fakse Bugt • Denmark 95 F14
Fakse Ladeplads • Denmark 95 F14
Falaise • France 10 E5
Falaise de Tiguidit • Niger 20 G5
Falam • Myanmar 31 A2
Falásama • Crete, Greece 93 E1
Falcade **Ski** • Italy 70 [223]
Falcade • Italy 90 B4
Falcon, Cap • Algeria 11 K9
Falcon Reservoir • TX, United States 40 G6
Falconara • Italy 91 E12
Falconara Marittima • Italy 12 H5
Falcone, Capo del • Sardinia, Italy 90 C1
Faléme • Mali/Senegal 22 B2
Falfurrias • TX, United States 119 N5
Faliráki • Rhodes, Greece 93 F2
Faliráki [Beach] • Rhodes, Greece 93 F2
Falkenberg **Beach** • Sweden 68 [4]
Falkenberg • Sweden 95 F7
Falkensee • Germany 81 F1
Falkirk • United Kingdom 74 B3
Falkland Is. • Atlantic Ocean 45 E6
Falköping • Sweden 95 F3
Fall River • MA, United States 118 H2
Fallingbostel • Germany 8 E4
Fallingbostel **Spa** • Germany 83 [61]
Fallon • NV, United States 117 F4
Falls Creek • VI, Australia 111 G3
Falmouth • United Kingdom 74 F4
Falmouth • Jamaica 124 C1
Falmouth • Antigua & Barbuda 125 F4
Falmouth Harbour • Antigua & Barbuda 125 F4
False Bay • South Africa 100 C5
Falster • Denmark 95 F14
Falsterbo • Sweden 95 F15
Falticeni • Romania 14 N2
Falun • Sweden 16 H6
Famagusta • Cyprus 93 J4
Famagusta Bay • Cyprus 93 J2
Familien-Freizeitpark Tolk-Schau **Park** • Germany 73 [51]
Fan Si Pan • Vietnam 31 C2
Fana • Mali 20 D6
Fana • Norway 94 C3
Fanári **Beach** • Greece 69 [196]
Fanári • Greece 92 D2
Fanchang • China 107 J3
Fang • Thailand 109 G1
Fanling • Hong Kong, China 107 H3
Fanø **Beach** • Denmark 68 [51]
Fano • Italy 91 E12
Fanø • Denmark 95 F13
Fanø Bugt • Denmark 95 F13
Fantasylandia • Ibiza, Spain 87 G2
Far East cruise area • Asia 59 A8
Faraday [Base] • Antarctica 46 (1) II3
Faradje • Dem. Rep. of Congo 23 D3
Farafra Oasis • Egypt 101 F3
Faráh • Afghanistan 18 H3
Faráh [Riv] • Afghanistan 18 H3
Faranah • Guinea 22 B2
Farasan, Jaza'ir • Saudi Arabia 18 D6
Farbairn Reservoir • QL, Australia 111 F3
Fareham • United Kingdom 7 K11
Farewell, Cape • New Zealand 35 D5
Farewell Spit • New Zealand 35 D5
Fargo • ND, United States 41 G2
Faribault • MN, United States 41 H3
Faridabad • India 105 C2
Farilhões, Is. • Portugal 11 B5
Farim • Guinea-Bissau 22 A2
Färjestaden • Sweden 95 F8
Farley Hill Park • Barbados 125 H1
Farmakonissi • Greece 92 D8
Farmington • NM, United States 118 J2
Färnebofjärden • Sweden 95 D1
Farnham • United Kingdom 74 E3
Fårö • Sweden 16 J8
Faro • Portugal 88 E7
Faro [Adm] • Portugal 88 E7
Faro, Punta del • Sicily, Italy 12 J10
Faroe Is. • Atlantic Ocean 4 I4
Fårösund • Sweden 16 J8
Farquhar, Atoll de • Seychelles 106 F3
Farrukhabad • India 105 C3
Fársala • Greece 15 D4
Farsø **Beach** • Denmark 68 [48]
Farsø • Denmark 95 F5
Farsund • Norway 16 D7
Farukolhufushi • Maldives 106 E4
Fårup • Denmark 95 F9
Fårup Aquapark & Sommerland **Park** • Denmark 73 [14]
Fårup Sommerland • Denmark 95 F5
Farvel, Kap • Greenland 39 W5
Fasano • Italy 12 L8
Fashir, Al • Sudan 21 E5
Fasil Ghebbi **Heritage C** • Ethiopia 63 [85]
Fasillar • Turkey 93 G2
Fatehpur • Rajasthan, India 105 C2
Fatehpur • Uttar Pradesh, India 105 C7
Fatehpur Sikri **Heritage C** • India 63 [120]
Fatehpur Sikri • India 105 C3
Fátima • Portugal 11 C5
Fatrade Beach • Goa, India 105 B2
Fatu Hiva • French Polynesia 33 N7
Faucigny • France 85 F2
Faugères • France 84 B4
Faurei • Romania 97 D1
Fauske • Norway 16 H3
Faute-sur-Mer, la **Beach** • France 68 [83]
Favara • Sicily, Italy 12 H11
Favàritx, Cap de • Minorca, Spain 87 F2
Favignana, I. • Italy 90 D1
Faw, Al • Iraq 21 I1
Fawn • OT, Canada 39 N6
Faxälven • Sweden 16 H5
Faya-Largeau • Chad 21 C4
Faye, Pas de la • France 85 H2
Fayetteville • NC, United States 41 K5
Fazao-Malfakassa, Parc nat. de **Park** • Togo 103 [30]
Fazilka • India 18 J3
Fazzan • Libya 21 B2
Fderick • Mauritania 20 C4
Feale • Ireland 79 F6
Fear, Cape • NC, United States 41 K5
Fécamp • France 10 F4
Federación • Argentina 45 E2
Federal Hall Nat. Mem. **Park** • NY, United States 121 [326]
Fedje • Norway 94 C3
Fehmarn • Germany 8 G2
Fehmarnbelt • Germany 8 G2
Feia, Lago • Brazil 127 C4
Feijó • Brazil 43 C5
Feilding • New Zealand 35 E5
Feira de Santana • Brazil 44 I1
Felanitx **Beach** • Majorca, Spain 68 [126]
Felanitx • Majorca, Spain 87 H4
Feldafing • Germany 82 J3
Feldberg **Ski** • Germany 70 [1]
Feldberg • Germany 82 G8
Feldkirch • Austria 89 H5
Feliceto • Corsica, France 85 L1
Félicité • Seychelles 106 F4
Felidu Atoll • Maldives 106 E1
Felixstowe • United Kingdom 74 E2
Fell Foot Park • United Kingdom 74 C4
Feltre • Italy 90 B4
Femer Bælt • Denmark/Germany 95 F14
Femund • Norway 16 F5
Fen He • China 29 E3
Fendek, El • Morocco 11 F9
Fengcheng • China 30 C4
Fenghua • China 107 J4
Fengjie • China 29 D4
Fengshui Shan • China 27 J6
Fengxian • China 107 J4
Fenit **Beach** • Ireland 68 [60]
Fenit • Ireland 79 F5
Fenouillèdes • France 85 K2
Fens, The • United Kingdom 7 M9
Fensfjorden • Norway 94 C3
Fenyang • China 29 E3
Fer, Cap de • Algeria 20 G1
Ferdows • Iran 18 G3
Fère-Champenoise • France 5 H6
Féres • Greece 15 H3
Ferfer • Ethiopia 23 H2
Fergana • Uzbekistan 18 J1
Fergana Basin • Uzbekistan 96 A3
Ferguson Lake • NU, Canada 38 J3
Fergusson • Papua New Guinea 35 (1) E2
Ferienzentrum Schloß Dankern **Park** • Germany 73 [53]
Ferkéssédougou • Côte d'Ivoire 22 C3
Ferlo • Senegal 20 C6
Ferlo [Riv] • Senegal 20 B5
Fermanagh • United Kingdom 75 A3
Fermo • Italy 12 H5
Fermoy • Ireland 79 F8
Fern Gully • Jamaica 124 C2
Fernandina • Galapagos Is. 43 (1) A2
Fernandina Beach • FL, United States 119 M3
Fernando de Noronha, Território de • Brazil 45 (1) E2
Fernando Póo • Equatorial Guinea 22 F4
Fernandópolis • Brazil 44 F3
Fernie Snow Valley **Ski** • BC, Canada 116 [10]
Fernmeldeturm • Germany 81 E3
Ferragudo • Portugal 88 E6
Ferrandina • Italy 12 K8
Ferrara **Heritage C** • Italy 64 [115]
Ferrara • Italy 91 E7
Ferraria, Ponta da • Azores 88 B1
Ferreira do Alentejo • Portugal 11 C6
Ferreiras • Portugal 88 E6
Ferreries **Beach** • Minorca, Spain 68 [127]
Ferreries • Minorca, Spain 87 F1
Ferret, Cap • France 85 G3
Ferru, Monte • Sardinia, Italy 90 C1
Ferrutx, Es Cap de • Majorca, Spain 11 O5
Ferté-Bernard, la • France 84 D2
Ferté-Macé, la • France 5 C6
Fès **Heritage C** • Morocco 64 [214]
Fès • Morocco 101 D2
Fesdu Fun I. • Maldives 106 E1
Feshi • Dem. Rep. of Congo 22 H6
Festós • Crete, Greece 93 E6
Fetesti • Romania 97 D2
Fethiye • Turkey 92 D9
Fethiye Körfezi • Turkey 15 J7
Fetlar • United Kingdom 6 L1
Fetsund • Norway 94 B2
Feuchtwangen • Germany 9 F7
Feuilles, Rivière aux • QU, Canada 39 Q5
Feurs • France 10 J8
Feyzabad • Afghanistan 18 J2
Fezzan • Libya 20 H3
Ffestiniog • United Kingdom 7 I9
Fiabilandia **Park** • Italy 73 [84]
Fianarantsoa • Madagascar 24 H4
Fiche • Ethiopia 23 F1
Fichtelgebirge • Germany 9 H6
Fichtenwalde • Germany 81 F3
Fidenza • Italy 91 E6
Fideris **Ski** • Switzerland 70 [112]
Fieberbrunn **Ski** • Austria 70 [155]
Fieberbrunn • Austria 89 H3
Fiemme, Val di • Italy 90 B3
Fier • Albania 15 A3
Fiesch **Ski** • Switzerland 70 [101]
Fiesch • Switzerland 89 G6
Fiésole • Italy 91 E11
Fife • United Kingdom 74 B2
Fife Ness • United Kingdom 6 J5
Fifi, Al • Sudan 23 D1
Fig Tree • St Kitts & Nevis 125 G4
Fig Tree Drive • Antigua & Barbuda 125 F3
Figari • Corsica, France 85 L4
Figeac • France 85 G4
Figeholm • Sweden 95 F8
Figueira da Foz • Portugal 11 C4
Figueira da Foz **Beach** • Portugal 68 [96]
Figueres • Spain 87 D2
Figuig • Morocco 101 D4
Fihalhohi • Maldives 106 E4
Fiji • Pacific Ocean 35 (2) D2
Filadelfia • Brazil 43 H5
Filchner Ice Shelf • Antarctica 46 (1) B2
Filey **Beach** • United Kingdom 75 [25]
Filfla • Malta 93 H4
Filiasi • Romania 14 K5
Filiátes • Greece 15 B4
Filiatrá • Greece 15 C6
Filicudi, I. • Italy 90 D2
Filingué • Niger 20 F6
Fílipi • Greece 92 D1
Filipiáda • Greece 15 B4
Filipstad • Sweden 16 H7
Fillefjell • Norway 94 C4
Filosorma • Corsica, France 85 L1
Filzmoos **Ski** • Austria 70 [180]
Filzmoos • Austria 89 H4
Fímaina • Greece 15 H6
Fimi • Dem. Rep. of Congo 23 B4
Finale Ligure • Italy 12 C4
Finale Ligure **Beach** • Italy 68 [141]
Findel [Apt] • Luxembourg 80 A20
Finestrat **Beach** • Spain 68 [118]
Finestrat • Spain 87 C2
Finger Lakes • NY, United States 122 B10
Fingly • BC, Canada 38 F5
Finhaut • Switzerland 89 G5
Finike • Turkey 93 G3
Finike Körfezi • Turkey 93 G3
Finikoúndas **Beach** • Greece 69 [181]
Finistère • France 84 C1
Finisterre, Cabo • Spain 11 B2
Finke • NT, Australia 112 H4
Finke Gorge Nat. Park • NT, Australia 112 H4
Finke, Mt • SA, Australia 34 F6
Finke [Riv] • NT/SA, Australia 112 H4
Finkenberg **Ski** • Austria 70 [142]
Finkenberg • Austria 89 H7
Finland • Europe 16
Finland, Gulf of • Europe 16 N7
Finnemarka • Norway 94 B1
Finnigan, Mt • QL, Australia 34 I3
Finnish Archipelago • Finland 94 A9
Finnish Lakeland • Finland 94 A9
Finniss, Cape • SA, Australia 34 F6
Finnmark • Norway 16 L2
Finnvede • Sweden 95 F7
Finschhafen • Papua New Guinea 35 (1) D2
Finse • Norway 94 C4
Finspång • Sweden 95 D3
Finsteraarhorn • Switzerland 89 G6
Finsterwalde • Germany 8 I5
Fionnphort • United Kingdom 6 F5
Fiordland • New Zealand 112 L1
Fiordland Nat. Park • New Zealand 112 L1
Firat • Turkey 18 C2
Fire I. Nat. Seashore **Park** • NY, United States 121 [333]
Firefly • Jamaica 124 C2
Firenze **Heritage C** • Italy 64 [118]
Firenze • Italy 91 E11
Firmat • Argentina 127 D1
Firminy • France 10 J8
Firozabad • India 105 C3
Firozpur • India 28 B2
Fischen • Germany 82 J6
Fischen **Spa** • Germany 83 [241]
Fish • Namibia 24 B4
Fish River Canyon • Namibia 24 B5
Fishbourne • United Kingdom 78 C8
Fisher Strait • NU, Canada 39 O4
Fishguard • United Kingdom 7 H10
Fishnish • United Kingdom 78 A2
Fiskárdo • Greece 92 C2
Fiskarhalvön • Russian Fed. 17 E1
Fiskebäckskil • Sweden 95 F2
Fisterra **Beach** • Spain 68 [92]
Fitou • France 84 B4
Fitri, Lac • Chad 22 H2
Fitzcarrald • Peru 127 B2
Fitzroy • WA, Australia 34 D3
Fitzroy • QL, Australia 111 F4
Fitzroy Crossing • WA, Australia 34 E3
Fitzroy I. • QL, Australia 111 F1
Fiumicino • Italy 91 F3
Fiumorbo • Corsica, France 85 L4
Five Islands Harbour • Antigua & Barbuda 125 F1
Five Islands Village • Antigua & Barbuda 125 F1
Fjällbacka • Sweden 95 F2
Fjäråsbräcka • Sweden 95 F6
Fjerritslev **Beach** • Denmark 68 [48]
Fjerritslev • Denmark 95 F5
Fjöllum, Jökulsá á • Iceland 16 (1) E2
Flå • Norway 94 B1
Flachau **Ski** • Austria 70 [173]
Flachau • Austria 89 H4
Flachauwinkel **Ski** • Austria 70 [171]
Flagstaff • AZ, United States 118 J1
Flagstaff Lake • ME, United States 118 G2
Flaine **Ski** • France 70 [19]
Flaine • France 85 F2
Flåm • Norway 94 C4
Flambards Victorian Village • United Kingdom 74 F4
Flamborough **Beach** • United Kingdom 75 [26]
Fläming • Germany 13 B5
Flanders • Belgium/France/Neths. 80 A13
Flandre-Zuydcoote **Beach** • France 68 [74]
Flannan Isles • United Kingdom 75 A1
Flåsjon • Sweden 16 I4
Flat I. • South China Sea 31 F4
Flateby • Norway 94 B2
Flathead Lake • MT, United States 117 E2
Flattery, Cape • WA, United States 117 E1
Flåvatn • Norway 94 B3
Flaxaflói • Iceland 16 (1) B2
Flèche, la • France 84 D1
Fleetwood • United Kingdom 7 I8
Flekkefjord • Norway 16 D7
Flen • Sweden 95 D3
Flensburg • Germany 8 E2
Flers • France 5 C6
Flesberg • Norway 94 B1
Flesland [Apt] • Norway 94 C3
Fleuve Maroni • French Guiana/Suriname 43 G3
Flevoland • Netherlands 80 A7
Flevoland [Adm] • Netherlands 80 A7
Flims **Ski** • Switzerland 70 [106]
Flims • Switzerland 89 G3
Flin Flon • MN, Canada 38 K6
Flinders • QL, Australia 34 H3
Flinders I. • TS, Australia 34 I8
Flinders Passage • QL, Australia 111 F1
Flinders Ranges • SA, Australia 34 G6
Flinders Reefs • CL, Australia 111 F1
Flint • United Kingdom 7 I8
Flint • Kiribati 33 L7
Flint • MI, United States 41 J3
Flintshire • United Kingdom 75 A4
Flisa • Norway 16 F6
Flix • Spain 10 F12
Flöha • Germany 9 I6
Florence • AL, United States 41 I5
Florence • SC, United States 41 K5
Florence **Heritage C** • Italy 64 [118]
Florence • Italy 91 E11
Florence • OR, United States 117 E3
Florencia • Colombia 43 B3
Florenville • Belgium 80 A19
Flores • Indonesia 32 (1) B4
Flores • Guatemala 37 C4
Flores • Azores 88 B1
Flores • Argentina 127 D3
Flores, I. de • Uruguay 127 D2
Flores, Laut • Indonesia 25 N10
Flores Sea • Indonesia 32 (1) B4
Floresti • Moldova 14 P2
Floresville • TX, United States 119 N5
Floriana • Malta 93 H4
Floriano • Brazil 45 (1) C3
Florianópolis • Brazil 44 G4
Florida • United States 119 M
Florida • Cuba 124 D7
Florida • Uruguay 127 D2
Florida Caverns State Park • FL, United States 119 M2
Florida Citrus Bowl • FL, United States 121 C2
Florida Citrus Tower • FL, United States 121 C1
Florida City • FL, United States 119 M8
Florida Keys • FL, United States 119 M8
Florida, Straits of • FL, United States 41 J7
Florida's Cypress Gardens • FL, United States 119 M5
Florida's Silver Springs • FL, United States 119 M3
Florida's Silver Springs **Park** • FL, United States 121 [AA]
Floridablanca • Colombia 43 C2
Flórina • Greece 15 C3
Florissant Fossil Beds Nat. Mon. **Park** • CO, United States 120 [93]
Florø • Norway 94 C1
Flower Forest • Barbados 125 H1
Flowers Cove • NF, Canada 39 T6
Flumendosa • Sardinia, Italy 90 C4
Flumserberg **Ski** • Switzerland 70 [105]
Flumserberg • Switzerland 89 G3
Flushing • Netherlands 80 A10
Fluviá • Spain 10 H11
Fly • Papua New Guinea 35 (1) C2
Flying Fish Cove • Indian Ocean 32 D5
Flying Tigers Warbird Air Museum • FL, United States 121 C2
Foca • Bosnia-Herz. 14 F6
Foça **Beach** • Turkey 69 [236]
Foça • Turkey 92 D5
Focsani • Romania 14 O4
Fogdön • Sweden 95 D3
Foggia • Italy 12 J7
Foggo • Nigeria 20 H6
Fogo • Cape Verde 22 (1) B2
Fogo • NF, Canada 123 D4
Fogo [I.] • NF, Canada 123 D4
Fohnsdorf • Austria 13 D10
Föhr • Germany 8 D2
Föhr **Spa** • Germany 83 [4]
Fóia • Portugal 88 E2
Foix • France 85 K1
Foix [Region] • France 85 K1
Folda • Norway 16 F4
Foldereid • Norway 16 G4
Folégrandos • Greece 92 D7
Folelli • Corsica, France 85 L2
Foley I. • NU, Canada 39 Q3
Folgaría **Ski** • Italy 70 [211]
Folgárida **Ski** • Italy 70 [206]
Folgefonn • Norway 94 C3
Folgoët, le • France 84 C1
Foligno • Italy 91 E12
Folkestone • United Kingdom 74 E4
Folkestone Underwater Park • Barbados 125 H3
Follónica • Italy 91 E11
Fomboni • Comoros 24 G2
Fomento • Cuba 124 D2
Fond Assau • St Lucia 125 J2
Fond d'Or Bay • St Lucia 125 J2
Fond du Lac • SA, Canada 38 J5
Fond du Lac • WI, United States 41 I3
Fond St Jacques • St Lucia 125 J3
Fondi • Italy 91 F4
Fonsagrada • Spain 11 D1
Fonseca, Golfo de • El Salvador/Nicaragua 37 D5
Font • Switzerland 89 G1
Font-Romeu • France 85 K2
Fontainebleau **Heritage C** • France 64 [57]
Fontainebleau • France 85 E4
Fontainebleau, Forêt de • France 85 E4
Fontana Rossa • Sicily, Italy 90 D4
Fontas • BC, Canada 38 G5
Fonte alla Róccia • Italy 90 B2
Fonte Boa • Brazil 43 D4
Fontenay **Heritage C** • France 64 [54]
Fontenay-le-Comte • France 84 D3
Fontevraud • France 84 D3
Fontur • Iceland 16 (1) F1
Fonualei • Tonga 35 (2) F2
Fóppolo • Italy 91 E2
Föra • Sweden 95 F8
Fora, I. de • Madeira 88 C2
Forbach • France 10 L4
Forbes • NS, Australia 111 G2
Forchheim • Germany 9 G7
Ford's Theatre Nat. Hist. Site **Park** • DC, United States 121 [284]
Førde • Sogn og Fjordane, Norway 94 C1
Førde • Rogaland, Norway 94 C5
Førdefjorden • Norway 94 C1
Fore Abbey • Ireland 79 E1
Forel, Mt • Greenland 39 X3
Forest Finland • Finland 94 A6
Forestville • QU, Canada 123 D1
Forez, Mts du • France 10 I8
Forfar • United Kingdom 74 B2
Forggensee • Germany 82 J6
Forillon Nat. Park • QU, Canada 123 D2
Forío • Italy 91 G3
Forlì • Italy 91 E7
Formby **Beach** • United Kingdom 75 [231]
Formentera **Beach** • Spain 68 [124]
Formentera • Spain 87 G4
Formentor • Majorca, Spain 87 H2
Formentor, Cap de • Majorca, Spain 87 H2
Formia • Italy 91 F4
Formiga • Brazil 127 C1
Formigas • Azores 88 B2
Formosa • Argentina 44 E4
Formosa • Brazil 44 G2
Formosa Strait • China 29 F6
Fornebu [Apt] • Norway 94 B2
Fornells • Minorca, Spain 87 F2
Forrest • WA, Australia 34 E6
Forrest City • AR, United States 41 H4
Fors • Sweden 95 D1
Forsayth • QL, Australia 34 H3
Forssa • Finland 95 E4
Forst • Germany 8 J5
Fort Albany • OT, Canada 39 O6
Fort Apache Indian Reservation • AZ, United States 118 J3
Fort Archambault • Chad 21 C6
Fort Augustus • United Kingdom 6 H4
Fort Beaufort • South Africa 100 C4
Fort Bragg • CA, United States 117 F1
Fort Chipewyan • AL, Canada 38 I5
Fort Collins • CO, United States 40 E3
Fort de France • Martinique 37 I5
Fort Dodge • IA, United States 41 H3
Fort Erie • OT, Canada 122 B9
Fort Fun Abenteuerland **Park** • Germany 73 [59]
Fort George • QU, Canada 39 P6
Fort Good Hope • NT, Canada 46 BB3
Fort Hope • OT, Canada 39 N6
Fort Kent • ME, United States 118 G2
Fort Lauderdale • FL, United States 119 M8
Fort Macleod • AL, Canada 122 C4
Fort McMurray • AL, Canada 38 I5
Fort McPherson • NT, Canada 38 E3
Fort Médoc • France 85 G1
Fort Miribel • Algeria 20 F3
Fort Myers • FL, United States 119 M5
Fort Nelson • BC, Canada 38 G5
Fort Nelson [Riv] • BC, Canada 38 G5
Fort Norman • NT, Canada 38 F4
Fort Peck Lake • MT, United States 40 E2
Fort Pierce • FL, United States 119 M6
Fort Providence • NT, Canada 38 H4
Fort Resolution • NT, Canada 38 I4
Fort Severn • OT, Canada 39 N5
Fort Shevchenko • Kazakhstan 17 I6
Fort Simpson • NT, Canada 38 G4
Fort Smith • NT, Canada 38 I4
Fort Smith • AR, United States 41 H4
Fort St James • BC, Canada 38 G6
Fort St John • BC, Canada 122 C1
Fort Steele • BC, Canada 122 C4
Fort Stockton • TX, United States 40 F5
Fort Union Trading Post Nat. Hist. Site **Park** • ND, United States 120 [147]
Fort Vermilion • AL, Canada 38 H5
Fort Walton Beach • FL, United States 119 M2
Fort Wayne • IN, United States 41 I3
Fort Wilderness • FL, United States 121 C1
Fort William • United Kingdom 6 G5
Fort Worth • TX, United States 119 N1
Fort Yukon • AK, United States 38 B3
Fortaleza • Brazil 45 (1) D2
Forte dei Marmi **Beach** • Italy 68 [144]
Forte dei Marmi • Italy 91 E10
Fortescue • WA, Australia 34 C4
Forth • United Kingdom 74 B3
Forth, Firth of • United Kingdom 74 B4
Fortin Coronel Eugenio Garay • Paraguay 44 D3
Fortress Mtn **Ski** • AL, Canada 116 [14]
Fortune • NF, Canada 123 D3
Fortune Bay • NF, Canada 123 D3
Fortuneswell • United Kingdom 74 F6
Fos-sur-Mer **Beach** • France 68 [132]
Fosforescente, Bahía • Puerto Rico 125 E3
Foshan • China 107 H1
Fosnvåg • Norway 94 C1
Fossano • Italy 12 B4
Fossanova, Abbazia di • Italy 91 F4
Fossil Bluff [Base] • Antarctica 46 (1) II2
Fossil Butte Nat. Mon. **Park** • WY, United States 120 [77]
Fossombrone • Italy 12 G5
Foster • VI, Australia 111 G3
Fougères • France 10 D5
Foula • United Kingdom 6 J1
Foulness • United Kingdom 5 D3
Foulness I. • United Kingdom 74 E2
Foulwind, Cape • New Zealand 35 C5
Foumban • Cameroon 22 G3
Fountain • St Kitts & Nevis 125 G4
Fountains Abbey **Heritage C** • United Kingdom 64 [17]
Fouras **Beach** • France 68 [84]
Fouras • France 85 G1
Fourfourás • Crete, Greece 93 E6
Foúrka **Beach** • Greece 69 [192]
Fourmies • France 5 H4
Foúrnoi • Greece 92 D8
Fouta • Senegal 22 A1
Fouta Djallon • Guinea 22 B2
Foux-d'Allos, la **Ski** • France 70 [70]
Foveaux Strait • New Zealand 112 L4
Fowey • United Kingdom 74 F4
Fowlers Bay • SA, Australia 34 F6
Fox • MN, Canada 38 M5
Fox Is. • AK, United States 36 (1) D2
Foxe Basin • NU, Canada 39 P3
Foxe Channel • NU, Canada 39 O4
Foxe Peninsula • NU, Canada 39 P4
Foxen • Sweden 94 B4
Foxford • Ireland 79 F2
Foyle, Lough • Ireland/UK 7 E6
Foynes • Ireland 79 F6
Foz **Beach** • Spain 68 [91]
Fôz do Cunene • Namibia 24 A3
Foz do Iguaçu • Brazil 44 F4
Frabosa • Italy 91 E5
Fraga • Spain 11 L3
Framura **Beach** • Italy 68 [143]
Franca • Brazil 44 G3
France • Europe 10
Francés, Punta • Cuba 124 D1
Franceville • Gabon 22 G5
Franche Comte • France 10 K6
Francis Case, Lake • SD, United States 40 G3
Francisco Beltrão • Brazil 44 F4
Franciscus Bay • Namibia 24 A5
Francistown • Botswana 24 D4
Franconia • NH, United States 118 G3
Franeker • Netherlands 8 A3
Frangokástelo • Crete, Greece 93 E6
Frankenberg • Germany 9 D5
Frankenberg • Germany 9 I6
Frankenstein, Burg • Germany 82 H4
Frankenwald • Germany 9 G6
Frankfort • KY, United States 41 J4
Frankfurt am Main • Germany 82 H4
Frankfurt an der Oder • Germany 8 J4
Fränkisch Alb • Germany 9 G7
Fränkische Saale • Germany 9 E6
Franklin Bay • NT, Canada 38 F3
Franklin, Benjamin, Nat. Mem. **Park** • PA, United States 121 [308]
Franklin Mtns • NT, Canada 38 G4
Franklin Strait • NU, Canada 38 L2
Frantiskovy Lazne • Czech Rep. 96 C1
Frantsa-Iosifa, Zemlya • Russian Fed. 96 A2
Franz Josef Land • Arctic Ocean 26 G1
Franz Joseph Strauss [Apt] • Germany 82 J3
Frasassi, Grotta di • Italy 91 E12
Frascati • Italy 91 F3
Fraser • BC, Canada 122 C3
Fraser I. **Heritage N** • QL, Australia 61 [135]
Fraser I. • QL, Australia 111 F6
Fraser Range • WA, Australia 34 D6
Fraser's Hill • Malaysia 108 D2
Fraserburgh • United Kingdom 6 K4
Fraserburgh • South Africa 100 C2
Frauenfeld • Switzerland 9 D9
Fray Bentos • Uruguay 127 D2
Frederica, Fort, Nat. Mon. **Park** • GA, United States 121 [216]
Fredericia **Beach** • Denmark 68 [46]
Fredericia • Denmark 95 F9
Fredericksburg • VA, United States 118 H3
Fredericksburg • TX, United States 119 N3
Fredericksburg & Spotsylvania County Battlefields Mem. • VA, United States 118 H3
Fredericksburg & Spotsylvania County Battlefields Mem. **Park** • VA, United States 121 [263]
Fredericton • NB, Canada 123 D7
Frederiksborg • Denmark 95 F10
Frederikshåb • Greenland 39 V4
Frederikshavn **Beach** • Denmark 68 [48]
Frederikshavn • Denmark 95 F6
Frederikssund • Denmark 95 F10
Frederiksted • US Virgin Is. 58 B7
Frederiksværk **Beach** • Denmark 68 [41]
Frederiksværk • Denmark 95 F10
Fredrikstad • Norway 94 B4

Free State • South Africa 24 D5
Freels, Cape • NF, Canada 123 D4
Freeport • TX, United States 119 N6
Freeport • Bahamas 124 B2
Freer • TX, United States 119 N5
Freetown • Sierra Leone 22 B3
Freetown • Antigua & Barbuda 125 F4
Frégate • Seychelles 106 F2
Fréhel, Cap • France 84 C2
Freiberg • Germany 9 I6
Freiberger Mulde • Germany 9 I6
Freiburg im Breisgau • Germany 82 G8
Freiburg im Breisgau Spa • Germany 83 [195]
Freilassing • Germany 82 J8
Freising • Germany 82 J3
Freistadt • Austria 13 D9
Freital • Germany 9 I6
Freizeit- und Miniaturpark Allgäu Park • Germany 73 [66]
Freizeit- und Miniaturpark Allgäu • Germany 82 J5
Freizeit-Land Park • Germany 73 [65]
Freizeitpark Lochmuhle • Germany 82 H2
Freizeitpark Schloß Beck • Germany 81 E1
Fréjus Beach • France 68 [133]
Fréjus • Var, France 85 F4
Fréjus • Hautes-Alpes, France 85 H4
Fréjus, Tunnel du • France/Italy 85 F4
Fremantle • WA, Australia 34 C6
Fremont • NE, United States 41 G3
Fremont • CA, United States 117 F3
Fremont Mtns • OR, United States 117 E3
French Guiana • S. America 43 G3
French I. • VI, Australia 111 G3
French Pass • New Zealand 35 D5
French Polynesia • Pacific Ocean 33 M8
Frenchman • SA, Canada 38 J7
Freshwater Beach • United Kingdom 75 [154]
Fresnillo • Mexico 37 (1) B1
Fresno • CA, United States 117 F3
Freu, Cap del • Majorca, Spain 11 O5
Freudenberg • Germany 9 C6
Freudenstadt • Germany 82 G6
Freudenstadt Spa • Germany 83 [186]
Fri • Greece 15 H8
Fria • Guinea 22 B2
Frías • Argentina 44 C4
Fribourg • Switzerland 89 G2
Fridlevstad • Sweden 95 F12
Fridtjof Nansen, Mt • Antarctica 46 (1) Y1
Friedberg • Hessen, Germany 9 D6
Friedberg • Bavaria, Germany 82 J2
Friedenweiler Spa • Germany 83 [210]
Friedrichroda Spa • Germany 83 [302]
Friedrichshafen • Germany 82 J5
Friedrichskoog Spa • Germany 83 [9]
Friendship Hill Nat. Hist. Site Park • PA, United States 121 [300]
Friesland • Germany/Neths. 5 K1
Friesland [Adm] • Netherlands 80 A3
Friesoythe • Germany 8 C3
Frigate Bay • St Kitts & Nevis 125 G2
Frigate Bay Beach • St Kitts & Nevis 125 G2
Frio, Cabo • Brazil 127 C4
Frisian Is. • Germany/Neths. 8 B3
Frisian Is., East • Germany 8 C3
Frisian Is., North • Germany 8 D2
Frisian Is., West • Netherlands 8 A3
Fristad • Sweden 95 F7
Fritzlar • Germany 9 E5
Friuli-Vénezia Giulia • Italy 91 E4
Frobisher Bay • NU, Canada 39 R4
Frobisher Bay [Bay] • NU, Canada 39 R4
Frobisher Lake • SA, Canada 38 J5
Frolovo • Russian Fed. 17 G5
Frome • United Kingdom 74 F3
Frome, Lake • SA, Australia 34 G6
Fronsac • France 84 B3
Frontenac Prov. Park • QU, Canada 122 B4
Frontignan Beach • France 68 [130]
Frosinone • Italy 91 F4
Frøya • Norway 16 E5
Frozen Strait • NU, Canada 39 O3
Frunzivka • Ukraine 14 Q2
Fruska Gora • F.R. of Yugoslavia 14 G4
Fruska Gora Nat. Park Park • Fed. Rep. of Yugoslavia 72 [115]
Frutal • Brazil 44 G3
Frydek Mistek • Czech Rep. 13 H8
Frydlant • Czech Rep. 96 C2
Fu Yang • China 107 J3
Fuah Mulah Atoll • Maldives 106 E3
Fuchskauten • Germany 5 L4
Fuchun Jiang • China 107 J3
Fucino, Piana del • Italy 91 F2
Fuding • China 29 G5
Fuengirola Beach • Spain 68 [114]
Fuengirola • Spain 86 B6
Fuente Alto • Chile 44 B5
Fuentesaúco • Spain 11 F3
Fuerteventura • Canary Is. 87 E2
Fügen • Austria 89 H3
Fuggerschloß • Germany 82 J2
Fuhai • China 26 O8
Fuji-san • Japan 30 J7
Fujian • China 107 G8
Fujin • China 29 I1
Fukagawa • Japan 30 K3
Fukuchiyama • Japan 30 H7
Fukue • Japan 30 E8
Fukue [I.] • Japan 30 E8
Fukueichiao • Taiwan 29 G5
Fukui • Japan 30 I6
Fukuoka • Japan 30 F8
Fukushima • Japan 30 K6
Fukuyama • Japan 30 G7
Fulda • Germany 9 E6
Fulda [Riv] • Germany 9 E5
Fuling • China 29 D5
Full Moon • Maldives 106 E4
Fulpmes • Austria 89 H6
Fulton • MO, United States 41 H4
Fulton • AR, United States 119 N2
Fumay • France 5 H4
Fuminimaggiore • Sardinia, Italy 12 C9
Fun Acres Park • United Kingdom 73 [37]
Fun I. • Maldives 106 E4
Funabashi • Japan 30 J7
Funafuti • Kiribati 33 I6
Funafuti [I.] • Kiribati 33 I6
Funchal Beach • Madeira 68 [108]
Funchal • Madeira 88 C2
Fundão • Portugal 11 D4
Fundy, Bay of • NB/NS, Canada 123 D7
Fundy Nat. Park • NB, Canada 123 D7
Fünen • Denmark 95 F14
Fünfkirchen • Hungary 71 A14
Fungus Rock • Malta 93 H1
Fur • Denmark 95 F5
Furana • Maldives 106 E4
Furancungo • Mozambique 24 E2
Furano • Japan 30 L3
Furat, Al • Iraq/Syria 18 D3
Furkapass • Switzerland 89 G3
Furnas • Azores 88 B1
Furnas Dam • Brazil 127 C1
Furnas, Represa de • Brazil 127 C1
Furneaux Group • TS, Australia 34 I8
Furness Abbey • United Kingdom 74 C3
Furness Fells • United Kingdom 74 C4
Fürstenfeld • Austria 14 D2
Fürstenfeldbruck • Germany 82 J3
Fürstenwalde • Germany 8 J4
Fürth • Germany 9 G7
Furth im Wald • Germany 9 H7
Furtwangen • Germany 82 G8
Furukawa • Japan 30 K5
Furuviksparken Park • Sweden 73 [8]
Fury & Hecla Strait • NU, Canada 39 O3
Fusa • Norway 94 C3
Fushë-Lura • Albania 15 B2
Fushun • China 29 G2
Fusong • China 30 D3
Füssen • Germany 82 J6
Füssen Spa • Germany 83 [244]
Futuna • Vanuatu 35 (2) C2
Futuna • Wallis & Futuna 35 (2) E1
Futuroscope Park • France 73 [74]
Futuroscope • France 84 D4
Fuxian • China 30 A5
Fuxin • China 29 G2
Fuyang • China 29 F4
Fuyu • China 27 J8
Fuyun • China 26 O8
Fuzhou • Fujian, China 29 F5
Fuzhou • Jiangxi, China 29 F5
Fyn [Adm] • Denmark 95 F14
Fyn [I.] • Denmark 95 F14
Fyne, Loch • United Kingdom 6 G6
Fynshav • Denmark 95 F13
Fyresdal • Norway 94 C6
Fyresvatn • Norway 94 C6
Gaafaru Atoll • Maldives 106 E2
Gabbs • NV, United States 117 F4
Gabela • Angola 23 A6
Gabès • Tunisia 101 E4
Gabès, Golfe de • Tunisia 101 E4
Gabicce Mare • Italy 91 E12
Gabon • Africa 22 G5
Gaborone • Botswana 24 D4
Gabriel Strait • NU, Canada 39 R4
Gabrovo • Bulgaria 97 D3
Gad • Jordan 98 A6
Gadag • India 106 D2
Gadara • Jordan 98 A4
Gäddede • Sweden 16 H4
Gadsden • AL, United States 41 I5
Gadsden, Fort, State Hist. Site • FL, United States 119 M2
Gaesti • Romania 97 D1
Gaeta • Italy 91 F4
Gaeta, Golfo di • Italy 12 H7
Gaferut • Fed. States of Micronesia 33 F5
Gafsa • Tunisia 101 E3
Gagarin • Russian Fed. 97 E3
Gaggenau Spa • Germany 83 [181]
Gagnoa • Côte d'Ivoire 22 C3
Gagnon • QU, Canada 39 R6
Gai Xian • China 30 B4
Gaillac • France 85 G4
Gaillimh • Ireland 79 F4
Gaitaler Alpen • Austria 89 H8
Gainer Wildlife Sanctuary • India 105 C1
Gainesville • FL, United States 119 M3
Gainesville • TX, United States 119 N1
Gainsborough • United Kingdom 7 L8
Gairdner, Lake • SA, Australia 34 G6
Gairloch • United Kingdom 6 G4
Gal Oya Nat. Park • Sri Lanka 106 D16
Gala Gölü • Turkey 15 H3
Galán, Cerro • Argentina 44 C4
Galana • Kenya 101 G4
Galanta • Slovak Rep. 13 G9
Galápagos Is. • Pacific Ocean 43 (1) A1
Galápagos, Parque Nac. Heritage N • Pacific Ocean 60 [30]
Galashiels • United Kingdom 74 B4
Galáta • Cyprus 93 J3
Galata • Bulgaria 97 D4
Galati • Romania 97 D2
Galatina • Italy 12 M8
Galdhøpiggen • Norway 94 C2
Galé, Costa da • Portugal 88 A3
Galeão • Brazil 127 C4
Galeota Point • Trinidad & Tobago 125 K4
Galera Point • Trinidad & Tobago 125 K2
Galgibaga Beach • Goa, India 105 B2
Galhak, El • Sudan 21 F5
Galicia • Spain 11 C2
Galicia • Poland 13 L8
Galicica Nat. Park Park • F.Y.R. of Macedonia 72 [123]
Galilee • Israel 98 A2
Galilee, Sea of • Israel 98 A4
Galilei, Galileo [Apt] • Italy 91 E11
Galina Point • Jamaica 124 C2
Galite, Canal de la • Tunisia 12 C11
Galite, La • Tunisia 101 E1
Galka'yo • Somalia 23 H2
Gallarus Oratory • Ireland 79 F5
Galle Heritage C • Sri Lanka 63 [139]
Galle • Sri Lanka 106 D15
Gallipoli • Italy 12 M8
Gallipoli • Turkey 92 D2
Gallipoli Peninsula • Turkey 92 D2
Gallivare • Sweden 16 K3
Gällö • Sweden 16 H5
Galloway, Mull of • United Kingdom 7 H7
Gallup • NM, United States 118 J2
Gallur • Spain 11 J3
Galtür • Austria 89 H5
Galty Mtns • Ireland 79 F6
Galveston • TX, United States 119 N6
Galveston Bay • TX, United States 119 N6
Galveston I. • TX, United States 119 N6
Gálvez • Argentina 44 D5
Galway • Ireland 79 F4
Galway [Adm] • Ireland 79 F4
Galway Bay • Ireland 79 F4
Galway City Beach • Ireland 68 [62]
Gamarra • Colombia 43 C2
Gamasa • Egypt 101 F2
Gambia [Riv] • Gambia/Senegal 20 B6
Gambia, The • Africa 20 B6
Gambie • Senegal 22 B2
Gambier • Bahamas 124 B3
Gamboma • Congo 22 H5
Gamkonora, Gunung • Indonesia 32 (1) C2
Gamla Uppsala • Sweden 95 D2
Gamleby • Sweden 95 F4
Gammarth • Tunisia 101 E2
Gammelstad Heritage C • Sweden 63 [72]
Gammertingen • Germany 82 J1
Gamph, Slieve • Ireland 79 F2
Gamud • Ethiopia 23 F3
Gamvik • Norway 16 O1
Gan • Maldives 106 E3
Gan Jiang • China 29 F5
Ganado • AZ, United States 40 E4
Gand • Belgium 80 A14
Gandadiwata, Bulu • Indonesia 32 (1) A3
Gandajika • Dem. Rep. of Congo 23 C5
Gandak • India 105 C8
Gander • NF, Canada 123 D4
Ganderkesee • Germany 5 L1
Gandhi Dam • India 105 C6
Gandhi, Indira [Apt] • India 105 C2
Gandhi, Indira, Nahar • India 105 C1
Gandhi, Indira, Wildlife Sanctury • India 106 D10
Gandhi Sagar • India 105 C6
Gandhinagar • India 28 B4
Gandia • Spain 11 K6
Gandia Beach • Spain 68 [119]
Gandria • Switzerland 89 G7
Gandu • Brazil 44 I1
Ganetti • Sudan 21 F4
Ganga • India 28 D3
Gangaikondacholapuram • India 106 D11
Gangaw • Myanmar 28 F4
Gangca • China 29 C3
Gangdhar • India 105 C6
Gangdisê Shan • China 28 D2
Ganges • India 28 D3
Ganges Plain • India 105 C7
Gangtok • India 28 E3
Gani • Indonesia 32 (1) C3
Gannett Peak • WY, United States 40 E3
Gansbaai • South Africa 100 C5
Gansu • China 107 G3
Ganta • Liberia 22 C3
Ganteng • China 107 J3
Ganzano di Roma • Italy 91 F3
Ganzhou • China 29 E5
Gao • Mali 20 E5
Gaochun • China 107 J1
Gaolan • Zhuhai, China 107 H3
Gaolan Dao • Zhuhai, China 107 H3
Gaotingzhen • China 107 J4
Gaoual • Guinea 22 B2
Gaoua • Burkina Faso 22 D2
Gaoyou Hu • China 29 F4
Gap • France 85 F3
Gara, Lough • Ireland 79 F2
Gara Muleta • Ethiopia 23 G2
Gara'ad • Somalia 23 H2
Garachico • Tenerife, Canary Is. 86 E1
Garajonay, Parque Nac. de Heritage N • Gomera, Canary Is. 61 [48]
Garajonay, Parque Nac. de Park • Gomera, Canary Is. 72 [77]
Garajonay, Parque Nac. de • Gomera, Canary Is. 87 E5
Garama • Libya 21 B2
Garamba, Parc nat. de la Heritage N • Dem. Rep. of Congo 61 [82]
Garamba, Parc nat. de la Park • Dem. Rep. of Congo 103 [54]
Garanhuns • Brazil 45 (1) D3
Garba • Central African Rep. 23 C2
Garbsen • Germany 8 E4
Garching bei München • Germany 82 J3
Garda, Lago di • Italy 91 E7
Gardaland Park • Italy 73 [83]
Gardaland • Italy 91 E7
Gardelegen • Germany 8 G4
Garden City • KS, United States 40 F4
Garden Route • South Africa 100 C7
Gardermoen [Apt] • Norway 94 B2
Gardez • Afghanistan 18 I3
Gardiki • Corfu, Greece 92 B1
Gardone Riviera • Italy 91 E7
Gärdsjö • Sweden 95 F3
Gärdslösa • Sweden 95 F8
Garfield, James A., Nat. Hist. Site Park • OH, United States 121 [188]
Gargaliáni • Greece 15 C6
Gargano • Italy 12 J7
Gargellen • Austria 89 H5
Garibaldi Prov. Park • BC, Canada 122 C3
Garicin Grad • F.R. of Yugoslavia 14 I7
Garigliano • Italy 91 F4
Garissa • Kenya 101 G4
Gariwerd • VI, Australia 111 E7
Garmisch-Partenkirchen Ski • Germany 70 [3]
Garmisch-Partenkirchen • Germany 82 J6
Garmisch-Partenkirchen Spa • Germany 83 [246]
Garonne • France 10 E9
Garonne, Canal latéral a la • France 10 F9
Garoua • Cameroon 22 G3
Garowe • Somalia 23 H2
Garphyttan Nat. Park Park • Sweden 72 [25]
Garrison • Barbados 125 H3
Garry Lake • NU, Canada 38 K3
Garsa, Chott el • Tunisia 101 E3
Garsen • Kenya 23 F4
Gärtringen • Germany 9 D8
Garut • Java, Indonesia 110 D6
Garvie Mtns • New Zealand 112 L2
Garwa • India 105 C8
Garwolin • Poland 13 K6
Gary • IN, United States 41 I3
Garyarsa • China 28 D2
Garzê • China 29 C4
Garzón • Colombia 43 B3
Gasan-Kuli • Turkmenistan 18 F2
Gaschurn Ski • Austria 70 [125]
Gaschurn • Austria 89 H5
Gascogne • France 10 F10
Gascony • France 84 A2
Gascoyne • WA, Australia 34 C5
Gasfinolhu • Maldives 106 E2
Gashaka Game Reserve Park • Nigeria 103 [35]
Gashua • Nigeria 22 G2
Gaspé • QU, Canada 123 D2
Gaspé, Cap • QU, Canada 123 D2
Gaspésie, Péninsule de • QU, Canada 123 D2
Gassol • Nigeria 22 G3
Gastonia • NC, United States 41 J4
Gastoúni • Greece 15 C6
Gastoúri • Corfu, Greece 92 B1
Gastre • Argentina 45 C4
Gata, Cabo de • Spain 86 B8
Gáta, Cape • Cyprus 93 J3
Gata, Sierra de • Spain 11 E4
Gatchina • Russian Fed. 97 E1
Gates of the Arctic Nat. Park & Preserve Park • AK, United States 120 [3]
Gateshead • United Kingdom 7 K7
Gateway Nat. Recreation Area Park • NJ/NY, United States 121 [327]
Gatineau • QU, Canada 122 B2
Gatineau Park • QU, Canada 122 B2
Gatorland • FL, United States 121 C2
Gatwick [Apt] • United Kingdom 74 E3
Gauja • Latvia 16 M8
Gauja Nat. Park Park • Latvia 72 [144]
Gauley River Nat. Recreation Area Park • WV, United States 121 [269]
Gaume, Fonte de • France 85 G2
Gaupne • Norway 94 C4
Gausta • Norway 94 B1
Gaustablikk • Norway 94 B1
Gauteng • South Africa 24 D5
Gavarnie • France 85 J2
Gavdopoúla • Greece 93 E5
Gávdos • Greece 92 D10
Gävle • Sweden 16 I6
Gävleborg • Sweden 16 I6
Gávrio • Greece 92 D7
Gawler • SA, Australia 34 G6
Gawler Ranges • SA, Australia 34 G6
Gaya • Niger 22 E2
Gaya • India 105 C8
Gayndah • QL, Australia 111 F6
Gayny • Russian Fed. 17 I2
Gaza • Palestine 18 B3
Gázi Beach • Crete, Greece 69 [214]
Gazi Beach • Kenya 101 G5
Gaziantep • Turkey 18 C2
Gazipasa • Turkey 93 G4
Gdansk • Poland 13 H3
Gdansk, Gulf of • Poland 13 I3
Gdynia • Poland 13 H3
Gê'gyai • China 28 D2
Gebiz • Turkey 93 G2
Gebze • Turkey 15 K3
Gedi • Kenya 23 F4
Gedi Nat. Mon. • Kenya 101 G5
Gediz • Turkey 15 K4
Gediz [Riv] • Turkey 92 D6
Gedser • Denmark 95 F14
Gedung • Malaysia 108 C4
Geel • Belgium 5 H3
Geelen • Netherlands 80 A16
Geelong • VI, Australia 111 G3
Geesthacht • Germany 8 F3
Géfira • Greece 15 D3
Geigar • Sudan 23 E1
Geilo • Norway 94 C4
Geiranger • Norway 94 C2
Geirangerfjorden • Norway 94 C2
Geislingelhof • Germany 82 H1
Geislingen an der Steige • Germany 9 E8
Geita • Tanzania 102 H1
Geithus • Norway 94 B1
Gejiu • China 29 C6
Gela • Sicily, Italy 90 D4
Gela, Golfo di • Sicily, Italy 90 D4
Geladi • Ethiopia 23 H2
Gelderland • Netherlands 80 A7
Geldermalsen • Netherlands 80 C4
Geldern • Germany 8 B5
Gélengdeng • Chad 23 B1
Gelibolu • Turkey 92 D2
Gelibolu Yarimadasi • Turkey 92 D2
Gelinsor • Somalia 23 H2
Gelnhausen • Germany 82 G2
Gelsenkirchen • Germany 81 E2
Gelsenkirchen: Buer • Germany 81 E2
Gelting Spa • Germany 83 [1]
Gelugur • Penang, Malaysia 108 C4
Gemas • Malaysia 108 D4
Gembloux • Belgium 71 A7
Gemena • Dem. Rep. of Congo 23 B3
Gemlik • Turkey 92 D3
Gemlik Körfezi • Turkey 15 J3
Gemünd Spa • Germany 83 [117]
Gemünden • Germany 9 E6
Genádio Beach • Rhodes, Greece 69 [211]
Genádio • Rhodes, Greece 93 F3
Genale • Ethiopia 23 G2
Gencek • Turkey 93 G2
General Acha • Argentina 45 D3
General Alvear • Argentina 44 C5
General Belgrano Station [Base] • Antarctica 46 (1) B2
General Bernardo O'Higgins [Base] • Antarctica 46 (1) JJ3
General Carrera, Lago • Chile 45 B5
General Lavalle • Argentina 127 D4
General Manuel Belgrano, Cerro • Argentina 44 C4
General Pico • Argentina 44 D6
General Pinedo • Argentina 44 D4
General Roca • Argentina 45 C3
General Santos • Philippines 31 H5
General Tosevo • Bulgaria 14 P6
General Villegas • Argentina 45 D3
Geneva • Switzerland 89 G5
Geneva, Lake • Switzerland/France 89 G5
Genève • Switzerland 89 G5
Gengenbach • Germany 82 G6
Genil • Spain 86 B2
Genk • Belgium 80 A15
Gennargentu, Monte del • Sardinia, Italy 90 C2
Genoa • Italy 91 E6
Génova • Italy 91 E6
Génova, Golfo di • France/Italy 91 E10
Genovesa • Galapagos Is. 43 (1) B1
Gent • Belgium 80 A14
Gent naar Oostende, Kanaal van • Belgium 80 B2
Genteng • Indonesia 110 D5
Genteng [I.] • Indonesia 110 D8
Genthin • Germany 8 H4
Genting Highlands • Malaysia 108 D4
Genyem • Indonesia 32 (1) F3
Geographe Bay • WA, Australia 34 C6
Geok-Tepe • Turkmenistan 18 G2
Georg von Neumayer [Base] • Antarctica 46 (1) E2
George, Zemlya • Russian Fed. 96 A2
George • QU, Canada 39 S5
George • South Africa 100 C7
George, Fort • OT, Canada 122 B9
George, Fort • Trinidad & Tobago 125 K1
George, Lake • NS, Australia 111 G2
George Sound • New Zealand 112 L1
George Town • TS, Australia 34 I8
George Town • Cayman Is. 37 E4
George Town • Penang, Malaysia 108 C2
George VI Sound • Antarctica 46 (1) II3
Georgetown • Ascension 19 C6
Georgetown • QL, Australia 34 H3
Georgetown • Guyana 43 F2
Georgetown • TX, United States 119 N3
Georgia • Asia 17 G6
Georgia • United States 41 J5
Georgia, Strait of • BC, Canada 38 G7
Georgian Bay • OT, Canada 39 O7
Georgian Bay Is. Nat. Park • OT, Canada 122 B5
Georgina • NT/QL, Australia 111 E3
Georgioúpoli • Crete, Greece 93 E2
Georgsmarienhütte • Germany 8 D4
Gera • Germany 9 H6
Gera [Riv] • Germany 9 G5
Géradmer • France 10 L5
Geráki • Greece 15 D7
Gerakiní Beach • Greece 69 [192]
Gerakiní • Greece 92 D1
Geral do Goiás, Serra • Brazil 45 (1) B4
Geral do Paraná, Serra • Brazil 44 G2
Geral, Serra • Brazil 44 F4
Geraldine • New Zealand 35 C7
Geraldton • WA, Australia 34 B5
Geraniou Beach • Crete, Greece 69 [212]
Gerasa • Jordan 98 A6
Gerbichi, gora • Russian Fed. 26 S3
Gerede • Turkey 15 N3
Gerede [Riv] • Turkey 15 N3
Gerês, Serra do • Portugal 11 D3
Gereshk • Afghanistan 18 H3
Geretsried • Germany 82 J3
Gérgeri • Crete, Greece 93 E7
Gerizim, Mount • Jordan 98 A6
Gerlachovsky Stit • Slovak Rep. 13 J8
Gerlos Ski • Austria 70 [145]
Gerlos • Austria 89 H7
Gerlovo • Bulgaria 14 N6
Germany • Europe 8/9
Germete Spa • Germany 83 [101]
Germi • Iran 18 F3
Germona del Friuli • Italy 12 H2
Gernsheim • Germany 82 H4
Gerolstein • Germany 82 H1
Geroskipou Beach • Cyprus 69 [217]
Gers • France 85 G4
Gersau • Switzerland 89 G3
Gersfeld Spa • Germany 83 [133]
Gersthofen • Germany 82 J2
Gertak Sanggul • Penang, Malaysia 108 C3
Gertak Sanggul, Tanjong • Penang, Malaysia 108 C3
Gerze • China 28 D2
Gesundaberget • Sweden 16 H6
Geta • Finland 95 E3
Getafe • Spain 11 H4
Getaria Beach • Spain 68 [87]
Gete • Belgium 5 I4
Gets, les Ski • France 70 [13]
Gets, les • France 85 F2
Gettysburg Nat. Military Park • PA, United States 118 H1
Gettysburg National Military Park Park • PA, United States 121 [305]
Getxo Beach • Spain 68 [88]
Geureudong, Gunung • Indonesia 110 B1
Gevelsberg • Germany 81 E2
Geyik Dagi • Turkey 15 N7
Geyikli • Turkey 15 H4
Geyve • Turkey 15 L3
Gezer • Israel 98 A5
Ggantija Heritage C • Malta 64 [196]
Ggantija • Malta 93 H1
Ghadamis • Libya 21 A1
Ghadamis Heritage C • Libya 64 [232]
Ghaghara • India 105 C8
Ghajn Tuffieha Bay • Malta 93 H3
Ghana • Africa 22 D3
Ghar Dalam • Malta 93 H4
Gharb • Malta 93 H1
Gharbi • Tunisia 101 E4
Gharbiyah, Al Istiwa'iyah al • Sudan 23 D2
Ghard Abu Muharik • Egypt 21 E2
Ghardaïa • Algeria 20 F2
Ghârib • Egypt 21 F2
Gharyan • Libya 21 B1
Ghat • Libya 21 A2
Ghats, Eastern • India 106 D3
Ghats, Western • India 106 D6
Ghazal, Bahr al • Sudan 23 E2
Ghazal, Bahr el • Chad 21 C5
Ghazaouet • Algeria 11 J9
Ghaziabad • India 105 C2
Ghazipur • India 105 C8
Ghazni • Afghanistan 18 I3
Ghent • Belgium 80 A14
Gherla • Romania 14 K2
Ghisonaccia • Corsica, France 85 L4
Ghisoni • Corsica, France 85 L4
Ghoumrassen • Tunisia 101 E6
Ghuzayyil, Sabkhat • Libya 21 C2
Giali • Greece 92 D8
Gianades Beach • Corfu, Greece 69 [170]
Gianades • Corfu, Greece 92 B1
Gianisáda • Greece 93 E4
Giannutri, I. di • Italy 90 A2
Giant's Castle Game Reserve Park • South Africa 103 [129]
Giant's Causeway • United Kingdom 7 F6
Giant's Causeway Heritage N • United Kingdom 61 [41]
Giants Ridge Ski • MN, United States 116 [109]
Gianyar • Bali, Indonesia 110 C4
Giao • Vietnam 31 D4
Giardini-Naxos • Sicily, Italy 90 D2
Giáros • Greece 92 D7
Giarre • Sicily, Italy 12 J11
Gibara • Cuba 124 D8
Gibb River • WA, Australia 34 E3
Gibbs Beach • Barbados 125 H1
Gibeon • Namibia 24 B5
Gibeon • Jordan 98 A5
Gibostad • Norway 16 I2
Gibraltar • Europe 86 B6
Gibraltar, Strait of • Morocco/Spain 11 F9
Gibson Desert • WA, Australia 34 D4
Gien • France 10 H6
Giens • France 85 H3
Gießen • Germany 82 G2
Giethoorn • Netherlands 80 A8
Gifford • NU, Canada 39 O2
Gifhorn • Germany 8 F4
Gifu • Japan 30 I7
Gigha • United Kingdom 78 A2
Giglio • Italy 12 E6
Gijón • Spain 11 F1
Gila • AZ/NM, United States 118 J4
Gila Bend • AZ, United States 118 J3
Gila Cliff Dwellings Nat. Mon. • NM, United States 118 J4
Gila Cliff Dwellings Nat. Mon. Park • NM, United States 120 [120]
Gilbert • QL, Australia 34 H3
Gilbert Is. • Kiribati 33 I6
Gilbo'a, Mount • Israel/Jordan 98 A4
Gilbués • Brazil 45 (1) B3
Giles Meteorological Station • WA, Australia 34 E5
Gilgit • Jammu & Kashmir 28 B1
Gilgit [Riv] • Jammu & Kashmir 28 B1
Gilimanuk • Bali, Indonesia 110 C1
Gill, Lough • Ireland 79 F2
Gillam • MN, Canada 38 M5
Gilleleje • Denmark 95 F10
Gillette • WY, United States 40 E3
Gillingham • United Kingdom 74 F3
Gimbi • Ethiopia 23 F2
Gimie, Mt • St Lucia 125 J3
Gin Gin • QL, Australia 111 F6
Gingin • WA, Australia 34 C6
Gingoog • Philippines 31 G5
Ginosa Beach • Italy 69 [156]
Gioia del Colle • Italy 12 K8
Gioúra • Greece 92 D4
Gippsland • VI, Australia 111 G3
Gippsland Lakes • VI, Australia 111 G3
Giraglia, I. de la • Corsica, France 85 L2
Girão, Cabo • Madeira 88 C1
Girard • St Lucia 125 J2
Girardot • Colombia 43 C3
Giravara • Maldives 106 E4
Giri • Dem. Rep. of Congo 23 B3
Girne • Cyprus 15 O8
Girolata, Golfe de Heritage N • Corsica, France 61 [45]
Girolata, Golfe de • Corsica, France 85 L1
Girona • Spain 87 D2
Gironde • France 85 G1
Gironde [Adm] • France 85 G3
Gisborne • New Zealand 35 G4
Gisborne [Adm] • New Zealand 112 J2
Gislaved • Sweden 95 F7
Gisors • France 85 E1
Gistel • Belgium 80 B1
Gitgit Waterfall • Bali, Indonesia 110 C2
Githio • Greece 15 D7
Githio Beach • Greece 69 [182]
Giulianova • Italy 91 E12
Giumalau, Virful • Romania 14 M2
Giurgeni • Romania 97 D2
Giurgiu • Romania 97 D1
Give • Denmark 95 F9
Givet • France 5 H4
Giza Pyramids • Egypt 101 F1
Gizhiga • Russian Fed. 27 R4
Gizhinskaya Guba • Russian Fed. 27 Q4
Gizo • Solomon Is. 35 (1) F2
Gizycko • Poland 13 K3
Gjerstad • Norway 94 B3
Gjirokastër • Albania 15 B3
Gjoa Haven • NU, Canada 38 L3
Gjøvik • Norway 16 F6
Gjuhëzës, Kep i • Albania 15 A3
Glace Bay • NS, Canada 123 D8
Glacier Bay • AK, United States 58 A2
Glacier Bay Nat. Park & Preserve Heritage N • AK, United States 60 [1]
Glacier Bay Nat. Park & Preserve Park • AK, United States 120 [13]
Glacier Nat. Park • MT, United States 117 E2
Glacier Nat. Park Park • MT, United States 120 [67]
Glacier Nat. Park • BC, Canada 122 C4
Glacier Peak • WA, United States 38 G7
Gladbeck • Germany 81 E1
Gladenbach • Germany 9 D6
Gladenbach Spa • Germany 83 [127]
Gladstone • QL, Australia 111 F4
Glåma • Norway 16 F6
Glamis Castle • United Kingdom 74 B2
Glamorgan • United Kingdom 75 A5
Glan • Germany 9 C7
Glan • Sweden 95 F4
Glanvilles • Antigua & Barbuda 125 F4
Glarner Alpen • Switzerland 89 G3
Glasgow • MT, United States 40 E2
Glasgow • United Kingdom 74 B3
Glashütte • Germany 9 I6
Glasriket • Sweden 95 F8
Glass Country • Sweden 95 F8
Glass Window Bridge • Bahamas 124 B1
Glasshouse Mtns Nat. Park • QL, Australia 111 F6
Glastonbury • United Kingdom 74 F3
Glastonbury Tor • United Kingdom 74 F3
Glauchau • Germany 13 B7
Glazov • Russian Fed. 17 I3
Glen • NH, United States 118 G3
Glen Canyon Dam • AZ, United States 118 J1
Glen Canyon Nat. Recreation Area • AZ/UT, United States 118 J1
Glen Canyon Nat. Recreation Area Park • AZ/UT, United States 120 [101]
Glen Eden Ski • OT, Canada 116 [23]
Glen Helen • NT, Australia 112 H1
Glen Innes • NS, Australia 34 J5
Glen Shee • United Kingdom 74 B2
Glenbeigh Beach • Ireland 68 [60]
Glenbeigh • Ireland 79 F7
Glencree • Ireland 79 E4
Glendalough • Ireland 79 E4
Glendive • MT, United States 40 F2
Gleneagles • United Kingdom 74 B1
Glengarriff • Ireland 79 F7
Glenmalure • Ireland 79 E4
Glenorchy • New Zealand 112 L2
Glenridding • United Kingdom 74 C2
Glenrothes • United Kingdom 74 B2
Glens Falls • NY, United States 118 G3
Glenveagh Nat. Park Park • Ireland 72 [38]
Glenwood Springs • CO, United States 40 E4
Gletsch • Switzerland 89 G3
Glifáda • Corfu, Greece 92 B1
Glifáda • Greece 92 D7
Glinde • Germany 8 F3
Glindow • Germany 81 F3
Glittertind • Norway 94 C2
Gliwice • Poland 13 H7
Globe • AZ, United States 118 J3
Glogów • Poland 13 F6
Glomfjord • Norway 16 G3
Glommersträsk • Sweden 16 J4
Glorenza • Italy 91 E3
Gloria Dei Church Nat. Hist. Site Park • PA, United States 121 [310]

Glorieuses • Réunion 24 H2
Gloucester • United Kingdom 74 D3
Gloucester • MA, United States 118 G3
Gloucester, Cape • Papua New Guinea 35 (1) D2
Gloucestershire • United Kingdom 74 D4
Glowno • Poland 13 I6
Glubokoye • Belarus 16 N9
Glucholazy • Poland 13 G7
Glücksburg **Spa** • Germany 83 [10]
Glückstadt • Germany 8 E3
Glurns • Italy 91 E3
Glyngøre • Denmark 95 F5
Gmund • Germany 82 J7
Gmünd • Austria 89 H8
Gmünd • Austria 96 C4
Gmunden • Austria 89 H4
Gnarp • Sweden 16 I5
Gnesen • Poland 71 A9
Gnesta • Sweden 95 D3
Gniezno • Poland 13 G5
Gnosjö • Sweden 95 F7
Gnowangerup • WA, Australia 34 C6
Goa **Heritage C** • India 63 [126]
Goa • India 105 B
Goa Lawah Cave • Bali, Indonesia 110 C4
Goba • Ethiopia 23 G2
Gobabis • Namibia 24 B4
Gobernador Gregores • Argentina 45 B5
Gobi • China/Mongolia 29 D2
Gobo • Japan 30 H8
Goch • Germany 8 B5
Gochas • Namibia 24 B4
Göd • Hungary 13 I10
Godavari • India 28 D5
Godavari, Mouths of the • India 106 D4
Godbout • QU, Canada 123 D1
Gode • Ethiopia 23 G2
Godelbukta Breidvika • Antarctica 46 (1) H2
Gödene • Turkey 93 G3
Godhavn • Greenland 39 U3
Godhra • India 28 B4
Godinne • Belgium 80 A15
Gödöllö • Hungary 13 I10
Godoy Cruz • Argentina 44 C5
Gods Lake • MN, Canada 38 M6
Godthåb • Greenland 39 U4
Goéland, Lac-au- • QU, Canada 39 P6
Goelo, Côte du • France 84 C2
Goeree **Beach** • Netherlands 68 [68]
Goeree • Netherlands 80 A10
Goes • Netherlands 5 G3
Gogrial • Sudan 23 D2
Göhren **Spa** • Germany 83 [280]
Goianésia • Brazil 44 G2
Goiânia • Brazil 44 G2
Goiás • Brazil 44 F2
Goiás [Adm] • Brazil 44 G1
Goiatuba • Brazil 44 G2
Goifulha Fehendhu Atoll • Maldives 106 E1
Going **Ski** • Austria 70 [153]
Göinge • Sweden 95 F11
Góis • Portugal 11 C4
Gök Tepe • Turkey 15 K7
Gokarn • India 106 D5
Gokayama **Heritage C** • Japan 63 [168]
Gökçe • Turkey 15 G3
Gökçeada • Turkey 92 D2
Gökdere • Turkey 15 N7
Gökova Körfezi • Turkey 15 I7
Göksu • Turkey 15 K3
Göktepe • Turkey 15 J6
Gokwe • Zimbabwe 102 J1
Gol • Norway 94 C4
Gola Forest Reserve **Park** • Sierra Leone 103 [16]
Golan Heights • Syria 98 A2
Golancz • Poland 13 G5
Golaninha • Brazil 45 (1) D3
Gölcük • Turkey 15 K3
Gold Beach • OR, United States 117 E3
Gold Coast • Ghana 22 D4
Gold Coast • QL, Australia 111 F6
Goldap • Poland 13 L3
Goldau • Switzerland 89 G3
Golden Bay • New Zealand 35 D5
Golden Bay • Malta 93 H3
Golden Coast • Sweden 95 F6
Golden Gate • CA, United States 40 B4
Golden Gate Nat. Recreation Area **Park** • CA, United States 120 [45]
Golden Horsehoe • OT, Canada 122 B9
Golden Ring • Russian Fed. 97 E4
Golden Rock [Apt] • St Kitts & Nevis 125 G1
Golden Sands • Bulgaria 97 D4
Golden Spike Nat. Hist. Site **Park** • UT, United States 120 [78]
Golden Triangle • India 105 C2
Golden Triangle • Laos/Myanmar/Thailand 108 A1
Golden Valley • United Kingdom 74 D3
Golden Winde • BC, Canada 40 A1
Goldsboro • NC, United States 41 K4
Goldsworthy • WA, Australia 34 C4
Goldthwaite • TX, United States 119 N3
Goléa, El • Algeria 20 F2
Goleniów • Poland 13 D4
Golfe-Juan • France 85 H4
Golfito • Costa Rica 37 E6
Golfo Aranci **Beach** • Sardinia, Italy 68 [137]
Golfo Aranci • Sardinia, Italy 90 C2
Golfo de Chiriqui • Panama 37 E6
Golija • F.R. of Yugoslavia 14 H6
Golm • Germany 81 F3
Gölmarmara • Turkey 15 I5
Golmud • China 28 F1
Golmud He • China 28 F1
Golo • Corsica, France 85 L2
Goma • Dem. Rep. of Congo 23 D4
Gombe • Nigeria 22 G2
Gombe Nat. Park • Tanzania 102 H1
Gombe Nat. Park **Park** • Tanzania 103 [93]
Gomera • Canary Is. 87 E5
Gómez Palacio • Mexico 40 F6
Gomi • Ethiopia/Sudan 21 F6
Gomo • China 28 E2
Gonabad • Iran 18 G3
Gonaïves • Haiti 37 G4
Gonarezhou Nat. Park • Zimbabwe 102 J4
Gonâve, I. de • Haiti 124 A2
Gonbad-e Qabus • Iran 18 G2
Gonder • Ethiopia 21 G5
Gonder monuments **Heritage C** • Ethiopia 63 [85]
Gondia • India 28 C4
Gondomar • Portugal 11 C3
Gönen • Turkey 92 D3
Gönen [Riv] • Turkey 15 I3
Gongbai • Zhuhai, China 107 H1
Gongbo'gyamda • China 28 F3
Gongga Shan • China 29 C5
Gonghe • China 29 C3
Gongola [Adm] • Nigeria 22 G3
Gongola [Riv] • Nigeria 22 G2
Gongshan • China 31 B1
Good Hope, Cape of • South Africa 100 C5
Goodenough • Papua New Guinea 35 (1) E2
Goodhouse • South Africa 24 B5
Gooding • ID, United States 117 E4
Goodrich • United Kingdom 74 D3
Goodwood • United Kingdom 74 E3
Goole • United Kingdom 7 L8
Goomalling • WA, Australia 34 C6
Goondiwindi • QL, Australia 111 F6
Goonhilly Downs • United Kingdom 74 F4
Goor • Netherlands 5 J2
Goose Bay • NF, Canada 39 S6
Goose Lake • CA/OR, United States 117 E3
Gooty • India 106 D2
Göppingen • Germany 9 E8
Gora • New Zealand 112 L4
Gora Stoj • Ukraine 13 M9
Gorakhpur • India 105 C4
Gorczanski Nat. Park **Park** • Poland 72 [96]
Gorda, Punta • CA, United States 117 F1
Gördes • Turkey 15 J5
Gordion • Turkey 15 N4
Gordonvale • QL, Australia 34 I3
Goré • Chad 22 H3
Gore • Ethiopia 23 F2
Gore Mtn **Ski** • NY, United States 116 [183]
Gorée, I. de **Heritage C** • Senegal 63 [95]
Göreme Nat. Park **Heritage N** • Turkey 61 [63]
Göreme Nat. Park **Heritage C** • Turkey 64 [193]
Görenez Dagi • Turkey 15 J5
Gorgan • Iran 18 F2
Gorgona • Colombia 43 B3
Gorgona, I. di • Italy 91 E10
Gorham • NH, United States 118 G3
Gorinchem • Netherlands 80 C4
Gorizia • Italy 91 E4
Gorjanci • Croatia/Slovenia 14 C4
Gorkovskoye Vdkhr. • Russian Fed. 17 G3
Gørlev **Beach** • Denmark 68 [43]
Gørlev • Denmark 95 F10
Gorlice • Poland 13 K8
Görlitz • Germany 9 J5
Gorna Orjahovica • Bulgaria 97 D3
Gorno-Altaysk • Russian Fed. 26 O7
Gornozavodsk • Russian Fed. 29 K1
Gorochan • Ethiopia 23 F2
Gorodets • Russian Fed. 17 G3
Gorodok • Ukraine 13 M8
Goroka • Papua New Guinea 35 (1) D2
Gorong, Kepulauan • Indonesia 32 (1) D3
Gorongosa, Parque Nac. da **Park** • Mozambique 103 [135]
Gorongoza, Serra da • Mozambique 24 E3
Gorontalo • Indonesia 32 (1) B2
Górowo Ilaweckie • Poland 13 J3
Gorran Haven **Beach** • United Kingdom 75 [119]
Gorriti, I. de • Uruguay 127 D2
Gorski Kotar • Croatia/Slovenia 14 B4
Gort • Ireland 79 F4
Gortipohl **Ski** • Austria 70 [126]
Górtis • Crete, Greece 93 E7
Gortyna • Crete, Greece 93 E7
Goru, Virful • Romania 14 N4
Gorumna I. • Ireland 79 F3
Gory Stolowe Nat. Park **Park** • Poland 72 [98]
Gorzów Wielkopolski • Poland 13 E5
Gosau **Ski** • Austria 70 [177]
Gosau • Austria 89 H4
Gosford • NS, Australia 111 G2
Goshen • Jamaica 124 C2
Goslar • Germany 8 F5
Goslar **Heritage C** • Germany 64 [35]
Gospic • Croatia 14 C5
Gosport • United Kingdom 7 K11
Gossi • Mali 20 E5
Gossilies [Apt] • Belgium 80 A14
Gostivar • F.Y.R. of Macedonia 15 B2
Gostyn • Poland 13 G6
Gostynin • Poland 13 I5
Göta älv • Sweden 95 F2
Göta kanal • Sweden 95 F4
Göteborg **Beach** • Sweden 68 [1]
Göteborg • Sweden 95 F6
Göteborg och Bohus • Sweden 95 F2
Gotel Mtns • Cameroon/Nigeria 22 G3
Gotene • Sweden 95 F3
Gotha • Germany 9 F6
Gothenburg • Sweden 95 F6
Gothèye • Niger 20 F6
Gotland • Sweden 16 J8
Goto-Retto • Japan 30 E8
Gotowasi • Indonesia 32 (1) C2
Gotse Delchev • Bulgaria 14 K8
Gotska Sandön • Sweden 16 J7
Gotsu • Japan 30 G7
Göttingen • Germany 8 E5
Gouda • Netherlands 80 C3
Goudiri • Senegal 20 C6
Goudoumaria • Niger 22 G2
Gough I. • Atlantic Ocean 19 C9
Gough I. Wildlife Reserve **Heritage N** • Atlantic Ocean 61 [101]
Gouin, Réservoir • QU, Canada 39 Q7
Goulburn • NS, Australia 111 G2
Goulburn [Riv] • VI, Australia 111 G3
Goulimine • Morocco 101 D5
Gouménissa • Greece 14 J9
Gouna • Cameroon 23 A2
Goundam • Mali 20 E5
Gourdon • France 10 G9
Gouré • Niger 20 H6
Gouritsmond • South Africa 100 C6
Gourma Rharous • Mali 20 E5
Gournay-en-Bray • France 85 E1
Gourniá • Crete, Greece 93 E8
Gourock • United Kingdom 78 A3
Gourock Range • NS, Australia 111 G2
Gourrama • Morocco 20 E2
Goúves **Beach** • Crete, Greece 69 [214]
Goúves • Crete, Greece 93 E3
Gouviá • Corfu, Greece 92 B1
Gov'Altyan Nuruu • Mongolia 29 C2
Gove Peninsula • NT, Australia 34 G2
Govena, mys • Russian Fed. 27 S5
Governador Valadares • Brazil 127 C2
Govind Ballabh Pant Sagar • India 105 C8
Goya • Argentina 44 E4
Göynük • Turkey 15 L3
Göynük **Beach** • Turkey 69 [228]
Göynük • Turkey 93 G3
Goz Beida • Chad 23 C1
Gozha Co • China 28 D1
Gozo • Malta 93 H1
Graaff-Reinet • South Africa 100 C4
Graal-Müritz • Germany 8 H2
Graal-Müritz **Beach** • Germany 68 [33]
Graal-Müritz **Spa** • Germany 83 [273]
Grabo • Côte d'Ivoire 22 C4
Grächen • Switzerland 89 G6
Gracias a Dios, Cabo • Nicaragua 37 E4
Graciosa **Beach** • Azores 68 [103]
Graciosa • Canary Is. 87 E3
Graciosa • Azores 88 B2
Gradaus, Serra dos • Brazil 43 G5
Grado • Spain 11 E1
Grado **Beach** • Italy 68 [166]
Grado • Italy 91 E8
Græsted-Gilleleje **Beach** • Denmark 68 [41]
Grafton • NS, Australia 34 J5
Grafton • ND, United States 41 G2
Graham • TX, United States 119 N1
Graham I. • BC, Canada 38 E6
Graham Land • Antarctica 46 (1) II3
Graham Moore, Cape • NU, Canada 39 P2
Grahamstown • South Africa 100 C8
Grain Coast • Liberia/Sierra Leone 22 B3
Grainau • Germany 82 J6
Grajau • Brazil 45 (1) B3
Grajewo • Poland 13 L4
Gram • Denmark 95 F13
Gramat, Causse de • France 85 G4
Grampian Mtns • United Kingdom 6 H5
Grampians, The • VI, Australia 111 E7
Gramvoúxa • Crete, Greece 93 E1
Gramvoúxa, Akria • Crete, Greece 93 E1
Gran • Hungary 71 A14
Gran • Norway 94 B2
Gran Canaria • Canary Is. 86 E4
Gran Chaco • Argentina/Paraguay 44 D3
Gran Paradiso • Italy 91 E5
Gran Paradiso, Parco Naz. del **Park** • Italy 72 [85]
Gran Paradiso, Parco Naz. del • Italy 91 E5
Gran Piedra • Cuba 124 D8
Gran Pilastro • Austria/Italy 90 B1
Gran San Bernardo • Italy/Switzerland 12 B3
Gran Sasso d'Italia • Italy 91 F2
Gran Tarajal • Fuerteventura, Canary Is. 87 E2
Granada • Nicaragua 37 D5
Granada **Heritage C** • Spain 64 [94]
Granada • Spain 86 B3
Granby • QU, Canada 122 B8
Grand Anse • St Lucia 125 J2
Grand Bahama I. • Bahamas 124 B2
Grand Ballon • France 9 C9
Grand Bank • NF, Canada 123 D3
Grand Bassam • Côte d'Ivoire 22 D3
Grand Brière • France 84 C4
Grand Canal • Ireland 7 E8
Grand Canal • China 29 F4
Grand Canyon • AZ, United States 118 J1
Grand Canyon Nat. Park **Heritage N** • AZ, United States 60 [12]
Grand Canyon Nat. Park • AZ, United States 118 J1
Grand Canyon Nat. Park **Park** • AZ, United States 120 [100]
Grand Canyon of Pennsylvania • PA, United States 118 H1
Grand Causses • France 10 I9
Grand Cayman • Cayman Is. 124 D6
Grand Cess • Liberia 22 C4
Grand Coulee • WA, United States 40 C2
Grand Coulee Dam • WA, United States 117 E2
Grand Erg Occidental • Algeria 20 F2
Grand Erg Oriental • Algeria/Tunisia 20 G2
Grand Falls • NB, Canada 123 D1
Grand Falls • NF, Canada 123 D3
Grand Forks • ND, United States 41 G2
Grand Harbour • Malta 93 H4
Grand Island • NE, United States 41 G3
Grand Isle • VT, United States 118 G3
Grand Junction • CO, United States 40 E4
Grand Junction • CO, United States 116 A
Grand Lake • Canada/United States 118 G2
Grand Lake • LA, United States 118 K3
Grand Lake • NF, Canada 123 D3
Grand Lake • NB, Canada 123 D7
Grand Manan I. • NB, Canada 123 D6
Grand Morin, Vallée du • France 85 E4
Grand Portage Nat. Mon. **Park** • MN, United States 121 [156]
Grand Prairie • TX, United States 119 N1
Grand Pré • NS, Canada 123 D7
Grand Pressigny, le [Château] • France 84 D4
Grand Rapids • MN, Canada 38 L6
Grand Rapids • MN, United States 41 H2
Grand Rapids • MI, United States 41 I3
Grand Ravine • St Lucia 125 J2
Grand Récif de Cook • New Caledonia 35 (2) A2
Grand St-Bernard, Col du • Italy/Switzerland 89 G6
Grand Teton • WY, United States 40 D3
Grand Teton Nat. Park **Park** • WY, United States 120 [76]
Grand-Bornand, le **Ski** • France 70 [20]
Grand-Motte, la **Beach** • France 68 [130]
Grand-Village-Plage, le **Beach** • France 68 [84]
Grandcamp-Maisy • France 10 D4
Grande • Brazil 44 G2
Grande, Bahía • Argentina 45 C6
Grande, Baia de I. • Brazil 127 C3
Grande Casse • France 10 L8
Grande Comore • Comoros 24 G2
Grande Cul de Sac Bay • St Lucia 125 J1
Grande, I. • Brazil 127 C3
Grande Lande, Ecomusée de la • France 85 G3
Grande Morin • France 5 G6
Grande Prairie • AL, Canada 122 C2
Grande, Rio • Mexico/United States 40 F6
Grande, Rio • Bolivia 44 D2
Grande, Rio • Jamaica 124 C4
Grande Rivière • Dennery, St Lucia 125 J2
Grande Rivière • Gros Islet, St Lucia 125 J2
Grande, Serra • Brazil 45 (1) C3
Grândola • Portugal 11 C6
Grândola **Beach** • Portugal 68 [99]
Grands-Jardins Prov. Park • QU, Canada 123 D1
Grange-over-Sands • United Kingdom 74 C4
Grangemouth • United Kingdom 74 B4
Granhult • Sweden 95 F8
Granit Rose, Côte de • France 84 C2
Granite Peak • NV, United States 117 F2
Granites, The • NT, Australia 34 F4
Grankulla • Finland 95 E4
Gränna • Sweden 95 F3
Granollers • Spain 87 D4
Grant, General, Nat. Mem. **Park** • NY, United States 121 [328]
Grant, Ulysses S., Nat. Hist. Site **Park** • MO, United States 121 [176]
Grant-Kohrs Ranch Nat. Hist. Site **Park** • MT, United States 120 [68]
Grantham • United Kingdom 7 L9
Grants Pass • OR, United States 117 E3
Granville • France 84 C2
Grasellenbach **Spa** • Germany 83 [149]
Graskop • South Africa 24 E4
Grasmere • United Kingdom 74 C2
Grassmoor • United Kingdom 74 C1
Gräsö • Sweden 16 J6
Grass I. • Hong Kong, China 107 H4
Grass Valley • CA, United States 117 F3
Grasse • France 85 H4
Gråsten • Denmark 95 F13
Grau-du-Roi, le **Beach** • France 68 [131]
Graus • Spain 11 L2
Grave [Battlefield] • Netherlands 80 A11
Grave, la **Ski** • France 70 [59]
Grave, la • France 85 F4
Grave, Pointe de • France 85 G1
Gravelines • France 5 F3
Gravenhurst • OT, Canada 122 B5
Graves • France 84 B3
Gravesend • United Kingdom 74 E1
Gravina in Puglia • Italy 12 K8
Gravonne • Corsica, France 85 L3
Grays Harbor • WA, United States 117 E1
Grays Peak • CO, United States 116 A
Graz • Austria 13 E10
Great Abaco • Bahamas 124 B1
Great Australian Bight • Australia 34 E6
Great Barrier I. • New Zealand 35 E3
Great Barrier Reef **Heritage N** • QL, Australia 61 [131]
Great Barrier Reef • QL, Australia 111 F
Great Barrier Reef Marine Park • QL, Australia 34 J4
Great Basin • NV, United States 117 F2
Great Basin Nat. Park • NV, United States 117 F4
Great Basin Nat. Park **Park** • NV, United States 120 [62]
Great Bear • NT, Canada 38 G4
Great Bear Lake • NT/NU, Canada 38 G3
Great Bend • KS, United States 40 G4
Great Bernera • United Kingdom 75 A1
Great Bird I. • Antigua & Barbuda 125 F2
Great Blasket I. • Ireland 79 F7
Great Coxwell Barn • United Kingdom 74 D4
Great Dividing Range • Australia 34 I4
Great Exhibition Bay • New Zealand 35 D2
Great Exuma • Bahamas 124 B3
Great Falls • MT, United States 40 D2
Great Fish • South Africa 100 C8
Great Gable • United Kingdom 74 C1
Great George Resort Action Park • NJ, United States 118 H1
Great Gorge Resort Action Park **Park** • NJ, United States 121 [LL]
Great Harbour Cay • Bahamas 124 B1
Great Harbour Deep • NF, Canada 123 D5
Great Inagua • Bahamas 124 B4
Great Karoo • South Africa 100 C3
Great Keppel I. • QL, Australia 111 F4
Great Lakes • Canada/United States 117 D4
Great Malvern • United Kingdom 74 D3
Great Nicobar • India 28 F7
Great Oasis, The • Egypt 101 F3
Great Palm I. • QL, Australia 111 F1
Great Pedro Bluff • Jamaica 124 C3
Great Plains • Canada/United States 40 E2
Great [Riv] • Jamaica 124 C1
Great Ruaha • Tanzania 102 H4
Great Salt Lake • UT, United States 40 D3
Great Salt Lake Desert • UT, United States 40 D3
Great Salt Pond • St Kitts & Nevis 125 G4
Great Sand Dunes Nat. Mon. **Park** • CO, United States 120 [97]
Great Sandy Desert • WA, Australia 34 D4
Great Sandy Desert • OR, United States 117 E4
Great Skellig • Ireland 79 F7
Great Slave Lake • NT, Canada 38 H4
Great Smoky Mtns Nat. Park **Heritage N** • NC/TN, United States 60 [16]
Great Smoky Mtns Nat. Park **Park** • NC/TN, United States 121 [232]
Great Torrington • United Kingdom 74 F2
Great Valley • TN/VA United States 41 J4
Great Victoria Desert • SA/WA, Australia 34 E5
Great Victoria Desert Nature Reserve • SA/WA, Australia 34 E5
Great Wall • China 29 D3
Great Wall **Heritage C** • China 63 [144]
Great White Heron Nat. Wildlife Refuge • FL, United States 119 M7
Great Yarmouth • United Kingdom 7 N9
Great Yarmouth **Beach** • United Kingdom 75 [39-40]
Great Zimbabwe Nat. Mon. **Heritage C** • Zimbabwe 63 [100]
Great Zimbabwe Nat. Mon. • Zimbabwe 102 J4
Greater Antilles • West Indies 37 G4
Greater St Lucia Wetland Park **Park** • South Africa 103 [127]
Greater Sunda Is. • Indonesia 32 E4
Greatstone-on-Sea **Beach** • United Kingdom 75 [66]
Grebbestad • Sweden 95 F2
Gréboun, Mt • Niger 20 G4
Greco, Cape • Cyprus 93 J4
Gredos, Sierra de • Spain 11 F4
Greece • Europe 17
Greek Peak **Ski** • NY, United States 116 [176]
Greeley • CO, United States 40 F3
Greem Bell, Ostrov • Russian Fed. 96 A3
Green Bay • WI, United States 41 I3
Green Bay [Bay] • WI, United States 39 N7
Green I. • QL, Australia 111 F1
Green I. • Antigua & Barbuda 125 F4
Green Meadows Petting Farm • FL, United States 121 C2
Green Mtns • VT, United States 118 G3
Green [Riv] • UT/WY, United States 40 E3
Green River • WY, United States 40 E3
Green Springs Hist. District **Park** • VA, United States 121 [260]
Green Turtle Cay • Bahamas 124 B1
Green Valley • AZ, United States 118 J3
Greenbelt Park **Park** • MD, United States 121 [280]
Greenland • N. America 36 M2
Greenland Sea • Arctic Ocean 46 P2
Greenock • United Kingdom 74 B3
Greensboro • NC, United States 41 K4
Greenville • Liberia 22 C3
Greenville • SC, United States 41 J5
Greenville • NC, United States 118 H5
Greenville • MS, United States 118 K2
Greenville • TX, United States 119 N2
Greenwich • United Kingdom 7 M10
Greenwood • MS, United States 118 K2
Greenwood Great House • Jamaica 124 C1
Gregorio • Brazil 43 C5
Gregory Lake • WA, Australia 34 E3
Gregory, Lake • SA, Australia 34 G5
Greifswald • Germany 8 I2
Greifswalder Bodden • Germany 8 I2
Grein • Austria 13 D9
Greiz • Germany 9 H6
Gremikha • Russian Fed. 17 F1
Grenå **Beach** • Denmark 68 [47]
Grenå • Denmark 95 F10
Grenada • West Indies 37 I5
Grenadines, The • St Vincent 37 I5
Grenen • Denmark 95 F6
Grenoble • France 85 F3
Grenville, Cape • QL, Australia 34 H2
Gréolières-les-Neiges • France 85 H2
Gresik • Java, Indonesia 110 D4
Gressåmoen Nat. Park **Park** • Norway 72 [11]
Gressoney-la-Trinité **Ski** • Italy 70 [202]
Gressoney-la-Trinité • Italy 91 E1
Gressoney-St Jean **Ski** • Italy 70 [202]
Greve **Beach** • Denmark 68 [38]
Greven • Germany 8 C4
Grevená • Greece 15 C3
Grevenbroich • Germany 81 E3
Grevesmühlen • Germany 8 G3
Grey Is. • NF, Canada 123 D5
Grey Range • QL, Australia 34 H5
Greymouth • New Zealand 35 C6
Greystones **Beach** • Ireland 68 [55]
Greystones • Ireland 79 E4
Greytown • New Zealand 35 E5
Gribës • Albania 15 A3
Gribingu • Central African Rep./Chad 22 H3
Grieben **Spa** • Germany 83 [278]
Griesheim • Germany 5 L5
Griesheim • Germany 82 H4
Griffin • GA, United States 41 J5
Griffith • NS, Australia 111 G1
Grimari • Central African Rep. 22 H3
Grimaud **Beach** • France 68 [133]
Grimentz • Switzerland 89 G6
Grimmen • Germany 8 I2
Grimsby • United Kingdom 7 L8
Grimselpass • Switzerland 89 G3
Grimsey • Iceland 16 (1) E1
Grímsstadir • Iceland 16 (1) E2
Grimstad • Norway 95 F1
Grindavik • Iceland 16 (1) B3
Grindelwald **Ski** • Switzerland 70 [97]
Grindelwald • Switzerland 89 G2
Grindsted • Denmark 95 F9
Grintavec • Slovenia 13 D11
Gripsholm • Sweden 95 D3
Gris-Nez, Cap • France 10 G3
Grise Fjord • NU, Canada 36 I2
Grisons • Switzerland 89 G4
Grisslehamn • Sweden 95 D2
Grizedale Forest • United Kingdom 74 C4
Grmec • Bosnia-Herz. 14 D5
Grodno • Belarus 13 M4
Grodzisk Mazowiecki • Poland 13 J5
Groix, I. de • France 84 C3
Grójec • Poland 13 J6
Grömitz **Spa** • Germany 83 [25]
Gröna Lunds Tivoli **Park** • Sweden 73 [7]
Gronant **Beach** • United Kingdom 75 [204]
Gronau • Germany 8 C4
Grönenbach • Germany 82 J2
Grönenbach **Spa** • Germany 83 [237]
Grong • Norway 16 G4
Groningen • Netherlands 80 A4
Groningen [Adm] • Netherlands 80 A4
Groot • South Africa 100 C7
Groot-Karasberge • Namibia 24 B5
Groote Eylandt • NT, Australia 34 G2
Grootfontein • Namibia 24 B3
Gros Islet • St Lucia 125 J2
Gros Morne • NF, Canada 123 D3
Gros Morne Nat. Park **Heritage N** • NF, Canada 60 [7]
Gros Morne Nat. Park • NF, Canada 123 D3
Gros Piton • St Lucia 125 J3
Gros Piton Point • St Lucia 125 J3
Groß-Gerau • Germany 82 H4
Großarl **Ski** • Austria 70 [170]
Großbeeren • Germany 81 F4
Großenbrode **Spa** • Germany 83 [23]
Großer Arber • Germany 9 I7
Großer Feldberg • Germany 82 H2
Großer Inselsberg • Germany 9 F6
Großer Müggelsee • Germany 81 F4
Großer Plöner See • Germany 8 F2
Großer Seddiner See • Germany 81 F3
Großer Zernsee • Germany 81 F3
Großerdhünne Stausee • Germany 81 E4
Grosseto • Italy 91 E11
Grosseto-Prugna **Beach** • Corsica, France 68 [135]
Grosseto-Prugna • Corsica, France 85 L3
Großglockner • Austria 89 H8
Großostheim • Germany 9 E7
Großräschen • Germany 8 J5
Großrotte • Austria 89 H7
Grosswardein • Romania 71 A14
Grotli • Norway 94 C2
Grottaglie • Italy 12 L8
Grottammare • Italy 12 G5
Grou • Morocco 101 D1
Groznyy • Russian Fed. 17 H6
Grudovo • Bulgaria 97 D3
Grudziadz • Poland 13 H4
Gruissan **Beach** • France 68 [129]
Grumeti • Tanzania 23 E4
Grünau • Namibia 24 B5
Grünberg • Germany 82 G2
Grundy Lake Prov. Park • OT, Canada 122 B1
Grunewald • Germany 81 F3
Grünstadt • Germany 82 G4
Grünthal • Germany 81 F2
Grüsch • Switzerland 89 G4
Gruyères • Switzerland 89 G2
Gryazovets • Russian Fed. 97 E2
Gryfice • Poland 13 E4
Gryfino • Poland 13 D4
Gryon **Ski** • Switzerland 70 [83]
Gryon • Switzerland 89 G6
Gryt • Sweden 95 F4
Grytviken • South Georgia 46 (1) B4
Gstaad • Switzerland 89 G6
Gstaad-Saanenland **Ski** • Switzerland 70 [86]
Guacanayabo, Golfo de • Cuba 124 D7
Guadalajara • Spain 11 H4
Guadalajara **Heritage C** • Mexico 62 [19]
Guadalcanal • Solomon Is. 35 (1) G2
Guadaleste • Spain 87 C2
Guadalimar • Spain 11 H6
Guadalope • Spain 11 K4
Guadalquivir • Spain 11 F7
Guadalupe • Spain 11 F5
Guadalupe • Mexico 37 A2
Guadalupe **Heritage C** • Spain 64 [89]
Guadalupe • TX, United States 119 N5
Guadalupe [I.] • Mexico 36 F7
Guadalupe Mtns Nat. Park **Park** • TX, United States 120 [136]
Guadarrama, Sierra de • Spain 11 G4
Guadeloupe • West Indies 37 I4
Guadiana • Portugal/Spain 11 D7
Guadiana, Bahía de • Cuba 124 D1
Guadix • Spain 86 B4
Guaíba • Brazil 44 F5
Guáimaro • Cuba 124 D7
Guaiquinima • Venezuela 43 E2
Guaíra • Brazil 44 F3
Guajaba, Cayo • Cuba 124 D3
Guajara Mirim • Brazil 43 D6
Guajataca • Puerto Rico 125 E1
Guajira, Península de • Colombia 43 C1
Guakolak, Tanjung • Java, Indonesia 110 D1
Gualdo Tadino • Italy 71 A13
Gualeguay • Argentina 127 D1
Gualeguaychu • Argentina 127 D1
Guam • Pacific Ocean 33 F4
Guamá Indian Village • Cuba 124 D2
Guampi, Sierra de • Venezuela 37 H6
Guanajay • Cuba 124 D1
Guanajuato **Heritage C** • Mexico 62 [15]
Guanajuato • Mexico 123 E1
Guanajuato [Adm] • Mexico 37 (1) B1
Guanare • Venezuela 43 D2
Guane • Cuba 124 D1
Guangde • China 107 J3
Guangdong • China 107 G7
Guangmao Shan • China 31 C1
Guangming Ding • China 107 J3
Guangxi Zhuangzu Zizhiqu • China 29 D6
Guangzhou • China 107 H1
Guangzhou East • China 107 H2
Guánica • Puerto Rico 125 E3
Guanimar, Playa • Cuba 124 D1
Guantánamo • Cuba 124 D8
Guantánamo Bay • Cuba 124 D8
Guapay • Bolivia 44 D2
Guapi • Colombia 43 B3
Guaporé • Bolivia/Brazil 43 E6
Guaqui • Bolivia 44 C2
Guarabira • Brazil 45 (1) D3
Guarapari • Brazil 127 C2
Guarapuava • Brazil 44 F4
Guarda • Portugal 11 D4
Guarda [Adm] • Portugal 88 A1
Guardalabarca, Playa • Cuba 124 D8
Guardamar del Segura **Beach** • Spain 68 [118]
Guardamar del Segura • Spain 87 C3
Guárdia Sanframondi • Italy 91 G2
Guarujá • Brazil 127 C3
Guarulhos • Brazil 127 C3
Guarulhos [Apt] • Brazil 127 C3
Guasave • Mexico 40 E6
Guatemala • C. America 37 C4
Guatemala City • Guatemala 37 C5
Guatuaro Point • Trinidad & Tobago 125 K4
Guaviare • Colombia 43 D3
Guaxupé • Brazil 127 C1
Guayaguayare • Trinidad & Tobago 125 K4
Guayama • Puerto Rico 125 E4
Guayaneco, Archipiélago • Chile 45 A5
Guayanilla, Bahía de • Puerto Rico 125 E3
Guayaquil • Ecuador 43 B4
Guayaquil, Golfo de • Ecuador 43 A4
Guaymas • Mexico 40 D6
Gubakha • Russian Fed. 26 I6
Guban • Somalia 23 H1
Gubbat Sawqirah • Oman 18 G6
Gúbbio • Italy 91 E12
Guben • Germany 8 J5
Gubin • Poland 8 J5
Gúdar, Sierra de • Spain 11 K4
Gudbrandsdalen • Norway 16 E6
Gudhjem • Denmark 95 F16
Güdül • Turkey 15 N3
Gudur • India 106 D7
Gudvangen • Norway 94 C4
Guebwiller • France 9 C9
Guédi, Mt • Chad 23 B1
Guellala • Tunisia 101 E6
Guelma • Algeria 20 G1
Guelph • OT, Canada 122 B9
Guelta Zemmur • Western Sahara 20 C3

Guéne

Guéne • Benin 20 F6
Guéra, Massif de • Chad 21 C5
Guérande • France 84 C4
Guéret • France 85 G2
Guernica • Spain 11 I1
Guernsey • Channel Is. 7 J12
Guerrero • Mexico 37 (1) B2
Guerrero Negro • Mexico 40 D6
Guge • Ethiopia 23 F2
Guglionesi • Italy 12 I7
Guiana Highlands • S. America 43 E3
Guiana I. • Antigua & Barbuda 125 F2
Guide • China 29 C3
Guidel Beach • France 68 [81]
Guidel • France 84 C3
Guider • Cameroon 23 A2
Guiglo • Côte d'Ivoire 22 C3
Guignes • France 85 E4
Guildford • United Kingdom 74 E3
Guilford Courthouse Nat. Military Park Park • NC, United States 121 [246]
Guilin • China 29 E5
Güimar • Tenerife, Canary Is. 86 E1
Guimarães • Portugal 11 C3
Guincho • Portugal 88 D1
Guinea • Africa 22 B2
Guinea, Gulf of • Africa 22 F4
Guinea-Bissau • Africa 20 B6
Güines • Cuba 124 D2
Guingamp • France 84 C2
Guiria • Venezuela 43 E1
Guitiriz • Spain 11 D1
Guiuan • Philippines 31 H4
Guixi • China 31 F1
Guiyang • China 29 D5
Guizhou • China 107 G7
Gujarat • India 28 B4
Gujranwala • Pakistan 28 B2
Gujrat • Pakistan 28 B2
Gulbarga • India 106 D2
Gulbene • Latvia 16 N8
Gulen • Norway 94 C3
Gulf Is. Nat. Seashore • MS, United States 118 K4
Gulf Is. Nat. Seashore • FL, United States 119 M1
Gulf Is. Nat. Seashore Park • FL/MS, United States 121 [218]
Gulf, The • Asia 18 F4
Gulfport • MS, United States 118 K4
Gulfstream Park • FL, United States 119 M8
Gulhi • Maldives 106 E4
Gulian • China 27 J6
Gulistan • Uzbekistan 26 K9
Gulkana • AK, United States 38 B4
Gullane Bents Beach • United Kingdom 75 [7]
Gullivers Kingdom Park • United Kingdom 73 [26]
Gullspång • Sweden 95 F3
Güllük • Turkey 92 D9
Güllük Körfezi • Turkey 15 I6
Gülnar • Turkey 15 O7
Gülpinar • Turkey 15 H4
Gulu • Uganda 23 E3
Gumbiri, Jabal • Sudan 23 E3
Gummersbach • Germany 81 E4
Gummi • Nigeria 20 G6
Gümüssu • Turkey 15 K5
Gun Hill Tower • Barbados 125 H3
Guna • Ethiopia 21 G5
Guna • India 105 C6
Gündogmus • Turkey 93 G4
Gungu • Dem. Rep. of Congo 23 B5
Gunnar • SA, Canada 38 J5
Gunnbjørns Fjeld • Greenland 46 S2
Gunnedah • NS, Australia 34 J6
Gunnislake • United Kingdom 74 F5
Gunstock Ski • NH, United States 116 [209]
Guntakal • India 106 D2
Guntur • India 106 D3
Gunung Kawi • Bali, Indonesia 110 C2
Gunungsitoli • Indonesia 110 B3
Günz • Germany 9 F8
Günzburg • Germany 82 J2
Gunzenhausen • Germany 9 F7
Gur, Lough • Ireland 79 F6
Guradu • Maldives 106 E4
Güre • Turkey 15 K5
Gurgel • Sudan 21 D5
Gurha • India 105 C5
Gurktaler Alpen • Austria 14 A3
Gurskøy • Norway 94 C1
Gurupá • Brazil 43 G4
Gurupi • Brazil 45 (1) B4
Gurupi [Riv] • Brazil 45 (1) B2
Gurupi, Serra do • Brazil 45 (1) B4
Guruvayur • India 106 D10
Guruve • Zimbabwe 102 J2
Gusau • Nigeria 22 F2
Gusev • Russian Fed. 13 L3
Gush Halav • Israel 98 A2
Gushan • China 30 B5
Gusinaya, Guba • Russian Fed. 27 P2
Gusinoozersk • Russian Fed. 27 G6
Guspini • Sardinia, Italy 12 C9
Güstrow • Germany 8 H3
Gusum • Sweden 95 F4
Gutach • Germany 82 G8
Güterfelde • Germany 81 F3
Gütersloh • Germany 8 D5
Guthega • NS, Australia 111 G4
Guttenberg, Burg • Germany 82 G4
Guwahati • India 28 F3
Guyana • S. America 43 F2
Guyang • China 29 E2
Guyenne • France 10 F9
Guymon • OK, United States 40 F4
Güzelsu • Turkey 93 G4
Güzelyurt • Cyprus 15 N8
Güzelyurt Körfezi • Cyprus 15 N8
Gvardeysk • Russian Fed. 13 K3
Gvarv • Norway 94 B3
Gwadar • Pakistan 18 H4
Gwalior • India 105 C7
Gwanda • Zimbabwe 102 J3
Gwda • Poland 13 F4
Gweebarra Bay • Ireland 7 D7
Gwei • Zimbabwe 102 J3
Gweru • Zimbabwe 102 J4
Gyaca • China 28 F3
Gyandzha • Azerbaijan 18 E1
Gyangze • China 28 E3
Gyaring Co • China 28 E2
Gyaring Hu • China 28 G2
Gyda • Russian Fed. 26 M3
Gydan Peninsula • Russian Fed. 96 A3
Gydanskiy Poluostrov • Russian Fed. 26 M3
Gympie • QL, Australia 111 F6
Gyoma • Hungary 13 J11
Gyöngyös • Hungary 13 I10
Györ • Hungary 13 G10
Gypsumville • MN, Canada 38 L6
Gyula • Hungary 13 K11
Gyumri • Armenia 18 D1

H

Ha Giang • Vietnam 31 C2
Ha Long Bay Heritage N • Vietnam 61 [121]
Ha Long Bay • Vietnam 108 A1
Ha Tien • Vietnam 108 B3
Ha Tinh • Vietnam 31 D3
Ha'apai Group • Tonga 35 (2) F2
Ha'il • Saudi Arabia 18 D4
Ha-ad Chao Samran • Thailand 109 H3
Haag • Germany 82 J4
Haan • Germany 81 E3
Haapsalu • Estonia 16 L7
Haardt • Germany 9 C7
Haarlem • Netherlands 80 C1
Haarlemmermeer Polder • Netherlands 80 C1
Haast • New Zealand 35 B6
Haast Bluff • NT, Australia 112 H1
Haast Pass • New Zealand 35 B7
Haasts Bluff Aboriginal Land • NT, Australia 112 H1
Habarane • Sri Lanka 106 D15
Habaswein • Kenya 23 F3
Haboro • Japan 30 K2
Hachijo • Japan 30 J8
Hachinohe • Japan 30 K4
Hacilar • Turkey 93 G1
Hackås • Sweden 16 H5
Hackleton's Cliff • Barbados 125 H4
Hadamar • Germany 82 H2
Hadaribah, Ra's al • Sudan 18 C5
Hadd, Al • Oman 18 G5
Hadd, Ra's al • Oman 18 G5
Hadded • Somalia 23 H1
Haddington • United Kingdom 74 B4
Haddumati Atoll • Maldives 106 E3
Hadejia • Nigeria 22 F2
Hadejia [Riv] • Nigeria 22 F2
Hadejia-Nguru Wetlands Park • Nigeria 103 [33]
Hadeland • Norway 94 B2
Haderslev Beach • Denmark 68 [45]
Haderslev • Denmark 95 F13
Hadijah • Saudi Arabia 18 C4
Hadim • Turkey 15 N7
Hadithah, Al • Iraq 18 D3
Hadjout • Algeria 11 N8
Hadley Bay • NU, Canada 38 J2
Hadramawt • Yemen 18 E6
Hadrian's Wall • United Kingdom 7 J6
Hadrian, Villa • Italy 91 F1
Hadrian's Wall Heritage C • United Kingdom 64 [15]
Hadsund Beach • Denmark 68 [48]
Hadsund • Denmark 95 F6
Hae, Ko • Thailand 109 K2
Haeinsa Temple Heritage C • Rep. of Korea 63 [159]
Haeju • D.P.R. of Korea 30 C6
Hafar al Batin • Saudi Arabia 18 E4
Hafibah, Ra's • Saudi Arabia 18 E4
Hafirat al 'Ayda • Saudi Arabia 18 C4
Hafnarfjördur • Iceland 16 (1) B2
Hafun, Râs • Somalia 23 I1
Hagadera • Kenya 23 G3
Hagby • Sweden 95 F12
Hagen • Germany 81 E2
Hagen: Hohen-Limburg • Germany 81 E2
Hagenow • Germany 8 G3
Hagerman Fossil Beds Nat. Mon. • ID, United States 117 E4
Hagerman Fossil Beds Nat. Mon. Park • ID, United States 120 [64]
Haghpat Heritage C • Armenia 63 [79]
Hagi • Japan 30 F7
Hagondange • France 10 L4
Hague, Cap de la • France 10 D4
Hague, The • Netherlands 80 C1
Haguenau • France 10 M5
Hagunia • Western Sahara 20 C3
Hahnenklee Spa • Germany 83 [77]
Hai Phong • Vietnam 31 D2
Hai'an • China 107 J2
Haifa • Israel 98 A3
Haiku • China 31 E2
Hailar • China 27 I7
Hailong • China 29 H2
Hailun • China 29 H1
Hailuoto • Finland 16 M4
Haimen • China 107 J2
Hainan • China 31 E3
Hainaut • Belgium 80 A14
Haines • AK, United States 46 CC4
Haines Junction • YT, Canada 38 D4
Hainichen • Germany 9 I6
Haining • China 107 J4
Haiti • West Indies 37 G4
Haïtien, Cap • Haiti 37 G4
Haixin Shan • China 29 C3
Haiyan • China 107 J4
Haizhou Wan • China 29 F3
Hajarah, Al • Iraq 18 D4
Hajdúböszörmény • Hungary 13 K10
Hajdúdorog • Hungary 13 K10
Hajdúhadház • Hungary 13 K10
Hajdúnánás • Hungary 13 K10
Hajla • F.R. of Yugoslavia 14 H7
Hajnówka • Poland 13 M5
Hakken • Japan 30 H7
Hakodate • Japan 30 K4
Haku • Japan 30 I6
Hal Saflieni Hypogeum Heritage C • Malta 64 [197]
Hal Saflieni Hypogeum • Malta 93 H4
Hala Sultan Tekke • Cyprus 93 J4
Hala'ib • Egypt 21 G3
Halab • Syria 18 C2
Halab Heritage C • Syria 64 [239]
Hålaveden • Sweden 95 F3
Halban • Mongolia 26 Q8
Halberstadt • Germany 8 G5
Halcon, Mt • Philippines 31 G4
Hald • Denmark 95 F9
Halden • Norway 94 B4
Haldensleben • Germany 8 G4
Hale, Mt • WA, Australia 34 C5
Haleakala Crater • HI, United States 119 L3
Haleakala Nat. Park • HI, United States 119 L3
Haleakala Nat. Park Park • HI, United States 120 [18]
Halebid • India 106 D6
Haleiwa • HI, United States 119 L1
Half Moon Bay • Antigua & Barbuda 125 F4
Half Moon I. • Antarctica 59 A10
Half Way Tree • St Kitts & Nevis 125 G1
Halfa, Wadi • Egypt 21 F3
Halfmoon Bay • New Zealand 35 B8
Haliburton Highlands • OT, Canada 122 B6
Halifax • NS, Canada 123 D7
Halifax Bay • QL, Australia 111 F1
Halifax, Mt • QL, Australia 111 F1
Halikarnassos • Turkey 92 D9
Halil • Iran 18 G4
Halim Perdana Kusuma [Apt] • Java, Indonesia 110 D1
Hálki • Greece 93 F1
Hálki [I.] • Greece 93 F1
Halkida • Greece 92 D4
Halkidiki • Greece 92 D1
Hall Beach • NU, Canada 39 O3
Hall in Tirol • Austria 89 H2
Hall Peninsula • NU, Canada 39 R4
Halla • Rep. of Korea 30 D8
Halland • Sweden 95 F7
Hallandsås • Sweden 95 F11
Halle • Belgium 5 H4
Halle • Germany 8 G5
Halleberg • Sweden 95 F3
Hälleforsnäs • Sweden 95 D3
Hallein • Austria 89 H4
Hallet, Cape • Antarctica 59 A10
Halley Bay • Antarctica 46 (1) C2
Hallingdalselva • Norway 16 E6
Hallingskarvet • Norway 94 C4
Halls Creek • WA, Australia 34 E3
Hallsberg • Sweden 95 F4
Hallstadt-Dachstein-Salzkammergut Heritage C • Austria 64 [106]
Hallstahammar • Sweden 95 D1
Hallstavik • Sweden 95 D2
Halmahera • Indonesia 32 (1) C2
Halmeu • Romania 14 K2
Halmstad Beach • Sweden 68 [5]
Halmstad • Sweden 95 F11
Haloze • Slovenia 14 C3
Hals Beach • Denmark 68 [48]
Hals • Denmark 95 F6
Halsskov • Denmark 95 F14
Halstatt • Austria 89 H4
Halti • Finland 16 K2
Halver • Germany 81 E4
Hamad, Al • Saudi Arabia 21 H1
Hamada de Tinrhert • Algeria 20 G3
Hamada el Haricha • Mali 20 E4
Hamadah al Hamrah, Al • Libya 21 B1
Hamadan • Iran 18 E3
Hamah • Syria 18 C2
Hamamatsu • Japan 30 I7
Hamar • Norway 16 F6
Hamat Gader • Israel 98 A4
Hamâta • Egypt 21 G3
Hamatonbetsu • Japan 30 L2
Hambantota • Sri Lanka 106 D15
Hamber Prov. Park • BC, Canada 122 C4
Hamburg • Germany 8 F3
Hamburg • AR, United States 118 K1
Hamburg [Adm] • Germany 81 D1
Hamburgisches Wattenmeer, Nationalpark Park • Germany 72 [56]
Hamd, Wadi al • Saudi Arabia 21 G2
Häme • Finland 95 E2
Hämeenlinna • Finland 95 E4
Hameln • Germany 8 E4
Hamero Hadad • Ethiopia 23 G2
Hamersley Range • WA, Australia 34 C4
Hamgyong-Sanmaek • D.P.R. of Korea 30 E4
Hamhung • D.P.R. of Korea 30 D5
Hami • China 26 P9
Hamilton • VI, Australia 34 H7
Hamilton • OH, United States 41 J4
Hamilton • Bermuda 58 A2
Hamilton • United Kingdom 74 B3
Hamilton • New Zealand 112 K1
Hamilton • OT, Canada 122 B9
Hamilton Grange Nat. Mem. Park • NY, United States 121 [329]
Hamilton I. • QL, Australia 111 F1
Hamina • Finland 16 N6
Hamm • Germany 8 C5
Hamm Spa • Germany 83 [106]
Hammam Lif • Tunisia 101 E2
Hammamet • Tunisia 101 E2
Hammamet, Golfe de • Tunisia 101 E2
Hammarsjön • Sweden 95 F11
Hammel • Denmark 95 F9
Hammelburg • Germany 9 E6
Hammerdal • Sweden 16 H5
Hammerfest • Norway 16 L1
Hammershus • Denmark 95 F16
Hammond • LA, United States 118 K4
Hamoyet, Jabal • Eritrea/Sudan 16 D8
Hampden • New Zealand 35 C7
Hampi Heritage C • India 63 [128]
Hampi • India 106 D2
Hampshire • United Kingdom 75 A6
Hampstead • United Kingdom 74 E1
Hampton • VA, United States 118 H3
Hampton Court • United Kingdom 74 E1
Hampton Nat. Hist. Site Park • MD, United States 121 [281]
Hamra Nat. Park Park • Sweden 72 [24]
Hamun-e Jaz Murian • Iran 18 G4
Han • Rep. of Korea 30 D6
Han Shui • China 29 E4
Han-sur-Lesse • Belgium 80 A19
Hana • HI, United States 119 L4
Hanamaki • Japan 30 K5
Hanang • Tanzania 102 H2
Hanau • Germany 82 G4
Hancesti • Moldova 14 P3
Handan • China 29 E3
Handen • Sweden 95 D4
Handlová • Slovak Rep. 13 H9
Hanford • CA, United States 117 F3
Hangklip, Cape • South Africa 100 C5
Hangö • Finland 95 E4
Hangzhou • China 107 J3
Hangzhou Wan • China 107 J4
Haniá • Crete, Greece 93 E1
Haniá [Adm] • Crete, Greece 93 E1
Haninge • Sweden 16 J7
Haniòn, Kólpos • Crete, Greece 93 E1
Haniótis Beach • Greece 69 [192]
Haniótis • Greece 92 D1
Hanita • Israel 98 A1
Hankey • South Africa 100 C8
Hanko • Finland 95 E4
Hanmer Springs • New Zealand 35 D6
Hann, Mt • WA, Australia 34 E3
Hanna • AL, Canada 38 I6
Hannover • Germany 8 E4
Hanöbukt • Germany 13 D2
Hanöbukten • Sweden 95 F12
Hanoi • Vietnam 31 D2
Hanover • NH, United States 118 G3
Hansapark Park • Germany 73 [52]
Hanshan • China 107 J1
Hansi • India 105 C2
Hantsholm • Denmark 95 F5
Hanumangarh • India 105 C2
Hanzhong • China 29 D4
Hao • French Polynesia 33 M7
Haora • India 28 E4
Haouaria, El • Tunisia 101 E2
Haparanda • Sweden 16 M4
Hapsu • D.P.R. of Korea 30 E4
Har Sai Shan • China 29 B3
Harad • Saudi Arabia 18 E5
Hárakas • Crete, Greece 15 G9
Haraki • Rhodes, Greece 93 F4
Haramachi • Japan 30 K6
Harare • Zimbabwe 102 J2
Haraz • Chad 22 H2
Harazah • Sudan 21 F4
Harazé Mangueigne • Chad 23 C2
Harbin • China 29 H1
Harbo • Sweden 95 D1
Harboør • Denmark 95 F9
Harbour Breton • NF, Canada 123 D3
Harbour Grace • NF, Canada 123 D4
Harbour, Lake • NU, Canada 39 R4
Harbour Park, Littlehampton Park • United Kingdom 73 [38]
Hardangerfjorden • Norway 94 C3
Hardangerjøkulen • Norway 94 C4
Hardangervidda • Norway 94 C4
Hardangervidda Nat. Park Park • Norway 72 [15]
Hardangervidda Nat. Park • Norway 94 C4
Hardenberg • Netherlands 5 J2
Harderwijk • Netherlands 80 A7
Harderwijk, Zeedierenpark • Netherlands 80 A7
Harding • South Africa 24 E6
Hardknott Pass • United Kingdom 74 C3
Hare Indian • NT, Canada 38 F3
Hareidlandet • Norway 94 C1
Haren • Germany 8 C4
Harer • Ethiopia 23 G2
Harestua • Norway 94 B2
Hargeysa • Somalia 23 G2
Hargeysa Nat. Park Park • Somalia 103 [67]
Harghita, Muntii • Romania 14 M3
Haria Beach • Lanzarote, Canary Is. 68 [111]
Haridwar • India 105 C3
Haringvliet • Netherlands 80 C3
Haringvliet Dam • Netherlands 80 C3
Harirud • Afghanistan 18 I3
Harjavalta • Finland 95 E1
Harlech Beach • United Kingdom 75 [191]
Harlingen • Netherlands 80 A3
Harlow • United Kingdom 74 E1
Harmal • Goa, India 105 B1
Harmancik • Turkey 15 K4
Harmil • Eritrea 21 H4
Harney Basin • OR, United States 117 E4
Harney Lake • OR, United States 117 E4
Harney Peak • SD, United States 40 F3
Härnösand • Sweden 16 I5
Harpalpur • India 105 C7
Harper • Liberia 22 C4
Harpers Ferry Nat. Hist. Park Park • WV, United States 121 [270]
Harrachov • Czech Rep. 96 C2
Harrah, Al • Saudi Arabia 21 G1
Harrat al 'Uwayrid • Saudi Arabia 21 G2
Harricana • QU, Canada 39 P6
Harrington Harbour • QU, Canada 39 T6
Harris • United Kingdom 6 F4
Harrisburgh • PA, United States 118 H1
Harrismith • South Africa 24 D5
Harrison Point • Barbados 125 H1
Harrison's Cave • Barbados 125 H3
Harrisonburg • VA, United States 41 K4
Harrogate • United Kingdom 7 K8
Harsho • Somalia 23 H1
Harstad • Norway 16 I2
Harsum • Germany 8 E4
Hart, Lake • FL, United States 121 C2
Harteigen • Norway 94 C4
Hartford • CT, United States 118 H2
Hartland Covered Bridge • NB, Canada 123 D6
Hartland Point • United Kingdom 74 F1
Hartlepool • United Kingdom 7 K7
Hartola • Finland 95 E2
Haruj al Aswad, Al • Libya 21 C2
Harun, Bukit • Indonesia 31 F6
Harun, Bukit • Indonesia 32 F2
Harvey • WA, Australia 34 C6
Harwich • United Kingdom 74 E2
Haryana • India 105 C2
Harz • Germany 8 F5
Hasa, Al • Saudi Arabia 18 E4
Hasakah, Al • Syria 18 D2
Hasbayya • Lebanon 98 A2
Hase • Germany 8 C4
Hasi Ausert • Western Sahara 20 C4
Haslemere • United Kingdom 7 L10
Haslev • Denmark 95 F14
Hassan • India 106 D6
Hasselt • Belgium 80 A15
Hassi Bel Guebbour • Algeria 20 G3
Hassi Messaoud • Algeria 20 G2
Hassi Serouenout • Algeria 20 G4
Hässleholm • Sweden 95 F11
Hastings • United Kingdom 74 E4
Hastings • New Zealand 112 K4
Hasvik • Norway 16 L1
Hat Yai • Thailand 31 C5
Hatfield • United Kingdom 74 E1
Hatgal • Mongolia 27 F6
Hathras • India 105 C3
Hatillo • Puerto Rico 125 E1
Hatra Heritage C • Iraq 64 [250]
Hatteras, Cape • NC, United States 118 H5
Hatteras, Cape, Nat. Seashore • NC, United States 118 H5
Hattiesburg • MS, United States 118 K2
Hattingen • Germany 81 E2
Hattula • Finland 95 E2
Hattusha Heritage C • Turkey 64 [192]
Hatvan • Hungary 13 I10
Haugesund • Norway 94 C5
Hauhungaroa Range • New Zealand 112 K4
Haukeligrend • Norway 16 D7
Haukipudas • Finland 16 M4
Haukivesi • Finland 16 O5
Hauraki Gulf • New Zealand 35 E3
Hauroko, Lake • New Zealand 112 L3
Haus in Ennstal Ski • Austria 70 [182]
Hausa • Western Sahara 20 C3
Haut Atlas • Morocco 101 D4
Haut Médoc • France 84 B3
Haut Zaïre • Dem. Rep. of Congo 23 D3
Haute Corse • Corsica, France 85 L2
Haute Normandie • France 84 A1
Haute Savoie • France 85 F2
Haute-Touche, Parc de la • France 84 D4
Hautefort • France 85 G2
Hautes Fagnes • Belgium 5 I4
Hautes Pyrénées • France 85 J2
Hautmont • France 5 G4
Hautot-sur-Mer Beach • France 68 [77]
Hauts Plateaux • Algeria 20 E2
Hauula • HI, United States 119 L1
Hauzenberg • Germany 9 I8
Havana Heritage C • Cuba 62 [34]
Havana • Cuba 124 D1
Havant • United Kingdom 7 L11
Havasu, Lake • AZ/NV, United States 118 J1
Havel • Germany 8 I3
Havelkanal • Germany 81 F1
Havelland • Germany 81 D2
Havelock North • New Zealand 112 K4
Havelte • Netherlands 80 A8
Haverthwaite • United Kingdom 74 C4
Havirov • Czech Rep. 13 H8
Havlickuv Brod • Czech Rep. 96 C4
Havnsø • Denmark 95 F10
Havøysund • Norway 16 M1
Havre • MT, United States 40 E2
Havre, le • France 10 F4
Havre-Aubert • QU, Canada 123 D2
Havre-St Pierre • QU, Canada 123 D2
Havsa • Turkey 15 H2
Haw Par Dragon World • Singapore 108 E3
Hawaii • Pacific Ocean 119 L
Hawaii [I.] • HI, United States 119 L8
Hawaii Volcanoes Nat. Park Heritage N • HI, United States 60 [8]
Hawaii Volcanoes Nat. Park • HI, United States 119 L8
Hawaii Volcanoes Nat. Park Park • HI, United States 120 [22]
Hawaiian Is. cruise area • Pacific Ocean 58 A1
Hawalli • Kuwait 18 E4
Hawd • Ethiopia/Somalia 23 H2
Hawea • New Zealand 112 L2
Hawea, Lake • New Zealand 112 L2
Hawera • New Zealand 112 K3
Haweswater Reservoir • United Kingdom 74 C2
Hawi • HI, United States 119 L8
Hawick • United Kingdom 6 J6
Hawke Bay • New Zealand 35 F4
Hawke's Bay [Adm] • New Zealand 112 K4
Hawkes, Mt • Antarctica 46 (1) J1
Hawkshead • United Kingdom 74 C4
Hawksbill Beach • Antigua & Barbuda 125 F1
Hawng Tuk • Myanmar 31 B2
Hawthorne • NV, United States 117 F4
Hawthorne, Mt • Antarctica 46 (1) F3
Hay • AL, Canada 38 H5
Hay • NS, Australia 111 G1
Hay River • NT, Canada 38 H4
Hay-on-Wye • United Kingdom 74 D3
Hayes • MN, Canada 38 M5
Hayes, Mt • AK, United States 38 B4
Hayle • United Kingdom 74 F4
Hayling I. Beach • United Kingdom 75 [77-78]
Hayman I. • QL, Australia 111 F1
Haymana • Turkey 15 N4
Haynesville • LA, United States 118 K1
Hayrabolu • Turkey 15 H2
Haystack Ski • VT, United States 116 [195]
Haywards Heath • United Kingdom 74 E3
Hayya • Sudan 21 G4
Hazebrouck • France 10 H3
Hazleton • PA, United States 118 H1
Hazor • Israel 98 A2
He Xian • China 107 J1
Heacham Beach • United Kingdom 75 [32-33]
Head of Bight • SA, Australia 34 F6
Head-Smashed-In Buffalo Jump Heritage C • AL, Canada 62 [2]
Healdsburg • CA, United States 117 F3
Heard I. • Indian Ocean 19 (1) B2
Heard I. Heritage N • Indian Ocean 61 [138]
Hearne • TX, United States 119 N3
Hearst San Simeon State Hist. Mon. • CA, United States 117 F3
Heart of England • United Kingdom 74 D
Heathrow [Apt] • United Kingdom 74 E1
Heavenly Ski • NV, United States 116 [68]
Hebbronville • TX, United States 119 N5
Hebei • China 107 G3
Hebi • China 29 E3
Hebrides, Inner • United Kingdom 6 F5
Hebrides, Outer • United Kingdom 6 E4
Hebrides, Sea of • United Kingdom 6 E4
Hebron • NF, Canada 39 S5
Hebron • Jordan 98 A7
Heby • Sweden 95 D1
Hecate Strait • BC, Canada 38 E6
Hechingen • Germany 9 D8
Hechuan • China 29 D4
Hed • Sweden 95 D1
Heddal stavkirke • Norway 94 B1
Heddalsvatnet • Norway 94 B3
Hede • Sweden 16 G5
Hedemora • Sweden 16 I6
Hedesundafjärden • Sweden 95 D1
Hedmark • Norway 16 F6
Heemstede • Netherlands 80 C1
Heerenlogement Cave • South Africa 100 C1
Heerenveen • Netherlands 80 A3
Heerlen • Netherlands 80 A16
Hefa • Israel 98 A3
Hefei • China 29 F4
Hegang • China 29 I1
Hegura • Japan 30 I6
Hei Ling Chau • Hong Kong, China 107 H5
Heide • Germany 8 E2
Heide-Park Park • Germany 73 [54]
Heidelberg • Germany 82 G4
Heidenheim an der Brenz • Germany 9 F8
Heikendorf Spa • Germany 83 [16]
Heilbad Heiligenstadt Spa • Germany 83 [297]
Heilbronn • Germany 82 G6
Heiligenberg, Schloß • Germany 82 J5
Heiligenblut • Austria 89 H8
Heiligendamm Beach • Germany 68 [3]
Heiligendamm Spa • Germany 83 [269]
Heiligenhafen • Germany 8 G2
Heiligenhafen Spa • Germany 83 [21]
Heiligenhaus • Germany 81 E1
Heiligenstadt • Germany 9 F5
Heilong Jiang • China 27 K7
Heilongjiang • China 107 G4
Heimaey • Iceland 16 (1) C3
Heimdal • Norway 16 F5
Heinola Beach • Finland 69 [28]
Heinola • Finland 95 E2
Heishan Xia • China 29 C3
Hekla • Iceland 16 (1) D2
Hel • Poland 13 H3
Helagsfjället • Sweden 16 G5
Helen Reef • Palau 32 (1) D2
Helena • MT, United States 40 D2
Helengeli • Maldives 106 E2
Helensburgh • United Kingdom 74 B3
Helgasjön • Sweden 95 F7
Helgeland • Norway 16 G3
Helgoland • Germany 8 C2
Helgoland Spa • Germany 83 [1]
Helgoländer Bucht • Germany 8 D2
Heliopolis • Egypt 101 F2
Hellendoorn, Avonturenpark • Netherlands 80 A8
Hellesylt • Norway 94 C2
Hellevoetsluis • Netherlands 80 C3
Hellin • Spain 11 J6
Hellinikon [Apt] • Greece 92 D4
Hells Canyon Nat. Recreation Area • ID/OR, United States 117 E4
Hells Gate Nat. Park • Kenya 101 G3
Hellshire Hills • Jamaica 124 C4
Helmand • Afghanistan 18 H3
Helme • Germany 8 G5
Helmond • Netherlands 80 A11
Helmstedt • Germany 8 G4
Helong • China 30 E3
Helsingborg Beach • Sweden 68 [10]
Helsingborg • Sweden 95 F11
Helsinge Beach • Denmark 68 [41]
Helsingfors Heritage C • Finland 64 [8]
Helsingfors • Finland 95 E4
Helsingør • Denmark 95 F11
Helsinki Beach • Finland 69 [27]
Helsinki Heritage C • Finland 64 [8]
Helsinki • Finland 95 E4
Helston • United Kingdom 74 F4
Helvellyn • United Kingdom 74 C2
Helwân • Egypt 101 F2
Hembadoo • Maldives 106 E2
Hemel Hempstead • United Kingdom 7 L10
Hemnes • Norway 94 B2
Hempstead • TX, United States 119 N4
Hemsedal • Norway 94 C4
Henan • China 107 G7
Henbury • NT, Australia 112 H4
Henbury meteorite craters • NT, Australia 112 H4
Hendaye • France 85 J1
Hendek • Turkey 15 L3
Henderson • NV, United States 117 F4
Henderson • TX, United States 119 N2
Henderson I. Heritage N • Pacific Ocean 60 [142]
Heng Shan • Shanxi, China 107 G3
Heng Shan • Hunan, China 107 G7
Hengduan Shan • China 31 B1
Hengelo • Netherlands 80 A8
Hengqin • China 107 H3
Hengshui • China 29 F3
Hengyang • China 29 E5
Hénin-Beaumont • France 5 F4
Hennebont • France 84 C4
Hennigsdorf • Germany 81 F1
Henrietta Maria, Cape • OT, Canada 39 O5
Henry, Cape • VA, United States 118 H5
Henzada • Myanmar 31 B3
Heping • China 29 F6
Heptapegon • Israel 98 A4
Héradsvötn • Iceland 16 (1) D2
Herakleion • Crete, Greece 93 E3
Herald Cays • CL, Australia 111 F1
Herat • Afghanistan 18 H3
Herborn • Germany 82 G2
Herbstein Spa • Germany 83 [135]
Herculaneum Heritage C • Italy 64 [128]
Herculaneum • Italy 91 G3
Herdecke • Germany 81 E2
Heredia • Costa Rica 37 E5
Hereford • TX, United States 40 F5
Hereford • United Kingdom 74 D3
Herefordshire • United Kingdom 74 D1
Hereke • Turkey 15 K3
Herentals • Belgium 80 A11
Herford • Germany 8 D4
Hergiswil • Switzerland 89 G3
Hergla • Tunisia 101 E2
Heringsdorf • Germany 8 J3
Heringsdorf Beach • Germany 69 [30]
Heringsdorf Spa • Germany 83 [285]
Herisau • Switzerland 9 E9
Heritage Quay • Antigua & Barbuda 125 F1
Herm • Channel Is. 75 A8
Hermannsburg • NT, Australia 112 H2
Hermannsburg Aboriginal Land • NT, Australia 112 H2
Hermanos • Venezuela 43 E1
Hermansverk • Norway 94 C4
Hermanus • South Africa 100 C5
Hermitage • France 84 B4
Hermitage, The • Bahamas 124 B2
Hermon, Mount • Lebanon/Syria 98 A2
Hermosillo • Mexico 40 D6
Hermsdorf • Germany 9 G6
Hernád • Slovak Rep. 13 K9
Hernani • Spain 11 J1
Herne • Germany 81 E2
Herne Bay • United Kingdom 74 E2
Herne Bay Beach • United Kingdom 75 [60]
Herne: Wanne-Eickel • Germany 81 E2
Herning • Denmark 95 F9
Herodium • Jordan 98 A8
Heroine's monument • Phuket, Thailand 109 K1
Herolds Bay • South Africa 100 C7
Heron I. • QL, Australia 111 F4
Herouval, le Bois • France 85 E1
Herräng • Sweden 95 D2
Herrenchiemsee, Schloß • Germany 82 J4
Herrera de Pisuerga • Spain 11 G2
Herrljunga • Sweden 95 F3
Herrnsheim • Germany 82 H4
Herrsching • Germany 82 J3
Hershey • PA, United States 118 H1
Hersheypark Park • PA, United States 121 [JJ]
Herstal • Belgium 5 I4
Herten • Germany 81 E2
Hertford • United Kingdom 74 E1
Hertfordshire • United Kingdom 74 E1

Hervey Bay • QL, Australia 111 F4
Herzberg • Germany 8 F5
Herzogenaurach • Germany 9 F7
Herzogenrath • Germany 5 J4
Hesdin • France 5 F4
Heshbon • Jordan 98 A6
Hesse • Germany 81 D3
Hessen • Germany 9 D6
Hessisch Lichtenau • Germany 9 E5
Hettstedt • Germany 8 G5
Hever Castle • United Kingdom 74 E3
Heves • Hungary 13 J10
Hewanorra [Apt] • St Lucia 125 J4
Hexham • United Kingdom 7 J7
Hexrivierberge • South Africa 100 C6
Heysham • United Kingdom 78 A5
Heyuan • China 29 E6
Heywood • VI, Australia 34 H7
Heywoods Beach • Barbados 125 H1
Heze • China 29 F3
Hialeah • FL, United States 119 M8
Hibbing • MN, United States 41 H2
Hicacos, Peninsula • Cuba 124 D2
Hida-Sanmyaku • Japan 30 I6
Hidaka-Sanmyaku • Japan 30 L3
Hidalgo • Mexico 37 B3
Hidalgo del Parral • Mexico 40 E6
Hidalgo, Miguel [Apt] • Mexico 123 E1
Hidcote Manor • United Kingdom 74 D4
Hidden Valley **Ski** • PA, United States 116 [159]
Hiddensee • Germany 8 I2
Hiddensee **Spa** • Germany 83 [278]
Hiddesen **Spa** • Germany 83 [95]
Hierakonopolis • Egypt 101 F5
Hierapolis • Turkey 92 D6
Hierapolis-Pamukkale **Heritage N** • Turkey 61 [62]
Hierapolis-Pamukkale **Heritage C** • Turkey 64 [189]
Hierro • Canary Is. 87 E5
High Island • TX, United States 119 N4
High Island Reservoir • Hong Kong, China 107 H6
High Plains • United States 117 D2
High Point • NC, United States 41 K4
High Rock • Bahamas 124 B2
High Street • United Kingdom 74 C2
High Willhays • United Kingdom 74 F5
High Wycombe • United Kingdom 7 L10
Highgate • Jamaica 124 C2
Highland Park • Ko Samui, Thailand 109 J1
Highlands Forest Reserve • Penang, Malaysia 108 C1
Highlands Hammock State Recreation Area • FL, United States 119 M5
Highlands, North West • United Kingdom 6 G4
Highveld • Zimbabwe 102 J4
Higüero, Punta • Puerto Rico 125 E1
Higüey • Dominican Rep. 37 H4
Hiitola • Russian Fed. 16 O6
Hiiumaa • Estonia 16 L7
Hijar • Spain 11 K3
Hijaz, Al • Saudi Arabia 18 C5
Hikkaduwa • Sri Lanka 106 D15
Hikurangi • New Zealand 35 E2
Hikurangi [Mtn] • New Zealand 35 G3
Hila • Indonesia 32 (1) C4
Hildburghausen • Germany 9 F6
Hilden • Germany 81 E3
Hildesheim • Germany 8 E4
Hildesheim **Heritage C** • Germany 64 [36]
Hilisimaetano • Indonesia 110 B3
Hill End • NS, Australia 111 G2
Hill Head **Beach** • United Kingdom 75 [79-80]
Hillaby, Mt • Barbados 125 H1
Hillah, Al • Iraq 18 D3
Hillah, Al • Saudi Arabia 18 E5
Hillegom • Netherlands 80 C1
Hillerød • Denmark 95 F10
Hillsboro • TX, United States 119 N1
Hillswick • United Kingdom 6 K1
Hilo • HI, United States 119 L8
Hilpoltstein • Germany 9 G7
Hilvarenbeek • Netherlands 80 A11
Hilversum • Netherlands 80 C2
Himachal Pradesh • India 28 C2
Himalaya • Asia 28 E3
Himarë • Albania 15 A3
Himeji • Japan 30 H7
Himeji **Heritage C** • Japan 63 [165]
Himmafushi • Maldives 106 E2
Himmerland • Denmark 95 F5
Himos • Finland 95 E2
Hin Khom, Laem • Ko Samui, Thailand 109 J2
Hinakiyah, Al • Saudi Arabia 18 D5
Hinca Renancó • Argentina 44 D5
Hinchinbrook I. • QL, Australia 111 F1
Hindelang • Germany 82 J6
Hindelang **Spa** • Germany 83 [243]
Hindsholm • Denmark 95 F10
Hindu Kush • Asia 28 B1
Hindupur • India 106 D6
Hindustan • India 28 C3
Hinganghat • India 28 C4
Hinggan Ling • China 25 M5
Hinlad Falls • Ko Samui, Thailand 109 J1
Hinnøya • Norway 16 H2
Hinojosa del Duque • Spain 11 F6
Hins • Syria 18 C3
Hinterglemm • Austria 89 H3
Hintertux **Ski** • Austria 70 [141]
Hintertux • Austria 89 H7
Hinterzarten **Spa** • Germany 83 [209]
Hios **Heritage C** • Greece 64 [184]
Hios • Greece 92 D5
Hios [I.] • Greece 92 D5
Hippos • Israel 98 A4
Hirado • Japan 30 E8
Hirara • Japan 29 H6
Hirebhasgar Reservoir • India 106 D6
Hirfanii Baraji Gölü • Turkey 15 O4
Hirhafok • Algeria 20 G4
Hiroo • Japan 30 L3
Hirosaki • Japan 30 K4
Hiroshima • Japan 30 G7
Hiroshima **Heritage C** • Japan 63 [163]
Hirschegg **Ski** • Austria 70 [128]
Hirschegg • Austria 89 H1
Hirson • France 10 J4
Hîrsova • Romania 97 D2
Hirtshals **Beach** • Denmark 68 [48]
Hirtshals • Denmark 95 F6
Hisar • India 105 C2
Hispaniola • West Indies 37 G3
Histria • Romania 97 D2
Hitachi • Japan 30 K6
Hitoyoshi • Japan 30 F8
Hitra • Norway 16 E5
Hjallerup • Denmark 95 F6
Hjälmaren • Sweden 95 D3
Hjelm Bugt • Denmark 95 F15
Hjelmeland • Norway 94 C5
Hjo • Sweden 95 F3
Hjørring **Beach** • Denmark 68 [48]
Hjørring • Denmark 95 F6
Hlane Game Sanctuary **Park** • Swaziland 103 [131]
Hlohovec • Slovak Rep. 13 G9
Hluboká • Czech Rep. 96 C4
Hluhluwe/Umfolozi Game Reserve **Park** • South Africa 103 [128]
Ho • Ghana 22 E3
Ho Chi Minh City • Vietnam 108 B1
Hoa Da • Vietnam 108 B2
Hoanib • Namibia 24 A3
Hobart • TS, Australia 34 I8
Hobbs • NM, United States 40 F5
Hobq Shamo • China 29 D3
Hobro • Denmark 95 F9
Hobya Obbia • Somalia 23 H2
Hoch Harz, Nationalpark **Park** • Germany 72 [63]
Hochbrig • Switzerland 89 G3
Höchenschwand **Spa** • Germany 83 [207]
Hochfeiler • Austria/Italy 90 B1
Hochgolling • Austria 9 I8
Hochgurgl **Ski** • Austria 70 [136]
Hochgurgl • Austria 89 H6
Höchneukirch • Germany 81 E3
Hochschwab • Austria 13 E10
Hochsölden • Austria 89 H6
Höchstadt an der Aisch • Germany 9 F7
Hockenheim • Germany 5 L5
Hockenheim • Germany 82 G4
Hodeida • Yemen 18 D7
Hodh • Mauritania 20 D5
Hódmezővásárhely • Hungary 13 J11
Hodna, Chott el • Algeria 20 F1
Hodonín • Czech Rep. 13 G9
Hoek van Holland • Netherlands 80 C3
Hoekse Waard • Netherlands 80 C3
Hof • Germany 9 G6
Hofgeismar • Germany 8 E5
Höfn • Iceland 16 (1) F2
Hofors • Sweden 16 I6
Hofsjökull • Iceland 16 (1) D2
Hofu • Japan 30 F7
Höganäs • Sweden 95 F11
Hogarth, Mt • NT, Australia 34 G4
Högby • Sweden 95 F8
Hoggar • Algeria 100 A1
Hogland • Russian Fed. 16 N6
Höglwörth • Germany 82 J8
Högsby • Sweden 95 F8
Høgsfjorden • Norway 94 C5
Hoh Xil Nur • China 28 F1
Hoh Zil Shan • China 28 E1
Hohe Acht • Germany 82 H1
Hohe Tauern, Nationalpark **Park** • Austria 72 [82]
Hohe Tauern, Nationalpark • Austria 89 H8
Hohe Wilde • Austria/Italy 90 B1
Hohegeiß **Spa** • Germany 83 [81]
Hohen Neuendorf • Germany 81 F1
Hoheneck **Spa** • Germany 83 [175]
Hohenschwangau • Germany 82 J6
Hohentwiel • Germany 82 G8
Hohenzollern, Schloß • Germany 82 G6
Hohhot • China 29 E2
Hohneck • France 10 L5
Hohneck, Burg • Germany 82 H4
Hohokam Pima Nat. Mon. **Park** • AZ, United States 120 [112]
Hohwacht **Spa** • Germany 83 [19]
Hoima • Uganda 23 E3
Højer • Denmark 95 F13
Hok-Kai • Japan 30 M2
Hokensås • Sweden 95 F3
Hokitika • New Zealand 35 C6
Hokkaido • Japan 30 M3
Hokksund • Norway 94 B1
Hol • Norway 94 C4
Holasovice • Czech Rep. 96 C4
Holbæk **Beach** • Denmark 68 [43]
Holbæk • Denmark 95 F10
Holbrook • AZ, United States 40 D5
Holburgen • Sweden 16 J8
Holeby **Beach** • Denmark 68 [37]
Holen • Norway 94 B4
Holetown • Barbados 125 H3
Holguín • Cuba 124 D8
Holiday Mtn **Ski** • NY, United States 116 [179]
Holiday Park **Park** • Germany 73 [63]
Holiday Park • Germany 82 G4
Holiday Valley **Ski** • NY, United States 116 [172]
Höljes • Sweden 16 G6
Hollabrunn • Austria 13 F9
Holland • United Kingdom 75 A5
Hollandse IJssel • Netherlands 80 C4
Hollant **Beach** • Goa, India 105 B2
Holleia • Norway 94 B1
Hollókö **Heritage C** • Hungary 64 [152]
Hollywood • CA, United States 117 F6
Hollywood • FL, United States 119 M8
Holman I. • NT, Canada 38 H2
Holmes Hill • St Kitts & Nevis 125 G4
Holmes Reefs • CL, Australia 33 F7
Holmestrand • Norway 94 B3
Holmsland **Beach** • Denmark 68 [50]
Holmsland Klit • Denmark 95 F9
Holmsund • Sweden 16 K5
Hölö • Sweden 95 D4
Holomóndas • Greece 15 E3
Holsnøy • Norway 94 C3
Holstebro • Denmark 95 F9
Holsteinsborg • Greenland 39 U3
Holsworthy • United Kingdom 74 F2
Holtyn-Daba • Mongolia 27 G7
Holy I. • England, UK 6 K6
Holy I. • Wales, UK 7 H8
Holy Island **Beach** • United Kingdom 75 [212-215]
Holy Land • Asia 98 A
Holyhead • United Kingdom 7 H8
Holywood Park **Park** • Germany 73 [58]
Holzgau • Austria 89 H2
Holzkirchen • Germany 82 J3
Holzminden • Germany 8 E5
Holzwickede • Germany 81 E2
Homa Bay • Kenya 101 G3
Homalin • Myanmar 31 B2
Homberg • Germany 9 E5
Hombori • Mali 20 E5
Homburg • Germany 9 C7
Home Bay • NU, Canada 39 R3
Home Hill • QL, Australia 111 F1
Homel • Belarus 17 E4
Homer • AK, United States 46 EE4
Homestead • FL, United States 119 M8
Homestead Nat. Mon. of America **Park** • NE, United States 121 [167]
Homewood **Ski** • CA, United States 116 [56]
Homoljske Planina • F.R. of Yugoslavia 14 I5
Homosassa Springs State Wildlife Park • FL, United States 119 M5
Homr, El • Algeria 20 F3
Hon Chong • Vietnam 108 B3
Hon Khoai • Vietnam 108 B3
Hon Lon • Vietnam 108 B2
Hon Quan • Vietnam 108 B1
Hon Tre • Vietnam 108 B2
Honakaa • HI, United States 119 L8
Honavar • India 106 D5
Honaz Dagi • Turkey 15 K6
Honda • Colombia 43 C2
Hondo • Japan 30 F8
Hondo • Belize/Mexico 37 D4
Honduras • C. America 37 D5
Honduras, Golfo de • C. America 37 D4
Hønefoss • Norway 94 B1
Honey Lake Resort • Shenzhen, China 107 H3
Honfleur • France 10 F4
Hong Kong Central • Hong Kong, China 107 H5
Hong Kong I. • Hong Kong, China 107 H6
Hong Kong Special Administrative Region • China 107 H2
Hong, Song • Vietnam 108 A1
Hongch'on • Rep. of Korea 30 D6
Hongor • Mongolia 29 E1
Hongqiao [Apt] • China 107 J2
Hongsong • Rep. of Korea 30 D6
Honguedo, Détroit d' • QU, Canada 123 D2
Hongwon • D.P.R. of Korea 30 D5
Honiara • Solomon Is. 35 (1) F2
Honister Pass • United Kingdom 74 C1
Honiton • United Kingdom 74 F2
Honjo • Japan 30 K5
Honkajoki • Finland 95 E1
Hønne Strand • Denmark 95 F9
Honningsvåg • Norway 16 M1
Honolulu • HI, United States 119 L6
Honrubia • Spain 11 I5
Hons • Syria 18 C3
Honshu • Japan 30 J5
Hood, Fort • TX, United States 119 N3
Hood, Mt • OR, United States 117 E3
Hoofddorp • Netherlands 80 C1
Hoogeveen • Netherlands 80 A8
Hoogezand • Netherlands 80 A4
Hoogvliet • Netherlands 80 C3
Hook I. • QL, Australia 111 F1
Hook of Holland • Netherlands 80 C3
Hoonah • AK, United States 38 D5
Hooper, Cape • NU, Canada 39 R3
Höör • Sweden 95 F11
Hoorn • Netherlands 80 A7
Hoover Dam • AZ/NV, United States 118 J1
Hoover, Herbert, Nat. Hist. Site **Park** • IA, United States 121 [169]
Hope • AR, United States 41 H5
Hope • BC, Canada 122 C3
Hope Bay • Antarctica 59 A10
Hope Bay • Jamaica 124 C2
Hope Town • Bahamas 124 B1
Hopes Advance, Cap • QU, Canada 39 R4
Hopetoun • WA, Australia 34 D6
Hopetoun • VI, Australia 34 H7
Hopewell Culture Nat. Hist. Park **Park** • OH, United States 121 [186]
Hopewell Furnace Nat. Hist. Site **Park** • PA, United States 121 [306]
Hopfen am See **Spa** • Germany 83 [244]
Hopfenberg **Spa** • Germany 83 [89]
Hopfgarten im Brixental **Ski** • Austria 70 [149]
Hopi Indian Reservation • AZ, United States 118 J1
Hopkins, Lake • WA, Australia 112 H3
Hóra • Greece 15 C6
Horain • Turkey 93 G3
Horb • Germany 9 D8
Horbat Ashdod Yam • Israel 98 A5
Hörby • Sweden 95 F11
Hordaland • Norway 94 C3
Horeftó • Greece 92 D4
Horezu **Heritage C** • Romania 64 [164]
Horlivka • Ukraine 17 F5
Hormigueros • Puerto Rico 125 E3
Hormoz, Küh-e • Iran 18 F4
Hormuz • Iran 98 B4
Hormuz, Strait of • Iran/Oman 18 G4
Horn • Iceland 16 (1) B1
Horn, Cape • Chile 45 C7
Horn, Is. de • Wallis & Futuna 35 (2) E1
Horn Plateau • NT, Canada 38 H4
Hornavan • Sweden 16 J3
Hornberg, Burg • Germany 82 G4
Horncastle • United Kingdom 5 C1
Hörnefors • Sweden 16 J5
Hornindalsvatn • Norway 94 C1
Hornisgrinde • Germany 82 G6
Hornos, Cabo de • Chile 45 C7
Hörnum **Spa** • Germany 83 [2]
Horovice • Czech Rep. 96 C1
Horqin Youyi Qianqqi • China 29 G1
Horqin Zuoyi Zhongqi • China 27 J8
Horred • Sweden 95 F7
Horse Is. • NF, Canada 123 D3
Horsens **Beach** • Denmark 68 [46]
Horsens • Denmark 95 F9
Horseshoe Bend Nat. Military Park **Park** • AL, United States 121 [205]
Horsham • VI, Australia 34 H7
Horsham • United Kingdom 74 E3
Horst, Schloß • Germany 81 E2
Horta • Azores 88 B1
Hortas do Tabual • Portugal 88 E5
Horten • Norway 94 B4
Hortobágyi Nat. Park **Park** • Hungary 72 [105]
Horton • NT, Canada 38 F3
Horumersiel **Spa** • Germany 83 [48]
Horyuji **Heritage C** • Japan 63 [166]
Hosaina • Ethiopia 23 F2
Hösbach • Germany 9 E6
Hoséré Vokré • Cameroon 22 G3
Hoskins • Papua New Guinea 35 (1) E2
Hospet • India 106 D2
Hospitalet de Llobregat, l' • Spain 11 N3
Hossegor • France 85 G3
Hossmo • Sweden 95 F8
Hoste, I. • Chile 45 C7
Hot • Thailand 109 G3
Hot Springs • SD, United States 40 F3
Hot Springs Nat. Park **Park** • AR, United States 121 [193]
Hotan • China 26 M10
Hotazel • South Africa 24 C5
Hoting • Sweden 16 I4
Hottah Lake • NT, Canada 38 H3
Hottentots Holland Nature Reserve • South Africa 100 C5
Hotton • Belgium 80 A15
Houdan • France 85 E3
Houlton • ME, United States 118 G2
Houma • LA, United States 118 K4
Houmt-Souk • Tunisia 101 E4
Houmt-Souq • Tunisia 101 E4
Houndé • Burkina Faso 22 D2
Hourtin **Beach** • France 68 [85]
Houston • TX, United States 119 N4
Houston • BC, Canada 122 C1
Houtribdijk • Netherlands 80 A7
Hov • Denmark 95 F10
Hovdehytta • Norway 94 C6
Hove • United Kingdom 7 L11
Hovenweep Nat. Mon. **Park** • CO, United States 120 [94]
Hovgården **Heritage C** • Sweden 64 [4]
Howa • Chad/Sudan 21 D4
Howe, Cape • NS/VI, Australia 111 G4
Howland • Pacific Ocean 33 J5
Howletts Park • United Kingdom 74 E3
Howth • Ireland 79 E2
Höxter • Germany 8 E5
Hoy • United Kingdom 6 I3
Høyanger • Norway 94 C3
Hoyerswerda • Germany 8 J5
Hpunhpu • Myanmar 31 B1
Hradec Králove • Czech Rep. 96 C2
Hrissi • Greece 93 E8
Hrissoúpoli • Greece 15 F3
Hristiani • Greece 92 D11
Hrodna • Belarus 13 M4
Hron • Slovak Rep. 13 H9
Hrubieszów • Poland 13 M7
Hruby Nisky Jesenik • Czech Rep. 13 G7
Hsinchu • Taiwan 29 G6
Hsophang • Myanmar 31 B2
Hu Men • China 107 H2
Hua Hin • Thailand 109 H3
Hua Shan • China 107 G3
Huacho • Peru 43 B6
Huacrachuco • Peru 43 B5
Huainan • China 29 F4
Huairen • China 29 E3
Huajuápan de León • Mexico 123 E4
Hualapai Indian Reservation • AZ, United States 118 J1
Hualien • Taiwan 29 G6
Huambo • Angola 23 B6
Huancabamba • Peru 43 B6
Huancapi • Peru 127 B1
Huancavelica • Peru 127 B1
Huancayo • Peru 127 B1
Huang Hai • Asia 29 G3
Huang He • China 29 E3
Huang Shan **Heritage N** • China 61 [114]
Huang Shan **Heritage C** • China 63 [154]
Huang Shan • China 107 J3
Huang Shui • China 29 C3
Huangqang Liang • China 27 I8
Huanglong **Heritage N** • China 61 [116]
Huangmao Jian • China 31 F1
Huangpu • China 107 H1
Huangshan • China 107 J3
Huangshi • China 29 F4
Huangtian [Apt] • China 107 H3
Huanren • China 30 C4
Huánta • Peru 127 B1
Huánuco • Peru 43 B6
Huaral • Peru 127 B1
Huaráz • Peru 43 B5
Huascarán • Peru 43 B5
Huascarán, Parque Nac. **Heritage N** • Peru 60 [32]
Huatabampo • Mexico 40 E6
Hubbell Trading Post Nat. Hist. Site • AZ, United States 118 J2
Hubbell Trading Post Nat. Hist. Site **Park** • AZ, United States 120 [104]
Hubei • China 107 G7
Hubli • India 106 D2
Hubsugul Nur • Mongolia 27 F6
Hückeswagen • Germany 81 E4
Hucknall • United Kingdom 7 K8
Hudaydah, Al • Yemen 18 D7
Huddersfield • United Kingdom 7 K8
Huddinge • Sweden 95 D4
Hudhuveli • Maldives 106 E2
Hudhuveli • Maldives 106 E4
Hudiksvall • Sweden 16 I6
Hudson • United States 41 L3
Hudson Bay • SA, Canada 38 K6
Hudson Bay [Bay] • Canada 39 N5
Hudson Strait • NU/QU, Canada 39 Q4
Hue • Vietnam 31 D3
Hue **Heritage C** • Vietnam 63 [169]
Huedin • Romania 14 K3
Huelgoat • France 84 C1
Huelva • Spain 86 B1
Huercal-Overa • Spain 86 B4
Huertas, Cabo de las • Spain 11 K6
Huesca • Spain 11 K2
Huéscar • Spain 86 B4
Huevos I. • Trinidad & Tobago 125 K1
Huexotla • Mexico 123 E4
Huftarøy • Norway 94 C3
Hufuf, Al • Saudi Arabia 18 E4
Hügel, Villa • Germany 81 E1
Hughenden • QL, Australia 34 H4
Hugo • OK, United States 119 N2
Hui • Brazil 43 C4
Hui Cheng • China 107 J3
Huiarau Range • New Zealand 112 K2
Huich'on • D.P.R. of Korea 29 H2
Huila • Colombia 43 B3
Huili • China 31 F2
Huiñamarca, Lago de • Bolivia/Peru 127 B4
Huisne • France 10 F5
Huitten Nur • China 28 F1
Huittinen • Finland 95 E2
Huiyang • China 107 H2
Huizen • Netherlands 80 C2
Huizhou • China 107 H2
Huka Falls • New Zealand 112 K2
Hukou • China 29 E3
Hukuntsi • Botswana 24 C4
Hula Valley • Israel 98 A2
Hulayfa' • Saudi Arabia 18 D4
Hulin • China 29 I1
Hull • QU, Canada 122 B7
Hüllhorst **Spa** • Germany 83 [85]
Hulst • Netherlands 5 H3
Hultsfred • Sweden 95 F8
Hulun Nur • China 27 I7
Humacao • Puerto Rico 125 E4
Humaita • Brazil 43 E5
Humber • United Kingdom 7 L8
Humboldt • New Caledonia 35 (2) B3
Humboldt • NV, United States 117 F2
Hume, Lake • NS, Australia 111 G3
Humen • China 107 H2
Humenné • Slovak Rep. 13 K9
Hümmling, Der • Germany 8 C4
Humphreys Peak • AZ, United States 118 J1
Humppila • Finland 95 E4
Hun • Libya 21 C2
Hun • China 30 C4
Húnaflói • Iceland 16 (1) C2
Hunan • China 107 G7
Hunchun • China 30 F3
Hundested **Beach** • Denmark 68 [41]
Hundested • Denmark 95 F10
Hunedoara • Romania 14 J4
Hünfeld • Germany 9 E6
Hungarian Plain • Hungary 96 B2
Hungary • Europe 13 I10
Hungnam • D.P.R. of Korea 30 D5
Hunjiang • China 30 D4
Hunneberg • Sweden 95 F3
Hunnebostrand • Sweden 95 F2
Hunsrück • Germany 82 H3
Hunstanton • United Kingdom 7 M9
Hunstanton **Beach** • United Kingdom 75 [34]
Hunte • Germany 8 D4
Hunter • New Caledonia 35 (2) C3
Hunter • NS, Australia 111 G2
Hunter Mtn **Ski** • NY, United States 116 [181]
Hunter Mtns • New Zealand 112 I5
Hunter Valley • NS, Australia 111 E8
Huntingdon • NY, United States 118 H2
Huntingdonshire • United Kingdom 75 A5
Huntington • WV, United States 41 J4
Huntly • New Zealand 112 K1
Huntsville • AL, United States 41 I5
Huntsville • TX, United States 119 N4
Huntsville • OT, Canada 122 B5
Hünxe • Germany 81 E1
Hunza • Jammu & Kashmir 28 B1
Hunze • Netherlands 5 J2
Huocheng • China 26 N9
Huon Gulf • Papua New Guinea 35 (1) D2
Huonville • TS, Australia 34 I8
Hura • Maldives 106 E2
Hurdalsjøen • Norway 94 B2
Hurdiyo • Somalia 23 I1
Hurghada • Egypt 101 F4
Huron • SD, United States 41 G3
Huron, Lake • Canada/United States 39 O7
Hürth • Germany 5 J4
Hurunui • New Zealand 35 D6
Húsavík • Iceland 16 (1) E1
Hushan • China 107 J4
Husi • Romania 14 P3
Huskvarna • Sweden 95 F7
Hust • Ukraine 14 K1
Husum • Germany 8 E2
Husum • Sweden 16 J5
Hutag • Mongolia 27 F7
Hutanopan • Indonesia 110 B4
Hutchinson • KS, United States 41 G4
Hutchinson • South Africa 100 C3
Huvhoyfun, gora • Russian Fed. 27 R5
Huwaimi, Al • Yemen 18 E7
Huxley, Mt • New Zealand 35 B7
Huy • Belgium 80 A15
Huzhou • China 107 J3
Hvaler • Norway 94 B4
Hvannadalshnúkur • Iceland 16 (1) E2
Hvar • Croatia 12 K5
Hvar [I.] • Croatia 12 K5
Hvarski kanal • Croatia 14 D6
Hveragerdi • Iceland 16 (1) C3
Hvidbjerg • Denmark 95 F5
Hvitá • Iceland 16 (1) C2
Hvitsten • Norway 94 B2
Hvittingfoss • Norway 94 B3
Hwang-Hae • Asia 29 G3
Hwange • Zimbabwe 102 J1
Hwange Nat. Park • Zimbabwe 102 J3
Hwange Nat. Park **Park** • Zimbabwe 103 [109]
Hyak **Ski** • WA, United States 116 [44]
Hyannis • MA, United States 118 H2
Hycklinge • Sweden 95 F4
Hyde Park • NY, United States 118 H2
Hyderabad • Pakistan 28 A3
Hyderabad • India 106 D3
Hydra • Greece 92 D7
Hyères **Beach** • France 68 [133]
Hyères • France 85 H3
Hyères, Is. d' • France 85 H3
Hyères-Plage • France 85 H3
Hyesan • D.P.R. of Korea 30 E4
Hyland Post • BC, Canada 122 C1
Hylestad • Norway 94 C6
Hyltebruk **Beach** • Sweden 68 [7]
Hyltebruk • Sweden 95 F7
Hyndman Peak • ID, United States 38 I8
Hythe • United Kingdom 74 E4
Hyuga • Japan 30 F8
Hyvinkää • Finland 95 E4
I-n-Abanrherit • Niger 20 G5
I-n-Afaleleh • Algeria 20 G4
I-n-Amenas • Algeria 20 G3
I-n-Azaoua • Niger 20 G5
I-n-Ezzane • Algeria 20 H4
I-n-Gall • Niger 20 G5
I-n-Guezzâm • Algeria 20 G5
I-n-Salah • Algeria 20 F3
I-n-Tabezas • Mali 20 F5
I-n-Tallak • Mali 20 F5
I-n-Techerène • Mali 20 E4
I-n-Tessoum • Niger 20 G5
Ialisos **Beach** • Rhodes, Greece 69 [211]
Ialisos • Rhodes, Greece 93 F2
Ialomita • Romania 14 O5
Iao Valley State Mon. • HI, United States 119 L3
Iar-Chonnacht • Ireland 79 F4
Iasi • Romania 14 O2
Ibadan • Nigeria 22 E3
Ibague • Colombia 43 B3
Ibarra • Ecuador 43 B3
Ibarranguelua **Beach** • Spain 68 [88]
Ibarreta • Argentina 44 E4
Ibbenbüren • Germany 8 C4
Ibérico, Sistema • Spain 11 I3
Ibi • Spain 11 K6
Ibi • Nigeria 21 A6
Ibicaraí • Brazil 44 I1
Ibiza • Ibiza, Spain 87 G2
Ibiza [I.] • Spain 87 G
Ibri • Oman 18 G5
Ica • Peru 127 B1
Icacos Point • Trinidad & Tobago 125 K3
Icama • Brazil 43 D3
Ice Age Nat. Scientific Reserve **Park** • WI, United States 121 [158]
Iceland • Atlantic Ocean 16 (1) D2
Ichinskaya Sopka, Vulkan • Russian Fed. 27 Q5
Ichkeul Nat. Park **Heritage N** • Tunisia 61 [67]
Ichkeul Nat. Park • Tunisia 101 E2
Icod de los Vinos **Beach** • Tenerife, Canary Is. 68 [109]
Icod de los Vinos • Tenerife, Canary Is. 86 E1
Idah • Nigeria 22 F3
Idaho • United States 40 C3
Idaho City • ID, United States 117 E4
Idaho Falls • ID, United States 40 D3
Idan • Somalia 23 H2
Idar-Oberstein • Germany 82 H3
Ideles • Algeria 20 G4
Idéon Antron • Crete, Greece 93 E6
Idfu • Egypt 101 F5
Idhan Awbari • Libya 21 B2
Idhan Murzuq • Libya 21 B3
Idi Oros • Crete, Greece 93 E6
Idra • Greece 15 E6
Idra [I.] • Greece 92 D7
Idstein • Germany 9 D6
Ieper • Belgium 80 A13
Ierápetra **Beach** • Crete, Greece 69 [215]
Ierápetra • Crete, Greece 93 E8
Ierisoú, Kólpos • Greece 15 E3
Ierissós • Greece 15 E3
Ifach, Peñon de • Spain 87 C2
Ifakara • Tanzania 102 H4
Ife • Nigeria 22 E3
Iferouâne • Niger 20 G5
Ifetesene • Algeria 20 F3
Ifrane • Morocco 101 D2
Igarapé Miri • Brazil 45 (1) B2
Igarka • Russian Fed. 26 O4
Iglesias • Sardinia, Italy 90 C3
Igloolik • NU, Canada 39 O3
Igls • Austria 89 H6
Ignalina Nat. Park **Park** • Lithuania 72 [146]
Igneada Burun • Turkey 15 I2
Igneado • Turkey 15 I2
Igombe • Tanzania 23 E4
Igoumenitsa • Greece 15 B4
Igoumenitsa **Beach** • Greece 69 [173]
Igrim • Russian Fed. 26 J5
Iguaçu • Brazil 44 F4
Iguaçu, Parque Nac. do **Heritage N** • Brazil 60 [36]
Iguaçu, Parque Nacional do • Brazil 44 F4
Iguala • Mexico 123 E4
Igualada • Spain 87 D3
Iguatu • Brazil 45 (1) D3
Iguazú, Cataratas del • Argentina/Brazil 44 F4
Iguazu, Parque Nac. de **Heritage N** • Argentina 60 [37]
Iguéla • Gabon 22 F5
Iguéla, Réserve d' **Park** • Gabon 103 [49]
Iguidi, Erg • Algeria/Mauritania 20 D3
Ih-Obo-Ula • Mongolia 26 Q9
Iharana • Madagascar 24 H2
Ihavandiffulu Atoll • Maldives 106 E1
Ihosy • Madagascar 24 H4
Ihuru • Maldives 106 E2
Iida • Japan 30 I7
Iide • Japan 30 J6
IJ-Meer • Netherlands 80 C2
Ijebu Ode • Nigeria 22 E3
IJmuiden • Netherlands 80 C1
IJssel • Netherlands 80 A8
IJsselmeer • Netherlands 80 A7
Ijuí • Brazil 44 F4
IJzendijke • Netherlands 80 A10
IJzer • Belgium 5 F4
Ikaalinen • Finland 95 E2
Ikali • Dem. Rep. of Congo 23 C4
Ikaria • Greece 92 D8
Ikast • Denmark 95 F9
Ikeda • Japan 30 L3
Ikej • Russian Fed. 27 F6
Ikeja • Nigeria 22 E3
Ikela • Dem. Rep. of Congo 23 C4
Ikopa • Madagascar 24 H3
Ilagan • Philippines 31 G3
Ilawa • Poland 13 I4
Ilbenge • Russian Fed. 27 K4
Ile de France • France 10 H4
Ilebo • Dem. Rep. of Congo 23 C4
Ilek • Kazakhstan/Russian Fed. 17 I6
Ilerh • Algeria 20 F4
Ilesha • Nigeria 22 E3
Ilfracombe • United Kingdom 74 F2
Ilgaz • Turkey 15 O3
Ilgaz Daglari • Turkey 15 O2
Ilgin • Turkey 15 M5
Ilha do Bananal • Brazil 45 (1) B4
Ilhabela • Brazil 127 C3
Ilhavo • Portugal 11 C4
Ilhavo **Beach** • Portugal 68 [95]
Ilhéus • Brazil 44 I1
Iligan • Philippines 31 G5
Ilir • Russian Fed. 27 F6
Ilîja • Romania 14 N2
Illapel • Chile 44 B5
Iller • Germany 82 J1
Illertissen • Germany 82 J1
Illetes • Majorca, Spain 87 H3
Illimani, Nevado del • Bolivia 44 C2
Illinois • United States 41 I4
Illinois & Michigan Canal Nat. Heritage Corridor **Park** • IL, United States 121 [179]
Illizi • Algeria 20 G3
Ilm • Germany 9 G6
Ilman, Ozero • Russian Fed. 97 E1
Ilmenau • Thüringen, Germany 9 F6
Ilmenau • Sachsen, Germany 9 H6
Ilo • Peru 127 B4
Iloilo • Philippines 31 G4
Ilomantsi • Finland 16 P5
Ilorin • Nigeria 22 E3
Ilulissat • Greenland 46 U3
Ilwaki • Indonesia 32 (1) C4
Imabari • Japan 30 G7
Imandra, Ozero • Russian Fed. 17 E1
Imari • Japan 30 E8
Imata • Peru 127 B4
Imatra • Finland 16 O6
Imbituba • Brazil 44 G4
Imeni Gastello • Russian Fed. 27 O4
Imi • Ethiopia 23 G2
Imilili • Western Sahara 20 B4
Imjin • D.P.R. of Korea 30 D5
Immenstadt • Germany 82 J6
Imo • Nigeria 22 F3
Imogiri • Java, Indonesia 110 D7
Imola • Italy 91 E7
Imotski • Croatia 14 E6

Imperatorskaya Gavan • Russian Fed. 27 M7
Imperatriz • Brazil 45 (1) B3
Imperia • Italy 91 E9
Impfondo • Congo 22 H4
Imphal • India 28 F4
Imst • Austria 89 H6
Imzouren • Morocco 11 H9
Ina • Japan 30 I7
Inambari • Peru 127 B2
Inangahua Junction • New Zealand 35 C5
Inanwatan • Indonesia 32 (1) D3
Iñapari • Peru 43 D6
Inari • Finland 16 N2
Inarijarvi • Finland 16 N2
Inca • Majorca, Spain 87 H1
Inca de Oro • Chile 44 C4
Incaguasi • Chile 44 B4
Ince Burun • Turkey 15 I3
Incekum • Turkey 93 G4
Inch'on • Rep. of Korea 30 D6
Incir Han • Turkey 93 G1
Indalsälven • Sweden 16 I5
Indawgyi • Myanmar 28 G3
Independence • MO, United States 41 H4
Independence Nat. Hist. Park **Park** • PA, United States 121 [311]
Independência • Brazil 45 (1) C3
Independencia, I. • Peru 127 B1
India • Asia 28
Indian Ocean • 3 S8
Indian Town Point • Antigua & Barbuda 125 F2
Indiana • United States 41 I4
Indiana Dunes Nat. Lakeshore **Park** • IN, United States 121 [181]
Indianapolis • IN, United States 41 I4
Indianhead Mtn **Ski** • MI, United States 116 [127]
Indianola • MS, United States 118 K2
Indiga • Russian Fed. 17 I1
Indigirka • Russian Fed. 27 O3
Indonesia • Asia 25 N10
Indore • India 28 C4
Indragiri • Indonesia 32 C3
Indramayu • Java, Indonesia 110 D2
Indravati • India 28 D5
Indre • France 84 D4
Indre [Adm] • France 84 D4
Indre Arna • Norway 94 C3
Indre-et-Loire • France 84 D2
Indus • Pakistan 28 A3
Inebolu • Turkey 15 O2
Inecik • Turkey 15 I3
Inegöl • Turkey 15 K3
Inezgane • Morocco 20 D2
Inezgane [Apt] • Morocco 101 D5
Infanta, Cape • South Africa 100 C6
Infantado • Portugal 88 D2
Ingelstad • Sweden 95 F8
Ingeniero Jacobacci • Argentina 45 C4
Ingenio • Gran Canaria, Canary Is. 86 E4
Ingenio Santa Ana • Argentina 44 C4
Ingenios, Valley de los **Heritage C** • Cuba 62 [35]
Ingham • QL, Australia 111 F1
Inglewood • QL, Australia 111 F6
Inglewood • New Zealand 112 K3
Ingolstadt • Germany 9 G8
Ingushetia • Russian Fed. 17 H6
Inhambane • Mozambique 24 F4
Inhambane, Baia de • Mozambique 24 F4
Inhisar • Turkey 15 L3
Inhumas • Brazil 44 G2
Inirida • Colombia 43 D3
Inishark • Ireland 79 F3
Inishbofin • Ireland 79 F3
Inishcrone **Beach** • Ireland 68 [64]
Inishcrone • Ireland 79 F2
Inisheer • Ireland 79 F3
Inishkea North • Ireland 79 F1
Inishkea South • Ireland 79 F1
Inishmaan • Ireland 79 F3
Inishmore • Ireland 79 F3
Inishmurray • Ireland 79 F2
Inishowan Peninsula • Ireland 79 D1
Inishturk • Ireland 79 F1
Injune • QL, Australia 111 F5
Inkisi • Dem. Rep. of Congo 23 B5
Inland Kaikoura Range • New Zealand 35 D5
Inland Sea • Japan 30 G7
Inland Sea • Malta 93 H1
Inn • Austria/Germany 9 I8
Innamincka • SA, Australia 34 H5
Innbygda • Norway 16 G6
Inner Hope **Beach** • United Kingdom 75 [112]
Inner Mongolia • China 29 E2
Inner Sound • United Kingdom 6 G4
Innfield • Ireland 79 E1
Innichen **Ski** • Italy 70 [239]
Innichen • Italy 90 B2
Innisfail • QL, Australia 111 F1
Innsbruck • Austria 89 H6
Innvikfjorden • Norway 94 C2
Inongo • Dem. Rep. of Congo 23 B4
Inönü • Turkey 15 L4
Inoússes • Greece 92 D5
Inowroclaw • Poland 13 H5
Inscription, Cape • WA, Australia 34 B5
Insuyu • Turkey 93 G1
Inta • Russian Fed. 26 J4
Intepe • Turkey 15 H4
Interlaken **Ski** • Switzerland 70 [93]
Interlaken • Switzerland 89 G2
International Drive • FL, United States 121 C2
International Peace Garden **Park** • ND, United States 120 [146]
Intracoastal Waterway • United States 118 K4
Inukjuak • QU, Canada 39 P5
Inuvik • NT, Canada 38 E3
Invercargill • New Zealand 112 L4
Invergordon • United Kingdom 59 D1
Inverness • United Kingdom 6 H4
Inverness • NS, Canada 123 D7
Inverness-shire • United Kingdom 75 A2
Investigator Group • SA, Australia 34 F6
Investigator Strait • SA, Australia 34 G7
Inya • Russian Fed. 27 N5
Inya [Riv] • Russian Fed. 27 N5
Inzia • Dem. Rep. of Congo 22 H5
Ioánina • Greece 15 B4
Ion Corvin • Romania 97 D2
Iona • United Kingdom 75 A2
Ionian Is. • Greece 92 B/C
Ionian Sea • Europe 4 N9
Iónion Pélagos • Greece 15 B6
Ios **Beach** • Greece 69 [208]
Ios • Greece 92 D8
Ios [I.] • Greece 92 D8
Iowa • United States 41 H3
Iowa City • IA, United States 41 H3
Ipameri • Brazil 44 G2
Ipanema • Brazil 127 C4
Ipatinga • Brazil 127 C2
Ipek • Fed. Rep. of Yugoslavia 71 A14
Ipiales • Colombia 43 B3
Ipiaú • Brazil 44 I1
Ipirós • Greece 92 A1
Ipixuna • Brazil 43 C5
Ipoh • Malaysia 108 D1
Ipoly • Slovak Rep. 14 G1
Iporá • Brazil 44 F2
Ipsala • Turkey 14 N9
Ipsos • Corfu, Greece 92 B1
Ipswich • United Kingdom 7 N9
Ipswich • QL, Australia 111 F6
Ipswich • Jamaica 124 C1
Iqaluit • NU, Canada 39 R4
Iquique • Chile 44 B3
Iquitos • Peru 43 C4
Iracoubo • French Guiana 43 G2
Iráklia • Greece 92 D8
Iráklio • Crete, Greece 93 E3
Iráklio [Adm] • Crete, Greece 93 E7
Iran • Asia 18 F3
Iranshahr • Iran 18 H4
Irapuato • Mexico 123 E1
Iraq • Asia 18 D3
Irati • Brazil 44 F4
Irazú, Volcán • Costa Rica 37 E5
Irbid • Jordan 18 C3
Irbit • Russian Fed. 26 J6
Irebu • Dem. Rep. of Congo 23 B4
Irecê • Brazil 45 (1) C4
Ireland • Europe 4 I6
Irelands Eye • Ireland 79 E2
Irgiz • Kazakhstan 26 J8
Irgiz [Riv] • Kazakhstan 26 J8
Iri • Rep. of Korea 30 D7
Irian [I.] • Indonesia 32 (1) E4
Irian Jaya • Indonesia 32 (1) E3
Iringa • Tanzania 102 H4
Irinya, gora • Russian Fed. 26 R6
Iriri • Brazil 43 G4
Irish Sea • Ireland/UK 7 H8
Irituia • Brazil 45 (1) B2
Irkutsk • Russian Fed. 27 F6
Iroise • France 84 C1
Ironbridge • United Kingdom 74 D1
Ironbridge Gorge **Heritage C** • United Kingdom 64 [18]
Ironwood • MI, United States 41 I2
Irouléguy • France 84 B3
Irqah, Al • Yemen 18 E7
Irrawaddy • Myanmar 31 B3
Irrsdorf • Austria 89 H4
Irtysh • Asia 26 L6
Irún • Spain 11 I1
Irurzun • Spain 11 J2
Irvine • United Kingdom 6 H6
Isa, Ra's • Yemen 21 H5
Isabela • Philippines 31 G5
Isabela • Galapagos Is. 43 (1) A2
Isabela • Puerto Rico 125 E1
Isabela de Sagua • Cuba 124 D2
Isabelia, Cordillera • Nicaragua 37 D5
Isafjördur • Iceland 16 (1) B1
Isalo, Massif de l' • Madagascar 24 H4
Isalo, Parc nat. de l' **Park** • Madagascar 103 [139]
Isangi • Dem. Rep. of Congo 23 C3
Isar • Germany 9 H8
Isarco • Italy 90 B1
Isarkanal • Germany 82 J3
Ischgl **Ski** • Austria 70 [134]
Ischgl • Austria 89 H6
Ischia • Italy 91 G3
Ischia, I. d' • Italy 91 G3
Ise • Japan 30 I7
Ise-Wan • Japan 30 I7
Isefjord • Denmark 95 F10
Isel • Austria 90 B2
Iseo, Lago d' • Italy 91 E2
Isère • France 85 F3
Isère [Adm] • France 85 F3
Iserlohn • Germany 81 E2
Iset • Russian Fed. 26 K6
Iseyin • Nigeria 22 E3
Isfahan • Iran 18 F3
Isfahan **Heritage C** • Iran 63 [108]
Isfendiyar Daglari • Turkey 15 O2
Isfjorden • Norway 94 C2
Isha Baydabo • Somalia 23 G3
Isherton • Guyana 43 F3
Ishikari-Wan • Japan 30 K3
Ishim • Russian Fed. 26 K6
Ishim [Riv] • Kazakhstan/Russian Fed. 26 K7
Ishimskaya Step • Russian Fed. 26 K6
Ishinomaki • Japan 30 K5
Ishodnaya, gora • Russian Fed. 27 W4
Ishøj **Beach** • Denmark 68 [39]
Isigny-sur-Mer • France 5 B5
Isilkul • Russian Fed. 26 L7
Isiolo • Kenya 101 G2
Isiro • Dem. Rep. of Congo 23 D3
Iskandariya, El • Egypt 101 F1
Iskenderun • Turkey 18 C2
Iskur • Bulgaria 14 L6
Isla Cristina **Beach** • Spain 68 [112]
Isla Cristina • Spain 86 B1
Islamabad • Pakistan 28 B2
Islamorada • FL, United States 119 M8
Island Lake • MN, Canada 38 M6
Islands, Bay of • NF, Canada 123 D3
Islantilla **Beach** • Spain 68 [112]
Islay • United Kingdom 6 F6
Isle • France 85 G1
Isle Royale Nat. Park **Park** • MI, United States 121 [159]
Islote de Hilario • Lanzarote, Canary Is. 87 E3
Ismâ'îlîya • Egypt 101 F2
Isna • Egypt 101 F4
Isny • Germany 82 J5
Isny **Spa** • Germany 83 [218]
Isoka • Zambia 24 E2
Isola 2000 • France 85 H2
Isonzo • Italy 91 E4
Isparta • Turkey 93 G1
Isparta [Adm] • Turkey 93 G2
Isparta [Riv] • Turkey 93 G1
Ispica • Sicily, Italy 12 I12
Ispico, Cava d' • Sicily, Italy 90 D4
Israel • Asia 18 B3
Issachar • Israel 98 A4
Issoire • France 10 I8
Issoudun • France 10 H7
Issum • Germany 81 E1
Issyk-Kul • Kyrgyzstan 26 M9
Issyk-Kul [Lake] • Kyrgyzstan 26 M9
Ist • Croatia 14 B5
Istanbul **Heritage C** • Turkey 64 [190]
Istanbul • Turkey 92 D3
Istanbul-Bakirköy • Turkey 15 J3
Istanbul-Kadiköy • Turkey 15 J3
Istiéa • Greece 15 E5
Isto, Mt • AK, United States 40 (2) G2
Istra • Croatia 14 A4
Istria • Croatia 96 B2
Itabaianinha • Brazil 44 I1
Itabapoana • Brazil 127 C2
Itaberaba • Brazil 44 H1
Itaberaí • Brazil 44 G2
Itabira • Brazil 127 C2
Itabuna • Brazil 44 I1
Itacoatiara • Brazil 43 F4
Itagüí • Colombia 43 B2
Itaipu, Reprêsa de • Brazil/Paraguay 44 F3
Itaituba • Brazil 43 F4
Itajaí • Brazil 44 G4
Itajubá • Brazil 127 C3
Italian Lake District • Italy 90 A1
Italy • Europe 12
Itambacuri • Brazil 44 H2
Itambé, Pico de • Brazil 44 H2
Itanagar • India 28 F3
Itanós • Crete, Greece 93 E8
Itapebi • Brazil 44 I2
Itaperuna • Brazil 127 C2
Itapetinga • Brazil 44 H2
Itapetininga • Brazil 44 G3
Itapicuru • Brazil 45 (1) C2
Itapicuru-Mirim • Brazil 45 (1) C2
Itapipoca • Brazil 45 (1) D2
Itaqui • Brazil 44 E4
Itarsi • India 28 C4
Itatiaia • Brazil 127 C3
Itaúna • Brazil 127 C1
Itbay • Egypt 21 F2
Itchan Kala **Heritage C** • Uzbekistan 63 [80]
Itéa **Beach** • Greece 69 [176]
Ithaca • NY, United States 41 K3
Ithaca • Greece 92 C2
Itháki • Greece 92 C2
Itháki [I.] • Greece 92 C2
Iti • Greece 15 D5
Iti Oros Nat. Park **Park** • Greece 72 [138]
Ito • Japan 30 J7
Iton • France 10 F5
Itremo, Massif de l' • Madagascar 24 H4
Itsukushima Shrine **Heritage C** • Japan 63 [164]
Itter • Austria 89 H3
Ituiutaba • Brazil 44 G2
Itumbiara • Brazil 44 G2
Iturup, Ostrov • Russian Fed. 27 O8
Itzehoe • Germany 8 E3
Iultin • Russian Fed. 27 V3
Iúna • Brazil 127 C2
Ivajlovgrad • Bulgaria 15 H2
Ivalo • Finland 16 N2
Ivalojoki • Finland 16 N2
Ivangorod • Russian Fed. 16 O7
Ivangrad • F.R. of Yugoslavia 14 G7
Ivanhoe • NS, Australia 111 G1
Ivano-Frankovsk • Ukraine 17 C5
Ivanovo **Heritage C** • Bulgaria 64 [169]
Ivanovo • Bulgaria 97 D3
Ivanovo • Russian Fed. 97 E4
Ivdel • Russian Fed. 26 J5
Iveragh Peninsula • Ireland 79 F7
Ivigtut • Greenland 39 V4
Ivindo • Congo/Gabon 22 G4
Ivory Coast • Africa 22 C4
Ivösjön • Sweden 95 F11
Ivrea • Italy 91 E5
Ivrindi • Turkey 15 I4
Ivujivik • QU, Canada 39 P4
Iwaki • Japan 30 K6
Iwaki [Mtn] • Japan 30 K4
Iwakuni • Japan 30 G7
Iwanai • Japan 30 K3
Iwate • Japan 30 K5
Iwate [Mtn] • Japan 30 K5
Iwo Jima • Japan 25 P7
Iwon • D.P.R. of Korea 30 E4
Ixiá • Rhodes, Greece 93 F2
Ixiá [Bay] • Rhodes, Greece 93 F2
Ixiamas • Bolivia 44 C1
Ixtapa • Mexico 123 E3
Ixtapan del Oro • Mexico 123 E4
Izabel, Lago de • Guatemala 37 D4
Izhevsk • Russian Fed. 17 I3
Izmail • Ukraine 14 P4
Izmir • Turkey 92 D5
Izmir Körfezi • Turkey 15 H5
Izmit • Turkey 15 K3
Izmit Körfezi • Turkey 15 K3
Iznajar, Embalse de • Spain 11 G7
Iznik • Turkey 92 D3
Iznik Gölü • Turkey 92 D3
Iztochni Rodópi • Bulgaria 14 M8
Izu • Japan 30 J7
Izu-Shoto • Japan 30 J8
Izúcar de Matamoros • Mexico 123 E4
Izuhara • Japan 30 E7
Izumo • Japan 30 G7
Izvestiy Tsik, Ostrova • Russian Fed. 26 N2
Izyum • Ukraine 17 F5

J

J.A.D. Jensens Nunatakker • Greenland 39 V4
Ja'el • Somalia 23 I1
Jabal al Qarantal • Jordan 98 A6
Jabal, Bahr al • Sudan 23 E2
Jabalpur • India 28 C4
Jabbeke **Beach** • Belgium 68 [70]
Jabbeke • Belgium 80 B2
Jabjabah, Wadi • Egypt 21 F3
Jablanica • Bosnia-Herz. 12 L5
Jablonec nad Nisou • Czech Rep. 13 E7
Jablonné v Podjestedi • Czech Rep. 96 C2
Jabonitski • Ukraine 14 L1
Jabridge Wilderness Area • NV, United States 117 F2
Jabuticabal • Brazil 44 G3
Jaca • Spain 11 K2
Jacarezinho • Brazil 44 G3
Jáchal • Argentina 44 C4
Jáchymov • Czech Rep. 96 C1
Jack Frost **Ski** • PA, United States 116 [168]
Jackson • WY, United States 40 D3
Jackson • TN, United States 41 I4
Jackson • MS, United States 118 K2
Jackson Head • New Zealand 35 B7
Jackson Hole, Teton **Ski** • WY, United States 116 [76]
Jackson, Mt • Antarctica 46 (1) II2
Jackson Prairie • MS, United States 118 K2
Jacksonville • IL, United States 41 H4
Jacksonville • NC, United States 41 K5
Jacksonville • NC, United States 118 H5
Jacksonville • FL, United States 119 M3
Jacksonville • TX, United States 119 N2
Jacob's Well • Jordan 98 A6
Jacobabad • Pakistan 28 A3
Jacobina • Brazil 45 (1) C4
Jacques-Cartier, Détroit de • QU, Canada 123 D2
Jacques-Cartier, Mt • QU, Canada 123 D2
Jacques-Cartier Prov. Park • QU, Canada 123 D1
Jacui, Rio • Brazil 44 F5
Jaddi, Ras • Pakistan 18 H4
Jadebusen • Germany 5 L1
Jadida, El • Morocco 101 D1
Jadu • Libya 21 B1
Jægerspris **Beach** • Denmark 68 [41]
Jaén • Spain 86 B3
Jaeren • Norway 16 C7
Jaffa • Israel 98 A5
Jaffa, Cape • SA, Australia 34 G7
Jâffar, Cirque de • Morocco 101 D4
Jaffna • Sri Lanka 106 D11
Jagaraga Temple • Bali, Indonesia 110 C2
Jagdalpur • India 28 D5
Jagodina • F.R. of Yugoslavia 14 I6
Jagst • Germany 9 E7
Jaguaquara • Brazil 44 I1
Jaguarão • Brazil 44 F5
Jagüey Grande • Cuba 124 D2
Jahrom • Iran 18 F4
Jailolo • Indonesia 32 (1) C2
Jaipur • India 105 C6
Jaisalmer • India 105 C1
Jajce • Bosnia-Herz. 12 L4
Jakarta • Java, Indonesia 110 D1
Jakobshavn • Greenland 46 U3
Jakobstad • Finland 16 L5
Jakupica • F.Y.R. of Macedonia 15 C2
Jalalabad • Afghanistan 28 B2
Jalapa • Mexico 123 E2
Jalasjärvi • Finland 16 L5
Jalgaon • India 28 C4
Jalisco • Mexico 37 (1) B1
Jalón • Spain 10 C12
Jalor • India 105 C5
Jamaare • Nigeria 20 G6
Jamaica • West Indies 124 C
Jamalpur • Bangladesh 28 E4
Jamame • Somalia 23 G3
Jamantau, gora • Russian Fed. 26 I7
Jambi • Indonesia 32 C3
Jameos del Agua • Lanzarote, Canary Is. 87 E3
James • ND/SD, United States 38 L8
James Bay • NU, Canada 39 O6
James, Fort • Antigua & Barbuda 125 F1
James, Fort • Trinidad & Tobago 125 K2
James Ross Strait • NU, Canada 38 L2
Jamestown • St Helena 19 D7
Jamestown • SA, Australia 34 G6
Jamestown • ND, United States 41 G2
Jamestown • NY, United States 41 K3
Jamestown Nat. Hist. Site • VA, United States 118 H3
Jamestown Nat. Hist. Site **Park** • VA, United States 121 [256]
Jammerbugten • Denmark 95 F5
Jammu • Jammu & Kashmir 28 B2
Jammu & Kashmir • Asia 28 C2
Jamnagar • India 28 B4
Jämsä • Finland 95 E2
Jämsänkoski • Finland 95 E2
Jamshedpur • India 28 E4
Jämtland • Sweden 16 G5
Jamtli Historieland **Park** • Sweden 73 [9]
Jan Mayen • Greenland Sea 4 I2
Janaucu • Brazil 43 H3
Jandia • Fuerteventura, Canary Is. 87 E2
Jandia Playa • Fuerteventura, Canary Is. 87 E2
Jandia, Punta de • Fuerteventura, Canary Is. 87 E2
Jane Peak • New Zealand 112 L2
Janesville • WI, United States 41 I3
Jánoshalma • Hungary 13 I11
Jánosháza • Hungary 12 L1
Janské Lázne • Czech Rep. 96 C2
Janúaria • Brazil 44 H2
Japan • Asia 30
Japan, Sea of • Asia 30 G4
Japan Trench • Pacific Ocean 30 M6
Japiim • Brazil 43 C5
Japura • Brazil 43 D4
Jaramillo • Argentina 45 C5
Jarandilla • Spain 11 F4
Jard-sur-Mer **Beach** • France 68 [83]
Jard-sur-Mer • France 84 D3
Jardim • Brazil 44 E3
Jardin d'Acclimation **Park** • France 73 [71]
Jardin de la France • France 84 B1
Jardines de la Reina, Archipiélago de los • Cuba 124 D7
Jaren • Norway 94 B2
Jari • Brazil 43 G3
Järlåsa • Sweden 95 D1
Jarmah • Libya 21 B2
Järna • Sweden 95 D4
Järnlunden • Sweden 95 F4
Jarny • France 5 I5
Jarocin • Poland 13 G6
Jaromer • Czech Rep. 96 C2
Jaroslaw • Poland 13 L8
Järvenpää • Finland 95 E4
Jarvis • Pacific Ocean 33 K5
Jask • Iran 18 G4
Jaslo • Poland 13 K8
Jasmund, Nationalpark **Park** • Germany 72 [59]
Jason Islands • Falkland Is. 45 D6
Jasper • TX, United States 119 N4
Jasper • AL, Canada 122 C2
Jasper Nat. Park • AL, Canada 122 C2
Jassy • Romania 71 A15
Jastrzebie Zdrój • Poland 13 H8
Jászárokszállás • Hungary 13 I10
Jászberény • Hungary 13 I10
Jatai • Brazil 44 F2
Jatibarang • Java, Indonesia 110 D2
Jatibonico • Cuba 124 D3
Jatijajar Caves • Java, Indonesia 110 D6
Jatiwangi • Java, Indonesia 110 D2
Jaú • Brazil 44 G3
Jauja • Peru 127 B1
Jaunpur • India 105 C8
Java • Indonesia 110 D
Java Sea • Indonesia 32 D3
Java Trench • Indonesia 32 C4
Jávia **Beach** • Spain 68 [118]
Jávia • Spain 87 C2
Javier • Spain 11 J2
Javor Osa • Bosnia-Herz. 14 F5
Javorov • Ukraine 13 M8
Jawa • Indonesia 32 D4
Jawa Barat • Java, Indonesia 110 D1
Jawa Tengah • Java, Indonesia 110 D3
Jawa Timur • Java, Indonesia 110 D8
Jawf, Al • Saudi Arabia 18 C4
Jawf, Al • Libya 21 D3
Jawi • Penang, Malaysia 108 C4
Jawor • Poland 13 F6
Jaworzno • Poland 13 I7
Jaxartes • Asia 98 B2
Jay Peak **Ski** • VT, United States 116 [205]
Jaya Ancol Dreamland • Java, Indonesia 110 D1
Jaya, Puncak • Indonesia 32 (1) E3
Jayaprana Grave • Bali, Indonesia 110 C1
Jayapura • Indonesia 32 (1) F3
Jayawijaya, Pegunungen • Indonesia 32 (1) E3
Jazirah, Al • Sudan 21 F5
Jazovir Iskar • Bulgaria 14 K7
Jebha • Morocco 11 G9
Jeddah • Saudi Arabia 18 C5
Jeddore Lake • NF, Canada 123 D3
Jedrzejów • Poland 13 J7
Jefferson • NH, United States 118 G3
Jefferson • TX, United States 119 N2
Jefferson City • MO, United States 41 H4
Jefferson, Fort • FL, United States 119 M7
Jefferson Nat. Expansion Mem. **Park** • MO, United States 121 [177]
Jefferson, Thomas, Mem. **Park** • DC, United States 121 [296]
Jeffrey's Bay • South Africa 100 C8
Jega • Nigeria 20 F6
Jekabpils • Latvia 16 M8
Jelai • Malaysia 108 D2
Jelena Góra • Poland 13 E7
Jelgava • Latvia 16 L8
Jelling **Heritage C** • Denmark 64 [9]
Jelling • Denmark 95 F9
Jeløy • Norway 94 B4
Jels • Denmark 95 F13
Jelutong • Penang, Malaysia 108 C2
Jem, El • Tunisia 101 E4
Jemaja • Indonesia 31 D6
Jember • Java, Indonesia 110 D8
Jemniste • Czech Rep. 96 C2
Jena • Germany 9 G6
Jendouba • Tunisia 12 C12
Jenner • Germany 82 J8
Jennings • LA, United States 118 K3
Jennings • Antigua & Barbuda 125 F3
Jenolan Caves • NS, Australia 111 G2
Jepara • Java, Indonesia 110 D3
Jequié • Brazil 44 H1
Jerada • Morocco 101 D2
Jerantut • Malaysia 108 D2
Jerba • Tunisia 101 E6
Jerejak • Malaysia 108 C4
Jeréz de la Frontera • Spain 86 B5
Jericho • Jordan 98 A6
Jericho • QL, Australia 111 F3
Jerid, Chott el • Tunisia 101 E5
Jersey • Channel Is. 7 J12
Jersey City • NJ, United States 118 H1
Jerusalem **Heritage C** • Israel/Jordan 64 [247]
Jerusalem • Israel/Jordan 98 A5
Jervis Bay • AC, Australia 111 G2
Jesenica • Slovenia 13 D11
Jesi • Italy 91 E12
Jésolo • Italy 12 G3
Jesperhus Blomsterpark • Denmark 95 F5
Jesperhus Blomsterhpark **Park** • Denmark 73 [13]
Jessheim • Norway 94 B2
Jestr, Wabe • Ethiopia 23 G2
Jesup • GA, United States 41 J5
Jesup, Fort • LA, United States 118 K1
Jesús **Heritage C** • Paraguay 62 [56]
Jever • Germany 8 C3
Jevnaker • Norway 94 B2
Jewel Cave Nat. Mon. **Park** • SD, United States 120 [150]
Jeypore • India 28 D5
Jezercës • Albania 15 A1
Jezioro Lebsko • Poland 13 G3
Jezioro Mamry • Poland 13 K3
Jezioro Sniardwy • Poland 13 L4
Jezreel, Valley of • Israel 98 A4
Jhajjar • India 105 C2
Jhalarapatan • India 105 C6
Jhalawar • India 105 C6
Jhang Sadar • Pakistan 28 B2
Jhansi • India 105 C7
Jhelum • Pakistan 28 B2
Jhelum [Riv] • Pakistan 28 B2
Jhunjhunun • India 105 C2
Ji'an • Jilin, China 30 D4
Ji'an • Jiangxi, China 31 F1
Jiading • China 107 J2
Jialing Jiang • China 29 D4
Jiamusi • China 29 I1
Jiangdu • China 107 J1
Jiangmen • China 107 H1
Jiangsu • China 107 G4
Jiangxi • China 107 G8
Jiangyin • China 107 J2
Jianyang • China 29 F5
Jiaozou • China 29 E3
Jiashan • China 107 J4
Jiaxing • China 107 J4
Jiayuguan • China 107 G2
Jibacoa • Cuba 124 D2
Jicín • Czech Rep. 96 C2
Jida • Zhuhai, China 107 H1
Jiddah • Saudi Arabia 18 C5
Jiddat al Harasis • Oman 18 G6
Jiesjavrre • Norway 16 M2
Jihlava • Czech Rep. 96 C4
Jijiga • Ethiopia 23 G2
Jilib • Somalia 23 G3
Jilin • China 29 H2
Jilin [Adm] • China 107 G4
Jima • Ethiopia 23 F2
Jimbaran Beach • Bali, Indonesia 110 C4
Jimbe • Angola 23 C6
Jimbolia • Romania 14 H4
Jimena de la Frontera • Spain 11 F8
Jiminy Peak **Ski** • MA, United States 116 [191]
Jin I. • Hong Kong, China 107 H6
Jinan • China 29 F3
Jindrichuv Hradec • Czech Rep. 96 C4
Jing Xian • China 107 J3
Jingde • China 107 J3
Jingdezhen • China 29 F5
Jinggang Shan • China 31 E1
Jinghe • China 26 N9
Jinghong • China 31 C2
Jingjiang • China 107 J2
Jingyu • China 30 D3
Jinhua • China 29 F5
Jining • Nei Monggol, China 29 E2
Jining • Shandong, China 29 F3
Jinja • Uganda 23 E3
Jinmen • Taiwan 31 F2
Jinsha • China 107 J2
Jinsha Jiang • China 31 C2
Jinshan • China 107 J4
Jintan • China 107 J1
Jinzhou • China 29 G2
Jiparaná • Brazil 43 E5
Jipijapa • Ecuador 43 A4
Jiuhua Shan • China 107 G8
Jiujiang • China 29 F5
Jiuquan • China 29 B3
Jiuzhaigou Valley **Heritage N** • China 61 [115]
Jiuzhou • Zhuhai, China 107 H1
Jiwa, Al • United Arab Emirates 18 F5
Jiwani, Ras • Pakistan 18 H4
Jixi • Heilongjiang, China 29 I1
Jixi • Anhui, China 107 J3
Jizan • Saudi Arabia 18 D6
Jizo-Zaki • Japan 30 G7
Jizzakh • Uzbekistan 26 K9
João Pessoa • Brazil 45 (1) E3
João Pinheiro • Brazil 44 G2
Jochberg **Ski** • Austria 70 [159]
Jochgrimm • Italy 90 B3
Jódar • Spain 11 H7
Jodhpur • India 105 C5
Joensuu • Finland 16 O5
Joetsu • Japan 30 J6
Jog Falls • India 106 D6
Jogeva • Estonia 16 N7
Johannesburg • South Africa 24 D5
John Day • OR, United States 38 H8
John Day Fossil Beds Nat. Mon. • OR, United States 117 E3
John Day Fossil Beds Nat. Mon. **Park** • OR, United States 120 [35]
John o'Groats • United Kingdom 6 I3
Johns Lake • FL, United States 121 C1
Johnson, Andrew, Nat. Hist. Site **Park** • TN, United States 121 [233]
Johnson, Lyndon B., Mem. Grove **Park** • DC, United States 121 [288]
Johnson, Lyndon B., Nat. Hist. Park • TX, United States 119 N3
Johnson, Lyndon B., Nat. Hist. Park **Park** • TX, United States 120 [140]
Johnson Space Center • TX, United States 119 N6
Johnsons Point • Antigua & Barbuda 125 F3
Johnsons Point Beach • Antigua & Barbuda 125 F3
Johnstown • PA, United States 41 K3
Johnstown Flood Nat. Mem. **Park** • PA, United States 121 [302]
Johor • Malaysia 31 C6
Johor Baharu • Malaysia 108 E1
Johor Strait • Malaysia/Singapore 108 E2
Joigny • France 10 I6
Joinvile • Brazil 44 G4
Joinville • France 10 K5
Jokkmokk • Sweden 16 J3
Jokulsargljufur Nat. Park **Park** • Iceland 72 [1]
Joliet • IL, United States 41 I3
Joliette • QU, Canada 122 B3
Jolly Harbour • Antigua & Barbuda 125 F3
Jolo • Philippines 31 G5
Jolo Group • Philippines 31 G5
Jølstravatnet • Norway 94 C1
Jombang • Java, Indonesia 110 D7
Jomfruland • Norway 94 B3
Jomsom • Nepal 105 C4
Jonava • Lithuania 13 N2
Jonesboro • AR, United States 41 H4
Jonesville • LA, United States 118 K1
Jonglei • Sudan 23 E2
Jonglei Canal • Sudan 23 E2
Jönköping • Sweden 95 F7
Jönköping [Adm] • Sweden 95 F7
Jonquera, la • Spain 87 D2
Jonquière • QU, Canada 123 D1
Joplin • MO, United States 41 H4
Joppa • Israel 98 A5
Jordan • Asia 18 B3
Jordan [Riv] • Israel/Jordan 98 A6
Jorhat • India 28 F3
Jörn • Sweden 16 K4
Jørpeland • Norway 94 C5
Jos • Nigeria 22 F3
Jos Plateau • Nigeria 22 F3
José de San Martín • Argentina 45 B4
José Miguel, Cuevas de • Cuba 124 D1
Joseph Bonaparte Gulf • WA, Australia 34 E2
Joseph, Lac • NF, Canada 39 R6
Joshua Tree Nat. Park • CA, United States 117 F6
Joshua Tree Nat. Park **Park** • CA, United States 120 [59]
Josselin • France 84 C4
Jostedalen • Norway 94 C2
Jostedalsbreen • Norway 94 C2
Jotunheimen • Norway 94 C2
Jotunheimen Nat. Park **Park** • Norway 72 [14]
Jotunheimen Nat. Park • Norway 94 C2
Joubertina • South Africa 100 C7
Joue du Loup, la **Ski** • France 70 [63]
Joumâa • Tunisia 101 E6
Joutsa • Finland 95 E2
Joutseno • Finland 16 O6
Jovellanos • Cuba 124 D2
Jowhar Giohar • Somalia 23 H3
Joya de Cerén **Heritage C** • El Salvador 62 [31]
Joyce's Country • Ireland 79 F3
Juan de Fuca, Strait of • Canada/United States 122 C3
Juan de Nova • Réunion 24 G3
Juan Fernandez, Archipiélago • Pacific Ocean 42 B8
Juan Francisco, Playa • Cuba 124 D3
Juan les Pins • France 85 H4
Juarez, Benito [Apt] • Mexico 123 E4
Juàzeiro • Brazil 45 (1) C3

Juàzeiro do Norte • Brazil **45** (1) D3
Juba • Sudan **23** E3
Jubaland • Somalia **23** G3
Jubba, Webi • Somalia **23** G3
Juby, Cap • Morocco **20** C3
Júcar • Spain **11** J5
Júcaro • Cuba **124** D3
Jüchen • Germany **81** E3
Judaberg • Norway **94** C5
Judaea • Israel/Jordan **98** A7
Judaea, Wilderness of • Israel/Jordan **98** A7
Judah • Jordan **98** A7
Judenburg • Austria **13** D10
Juegang • China **107** J2
Juelsminde **Beach** • Denmark **68** [46]
Juelsminde • Denmark **95** F10
Jui • Romania **14** K5
Juist • Germany **8** B3
Juist **Spa** • Germany **83** [37]
Juiz de Fora • Brazil **127** C4
Jukleegga • Norway **94** C4
Juli • Peru **127** B4
Julia Creek • QL, Australia **34** H4
Juliaca • Peru **127** B4
Julian Alps • Slovenia **96** B2
Juliana Kanaal • Netherlands **5** I3
Juliana Top • Suriname **43** F3
Julianehåb • Greenland **39** V4
Jülich • Germany **9** B6
Julijske Alpe • Slovenia **12** H2
Julita • Sweden **95** D3
Jullundur • India **28** C2
Juma, Pampas de **Heritage C** • Peru **62** [52]
Jumba • Kenya **101** G5
Jumilla • Spain **87** C1
Junagadh • India **28** B4
Junaynah, Al • Sudan **21** D5
Junction • TX, United States **40** G5
Junction City • KS, United States **41** G4
June Mtn **Ski** • CA, United States **116** [62]
Juneau • AK, United States **38** E5
Junee • NS, Australia **111** G1
Jungfrau • Switzerland **89** G2
Junggar Basin • China **107** G1
Junggar Pendi • China **26** O8
Jungutbatu • Indonesia **110** C4
Junín • Argentina **127** D1
Junsele • Sweden **16** I5
Jupiá, Represa de • Brazil **44** F3
Jupiter • Romania **97** D2
Jura • United Kingdom **6** F6
Jura, Sound of • United Kingdom **6** G6
Juradó • Colombia **43** B2
Jurançon • France **84** B3
Jurbarkas • Lithuania **16** L9
Jurilovca • Romania **97** D2
Jurmala • Latvia **16** L8
Jurong • China **107** J1
Jurong Bird Park • Singapore **108** E1
Jurong New Town • Singapore **108** E1
Juru • Penang, Malaysia **108** C4
Jurua • Brazil **43** C5
Juruena • Brazil **43** F6
Juruena [Riv] • Brazil **43** F6
Juruti • Brazil **43** F4
Justo Daract • Argentina **44** C5
Jutai • Brazil **43** D5
Jutai [Riv] • Brazil **43** D4
Jüterbog • Germany **8** I5
Jutland • Denmark **95** F9
Juuka • Finland **16** O5
Juva • Finland **16** N6
Juventud, I. de la • Cuba **124** D1
Jyderup • Denmark **95** F10
Jylland • Denmark **95** F9
Jyväskylä • Finland **95** E2

K2 • China/Kashmir **28** C1
Ka • Nigeria **22** E2
Ka, Laem • Phuket, Thailand **109** K2
Kaabong • Uganda **23** E3
Kaakhka • Turkmenistan **18** G2
Kaala • HI, United States **119** L5
Kaamanen • Finland **16** N2
Kaarst • Germany **81** E3
Kaarta • Mali **22** C2
Kaatsheuvel • Netherlands **80** A11
Kabaena • Indonesia **32** (1) B4
Kabala • Sierra Leone **22** B3
Kabale • Uganda **102** H1
Kabalega Falls • Uganda **23** E3
Kabalo • Dem. Rep. of Congo **23** D5
Kabanjahe • Indonesia **110** B2
Kabardino-Balkaria • Russian Fed. **17** G6
Kabba • Nigeria **22** F3
Kåbdalis • Sweden **16** K3
Kabin Buri • Thailand **109** H2
Kabinda • Dem. Rep. of Congo **23** C5
Kableshkovo • Bulgaria **15** I1
Kablow-Ziegelei • Germany **81** F4
Kabo • Central African Rep. **22** H3
Kabompo • Zambia **24** C2
Kabongo • Dem. Rep. of Congo **23** D5
Kabul • Afghanistan **18** I3
Kabunda • Dem. Rep. of Congo **24** D2
Kabwe • Zambia **24** D2
Kacanik • F.R. of Yugoslavia **15** C1
Kachin • Myanmar **31** B1
Kachug • Russian Fed. **27** G6
Kacina • Czech Rep. **96** C2
Kackar Dagi • Turkey **18** D1
Kadamatt I. • India **106** D9
Kadan • Czech Rep. **96** C1
Kadan Kyun • Myanmar **31** B4
Kadei • Cameroon/Central African Rep. **22** G4
Kadinhani • Turkey **15** N5
Kadoma • Zimbabwe **102** J2
Kaduna • Nigeria **22** F2
Kaduna Plateau • Nigeria **22** F2
Kaduna [Riv] • Nigeria **22** F2
Kaduqli • Sudan **21** E5
Kaduy • Russian Fed. **97** E2
Kadzherom • Russian Fed. **17** J2
Kaédi • Mauritania **20** C5
Kaena Point • HI, United States **119** L5
Kaesong • D.P.R. of Korea **30** D6
Kaew Noi, Ko • Thailand **109** K1
Kaew Yai, Ko • Thailand **109** K2
Kafakumba • Dem. Rep. of Congo **24** C1
Kaffrine • Senegal **20** B6
Kafiréa, Stenó • Greece **15** F6
Kafiréas, Akra • Greece **15** F5
Kafue • Zambia **24** D3
Kafue Dam • Zambia **24** D3
Kafue Flats • Zambia **24** D3
Kafue Nat. Park **Park** • Zambia **103** [105]
Kaga • Japan **30** I6
Kaga Bandoro • Central African Rep. **23** B2
Kagan • Uzbekistan **18** H2
Kagera • Africa **23** E4
Kagera • Rwanda/Tanzania **102** H1
Kagoshima • Japan **30** F9
Kahaluu • HI, United States **119** L6
Kahama • Tanzania **102** H1
Kahana Valley State Park • HI, United States **119** L5
Kahemba • Dem. Rep. of Congo **23** B5
Kahla • Germany **9** G6
Kahler Asten • Germany **9** D5
Kahoolawe • HI, United States **119** L7
Kahovka • Ukraine **17** E5
Kahuku Point • HI, United States **119** L1
Kahului • HI, United States **119** L3
Kahuzi-Biega, Parc nat. du **Heritage N** • Dem. Rep. of Congo **61** [85]
Kahuzi-Biega, Parc nat. du **Park** • Dem. Rep. of Congo **103** [58]
Kai Besar • Indonesia **35** (1) A2
Kai, Kepulauan • Indonesia **32** (1) D4
Kaiama • Nigeria **22** E3
Kaiapoi • New Zealand **35** D6
Kaieteur Falls • Guyana **43** F2
Kaifeng • China **29** E4
Kaikohe • New Zealand **35** D2
Kaikoura • New Zealand **35** D6
Kailu • China **27** J8
Kailua • HI, United States **119** L6
Kailua Kona • HI, United States **119** L8
Kaimana • Indonesia **32** (1) D3
Kaimanawa Mtns • New Zealand **112** K4
Kainantu • Papua New Guinea **35** (1) D2
Kainji Reservoir • Nigeria **22** E2
Kainuu • Finland **94** A6
Kairouan **Heritage C** • Tunisia **64** [231]
Kairouan • Tunisia **101** E4
Kaiserslautern • Germany **82** G4
Kaiserstuhl • Germany **82** G7
Kaitaia • New Zealand **35** D2
Kaiwi Channel • HI, United States **119** L3
Kaiyuan • China **31** C2
Kajaani • Finland **16** N4
Kajaapu • Indonesia **32** C4
Kajabbi • QL, Australia **34** H3
Kajang • Malaysia **108** D4
Kajmakcalan • Greece/F.Y.R. of Macedonia **15** C2
Kaka • Ethiopia **23** F2
Kakadu Nat. Park • NT, Australia **34** F2
Kakadu Nat. Park **Heritage N** • NT, Australia **61** [128]
Kakadu Nat. Park **Heritage C** • Australia **63** [180]
Kakamega • Kenya **101** G1
Kakamega Forest Game Reserve • Kenya **101** G1
Kakar Range • Pakistan **28** A2
Kakata • Liberia **22** B3
Kakinada • India **106** D4
Kakopetriá • Cyprus **93** J3
Kaktovik • AK, United States **38** C2
Kakum Nature Park **Park** • Ghana **103** [27]
Kala • Phuket, Thailand **109** K1
Kala, El • Algeria **12** C12
Kalaâ Kasbah • Tunisia **101** E3
Kalaallit Nunaat • Greenland **39** V3
Kalabahi • Indonesia **32** (1) B4
Kalabsha • Egypt **101** F5
Kalacha Beach • Goa, India **105** B1
Kaladan • India/Myanmar **28** F4
Kaladar • OT, Canada **122** B6
Kalahari Desert • Botswana **24** C4
Kalahari Gemsbok Nat. Park **Park** • South Africa **103** [113]
Kalai Mor • Turkmenistan **26** J10
Kalajoki • Finland **16** L4
Kalajoki **Beach** • Finland **69** [25]
Kalakan • Russian Fed. **27** I5
Kalalau Lookout • HI, United States **119** L2
Kalamáki • Greece **15** E6
Kalamáki • Zante, Greece **92** C3
Kalamáta • Greece **15** D6
Kalamáta **Beach** • Greece **69** [181]
Kalamazoo • MI, United States **41** I3
Kalambo Falls • Tanzania **102** H3
Kalámi • Crete, Greece **93** E1
Kálamos • Greece **92** C1
Kalamunda • WA, Australia **34** C6
Kalándra **Beach** • Greece **69** [192]
Kalándra • Greece **92** D1
Kalao • Indonesia **32** (1) B4
Kalapana • HI, United States **119** L8
Kalasin • Indonesia **32** E2
Kalat • Pakistan **28** A3
Kálathos **Beach** • Rhodes, Greece **69** [211]
Kálathos • Rhodes, Greece **93** F4
Kalaupapa Nat. Hist. Park • HI, United States **119** L3
Kalaupapa Nat. Hist. Park **Park** • HI, United States **120** [17]
Kalavárda • Rhodes, Greece **93** F1
Kale • Denizli, Turkey **15** J6
Kale • Alanya, Turkey **93** G3
Kale • Antalya, Turkey **93** G4
Kalecik • Turkey **15** O3
Kalemie • Dem. Rep. of Congo **23** D5
Kalevala • Russian Fed. **16** P4
Kalewa • Myanmar **31** A2
Kalgoorlie • WA, Australia **34** D6
Kalí Liménes • Crete, Greece **93** E6
Kaliakoúda • Greece **15** C5
Kaliakra, Nos • Bulgaria **14** P6
Kalima • Dem. Rep. of Congo **23** D4
Kalimantan • Indonesia **32** E3
Kálimnos • Greece **15** I7
Kálimnos [I.] • Greece **92** D8
Kaliningrad • Russian Fed. **13** J3
Kalinjar • India **105** C7
Kalispell • MT, United States **117** E2
Kaliste • Czech Rep. **96** C4
Kalisz • Koszalinskie, Poland **13** E4
Kalisz • Kaliskie, Poland **13** H6
Kalithéa **Beach** • Greece **69** [192]
Kalithiés **Beach** • Rhodes, Greece **69** [211]
Kalithiés • Rhodes, Greece **93** F2
Kaliua • Tanzania **102** H1
Kaliurang • Java, Indonesia **110** D7
Kalíves **Beach** • Crete, Greece **69** [212]
Kalíves • Crete, Greece **93** E1
Kalix • Sweden **16** L4
Kalix älv • Sweden **16** L3
Kalkan • Turkey **92** D9
Kalkim • Turkey **15** I4
Kalkrand • Namibia **24** B4
Kalkudah • Sri Lanka **106** D16
Kållandsö • Sweden **95** F3
Kallavesi • Finland **16** N5
Kallirhoe • Jordan **98** A8
Kalloní **Beach** • Greece **69** [199]
Kalloní • Greece **92** D5
Kallsjön • Sweden **16** G5
Kalmar • Sweden **95** F8
Kalmar [Adm] • Sweden **95** F8
Kalmarsund • Sweden **95** F8
Kalmykia • Russian Fed. **17** G5
Kaló Horió **Beach** • Crete, Greece **69** [215]
Kaló Horío • Crete, Greece **93** E8
Kalocsa • Hungary **13** H11
Kalofer • Bulgaria **14** L7
Kaloko-Honokohau Nat. Hist. Park • HI, United States **119** L8
Kaloko-Honokohau Nat. Hist. Park **Park** • HI, United States **120** [20]
Kalólimnos • Greece **92** D8
Kalomo • Zambia **102** J1
Kalopanayiotis • Cyprus **93** J3
Kalpáki • Greece **15** B4
Kalpeni I. • India **106** D9
Kalsubai • India **25** I8
Kaluga • Russian Fed. **17** F4
Kalumburu Mission • WA, Australia **34** E2
Kalundborg **Beach** • Denmark **68** [43]
Kalundborg • Denmark **95** F10
Kalvåg • Norway **94** C1
Kalvarija • Lithuania **13** M3
Kalyazin • Russian Fed. **97** E4
Kam Shan Country Park • Hong Kong, China **107** H5
Kama • Russian Fed. **26** H6
Kamai • Chad **20** I4
Kamaishi • Japan **30** K5
Kaman • Turkey **15** O4
Kamanjab • Namibia **24** A3
Kamaran • Yemen **18** D6
Kamarang • Guyana **43** E2
Kamáres • Greece **92** D7
Kamári **Beach** • Greece **69** [209]
Kamativi • Zimbabwe **102** J1
Kambalda • WA, Australia **34** D6
Kambalnaya Sopka, Vulkan • Russian Fed. **27** Q6
Kambanós, Akra • Greece **15** F6
Kamchatka Peninsula • Russian Fed. **97** A7
Kamchatka, Poluostrov • Russian Fed. **27** Q5
Kamchatka [Riv] • Russian Fed. **27** Q6
Kamchatka volcanoes **Heritage N** • Russian Fed. **61** [66]
Kamchatskiy Zaliv • Russian Fed. **27** R5
Kamchiya • Bulgaria **97** D4
Kamchiya [Riv] • Bulgaria **14** O6
Kamen • Germany **81** E2
Kámen • Czech Rep. **96** C4
Kamen-na-Obi • Russian Fed. **26** N7
Kaména Voúrla **Beach** • Greece **69** [187]
Kaména Voúrla • Greece **92** D4
Kamenka • Ukraine **17** E5
Kamenka • Russian Fed. **17** G4
Kamensk-Uralskiy • Russian Fed. **26** J6
Kamenz • Germany **9** J5
Kamet • India **28** C2
Kamien Pomorski • Poland **13** D4
Kamina • Dem. Rep. of Congo **23** C5
Kámiros • Rhodes, Greece **93** F1
Kámiros Skala • Rhodes, Greece **93** F1
Kamloops • BC, Canada **122** C3
Kammam • India **106** D3
Kamnarok Game Reserve • Kenya **101** G1
Kamp-Lintfort • Germany **81** E1
Kampala • Uganda **23** E3
Kampar • Malaysia **31** C6
Kampar • Indonesia **32** C2
Kampen • Netherlands **80** A7
Kampen **Spa** • Germany **83** [2]
Kampenwand • Germany **82** J8
Kampinoski Nat. Park **Park** • Poland **72** [91]
Kâmpong Saôm • Cambodia **31** C4
Kamrau, Teluk • Indonesia **35** (1) A1
Kamuela • HI, United States **119** L8
Kamui-Misaki • Japan **30** K3
Kamuku Wildlife Reserve **Park** • Nigeria **103** [32]
Kamvoúnia Ori • Greece **15** C4
Kamyshin • Russian Fed. **17** H4
Kanaaupscow • QU, Canada **39** P6
Kanairiktok • NF, Canada **39** S6
Kanáli • Corfu, Greece **92** B1
Kananga • Dem. Rep. of Congo **23** C5
Kanazawa • Japan **30** I6
Kanchanaburi • Thailand **109** H1
Kanchenjunga • India **28** E3
Kanchipuram • India **106** D7
Kandalaksha • Russian Fed. **17** E1
Kandalakshskaya Guba • Russian Fed. **17** E1
Kandangan • Indonesia **32** F3
Kandanghaur • Java, Indonesia **110** D2
Kándanos • Crete, Greece **93** E1
Kandavu • Fiji **35** (2) D2
Kandel • Germany **82** G8
Kandersteg • Switzerland **89** G6
Kandi • Benin **22** E2
Kandira • Turkey **15** L2
Kandla • India **28** B4
Kandooma • Maldives **106** E4
Kandrian • Papua New Guinea **35** (1) D2
Kandy **Heritage C** • Sri Lanka **63** [138]
Kandy • Sri Lanka **106** D15
Kanem • Chad **21** B5
Kaneohe • HI, United States **119** L6
Kaneohe Bay • HI, United States **119** L6
Kánestron, Akra • Greece **15** E4
Kang • Botswana **24** C4
Kang Kra Chan • Thailand **109** H3
Kangaba • Mali **20** D6
Kangar • Malaysia **32** C1
Kangaroo I. • SA, Australia **34** G7
Kangasniemi • Finland **16** N6
Kangean, Kepulauan • Indonesia **32** F4
Kangerlussaq • Greenland **46** U3
Kanggye • D.P.R. of Korea **30** D4
Kangiqsualujjuaq • QU, Canada **39** R5
Kangirsuk • QU, Canada **39** R4
Kangmar • India **28** E3
Kangnung • Rep. of Korea **30** E6
Kango • Gabon **22** G4
Kangrinboqê Feng • China **28** D2
Kanifinolhu • Maldives **106** E2
Kanin Nos • Russian Fed. **17** G1
Kanin Nos, mys • Russian Fed. **17** G1
Kanin, Poluostrov • Russian Fed. **17** I1
Kanjiza • F.R. of Yugoslavia **13** J11
Kankaanpää • Finland **95** E1
Kankan • Guinea **22** C2
Kankesanturai • Sri Lanka **106** D11
Kankroli • India **105** C6
Kankunskiy • Russian Fed. **27** K5
Kannauj • India **105** C3
Kanniyakumari • India **106** D14
Kano • Nigeria **22** F2
Kano [Adm] • Nigeria **22** F2
Kanona • Zambia **23** E6
Kanoya • Japan **30** F9
Kanpur • India **105** C7
Kansas • United States **40** G4
Kansas City • KS/MO, United States **41** H4
Kansk • Russian Fed. **26** Q6
Kansong • Rep. of Korea **30** E5
Kansyat • Indonesia **32** (1) E3
Kantara Castle • Cyprus **93** J2
Kantchari • Burkina Faso **20** F6
Kante • Togo **22** E3
Kanturk Castle • Ireland **79** F6
Kanye • Botswana **24** D4
Kanyemba • Zimbabwe **102** J2
Kanyu • Botswana **24** C4
Kaohsiung • Taiwan **29** G6
Kaolack • Senegal **22** A2
Kaole • Tanzania **102** H4
Kapaa • HI, United States **119** L2
Kapanga • Dem. Rep. of Congo **23** C5
Kapchagay • Kazakhstan **26** M9
Kapellskär • Sweden **95** D2
Kapenguria • Kenya **101** G1
Kapfenberg • Austria **13** E10
Kapidagi Yarim Adasi • Turkey **15** I3
Kapit • Malaysia **32** E2
Kapka, Massif du • Chad/Sudan **21** D5
Kapos • Hungary **13** H11
Kappeln • Germany **8** E2
Kaprun **Ski** • Austria **70** [163]
Kaprun • Austria **89** H4
Kapsan • D.P.R. of Korea **30** E4
Kapuas • Indonesia **32** E2
Kapuskasing • OT, Canada **39** O7
Kapuvár • Hungary **13** F10
Kara • Togo **22** E3
Kara Bogaz Gol • Turkmenistan **26** H9
Kara Burun • Turkey **15** J7
Kara Dag • Turkey **15** O6
Kara Dong • China **26** N10
Kara Gölü • Turkey **15** K7
Kara Kum • Turkmenistan **18** G2
Kara Sea • Arctic Ocean **26** J3
Kara Strait • Russian Fed. **26** I4
Karabiga • Turkey **15** I3
Karaburun • Istanbul, Turkey **15** H5
Karaburun • Izmir, Turkey **15** J2
Karabutak • Kazakhstan **26** J8
Karacabey • Turkey **15** J3
Karacaoglan • Turkey **15** I2
Karachay-Cherkessia • Russian Fed. **17** G6
Karachi • Pakistan **28** A3
Karadeniz Bogazi • Turkey **92** D3
Karaganda • Kazakhstan **26** L8
Karaginskiy, Ostrov • Russian Fed. **27** R5
Karaginskiy Zaliv • Russian Fed. **27** R5
Karagos, gora • Russian Fed. **26** O7
Karaikal • India **106** D11
Karain • Turkey **93** G1
Karak • Kazakhstan **26** J9
Karakalpakstan • Uzbekistan **26** I9
Karakax He • China **28** C1
Karakelong • Indonesia **32** (1) C2
Karakol • Kyrgyzstan **26** M9
Karakoram • Asia **28** C1
Karakorum • Mongolia **98** B3
Karakul, Ozero • China **18** J2
Karakumskiy Kanal • Turkmenistan **18** H2
Karam • Russian Fed. **27** G5
Karaman • Turkey **15** O6
Karamanli • Turkey **93** G1
Karamay • China **26** N8
Karamea • New Zealand **35** D5
Karamea Bight • New Zealand **35** C5
Karamiran He • China **28** E1
Karamiran Shankou • China **26** O10
Karamürsel • Turkey **15** K3
Karangsari Cave • Indonesia **110** C4
Karasburg • Namibia **24** B5
Karasjok • Norway **16** M2
Karasu • Turkey **15** L2
Karasu [Riv] • Turkey **18** C2
Karasuk • Russian Fed. **26** M7
Karatas • Turkey **15** J5
Karatau • Kazakhstan **26** L9
Karatsu • Japan **30** E8
Karaul • Russian Fed. **26** N3
Karauli • India **105** C6
Karavastase, Gjiri i • Albania **14** G9
Karavostási • Cyprus **93** J1
Karawang • Java, Indonesia **110** D1
Karawanken • Austria/Slovenia **13** D11
Karbala • Iraq **18** D3
Kårbole • Sweden **16** H6
Karcag • Hungary **13** K10
Kardam • Bulgaria **97** D2
Kardámena **Beach** • Greece **69** [210]
Kardámena • Greece **92** D8
Kardámila • Greece **15** H5
Kardámila **Beach** • Greece **69** [200]
Karditsa • Greece **15** C4
Kärdla • Estonia **16** L7
Kareedouw • South Africa **100** C7
Kareha, Jbel • Morocco **11** F9
Karelia • Russian Fed. **17** E2
Karelia [Adm] • Russian Fed. **17** E1
Karelia, Northern • Finland **94** A6
Karelska Naset • Russian Fed. **17** D2
Karen • India **28** F6
Karen • Myanmar **31** B3
Karesuando • Sweden **16** L2
Kargilik • China **28** C1
Kargopol • Russian Fed. **17** F2
Karhula • Finland **16** N6
Kari • Nigeria **20** H6
Kariai • Greece **15** F3
Karianí **Beach** • Greece **69** [194]
Karianous Nat. Park • Kenya **101** G3
Kariba • Zimbabwe **102** J1
Kariba Dam • Zambia/Zimbabwe **102** J1
Kariba, Lake • Zambia/Zimbabwe **102** J1
Karibib • Namibia **24** B4
Karidu Atoll • Maldives **106** E1
Kariega • South Africa **100** C3
Karigasniemi • Finland **17** D1
Karikari, Cape • New Zealand **35** D2
Karimata, Kepulauan • Indonesia **32** D3
Karimnagar • India **28** C5
Karimunjawa, Kepulauan • Indonesia **110** D3
Karin • Somalia **23** H1
Karis • Finland **95** E4
Karisimbi • Rwanda **23** D4
Káristos • Greece **92** D4
Karjaa • Finland **95** E4
Karjala • Russian Fed. **17** E2
Karkar • Papua New Guinea **35** (1) D1
Karkinitskiy Zaliv • Ukraine **17** E5
Karkonoski Nat. Park **Park** • Poland **72** [98]
Karleby • Finland **16** L5
Karlik Shan • China **29** A2
Karlobag • Croatia **12** J4
Karlovac • Croatia **14** C4
Kárlovássi • Greece **92** D8
Karlovo • Bulgaria **14** L7
Karlovy Vary • Czech Rep. **96** C1
Karlsbad • Czech Rep. **96** C1
Karlsborg • Sweden **95** F3
Karlshamn • Sweden **95** F12
Karlskoga • Sweden **16** H7
Karlskrona • Sweden **95** F12
Karlslunde • Denmark **95** F10
Karlsruhe • Germany **82** G6
Karlstad • Sweden **16** G7
Karlstadt • Germany **9** E7
Karlstein-Nonn **Spa** • Germany **83** [261]
Karlstejn • Czech Rep. **96** C2
Karmah • Sudan **21** F4
Karmøy • Norway **94** C5
Karnak • Egypt **101** F4
Karnal • India **105** C2
Karnataka • India **106** D2
Karnataka Plateau • India **106** D2
Karnishe Skiregion **Ski** • Austria **70** [190]
Karnobat • Bulgaria **97** D3
Kärnten • Austria **13** C11
Karo Batak Villages • Indonesia **110** B2
Karoi • Zimbabwe **102** J2
Karon • Phuket, Thailand **109** K2
Karon Beach • Phuket, Thailand **109** K2
Karonga • Malawi **24** E2
Karoo, Great • South Africa **100** C3
Karoo, Little • South Africa **100** C6
Karoo Nat. Park • South Africa **100** C3
Karoo Nat. Park **Park** • South Africa **103** [119]
Karora • Sudan **21** G4
Karpackie, Pogórze • Poland **13** J8
Karpas Peninsula • Cyprus **93** J2
Kárpathos • Greece **92** D11
Kárpathos [I.] • Greece **92** D11
Karpathou, Stenó • Greece **15** I8
Karratha • WA, Australia **34** C4
Kars • Turkey **92** A4
Karsakpay • Kazakhstan **26** K8
Kärsämäki • Finland **16** M4
Karsiyaka • Turkey **15** I5
Karskiye Vorota, Proliv • Russian Fed. **26** I3
Karskoye More • Russian Fed. **46** H2
Kartal • Turkey **15** K3
Kartuzy • Poland **13** H3
Karumba • QL, Australia **34** H3
Karun • Iran **18** E3
Karungi • Sweden **16** L3
Karungu • Kenya **23** E4
Karup • Denmark **95** F9
Karur • India **106** D11
Karviná • Czech Rep. **13** H8
Karwandelgebirge • Austria **9** G9
Karwar • India **106** D1
Karymskoye • Russian Fed. **27** H6
Kas **Beach** • Turkey **69** [231]
Kas • Turkey **93** G3
Kasaba • Zambia **23** E6
Kasai • Dem. Rep. of Congo **23** C4
Kasai [Riv] • Dem. Rep. of Congo **23** C5
Kasama • Zambia **24** E2
Kasanga • Tanzania **102** H3
Kasaragod • India **106** D6
Kasba Lake • NT/NU, Canada **38** K4
Kasba Tatla • Morocco **20** D2
Kasempa • Zambia **24** D2
Kasenga • Dem. Rep. of Congo **23** D6
Kasese • Uganda **23** E3
Kashan • Iran **18** F3
Kashgar • China **18** K2
Kashi • China **26** M10
Kashin • Russian Fed. **97** E4
Kashiwazaki • Japan **30** J6
Kashmar • Iran **18** G2
Kasimov • Russian Fed. **17** G3
Kaskinen • Finland **95** E1
Kaskö • Finland **95** E1
Kasongo • Dem. Rep. of Congo **23** D4
Kasongo-Lunda • Dem. Rep. of Congo **23** B5
Kaspiyskiy • Russian Fed. **17** H5
Kasr, Ra's • Sudan **21** G4
Kassala • Sudan **21** G4
Kassándra • Greece **92** D1
Kassándras, Akra • Greece **15** E4
Kassándras, Kólpos • Greece **15** E3
Kassándria **Beach** • Greece **69** [192]
Kassel • Germany **9** E5
Kassel-Wilhelmshöhe **Spa** • Germany **83** [123]
Kasselburg • Germany **82** H1
Kasserine • Tunisia **101** E3
Kassiópi **Beach** • Corfu, Greece **69** [170]
Kassiópi • Corfu, Greece **92** B1
Kássos • Greece **92** D11
Kastamonu • Turkey **15** O2
Kastaniés • Greece **15** H2
Kastelholm • Finland **95** E3
Kastéli • Crete, Greece **93** E7
Kastelruth • Italy **90** B1
Kasterlee **Beach** • Belgium **68** [71]
Kasterlee • Belgium **80** A11
Kastoriá • Greece **15** C3
Kastoriás, Límni • Greece **15** C3
Kastós • Greece **92** C1
Kástro **Beach** • Greece **69** [180]
Kástro • Greece **92** D4
Kastrup [Apt] • Denmark **95** F11
Kasumiga-ura • Japan **30** K6
Kasungu • Malawi **24** E2
Kasungu Nat. Park **Park** • Malawi **103** [97]
Kasur • Pakistan **18** J3
Kata • Phuket, Thailand **109** K2
Kata Noi Beach • Phuket, Thailand **109** K2
Kata Yai Beach • Phuket, Thailand **109** K2
Kataba • Zambia **24** D3
Katahdin, Mt • ME, United States **118** G2
Katanga • Dem. Rep. of Congo **23** C5
Katanning • WA, Australia **34** C6
Katápola • Greece **92** D8
Katavi Nat. Park • Tanzania **102** H3
Katavia • Rhodes, Greece **93** F3
Katchall • India **28** F7
Kateríni • Greece **15** D3
Kateríni **Beach** • Greece **69** [190]
Katha • Myanmar **31** B2
Katherina • Egypt **21** F2
Katherine • NT, Australia **34** F2
Kathiawar • India **28** B4
Kathmandu • Nepal **28** E3
Kathmandu Valley **Heritage C** • Nepal **63** [141]
Kati • Mali **20** D6
Katikati • New Zealand **112** K2
Katiola • Côte d'Ivoire **22** C3
Katiti Aboriginal Land • NT, Australia **112** H3
Katlabukh, Ozero • Ukraine **14** P4
Katmai Nat. Park & Preserve **Park** • AK, United States **120** [9]
Kátó Ahaía • Greece **15** C5
Káto Korakiana **Beach** • Corfu, Greece **69** [170]
Káto Stavrós **Beach** • Greece **69** [193]
Káto Zákros • Crete, Greece **93** E8
Katong • Singapore **108** E2
Katoomba • NS, Australia **111** G2
Katowice • Poland **13** H7
Katrine, Loch • United Kingdom **74** B1
Katrineholm • Sweden **95** D3
Katsina • Nigeria **22** F2
Katsuura • Japan **30** K7
Kattakurgan • Uzbekistan **18** I2
Kattegat • Denmark/Sweden **95** F6
Katu • Phuket, Thailand **109** K2
Katun • Russian Fed. **26** O7
Katunayake • Sri Lanka **106** D15
Katwijk • Netherlands **80** C1
Katwijkse Duinen • Netherlands **80** C1
Katz, Burg • Germany **82** H2
Kau • Indonesia **32** (1) C2
Kau Paulatmada, Gunung • Indonesia **32** (1) C3
Kau Sai Chau • Hong Kong, China **107** H6
Kauai • HI, United States **119** L2
Kauai Channel • HI, United States **119** L2
Kaub • Germany **82** H4
Kaufbeuren • Germany **82** J2
Kaufungen • Germany **9** E5
Kauhajoki • Finland **16** L5
Kaukauveld • Botswana/Namibia **24** C3
Kaukiainen • Finland **95** E4
Kaula I. • HI, United States **119** L1
Kaunakakai • HI, United States **119** L3
Kaunas • Lithuania **13** M3
Kaunos • Turkey **92** D9
Kaupanger • Norway **94** C4
Kausambi • India **105** C7
Kautokeino • Norway **16** L2
Kavadarci • F.Y.R. of Macedonia **14** J8
Kavajë • Albania **14** G8
Kavak • Turkey **15** H3
Kavála **Beach** • Greece **69** [194]
Kavála • Greece **92** D1
Kavális, Kólpos • Greece **15** F3
Kavalerovo • Russian Fed. **30** H2
Kavali • India **106** D3
Kavaratti • India **106** D9
Kavaratti I. • India **106** D9
Kavarna **Beach** • Bulgaria **69** [243]
Kavarna • Bulgaria **97** D4
Kavendou, Mt • Guinea **22** B2
Kavieng • Papua New Guinea **35** (1) E1
Kavir, Dasht-e • Iran **18** G3
Kávos • Corfu, Greece **92** B1
Kavoúri • Greece **92** D7
Kavoúsi • Crete, Greece **93** E8
Kawa • Sudan **21** F4
Kawaikini • HI, United States **119** L2
Kawambwa • Zambia **24** D1
Kawasaki • Japan **30** J7
Kaweka Range • New Zealand **112** K4
Kawerau • New Zealand **112** K2
Kawhia • New Zealand **112** K1
Kawhia Harbour • New Zealand **112** K1
Kaxgar He • China **26** M10
Kaya • Burkina Faso **20** E6
Kayah • Myanmar **31** B3
Kayak • Russian Fed. **26** R3
Kayali Dagi • Turkey **15** H4
Kayan • Indonesia **32** F2
Kayes • Mali **22** B2
Kayseri • Turkey **18** C2
Kazachye • Russian Fed. **27** M2
Kazakhstan • Asia **26** K8
Kazan • Russian Fed. **17** H3
Kazan • NU, Canada **38** L4
Kazan Retto • Japan **25** P7
Kazandzik • Turkmenistan **18** G2
Kazanluk **Heritage C** • Bulgaria **64** [172]
Kazanluk • Bulgaria **97** D3
Kazerun • Iran **18** F4
Kazincbarcika • Hungary **13** J9
Kaziranga Nat. Park **Heritage N** • India **61** [108]
Kazuma Pan Nat. Park • Zimbabwe **102** J1
Ké • Chad **20** I5
Kéa • Greece **92** D7
Kearney • NE, United States **40** G3
Kebili • Tunisia **101** E5
Kebnekaise • Sweden **16** J3
Kebumen • Java, Indonesia **110** D6
Kecel • Hungary **13** I11
Kechika • BC, Canada **38** F5
Kecskemét • Hungary **13** I11
Kedah • Malaysia **31** C5
Kedainiai • Lithuania **13** N2
Kédia d'Idjil • Mauritania **20** C4
Kediri • Java, Indonesia **110** D7
Kédougou • Senegal **22** B2
Kedzierzyn-Kozle • Poland **13** G7
Keekorok Lodge • Kenya **101** G3
Keel • Ireland **79** F1
Keele Peak • YT, Canada **38** E4
Keene • NH, United States **118** G3
Keetmanshoop • Namibia **24** B5
Kef Lakhdar Chergui • Algeria **11** O9
Kefaloniá • Greece **92** C2
Kefaloniá Nat. Park • Greece **92** C2
Keflavík • Iceland **16** (1) B2
Kehl • Germany **9** C8
Kehlheim • Germany **9** G8
Kehlstein • Germany **82** J8
Keighley • United Kingdom **7** K8
Keilah • Jordan **98** A7
Keitele • Finland **16** M5
Keith • SA, Australia **34** H7
Keith Arm • NT, Canada **38** G3
Keitum **Spa** • Germany **83** [2]
Kejimkujik Nat. Park • NS, Canada **123** D7
Kek Lok Si Temple • Penang, Malaysia **108** C1
Kekaha • HI, United States **119** L2
Kekes • Hungary **13** I10
Kekova • Turkey **93** G3
Kel Tepe • Izmit, Turkey **15** L3
Kel Tepe • Zonguldak, Turkey **15** N2
Kelafo • Ethiopia **23** G2
Kelang • Malaysia **108** D3
Kelang [I.] • Malaysia **108** D3
Kelantan • Malaysia **31** C5
Keld Chapel • United Kingdom **74** C2
Kelem • Ethiopia **23** F2
Kelibia • Tunisia **101** E2
Kellberg **Spa** • Germany **83** [265]
Kelle • Congo **22** G4
Kellenhusen **Spa** • Germany **83** [24]
Kellerwand • Austria/Italy **89** H8
Kellet, Cape • NT, Canada **38** F2
Kellie's Castle • Malaysia **108** D1
Kellog • Russian Fed. **27** C4
Kellogg • MT, United States **117** E2

Kells • Ireland 79 E1
Kélo • Chad 22 H3
Kelowna • BC, Canada 122 C4
Kelsey • MN, Canada 38 L5
Kelsey Bay • BC, Canada 38 F6
Kelti, Jbel • Morocco 11 F9
Keluang • Malaysia 31 C6
Kem • Russian Fed. 17 E2
Kemalpasa • Turkey 15 J4
Kemaman • Malaysia 108 A4
Kemer • Turkey 15 J6
Kemer • Mugla, Turkey 15 K7
Kemer **Beach** • Turkey 69 [229]
Kemer • Antalya, Turkey 93 G3
Kemer Barji • Turkey 15 J6
Kemerovo • Russian Fed. 26 O6
Kemijärvi • Finland 16 N3
Kemijärvi [Lake] • Finland 16 N3
Kemijoki • Finland 16 N3
Kemiö • Finland 95 E3
Kempen • Belgium 5 I3
Kempen • Germany 81 E1
Kempendyay • Russian Fed. 27 J4
Kempens Kanaal • Belgium 5 H3
Kempsey • NS, Australia 34 J6
Kempt, Lac • QU, Canada 39 Q7
Kempten • Germany 82 J6
Kenai • AK, United States 46 EE3
Kenai Fjords Nat. Park **Park** • AK, United States 120 [11]
Kenai Peninsula • AK, United States 40 (2) G2
Kendal • United Kingdom 74 C4
Kendari • Indonesia 32 (1) B3
Kendawangan • Indonesia 32 E3
Kenema • Sierra Leone 22 B3
Keng Tung • Myanmar 31 B2
Kenge • Dem. Rep. of Congo 23 B4
Kengur Shan • China 26 M10
Kenhardt • South Africa 24 C5
Kenitra • Morocco 101 D1
Kenkoure • Guinea 22 B2
Kenmare • Ireland 79 F7
Kenmare [Riv] • Ireland 79 F7
Kennack Sands **Beach** • United Kingdom 75 [120]
Kennacraig • United Kingdom 78 A2
Kennebec • ME, United States 118 G2
Kennebunkport • ME, United States 118 G3
Kennedy, John F. [Apt] • NY, United States 118 H2
Kennedy, John F., Nat. Hist. Site **Park** • MA, United States 121 [347]
Kennedy, John F., Space Center • FL, United States 119 M6
Kennemerduinen, Nat. Park de • Netherlands 80 C1
Kennesaw Mtn Nat. Battlefield Park **Park** • GA, United States 121 [209]
Kennet • United Kingdom 5 B3
Kennewick • WA, United States 117 E2
Keno Hill • YT, Canada 38 D4
Kenogami • OT, Canada 39 N6
Kenora • OT, Canada 38 M7
Kenosha • WI, United States 41 I3
Kensington • United Kingdom 74 E1
Kensington Oval • Barbados 125 H3
Kent • United Kingdom 74 E4
Kent Peninsula • NU, Canada 38 J3
Kentau • Kazakhstan 26 K9
Kentucky • United States 41 I4
Kentucky Kingdom **Park** • KY, United States 121 [W]
Kentwood • LA, United States 118 K4
Kenya • Africa 101 G
Kenya, Mt • Kenya 101 G3
Kenya, Mt, Nat. Park **Heritage N** • Kenya 61 [89]
Kenyatta, Jomo [Apt] • Kenya 101 G3
Keoladeo Nat. Park **Heritage N** • India 61 [106]
Keoladeo Nat. Park • India 105 C2
Kepi • Indonesia 32 (1) E4
Kepice • Poland 13 F3
Kepler Mtns • New Zealand 112 L1
Kepno • Poland 13 G6
Kepsut • Turkey 15 J4
Kerala • India 106 D10
Kéran, Parc nat. de la **Park** • Togo 103 [29]
Kerang • VI, Australia 111 G1
Kerava • Finland 95 E4
Keraz • Algeria 20 E3
Kerch • Ukraine 17 F5
Kerema • Papua New Guinea 35 (1) D2
Kerempe Burun • Turkey 15 O1
Keren • Eritrea 21 G4
Kerguelen Is. • Indian Ocean 19 (1) A1
Kerí • Greece 92 C3
Kerinci, Gunung • Indonesia 32 C3
Kerio Valley Game Reserve • Kenya 101 G1
Keriya • China 28 D1
Keriya He • China 28 D1
Kerken • Germany 81 E1
Kerki • Turkmenistan 18 I2
Kérkira **Beach** • Corfu, Greece 69 [170]
Kérkira • Corfu, Greece 92 B1
Kérkira [I.] • Greece 92 B1
Kerkouane **Heritage C** • Tunisia 64 [228]
Kerkouane • Tunisia 101 E2
Kermadec Is. • New Zealand 33 J9
Kerman • Iran 18 G3
Kerme • Turkey 15 J6
Kerni • Finland 16 M4
Kéros • Greece 92 D8
Kérouane • Guinea 22 C3
Kerpen • Germany 9 B6
Kerry • Ireland 79 F5
Kerry Head • Ireland 79 F5
Kerry, Ring of • Ireland 79 F7
Kerrykeel **Beach** • Ireland 68 [65]
Kerteminde • Denmark 95 F14
Kertosono • Java, Indonesia 110 D7
Kesan • Turkey 15 H3
Kesen'numa • Japan 30 K5
Keski-Suomi • Finland 16 M5
Keski-Suomi • Finland 94 A9
Keskin • Turkey 15 O4
Kessingland **Beach** • United Kingdom 75 [44]
Kestel **Beach** • Turkey 69 [221]
Kesteven • United Kingdom 75 A4
Keswick • United Kingdom 74 C2
Keszthely • Hungary 13 G11
Ket • Russian Fed. 26 O6
Ketapang • Borneo, Indonesia 32 E3
Ketapang • Java, Indonesia 110 D8
Ketchikan • AK, United States 38 E5
Ketou • Benin 22 E3
Ketrzyn • Poland 13 K3
Kettering • United Kingdom 7 L9
Ketzin • Germany 81 F3
Keukenhof • Netherlands 80 C1
Keurusselka • Finland 95 E2
Keuruu • Finland 95 E2
Keweenaw Nat. Hist. Park **Park** • MI, United States 121 [160]
Key • St Kitts & Nevis 125 G1
Key Biscayne • FL, United States 119 M8
Key Deer Nat. Wildlife Refuge • FL, United States 119 M8
Key Largo • FL, United States 119 M8
Key, Lough • Ireland 79 F2
Key West • FL, United States 119 M7
Keystone **Ski** • CO, United States 116 [93]
Kezhma • Russian Fed. 26 R6
Kezmarok • Slovak Rep. 13 J8
Khabarovsk • Russian Fed. 27 M7
Khaburah, Al • Oman 18 G5
Khadra • Algeria 11 L8
Khairpur • Pakistan 28 A3
Khajuraho **Heritage C** • India 63 [121]
Khajuraho • India 105 C7
Khakassia • Russian Fed. 26 O7
Khalesavey • Russian Fed. 26 M5
Khalij Sirt • Libya 21 C1
Khaluf • Oman 18 G5
Khambhat, Gulf of • India 28 B4
Khami Ruins Nat. Mon. **Heritage C** • Zimbabwe 63 [101]
Khami Ruins Nat. Mon. • Zimbabwe 102 J3
Khamir • Yemen 18 D6
Khamis, Ash Shallal al • Sudan 21 F4
Khamra • Russian Fed. 27 H4
Khan al Ahmar • Jordan 98 A6
Khandwa • India 28 C4
Khanka, Ozero • Russian Fed. 27 L8
Khanpur • Pakistan 28 B3
Khanty-Mansiysk • Russian Fed. 26 K5
Khao Chamao • Thailand 109 H4
Khao Kheaw • Thailand 109 H2
Khao Kheaw Zoo • Thailand 109 H4
Khao Laem • Thailand 109 H2
Khao Mokochu • Thailand 31 B3
Khao Saming • Thailand 31 C4
Khao Yai • Thailand 109 H2
Kharabali • Russian Fed. 17 H5
Kharagpur • India 28 E4
Kharevaddo Beach • Goa, India 105 B1
Khârga, El • Egypt 101 F3
Kharkov • Ukraine 17 F4
Kharmanli • Bulgaria 14 M8
Kharovsk • Russian Fed. 17 F3
Khartoum • Sudan 21 F4
Khasan • Russian Fed. 30 F3
Khash • Afghanistan 18 H3
Khaskovo • Bulgaria 97 D3
Khatangha • Russian Fed. 26 R3
Khatt Atoui • Mauritania 20 B4
Khemis Miliana • Algeria 11 N8
Khemisset • Morocco 20 D2
Khenchela • Algeria 20 G1
Khenifra • Morocco 101 D1
Kherson • Ukraine 17 E5
Kheta • Russian Fed. 27 E2
Kheta [Riv] • Russian Fed. 26 R3
Khilok • Russian Fed. 27 H6
Khilok [Riv] • Russian Fed. 27 H6
Khimki • Russian Fed. 97 E4
Khionótripa • Greece 15 F2
Khiva • Uzbekistan 18 H1
Khizi Pogost **Heritage C** • Russian Fed. 63 [77]
Khizi Pogost • Russian Fed. 96 A2
Khmel'nitskiy • Ukraine 17 D5
Kho Khot Kra • Myanmar 31 B4
Khodzheyli • Uzbekistan 18 G1
Khok Pip • Thailand 109 H2
Kholm • Afghanistan 28 A1
Kholm • Russian Fed. 97 E3
Kholmsk • Russian Fed. 27 N7
Khon Kaen • Thailand 31 C3
Khonuu • Russian Fed. 27 N3
Khoper • Russian Fed. 17 G4
Khor • Russian Fed. 27 M7
Khorasan • Iran 18 G3
Khorat • Thailand 109 F2
Khorog • Tajikistan 18 J2
Khorramabad • Iran 18 E3
Khorranshahr • Iran 18 E3
Khotan • China 98 B2
Khouribga • Morocco 101 D1
Khram, Ko • Thailand 109 H4
Khrysokhou Bay • Cyprus 93 J1
Khufayfiyah, Al • Saudi Arabia 18 D5
Khulna • Bangladesh 28 E4
Khun Yuam • Thailand 109 G1
Khuriya Muriya, Jaza'ir • Oman 18 G6
Khurtum, Al • Sudan 21 F4
Khurtum Bahri, Al • Sudan 21 F4
Khwae Noi • Thailand 109 H1
Khyber Pass • Pakistan 28 B2
Kiamba • Philippines 31 G5
Kiang West Nat. Park **Park** • Gambia 103 [12]
Kiangarow, Mt • QL, Australia 34 J5
Kiantajärvi • Finland 16 O4
Kiáton • Greece 15 D6
Kiboko • Kenya 23 F4
Kibombo • Dem. Rep. of Congo 23 D4
Kibondo • Tanzania 102 H1
Kicevo • F.Y.R. of Macedonia 15 B2
Kicking Horse Pass • AL/BC, Canada 122 C4
Kidal • Mali 20 F5
Kidderminster • United Kingdom 74 D1
Kidira • Senegal 22 B2
Kidnappers, Cape • New Zealand 112 K4
Kiedrich • Germany 82 H4
Kiel • Germany 8 F2
Kielce • Poland 13 J7
Kieler Bucht • Germany 8 F2
Kierspe • Germany 81 E4
Kieta • Papua New Guniea 35 (1) F2
Kiev • Ukraine 17 E4
Kiev **Heritage C** • Ukraine 64 [204]
Kiffa • Mauritania 20 C5
Kifisós • Greece 15 D5
Kigoma • Tanzania 102 H1
Kihei • HI, United States 119 L3
Kihnu • Estonia 16 L7
Kii-Suido • Japan 30 H8
Kiikoinen • Finland 95 E1
Kikai • Japan 29 H5
Kikambala • Kenya 101 G5
Kikinda • F.R. of Yugoslavia 14 H4
Kikladés • Greece 15 F6
Kikonai • Japan 30 K4
Kikori • Papua New Guinea 35 (1) C2
Kikori [Riv] • Papua New Guinea 35 (1) C2
Kikwit • Dem. Rep. of Congo 23 B5
Kil-Sanchi • Japan 30 H7
Kilauea Caldera • HI, United States 119 L8
Kilchoan • United Kingdom 78 A2
Kilchu • D.P.R. of Korea 30 E4
Kilcock • Ireland 79 E1
Kilconnell Friary • Ireland 79 F4
Kilcrea Abbey • Ireland 79 F8
Kilcreggan • United Kingdom 78 A3
Kilcullen • Ireland 79 E3
Kildare • Ireland 79 E3
Kildare [Adm] • Ireland 79 E3
Kilfenora • Ireland 79 F4
Kilgore • TX, United States 119 N2
Kilifi • Kenya 101 G5
Kilimanjaro, Mt • Tanzania 102 H2
Kilimanjaro Nat. Park **Heritage N** • Tanzania 61 [92]
Kilimanjaro Nat. Park • Tanzania 102 H2
Kilimanjaro Nat. Park **Park** • Tanzania 103 [90]
Kilindoni • Tanzania 102 H4
Kilíni • Greece 15 D6
Kiliya • Ukraine 14 Q4
Kilkee • Ireland 79 F5
Kilkenny • Ireland 7 E9
Kilkenny [Adm] • Ireland 79 D2
Kilkís • Greece 15 D3
Killala **Beach** • Ireland 68 [63]
Killala • Ireland 79 F2
Killala Bay • Ireland 79 F2
Killaloe • Ireland 79 F6
Killarney • Ireland 79 F7
Killarney, Lake • Bahamas 124 B3
Killarney, Lakes of • Ireland 79 F7
Killarney Nat. Park **Park** • Ireland 72 [40]
Killarney Nat. Park • Ireland 79 F7
Killary Harbour • Ireland 79 F3
Killerton House • United Kingdom 74 F2
Killiecrankie, Pass of • United Kingdom 74 B1
Killiney **Beach** • Ireland 68 [54]
Killiney • Ireland 79 E4
Killington **Ski** • VT, United States 116 [199]
Killington • VT, United States 118 G3
Killorglin • Ireland 79 F7
Killybegs **Beach** • Ireland 68 [65]
Kilmacduagh • Ireland 79 F4
Kilmallock • Ireland 79 F6
Kilmichael Point • Ireland 79 E4
Kilombero • Tanzania 23 F5
Kilosa • Tanzania 102 H4
Kilpisjärvi • Finland 16 K2
Kilronan **Beach** • Ireland 68 [62]
Kilronan • Ireland 79 F3
Kilrush **Beach** • Ireland 68 [61]
Kilrush • Ireland 79 F6
Kilttan I. • India 106 D9
Kilwa • Dem. Rep. of Congo 24 D1
Kilwa Kisiwani **Heritage C** • Tanzania 63 [99]
Kilwa Kisiwani • Tanzania 102 H4
Kilwa Kivinje • Tanzania 102 H4
Kilwa Masoko • Tanzania 102 H4
Kilyos • Turkey 92 D3
Kimbe • Papua New Guinea 35 (1) D2
Kimbe Bay • Papua New Guinea 35 (1) E1
Kimberley • South Africa 24 C5
Kimberley **Ski** • BC, Canada 116 [9]
Kimberley Plateau • WA, Australia 34 E3
Kimch'aek • D.P.R. of Korea 30 E4
Kimch'on • Rep. of Korea 30 D6
Kími • Greece 92 D4
Kimito • Finland 95 E3
Kimito [I.] • Finland 16 L6
Kímolos • Greece 92 D7
Kimry • Russian Fed. 97 E4
Kinabalu, Gunung • Malaysia 32 F1
Kinabatangan • Malaysia 32 F1
Kínaros • Greece 92 D8
Kinbasket Lake • BC, Canada 122 C4
Kincardine • OT, Canada 39 O8
Kincardine • United Kingdom 74 B4
Kincardineshire • United Kingdom 75 A2
Kind • Sweden 95 F7
Kinda • Sweden 95 F4
Kinder • LA, United States 118 K3
Kinder Scout • United Kingdom 5 B1
Kinderdijk • Netherlands 80 C3
Kinderdijk-Elshout **Heritage C** • Netherlands 64 [28]
Kindersley • SA, Canada 38 J6
Kindia • Guinea 22 B2
Kindu • Dem. Rep. of Congo 23 D4
Kineshma • Russian Fed. 17 G3
King Country, The • New Zealand 112 K1
King George, Fort • Trinidad & Tobago 125 K2
King George I. • Antarctica 59 A10
King I. • TS, Australia 34 H7
King Jr., Martin Luther, Nat. Historic Site **Park** • GA, United States 121 [211]
King Leopold • WA, Australia 34 E3
King Ridge **Ski** • NH, United States 116 [207]
King Sound • WA, Australia 34 D3
King William I. • NU, Canada 38 L3
King William's Town • South Africa 24 D6
King's Bay Waterfall • Trinidad & Tobago 125 K2
King's Lynn • United Kingdom 7 M9
Kingaroy • QL, Australia 111 F6
Kingisepp • Russian Fed. 16 O7
Kingman • Pacific Ocean 33 K5
Kingman • AZ, United States 118 J1
Kingoonya • SA, Australia 34 G6
Kings Canyon • NT, Australia 112 H3
Kings Canyon Nat. Park • CA, United States 117 F4
Kings Canyon Nat. Park **Park** • CA, United States 120 [53]
Kings Landing • NB, Canada 123 D6
Kings Mtn Nat. Military Park **Park** • SC, United States 121 [242]
Kings, Valley of the • Egypt 101 F4
Kingsbarns **Beach** • United Kingdom 75 [5]
Kingsbridge • United Kingdom 74 F5
Kingscote • SA, Australia 34 G7
Kingsford Smith [Apt] • NS, Australia 111 G2
Kingston • New Zealand 112 L2
Kingston • NY, United States 118 H1
Kingston • OT, Canada 122 B6
Kingston • Jamaica 124 C4
Kingston South East • SA, Australia 34 G7
Kingston upon Hull • United Kingdom 7 L8
Kingston-upon-Thames • United Kingdom 74 E1
Kingstown • St Vincent 37 I5
Kingsville • TX, United States 119 N5
Kingussie • United Kingdom 6 H4
Kinik • Turkey 15 I4
Kinna • Sweden 95 F7
Kinnairds Head • United Kingdom 6 K4
Kinnegad • Ireland 79 E1
Kinnekulle • Sweden 95 F3
Kinoosao • MN, Canada 38 K5
Kinross • United Kingdom 74 B2
Kinross-shire • United Kingdom 74 B2
Kinsale • Ireland 79 F8
Kinsarvik • Norway 94 C4
Kinshasa • Dem. Rep. of Congo 23 B4
Kinston • NC, United States 118 H5
Kintap • Indonesia 32 F3
Kintyre • United Kingdom 6 G6
Kintyre, Mull of • United Kingdom 7 G6
Kinvarra **Beach** • Ireland 68 [62]
Kinvarra • Ireland 79 F4
Kinyeti • Sudan 23 E3
Kinzig • Germany 9 D8
Kióni • Greece 92 C2
Kiparissiakós Kolpos • Greece 15 C6
Kipembawe • Tanzania 102 H3
Kipengere Range • Tanzania 102 H3
Kipili • Tanzania 102 H3
Kipushi • Dem. Rep. of Congo 24 D2
Kirakira • Solomon Is. 35 (1) G3
Kirazli • Turkey 15 H3
Kirbyville • TX, United States 119 N4
Kirchberg in Tirol **Ski** • Austria 70 [156]
Kirchdorf • Austria 89 H3
Kirchhain • Germany 82 G2
Kirchheim bei München • Germany 82 J3
Kirchheim unter Teck • Germany 9 E8
Kirchheim-Bolanden • Germany 82 H4
Kireç • Turkey 15 J4
Kireli • Turkey 93 G2
Kirensk • Russian Fed. 27 G5
Kirghiz Steppe • Kazakhstan 26 I8
Kirgöz Hani • Turkey 93 G1
Kiri • Dem. Rep. of Congo 22 H5
Kiribati • Pacific Ocean 33 J6
Kirikkale • Turkey 15 O4
Kirinyaga • Kenya 23 F3
Kirishi • Russian Fed. 97 E1
Kiritimati • Kiribati 33 L5
Kirkagaç • Turkey 15 I4
Kirkby Lonsdale • United Kingdom 7 J7
Kirkcaldy • United Kingdom 74 B4
Kirkcudbrightshire • United Kingdom 75 A3
Kirkenær • Norway 94 B2
Kirkenes • Norway 16 P2
Kirkintilloch • United Kingdom 74 B3
Kirkjubæjarklaustur • Iceland 16 (1) D3
Kirkkonummi • Finland 95 E4
Kirkland Lake • OT, Canada 39 O7
Kirklareli • Turkey 15 I2
Kirkpatrick, Mt • Antarctica 46 (1) V1
Kirkstone Pass • United Kingdom 74 C2
Kirkuk • Iraq 18 D2
Kirkwall • United Kingdom 6 J3
Kirkwood • South Africa 100 C8
Kirkwood **Ski** • CA, United States 116 [59]
Kirn • Germany 5 K5
Kirov • Russian Fed. 17 E4
Kirovograd • Ukraine 17 E5
Kirovsk • Russian Fed. 17 E1
Kirovskiy • Russian Fed. 27 K6
Kirriemuir • United Kingdom 74 B2
Kirs • Russian Fed. 17 I3
Kiruna • Sweden 16 K3
Kisa • Sweden 95 F4
Kisalföld • Hungary 13 G10
Kisangani • Dem. Rep. of Congo 23 D3
Kishangarh • India 105 C6
Kishiwada • Japan 30 H7
Kisii • Kenya 101 G3
Kisite Nat. Park • Kenya 101 G5
Kiska • AK, United States 36 (1) B2
Kiskörei Víztároló • Hungary 13 J10
Kiskörös • Hungary 13 I11
Kiskunfélegyháza • Hungary 13 I11
Kiskunhalas • Hungary 13 I11
Kiskunmajsa • Hungary 13 I11
Kiskunság Nat. Park **Park** • Hungary 72 [106]
Kislovodsk • Russian Fed. 17 G6
Kismanyo • Somalia 23 G4
Kismayo Nat. Park **Park** • Somalia 103 [68]
Kismayu • Somalia 23 G4
Kiso • Japan 30 I7
Kissámou Kastéli • Crete, Greece 93 E1
Kissámou, Kólpos • Crete, Greece 93 E1
Kissidougou • Guinea 22 B3
Kissimmee • FL, United States 121 C2
Kissing Bridge **Ski** • NY, United States 116 [173]
Kisújszállás • Hungary 13 J10
Kisumu • Kenya 101 G3
Kisvárda • Hungary 13 L9
Kita • Mali 22 C2
Kitakyushu • Japan 30 F8
Kitale • Kenya 101 G1
Kitami • Japan 30 L3
Kitami-Sanchi • Japan 30 L2
Kitay, Ozero • Ukraine 14 Q4
Kitchener-Waterloo • OT, Canada 122 B9
Kitee • Finland 16 P5
Kitessa • Central African Rep. 23 D2
Kitgum • Uganda 23 E3
Kíthira • Greece 92 D10
Kíthira [I.] • Greece 92 D7
Kíthnos • Greece 92 D7
Kithnou, Stenó • Greece 15 F6
Kíti • Cyprus 93 J4
Kíti, Cape • Cyprus 93 J4
Kitimat • BC, Canada 38 F6
Kitimat Ranges • BC, Canada 38 F6
Kitridge Point • Barbados 125 H4
Kitros • Greece 15 D3
Kittilä • Finland 16 M3
Kitui • Kenya 23 F4
Kitunda • Tanzania 102 H3
Kitwe-Nkana • Zambia 24 D2
Kitzbühel **Ski** • Austria 70 [157]
Kitzbühel • Austria 89 H3
Kitzbüheler Alpen • Austria 89 H3
Kitzingen • Germany 9 F7
Kiu Tsui Chau • Hong Kong, China 107 H6
Kiunga • Kenya 23 G4
Kiunga • Papua New Guinea 35 (1) C2
Kiunga Marine Game Reserve • Kenya 101 G4
Kiuruvesi • Finland 16 N5
Kivéri **Beach** • Greece 69 [184]
Kivijärvi • Finland 16 M5
Kivik • Sweden 95 F11
Kivioli • Estonia 16 N7
Kivu • Dem. Rep. of Congo 23 D4
Kivu, Lac • Rwanda/Dem. Rep. of Congo 23 D4
Kiwai • Papua New Guinea 35 (1) C2
Kizel • Russian Fed. 26 I6
Kizikkaya • Turkey 93 G1
Kizil Adalar • Turkey 92 D3
Kizil Dag • Turkey 15 N7
Kizil Irmak • Turkey 18 B1
Kizilcahaman • Turkey 15 N3
Kizilhisar • Turkey 15 K6
Kizilkadag • Turkey 93 G1
Kizimen Sopka, Vulkan • Russian Fed. 27 R5
Kizyl-Arvat • Turkmenistan 18 G2
Kjellerup • Denmark 95 F9
Kjevik [Apt] • Norway 95 F1
Kladanj • Bosnia-Herz. 14 F5
Kladno • Czech Rep. 96 C2
Kladruby • Czech Rep. 96 C3
Klaeng • Thailand 109 H4
Klagenfurt • Austria 13 D11
Klaiped • Lithuania 13 K2
Klamath • CA/OR, United States 117 F1
Klamath Falls • OR, United States 117 E3
Klamath Mtns • CA, United States 117 F1
Klamono • Indonesia 32 (1) D3
Klarälven • Sweden 16 G6
Klating Beach • Bali, Indonesia 110 C4
Klatovy • Czech Rep. 96 C3
Klausen • Italy 90 B1
Klawer • South Africa 100 C1
Kleinarl **Ski** • Austria 70 [172]
Kleinburg • OT, Canada 122 B9
Kleinmachnow • Germany 81 F3
Kleinwalsertal **Ski** • Austria 70 [128]
Klencí pod Cerchovem • Czech Rep. 96 C3
Klerksdorp • South Africa 24 D5
Kleve • Germany 8 B5
Klibreck, Ben • United Kingdom 6 H3
Klin • Russian Fed. 97 E4
Klincy • Russian Fed. 17 E4
Klingenbuerg • Germany 82 G4
Klingenthal • Germany 13 B7
Klínovec • Czech Rep. 96 C1
Klintehamn • Sweden 16 J8
Klió **Beach** • Greece 69 [199]
Klippan • Sweden 95 F11
Klitmøller • Denmark 95 F5
Klobuck • Poland 13 H7
Klodzko • Poland 13 F7
Klöfta • Norway 94 B2
Klondike • YT, Canada 38 D4
Klondike Gold Rush Nat. Hist. Park **Park** • AK, United States 120 [15]
Klosterneuburg • Austria 13 F9
Klosters **Ski** • Switzerland 70 [112]
Klosters • Switzerland 89 G4
Kloten • Switzerland 9 D9
Kluane Nat. Park **Heritage N** • YT, Canada 60 [1]
Kluczbork • Poland 13 H7
Klungkung • Bali, Indonesia 110 C4
Klyuchevskaya Sopka, Vulkan • Russian Fed. 27 R5
Knäred • Sweden 95 F11
Knarvik • Norway 94 C3
Knebworth House • United Kingdom 74 E1
Knechtsteden • Germany 81 E3
Knife River Indian Villages Nat. Hist. Site **Park** • ND, United States 120 [149]
Knightshayes Court • United Kingdom 74 F2
Knin • Croatia 12 K4
Knislinge • Sweden 95 F11
Knittelfeld • Austria 13 D10
Knivskjellodden • Norway 16 M1
Knivsta • Sweden 95 D2
Knock • Ireland 79 F2
Knock [Apt] • Ireland 79 F2
Knockmealdown Mtns • Ireland 7 E9
Knoebels Grove • PA, United States 118 H1
Knokke-Heist • Belgium 80 B2
Knossós • Crete, Greece 93 E7
Knott's Berry Farm **Park** • CA, United States 120 [G]
Knott's Camp Snoopy **Park** • MN, United States 121 [R]
Knowth • Ireland 79 E2
Knox, Cape • BC, Canada 38 E6
Knoxville • TN, United States 41 J4
Knutby • Sweden 95 D2
Knuthenborg Park • Denmark 95 F14
Knysna • South Africa 100 C7
Knysna Nat. Lake Area • South Africa 100 C7
Ko • Japan 30 J4
Kobayashi • Japan 30 F9
Kobe • Japan 30 H7
København **Beach** • Denmark 68 [40]
København • Denmark 95 F11
Kobern-Gondorf • Germany 82 H1
Kobetdag • Turkmenistan 18 G2
Koblenz • Germany 82 H2
Kobrin • Belarus 13 N5
Kobuk Valley Nat. Park **Park** • AK, United States 120 [4]
Kobyay • Russian Fed. 27 K4
Koca • Balikesir, Turkey 15 I3
Koca • Zonguldak, Turkey 15 N2
Kocabas • Turkey 15 I3
Kocain • Turkey 93 G1
Kocevje • Slovenia 12 I3
Koch I. • NU, Canada 39 P3
Kochechum • Russian Fed. 26 Q4
Kochel • Germany 82 J7
Kochelsee • Germany 82 J7
Kocher • Germany 9 E7
Kochi • Japan 30 G8
Kochisar Ovasi • Turkey 15 O5
Kochubey • Russian Fed. 17 H6
Kodagu • India 106 D6
Kodaikanal • India 106 D10
Kodiak I. • AK, United States 40 (2) F2
Kodikkarai Bird Sanctuary • India 106 D11
Kodok • Sudan 21 F5
Kodungallur • India 106 D10
Kodyma • Ukraine 14 Q1
Kodyma [Riv] • Ukraine 14 Q1
Kodzha Balkan • Bulgaria 14 N7
Koës • Namibia 24 B5
Köflach • Austria 13 E10
Kofu • Japan 30 J7
Kogalniceanu, Mihail [Apt] • Romania 97 D2
Køge • Denmark 95 F14
Køge Bugt • Denmark 95 F15
Kohat • Pakistan 28 B2
Kohima • India 28 F3
Kohtla-Järve • Estonia 16 N7
Kohu Dagi • Turkey 15 K7
Koje • Rep. of Korea 30 E7
Kojo • D.P.R. of Korea 30 D5
Kok • Thailand 109 G2
Kök Shal Tau • Kyrgyzstan 26 M9
Kok-Yangak • Kyrgyzstan 18 J1
Kokand • Uzbekistan 18 J1
Kokas • Indonesia 32 (1) D3
Kokchetav • Kazakhstan 26 K7
Kokemäenjoki • Finland 95 E2
Kokemäki • Finland 95 E1
Kokini Hani • Crete, Greece 93 E3
Kokkina • Cyprus 15 (1) B1
Kokkola • Finland 16 L5
Kokkoni **Beach** • Greece 69 [178]
Koko • Nigeria 22 E2
Koko Head Natural Park • HI, United States 119 L6
Koko Nor • China 29 C3
Kokoda • Papua New Guinea 34 I1
Kokonau • Indonesia 32 (1) E3
Kokorín • Czech Rep. 96 C2
Koksijde-Bad • Belgium 80 B1
Koksoak • QU, Canada 39 R5
Kol'skiy Poluostrov • Russian Fed. 17 F1
Kola • Russian Fed. 16 Q2
Kola Peninsula • Russian Fed. 17 F1
Kolaka • Indonesia 32 (1) B3
Kolar • India 106 D7
Kolar Gold Fields • India 106 D7
Kolari • Finland 16 L3
Kolárovo • Slovak Rep. 13 G10
Kolayat • India 105 C1
Kolbäck • Sweden 95 D1
Kolbermoor • Germany 82 J3
Kolda • Senegal 22 A2
Kolding **Beach** • Denmark 68 [46]
Kolding • Denmark 95 F9
Koléa • Algeria 11 N8
Kolente • Guinea/Sierra Leone 22 B3
Kolguyev, Ostrov • Russian Fed. 17 I1
Kolhapur • India 106 D1
Kolímbia • Rhodes, Greece 93 F2
Kolímbia [Beach] • Rhodes, Greece 93 F2
Kolimvári • Crete, Greece 93 E1
Kolín • Czech Rep. 96 C2
Kollfuschg • Italy 90 B2
Kolmården • Sweden 95 D3
Kolmårdens Djurpark • Sweden 95 D3
Köln **Heritage C** • Germany 64 [38]
Köln • Germany 81 E3
Kolo • Poland 13 H5
Kolobrzeg • Poland 13 E3
Kolokani • Mali 22 C2
Kololo • Ethiopia 21 H6
Kolomna • Russian Fed. 97 E4
Kolomyya • Ukraine 17 C5
Kolonodale • Indonesia 32 (1) B3
Kolpashevo • Russian Fed. 26 N6
Kolpino • Russian Fed. 97 E1
Kölpinsee **Spa** • Germany 83 [284]
Kolsva • Sweden 95 D1
Kolumadulu Atoll • Maldives 106 E3
Kolwezi • Dem. Rep. of Congo 23 D6
Kolyma • Russian Fed. 27 O4
Kolyma Lowlands • Russian Fed. 97 A7
Kolymskaya Nizmennost • Russian Fed. 27 P3
Kolymskoye Nagorye • Russian Fed. 27 Q4
Kom • Bulgaria 14 K6
Kom • Africa 22 G4
Kom Ombo • Egypt 101 F5
Kóma tou Yialoú • Cyprus 93 J2
Komadugu Gana • Nigeria 20 H6
Komandorskiye Ostrova • Russian Fed. 27 S5
Komárno • Slovak Rep. 14 F2
Komárom • Hungary 14 F2
Komi • Russian Fed. 17 J2
Komi virgin forests **Heritage N** • Russian Fed. 61 [64]
Komló • Hungary 13 H11
Kommunizm, Qullai • Tajikistan 18 J2
Komodo • Indonesia 32 (1) A4
Komodo Nat. Park **Heritage N** • Indonesia 61 [126]
Komoé • Burkina Faso/Côte d'Ivoire 22 D3
Komoran • Indonesia 32 (1) E4
Komotiní • Greece 92 D2
Kompong Cham • Cambodia 108 B1
Kompong Chhnang • Cambodia 108 B1
Komsa • Russian Fed. 26 O5
Komsomol'sk-na-Amure • Russian Fed. 27 M6
Komsomolets, Ostrov • Russian Fed. 96 A4
Komsomolskiy • Russian Fed. 27 T3
Kömür Burnu • Turkey 15 H5
Kona • Mali 20 E6
Konakovo • Russian Fed. 97 E4
Konar • Afghanistan 28 B1
Konarak • India 28 E5
Konarak **Heritage C** • India 63 [131]
Kondagaon • India 28 D5
Kondinin • WA, Australia 34 C6
Kondoa • Tanzania 102 H2
Kondopoga • Russian Fed. 17 E2
Koné • New Caledonia 35 (2) B3
Kong Christian IX Land • Greenland 39 W3
Kong Frederik VI Kyst • Greenland 39 W4
Kongolo • Dem. Rep. of Congo 23 D5
Kongsberg • Norway 94 B1
Kongsvinger • Norway 94 B2
Königs Wusterhausen • Germany 81 F4
Königsberg • Russian Fed. 71 A4
Königsbrunn • Germany 82 J2
Königsfeld **Spa** • Germany 83 [198]
Königsleiten **Ski** • Austria 70 [146]
Königssee • Germany 82 J8
Königssee **Spa** • Germany 83 [262]
Königstein • Germany 82 H2
Königstein **Spa** • Germany 83 [143]
Königswinter • Germany 82 H1
Konin • Poland 13 H5
Konispol • Albania 15 B4
Konjic • Bosnia-Herz. 14 E6
Konkan • India 105 A3
Konopiste • Czech Rep. 96 C2
Konosha • Russian Fed. 17 F2
Konskie • Poland 13 J6
Konstanz • Germany 82 G8
Kontagora • Nigeria 22 F2
Kontcha • Cameroon 22 G3
Kontich • Belgium 5 H3
Kontiomäki • Finland 16 O4
Kontókali • Corfu, Greece 92 B1
Kontum Plateau • Vietnam 108 A2
Konya • Turkey 15 N6
Konya Ovasi • Turkey 15 N6
Konyaalti **Beach** • Turkey 69 [226]
Konz • Germany 5 J5
Konz • Germany 82 H3
Koolau Range • HI, United States 119 L5
Koorda • WA, Australia 34 C6
Kootenay • Canada/United States 122 C4
Kootenay Nat. Park • BC, Canada 122 C4
Kopaonik • F.R. of Yugoslavia 14 H6
Kópavogur • Iceland 16 (1) C2
Koper • Slovenia 12 H3

Kopervik • Norway **94** C5
Kopeysk • Russian Fed. **26** J6
Köping • Sweden **95** D1
Kopliku • Albania **15** A1
Koppang • Norway **16** F6
Kopparberg • Sweden **16** H7
Koprivnica • Croatia **12** K2
Köprülü • Turkey **93** G4
Kora Nat. Park • Kenya **101** G4
Korabük • Turkey **15** N2
Korahe • Ethiopia **23** G2
Koraka • Crete, Greece **93** E6
Korat Plateau • Thailand **109** F2
Korba • Tunisia **12** E12
Korba • India **28** D4
Korbach • Germany **9** D5
Korbous • Tunisia **101** E2
Korbroor • Indonesia **32** (1) D4
Korçë • Albania **15** B3
Korcula • Croatia **12** L6
Korcula [I.] • Croatia **12** L6
Korculanski kanal • Croatia **14** D6
Korea, Democratic People's Republic of • Asia **30** D6
Korea, Republic of • Asia **30** D5
Korea Strait • Japan/Rep. of Korea **30** E8
Korea War Veterans Memeorial **Park** • DC, United States **121** [286]
Köreglu Daglari • Turkey **15** M3
Korf • Russian Fed. **46** II3
Korhogo • Côte d'Ivoire **22** C3
Korinós **Beach** • Greece **69** [190]
Korinthiakós Kólpos • Greece **15** D5
Kórinthos • Greece **92** D4
Koriolei • Somalia **23** G3
Koríthi • Greece **92** C3
Koritnik • Albania/F.R. of Yugoslavia **14** H7
Koriyama • Japan **30** K6
Korkuteli • Turkey **93** G1
Korla • China **26** O9
Kormakiti Burun • Cyprus **15** (1) B1
Kormakíti, Cape • Cyprus **93** J1
Körmend • Hungary **13** F10
Kormy, gora • Russian Fed. **26** S5
Kornati • Croatia **14** C6
Kornati Nat. Park **Park** • Croatia **72** [111]
Kornelimünster • Germany **82** G1
Kornsjø • Norway **94** B4
Koro Sea • Fiji **35** (2) D2
Koro Toro • Chad **20** I5
Koroba • Papua New Guinea **35** (1) C2
Köroglu Tepe • Turkey **15** M3
Korogwe • Tanzania **102** H2
Korónia, Límni • Greece **15** E3
Koronída **Beach** • Greece **69** [206]
Koronowo • Poland **13** G4
Koror • Palau **33** E5
Körös • Hungary **13** J11
Korosten • Ukraine **17** D4
Korpilahti • Finland **95** E2
Korpo • Finland **95** E3
Korppoo • Finland **95** E3
Korsakov • Russian Fed. **27** N7
Korschenbroich • Germany **81** E3
Korsnäs • Finland **16** K5
Korsør **Beach** • Denmark **68** [43]
Korsør • Denmark **95** F14
Kortrijk • Belgium **80** A13
Koru Dagi • Turkey **15** H3
Korucu • Turkey **15** I4
Korup, Parc nat. du **Park** • Cameroon **103** [38]
Koryakskiy Nagorye • Russian Fed. **27** T4
Koryapskaya, Vulkan • Russian Fed. **27** Q6
Koryazhma • Russian Fed. **17** H2
Kos **Beach** • Greece **69** [210]
Kos • Greece **92** D8
Kos [I.] • Greece **92** D8
Koscian • Poland **13** F5
Koscierzyna • Poland **13** G3
Kosciusko • MS, United States **118** K2
Kosciusko, Mt • NS, Australia **111** G4
Kosciuszko, Thaddeus, Nat. Mem. **Park** • PA, United States **121** [312]
Koserow **Spa** • Germany **83** [284]
Koshiki-Retto • Japan **30** E9
Kosice • Slovak Rep. **13** K9
Koski • Finland **95** E4
Koskinoú **Beach** • Rhodes, Greece **69** [211]
Koskinoú • Rhodes, Greece **93** F2
Koslan • Russian Fed. **17** H2
Kosong • D.P.R. of Korea **30** E5
Kosovo • F.R. of Yugoslavia **14** I7
Kosovska Mitrovica • F.R. of Yugoslavia **14** H7
Kosrae • Fed. States of Micronesia **33** H5
Kossou, Barrage de • Côte d'Ivoire **22** C3
Kosta • Sweden **95** F8
Koster • Sweden **95** F2
Kostomuksha • Russian Fed. **16** P4
Kostroma • Russian Fed. **97** E2
Kostromskoye Vdkhr. • Russian Fed. **97** E2
Kostrzyn • Gorzowskie, Poland **13** D5
Kostrzyn • Poznanskie, Poland **13** G5
Koszalin • Poland **13** F3
Köszeg • Hungary **13** F10
Kota • India **105** C6
Kota Baharu • Malaysia **32** C1
Kota Kinabalu • Malaysia **32** F1
Kotabaru • Indonesia **32** F3
Kotabumi • Indonesia **32** D3
Kotadabok • Indonesia **32** C3
Kotare Gorge • New Zealand **112** K3
Kotel • Bulgaria **14** N7
Kotelnich • Russian Fed. **17** H3
Kotelnyy, Ostrov • Russian Fed. **27** M1
Köthen • Germany **8** G5
Kotka • Finland **16** N6
Kotlas • Russian Fed. **17** H2
Kotlin, Ostrov • Russian Fed. **97** E1
Kotlina Sandomierska • Poland **13** K7
Kotopasa, Gunung • Indonesia **32** (1) B3
Kotor **Heritage N** • F.R. of Yugoslavia **61** [54]
Kotor **Heritage C** • F.R. of Yugoslavia **64** [159]
Kotovo • Russian Fed. **17** G4
Kotovsk • Ukraine **14** Q2
Kotsifoú, Farági • Crete, Greece **93** E6
Kottayam • India **106** D10
Kotte • Sri Lanka **106** D15
Kotto • Central African Rep. **23** C2
Kotuy • Russian Fed. **26** R3
Kotzebue • AK, United States **46** FF3
Kötzting **Spa** • Germany **83** [232]
Kouba Modounga • Chad **22** H1
Kouchibouguac Nat. Park • NB, Canada **123** D7
Koudougou • Burkina Faso **22** D2
Koufonísi • Aegean Sea, Greece **92** D8
Koufonisi • Mediterranean Sea, Greece **93** E8
Kougaberge • South Africa **100** C7
Koukdjuak, Great Plain of the • NU, Canada **39** Q3
Koulamoutou • Gabon **22** G5
Koulikoro • Mali **20** D6
Koumbi-Saleh • Mauritania **20** D5
Koumpentoum • Senegal **20** C6
Koupéla • Burkina Faso **22** D2
Kourim • Czech Rep. **96** C2
Kourou • French Guiana **43** G2
Kouroussa • Guinea **20** D6
Kourtaliótiko Farági • Crete, Greece **93** E6
Koutiala • Mali **22** C2
Koutsounari • Crete, Greece **93** E8
Kouvola • Finland **16** N6
Kovalam • India **106** D14
Kovdor • Russian Fed. **16** P3
Kovdozero • Russian Fed. **16** P3
Kovel • Ukraine **17** C4
Kovriga, gora • Russian Fed. **26** P5
Kovrov • Russian Fed. **17** G3
Kowloon • Hong Kong, China **107** H6
Kowloon City • Hong Kong, China **107** H6
Kowon • D.P.R. of Korea **30** D5
Köycegiz • Turkey **15** J7
Koytezek • Tajikistan **26** L10
Kozagaci • Turkey **93** G3
Kozáni • Greece **15** C3
Kozara • Bosnia-Herz. **14** D4
Kozhim • Russian Fed. **17** J1
Kozienice • Poland **13** K6
Kozlu • Turkey **15** M2
Kozu • Japan **30** J7
Kozuf • F.Y.R. of Macedonia **14** J8
Kpalimé • Togo **22** E3
Kra, Isthmus of • Thailand **109** F3
Kraaifontein • South Africa **100** C5
Krabbfjärden • Sweden **95** D4
Krâchéh • Cambodia **31** D4
Kragerø • Norway **94** B3
Kragujevac • F.R. of Yugoslavia **14** H5
Krajiste • Bulgaria/F.R. of Yugoslavia **14** J7
Krakatau • Java, Indonesia **110** D1
Krakatau Nature Reserve **Heritage N** • Indonesia **61** [125]
Kraków • Poland **13** I8
Kraków **Heritage C** • Poland **64** [141]
Kraljevo • F.R. of Yugoslavia **14** H6
Kralupy nad Vltavou • Czech Rep. **13** D7
Kramsach • Austria **89** H3
Kramsfors • Sweden **16** I5
Kranebitten [Apt] • Austria **89** H2
Kranídi • Greece **15** E6
Kranj • Slovenia **13** D11
Krapina • Croatia **12** J2
Krapkowice • Poland **13** G7
Krasavino • Russian Fed. **17** H2
Kraskino • Russian Fed. **30** F3
Krasnik • Poland **13** L7
Krasnodar • Russian Fed. **17** F5
Krasnogorsk • Russian Fed. **27** N7
Krasnokamensk • Russian Fed. **27** I7
Krasnokamsk • Russian Fed. **17** J3
Krasnoselkup • Russian Fed. **26** N4
Krasnoufimsk • Russian Fed. **26** I6
Krasnoural'sk • Russian Fed. **26** J6
Krasnovishersk • Russian Fed. **26** I5
Krasnoyarsk • Russian Fed. **26** P6
Krasnozatonskiy • Russian Fed. **17** I2
Krasnystaw • Poland **13** M7
Krasnyy Chikoy • Russian Fed. **27** G6
Kratochvíle • Czech Rep. **96** C4
Kratovo • F.Y.R. of Macedonia **14** J7
Krazh Khara-Tas • Russian Fed. **26** S3
Krefeld • Germany **81** E1
Kremastí • Rhodes, Greece **93** F2
Kremastón, Tehnití Límni • Greece **15** C5
Kremenchug • Ukraine **17** E5
Kremenchugskoye Vdkhr. • Ukraine **17** E5
Kremna • Turkey **93** G1
Krems • Austria **14** C1
Kresta, Zaliv • Russian Fed. **27** V3
Kretinga • Lithuania **13** K2
Kreuzlingen • Switzerland **9** E9
Kreuztal • Germany **9** D6
Kribi • Cameroon **22** F4
Krichev • Belarus **17** E4
Krichim • Bulgaria **15** F1
Krim • Ukraine **17** E5
Krimpenerwaard • Netherlands **80** C4
Krimskiye Gory • Ukraine **17** E6
Kriopigí **Beach** • Greece **69** [192]
Kriopigí • Greece **92** D1
Krios, Akra • Crete, Greece **93** E5
Krishna • India **106** D3
Krishna, Mouths of the • India **106** D3
Krishnagiri • India **106** D7
Kristdala • Sweden **95** F8
Kristianopel • Sweden **95** F12
Kristiansand • Norway **95** F1
Kristiansand Dyrepark **Park** • Norway **73** [1]
Kristiansand Dyrepark • Norway **95** F1
Kristianstad **Beach** • Sweden **69** [14]
Kristianstad • Sweden **95** F11
Kristiansund • Norway **16** D5
Kristiinankaupunki • Finland **95** E1
Kristinestad • Finland **95** E1
Kritinía • Rhodes, Greece **93** F1
Kritsá • Crete, Greece **93** E7
Krivoklát • Czech Rep. **96** C1
Krivolátska Vrchovina • Czech Rep. **96** C1
Krivoy Rog • Ukraine **17** E5
Krk • Croatia **14** B4
Krk [I.] • Croatia **14** B4
Krka Nat. Park **Park** • Croatia **72** [112]
Krkonose Nat. Park **Park** • Czech Rep. **72** [99]
Krkonose Nat. Park • Czech Rep. **96** C2
Krnov • Czech Rep. **13** G7
Krøderen • Norway **94** B1
Krøderen [Lake] • Norway **94** B1
Krokek • Sweden **95** D3
Krokom • Sweden **16** H5
Kromeriz • Czech Rep. **13** G8
Kronach • Germany **9** G6
Kronberg • Germany **82** H2
Kronoberg • Sweden **95** F7
Kronoki • Russian Fed. **27** R6
Kronotskaya Sopka, Vulkan • Russian Fed. **27** R5
Kronotskiy Zaliv • Russian Fed. **27** R6
Kronshagen • Germany **8** F2
Kronstadt • Russian Fed. **97** E1
Kroonstad • South Africa **24** D5
Kropotkin • Russian Fed. **17** G5
Kropotkin • Russian Fed. **27** I5
Kroppefjäll • Sweden **95** F2
Krosno • Poland **13** K8
Krotoszyn • Poland **13** G6
Kroussónas • Crete, Greece **93** E7
Kröv • Germany **82** H3
Kroya • Java, Indonesia **110** D6
Krsko • Slovenia **14** C4
Kruger Nat. Park • South Africa **24** E4
Kruger Nat. Park **Park** • South Africa **103** [124]
Krugersdorp • South Africa **24** D5
Krujë • Albania **14** G8
Krumbach • Germany **82** J2
Krumbad • Germany **82** J2
Krumbad **Spa** • Germany **83** [234]
Krumovgrad • Bulgaria **14** M8
Krung Thep • Thailand **109** H1
Krüpelsee • Germany **81** F4
Krusevac • F.R. of Yugoslavia **14** I6
Krusne Hory • Czech Rep. **96** C1
Krykslätt • Finland **95** E4
Krynica • Poland **13** J8
Krzyz • Poland **13** F5
Ksar el Boukhari • Algeria **11** N9
Ksar el Kebir • Morocco **101** D1
Ksar es Srhir • Morocco **11** F9
Ksar Hadada • Tunisia **101** E6
Ksar Hellal • Tunisia **101** E4
Ksar Ouled Soltane • Tunisia **101** E6
Ksour, Mts des • Algeria **20** E2
Ktikados **Beach** • Greece **69** [202]
Ku-Ring-Gai Chase Nat. Park • NS, Australia **111** G2
Kuala Belait • Brunei **32** E2
Kuala Dungun • Malaysia **32** C2
Kuala Kelawang • Malaysia **108** D4
Kuala Kerai • Malaysia **32** C1
Kuala Kubu Baharu • Malaysia **108** D2
Kuala Lipis • Malaysia **108** D2
Kuala Lumpur • Malaysia **108** D4
Kuala Selangor • Malaysia **108** D3
Kuala Terengganu • Malaysia **32** C1
Kuandang • Indonesia **32** (1) B2
Kuandian • China **30** C4
Kuantan • Malaysia **32** C2
Kuba • Azerbaijan **17** H6
Kuban • Russian Fed. **17** G5
Kubenskoye, Ozero • Russian Fed. **97** E2
Kubokawa • Japan **30** G8
Kubutambahan • Bali, Indonesia **110** C2
Kuching • Malaysia **32** E2
Kucova • Albania **15** A3
Küçük Menderes • Turkey **15** I5
Kucurgan • Ukraine **14** Q2
Kudahithi • Maldives **106** E2
Kudat • Malaysia **32** F1
Kudus • Java, Indonesia **110** D3
Kudymkar • Russian Fed. **17** I3
Kuenga • Russian Fed. **97** A5
Kufrah Oasis • Libya **21** D3
Kufstein • Austria **89** H3
Kugluktuk • NU, Canada **38** H3
Kühlungsborn • Germany **8** G2
Kühlungsborn **Beach** • Germany **68** [34]
Kühlungsborn **Spa** • Germany **83** [268]
Kuhmo • Finland **16** O4
Kuito • Angola **23** B6
Kujani Game Reserve **Park** • Ghana **103** [24]
Kujawy • Poland **13** H5
Kuji • Japan **30** K4
Kuju • Japan **30** F8
Kul • Iran **18** F4
Kula • F.R. of Yugoslavia **14** G4
Kula • Bulgaria **14** J6
Kula • Turkey **15** J5
Kular • Russian Fed. **27** M2
Kulata • Bulgaria **14** K8
Kuldiga • Latvia **16** K8
Kulgera • NT, Australia **112** H4
Kulmbach • Germany **9** G6
Kulob • Tajikistan **18** I2
Kulsary • Kazakhstan **26** H8
Kulu • Turkey **15** O4
Kulu • Russian Fed. **27** O4
Kulunda • Russian Fed. **26** M7
Kum-Dag • Turkmenistan **18** F2
Kuma • Russian Fed. **4** T7
Kumagaya • Japan **30** J6
Kumai • Indonesia • **32** E3
Kumamoto • Japan **30** F8
Kumano • Japan **30** H8
Kumanovo • F.Y.R. of Macedonia **14** I7
Kumasi • Ghana **22** D3
Kumaun • India **105** C3
Kumba • Cameroon **22** F4
Kumbakonam • India **106** D11
Kumbe • Indonesia **32** (1) F4
Kumbhalgarh • India **105** C5
Kumdah • Saudi Arabia **21** I3
Kume • Japan **29** H5
Kumhwa • Rep. of Korea **30** D5
Kumköy • Turkey **15** K2
Kumkuduk • China **26** P9
Kumla • Orebro, Sweden **16** H7
Kumla • Västmanland, Sweden **95** D1
Kumluca • Turkey **93** G3
Kumo älv • Finland **95** E2
Kumul • China **29** A2
Kunashir, Ostrov • Russian Fed. **27** O8
Kunashiri-To • Russian Fed. **27** O8
Kunashirskiy Proliv • Russian Fed. **27** O8
Kundapura • India **106** D6
Kundelungu, Mtns • Dem. Rep. of Congo **23** D6
Kundelungu, Parc nat. de **Park** • Dem. Rep. of Congo **103** [60]
Kundiawa • Papua New Guinea **35** (1) C2
Kunduchi • Tanzania **102** H4
Künes He • China **26** N9
Kung Bay • Phuket, Thailand **109** K1
Kungagraven • Sweden **95** F11
Kungälv • Sweden **95** F6
Kungey-Alatau • Kazakhstan **26** M9
Kungsbacka • Sweden **95** F6
Kungshamn • Sweden **95** F2
Kungsör • Sweden **95** D3
Kungu • Dem. Rep. of Congo **23** B3
Kungur • Russian Fed. **17** J3
Kunhing • Myanmar **31** B2
Kunlun Shan • China **28** E1
Kunlun Shankou • China **28** F1
Kunming • China **29** C5
Kunsan • Rep. of Korea **30** D7
Kunshan • China **107** J2
Kununurra • WA, Australia **34** E3
Künzelsau • Germany **9** E7
Kuopio • Finland **16** N5
Kuopio **Beach** • Finland **69** [29]
Kuopio [Adm] • Finland **16** N5
Kuopio [Adm] • Finland **94** A6
Kupa • Croatia **12** J3
Kupang • Indonesia **32** (1) B5
Kupiano • Papua New Guinea **35** (1) D3
Kupino • Russian Fed. **26** M7
Kupiskis • Lithuania **13** O2
Kupreanof Is. • AK, United States **38** E5
Kuqa • China **26** N9
Kura • Azerbaijan **18** E1
Kuramathi • Maldives **106** E1
Kuranda • QL, Australia **111** F1
Kurashiki • Japan **30** G7
Kuraymah • Sudan **21** F4
Kurdistan • Asia **18** D2
Kurdufan al Janubiyah • Sudan **23** D1
Kurdzhali • Bulgaria **14** M8
Küre • Turkey **15** O2
Kure • Japan **30** G7
Kuressaare • Estonia **16** L7
Kurgan • Russian Fed. **26** K6
Kuri Bay • WA, Australia **34** D3
Kurikka • Finland **16** L5
Kuril Is. • Russian Fed. **27** P7
Kuril'sk • Russian Fed. **27** O7
Kurilskiye Ostrova • Russian Fed. **25** P5
Kurland • Latvia **16** K8
Kurmuk • Sudan **23** E1
Kurnool • India **106** D3
Kurobe • Japan **30** I6
Kuroishi • Japan **30** K4
Kurort Krakow am See **Spa** • Germany **83** [286]
Kurort Oberwiesenthal **Spa** • Germany **83** [317]
Kurort Schmalkalden • Germany **9** F6
Kurpfalzpark • Germany **82** G4
Kursenai • Lithuania **13** L1
Kursk • Russian Fed. **17** F4
Kurski Zaliv • Lithuania/Russian Fed. **13** J2
Kürten • Germany **81** E4
Kuru • Finland **95** E2
Kurucasile • Turkey **15** N2
Kurukshetra • India **105** C2
Kuruman • South Africa **24** C5
Kurumbu • Maldives **106** E4
Kurume • Japan **30** F8
Kurunegala • Sri Lanka **106** D15
Kurutag • China **26** O9
Kus Gölü • Turkey **92** D3
Kusadasi • Turkey **92** D8
Kusadasi Körfezi • Turkey **15** H6
Kusamba • Bali, Indonesia **110** C4
Kushikino • Japan **30** F9
Kushimoto • Japan **30** H8
Kushinagar • India **105** C4
Kushiro • Japan **30** M3
Kushka • Turkmenistan **18** H2
Kushmurun • Kazakhstan **26** J7
Kusong • D.P.R. of Korea **30** C5
Kussharo-Ko • Japan **30** M3
Küssnacht • Switzerland **89** G3
Kustanay • Russian Fed. **26** J7
Kusti • Sudan **21** F5
Kusva • Russian Fed. **26** I6
Kut, Al • Iraq **18** E3
Kut, Ko • Thailand **31** C4
Kuta • Bali, Indonesia **110** C4
Kuta Beach • Bali, Indonesia **110** C4
Kútaha • Turkey **15** K4
Kutaisi • Georgia **17** G6
Kutaisi **Heritage C** • Georgia **64** [212]
Kutch, Gulf of • India **28** A4
Kutch, Rann of • India **28** A4
Kutina • Croatia **14** D4
Kutná Hora **Heritage C** • Czech Rep. **64** [144]
Kutná Hora • Czech Rep. **96** C2
Kutno • Poland **13** I5
Kuttanad • India **106** D10
Kutu • Dem. Rep. of Congo **23** B4
Kuty • Ukraine **14** M1
Kuujjuaq • QU, Canada **39** R5
Kuujjuarapik • QU, Canada **39** P5
Kuusamo • Finland **16** O3
Kuwait • Asia **18** E4
Kuwait City • Kuwait **18** E4
Kuygan • Kazakhstan **26** L8
Kuytun • China **26** O9
Kuznetsk • Russian Fed. **17** H4
Kuznetskiy Alatau • Russian Fed. **26** O7
Kuzomen • Russian Fed. **17** F1
Kvænangen • Norway **16** K1
Kvaløy • Norway **16** J2
Kvaløya • Norway **16** L1
Kvarner • Croatia **14** B5
Kvarneric • Croatia **14** B5
Kvicksund • Sweden **95** D3
Kvikkjokk • Sweden **16** I3
Kviteseid • Norway **94** C6
Kwa • Dem. Rep. of Congo **23** B4
Kwahu Plateau • Ghana **22** D3
Kwai Chung Port • Hong Kong, China **107** H5
Kwajalein • Marshall Is. **33** H5
Kwakoegron • Suriname **43** F2
Kwale • Kenya **101** G5
Kwando • Africa **24** C3
Kwangju • Rep. of Korea **30** D7
Kwango • Dem. Rep. of Congo **23** B4
Kwanmo • D.P.R. of Korea **30** E4
Kwara • Nigeria **22** F3
Kwazulu Natal • South Africa **24** E4
Kwekwe • Zimbabwe **102** J2
Kwidzyn • Poland **13** H4
Kwikila • Papua New Guinea **34** I1
Kwilu • Dem. Rep. of Congo **23** B4
Kwoka, Gunung • Indonesia **32** (1) D3
Kyabé • Chad **21** C6
Kyaikkami • Myanmar **31** B3
Kyakhta • Russian Fed. **27** G6
Kyancutta • SA, Australia **34** G6
Kyaukpyu • Myanmar **28** F5
Kyelang • India **28** C2
Kyjov • Czech Rep. **13** G9
Kykko Monastery • Cyprus **93** J3
Kyle, Lake • Zimbabwe **102** J4
Kyle of Lochalsh • United Kingdom **6** G4
Kyleakin • United Kingdom **78** A1
Kyles Scalpay • United Kingdom **78** A1
Kyll • Germany **82** H3
Kyllburg **Spa** • Germany **83** [159]
Kymi • Finland **16** N6
Kymi • Finland **94** A9
Kymijoki • Finland **16** N6
Kymmene älv • Finland **16** N6
Kynnefjäll • Sweden **95** F2
Kyoga, Lake • Uganda **23** E3
Kyoga-Misaki • Japan **30** H7
Kyonggi-man • Rep. of Korea **30** C6
Kyongju • Rep. of Korea **30** E7
Kyongju **Heritage C** • Rep. of Korea **63** [161]
Kyongsong • D.P.R. of Korea **30** E4
Kyoto • Japan **30** H7
Kyoto **Heritage C** • Japan **63** [167]
Kyperoúda • Cyprus **93** J3
Kyren • Russian Fed. **27** F6
Kyrenia • Cyprus **93** J1
Kyrenia Mtns • Cyprus **93** J2
Kyrgyzstan • Asia **26** L9
Kyrkhult • Sweden **95** F11
Kythréa • Cyprus **93** J2
Kyushu • Japan **30** F8
Kyushu-Sanchi • Japan **30** F8
Kyustendil • Bulgaria **14** J7
Kyusyur • Russian Fed. **27** K2
Kyyiv • Ukraine **17** E4
Kyyiv **Heritage C** • Ukraine **64** [204]
Kyzyl • Russian Fed. **26** P7
Kyzyl-Kum • Kazakhstan/Uzbekistan **26** J9
Kyzylart • China **26** M10
Kyzylkum • Uzbekistan **18** H1
Kzilca Dagi • Turkey **15** K7
Kzyl-Orda • Kazakhstan **26** K9
Kzyltu • Kazakhstan **26** L7

L'Abbaye • St Lucia **125** J1
L'Ancresse Bay **Beach** • Channel Is. **75** [246]
L'Anse au Loup • NF, Canada **123** D5
L'Anse aux Meadows • NF, Canada **123** D5
L'Anse aux Meadows Hist. Park **Heritage C** • NF, Canada **62** [5]
L'Aquila • Italy **91** F2
L'Erée Bay **Beach** • Channel Is. **75** [243]
L'Europa • Reunion **24** G4
L'gov • Russian Fed. **17** F4
L'île Rousse • Corsica, France **85** L1
La Almunia de Doña Godina • Spain **11** J3
La Ametlla de Mar • Spain **11** L4
La Amistad, Parque Int. **Heritage N** • Costa Rica/Panama **60** [24]
La Antilla • Spain **86** B1
La Banda • Argentina **44** D4
La Bañeza • Spain **11** F2
La Borne • St Lucia **125** J2
La Brea • Trinidad & Tobago **125** K3
La Cadena • Puerto Rico **125** E1
La Canal • Ibiza, Spain **87** G3
La Ceiba • Honduras **37** D4
La Chaux-de-Fonds • Switzerland **89** G1
La Chorrera • Panama **43** B2
La Chorrera • Colombia **43** C4
La Croix Maingot • St Lucia **125** J1
La Crosse • WI, United States **41** H3
La Dorada • Colombia **43** C2
La Esmeralda • Venezuela **43** D3
La Española • West Indies **37** G3
La Esperanza • Cuba **124** D1
La Estrada • Spain **11** C2
La Fé • Cuba **124** D1
La Fortaleza **Heritage C** • Puerto Rico **62** [39]
La Fortaleza • Puerto Rico **125** E2
La Goulette • Tunisia **101** E2
La Gran Sabana • Venezuela **43** E2
La Grande • OR, United States **117** E4
La Grande Rivière • QU, Canada **39** P6
La Grita • Venezuela **43** C2
La Guaira • Venezuela **37** H5
La Guardia • Portugal **11** C3
La Habana **Heritage C** • Cuba **62** [34]
La Habana • Cuba **124** D1
La Isleta • Lanzarote, Canary Is. **87** E3
La Laguna • Tenerife, Canary Is. **86** E1
La Línea • Spain **86** B6
La Línea de la Concepción **Beach** • Spain **68** [113]
La Maddalena **Beach** • Sardinia, Italy **68** [137]
La Mancha • Spain **11** H5
La Manche • France/UK **10** D3
La Manga del Mar Menor • Spain **87** C3
La Mármora, Punta • Sardinia, Italy **90** C4
La Marsa • Tunisia **101** E2
La Montaña • Peru **43** C5
La Neuveville • Switzerland **89** G2
La Oliva • Fuerteventura, Canary Is. **87** E2
La Orotava • Tenerife, Canary Is. **86** E1
La Oroya • Peru **127** B1
La Palma • Panama **37** F6
La Palma • Canary Is. **87** E5
La Panchita • Cuba **124** D2
La Paragua • Venezuela **43** E2
La Pared, Istmo de • Fuerteventura, Canary Is. **87** E2
La Paz • Mexico **40** D7
La Paz • Bolivia **44** C2
La Paz • Mendoza, Argentina **44** C5
La Paz • Entre Ríos, Argentina **44** E5
La Pedrera • Colombia **43** D4
La Peraleja • Spain **11** I4
La Pérouse Strait • Russian Fed. **27** N7
La Plata • Argentina **127** D2
La Plata, Río de • Argentina/Uruguay **127** D2
La Playa de Mogán • Gran Canaria, Canary Is. **86** E4
La Point Beach • St Lucia **125** J3
La Puntilla • Ecuador **43** A4
La Purisma Mission State Hist. Park • CA, United States **117** F5
La Quiaca • Argentina **44** C3
La Rapita • Majorca, Spain **87** H4
La Ressource • St Lucia **125** J2
La Rioja • Spain **11** I2
La Rioja • Argentina **44** C4
La Robla • Spain **11** F2
La Roche-en-Ardenne • Belgium **80** A19
La Rochelle **Beach** • France **68** [84]
La Rochelle • France **84** D3
La Roda • Spain **11** I5
La Romana • Dominican Rep. **37** H4
La Ronge • SA, Canada **38** J5
La Sabana • Colombia **43** D3
La Serena • Spain **11** F6
La Serena • Chile **44** B4
La Solana • Spain **11** H6
La Spézia • Italy **91** E10
La Tagua • Colombia **43** C4
La Tzoumas **Ski** • Switzerland **70** [79]
La Unión • Chile **45** B4
La Unión • Spain **87** C3
La Vache Bay • Trinidad & Tobago **125** K1
La Veguita • Lanzarote, Canary Is. **87** E3
La Vela • Venezuela **43** D1
La Verna, Abbazia • Italy **91** E11
La Victoria • Venezuela **43** D2
La Vila Joiosa **Beach** • Spain **68** [118]
La Viña • Peru **43** B5
La'nga Co • China **28** D2
La-Punt-Chaumes-ch. **Ski** • Switzerland **70** [115]
Laarne • Belgium **80** A14
Laax **Ski** • Switzerland **70** [107]
Laax • Switzerland **89** G3
Labe • Guinea **22** B2
Labe • Czech Rep. **96** C2
Labezanga • Niger **20** F6
Laboe **Spa** • Germany **83** [17]
Laborie • St Lucia **125** J3
Laborie Bay • St Lucia **125** J3
Labota • Indonesia **32** (1) B3
Labouheyre • France **85** G3
Laboulaye • Argentina **44** D5
Labrador • NF/QU, Canada **39** R6
Labrador City • NF, Canada **39** R6
Labrador, Coast of • NF, Canada **39** S5
Labrador Mtn **Ski** • NY, United States **116** [177]
Labrador Sea • Atlantic Ocean **36** M4
Lábrea • Brazil **43** E5
Labuha • Indonesia **32** (1) C3
Labuhan • Java, Indonesia **110** D1
Labuhanbajo • Indonesia **32** (1) A4
Labuhanbalai • Indonesia **110** B2
Labuk, Teluk • Malaysia **31** F5
Labutta • Myanmar **31** A3
Labytnangi • Russian Fed. **26** K4
Lac • Albania **15** A2
Lac la Biche • AL, Canada **38** I6
Lac la Martre • NT, Canada **38** H4
Lac Mégantic • QU, Canada **122** B4
Lacanau • France **85** G1
Laccadive Is. • India **25** H8
Lacepede Bay • SA, Australia **34** G7
Lachay, Punta • Peru **43** B6
Lachi • Cyprus **93** J3
Lachlan • NS, Australia **111** G1
Lachute • QU, Canada **122** B3
Lacken Reservoir • Ireland **79** E4
Läckö • Sweden **95** F3
Ladakh • Jammu & Kashmir **28** C2
Ladhiqiyah, Al • Syria **18** C2
Ladiko • Rhodes, Greece **93** F2
Ladispoli • Italy **91** F1
Ladoga, Lake • Russian Fed. **17** E2
Ladozhskoye, Ozero • Russian Fed. **17** E2
Lady Ann Strait • NU, Canada **39** P1
Lady Elliot I. • QL, Australia **111** F4
Ladysmith • South Africa **24** E5
Lae • Papua New Guinea **35** (1) D2
Laem Chabang • Thailand **109** H4
Laem So Pagoda • Ko Samui, Thailand **109** J2
Lærdalsøyri • Norway **94** C4
Læsø **Beach** • Denmark **68** [48]
Læsø • Denmark **95** F6
Læsø Rende • Denmark **95** F6
Lafayette • LA, United States **118** K3
Lafia • Nigeria **22** F3
Lafiagi • Nigeria **22** F3
Lafite, Château • France **85** G1
Lafitte, Jean, Nat. Hist. Park • LA, United States **118** K4
Lafitte, Jean, Nat. Hist. Park **Park** • LA, United States **121** [198]
Lågan • Sweden **95** F7
Laganás • Greece **92** C3
Lågen • Norway **16** F6
Laghouat • Algeria **20** F2
Laghy **Beach** • Ireland **68** [65]
Lago de Moreno • Mexico **123** E1
Lagoa **Beach** • Portugal **68** [100]
Lagoa **Beach** • São Miguel, Azores **68** [105]
Lagoa • Azores **88** B1
Lagoa • Portugal **88** E6
Lagoa Vermelha • Brazil **44** F4
Lagonissi • Greece **92** D7
Lagos • Nigeria **22** E3
Lagos **Beach** • Portugal **68** [100]
Lagos • Portugal **88** E6
Lágos • Greece **92** D2
Lagos [Adm] • Nigeria **22** E3
Lagos, Baía de • Portugal **88** E6
Lagosa • Tanzania **102** H1
Laguardia • Spain **11** I2
LaGuardia [Apt] • NY, United States **118** H2
Laguna • Brazil **44** G4
Laguna • NM, United States **118** J2
Lagunillas • Bolivia **44** D2
Lahad Datu • Malaysia **32** F1
Lahaina • HI, United States **119** L3
Lahat • Indonesia **32** C3
Lahemaa Nat. Park **Park** • Estonia **72** [143]
Lahewa • Indonesia **110** B3
Lahn • Germany **82** G2
Lahnstein • Germany **82** H2
Lahnstein **Spa** • Germany **83** [155]
Laholm **Beach** • Sweden **68** [6]
Laholm • Sweden **95** F11
Laholmsbukten • Sweden **95** F11
Lahore • Pakistan **28** B2
Lahore **Heritage C** • Pakistan **63** [115]
Lahr • Germany **82** G6
Lahti • Finland **95** E4
Lai • Chad **23** B2
Lai Chau • Vietnam **31** C2
Lai'an • China **107** J1
Laiagam • Papua New Guinea **35** (1) C2
Laie • HI, United States **119** L1
Laiguéglia **Beach** • Italy **68** [141]
Laiguéglia • Italy **91** E9
Laikipia Game Reserve • Kenya **101** G1
Laingsburg • South Africa **100** C6
Lainio älv • Sweden **16** K2
Laitila • Finland **95** E3
Laiwui • Indonesia **32** (1) C3
Laja • Chile **44** B6
Lajes • Brazil **44** F4
Lajes do Pico • Azores **88** B1
Lajosmizse • Hungary **13** I10
Lake Bogoria Game Reserve • Kenya **101** G1
Lake Buena Vista • FL, United States **121** C2
Lake Charles • LA, United States **118** K3
Lake Chelan Nat. Recreation Area • WA, United States **117** E1
Lake Chelan Nat. Recreation Area **Park** • WA, United States **120** [28]
Lake City • FL, United States **119** M3
Lake Clark Nat. Park & Preserve **Park** • AK, United States **120** [8]
Lake District • United Kingdom **74** C
Lake District Nat. Park **Park** • United Kingdom **72** [43]
Lake District Nat. Park • United Kingdom **74** C
Lake Grace • WA, Australia **34** C6
Lake Havasu City • AZ, United States **118** J1
Lake King • WA, Australia **34** C6

Lake Louise **Ski** • AL, Canada 116 [12]
Lake Louise • AL, Canada 122 C4
Lake Mackay Aboriginal Land • NT, Australia 112 H1
Lake Malawi Nat. Park **Heritage N** • Malawi 61 [94]
Lake Malawi Nat. Park **Park** • Malawi 103 [98]
Lake Mead Nat. Recreation Area **Park** • NV, United States 120 [61]
Lake Meredith Nat. Recreation Area **Park** • TX, United States 120 [133]
Lake Monroe • FL, United States 119 M4
Lake Murray • Papua New Guinea 35 (1) C2
Lake Nakuru Nat. Park • Kenya 101 G3
Lake Nakuru Nat. Park **Park** • Kenya 103 [81]
Lake Placid • NY, United States 41 L3
Lake Placid • NY, United States 116 C
Lake River • OT, Canada 39 O6
Lake Tekapo • New Zealand 35 C7
Lake Wales • FL, United States 119 M5
Lakefield Nat. Park • QL, Australia 34 H3
Lakeland • FL, United States 119 M5
Lakemba • Fiji 35 (2) E2
Lakes Beach • Barbados 125 H1
Lakes Entrance • VI, Australia 111 G3
Lakeview • OR, United States 117 E3
Lákmos • Greece 15 C4
Lakonikós Kólpos • Greece 15 D7
Lakópetra **Beach** • Greece 69 [179]
Laksamana Forest Reserve • Penang, Malaysia 108 C1
Laksefjorden • Norway 16 N1
Lakselv • Norway 16 M1
Lakshadweep • India 106 D9
Lakshadweep Sea • India 106 D10
Lalapasa • Turkey 15 H2
Lalibela • Ethiopia 21 G5
Lalibela **Heritage C** • Ethiopia 63 [86]
Lalitpur • India 105 C7
Lalzit, Gjiri i • Albania 14 G8
Lam Po Reservoir • Thailand 109 F2
Lam Tseun Country Park • Hong Kong, China 107 H3
Lamai Beach • Ko Samui, Thailand 109 J2
Lamar • CO, United States 40 F4
Lambarené • Gabon 22 G5
Lambari • Brazil 127 C3
Lambasa • Fiji 35 (2) D2
Lambay I. • Ireland 79 E2
Lambert's Bay • South Africa 100 C1
Lambton, Cape • NT, Canada 38 G2
Lamego • Portugal 11 D3
Lamèque, I. • NB, Canada 123 D2
Lamesa • TX, United States 40 F5
Lamézia Terme • Italy 12 K10
Lamía • Greece 15 D5
Lamington Nat. Park • QL, Australia 111 F6
Lamma I. • Hong Kong, China 107 H5
Lammermuir Hills • United Kingdom 74 B4
Lammhult • Sweden 95 F7
Lamon Bay • Philippines 31 G4
Lamongan • Java, Indonesia 110 D4
Lampang • Thailand 109 G4
Lampasas • TX, United States 119 N3
Lampedusa • Italy 12 G13
Lampertheim • Germany 9 D7
Lamphun • Thailand 109 G3
Lamu • Kenya 101 G4
Lamu I. • Kenya 101 G4
Lan Hsu • Taiwan 29 G6
Lan, Ko • Thailand 109 H4
Lanai • HI, United States 119 L3
Lanai City • HI, United States 119 L3
Lanao, Lake • Philippines 31 G5
Lanark • United Kingdom 74 B3
Lanarkshire • United Kingdom 75 A3
Lancang Jiang • China 29 B5
Lancashire • United Kingdom 7 J8
Lancaster • United Kingdom 7 J7
Lancaster • PA, United States 118 H1
Lancaster Sound • NU, Canada 39 O2
Lancelin • WA, Australia 34 C6
Lancha He • China 29 F2
Lanciano • Italy 12 I6
Lancut • Poland 13 L7
Land of the Midnight Sun cruise area • Norway 59 A4
Land van Altena • Netherlands 80 C4
Landau an der Isar • Germany 13 B9
Landau in der Pfalz • Germany 82 G6
Landeck • Austria 89 H6
Lander • NT, Australia 34 F4
Landes, les • France 85 G3
Landete • Spain 11 J5
Lands End • United Kingdom 74 F4
Landsberg am Lech • Germany 82 J2
Landshut • Germany 9 H8
Landskrona • Sweden 95 F11
Landsort • Sweden 95 D4
Landvetter [Apt] • Sweden 95 F6
Lanerbach • Austria 89 H7
Lang Son • Vietnam 31 D2
Langada • Greece 92 D5
Langano & Shala-Abiyata Lakes Nat. Park **Park** • Ethiopia 103 [64]
Langara • Indonesia 32 (1) B3
Langcang Jiang • China 28 G2
Langdale Fell • United Kingdom 74 C2
Langeais [Château] • France 84 D2
Langeberg • South Africa 100 C6
Langeland • Denmark 95 F14
Längelmävesi • Finland 95 E2
Langen • Germany 8 D3
Langenfeld • Germany 81 E3
Langenhagen • Germany 8 E4
Langenselbold • Germany 9 E6
Langeoog • Germany 8 C3
Langeoog **Spa** • Germany 83 [40]
Langer See • Germany 81 F4
Langesund • Norway 94 B3
Langevåg • More og Romsdal, Norway 94 C1
Langevåg • Rogaland, Norway 94 C5
Langfjorden • Norway 94 C2
Langjökull • Iceland 16 (1) C2
Langkawi • Malaysia 32 B1
Langnau • Switzerland 89 G2
Langogne • France 10 I9
Langon • France 85 G3
Langøya • Norway 16 H2
Langreo • Spain 11 F1
Langres • France 10 K6
Langsa • Indonesia 110 B1
Langsele • Sweden 16 I5
Langue de Barbarie, Parc nat. de la **Park** • Senegal 103 [7]
Languedoc • France 10 I10
Languedoc-Roussillon • France 84 A2
Langwedel • Germany 8 E4
Langxi • China 107 J1
Langzhong • China 29 D4
Lanhydrock House • United Kingdom 74 F4
Lanin, Volcán • Argentina 45 B3
Lankanfinolhu • Maldives 106 E2
Lannemezan • France 85 J2
Lannion • France 84 C1
Lansing • MI, United States 41 J3
Lanta, Ko • Thailand 109 F4
Lantau I. • Hong Kong, China 107 H5
Lantau Peak • Hong Kong, China 107 H5
Lante, Villa • Italy 91 F1
Lanton **Beach** • France 68 [85]
Lanzarote • Canary Is. 87 E3
Lanzhou • China 29 C3
Lao • Thailand 109 G2
Lao Cai • Vietnam 31 C2
Lao Ling • China 30 D4
Laoag • Philippines 31 G3
Laocheng • China 29 F3
Laodicea • Turkey 15 K6
Laois • Ireland 79 D2
Laon • France 10 I4
Laos • Asia 31 C2
Laou • Morocco 11 F9
Lapa • Brazil 44 G4
Lápithos • Cyprus 93 J1
Lappeenranta • Finland 16 O6
Lappersdorf • Germany 9 H7
Lappi • Finland 16 N3
Lappijärvi • Finland 16 L5
Lapponian area **Heritage N** • Sweden 61 [39]
Lapponian area **Heritage C** • Sweden 63 [71]
Laprida • Argentina 127 D3
Lapseki • Turkey 15 H3
Laptev Sea • Arctic Ocean 46 C2
Laptevykh, More • Arctic Ocean 46 C2
Lapua • Finland 16 L5
Lapy • Poland 13 L4
Laquiat al Arba'in • Sudan 21 E3
Lar • Iran 18 F4
Lara, Plaj • Turkey 93 G3
Larache • Morocco 101 D1
Laramie • WY, United States 40 E3
Laramie, Fort, Nat. Hist. Site **Park** • WY, United States 120 [73]
Laramie Mtns • WY, United States 40 E3
Larantuka • Indonesia 32 (1) B4
Larat • Indonesia 32 (1) D4
Larba • Algeria 11 O8
Lárdos **Beach** • Rhodes, Greece 69 [211]
Lárdos • Rhodes, Greece 93 F4
Lárdos, Akra • Rhodes, Greece 93 F4
Laredo • Spain 11 H1
Laredo • TX, United States 40 G6
Laredo **Beach** • Spain 68 [89]
Laren • Netherlands 80 C2
Larestan • Iran 18 G4
Largo, Cayo • Cuba 124 D2
Largs • United Kingdom 74 B3
Larino • Italy 14 B8
Lárissa • Greece 15 D4
Larkana • Pakistan 28 A3
Larnaca **Beach** • Cyprus 69 [219]
Larnaca • Cyprus 93 J4
Larnaca Bay • Cyprus 93 J4
Larne • United Kingdom 7 G7
Larned, Fort, Nat. Hist. Site **Park** • KS, United States 120 [170]
Larochette • Luxembourg 80 A20
Larrau • France 85 J1
Larrimah • NT, Australia 34 F3
Larsen Ice Shelf • Antarctica 46 (1) II3
Larsen, Mt • Antarctica 46 (1) V2
Larvik • Norway 94 B3
Las Aves, Is. • Venezuela 124 A5
Las Casitas • Mexico 40 E7
Las Cruces • NM, United States 118 J4
Las Cuevas Bay • Trinidad & Tobago 125 K1
Las Flores • Argentina 127 D3
Las Galletas • Tenerife, Canary Is. 86 E1
Las Heras • Argentina 44 C5
Las Lajas • Argentina 45 B3
Las Marécottes • Switzerland 89 G5
Las Marismas • Spain 86 B1
Las Médulas **Heritage C** • Spain 64 [79]
Las Navas de Tolosa • Spain 71 A16
Las Palmas de Gran Canaria **Beach** • Gran Canaria, Canary Is. 68 [110]
Las Palmas de Gran Canaria • Gran Canaria, Canary Is. 86 E4
Las Piedras • Uruguay 44 E5
Las Piedras, Rio de • Peru 44 C1
Las Pipinas • Argentina 127 D4
Las Plumas • Argentina 45 C4
Las Qoray • Somalia 23 H1
Las Vegas • NM, United States 40 E4
Las Vegas • NV, United States 117 F4
Las'anod • Somalia 23 H2
Lascaux, Grotte de • France 85 G2
Lash-e Joveyn • Afghanistan 18 H3
Lashio • Myanmar 31 B2
Lashkar Gah • Afghanistan 18 H3
Lask • Poland 13 I6
Lassen Volcanic Nat. Park • CA, United States 117 F1
Lassen Volcanic Nat. Park **Park** • CA, United States 120 [41]
Lassíthi • Crete, Greece 93 E7
Lassíthi [Adm] • Crete, Greece 93 E8
Last Mountain Lake • SA, Canada 38 J6
Lastovo • Croatia 14 D7
Latakia • Syria 18 C2
Late • Tonga 35 (2) F2
Látemar • Italy 90 B3
Latín • Spain 11 C2
Latina • Italy 91 F4
Lató • Crete, Greece 93 E8
Latorica • Ukraine 13 L9
Latrobe Valley • VI, Australia 111 G3
Lattari, Monti • Italy 91 G3
Latur • India 28 C5
Latvia • Europe 16 M8
Lau Group • Fiji 35 (2) E2
Lauchammer • Germany 8 I5
Lauenburg • Germany 8 F3
Lauf • Germany 9 G7
Laufen • Germany 82 J4
Laughlin • NV, United States 117 F6
Laukaa • Finland 95 E2
Launceston • TS, Australia 34 I8
Launceston • United Kingdom 74 F5
Laupheim • Germany 82 J1
Laurel • MS, United States 118 K2
Laurentians • QU, Canada 122 B3
Laurentides, Plateau • QU, Canada 39 R6
Laurentides Prov. Reserve • QU, Canada 123 D1
Lauria • Italy 12 J8
Lausanne • Switzerland 89 G5
Laut • Indonesia 32 F3
Lautem • East Indies 32 (1) C4
Lauter • Germany 9 C7
Lauterbach • Germany 82 G2
Lauterbrunnen **Ski** • Switzerland 70 [94]
Lauterbrunnen • Switzerland 89 G2
Lauttawar, Danau • Indonesia 110 B1
Lava Beds Nat. Mon. • CA, United States 117 F1
Lava Beds Nat. Mon. **Park** • CA, United States 120 [39]
Lavagna **Beach** • Italy 68 [142]
Lavagna • Italy 91 E6
Laval • France 84 D1
Lavandou, le **Beach** • France 68 [133]
Lavandou, le • France 85 H3
Lavapié, Punta • Chile 44 B6
Lavarone **Ski** • Italy 70 [212]
Lavayai, Ko • Thailand 109 K1
Laverton • WA, Australia 34 D5
Lavezzi, I. • Corsica, France 85 L4
Lavik • Norway 94 C3
Lavon Lake • TX, United States 119 N1
Lavras • Brazil 127 C1
Lávrio • Greece 92 D7
Lavumisa • Swaziland 24 E5
Lawang • Java, Indonesia 110 D8
Lawit, Gunung • Indonesia 32 E2
Lawra • Burkina Faso 20 E6
Lawrah • Afghanistan 28 A2
Lawrence • KS, United States 41 G4
Lawson • Papua New Guinea 35 (1) D2
Lawton • OK, United States 40 G5
Lawu, Gunung • Java, Indonesia 110 D7
Lawz • Saudi Arabia 21 G2
Laxå • Sweden 95 F3
Laxe **Beach** • Spain 68 [92]
Laycock Abbey • United Kingdom 74 F3
Layla • Saudi Arabia 18 E5
Lázaro Cárdenas • Mexico 123 E3
Lazdijai • Lithuania 13 M3
Lazio • Italy 91 F1
Le Bourget [Apt] • France 85 E2
Le Brassus • Switzerland 89 G1
Le Châble **Ski** • Switzerland 70 [77]
Le Havre • France 10 F4
Le Kef • Tunisia 101 E1
Le Locle • Switzerland 89 G1
Le Mans • France 84 D2
Le Phang Bay • Phuket, Thailand 109 K1
Le Relais **Ski** • QU, Canada 116 [36]
Le Rœulx • Belgium 80 A14
Le Vaud • Switzerland 89 G5
Lea • United Kingdom 5 C3
Leap • Ireland 79 F8
Learmonth • WA, Australia 34 B4
Leba • Poland 13 G3
Lebanon • Asia 18 B3
Lebanon • NH, United States 118 G3
Leblon • Brazil 127 C4
Lebombo Mtns • South Africa 24 E4
Lebork • Poland 13 G3
Lebrija • Spain 11 E8
Lebu • Chile 45 B3
Lecce • Italy 12 M8
Lecco • Italy 91 E2
Lech **Ski** • Austria 70 [129]
Lech • Austria 89 H5
Lech [Riv] • Austria/Germany 82 J6
Lechtaler Alpen • Austria 89 H2
Leczna • Poland 13 L6
Leczyca • Poland 13 I5
Ledbury • United Kingdom 74 D3
Ledesma • Spain 11 F3
Lednice-Valtice **Heritage C** • Czech Rep. 64 [148]
Lédo, Cabo • Angola 24 A1
Ledyanaya, gora • Russian Fed. 27 T4
Lee • Ireland 79 F8
Lee, Robert E., Mem. **Park** • VA, United States 121 [268]
Leeds • United Kingdom 7 K8
Leeds Castle • United Kingdom 74 E4
Leegebruch • Germany 81 F1
Leer • Germany 8 C3
Leerdam • Netherlands 80 C4
Leeuwarden • Netherlands 80 A3
Leeuwin, Cape • WA, Australia 34 C6
Leeward Is. • West Indies 37 I4
Lefká Ori • Crete, Greece 93 E1
Lefká Ori Nat. Park • Crete, Greece 93 E5
Lefkáda • Greece 92 C1
Lefkáda [I.] • Greece 92 C1
Léfkara • Cyprus 93 J3
Lefkími **Beach** • Corfu, Greece 69 [170]
Lefkími • Corfu, Greece 92 B1
Lefkóniko • Cyprus 93 J2
Leganés • Spain 11 H4
Legazpi • Philippines 31 G4
Lège-Cap-Ferret **Beach** • France 68 [85]
Legendes, Côte des • France 84 C1
Leghorn • Italy 91 E11
Legian Beach • Bali, Indonesia 110 C4
Legionowo • Poland 13 J5
Legnano • Lombardia, Italy 12 C3
Legnano • Véneto, Italy 91 E7
Legnica • Poland 13 F6
Legoland **Park** • Denmark 73 [16]
Legoland **Park** • United Kingdom 73 [34]
Legoland • United Kingdom 74 E1
Legoland • Denmark 95 F9
Legundi • Indonesia 110 D1
Leh • Jammu & Kashmir 28 C2
Lehená • Greece 15 C6
Lehinch **Beach** • Ireland 68 [61]
Lehinch • Ireland 79 F4
Lehrte • Germany 8 E4
Leicester • United Kingdom 74 D2
Leicestershire • United Kingdom 75 A5
Leichlingen • Germany 81 E3
Leiden • Netherlands 80 C1
Leie • Belgium 5 G4
Leigh Creek • SA, Australia 34 G6
Leigh-on-Sea **Beach** • United Kingdom 75 [56]
Leignitz • Poland 71 A9
Leikanger • Norway 94 C4
Leine • Germany 8 E4
Leinefelde • Germany 9 F5
Leinster • Ireland 7 E8
Leipnitzsee • Germany 81 F2
Leipzig • Germany 9 H5
Leiria • Portugal 11 C5
Leiria **Beach** • Portugal 68 [97]
Leiria [Adm] • Portugal 88 A2
Leirvik • Norway 94 C5
Leisure I. • Maldives 106 E2
Leith • United Kingdom 74 B4
Leitha • Austria 13 F10
Leitrim • Ireland 79 D1
Leiva • Colombia 43 C3
Leixlip • Ireland 79 E2
Lejre **Beach** • Denmark 68 [42]
Lek • Netherlands 80 A7
Leka • Norway 94 A5
Lekánis • Greece 15 F2
Lékéti, Mts de la • Congo 22 G5
Lekitobi • Indonesia 32 (1) B3
Leknes • Norway 16 G2
Leksozero • Russian Fed. 16 P5
Leksula • Indonesia 32 (1) C3
Lelång • Sweden 94 B4
Lelystad • Netherlands 80 C2
Léman, Lac • Switzerland 89 G5
Lemba Harau Reserve • Indonesia 110 B4
Lemesós • Cyprus 93 J3
Lemgo • Germany 8 D4
Lemieux Is. • NU, Canada 39 S4
Lemland • Finland 95 E3
Lemmenjoki Nat. Park **Park** • Finland 72 [29]
Lemmer • Netherlands 5 I2
Lemnos • Greece 92 D2
Lemsid • Western Sahara 20 C3
Lemvig **Beach** • Denmark 68 [50]
Lemvig • Denmark 95 F9
Lena • Russian Fed. 27 J3
Lena Delta • Russian Fed. 97 A6
Léndas • Crete, Greece 93 E7
Lengerich • Germany 8 C4
Lenggries • Germany 82 J7
Lengua de Vaca, Punta • Chile 44 B5
Lengwe Nat. Park **Park** • Malawi 103 [101]
Lenina, pik • Kyrgyzstan 18 J2
Leningradskaya [Base] • Antarctica 46 (1) U3
Leningradskiy • Russian Fed. 46 HH3
Leninsk-Kuznetskiy • Russian Fed. 26 O7
Lenk **Ski** • Switzerland 70 [89]
Lenk • Switzerland 89 G6
Lenkoran • Azerbaijan 18 E2
Lenne • Germany 9 C5
Lennox, Fort • QU, Canada 122 B8
Leno-Angarskoye Plato • Russian Fed. 27 F6
Lens • France 10 H3
Lensk • Russian Fed. 27 I4
Lenti • Hungary 14 D3
Lentini • Sicily, Italy 12 J11
Lentua • Finland 16 O4
Lenzerheide • Switzerland 89 G4
Lenzerheide-Valbella **Ski** • Switzerland 70 [110]
Lenzkirch **Spa** • Germany 83 [209]
Léo • Burkina Faso 22 D2
Leoben • Austria 13 E10
Leogang **Ski** • Austria 70 [162]
Leok • Indonesia 32 (1) B2
Leominster • United Kingdom 74 D1
Leominster • MA, United States 118 G3
Léon • France 10 D10
León • Spain 11 F2
León • Nicaragua 37 D5
León • Mexico 123 E1
León, Montes de • Spain 11 E2
Léon, Pays de • France 84 C1
Leonardville • Namibia 24 B4
Leonberg • Germany 9 E8
Leone, Monte • Italy/Switzerland 89 G6
Leonídio **Beach** • Greece 69 [183]
Leonora • WA, Australia 34 D5
Leontes • Lebanon 98 A2
Leopardstown • Ireland 79 E2
Leopoldina • Brazil 127 C2
Leova • Moldova 14 P3
Lepanto • Greece 71 A20
Lepe • Spain 86 B1
Lepe Country Park **Beach** • United Kingdom 75 [81]
Lephepe • Botswana 24 D4
Lepini, Monti • Italy 91 F4
Lepsy • Kazakhstan 26 M8
Leptis Magna • Libya 21 B1
Leptis Magna **Heritage C** • Libya 64 [234]
Lercara Fridi • Sicily, Italy 12 H11
Léré • Chad 22 G3
Lérici • Italy 91 E10
Lérida • Spain 11 L3
Lérida • Colombia 43 C4
Lérins, Is. de • France 85 H4
Lerma • Spain 10 B11
Lermoos **Ski** • Austria 70 [138]
Lermoos • Austria 89 H2
Léros • Greece 92 D8
Lerum • Sweden 95 F6
Lerwick • United Kingdom 6 K1
Les Amirantes • Seychelles 106 F2
Les Bioux • Switzerland 89 G1
Les Cayes • Haiti 37 G4
Les Collons **Ski** • Switzerland 70 [82]
Les Crosets **Ski** • Switzerland 70 [76]
Les Diablerets **Ski** • Switzerland 70 [84]
Les Diablerets • Switzerland 89 G6
Les Mosses • Switzerland 89 G6
Lesbos • Greece 92 D5
Leshan • China 29 C5
Leshan Giant Buddha **Heritage N** • China 61 [117]
Leshan Giant Buddha **Heritage C** • China 63 [156]
Lésina, Lago di • Italy 12 J7
Lesjaskog • Norway 94 C2
Lesjaskogsvatnet • Norway 94 C2
Lesjöfors • Sweden 16 H7
Leskovac • F.R. of Yugoslavia 14 I7
Leskovik • Albania 15 B3
Lesneven • France 84 C1
Lesnoy • Russian Fed. 17 I3
Lesosibirsk • Russian Fed. 26 P6
Lesotho • Africa 24 D5
Lesozavodsk • Russian Fed. 27 L7
Lesser Antilles • West Indies 37 I5
Lesser Sunda Is. • Indonesia 32 (1) B4
Lésvos • Greece 92 D5
Leszno • Poland 13 F6
Lethbridge • AL/Canada 38 I7
Lethem • Guyana 43 F3
Leti, Kepulauan • Indonesia 110 A7
Leticia • Colombia 43 D4
Letmathe • Germany 81 E2
Letoon • Turkey 92 D9
Letpadan • Myanmar 31 B3
Letterfrack • Ireland 79 F3
Letterkenny • United Kingdom 7 E7
Lettermore I. • Ireland 79 F3
Leu • Romania 14 L5
Leu, H.P. Leu, Botanical Gardens • FL, United States 121 C2
Leucate **Beach** • France 68 [129]
Leucate • France 85 K2
Leucate, Etang de • France 85 K2
Leuk • Switzerland 89 G6
Leukerbad • Switzerland 89 G6
Leuna • Germany 9 H5
Leuser, Gunung • Indonesia 110 B1
Leutkirch • Germany 82 J5
Leutze **Spa** • Germany 83 [176]
Leuven • Belgium 80 A15
Levanger • Norway 16 F5
Levant • Asia 59 C8
Levant, I. du • France 85 H3
Lévanto • Italy 91 E6
Lévanzo, I. de • Italy 90 D1
Leven, Loch • United Kingdom 74 B2
Levens Hall • United Kingdom 74 C4
Lévêque, Cape • WA, Australia 34 D3
Leverkusen • Germany 81 E3
Levern **Spa** • Germany 83 [87]
Levice • Slovak Rep. 13 H9
Lévico Terme • Italy 90 B3
Levin • New Zealand 35 E5
Lévis • QU, Canada 122 B4
Levítha • Greece 92 D8
Levkas • Greece 92 C1
Levkosia • Cyprus 93 J2
Levoca • Slovak Rep. 13 J8
Levski • Bulgaria 97 D3
Lewes • United Kingdom 74 E3
Lewes • DE, United States 118 H3
Lewis • United Kingdom 6 F3
Lewis Hills • NF, Canada 123 D3
Lewis Pass • New Zealand 35 D6
Lewis Range • Canada/United States 38 I7
Lewiston • ID, United States 117 E2
Lewiston • ME, United States 118 G4
Lewistown • MT, United States 40 E2
Lewisville • TX, United States 119 N1
Lexington • KY, United States 41 J4
Leyre • France 10 E9
Leysdown-on-Sea **Beach** • United Kingdom 75 [59]
Leysin • Switzerland 89 G5
Leyte • Philippines 31 H4
Lezha • Albania 15 A2
Lhasa • China 28 F3
Lhasa **Heritage C** • China 63 [142]
Lhaze • China 28 E3
Lhazhong • China 28 E2
Lho-Nga Beach • Indonesia 110 B1
Lhohifushi • Maldives 106 E2
Lhokseumawe • Indonesia 110 B1
Lhozhag • China 28 F3
Liákoura • Greece 15 D5
Liamuga, Mt • St Kitts & Nevis 125 G1
Liangspran, Gunung • Indonesia 32 E2
Lianhuashan • China 107 H2
Lianxian • China 29 E5
Lianyungang • China 29 F4
Liao He • China 29 G2
Liaodong • China 29 G2
Liaodong Wan • China 29 G2
Liaoning • China 107 G4
Liaoyang • China 29 G2
Liard • Canada 38 G4
Liard River • BC, Canada 38 F5
Libby • MT, United States 40 C2
Libechov • Czech Rep. 96 C2
Libenge • Dem. Rep. of Congo 23 B3
Liberal • KS, United States 40 F4
Liberec • Czech Rep. 96 C2
Liberia • Africa 22 B3
Liberia • Costa Rica 37 D5
Liberta • Antigua & Barbuda 125 F3
Liberty • TX, United States 119 N4
Libiyah, As Sahra al • Africa 21 E2
Libobo, Tanjung • Indonesia 32 (1) C3
Liboi • Kenya 23 G3
Libournais • France 84 B3
Libourne • France 85 G1
Libreville • Gabon 22 F4
Libya • Africa 21 C2
Libyan Desert • Egypt 21 E2
Licantén • Chile 45 B2
Licata • Sicily, Italy 12 H11
Lichfield • United Kingdom 74 D2
Lichinga • Mozambique 24 F2
Lichnice • Czech Rep. 96 C2
Lichtenfels • Germany 9 G6
Licosa, Punta • Italy 12 I8
Lida • Belarus 16 M10
Lidice • Czech Rep. 96 C2
Lidingö • Sweden 95 D4
Lidköping • Sweden 95 F3
Lido de Camaiore • Italy 91 E10
Lido de Jésolo • Italy 91 E8
Lido di Ostia • Italy 12 G7
Lidoríki • Greece 15 D5
Lidzbark Warminski • Poland 13 J3
Liebeneck, Burg • Germany 82 H2
Liebenstein, Burg • Germany 82 H2
Liebig, Mt • NT, Australia 112 H1
Liechtenstein • Europe 89 H5
Liège • Belgium 80 A15
Liège [Adm] • Belgium 80 A16
Lieksa • Finland 16 P5
Lienz • Austria 89 H8
Liepaja • Latvia 13 J1
Lier • Belgium 80 A11
Lierbyen • Norway 94 B1
Liesjärvi Nat. Park **Park** • Finland 72 [36]
Liesjärvi Nat. Park • Finland 95 E4
Lièvin • France 10 H3
Liezen • Austria 13 D10
Liffey • Ireland 79 E1
Lifford • Ireland 7 E7
Lifiyah, Al • Saudi Arabia 21 H1
Lifjell • Norway 94 B3
Lifou • New Caledonia 35 (2) B3
Ligeni Shkodrés • Albania 14 G7
Lightbourne Cay • Bahamas 124 B2
Lightwater Valley **Park** • United Kingdom 73 [24]
Lignano • Italy 91 E8
Lignano Sabbiadoro **Beach** • Italy 68 [165]
Ligny-en-Barrois • France 5 I6
Ligórtinos • Crete, Greece 93 E7
Liguria • Italy 91 E6
Ligurian Sea • Italy 12 C5
Lihir • Papua New Guinea 35 (1) E1
Lihou Reef & Cays • CL, Australia 111 F2
Lihue • HI, United States 119 L2
Lijiang • China 29 C5
Lijiang **Heritage C** • China 63 [157]
Lijoki • Finland 16 M4
Likasi • Dem. Rep. of Congo 23 D6
Likoni • Kenya 101 G5
Likouala • Congo 22 G4
Lilla Edet • Sweden 95 F2
Lille • France 10 H3
Lille **Beach** • Belgium 68 [71]
Lille • Belgium 80 A11
Lille Bælt • Denmark 95 F13
Lillebonne • France 7 M12
Lillehammer • Norway 16 F6
Lillers • France 5 F4
Lillesand • Norway 95 F1
Lillestrøm • Norway 94 B2
Lillhärdal • Sweden 16 H6
Lillooet • BC, Canada 122 C3
Lilongwe • Malawi 24 E2
Lim • F.R. of Yugoslavia 14 G6
Lima **Heritage C** • Peru 62 [49]
Lima • Peru 127 B1
Limassol • Cyprus 93 J3
Limay • Argentina 45 C3
Limbe • Cameroon 22 F4
Limburg • Netherlands 80 A12
Limburg • Belgium 80 A15
Limburg an der Lahn • Germany 82 H2
Limeira • Brazil 44 G3
Limenas Hersonissou **Beach** • Crete, Greece 69 [214]
Limenas Hersonissou • Crete, Greece 93 E3
Limerick • Ireland 79 F6
Limerick [Adm] • Ireland 79 F6
Limes • Germany 71 A8
Limfjorden • Denmark 95 F5
Limingen • Norway 16 G4
Liminka • Finland 16 M4
Límni • Greece 92 D4
Límnos • Greece 92 D2
Limoeiro • Brazil 45 (1) D3
Limoges • France 85 G2
Limogne, Causse de • France 85 G4
Limone Piemonte **Ski** • Italy 70 [191]
Limone Piemonte • Italy 91 E5
Limousin • France 10 G8
Limoux • France 11 N1
Limoux • France 84 B3
Limpopo • Africa 24 D4
Lin'an • China 107 J3
Linares • Spain 11 H6
Linares • Mexico 37 B3
Linares • Chile 44 B6
Linariá • Greece 92 D4
Linaro, Capo • Italy 91 F1
Linate [Apt] • Italy 91 E6
Lincang • China 29 C6
Lincoln • United Kingdom 7 L8
Lincoln • NE, United States 41 G3
Lincoln • ME, United States 118 G2
Lincoln • Argentina 127 D1
Lincoln, Abraham, Birthplace Nat. Hist. Site **Park** • KY, United States 121 [236]
Lincoln Boyhood Nat. Mem. **Park** • IN, United States 121 [183]
Lincoln City • OR, United States 117 E3
Lincoln Home Nat. Hist. Site **Park** • IL, United States 121 [178]
Lincoln Mem. **Park** • DC, United States 121 [287]
Lincolnshire • United Kingdom 75 A4
Lindås • Norway 94 C3
Lindau • Germany 82 J5
Lindbergh Field [Apt] • CA, United States 117 F6
Lindeman I. • QL, Australia 111 F1
Linden • Guyana 43 F2
Lindenberg • Germany 81 F2
Lindenberg • Germany 82 J5
Lindenfels • Germany 82 G4
Lindenfels **Spa** • Germany 83 [148]
Linderhof, Schloß • Germany 82 J6
Linderödsåsen • Sweden 95 F11
Lindesberg • Sweden 16 H7
Lindesnes • Norway 16 D7
Lindi • Dem. Rep. of Congo 23 D3
Lindi • Tanzania 102 H4
Lindis Pass • New Zealand 112 L2
Lindisfarne • United Kingdom 6 K6
Lindlar • Germany 81 E4
Líndos **Beach** • Rhodes, Greece 69 [211]
Líndos • Rhodes, Greece 93 F4
Lindsay • OT, Canada 122 B5
Lindsdal • Sweden 95 F8
Lindsey • United Kingdom 75 A4
Line Is. • Kiribati 33 L6
Linfen • China 29 E3
Lingayen • Philippines 31 G3
Lingayen Gulf • Philippines 31 G3
Lingding I. • Zhuhai, China 107 H4
Lingen • Germany 8 C4
Lingga • Indonesia 32 C3
Lingga, Kepulauan • Indonesia 32 D3
Lingling • China 29 E5
Lingsugur • India 106 D2
Linguére • Senegal 22 A1
Linhai • China 29 G5
Linhares • Brazil 44 I2
Linjiang • China 30 D4
Linköping • Sweden 95 F4
Linlithgow Palace • United Kingdom 74 B4
Linn, Burg • Germany 81 E1
Linnanmaki **Park** • Finland 73 [12]
Linnansaari Nat. Park **Park** • Finland 72 [34]
Linnhe, Loch • United Kingdom 6 G5
Linping • China 107 J4
Lins • Brazil 44 G3
Linstead • Jamaica 124 C4
Lintorf • Germany 81 E1
Linxi • China 29 F2
Linyi • China 29 F3
Linz • Austria 13 D9
Linz • Germany 82 H1
Lion, Golfe du • Mediterranean Sea 10 J11
Lion Rock Country Park • Hong Kong, China 107 H6
Lioppa • Indonesia 32 (1) C4
Liouesso • Congo 22 H4
Lipa • Philippines 31 G4
Lípari, I. • Italy 90 D2
Lípari, Is. • Italy 90 D2
Lipcani • Moldova 14 N1
Lipenská Prehradní Nádrz • Czech Rep. 96 C4
Liperi • Finland 16 O5
Lipetsk • Russian Fed. 17 F4
Lipez, Cordillera de • Bolivia 44 C3
Lipnice nad Sázavou • Czech Rep. 96 C4
Lipno • Poland 13 I5
Lipova • Romania 14 I3
Lippe • Germany 8 D5
Lippstadt • Germany 8 D5
Lipsí • Greece 92 D8
Liptovsky Mikulás • Slovak Rep. 13 I8
Lira • Uganda 23 E3
Liranga • Congo 22 H5
Liri • Italy 12 H7
Lisala • Dem. Rep. of Congo 23 C3
Lisalmi • Finland 16 N5
Lisboa **Heritage C** • Portugal 64 [100]
Lisboa • Portugal 88 D2
Lisboa [Adm] • Portugal 88 A2
Lisboa, Costa de • Portugal 88 A3
Lisbon **Heritage C** • Portugal 64 [100]

Lisbon • Portugal 88 D2
Lisburn • United Kingdom 7 F7
Lisdoonvarna • Ireland 79 F4
Liseberg **Park** • Sweden 73 [5]
Lishui • Zhejiang, China 31 F1
Lishui • Jiangsu, China 107 J1
Lisichansk • Ukraine 17 F5
Lisieux • France 10 F4
Liskeard • United Kingdom 74 F5
Liski • Romania 14 N3
Lismore • United Kingdom 75 A2
Lismore • NS, Australia 111 F6
Lissadell House • Ireland 79 F2
Lisse • Netherlands 80 C1
List **Spa** • Germany 83 [2]
Lista • Norway 16 D7
Lister, Mt • Antarctica 46 (1) V2
Listowel • Ireland 79 F5
Lit-et-Mixe, Fôret de • France 85 G3
Litani • Lebanon 98 A2
Liternum • Italy 91 G1
Lith, Al • Saudi Arabia 18 D5
Lithgow • NS, Australia 111 G2
Lithino, Akra • Crete, Greece 93 E6
Lithuania • Europe 16 M9
Litle Abaco • Bahamas 124 B1
Litohóro **Beach** • Greece 69 [190]
Litomerice • Czech Rep. 96 C2
Little • TX, United States 119 N3
Little Andaman • India 28 F6
Little Bighorn Battlefield Nat. Mon. **Park** • MT, United States 120 [71]
Little Cayman • Cayman Is. 124 D6
Little Current • OT, Canada 39 O7
Little Exuma • Bahamas 124 B4
Little Hura • Maldives 106 E2
Little Inagua • Bahamas 124 B4
Little Karoo • South Africa 100 C6
Little Missouri • United States 38 K7
Little Nicobar • India 28 F7
Little River Canyon Nat. Preserve **Park** • AL, United States 121 [206]
Little Rock • AR, United States 41 H5
Little Skellig • Ireland 79 F7
Little Tobago • Trinidad & Tobago 125 K2
Littlehampton • United Kingdom 74 E3
Littlehampton **Beach** • United Kingdom 75 [75]
Litvínov • Czech Rep. 96 C1
Liuhe • China 30 C3
Liullaillaco, Volcán • Argentina/Chile 44 C3
Liuzhou • China 29 D6
Livadiá • Greece 15 D5
Livanates **Beach** • Greece 69 [187]
Liverpool • United Kingdom 7 J8
Liverpool • NS, Canada 123 D7
Liverpool Bay • United Kingdom 7 I8
Liverpool Bay • NT, Canada 38 E3
Livigno **Ski** • Italy 70 [204]
Livigno • Italy 91 E2
Livingston • MT, United States 40 D2
Livingston • United Kingdom 74 B4
Livingston • TX, United States 119 N4
Livingston, Lake • TX, United States 119 N4
Livingstone • Zambia 24 D3
Livingstone, Chutes de • Dem. Rep. of Congo 23 A5
Livingstone Falls • Dem. Rep. of Congo 23 A5
Livingstone Mtns • Tanzania 23 E5
Livingstone Mtns • New Zealand 112 L2
Livingstonia • Malawi 23 E6
Livland • Estonia/Latvia 16 N8
Livno • Bosnia-Herz. 14 D6
Livorno • Italy 91 E11
Liwale • Tanzania 102 H4
Liwonde Nat. Park **Park** • Malawi 103 [99]
Lixoúri • Greece 92 C2
Liyang • China 107 J1
Liyuan • China 107 J2
Lizard Point • United Kingdom 74 F4
Ljubinje • Bosnia-Herz. 14 F7
Ljubisnja • Bosnia-Herz./F.R. of Yugoslavia 14 F6
Ljubljana • Slovenia 13 D11
Ljugarn • Sweden 16 J8
Ljungan • Sweden 16 I5
Ljungby • Sweden 95 F7
Ljungsbro • Sweden 95 F4
Ljusdal • Sweden 16 I6
Ljusnan • Sweden 16 I6
Ljusterö • Sweden 95 D2
Ljusterö [I.] • Sweden 95 D2
Llançà **Beach** • Spain 68 [123]
Llançà • Spain 87 D2
Llandanwg **Beach** • United Kingdom 75 [190]
Llanddona **Beach** • United Kingdom 75 [228]
Llandrindod Wells • United Kingdom 7 I9
Llandudno **Beach** • United Kingdom 75 [199]
Llaneilian **Beach** • United Kingdom 75 [223]
Llanelli • United Kingdom 7 H10
Llanenddwyn **Beach** • United Kingdom 75 [189]
Llanes • Spain 11 G1
Llanes **Beach** • Spain 68 [90]
Llanfaelog **Beach** • United Kingdom 75 [207-209]
Llanfaethlu **Beach** • United Kingdom 75 [217-218]
Llanfairfechan **Beach** • United Kingdom 75 [197]
Llanfwrog **Beach** • United Kingdom 75 [216]
Llangennith **Beach** • United Kingdom 75 [145]
Llangollen • United Kingdom 7 I9
Llangrannog **Beach** • United Kingdom 75 [173-174]
Llano • TX, United States 119 N3
Llano Estacado • NM/TX, United States 40 F5
Llano [Riv] • TX, United States 119 N3
Llanos • Colombia/Venezuela 43 D2
Llanos de Concepcion • Fuerteventura, Canary Is. 87 E2
Llanrhystud **Beach** • United Kingdom 75 [180]
Llantwit Major • United Kingdom 74 F2
Llerena • Spain 11 F6
Llevant, Costa de • Spain 87 D2
Llevant, Serra de • Majorca, Spain 87 H4
Lliria • Spain 11 K5
Llivia • Spain 87 D1
Llobregat • Spain 87 D1
Llogara Nat. Park **Park** • Albania 72 [127]
Lloret de Mar **Beach** • Spain 68 [123]
Lloret de Mar • Spain 87 D4
Lloyd George, Mt • BC, Canada 38 F5
Lloydminster • SA, Canada 38 J6
Lluc Alcari • Majorca, Spain 87 H1
Lluc, Monestir de • Majorca, Spain 87 H1
Llucmajor • Majorca, Spain 87 H3
Lo Wu • Hong Kong, China 107 H3
Loa • Chile 44 C3
Loano • Italy 12 C4
Lôbau • Germany 9 J5
Lobaye • Central African Rep. 23 B2
Lobéria • Argentina 127 D3
Lobito • Angola 23 A6
Lobo • Indonesia 32 (1) D3
Lobos • Canary Is. 87 E2
Lobos • Argentina 127 D1
Lobos, I. de • Uruguay 127 D2
Locarno • Switzerland 89 G7
Lochaline • United Kingdom 78 A2
Lochboisdale • United Kingdom 6 E4
Loches [Château] • France 84 D4
Lochgilphead • United Kingdom 6 G5
Lochinver • United Kingdom 6 G3
Lochmaddy • United Kingdom 6 E4
Lochnagar • United Kingdom 6 I5
Lochranza • United Kingdom 78 A2
Lochy, Loch • United Kingdom 6 H5
Lockhart • TX, United States 119 N3
Locmariaquer **Beach** • France 68 [81]
Locmariaquer • France 84 C4
Locminé • France 10 C6
Locri • Italy 12 K10
Locronan • France 84 C3
Lod • Israel 98 A5
Lodève • France 10 I10
Lodeynoye Pole • Russian Fed. 17 E2
Lodi • Italy 91 E6
Lødingen • Norway 16 H2
Lodja • Dem. Rep. of Congo 23 C4
Lodore Falls • United Kingdom 74 C2
Lodwar • Kenya 101 G1
Lódz • Poland 13 I6
Loei • Thailand 109 G4
Loerie • South Africa 100 C8
Loffa • Liberia 22 B3
Lofoten • Norway 16 G2
Loftahammar • Sweden 95 F4
Lofthus • Norway 94 C4
Logan • UT, United States 40 D3
Logan [Apt] • MA, United States 118 G3
Logan, Mt • YT, Canada 38 C4
Logansport • LA, United States 118 K1
Loge • Angola 23 A5
Logone • Chad 21 C5
Logroño • Spain 11 I2
Løgstør **Beach** • Denmark 68 [48]
Løgstør • Denmark 95 F5
Logudoro • Sardinia, Italy 12 C8
Løgumkloster • Denmark 95 F13
Lögurinn • Iceland 16 (1) F2
Lohja • Finland 95 E4
Lohmar • Germany 82 G1
Löhne • Germany 8 D4
Lohne • Germany 8 D4
Lohr • Germany 9 E6
Lohria • Crete, Greece 93 E6
Loi-kaw • Myanmar 31 B3
Loibl • Slovenia 13 D11
Loimaa • Finland 95 E4
Loir • France 84 D2
Loir-et-Cher • France 84 D2
Loire • France 10 G6
Loix **Beach** • France 68 [84]
Loiza Aldea • Puerto Rico 125 E2
Loíza, Rio Grande de • Puerto Rico 125 E4
Loja • Ecuador 43 B4
Loja • Spain 86 B3
Lokan tekojärri • Finland 16 N3
Løken • Norway 94 B2
Lokeren • Belgium 5 G3
Loket • Czech Rep. 96 C1
Lokitaung • Kenya 23 F3
Løkken • Denmark 95 F5
Løkken-Vrå **Beach** • Denmark 68 [48]
Lokoja • Nigeria 22 F3
Lokomo • Cameroon 23 B3
Loks Land • NU, Canada 39 S4
Lokwe Kangole • Kenya 101 G1
Lolland • Denmark 95 F14
Lolo Pass • MT, United States 117 E2
Lom • Bulgaria 14 K6
Lom • Norway 94 C2
Lom Sak • Thailand 109 G4
Loma Mtns • Guinea/Sierra Leone 22 B3
Lomami • Dem. Rep. of Congo 23 C5
Lombarda, Serra • Brazil 43 G3
Lombardia • Italy 91 E6
Lombardsijde-Bad • Belgium 80 B1
Lombardy • Italy 90 A1
Lombok • Indonesia 32 F4
Lomé • Togo 22 E3
Lomela • Dem. Rep. of Congo 23 C4
Lomié • Cameroon 22 G4
Lommel • Belgium 5 I3
Lomond, Loch • United Kingdom 74 B3
Lomonosov • Russian Fed. 17 D3
Lomza • Poland 13 L4
Lon, Ko • Thailand 109 K2
Londe-les-Maures, la **Beach** • France 68 [133]
Londerzeel **Beach** • Belgium 68 [73]
Londerzeel • Belgium 80 A14
London • OT, Canada 39 O8
London **Heritage C** • United Kingdom 64 [22-24]
London • United Kingdom 74 E1
London City [Apt] • United Kingdom 74 E1
Londonderry • United Kingdom 7 E7
Londonderry, Cape • WA, Australia 34 E2
Long Akah • Malaysia 31 E6
Long Bay • Jamaica 124 C4
Long Bay • Antigua & Barbuda 125 F2
Long Bay • Barbados 125 H4
Long Bay [Bay] • Jamaica 124 C3
Long Beach • CA, United States 117 F6
Long Branch • NJ, United States 118 H1
Long Cay • Bahamas 124 B4
Long Hai • Vietnam 108 B4
Long I. • Papua New Guinea 35 (1) D2
Long I. • QL, Australia 111 F1
Long I. • New Zealand 112 L3
Long I. • NY, United States 118 H2
Long I. • Bahamas 124 B4
Long I. • Antigua & Barbuda 125 F2
Long Island Sound • CT/NY, United States 41 L3
Long Kloof • South Africa 100 C7
Long Mynd, The • United Kingdom 74 D1
Long Point • New Zealand 112 L3
Long Point • OT, Canada 122 B9
Long Range Mtns • NF, Canada 123 D3
Long Xuyen • Vietnam 108 B3
Longa, Proliv • Russian Fed. 27 U3
Longarone • Italy 90 B4
Longboat Key • FL, United States 119 M5
Longchamp • France 85 E3
Longeville-sur-Mer **Beach** • France 68 [83]
Longfellow Nat. Hist. Site **Park** • MA, United States 121 [348]
Longford • Ireland 7 E8
Longford [Adm] • Ireland 79 D1
Longgang • China 107 H2
Longlac • OT, Canada 39 N7
Longleat House & Safari Park • United Kingdom 74 F3
Longmalinau • Indonesia 32 F2
Longmont • CO, United States 40 F3
Longnan • China 31 E2
Longonot Nat. Park • Kenya 101 G3
Longpujungan • Indonesia 32 F2
Longreach • QL, Australia 34 H4
Longs Peak • CO, United States 40 E3
Longue, I. • Seychelles 106 F1
Longuyon • France 10 K4
Longview • WA, United States 117 E1
Longview • TX, United States 119 N2
Longwood Gardens • PA, United States 118 H3
Longwy • France 5 I5
Longxi • China 29 C3
Longxi Shan • China 31 F1
Longyearbyen • Svalbard 46 N2
Löningen • Germany 8 C4
Lons-le-Saunier • France 10 K7
Looe • United Kingdom 74 F5
Looe Key Nat. Marine Sanctuary • FL, United States 119 M8
Lookout, Cape • NC, United States 118 H5
Lookout, Cape, Nat. Seashore • NC, United States 118 H5
Lookout Pass • MT, United States 40 C2
Loolmalassin • Tanzania 23 F4
Loon **Ski** • NH, United States 116 [214]
Loop Head • Ireland 79 F5
Loosdrechtse Plassen • Netherlands 80 C2
Lop Buri • Thailand 31 C4
Lop Nur • China 26 P9
Lopatina, gora • Russian Fed. 27 N6
Lopatka, mys • Russian Fed. 25 Q4
Lopé, Réserve de **Park** • Gabon 103 [47]
Lopez, Cap • Gabon 22 F5
Lopez, Cap, Baie du • Gabon 22 F5
Lopikerwaard • Netherlands 80 C4
Loppem • Belgium 80 B2
Lora del Rio • Spain 11 F7
Lorain • OH, United States 41 J3
Lorca • Spain 11 J7
Lorch • Germany 82 H4
Lord Howe I. • NS, Australia 34 K6
Lord Howe I. **Heritage N** • NS, Australia 61 [137]
Lordsburg • NM, United States 118 J4
Loreley • Germany 82 H4
Lorengau • Papua New Guinea 35 (1) D1
Loreto • Bolivia 44 D2
Loreto **Heritage C** • Argentina 62 [64]
Loreto • Italy 91 E12
Loreto • Mexico 123 E1
Lorian Swamp • Kenya 101 G2
Lorient • France 84 C3
Lörinci • Hungary 13 I10
Lorn, Firth of • United Kingdom 6 G5
Lörrach • Germany 82 G7
Lorraine • France 10 K4
Lorsach • Germany 82 J3
Lorsch **Heritage C** • Germany 64 [44]
Lorsch • Germany 82 H4
Los Alamos • NM, United States 118 J2
Los Alcázares **Beach** • Spain 68 [117]
Los Alcázares • Spain 87 C3
Los Angeles • Chile 45 B3
Los Angeles • CA, United States 117 F6
Los Arenales del Sol • Spain 87 C1
Los Blancos • Argentina 44 D3
Los Cristianos • Tenerife, Canary Is. 86 E1
Los Gigantes • Tenerife, Canary Is. 86 E1
Los Glaciares, Parque Nac. **Heritage N** • Argentina 60 [38]
Los, Is. de • Guinea 22 B3
Los Katios, Parque Nac. **Heritage N** • Colombia 60 [28]
Los Mochis • Mexico 40 E6
Los Monegros • Spain 11 K3
Los Monos • Mexico 123 E3
Los Padres, Laguna de • Argentina 127 D4
Los Palacios • Cuba 124 D1
Los Palacios y Villafranca • Spain 11 F7
Los Pinos, Costa de • Majorca, Spain 87 H2
Los Pocillos • Lanzarote, Canary Is. 87 E3
Los Rodeos [Apt] • Tenerife, Canary Is. 86 E1
Los Teques • Venezuela 43 D2
Los Vilos • Chile 44 B5
Losai Game Reserve • Kenya 101 G2
Losinj • Croatia 14 B5
Lost Trail Pass • MT, United States 117 E2
Lostwithiel • United Kingdom 74 F4
Lot • France 10 G9
Lot • Sudan 21 E6
Lot [Adm] • France 85 G4
Lota • Chile 44 B6
Lotkipi Plain • Kenya 101 G1
Loto • Dem. Rep. of Congo 23 C4
Lotuka, Jabal • Sudan 23 E3
Lotus Mtn • China 107 H2
Louangphrabang • Laos 31 C3
Louangphrabang **Heritage C** • Laos 63 [170]
Loubomo • Congo 22 G5
Loudéac • France 84 C2
Loudima • Congo 22 G5
Loudun • France 84 D3
Loué • France 10 E6
Louga • Senegal 22 A1
Loughborough • United Kingdom 74 D2
Loughrea **Beach** • Ireland 68 [62]
Loughrea • Ireland 79 F4
Loughwood Meeting House • United Kingdom 74 F3
Louisa, Lake • FL, United States 121 C1
Louisa, Lake, State Park • FL, United States 121 C1
Louisbourg, Fortress of • NS, Canada 123 D8
Louisburgh **Beach** • Ireland 68 [63]
Louisburgh • Ireland 79 F1
Louisiade Archipelago • Papua New Guinea 35 (1) E2
Louisiana • United States 118 K1
Louisville • KY, United States 41 I4
Louisville • MS, United States 118 K2
Loulan • China 98 B3
Loulan Yiji • China 26 O9
Loulé **Beach** • Portugal 68 [100]
Loulé • Portugal 88 E7
Louny • Czech Rep. 96 C1
Loup • France 85 H2
Loup, Gorges du • France 85 H2
Lourdes • France 85 J2
Louth • United Kingdom 7 M8
Louth • Ireland 79 D1
Loutrá • Greece 92 D7
Loutrá Edipsoú • Greece 92 D4
Loutráki **Beach** • Greece 69 [178]
Louvière, la • Belgium 5 H4
Louviers • France 10 G4
Lövånger • Sweden 16 K4
Lovat • Russian Fed. 97 E3
Lovat • Bulgaria 14 F7
Lovcen Nat. Park **Park** • Fed. Rep. of Yugoslavia 72 [120]
Lovech • Bulgaria 14 L6
Loveland **Ski** • CO, United States 116 [91]
Lovelock • NV, United States 117 F2
Lover's Leap • Jamaica 124 C3
Lovina Beach • Bali, Indonesia 110 C2
Lovoi • Dem. Rep. of Congo 23 D5
Lovosice • Czech Rep. 96 C1
Lövstad • Sweden 95 F4
Low, Cape • NU, Canada 39 N4
Low Newton **Beach** • United Kingdom 75 [12]
Lowa • Dem. Rep. of Congo 23 D4
Lowell • MA, United States 118 G3
Lowell Nat. Hist. Park **Park** • MA, United States 121 [351]
Lower Austria • Austria 89 F4
Lower Egypt • Egypt 101 F1
Lower Hutt • New Zealand 35 E5
Lower Post • YT, Canada 38 F4
Lower Saxony • Germany 81 D2
Lower Zambezi Nat. Park **Park** • Zambia 103 [106]
Lowestoft • United Kingdom 7 N9
Lowestoft **Beach** • United Kingdom 75 [41-43]
Loweswater • United Kingdom 74 C1
Lowicz • Poland 13 I5
Loxstedt • Germany 5 L1
Loxstedt • Germany 8 D3
Loxton • South Africa 100 C3
Loyalty Is. • New Caledonia 35 (2) B3
Loyangalani • Kenya 101 G1
Loyauté, Is. • New Caledonia 35 (2) B3
Lozenets • Bulgaria 97 D4
Lozère, Mt • France 10 I9
Loznica • F.R. of Yugoslavia 14 G5
Lu Shan **Heritage C** • China 63 [155]
Lu'an • China 29 F4
Lua • Dem. Rep. of Congo 22 H4
Luacano • Angola 24 C2
Luachimo • Angola 23 C5
Luachimo [Riv] • Angola 23 C5
Luahasibuka • Indonesia 110 B4
Lualaba • Dem. Rep. of Congo 23 D5
Luama • Dem. Rep. of Congo 23 D4
Luana Point • Jamaica 124 C3
Luanda • Angola 23 A5
Luando • Angola 23 B6
Luang Po Ban Laem • Thailand 109 H3
Luang Prabang **Heritage C** • Laos 63 [170]
Luang Prabang Range • Laos/Thailand 109 G4
Luanginga • Angola/Zambia 24 C2
Luangwa • Zambia 102 J2
Luangwa [Riv] • Zambia 24 E2
Luanshya • Zambia 24 D2
Luao • Angola 23 C6
Luapula • Dem. Rep. of Congo/Zambia 23 D6
Luarca • Spain 11 E1
Luba • Equatorial Guinea 22 F4
Luban • Poland 13 E6
Lubang • Philippines 31 G4
Lubango • Angola 24 A2
Lubao • Dem. Rep. of Congo 23 D5
Lubartow • Poland 13 L6
Lübbecke • Germany 8 D4
Lübben • Germany 8 I5
Lübbenau • Germany 8 I5
Lubbock • TX, United States 40 F5
Lübeck • Germany 8 F3
Lübeck **Heritage C** • Germany 64 [30]
Lübecker Bucht • Germany 8 G2
Lubenec • Czech Rep. 9 I6
Lubilash • Dem. Rep. of Congo 23 C5
Lublin • Poland 13 F6
Lublin • Poland 13 L6
Lubliniec • Poland 13 H7
Lubmin **Spa** • Germany 83 [282]
Lubnān, Jabal • Lebanon 18 C3
Lubny • Ukraine 17 E4
Lubon • Poland 13 F5
Lubsko • Poland 13 D6
Lubudi • Dem. Rep. of Congo 23 C6
Lubuklinggau • Indonesia 32 C3
Lubumbashi • Dem. Rep. of Congo 23 D6
Luc • France 85 F3
Luc, le • France 85 H3
Lucala • Angola 22 H6
Lucala [Riv] • Angola 22 H6
Lucan • Ireland 79 E2
Lucapa • Angola 23 C5
Lucaya • Bahamas 124 B2
Lucaya Estates • Bahamas 124 B2
Lucca • Italy 91 E11
Luce Bay • United Kingdom 7 H7
Lucea • Jamaica 124 C1
Lucena • Spain 11 G7
Lucena del Cid • Spain 11 K4
Lucenec • Slovak Rep 13 I9
Lucera • Italy 14 C8
Lucerne • Switzerland 89 G3
Lucerne, Lake of • Switzerland 89 G3
Lucheringo • Mozambique 23 F6
Lucira • Angola 24 A2
Luckau • Germany 8 I5
Luckenwalde • Germany 8 I4
Lucknow • India 105 C3
Luçon • France 84 D3
Lucrecia, Cabo • Cuba 124 D8
Lucusse • Angola 23 C6
Lüda • China 29 G3
Lude, le • France 84 D1
Lüdenscheid • Germany 81 E4
Lüderitz • Namibia 24 B5
Lüderitz Bay • Namibia 24 B5
Ludhiana • India 28 C2
Ludlow • United Kingdom 74 D1
Ludogorije • Bulgaria 14 O6
Ludogorsko Plato • Bulgaria 14 O6
Ludus • Romania 14 L3
Ludvika • Sweden 16 H6
Ludwigsburg • Germany 82 G6
Ludwigsfelde • Germany 81 F3
Ludwigshafen • Germany 82 G4
Ludwigslust • Germany 8 G3
Luebo • Dem. Rep. of Congo 23 C5
Luena • Angola 24 C2
Luena [Riv] • Zambia 24 C2
Luenha • Mozambique/Zimbabwe 24 E3
Lufira • Dem. Rep. of Congo 23 D6
Lufkin • TX, United States 119 N4
Luga • Russian Fed. 17 D3
Lugano • Switzerland 89 G7
Lugano, Lago di • Italy/Switzerland 89 G7
Lugansk • Ukraine 17 F5
Luganville • Vanuatu 35 (2) B2
Lugenda • Mozambique/Tanzania 24 F2
Lugnaquillia • Ireland 79 E4
Lugo • Spain 11 D1
Lugo • Italy 12 F4
Lugoj • Romania 14 I4
Luhayyah, Al • Yemen 18 D6
Luhe • China 107 J1
Luhit • India 28 G3
Luhur Batukau Temple • Bali, Indonesia 110 C2
Lui • Angola 22 H6
Luiana • Angola 24 C3
Luiana [Riv] • Africa 24 C3
Luilaka • Dem. Rep. of Congo 23 C4
Luimneach • Ireland 79 F6
Luing • United Kingdom 75 A2
Luján • Argentina 127 D1
Lukenie • Dem. Rep. of Congo 23 C4
Lukolela • Dem. Rep. of Congo 22 H5
Lukovit • Bulgaria 14 L6
Luków • Poland 13 L6
Lukuga • Dem. Rep. of Congo 23 D5
Lukulu • Zambia 24 C2
Lule älv • Sweden 16 K4
Lulea • Sweden 16 L4
Luleå **Heritage C** • Sweden 63 [72]
Lüleburgaz • Turkey 15 I2
Lulimba • Dem. Rep. of Congo 23 D4
Lulonga • Dem. Rep. of Congo 23 B3
Lulua • Dem. Rep. of Congo 23 C5
Lumajang • Java, Indonesia 110 D8
Lumajangdong Co • China 28 D2
Lumbala • Angola 24 C2
Lumberton • NC, United States 41 K5
Lumbini **Heritage C** • Nepal 63 [140]
Lumi • Papua New Guinea 35 (1) C1
Lumjiag, Laem • Phuket, Thailand 109 K2
Lumsden • New Zealand 112 L4
Lumut • Malaysia 108 D1
Lumut • Malaysia 108 D3
Lunar Crater • NV, United States 117 F4
Lund • Sweden 95 F11
Lunda • Angola 23 B5
Lundazi • Zambia 24 E2
Lunde • Norway 94 B3
Lunds Tivoli **Park** • Norway 73 [3]
Lundu • Malaysia 32 D2
Lundy • United Kingdom 74 F1
Lüneburg • Germany 8 F3
Lüneburg **Spa** • Germany 83 [57]
Lüneburger Heide • Germany 8 F3
Lünen • Germany 5 K3
Lünen • Germany 81 E2
Lunenburg **Heritage C** • NS, Canada 62 [4]
Lunenburg • NS, Canada 123 D7
Luneur **Park** • Italy 73 [85]
Lunéville • France 10 L5
Lung Kwu Chau • Hong Kong, China 107 H5
Luni • India 105 C5
Luo He • China 29 D3
Luohe • China 29 E4
Luoyang • China 29 E4
Lupeni • Romania 14 K4
Lupilichi • Mozambique 24 F2
Luputa • Dem. Rep. of Congo 23 C5
Luq • Somalia 23 G3
Luqa [Apt] • Malta 93 H4
Luque • Paraguay 44 E4
Luquillo • Puerto Rico 125 E2
Luquillo, Sierra de • Puerto Rico 125 E2
Lura Nat. Park **Park** • Albania 72 [125]
Lure • France 9 B9
Luremo • Angola 23 B5
Lurgan • United Kingdom 7 F7
Lúrio • Mozambique 24 F2
Lusaka • Zambia 24 D3
Lusambo • Dem. Rep. of Congo 23 C4
Luserna **Ski** • Italy 70 [212]
Lushnjë • Albania 14 G9
Lushoto • Tanzania 102 H2
Lushui • China 29 B5
Lüshun • China 29 G3
Lussac-les-Châteaux • France 84 D4
Lut, Dasht-e • Iran 18 G3
Lutembo • Angola 24 C2
Lutolim • Goa, India 105 B2
Luton • United Kingdom 74 E1
Lutselk'e • NT, Canada 38 I4
Lutsk • Ukraine 17 D4
Lützen • Germany 9 H5
Lützow-Holmbukta • Antarctica 46 (1) I3
Luvua • Dem. Rep. of Congo 23 D5
Luwaymi, Al • Saudi Arabia 18 D4
Luwego • Tanzania 23 F5
Luwuk • Indonesia 32 (1) B3
Luxembourg • Europe 80 A20
Luxembourg [Adm] • Belgium 80 A19
Luxembourg-Ville **Heritage C** • Luxembourg 64 [29]
Luxembourg-Ville • Luxembourg 80 A20
Luxeuil-les-Bains • France 10 L6
Luxi • China 29 B6
Luxor • Egypt 101 F4
Luxu • Morocco 101 D1
Luy • France 10 E10
Luz • France 85 J2
Luz, Costa de la • Spain 86 B5
Luza • Russian Fed. 17 H2
Luzern • Switzerland 89 G3
Luzhou • China 29 D5
Luziânia • Brazil 44 G2
Luznice • Czech Rep. 96 C4
Luzon • Philippines 31 G3
Luzon Strait • Philippines 31 G2
Lviv • Ukraine 17 C5
Lvov • Ukraine 17 C5
Lyakhovskiy Ostrova • Russian Fed. 97 A5
Lyall, Mt • New Zealand 112 L1
Lycksele • Sweden 16 J4
Lydd • United Kingdom 5 D4
Lydd [Apt] • United Kingdom 74 E4
Lydford Cay • Bahamas 124 B3
Lydië • Turkey 15 I5
Lydstep **Beach** • United Kingdom 75 [151]
Lyme Bay • United Kingdom 74 F6
Lyme Regis • United Kingdom 74 F3
Lymington • United Kingdom 7 K11
Lymira • Turkey 93 G3
Lyna Alie • Poland 13 J3
Lynchburg • VA, United States 41 K4
Lynd • QL, Australia 34 H3
Lynn Lake • MN, Canada 38 L5
Lynnay, gora • Russian Fed. 27 R4
Lynton • United Kingdom 74 F2
Lynx Lake • NT, Canada 38 J4
Lyon • France 85 F1
Lyons • WA, Australia 34 C4
Lys • France 5 F4
Lysebotn • Norway 94 C6
Lysefjorden • Norway 94 C5
Lysekil • Sweden 95 F2
Lysva • Russian Fed. 26 I6
Lytham St Anne's • United Kingdom 7 I8
Lyubertsy • Russian Fed. 97 E4
Lyubimets • Bulgaria 15 H2

M'Sila • Algeria 20 F1
M'Zab Valley **Heritage C** • Algeria 64 [224]
Ma On Shan Country Park • Hong Kong, China 107 H6
Ma, Oued el • Mauritania 20 D4
Ma Wan • Hong Kong, China 107 H5
Ma'an • Jordan 18 B3
Ma'anshan • China 107 J1
Ma'aza Plateau • Egypt 101 F4
Ma'tan as Sarra • Libya 21 D3
Maafushi • Maldives 106 E4
Maam Turk Mtns • Ireland 79 F3
Maarianhamina • Finland 95 E3
Maarssen • Netherlands 80 C2
Maas • Netherlands 80 A12
Maas en Waal, Land van • Netherlands 80 C4
Maaseik • Belgium 5 I3
Maassluis • Netherlands 80 C3
Maastricht • Netherlands 80 A15
Maasvlakte • Netherlands 80 C3
Mablethorpe **Beach** • United Kingdom 75 [28]
Mabote • Mozambique 24 E4
Macaé • Brazil 127 C4
Maçanet • Spain 87 D2
Macapá • Brazil 43 G3
Macará • Ecuador 43 B4
Macas • Ecuador 43 B4
Macau • Brazil 45 (1) D2
Macau • Asia 107 H1
Macaúbas • Brazil 44 H1
Macauley • New Zealand 33 J9
Macclesfield • United Kingdom 7 J8
Macclesfield Bank • South China Sea 107 G8
Macdhui, Ben • United Kingdom 6 I4
Macdonald, Lake • NT/WA, Australia 112 H1
Macdonnell Ranges • NT, Australia 112 H2
Macedo de Cavaleiros • Portugal 11 E3
Macedonia • Greece 92 A1
Macedonia, F.Y.R. of • Europe 14 I8
Maceió • Brazil 45 (1) D3
Macenta • Guinea 22 C3
Macerata • Italy 12 H5
Macfarlane, Lake • SA, Australia 34 G6
Macgillicuddy's Reeks • Ireland 79 F7
Machaerus • Jordan 98 A8
Machakos • Kenya 101 G3
Machala • Ecuador 43 B4
Machareti • Bolivia 44 D3
Macheng • China 29 F4
Mácher • Lanzarote, Canary Is. 87 E3
Machico • Madeira 88 C2
Machilipatnam • India 106 D3
Machiques • Venezuela 43 C2
Machu Picchu • Peru 127 B2
Machu Picchu, Santuario histórico **Heritage N** • Peru 60 [33]
Machu Picchu, Santuario histórico **Heritage C** • Peru 62 [50]
Macia • Mozambique 24 E4
Macina Gourma • Mali 22 D1
Macinaggio • Corsica, France 85 L2
Macizo Galaico • Spain 11 D2
Mackay • QL, Australia 111 F3
Mackay, Lake • NT/WA, Australia 112 H1
Mackenzie • NT, Canada 38 E3
Mackenzie Bay • YT, Canada 38 D3
Mackenzie Bay • Kerguelen Is. 46 (1) L3
Mackenzie Delta • NT, Canada 122 A1
Mackenzie Mtns • NT/YT, Canada 38 F4
Mackerricher State Park • CA, United States 117 F1
Mackinac, Strait of • MI, United States 39 O7
Mackinnon Road • Kenya 101 G5
Maclear • South Africa 24 D6
MacLeod, Lake • WA, Australia 34 B4
Macmillan • YT, Canada 38 E4
Macomer • Sardinia, Italy 90 C1
Macon • GA, United States 41 J5
Mâcon • France 85 F1
Macondo • Angola 24 C2
Mâconnais • France 84 B2
Macquarie I. • Pacific Ocean 3 X10
Macquarie I. **Heritage N** • Southern Ocean 61 [139]
Macroom • Ireland 79 F8
Macugnaga • Italy 91 E1
Macujer • Colombia 43 C3
Macusani • Peru 127 B2
Madaba • Jordan 98 A8
Madagascar • Indian Ocean 24 H3
Madama • Niger 20 H4
Madan • Bulgaria 14 M8
Madang • Papua New Guinea 35 (1) D2
Madaoua • Niger 20 G6
Madara **Heritage C** • Bulgaria 64 [170]
Madara • Bulgaria 97 D3
Maddalena, I. • Sardinia, Italy 90 C2
Madeira • Brazil 43 E5
Madeira • Atlantic Ocean 88 C
Mädelegabel • Austria/Germany 82 J6
Madeleine, Is. de la • QU, Canada 123 D2
Madera • CA, United States 40 B4
Madera • Mexico 40 E6

Madésimo

Madésimo • Italy 91 E2
Madhar, Ra's • Saudi Arabia 21 G2
Madhya Pradesh • India 28 C4
Madikeri • India 106 D6
Madinah, Al • Saudi Arabia 18 C5
Madiran • France 84 B3
Madison • WI, United States 41 I3
Madison • IN, United States 41 I4
Madiun • Java, Indonesia 110 D7
Madoi • China 28 G1
Madone d'Utelle • France 85 H2
Madonie • Sicily, Italy 90 D2
Madonna di Campíglio **Ski** • Italy 70 [209]
Madonna di Campíglio • Italy 91 E3
Madra Dagi • Turkey 15 I4
Madrakah, Ra's al • Oman 18 G6
Madras • India 106 D7
Madre de Dios • Peru 127 B2
Madre de Dios [Riv] • Bolivia/Peru 44 C1
Madre Occidental, Sierra • Mexico 40 E6
Madre Oriental, Sierra • Mexico 40 F7
Madre, Sierra • Mexico 37 C4
Madrid • Spain 11 H4
Madrid, Comunidad de • Spain 11 H4
Madridejos • Spain 11 H5
Madura • Indonesia 110 D4
Madura, Selat • Java, Indonesia 110 D8
Madurai • India 106 D11
Madurodam • Netherlands 80 C3
Madyan • Saudi Arabia 21 G2
Mae Hong Son • Thailand 109 G1
Mae La Noi • Thailand 109 G3
Mae Ping Nat. Park • Thailand 109 G3
Mae Rim • Thailand 109 G1
Mae Sai • Thailand 109 G2
Mae Sariang • Thailand 109 G3
Mae Suai • Thailand 109 G2
Mae Taeng • Thailand 109 G1
Maebashi • Japan 30 J6
Mæl • Norway 94 B1
Maenam Beach • Ko Samui, Thailand 109 J1
Maestra, Sierra • Cuba 124 D8
Maevatanana • Madagascar 24 H3
Maéwo • Vanuatu 35 (2) B1
Mafeteng • Lesotho 24 D5
Mafia I. • Tanzania 102 H4
Mafikeng • South Africa 24 D5
Mafra • Brazil 44 G4
Mafra • Portugal 88 D1
Magadan • Russian Fed. 27 P5
Magadi • Kenya 101 G3
Magadino • Switzerland 89 G7
Magalluf • Majorca, Spain 87 H3
Magangué • Colombia 43 C2
Magaria • Niger 22 F2
Magarida • Papua New Guinea 34 I2
Magda Plateau • NU, Canada 39 O2
Magdagachi • Russian Fed. 27 K6
Magdalena • Mexico 40 D5
Magdalena • Colombia 43 C2
Magdalena • Bolivia 44 D1
Magdalena • Argentina 127 D2
Magdalena, I. • Mexico 123 E3
Magdeburg • Germany 8 G4
Magdelaine Cays • CL, Australia 34 J3
Magelang • Java, Indonesia 110 D7
Magellan, Strait of • Chile 45 B6
Magerøya • Norway 16 N1
Maggiore, Lago • Italy 91 E2
Maghâgha • Egypt 101 F3
Maghnia • Algeria 20 E2
Magic Hill Farm • OT, Canada 122 B5
Magic Kingdom • FL, United States 121 C1
Magic Valley • NS, Canada 123 D7
Magical World of Fantasy Island **Park** • United Kingdom 73 [28]
Maglaj • Bosnia-Herz. 12 M4
Maglic • F.R. of Yugoslavia 14 F6
Maglie • Italy 12 M8
Máglie • Italy 12 M9
Magnetic I. • QL, Australia 111 F1
Magnitogorsk • Russian Fed. 26 I7
Magnor • Norway 94 B2
Magny-en-Vexin • France 85 E1
Mago • Russian Fed. 27 N6
Mago Nat. Park **Park** • Ethiopia 103 [66]
Magoebaskloof • South Africa 24 D4
Magoulades **Beach** • Corfu, Greece 69 [170]
Magouládes • Corfu, Greece 92 B1
Maguarinho, Cabo • Brazil 45 (1) B2
Magwe • Myanmar 31 B2
Maha Sarakhan • Thailand 31 C3
Mahabad • Iran 18 E2
Mahabalipuram **Heritage C** • India 63 [130]
Mahabalipuram • India 106 D7
Mahafaly, Plateau • Madagascar 24 G4
Mahajan • India 105 C2
Mahajanga • Madagascar 24 H3
Mahakam • Indonesia 32 F3
Mahalapye • Botswana 24 D4
Mahanadi • India 28 D4
Maharashtra • India 28 C4
Mahaweli Ganga • Sri Lanka 106 D15
Mahbubnagar • India 106 D3
Mahdia • Guyana 43 F2
Mahdia • Tunisia 101 E4
Mahe • India 106 D10
Mahé • Seychelles 106 F1
Mahenge • Tanzania 102 H4
Mahesana • India 28 B4
Mahi • India 28 B4
Mahia Peninsula • New Zealand 35 F4
Mahilov • Belarus 17 E4
Mahlow • Germany 81 F4
Mahón **Beach** • Minorca, Spain 68 [127]
Mahón • Minorca, Spain 87 F4
Mähren • Czech Rep. 13 F8
Mahrès • Tunisia 101 E4
Mai Khao Beach • Phuket, Thailand 109 K1
Mai Ndombe, Lac • Dem. Rep. of Congo 23 B4
Mai Po Marsh • Hong Kong, China 107 H3
Mai-Ndombe, Lac • Dem. Rep. of Congo 22 H5
Maicao • Colombia 43 C1
Maiden Castle • United Kingdom 74 F3
Maiden I. • Antigua & Barbuda 125 F2
Maidstone • United Kingdom 74 E4
Maiduguri • Nigeria 22 G2
Maihar • India 105 C7
Maiko, Parc nat. de la **Park** • Dem. Rep. of Congo 103 [57]
Maikona • Kenya 23 F3
Maili • HI, United States 119 L5
Main • Germany 9 E7
Main Barrier Range • NS, Australia 34 H6
Main-Donau-Kanal • Germany 9 G7
Maínalon • Greece 15 D6
Mainau • Germany 82 J5
Mainburg • Germany 9 G8
Maine • France 10 D5
Maine • United States 118 G2
Maine, Gulf of • Canada/United States 39 R8
Maine-et-Loire • France 84 D1
Mainique, Pongo • Peru 127 B2
Mainland • Orkney, UK 6 I2
Mainland • Shetland, UK 6 K1
Maintenon • France 85 E3
Mainz • Germany 82 H4
Maio • Cape Verde 22 (1) B1
Maipo, Volcá • Argentina 44 C5
Maipú • Argentina 127 D4
Maira • Italy 10 M9
Maisi, Cabo • Cuba 124 D8
Maitland • NS, Australia 111 G2
Maíz, Is. del • Nicaragua 43 A1
Maizhokunggar • China 28 F3
Maizuru • Japan 30 H7
Majalengka • Java, Indonesia 110 D2
Majene • Indonesia 32 (1) A3
Majerten • Somalia 23 H2
Majete Game Reserve **Park** • Malawi 103 [100]
Majevica • Bosnia-Herz. 14 F5
Maji • Ethiopia 23 F2
Major, Puig • Majorca, Spain 87 H1
Major's Bay • St Kitts & Nevis 125 G4
Majorca • Spain 87 H
Majorda • Goa, India 105 B2
Majorda Beach • Goa, India 105 B2
Majuro • Marshall Is. 33 I5
Makaha • HI, United States 119 L5
Makakan • Indonesia 32 F3
Makakilo City • HI, United States 119 L5
Makale • Indonesia 32 (1) A3
Makallé • Argentina 44 E4
Makalondi • Niger 20 F6
Makambako • Tanzania 102 H3
Makanza • Dem. Rep. of Congo 23 B3
Makari Mtns • Tanzania 102 H1
Makarikari • Botswana 24 D4
Makarov • Russian Fed. 27 N7
Makarska • Croatia 14 E6
Makassar, Selat • Indonesia 25 M10
Makassar Strait • Indonesia 32 F3
Makat • Kazakhstan 17 I5
Makaw • Myanmar 31 B1
Makaza • Bulgaria/Greece 14 M8
Makedonía • Greece 15 D3
Makeni • Sierra Leone 22 B3
Makgadikgadi Pans • Botswana 24 D3
Makgadikgadi Pans Game Reserve **Park** • Botswana 103 [112]
Makhachkala • Russian Fed. 17 H6
Makhan • Phuket, Thailand 109 K2
Makhan Bay • Phuket, Thailand 109 K2
Makhan Beach • Phuket, Thailand 109 K2
Makheras Monastery • Cyprus 93 J3
Makinsk • Kazakhstan 26 L7
Makkah • Saudi Arabia 18 C5
Makó • Hungary 13 J11
Makokou • Gabon 22 G4
Makongolosi • Tanzania 102 H3
Makorako, Mt • New Zealand 112 K4
Makoua • Congo 22 H4
Makran • Iran/Pakistan 18 H4
Makrigialós **Beach** • Greece 69 [190]
Makrigialós • Crete, Greece 93 E8
Makthar • Tunisia 101 E1
Makunudhoo • Maldives 106 E2
Makunudu Atoll • Maldives 106 E1
Makurazaki • Japan 30 F9
Makurdi • Nigeria 22 F3
Malå • Sweden 16 J4
Mala Kapela • Croatia 14 C5
Mala, Punta • Panama 37 E6
Malabang • Philippines 31 G5
Malabar Coast • India 106 D10
Malabo • Equatorial Guinea 22 F4
Malacca • Malaysia 108 A4
Malacca, Strait of • Indonesia/Malaysia 32 B2
Malacky • Slovak Rep. 13 G9
Málaga • Colombia 43 C2
Málaga **Beach** • Spain 68 [114]
Málaga • Spain 86 B7
Malagarasi • Tanzania 102 H1
Malahide • Ireland 79 E2
Malaimbandy • Madagascar 24 H4
Malaita • Solomon Is. 35 (1) G2
Malakal • Sudan 23 E2
Malakula • Vanuatu 35 (2) B2
Malan, D.F. [Apt] • South Africa 100 C5
Malang • Java, Indonesia 110 D8
Malanje • Angola 23 B5
Malanville • Benin 20 F6
Mälaren • Sweden 95 D3
Malatya • Turkey 18 C2
Malawi • Africa 24 E2
Malawi, Lake • Africa 24 E2
Malay Peninsula • Malaysia 31 C5
Malaya Vishera • Russian Fed. 97 E1
Malaybalay • Philippines 31 G5
Malaysia • Asia 31 C6
Malbork • Poland 13 I3
Malbork **Heritage C** • Poland 64 [136]
Malbun • Liechtenstein 89 H5
Malcésine • Italy 91 E3
Malchin • Germany 8 H3
Malchow • Germany 8 H3
Malden • Kiribati 33 L6
Maldives • Indian Ocean 106 E
Maldon • United Kingdom 7 M10
Maldonado • Uruguay 127 D2
Malé • Maldives 106 E4
Malé Atoll • Maldives 106 E2
Maléas, Akra • Greece 92 D7
Malegaon • India 28 B4
Máleme **Beach** • Crete, Greece 69 [212]
Máleme • Crete, Greece 93 E1
Målerås • Sweden 95 F8
Malgomaj • Sweden 16 H4
Malgrat de Mar **Beach** • Spain 68 [122]
Malgrat de Mar • Spain 87 D4
Malha Wells • Sudan 21 E4
Malhalla el Kubra, El • Egypt 101 F1
Malheur Lake • OR, United States 117 E4
Mali • Africa 20 E5
Mali i Krabit • Albania 14 G7
Mália **Beach** • Crete, Greece 69 [214]
Mália • Crete, Greece 93 E7
Mália [Hist.] • Crete, Greece 93 E7
Malibu • CA, United States 117 F6
Malik, Wadi al • Sudan 21 E4
Malimba, Mtns • Dem. Rep. of Congo 23 D5
Malin Head • Ireland 6 E6
Malindi • Kenya 101 G3
Malindi Marine Game Reserve • Kenya 101 G5
Malindi Marine Nat. Park • Kenya 101 G3
Malindidzimu • Zimbabwe 102 J3
Malino, Bukit • Indonesia 32 (1) B2
Malion, Kólpos • Crete, Greece 93 E3
Maljen • F.R. of Yugoslavia 14 G5
Malkara • Turkey 15 H3
Malko Turnovo • Bulgaria 15 I2
Mallacoota • VI, Australia 111 G4
Mallaig • United Kingdom 6 G4
Mallawi • Egypt 18 A4
Mallorca • Spain 87 H
Mallow • Ireland 79 F8
Malmberget • Sweden 16 K3
Malmédy • Belgium 5 J4
Malmesbury • United Kingdom 74 D4
Malmesbury • South Africa 100 C5
Malmköping • Sweden 95 D3
Malmö **Beach** • Sweden 68 [11]
Malmö • Sweden 95 F11
Malo • Vanuatu 35 (2) B2
Maloja **Ski** • Switzerland 70 [121]
Malolotja Nature Reserve **Park** • Swaziland 103 [132]
Malónas • Rhodes, Greece 93 F2
Malonga • Dem. Rep. of Congo 24 C2
Malosmadulu Atoll North • Maldives 106 E1
Malosmadulu Atoll South • Maldives 106 E1
Måløy • Norway 94 C1
Malpelo • Colombia 43 A3
Malpensa [Apt] • Italy 91 E6
Malpica **Beach** • Spain 68 [92]
Malprabha • India 28 C5
Malsch • Germany 82 G6
Malta • MT, United States 40 E2
Malta • Europe 93 H
Malta Channel • Italy/Malta 12 I12
Maltepe • Turkey 15 K3
Maluku, Kepulauan • Indonesia 32 (1) C2
Malunda • Indonesia 32 (1) A3
Malung • Sweden 16 G6
Malut • Sudan 23 E1
Maluu • Solomon Is. 35 (1) G2
Malvasia • Greece 71 A20
Malveira da Serra • Portugal 88 D1
Malvern Hills • United Kingdom 74 D3
Malvinas, Is. • Atlantic Ocean 45 E6
Malwan • India 106 D1
Maly Karmakuly • Russian Fed. 26 H3
Malyy Lyakhovskiy, Ostrov • Russian Fed. 27 N2
Mama • Russian Fed. 27 H5
Mamaia-Bai • Romania 97 D2
Mamaia-Sat • Romania 97 D2
Mambéré • Africa 23 A2
Mambrui • Kenya 101 G3
Mammoth Cave Nat. Park **Heritage N** • KY, United States 60 [15]
Mammoth Cave Nat. Park **Park** • KY, United States 121 [235]
Mammoth Lakes • CA, United States 117 F4
Mammoth Mtn **Ski** • CA, United States 116 [63]
Mamonovo • Russian Fed. 13 J3
Mamoré • Bolivia 44 C1
Mamou • Guinea 22 B2
Mamoutzou • Mayotte 23 H6
Mamuju • Indonesia 32 (1) A3
Mamuno • Botswana 24 C4
Mamunta-Mayoso Wildlife Sanctuary **Park** • Sierra Leone 103 [15]
Man • Côte d'Ivoire 22 C3
Man, Isle of • Europe 7 H7
Man of War Bay • Trinidad & Tobago 125 K2
Mana Pools Nat. Park **Heritage N** • Zimbabwe 61 [96]
Mana Pools Nat. Park • Zimbabwe 102 J2
Mana Pools Nat. Park **Park** • Zimbabwe 103 [107]
Manacapuru • Brazil 43 E4
Manacor **Beach** • Majorca, Spain 68 [126]
Manacor • Majorca, Spain 87 H2
Manado • Indonesia 32 (1) B2
Managua • Nicaragua 37 D5
Manakara • Madagascar 24 H4
Manamah, Al • Bahrain 18 F4
Manambolo • Madagascar 24 H3
Manapouri • New Zealand 112 L3
Manapouri, Lake • New Zealand 112 L3
Manar • Yemen 21 H5
Manas • China 26 O9
Manas Wildlife Sanctuary **Heritage N** • India 61 [107]
Manassas Nat. Battlefield Park **Park** • VA, United States 121 [265]
Manasseh • Israel/Jordan 98 A4
Manatí • Puerto Rico 125 E1
Manatí, Río Grande de • Puerto Rico 125 E2
Manaus • Brazil 43 E4
Manavgat **Beach** • Turkey 69 [222]
Manavgat • Turkey 93 G4
Manche, la • France/UK 10 D3
Manchester • United Kingdom 7 J8
Manchskaya Vpadina • Russian Fed. 17 G5
Manchuria • China 107 G4
Mand • Iran 18 F4
Manda • Sudan 21 D6
Manda • Tanzania 102 H3
Manda I. • Kenya 101 G4
Manda, Jabal • Sudan 23 C2
Mandab, Bab al • Africa/Asia 21 H5
Mandaguari • Brazil 44 F3
Mandal • Norway 95 F1
Mandala, Puncak • Indonesia 32 (1) F3
Mandalay • Myanmar 31 B2
Mandalgovi • Mongolia 29 D1
Mandalselva • Norway 95 F1
Mandan • ND, United States 40 F2
Mandara, Mts • Cameroon 21 B5
Mandas • Sardinia, Italy 12 D9
Mandawa • India 105 C2
Mandelieu **Beach** • France 68 [134]
Mandera • Kenya 101 G2
Mandera [Region] • Kenya 101 G2
Manderscheid • Germany 82 H3
Manderscheid **Spa** • Germany 83 [160]
Mandeville • Jamaica 124 C3
Mandingues, Mts • Mali 22 B2
Mandla • India 28 C4
Mandore • India 105 C5
Mandoúdi • Greece 15 E5
Mandrem Beach • Goa, India 105 B1
Mandritsara • Madagascar 24 H3
Mandsaur • India 105 C6
Mandurah • WA, Australia 34 C6
Manduria • Italy 12 L8
Mandvi • India 18 I5
Mandzavinata **Beach** • Greece 69 [171]
Mandzavinata • Greece 92 C2
Manendragarh • India 28 D4
Manfalût • Egypt 18 A4
Manfredonia • Italy 12 J7
Manfredonia, Golfo di • Italy 12 K7
Manga • Niger 20 H6
Manga • Brazil 45 (1) C4
Mangalia • Romania 97 D2
Mangalore • India 106 D6
Mángana **Beach** • Greece 69 [195]
Mangaratiba • Brazil 127 C3
Mangareva • French Polynesia 33 N8
Manger • Norway 94 C3
Mangfall • Germany 82 J3
Manggar • Indonesia 32 D3
Mangin Yoma • Myanmar 31 B2
Mangnai • China 28 F1
Mangoky • Madagascar 24 G4
Mangole • Indonesia 32 (1) C3
Mangueira, Lagoa • Brazil 44 F5
Mangueni, Plateau de • Niger 20 H4
Mangui • China 27 J6
Manhattan • NY, United States 118 H2
Manhuaçu • Brazil 127 C2
Mani • Colombia 43 C3
Manía • Madagascar 24 H3
Manica • Mozambique 102 J2
Manicaland • Zimbabwe 102 J2
Manicouagan • QU, Canada 39 R6
Manicouagan, Réservoir • QU, Canada 39 R6
Manihiki • Cook Is. 33 K7
Manila • Philippines 31 G4
Manila **Heritage C** • Philippines 63 [176]
Manila Bay • Philippines 31 G4
Manilva **Beach** • Spain 68 [114]
Manilva • Spain 86 B6
Maningrida Settlement • NT, Australia 34 F2
Maninjau, Danau • Indonesia 110 B4
Manipur • India 28 F4
Manises • Spain 11 K5
Manitoba • Canada 38 L5
Manitoba, Lake • MN, Canada 38 L6
Manitoulin • OT, Canada 39 O7
Maniwaki • QU, Canada 122 B2
Manizales • Colombia 43 B3
Manja • Madagascar 24 G4
Manjimup • WA, Australia 34 C6
Manjira • India 28 C5
Månkarbo • Sweden 95 D1
Mankato • MN, United States 41 H3
Mankono • Côte d'Ivoire 22 C3
Manley, Norman [Apt] • Jamaica 124 C4
Manlleu • Spain 11 N3
Manly • Russian Fed. 27 S4
Manmanoc, Mt • Philippines 31 G3
Mann • NT, Australia 34 F2
Mann Ranges • NT/SA, Australia 112 H3
Manna • Indonesia 32 C3
Mannar • Sri Lanka 106 D11
Mannar, Gulf of • India/Sri Lanka 106 D15
Mannheim • Germany 82 G4
Manning • AL, Canada 38 H5
Mannu, Capu • Sardinia, Italy 12 C8
Mannu, Rio • Sardinia, Italy 12 C8
Manoa • Bolivia 43 D6
Manokwari • Indonesia 32 (1) D3
Manombo • Madagascar 24 G4
Mañón **Beach** • Spain 68 [92]
Manono • Dem. Rep. of Congo 23 D5
Manorbier **Beach** • United Kingdom 75 [153]
Manosque • France 85 H1
Manovo-Gounda St Floris, Parc nat. de **Heritage N** • Central African Rep. 61 [79]
Manovo-Gounda-St Floris, Parc nat. **Park** • Central African Rep. 103 [44]
Manp'ojin • D.P.R. of Korea 30 D4
Manra • Kiribati 33 J6
Manresa • Spain 87 D3
Mans, le • France 84 D2
Mansa Konko • Gambia 22 A2
Mansel I. • NU, Canada 39 P4
Mansfield • United Kingdom 7 K8
Mansfield • OH, United States 41 J3
Mansfield • LA, United States 118 K1
Mansion • St Kitts & Nevis 125 G1
Mansura • LA, United States 118 K3
Mansûra, El • Egypt 101 F2
Manta • Ecuador 43 A4
Manta, Bahía de • Ecuador 43 A4
Mantaro • Peru 127 B1
Mantes-la-Jolie • France 85 E1
Mantiqueira, Serra da • Brazil 127 C3
Mantova • Italy 91 E7
Mäntsälä • Finland 95 E4
Mänttä • Finland 95 E2
Mantua • Italy 91 E7
Manturovo • Russian Fed. 17 G3
Manú • Peru 127 B2
Manu Bay • New Zealand 112 K1
Manú, Parque Nac. **Heritage N** • Peru 60 [34]
Manú, Parque Nac. • Peru 127 B2
Manua • American Samoa 35 (2) G1
Manukau • New Zealand 35 E3
Manuoha, Mt • New Zealand 112 K2
Many • LA, United States 118 K1
Manyara Nat. Park • Tanzania 102 H2
Manyas-Kuscenneti Nat. Park **Park** • Turkey 72 [142]
Manyas-Kuscenneti Nat. Park • Turkey 92 D3
Manyoni • Tanzania 102 H1
Manzanar Nat. Hist. Site **Park** • CA, United States 120 [54]
Manzanares • Spain 11 H5
Manzanilla Point • Trinidad & Tobago 125 K4
Manzanillo • Mexico 123 E3
Manzanillo • Cuba 124 D7
Manzhouli • China 27 I7
Mao • Chad 21 B5
Maó **Beach** • Minorca, Spain 68 [127]
Maó • Minorca, Spain 87 F4
Mao Shan • China 107 J1
Maoke, Pegunungan • Indonesia 32 (1) E3
Maomao Shan • China 29 C3
Maoming • China 29 E6
Maotou Shan • China 31 C2
Mapi • Indonesia 32 (1) E4
Mapi [Riv] • Indonesia 32 (1) E4
Mapia, Kepulauan • Indonesia 32 (1) D2
Maple Creek • SA, Canada 38 J7
Mapou, Ko • Thailand 109 K2
Maprik • Papua New Guinea 35 (1) C1
Mapuera • Brazil 43 F4
Mapusa • Goa, India 105 B1
Maputo • Mozambique 24 E5
Maputo, Baia de • Mozambique 24 E5
Maputo Elephant Reserve **Park** • Mozambique 103 [134]
Maqaman Nabi Musá • Jordan 98 A8
Maquan He • China 28 D3
Maquinchao • Argentina 45 C4
Mar Chiquita, Lago • Argentina 127 D4
Mar Chiquita, Laguna • Argentina 44 D5
Mar del Plata • Argentina 127 D4
Mar del Tuyú • Argentina 127 D4
Mar, Serra do • Brazil 127 C3
Mara • Kenya/Tanzania 23 E4
Marabá • Brazil 43 H5
Maracá • Brazil 43 G3
Maracaibo • Venezuela 43 C1
Maracaibo, Lago de • Venezuela 43 C2
Maracaju • Brazil 44 E3
Maracaju, Serra de • Brazil 44 E3
Maracás • Brazil 44 H1
Maracas Bay • Trinidad & Tobago 125 K1
Maracay • Venezuela 43 D1
Maradi • Niger 20 G6
Marahoué, Parc nat. de la **Park** • Côte d'Ivoire 103 [20]
Marahuaca • Venezuela 43 D3
Marajó, Baía de • Brazil 45 (1) B2
Marajó, I. de • Brazil 43 G4
Maralal Game Reserve • Kenya 101 G1
Maralinga • SA, Australia 34 F6
Maramba • Zambia 24 D3
Marand • Iran 18 E2
Maranhão • Brazil 45 (1) B3
Marano, Laguna di • Italy 12 H3
Marañón • Peru 43 B4
Marão, Serra do • Portugal 11 D3
Maratea • Italy 12 J8
Maratea **Beach** • Italy 69 [150]
Maratea • Italy 90 A2
Marateca • Portugal 88 D2
Marathiá, Akra • Greece 92 C3
Marathon • OT, Canada 39 N7
Marathon • OT, Canada 41 I2
Marathón • Greece 92 D4
Marathon • FL, United States 119 M8
Márathospilo • Crete, Greece 93 E2
Marawi • Sudan 21 F4
Marbella **Beach** • Spain 68 [114]
Marbella • Spain 86 B6
Marble Bar • WA, Australia 34 C4
Marble Canyon • AZ, United States 118 J1
Marburg • Germany 82 G2
Marcali • Hungary 12 L2
March • United Kingdom 7 M9
March • Austria 13 F9
Marche • France 10 G7
Marche • Italy 91 E12
Marche-en-Famenne • Belgium 80 A19
Marchena • Spain 11 F7
Marchena • Galapagos Is. 43 (1) A1
Märchenwald im Isartal • Germany 82 J3
Marches, The • United Kingdom 74 D1
Marcianise • Italy 91 G1
Marco I. • FL, United States 119 M7
Marconi, G [Apt] • Italy 91 E7
Marcos Juárez • Argentina 44 D5
Marcus • Pacific Ocean 33 G3
Marcy • NY, United States 41 L3
Mardan • Pakistan 28 B2
Mardin • Turkey 92 A4
Maré • New Caledonia 35 (2) B3
Maree, Loch • United Kingdom 6 G4
Mareeba • QL, Australia 111 F1
Mareg • Somalia 23 H3
Maremma • Italy 91 E11
Marennes • France 85 G1
Mareth • Tunisia 101 E6
Maréttimo, I. • Italy 90 D1
Marfa Point • Malta 93 H1
Margai Caka • China 28 E1
Margao • Goa, India 105 B2
Margaret • WA, Australia 34 C6
Margarita • Venezuela 43 E1
Margaríti • Greece 15 B4
Margate • United Kingdom 74 E2
Margate **Beach** • United Kingdom 75 [62]
Margaux • France 85 G1
Margeride, Mts de la • France 10 I8
Marguerite Bay • Antarctica 46 (1) HH3
Mari-El • Russian Fed. 17 H3
Maria • Tubuai Is., French Polynesia 33 L8
Maria • Gambier Is., French Polynesia 33 N8
Maria Alm **Ski** • Austria 70 [165]
María Elena • Chile 44 C3
Maria Is. • St Lucia 125 J4
Maria Laach • Germany 82 H1
Mariana • Brazil 127 C2
Marianao • Cuba 37 E3
Marianas Trench • Pacific Ocean 25 Q8
Mariankani • Kenya 101 G5
Marianna • FL, United States 119 M2
Marianne • Seychelles 106 F4
Mariannelund • Sweden 95 F8
Mariánské Lázne • Czech Rep. 96 C1
Mariapfarr **Ski** • Austria 70 [186]
Marias, I. • Mexico 123 E7
Marias, Is • Mexico 37 (1) A1
Mariato, Punta • Panama 37 E6
Marib • Yemen 18 E6
Maribo • Denmark 95 F14
Maribor • Slovenia 13 E11
Marie Byrd Land • Antarctica 46 (1) BB2
Marie Louise • Seychelles 106 F2
Marie-Galante • Guadeloupe 37 I4
Mariedamm • Sweden 95 F4
Mariefred • Sweden 95 D3
Mariehamn • Finland 95 E3
Mariel • Cuba 124 D1
Marienbad • Czech Rep. 96 C1
Marienheide • Germany 81 E4
Mariental • Namibia 24 B4
Mariestad • Sweden 95 F3
Marietta • GA, United States 41 J5
Marignane [Apt] • France 85 H3
Marigot Bay • St Lucia 125 J1
Marigot Harbour • St Lucia 125 J1
Mariinsk • Russian Fed. 26 O6
Marijampolé • Lithuania 13 M3
Marília • Brazil 44 F3
Marilléva **Ski** • Italy 70 [207]
Marilléva • Italy 91 E3
Marimba • Angola 24 B1
Marín • Spain 11 C2
Marín **Beach** • Spain 68 [93]
Marin, Luis Muñoz [Apt] • Puerto Rico 125 E2
Marina Bay • Singapore 108 E4
Marina del Rey • CA, United States 117 F6
Marina di Massa • Italy 91 E10
Marina di Pietrasanta • Italy 91 E10
Marina di Pisa • Italy 12 E5
Marinduque • Philippines 31 G4
Marine World Africa USA **Park** • CA, United States 120 [A]
Marineland of Florida • FL, United States 119 M4
Marinella, Golfo di • Sardinia, Italy 90 C2
Maringa • Dem. Rep. of Congo 23 C3
Maringá • Brazil 44 F3
Marinha Grande • Portugal 11 C5
Marinha Grande **Beach** • Portugal 68 [97]
Marino • Italy 12 G7
Marion Reef • CL, Australia 111 F2
Maripa • Venezuela 43 D2
Mariposa • CA, United States 117 F3
Marisa • Indonesia 32 (1) B2
Mariscal Estigarribia • Paraguay 44 D3
Marismas, Las • Spain 86 B1
Maritime Museum • Singapore 108 E4
Maritsa • Europe 14 M7
Mariupol • Ukraine 17 F5
Marj, Al • Libya 21 D1
Marka • Somalia 23 G3
Markaryd • Sweden 95 F11
Marken • Netherlands 80 C2
Markermeer • Netherlands 80 C2
Market Harborough • United Kingdom 7 L9
Markha • Russian Fed. 27 J4
Markha [Riv] • Russian Fed. 27 I3
Markham, Mt • Antarctica 46 (1) V1
Marki • Poland 13 K5
Märkisch Wilmersdorf • Germany 81 F3
Markópoulo **Beach** • Greece 69 [185]
Markounda • Central African Rep. 22 H3
Markovo • Russian Fed. 27 T4
Markschellenberg **Spa** • Germany 83 [262]
Marktheidenfeld • Germany 9 E7
Marktoberdorf • Germany 82 J6
Marktredwitz • Germany 9 H6
Marl • Germany 5 K3
Marl • Germany 81 E2
Marlboro • VT, United States 118 G3
Marlborough • QL, Australia 111 F4
Marlborough • New Zealand 112 J4
Marle • France 5 G5
Marlin • TX, United States 119 N3
Marlin Coast • QL, Australia 111 F1
Marloes **Beach** • United Kingdom 75 [159]
Marlow • United Kingdom 74 E1
Marmalete • Portugal 88 E1
Marmande • France 85 G3
Marmara • Turkey 15 I3
Marmara Adasi • Turkey 92 D3
Marmara Ereglisi • Turkey 15 I3
Marmara Gölü • Turkey 15 I5
Marmara, Sea of • Turkey 92 D3
Marmári • Greece 92 D4
Marmaris **Beach** • Turkey 69 [232]
Marmaris • Turkey 92 D9
Mármaro • Greece 92 D5
Marmarole, Gruppo delle • Italy 90 B4
Marmolada • Italy 90 B4
Marmot Basin **Ski** • AL, Canada 116 [11]
Marne • France 10 I4
Marne au Rhin, Canal de la • France 10 J5
Maro • Chad 21 C6
Maro [Riv] • Chad 20 I5
Maroantsetra • Madagascar 24 H3
Maromokotro • Madagascar 24 H2
Marondera • Zimbabwe 102 J2
Marónia • Greece 92 D2
Maroochydore • QL, Australia 111 F6
Maroua • Cameroon 22 G2
Márpissa **Beach** • Greece 69 [205]
Marquesas • French Polynesia 33 N6
Marquette • MI, United States 41 I2
Marquette, Father, Nat. Mem. & Museum **Park** • MI, United States 121 [162]
Marquis • St Lucia 125 J2
Marquis, Cape • St Lucia 125 J2
Marrah • Sudan 21 D5
Marrah, Jabal • Sudan 21 D5
Marrakech **Heritage C** • Morocco 64 [217]
Marrakech • Morocco 101 D3
Marree • SA, Australia 34 G5
Marromeu • Mozambique 24 F3
Marromeu, Reserve de **Park** • Mozambique 103 [136]
Marsá al Burayquah • Libya 21 C1
Marsa Alam • Egypt 101 F5
Marsa, El • France 11 L8
Marsabit • Kenya 101 G2
Marsabit Game Reserve • Kenya 101 G2
Marsabit Nat. Park • Kenya 101 G2
Marsabit Nat. Park **Park** • Kenya 103 [75]
Marsala • Sicily, Italy 90 D1
Marsalforn • Malta 93 H1
Marsalforn Bay • Malta 93 H1
Marsaskala • Malta 93 H4
Marsaxlokk • Malta 93 H4
Marsaxlokk Bay • Malta 93 H4
Marsberg • Germany 8 D5
Marseille • France 85 H3
Marsh Harbour • Bahamas 124 B1
Marsh I. • LA, United States 118 K3
Marshall • MN, United States 41 G3
Marshall • TX, United States 119 N2
Marshall Is. • Pacific Ocean 33 H4
Marshfield • WI, United States 41 H3
Marssum • Netherlands 80 A3
Märsta • Sweden 95 D2
Marstal **Beach** • Denmark 68 [44]
Marstal • Denmark 95 F14
Marston Moor • United Kingdom 71 A7
Marstrand • Sweden 95 F6
Martaban, Gulf of • Myanmar 31 B3
Martha Brae • Jamaica 124 C1
Martha's Vineyard • MA, United States 118 H2
Marthaville • LA, United States 118 K1
Martí • Cuba 124 D7
Martí,José [Apt] • Cuba 124 D2
Martigny • Switzerland 89 G6
Martigues • France 10 K10
Martigues **Beach** • France 68 [132]
Martil • Morocco 101 D2
Martim Longo • Portugal 88 E4
Martin • Slovak Rep. 13 H8
Martin Vaz, Is. • Atlantic Ocean 19 B8
Martin Vaz, Is. • Brazil 127 A2
Martin's Haven **Beach** • United Kingdom 75 [160]
Martinique • West Indies 37 I5
Martins Bay • New Zealand 112 L2
Marton • New Zealand 35 E5
Martorell • Spain 87 D3
Martos • Spain 11 H7
Martre, Lac la • NT, Canada 38 H4
Martti • Finland 16 O3

Marungu, Mtns •
Dem. Rep. of Congo 23 D5
Marv-Dasht • Iran 18 F4
Marvão • Portugal 11 D5
Marwar • India 105 C5
Mary • Turkmenistan 18 H2
Mary Jane **Ski** •
CO, United States 116 [90]
Maryborough • QL, Australia 111 F6
Maryborough • VI, Australia 111 G3
Maryport • United Kingdom 74 C1
Marysville • CA, United States 40 B4
Maryville • MO, United States 41 H3
Maryville • TN, United States 41 J4
Masada • Israel 98 A8
Masai • Malaysia 108 E2
Masai Mara Game Reserve • Kenya 101 G3
Masai Mara Nat. Reserve **Park** •
Kenya 103 [82]
Masai Steppe • Tanzania 102 H2
Masaka • Uganda 23 E4
Masalembo, Kepulauan •
Indonesia 110 D4
Masan • Rep. of Korea 30 E7
Másari • Rhodes, Greece 93 F2
Masasi • Tanzania 102 H4
Masbate • Philippines 31 G4
Masbate [I.] • Philippines 31 G4
Mascara • Algeria 20 F1
Maseru • Lesotho 24 D5
Mashabih • Saudi Arabia 21 G2
Mashhad • Iran 18 G2
Mashonaland • Zimbabwe 102 J2
Masindi • Uganda 23 E3
Masirah, Jazirat • Oman 18 G5
Masirah, Khalij • Oman 18 G6
Mask, Lough • Ireland 79 F4
Maskad, Al • Somalia 23 H1
Mason City • IA, United States 41 H3
Mason's Limestone Valley •
New Zealand 112 K1
Maspalomas •
Gran Canaria, Canary Is. 86 E4
Massa • Italy 12 E4
Massa Lubrense • Italy 91 G3
Massa Marittima • Italy 91 E11
Massachusetts • United States 41 L3
Massafra • Italy 12 L8
Massaguet • Chad 23 B1
Massangena • Mozambique 24 E4
Massanutten **Ski** •
VA, United States 116 [157]
Massawa • Eritrea 21 G4
Massénya • Chad 20 I6
Masserberg **Spa** • Germany 83 [307]
Masset • BC, Canada 38 E6
Massif Central • France 10 H8
Massinga • Mozambique 24 F4
Massy • France 85 E3
Masterton • New Zealand 35 E5
Mastigouche Prov. Park •
QU, Canada 122 B3
Masuda • Japan 30 F7
Masuguru • Tanzania 102 H4
Masurai, Gunung • Indonesia 32 C3
Masuria • Poland 96 B1
Masuriska Sjöarna • Poland 13 K4
Masvingo • Zimbabwe 102 J4
Mat Lang, Ko • Thailand 109 J1
Mata-Utu • Wallis & Futuna 35 (2) E1
Matabeleland • Zimbabwe 102 J3
Matadi • Dem. Rep. of Congo 23 A5
Matagalpa • Nicaragua 37 D5
Matagami • QU, Canada 39 P7
Matagorda • TX, United States 119 N6
Matagorda Bay •
TX, United States 119 N5
Matagorda I. •
TX, United States 119 N5
Matagorda Peninsula •
TX, United States 119 N6
Matakana I. • New Zealand 112 K2
Matala • Angola 24 B2
Matala • Crete, Greece 93 E6
Matalascanas, Playa de • Spain 86 B5
Matale • Sri Lanka 106 D15
Matam • Senegal 20 C5
Matamata • New Zealand 112 K2
Matamoros • Mexico 37 B2
Matane • QU, Canada 123 D1
Matanzas • Cuba 124 D2
Matanzas, Fort, Nat. Mon. •
FL, United States 119 M4
Matanzas, Fort, Nat. Mon. **Park** •
FL, United States 121 [222]
Matapédia • QU, Canada 123 D2
Matara • Eritrea 21 G5
Matara • Sri Lanka 106 D15
Mataram • Indonesia 32 F4
Matarani • Peru 127 B4
Mataranka • NT, Australia 34 F2
Mataró • Spain 87 D4
Mataura • New Zealand 112 L4
Mataura [Riv] • New Zealand 112 L4
Matehuala • Mexico 123 E1
Matélica • Italy 91 E12
Matelot • Trinidad & Tobago 125 K2
Matera • Italy 12 K8
Matera **Heritage C** • Italy 64 [131]
Matese, Monti del • Italy 91 G1
Mátészalka • Hungary 13 L10
Mateur • Tunisia 101 E2
Mathura • India 105 C2
Mati • Albania 14 H8
Mati • Philippines 31 H5
Matlock • United Kingdom 7 K8
Matmata • Tunisia 101 E6
Mato Grosso • Brazil 44 E2
Mato Grosso [Adm] • Brazil 44 E1
Mato Grosso do Sul • Brazil 44 E2
Mato Grosso, Planalto do •
Brazil 42 E6
Matobo Nat. Park • Zimbabwe 102 J3
Matochkin Shar • Russian Fed. 26 I3
Matosinhos • Portugal 11 C3
Matra • Hungary 13 I10
Matrah • Oman 18 G5
Matre • Norway 94 C3
Matrei • Austria 89 H7
Matrûh • Egypt 101 F1
Matsu Liehtao • Taiwan 29 G5
Matsudona Nat. Park • Zimbabwe 102 J1
Matsue • Japan 30 G7
Matsumoto • Japan 30 I6
Matsuyama • Japan 30 G8
Mattagami • OT, Canada 39 O7
Mattancheri • India 106 D10
Mattawa • OT, Canada 122 B1
Matterdale • United Kingdom 74 C2
Matterhorn • Italy/Switzerland 89 G6
Matthew Town • Bahamas 124 B4
Matthews Ridge • Guyana 43 E2
Matucana • Peru 127 B1
Matuku • Fiji 35 (2) D2
Matura Bay • Trinidad & Tobago 125 K2
Maturín • Venezuela 43 E2
Mau • India 105 C8
Mau Escarpment • Kenya 23 F4
Mau Kyun • Myanmar 31 B4
Maubeuge • France 10 I3
Maubuisson • France 85 G1
Mauganj • India 105 C8
Mauguio **Beach** • France 68 [130]
Maui • HI, United States 119 L3
Maulbronn **Heritage C** • Germany 64 [42]
Mauléon • France 85 J1
Maullín • Chile 45 B4
Maumere • Indonesia 32 (1) B4
Maun • Botswana 24 C3
Mauna Kea • HI, United States 119 L8
Mauna Loa • HI, United States 119 L8
Maunoir, Lac • NT, Canada 38 F3
Maurepas, Lake •
LA, United States 118 K4
Maures, Massif des • France 85 H3
Maurice, Lake • SA, Australia 34 F5
Mauricie, la, Nat. Park •
QU, Canada 122 B4
Maurienne • France 85 F4
Mauritania • Africa 20 C5
Mauritius • Africa 24 (1) B2
Maus, Burg • Germany 82 H2
Mäuseturm • Germany 82 H4
Mauterndorf **Ski** • Austria 70 [186]
Mavinga • Angola 24 C3
Mavrovo Nat. Park **Park** •
F.Y.R. of Macedonia 72 [122]
Mavrovoúni • Greece 14 K8
Mawan • Shenzhen, China 107 H3
Mawgan Porth **Beach** •
United Kingdom 75 [126]
Mawkmai • Myanmar 109 G1
Mawlaik • Myanmar 28 F4
Mawsil, Al • Iraq 18 D2
Mawson [Base] • Antarctica 46 (1) L3
Maxglan [Apt] • Austria 89 H4
Máximo Gómez • Cuba 124 D3
May, Cape • NJ, United States 118 H3
May Day Mtns • Jamaica 124 C3
May Pen • Jamaica 124 C4
Maya • Russian Fed. 27 M5
Maya • Indonesia 32 D3
Mayaguana • Bahamas 124 B4
Mayagüez • Puerto Rico 125 E3
Mayagüez, Bahía de •
Puerto Rico 125 E3
Mayapán • Mexico 37 D3
Mayarí • Cuba 124 D8
Mayaro Bay • Trinidad & Tobago 125 K4
Maychew • Ethiopia 18 C7
Mayen • Germany 82 H1
Mayenne • France 10 E5
Mayenne [Riv] • France 10 E6
Mayens-de-l'Ours **Ski** •
Switzerland 70 [81]
Mayens-de-Riddes **Ski** •
Switzerland 70 [79]
Maykain • Kazakhstan 26 M7
Maykop • Russian Fed. 17 G6
Maynas • Peru 43 B4
Maynooth • Ireland 79 E1
Mayo • Ireland 79 F2
Mayo, Plains of • Ireland 79 F2
Mayon, Mt • Philippines 25 N8
Mayor I. • New Zealand 112 K2
Mayrhofen **Ski** • Austria 70 [143]
Mayrhofen • Austria 89 H7
Mayshoß • Germany 82 H1
Mazabuka • Zambia 24 D3
Mazagão • Brazil 43 G4
Mazagón • Spain 86 B1
Mazamet • France 10 H10
Mazar • China 26 M10
Mazar-e Sharif • Afghanistan 18 I2
Mazara del Vallo •
Sicily, Italy 12 G11
Mazara, Val di • Sicily, Italy 90 D1
Mazarrón **Beach** • Spain 68 [117]
Mazarrón • Spain 87 C3
Mazarrón, Golfo de • Spain 11 J7
Mazartag • China 26 N10
Mazatenango • Guatemala 37 C5
Mazatlán • Mexico 37 (1) A1
Mazeikiai • Lithuania 13 L1
Mazong Shan • China 29 B2
Mazowe • Zimbabwe 102 J2
Mazowe [Riv] •
Mozambique/Zimbabwe 102 J2
Mazurski Nat. Park **Park** •
Poland 72 [92]
Mazzarò • Sicily, Italy 90 D2
Mbabane • Swaziland 24 E5
Mbaiki • Central African Rep. 23 B3
Mbala • Zambia 23 E5
Mbalabala • Zimbabwe 24 D4
Mbale • Uganda 23 E3
Mbalmayo • Cameroon 22 G4
Mbamba Bay • Tanzania 102 H3
Mbandaka • Dem. Rep. of Congo 23 B3
Mbanga • Cameroon 22 F4
Mbanza Congo • Angola 23 A5
Mbanza-Ngungu •
Dem. Rep. of Congo 23 A5
Mbé • Cameroon 23 A2
Mbéré •
Cameroon/Central African Rep. 22 H3
Mbeya • Tanzania 102 H3
Mbinda • Congo 22 G5
Mbomou • Central African Rep./Dem. Rep. of Congo 23 D2
Mbour • Senegal 22 A2
Mbout • Mauritania 20 C5
Mbua • Fiji 35 (2) D2
Mbuji-Mayi • Dem. Rep. of Congo 23 C5
Mbulu • Tanzania 102 H2
Mbwemburu • Tanzania 24 F2
McAlester • OK, United States 41 G5
McAllen • TX, United States 40 G6
McCall • ID, United States 117 E4
McCarran [Apt] •
NV, United States 117 F4
McClintock Channel • NU, Canada 38 K2
McClintock, Mt • Antarctica 46 (1) V1
McClure Strait • NT, Canada 36 E2
McComb • MS, United States 118 K2
McCook • NE, United States 40 F3
McDonald I. • Indian Ocean 3 R10
McDonald I. **Heritage N** •
Indian Ocean 61 [138]
McHenry, Fort, Nat. Mon. & Hist. Shrine **Park** • MD, United States 121 [279]
Mchinga • Tanzania 102 H4
McIlwraith Range •
QL, Australia 34 H2
McKerrow, Lake • New Zealand 112 L2
McKinley, Mt •
AK, United States 40 (2) F2
McKinney • TX, United States 119 N1
McLean's Town • Bahamas 124 B2
McLoughlin House Nat. Hist. Site **Park** •
OR, United States 120 [34]
McMinnville • OR, United States 117 E3
McMurdo [Base] • Antarctica 46 (1) V2
Mdennah • Algeria/Mali 20 D4
Mdina • Malta 93 H4
Mdiq • Morocco 101 D1
Me'arot Hever • Israel 98 A8
Mead, Lake •
AZ/NV, United States 118 J1
Mead, Lake, Nat. Recreation Area •
AZ/NV, United States 118 J1
Meadow Lake • SA, Canada 38 J6
Mealhada • Portugal 11 C4
Mealy Mtns • NF, Canada 39 T6
Meander • AL, Canada 38 H5
Meath • Ireland 79 E1
Meaux • France 85 E2
Mebrigede • Angola 23 A5
Mecca • Saudi Arabia 18 C5
Mechelen • Belgium 80 A14
Mecheria • Algeria 20 E2
Mecidiye • Turkey 15 H3
Meckenheim • Germany 82 H1
Mecklenburg-Vorpommern •
Germany 8 H3
Mecklenburger Bucht • Germany 8 G2
Mecklenburgische Seenplatte •
Germany 8 H3
Mecsek • Hungary 13 H11
Mecula • Mozambique 24 F2
Medan • Indonesia 110 B2
Médéa • Algeria 11 N8
Medellín • Colombia 43 B2
Medenine • Tunisia 101 E6
Mederdra • Mauritania 20 B5
Medewi Beach • Bali, Indonesia 110 C1
Medford • OR, United States 117 E3
Medgidia • Romania 97 D2
Media Luna • Cuba 124 D7
Medias • Romania 14 L3
Medicine Hat • AL, Canada 38 I6
Medina • Saudi Arabia 18 C5
Medina de Rioseco • Spain 11 F3
Medina del Campo • Spain 11 G3
Medina-Sidonia • Spain 11 F8
Medinaceli • Spain 11 I3
Mediterranean cruise area •
Africa/Europe 59 C
Mediterranean Sea • Europe 4 N11
Medjerda, Mts de la •
Algeria/Tunisia 12 C12
Mednogorsk • Russian Fed. 26 I7
Mednyy, Ostrov • Russian Fed. 27 S6
Médoc • France 85 G1
Medon • France 10 L5
Medouneu • Gabon 22 G4
Medveditsa • Russian Fed. 17 G4
Medvednica • Croatia 14 C4
Medvezh'yegorsk • Russian Fed. 17 E2
Medvezhi, Ostrovo •
Russian Fed. 27 R2
Meekatharra • WA, Australia 34 C5
Meelpaeg lake • NF, Canada 123 D3
Meerane • Germany 9 H6
Meerbusch • Germany 81 E3
Meersburg • Germany 82 J5
Meerufenfushi • Maldives 106 E2
Meerut • India 105 C3
Mega • Ethiopia 23 F3
Mega • Indonesia 32 (1) D3
Megalon Khorion • Greece 15 I7
Megalópolis • Greece 15 D6
Meganissi • Greece 92 C1
Meganom, mys • Ukraine 17 F6
Mégara • Greece 15 E6
Megève **Ski** • France 70 [23]
Megève • France 85 F2
Meghalaya • India 28 F3
Megisti • Greece 93 G3
Meharry, Mt • WA, Australia 34 C4
Mehdiya-Plage • Morocco 101 D1
Mehran • Iran 18 F4
Mei Yuan • China 107 J1
Meiganga • Cameroon 22 G3
Meiktila • Myanmar 31 B2
Meinershagen • Germany 81 E4
Meiningen • Germany 9 F6
Meiringen • Switzerland 89 G2
Meiringspoort • South Africa 100 C7
Meisenheim • Germany 82 H4
Meißen • Germany 9 I5
Meizhou • China 29 F6
Mejez el Bab • Tunisia 101 E2
Mékambo • Gabon 22 G4
Mekele • Ethiopia 21 G5
Mekherrhane, Sebkha • Algeria 20 F3
Meknassy • Tunisia 101 E3
Meknès **Heritage C** • Morocco 64 [216]
Meknès • Morocco 101 D1
Mekong • Asia 31 D3
Mekong, Mouths of the • Vietnam 108 B3
Mekongga, Gunung • Indonesia 32 (1) B3
Mékrou • Africa 22 E2
Melaka • Malaysia 32 C2
Melamo, Cabo • Mozambique 24 G2
Melanesia • Pacific Ocean 33 H6
Melaque • Mexico 123 E2
Melaselkä • Russian Fed. 16 P5
Melawi • Indonesia 32 E3
Melbourne • VI, Australia 111 G3
Melbourne • FL, United States 119 M6
Melbu • Norway 16 H2
Melchsee-Frutt • Switzerland 89 G3
Meldorf • Germany 8 E2
Melela • Mozambique 24 F3
Melendugno • Italy 12 M8
Melfi • Italy 12 J8
Melfi • Chad 23 B1
Meli Park **Park** • Belgium 73 [46]
Meli Park • Belgium 80 B1
Melidoni • Crete, Greece 93 E2
Melilla • Africa 101 D2
Melincué • Argentina 127 D1
Melipilla • Chile 44 B5
Melissáni • Greece 92 C2
Melita [Apt] • Tunisia 101 E4
Melitopol' • Ukraine 17 F5
Melivia • Greece 92 D1
Melk • Austria 14 C1
Melle **Spa** • Germany 83 [66]
Mellègue • Algeria/Tunisia 101 E1
Mellerud • Sweden 95 F3
Mellieha • Malta 93 H1
Mellieha Bay • Malta 93 H1
Mellifont Abbey • Ireland 79 E2
Melnik • Czech Rep. 96 C2
Melo • Uruguay 44 F5
Melsungen • Germany 9 E5
Meltaus • Finland 16 M3
Melton Mowbray • United Kingdom 7 L9
Melun • France 85 E4
Melville • SA, Canada 38 K6
Melville Bay • NT, Australia 34 G2
Melville, Cape • QL, Australia 34 H2
Melville Hills • NT/NU, Canada 38 G3
Melville I. • NT, Australia 34 F2
Melville I. • NT/NU, Canada 36 F2
Melville, Lake • NF, Canada 39 T6
Melville Peninsula • NU, Canada 39 O3
Memba, Baia de • Mozambique 24 G2
Memberamo • Indonesia 32 (1) E3
Memboro • Indonesia 32 (1) A4
Memmert • Germany 8 B3
Memmingen • Germany 82 J2
Memphis • TN, United States 41 I4
Memphis **Heritage C** • Egypt 64 [238]
Memphis • Egypt 101 F1
Menabe • Madagascar 24 G4
Menaggio • Italy 91 E2
Ménaka • Mali 20 F5
Menangalaku • Indonesia 32 (1) A4
Menara [Apt] • Morocco 101 D3
Mendaya • Bali, Indonesia 110 C1
Mende • France 10 I9
Mendebo • Ethiopia 23 F2
Menden • Germany 8 C5
Menderes, Adnan [Apt] • Turkey 92 D5
Mendi • Papua New Guinea 35 (1) C2
Mendip Hills • United Kingdom 74 F3
Mendocino • CA, United States 117 F3
Mendocino, Cape •
CA, United States 40 B3
Mendoza • Argentina 44 C5
Menemen • Turkey 15 I5
Menen • Belgium 5 G4
Menfi • Sicily, Italy 12 G11
Menfi **Beach** • Sicily, Italy 68 [152]
Mengen • Germany 82 J1
Menggala • Indonesia 32 D3
Mengkalihat, Tanjung •
Indonesia 32 (1) A2
Meníkio • Greece 15 E2
Menindee • NS, Australia 34 H6
Meningie • SA, Australia 34 G7
Menjangan • Bali, Indonesia 110 C1
Menjapa, Gunung • Indonesia 32 F2
Menongue • Angola 24 B2
Menor, Mar • Spain 87 C3
Menorca • Spain 87 F
Mensk • Belarus 17 D4
Mentakab • Malaysia 108 D4
Mentawai, Kepulauan • Indonesia 32 B3
Mentawai, Selat • Indonesia 32 B3
Mentigi • Indonesia 110 C4
Menton **Beach** • France 68 [134]
Menton • France 85 H2
Menuires, les **Ski** • France 70 [41]
Menuires, les • France 85 F4
Menzel Bourguiba • Tunisia 12 D11
Menzies • WA, Australia 34 D5
Menzies, Mt • Antarctica 46 (1) L2
Meppel • Netherlands 80 A8
Meppen • Germany 8 C4
Mequinenza, Embalse de • Spain 11 K3
Mer de Sable, la **Park** • France 73 [69]
Mer de Sable, la • France 85 E2
Merak • Java, Indonesia 110 D1
Meran • Italy 90 B1
Merano • Italy 90 B1
Merapi, Gunung • Indonesia 110 B4
Merauke • Indonesia 32 (1) F4
Merbabu, Gunung •
Java, Indonesia 110 D7
Mercantour, Parc nat. du **Park** •
France 72 [68]
Mercantour, Parc nat. du •
France 85 H2
Mercato • Italy 91 G4
Merced • CA, United States 40 B4
Mercedario, Cerro • Argentina 44 C5
Mercedes • San Luis, Argentina 44 C5
Mercedes •
Corrientes, Argentina 44 E4
Mercedes • Uruguay 127 D2
Mercers Creek Bay •
Antigua & Barbuda 125 F2
Mercier Dam • QU, Canada 122 B2
Mercury I. • New Zealand 35 E3
Mercy, Cape • NU, Canada 39 S4
Méré Lava • Vanuatu 35 (2) B1
Meredoua • Algeria 20 F3
Merefa • Ukraine 17 F5
Merenga • Russian Fed. 27 Q4
Merengev • Kazakhstan 17 I5
Mergui • Myanmar 31 B4
Mergui Archipelago • Myanmar 31 B4
Méribel **Ski** • France 70 [39]
Méribel • France 85 F4
Mérida • Spain 11 E6
Mérida • Mexico 37 D3
Mérida • Venezuela 43 C2
Mérida **Heritage C** • Spain 64 [91]
Mérida, Cordillera de •
Venezuela 43 C2
Meridian • MS, United States 118 K2
Mérig • Vanuatu 35 (2) B1
Mérignac • France 10 E9
Mérignac [Apt] • France 85 G3
Merikarvia • Finland 95 E1
Merimbula • NS, Australia 111 G4
Mering • Germany 82 J2
Merioneth • United Kingdom 75 A5
Merlette • France 85 F4
Merlimau • Singapore 108 E3
Merlimont **Beach** • France 68 [75]
Meroe • Sudan 21 F4
Meroe [Adm] • Sudan 21 F4
Meron • Israel 98 A2
Merredin • WA, Australia 34 C6
Merrick • United Kingdom 7 H6
Merrimack •
MA/NH, United States 118 G3
Merritt I. Nat. Wildlife Refuge •
FL, United States 119 M6
Merryville • LA, United States 118 K3
Mersa Fatma • Eritrea 18 D7
Mersch • Luxembourg 80 A20
Mersea I. • United Kingdom 74 E2
Merseburg • Germany 9 H5
Mersin • Turkey 18 B2
Mersing • Malaysia 32 C2
Merta Road • India 18 J4
Mertert • Luxembourg 5 J5
Merthyr Tydfil • United Kingdom 7 I10
Merti • Kenya 23 F3
Mértola • Portugal 11 D7
Meru • Kenya 101 G2
Meru, Mt • Tanzania 102 H2
Meru Nat. Park • Kenya 101 G2
Meru Nat. Park **Park** • Kenya 103 [78]
Merv • Turkmenistan 98 B2
Meryemana • Turkey 92 D9
Merzig • Germany 82 H5
Mesa • AZ, United States 118 J3
Mesa Verde Nat. Park **Heritage C** •
CO, United States 62 [6]
Mesa Verde Nat. Park •
CO, United States 118 J2
Mesa Verde Nat. Park **Park** •
CO, United States 120 [96]
Mesagne • Italy 12 L8
Meschede • Germany 5 L3
Meschers-sur-Gironde **Beach** •
France 68 [84]
Meset • Turkey 15 O2
Meski • Morocco 101 D4
Mesklá • Crete, Greece 93 E1
Meso Gerakari **Beach** • Greece 69 [172]
Mesopotamia • Iraq/Syria 18 D3
Mesopotamia • Trinidad & Tobago 125 K2
Mesquer **Beach** • France 68 [82]
Mesquer • France 84 C4
Messalo • Mozambique 23 F6
Messanges • France 85 G3
Messaória Plain • Cyprus 93 J3
Messarás, Ormos • Crete, Greece 93 E6
Messel • Germany 82 G4
Messel Pit **Heritage N** • Germany 61 [42]
Messina • South Africa 24 E4
Messina • Sicily, Italy 90 D2
Messina, Stretto di • Italy 90 D2
Messíni • Greece 15 C6
Messíni **Beach** • Greece 69 [181]
Messiniakós Kólpos • Greece 15 D7
Messolóngi • Greece 15 C5
Messolóngi **Beach** • Greece 69 [175]
Messongi • Corfu, Greece 92 B1
Messótopos **Beach** • Greece 69 [199]
Mesta • Bulgaria 15 E2
Mestá • Greece 92 D5
Mesuji • Indonesia 32 D3
Meta • Colombia 43 C2
Meta • Italy 91 G3
Meta Incognita Peninsula •
NU, Canada 39 R4
Métabief **Ski** • France 70 [7]
Metamórfossi **Beach** • Greece 69 [192]
Metán • Argentina 44 D4
Metaponto • Italy 12 K8
Metéora **Heritage N** • Greece 61 [59]
Metéora **Heritage C** • Greece 64 [177]
Méthana • Greece 15 E6
Méthana [Peninsula] • Greece 92 D7
Methil • United Kingdom 74 B2
Methóni **Beach** • Greece 69 [181]
Methven • New Zealand 35 C6
Metkovic • Croatia 12 L5
Metlika • Slovenia 12 J3
Metmárfág • Western Sahara 20 C3
Metóhi **Beach** • Greece 69 [179]
Metohija • F.R. of Yugoslavia 14 H7
Mettlach • Germany 82 G3
Mettmann • Germany 81 E3
Metz • France 10 L4
Meulaboh • Indonesia 110 B1
Meurthe • France 10 L5
Meurudu • Indonesia 110 B1
Meuse • Belgium/France 80 A15
Meuse Valley • Belgium 80 A15
Meuselwitz • Germany 9 H5
Mevagissey • United Kingdom 74 F4
Mexiana • Brazil 43 H4
Mexicali • Mexico 40 C5
Mexican Riviera cruise area •
Mexico/United States 58 A3
Mexicana, Altiplanicie • Mexico 40 F6
Mexico • N. America 36 G8
Mexico City **Heritage C** • Mexico 62 [21]
Mexico City • Mexico 123 E4
Mexico, Gulf of • N. America 37 C2
Meymaneh • Afghanistan 18 H2
Mezen • Russian Fed. 17 G1
Mezen [Riv] • Russian Fed. 17 H2
Mezenskaya Guba • Russian Fed. 17 G1
Mezőkövesd • Hungary 13 J10
Mezőtúr • Hungary 13 J10
Mfanganu I. • Uganda 101 G3
Mgarr • Malta 93 H1
Mhamid • Morocco 101 D6
Mi • Japan 30 F7
Miami • FL, United States 119 M8
Miami Beach • FL, United States 119 M8
Miami Seaquarium •
FL, United States 119 M8
Miami Seaquarium **Park** •
FL, United States 121 [FF]
Mianyang • China 29 C4
Miarinarivo • Madagascar 24 H3
Miass • Russian Fed. 26 J6
Miastko • Poland 13 F3
Michalovce • Slovak Rep. 13 K9
Michelstadt • Germany 82 G4
Michendorf • Germany 81 F3
Michigan • United States 41 I2
Michigan, Lake • United States 41 I3
Michipicoten • OT, Canada 39 N7
Michoacán • Mexico 37 (1) B2
Michurin • Bulgaria 97 D4
Michurinsk • Russian Fed. 17 G4
Micoud • St Lucia 125 J4
Micra [Apt] • Greece 92 D1
Micronesia • Pacific Ocean 33 H5
Micronesia, Federated States of •
Pacific Ocean 33 F5
Middelburg • South Africa 24 D5
Middelburg • Netherlands 80 A10
Middelfart **Beach** • Denmark 68 [44]
Middelfart • Denmark 95 F9
Middelharnis • Netherlands 80 C3
Middelkirke-Bad • Belgium 80 B1
Middle Andaman • India 28 F6
Middle Island •
St Kitts & Nevis 125 G1
Middlesbrough • United Kingdom 7 K7
Middlesex • United Kingdom 74 E1
Middlesex • Jamaica 124 C2
Middleton • NS, Canada 123 D7
Middleton Reef • Australia 33 H8
Midelt • Morocco 20 E2
Midès • Tunisia 101 E3
Midi • France 84 B4
Midi, Canal du • France 10 G10
Midi-Pyrénées • France 84 A2
Midland • TX, United States 40 F5
Midland • OT, Canada 122 B5
Midleton • Ireland 79 F8
Midlothian • United Kingdom 74 B4
Midnight Sun Coast • Sweden 94 A5
Midongy Atsimo • Madagascar 24 H4
Midzor • F.R. of Yugoslavia 14 J6
Miedzyrzecz • Poland 13 E5
Miélan • France 85 J2
Mielec • Poland 13 K7
Miercurea Cuic • Romania 14 M3
Mieres • Spain 11 F1
Miesbach • Germany 82 J7
Migjorn, Platja de •
Formentera, Spain 87 G4
Mihaliççik • Turkey 15 M4
Mijares • Spain 11 K4
Mijas **Beach** • Spain 68 [114]
Mijas Costa • Spain 86 B6
Mijdrecht • Netherlands 80 C2
Mikhaylovka • Russian Fed. 17 G4
Mikines • Greece 15 D6
Mikkeli • Finland 16 N6
Mikkeli [Adm] • Finland 16 N6
Mikkeli [Adm] • Finland 94 A9
Mikonos **Beach** • Greece 69 [204]
Mikonos • Greece 92 D8
Mikonou, Stenó • Greece 15 G6
Mikrá Préspa, Límni • Greece 15 C3
Mikumi • Tanzania 102 H4
Mikumi Nat. Park • Tanzania 102 H4
Mikun • Russian Fed. 17 I2
Mikuni-Sanmyaku • Japan 30 J6
Mikura • Japan 30 J8
Milan **Heritage C** • Italy 64 [109]
Milan • Italy 91 E6
Milange • Mozambique 24 F3
Milano **Heritage C** • Italy 64 [109]
Milano • Italy 91 E6
Milano Marittima • Italy 91 E8
Milas • Turkey 92 D9
Milatos • Crete, Greece 93 E3
Milazzo • Sicily, Italy 90 D2
Mildura • NS, Australia 34 H6
Miles • QL, Australia 111 F6
Miles City • MT, United States 40 E2
Milet • Turkey 92 D8
Milevsko • Czech Rep. 96 C4
Milford Haven • United Kingdom 7 G10
Milford Sound • New Zealand 112 L2
Milford Sound [Fiord] •
New Zealand 112 L1
Milford Track • New Zealand 112 L2
Milh, Ra's al • Libya 21 D1
Miliana • Algeria 11 N8
Miliés • Greece 15 E4
Milikapiti • NT, Australia 34 F2
Milk • Canada/United States 38 I7
Milk River Spa • Jamaica 124 C3
Milkovo • Russian Fed. 27 Q6
Mill I. • NU, Canada 39 P4
Millau • France 10 I9
Millerovo • Russian Fed. 17 G5
Millevaches, Plateau de •
France 85 G2
Millicent • SA, Australia 34 H7
Millinocket • ME, United States 118 G2
Millom • United Kingdom 74 C3
Millstatt • Austria 89 H8
Millstätter See • Austria 89 H8
Millstreet • Ireland 79 F8
Milltown Malbay • Ireland 79 F6
Milltown-Malbay **Beach** • Ireland 68 [61]
Milnthorpe • United Kingdom 74 C4
Milos **Beach** • Greece 69 [207]
Milos • Greece 92 D7
Milparinka • NS, Australia 34 H5
Miltenberg • Germany 82 G4
Milton • New Zealand 35 B8
Milton • FL, United States 119 M1
Milton Keynes • United Kingdom 7 L9
Milwaukee • WI, United States 41 I3
Milyas • Turkey 93 G1
Mimaland • Malaysia 108 D4
Mimizan • France 85 G3
Mimizan, Fôret de • France 85 G3
Min • China 31 F1
Min Shan • China 29 C4
Mina • Algeria 11 L9
Mina Sa'ud • Kuwait 18 E4
Minami-Tori-Shima •
Pacific Ocean 33 G3
Minas • Uruguay 127 D2
Minas Gerais • Brazil 44 G2
Minbu • Myanmar 31 A2
Minch, Little • United Kingdom 6 F4
Minch, North • United Kingdom 6 G3
Minchinmávida, Volcán • Chile 45 B4
Mincio • Italy 91 E7
Mindanao • Philippines 31 H5
Mindel • Germany 9 F8
Mindelheim • Germany 82 J2
Mindelo • Cape Verde 22 (1) B1
Minden • Germany 8 D4
Minden **Spa** • Germany 83 [90]
Minden • LA, United States 118 K1
Mindoro • Philippines 31 G4
Mindoro Strait • Philippines 31 G4
Minehead • United Kingdom 74 F2
Mineiros • Brazil 44 F2
Mineola • TX, United States 119 N2
Mineral Wells •
TX, United States 119 N1
Minerva Reefs • Pacific Ocean 33 J8
Minervois • France 84 B3
Minfeng • China 28 D1
Ming Village • Singapore 108 E3
Mingan • QU, Canada 123 D2
Mingan Archipelago • QU, Canada 123 D2
Mingenew • WA, Australia 34 C5
Minglanilla • Spain 11 J5
Minho • Portugal 11 C3
Minho, Rio • Jamaica 124 C4
Minicoy I. • India 106 D13
Minilya • WA, Australia 34 B4
Minna • Nigeria 22 F3
Minneapolis • MN, United States 41 H3
Minnehaha, Lake •
FL, United States 121 C1
Minnesota • United States 41 H2
Miño • Spain 11 D2
Miño **Beach** • Spain 68 [92]
Minorca • Spain 87 F
Minot • ND, United States 40 F2
Minquiers, les • Channel Is. 75 A8
Minsk • Belarus 17 D4
Minsk Mazowiecki • Poland 13 K5
Minto, Lac • QU, Canada 39 P5
Minto, Mt • Antarctica 46 (1) V2
Minusinsk • Russian Fed. 26 P7
Minute Man Nat. Hist. Park **Park** •
MA, United States 121 [352]
Minya, El • Egypt 101 F3
Mira • Italy 12 G3
Mira **Beach** • Portugal 68 [96]
Mira • Portugal 88 E2
Mirabad • Afghanistan 18 H3
Mirabel [Apt] • QU, Canada 122 B3
Miracema • Brazil 127 C2
Miraflores • Boyaca, Colombia 43 C2
Miraflores • Guaviare, Colombia 43 C3
Miraj • India 106 D2
Miramar • Argentina 127 D4
Miramar Beach • Goa, India 105 B1
Mirambeau • France 10 E8
Mirambélou, Kólpos •
Crete, Greece 93 E8
Miranda de Ebro • Spain 11 H2
Mirándela • Portugal 11 D3
Mirándola • Italy 91 E7
Mirapolis **Park** • France 73 [68]
Mirapolis • France 85 E1
Mirbat • Oman 18 F6
Mirdita • Albania 14 H8
Mirepoix • France 11 M1
Mires • Crete, Greece 15 F8
Miri • Malaysia 32 E2
Miria • Niger 20 G6
Mirim, Lagoa • Brazil/Uruguay 44 F5

Mírina **Beach** • Greece 69 [198]
Mírina • Greece 92 D2
Mirny [Base] • Antarctica 46 (1) O3
Mirnyy • Russian Fed. 27 H4
Mirpur Khas • Pakistan 28 A3
Mirs Bay • China 107 H4
Mirtoan Sea • Greece 92 D7
Mirtóo Pélagos • Greece 15 E7
Mírtos • Crete, Greece 93 E7
Mirzapur • India 105 C8
Misano Adriático • Italy 91 E12
Miscou I. • NB, Canada 123 D2
Miseno, Capo • Italy 91 G3
Mish, Slieve • Ireland 79 F5
Mishan • China 27 L7
Misima • Papua New Guinea 35 (1) E3
Miskito, Cayos • Nicaragua 124 A4
Miskitos, Costa de • Nicaragua 37 E5
Miskolc • Hungary 13 J9
Misoöl • Indonesia 32 (1) D3
Misratah • Libya 21 B1
Misrikh • India 105 C3
Mission Beach • QL, Australia 111 F1
Mississauga • OT, Canada 122 B9
Mississippi [Adm] • United States 41 I5
Mississippi [Riv] • United States 41 H5
Mississippi River Delta • LA, United States 118 K4
Missoula • MT, United States 117 E2
Missouri [Adm] • United States 41 H4
Missouri [Riv] • United States 40 E2
Mistassibi • QU, Canada 39 Q6
Mistassini • QU, Canada 39 Q6
Mistassini, Lac • QU, Canada 39 Q6
Mistassini [Riv] • QU, Canada 39 Q7
Misterhult • Sweden 95 F8
Místrás • Greece 15 D6
Místrás **Heritage C** • Greece 64 [181]
Misty Fjords • AK, United States 58 A2
Mitchell • SD, United States 41 G3
Mitchell • QL, Australia 111 F5
Mitchell, Mt • NC, United States 41 J4
Mitchell [Riv] • QL, Australia 34 H3
Mitchell River Mission • QL, Australia 34 H3
Mitchelstown • Ireland 79 F6
Míthimna **Beach** • Greece 69 [199]
Míthimna • Greece 92 D5
Mítikas **Beach** • Epirus, Greece 69 [174]
Mítikas **Beach** • Ditiki Elláda, Greece 69 [175]
Mítikas • Epirus, Greece 92 C1
Mítikas • Ditiki Elláda, Greece 92 C1
Mitilíni **Beach** • Greece 69 [199]
Mitilíni • Greece 92 D5
Mitla • Mexico 123 E4
Mito • Japan 30 K6
Mittelberg **Ski** • Austria 70 [128]
Mittelfranken • Germany 9 G7
Mittelland • Switzerland 89 G2
Mittellandkanal • Germany 8 D4
Mittenwald • Germany 82 J7
Mittenwalde • Germany 81 F4
Mittersill **Ski** • Austria 70 [160]
Mittweida • Germany 9 H6
Mitú • Colombia 43 C3
Mitumba, Mtns • Dem. Rep. of Congo 23 D5
Mitwaba • Dem. Rep. of Congo 23 D5
Mitzic • Gabon 22 G4
Miyake • Japan 30 J7
Miyako • Japan 30 K5
Miyakonojo • Japan 30 F9
Miyanoura • Japan 30 F9
Miyazaki • Japan 30 F9
Miyoshi • Japan 30 G7
Mizdah • Libya 21 B1
Mizen Head • Wicklow, Ireland 79 E4
Mizen Head • Cork, Ireland 79 F7
Mizil • Romania 14 N5
Mizoram • India 28 F4
Mizuho [Base] • Antarctica 46 (1) J2
Mjölby • Sweden 95 F4
Mjøndalen • Norway 94 B1
Mjörn • Sweden 95 F3
Mjøsa • Norway 16 F6
Mkhaya Nature Reserve **Park** • Swaziland 103 [133]
Mkushi • Zambia 24 D2
Mkuzi Game Reserve **Park** • South Africa 103 [126]
Mladá Boleslav • Czech Rep. 96 C2
Mlawa • Poland 13 J4
Mlibizi • Zimbabwe 102 J1
Mljet • Croatia 14 E7
Mljet Nat. Park **Park** • Croatia 72 [113]
Mmabatho • South Africa 24 D5
Mnajdra • Malta 93 H4
Mnarani • Kenya 101 G5
Mnichovo Hradiste • Czech Rep. 96 C2
Mo i Rana • Norway 16 H3
Moa • Sierra Leone 22 B3
Moa • QL, Australia 34 H2
Moa • Cuba 124 D8
Moab • UT, United States 40 D4
Moab • Jordan 98 A8
Moala • Fiji 35 (2) D2
Moanda • Dem. Rep. of Congo 23 A5
Moba • Dem. Rep. of Congo 23 D5
Mobaye • Central African Rep. 23 C3
Mobayi-Mbongo • Dem. Rep. of Congo 23 C3
Mobile • AL, United States 119 M1
Mobile Bay • AL, United States 119 M1
Mobor Beach • Goa, India 105 B2
Mobridge • SD, United States 40 F2
Moçambique • Mozambique 24 F3
Moçambique, Canal de • Madagascar/Mozambique 24 G3
Moçambique, Ilha da **Heritage N** • Mozambique 61 [97]
Mochudi • Botswana 24 D4
Mocimboa da Praia • Mozambique 23 G6
Mocka • Yemen 18 D7
Möckeln • Sweden 95 F11
Môco, Serra • Angola 23 B6
Mocoa • Colombia 43 B3
Mocuba • Mozambique 24 F3
Modane • France 85 F4
Modave • Belgium 80 A15
Modena **Heritage C** • Italy 64 [117]
Modena • Italy 91 E7
Moder • France 9 C8
Modica • Sicily, Italy 12 I12
Mödling • Austria 13 F9
Moe • VI, Australia 111 G3
Moelfre **Beach** • United Kingdom 75 [225]
Moelv • Norway 16 F6
Moena • Italy 90 B3
Moena di Fassa **Ski** • Italy 70 [218]
Moengo • Suriname 43 G2
Moers • Germany 80 A12
Moers • Germany 81 E1
Mogadishu • Somalia 23 H3
Mogadouro • Portugal 11 E3
Mogadouro, Serra do • Portugal 11 E3
Mogami • Japan 30 K5
Mogán **Beach** • Gran Canaria, Canary Is. 68 [110]
Mogán • Gran Canaria, Canary Is. 86 E4
Mogao Caves **Heritage C** • China 63 [143]
Mogho • Ethiopia 23 G3
Mogoca • Russian Fed. 27 I6
Moguer **Beach** • Spain 68 [112]
Moguer • Spain 86 B1
Mohács • Hungary 13 H12
Mohammadia • Algeria 11 L9
Mohammed V [Apt] • Morocco 101 D1
Mohammedia • Morocco 101 D1
Moharraq, El • Egypt 101 F5
Mohave, Lake • AZ/NV, United States 118 J1
Mohawk Mtn **Ski** • CT, United States 116 [186]
Mohéli • Comoros 24 G2
Mohenjodaro • Pakistan 28 A3
Mohenjodaro **Heritage C** • Pakistan 63 [111]
Moher, Cliffs of • Ireland 79 F4
Mohinora • Mexico 40 E6
Möhne • Germany 8 D5
Moi • Myanmar/Thailand 109 G3
Moi [Apt] • Kenya 101 G5
Moinesti • Romania 14 N3
Mointy • Kazakhstan 26 L8
Moisie • QU, Canada 39 R6
Moissac • France 85 G4
Moïta • Corsica, France 85 L2
Möja • Sweden 95 D4
Mojácar **Beach** • Spain 68 [116]
Mojácar • Spain 86 B4
Mojave Desert • CA, United States 117 F6
Mojave Nat. Preserve • CA, United States 117 F6
Mojave Nat. Preserve **Park** • CA, United States 120 [60]
Mojokerto • Java, Indonesia 110 D8
Mojos, Llanos de • Bolivia 44 C1
Mokapu Peninsula • HI, United States 119 L6
Mokau • New Zealand 112 K3
Mokau [Riv] • New Zealand 112 K1
Moknine • Tunisia 101 E4
Mokp'o • Rep. of Korea 30 D7
Mokuleia Baech • HI, United States 119 L1
Mol • Belgium 5 I3
Mola di Bari • Italy 12 L7
Molái • Greece 15 D7
Mólai **Beach** • Greece 69 [182]
Molara, I. • Sardinia, Italy 90 C2
Molat • Croatia 14 B5
Molatón • Spain 11 J5
Mold • United Kingdom 7 I8
Moldau • Czech Rep. 13 D8
Moldavia • Romania 14 N2
Moldavia **Heritage C** • Romania 64 [166]
Molde • Norway 94 C2
Moldova • Europe 15 D5
Moldova Noua • Romania 14 I5
Moldova [Riv] • Romania 14 M2
Moldoveanu, Virful • Romania 14 L4
Mole Nat. Park **Park** • Ghana 103 [22]
Molepolole • Botswana 24 D4
Molfetta • Italy 12 K7
Molina de Aragón • Spain 11 J4
Molina de Segura • Spain 11 J6
Molise • Italy 12 I7
Mollafeneri • Turkey 15 K3
Mölle • Sweden 95 F11
Mollendo • Peru 127 B4
Mölln • Germany 8 F3
Mölln **Spa** • Germany 83 [35]
Mollösund • Sweden 95 F2
Mölndal • Sweden 95 F6
Molodechno • Belarus 16 N9
Molodezhnaya [Base] • Antarctica 46 (1) J3
Molokai • HI, United States 119 L3
Molong • NS, Australia 111 G2
Molopo • Botswana/South Africa 24 C5
Moloundou • Cameroon 22 H4
Molucca • Indonesia 32 (1) C3
Molucca Sea • Indonesia 32 (1) C2
Molygino • Russian Fed. 27 D5
Molyneux • St Kitts & Nevis 125 G1
Moma • Mozambique 24 F3
Moma • Russian Fed. 27 O3
Mombasa • Kenya 101 G5
Mombasa Marine Game Reserve • Kenya 101 G5
Mombasa Marine Nat. Park • Kenya 101 G5
Mombetsu • Japan 30 L2
Mompós • Colombia 43 C2
Mompós **Heritage C** • Colombia 62 [43]
Momski Khrebet • Russian Fed. 27 O3
Møn • Denmark 95 F15
Mon Repos • St Lucia 125 J4
Mona, Isla • Puerto Rico 124 A2
Monaco • Europe 85 H2
Monadhliath Mtns • United Kingdom 6 H4
Monadnock • NH, United States 118 G3
Monaghan • Ireland 7 F7
Monaghan [Adm] • Ireland 79 D1
Monasterevin • Ireland 79 E3
Monastir • Tunisia 101 E4
Monbetsu • Japan 30 L3
Moncalieri • Italy 12 B4
Monção • Portugal 11 C2
Moncarapacho • Portugal 88 E8
Moncayo • Spain 11 J3
Monchegorsk • Russian Fed. 17 E1
Mönchengladbach • Germany 81 E3
Monchique • Portugal 88 E2
Monchique, Serra de • Portugal 88 E2
Monchy • St Lucia 125 J2
Monclova • Mexico 37 A2
Moncófar **Beach** • Spain 68 [120]
Moncton • NB, Canada 123 D7
Mondego • Portugal 11 D4
Mondello • Sicily, Italy 90 D1
Mondo • Chad 22 H2
Mondorf-les-Bains • Luxembourg 80 A20
Mondovi • Italy 91 E5
Mondragone • Italy 91 G1
Mondsee • Austria 89 H4
Mondsee [Lake] • Austria 89 H4
Mondy • Russian Fed. 27 F6
Monéglia • Italy 91 E6
Monemvassia • Greece 92 D7
Monfalcone • Italy 12 H3
Monforte de Lemos • Spain 11 D2
Mong Hang • Myanmar 109 G1
Mong Kok • Hong Kong, China 107 H5
Monga • Dem. Rep. of Congo 23 C3
Mongalla • Sudan 23 E2
Monghyr • India 28 E3
Mongie, la • France 85 J2
Mongo • Chad 21 C5
Mongoito • Russian Fed. 27 H6
Mongol Altayn Nuruu • China/Mongolia 26 O8
Mongolia • Asia 25 L5
Mongonu • Nigeria 22 G2
Mongororo • Chad 23 C1
Mongouge • St Lucia 125 J3
Mongstad • Norway 94 C3
Mongu • Zambia 24 C3
Monheim • Germany 81 E3
Monjes • West Indies 43 C1
Monkey Hill • St Kitts & Nevis 125 G1
Monmouth • United Kingdom 74 D3
Monmouthshire • United Kingdom 74 D3
Monnickendam • Netherlands 80 C2
Mono Lake • CA, United States 117 F4
Monocacy Nat. Battlefield **Park** • MD, United States 121 [272]
Monólithos • Rhodes, Greece 93 F3
Monopoli • Italy 12 L8
Monor • Hungary 13 I10
Monos I. • Trinidad & Tobago 125 K1
Monóvar • Spain 11 K6
Monowai, Lake • New Zealand 112 L3
Monpazier • France 85 G4
Monreal del Campo • Spain 11 J4
Monreale • Sicily, Italy 90 D1
Monroe • LA, United States 118 K1
Monrovia • Liberia 22 B3
Mons • Belgium 80 A14
Møns Klint • Denmark 95 F15
Monschau • Germany 82 G1
Monselice • Italy 12 F3
Monsheim • Germany 82 H4
Monster • Netherlands 80 C3
Mönsteras • Sweden 95 F8
Mont Blanc • France/Italy 85 F2
Mont Blanc **Ski** • QU, Canada 116 [32]
Mont Blanc, Tunnel du • France/Italy 85 F2
Mont Cenis, Col du • France 85 F4
Mont d'Or, le **Ski** • France 70 [7]
Mont de Marsan • France 85 G3
Mont Gabriel **Ski** • QU, Canada 116 [27]
Mont Joli • QU, Canada 123 D1
Mont Laurier • QU, Canada 122 B3
Mont Louis • France 11 N2
Mont Mégantic Prov. Park • QU, Canada 122 B8
Mont Olympia **Ski** • QU, Canada 116 [28]
Mont Orford **Ski** • QU, Canada 116 [41]
Mont Orford Prov. Park • QU, Canada 122 B8
Mont St Bruno Prov. Park • QU, Canada 122 B8
Mont St Michel **Heritage N** • France 61 [43]
Mont St Michel **Heritage C** • France 64 [48]
Mont St Michel, Baie du • France 5 B6
Mont St Michel, le • France 84 C2
Mont Ste Anne **Ski** • QU, Canada 116 [35]
Mont Ste Anne Prov. Park • QU, Canada 123 D1
Mont Ste Saveur **Ski** • QU, Canada 116 [29]
Mont Sutton **Ski** • QU, Canada 116 [39]
Mont Tremblant Prov. Park • QU, Canada 122 B3
Mont Video **Ski** • QU, Canada 116 [25]
Mont-roig del Camp **Beach** • Spain 68 [121]
Montabaur • Germany 82 H2
Montacute House • United Kingdom 74 F3
Montagnana • Italy 91 E7
Montagnes Noires • France 84 C3
Montagu • South Africa 100 C6
Montalbán • Spain 11 K4
Montalegre • Portugal 11 D3
Montana • Bulgaria 14 K6
Montana • United States 40 E2
Montaña Blanca • Lanzarote, Canary Is. 87 E3
Montaña Clara • Canary Is. 87 E3
Montanhãs • Portugal 88 A1
Montargis • France 10 H6
Montauban • France 85 G4
Montauk • NY, United States 118 H2
Montbéliard • France 10 L6
Montblanc • Spain 87 D3
Montchavin **Ski** • France 70 [33]
Montchavin • France 85 F2
Monte Albán **Heritage C** • Mexico 62 [24]
Monte Albán • Mexico 123 E4
Monte Alegre • Brazil 43 G4
Monte Azul • Brazil 45 (1) C4
Monte Carlo • Monaco 85 H2
Monte Caseros • Argentina 44 E5
Monte Fogo, Serra de • Portugal 88 E7
Monte Gordo • Portugal 88 E8
Monte Lindo • Paraguay 44 E3
Monte Oliveto Maggiore, Abbazia di • Italy 91 E11
Monte Quemado • Argentina 44 D4
Monte Sant' Angelo • Italy 12 J7
Monte Santu, Capo di • Sardinia, Italy 12 D8
Montealegre del Castillo • Spain 11 J6
Montebelluno • Italy 91 E3
Montecassino, Abbazia di • Italy 91 F4
Montecatini • Italy 91 E11
Montechoro • Portugal 88 E6
Montecorvino • Italy 91 G4
Montecristo • Italy 12 E6
Montefalco • Italy 91 E12
Montego Bay • Jamaica 124 C1
Montegrotto • Italy 91 E7
Montélimar • France 85 F3
Montella • Italy 91 G2
Montemor-o-Novo • Portugal 11 C6
Montenegro • F.R. of Yugoslavia 14 G7
Montenegro • Brazil 44 F4
Montepulciano • Italy 91 E11
Montereau-Faut-Yonne • France 85 E4
Monterey • CA, United States 117 F3
Monterey Bay • CA, United States 117 F3
Montería • Colombia 43 B2
Monteriggioni • Italy 91 E11
Montero • Bolivia 44 D2
Monterosso **Beach** • Italy 68 [143]
Monterotondo • Italy 12 G6
Monterrey • Mexico 37 A2
Montes Claros • Brazil 44 H2
Montesárchio • Italy 91 G2
Montevarchi • Italy 12 F5
Montevideo • Uruguay 127 D2
Montezuma Castle Nat. Mon. • AZ, United States 118 J1
Montezuma Castle Nat. Mon. **Park** • AZ, United States 120 [109]
Montfort • Israel 98 A1
Montgenèvre **Ski** • France 70 [62]
Montgenèvre • France 85 F4
Montgeoffroy [Château] • France 84 D1
Montgomery • AL, United States 41 I5
Montgomery • United Kingdom 74 D1
Montgomeryshire • United Kingdom 75 A5
Monthey • Switzerland 89 G5
Monticello • Corsica, France 85 L1
Montignac • France 85 G2
Montigny-lès-Metz • France 10 L4
Montijo • Spain 11 E6
Montijo • Portugal 88 D2
Montilla • Spain 86 B2
Montivilliers • France 5 D5
Montlouis • France 84 B1
Montluçon • France 10 H7
Montmagny • QU, Canada 118 G1
Montmédy • France 5 I5
Montmélian • France 85 F1
Monto • QL, Australia 111 F4
Montoro • Spain 11 G6
Montpelier • VT, United States 118 G3
Montpellier • France 10 I10
Montpoupon [Château] • France 84 D2
Montréal • QU, Canada 122 B7
Montreuil • France 5 E4
Montreux • Switzerland 89 G5
Montrose • United Kingdom 6 J5
Montrose • CO, United States 40 E4
Monts Chic-Chocs prov. parks • QU, Canada 123 D2
Montsen • Spain 11 L2
Montserrat • West Indies 37 I4
Montserrat Hills • Trinidad & Tobago 125 K3
Montserrat, Monestir de • Spain 87 D3
Monywa • Myanmar 31 B2
Monza • Italy 91 E6
Monzón • Spain 11 L3
Moone • Ireland 79 E3
Moonie • QL, Australia 111 F6
Moonstone **Ski** • OT, Canada 116 [17]
Moor Abbey • Ireland 79 F6
Moora • WA, Australia 34 C6
Moorbad Lobenstein **Spa** • Germany 83 [308]
Moore, Lake • WA, Australia 34 C5
Mooréa • French Polynesia 58 A1
Moores Creek Nat. Battlefield **Park** • NC, United States 121 [247]
Moorfoot Hills • United Kingdom 74 B4
Moorhead • MN, United States 41 G2
Moosburg • Germany 82 J3
Moose • OT, Canada 39 O6
Moose Jaw • SA, Canada 38 J6
Moosehead • ME, United States 118 G2
Moosehead Lake • ME, United States 118 G2
Moosonee • OT, Canada 39 O6
Mopti • Mali 20 E6
Moquegua • Peru 127 B4
Mór • Hungary 13 H10
Mora • Portugal 11 C6
Mora • Spain 11 H5
Mora • Sweden 16 H6
Mora • Cameroon 22 G2
Móra d'Ebre • Spain 11 L3
Moradabad • India 105 C3
Morag • Poland 13 I4
Moraira • Spain 87 C2
Moraïtika • Corfu, Greece 92 B1
Morane • French Polynesia 33 N8
Morant Bay • Jamaica 124 C4
Morant Point • Jamaica 124 C4
Morar, Loch • United Kingdom 6 G5
Moratalla • Spain 11 J6
Moratuwa • Sri Lanka 106 D15
Morava • Czech Rep. 13 G9
Moravia • Czech Rep. 96 B1
Morawa • WA, Australia 34 C5
Morawhanna • Guyana 43 F2
Moray Firth • United Kingdom 6 I4
Morayshire • United Kingdom 75 A1
Morbach • Germany 82 H3
Morbihan • France 84 C4
Morbihan, Golfe du • France 84 C4
Mörbylånga • Sweden 95 F12
Morcenx • France 85 G3
Morcote • Switzerland 89 G7
Mordovia • Russian Fed. 17 G4
Möre • Sweden 95 F12
More, Glen • United Kingdom 6 H4
Møre og Romsdal • Norway 16 D5
Morecambe • United Kingdom 7 J7
Morecambe Bay • United Kingdom 7 J7
Moree • NS, Australia 34 I5
Morehead • Papua New Guinea 35 (1) C2
Moreiz, gora • Russian Fed. 26 J4
Mörel-Breiten **Ski** • Switzerland 70 [100]
Morelia **Heritage C** • Mexico 62 [20]
Morelia • Mexico 123 E1
Morella • Spain 11 K4
Moremi Wildlife Reserve **Park** • Botswana 103 [111]
Morena, Sierra • Spain 11 G6
Moreni • Romania 97 D1
Moresby I. • BC, Canada 38 E6
Moreton Bay • QL, Australia 34 J5
Moreton I. • QL, Australia 111 F6
Moreton-in-Marsh • United Kingdom 74 D4
Moreuil • France 5 F5
Mörfelden • Germany 5 L5
Morgan • UT, United States 116 B
Morgan City • LA, United States 118 K4
Morgan Lewis Beach • Barbados 125 H1
Morgan Lewis Mill • Barbados 125 H1
Morgan, Mt • QL, Australia 34 J4
Morges • Switzerland 89 G5
Morghab • Afghanistan 18 I2
Morgins **Ski** • Switzerland 70 [75]
Morgins • Switzerland 89 G5
Morhange • France 9 B8
Mori • China 26 P9
Mori • Japan 30 K3
Morib • Malaysia 108 D3
Morillon les Essert **Ski** • France 70 [15]
Morioka • Japan 30 K5
Morjärv • Sweden 16 L3
Morjim Beach • Goa, India 105 B1
Mörkö • Sweden 95 D4
Morlaix • France 84 C1
Mörlunda • Sweden 95 F8
Mormagao • Goa, India 105 B1
Morne Fortune • St Lucia 125 J1
Morne Seychellois • Seychelles 106 F1
Morne Seychellois Nat. Park • Seychelles 106 F1
Morne Trois Pitons Nat. Park **Heritage N** • Dominica 60 [26]
Mornington I. • QL, Australia 34 G3
Morobe • Papua New Guinea 35 (1) D2
Morocco • Africa 101 D
Morogoro • Tanzania 102 H4
Morombe • Madagascar 24 G4
Mörön • Mongolia 27 F7
Morón • Cuba 124 D3
Morón de la Frontera • Spain 11 F7
Moron Us He • China 28 F2
Moroni • Comoros 24 G2
Morotai • Indonesia 32 (1) C2
Moroto • Uganda 23 F3
Morotu • Japan 30 H8
Morpeth • United Kingdom 7 K6
Mórphou • Cyprus 93 J1
Mórphou Bay • Cyprus 93 J1
Morrinhos • Brazil 44 G2
Morrinsville • New Zealand 112 K2
Morris Jessup, Kap • Greenland 36 N1
Morristown Nat. Hist. Park **Park** • NJ, United States 121 [335]
Morro Bay State Park • CA, United States 117 F5
Morro de Chapéu • Brazil 44 H1
Mörrum • Sweden 95 F12
Mors **Beach** • Denmark 68 [49]
Mors • Denmark 95 F5
Morshansk • Russian Fed. 17 G4
Mort, Costa de la • Spain 87 D2
Mortagne • France 10 L5
Mortain • France 5 C6
Moruga • Trinidad & Tobago 125 K3
Morvan • France 10 J6
Morven • QL, Australia 111 F5
Morwell • VI, Australia 111 G3
Morzine **Ski** • France 70 [12]
Morzine • France 85 F2
Mosbach • Germany 82 G4
Moscow **Heritage C** • Russian Fed. 64 [207-208]
Moscow • Russian Fed. 97 E4
Moscow • ID, United States 117 E2
Mosel • Germany 82 H3
Mosel Valley • Germany 82 H3
Moselle • France 10 L5
Moses Lake • WA, United States 40 C2
Mosgiel • New Zealand 35 C7
Moshi • Tanzania 102 H2
Mosi-oa-Tunya **Heritage N** • Zambia/Zimbabwe 61 [95]
Mosjøen • Norway 16 G4
Moskenesøya • Norway 16 G3
Moskva **Heritage C** • Russian Fed. 64 [207-208]
Moskva • Russian Fed. 97 E4
Moskva [Riv] • Russian Fed. 97 E4
Moskviy, Kanal im • Russian Fed. 97 E4
Moslavacka Gora • Croatia 14 D4
Mosonmagyaróvár • Hungary 13 G10
Mosquito Bluff • St Kitts & Nevis 125 G4
Mosquitos, Costa de • Nicaragua 58 B9
Mosquitos, Golfo de • Costa Rica/Panama 37 E6
Moss • Norway 94 B4
Moss Park • FL, United States 121 C2
Moss Town • Bahamas 124 B3
Mossaka • Congo 23 B4
Mossel Bay • South Africa 100 C7
Mossendjo • Congo 22 G5
Mossman • QL, Australia 34 I3
Mossoró • Brazil 45 (1) D3
Most • Czech Rep. 96 C1
Mosta • Malta 93 H4
Mostaganem • Algeria 20 F1
Mostar • Bosnia-Herz. 14 E6
Mosul • Iraq 18 D2
Møsvatn • Norway 94 C6
Mota Lava • Vanuatu 35 (2) B1
Motaba • Congo 22 H4
Motagua • Guatemala 37 D4
Motala **Beach** • Sweden 69 [19]
Motala • Sweden 95 F4
Motherwell • United Kingdom 74 B3
Motihari • India 105 C8
Motilla del Palancar • Spain 11 J5
Motiti I. • New Zealand 112 K2
Motril • Spain 86 B7
Motru • Romania 14 J5
Motu One • French Polynesia 33 L7
Motueka • New Zealand 35 D5
Motuhora I. • New Zealand 112 K2
Mouchard • France 10 K7
Mouche, Anse a la • Seychelles 106 F1
Moudjéra • Mauritania 20 C5
Moúdros • Greece 92 D2
Mouila • Gabon 22 G5
Moukalaba, Réserve de la **Park** • Gabon 103 [51]
Moul • Niger 20 H5
Moulay Bousselham • Morocco 101 D1
Moulay Idriss • Morocco 101 D1
Moule à Chique, Cape • St Lucia 125 J4
Moulin [Château] • France 84 D2
Moulins • France 10 I7
Moulmein • Myanmar 31 B3
Moulouya • Morocco 101 D2
Moúnda, Akra • Greece 92 C2
Moundou • Chad 21 C6
Mount Abu • India 105 C5
Mount Aspiring Nat. Park • New Zealand 112 L2
Mount Bachelor **Ski** • OR, United States 116 [49]
Mount Baker **Ski** • WA, United States 116 [42]
Mount Barker • WA, Australia 34 C6
Mount Brighton **Ski** • MI, United States 116 [138]
Mount Buffalo • VI, Australia 111 G3
Mount Buller • VI, Australia 111 G3
Mount Carleton Prov. Park • NB, Canada 123 D2
Mount Darwin • Zimbabwe 102 J2
Mount Desert I. • ME, United States 118 G4
Mount Douglas • QL, Australia 34 I4
Mount Elgon Nat. Park • Kenya 101 G1
Mount Elgon Nat. Park **Park** • Kenya 103 [76]
Mount Gambier • SA, Australia 34 H7
Mount Hagen • Papua New Guinea 35 (1) C2
Mount Holly **Ski** • MI, United States 116 [139]
Mount Hood Meadows **Ski** • OR, United States 116 [47]
Mount Isa • QL, Australia 34 G4
Mount Kato **Ski** • MN, United States 116 [115]
Mount Kenya Nat. Park • Kenya 101 G3
Mount Kenya Nat. Park **Park** • Kenya 103 [79]
Mount Lavinia • Sri Lanka 106 D15
Mount Magnet • WA, Australia 34 C5
Mount Mansfield **Ski** • VT, United States 116 [203]
Mount Maunganui • New Zealand 112 K2
Mount Pleasant • MI, United States 41 J3
Mount Rainier Nat. Park • WA, United States 117 E1
Mount Rainier Nat. Park **Park** • WA, United States 120 [31]
Mount Revelstoke Nat. Park • BC, Canada 122 C4
Mount Robson Prov. Park • AL, Canada 122 C2
Mount Rose **Ski** • NV, United States 116 [67]
Mount Rushmore Nat. Mem. **Park** • SD, United States 120 [151]
Mount Snow **Ski** • VT, United States 116 [195]
Mount St Helens Nat. Volcanic Mon. • WA, United States 117 E1
Mount St Louis **Ski** • OT, Canada 116 [16]
Mount Sunapee **Ski** • NH, United States 116 [208]
Mount Tom **Ski** • MA, United States 116 [189]
Mount Vernon • WA, Australia 34 C4
Mount Vernon • WA, United States 40 B2
Mount Vernon • IL, United States 41 I4
Mount Washington **Ski** • BC, Canada 116 [1]
Mount's Bay • United Kingdom 74 F4
Mountain High **Ski** • CA, United States 116 [64]
Mountain Zebra Nat. Park • South Africa 100 C4
Mountain Zebra Nat. Park **Park** • South Africa 103 [120]
Mountshannon • Ireland 79 F4
Moura • Portugal 11 D6
Moura • QL, Australia 111 F4
Mourão • Portugal 11 D6
Mourdi, Dépression du • Chad 21 D4
Mourdiah • Mali 20 D6
Mourési **Beach** • Greece 69 [188]
Mourne Mtns • United Kingdom 7 G7
Mouscron • Belgium 5 G4
Moussoro • Chad 22 H2
Moutiers • France 85 F2
Mouton, Château • France 85 G1
Moutong • Indonesia 32 (1) B2
Mouydir • Algeria 20 F3
Moxey Town • Bahamas 124 B1
Moy • Ireland 79 F2
Moyale • Kenya 101 G2
Moyen Atlas • Morocco 101 D2
Moyne Abbey • Ireland 79 F2
Moyobamba • Peru 43 B5
Moyto • Chad 20 I6
Mozambique • Africa 24 E3
Mozambique, Canal de • Madagascar/Mozambique 24 G3
Mozambique Channel • Madagascar/Mozambique 24 G3
Mozyr • Belarus 17 D4
Mpanda • Tanzania 102 H1
Mpika • Zambia 24 E2
Mpouya • Congo 23 B4
Mpulungu • Zambia 24 E1
Mpumalanga • South Africa 24 D5
Mpungu Marine Nat. Park • Kenya 101 G5
Mragowo • Poland 13 K4
Mrâyer, El • Mauritania 20 D4
Mreiti, El • Mauritania 20 D4
Mrewa • Zimbabwe 102 J2
Mreyyé, El • Mali/Mauritania 20 D5
Msasani • Tanzania 102 H4
Msta • Russian Fed. 97 E1
Mtarazi Falls Nat. Park • Zimbabwe 102 J2
Mtelo • Kenya 23 F3
Mtsensk • Russian Fed. 17 F4
Mtskheta **Heritage C** • Georgia 63 [78]
Mtwara • Tanzania 102 H4
Muang Khammouan • Laos 31 C3
Muang Khong • Laos 31 D4
Muang Mai • Phuket, Thailand 109 K1
Muang Pakxan • Laos 31 C3
Muang Sing • Laos 31 C2
Muang Xaignabouri • Laos 31 C3
Muar • Malaysia 32 C2
Muarasiberut • Indonesia 32 B3
Muaratebo • Indonesia 32 C3
Muaratewe • Indonesia 32 E3
Muaro Takus • Indonesia 110 B4
Mubarraz, Al • Saudi Arabia 18 E4
Mubi • Nigeria 22 G2
Muchinga Mtns • Zambia 24 E2
Muck • United Kingdom 75 A2
Muckross Abbey • Ireland 79 F7
Muconda • Angola 23 C6
Mudan Jiang • China 29 H2
Mudanjiang • China 29 H2
Mudanya • Turkey 92 D3
Muddus Nat. Park **Park** • Sweden 72 [18]
Mudgee • NS, Australia 111 G2
Mudug • Somalia 23 H2
Mudumalai Wildlife Sanctuary • India 106 D10
Mudurnu • Turkey 15 L3
Mueda • Mozambique 24 F2
Muela de San Juan • Spain 11 J4
Muertos, I. Caja de • Puerto Rico 125 E3
Muezenti • Chad 20 I5
Mufulira • Zambia 24 D2
Mugila, Mtns • Dem. Rep. of Congo 23 D5
Mugla • Turkey 92 D9
Mugodzhary • Kazakhstan 26 I8
Muhammad 'Qawl • Sudan 21 G3
Muhammad, Râs • Egypt 101 F4
Mühlacker • Germany 9 D8
Mühlberg • Germany 71 A8
Mühldorf am Inn • Germany 82 J4
Mühlenbeck • Germany 81 F2
Mühlhausen • Germany 9 F5
Mühltal **Ski** • Austria 70 [147]
Muhos • Finland 16 N4
Muhu • Estonia 16 L7
Mui Wo • Hong Kong, China 107 H5
Muiden • Netherlands 80 C2
Muiderslot • Netherlands 80 C2
Muir, John, Nat. Hist. Site **Park** • CA, United States 120 [48]
Muir Woods Nat. Mon. **Park** • CA, United States 120 [43]
Muirfield • United Kingdom 74 B4
Muite • Mozambique 24 F2
Muizenberg • South Africa 100 C5

Mujeres, I. • Mexico 123 E6
Muji • China 28 C1
Muka Head • Penang, Malaysia 108 C1
Mukaceve • Ukraine 14 J1
Mukacevo • Ukraine 13 L9
Mukah • Malaysia 32 E2
Mukalla, Al • Yemen 18 E7
Mukawwar • Sudan 21 G3
Mukdahan • Thailand 31 C3
Mukha, Al • Yemen 18 D7
Mukinbudin • WA, Australia 34 C6
Mula • Spain 11 J6
Mulaku Atoll • Maldives 106 E3
Mulan • China 27 K7
Mulanje Mtns • Malawi 24 F3
Mulde • Germany 8 H5
Mulgrave I. • Australia 32 (1) F4
Mulhacén • Spain 86 B3
Mülheim an der Ruhr • Germany 81 E1
Mulhouse • France 10 M6
Mull • United Kingdom 6 G5
Mullaghareirk Mtns • Ireland 79 F6
Mullaghmore **Beach** • Ireland 68 [64]
Mullaittivu • Sri Lanka 106 D11
Mullet Peninsula • Ireland 79 F1
Mullewa • WA, Australia 34 C5
Müllheim • Germany 9 C9
Mullingar • Ireland 7 E8
Mullingar **Beach** • Ireland 68 [57]
Mullsjö • Sweden 95 F3
Mulobezi • Zambia 102 J1
Mulranny **Beach** • Ireland 68 [63]
Mulranny • Ireland 79 F1
Multan • Pakistan 28 B2
Mumbué • Angola 24 B2
Mummelsee • Germany 82 G6
Mun • Thailand 109 F2
Mun, Ko • Thailand 109 K2
Muna • Russian Fed. 27 J3
Muna • Indonesia 32 (1) B3
Munabao • India 18 J4
Münchberg • Germany 9 G6
München • Germany 82 J3
Muncie • IN, United States 41 I3
Munda • Solomon Is. 35 (1) F2
Mundaring • WA, Australia 34 C6
Münden • Germany 8 E5
Mundesley **Beach** •
United Kingdom 75 [37]
Mundiwindi • WA, Australia 34 D4
Mundo Nôvo • Brazil 44 H1
Munellës • Albania 15 B2
Mungbere • Dem. Rep. of Congo 23 D3
Müngstener Brücke • Germany 81 E4
Munh-Hajrhan-Ula • Mongolia 26 P8
Munhango • Angola 23 B6
Munich • Germany 82 J3
Muniesa • Spain 11 K3
Munifah • Saudi Arabia 18 E4
Munkedal • Sweden 95 F2
Munku Sardyk, gora •
Mongolia/Russian Fed. 27 F6
Munnar • India 106 D10
Munster • Ireland 7 C9
Münster • Germany 8 C5
Münsterland • Germany 8 C5
Muntenia • Romania 97 D1
Muntii Apuseni • Romania 14 J3
Muntok • Indonesia 32 D3
Munyati • Zimbabwe 102 J1
Münzenberg • Germany 82 G2
Muojärvi • Finland 16 O3
Muong Sen • Vietnam 31 C3
Muonio • Finland 16 L3
Muonio älv • Sweden 16 L2
Muonionjoki • Finland 16 L2
Muqdisho • Somalia 23 H3
Mur • Austria 13 D10
Mur, la • France 10 K9
Mura • Croatia 13 F11
Murad, Gunong • Malaysia 32 F2
Muranga • Kenya 101 G3
Murashi • Russian Fed. 17 H3
Murat • Turkey 18 D2
Murat Dagi • Turkey 15 K5
Muratli • Turkey 15 I2
Muratpasa **Beach** • Turkey 69 [225]
Murau • Austria 14 B2
Murchison Falls • Uganda 23 E3
Murchison • WA, Australia 34 C5
Murchison, Mt • New Zealand 35 C6
Murcia • Spain 87 C3
Murcia [Adm] • Spain 11 J7
Mure, la • France 10 K9
Mürefte • Turkey 15 I3
Mures • Romania 14 K4
Muret • France 10 G10
Murg • Germany 9 D8
Murgab • Turkmenistan 18 H2
Murgab • Tajikistan 18 J2
Murgon • QL, Australia 111 F6
Müritz • Germany 8 H3
Müritz, Nationalpark **Park** •
Germany 72 [60]
Muriaé • Brazil 127 C2
Murmansk • Russian Fed. 17 E1
Murmashi • Russian Fed. 17 E1
Murnau • Germany 82 J7
Murnau **Spa** • Germany 83 [250]
Muro **Beach** • Majorca, Spain 68 [126]
Muro • Majorca, Spain 87 H2
Murom • Russian Fed. 17 G3
Muroran • Japan 30 K3
Muros • Spain 11 B2
Muros **Beach** • Spain 68 [92]
Muros y Noya, Ria de • Spain 11 B2
Muroto-Zaki • Japan 30 H8
Murray • Australia 34 H6
Murray Bridge • SA, Australia 34 G7
Murray, Lake • Papua New Guinea 32 (1) F4
Murraysburg • South Africa 100 C3
Mürren **Ski** • Switzerland 70 [96]
Mürren • Switzerland 89 G2
Murrisk **Beach** • Ireland 68 [63]
Murrisk • Ireland 79 F1
Murrumbidgee • NS, Australia 111 G1
Murten • Switzerland 89 G2
Murtensee • Switzerland 89 G2
Murter • Croatia 14 C6
Murtosa **Beach** • Portugal 68 [95]
Murupara • New Zealand 112 K2
Mururoa • French Polynesia 33 N8
Murwara • India 105 C7
Murwillumbah • NS, Australia 111 F6
Murzuq • Libya 21 B2
Mürzzuschlag • Austria 13 E10
Mus • Turkey 18 D2
Mus-Haya • Russian Fed. 27 N4
Musa • Lithuania 13 N1
Musala • Bulgaria 14 K7
Musala • Indonesia 110 B4
Musan • D.P.R. of Korea 30 E3
Muscadet • France 84 B1
Muscat • Oman 18 G5
Muscatine • IA, United States 41 H3
Musgrave • QL, Australia 34 H2
Musgrave Ranges • SA, Australia 112 H3
Mushie • Dem. Rep. of Congo 23 B4
Muskegon • MI, United States 41 I3
Muskö • Sweden 95 D4
Muskö [I.] • Sweden 95 D4
Musoma • Tanzania 102 H1
Musselshell • MT, United States 38 J7
Mussende • Angola 23 B6
Mustafa Kemalpasa • Turkey 15 J3
Müstair **Heritage C** •
Switzerland 64 [104]
Müstair • Switzerland 89 G4
Mustvee • Estonia 16 N7
Musu-dan • D.P.R. of Korea 30 E4
Mut • Turkey 15 O7
Mut • Egypt 101 F3
Mutaf, Ra's al • Iran 18 F4
Mutare • Zimbabwe 102 J4
Muting • Indonesia 32 (1) F4
Mutirikwi, Lake • Zimbabwe 102 J4
Mutis, Gunung • Indonesia 32 (1) B4
Mutoko • Zimbabwe 24 E3
Mutoray • Russian Fed. 26 R5
Mutsamudu • Comoros 24 G2
Mutshatsha • Dem. Rep. of Congo 24 C2
Mutsu • Japan 30 K4
Mutsu-Wan • Japan 30 K4
Mutters • Austria 89 H6
Muwayh, Al • Saudi Arabia 21 H3
Muyinga • Burundi 23 E4
Muynak • Uzbekistan 26 I9
Muyun Kum • Kazakhstan 26 L9
Muzaffarnagar • India 105 C3
Muzaffarpur • India 105 C8
Muzhi • Russian Fed. 26 J4
Muztag • China 26 N10
Muztag • China 26 O10
Mvuma • Zimbabwe 102 J4
Mwabvi Game Reserve **Park** •
Malawi 103 [102]
Mwanza • Tanzania 102 H1
Mwaya • Tanzania 102 H3
Mwea Game Reserve • Kenya 101 G4
Mweelrea • Ireland 79 F3
Mweka • Dem. Rep. of Congo 23 C4
Mwene-Ditu • Dem. Rep. of Congo 23 C5
Mwense • Zambia 23 D6
Mweru, Lake •
Dem. Rep. of Congo/Zambia 23 D5
Mwinilunga • Zambia 24 C2
Mwnt **Beach** • United Kingdom 75 [170]
My Tho • Vietnam 108 B3
Myakit • Russian Fed. 27 P4
Myakka River State Park •
FL, United States 119 M5
Myako-Retto • Japan 29 H6
Myanaung • Myanmar 31 B3
Myanmar • Asia 31 B2
Mycene • Greece 15 D6
Myingyan • Myanmar 31 B2
Myinmoletkat Taung • Myanmar 31 B4
Myitkyina • Myanmar 31 B1
Mymensingh • Bangladesh 28 E4
Myra • Turkey 93 G3
Myrdal • Norway 94 C4
Myrdalsjökull • Iceland 16 (1) D3
Myre • Norway 16 H2
Myrtle Beach •
SC, United States 41 K5
Mys Shmidta • Russian Fed. 27 V3
Mysen • Norway 94 B4
Mysië • Turkey 15 I4
Myslenice • Poland 13 I8
Mysore • India 106 D6
Mystic • CT, United States 118 H2
Myszkow • Poland 13 I7
Myszyniec • Poland 13 K4
Mytishchi • Russian Fed. 97 E4
Myvatn • Iceland 16 (1) E2
Mze • Czech Rep. 96 C1

N

N'Djamena • Chad 21 B5
Na Cailleighe, Sliabh • Ireland 79 E1
Na Pali Coast State Park •
HI, United States 119 L2
Na Phra Lan, Laem •
Ko Samui, Thailand 109 J1
Naab • Germany 9 H7
Naalehu • HI, United States 119 L8
Naantali • Finland 95 E3
Naarden • Netherlands 80 C2
Naas • Ireland 79 E3
Nabadid • Somalia 21 H6
Naberezhnyye Chelny •
Russian Fed. 17 I3
Nabeul • Tunisia 101 E2
Nabi Shu'ayb • Yemen 25 F8
Nabi Shu'ayb, Jabal an • Yemen 21 H4
Nabire • Indonesia 32 (1) E3
Nablus • Jordan 98 A6
Nacala • Mozambique 24 G2
Nachingwea • Tanzania 102 H4
Nachod • Czech Rep. 13 F7
Nachuge • India 28 F6
Nacka • Sweden 95 D4
Nacogdoches • TX, United States 119 N4
Nådendal • Finland 95 E3
Nadiad • India 28 B4
Nador • Morocco 101 D2
Nadur • Malta 93 H1
Nadvoitsy • Russian Fed. 17 E2
Nadym • Russian Fed. 26 L4
Nadym [Riv] • Russian Fed. 26 L5
Nærøyfjorden • Norway 94 C4
Næstved **Beach** • Denmark 68 [37]
Næstved • Denmark 95 F14
Náfpaktos • Greece 15 C5
Náfpaktos **Beach** • Greece 69 [175]
Náfplio • Greece 15 D6
Náfplio **Beach** • Greece 69 [184]
Nafud, An • Saudi Arabia 18 D4
Nafusah, Jabal • Libya 21 B1
Nag's Head • St Kitts & Nevis 125 G4
Naga • Philippines 31 G4
Naga Hills • India 105 A2
Nagaland • India 28 F3
Nagano • Japan 30 J6
Nagaoka • Japan 30 J6
Nagappattinam • India 106 D11
Nagar Haveli • India 28 B4
Nagarhole Nat. Park • India 106 D6
Nagarjuna Sagar • India 106 D3
Nagarjunakona • India 106 D3
Nagasaki • Japan 30 E8
Nagato • Japan 30 F7
Nagaur • India 105 C1
Nagda • India 105 C5
Nagercoil • India 106 D14
Nagina • India 105 C3
Nago • Japan 29 H5
Nagold • Germany 82 G6
Nagornyy • Russian Fed. 27 J5
Nagoya • Japan 30 I7
Nagpur • India 28 C4
Nagqu • China 28 F2
Nagruawahia • New Zealand 112 K1
Nags Head • NC, United States 118 H5
Nagy-Milic • Slovak Rep. 14 I1
Nagyatád • Hungary 13 G11
Nagykálló • Hungary 13 K10
Nagykanisza • Hungary 13 G11
Nagykáta • Hungary 13 I10
Nagykörös • Hungary 13 I10
Naha • Japan 29 H5
Nahanni Butte • NT, Canada 38 G4
Nahanni Nat. Park **Heritage N** •
NT, Canada 60 [2]
Nahariyya • Israel 98 A1
Nahe • Germany 9 C7
Nahr Ouassel • Algeria 11 N9
Nai, Dong • Vietnam 108 B2
Nai Ham Beach •
Phuket, Thailand 109 K2
Nai Yang • Phuket, Thailand 109 K1
Nai Yang Beach •
Phuket, Thailand 109 K1
Nailsworth • United Kingdom 74 D3
Naimisharanya • India 105 C3
Nain • NF, Canada 39 S5
Naintal • India 105 C3
Nairn **Beach** • United Kingdom 75 [3]
Nairnshire • United Kingdom 75 A1
Nairobi • Kenya 101 G3
Nairobi Nat. Park • Kenya 101 G3
Nairobi Nat. Park **Park** • Kenya 103 [83]
Najaf, An • Iraq 18 D3
Najd • Saudi Arabia 21 H2
Najin • D.P.R. of Korea 30 F3
Najran • Saudi Arabia 18 D6
Naka Noi, Ko • Thailand 109 K1
Naka Yai, Ko • Thailand 109 K1
Naka-No • Japan 30 G6
Nakaina Mtns • Papua New Guinea 35 (1) E1
Nakajo • Japan 30 J5
Nakamura • Japan 30 G8
Nakasongola • Uganda 23 E3
Nakatchafushi • Maldives 106 E2
Nakatsu • Japan 30 F8
Nakatsugawa • Japan 30 I7
Nakhichen • Iran 18 E2
Nakhodka • Russian Fed. 27 L8
Nakhon Nayok • Thailand 109 H2
Nakhon Pathom • Thailand 109 H1
Nakhon Phanom • Thailand 31 C3
Nakhon Ratchasima • Thailand 31 C3
Nakhon Sawan • Thailand 31 C3
Nakhon Si Thammarat • Thailand 31 C5
Nakina • OT, Canada 39 N6
Nakiska **Ski** • AL, Canada 116 [15]
Naklo • Poland 13 G4
Nakonde • Zambia 23 E5
Nakskov **Beach** • Denmark 68 [37]
Nakskov • Denmark 95 F14
Naktong • Rep. of Korea 30 E7
Nakuru • Kenya 101 G3
Nal • Pakistan 18 I4
Nalayha • Mongolia 27 G7
Nalchik • Russian Fed. 17 G6
Nalgonda • India 106 D3
Nallamalla Range • India 106 D3
Nallihan • Turkey 15 M3
Nalón • Spain 11 F1
Nalut • Libya 21 B1
Nam Cat Tien Nat. Park •
Vietnam 108 B2
Nam Co • China 28 F2
Nam Dinh • Vietnam 31 D2
Nam Tok Surin Nat. Park •
Thailand 109 G1
Nam Wu Wu • Phuket, Thailand 109 K1
Namakwaland • South Africa 24 B6
Namangan • Uzbekistan 18 J1
Namatanai • Papua New Guinea 35 (1) E1
Namatjira Mem. • NT, Australia 112 H2
Namber • Indonesia 32 (1) D3
Nambour • QL, Australia 111 F6
Namdalen • Norway 16 G4
Nämdö • Sweden 95 D4
Nametil • Mozambique 24 F3
Namib Desert • Namibia 24 A3
Namib-Naukluft Nat. Park **Park** •
Namibia 103 [116]
Namibe • Angola 24 A3
Namibia • Africa 24 B4
Namja Namse La Shankou •
China/Nepal 28 D2
Namkham • Myanmar 31 B2
Namlea • Indonesia 32 (1) C3
Namous • Algeria 20 E2
Namp'o • D.P.R. of Korea 30 C5
Nampa • ID, United States 117 E4
Nampala • Mali 22 C1
Nampula • Mozambique 24 F3
Namrud • Syria 98 A2
Namsen • Norway 16 F4
Namsos • Norway 16 F4
Namuang Falls •
Ko Samui, Thailand 109 J2
Namuli, Serra • Mozambique 24 F3
Namur • Belgium 80 A15
Namur [Adm] • Belgium 80 A15
Namwon • Rep. of Korea 30 D7
Namyslow • Poland 13 G6
Nan • Thailand 109 G2
Nan Hai • China 29 F6
Nan Hulsan Hu • China 28 G1
Nan Jing • China 107 J1
Nan Ling • China 29 E5
Nan [Riv] • Thailand 109 G2
Nanaimo • BC, Canada 122 C3
Nanam • D.P.R. of Korea 30 E4
Nanango • QL, Australia 111 F6
Nanao • Japan 30 I6
Nanchang • China 29 F5
Nanchong • China 29 D4
Nancowry • India 28 F7
Nancy • France 10 L5
Nancy **Heritage C** • France 64 [51]
Nancy Sound • New Zealand 112 L1
Nanda Devi • India 25 I7
Nanda Devi Nat. Park **Heritage N** •
India 61 [105]
Nanded • India 28 C5
Nandi • Fiji 35 (2) D2
Nandikanima Pass • India 106 D3
Nandyal • India 106 D3
Nanfen • China 30 B4
Nanga Parbat • Jammu & Kashmir 28 B1
Nangapinoh • Indonesia 32 E3
Nangatayap • Indonesia 32 E3
Nangis • France 85 E4
Nangnim • D.P.R. of Korea 30 D4
Nangnim-Sanmaek •
D.P.R. of Korea 30 D4
Nanhui • China 107 J4
Naning • China 29 D6
Nankoku • Japan 30 G8
Nanling • China 107 J3
Nannup • WA, Australia 34 C6
Nanpan Jiang • China 29 C6
Nanping • China 29 F5
Nanqiao • China 107 J4
Nansei-Shoto • Japan 31 H1
Nansha • China 107 H2
Nansha Qundao • South China Sea 31 E5
Nanshan • Shenzhen, China 107 H3
Nantais, Lac • QU, Canada 39 Q4
Nantes • France 84 D1
Nanton Point •
Antigua & Barbuda 125 F4
Nantong • China 107 J2
Nantucket • MA, United States 58 A2
Nantucket I. •
MA, United States 118 H2
Nanumea • Tuvalu 33 I6
Nanuque • Brazil 44 H2
Nanus Fort • Goa, India 105 B1
Nanwei Dao • South China Sea 31 E5
Nanyandang Shan • China 29 G5
Nanyang • China 29 E4
Nanyo • Japan 30 K5
Nanyuki • Kenya 101 G1
Nao, Cabo de la • Spain 87 C2
Naococane, Lac • QU, Canada 39 Q6
Náoussa • Greece 15 D3
Napa Valley • CA, United States 117 F3
Napata • Sudan 21 F4
Naphtali • Israel/Lebanon 98 A2
Napier • New Zealand 112 K4
Naples **Heritage C** • Italy 64 [127]
Naples • Italy 91 G3
Naples • FL, United States 119 M7
Napo • Peru 43 C4
Napoléon, Route • France 85 H1
Nápoli **Heritage C** • Italy 64 [127]
Nápoli • Italy 91 G3
Nápoli, Golfo di • Italy 91 G3
Napoule-Plage, la • France 85 H4
Nar • United Kingdom 5 D2
Nar'yan Mar • Russian Fed. 17 I1
Nara • Mali 22 C1
Nara • Pakistan 28 A3
Nara • Japan 30 H7
Naracoorte **Heritage N** •
SA, Australia 61 [133]
Narayanganj • Bangladesh 28 F4
Narbonne • France 10 I10
Narbonne **Beach** • France 68 [129]
Narca, Punta da • Angola 22 G6
Narcondam • India 28 F6
Nardò • Italy 12 M8
Nares Strait • Canada/Greenland 46 V1
Narew • Poland 13 K4
Narin Gol • China 28 F1
Narithiwat • Thailand 109 F4
Nariva Swamp •
Trinidad & Tobago 125 K4
Narmada • India 28 C4
Narnaul • India 105 C2
Narni • Italy 12 G6
Naro • Sicily, Italy 90 D3
Narodnaya, gora • Russian Fed. 17 J1
Narrabri • NS, Australia 34 I6
Narrandera • NS, Australia 111 G1
Narrogin • WA, Australia 34 C6
Narromine • NS, Australia 34 I6
Narrows, The • St Kitts & Nevis 125 G4
Narsarsuaq • Greenland 39 V4
Narsimhapur • India 28 C4
Narva • Estonia 16 N7
Narvik • Norway 16 I2
Narym • Russian Fed. 26 N6
Naryn • Kazakhstan 26 M9
Naryn [Riv] •
Kazakhstan/Uzbekistan 26 M9
Narynkol • Kazakhstan 26 M9
Näsåker • Sweden 16 I5
Nasalot Game Reserve • Kenya 101 G1
Naseby • United Kingdom 71 A7
Nash Point • United Kingdom 74 F2
Nashoba Valley **Ski** •
MA, United States 116 [194]
Nashua • NH, United States 118 G3
Nashville • TN, United States 41 I4
Nasice • Croatia 12 M3
Näsijärvi • Finland 95 E2
Nasik • India 28 B4
Nasir • Sudan 23 E2
Nasiriyah, An • Iraq 18 E3
Nass • BC, Canada 38 F5
Nassau • Cook Is. 33 K7
Nassau • Bahamas 124 B3
Nasser, Lake • Egypt 101 F5
Nässjö • Sweden 95 F7
Nata • Botswana 24 D4
Nata [Riv] • Botswana/Zimbabwe 24 D3
Natal • Brazil 45 (1) D3
Natal • Indonesia 110 B4
Natashquan • QU, Canada 123 D2
Natashquan [Riv] • QU, Canada 39 S6
Natchez • MS, United States 118 K1
Natchez Nat. Hist. Park **Park** •
MS, United States 121 [199]
Natchez Trace Parkway •
United States 118 K2
Natchez Trace Parkway **Park** •
United States 121 [201]
Natchitoches •
LA, United States 118 K1
Nathdwara • India 105 C5
Nathon • Ko Samui, Thailand 109 J1
National Agricultural Centre •
United Kingdom 74 D2
National Birds of Prey Centre •
United Kingdom 74 D3
National Capital parks **Park** •
DC, United States 121 [290]
National Exhibition Centre •
United Kingdom 74 D2
National Mall **Park** •
DC, United States 121 [291]
National Park • New Zealand 112 K3
National Stadium • Singapore 108 E4
Natitingou • Benin 22 E2
Natividade • Brazil 43 H6
Natori • Japan 30 K5
Natron, Lake • Tanzania 102 H2
Nattawasaga Bay • OT, Canada 122 B5
Natuna Besar • Indonesia 32 D2
Natuna Is. • Indonesia 31 D6
Natuna, Kepulauan • Indonesia 110 A2
Natural Bridges Nat. Mon. **Park** •
UT, United States 120 [85]
Naturaliste, Cape •
WA, Australia 34 C6
Nature's Valley • South Africa 100 C7
Nauders • Austria 89 H6
Nauen • Germany 81 F1
Naujoji-Akmene • Lithuania 13 L1
Naukluft Mtns • Namibia 24 B4
Naul • Ireland 79 E2
Naumburg • Germany 9 G5
Naumburg **Spa** • Germany 83 [122]
Nauplia • Greece 71 A20
Nauru • Pacific Ocean 33 H6
Nauta • Peru 43 C4
Navahermosa • Spain 11 G5
Navajo Indian Reservation •
AZ/NM, United States 118 J2
Navajo Nat. Mon. •
AZ, United States 118 J1
Navajo Nat. Mon. **Park** •
AZ, United States 120 [102]
Navajo Reservoir •
CO/NM, United States 118 J2
Navalmoral de la Mata • Spain 11 F5
Navan • Ireland 79 E1
Navarin, mys • Russian Fed. 27 U4
Navarino • Greece 71 A20
Navarino, I. • Chile 45 C7
Navarra • Spain 11 J2
Navasota • TX, United States 119 N4
Navian, Pointe • New Caledonia 35 (2) A3
Navoi • Uzbekistan 18 I1
Navrongo • Ghana 22 D2
Nawabshah • Pakistan 28 A3
Nawalgarh • India 105 C2
Nawiliwili • HI, United States 119 L2
Náxos • Greece 92 D8
Náxos [I.] • Greece 92 D8
Nayarit • Mexico 37 (1) A1
Nayoro • Japan 30 L2
Nazaré • Portugal 11 B5
Nazaré • Brazil 44 I1
Nazaré **Beach** • Portugal 68 [97]
Nazareth • Israel 98 A4
Nazarovo • Russian Fed. 26 P6
Nazca **Heritage C** • Peru 62 [52]
Nazca • Peru 127 B1
Nazca Lines • Peru 127 B1
Naze • Japan 29 H5
Nazilli • Turkey 15 J6
Nazimovo • Russian Fed. 26 P6
Nazran • Russian Fed. 17 G6
Nazret • Ethiopia 23 F2
Nazwa • Oman 18 G5
Nchelenge • Zambia 23 D5
Ndalatando • Angola 23 B5
Ndali • Benin 22 E3
Ndélé • Central African Rep. 23 C2
Ndendé, Réserve de **Park** • Gabon 103 [52]
Ndere I. Nat. Park • Kenya 101 G3
Ndola • Zambia 24 D2
Ndrhamcha, Sebkha du •
Mauritania 20 B5
Nduindui • Solomon Is. 35 (1) F2
Ndumo Game Reserve **Park** •
South Africa 103 [125]
Nea • Norway 16 F5
Néa Artáki • Greece 15 E5
Néa Fókea **Beach** • Greece 69 [192]
Néa Ionia • Greece 92 D4
Néa Kidonia **Beach** •
Crete, Greece 69 [212]
Néa Moni • Greece 92 D5
Néa Póri **Beach** • Greece 69 [190]
Néa Róda **Beach** • Greece 69 [192]
Néa Skióni **Beach** • Greece 69 [192]
Néa Stíra • Greece 92 D4
Néa Zíhni • Greece 15 E2
Neagh, Lough • United Kingdom 7 F7
Neale, Lake • NT, Australia 112 H3
Neanderthal • Germany 81 E3
Neápoli • Macedonia, Greece 15 C3
Neápoli • Pelopónnisos, Greece 15 E7
Neápoli **Beach** • Greece 69 [182]
Neápoli • Crete, Greece 93 E7
Neapolitan Riviera • Italy 91 G4
Neath • United Kingdom 7 I10
Nebbio • Corsica, France 85 L2
Nebbou • Burkina Faso 20 E6
Nebel **Spa** • Germany 83 [3]
Nebit-Dag • Turkmenistan 18 F2
Neblina • Brazil/Venezuela 43 D3
Nebo • QL, Australia 111 F3
Nebo, Mount • Jordan 98 A8
Nebraska • United States 40 F3
Nebrodi • Sicily, Italy 12 I11
Necessity, Fort, Nat. Battlefield **Park** •
PA, United States 121 [301]
Nechako • BC, Canada 122 C1
Neches • TX, United States 119 N4
Neckar • Germany 82 G6
Neckargemünd • Germany 5 L5
Neckarsulm • Germany 9 E7
Necochea • Argentina 127 D3
Neder-Rijn • Netherlands 5 I3
Nedong • China 28 F3
Nedstrand • Norway 94 C5
Needham's Point • Barbados 125 H3
Needles • CA, United States 117 F6
Needles, The • United Kingdom 5 B4
Nefedova • Russian Fed. 26 L6
Nefta • Tunisia 101 E3
Neftekamsk • Russian Fed. 17 I3
Nefteyugansk • Russian Fed. 26 L5
Nefza • Tunisia 12 D12
Negage • Angola 22 H6
Negara • Bali, Indonesia 110 C1
Negele • Ethiopia 23 F2
Negeri Sembilan • Malaysia 31 C6
Negev • Israel 21 F1
Negomano • Mozambique 24 F2
Negombo • Sri Lanka 106 D15
Negra • Peru 43 A5
Negra, Punta • Peru 43 A5
Negrais, Cape • Myanmar 31 A3
Negreira • Spain 11 C2
Negril • Jamaica 124 C1
Negro • Brazil 43 E4
Negro • Uruguay 44 E5
Negro • Argentina 45 D4
Negroponte • Greece 71 A20
Negros • Philippines 31 G4
Negru Voda • Romania 97 D2
Nehe • China 27 J7
Neheim-Hüsten • Germany 8 C5
Nei Mongol Zizhiqu • China 29 E2
Neiderau **Ski** • Austria 70 [147]
Neidpath Castle •
United Kingdom 74 B4
Neijiang • China 29 D5
Neiva • Colombia 43 B3
Nekemt • Ethiopia 23 F2
Nekhen • Egypt 101 F5
Neksø • Denmark 95 F16
Nelichu • Sudan 23 E2
Nelidovo • Russian Fed. 97 E3
Nellore • India 106 D7
Nelma • Russian Fed. 27 M7
Nelson • New Zealand 35 D5
Nelson • BC, Canada 38 H7
Nelson • MN, Canada 38 L5
Nelson, Cape • VI, Australia 34 H7
Nelson Museum •
St Kitts & Nevis 125 G4
Nelson's Dockyard •
Antigua & Barbuda 125 F4
Nelspoort • South Africa 100 C3
Nelspruit • South Africa 24 E5
Nelyaty • Russian Fed. 27 I5
Néma • Mauritania 20 D5
Neman • Russian Fed. 13 K2
Neman [Riv] • Belarus 16 M10
Nembrala • Indonesia 32 (1) B5
Neméa • Greece 15 D6
Neméa [Adm] • Greece 15 D6
Nëmërçkë • Albania 15 B3
Nemi, Lagi di • Italy 91 F3
Nemours • France 85 E4
Nemrut Dag **Heritage C** • Turkey 64 [195]
Nemunas • Lithuania 13 L2
Nemuro • Japan 30 M3
Nen Jiang • China 27 K6
Nenagh • Ireland 79 F6
Nenana • AK, United States 38 B4
Nendaz **Ski** • Switzerland 70 [80]
Nene • United Kingdom 7 M9
Nenjiang • China 27 K7
Néo Itilo **Beach** • Greece 69 [182]
Neohóri **Beach** • Greece 69 [200]
Néos Marmarás **Beach** • Greece 69 [192]
Néos Marmarás • Greece 92 D1
Nepal • Asia 28 D3
Nepalganj • Nepal 28 D3
Nephi • UT, United States 40 D4
Nephin Beg Range • Ireland 79 F1
Neport Beach •
CA, United States 40 C5
Neptun-Olimp • Romania 97 D2
Nera • Italy 91 F1
Neratovice • Czech Rep. 13 D7
Neretva • Bosnia-Herz. 12 L5
Neringa • Lithuania 13 J2
Nerja **Beach** • Spain 68 [114]
Nerja • Spain 86 B7
Nerpio • Spain 11 I6
Nerva • Spain 11 E7
Nesbyen • Norway 94 C4
Nesebur **Beach** • Bulgaria 69 [242]
Nesebur **Heritage C** • Bulgaria 64 [171]
Nesebur • Bulgaria 97 D3
Neskaupstadur • Iceland 16 (1) F2
Neslandsvatn • Norway 94 B3
Nesna • Norway 16 G3
Ness, Loch • United Kingdom 6 H4
Nessebar **Beach** • Bulgaria 69 [242]
Nessebar **Heritage C** • Bulgaria 64 [171]
Nessebar • Bulgaria 97 D3
Nesselwang • Germany 82 J6
Neßmersiel **Spa** • Germany 83 [44]
Nesterov • Russian Fed. 13 L3
Nesterov • Ukraine 13 N8
Néstos • Greece 15 F2
Nesttun • Norway 94 C3
Nesvizh • Belarus 16 N10
Netanya • Israel 98 A3
Netherlands • Europe 5 I2
Netherlands Antilles •
West Indies 37 H5
Neto • Italy 12 K9
Nette • Germany 82 H1
Nettiling Lake • NU, Canada 39 Q3
Nettuno • Italy 91 F3
Nettuno, Grotta di •
Sardinia, Italy 90 C1
Neu-Anspach • Germany 82 H2
Neu-Ulm • Germany 82 J1
Neubrandenburg • Germany 8 I3
Neuburg • Germany 9 G8
Neuchâtel • Switzerland 89 G1
Neuchâtel, Lac de • Switzerland 89 G1
Neuendorf **Spa** • Germany 83 [278]
Neuenhagen bei Berlin • Germany 81 F2
Neufchâteau • France 10 K5
Neufchâteau • Belgium 80 A19
Neufchâtel-en-Bray • France 10 G4
Neuharlingersiel **Spa** • Germany 83 [46]
Neuhaus **Spa** • Germany 83 [55]
Neuhof • Germany 9 E6
Neukirchen • Germany 81 E1
Neukirchen **Spa** • Germany 83 [132]
Neuleiningen • Germany 82 G4
Neumagen-Dhron • Germany 82 H3
Neumarkt in der Oberpfalz •
Germany 9 G7
Neumarkt-St Veit • Germany 82 J4
Neumarkter Sattel • Austria 14 B2
Neumünster • Germany 8 E2
Neunkirchen • Germany 9 D6
Neunkirchen • Austria 13 F10
Neunkirchen • Germany 82 G3
Neuquén • Argentina 45 C3
Neuruppin • Germany 8 H4
Neuschwanstein • Germany 82 J6
Neusiedler See • Austria 13 F10
Neuss • Germany 81 E3
Neustadt **Spa** • Germany 83 [26]
Neustadt am Rübenberge •
Germany 8 E4
Neustadt an der Aisch • Germany 9 F7
Neustadt an der Weinstraße •
Germany 82 G4
Neustadt bei Coburg • Germany 9 G6
Neustadt in Holstein • Germany 8 F2
Neustift • Austria 89 H6
Neustift im Stubaital **Ski** •
Austria 70 [140]
Neustrelitz • Germany 8 I3
Neuwied • Germany 82 H1
Nevada • United States 117 F
Nevada City • CA, United States 117 F3
Nevada, Sierra • Colombia 43 C1
Nevada, Sierra • Spain 86 B3
Nevada, Sierra •
CA, United States 117 F3
Nevado • Colombia 43 C3
Neve, Serra da • Angola 24 A2
Nevel • Russian Fed. 17 D3
Nevers • France 10 I7
Nevesinje • Bosnia-Herz. 14 F6
Neviges • Germany 81 E2
Nevinnomyssk • Russian Fed. 17 G6
Nevis • St Kitts & Nevis 125 G4
Nevis, Ben • United Kingdom 6 H5
Nevis Peak • St Kitts & Nevis 125 G4
Nevyansk • Russian Fed. 26 J6
New Amsterdam • Suriname 43 F2
New Bedford • MA, United States 118 H2
New Bern • NC, United States 118 H5
New Braunfels •
TX, United States 119 N3
New Brighton • New Zealand 35 D6
New Britain • Papua New Guinea 35 (1) E2
New Brunswick • Canada 123 D2
New Caledonia • Pacific Ocean 35 (2) B3
New Castle • DE, United States 118 H3
New Delhi • India 105 C2
New Forest • United Kingdom 5 B4
New Georgia • Solomon Is. 35 (1) F2
New Georgia Sound • Solomon Is. 35 (1) F2

New Glasgow • NS, Canada 123 D7
New Guinea • Oceania 35 (1) C2
New Hampshire • United States 118 G3
New Hanover • Papua New Guinea 35 (1) E1
New Haven • CT, United States 118 H2
New Hazleton • BC, Canada 122 C1
New Hebrides • Vanuatu 35 (2) B2
New Iberia • LA, United States 118 K3
New Ireland • Papua New Guinea 35 (1) E1
New Jersey • United States 118 H1
New London • CT, United States 118 H2
New Mexico • United States 40 E5
New Norfolk • TS, Australia 34 I8
New Orleans • LA, United States 118 K4
New Orleans Jazz Nat. Hist. Park **Park** • LA, United States 121 [197]
New Paltz • NY, United States 118 H1
New Plymouth • New Zealand 112 K3
New Providence • Bahamas 124 B3
New Quay **Beach** • United Kingdom 75 [176-178]
New Ross • Ireland 7 F9
New Siberian Is. • Russian Fed. 27 N1
New South Wales • NS, Australia 34 I6
New Territories • Hong Kong, China 107 H5
New Ulm • MN, United States 41 H3
New Valley, The • Egypt 101 F3
New Westminster • BC, Canada 38 G7
New York • NY, United States 118 H2
New York [Adm] • United States 41 K3
New Zealand • Oceania 35
Newark • NJ, United States 118 H1
Newark-on-Trent • United Kingdom 7 L8
Newborough **Beach** • United Kingdom 75 [205]
Newbury • United Kingdom 7 K10
Newcastle • United Kingdom 7 G7
Newcastle • South Africa 24 E5
Newcastle • WY, United States 40 F3
Newcastle • NS, Australia 111 G2
Newcastle • NB, Canada 123 D2
Newcastle • Jamaica 124 C4
Newcastle • St Kitts & Nevis 125 G4
Newcastle Creek • NT, Australia 34 F3
Newcastle under Lyme • United Kingdom 7 J8
Newcastle upon Tyne • United Kingdom 7 K7
Newcastle West • Ireland 79 F6
Newfield • Antigua & Barbuda 125 F4
Newfoundland • NF, Canada 123 D3
Newfoundland & Labrador • Canada 39 T6
Newgale **Beach** • United Kingdom 75 [163]
Newgrange • Ireland 79 E2
Newhaven • United Kingdom 74 E3
Newman • WA, Australia 34 C4
Newmarket • United Kingdom 7 M9
Newmarket • Ireland 79 F6
Newmarket • OT, Canada 122 B5
Newmarket on Fergus • Ireland 79 F6
Newport • Isle of Wight, UK 7 K11
Newport • Wales, UK 74 D3
Newport **Beach** • United Kingdom 75 [168]
Newport • Ireland 79 F1
Newport • OR, United States 117 E3
Newport • VT, United States 118 G1
Newport • RI, United States 118 H2
Newport Beach • CA, United States 40 C5
Newport News • VA, United States 118 H5
Newquay • United Kingdom 74 F4
Newquay **Beach** • United Kingdom 75 [124-125]
Newry • United Kingdom 7 F7
Newton • KS, United States 41 G4
Newton Abbot • United Kingdom 74 F5
Newton Ground • St Kitts & Nevis 125 G1
Newtontoppen • Svalbard 46 N2
Newtown • United Kingdom 7 I9
Newtownabbey • United Kingdom 7 G7
Newtownards • United Kingdom 7 G7
Neya • Russian Fed. 17 G3
Neyshabur • Iran 18 G2
Neyveli • India 106 D11
Nez Perce Nat. Hist. Park • ID, United States 117 E2
Nez Perce Nat. Hist. Park **Park** • ID, United States 120 [66]
Nga, Laem • Phuket, Thailand 109 K2
Ngabé • Congo 22 H5
Ngami, Lake • Botswana 24 C4
Ngamiland • Botswana 24 C3
Ngangerabeli Plain • Kenya 23 G4
Ngangla Ringco • China 28 D2
Nganglong Kangri • China 28 D2
Nganze Co • China 28 E2
Ngao • Thailand 109 G2
Ngaoundéré • Cameroon 22 G3
Ngaruroro • New Zealand 112 K4
Ngauruhoe, Mt • New Zealand 112 K4
Ngo • Congo 22 H5
Ngoan Muc Pass • Vietnam 108 B2
Ngoc Linh • Vietnam 25 L8
Ngoko • Cameroon/Congo 23 B3
Ngola Shankou • China 29 B3
Ngoma • Zambia 24 D3
Ngoring Hu • China 28 G2
Ngorongoro Conservation Area **Heritage N** • Tanzania 61 [91]
Ngorongoro Conservation Area • Tanzania 102 H2
Ngorongoro Conservation Area **Park** • Tanzania 103 [89]
Ngorongoro Crater • Tanzania 102 H2
Ngounie • Gabon 22 G5
Ngourti • Niger 20 H5
Nguigmi • Niger 20 H6
Ngum, Ko • Thailand 109 K1
Nguni • Kenya 23 F4
Ngurah Rai [Apt] • Bali, Indonesia 110 C4
Nguru • Nigeria 22 H2
Nha Trang • Vietnam 108 B2
Nhulunbuy • NT, Australia 34 G2
Nia-Nia • Dem. Rep. of Congo 23 D3
Niafounké • Mali 20 E5
Niagara Falls • NY, United States 122 B9
Niagara Falls • OT, Canada 122 B9
Niagara Falls [Waterfall] • Canada/United States 122 B9
Niah • Malaysia 32 E2
Niamey • Niger 20 F6
Niangara • Dem. Rep. of Congo 23 D3
Niangay, Lac • Mali 20 E5
Niangoloko • Burkina Faso 22 D2
Nianzishan • China 27 J7
Niao Dao • China 29 B3
Nias • Indonesia 110 B3
Nibe • Denmark 95 F5
Nicaragua • C. America 37 D5
Nicaragua, Lago de • Nicaragua 37 D5
Nice • France 85 H2
Nice-Côte d'Azur [Apt] • France 85 H2
Nichicun, Lac • QU, Canada 39 Q6
Nicholls Town • Bahamas 124 B1
Nicholson • WA, Australia 34 E3
Nicobar Is. • India 28 F7
Nicosia • Cyprus 93 J2
Nidda • Germany 5 M4
Nidda • Germany 9 E6
Nidda [Riv] • Germany 9 E6
Nideggen • Germany 82 G1
Nidersächsisches Wattenmeer, Nationalpark **Park** • Germany 72 [55]
Nidri • Greece 92 C1
Nidzica • Poland 13 J4
Nieblum **Spa** • Germany 83 [4]
Niebüll • Germany 8 D2
Niecka Sieradzka • Poland 13 H6
Nied • France 5 J5
Niederau • Austria 89 H3
Niederbayern • Germany 9 H8
Niederdorf **Ski** • Italy 70 [238]
Niederlausitz • Germany 81 D2
Niederösterreich • Austria 13 E10
Niedersachsen • Germany 8 E4
Nienburg • Germany 8 E4
Nienhagen **Spa** • Germany 83 [270]
Niers • Germany 5 J3
Nieuw Amsterdam • Suriname 43 F2
Nieuwpoort • Belgium 80 B1
Nieuwpoort-aan-Zee • Belgium 80 B1
Nieves, Pico de las • Gran Canaria, Canary Is. 86 E4
Niger • Africa 20 G5
Niger [Adm] • Africa 22 F3
Niger Delta • Nigeria 22 F3
Niger [Riv] • Africa 22 D1
Nigrán **Beach** • Spain 68 [93]
Nigrita • Greece 14 K9
Nii • Japan 30 J7
Niigata • Japan 30 J6
Niihama • Japan 30 G8
Niihau • HI, United States 119 L2
Niimi • Japan 30 G7
Níjar **Beach** • Spain 68 [116]
Níjar • Spain 86 B4
Nijmegen • Netherlands 80 A11
Nika • Maldives 106 E1
Nikel' • Russian Fed. 17 E1
Nikitas **Beach** • Greece 69 [192]
Nikitas • Greece 92 D1
Nikki • Benin 22 E3
Nikolayev • Ukraine 17 E5
Nikolayevsk-na-Amure • Russian Fed. 27 N6
Nikolsk • Russian Fed. 17 H3
Nikopol • Ukraine 17 E5
Nikópoli • Greece 15 B4
Nikšic • F.R. of Yugoslavia 14 F7
Nîl, Bahr el • Africa 21 F2
Nilandu Atoll North • Maldives 106 E1
Nilandu Atoll South • Maldives 106 E3
Nilaveli • Sri Lanka 106 D11
Nile • Africa 21 F2
Nile Delta • Egypt 101 F1
Nilgiri Hills • India 106 D10
Nilometer • Egypt 101 F5
Nilüfer • Turkey 15 J3
Nimba, Mts • Africa 22 C3
Nimba, Réserve du Monts **Heritage N** • Côte d'Ivoire/Guinea 61 [73]
Nîmes • France 10 J10
Nin • Croatia 12 J4
Nine Degree Channel • Indian Ocean 106 D9
Ninety Mile Beach • New Zealand 35 D2
Ninety Mile Beach • VI, Australia 111 G3
Ninety Six Nat. Hist. Site **Park** • SC, United States 121 [240]
Nineveh • Iraq 18 D2
Ning Zhen Shan • China 107 J1
Ningbo • China 107 J4
Ningde • China 29 F5
Ningguo • China 107 J3
Ninghai • China 107 J4
Ningjing Shan • China 28 G2
Ningwu • China 29 E3
Ningxia Huizu Zizhiqu • China 29 D3
Ninh Hoa • Vietnam 108 B2
Niobrara • NE/WY, United States 38 K8
Niokolo Koba, Parc nat. de **Park** • Senegal 103 [10]
Niokolo Koba, Parc nat. du **Heritage N** • Senegal 61 [72]
Niolo • Corsica, France 85 L1
Nioro du Sahel • Mali 20 D5
Niort • France 84 D3
Nipigon, Lake • OT, Canada 39 N7
Nipissing, Lake • OT, Canada 122 B1
Niquelândia • Brazil 44 G1
Niquero • Cuba 124 D7
Nirmal • India 28 C5
Niš • F.R. of Yugoslavia 14 I6
Nisab • Yemen 18 E7
Nisava • F.R. of Yugoslavia 14 J6
Nisbet Plantation Inn • St Kitts & Nevis 125 G4
Niscemi • Sicily, Italy 12 I11
Nishi-No • Japan 30 G6
Nishino'omote • Japan 30 F9
Nisiporeni • Moldova 14 P2
Nisko • Poland 13 L7
Nissáki • Corfu, Greece 92 B1
Nissedal • Norway 94 C6
Nisser • Norway 94 C6
Nissiros • Greece 92 D8
Nissum Bredning • Denmark 95 F5
Nissum Fjord • Denmark 95 F9
Niterói • Brazil 127 C4
Nith • United Kingdom 7 I6
Nithavris • Crete, Greece 93 E6
Nitra • Slovak Rep. 13 H9
Nitra [Riv] • Slovak Rep. 13 H9
Nitray [Château] • France 84 D2
Nittedal • Norway 94 B2
Niuafo'ou • Tonga 35 (2) E2
Niuatoputapu • Tonga 35 (2) F2
Niue • Pacific Ocean 35 (2) G2
Niut, Gunung • Indonesia 32 D2
Nivala • Finland 16 M5
Nivelles • Belgium 80 A14
Nivernais • France 10 I6
Niya • China 28 D1
Nizamabad • India 28 C5
Nizhneangarsk • Russian Fed. 27 G5
Nizhnekamsk • Russian Fed. 17 I3
Nizhneudinsk • Russian Fed. 26 Q7
Nizhnevartovsk • Russian Fed. 26 M5
Nizhneyansk • Russian Fed. 27 M2
Nizhniy Novgorod • Russian Fed. 17 G3
Nizhniy Tagil • Russian Fed. 26 I6
Nizhnyaya Pesha • Russian Fed. 17 H1
Nizhnyaya Tunguska • Russian Fed. 26 P5
Nizina • Slovak Rep. 14 E2
Nizina Podlaska • Poland 13 L4
Nizke Tatry • Slovak Rep. 13 I9
Nizke Tatry Nat. Park **Park** • Slovak Rep. 72 [101]
Njandoma • Russian Fed. 17 G2
Njinjo • Tanzania 24 F1
Njombe • Tanzania 102 H3
Njudung • Sweden 95 F8
Njunes • Norway 16 J2
Nkayi • Congo 23 A4
Nkongsamba • Cameroon 22 F4
Nkululu • Tanzania 23 E5
No Name City • Germany 82 J3
Noatak Nat. Preserve **Park** • AK, United States 120 [2]
Nobeoka • Japan 30 F8
Noce • Italy 90 B3
Nockberge, Nationalpark **Park** • Austria 72 [83]
Noën • Mongolia 29 C2
Nogales • AZ, United States 118 J3
Nogent-le-Rotrou • France 84 D2
Noginsk • Siberia, Russian Fed. 26 P5
Noginsk • Moscow, Russian Fed. 97 E4
Nogliki • Russian Fed. 27 N6
Nogoa • QL, Australia 111 F3
Nogoyá • Argentina 44 E5
Nogueira, Serra da • Portugal 11 E3
Nohfelden • Germany 5 K5
Noia • Spain 11 C2
Noirmoutier, I. de • France 10 C7
Noirmoutier-en-l'Ile **Beach** • France 68 [83]
Noja **Beach** • Spain 68 [89]
Nok Kundi • Pakistan 18 H4
Nokaneng • Botswana 24 C3
Nokhra • India 105 C1
Nokia • Finland 95 E2
Nola • Central African Rep. 23 B3
Nola • Italy 91 G1
Noli **Beach** • Italy 68 [141]
Noli • Italy 91 E5
Nolinsk • Russian Fed. 17 H3
Nomad • Papua New Guinea 35 (1) C2
Nome • AK, United States 40 (2) E2
Nomuka Group • Tonga 35 (2) F3
Non, Val di • Italy 90 B3
Nonacho Lake • NT, Canada 38 J4
Nong Khai • Thailand 31 C3
Nong Nooch Garden • Thailand 109 H4
Nonnweiler **Spa** • Germany 83 [168]
Nonsuch Bay • Antigua & Barbuda 125 F4
Nonthaburi • Thailand 109 H1
Noord-Beveland • Netherlands 80 A10
Noord-Brabant • Netherlands 80 A11
Noord-Holland • Netherlands 80 A7
Noordoostpolder • Netherlands 80 A7
Noordwijk **Beach** • Netherlands 68 [68]
Noordwijk • Netherlands 80 C1
Noordzee Kanaal • Netherlands 80 C2
Noormarkku • Finland 95 E1
Noosa Heads • QL, Australia 111 F6
Nora • Sardinia, Italy 90 C4
Noranda • QU, Canada 39 P7
Norberg • Sweden 95 D1
Nord, I. du • Seychelles 106 F2
Nord-Ostsee-Kanal • Germany 8 E2
Nord-Pas de Calais • France 84 A1
Nord-Trøndelag • Norway 16 G4
Nordagutu • Norway 94 B3
Nordborg **Beach** • Denmark 68 [45]
Nordborg • Denmark 95 F13
Nordby • Denmark 95 F9
Norddeich • Germany 8 C3
Norddorf **Spa** • Germany 83 [3]
Norden • Germany 8 C3
Norden **Spa** • Germany 83 [43]
Nordenham • Germany 8 D3
Nordenskjöld [Base] • Antarctica 46 (1) D2
Norderney • Germany 8 C3
Norderney **Spa** • Germany 83 [38]
Norderstadt • Germany 8 F3
Nordeste **Beach** • São Miguel, Azores 68 [105]
Nordeste • Azores 88 B2
Nordfjord • Norway 94 C1
Nordfjordeid • Norway 94 C1
Nordfriesische Inseln • Germany 8 D2
Nordfriesland • Germany 8 D2
Nordfriska Öarna • Denmark/Germany 16 E9
Nordhausen • Germany 8 F5
Nordhorn • Germany 8 C4
Nordic Mtn **Ski** • WI, United States 116 [121]
Nordjylland • Denmark 95 F5
Nordkapp • Norway 16 M1
Nordkinn • Norway 16 N1
Nordkinn-Halvøya • Norway 16 N1
Nordkjosbotn • Norway 16 J2
Nordland • Norway 16 G3
Nördlingen • Germany 9 F8
Nordrhein-Westfalen • Germany 8 C5
Nordstrand • Germany 8 D2
Nordstrand **Spa** • Germany 83 [6]
Nore • Norway 94 B1
Nore og Uvdal • Norway 94 B1
Norefjell • Norway 94 B1
Noresund • Norway 94 B1
Norfolk • United Kingdom 7 M9
Norfolk • Australia 33 H8
Norfolk • NE, United States 41 G3
Norfolk • VA, United States 118 H5
Norheimsund • Norway 94 C3
Noril'sk • Russian Fed. 26 O4
Norman • OK, United States 41 G4
Norman Wells • NT, Canada 38 F3
Normanby • Papua New Guinea 35 (1) E2
Normandie • France 10 E5
Normandie, Collines de • France 10 E5
Normanton • QL, Australia 34 H3
Norra Kvarken • Finland/Sweden 16 K5
Norra Storfjället • Sweden 16 H4
Norrbotten • Sweden 16 K3
Norre Aby **Beach** • Denmark 68 [44]
Nørre Djurs **Beach** • Denmark 68 [47]
Nørre Nebel • Denmark 95 F9
Nørre Snede • Denmark 95 F9
Nørre Vorupør • Denmark 95 F5
Nørresundby • Denmark 95 F5
Norrhult • Sweden 95 F8
Norrköping • Sweden 95 F4
Norrland Riviera • Sweden 94 A5
Norrtälje **Beach** • Sweden 69 [23]
Norrtälje • Sweden 95 D2
Norseman • WA, Australia 34 D6
Norsjö • Sweden 16 J4
Norsjø • Norway 94 B3
Norsk • Russian Fed. 27 L6
Norsoup • Vanuatu 35 (2) B2
Norte, Cabo • Brazil 43 G3
Norte, Punta • Argentina 45 D4
North Andaman • India 28 F6
North Arm • NT, Canada 38 I4
North Battleford • SA, Canada 38 J6
North Bay • OT, Canada 122 B1
North Belcher Is. • NU, Canada 39 P5
North Berwick • United Kingdom 74 B4
North Cape • Norway 16 M1
North Cape • New Zealand 35 D2
North, Cape • NS, Canada 123 D3
North Cape cruise area • Norway 59 A4
North Caribou Lake • OT, Canada 39 M6
North Carolina • United States 41 K4
North Cascades Nat. Park • WA, United States 117 E1
North Cascades Nat. Park **Park** • WA, United States 120 [26]
North Channel • United Kingdom 7 G7
North Channel • OT, Canada 39 O7
North Conway • NH, United States 118 G3
North Dakota • United States 40 F2
North Downs • United Kingdom 74 E3
North Foreland • United Kingdom 7 N10
North Fork Pass • YT, Canada 38 D4
North Friar's Bay • St Kitts & Nevis 125 G2
North Frigate Bay • St Kitts & Nevis 125 G2
North Geomagnetic Pole • Greenland 46 V2
North I. • New Zealand 35 E4
North Kitui Game Reserve • Kenya 101 G4
North Land • Russian Fed. 97 A5
North Luangwa Nat. Park **Park** • Zambia 103 [103]
North Magnetic Pole • Canada 46 Z2
North Negril Point • Jamaica 124 C1
North Ossetia • Russian Fed. 17 G6
North Platte • NE, United States 40 F3
North Point • Seychelles 106 F1
North Point • Barbados 125 H1
North Riding • United Kingdom 75 A4
North Rona • United Kingdom 6 G2
North Ronaldsay • United Kingdom 75 A7
North Saskatchewan • AL, Canada 38 I6
North Sea • Europe 4 K6
North Sentinel • India 28 F6
North Siberian Lowlands • Russian Fed. 97 A5
North Stradbroke I. • QL, Australia 111 F6
North Sydney • NS, Canada 123 D8
North Uist • United Kingdom 6 E4
North West • South Africa 24 D5
North West Cape • WA, Australia 34 B4
North York Moors Nat. Park **Park** • United Kingdom 72 [45]
North York Moors Nat. Park • United Kingdom 75 A3
Northam • WA, Australia 34 C6
Northampton • United Kingdom 7 L9
Northampton • WA, Australia 34 B5
Northamptonshire • United Kingdom 75 A5
Northeast Aegean Is. • Greece 92 D5
Northeast Passage cruise area • N. America 58 A2
Northeim • Germany 8 F5
Northern Cape • South Africa 24 C6
Northern Capitals cruise area • Europe 59 A4
Northern Hills • Thailand 109 F1
Northern Indian Lake • MN, Canada 38 L5
Northern Ireland • United Kingdom 7 F7
Northern Mariana Is. • Pacific Ocean 33 F4
Northern Province • South Africa 24 D4
Northern Range • Trinidad & Tobago 125 K1
Northern Territory • Australia 34 F3
Northfield • MN, United States 41 H3
Northland • New Zealand 112 J2
Northstar-at-Tahoe **Ski** • CA, United States 116 [52]
Northumberland • United Kingdom 75 A3
Northumberland Is. • QL, Australia 111 F4
Northumberland Nat. Park **Park** • United Kingdom 72 [42]
Northumberland Nat. Park • United Kingdom 75 A3
Northumbria • United Kingdom 75 A3
Northway • AK, United States 38 C4
Northwest Territories • Canada 38 F4
Norton Sound • AK, United States 40 (2) E2
Norway • Europe 16
Norwegian Fjords cruise area • Norway 59 A4
Norwegian Sea • Europe 4 K3
Norwich • United Kingdom 7 N9
Norwich • CT, United States 118 H2
Noshiro • Japan 30 J4
Nosratabad • Iran 18 G4
Nossa Senhora das Candeias • Brazil 44 I1
Nossebro • Sweden 95 F3
Nossob • Africa 24 B4
Nostalgia Town • QL, Australia 111 F6
Nostra Señora de Guadelupe • Portugal 88 E5
Nostra Senyora de Cura, Santuari de • Majorca, Spain 87 H4
Nosy Bé • Madagascar 24 H2
Nosy Ste Marie • Madagascar 24 H3
Notec • Poland 13 F5
Noto • Sicily, Italy 12 J12
Noto • Japan 30 I6
Noto [Adm] • Japan 30 I6
Noto, Golfo di • Sicily, Italy 90 D4
Noto, Val di • Sicily, Italy 90 D4
Notodden • Norway 94 B3
Notre-Dame Bay • NF, Canada 123 D3
Notre-Dame, Monts • QU, Canada 123 D1
Notre-Dame-de-Bellecombe **Ski** • France 70 [22]
Nottaway • QU, Canada 39 P6
Nottekanal • Germany 81 F4
Nottingham • United Kingdom 7 K9
Nottingham I. • NU, Canada 39 P4
Nottinghamshire • United Kingdom 75 A4
Nouadhibou • Mauritania 20 B4
Nouadhibou, Dakhet • Mauritania 20 B4
Nouadhibou, Ras • Mauritania 20 B4
Nouakchott • Mauritania 20 B5
Nouamrhar • Mauritania 20 B5
Nouméa • New Caledonia 35 (2) B3
Nouna • Burkina Faso 22 D2
Nouvelle Caledonie • Pacific Ocean 35 (2) A3
Nouvelle France, Cap de • QU, Canada 39 Q4
Nouvelles Hébrides • Vanuatu 35 (2) B2
Nouzha, El [Apt] • Egypt 101 F1
Nova Friburgo • Brazil 127 C4
Nova Gaia • Angola 23 B6
Nova Iguaçu • Brazil 127 C3
Nova Lamego • Guinea-Bissau 22 B2
Nova Levante • Italy 90 B3
Nova Lima • Brazil 127 C1
Nova Lisboa • Angola 24 B2
Nova Mambone • Mozambique 24 E4
Nova Scotia • Canada 123 D7
Nova Zagora • Bulgaria 97 D3
Novara • Italy 91 E6
Novaya Sibir, Ostrov • Russian Fed. 27 O1
Novaya Zemlya • Russian Fed. 26 H3
Nové Zámky • Slovak Rep. 13 H10
Novelda • Spain 87 C1
Novgorod **Heritage C** • Russian Fed. 64 [206]
Novgorod • Russian Fed. 97 E1
Novi Ligure • Italy 12 C4
Novi Pazar • F.R. of Yugoslavia 14 H6
Novi Pazar • Bulgaria 97 D3
Novi Sad • F.R. of Yugoslavia 14 G4
Novo Gradiska • Croatia 12 L3
Nôvo Hamburgo • Brazil 44 F4
Novo Mesto • Slovak Rep. 13 G9
Novo Mesto • Slovenia 14 C4
Novo Orjahovo • Bulgaria 97 D4
Novocherkassk • Russian Fed. 17 G5
Novodvinsk • Russian Fed. 17 G2
Novojoa • Mexico 40 E6
Novokachalinsk • Russian Fed. 29 I1
Novokuybyshev • Russian Fed. 17 H4
Novokuznetsk • Russian Fed. 26 O7
Novolazarevskaya [Base] • Antarctica 46 (1) G2
Novomoskovsk • Russian Fed. 17 F4
Novomoskovsk • Ukraine 17 F5
Novorossiysk • Russian Fed. 17 F6
Novorybnoye • Russian Fed. 26 S3
Novosaya • Russian Fed. 17 I1
Novoshakhtinsk • Russian Fed. 17 F5
Novosibirskiye Ostrova • Russian Fed. 27 N1
Novouzensk • Russian Fed. 17 H4
Novovolynsk • Ukraine 13 N7
Novoyeniseysk • Russian Fed. 26 P6
Novoyerudinskiy • Russian Fed. 26 P6
Novy Jicin • Czech Rep. 13 H8
Novyy Port • Russian Fed. 26 L4
Novyy Uzen • Kazakhstan 26 H9
Novyy Vasyugan • Russian Fed. 26 M6
Nowa Ruda • Poland 13 F7
Nowa Sól • Poland 13 E6
Nowgong • India 105 C7
Nowogard • Poland 13 E4
Nowra • NS, Australia 111 G2
Nowy Dwór Mazowiecki • Poland 13 J5
Nowy Sacz • Poland 13 J8
Nowy Targ • Poland 13 I8
Noyon • France 10 H4
Nsukka • Nigeria 22 F3
Ntem • Cameroon/Equatorial Guinea 22 G4
Nu Jiang • China 28 F2
Nub's Nob **Ski** • MI, United States 116 [130]
Nubah, Jibal an • Sudan 21 F5
Nubian Desert • Sudan 21 F3
Nubiyah, As Sahra an • Sudan 21 F3
Nudow • Germany 81 F3
Nueces • TX, United States 119 N5
Nueltin Lake • NU, Canada 38 L4
Nueva Gerona • Cuba 124 D1
Nueva Palmira • Uruguay 127 D1
Nueva San Salvador • El Salvador 37 D5
Nueve (9) de Julio • Argentina 127 D3
Nuevitas • Cuba 124 D3
Nuevo Casas Grandes • Mexico 40 E5
Nuevo, Golfo • Argentina 45 D4
Nuevo Laredo • Mexico 37 B2
Nuevo Leon • Mexico 37 A2
Nuevo Mundo, Cerro • Bolivia 44 C3
Nuevo Rocafuerte • Ecuador 43 B4
Nuevo Rosita • Mexico 37 A2
Nugal • Somalia 23 H2
Nugget Point • New Zealand 35 B8
Nugssuaq • Greenland 39 U2
Nuhud, An • Sudan 21 E5
Nui Ba Den • Vietnam 108 B1
Nui Sam • Vietnam 108 B3
Nuiu'Erhu Shan • China 29 F2
Nukhaylah • Sudan 21 E4
Nuku Hiva • French Polynesia 33 M6
Nuku'alofa • Tonga 35 (2) E3
Nukunonu • Tokelau 33 J6
Nukus • Uzbekistan 18 G1
Nullagine • WA, Australia 34 D4
Nullarbor • SA, Australia 34 F6
Nullarbor Plain • SA/WA, Australia 34 E6
Numan • Nigeria 22 G3
Numancia • Philippines 31 H4
Numazu • Japan 30 J7
Nümbrecht **Spa** • Germany 83 [114]
Numedal • Norway 94 B1
Numedalslågen • Norway 94 B1
Numfoor • Indonesia 35 (1) A1
Nummela • Finland 95 E4
Nunavut • Canada 38 L3
Nuneaton • United Kingdom 74 D2
Nungarin • WA, Australia 34 C6
Nungnain Sum • China 27 I7
Nungo • Mozambique 24 F2
Nunivak I. • AK, United States 40 (2) E2
Nuoro • Sardinia, Italy 90 C2
Nuquí • Colombia 43 B2
Nura • Kazakhstan 26 L7
Nuraghe Santu Antine • Sardinia, Italy 12 C8
Nürburg • Germany 82 H1
Nürburgring • Germany 82 H1
Nuri • Sudan 21 F4
Nurkii • Russian Fed. 27 M5
Nurmes • Finland 16 O5
Nürnberg • Germany 9 G7
Nurra, la • Sardinia, Italy 90 C1
Nusa Dua • Bali, Indonesia 110 C4
Nusa Dua Beach • Bali, Indonesia 110 C4
Nusa Penida • Indonesia 110 C4
Nusa Tenggara • Indonesia 25 N10
Nusa Tenggara Barat • Indonesia 110 A6
Nusa Tenggara Timur • Indonesia 110 A7
Nutak • NF, Canada 39 S5
Nuthe • Germany 81 F3
Nuuk • Greenland 39 U4
Nuwara Eliya • Sri Lanka 106 D15
Nuweiba • Egypt 101 F2
Nuweveldberge • South Africa 100 C2
Nyainqentanglha Feng • China 28 E2
Nyainqentanglha Shan • China 28 F2
Nyaka • Zimbabwe 102 J1
Nyala • Sudan 21 D5
Nyali • Kenya 101 G5
Nyali Beach • Kenya 101 G5
Nyamlett • Sudan 23 D2
Nyampanda • Zimbabwe 102 J2
Nyanga • Congo/Gabon 22 G5
Nyanga Nat. Park • Zimbabwe 102 J2
Nyangani • Zimbabwe 102 J2
Nyanza-Lac • Burundi 23 D4
Nyborg • Denmark 95 F14
Nybro • Sweden 95 F8
Nyda • Russian Fed. 26 L4
Nydala • Sweden 95 F7
Nyeri • Kenya 101 G3
Nyika Nat. Park **Park** • Malawi 103 [96]
Nyíregyháza • Hungary 13 K10
Nyírség • Hungary 14 J2
Nyiru • Kenya 23 F3
Nykarleby • Finland 16 L5
Nykøbing • Sjælland, Denmark 95 F10
Nykøbing • Falster, Denmark 95 F14
Nykøbing • Mors, Denmark 95 F5
Nykøbing Rørvig **Beach** • Denmark 68 [43]
Nyköping • Sweden 95 D3
Nynäshamn • Sweden 95 D4
Nyngan • NS, Australia 34 I6
Nyon • Switzerland 89 G5
Nyong • Cameroon 22 G4
Nyrud • Norway 16 O2
Nysa • Poland 13 G7
Nysh • Russian Fed. 27 N6
Nyslott • Finland 16 O6
Nystad • Finland 95 E3
Nysted • Denmark 95 F14
Nyudo-Zaki • Japan 30 J5
Nyurba • Russian Fed. 27 I4
Nyuya • Russian Fed. 27 I4
Nzega • Tanzania 102 H1
Nzérékoré • Côte d'Ivoire 22 C3
Nzeto • Angola 23 A5
Nzi • Côte d'Ivoire 22 D3
Nzilo, Barrage de • Dem. Rep. of Congo 24 D2

O • Sea of Japan, Japan 30 J4
O • Izu-Shoto, Japan 30 J7
O Grove **Beach** • Spain 68 [93]
O'Neill, Eugene, Nat. Hist. Site **Park** • CA, United States 120 [49]
Oahe, Lake • SD, United States 40 F2
Oahu • HI, United States 119 L5
Oak Harbor • WA, United States 40 B2
Oak Ridge • TN, United States 41 J4
Oakland • CA, United States 117 F3
Oakley • KS, United States 40 F4
Oakura • New Zealand 112 K3
Oakwood Adventure **Park** • United Kingdom 73 [31]
Oamaru • New Zealand 35 C7
Oaro • New Zealand 35 D6
Oasis de Nazaret • Lanzarote, Canary Is. 87 E3
Oaxaca **Heritage C** • Mexico 62 [24]
Oaxaca • Mexico 123 E4
Ob • Russian Fed. 26 K4
Ob Estuary • Russian Fed. 96 A3
Obala • Cameroon 22 G4
Obama • Japan 30 H7
Oban • United Kingdom 6 G5
Oban • New Zealand 35 B8
Oban Hills • Nigeria 22 F3
Obando • Colombia 43 D3
Ober Engadin • Switzerland 89 G8
Ober Gatlinburg **Ski** • TN, United States 116 [150]
Oberá • Argentina 44 E4
Oberammergau • Germany 82 J6
Oberasbach • Germany 9 F7
Oberau **Ski** • Austria 70 [147]
Oberau **Spa** • Germany 83 [262]
Oberau • Austria 89 H3
Oberaudorf • Germany 82 J8
Oberbayern • Germany 82 J3
Obereggen **Ski** • Italy 70 [214]
Obereggen • Italy 90 B3
Oberfranken • Germany 9 G6
Obergurgl **Ski** • Austria 70 [136]
Obergurgl • Austria 89 H6
Oberharz **Spa** • Germany 83 [79]
Oberhausen • Germany 81 E1
Oberhausen: Sterkrade • Germany 81 E1
Oberhof • Germany 9 F6
Oberinntal • Austria 89 H6
Oberjoch • Germany 82 J6
Oberkirch • Germany 82 G6
Oberlausitz • Germany 81 D2
Oberlech **Ski** • Austria 70 [129]
Oberndorf • Germany 9 D8
Oberndorf • Austria 89 H4
Oberösterreich • Austria 13 D10
Oberpfalz • Germany 9 H7
Oberpfalzerwald • Germany 9 H7
Obersaxen • Switzerland 89 G3
Oberschleißheim • Germany 82 J3
Oberstaufen • Germany 82 J5
Oberstaufen **Spa** • Germany 83 [240]
Oberstdorf **Ski** • Germany 70 [2]
Oberstdorf • Germany 82 J6
Oberstdorf **Spa** • Germany 83 [242]
Obertauern **Ski** • Austria 70 [185]
Obertauern • Austria 89 H8
Obertraun • Austria 89 H4
Obervellach • Austria 89 H8
Oberwesel • Germany 82 H4
Obi • Indonesia 32 (1) C3
Obidos • Brazil 43 F4
Obihiro • Japan 30 L3
Obninsk • Russian Fed. 97 E4
Obo • Central African Rep. 23 D2
Obock • Djibouti 23 G1
Oborniki • Poland 13 F5
Obozerskiy • Russian Fed. 17 G2
Obrenovac • F.R. of Yugoslavia 14 H5
Obskaya Guba • Russian Fed. 26 L4
Obuasi • Ghana 22 D3
Obzor • Bulgaria 97 D4
Oc, d' • France 84 B4
Ocajón, Pico • Spain 10 B12
Ocala • FL, United States 119 M3
Ocaña • Spain 11 H5
Ocaña • Colombia 43 C2
Ocean City • NJ, United States 118 H3
Ocean City • MD, United States 118 H3
Ocean Falls • BC, Canada 38 F6
Ocean Hole • Bahamas 124 B1
Ocean I. • Kiribati 33 I6

Ocean Park • Hong Kong, China 107 H6
Ocean World Water Park • Thailand 109 H4
Oceanside • CA, United States 40 C5
Ochagavia • Spain 11 J2
Ochils, The • United Kingdom 74 B2
Ocho Rios • Jamaica 124 C2
Ochrid • F.Y.R. of Macedonia 71 A19
Ochsenfurt • Germany 9 F7
Ochsenhausen • Germany 82 J1
Oclini • Italy 90 B3
Ocmulgee Nat. Mon. **Park** • GA, United States 121 [212]
Ocnita • Moldova 14 O1
Ocoee • FL, United States 121 C1
Oda • Sudan 21 G3
Oda • Ghana 22 D3
Oda • Japan 30 G7
Odádahraun • Iceland 16 (1) E2
Odate • Japan 30 K4
Odda • Norway 94 C4
Odder **Beach** • Denmark 68 [47]
Odder • Denmark 95 F10
Odeborg • Sweden 95 F2
Odeceixe • Portugal 88 E1
Odelette • Portugal 88 E4
Odelouca • Portugal 88 E2
Odemis • Turkey 92 D6
Odense • Denmark 95 F14
Odenthal • Germany 81 E4
Odenwald • Germany 82 G4
Oder • Germany 8 J4
Oderhaff • Germany/Poland 16 H10
Oderzo • Italy 13 B12
Odesa • Ukraine 17 E5
Odeshög • Sweden 95 F3
Odessa • Ukraine 17 E5
Odessa • TX, United States 40 F5
Odessa • DE, United States 118 H3
Odiáxere • Portugal 88 E6
Odienne • Côte d'Ivoire 22 C3
Odle, Le • Italy 90 B1
Odorheiu Secuiesc • Romania 14 M3
Odra • Poland 13 G6
Odzani Falls • Zimbabwe 102 J2
Oeiras • Portugal 11 B6
Oeiras • Brazil 45 (1) C3
Oelsnitz • Germany 9 H6
Oelsnitz • Germany 9 H6
Oer-Erkenschwick • Germany 81 E2
Ofanto • Italy 12 J7
Offaly • Ireland 79 D2
Offenbach • Germany 9 D6
Offenbach am Main • Germany 82 G4
Offenburg • Germany 82 G6
Ofidoússa • Greece 92 D8
Ofunato • Japan 30 K5
Oga • Japan 30 J5
Oga [Peninsula] • Japan 30 J5
Ogaden • Ethiopia 23 H2
Ogaki • Japan 30 I7
Ogbomosho • Nigeria 22 E3
Ogden • UT, United States 40 D3
Ogden, Mt • UT, United States 116 B
Ogdensburg • NY, United States 41 K3
Ogilvie Mtns • YT, Canada 38 C3
Oglio • Italy 91 E6
Ognon • France 10 L6
Ogo • Somalia 23 H1
Ogoamas, Bulu • Indonesia 32 (1) B2
Ogoja • Nigeria 22 F3
Ogoki • OT, Canada 39 N6
Ogonëk • Russian Fed. 27 M5
Ogooué • Gabon 22 G5
Ogosta • Bulgaria 14 K6
Ograzden Belasica • Europe 15 D2
Ogre • Latvia 16 M8
Ogun • Nigeria 22 E3
Ohai • New Zealand 112 L4
Ohakune • New Zealand 112 K3
Ohanet • Algeria 20 G3
Ohata • Japan 30 K4
Ohio • United States 41 J3
Ohio [Riv] • United States 41 J4
Ohlstadt • Germany 82 J7
Ohope • New Zealand 112 K2
Ohopoho • Namibia 24 A3
Ohre • Czech Rep. 96 C1
Ohrid • F.Y.R. of Macedonia 14 H8
Ohrid, Lake • Albania/F.Y.R. of Macedonia 15 B2
Ohrid Lake **Heritage N** • F.Y.R. of Macedonia 61 [55]
Ohrid Lake **Heritage C** • F.Y.R. of Macedonia 64 [162]
Ohridsko jezero • Albania/F.Y.R. of Macedonia 15 B2
Ohringen • Germany 9 E7
Ohthoniá, Akra • Greece 15 F5
Oiapoque • Brazil 43 G3
Oinoanda • Turkey 93 G3
Oise • France 10 H4
Oise [Adm] • France 85 E2
Oiseaux, Parc des • France 85 F1
Oistins • Barbados 125 H3
Oistins Bay • Barbados 125 H3
Oit • Romania 14 L5
Oita • Japan 30 F8
Oituz • Romania 14 N3
Ojcowski Nat. Park **Park** • Poland 72 [97]
Ojinaga • Mexico 40 F6
Ojos del Salado, Nevado • Argentina/Chile 44 C4
Oka • Russian Fed. 17 G3
Okaba • Indonesia 32 (1) E4
Okahandja • Namibia 24 B4
Okanagan • Canada/United States 122 C4
Okanda, Parc nat. de l' **Park** • Gabon 103 [48]
Okapa • Papua New Guinea 35 (1) D2
Okapi, Réserve du **Heritage N** • Dem. Rep. of Congo 61 [83]
Okapi, Réserve du **Park** • Dem. Rep. of Congo 103 [55]
Okara • Pakistan 28 B2
Okarem • Turkmenistan 18 F2
Okaukuejo • Namibia 24 B3
Okavango • Africa 24 C3
Okavango Swamp • Botswana 24 C3
Okayama • Japan 30 G7
Okazaki • Japan 30 I7
Okeechobee, Lake • FL, United States 119 M6
Okefenokee Swamp • GA, United States 119 M3
Okehampton • United Kingdom 74 F2
Okemo Mtn **Ski** • VT, United States 116 [198]
Okha • Russian Fed. 27 N6
Okha • India 28 A4
Okhota • Russian Fed. 27 N4
Okhotsk • Russian Fed. 27 N5
Okhotsk, Sea of • Russian Fed. 27 O5
Oki-Shoto • Japan 30 G6
Okinawa-Shoto • Japan 29 H5
Okinoerabu • Japan 29 H5
Oklahoma • United States 41 G5
Oklahoma City • OK, United States 41 G4
Okomo Sanctuary **Park** • Nigeria 103 [36]
Okondja • Gabon 22 G5
Oksbøl • Denmark 95 F9
Oktya'birskiy • Bashkortostan, Russian Fed. 17 I4
Oktyabr'sk • Kazakhstan 26 I8
Oktyabr'skiy • Kamchatka, Russian Fed. 27 Q6
Oktyabr'skoy Revolyutsii, Ostrov • Russian Fed. 96 A4
Oktyabr'skoye • Russian Fed. 26 K5
Okulovka • Russian Fed. 97 E1
Okushiri • Japan 30 J3
Okwa • Botswana/Namibia 24 C4
Ol-Doinyo Sapuk Nat. Park • Kenya 101 G3
Ola • Russian Fed. 27 P5
Olaine • Latvia 16 L8
Oland • Sweden 95 F8
Olanesti • Moldova 14 Q3
Olang **Ski** • Italy 70 [236]
Olang • Italy 90 B2
Olanga • Russian Fed. 16 P3
Olavarría • Argentina 127 D3
Olawa • Poland 13 G7
Olbia • Sardinia, Italy 90 C2
Old Goa • Goa, India 105 B1
Old Harbour • Jamaica 124 C4
Old Head of Kinsale **Beach** • Ireland 68 [59]
Old Head of Kinsale • Ireland 79 F8
Old Kilcullen • Ireland 79 E3
Old Man of Coniston • United Kingdom 74 C4
Old Orchard Beach • ME, United States 118 G4
Old Road • Antigua & Barbuda 125 F3
Old Road Bay • St Kitts & Nevis 125 G1
Old Road Bluff • Antigua & Barbuda 125 F3
Old Road Town • St Kitts & Nevis 125 G1
Old Sarai • Russian Fed. 98 B1
Old Sarum • United Kingdom 74 F3
Olden • Norway 94 C2
Oldenburg • Germany 8 D3
Oldenburg in Holstein • Germany 8 F2
Oldenzaal • Netherlands 5 J2
Oldham • United Kingdom 7 J8
Olduvai Gorge • Tanzania 102 H2
Olean • NY, United States 41 K3
Olecko • Poland 13 L3
Oleiros **Beach** • Spain 68 [92]
Olekma • Russian Fed. 27 J5
Olëkminsk • Russian Fed. 27 J4
Olen • Norway 94 C5
Olenegorsk • Russian Fed. 17 E1
Olenëk • Russian Fed. 27 J2
Olenëkskiy Zaliv • Russian Fed. 27 J2
Oleniy, Ostrov • Russian Fed. 26 M3
Oléron, I. de • France 85 G1
Olesnica • Poland 13 G6
Oletta • Corsica, France 85 L2
Olga • Russian Fed. 27 M8
Olga, Mt • NT, Australia 112 H3
Olgod • Denmark 95 F9
Olhão • Portugal 88 E7
Olhos de Agua • Portugal 88 E7
Olhuveli • Maldives 106 E4
Oliana • Spain 11 M2
Olib • Croatia 14 B5
Oliena • Sardinia, Italy 90 C2
Olifants • Namibia 24 B4
Olifants • South Africa 100 C1
Olifants • South Africa 100 C7
Olimbía • Greece 15 C6
Olimbía **Heritage N** • Greece 61 [60]
Olimbía **Heritage C** • Greece 64 [179]
Olimbiáda **Beach** • Greece 69 [192]
Olimbos • Macedonia/Thessaly, Greece 15 D3
Olimbos • Lesbos, Greece 15 H4
Olimbos • Kárpathos, Greece 92 D11
Olimbos Nat. Park **Park** • Greece 72 [134]
Olinda • Brazil 45 (1) E3
Olinda **Heritage C** • Brazil 62 [60]
Olite • Spain 11 J2
Oliva • Spain 11 K6
Oliva • Argentina 44 D5
Oliva **Beach** • Spain 68 [119]
Oliva de la Frontera • Spain 11 E6
Oliveira do Brejinhos • Brazil 44 H1
Olkhon, Ostrov • Russian Fed. 97 A5
Olkusz • Poland 13 I7
Ollantayambo • Peru 127 B2
Olmedo • Spain 11 G3
Olmeto • Corsica, France 85 L3
Olmos • Peru 43 B5
Olmsted, Frederick Law, Nat. Hist. Site **Park** • MA, United States 121 [346]
Olmütz • Czech Rep. 71 A9
Olney • TX, United States 119 N1
Olofstrom • Sweden 95 F11
Olombo • Congo 23 B4
Olomouc • Czech Rep. 13 G8
Olonets • Russian Fed. 17 E2
Olonne-sur-Mer **Beach** • France 68 [83]
Olopango • Philippines 31 G3
Oloron, Gave d' • France 10 E10
Oloron-Ste Marie • France 85 J1
Olot • Spain 87 D2
Oloús • Crete, Greece 93 E8
Olpe • Germany 9 C5
Olsberg • Germany 9 D5
Olsberg **Spa** • Germany 83 [108]
Olsztyn • Poland 13 J4
Olsztynek • Poland 13 J4
Olt • Romania 14 M4
Olten • Switzerland 9 C9
Oltenia • Romania 14 J5
Oltenita • Romania 97 D1
Oltet • Romania 14 L5
Oltta • Russian Fed. 16 O2
Oluanpi • Taiwan 29 G6
Olüdeniz • Turkey 92 D9
Olympía • Greece 15 C6
Olympía **Heritage N** • Greece 61 [60]
Olympía **Heritage C** • Greece 64 [179]
Olympia • WA, United States 117 E1
Olympiastadion, Berlin • Germany 81 F1
Olympic Nat. Park **Heritage N** • WA, United States 60 [9]
Olympic Nat. Park • WA, United States 117 E1
Olympic Nat. Park **Park** • WA, United States 120 [24]
Olympos • Turkey 93 G3
Olympus • Greece 15 D3
Olympus • Cyprus 93 J3
Olympus, Mt • WA, United States 117 E1
Olympus Nat. Park **Park** • Greece 72 [134]
Olyutorskiy, mys • Russian Fed. 27 T5
Olyutorskiy Zaliv • Russian Fed. 27 S4
Om • Russian Fed. 26 L6
Omagh • United Kingdom 7 E7
Omaha • NE, United States 41 G3
Oman • Asia 18 G5
Oman, Gulf of • Iran/Oman 18 G5
Omarama • New Zealand 35 B7
Omatako • Namibia 24 B4
Ombo • Norway 94 C5
Ombrone • Italy 12 F6
Ombu • China 28 E2
Omchak • Russian Fed. 27 O4
Omdurman • Sudan 21 F4
Omeo • VI, Australia 111 G3
Omerköy • Turkey 15 J4
Ometepec • Mexico 37 B4
Omihi • New Zealand 35 D6
Ominec Mtns • BC, Canada 38 F5
Omiroúpoli **Beach** • Greece 69 [200]
Omis • Croatia 12 K5
Omiya • Japan 30 J7
Ommanney Bay • NU, Canada 38 K2
Ommen • Netherlands 80 A8
Omo • Ethiopia 23 F2
Omo Lower Valley **Heritage C** • Ethiopia 63 [89]
Omo Nat. Park **Park** • Ethiopia 103 [66]
Omokoroa • New Zealand 112 K2
Omolon • Russian Fed. 27 R3
Omolon [Riv] • Russian Fed. 27 Q3
Omsk • Russian Fed. 26 L7
Omsukchan • Russian Fed. 27 Q4
Omura • Japan 30 E8
Omuramba Omatako • Namibia 24 B3
Omuta • Japan 30 F8
Omutninsk • Russian Fed. 17 I3
Oña • Spain 10 B11
Onda • Spain 11 K5
Ondangua • Namibia 24 B3
Ondara • Slovak Rep. 13 K8
Ondo • Nigeria 22 F3
Ondöl Ondörhaan • Mongolia 29 E1
Onega, Lake • Russian Fed. 17 F2
Oneida Lake • NY, United States 122 B10
Onekotan, Ostrov • Russian Fed. 27 P7
Onezhskaya Guba • Russian Fed. 17 F2
Onezhskoye, Ozero • Russian Fed. 17 F2
Ongjin • D.P.R. of Korea 30 C6
Ongole • India 106 D3
Onilany • Madagascar 24 G4
Onitsha • Nigeria 22 F3
Ono • Japan 30 I7
Ono • Fiji 35 (2) D2
Ono-i-Lau • Fiji 35 (2) E3
Onon • Mongolia 27 H7
Onsala • Sweden 95 F6
Onsalalandet • Sweden 95 F6
Onslow • WA, Australia 34 C4
Onslow Bay • NC, United States 118 H5
Ontake • Japan 30 I7
Ontario • OT, Canada 39 N6
Ontario, Lake • Canada/United States 122 B10
Onteniente • Spain 11 K6
Ontong Java Atoll • Solomon Is. 35 (1) F2
Oodnadatta • SA, Australia 34 G5
Ooldea • SA, Australia 34 F6
Oost-Vlaanderen • Belgium 80 A14
Oostduinkerke-Bad • Belgium 80 B1
Oostende • Belgium 80 B1
Oosterbeek [Battlefield] • Netherlands 80 A7
Oosterhout • Netherlands 5 H3
Oosterschelde • Netherlands 5 G3
Oostvaarders Plassen • Netherlands 80 C2
Ooty • India 106 D10
Opatija • Croatia 12 I3
Opava • Czech Rep. 13 G8
Opelousas • LA, United States 118 K3
Opochka • Russian Fed. 17 D3
Opoczno • Poland 13 J6
Opole • Poland 13 G7
Oporto • Portugal 11 C3
Oporto **Heritage C** • Portugal 64 [95]
Opotiki • New Zealand 112 K2
Oppdal • Norway 16 E5
Oppegård • Norway 94 B2
Oppenheim • Germany 82 H4
Oppland • Norway 16 E6
Opryland USA **Park** • TN, United States 121 [X]
Opunake • New Zealand 112 K3
Ora • Italy 90 B3
Oracabessa • Jamaica 124 C2
Oradea • Romania 14 I2
Oradour-sur-Glane • France 85 G2
Orai • India 105 C7
Orakei Korako • New Zealand 112 K2
Oral • Kazakhstan 17 I4
Oran • Algeria 20 E1
Orange • France 10 J9
Orange • Namibia/South Africa 24 B5
Orange **Heritage C** • France 64 [66]
Orange • NS, Australia 111 G2
Orange • TX, United States 119 N4
Orange, Cabo • Brazil 43 G3
Orange County • FL, United States 121 C1
Orangeburg • SC, United States 41 J5
Orangeville • OT, Canada 122 B5
Orango • Guinea-Bissau 22 A2
Oranienburg • Germany 81 F1
Oranje • Namibia/South Africa 24 B5
Oranjestad • Aruba 43 D1
Orapa • Botswana 24 D4
Oravita • Romania 14 I4
Orayská priehradni nádrz • Slovak Rep. 13 I8
Orbe • Switzerland 89 G1
Orbetello • Italy 12 F6
Orbost • VI, Australia 111 G4
Orcadas [Base] • Antarctica 46 (1) A3
Orchha • India 105 C7
Orchila • Venezuela 43 D1
Orcières-Merlette **Ski** • France 70 [65]
Ord, Mt • WA, Australia 34 E3
Ordenes • Spain 11 C1
Ordesa, Parque Nac. de **Park** • Spain 72 [72]
Ordos • China 107 G3
Orebro • Sweden 16 H7
Orebro [Adm] • Sweden 16 H7
Oregon • United States 117 E3
Oregon Caves Nat. Mon. • OR, United States 117 E3
Oregon Caves Nat. Mon. **Park** • OR, United States 120 [37]
Oregon City • OR, United States 117 E3
Oregon Dunes Nat. Recreation Area • OR, United States 117 E3
Oregrund • Sweden 95 D2
Orekhovo-Zuyevo • Russian Fed. 97 E4
Orel • Russian Fed. 17 F4
Orel, gora • Russian Fed. 27 M6
Orellana • Amazonas, Peru 43 B4
Orellana • Loreto, Peru 43 B5
Orem • UT, United States 40 D3
Oren • Turkey 15 I6
Orenburg • Russian Fed. 17 J4
Orenburg • Russian Fed. 26 I7
Orepuki • New Zealand 112 L3
Orestiáda • Greece 14 N8
Oresund • Denmark/Sweden 95 F11
Oreti • New Zealand 112 L4
Orford Ness • United Kingdom 5 E2
Organ Pipe Cactus Nat. Mon. • AZ, United States 118 J3
Organ Pipe Cactus Nat. Mon. **Park** • AZ, United States 120 [114]
Organos, Sierra de los • Cuba 124 D1
Orgãos, Serra dos • Brazil 127 C4
Orhaneli • Turkey 15 K4
Orhangazi • Turkey 15 K3
Orhei • Moldova 14 P2
Orhon • Mongolia 27 F7
Orient • Majorca, Spain 87 H1
Orientale, Plaine • Corsica, France 85 L4
Orihuela **Beach** • Spain 68 [118]
Orihuela • Spain 87 C3
Oriku • Albania 15 A3
Orimattila • Finland 95 E4
Orinoco • Colombia/Venezuela 43 D2
Orinoco, Delta del • Venezuela 43 E2
Orissa • India 28 D4
Orissaare • Estonia 16 L7
Oristano • Sardinia, Italy 90 C3
Oristano, Golfo di • Sardinia, Italy 90 C3
Orives • Finland 16 O5
Orivesi • Finland 95 E2
Orizaba • Mexico 37 B4
Orizaba, Pico de • Mexico 123 E4
Orje • Norway 94 B4
Orjiva • Spain 11 H8
Orkanger • Norway 16 E5
Orkelljunga • Sweden 95 F11
Orkney • South Africa 24 D5
Orkney • United Kingdom 75 A7
Orkney Is. • United Kingdom 6 J3
Orlando • FL, United States 121 C2
Orlando Arena • FL, United States 121 C2
Orlando Museum of Art • FL, United States 121 C2
Orlando Science Center • FL, United States 121 C2
Orleanais • France 10 G6
Orléans • France 84 D2
Orléans, I. d' • QU, Canada 122 B4
Orlicke Hory • Czech Rep. 13 F7
Orlik • Russian Fed. 27 F6
Orlik • Czech Rep. 96 C4
Orlovista • FL, United States 121 C2
Orly [Apt] • France 85 E3
Ormara • Pakistan 18 H4
Ormea • Italy 91 E5
Ormília **Beach** • Greece 69 [192]
Ormiston Gorge Nat. Park • NT, Australia 112 H1
Ormoc • Philippines 31 G4
Ormond Beach • FL, United States 119 M4
Ormuz • Iran 98 B4
Orne • Lorraine, France 5 J5
Orne • Normandie, France 10 E4
Orneta • Poland 13 J3
Ornö • Sweden 95 D4
Ornö [I.] • Sweden 95 D4
Ornsköldsvik • Sweden 16 J5
Orocué • Colombia 43 C3
Orodara • Burkina Faso 22 D2
Orona • Kiribati 33 J6
Oropesa **Beach** • Spain 68 [120]
Oroqen Zizhiqi • China 27 J6
Oroquita • Philippines 31 G5
Oros Falakró • Greece 14 K8
Orosei • Sardinia, Italy 90 C2
Orosei, Golfo di • Sardinia, Italy 90 C2
Orosháza • Hungary 13 J11
Oroszlány • Hungary 13 H10
Orotukan • Russian Fed. 27 P4
Orpheus I. • QL, Australia 111 F1
Orrefors • Sweden 95 F8
Orres, les **Ski** • France 70 [68]
Orres, les • France 85 F4
Orsha • Belarus 17 E4
Orsk • Russian Fed. 26 I7
Orsoy • Germany 81 E1
Orsta • Norway 94 C1
Orsundsbro • Sweden 95 D1
Orta • Italy 91 E2
Ortaca • Turkey 15 J7
Ortakent • Turkey 15 I6
Orte • Italy 91 F1
Ortegal, Cabo • Spain 11 D1
Orthez • France 85 J1
Ortigueira • Spain 11 D1
Ortisei **Ski** • Italy 70 [230]
Ortisei • Italy 90 B1
Ortles • Italy 12 E2
Ortoire • Trinidad & Tobago 125 K4
Ortona • Italy 12 I6
Orumiyeh • Iran 18 D2
Orumiyeh, Daryacheh-ye • Iran 18 E2
Oruro • Bolivia 44 C2
Orust • Sweden 95 F2
Orval, Abbaye-d' • Belgium 80 A19
Orvieto • Italy 91 F1
Orzola • Lanzarote, Canary Is. 87 E3
Osaka • Japan 30 H7
Osaka-Wan • Japan 30 H7
Osan • Sweden 95 F3
Osby • Sweden 95 F11
Osceola County • FL, United States 121 C1
Oschiri • Sardinia, Italy 12 D8
Ose-Zaki • Japan 30 E8
Oserøya • Norway 94 C3
Osh • Kyrgyzstan 18 J1
Oshawa • OT, Canada 122 B9
Oshika • Japan 30 K5
Oshkosh • WI, United States 41 I3
Oshmyany • Belarus 16 M9
Oshogbo • Nigeria 22 E3
Oshwe • Dem. Rep. of Congo 22 H5
Osian • India 105 C5
Osijek • Croatia 14 F4
Osimo • Italy 12 H5
Oskarshamn • Sweden 95 F8
Oskerström • Sweden 95 F7
Oslo • Norway 94 B2
Oslofjorden • Norway 94 B4
Osmaneli • Turkey 15 L3
Osmo • Sweden 95 D4
Osnabrück • Germany 8 D4
Osogovske Planine • F.Y.R. of Macedonia 15 D1
Osorno • Chile 45 B4
Osøyro • Norway 94 C3
Ospedaletti • Italy 91 E9
Oss • Netherlands 5 I3
Ossa • Greece 15 D4
Ossa, Mt • TS, Australia 34 I8
Ossora • Russian Fed. 27 R5
Ossun [Apt] • France 85 J2
Ostashkov • Russian Fed. 97 E3
Oste • Germany 8 E3
Ostend • Belgium 80 B1
Oster Hurup • Denmark 95 F6
Osterbymo • Sweden 95 F8
Osterdalälven • Sweden 16 G6
Osterdalen • Norway 16 F6
Ostergötland • Sweden 95 F4
Osterholz-Scharmbeck • Germany 8 D3
Osterode • Germany 8 F5
Ostersjön • Sweden 16 J7
Ostersund • Sweden 16 H5
Ostervåla • Sweden 95 D1
Ostfold • Norway 94 B4
Ostfriesische Inseln • Germany 8 C3
Ostfriesland • Germany 8 C3
Osthammar • Sweden 95 D2
Ostia • Italy 91 F3
Ostpreussen • Poland/Russian Fed. 16 K9
Ostrach • Germany 82 J1
Ostrava • Czech Rep. 13 H8
Ostrobothnia • Finland 94 A6
Ostróda • Poland 13 I4
Ostrogozhsk • Russian Fed. 17 F4
Ostroleka • Poland 13 K4
Ostrov • Russian Fed. 16 O8
Ostrov • Czech Rep. 96 C1
Ostrovul Delta Dunarii • Romania 14 Q4
Ostrów Mazowiecka • Poland 13 K5
Ostrów Wielkopolski • Poland 13 G6
Ostrowiec Swietokrzyski • Poland 13 K7
Ostrzeszów • Poland 13 G6
Osttirol • Austria 89 H7
Ostuni • Italy 12 L8
Ostuni **Beach** • Italy 69 [157]
Osumi-Shoto • Japan 30 E9
Osuna • Spain 11 F7
Oswego • NY, United States 122 B10
Oswego [Riv] • NY, United States 122 B10
Oswestry • United Kingdom 7 I9
Oswiecim • Poland 13 I7
Oswiecim **Heritage C** • Poland 64 [142]
Otago • New Zealand 112 J3
Otago Peninsula • New Zealand 35 C7
Otaki • New Zealand 35 E5
Otaru • Japan 30 K3
Otautau • New Zealand 112 L4
Otava • Czech Rep. 9 I7
Otavi • Namibia 24 B3
Otawara • Japan 30 J6
Othris • Greece 15 D4
Otira • New Zealand 35 C6
Otish, Mtns • QU, Canada 39 Q6
Otjiwarongo • Namibia 24 B4
Otopeni [Apt] • Romania 97 D1
Otorohanga • New Zealand 112 K1
Otra • Norway 16 D7
Otranto • Italy 12 M8
Otranto, Canal d' • Italy 12 M8
Otrøy • Norway 94 C2
Otsu • Japan 30 H7
Otta • Norway 16 E6
Ottadalen • Norway 94 C2
Ottaviano • Italy 91 G3
Ottawa • OT, Canada 122 B7
Ottawa [Riv] • OT/QU, Canada 122 B3
Otterøya • Norway 16 F4
Otterup • Denmark 95 F10
Ottobeuren • Germany 82 J2
Ottobeuren **Spa** • Germany 83 [236]
Ottumwa • IA, United States 41 H3
Otway, Cape • VI, Australia 111 G3
Otwock • Poland 13 K5
Otztal • Austria 89 H6
Otztaler Alpen • Austria/Italy 89 H6
Ou-Sanmyaku • Japan 30 K5
Ouachita • AR/LA, United States 118 K1
Ouadane **Heritage C** • Mauritania 63 [92]
Ouadda • Central African Rep. 23 C2
Ouaddai • Chad 21 C5
Ouagadougou • Burkina Faso 22 D2
Ouahigouya • Burkina Faso 22 D2
Ouaka • Central African Rep. 23 C2
Oualata • Mauritania 20 D5
Oualata **Heritage C** • Mauritania 63 [92]
Oualidia • Morocco 20 D2
Ouanne, l' • France 10 I6
Ouargla • Algeria 20 G2
Ouarkziz, Jebel • Algeria/Morocco 20 D3
Ouarsenis, Massif de l' • Spain 11 M9
Ouarzazate • Morocco 101 D6
Ouatagouna • Mali 20 F5
Oubangi Chari • Central African Rep. 23 B2
Oubangui • Central African Rep./Congo 22 H4
Oud-Beijerland • Netherlands 80 C3
Oude Rijn • Netherlands 80 C4
Oudenaarde • Belgium 80 A14
Oudewater • Netherlands 80 C4
Oudna • Tunisia 101 E2
Oudon • France 10 E6
Oudong • Cambodia 108 B1
Oudref • Tunisia 101 E4
Oudtshoorn • South Africa 100 C7
Oued, El • Algeria 20 G2
Oued Rhiou • Algeria 11 L9
Oued Zem • Morocco 101 D1
Ouémé • Benin 22 E3
Ouerrha • Morocco 101 D2
Ouessant, I. d' • France 84 C1
Ouesso • Congo 23 B3
Oughterard • Ireland 79 F4
Oughterson Wildlife Park • Barbados 125 H4
Ouham • Central African Rep./Chad 23 B2
Ouieft • Mauritania 20 C4
Ouistreham • France 10 E4
Oujda • Morocco 101 D2
Oukaïmeden • Morocco 101 D5
Oulanka Nat. Park **Park** • Finland 72 [32]
Oulmès • Morocco 101 D1
Oulu • Finland 16 M4
Oulu [Adm] • Finland 16 N4
Oulu [Adm] • Finland 94 A6
Oulujärvi • Finland 16 N4
Oulujoki • Finland 16 N4
Oum Hadjer • Chad 22 H2
Oumm ed Droûs Guebli, Sebkhet • Mauritania 20 C4
Oumm ed Droûs Telli, Sebkhet • Mauritania 20 C4
Ounasjoki • Finland 16 M3
Oupeye • Belgium 5 I4
Our • Europe 5 J4
Our • Germany/Luxembourg 10 K3
Ouranópoli **Beach** • Greece 69 [192]
Ouranópoli • Greece 92 D1
Ourense • Spain 11 D2
Oureq • France 5 G5
Ourinhos • Brazil 44 G3
Ouro Prêto **Heritage C** • Brazil 62 [62]
Ouro Prêto • Brazil 127 C1
Ourthe • Belgium 80 A15
Ouse • United Kingdom 7 M9
Oust • France 10 C5
Outamba-Kilimi Nat. Park **Park** • Sierra Leone 103 [13]
Outão • Portugal 88 D2
Outeniqua Mtns • South Africa 100 C7
Outeniqua Pass • South Africa 100 C7
Outer Hope **Beach** • United Kingdom 75 [113]
Outjo • Namibia 24 B4
Outokumpu • Finland 16 O5
Ouvéa • New Caledonia 35 (2) B3
Ouyen • VI, Australia 34 H7
Ova • Turkey 15 N3
Ovalle • Chile 44 B5
Ovamboland • Namibia 24 B3
Ovar • Portugal 11 C4
Ovar **Beach** • Portugal 68 [95]
Overbecks • United Kingdom 74 F5
Overflakkee • Netherlands 80 C3
OverlJssel • Netherlands 80 A8
Overkalix • Sweden 16 L3
Overlida • Sweden 95 F7
Overloon • Netherlands 80 A11
Overton • NV, United States 117 F4
Overtorneå • Sweden 16 L3
Overum • Sweden 95 F4
Overuman • Sweden 16 H3
Oviedo • Spain 11 F1
Ovre Anarjokka Nat. Park **Park** • Norway 72 [5]
Ovre Ardal • Norway 94 C4
Ovre Dividal Nat. Park **Park** • Norway 72 [7]
Ovre Pasvik Nat. Park **Park** • Norway 72 [3]
Ovre Sirdal • Norway 94 C6
Ovre Soppero • Sweden 16 K2
Owabi Wildlife Sanctuary **Park** • Ghana 103 [25]
Owaka • New Zealand 112 L4
Owando • Congo 22 H5
Owasco Lake • NY, United States 122 B10
Owase • Japan 30 I7
Owatonna • MN, United States 41 H3
Owen, Mt • New Zealand 35 D5
Owen Sound • OT, Canada 39 O8
Owen Stanley Range • Papua New Guinea 35 (1) D2
Owensboro • KY, United States 41 I4
Owerri • Nigeria 22 F3
Owl's Head **Ski** • QU, Canada 116 [40]
Owo • Nigeria 22 F3
Owyhee • United States 117 E4
Ox Mtns • Ireland 79 F2
Oxelösund • Sweden 95 D3
Oxford • United Kingdom 74 D4
Oxfordshire • United Kingdom 74 D4
Oxnard • CA, United States 117 F5
Oxus • Asia 98 B2
Oy Mittelberg • Germany 82 J6
Oy Peter I. • Antarctica 46 (1) FF3
Oy-Mittelberg **Spa** • Germany 83 [247]
Oyahue • Chile 44 C3
Oyem • Gabon 22 G4
Oyeren • Norway 94 B2
Oykel • United Kingdom 6 H4
Oymyakon • Russian Fed. 27 N4
Oyo • Nigeria 22 E3
Oyster Bay • South Africa 100 C8
Oyten • Germany 8 E3
Oz-en-Oisans **Ski** • France 70 [56]
Ozamis • Philippines 31 G5
Ozark • AL, United States 41 I5
Ozark Plateau • AR/MO, United States 41 H4
Ozd • Hungary 13 J9
Ozeblin • Croatia 14 C5
Ozernovskiy • Russian Fed. 27 Q6
Ozernoye, Zaliv • Russian Fed. 27 R5
Ozieri • Sardinia, Italy 12 D8
Ozinki • Russian Fed. 17 H4
Ozorków • Poland 13 I6
Ozouri • Gabon 22 F5

P

P'ohang • Rep. of Korea 30 E7
P'ungsan • D.P.R. of Korea 30 E4
P'yongyang • D.P.R. of Korea 30 C5
Pa Sang • Thailand 109 G3
Pa-an • Myanmar 31 B3
Paar • Germany 9 G8
Paarl • South Africa 100 C5
Pabianice • Poland 13 I6
Pacaraima Mtns • Brazil/Guyana 43 E2
Pacaraima, Serra • Brazil/Venezuela 43 E3
Pachala • Sudan 23 E2
Pachino • Sicily, Italy 12 J12
Pachuca • Mexico 123 E2
Pacific Ocean • 2 C6
Pacific Palisades • HI, United States 119 L5
Pacific Ranges • BC, Canada 38 G6
Pacific Rim Nat. Park Reserve • BC, Canada 122 C3
Pacitan • Java, Indonesia 110 D7
Padang • Indonesia 110 B4
Padangbai • Bali, Indonesia 110 C4
Padanglawas • Indonesia 110 B4
Padangpanjang • Indonesia 110 B4
Padangsidempuan • Indonesia 110 B4
Padangtikar • Indonesia 32 D3
Padasjoki • Finland 95 E2
Paderborn • Germany 8 D5
Paderne • Portugal 88 E7
Pades, Virful • Romania 14 J4
Padirac, Gouffre de • France 85 G4
Padjelanta Nat. Park **Park** • Sweden 72 [19]
Padmanabhapuram • India 106 D14
Pádova **Heritage C** • Italy 64 [113]
Pádova • Italy 91 E7
Padre I. • TX, United States 119 N5
Padre I. Nat. Seashore • TX, United States 119 N5
Padre I. Nat. Seashore **Park** • TX, United States 121 [143]
Padstow • United Kingdom 74 F4
Padstow Bay • United Kingdom 74 F4
Padua **Heritage C** • Italy 64 [113]
Padua • Italy 91 E7
Paducah • KY, United States 41 I4
Paegam • D.P.R. of Korea 30 D4
Paengnyong • Rep. of Korea 30 C6
Paeroa • New Zealand 35 E3
Paestum • Italy 91 G4
Pafuri • Mozambique 24 E4
Pag • Croatia 14 C5
Pag [I.] • Croatia 14 B5
Pagadian • Philippines 31 G5
Pagai, Kepulauan • Indonesia 32 B3
Pagai Selatan • Indonesia 32 C3
Pagai Utara • Indonesia 32 C3
Pagalu • Equatorial Guinea 22 F5
Pagan • Northern Mariana Is. 33 F4
Pagassitikós Kólpos • Greece 15 D4
Pagatan • Indonesia 32 F3
Page • AZ, United States 118 J1
Paget, Mt • South Georgia 46 (1) B4
Págí **Beach** • Corfu, Greece 69 [170]
Pago Pago • American Samoa 35 (2) F1
Pahang [Adm] • Malaysia 31 C6
Pahang [Riv] • Malaysia 32 C2
Paharpur **Heritage C** • Bangladesh 63 [132]
Pahiatua • New Zealand 35 E5
Páhnes • Crete, Greece 93 E5
Pai • Thailand 109 G1
Paia • Vanuatu 35 (2) B2
Paide • Estonia 16 M7
Paignton • United Kingdom 74 F5
Paignton **Beach** • United Kingdom 75 [103]

Päijanne

Päijanne • Finland 95 E2
Paimpol • France 84 C2
Paine, Cerro • Chile 45 B6
Paine, Mt • Antarctica 46 (1) AA1
Painted Desert • AZ, United States 118 J1
País-Vasco • Spain 11 I1
Paisley • United Kingdom 74 B3
Paita • Peru 43 A5
Pajala • Sweden 16 L3
Pájara • Fuerteventura, Canary Is. 87 E2
Pajarito Mtn Ski • NM, United States 116 [103]
Pajaten • Peru 43 B5
Pakch'on • D.P.R. of Korea 30 C4
Pakhachi • Russian Fed. 46 II3
Paki • Nigeria 20 G6
Pakistan • Asia 18 I4
Paklenica Nat. Park Park • Croatia 72 [110]
Pakokku • Myanmar 31 B2
Pakrac • Croatia 12 L3
Paks • Hungary 13 H11
Pakse • Laos 108 A2
Pakwach • Uganda 23 E3
Pakxé • Laos 31 D3
Pala • Chad 23 A2
Palafrugell Beach • Spain 68 [123]
Palafrugell • Spain 87 D2
Palagruza • Croatia 14 D7
Palamau Nat. Park • India 105 C8
Palamós Beach • Spain 68 [123]
Palamós • Spain 87 D2
Palana • Russian Fed. 27 Q5
Palanga • Lithuania 13 J2
Palangkaraya • Indonesia 32 E3
Palani • India 106 D10
Palanpur • India 105 C5
Palapye • Botswana 24 D4
Palatka • FL, United States 119 M3
Palau • Pacific Ocean 33 E5
Palau • Sardinia, Italy 90 C2
Palauli • Western Samoa 35 (2) F1
Palawan • Philippines 31 F4
Paldiski • Estonia 16 M7
Palea Paphos • Cyprus 93 J3
Palékastro Beach • Crete, Greece 69 [215]
Palékastro • Crete, Greece 93 E8
Palembang • Indonesia 32 C3
Palencia • Spain 11 G3
Paléndria • Cyprus 93 J3
Palenque • Mexico 37 C4
Palenque Heritage C • Mexico 62 [25]
Paleo Falíro • Greece 92 D7
Paleohóra Beach • Crete, Greece 69 [212]
Paleohóra • Crete, Greece 93 E5
Paleokastrítsa • Corfu, Greece 92 B1
Paleókipos Beach • Greece 69 [199]
Palermo • Sicily, Italy 90 D1
Páleros • Greece 92 C1
Palestine • TX, United States 119 N4
Palestrina • Italy 91 F4
Palghat • India 106 D10
Pali • India 105 C5
Palioúri • Greece 92 D1
Palisades • NJ/NY, United States 118 H1
Palisadles • Jamaica 124 C4
Palk Bay • Sri Lanka 106 D11
Palk Strait • India/Sri Lanka 106 D11
Palkane • Finland 95 E2
Pallas-Ounastunturi Nat. Park Park • Finland 72 [28]
Pallasovka • Russian Fed. 17 H4
Palliser, Cape • New Zealand 35 E5
Palliser, Is. • French Polynesia 33 M7
Palm Beach • FL, United States 119 M6
Palm Springs • CA, United States 117 F6
Palm Valley • NT, Australia 112 H4
Palma • Mozambique 24 G2
Palma, Badia de • Majorca, Spain 87 H3
Palma de Mallorca Beach • Majorca, Spain 68 [126]
Palma de Mallorca • Majorca, Spain 87 H1
Palma del Rio • Spain 86 B2
Palma Nova • Majorca, Spain 87 H3
Palma, Playa de • Majorca, Spain 87 H3
Palma Soriana • Cuba 124 D8
Palma Sur • Costa Rica 43 A2
Palmanova • Italy 91 E4
Palmares • Brazil 45 (1) D3
Palmária, I. Heritage C • Italy 64 [119]
Palmarito • Venezuela 43 C2
Palmas, Cape • Liberia 22 C4
Pálmas, Golfo di • Sardinia, Italy 90 C3
Palmeira das Missões • Brazil 44 F4
Palmela • Portugal 88 D2
Palmer Station [Base] • Antarctica 46 (1) II3
Palmerston • Cook Is. 33 K7
Palmerston • New Zealand 35 C7
Palmerston North • New Zealand 35 E5
Palmi • Italy 12 J10
Palmira • Colombia 43 B3
Palmyra • Syria 18 C3
Palmyra Atoll • Pacific Ocean 33 K5
Palo Alto Battlefield Nat. Hist. Site Park • TX, United States 121 [142]
Paloh • Indonesia 32 D2
Palolem Beach • Goa, India 105 B2
Palomani, Nevado • Bolivia/Peru 127 B2
Palopo • Indonesia 32 (1) B3
Palos, Cabo de • Spain 87 C3
Palpa • Peru 127 B1
Palpala • Argentina 44 C3
Palu • Indonesia 32 (1) A3
Palyavaam • Russian Fed. 27 T3
Pama • Burkina Faso 22 E2
Pamekasan • Indonesia 110 D4
Pameungpeuk • Java, Indonesia 110 D6
Pamiers • France 10 G10
Pamir • Tajikistan 18 J2
Pâmiut • Greenland 39 V4
Pamlico Sound • NC, United States 118 H5
Pampa • TX, United States 40 F4
Pampa Húmida • Argentina 127 D3
Pampas • Argentina 45 D3
Pampas • Peru 127 B1
Pamplona • Spain 11 J2
Pamplona • Colombia 43 C2
Pamporovo • Bulgaria 96 B2
Pampus • Netherlands 80 C2
Pamukkale • Turkey 92 D6
Pamukova • Turkey 15 L3
Panagiá Beach • Greece 69 [194]
Panagyurishte • Bulgaria 15 F1
Panaitan • Indonesia 110 D1
Panaji • Goa, India 105 B1
Panajia Kerá • Crete, Greece 93 E8
Panalanes, Canal des • Madagascar 24 H4
Panama • C. America 37 E6
Panama Canal • Panama 37 F6
Panama City • Panama 37 F6
Panama City Heritage C • Panama 62 [33]
Panama City • FL, United States 119 M2
Panamá, Golfo de • Panama 43 B2
Panamá, Istmo de • Panama 43 B2
Panao • Peru 43 B6
Panarea • Italy 12 J10
Panarea, I. • Italy 90 D2
Panaro • Italy 91 E7
Panay • Philippines 31 G4
Pancevo • F.R. of Yugoslavia 14 H5
Pancicav vrh • F.R. of Yugoslavia 14 H6
Pandan • Philippines 31 G4
Pandava Caves • Goa, India 105 B2
Pandean • Indonesia 110 C1
Pandeleimónas Beach • Greece 69 [190]
Pandharpur • India 28 C5
Pándheon • Greece 15 D4
Pando • Uruguay 44 E5
Pandrup Beach • Denmark 68 [48]
Panevezys • Lithuania 13 N2
Panfilov • Kazakhstan 26 M9
Pangan • Tanzania 23 F4
Pangandaran • Java, Indonesia 110 D6
Pangéo • Greece 15 F3
Panggoe • Solomon Is. 35 (1) F2
Pangkalanbrandan • Indonesia 110 B1
Pangkalaseang, Tanjung • Indonesia 32 (1) B3
Pangkalpinang • Indonesia 32 D3
Pangkor • Malaysia 108 D1
Pangnirtung • NU, Canada 39 R3
Pangrago, Gunung • Java, Indonesia 110 D1
Pangutaran Group • Philippines 32 (1) B1
Panhala • India 106 D1
Panié • New Caledonia 35 (2) A3
Panipat • India 105 C2
Panja • Afghanistan/Tajikistan 28 A1
Panjang • Indonesia 110 D1
Panmunjom • D.P.R. of Korea 30 D6
Panna • India 105 C7
Pannonhalma Heritage C • Hungary 64 [154]
Panorama • Brazil 44 F3
Panorama Ski • BC, Canada 116 [8]
Panoramapark Sauerland Park • Germany 73 [60]
Pánormos • Crete, Greece 93 E2
Panshan • China 30 B4
Pantai Aceh Forest Reserve • Penang, Malaysia 108 C1
Pantai Suluban • Bali, Indonesia 110 C4
Pantanal • Brazil 44 E2
Pantar • Indonesia 110 A7
Pante Makassar • Indonesia 32 (1) B4
Pantelleria • Italy 12 G12
Pantoja • Peru 43 B4
Panuco • Mexico 37 B3
Pánuco • Mexico 123 E2
Panug, Ko • Thailand 109 K1
Panyu • China 107 H1
Panzi • Dem. Rep. of Congo 22 H6
Paola • Italy 12 K9
Paola • Malta 93 H4
Paoli Peaks Ski • IN, United States 116 [145]
Pápa • Hungary 13 G10
Papago Indian Reservation • AZ, United States 118 J3
Papatowai • New Zealand 112 L4
Papeete • French Polynesia 33 M7
Papenburg • Germany 8 C3
Papendorp • South Africa 100 C1
Papey • Iceland 16 (1) F2
Paphos Beach • Cyprus 69 [217]
Paphos Heritage C • Cyprus 64 [199]
Paphos • Cyprus 93 J3
Papija • Bulgaria 15 I1
Papineau-Labelle Prov. Reserve • QU, Canada 122 B3
Papua, Gulf of • Papua New Guinea 35 (1) C2
Papua New Guinea • Oceania 35 (1) C1
Papuk • Croatia 14 E4
Papun • Myanmar 109 G3
Papunya • NT, Australia 112 H1
Par Beach • United Kingdom 75 [117]
Pará • Brazil 43 G4
Paraburdoo • WA, Australia 34 C4
Paracatu • Brazil 44 G2
Paracel Is. • South China Sea 107 G7
Paradise Bay • Antarctica 59 A10
Paradise Bay • Malta 93 H1
Paradise I. • Bahamas 124 B3
Paradise Sea-Side Resort • BC, Canada 122 C3
Paradísi [Apt] • Rhodes, Greece 93 F2
Paragould • AR, United States 41 H4
Paragua • Venezuela 43 E2
Paragua • Bolivia 44 D1
Paraguarí • Paraguay 44 E4
Paraguay • S. America 44 E3
Paraguay [Riv] • S. America 44 E3
Paraíba • Brazil 45 (1) D3
Paraíba do Sul • Brazil 127 C4
Parainen • Finland 95 E3
Parakou • Benin 22 E3
Paralímni Beach • Cyprus 69 [220]
Paralímni • Cyprus 93 J4
Parálio Astros Beach • Greece 69 [183]
Paramaribo • Suriname 43 F2
Paramo Frontino • Colombia 43 B2
Paramount Canada's Wonderland • OT, Canada 122 B9
Paramount's Great America • CA, United States 117 F3
Paramount's Great America Park • CA, United States 120 [B]
Paramount's Kings Dominion • VA, United States 118 H3
Paramount's Kings Dominion Park • VA, United States 121 [HH]
Paramount's Kings I. Park • OH, United States 121 [V]
Paramushir, Ostrov • Russian Fed. 27 Q6
Paraná • Argentina 44 D5
Paraná [Adm] • Brazil 44 F3
Paraná [Riv] • S. America 44 E4
Paraná [Riv] • Brazil 45 (1) B4
Paranaguá • Brazil 44 G4
Paranaíba • Brazil 44 G2
Paranapanema • Brazil 44 F3
Paranavaí • Brazil 44 F3
Parangtritis • Java, Indonesia 110 D7
Parati • Brazil 127 C3
Parbati • India 28 C4
Parbhani • India 28 C5
Parc Astérix Park • France 73 [70]
Parc Astérix • France 85 E2
Parc des Princes, Paris • France 85 E3
Parc Floral Park • France 73 [72]
Parchim • Germany 8 G3
Pardo • Brazil 45 (1) C5
Pardubice • Czech Rep. 96 C2
Parecis, Chapada dos • Brazil 43 E6
Paren • Russian Fed. 27 R4
Parepare • Indonesia 32 (1) A3
Pares • Antigua & Barbuda 125 F2
Párga • Greece 15 B4
Pargas • Finland 95 E3
Pargo, Ponta do • Madeira 88 C1
Parguera • Puerto Rico 125 E3
Parham • Antigua & Barbuda 125 F2
Parham Harbour • Antigua & Barbuda 125 F2
Paria, Gulf of • Trinidad & Tobago 125 K3
Pariaguán • Venezuela 43 E2
Pariaman • Indonesia 110 B4
Parika • Guyana 43 F2
Parima, Serra • Brazil/Venezuela 43 E3
Pariñas, Punta • Peru 43 A4
Parintins • Brazil 43 F4
Paris Heritage N • France 61 [44]
Paris Heritage C • France 64 [58]
Paris • France 85 E3
Paris • TX, United States 119 N2
Parish Closes • France 84 C1
Park City • UT, United States 116 B
Park City Ski • UT, United States 116 [80]
Park West Ski • UT, United States 116 [81]
Parkano • Finland 95 E2
Parken Zoo i Eskilstuna Park • Sweden 73 [6]
Parker • AZ, United States 118 J3
Parker Dam • AZ/NV, United States 118 J3
Parkes • NS, Australia 111 G2
Parma • Italy 91 E7
Parnaiba • Brazil 45 (1) C2
Parnaiba [Riv] • Brazil 45 (1) C3
Parnassós • Greece 15 D5
Parnassós Nat. Park Park • Greece 72 [139]
Parnassus • New Zealand 35 D6
Párnitha Nat. Park Park • Greece 72 [140]
Párnitha, Oros • Greece 15 E5
Párnonas, Oros • Greece 15 D6
Pärnu • Estonia 16 M7
Páros • Greece 92 D8
Páros [I.] • Greece 92 D8
Parpaillon • France 12 A4
Parpan Ski • Switzerland 70 [111]
Parral • Chile 44 B6
Parramatta • NS, Australia 111 G2
Parrett • United Kingdom 74 F3
Parry Is. • NT/NU, Canada 38 L2
Parry Peninsula • NT, Canada 38 F2
Parry Sound • OT, Canada 122 B5
Parsons • KS, United States 41 G4
Partenen Ski • Austria 70 [124]
Partenen • Austria 89 H5
Parthenay • France 84 D3
Partinico • Sicily, Italy 12 H10
Partnachklamm • Germany 82 J6
Partry Mtns • Ireland 79 F4
Paru • Brazil 43 G4
Pas de la Casa • Andorra 85 K1
Pasadena • CA, United States 117 F6
Pasadena • TX, United States 119 N4
Pascagoula • MS, United States 119 M1
Pascani • Romania 14 N2
Pasco • WA, United States 117 E2
Pascoal, Mt • Brazil 44 I2
Pascua, I. de • Pacific Ocean 33 Q8
Pasewalk • Germany 8 I3
Pasir Panjang • Penang, Malaysia 108 C3
Pasir Ras New Town • Singapore 108 E2
Pasirputih • Java, Indonesia 110 D8
Påskallavik • Sweden 95 F8
Pasni • Pakistan 18 H4
Paso de Indios • Argentina 45 C4
Paso de los Libres • Argentina 44 E4
Paso de los Toros • Uruguay 127 D2
Paso Real • Costa Rica 37 E6
Passage to India cruise area • Indian Ocean 59 A5/8
Pássaro, Capo • Sicily, Italy 90 D4
Passau • Germany 9 I8
Passendale [Battlefield] • Belgium 80 A13
Passer • Italy 90 B1
Passo Fundo • Brazil 44 F4
Passo Rolle Ski • Italy 70 [220]
Passo Tonale Ski • Italy 70 [208]
Passos • Brazil 127 C1
Pasto • Colombia 43 B3
Pastos Bons • Brazil 45 (1) C3
Pasuruan • Java, Indonesia 110 D8
Pasut Beach • Bali, Indonesia 110 C4
Pasvikelva • Norway 16 O2
Pat Sin Leng Country Park • Hong Kong, China 107 H4
Patagonia • Argentina 45 B5
Patagonica, Cordillera • Argentina/Chile 45 B5
Patan • Nepal 28 E3
Patani • Indonesia 32 (1) C2
Patara • Turkey 92 D9
Pate I. • Kenya 101 G4
Pate Manda • Kenya 23 G4
Patea • New Zealand 112 K3
Paternò • Sicily, Italy 12 I11
Paterson • South Africa 100 C8
Paterson Range • WA, Australia 34 D4
Patia • Colombia 43 B3
Patillas, Puerto • Puerto Rico 125 E4
Pativilca • Peru 43 B6
Pátmos • Greece 92 D8
Patna • India 105 C8
Patnem Beach • Goa, India 105 B2
Pato Branco • Brazil 44 F4
Patomskoye Nagorye • Russian Fed. 27 I5
Patong • Phuket, Thailand 109 K2
Patong Bay • Phuket, Thailand 109 K2
Patong Beach • Phuket, Thailand 109 K2
Patos • Brazil 45 (1) D3
Patos de Minas • Brazil 44 G2
Patos, Lagoa dos • Brazil 44 F5
Patquía • Argentina 44 C4
Pátra • Greece 15 C5
Patras • Greece 15 C5
Patrocinio • Brazil 44 G2
Pats Peak Ski • NH, United States 116 [206]
Pattadakal Heritage C • India 63 [127]
Pattadakal • India 106 D2
Pattaya • Thailand 109 H4
Patterdale • United Kingdom 74 C2
Patti • Sicily, Italy 12 I10
Patuca • Honduras 37 E4
Pátzcuaro • Mexico 123 E3
Pau • France 85 J2
Pauillac • France 85 G1
Pauini • Brazil 43 D5
Pauini [Riv] • Brazil 43 D5
Paul de Serra • Madeira 88 C1
Paul Sauer Bridge • South Africa 100 C7
Paulet I. • Antarctica 59 A10
Paulo Alfonso • Brazil 45 (1) D3
Pavia • Italy 91 E6
Pavia, Certosa di • Italy 91 E6
Pavlodar • Kazakhstan 26 M7
Pavlovsk • Russian Fed. 97 E1
Pawai • Singapore 108 E3
Paxí • Greece 15 B4
Paximada • Greece 93 E4
Paximádia • Greece 93 E6
Payakumbuh • Indonesia 110 B4
Payangan • Bali, Indonesia 110 C2
Payerne • Switzerland 89 G1
Paynesville • VI, Australia 111 G3
Pays de la Loire • France 84 A1
Paysandú • Uruguay 44 E5
Payyer, gora • Russian Fed. 26 J4
Pazarbasi Burun • Turkey 15 L2
Pazardzik • Bulgaria 14 L7
Pazaryeri • Turkey 15 K4
Pazin • Croatia 14 A4
Pea Ridge Nat. Military Park Park • AR, United States 121 [191]
Peace [Riv] • AL/BC, Canada 38 G5
Peace River • AL, Canada 122 C2
Peak District Nat. Park Park • United Kingdom 72 [46]
Peak District Nat. Park • United Kingdom 75 A4
Pearl • MS, United States 118 K2
Pearl City • HI, United States 119 L5
Pearl Harbor • HI, United States 119 L5
Pearl Land • Zhuhai, China 107 H2
Pearson, Lester B. [Apt] • OT, Canada 122 B9
Pearston • South Africa 100 C4
Peary Land • Greenland 36 O1
Peatland World • Ireland 79 E1
Peaugres, Safari de • France 85 F3
Pebane • Mozambique 24 F3
Pebas • Peru 43 C4
Pec • F.R. of Yugoslavia 14 H7
Peche-Merle, Grotte du • France 85 G4
Pechenga • Russian Fed. 17 E1
Pechora • Russian Fed. 17 J1
Pechora [Riv] • Russian Fed. 17 I1
Pechorskaya Guba • Russian Fed. 17 I1
Pechorskoye More • Russian Fed. 26 H4
Pecos • TX, United States 40 F5
Pecos Nat. Hist. Park • NM, United States 118 J2
Pecos Nat. Hist. Park Park • NM, United States 120 [130]
Pecos [Riv] • NM/TX, United States 40 F5
Pécs • Hungary 13 H11
Pedde Beach • Goa, India 105 B2
Pedra Azul • Brazil 44 H2
Pedráces Ski • Italy 70 [233]
Pedráces • Italy 90 B2
Pedraisches • Italy 90 B2
Pedreiras • Brazil 45 (1) C2
Pedro Afonso • Brazil 45 (1) B3
Pedro Juan Caballero • Paraguay 44 E3
Pedro Luro • Argentina 45 D3
Pedro Osorio • Brazil 44 F5
Peebles • United Kingdom 74 B4
Peeblesshire • United Kingdom 74 B4
Peek'n Peak Ski • NY, United States 116 [171]
Peel • YT, Canada 38 D3
Peel Sound • NU, Canada 38 L2
Peel's Grave, John • United Kingdom 74 C2
Peene • Germany 8 I3
Peera Peera Poolanna Lake • SA, Australia 34 G5
Pefka • Rhodes, Greece 93 F4
Péfki Beach • Crete, Greece 69 [215]
Péfki • Crete, Greece 93 E8
Pefkohóri Beach • Greece 69 [192]
Pefkohóri • Greece 92 D1
Péfkos • Crete, Greece 93 E7
Peg Barisan • Indonesia 25 L10
Pegasus Bay • New Zealand 35 D6
Peggys Cove • NS, Canada 123 D7
Pegnitz • Germany 9 G7
Pegnitz [Riv] • Germany 9 G7
Pegu • Myanmar 31 B3
Pegu Yoma • Myanmar 31 B2
Peguera • Majorca, Spain 87 H3
Pegunungan Iran • Indonesia/Malaysia 31 F6
Pehlivanköy • Turkey 15 H2
Pehuajó • Argentina 127 D3
Peillon • France 85 H2
Peine • Germany 8 F4
Peipsi jarv • Estonia/Russian Fed. 16 N7
Peipus, Lake • Estonia/Russian Fed. 17 D3
Peisey-Nancroix-Vallandry Ski • France 70 [30]
Peißenberg • Germany 82 J6
Peixe • Brazil 45 (1) B4
Peixoto, Represa de • Brazil 44 G3
Pekalongan • Java, Indonesia 110 D2
Pekan • Malaysia 32 C2
Pekanbaru • Indonesia 110 B4
Peking • China 29 F3
Peking Heritage C • China 63 [146]
Pekulney, Khrebet • Russian Fed. 27 U3
Péla • Greece 15 D3
Pelabuhan Kelang • Malaysia 108 D3
Pelabuhanratu • Java, Indonesia 110 D1
Pelagonija • F.Y.R. of Macedonia 14 I8
Pélagos • Greece 92 D4
Pelat, Mont • France 85 H2
Pelawanbesar • Indonesia 32 F2
Peleaga, Virful • Romania 14 J4
Peleduy • Russian Fed. 27 H5
Peleé, Montagne • Martinique 37 I5
Pélekas Beach • Corfu, Greece 69 [170]
Peleng • Indonesia 32 (1) B3
Pelhrimov • Czech Rep. 96 C4
Pelican Cay Nat. Park • Bahamas 124 B1
Pelican I. • Antigua & Barbuda 125 F2
Pelinaion • Greece 15 H5
Pelister Nat. Park Park • F.Y.R. of Macedonia 72 [124]
Peljesac • Croatia 14 E7
Pelkosenniemi • Finland 16 N3
Pella • Jordan 98 A4
Pello • Finland 16 M3
Pellworm • Germany 8 D2
Pellworm Spa • Germany 83 [5]
Pelly • YT, Canada 38 E4
Pelly Mtns • YT, Canada 38 E4
Pelopónnisos • Greece 15 D6
Pelotas • Brazil 44 F5
Pelusium • Egypt 101 F2
Pemalang • Java, Indonesia 110 D2
Pematangsiantar • Indonesia 110 B2
Pemba • Mozambique 24 G2
Pemba I. • Tanzania 102 H2
Pemberton • WA, Australia 34 C6
Pembina • Canada/United States 38 L7
Pembrey Country Park Beach • United Kingdom 75 [146]
Pembroke Beach • Channel Is. 75 [246]
Pembroke • OT, Canada 122 B2
Pembrokeshire • United Kingdom 75 A5
Pembrokeshire Coast Nat. Park • United Kingdom 75 A5
Pembrokeshire Nat. Park Park • United Kingdom 72 [48]
Pembuang • Indonesia 32 E3
Peña Nevada • Mexico 40 F7
Peña, Sierra de la • Spain 11 K2
Penang • Malaysia 108 C
Penang Bird Park • Penang, Malaysia 108 C2
Penang Botanic Gardens • Penang, Malaysia 108 C1
Penang Hill • Penang, Malaysia 108 C1
Penang I. Bridge • Penang, Malaysia 108 C4
Penara Bukit Forest Reserve • Penang, Malaysia 108 C3
Peñarroya-Pueblonuevo • Spain 11 F6
Peñas, Cabo de • Spain 11 F1
Pend Oreille • Canada/United States 38 H7
Pend Oreille Lake • ID, United States 117 E2
Pendennis Castle • United Kingdom 74 F4
Pendik • Turkey 15 K3
Pendjari, Parc nat. de la Park • Benin 103 [31]
Pendleton • OR, United States 117 E4
Penebel • Bali, Indonesia 110 C2
Peneda, Serra da • Portugal 88 A1
Peneda-Gerês, Parque Nac. da Park • Portugal 72 [80]
Penedo • Brazil 45 (1) D4
Penelokan • Bali, Indonesia 110 C2
Penetanguishene • OT, Canada 122 B5
Peng Chau • Hong Kong, China 107 H5
Pengambengan • Bali, Indonesia 110 C1
Penganga • India 28 C5
Pengastulan • Bali, Indonesia 110 C1
Penghu • Taiwan 107 G8
Penghu Liehtao • Taiwan 31 F2
Penibético, Sistema • Spain 11 G8
Peniche • Portugal 11 B5
Peniche Beach • Portugal 68 [97]
Penicuik • United Kingdom 6 I6
Peninsula [Apt] • CA, United States 117 F3
Peñiscola • Spain 11 L4
Peñíscola Beach • Spain 68 [120]
Penjat, I. des • Formentera, Spain 87 G4
Penmaenmawr Beach • United Kingdom 75 [198]
Penmarc'h, Pointe de • France 84 C3
Penmon Beach • United Kingdom 75 [229]
Penn's Cave • PA, United States 118 H1
Penne • India 106 D3
Penne, Punta • Italy 12 L8
Pennekamp, John, Coral Reef State Park • FL, United States 119 M8
Pennines • United Kingdom 7 J7
Pennsylvania • United States 41 K3
Pennsylvania Avenue Nat. Hist. Site Park • DC, United States 121 [292]
Penny Highland • NU, Canada 39 R3
Penobscot • ME, United States 118 G2
Penobscot Bay • ME, United States 118 G4
Penola • SA, Australia 34 H7
Penong • SA, Australia 34 F6
Penrhyn • Cook Is. 33 L6
Penrith • NS, Australia 34 J6
Penrith • United Kingdom 74 C2
Pensacola • FL, United States 119 M1
Penshurst Place • United Kingdom 74 E3
Pensiangan • Malaysia 32 F2
Pentecôte • Vanuatu 35 (2) B2
Penticton • BC, Canada 122 C4
Pentland Firth • United Kingdom 6 I3
Pentland Hills • United Kingdom 74 B4
Pentraeth Beach • United Kingdom 75 [227]
Penukonda • India 106 D6
Penza • Russian Fed. 17 G4
Penzance • United Kingdom 74 F4
Penzberg • Germany 82 J7
Penzhinskaya Guba • Russian Fed. 27 R4
Peoria • IL, United States 41 I3
Pequeno I. • Goa, India 105 B1
Perabumulih • Indonesia 32 C3
Peraea • Jordan 98 A6
Perai • Penang, Malaysia 108 C2
Perak [Adm] • Malaysia 31 C5
Perak [Riv] • Malaysia 108 D1
Pérama • Corfu, Greece 92 B1
Pérama • Crete, Greece 93 E2
Percé • QU, Canada 123 D2
Perche, Collines du • France 5 D6
Perdido, Monte Heritage N • France/Spain 61 [46]
Perdido, Monte Heritage C • France/Spain 64 [70]
Perdido, Mt • France/Spain 11 L2
Peréa Beach • Greece 69 [191]
Pereira • Colombia 43 B3
Pereiro • Portugal 88 E4
Perenjori • WA, Australia 34 C5
Pereyaslav • Ukraine 71 A10
Perfect North Slopes Ski • IN, United States 116 [146]
Pergamino • Argentina 127 D1
Pergamon • Turkey 92 D5
Perge • Turkey 93 G1
Péribonca • QU, Canada 39 Q7
Perico • Argentina 44 C3
Périgord Blanc • France 85 G2
Périgord Noir • France 85 G2
Périgord Vert • France 85 G2
Périgueux • France 85 G2
Perija, Sierra de • Colombia/Venezuela 43 C2
Perim • Djibouti 21 H5
Perinet, Réserve de Park • Madagascar 103 [137]
Perisher Blue • NS, Australia 111 G4
Perístasi Beach • Greece 69 [190]
Peristéra • Greece 92 D4
Periyar Wildlife Sanctuary • India 106 D10
Perkam, Tanjung • Indonesia 32 (1) E3
Perks Pleasure Park Park • Ireland 73 [19]
Perl • Germany 82 G3
Perlak, Kuala • Malaysia 108 D1
Perleberg • Brandenburg, Germany 8 G3
Perleberg • Niedersachsen, Germany 8 G4
Perlis • Malaysia 31 C5
Pernambuco • Brazil 45 (1) C3
Pernem • Goa, India 105 B1
Pernik • Bulgaria 14 K7
Perniö • Finland 95 E4
Pernis • Netherlands 80 C3
Péronne • France 5 F5
Peroulades Beach • Corfu, Greece 69 [170]
Perpignan • France 85 K2
Perranporth • United Kingdom 74 F4
Perros-Guirec • France 84 C1
Perry's Victory & Int. Peace Mem. Park • OH, United States 121 [187]
Persenk • Bulgaria 15 F2
Persepolis Heritage C • Iran 63 [109]
Perseverancia • Bolivia 44 D1
Perstorp • Sweden 95 F11
Perth • WA, Australia 34 C6
Perth • United Kingdom 74 B2
Perth • OT, Canada 122 B6
Perthshire • United Kingdom 74 B1
Pertuis • France 85 H1
Pertusato, Capo • Corsica, France 85 L4
Peru • S. America 42 C5
Peru, Altiplano del • Peru 127 B2
Peru-Chile Trench • Pacific Ocean 44 B3
Perúgia • Italy 91 E12
Perumal Par I. • India 106 D9
Pervomay • Bulgaria 15 G1
Pésaro • Italy 91 E12
Pescadores • Taiwan 107 G8
Pescara • Italy 12 I6
Pescara [Riv] • Italy 12 H6
Peschanyy, Ostrov • Russian Fed. 27 I2
Pesek • Singapore 108 E3
Peshawar • Pakistan 28 B2
Peshkoni • Albania 15 B2
Pessac • France 10 E9
Pessac-Léognan • France 84 B3
Pessáda • Greece 92 C2
Pest • Hungary 71 A14
Pestovo • Russian Fed. 97 E2
Petäjävesi Heritage C • Finland 63 [74]
Petäjävesi • Finland 95 E2
Petaling Jaya • Malaysia 108 D4
Petalión, Kólpos • Greece 15 F5
Petaloudes • Rhodes, Greece 93 F2
Petaluma • CA, United States 117 F3
Petare • Venezuela 43 D1
Petauke • Zambia 24 E2
Petchaburi • Thailand 109 H3
Peterborough • United Kingdom 7 L9
Peterborough • SA, Australia 34 G6
Peterborough • OT, Canada 122 B5
Peterhead • United Kingdom 6 K4
Peterlee • United Kingdom 7 K7
Petermann Aboriginal Land • NT, Australia 112 H3
Petermann Ranges • NT/WA, Australia 112 H3
Petersburg • AK, United States 38 E5
Petersburg • VA, United States 118 H3
Petersburg Nat. Battlefield Park • VA, United States 121 [255]
Petersmanns Bjerg • Greenland 36 O2
Petiot • BC, Canada 38 G5
Petit Mécatina, Rivière du • NF/QU, Canada 39 S6
Petit Piton • St Lucia 125 J3
Petit St Bernard, Col du • France/Italy 85 F2
Petit-Loango, Réserve de Park • Gabon 103 [50]
Petites Pyrénées • France 11 M1
Petitsikapau Lake • NF, Canada 39 R6
Petkeljärvi Nat. Park Park • Finland 72 [33]
Pétra Beach • Greece 69 [199]
Petra Heritage C • Jordan 64 [249]
Petra Velikogo, Zaliv • Russian Fed. 30 F3
Petralona • Greece 92 D1
Petre, Point • OT, Canada 122 B10
Petrel [Base] • Antarctica 46 (1) JJ3
Petreto-Bicchisano • Corsica, France 85 L3
Petrich • Bulgaria 14 K8
Pétrie, Récifs • New Caledonia 35 (2) A2
Petrified Forest Nat. Park • AZ, United States 118 J2
Petrified Forest Nat. Park Park • AZ, United States 120 [110]
Petrila • Romania 14 K4
Petroglyph Nat. Mon. Park • NM, United States 120 [128]
Petrolina • Brazil 45 (1) C3
Petropavl • Kazakhstan 26 K7
Petropavlovsk-Kamchatskiy • Russian Fed. 27 Q6
Petrópolis • Brazil 127 C4
Petrosani • Romania 14 K4
Petrovsk-Zabaykalskiy • Russian Fed. 27 G6
Petrozavodsk • Russian Fed. 17 E2
Petsamo • Russian Fed. 17 E1
Peuetsagoe, Gunung • Indonesia 110 B1
Pevek • Russian Fed. 27 T3
Péyia Beach • Cyprus 69 [217]
Peyia Basilica • Cyprus 93 J3
Peyriac-de-Mer Beach • France 68 [129]
Pezinok • Slovak Rep. 13 G9
Pfalz • Germany 82 H4
Pfälzer Wald • Germany 82 G4
Pfarrkirchen • Germany 82 J4
Pfeiffer Big Sur State Park • CA, United States 117 F3
Pforzheim • Germany 82 G6
Pfronten • Germany 82 J6
Pfullendorf • Germany 82 J1
Pfullingen • Germany 9 E8
PGA National • FL, United States 119 M6
Pha Tai Caves • Thailand 109 G4
Phaestos • Crete, Greece 93 E6
Phai Rong Wua, Wat • Thailand 109 H1
Phalodi • India 105 C1
Phan • Thailand 109 G2
Phan Rang • Vietnam 108 B2
Phan Thiet • Vietnam 108 B2
Phanat Nikhom • Thailand 109 H4
Phangan, Ko • Thailand 31 C5
Phangnga • Thailand 31 B5
Phanom Dong Rak • Cambodia/Thailand 31 C4
Phanom Rung • Thailand 109 F2
Phantasialand Park • Germany 73 [61]
Phantasialand • Germany 82 G1
Phara • Phuket, Thailand 109 K1
Phaselis • Turkey 93 G3
Phayao • Thailand 109 G2
Phi Phi, Ko • Thailand 109 K2
Philadelphia Heritage C • PA, United States 62 [11]
Philadelphia • Jordan 98 A6
Philadelphia • PA, United States 118 H1
Philadelphia • MS, United States 118 K2
Philae Heritage C • Egypt 63 [83]
Philae • Egypt 101 F5
Philippeville • Belgium 5 H4
Philippi • Greece 92 D1
Philippine Trench • Philippines 31 H4
Philippines • Asia 31 G4
Philippopolis • Bulgaria 71 A15
Philipsburg • St Maarten 58 B7
Philistia • Israel 98 A7
Phillip I. • VI, Australia 111 G3
Phillippsburg • Germany 5 L5
Phimai • Thailand 109 F2

Phitsanulok • Thailand 109 G4
Phlu, Khao • Ko Samui, Thailand 109 J2
Phnom Penh • Cambodia 108 B1
Phoenicia • Israel/Lebanon 98 A1
Phoenix • AZ, United States 118 J3
Phoenix Is. • Kiribati 33 K6
Phoenix Park • Ireland 79 E2
Phoi, Ko • Thailand 109 H4
Phôngsali • Laos 31 C2
Phou Bia • Laos 31 C3
Phra Buddha Sothorp • Thailand 109 H2
Phra Pathom Chedi • Thailand 109 H1
Phra Phutthabat • Thailand 109 H2
Phra Sriratana Mahathat, Wat • Thailand 109 H3
Phra Thong, Ko • Thailand 109 F4
Phra Thong, Wat • Phuket, Thailand 109 K1
Phrae • Thailand 109 G4
Phu Hin Rongkla Nat. Park • Thailand 109 G4
Phu Luang Nat. Park • Thailand 109 G4
Phu Rua Nat. Park • Thailand 109 G4
Phuket • Thailand 109 K
Phumi Mlu Prey • Cambodia 31 D4
Piacenza • Italy 91 E6
Piana • Corsica, France 85 L1
Piancavallo • Italy 90 B4
Pianosa • Tyrrhenian Sea, Italy 12 E6
Pianosa • Adriatic Sea, Italy 12 J6
Piarco [Apt] • Trinidad & Tobago 125 K3
Piaseczno • Poland 13 K5
Piatra Neamt • Romania 14 N3
Piau-Engaly • France 85 J2
Piauí • Brazil 45 (1) C3
Piave • Italy 91 E3
Piaye • St Lucia 125 J3
Piazza Armerina • Sicily, Italy 90 D4
Pibor • Sudan 23 E2
Pibor Post • Sudan 23 E2
Pic Touside • Chad 21 C3
Picardie • France 10 H4
Picardy • France 84 A1
Piceno • Italy 12 H6
Picentini, Monti • Italy 91 G4
Pichilemu • Chile 44 B5
Pickens, Fort • FL, United States 119 M1
Pickle Lake • OT, Canada 39 M6
Pico **Beach** • Azores 68 [102]
Pico • Azores 88 B1
Pico **Ski** • VT, United States 116 [200]
Pico dei Tre Signori • Austria/Italy 90 B2
Pico Truncado • Argentina 45 C5
Picos • Brazil 45 (1) C3
Picton • New Zealand 35 E5
Picton • OT, Canada 122 B6
Pictured Rocks Nat. Lakeshore **Park** • MI, United States 121 [161]
Pidurutalagala • Sri Lanka 106 D15
Piedade, Ponta da • Portugal 88 E6
Piedmont • Italy 90 A1
Piedmonte Matese • Italy 91 G1
Piedras • Peru 43 C6
Piedras Negras • Mexico 37 A2
Piedras, Punta • Argentina 127 D4
Piekary Slaskie • Poland 13 H7
Pieksämäki • Finland 16 N5
Pielavesi • Finland 16 N5
Pielavesi [Lake] • Finland 94 A6
Pielinen • Finland 16 P5
Pieljekaise Nat. Park **Park** • Sweden 72 [20]
Piemonte • Italy 91 E5
Pieninski Nat. Park **Park** • Poland 72 [96]
Pieninsky Nat. Park **Park** • Slovak Rep. 72 [102]
Pienza **Heritage C** • Italy 64 [123]
Pienza • Italy 91 E11
Pierce Reservoirs • Singapore 108 E1
Piéria • Greece 15 D3
Pierre • SD, United States 40 F3
Pierrefonds • France 85 E2
Pierreville • Trinidad & Tobago 125 K4
Piest'any • Slovak Rep. 13 G9
Pietarsaari • Finland 16 L5
Pietermaritzburg • South Africa 24 E5
Pietersburg • South Africa 24 D4
Pietra Ligure • Italy 91 E9
Pietrasanta • Italy 12 E5
Pietrosu, Virful • Romania 14 M2
Pieve di Cadore • Italy 90 B4
Pigeon I. Nat. Park • St Lucia 125 J2
Piggotts • Antigua & Barbuda 125 F1
Pigi **Beach** • Crete, Greece 69 [213]
Pigi • Crete, Greece 93 E2
Pigs, Bay of • Cuba 124 D2
Pihlajavesi • Finland 16 O6
Piilanihale Heiau Temple • HI, United States 119 L4
Pikes Peak • CO, United States 116 A
Piketberg • South Africa 100 C1
Pila • Poland 13 F4
Pila • Italy 91 E1
Pilanesberg Nat. Park **Park** • South Africa 103 [123]
Pilar • Paraguay 44 E4
Pilar de la Horadada **Beach** • Spain 68 [118]
Pilar de la Horadada • Spain 87 C3
Pilaya • Bolivia 44 D3
Pilbara • WA, Australia 111 E1
Pilcomaya • S. America 44 D3
Pilibhit • India 105 C3
Pilica • Poland 13 I7
Pilio • Greece 92 D4
Pilón • Cuba 124 D7
Pilónas • Rhodes, Greece 93 F4
Pilos • Greece 15 C7
Pilsen • Czech Rep. 96 C1
Pinamar • Argentina 127 D4
Pinang • Malaysia 108 C
Pinar • Spain 11 F8
Pinar, Cap d'es • Majorca, Spain 87 H2
Pinar del Rio • Cuba 124 D1
Pinarellu • Corsica, France 85 L4
Pinarhisar • Turkey 15 I2
Pinatubo, Mt • Philippines 31 G3
Pinckney, Charles, Nat. Hist. Site **Park** • SC, United States 121 [238]
Pinçon, Mt • France 5 C6
Pindos Nat. Park **Park** • Greece 72 [135]
Pindos Oros • Greece 15 C4
Pine Bluff • AR, United States 41 H5
Pine Castle • FL, United States 121 C2
Pine Creek • NT, Australia 34 F2
Pine Hills • FL, United States 121 C2
Pine I. • FL, United States 119 M5
Pine I. Bay • Antarctica 46 (1) EE2
Pine Keys • FL, United States 119 M7
Pine Knob **Ski** • MI, United States 116 [140]
Pine Pass • BC, Canada 38 G5
Pineda de Mar **Beach** • Spain 68 [122]
Pineda de Mar • Spain 87 D4
Pineda, la • Spain 87 D3
Pinega • Russian Fed. 17 G2
Pinega [Riv] • Russian Fed. 17 H2
Pinehouse Lake • SA, Canada 38 J5
Pinelands Nat. Reserve **Park** • NJ, United States 121 [336]
Pinerolo • Italy 91 E5
Pineta • Sardinia, Italy 90 C4
Ping • Thailand 109 G3
Ping Chau • Hong Kong, China 107 H4
Pingding Shan • China 29 H1
Pinghu • China 107 J4
Pingliang • China 29 D3
Pingtung • Taiwan 29 G6
Pingvallavatn • Iceland 16 (1) C2
Pingvellir • Iceland 16 (1) C2
Pingwu • China 29 C4
Pingxiang • Guangxi, China 29 D6
Pingxiang • Jiangxi, China 29 E5
Pingyao **Heritage C** • China 63 [148]
Pinhel • Portugal 11 D4
Pini • Indonesia 110 B4
Piniós • Greece 15 C6
Pinnacles Nat. Mon. **Park** • CA, United States 120 [50]
Pinnacles, The • WA, Australia 111 E5
Pinneberg • Germany 8 E3
Pinnes, Akra • Greece 15 F3
Pinney's Beach • St Kitts & Nevis 125 G4
Pino • Corsica, France 85 L2
Pinolosean • Indonesia 32 (1) B2
Pinos, I. de • Cuba 124 D1
Pins, Anse aux • Seychelles 106 F1
Pins, I. des • New Caledonia 35 (2) B3
Pinsk • Belarus 17 D4
Pinta • Galapagos Is. 43 (1) A1
Pinto • Argentina 44 D4
Pintu Gedong • Malaysia 108 D3
Piombino • Italy 91 E11
Pioneer Territory • NV, United States 117 F4
Pioner, Ostrov • Russian Fed. 96 A4
Pionerskiy • Russian Fed. 13 J3
Pionki • Poland 13 K6
Piopio • New Zealand 112 K1
Piotrków Trybunalski • Poland 13 I6
Pipa Dingzi • China 29 H2
Pipalyatjara • SA, Australia 112 H3
Pipamuanan, Réservoir • QU, Canada 123 D1
Pipe Spring Nat. Mon. • AZ, United States 118 J1
Pipe Spring Nat. Mon. **Park** • AZ, United States 120 [99]
Pipestone Nat. Mon. **Park** • MN, United States 121 [154]
Pipiriki • New Zealand 112 K3
Pipri Dam • India 105 C8
Piquiri • Brazil 44 F3
Piracicaba • Brazil 44 G3
Piraeus • Greece 92 D4
Piran • Slovenia 12 H3
Piran **Beach** • Slovenia 69 [168]
Pirapora • Brazil 44 H2
Pireás • Greece 92 D4
Pírgos • Pelopónnisos, Greece 15 C6
Pírgos • Greece 15 D3
Pírgos • Crete, Greece 93 E7
Piriac-sur-Mer **Beach** • France 68 [82]
Piriac-sur-Mer • France 84 C4
Piriápolis • Uruguay 127 D2
Pirin • Bulgaria 14 K8
Pirin Nat. Park **Heritage N** • Bulgaria 61 [58]
Pirin Nat. Park **Park** • Bulgaria 72 [132]
Pirineos • Spain 11 L2
Piripiri • Brazil 45 (1) C2
Pirmasens • Germany 82 G5
Pirna • Germany 9 J6
Pirongia, Mt • New Zealand 112 K1
Pirot • F.R. of Yugoslavia 14 J6
Piru • Indonesia 32 (1) C3
Pisa **Heritage C** • Italy 64 [120]
Pisa • Italy 91 E11
Pisa Range • New Zealand 112 L2
Pisac • Peru 127 B2
Piscataway Park **Park** • MD, United States 121 [276]
Pisco • Peru 127 B1
Písek • Czech Rep. 96 C4
Pissoúri **Beach** • Cyprus 69 [218]
Pissoúri • Cyprus 93 J3
Pisticci • Italy 12 K8
Pistilfjördur • Iceland 16 (1) F1
Pistóia • Italy 91 E11
Pisz • Poland 13 K4
Pit • CA, United States 117 F1
Pitalito • Colombia 43 B3
Pitcairn • Pitcairn Is. 33 O8
Pitcairn Is. • Pacific Ocean 33 O8
Pitch Lake • Trinidad & Tobago 125 K3
Pite älv • Sweden 16 K4
Piteå • Sweden 16 K4
Pitesti • Romania 14 L5
Pithagório **Beach** • Greece 69 [201]
Pitjantjatjara Aboriginal Land • SA, Australia 112 H3
Pitkyaranta • Russian Fed. 17 E2
Pitlochry • United Kingdom 74 B1
Pitsidia **Beach** • Cyprus 69 [216]
Pitt I. • New Zealand 35 (3) A2
Pitt I. • BC, Canada 38 E6
Pitti I. • India 106 D9
Pittsburgh • PA, United States 41 K3
Pittsfield • MA, United States 118 G3
Pitu • Indonesia 32 (1) C2
Piura • Peru 43 A5
Pjórsá • Iceland 16 (1) D2
Placentia Bay • NF, Canada 123 D4
Placetas • Cuba 124 D2
Plackovica • F.Y.R. of Macedonia 15 D2
Plage de la Corniche • Tunisia 101 E2
Plage des Nations • Morocco 101 D1
Plagne, la **Ski** • France 70 [33]
Plagne, la • France 85 F2
Plagne Montalbert **Ski** • France 70 [33]
Pláka **Beach** • Crete, Greece 69 [212]
Pláka, Akra • Greece 15 G3
Plake • F.Y.R. of Macedonia 15 C2
Plakiás • Crete, Greece 93 E6
Plana Cays • Bahamas 124 B4
Planachaux • Switzerland 89 G5
Planicies • Portugal 88 A3
Plano • TX, United States 119 N1
Plános **Beach** • Greece 69 [172]
Plános • Greece 92 C3
Plasencia • Spain 11 E4
Plastun • Russian Fed. 30 I2
Plasy • Czech Rep. 96 C1
Platamónas **Beach** • Greece 69 [190]
Platanés • Crete, Greece 93 E2
Plátani • Sicily, Italy 90 D3
Plataniás **Beach** • Crete, Greece 69 [212]
Plataniás • Crete, Greece 93 E1
Platanos • Crete, Greece 93 E1
Plate, I. • Seychelles 106 F2
Plate, River • Argentina/Uruguay 127 D2
Plati • Greece 15 D3
Platja d'Aro • Spain 87 D2
Platja d'En Bossa • Ibiza, Spain 87 G3
Platja de Muro • Majorca, Spain 87 H2
Platja dels Dols • Majorca, Spain 87 H4
Platja Talamanca • Ibiza, Spain 87 G2
Plato • Colombia 43 C2
Plátres • Cyprus 93 J3
Platte • CO/NE, United States 40 G3
Plattsburgh • NY, United States 118 G3
Plau • Germany 8 H3
Plauen • Germany 9 H6
Plauer See • Germany 8 H3
Playa Azul • Mexico 123 E3
Playa Blanca • Lanzarote, Canary Is. 87 E3
Playa de Fajardo • Puerto Rico 125 E2
Playa de Guayanés • Puerto Rico 125 E4
Playa de Guyanilla • Puerto Rico 125 E3
Playa de las Americas • Tenerife, Canary Is. 86 E1
Playa del Inglés • Gran Canaria, Canary Is. 86 E4
Playa Girón • Cuba 124 D2
Playa Larga • Cuba 124 D2
Playa Paraiso • Tenerife, Canary Is. 86 E1
Pleasure I. • FL, United States 121 C2
Pleasurewood Hills **Park** • United Kingdom 73 [30]
Plechy • Czech Rep. 96 C3
Pleiku • Vietnam 31 D4
Pleiney, le **Ski** • France 70 [51]
Plenty • NT, Australia 112 H2
Plenty, Bay of • New Zealand 35 F3
Plérin • France 84 C2
Plesetsk • Russian Fed. 17 G2
Plessis-Bourré, le [Château] • France 84 D1
Pleszew • Poland 13 G6
Plettenberg • Germany 9 C5
Plettenberg Bay • South Africa 100 C7
Pleven • Bulgaria 14 L6
Plimiri • Rhodes, Greece 93 F3
Pliska • Bulgaria 97 D3
Plitvica • Croatia 12 J4
Plitvice Lakes Nat. Park **Heritage N** • Croatia 61 [52]
Plitvice Lakes Nat. Park **Park** • Croatia 72 [109]
Pljesevica • Bosnia-Herz./Croatia 14 C5
Pljevlja • F.R. of Yugoslavia 14 G6
Ploca, Rt • Croatia 14 C6
Ploce • Croatia 12 L5
Ploce • Bosnia-Herz. 12 L5
Plock • Poland 13 I5
Plöckenstein • Austria/Czech Rep. 9 I8
Ploërmel • France 84 C4
Plogshagen **Spa** • Germany 83 [278]
Ploiesti • Romania 97 D1
Plomári **Beach** • Greece 69 [199]
Plomb du Cantal • France 10 H8
Plön • Germany 8 F2
Plonsk • Poland 13 J5
Plötzin • Germany 81 F3
Plougerneau • France 10 A5
Plouha • France 84 C2
Ploumanac'h • France 84 C1
Plovdiv • Bulgaria 14 L7
Plover Cove Country Park • Hong Kong, China 107 H4
Plover Cove Reservoir • Hong Kong, China 107 H4
Plumtree • Zimbabwe 102 J3
Plunge • Lithuania 13 K2
Plymouth • Montserrat 58 B7
Plymouth • United Kingdom 74 F5
Plymouth • Trinidad & Tobago 125 K2
Plzen • Czech Rep. 96 C1
Po • Italy 91 E7
Po Basin • Italy 90 A1
Po, Colline del • Italy 91 E5
Po, Foci del • Italy 91 E8
Po Lin Monastery • Hong Kong, China 107 H5
Po Toi • Hong Kong, China 107 H6
Poarta Orientala • Romania 14 J4
Pobeda, gora • Russian Fed. 25 P3
Pobedy, Pik • Kyrgyzstan 26 N9
Pobla de Segur, la • Spain 11 M2
Poblet **Heritage C** • Spain 64 [73]
Poblet, Reial Monestir de • Spain 87 D3
Pobrezije • Bulgaria 14 N6
Pocano Mtns • PA, United States 118 H1
Pocatello • ID, United States 40 D3
Pochentong [Apt] • Cambodia 108 B1
Poço das Antas, Reserva biológica • Brazil 127 C4
Poções • Brazil 44 H1
Poços de Caldas • Brazil 127 C3
Podebrady • Czech Rep. 96 C2
Podgorica • F.R. of Yugoslavia 14 G7
Podkammennaya Tunguska • Russian Fed. 26 P5
Podolsk • Russian Fed. 97 E4
Podor • Senegal 20 C5
Podporozh'ye • Russian Fed. 17 E2
Podravina • Croatia 14 E4
Podrima • F.R. of Yugoslavia 14 H7
Podunajska • Slovak Rep. 14 E1
Poe, Edgar Allen, Nat. Hist. Site **Park** • PA, United States 121 [309]
Poel • Germany 8 G2
Pogradec • Albania 15 B3
Pohjois-Karjala • Finland 16 O5
Pohjois-Karjala • Finland 94 A6
Pohnpei • Fed. States of Micronesia 33 G5
Pohorje • Slovenia 13 E11
Point au Fer I. • LA, United States 118 K4
Point, Fort, Nat. Hist. Site **Park** • CA, United States 120 [44]
Point Fortin • Trinidad & Tobago 125 K3
Point Lake • NT, Canada 38 I3
Point Lisas • Trinidad & Tobago 125 K3
Point Pleasant • NJ, United States 118 H1
Point Reyes Nat. Seashore **Park** • CA, United States 120 [42]
Pointe à Pierre • Trinidad & Tobago 125 K3
Pointe à Pitre • Guadeloupe 37 I4
Pointe au Sel • Seychelles 106 F1
Pointe du Cap • St Lucia 125 J2
Pointe Noire • Congo 22 G5
Pointe Seraphine • St Lucia 125 J1
Poissy • France 5 F6
Poitevin, Marais • France 84 D3
Poitiers • France 84 D4
Poitou • France 84 D3
Poitou-Charentes • France 84 A1
Poivre • Seychelles 106 F2
Poix-de-Picardie • France 10 G4
Pojezierze Chelminskie • Poland 13 I4
Pojezierze Dobrzynskie • Poland 13 I5
Pojezierze Mazurskie • Poland 13 J4
Pojezierze Pomorskie • Poland 13 F4
Pojezierze Wielkopolsko-Kujawskie • Poland 13 F5
Pok Pu Lam Country Park • Hong Kong, China 107 H5
Pokaran • India 105 C1
Pokhara • Nepal 28 D3
Poko • Dem. Rep. of Congo 23 D3
Pol-e Khomri • Afghanistan 26 K10
Pola de Laviana • Spain 11 F1
Pola de Lena • Spain 11 F1
Pola de Siero • Spain 11 F1
Poland • Europe 13
Polatli • Turkey 15 N4
Polem Beach • Goa, India 105 B2
Polesine • Italy 91 E7
Polessje • Ukraine 13 N6
Polessk • Russian Fed. 13 K3
Poli • Cameroon 22 G3
Poliçan • Albania 15 B3
Policastro, Golfo di • Italy 12 J9
Police • Poland 13 D4
Police, Pointe • Seychelles 106 F3
Policoro • Italy 12 K8
Policoro **Beach** • Italy 69 [155]
Poliegos • Greece 92 D7
Poligny • France 10 K7
Poligus • Russian Fed. 26 P5
Polihnitos • Greece 15 H4
Polihnitos **Beach** • Greece 69 [199]
Polihrono **Beach** • Greece 69 [192]
Polikastro • Greece 15 D2
Polillo • Philippines 31 G4
Polirinia • Crete, Greece 93 E1
Pólis **Beach** • Cyprus 69 [217]
Pólis • Cyprus 93 J3
Polistena • Italy 12 K10
Polk, Fort • LA, United States 118 K3
Polkowice • Poland 13 F6
Pollachi • India 106 D10
Pollença • Majorca, Spain 87 H2
Póllica • Italy 12 J8
Póllica **Beach** • Italy 69 [149]
Polo, Marco [Apt] • Italy 91 E8
Polonia [Apt] • Indonesia 110 B2
Polonnaruwa **Heritage C** • Sri Lanka 63 [136]
Polonnaruwa • Sri Lanka 106 D15
Polotsk • Belarus 17 D3
Polousnyy Kryazh • Russian Fed. 27 N3
Polson • MT, United States 117 E2
Poltava • Ukraine 17 E5
Polyarnyy • Russian Fed. 17 E1
Polynesia • Pacific Ocean 33 K6
Polzeath **Beach** • United Kingdom 75 [130]
Pomarkku • Finland 95 E1
Pomerania • Poland 96 B1
Pomerol • France 84 B3
Pomio • Papua New Guinea 35 (1) E2
Pommersche Bucht • Germany/Poland 8 J2
Pomongwe Cave • Zimbabwe 102 J3
Pomorie • Bulgaria 97 D3
Pomorska, Zatoka • Germany/Poland 8 J2
Pomorskiy Proliv • Russian Fed. 17 I1
Pompadour, Château de • France 85 G2
Pompano Beach • FL, United States 119 M8
Pompei • Italy 91 G3
Pompei and **Heritage C** • Italy 64 [128]
Pomposa Abbazia • Italy 91 E8
Ponape • Fed. States of Micronesia 33 G5
Ponca City • OK, United States 41 G4
Ponce • Puerto Rico 125 E3
Pond Inlet • NU, Canada 39 P2
Ponda • Goa, India 105 B1
Pondicherry • India 106 D7
Ponferrada • Spain 11 E2
Pong Qu • China/Nepal 28 E3
Pongola • Mozambique/South Africa 24 E5
Ponmudi • India 106 D10
Ponoy • Russian Fed. 17 G1
Pons • Spain 10 G12
Pont-à-Mousson • France 5 J6
Pont-Audemer • France 10 F4
Pont-Aven • France 84 C3
Pont-l'Abbé • France 84 C2
Ponta Delgada **Beach** • São Miguel, Azores 68 [105]
Ponta Delgada • Azores 88 B1
Ponta do Sol • Madeira 88 C1
Ponta Grossa • Brazil 44 F4
Ponta Porã • Brazil 44 E3
Pontal • Portugal 88 E5
Pontarlier • France 89 G1
Pontchartrain, Lake • LA, United States 118 K4
Ponte de Lima **Beach** • Portugal 68 [94]
Ponte di Legno • Italy 91 E3
Ponte Leccia • Corsica, France 85 L2
Ponte Nova • Brazil 127 C2
Pontecagnano • Italy 91 G4
Pontevedra • Spain 11 C2
Pontevedra, Ria de • Spain 11 C2
Pontiac • MI, United States 41 J3
Pontianak • Indonesia 32 D3
Pontivy • France 84 C4
Pontorson • France 5 B6
Pontrémoli • Italy 91 E6
Pontresina **Ski** • Switzerland 70 [122]
Pontresina • Switzerland 89 G8
Pontypool • United Kingdom 7 I10
Pony Express Territory • NV, United States 117 F2
Ponypark **Park** • Netherlands 73 [39]
Ponypark • Netherlands 80 A8
Ponza • Italy 12 G8
Ponziane, Is. • Italy 12 G8
Pool Plateau • Antarctica 46 (1) A1
Poole • United Kingdom 74 F3
Poole **Beach** • United Kingdom 75 [84]
Poona • India 28 B5
Poopó • Bolivia 44 C2
Poopó, Lago de • Bolivia 44 C2
Popayán • Colombia 43 B3
Poperinge • Belgium 80 A13
Popeye Village • Malta 93 H1
Popigay • Russian Fed. 27 H2
Poplar Bluff • MO, United States 41 H4
Popocatépetl **Heritage C** • Mexico 62 [22]
Popocatépetl • Mexico 123 E4
Pópoli • Italy 91 F2
Popondetta • Papua New Guinea 35 (1) D2
Popovo • Bulgaria 97 D3
Poprad • Slovak Rep. 13 J8
Porbandar • India 28 B4
Porcupine • Canada/United States 38 C3
Porcupine Plain • YT, Canada 38 D3
Pordenone • Italy 90 B4
Porec • Croatia 14 A4
Porec **Heritage C** • Croatia 64 [155]
Poretta [Apt] • Corsica, France 85 L2
Pori • Finland 95 E1
Porirua • New Zealand 35 E5
Pórisvatn • Iceland 16 (1) D2
Porkkala • Finland 95 E4
Porlamar • Venezuela 43 E1
Porlock • United Kingdom 74 F2
Pornic **Beach** • France 68 [82]
Pornichet • France 84 C4
Poronaysk • Russian Fed. 27 N7
Póros • Greece 15 E6
Póros **Beach** • Greece 69 [171]
Póros • Cephalonia, Greece 92 C2
Póros [I.] • Greece 92 D7
Porpoise Bay • Antarctica 46 (1) R3
Porpoise Bay • New Zealand 112 L4
Porquerolles, I. de • France 85 H3
Porsangen • Norway 16 M1
Porsanger-Halvøya • Norway 16 M1
Porsgrunn • Norway 94 B3
Pórshöfn • Iceland 16 (1) F1
Porsuk • Turkey 15 M4
Porsuk Baraji • Turkey 15 L4
Port Alberni • BC, Canada 122 C3
Port Alfred • South Africa 24 D6
Port Alice • BC, Canada 38 F6
Port Angeles • WA, United States 117 E1
Port Antonio • Jamaica 124 C2
Port Aransas • TX, United States 119 N5
Port Arthur • China 29 G3
Port Arthur • TS, Australia 34 I8
Port Arthur • TX, United States 119 N4
Port Askaig • United Kingdom 6 F6
Port au Choix • NF, Canada 123 D5
Port au Prince • Haiti 37 G4
Port Augusta • SA, Australia 34 G6
Port aux Français • Kerguelen Is. 19 (1) B1
Port Aventura **Park** • Spain 73 [76]
Port Aventura • Spain 87 D3
Port Barcarès • France 85 K2
Port Beaufort • South Africa 100 C6
Port Blair • India 28 F6
Port Burwell • NU, Canada 39 S4
Port Campbell Nat. Park • VI, Australia 111 G3
Port Canaveral • FL, United States 119 M6
Port Cartier • QU, Canada 39 R6
Port Chalmers • New Zealand 35 C7
Port Charlotte • FL, United States 119 M5
Port Chicago Naval Magazine Nat. Mem. **Park** • CA, United States 120 [47]
Port Cros, I. de • France 85 H3
Port Cros, Parc nat. de **Park** • France 72 [69]
Port Cros, Parc nat. de • France 85 H3
Port d'Addaia • Minorca, Spain 87 F2
Port d'es Torrent • Ibiza, Spain 87 G1
Port Daniel Prov. Reserve • QU, Canada 123 D2
Port de Alcúdia • Majorca, Spain 87 H2
Port de Andratx • Majorca, Spain 87 H3
Port de Bouc • France 10 K10
Port de Pollença • Majorca, Spain 87 H2
Port de Sóller • Majorca, Spain 87 H1
Port de St Miquel • Ibiza, Spain 87 G2
Port des Barques **Beach** • France 68 [84]
Port Dickson • Malaysia 108 D4
Port el Kantaoui • Tunisia 101 E2
Port Elizabeth • South Africa 100 C8
Port Ellen • United Kingdom 6 F6
Port Erin • Isle of Man 7 H7
Port Eynon **Beach** • United Kingdom 75 [144]
Port Fitzroy • New Zealand 35 E3
Port Gentil • Gabon 22 F5
Port Gibson • MS, United States 118 K2
Port Grimaud • France 85 H4
Port Harcourt • Nigeria 22 F4
Port Hardy • BC, Canada 38 F6
Port Hawkesbury • NS, Canada 123 D7
Port Hedland • WA, Australia 34 C4
Port Hope • OT, Canada 122 B5
Port Hope Simpson • NF, Canada 39 T6
Port Huron • MI, United States 41 J3
Port I. • Hong Kong, China 107 H4
Port Jackson • NS, Australia 111 G2
Port Kelang • Malaysia 108 D3
Port Kembla • NS, Australia 111 G2
Port la Nouvelle • France 11 O2
Port la Nouvelle **Beach** • France 68 [129]
Port Láirge • Ireland 7 E9
Port Lavaca • TX, United States 119 N5
Port Leucate • France 85 K2
Port Lincoln • SA, Australia 34 G6
Port Lockroy • Antarctica 59 A10
Port Louis • Mauritius 24 (1) B2
Port Lympne Wildlife Park • United Kingdom 74 E3
Port Macquarie • NS, Australia 34 J6
Port Maria • Jamaica 124 C2
Port Menier • QU, Canada 123 D2
Port Morant • Jamaica 124 C4
Port Moresby • Papua New Guinea 35 (1) D2
Port O'Connor • TX, United States 119 N5
Port of Spain • Trinidad & Tobago 125 K3
Port Phillip Bay • VI, Australia 111 G3
Port Pirie • SA, Australia 34 G6
Port Royal • Jamaica 124 C4
Port Royal des Champs, Abbaye de • France 85 E3
Port Said • Egypt 101 F2
Port Saunders • NF, Canada 123 D5
Port Shelter • Hong Kong, China 107 H6
Port Shepstone • South Africa 100 B2
Port Soif Bay **Beach** • Channel Is. 75 [245]
Port Stanley • Falkland Is. 59 A10
Port Stephens • NS, Australia 111 E8
Port Sudan • Sudan 21 G4
Port Talbot • United Kingdom 7 I10
Port Vendres • France 10 I11
Port Vendres **Beach** • France 68 [128]
Port Vila • Vanuatu 35 (2) B2
Port Wakefield • SA, Australia 34 G6
Porta, la • Corsica, France 85 L2
Porta Westfalica **Spa** • Germany 83 [91]
Portadown • United Kingdom 7 F7
Portage la Prairie • MN, Canada 38 L6
Portalegre • Portugal 11 D5
Portalegre [Adm] • Portugal 88 A2
Portales • NM, United States 40 F5
Portals Nous • Majorca, Spain 87 H3
Portals Vells • Majorca, Spain 87 H3
Portarlington • Ireland 79 E3
Portbou **Beach** • Spain 68 [123]
Portbou • Spain 87 D2
Porté Puymorens • France 85 K1
Portel • Brazil 43 G4
Portel, le **Beach** • France 68 [75]
Portela • Madeira 88 C2
Portela de Sacavém [Apt] • Portugal 88 D2
Portelet Bay **Beach** • Channel Is. 75 [247]
Porterville • South Africa 24 B6
Porterville • CA, United States 117 F3
Portes du Soleil • France 85 F2
Portes, Punta de ses • Ibiza, Spain 87 G3
Porthcawl • United Kingdom 74 F2
Porthcawl **Beach** • United Kingdom 75 [142]
Porthmadog • United Kingdom 7 H9
Porticcio • Corsica, France 85 L3
Portici • Italy 91 G3
Portigliolo • Corsica, France 85 L3
Portimão **Beach** • Portugal 68 [100]
Portimão • Portugal 88 E6
Portinão da Arrábida • Portugal 88 D2
Portinatx • Ibiza, Spain 87 G2
Portland • VI, Australia 34 H7
Portland • OR, United States 117 E3
Portland • ME, United States 118 G4
Portland Bight • Jamaica 124 C4
Portland Bill • United Kingdom 74 F6
Portland, Isle of • United Kingdom 74 F6
Portland Point • Jamaica 124 C4
Portlaoise • Ireland 7 E8
Portmarnock • Ireland 79 E2
Portmore • Jamaica 124 C4
Portnoo **Beach** • Ireland 68 [65]
Porto • Portugal 11 C3
Porto **Heritage C** • Portugal 64 [95]
Porto • Corsica, France 85 L1
Porto Acre • Brazil 43 D5
Porto [Adm] • Portugal 88 A1
Pôrto Alegre • Brazil 44 F5
Porto Amboim • Angola 23 A6
Porto Azzurro • Italy 91 E11
Porto Cervo • Sardinia, Italy 90 C2
Porto Colom • Majorca, Spain 87 H4
Porto Conte • Sardinia, Italy 90 C1
Porto Cristo • Majorca, Spain 87 H2
Porto da Cruz • Madeira 88 C2
Porto de Moz • Brazil 43 G4
Porto Empédocle • Sicily, Italy 90 D4
Porto Franco • Brazil 45 (1) B3
Porto Garibaldi • Italy 91 E8
Porto, Golfe de **Heritage N** • Corsica, France 61 [45]
Porto, Golfe de • Corsica, France 85 L1
Porto Moniz **Beach** • Madeira 68 [108]
Porto Moniz • Madeira 88 C1
Porto Novo • Cape Verde 22 (1) A1
Porto Petro • Majorca, Spain 87 H4
Porto Potenza Picena • Italy 91 E12
Porto Rafael • Sardinia, Italy 90 C2
Pórto Ráfti • Greece 92 D7
Porto Recanati • Italy 91 E12
Porto Rotondo • Sardinia, Italy 90 C2
Porto San Giórgio • Italy 12 H5
Pôrto Santana • Brazil 43 G4
Porto Santo • Madeira 20 B2
Porto Santo **Beach** • Madeira 68 [107]
Porto Santo Stefano • Italy 12 F6
Porto Seguro • Brazil 44 I2
Porto Tolle • Italy 12 G4
Porto Tórres • Sardinia, Italy 90 C1
Porto Válter • Brazil 43 C5
Porto Vecchio • Corsica, France 85 L4
Porto Velho • Brazil 43 E5
Portobelo **Heritage C** • Panama 62 [32]
Portoferráio • Italy 91 E10
Portofino **Beach** • Italy 68 [142]
Portofino • Italy 91 E6
Portogruaro • Italy 12 G3
Portohéli **Beach** • Greece 69 [184]
Portohéli • Greece 92 D7
Portonovo • Benin 22 E3
Portoroz **Beach** • Slovenia 69 [169]
Portoroz • Slovenia 96 B2
Portoscuso • Sardinia, Italy 90 C3
Portovénere **Heritage C** • Italy 64 [119]
Portovénere • Italy 91 E10
Portoviejo • Ecuador 43 A4
Portree • United Kingdom 6 F4
Portrush **Beach** • United Kingdom 75 [236-237]
Portsmouth • United Kingdom 7 K11
Portsmouth • OH, United States 41 J4
Portsmouth • Dominica 58 B11
Portsmouth • NH, United States 118 G3
Portsmouth • VA, United States 118 H5
Portstewart **Beach** • United Kingdom 75 [235]
Porttipahdan tekojarvi • Finland 16 N2
Portugal • Europe 11
Portugalete • Spain 11 H1
Portumna • Ireland 79 F4
Porvenir • Bolivia 43 D6
Porvenir • Chile 45 B6
Porvoo • Finland 95 E4
Posada • Sardinia, Italy 90 C2
Posadas • Argentina 44 E4
Posavina • Bosnia-Herz./Croatia 14 F5
Poschiavo • Switzerland 89 G8
Poseidon, Temple of • Greece 92 D7
Posillipo • Italy 91 G3
Posio • Finland 16 O3
Positano **Beach** • Italy 69 [149]
Positano • Italy 91 G3
Poso • Indonesia 32 G3
Poso, Danau • Indonesia 32 (1) B3
Posse • Brazil 45 (1) B4
Postavy • Belarus 16 N9
Postojna • Slovenia 14 B4
Potamiés • Crete, Greece 93 E7
Potenza • Italy 12 J8
Potenza [Riv] • Italy 12 H5
Poteriteri, Lake • New Zealand 112 L3
Poti • Georgia 17 G6
Potiskum • Nigeria 22 G2
Potnarvin • Vanuatu 35 (2) B2
Poto • Peru 127 B2
Potomac • MD/VI, United States 118 H3
Potosí • Bolivia 44 C2
Potosí **Heritage C** • Bolivia 62 [53]
Potsdam **Heritage C** • Germany 64 [31]
Potsdam • Germany 81 F3
Potsdam Neues Palais • Germany 81 F3
Potters Village • Antigua & Barbuda 125 F1
Pottsville • PA, United States 41 K3
Pottuvil • Sri Lanka 106 D16
Potworks Dam • Antigua & Barbuda 125 F4
Poughkeepsie • NY, United States 118 H2
Pouilly-Fumé • France 84 B2
Pouso Alegre • Brazil 127 C3
Pouthisat • Cambodia 31 C4
Povazská Bystrica • Slovak Rep. 13 H8
Poverty Bay • New Zealand 35 F4
Poverty Point Nat. Mon. • LA, United States 118 K1
Poverty Point Nat. Mon. **Park** • LA, United States 121 [195]
Póvoa de Varzim • Portugal 11 C3
Povoação • Azores 88 B1
Powder • MT/WY, United States 38 J7
Powder Mtn **Ski** • UT, United States 116 [77]
Powell • WY, United States 40 E3

Powell, Lake • AZ/UT, United States 118 J1
Powell River • BC, Canada 38 G7
Powerscourt House • Ireland 79 E4
Poyang Hu • China 29 F5
Pöytyä • Finland 95 E3
Poza Rica • Mexico 123 E2
Pozarevac • F.R. of Yugoslavia 14 I5
Poznan • Poland 13 F5
Pozoblanco • Spain 11 G6
Pozos, Punta • Argentina 45 C5
Pozuelos • Venezuela 43 E2
Pozza di Fassa **Ski** • Italy 70 [221]
Pozza di Fassa • Italy 90 B3
Pozzallo • Sicily, Italy 90 D4
Pozzuoli • Italy 91 G3
Pra • Ghana 22 D3
Pra-Loup **Ski** • France 70 [69]
Pra-Loup • France 85 H2
Prachatice • Czech Rep. 96 C3
Prachin Buri • Thailand 109 H2
Prachuap Kiri Khan • Thailand 31 B4
Praded • Czech Rep. 13 G7
Prades • France 85 K2
Præstø • Denmark 95 F14
Prague **Heritage C** • Czech Rep. 64 [143]
Prague • Czech Rep. 96 C2
Praha **Heritage C** • Czech Rep. 64 [143]
Praha • Czech Rep. 96 C2
Praia • Cape Verde 22 (1) B2
Praia da Falésia • Portugal 88 E7
Praia da Luz • Portugal 88 E5
Praia da Oura • Portugal 88 E7
Praia da Rocha • Portugal 88 E6
Praia das Macas • Portugal 88 D1
Praia de Balaia • Portugal 88 E7
Praia de Castelo • Portugal 88 E6
Praia de Galé • Portugal 88 E6
Praia de Vale do Lobo • Portugal 88 E7
Praia Grande • Portugal 88 D1
Praia Parede • Portugal 88 D1
Praia Verde • Portugal 88 E8
Prainha • Brazil 43 G4
Prainha • Madeira 88 C2
Prambanan **Heritage C** • Java, Indonesia 63 [178]
Prambanan • Java, Indonesia 110 D7
Pranauron **Ski** • Italy 70 [231]
Pranita • India 28 C5
Prapat • Indonesia 110 B2
Prapoutel **Ski** • France 70 [51]
Praslin • Seychelles 106 F4
Praslin Bay • St Lucia 125 J4
Prasonísi, Akra • Rhodes, Greece 93 F3
Prat Mataou • France 85 K1
Prata • Brazil 44 G2
Prata, Costa de • Portugal 88 A2
Pratas Is. • China 107 G8
Prato • Italy 91 E11
Prats-de-Mollo • France 85 K2
Pravdinsk • Russian Fed. 13 K3
Pravia • Spain 11 E1
Prawl Point • United Kingdom 74 F5
Praz de Lys, le **Ski** • France 70 [14]
Prazeres • Madeira 88 C1
Predazzo **Ski** • Italy 70 [217]
Predazzo • Italy 90 B3
Preetz • Germany 8 F2
Pregolya • Russian Fed. 13 J3
Prekmurje • Slovenia 14 D3
Premnitz • Germany 8 H4
Premuda • Croatia 14 B5
Prenj • Bosnia-Herz. 14 E6
Prenn Falls • Vietnam 108 B2
Prenzlau • Germany 8 I3
Preobrazhenka • Russian Fed. 27 G5
Preparis North Channel • Myanmar 31 A3
Prerov • Czech Rep. 13 G8
Prerov nad Labem • Czech Rep. 96 C2
Prerow **Beach** • Germany 68 [32]
Prerow **Spa** • Germany 83 [276]
Prescott • AZ, United States 118 J1
Preservation Inlet • New Zealand 112 L3
Presidencia Roque Sáenz Peña • Argentina 44 D4
Presidente Epitácio • Brazil 44 F3
Presidente Frei [Base] • Antarctica 46 (1) JJ4
Presidente Prudente • Brazil 44 F3
Presidio • TX, United States 40 F6
Preslav • Bulgaria 97 D3
Presov • Slovak Rep. 13 K8
Préspa Nat. Park **Park** • Greece 72 [133]
Presque Isle • ME, United States 118 G2
Pressburg • Slovak Rep. 71 A14
Prestatyn **Beach** • United Kingdom 75 [203]
Prestice • Czech Rep. 9 I7
Preston • United Kingdom 7 J8
Prestwick [Apt] • United Kingdom 6 H6
Pretoria • South Africa 24 D5
Pretorius, Willem Game Reserve **Park** • South Africa 103 [122]
Preußisch-Oldendorf **Spa** • Germany 83 [86]
Prevel, Fort • QU, Canada 123 D2
Préveza • Greece 92 C1
Priboj • F.R. of Yugoslavia 14 G6
Príbram • Czech Rep. 96 C3
Pribyslav • Czech Rep. 96 C4
Price • UT, United States 40 D4
Prickley Pear I. • Antigua & Barbuda 125 F1
Pridz Bay • Antarctica 46 (1) M3
Priego • Spain 11 I4
Priego de Córdoba • Spain 11 G7
Prien • Germany 82 J4
Prien **Spa** • Germany 83 [256]
Priene • Turkey 92 D9
Prieros • Germany 81 F4
Prieska • South Africa 24 C5
Prievidza • Slovak Rep. 13 H9
Prignitz • Germany 81 D1
Prijedor • Bosnia-Herz. 12 K4
Prilep • F.Y.R. of Macedonia 14 I8
Priluki • Ukraine 17 E4
Primavera [Base] • Antarctica 46 (1) II3
Primeira Cruz • Brazil 45 (1) C2
Primorsk • Russian Fed. 16 O6
Primorsko **Beach** • Bulgaria 69 [242]
Primorsko • Bulgaria 97 D3
Primorsko-Akhtarsk • Russian Fed. 17 F5
Primosten • Croatia 12 J5
Prince Albert • SA, Canada 38 J6
Prince Albert • South Africa 100 C7
Prince Albert Peninsula • NT, Canada 38 H2
Prince Albert Road • South Africa 100 C2
Prince Albert Sound • NT, Canada 38 H2
Prince Alfreds Pass • South Africa 100 C7
Prince Charles I. • NU, Canada 39 P3
Prince Charles Mtns • Antarctica 46 (1) L2
Prince de Galles, Cap du • QU, Canada 39 Q4
Prince Edward I. • Canada 123 D7
Prince Edward I. Nat. Park • PE, Canada 123 D7
Prince Edward Is. • Indian Ocean 19 H10
Prince George • BC, Canada 122 C1
Prince of Wales, Cape • AK, United States 36 A3
Prince of Wales I. • QL, Australia 34 H2
Prince of Wales I. • AK, United States 38 E5
Prince of Wales I. • NU, Canada 38 L2
Prince of Wales Strait • NT, Canada 38 H2
Prince Regent Inlet • NU, Canada 39 N2
Prince Rupert • BC, Canada 38 F6
Prince Rupert Bay • Dominica 58 B11
Princes Is. • Turkey 92 D3
Princes Town • Trinidad & Tobago 125 K3
Princess Charlotte Bay • QL, Australia 34 H2
Princess Royal I. • BC, Canada 38 F6
Princeton • NJ, United States 118 H1
Príncipe • Sao Tomé e Príncipe 22 F4
Prínos **Beach** • Kavála, Greece 69 [194]
Prínos **Beach** • Crete, Greece 69 [213]
Prínos • Crete, Greece 93 E2
Prinzapolka • Nicaragua 43 A1
Pripyat • Belarus 17 D4
Priskaspiyskaya Nizmennost • Kazakhstan 17 I5
Pristina • F.R. of Yugoslavia 14 I7
Pritzwalk • Germany 8 H3
Privas • France 10 J9
Priverno • Italy 91 F4
Prizren • F.R. of Yugoslavia 14 H7
Probolinggo • Java, Indonesia 110 D8
Prócida, I. di • Italy 91 G3
Procópio • Brazil 44 F3
Pródhromos • Cyprus 93 J3
Profitis Ilías • Greece 15 D7
Profondeville • Belgium 80 A15
Progonati • Albania 15 A3
Progress [Base] • Antarctica 46 (1) N3
Prokop'yevsk • Russian Fed. 26 O7
Prokuplje • F.R. of Yugoslavia 14 I6
Prome • Myanmar 31 B3
Promthep, Laem • Phuket, Thailand 109 K2
Propriá • Brazil 45 (1) D4
Propriano • Corsica, France 85 L3
Proserpine • QL, Australia 111 F1
Prosna • Poland 13 G5
Prosperidad • Philippines 31 H5
Prostejov • Czech Rep. 13 G8
Provadiya • Bulgaria 97 D3
Provence • France 85 H1
Provence-Alpes-Côte d'Azur • France 84 A2
Providence • Seychelles 106 F3
Providence • RI, United States 118 H2
Providence, Bancs • Seychelles 106 F3
Providencia • Colombia 37 E5
Provideniya • Russian Fed. 46 GG3
Provins • France 85 E4
Provo • UT, United States 40 D3
Provost • AL, Canada 38 I6
Prozor • Bosnia-Herz. 12 L5
Prudnik • Poland 13 G7
Prüm • Germany 82 G1
Pruszcz Gdanski • Poland 13 H3
Pruszków • Poland 13 J5
Prut • Ukraine 14 L1
Pruzhany • Belarus 13 N5
Przasnysz • Poland 13 J4
Przemysl • Poland 13 L8
Psará • Greece 92 D5
Psérimos • Greece 92 D8
Psiloritis • Crete, Greece 93 E6
Psínthos • Rhodes, Greece 93 F2
Pskov • Russian Fed. 17 D3
Ptolemais • Libya 21 D1
Ptolemais • Israel 98 A1
Pu'er • China 29 C6
Pu'uhonua o Honaunau Nat. Hist. Park • HI, United States 119 L8
Pu'uhonua o Honaunau Nat. Hist. Park **Park** • HI, United States 120 [21]
Pucallpa • Peru 43 C5
Puck • Poland 13 H3
Pudasjärvi • Finland 16 N4
Pudent, Estany • Formentera, Spain 87 G4
Pudoz • Russian Fed. 17 F2
Pudukkottai • India 106 D11
Puebla **Heritage C** • Mexico 62 [23]
Puebla • Mexico 123 E4
Pueblo • CO, United States 40 F4
Pueblo de Taos **Heritage C** • NM, United States 62 [8]
Puelches • Argentina 45 C3
Puente Genil • Spain 11 G7
Puenteáreas • Spain 11 C2
Puerto Acosta • Bolivia 44 C2
Puerto Aisén • Chile 45 B5
Puerto Alegre • Bolivia 44 D1
Puerto Angel • Mexico 123 E4
Puerto Armuelles • Panama 37 E6
Puerto Asis • Colombia 43 B3
Puerto Ayacucho • Venezuela 43 D2
Puerto Ayora • Galapagos Is. 43 (1) A2
Puerto Banús • Spain 86 B6
Puerto Baquerizo Morena • Galapagos Is. 43 (1) B2
Puerto Barrios • Guatemala 37 D4
Puerto Berrio • Colombia 43 C2
Puerto Cabello • Venezuela 37 H5
Puerto Cabezas • Nicaragua 37 E5
Puerto Caldera • Costa Rica 58 B9
Puerto Carreño • Colombia 43 D2
Puerto Cumarebo • Venezuela 43 D1
Puerto de la Cruz **Beach** • Tenerife, Canary Is. 68 [109]
Puerto de la Cruz • Tenerife, Canary Is. 86 E1
Puerto de la Peña • Fuerteventura, Canary Is. 87 E2
Puerto de Lajas • Mexico 40 E6
Puerto de Mazarrón • Spain 87 C3
Puerto de Santiago • Tenerife, Canary Is. 86 E1
Puerto del Carmen • Lanzarote, Canary Is. 87 E3
Puerto del Rosario • Fuerteventura, Canary Is. 87 E2
Puerto del Santiago **Beach** • Tenerife, Canary Is. 68 [109]
Puerto Deseado • Argentina 45 C5
Puerto Escondido • Mexico 123 E4
Puerto Francisco de Orellana • Ecuador 43 B4
Puerto Heath • Bolivia 43 D6
Puerto Huasco • Chile 44 B4
Puerto Huitoto • Colombia 43 C3
Puerto Inca • Peru 127 B3
Puerto la Concordia • Colombia 43 C3
Puerto la Cruz • Venezuela 43 E1
Puerto Leguizamo • Colombia 43 C4
Puerto Limón • Costa Rica 37 E6
Puerto Limón • Colombia 43 B3
Puerto Lopez • Colombia 43 C3
Puerto Madryn • Argentina 58 A3
Puerto Maldonado • Peru 127 B2
Puerto Maunabo • Puerto Rico 125 E4
Puerto Montt • Chile 45 B4
Puerto Nariño • Venezuela 43 D3
Puerto Natales • Chile 45 B6
Puerto Ordaz • Venezuela 43 E2
Puerto Padre • Cuba 124 D8
Puerto Paez • Venezuela 43 D2
Puerto Plata • Dominican Rep. 37 G4
Puerto Portals • Majorca, Spain 87 H3
Puerto Prado • Peru 127 B1
Puerto Princesa • Philippines 31 F5
Puerto Providencia • Peru 127 B2
Puerto Real • Spain 11 E8
Puerto Rico • Colombia 43 B3
Puerto Rico • Bolivia 43 D6
Puerto Rico • Gran Canaria, Canary Is. 86 E4
Puerto Rico • West Indies 125 E
Puerto Rico Trench • West Indies 37 H4
Puerto San José • Guatemala 37 C5
Puerto Santa Cruz • Argentina 45 C6
Puerto Siles • Bolivia 44 C1
Puerto Suárez • Bolivia 44 E2
Puerto Vallarta • Mexico 123 E1
Puerto Varas • Chile 45 B4
Puertollano • Spain 11 G6
Puesti • Romania 14 O3
Puglia • Italy 12 K8
Puigcerdà • Spain 87 D1
Puigmal • France/Spain 11 N2
Puk'chong • D.P.R. of Korea 30 E4
Puka • Albania 15 A1
Pukapuka • French Polynesia 33 N7
Puksoozero • Russian Fed. 17 G2
Puksubaek • D.P.R. of Korea 30 D4
Pula • Croatia 12 H4
Pulaski, Fort, Nat. Mon. **Park** • GA, United States 121 [215]
Pulau Pinang [Adm] • Malaysia 31 C5
Pulau Tikus • Penang, Malaysia 108 C2
Pulawy • Poland 13 K6
Pulguksa Temple **Heritage C** • Rep. of Korea 63 [162]
Pulheim • Germany 81 E3
Pulicat Lake • India 106 D7
Pulkkila • Finland 16 M4
Pulkovo [Apt] • Russian Fed. 97 E1
Pullman • WA, United States 117 E2
Pulog, Mt • Philippines 31 G3
Pulpí **Beach** • Spain 68 [116]
Pultusk • Poland 13 K5
Puma Yumco • China 28 E3
Pump Bay • St Kitts & Nevis 125 G1
Puná • Ecuador 43 A4
Punchestown • Ireland 79 E3
Pune • India 28 B5
Punggol • Singapore 108 E2
Púngoe • Mozambique 24 E3
Punia • Dem. Rep. of Congo 23 D4
Punjab • India/Pakistan 28 B2
Punjab [Adm] • Pakistan 28 B2
Punjab [Adm] • India 28 C2
Puno • Peru 127 B4
Punta Almina • Spain 11 F9
Punta Alta • Argentina 45 D3
Punta Arenas • Chile 45 B6
Punta, Cerro de • Puerto Rico 125 E3
Punta del Este • Uruguay 127 D2
Punta Gorda • Belize 37 D4
Punta Prieta • Mexico 40 D6
Punta Prima • Minorca, Spain 87 F4
Punta Ráisi [Apt] • Sicily, Italy 90 D1
Punta Umbría **Beach** • Spain 68 [112]
Punta Umbría • Spain 86 B1
Puntarenas • Costa Rica 37 E6
Punto Fijo • Venezuela 43 C1
Puolanka • Finland 16 N4
Pupapuka • Cook Is. 33 K7
Puquio • Peru 127 B1
Pur • Russian Fed. 26 M4
Purace, Volcán • Colombia 43 B3
Purbeck, Isle of • United Kingdom 74 F6
Purbolinggo • Java, Indonesia 110 D6
Purcell Mtns • AL/BC, Canada 38 I7
Pureora Foreat Park • New Zealand 112 K2
Purgatory **Ski** • CO, United States 116 [102]
Purmerend • Netherlands 80 C2
Purnia • India 28 E3
Purulya • India 28 E4
Purus • Brazil 43 E5
Purwakarta • Java, Indonesia 110 D1
Purwodadi • Java, Indonesia 110 D3
Purwokerto • Java, Indonesia 110 D6
Pusan • Rep. of Korea 30 E7
Pushkar • India 105 C6
Pushkin • Russian Fed. 17 E3
Puspökladany • Hungary 13 K10
Pustería, Val • Italy 90 B2
Pustertal • Austria/Italy 90 B2
Pusula Dagi • Turkey 15 N6
Puszcza Notecka • Poland 13 F5
Putao • Myanmar 31 B1
Putaruru • New Zealand 112 K2
Puteran • Indonesia 110 D4
Putian • China 29 F5
Putila • Ukraine 14 M2
Putorana, Plato • Russian Fed. 26 P4
Putsborough Sands **Beach** • United Kingdom 75 [136]
Puttalam • Sri Lanka 106 D15
Puttaparthy • India 106 D6
Putten • Netherlands 80 C3
Puttgarden • Germany 8 G2
Putumayo • S. America 43 C4
Putuo Shan • China 107 J4
Putussibau • Indonesia 32 E2
Puukohola Heiau Nat. Hist. Site • HI, United States 119 L8
Puukohola Heiau Nat. Hist. Site **Park** • HI, United States 120 [19]
Puulavesi • Finland 16 N6
Puuwai • HI, United States 119 L2
Puy, le • France 10 I8
Puy-l'Evêque • France 85 G4
Puysegur Point • New Zealand 112 L3
Pweto • Dem. Rep. of Congo 23 D5
Pwllheli • United Kingdom 7 H9
Pwllheli **Beach** • United Kingdom 75 [193]
Pyalma • Russian Fed. 17 F2
Pyanskiy Zaliv • Russian Fed. 26 N3
Pyaozero • Russian Fed. 16 P3
Pyapon • Myanmar 28 G5
Pyasina • Russian Fed. 26 P3
Pyhä-Häkki Nat. Park **Park** • Finland 72 [35]
Pyhäjärvi • Finland 95 E3
Pyhäjoki • Finland 16 L4
Pyhätunturi • Finland 16 N3
Pyhätunturi Nat. Park **Park** • Finland 72 [31]
Pyhrnpaß • Austria 14 B2
Pyräjoki • Finland 16 M4
Pyramid Canyon • AZ/NV, United States 118 J1
Pyramid Lake • NV, United States 117 F1
Pyrénées Occidentales, Parc nat. des **Park** • France 72 [71]
Pyrénées-Occidentales • France 85 J
Pyrénées-Occidentales, Parc nat. des • France 85 J2
Pyrénées-Orientales • France 85 K
Pyrénées-Orientales [Adm] • France 85 K2
Pyrgos **Beach** • Cyprus 69 [218]
Pyrzice • Poland 13 D4
Pyu • Myanmar 31 B3

Q

Qaanaaq • Greenland 36 K2
Qadarif, Al • Sudan 21 G5
Qadimah, Al • Saudi Arabia 21 G3
Qadub • Yemen 18 F7
Qâhira, El • Egypt 101 F1
Qaidam Basin • China 107 G2
Qaidam He • China 28 G1
Qaidam Pendi • China 28 G1
Qairouan **Heritage C** • Tunisia 64 [231]
Qairouan • Tunisia 101 E4
Qal'at al Jundi • Egypt 101 F2
Qal'at Bishah • Saudi Arabia 18 D6
Qal'eh-ye Now • Afghanistan 18 H3
Qala • Malta 93 H1
Qalat • Afghanistan 18 I3
Qalibah, Al • Saudi Arabia 18 C4
Qamdo • China 29 B4
Qandahar • Afghanistan 18 I3
Qang Ngai • Vietnam 31 D3
Qang Tri • Vietnam 31 D3
Qaqortoq • Greenland 39 V4
Qar Wager • Somalia 23 H1
Qarabulli, Al • Libya 20 H2
Qarat as Sab'ah • Libya 21 C2
Qardo • Somalia 23 H2
Qarqan • China 28 E1
Qarqan He • China 26 O10
Qarshi • Uzbekistan 18 I2
Qasigianguit • Greenland 39 U3
Qasr Amra **Heritage C** • Jordan 64 [248]
Qasr, El • Egypt 101 F3
Qasr Farâfra • Egypt 21 E2
Qasr Haman • Saudi Arabia 18 E5
Qasr Ibrîm • Egypt 101 F5
Qasserine • Tunisia 101 E3
Qatar • Asia 18 F4
Qatif, Al • Saudi Arabia 18 E4
Qâttara • Egypt 21 E2
Qattâra Depression • Egypt 101 F1
Qattâra, Munkhaffad al • Egypt 21 E2
Qawra • Malta 93 H2
Qayihah, Al • Saudi Arabia 18 D5
Qazrin • Syria 98 A2
Qazvin • Iran 18 E2
Qena • Egypt 101 F4
Qeqertarssuaq • Greenland 39 U3
Qerqenah Is. • Tunisia 101 E4
Qeshm • Iran 18 G4
Qezel Owzan • Iran 18 E2
Qian Gorlos • China 29 G1
Qian Shan • China 29 G2
Qianshan • Zhuhai, China 107 H1
Qiao Dao • Zhuhai, China 107 H2
Qiaowan • China 29 B2
Qidong • China 107 J2
Qiemo • China 28 E1
Qikiqtaluk • NU, Canada 122 A3
Qilian Shan • China 29 B3
Qin Ling • China 29 D4
Qingdao • China 29 G3
Qinghai • China 107 G2
Qinghai Hu • China 29 C3
Qingpu • China 107 J2
Qingyang • China 29 D3
Qingyi Jiang • China 107 J3
Qingyuan • China 30 C3
Qinhuangdao • China 29 F2
Qinzhou • China 31 D2
Qionghai • China 31 E3
Qiqihar • China 29 G1
Qishn • Yemen 18 F6
Qitai • China 26 O9
Qitaihe • China 27 L7
Qixiashan • China 107 J1
Qogir Feng • China/Kashmir 28 C1
Qolleh-ye Damavand • Iran 18 F2
Qom • Iran 18 F3
Qomolangma Feng • China/Nepal 28 E3
Qomsheh • Iran 18 F3
Qonduz • Afghanistan 18 I2
Qu'Appelle • MN/SA, Canada 38 K6
Quadane • Mauritania 20 C4
Quakenbrück • Germany 8 C4
Quan Long • Vietnam 108 B3
Quanjiao • China 107 J1
Quantock Hills • United Kingdom 74 F2
Quanzhou • Guangxi, China 29 E5
Quanzhou • Fujian, China 29 F6
Quaqtaq • QU, Canada 39 R4
Quarry Bay • Hong Kong, China 107 H6
Quarteira • Portugal 88 E7
Quartu San'Elena **Beach** • Sardinia, Italy 68 [139]
Quartu Sant' Elena • Sardinia, Italy 12 D9
Quatre Bornes • Seychelles 106 F3
Quchan • Iran 18 G2
Queanbeyan • NS, Australia 111 G2
Québec **Heritage C** • QU, Canada 62 [3]
Québec • QU, Canada 122 B4
Québec [Adm] • Canada 39 P6
Qued el Kehir • Algeria 12 C12
Quedlinburg • Germany 8 G5
Quedlinburg **Heritage C** • Germany 64 [34]
Queen Alexandra Range • Antarctica 46 (1) U1
Queen, Cape • NU, Canada 39 P4
Queen Charlotte Is. • BC, Canada 38 E6
Queen Charlotte Sound • BC, Canada 38 E6
Queen Charlotte Strait • BC, Canada 38 F6
Queen Elizabeth Is. • NU, Canada 38 K2
Queen Elizabeth Nat. Park **Park** • Uganda 103 [70]
Queen Maud Gulf • NU, Canada 38 K3
Queen Maud Land • Antarctica 46 (1) G2
Queen Maud Mtns • Antarctica 46 (1) CC1
Queen of Spains Valley • Jamaica 124 C1
Queens • NY, United States 118 H2
Queensland • Australia 34 H4
Queensland wet tropics **Heritage N** • QL, Australia 61 [129]
Queenstown • South Africa 24 D6
Queenstown • TS, Australia 34 I8
Queenstown • New Zealand 112 L2
Queenstown New Town • Singapore 108 E2
Quela • Angola 22 H6
Quelimane • Mozambique 24 F3
Quelpart • Rep. of Korea 30 D7
Queluz • Portugal 88 D1
Quemoy • Taiwan 31 F2
Quenza • Corsica, France 85 L4
Quepem • Goa, India 105 B2
Quequén • Argentina 127 D3
Quercianella • Italy 91 E11
Querétaro **Heritage C** • Mexico 62 [16]
Querétaro • Mexico 123 E2
Querim Beach • Goa, India 105 B1
Queseda • Spain 11 H7
Quesnel • BC, Canada 122 C1
Quesnel Lake • BC, Canada 38 G6
Quetta • Pakistan 28 A2
Quevedo • Ecuador 43 B4
Queyras • France 85 F4
Quezaltenango • Guatemala 37 C5
Quezon • Palawan, Philippines 31 F5
Quezon City • Luzon, Philippines 31 G3
Qufu **Heritage C** • China 63 [152]
Qui Nhon • Vietnam 31 D4
Quibdó • Colombia 43 B2
Quiberon • France 84 C4
Quickborn • Germany 8 E3
Quilán, Cabo • Chile 45 B4
Quill Lakes • SA, Canada 38 K6
Quillabamba • Peru 127 B2
Quillacollo • Bolivia 44 C2
Quillan • France 85 K2
Quillota • Chile 44 B5
Quilmes • Argentina 44 E5
Quilon • India 106 D10
Quilpie • QL, Australia 34 H5
Quilpué • Chile 44 B5
Quimbele • Angola 23 B5
Quimili • Argentina 44 D4
Quimper • France 84 C3
Quimperlé • France 84 C3
Quincy • IL, United States 41 H4
Quincy • France 84 B1
Quincy • CA, United States 117 F1
Quinta do Palheiro Ferreiro • Madeira 88 C2
Quintana Roo • Mexico 37 D4
Quiriguá **Heritage C** • Guatemala 62 [29]
Quirihue • Chile 45 B3
Quirima • Angola 24 B2
Quiterajo • Mozambique 23 G6
Quito • Ecuador 43 B4
Quito **Heritage C** • Ecuador 62 [46]
Qumar He • China 28 F1
Qumran • Jordan 98 A8
Qunfudhah, Al • Saudi Arabia 18 D6
Quoin I. • QL, Australia 111 F4
Qurdud • Sudan 23 E1
Qurghoteppa • Tajikistan 18 I2
Quseir • Egypt 101 F4
Quthing • Lesotho 24 D6
Quxian • China 29 F5
Qüxü • China 28 F3

R

R'as al Khaymah • United Arab Emirates 18 G4
Ra's al Unif • Libya 21 C1
Ra's as Saffaniyah • Saudi Arabia 18 E4
Råå • Sweden 95 F11
Raab • Austria 13 F11
Raabs • Austria 96 C4
Raahe • Finland 16 M4
Raalte • Netherlands 5 J2
Raas • Indonesia 110 D4
Raasay • United Kingdom 75 A1
Raasay, Sound of • United Kingdom 6 F4
Rab • Croatia 14 B5
Rába • Hungary 13 G10
Raba • Indonesia 32 (1) A4
Rabat • Malta 93 H4
Rabat • Morocco 101 D1
Rabaul • Papua New Guinea 35 (1) E1
Rabbah • Jordan 98 A6
Rabí • Czech Rep. 96 C3
Rabi, Ash Shallal ar • Sudan 21 F4
Rabigh • Saudi Arabia 18 C5
Rabka • Poland 13 I8
Race, Cape • NF, Canada 123 D4
Rach Gia • Vietnam 108 B3
Racibórz • Poland 13 H7
Racine • WI, United States 41 I3
Rad, Ko • Thailand 109 K1
Radan • F.R. of Yugoslavia 14 I7
Radbuza • Czech Rep. 96 C3
Råde • Norway 94 B4
Radeberg • Germany 13 C6
Radebeul • Germany 9 I5
Radevormwald • Germany 81 E4
Radium Hot Springs • BC, Canada 122 C4
Radnor Forest • United Kingdom 74 D1
Radnorshire • United Kingdom 75 A5
Radolfzell • Germany 9 E9
Radolfzell **Spa** • Germany 83 [211]
Radom • Poland 13 K6
Radomir • Bulgaria 15 D1
Radomsko • Poland 13 I6
Radovis • F.Y.R. of Macedonia 15 D2
Radøy • Norway 94 C3
Radstadt **Ski** • Austria 70 [176]
Radviliskis • Lithuania 13 M2
Radzyn Podlaski • Poland 13 L6
Rae • NT, Canada 38 H4
Raetea • New Zealand 35 D2
Raetihi • New Zealand 112 K3
Raevavae • French Polynesia 33 M8
Raf-Raf • Tunisia 101 E2
Rafaela • Argentina 44 D5
Rafaï • Central African Rep. 23 C2
Raffles Lighthouse • Singapore 108 E3
Rafha • Saudi Arabia 18 D4
Rafína • Greece 92 D4
Rafsanjan • Iran 18 G3
Ragged I. • Bahamas 124 B4
Ragged I. Range • Bahamas 124 B3
Ragged, Mt • WA, Australia 34 D6
Ragged Point • Barbados 125 H4
Raging Waters **Park** • CA, United States 120 [F]
Raglan • New Zealand 112 K1
Raglan Castle • United Kingdom 74 D3
Raglan Harbour • New Zealand 112 K1
Ragley Hall • United Kingdom 74 D2
Ragusa • Croatia 71 A14
Ragusa • Sicily, Italy 90 D4
Raha • Indonesia 32 (1) B3
Rahad, Ar • Sudan 21 F5
Ráhes **Beach** • Greece 69 [187]
Rahimyar Khan • Pakistan 28 B3
Rahole Game Reserve • Kenya 101 G2
Raichur • India 106 D2
Raigarh • India 28 D4
Rainbow Bridge Nat. Mon. • UT, United States 118 J1
Rainbow Bridge Nat. Mon. **Park** • UT, United States 120 [84]
Rainbow Springs • New Zealand 112 K2
Rainier, Mt • WA, United States 117 E1
Rainy Lake • Canada/United States 38 M7
Raippaluoto • Finland 16 K5
Raipur • India 28 D4
Raisio • Finland 95 E3
Raja • Indonesia 110 D8
Raja Noi, Ko • Thailand 109 K2
Raja Yai, Ko • Thailand 109 K2
Rajahmundry • India 106 D4
Rajang • Malaysia 32 E2
Rajapalaiyam • India 106 D10
Rajasthan • India 105 C2
Rajasthan Canal • India 105 C1
Rajbag Beach • Goa, India 105 B2
Rajkot • India 28 B4
Rajshahi • Bangladesh 28 E4
Raka Zangbo • China 28 E3
Rakhine • Myanmar 31 A2
Rakhiv • Ukraine 14 L1
Rakhmanovskiye Klyuchi • Russian Fed. 26 O8
Rakit • Indonesia 110 D2
Rakitovo • Bulgaria 14 L8
Rakkestad • Norway 94 B4
Rakoniewice • Poland 13 F5
Rakops • Botswana 24 C4
Rakovnik • Czech Rep. 9 I6
Råkvåg • Norway 16 F5
Rakvere • Estonia 16 N7
Raleigh • NC, United States 41 K4
Raleigh, Fort, Nat. Hist. Site • NC, United States 118 H5
Raleigh, Fort, Nat. Hist. Site **Park** • NC, United States 121 [250]
Ralik Chain • Marshall Is. 33 H5
Rama • Nicaragua 43 A1
Ramadi, Ar • Iraq 18 D3
Ramatuelle • France 85 H4
Rambervillers • France 9 B8
Rambouillet • France 85 E3
Rambouillet, Forêt de • France 85 E3
Rambut Siwi Temple • Bali, Indonesia 110 C1
Rameswaram • India 106 D11
Ramgarh • India 105 C1
Ramiers Hist. Park **Heritage C** • Haiti 62 [37]
Ramisi • Kenya 101 G5
Ramla • Israel 98 A5
Ramla Bay • Malta 93 H1
Ramlat Dahm • Saudi Arabia 21 I4
Ramlu • Ethiopia 18 D7
Ramnagar • India 105 C8
Ramnäs • Sweden 95 D1
Rampur • India 105 C3
Ramree • Myanmar 31 A3
Ramsau • Germany 82 J8
Ramsau **Spa** • Germany 83 [262]
Ramsau am Dachstein **Ski** • Austria 70 [183]
Ramsele • Sweden 16 I5
Ramsgate • United Kingdom 74 E2
Ramsjö • Sweden 16 H5
Ran • Laos 31 C2
Rana • Norway 16 H3
Ranai • Indonesia 32 D2
Ranakpur • India 105 C5
Rånåsfoss • Norway 94 B2
Ranau • Malaysia 32 F1
Rancagua • Chile 45 B2
Rance • France 84 C2
Ranchi • India 28 D4
Rancho Luna, Playa • Cuba 124 D2
Randaberg • Norway 94 C5
Randers • Denmark 95 F10
Random I. • NF, Canada 123 D4
Randringhausen **Spa** • Germany 83 [85]
Ranfurly • New Zealand 35 C7
Rangiora • New Zealand 35 D6
Rangitaiki • New Zealand 112 K2
Rangitikei • New Zealand 112 K4
Rangkasbitung • Java, Indonesia 110 D1
Rangoon • Myanmar 31 B3
Rangpur • Bangladesh 28 E3
Rangsdorf • Germany 81 F4
Rangsdorfer See • Germany 81 F4
Ranikhet • India 105 C3
Rannalhi • Maldives 106 E4
Rannoch, Loch • United Kingdom 74 B1
Ranomafana, Parc nat. de **Park** • Madagascar 103 [138]
Ranong • Thailand 31 B5
Ransdfjorden • Norway 94 B2
Ransiki • Indonesia 32 (1) D3
Rantaupanjang • Indonesia 32 E3
Rantauprapat • Indonesia 110 B4
Ranthambor Nat. Park • India 105 C6
Rantum **Spa** • Germany 83 [2]
Ranua • Finland 16 N4
Ranyah, Wadi • Saudi Arabia 21 H3
Raoul • New Zealand 33 J8
Rapa • French Polynesia 33 M8
Rapa Nui • Pacific Ocean 33 Q8
Rapa Nui, Parque Nac. **Heritage C** • Pacific Ocean 62 [66]
Rapallo • Italy 91 E6
Raper, Cape • NU, Canada 39 R3
Rapid City • SD, United States 40 F3
Rapla • Estonia 16 N7
Raposeira • Portugal 88 E5
Rapperswil • Switzerland 89 G3
Rápulo • Bolivia 44 C1
Raroia • French Polynesia 33 M7
Rarotonga • Cook Is. 33 L8
Ras Beddouza • Morocco 20 D2
Râs el Bar • Egypt 101 F2
Râs el Mâ • Mali 20 E5
Râs el Ma Niafounke • Mali 22 D1
Râs Ghârib • Egypt 101 F4
Râs Jumbo • Somalia 23 G4
Râs Sidi Ali el Mekki • Tunisia 12 E11
Rasa, Punta • Argentina 45 D4
Rasa, Punta • Argentina 127 D4
Rascani • Moldova 14 O2
Rasdhu Atoll • Maldives 106 E1
Raseiniai • Lithuania 13 M2
Rashîd • Egypt 101 F1
Rasht • Iran 18 E2
Raso, Cabo • Portugal 88 D1
Rason Lake • WA, Australia 34 D5
Rastatt • Germany 82 G6
Rastede • Germany 8 D3
Rat I. • St Lucia 125 J1
Rat Is. • AK, United States 36 (1) B2
Ratak Chain • Marshall Is. 33 I5
Ratangarh • India 18 J4
Ratchaburi • Thailand 109 H1
Ráth Luirc • Ireland 79 F6
Rathangan • Ireland 79 E3
Rathcoole • Ireland 79 E2
Rathdrum • Ireland 79 E4
Rathenow • Germany 8 H4
Rathkeale • Ireland 79 F6
Rathlin I. • United Kingdom 7 F6

Rathvilly • Ireland **79** E3
Ratiborice • Czech Rep. **96** C2
Ratingen • Germany **81** E3
Ratlam • India **28** C4
Ratnagiri • India **106** D1
Ratno • Ukraine **13** N6
Raton • NM, United States **40** F4
Ratta • Russian Fed. **26** N5
Rattenberg • Austria **89** H3
Rattlesnake Nat. Recreation Area • MT, United States **117** E2
Ratz, Mt • BC, Canada **38** E5
Ratzeburg • Germany **8** F3
Raub • Malaysia **108** D2
Rauch • Argentina **127** D3
Rauland • Norway **94** C6
Rauma **Heritage C** • Finland **63** [73]
Rauma • Norway **94** C2
Rauma • Finland **95** E1
Raung, Gunung • Java, Indonesia **110** D8
Raurkela • India **28** D4
Ravascletto • Italy **91** E4
Ravello • Italy **91** G4
Ravenglass • United Kingdom **74** C3
Ravenglass & Eskdale Railway • United Kingdom **74** C3
Ravenglass Estuary • United Kingdom **74** C3
Ravenna **Heritage C** • Italy **64** [116]
Ravenna • Italy **91** E8
Ravensburg • Germany **82** J5
Ravenshoe • QL, Australia **111** F1
Ravensthorpe • WA, Australia **34** D6
Ravi • Pakistan **28** B2
Ravnina • Turkmenistan **18** H2
Rawa Mazowiecka • Poland **13** J6
Rawai • Phuket, Thailand **109** K2
Rawai Beach • Phuket, Thailand **109** K2
Rawaki • Kiribati **33** J6
Rawalpindi • Pakistan **28** B2
Rawicz • Poland **13** F6
Rawlinna • WA, Australia **34** E6
Rawlins • WY, United States **40** E3
Rawlinson Ranges • NT/WA, Australia **34** E5
Rawson • Argentina **45** C4
Raxaul • India **105** C4
Raya, Bukit • Indonesia **32** E3
Rayburn, Sam, Reservoir • TX, United States **119** N4
Raychikhinsk • Russian Fed. **27** K7
Rayong • Thailand **109** H4
Rayy • Iran **98** B4
Raz, Pointe de • France **84** C3
Razelm, Lacul • Romania **97** D2
Razgrad • Bulgaria **97** D3
Razlog • Bulgaria **14** K8
Ré, I. de • France **84** D3
Reach Falls • Jamaica **124** C4
Reading • PA, United States **118** H1
Realico • Argentina **44** D5
Reboly • Russian Fed. **16** P5
Rebord Manambien • Madagascar **24** H4
Rebun • Japan **30** K2
Recherche, Archipelago of the • WA, Australia **34** D6
Recife • Brazil **45** (1) E3
Recife, Cape • South Africa **100** C8
Recklinghausen • Germany **81** E2
Recknitz • Germany **8** H2
Reconquista • Argentina **44** E4
Recreo • Argentina **44** C4
Red • China/Vietnam **29** C6
Red Basin • China **107** G7
Red Bluff • CA, United States **117** F1
Red Centre, The • NT, Australia **112** H
Red Cliff • St Kitts & Nevis **125** G4
Red Deer • AL, Canada **122** C4
Red Deer [Riv] • AL, Canada **38** I6
Red Hill Patrick Henry Nat. Mem. **Park** • VA, United States **121** [253]
Red Lodge Mtn **Ski** • MT, United States **116** [75]
Red Mtn **Ski** • BC, Canada **116** [7]
Red River • United States **40** G5
Red River **Ski** • NM, United States **116** [104]
Red River of the North • United States **41** G2
Red Sea • Africa/Asia **21** G3
Red Sea cruise area • Africa/Asia **59** A5/7
Redcar • United Kingdom **7** K7
Redding • CA, United States **117** F1
Redditch • United Kingdom **7** J9
Redeyef • Tunisia **101** E3
Redon • France **84** C4
Redondo • Portugal **11** D6
Redondo, Monte • Corsica, France **85** L2
Redruth • United Kingdom **74** F4
Réduit Beach • St Lucia **125** J2
Redwood Nat. Park **Heritage N** • CA, United States **60** [10]
Redwood Nat. Park • CA, United States **117** F1
Redwood Nat. Park **Park** • CA, United States **120** [38]
Ree, Lough • Ireland **7** D8
Reethi Rah • Maldives **106** E2
Refugio • TX, United States **119** N5
Regen • Germany **9** I8
Regen [Riv] • Germany **9** H7
Regensburg • Germany **9** H7
Regenstauf • Germany **9** H7
Reggane • Algeria **20** F3
Regge • Netherlands **5** J2
Réggio di Calabria • Italy **90** D2
Réggio nell' Emília • Italy **91** E7
Reghin • Romania **14** L3
Regina • SA, Canada **38** K6
Regina • French Guiana **43** G3
Regnitz • Germany **9** G7
Reguengos de Monsaraz • Portugal **11** D6
Rehoboth • Namibia **24** B4
Rehoboth Beach • DE, United States **118** H3
Rei, Costa • Sardinia, Italy **90** C4
Reichenbach • Germany **9** H6
Reichenstein, Burg • Germany **82** H4
Reichstag • Germany **81** F2
Reigate • United Kingdom **74** E3
Reims • France **10** J4
Reims **Heritage C** • France **64** [50]
Reina Adelaida, Archipiélago • Chile **45** A6
Reina Sofia [Apt] • Tenerife, Canary Is. **86** E1
Reindeer • SA, Canada **38** K5
Reindeer Lake • MN/SA, Canada **38** K5
Reiner's Beach • Goa, India **105** B2
Reinga, Cape • New Zealand **35** D2
Reinhardstein, Château de • Belgium **80** A16
Reis Magos Fort • Goa, India **105** B1
Reisa Nat. Park **Park** • Norway **72** [6]
Reisaelva • Norway **16** K2
Reischach **Ski** • Italy **70** [235]
Reischach • Italy **90** B2
Reit im Winkl **Ski** • Germany **70** [5]
Reit im Winkl • Germany **82** J8
Rejmyre • Sweden **95** D3
Rekarne • Sweden **95** D3
Reliance • NT, Canada **38** J4
Relizane • Algeria **20** F1
Remada • Tunisia **101** E6
Remagen • Germany **82** H1
Remarkables, The • New Zealand **112** L2
Rembang • Java, Indonesia **110** D3
Rembau • Malaysia **108** D4
Remich • Luxembourg **80** A20
Rémire • Seychelles **106** F2
Remiremont • France **10** L5
Remoulins **Heritage C** • France **64** [65]
Remscheid • Germany **81** E4
Rémuzat • France **10** K9
Rendsburg • Germany **8** E2
Renfrew • OT, Canada **39** P7
Renfrewshire • United Kingdom **74** B3
Rengat • Indonesia **32** C3
Rengo • Chile **44** B5
Rengsdorf **Spa** • Germany **83** [152]
Reni • Ukraine **14** P4
Renmark • SA, Australia **34** H6
Rennell • Solomon Is. **33** H7
Rennes • France **84** C4
Rennesøy • Norway **94** C5
Reno • Italy **12** F4
Reno • NV, United States **117** F1
Renon • Italy **90** B1
Renqiu • China **29** F3
Reo • Indonesia **32** (1) B4
Réole, la • France **85** G3
Reposaari • Finland **95** E1
Repulse Bay • NU, Canada **46** X3
Repulse Bay • Hong Kong, China **107** H6
Repulse Bay • QL, Australia **111** F3
Repvåg • Norway **16** M1
Requena • Spain **11** J5
Requena • Peru **43** C5
Réquista • France **10** H9
Rerik **Spa** • Germany **83** [267]
Rësheni • Albania **14** G8
Resistencia • Argentina **44** E4
Resita • Romania **14** I4
Resolute • NU, Canada **38** M2
Resolution I. • NU, Canada **39** S4
Resolution I. • New Zealand **112** L3
Restonica, Gorges de la • Corsica, France **85** L2
Retezat Nat. Park **Park** • Romania **72** [129]
Rethel • France **10** J4
Réthimno **Beach** • Crete, Greece **69** [213]
Réthimno • Crete, Greece **93** E2
Réthimno [Adm] • Crete, Greece **93** E6
Rettenberg • Germany **82** J6
Retz • Austria **96** C4
Reuben • Jordan **98** A8
Reuilly • France **84** B1
Réunion, la • Seychelles **106** F4
Reus • Spain **87** D3
Reuss • Switzerland **89** G3
Reutlingen • Germany **82** G6
Reval • Estonia **71** A4
Revelstoke • BC, Canada **122** C4
Revillagigedo, Is. • Mexico **36** F8
Revin • France **10** J4
Rewa • India **105** C7
Rewari • India **105** C2
Rex, Mt • Antarctica **46** (1) HH2
Rexburg • ID, United States **40** D3
Rey • Iran **18** F2
Rey • Panama **43** B2
Reyes, Point • CA, United States **117** F3
Reykjahlid • Iceland **16** (1) E2
Reykjanes • Iceland **16** (1) B3
Reykjavik • Iceland **16** (1) B2
Reynolds Range • NT, Australia **112** H2
Reynosa • Mexico **37** B2
Rezé • France **10** D6
Rezekne • Latvia **16** N8
Rezovo • Bulgaria **97** D4
Rezveya • Bulgaria/Turkey **15** I2
Rheda-Wiedenbrück • Germany **8** D5
Rhein • Germany/Switzerland **9** C6
Rhein-Main [Apt] • Germany **82** H4
Rheinbach • Germany **82** H1
Rheinberg • Germany **81** E1
Rheine • Germany **8** C4
Rheineck, Burg • Germany **82** H1
Rheinfelden • Germany **82** G8
Rheinfels, Burg • Germany **82** H2
Rheingau • Germany **82** H4
Rheinhessen • Germany **82** H4
Rheinisches Schiefergebirge • Germany **5** K4
Rheinland-Pfalz • Germany **9** C6
Rheinsberg • Germany **8** H3
Rheinturm • Germany **81** E3
Rhenen • Netherlands **80** A11
Rhens • Germany **82** H2
Rheris • Morocco **20** E2
Rheurdt • Germany **81** E1
Rheydt, Schloß • Germany **81** E3
Rhin • France **10** M5
Rhine • Europe **82** G6
Rhine Gorge • Germany **82** H2
Rhineland-Palatinate • Germany **81** D3
Rhir, Cap • Morocco **101** D5
Rhode I. • United States **118** H2
Rhodes **Beach** • Rhodes, Greece **69** [211]
Rhodes **Heritage C** • Greece **64** [187]
Rhodes • Rhodes, Greece **93** F2
Rhodes' Grave • Zimbabwe **102** J3
Rhodes [I.] • Greece **93** F
Rhodopi • Bulgaria/Greece **14** L8
Rhön • Germany **81** D3
Rhön, Hohe • Germany **9** F6
Rhondda • United Kingdom **7** I10
Rhône • France/Switzerland **10** J9
Rhône au Rhin, Canal du • France **9** C8
Rhône-Alpes • France **84** A2
Rhos-on-Sea **Beach** • United Kingdom **75** [200]
Rhosneigr **Beach** • United Kingdom **75** [210-211]
Rhossili **Beach** • United Kingdom **75** [145]
Rhubodach • United Kingdom **78** A2
Rhyl • United Kingdom **7** I8
Rhyl **Beach** • United Kingdom **75** [202]
Riaño • Spain **11** F2
Riau • Indonesia **110** B4
Riau, Kepulauan • Indonesia **32** C2
Riaza • Spain **10** B12
Rib Mtn **Ski** • WI, United States **116** [120]
Ribadeo • Spain **11** D1
Ribadeo **Beach** • Spain **68** [91]
Ribatejo • Portugal **11** C5
Ribble • United Kingdom **7** J8
Ribe • Denmark **95** F13
Ribe [Adm] • Denmark **95** F9
Ribeira • Spain **11** C2
Ribeira Grande • Azores **88** B1
Ribeirão Prêto • Brazil **44** G3
Ribnica • Slovenia **14** B4
Ribnitz-Damgarten • Germany **8** H2
Ricabayo, Embalse de • Spain **11** F3
Ricard, Circuit Paul • France **85** H3
Riccione • Italy **91** E12
Rich • Morocco **20** E2
Richard Collinson Inlet • NT, Canada **38** I2
Richard Toll • Senegal **20** B5
Richard's Bay • South Africa **24** E5
Richardson Mtns • NT/YT, Canada **38** D3
Richardson Mtns • New Zealand **112** L2
Richat, Guelb er • Mauritania **20** C4
Richborough Castle • United Kingdom **74** E2
Richelieu • France **10** F7
Richelieu • QU, Canada **122** B8
Richfield • UT, United States **40** D4
Richland • WA, United States **117** E2
Richmond • New Zealand **35** D5
Richmond • KY, United States **41** J4
Richmond • South Africa **100** C3
Richmond • VA, United States **118** H3
Richmond, Mt • New Zealand **35** D5
Richmond Nat. Battlefield Park **Park** • VA, United States **121** [259]
Ridderkerk • Netherlands **80** C3
Ried • Austria **13** C9
Riederalp **Ski** • Switzerland **70** [98]
Riederalp • Switzerland **89** G6
Riedlingen • Germany **82** J1
Rienz • Italy **90** B1
Riesa • Germany **9** I5
Riesco, I. • Chile **45** B6
Rieti • Italy **91** F2
Rietini, Monti • Italy **91** F2
Riezlern **Ski** • Austria **70** [128]
Riezlern • Austria **89** H1
Rif • Morocco **101** D2
Rifstangi • Iceland **16** (1) E1
Rift Valley • Africa **100** A3
Riga • Latvia **16** M8
Riga **Heritage C** • Latvia **64** [202]
Riga, Gulf of • Estonia/Latvia **16** M8
Rigestan • Afghanistan **18** I3
Rihiveli Beach • Maldives **106** E4
Riihimäki • Finland **95** E4
Rijeka • Croatia **14** B4
Rijnsburg • Netherlands **80** C1
Rijswijk • Netherlands **80** C3
Rika • Ukraine **14** K1
Rila • Bulgaria **14** K7
Rila **Heritage C** • Bulgaria **64** [173]
Rima • Nigeria **20** G6
Rimau • Malaysia **108** C3
Rimavská Sobota • Slovak Rep. **13** J9
Rimbo • Sweden **95** D2
Rimbo Panti Reserve • Indonesia **110** B4
Rimforsa • Sweden **95** F4
Rímini • Italy **91** E12
Rîmnicu Sarat • Romania **14** O4
Rîmnicu Vîlcea • Romania **14** L4
Rimouski • QU, Canada **123** D1
Rimouski Prov. Reserve • QU, Canada **123** D1
Rincón, Bahía de • Puerto Rico **125** E4
Rincon del Bonete, Lago Artificial de • Uruguay **127** D2
Ringe • Denmark **95** F14
Ringerike • Norway **94** B1
Ringkøbing **Beach** • Denmark **68** [50]
Ringkøbing • Denmark **95** F9
Ringkøbing [Adm] • Denmark **95** F9
Ringkøbing Fjord • Denmark **95** F9
Ringlades • Corfu, Greece **15** A4
Ringsjön • Sweden **95** F11
Ringsted **Beach** • Denmark **68** [43]
Ringsted • Denmark **95** F14
Ringvassøy • Norway **16** J1
Rínia • Greece **92** D8
Rinjani, Gunung • Indonesia **32** F4
Rinteln • Germany **8** E4
Rio Abiseo, Parque Nac. **Heritage N** • Peru **60** [31]
Rio Branco • Brazil **43** D6
Rio Bueno • Jamaica **124** C1
Rio Caribe • Venezuela **43** E1
Rio Claro • Trinidad & Tobago **125** K4
Rio Colorado • Argentina **45** D3
Rio Cuarto • Argentina **44** D5
Rio das Ostras • Brazil **127** C4
Rio de Janeiro • Brazil **127** C4
Rio de Janeiro [Adm] • Brazil **127** C4
Río de la Plata • Puerto Rico **125** E2
Rio de Oro, Bahía de • Western Sahara **20** B4
Rio do Sul • Brazil **44** G4
Rio Formosa • Portugal **88** E7
Rio Gallegos • Argentina **45** C6
Rio Grande • Brazil **44** F5
Rio Grande • Argentina **45** C6
Rio Grande do Norte • Brazil **45** (1) D3
Rio Grande do Sul • Brazil **44** F4
Rio Marina • Italy **91** E11
Rio Mayo • Argentina **45** B5
Rio Negro • Brazil **44** G4
Rio Pardo • Brazil **44** F4
Rio Platano, Reserva de la Biósfera **Heritage N** • Honduras **60** [22]
Rio Rancho • NM, United States **118** J2
Rio Tercero • Argentina **44** D5
Rio Verde • Brazil **44** F2
Rio Verde • Mexico **123** E2
Riobamba • Ecuador **43** B4
Riohacha • Colombia **43** C1
Riom • France **10** I8
Rionere in Vulture • Italy **12** J8
Ripoll • Spain **11** N2
Ripon • United Kingdom **7** K7
Riposto • Sicily, Italy **12** J11
Riscone **Ski** • Italy **70** [235]
Riscone • Italy **90** B2
Rishiri • Japan **30** K2
Risle • France **5** D6
Risnjak • Croatia **14** B4
Risnjak Nat. Park **Park** • Croatia **72** [108]
Risør • Norway **95** F1
Risoul **Ski** • France **70** [66]
Risoul • France **85** F4
Ritchie's Archipelago • India **28** F6
Riva del Garda • Italy **91** E3
Rivadavia • Argentina **44** C5
River Cess • Liberia **22** C3
River Kwai Bridge • Thailand **109** H1
Rivera • Argentina **44** D6
Rivera • Uruguay **44** E5
Riverina • NS, Australia **111** G1
Rivers • Nigeria **22** F3
Riversdale • South Africa **100** C6
Riverside • CA, United States **117** F6
Riverside [Apt] • United Kingdom **74** B2
Riversleigh **Heritage N** • QL, Australia **61** [133]
Riverton • WY, United States **40** E3
Riverton • New Zealand **112** L4
Rivesultes [Apt] • France **85** K2
Riviera • France/Italy **91** E10
Riviera di Levante • Italy **91** E10
Riviera di Ponente • Italy **91** E9
Rivière du Loup • QU, Canada **123** D1
Rivoli • Italy **12** B3
Rixensart • Belgium **80** A14
Riyadh • Saudi Arabia **18** E5
Rizhao • China **29** F3
Rizokarpásso • Cyprus **93** J2
Rjukan • Norway **94** B1
Roa • Spain **11** H3
Roa • Norway **94** B2
Road Bay • Anguilla **58** B7
Roanne • France **10** J7
Roanoke • VA, United States **41** K4
Roanoke • NC, United States **118** H5
Roatán • Honduras **37** D4
Rob Roy's Grave • United Kingdom **74** B1
Robben I. • South Africa **100** C5
Robe • Ireland **79** F4
Robe, Mt • NS, Australia **34** H6
Röbel • Germany **8** H3
Roberts, Mt • QL, Australia **111** F6
Robertsfors • Sweden **16** K4
Robertsganj • India **105** C8
Robertson • South Africa **100** C6
Robertstown • Ireland **79** E3
Roberval • QU, Canada **123** D1
Robin Hood's Bay **Beach** • United Kingdom **75** [22]
Robinson Range • WA, Australia **34** C5
Robson, Mt • AL, Canada **122** C2
Roca, Cabo da • Portugal **88** D1
Rocamadour, Château de • France **85** G4
Rocas, Atol das • Brazil **127** A1
Rocca di Papa • Italy **91** F3
Rocha • Uruguay **44** F5
Rochdale • United Kingdom **7** J8
Roche-Guyon, la • France **85** E1
Roche-Racan [Château] • France **84** D2
Roche-sur-Yon, la • France **84** D3
Rochefort • Belgium **80** A19
Rochefort • France **85** G1
Rochefoucauld, la • France **85** G2
Rochegda • Russian Fed. **17** G2
Rochehaut • Belgium **80** A19
Rochelle, la **Beach** • France **68** [84]
Rochelle, la • France **84** D3
Rocher River • NT, Canada **38** I4
Rochester • MN, United States **41** H3
Rochester • NY, United States **41** K3
Rochester • United Kingdom **74** E2
Rochester • NH, United States **118** G3
Rochford [Apt] • United Kingdom **74** E2
Rock Creek Park **Park** • DC, United States **121** [293]
Rock Hill • SC, United States **41** J5
Rock Sound • Bahamas **124** B1
Rock Springs • WY, United States **40** E3
Rockall • Atlantic Ocean **4** H5
Rockefeller Jr., John D., Mem. Parkway **Park** • WY, United States **120** [75]
Rockefeller Plateau • Antarctica **46** (1) BB1
Rockford • IL, United States **41** I3
Rockhampton • QL, Australia **111** F4
Rockingham • WA, Australia **34** C6
Rockland • ME, United States **118** G4
Rockley Beach • Barbados **125** H3
Rockport • TX, United States **119** N5
Rocky Mtn Nat. Park **Park** • CO, United States **120** [89]
Rocky Mtns • Canada/United States **36** F5
Rocky Point • Jamaica **124** C4
Rocque-Gageac, la • France **85** G4
Rocquefort • France **85** G3
Rocroi • France **5** H5
Rod Hill, Fort • BC, Canada **122** C3
Róda • Corfu, Greece **92** B1
Rodach **Spa** • Germany **83** [223]
Rødby • Denmark **16** F9
Rødby **Beach** • Denmark **68** [37]
Rødbyhavn • Denmark **95** F14
Rødeberg • Norway **94** B1
Rødenes • Norway **94** B2
Rødenessjøen • Norway **94** B4
Rödental • Germany **9** G6
Rodez • France **10** H9
Rodgau • Germany **5** L5
Rodi Gargánico • Italy **12** J7
Rodi Gargánico **Beach** • Italy **69** [158]
Rodiá **Beach** • Crete, Greece **69** [214]
Rodiá • Crete, Greece **93** E3
Roding • United Kingdom **5** D3
Roding • Germany **9** H7
Rodnei, Muntii • Romania **14** L2
Rodney Bay • St Lucia **125** J2
Rodolívos • Greece **15** E3
Rodonit, Kep i • Albania **14** G8
Rodopi • Greece **14** L8
Rodopi Planina • Bulgaria/Greece **14** L8
Rodópoi, Hersónisos • Crete, Greece **93** E1
Ródos **Beach** • Rhodes, Greece **69** [211]
Ródos **Heritage C** • Greece **64** [187]
Ródos • Rhodes, Greece **93** F2
Ródos [I.] • Greece **93** F
Rodrigues • Indian Ocean **19** K8
Roebourne • WA, Australia **34** C4
Roermond • Netherlands **80** A12
Roes Welcome Sound • NU, Canada **39** N4
Roeselare • Belgium **5** G4
Rogaguado, Laguna • Bolivia **44** C1
Rogaland • Norway **16** D7
Rogliano • Corsica, France **85** L2
Rohtak • India **105** C2
Rohtas **Heritage C** • Pakistan **63** [114]
Rohtas • India **105** C8
Rojo, Cabo • Puerto Rico **125** E3
Rokan • Indonesia **110** B4
Rokitnokärren • Belarus **13** N5
Rokycany • Czech Rep. **96** C1
Rola Co • China **28** E1
Rolandsbogen • Germany **82** H1
Røldal • Norway **94** C6
Rolla • MO, United States **41** H4
Rollag • Norway **94** B1
Rolle, Passo di • Italy **90** B3
Rolvsøya • Norway **94** A3
Roma **Heritage C** • Italy **64** [125]
Roma • Italy **91** F3
Roma • QL, Australia **111** F5
Romainmôtier • Switzerland **89** G1
Roman • Romania **14** N3
Romang • Indonesia **32** (1) C4
Romania • Europe **14** M4
Romans-sur-Isère • France **10** J8
Romanshorn • Switzerland **89** H1
Romantische Straße • Germany **82** J2
Rombo Pass • Austria/Italy **90** B1
Rome • GA, United States **41** J5
Rome **Heritage C** • Italy **64** [125]
Rome • Italy **91** F3
Rome • NY, United States **122** B10
Romeleåsen • Sweden **95** F11
Romerike • Norway **94** B2
Romilly-sur-Seine • France **10** I5
Romkamhaeng Nat. Park • Thailand **109** G4
Romney • United Kingdom **71** A7
Romney, Hythe & Dymchurch Light Railway • United Kingdom **74** E3
Romney Manor • St Kitts & Nevis **125** G1
Romny • Ukraine **17** E4
Rømø • Denmark **95** F13
Romoranthin-Lanthenay • France **84** D2
Romsdalfjorden • Norway **94** C2
Roncador, Serra do • Brazil **44** F1
Roncesvalles • Spain **11** J1
Ronda • Spain **86** B6
Ronda, Serranía de • Spain **86** B6
Rondane • Norway **16** E6
Rondane Nat. Park **Park** • Norway **72** [13]
Rønde • Denmark **95** F10
Ronde, I. • Seychelles **106** F4
Rondón • Brazil **43** E3
Rondônia • Brazil **43** E6
Rondonópolis • Brazil **44** F2
Ronge, Lac la • SA, Canada **38** K5
Rønne • Denmark **95** F16
Ronne Bay • Antarctica **46** (1) HH2
Ronne Ice Shelf • Antarctica **46** (1) JJ2
Ronneby • Sweden **95** F12
Ronse • Belgium **5** G4
Roosendaal • Netherlands **80** A10
Roosevelt • Brazil **43** E6
Roosevelt Campobello Int. Park **Park** • NB, Canada **121** [356]
Roosevelt Campobello Int. Park • NB, Canada **123** D6
Roosevelt, Eleanor, Nat. Hist. Site **Park** • NY, United States **121** [321]
Roosevelt, Franklin D., Lake • WA, United States **117** E2
Roosevelt, Home of F.D., Nat. Hist. Site **Park** • NY, United States **121** [323]
Roosevelt, Mt • BC, Canada **38** F5
Roosevelt, Theodore, Birthplace Nat. Hist. Site **Park** • NY, United States **121** [332]
Roosevelt, Theodore, Dam • AZ, United States **118** J3
Roosevelt, Theodore, Inaugural Nat. Hist. Site **Park** • NY, United States **121** [316]
Roosevelt, Theodore, Island **Park** • DC, United States **121** [295]
Roosevelt, Theodore, Lake • AZ, United States **118** J3
Roosevelt, Theodore, Nat. Park **Park** • ND, United States **120** [148]
Roper • NT, Australia **34** F2
Roques • Venezuela **43** D1
Roquetas de Mar **Beach** • Spain **68** [116]
Roquetas de Mar • Spain **86** B8
Roraima [Adm] • Brazil **43** E3
Roraima [Mtn] • S. America **43** E2
Røros • Norway **16** F5
Røros **Heritage C** • Norway **63** [69]
Rørvig • Denmark **95** F10
Rørvik • Norway **16** F4
Rosa, Lake • Bahamas **124** B4
Rosa, Monte • Italy/Switzerland **89** G6
Rosario • Paraguay **44** E3
Rosário • Brazil **45** (1) C2
Rosario • Argentina **127** D1
Rosario • Uruguay **127** D2
Rosario de Arriba • Mexico **40** C5
Rosario de Lerma • Argentina **44** C3
Rosário do Sul • Brazil **44** F5
Rosário Oeste • Brazil **44** E1
Rosario, Sierra del • Cuba **124** D1
Rosarno • Italy **12** K10
Roscoff • France **84** C1
Roscommon • Ireland **79** F4
Roscommon [Adm] • Ireland **79** F2
Roscrea • Ireland **7** E9
Rose Hall • Jamaica **124** C1
Roseau • Dominica **37** I4
Rosebery • TS, Australia **34** I8
Roseburg • OR, United States **40** B3
Rosenberg • TX, United States **119** N6
Rosendal • Norway **94** C5
Rosenheim • Germany **82** J3
Rosenholm • Denmark **95** F10
Roses **Beach** • Spain **68** [123]
Roses • Spain **87** D2
Roses, Golf de • Spain **11** O2
Roses, Valley of • Bulgaria **97** D3
Rosethern • SA, Canada **38** J6
Roseto Capo **Beach** • Italy **69** [154]
Rosetown • SA, Canada **38** J6
Rosetta • Egypt **101** F1
Rosetta Mouth • Egypt **101** F1
Rosetto degli Abruzzi • Italy **12** I6
Rosière, la **Ski** • France **70** [37]
Rosière, la • France **85** F4
Rosignano Marittimo **Beach** • Italy **68** [146]
Rosignano Marittimo • Italy **91** E11
Rosiori de Vede • Romania **97** D1
Roskilde **Beach** • Denmark **68** [42]
Roskilde **Heritage C** • Denmark **64** [10]
Roskilde • Denmark **95** F10
Roskilde [Adm] • Denmark **95** F10
Roslagen • Sweden **95** D2
Roslavl • Russian Fed. **17** E4
Ross • TS, Australia **34** I8
Ross • New Zealand **35** C6
Ross Abbey • Ireland **79** F4
Ross Carbery **Beach** • Ireland **68** [59]
Ross Carbery • Ireland **79** F8
Ross, Fort, State Hist. Park • CA, United States **117** F3
Ross Ice Shelf • Antarctica **46** (1) Z1
Ross Lake Nat. Recreation Area • WA, United States **117** E1
Ross Lake Nat. Recreation Area **Park** • WA, United States **120** [27]
Ross, Mt • Kerguelen Is. **46** (1) L5
Ross River • NT, Australia **112** H2
Ross Sea • Antarctica **46** (1) Y2
Ross-on-Wye • United Kingdom **74** D3
Ross-shire & Cromartyshire • United Kingdom **75** A1
Rossan Point • Ireland **7** D7
Rossano • Italy **12** K9
Rosses Point **Beach** • Ireland **68** [64]
Rosses Point • Ireland **79** F2
Rossignol, Lake • NS, Canada **123** D7
Rosslare **Beach** • Ireland **68** [56]
Rosslare Harbour • Ireland **7** F9
Rosslau • Germany **8** H5
Rossnowlagh **Beach** • Ireland **68** [65]
Rosso • Mauritania **20** B5
Rossosh • Russian Fed. **17** F4
Røssvatnet • Norway **16** G4
Røst • Norway **16** G3
Rostock • Germany **8** H2
Rostocze • Poland **13** M7
Rostov • Russian Fed. **97** E4
Rostov-na-Donu • Russian Fed. **17** F5
Rostrenen • France **84** C1
Roswell • NM, United States **40** F5
Rot • Germany **82** J1
Rota • Northern Mariana Is. **33** F4
Rota **Beach** • Spain **68** [113]
Rota • Spain **86** B5
Rote • Indonesia **110** A7
Rotenburg • Germany **8** E3
Rotenburg an der Fulda • Germany **9** E5
Roth • Germany **9** G7
Rothaargebirge • Germany **9** D5
Rothenburg ob der Tauber • Germany **9** F7
Rothenuffeln **Spa** • Germany **83** [88]
Rothera [Base] • Antarctica **46** (1) II3
Rotherham • United Kingdom **7** K8
Rothesay • United Kingdom **78** A2
Roti • Indonesia **34** D2
Rotoehu, Lake • New Zealand **112** K2
Rotoiti, Lake • New Zealand **112** K2
Rotoma, Lake • New Zealand **112** K2
Rotorua • New Zealand **112** K2
Rotorua, Lake • New Zealand **112** K2
Rott • Germany **9** I8
Rottach-Egern • Germany **82** J7
Rottach-Egern **Spa** • Germany **83** [258]
Rottal • Germany **82** J4
Rottenbuch • Germany **82** J6
Rottenburg am Neckar • Germany **82** G6
Rotterdam • Netherlands **80** C3
Rottnen • Sweden **95** F8
Rottumerplaat • Netherlands **8** B3
Rottweil • Germany **82** G8
Rotuma • Fiji **35** (2) D1
Roubaix • France **10** I3
Roudnice nad Labem • Czech Rep. **13** D7
Rouen • France **10** G4
Rouergue • France **85** G4
Rouge-Matawan Prov. Reserve • QU, Canada **122** B3
Rougemont • Switzerland **89** G6
Rougsø **Beach** • Denmark **68** [47]
Round Mountain, The • NS, Australia **34** J6
Roundstone • Ireland **79** F3
Rousay • United Kingdom **6** I2
Roussillon • France **85** K2
Rouyn • QU, Canada **39** P7
Rovaniemi • Finland **16** M3
Rovereto • Italy **91** E3
Roviés • Greece **92** D4
Rovigo • Italy **91** E7
Rovinj • Italy **12** H3
Rovno • Ukraine **17** D4
Rovuma • Mozambique **23** G6
Rowley I. • NU, Canada **39** P3
Rowley Shoals • QL, Australia **33** C7
Roxas • Palawan, Philippines **31** F4
Roxas • Panay, Philippines **31** G4
Roxborough • Trinidad & Tobago **125** K2
Roxburgh • New Zealand **112** L4
Roxburgh, Lake • New Zealand **112** L2
Roxburghshire • United Kingdom **75** A3
Roxen • Sweden **95** F4
Roxo, Cap • Senegal **20** B6
Roy Hill • WA, Australia **34** C4
Roya • France **85** H2
Royal & Ancient, The • United Kingdom **74** B2
Royal Canal • Ireland **7** E8
Royal Chitwan Nat. Park **Heritage N** • Nepal **61** [104]
Royal Dockyard • Bermuda **58** A2
Royal Leamington Spa • United Kingdom **74** D2
Royal St George's • United Kingdom **74** E4
Royal Tunbridge Wells • United Kingdom **74** E3
Royan • France **85** G1
Royaumont, Abbaye de • France **85** E1
Roye • France **5** F5
Røyrvik • Norway **16** G4
Røysheim • Norway **94** C2
Rózan • Poland **13** K5
Rozmberk • Czech Rep. **96** C4
Roznava • Slovak Rep. **13** J9
Rtishchevo • Russian Fed. **17** G4
Ruaha Nat. Park • Tanzania **102** H3
Ruaha Nat. Park **Park** • Tanzania **103** [94]
Ruahine Range • New Zealand **112** K4
Ruapehu, Mt • New Zealand **112** K4
Ruapuke I. • New Zealand **35** B8
Rub 'al Khali, Ar • Saudi Arabia **18** E6
Rubiku • Albania **15** A2
Rubio • Venezuela **43** C2
Rubondo I. Nat. Park • Tanzania **102** H1
Rubondo I. Nat. Park **Park** • Tanzania **103** [87]
Rubtsovsk • Russian Fed. **26** N7
Ruby Mtns • NV, United States **117** F2
Ruda Slaska • Poland **13** H7
Rudall River Nat. Park • WA, Australia **34** D4
Rudbar • Afghanistan **18** H3
Rudbjerg **Beach** • Denmark **68** [37]
Rüdersdorf • Germany **8** I4
Rüdesheim • Germany **82** H4
Rudkøbing **Beach** • Denmark **68** [44]
Rudkøbing • Denmark **95** F14
Rudnaya Pristan • Russian Fed. **27** M8
Rudnik • F.R. of Yugoslavia **14** H5
Rudnik • Bulgaria **15** I1
Rüdnitz • Germany **81** F2
Rudnyy • Kazakhstan **26** J7
Rudolf, Lake • Kenya **23** F3
Rudolstadt • Germany **9** G6
Rudong • China **107** J2
Rudozem • Bulgaria **15** F2
Rue • France **5** E4
Rueil Malmaison • France **85** E3
Ruffec • France **85** G1
Rufiji • Tanzania **102** H4
Rufino • Argentina **44** D5
Rufisque • Senegal **22** A2
Rufunsa • Zambia **24** D3
Rugao • China **107** J2
Rugby • United Kingdom **74** D2
Rügen • Germany **8** I2
Rügen **Spa** • Germany **83** [279-281]
Ruhnu • Estonia **16** L8
Ruhpolding • Germany **82** J8
Ruhr • Germany **9** D5
Ruhrgebiet • Germany **81** E
Ruien • Bulgaria/F.Y.R. of Macedonia **15** D1
Ruijin • China **31** F1
Ruivo, Pico • Madeira **88** C1
Ruki • Dem. Rep. of Congo **23** B4
Rukwa, Lake • Tanzania **102** H3
Rum • United Kingdom **6** F4
Rum Cay • Bahamas **124** B4
Rum Jungle • NT, Australia **34** F2
Ruma • F.R. of Yugoslavia **14** G4
Ruma Nat. Park • Kenya **101** G3
Rumbek • Sudan **23** D2
Rumburk • Czech Rep. **96** C2
Rumia • Poland **13** H3
Rumija • F.R. of Yugoslavia **15** A1
Rummah, Wadi ar • Saudi Arabia **21** H2
Rumoi • Japan **30** K3
Runanga • New Zealand **35** C6
Runaway Bay • Jamaica **124** C1
Runaway Bay • Antigua & Barbuda **125** F1
Runaway, Cape • New Zealand **35** F3
Runde • Zimbabwe **102** J4
Rundu • Namibia **24** B3
Rung, Ko • Thailand **109** K2
Rungwa • Tanzania **102** H3
Rungwa [Riv] • Tanzania **23** E5
Runhällen • Sweden **95** D1
Runkel • Germany **82** H2
Runmarö • Sweden **95** D4
Runnymede • United Kingdom **74** E1
Runö • Estonia **16** L8

Runswick Bay

Runswick Bay **Beach** • United Kingdom 75 [20]
Ruo Shui • China 29 C2
Ruokolahti • Finland 16 D6
Ruoqiang • China 26 O10
Ruovesi • Finland 95 E2
Rupat • Indonesia 110 B4
Rupert • QU, Canada 39 P6
Ruppiner Kanal • Germany 81 F1
Rur • Germany 9 B5
Rurutu • French Polynesia 33 L8
Rusalka • Bulgaria 97 D4
Rusape • Zimbabwe 102 J2
Rusayris, Ar • Sudan 21 F5
Rusayris, Khazzan ar • Sudan 21 F5
Rusayris, Lake • Sudan 23 E1
Ruse • Bulgaria 97 D1
Rusenski Lom Nat. Park **Park** • Bulgaria 72 [130]
Rusenski Lom Nat. Park • Romania 97 D1
Rush • Ireland 79 E2
Rusk • TX, United States 119 N4
Rußbach **Ski** • Austria 70 [178]
Russborough House • Ireland 75 E3
Russel I. • NU, Canada 38 L2
Russell • New Zealand 35 E2
Russell Cave Nat. Mon. **Park** • AL, United States 121 [207]
Rüsselsheim • Germany 9 D6
Russian Black Sea Coast • Russian Fed. 96 A2
Russian Federation • Europe/Asia 25 I3
Russkaya [Base] • Antarctica 46 (1) BB2
Rustavi • Georgia 17 H6
Ruston • LA, United States 118 K1
Rutanzige, Lac • Uganda/Dem. Rep. of Congo 23 D4
Rutbah, Ar • Iraq 18 C3
Ruteng • Indonesia 32 (1) B4
Rutenga • Zimbabwe 102 J4
Rutland • India 28 F6
Rutland • United Kingdom 75 A5
Rutland • VT, United States 118 G3
Rutog • China 28 C2
Ruvu • Tanzania 102 H2
Ruvuma • Mozambique/Tanzania 102 H4
Ruwenzori Mtns Nat. Park **Heritage N** • Uganda 61 [86]
Ruwenzori Nat. Park **Park** • Uganda 103 [69]
Ruya • Mozambique/Zimbabwe 24 E3
Ruzomberok • Slovak Rep. 13 I8
Ruzyne [Apt] • Czech Rep. 96 C2
Rwanda • Africa 23 E4
Ry **Beach** • Denmark 68 [47]
Ry • Denmark 95 F9
Ryazan • Russian Fed. 17 F4
Rybachiy, Poluostrov • Russian Fed. 16 Q2
Rybinsk • Russian Fed. 97 E2
Rybinskoye Vdkhr. • Russian Fed. 97 E2
Rybnik • Poland 13 H7
Rydaholm • Sweden 95 F7
Rydal Mt • United Kingdom 74 C2
Ryde **Beach** • United Kingdom 75 [89]
Ryde • United Kingdom 78 C8
Rye • United Kingdom 74 E4
Ryfylke • Norway 94 C6
Rygge • Norway 94 B4
Ryotsu • Japan 30 J5
Rypin • Poland 13 I4
Ryukyu Is. • Japan 29 H5
Ryukyu-Shoto • Japan 29 H5
Rzepin • Poland 13 D5
Rzeszów • Poland 13 L8
Rzhev • Russian Fed. 97 E3

S'Albufeira • Minorca, Spain 87 F2
S'Albufeira • Majorca, Spain 87 H2
S'Algar • Minorca, Spain 87 F4
S'Arenal • Majorca, Spain 87 H3
S'Argamassa • Ibiza, Spain 87 G2
S'Horta • Majorca, Spain 87 H2
S'Illot • Majorca, Spain 87 H2
s-Gravenhage • Netherlands 80 C1
s-Hertogenbosch • Netherlands 80 A11
Sa Calobra • Majorca, Spain 87 H1
Sa Conillera • Ibiza, Spain 87 G1
Sa Keo • Thailand 109 H2
Sa Talaiassa de Sant Josep • Ibiza, Spain 87 G1
Sa'dah • Yemen 18 D6
Sa'idabad • Iran 18 G4
Saalach • Austria/Germany 82 J8
Saalbach • Austria 89 H3
Saalbach Hinterglemm **Ski** • Austria 70 [161]
Saale • Germany 8 G5
Saalfeld • Germany 9 G6
Saalfelden • Austria 89 H4
Saane • Switzerland 10 M7
Saanen • Switzerland 89 G6
Saanenmöser • Switzerland 89 G6
Saar • Germany 82 G3
Saarbrücken • Germany 82 G3
Saarburg • Germany 82 G3
Saaremaa • Estonia 16 L7
Saarijärvi • Finland 16 M5
Saaristomeri Nat. Park **Park** • Finland 72 [37]
Saaristomeri Nat. Park • Finland 95 E3
Saarland • Germany 82 G3
Saarlouis • Germany 82 G3
Saas Fee **Ski** • Switzerland 70 [92]
Saas Fee • Switzerland 89 G6
Saba • West Indies 37 I4
Sabac • F.R. of Yugoslavia 14 G5
Sabadell • Spain 87 D3
Sabah • Malaysia 32 F2
Sabaki • Kenya 101 G5
Saban, Archipiélago de • Cuba 124 D2
Sabang • Sulawesi, Indonesia 32 (1) A2
Sabang • Indonesia 110 B1
Sabanözü • Turkey 15 O3
Sabará • Brazil 127 C1
Sabarei • Kenya 23 F3
Sabáudia • Italy 91 F4
Sabáudia, Lago di • Italy 91 F4
Sabha • Libya 21 B2
Sabi • Mozambique/Zimbabwe 102 J4
Sabina • Italy 91 F1
Sabinal, Cayo • Cuba 124 D3
Sabiñánigo • Spain 11 K2
Sabine • LA/TX, United States 119 N2
Sabine Lake • LA/TX, United States 118 K3
Sabkhat Tawurgha • Libya 21 B1
Sable, Cape • FL, United States 119 M8
Sable, Cape • NS, Canada 123 D7
Sable I. • NS, Canada 123 D8
Sablé-sur-Sarthe • France 84 D1
Sables d'Olonne, les • France 10 D7
Sablukah, Ash Shallal as • Sudan 21 F4
Sabrata • Libya 21 B1
Sabratha **Heritage C** • Libya 64 [233]
Sabya • Saudi Arabia 18 D6
Sabzevar • Iran 18 G2
Saché [Château] • France 84 D2
Sachigo • OT, Canada 39 M6
Sachs Harbour • NT, Canada 38 G2
Sachsen • Germany 9 I5
Sachsen-Anhalt • Germany 8 G4
Sachsische Schweiz • Germany 9 J5
Sächsische Schweiz, Nationalpark **Park** • Germany 72 [62]
Sacramento • Brazil 44 G2
Sacramento • CA, United States 117 F3
Sacramento, Pampa del • Peru 43 B5
Sacramento [Riv] • CA, United States 117 F1
Sacramento Valley • CA, United States 40 B3
Sacred Falls State Park • HI, United States 119 L5
Sada Temple • Bali, Indonesia 110 C4
Sádaba • Spain 11 J2
Sadani • Tanzania 102 H2
Sadao • Thailand 109 F4
Sadiklar • Turkey 93 G4
Sadiya • India 28 G3
Sadlers • St Kitts & Nevis 125 G1
Sado • Portugal 11 C6
Sado • Japan 30 J5
Sado • Portugal 88 D2
Sadr, As • United Arab Emirates 18 F5
Sadung • Thailand 109 H1
Sæby **Beach** • Denmark 68 [48]
Sæby • Denmark 95 F6
Safad • Israel 98 A2
Safari- und Abenteuerpark **Park** • Austria 73 [82]
Säffle • Sweden 16 G7
Saffron Walden • United Kingdom 7 M9
Safi • Morocco 101 D3
Safid • Iran 18 E2
Safonovo • Russian Fed. 17 E3
Safranbolu • Turkey 15 N2
Safranbolu **Heritage C** • Turkey 64 [191]
Sag Harbor • NY, United States 118 H2
Saga • Japan 30 F8
Sagaing • Myanmar 31 B2
Sagalassos • Turkey 93 G1
Sagaminada • Japan 30 J7
Sagamore Hill Nat. Hist. Site **Park** • NY, United States 121 [324]
Sagar • India 105 C7
Sagarmatha • China/Nepal 28 E3
Sagarmatha Nat. Park **Heritage N** • Nepal 61 [103]
Saggat • Sweden 16 I3
Saginaw • MI, United States 41 J3
Saginaw Bay • MI, United States 39 O8
Sagiz • Kazakhstan 26 H8
Saglouc • QU, Canada 36 J3
Sagone • Corsica, France 85 L3
Sagone, Golfe de • Corsica, France 85 L3
Sagres • Portugal 88 E5
Sagres, Ponta de • Portugal 88 E5
Sagua de Tánamo • Cuba 124 D8
Sagua Grande • Cuba 124 D2
Saguaro Nat. Park • AZ, United States 118 J3
Saguaro Nat. Park **Park** • AZ, United States 120 [117]
Saguenay • QU, Canada 39 Q7
Saguenay Prov. Park • QU, Canada 123 D1
Saguia el-Hamra • Western Sahara 20 C3
Sagunto • Spain 11 K5
Sagunto **Beach** • Spain 68 [119]
Sahagún • Spain 11 F2
Saharanpur • India 28 C2
Sahel • Tunisia 101 E4
Sahiwal • Pakistan 28 B2
Sahlabad • Iran 18 G3
Sahr-i-Bahlol **Heritage C** • Pakistan 63 [112]
Sahra Bayyudah • Sudan 21 F4
Sahra Murzuq • Libya 21 B3
Sahra Rabyanah • Libya 21 C3
Sahuayo • Mexico 123 E1
Sahyadri • India 28 B5
Sai Gon [Riv] • Vietnam 108 B1
Sai Kung • Hong Kong, China 107 H6
Sai Kung Country Park • Hong Kong, China 107 H6
Sai, Laem • Ko Samui, Thailand 109 J1
Saïda • Algeria 20 F2
Saïdia • Morocco 101 D2
Saidor • Papua New Guinea 35 (1) D2
Saigon • Vietnam 108 B1
Saiki • Japan 30 F8
Saima Kanal • Finland/Russian Fed. 16 O6
Saimaa • Finland 16 N6
Saimaan Kanava • Finland/Russian Fed. 16 O6
St Agnes • United Kingdom 74 F4
St Alban's Head • United Kingdom 74 F6
St Albans • United Kingdom 74 E1
St Albans • VT, United States 118 G1
St Aldhelm's Head • United Kingdom 74 F6
St André, Cap • Madagascar 24 G3
St Andreasberg **Spa** • Germany 83 [80]
St Andrews • United Kingdom 74 B2
St Andrews **Beach** • United Kingdom 75 [4]
St Andrews • NB, Canada 123 D6
St Ann's Bay • Jamaica 124 C2
St Anne-de-Beaupré • QU, Canada 123 D1
St Annes • Channel Is. 7 J12
St Anthony • NF, Canada 123 D5
St' Antioco • Sardinia, Italy 90 C3
St' Antioco, I. di • Sardinia, Italy 90 C3
St Anton am Arlberg **Ski** • Austria 70 [132]
St Anton am Arlberg • Austria 89 H6
St Arnaud • VI, Australia 111 G3
St Augustin • Germany 9 C6
St Augustin-Saguenay • QU, Canada 39 T6
St Augustine • FL, United States 119 M4
St Augustine, Baie de • Madagascar 24 G4
St Austell • United Kingdom 74 F4
St Austell **Beach** • United Kingdom 75 [118]
St Avold • France 5 J5
St Bad Cannstadt **Spa** • Germany 83 [176]
St Barbe • NF, Canada 123 D5
St Barthélemy • West Indies 37 I4
St Bee's Head • United Kingdom 74 C1
St Berg **Spa** • Germany 83 [176]
St Blais, Cape • South Africa 100 C6
St Blaise • Switzerland 89 G1
St Blasien • Germany 82 G8
St Blasien **Spa** • Germany 83 [206]
St Boniface • MN, Canada 38 L7
St Brevin • France 84 C4
St Brévin-les-Pins **Beach** • France 68 [82]
St Brides Haven **Beach** • United Kingdom 75 [161]
St Brieuc • France 84 C2
St Brieuc, Baie de • France 10 C5
St Calais • France 84 D2
St Cast • France 84 C2
St Catharines • OT, Canada 122 B9
St Catherine, Monastery of • Egypt 101 F4
St Catherine's Point • United Kingdom 5 B4
St Chamond • France 10 J8
St Charles • MO, United States 41 H4
St Chinian • France 84 B4
St Christina in Gröden • Italy 90 B1
St Christoph am Arlberg **Ski** • Austria 70 [133]
St Christoph am Arlberg • Austria 89 H5
St Christopher • St Kitts & Nevis 125 G1
St Christopher, Rocque • France 85 G2
St Cirq-Lapopie • France 85 G4
St Cloud • MN, United States 41 H2
St Croix • WI, United States 39 M7
St Croix I. Int. Hist. Site **Park** • ME, United States 121 [355]
St Croix I. Int. Hist. Site • Canada/United States 123 D6
St Cyprien **Beach** • France 68 [128]
St Cyr-sur-Mer **Beach** • France 68 [133]
St Cyr-sur-Mer • France 85 H3
St David's **Beach** • United Kingdom 75 [164-165]
St David's Head • United Kingdom 7 G10
St Denis • Réunion 24 (1) B2
St Denis • France 85 E1
St Denis d'Oléron **Beach** • France 68 [84]
St Dié • France 10 L5
St Dizier • France 10 J5
St Dogmael **Beach** • United Kingdom 75 [169]
St Elias, Mt • YT, Canada 38 C4
St Elias Mtns • Canada/United States 38 D4
St Elie • French Guiana 43 G3
St Emilion • France 85 G1
St Estephe • France 84 B3
St Etienne • France 10 J8
St Étienne-de-Tinée **Ski** • France 70 [71]
St Etienne-du-Rouvray • France 5 E5
St Eustatius • West Indies 37 I4
St Florent • Corsica, France 85 L2
St Florent, Golfe de • Corsica, France 85 L2
St Florentin • France 10 I6
St Flour • France 10 I8
St Francis Bay • South Africa 100 C8
St Francis, Cape • South Africa 100 C8
St Francisville • LA, United States 118 K4
St François • Seychelles 106 F4
St Francois • QU, Canada 122 B4
St François-Longchamp **Ski** • France 70 [45]
St Gallen • Switzerland 9 E9
St Gallen **Heritage C** • Switzerland 64 [103]
St Gallenkirch **Ski** • Austria 70 [127]
St Gaudens • France 85 J2
St Gaudens Nat. Hist. Site • NH, United States 118 G3
St Gaudens Nat. Hist. Site **Park** • NH, United States 121 [353]
St George • UT, United States 40 D4
St George • QL, Australia 111 F5
St George, Cape • Papua New Guinea 35 (1) E1
St George I. • FL, United States 119 M2
St George, Monastery of • Jordan 98 A6
St George's • Grenada 37 I5
St George's • Bermuda 58 A2
St George's Bay • NF, Canada 123 D3
St George's Channel • Ireland/UK 7 F10
St George's Church • Barbados 125 H3
St Georges-de-la-Rivière **Beach** • France 68 [78]
St Germain, Forêt de • France 85 E1
St Germain-en-Laye • France 85 E1
St Gervais **Ski** • France 70 [25]
St Gervais-les-Bains • France 85 F2
St Gilgen • Austria 89 H4
St Gilles-Croix-de-Vie **Beach** • France 68 [83]
St Girons • France 85 K1
St Goar • Germany 82 H2
St Helena • Atlantic Ocean 19 D7
St Helena Bay • South Africa 100 C1
St Helens • United Kingdom 7 J8
St Helens • TS, Australia 34 I8
St Helens **Beach** • United Kingdom 75 [91]
St Helens, Mt • WA, United States 117 E1
St Helier • Channel Is. 7 J12
St Hilaire-de-Riez **Beach** • France 68 [83]
St Hilarion Castle • Cyprus 93 J1
St Hubert • Belgium 5 I4
St Hyacinthe • QU, Canada 122 B4
St Idesbald • Belgium 80 B1
St Ingbert • Germany 5 K5
St Ives • United Kingdom 74 F4
St Ives **Beach** • United Kingdom 75 [122-123]
St Ives Bay • United Kingdom 74 F4
St Jacut • France 84 C2
St Jakob am Arlberg **Ski** • Austria 70 [132]
St James, Cape • BC, Canada 38 E6
St James, The Way of **Heritage C** • Spain 64 [80]
St Jean • QU, Canada 122 B8
St Jean d'Arves **Ski** • France 70 [48]
St Jean, Lac • QU, Canada 123 D1
St Jean-Cap-Ferrat • France 85 H2
St Jean-d'Angély • France 85 G1
St Jean-d'Aulps **Ski** • France 70 [11]
St Jean-de-Luz • France 85 J1
St Jean-Pied-de-Port • France 85 J1
St Jérôme • QU, Canada 39 P7
St Johann im Pongau **Ski** • Austria 70 [167]
St Johann im Pongau • Austria 89 H4
St Johann in Tirol **Ski** • Austria 70 [154]
St Johann in Tirol • Austria 89 H3
St John • NB, Canada 123 D7
St John [Riv] • Canada/United States 123 D6
St John's • NF, Canada 123 D4
St John's • Antigua & Barbuda 125 F1
St John's Church • Barbados 125 H4
St John's Harbour • Antigua & Barbuda 125 F1
St Johns • AZ, United States 118 J2
St Johnsbury • VT, United States 118 G3
St Johnstone Village • Antigua & Barbuda 125 F1
St Joseph • Réunion 24 (1) B2
St Joseph • MO, United States 41 H4
St Joseph • France 84 B4
St Joseph • Seychelles 106 F2
St Joseph, Lake • OT, Canada 39 M6
St Julian's • Malta 93 H4
St Julien • France 84 B3
St Just • United Kingdom 74 F4
St Kassian **Ski** • Italy 70 [233]
St Kassien • Italy 90 B2
St Kilda • United Kingdom 6 D4
St Kilda • New Zealand 35 C7
St Kilda **Heritage N** • United Kingdom 61 [40]
St Kitts • St Kitts & Nevis 125 G1
St Kitts & Nevis • West Indies 125 G
St Lary Soulan • France 85 J2
St Laurent • QU, Canada 39 R7
St Laurent • French Guiana 43 G2
St Lawrence • QU, Canada 39 R7
St Lawrence • QL, Australia 111 F3
St Lawrence • Barbados 125 H3
St Lawrence, Gulf of • QU, Canada 123 D2
St Lawrence I. • Bering Sea 40 (2) D2
St Lawrence Is. Nat. Park • OT, Canada 122 B6
St Lazaire • France 10 I11
St Léonard-de-Noblat • France 85 G2
St Leonhard **Ski** • Italy 70 [233]
St Leonhard in Passeier • Italy 90 B1
St Lizier • France 85 K1
St Lô • France 10 D4
St Louis • France 9 C9
St Louis • Senegal 22 A1
St Louis • MO, United States 41 H4
St Lucia • West Indies 125 J
St Lucia, Cape • South Africa 24 E5
St Maarten • West Indies 37 I4
St Malo • France 84 C2
St Malo, Golfe de • France 84 C2
St Margarethen im Lungau **Ski** • Austria 70 [187]
St Märgen • Germany 82 G8
St Marie, Cap • Madagascar 24 H5
St Martin-de-Belleville **Ski** • France 70 [40]
St Martinville • LA, United States 118 K3
St Mary Peak • SA, Australia 34 G6
St Mary's, Cape • NF, Canada 123 D4
St Marys • United Kingdom 7 F12
St Marys • TS, Australia 34 I8
St Marys City • MD, United States 118 H3
St Mathieu, Point de • France 84 C1
St Maur-des-Fossés • France 5 F6
St Maurice • QU, Canada 39 Q7
St Maurice Prov. Reserve • QU, Canada 122 B4
St Mawes • United Kingdom 74 F4
St Maximin la Ste Baume • France 85 H3
St Memmie • France 5 H6
St Merryn **Beach** • United Kingdom 75 [127-129]
St Michael im Lungau **Ski** • Austria 70 [188]
St Michael's Mount • United Kingdom 74 F4
St Michel • Finland 16 N6
St Michel-Chef-Chef **Beach** • France 68 [82]
St Mihiel • France 5 I6
St Moritz **Ski** • Switzerland 70 [118]
St Moritz • Switzerland 89 G8
St Nazaire • France 84 C4
St Nicholas' Abbey • Barbados 125 H1
St Nicolas-de-Port • France 5 J6
St Nicolas-de-Véroce **Ski** • France 70 [27]
St Niklaas • Belgium 80 A10
St Omer • France 10 H3
St Paul • Réunion 24 (1) B2
St Paul • AL, Canada 38 I6
St Paul • MN, United States 41 H2
St Paul • France 85 H2
St Paul I. • NS, Canada 123 D3
St Paul, Monastery of • Egypt 101 F4
St Paul's • St Kitts & Nevis 125 G1
St Paul's Bay • Malta 93 H2
St Paul's Church Nat. Hist. Site **Park** • NY, United States 121 [330]
St Paul's Is. • Malta 93 H2
St Pé, Parc zoologique • France 85 J2
St Peter • Germany 82 G8
St Peter Ording • Germany 8 D2
St Peter Ording **Spa** • Germany 83 [7]
St Peter Port • Channel Is. 7 J12
St Peterburg • Russian Fed. 97 E1
St Petersburg **Heritage C** • Russian Fed. 64 [205]
St Petersburg • Russian Fed. 97 E1
St Petersburg • FL, United States 119 M5
St Philips • Antigua & Barbuda 125 F4
St Phillip • St Lucia 125 J3
St Pierre • Réunion 24 (1) B2
St Pierre • Seychelles 106 F3
St Pierre • St Pierre et Miquelon 123 D3
St Pierre et Miquelon • N. America 123 D3
St Pierre, Lac • QU, Canada 122 B4
St Pieters-Leeuw • Belgium 5 H4
St Pölten • Austria 13 E9
St Quay-Portrieux **Beach** • France 68 [80]
St Quay-Portrieux • France 84 C2
St Quentin • France 10 I4
St Raphaël • France 85 H4
St Sauveur-des-Monts • QU, Canada 122 B3
St Savin • France 84 D4
St Savin-sur-Gartempe **Heritage C** • France 64 [62]
St Sebastien, Cap • Réunion 24 H2
St Siméon • QU, Canada 123 D1
St Stephen • NB, Canada 123 D6
St Thégonnec • France 84 C1
St Thomas Bay • Malta 93 H4
St Trojan-les-Bains **Beach** • France 68 [84]
St Tropez • France 85 H4
St Truiden • Belgium 5 I4
St Ulrich **Ski** • Italy 70 [230]
St Ulrich • Italy 90 B1
St Vaast-la-Hougue **Beach** • France 68 [78]
St Valéry-en-Caux • France 5 D5
St Veit an der Glan • Austria 13 D11
St Vigil in Enneberg • Italy 90 B2
St Vincent, Gulf • SA, Australia 34 G6
St Vincent I. • FL, United States 119 M2
St Vincent & the Grenadines • West Indies 37 I5
St Vincent-sur-Jard **Beach** • France 68 [83]
St Vith • Belgium 80 A16
St Wendel • Germany 9 C7
St Wolfgang • Austria 89 H4
Ste Agathe-des-Monts • QU, Canada 122 B3
Ste Anne • Seychelles 106 F1
Ste Anne Marine Nat. Park • Seychelles 106 F1
Ste Anne-des-Monts • QU, Canada 123 D2
Ste Croix • Switzerland 89 G1
Ste Engrâce • France 85 J1
Ste Foy • QU, Canada 122 B4
Ste Foy-la-Grande • France 85 G3
Ste Maxime • France 85 H4
Ste Menehould • France 5 H5
Stes Maries-de-la-Mer • France 10 J10
Saintes • France 85 G1
Saintonge • France 10 E8
Saipan • Northern Mariana Is. 33 F4
Sairecabur, Cerro • Bolivia 44 C3
Sais [Apt] • Morocco 101 D2
Saiwa Swamp Nat. Park • Kenya 101 G1
Sajak • Kazakhstan 26 M8
Sajama • Bolivia 44 C2
Sajama, Nevado de • Bolivia 44 C2
Sajó • Hungary 13 J9
Sajószentpéter • Hungary 13 J9
Sakai • Japan 30 H7
Sakakah • Saudi Arabia 18 C4
Sakakawea, Lake • ND, United States 40 F2
Sakar • Bulgaria 15 H2
Sakaraha • Madagascar 24 G4
Sakarya • Turkey 15 L3
Sakata • Japan 30 J5
Sakenan Temple • Bali, Indonesia 110 C4
Sakha • Russian Fed. 27 H3
Sakhalin, Ostrov • Russian Fed. 27 N6
Sakhalinskiye Zaliv • Russian Fed. 27 N6
Sakhira • Tunisia 101 E4
Sakishima-Shoto • Japan 31 G2
Sakjiang • Singapore 108 E4
Sakra • Singapore 108 E3
Sakskøbing • Denmark 95 F14
Sal • Cape Verde 22 (1) B1
Sal'a • Slovak Rep. 13 G9
Sala • Chad 21 D4
Sala • Sweden 95 D1
Sala Consilina • Italy 12 J8
Sala y Gómez • Pacific Ocean 33 Q8
Salabangka, Kepulauan • Indonesia 32 (1) B3
Salacgriva • Latvia 16 M8
Saladillo • Argentina 127 D3
Salado • Argentina 44 C5
Salado • Argentina 44 D4
Salado • Cuba 124 D1
Salado • Argentina 127 D1
Salagle • Somalia 23 G3
Sálakos • Rhodes, Greece 93 F1
Salal • Chad 22 H2
Salalah • Oman 18 F6
Salamanca • Spain 11 F4
Salamanca **Heritage C** • Spain 64 [84]
Salamanca • Mexico 123 E1
Salamat, Bahr • Chad 21 C5
Salamina • Greece 15 E6
Salamina [I.] • Greece 92 D4
Salamis • Cyprus 93 J2
Salamiyah, As • Saudi Arabia 18 E5
Salas • Spain 11 E1
Salas de los Infantes • Spain 11 H2
Salatiga • Java, Indonesia 110 D7
Salavat • Russian Fed. 4 V6
Salawati • Indonesia 32 (1) D3
Salbris • France 10 H6
Salcantay, Nevado de • Peru 127 B2
Salcombe • United Kingdom 74 F5
Salcombe **Beach** • United Kingdom 75 [110-111]
Salda Gölü • Turkey 93 G1
Saldaña • Spain 11 G2
Saldanha • South Africa 100 C1
Saldanha Bay • South Africa 100 C1
Saldus • Latvia 16 L8
Salé • Morocco 101 D1
Sale • VI, Australia 111 G3
Salé [Apt] • Morocco 101 D1
Salekhard • Russian Fed. 26 K4
Salem • India 106 D11
Salem • OR, United States 117 E3
Salem • MA, United States 118 H2
Salem Maritime Nat. Hist. Site **Park** • MA, United States 121 [350]
Salema • Portugal 88 E5
Salemi • Sicily, Italy 12 G11
Salerno • Italy 91 G4
Salerno, Golfo di • Italy 91 G4
Salgotarján • Hungary 13 I9
Salgueiro • Brazil 45 (1) D3
Salîm • Egypt 21 E1
Salina • KS, United States 41 G4
Salina Bay • Malta 93 H2
Salina Cruz • Mexico 123 E4
Salina, I. • Italy 90 D2
Salinas • Ecuador 43 A4
Salinas • Puerto Rico 125 E4
Salinas, Bahia • Puerto Rico 125 E3
Salinas Cliff Dwellings Nat. Mon. • NM, United States 118 J4
Salinas Grandes • Argentina 44 D4
Salinas Pueblo Missions Nat. Mon. **Park** • NM, United States 120 [123]
Salines, Cap de ses • Majorca, Spain 11 O5
Salir • Portugal 88 E3
Salisbury • United Kingdom 74 F3
Salisbury • MD, United States 118 H3
Salisbury I. • NU, Canada 39 P4
Salisbury Plain • United Kingdom 74 F3
Salla • Finland 16 O3
Sallingsund **Beach** • Denmark 68 [49]
Sallins • Ireland 79 E3
Salluit • QU, Canada 39 P4
Sallyana • Nepal 105 C4
Salmon • ID, United States 117 E4
Salmon Arm • BC, Canada 38 G6
Salmon Falls • ID, United States 117 E4
Salmon River Mtns • ID, United States 117 E4
Salmonsdam Nature Reserve • South Africa 100 C6
Salò • Italy 91 E7
Salo • Finland 95 E4
Salobreña • Spain 86 B7
Salon-de-Provence • France 10 K10
Salonga, Parc nat. de la **Heritage N** • Dem. Rep. of Congo 61 [81]
Salonga, Parc nat. de la **Park** • Dem. Rep. of Congo 103 [53]
Salonika **Heritage C** • Greece 64 [175]
Salonika • Greece 92 D1
Salonta • Romania 14 I3
Salor • Spain 11 E5
Salou **Beach** • Spain 68 [121]
Salou • Spain 87 D3
Saloum • Senegal 22 A2
Salseleh-ye Safid Kuh • Afghanistan 18 H3
Salsk • Russian Fed. 17 G5
Salso • Sicily, Italy 90 D4
Salsomaggiore • Italy 91 E6
Salt • Spain 11 N3
Salt • AZ, United States 118 J3
Salt Cay • Bahamas 124 B3
Salt Lake City • UT, United States 40 D3
Salt Pond Estate • St Kitts & Nevis 125 G4
Salta • Argentina 44 C3
Saltash • United Kingdom 74 F5
Saltburn-by-the-Sea • United Kingdom 7 L7
Salten • Norway 16 H3
Saltfjellet-Svartisen Nat. Park **Park** • Norway 72 [9]
Saltholm • Denmark 95 F11
Saltibus • St Lucia 125 J3
Saltillo • Mexico 37 A2
Salto • Uruguay 44 E5
Salto • Italy 91 F2
Salto Angostura • Colombia 43 C3
Salton Sea • CA, United States 117 F6
Saltram • United Kingdom 74 F5
Saltsjöbaden • Sweden 95 D4
Salut, Is. du • French Guiana 58 A3
Saluzzo • Italy 10 M9
Salvador de Bahia • Brazil 44 I1
Salvador de Bahia **Heritage C** • Brazil 62 [61]
Salween • Myanmar 31 B2
Salzach • Austria/Germany 9 H9
Salzburg **Heritage C** • Austria 64 [105]
Salzburg • Austria 89 H4
Salzburg [Adm] • Austria 89 H4
Salzburger Alpen • Austria/Germany 82 J8
Salzelmen **Spa** • Germany 83 [293]
Salzgitter • Germany 8 F4
Salzgitter Bad **Spa** • Germany 83 [76]
Salzhemmendorf **Spa** • Germany 83 [72]
Salzkammergut • Austria 89 H4
Salzwedel • Germany 8 G4
Sam • India 105 C1
Sam Lord's Castle • Barbados 125 H4
Sam Ngao • Thailand 109 G3
Samae San • Thailand 109 H4
Samae San, Ko • Thailand 109 H4
Samaipata • Bolivia 44 D2
Samana Cay • Bahamas 124 B4
Samani • Japan 30 L3
Samar • Philippines 31 H4
Samara • Russian Fed. 17 I4
Samara [Riv] • Russian Fed. 26 H7
Samaria • Jordan 98 A5
Samaria [Region] • Israel/Jordan 98 A5
Samariás, Farági • Crete, Greece 93 E5
Samarinda • Indonesia 32 F3
Samarkand • Uzbekistan 18 I2
Samarra • Iraq 18 D3
Samate • Indonesia 32 (1) D3
Samawah, As • Iraq 18 D3
Samba-Caju • Angola 22 H6
Sambalpur • India 28 D4
Sambas • Indonesia 32 D2
Sambhal • India 105 C3
Sambir • Ukraine 17 C5
Samborombón, Bahía • Argentina 127 D4
Sambre • Belgium 80 A14
Samburg • Russian Fed. 26 M4
Samburu Game Reserve • Kenya 101 G2
Samburu Nat. Reserve **Park** • Kenya 103 [77]
Samch'ongp'o • Rep. of Korea 30 D7
Samdong-ni • D.P.R. of Korea 30 D5
Same • Tanzania 102 H2
Samedan **Ski** • Switzerland 70 [117]
Samedan • Switzerland 89 G4
Samet, Ko • Thailand 109 H4
Samfya-Mwamfuli • Zambia 23 D6
Sámi • Greece 92 C2
Samnaun **Ski** • Switzerland 70 [123]
Samnaun • Switzerland 89 G4
Samnaun • Austria 89 H6
Samoa Is. • Pacific Ocean 35 (2) F1
Samode • India 105 C2
Samoeng • Thailand 109 G1
Samoëns **Ski** • France 70 [16]
Samoëns • France 85 F2
Samokov • Bulgaria 14 K7
Samora • Portugal 88 D2
Sámos **Beach** • Greece 69 [201]
Sámos **Heritage C** • Greece 64 [185]
Sámos • Greece 92 D8
Sámos [I.] • Greece 92 D8
Samosir • Indonesia 110 B2
Samothrace • Greece 92 D2
Samothráki • Greece 15 G3
Samothráki [I.] • Greece 92 D2
Sampang • Java, Indonesia 110 D8
Sampit • Indonesia 32 E3
Sampwe • Dem. Rep. of Congo 24 D1
Samrong, Laem • Ko Samui, Thailand 109 J1
Samsø • Denmark 95 F10
Samsø Bælt • Denmark 95 F10
Samuel, Mt • NT, Australia 34 F3
Samut Prakan • Thailand 109 H2
Samut Sakhon • Thailand 109 H1
Samut Songkhram • Thailand 109 H3
San • Poland 13 L7
San Agustín • Gran Canaria, Canary Is. 86 E4
San Agustín, Parque Arqueológico **Heritage C** • Colombia 62 [45]
San Ambrosio • Pacific Ocean 42 C7
San Andrés • Colombia 37 E5
San Andrés del Rabanedo • Spain 11 F2
San Angelo • TX, United States 40 F5
San Antonio • Chile 44 B5
San Antonio • TX, United States 119 N5
San Antonio Bay • TX, United States 119 N5
San Antonio, Cabo • Cuba 124 D1
San Antonio, Cabo • Argentina 127 D4
San Antonio de los Cobres • Argentina 44 C3
San Antonio Missions Nat. Hist. Park • TX, United States 119 N5
San Antonio Missions Nat. Hist. Park **Park** • TX, United States 120 [141]
San Antonio Oeste • Argentina 45 D4
San Augustin, Cap • Philippines 31 H5
San Augustine • TX, United States 119 N4
San Bartolomé de Tirajana **Beach** • Gran Canaria, Canary Is. 68 [110]
San Bartolomé de Tirajana • Gran Canaria, Canary Is. 86 E4
San Bartolomeo al Mare **Beach** • Italy 68 [140]

San Benedetto del Tronto • Italy 91 E12
San Bernardino • Switzerland 89 G7
San Bernardino • CA, United States 117 F6
San Bernardino, Passo del • Switzerland 89 G7
San Bernardo • Chile 44 B5
San Blas • Mexico 123 E1
San Blas Bay • Malta 93 H1
San Blas, Cape • FL, United States 119 M2
San Borja • Bolivia 44 C1
San Cándido **Ski** • Italy 70 [239]
San Cándido • Italy 90 B2
San Carlos • Philippines 31 G4
San Carlos • Nicaragua 37 E5
San Carlos • Venezuela 43 D2
San Carlos • Chile 44 B6
San Carlos • Uruguay 44 F5
San Carlos de Bariloche • Argentina 45 B4
San Carlos de Bolívar • Argentina 127 D3
San Carlos del Zulia • Venezuela 43 C2
San Carlos Indian Reservation • AZ, United States 118 J4
San Cassiano **Ski** • Italy 70 [233]
San Cassiano • Italy 90 B2
San Cataldo • Sicily, Italy 12 H11
San Clemente • Spain 11 I5
San Clemente del Tuyú • Argentina 127 D4
San Clemente I. • CA, United States 117 F6
San Cristóbal • Solomon Is. 35 (1) G3
San Cristóbal • Galapagos Is. 43 (1) A2
San Cristóbal • Venezuela 43 C2
San Cristóbal • Argentina 44 D5
San Diego • CA, United States 117 F6
San Diego, Cabo • Argentina 45 C6
San Donà di Piave • Italy 12 G3
San Esteban de Gormaz • Spain 11 H3
San Felice Circéo • Italy 91 F4
San Felipe • Venezuela 43 D1
San Felipe • Colombia 43 D3
San Felipe • Chile 44 B5
San Felix • Pacific Ocean 42 C7
San Fernando • Philippines 31 G3
San Fernando • Mexico 40 G7
San Fernando • Chile 44 B5
San Fernando **Beach** • Spain 68 [113]
San Fernando • Spain 86 B5
San Fernando • Trinidad & Tobago 125 K3
San Fernando de Apure • Venezuela 43 D2
San Fernando de Atabapo • Venezuela 43 D3
San Floriano • Italy 90 B3
San Francique • Trinidad & Tobago 125 K3
San Francisco • Argentina 44 D5
San Francisco • CA, United States 117 F3
San Francisco Maritime Nat. Hist. Park **Park** • CA, United States 120 [46]
San Francisco, Sierra de la **Heritage C** • Mexico 62 [13]
San Galgano • Italy 91 E11
San Gallán, I. • Peru 127 B1
San Germán • Puerto Rico 125 E3
San Gil • Colombia 43 C2
San Gimignano **Heritage C** • Italy 64 [121]
San Gimignano • Italy 91 E11
San Gottardo, Passo del • Switzerland 89 G3
San Ignacio • Paraguay 44 E4
San Ignacio Mini **Heritage C** • Argentina 62 [64]
San Isidro • Argentina 44 E5
San Javier • Chile 44 B6
San Javier **Beach** • Spain 68 [117]
San Javier • Spain 87 C3
San Joaquín • Bolivia 44 D2
San Joaquin • CA, United States 117 F3
San Joaquin Valley • CA, United States 40 B4
San Jorge • Argentina 44 D5
San Jorge, Golfo de • Argentina 45 C5
San Jose • Philippines 31 G4
San José • Costa Rica 37 E6
San José • Mexico 40 D7
San José • Venezuela 43 E2
San José • Bolivia 44 D2
San José • Spain 86 B8
San Jose • CA, United States 117 F3
San José de Jachal • Argentina 44 C5
San José de Mayo • Uruguay 127 D2
San José de Ocune • Colombia 43 D3
San José del Guaviare • Colombia 43 C3
San Juan • Costa Rica/Nicaragua 37 E5
San Juan • Argentina 44 C5
San Juan **Heritage C** • Puerto Rico 62 [39]
San Juan • CO/UT, United States 118 J2
San Juan • Puerto Rico 125 E2
San Juan • Trinidad & Tobago 125 K3
San Juan • Peru 127 B3
San Juan Bautista • CA, United States 117 F3
San Juan, Cabo • Equatorial Guinea 22 F4
San Juan de los Morros • Venezuela 43 D2
San Juan del Norte • Nicaragua 43 A1
San Juan I. Nat. Hist. Park • WA, United States 117 E1
San Juan I. Nat. Hist. Park **Park** • WA, United States 120 [23]
San Juan, Pico • Cuba 124 D2
San Juan y Martinez • Cuba 124 D1
San Julián • Argentina 45 C5
San Just, Sierra de • Spain 11 K4
San Lázaro • Paraguay 44 E3
San Lázaro, Cabo • Mexico 40 D7
San Leo • Italy 91 E12
San Leonardo **Ski** • Italy 70 [233]
San Leonardo in Passiria • Italy 90 B1
San Lorenzo **Heritage C** • Panama 62 [32]
San Lorenzo, I. • Peru 127 B1
San Lucas, Cabo • Mexico 40 E7
San Luis • Argentina 44 C5
San Luis • Cuba 124 D8
San Luis Capistrano, Mission • CA, United States 117 F6
San Luis Obispo • CA, United States 117 F5
San Luis Potosí • Mexico 123 E1
San Luis Potosí [Adm] • Mexico 37 (1) B1
San Luis Río Colorado • Mexico 40 D5
San Mamete • Italy 91 E2
San Marcos • Colombia 43 B2
San Marcos • TX, United States 119 N3
San Marino • Europe 91 E12
San Martín • Argentina 44 C5
San Martín • Bolivia 44 D1
San Martin [Base] • Antarctica 46 (1) II3
San Martin, Lago • Argentina/Chile 45 B5
San Martino de Lota • Corsica, France 85 L2
San Martino di Castrozza **Ski** • Italy 70 [220]
San Martino di Castrozza • Italy 90 B3
San Mateo • CA, United States 117 F3
San Matías, Golfo • Argentina 45 D4
San Michele, Grotta di • Italy 91 G2
San Miguel • El Salvador 37 D5
San Miguel • Bolivia 44 D2
San Miguel • CA, United States 117 F3
San Miguel de Allende • Mexico 123 E1
San Miguel de Tucumán • Argentina 44 C4
San Miguel I. • CA, United States 117 F5
San Millán **Heritage C** • Spain 64 [77]
San Miniato • Italy 12 E5
San Nicolás de los Arroyos • Argentina 127 D1
San Nicolás de Tolentino • Gran Canaria, Canary Is. 86 E4
San Nicolas I. • CA, United States 117 F5
San Pablo • Philippines 31 G4
San Pawl il-Bahar • Malta 93 H2
San Pedro • Jujuy, Argentina 44 D3
San Pedro • Buenos Aires, Argentina 127 D1
San Pedro Alcántara • Spain 86 B6
San Pedro de Lloc • Peru 43 B5
San Pedro de Macorís • Dominican Rep. 37 H4
San Pedro del Pinatar • Spain 87 C3
San Pedro Sula • Honduras 37 D4
San Philippe, Cayos de • Cuba 124 D1
San Pietro, I. di • Sardinia, Italy 90 C3
San Quintín • Mexico 40 C5
San Rafael • Argentina 44 C5
San Ramón de la Nueva Oran • Argentina 44 D3
San Remo • Italy 91 E9
San Rocque • Spain 86 B6
San Saba • TX, United States 119 N3
San Salvador • El Salvador 37 D5
San Salvador • Galapagos Is. 43 (1) A2
San Salvador de Jujuy • Argentina 44 C3
San Salvador I. • Bahamas 124 B4
San Sebastián • Spain 11 J1
San Sebastián • Gomera, Canary Is. 87 E5
San Sebastian • Puerto Rico 125 E1
San Severo • Italy 12 J7
San Sicário **Ski** • Italy 70 [192]
San Tin • Hong Kong, China 107 H3
San Valentin • Chile 45 B5
San Vicente de Cañete • Peru 127 B1
San Vicente de la Barquera • Spain 11 G1
San Vicente de la Barquera **Beach** • Spain 68 [89]
San Vicente del Raspeig • Spain 11 K6
San Vigilio di Marebbe **Ski** • Italy 70 [234]
San Vigilio in Marebbe • Italy 90 B2
San Vincente del Caguán • Colombia 43 C3
San Vincenzo • Italy 91 E11
San Vito, Capo • Sicily, Italy 12 G10
San Vito lo Capo • Sicily, Italy 90 D1
San'a • Yemen 18 D6
San'a **Heritage C** • Yemen 63 [103]
Sanae [Base] • Antarctica 46 (1) E2
Sanaga • Cameroon 22 G4
Sanana • Indonesia 32 (1) C3
Sanana [I.] • Indonesia 32 (1) C3
Sanandaj • Iran 18 E2
Sanary-sur-Mer • France 85 H3
Sancai • Ethiopia 21 G5
Sanchi **Heritage C** • India 63 [122]
Sancti-Spíritus • Cuba 124 D3
Sancy, Puy de • France 10 H8
Sand • Hedmark, Norway 94 B2
Sand • Rogaland, Norway 94 C5
Sand Cay • Seychelles 106 F2
Sand Hills • NE, United States 40 F3
Sand in Taufers • Italy 90 B2
Sand Key • FL, United States 119 M5
Sandakan • Malaysia 32 F1
Sandane • Norway 94 C1
Sandanski • Bulgaria 14 K8
Sandare • Mali 20 C6
Sanday • United Kingdom 6 J2
Sandburg, Carl, Home Nat. Hist. Site **Park** • NC, United States 121 [244]
Sande • Norway 94 B3
Sandefjord • Norway 94 B3
Sandhamn • Sweden 95 D4
Sandhornøya • Norway 16 G3
Sandikli • Turkey 15 L5
Sandlings • United Kingdom 5 E2
Sandnes • Norway 94 C5
Sandnessjøen • Norway 16 G3
Sandoa • Dem. Rep. of Congo 23 C5
Sandomierz • Poland 13 K7
Sandoná • Colombia 43 B3
Sandover • NT, Australia 112 H2
Sandown • United Kingdom 7 K11
Sandown **Beach** • United Kingdom 75 [92]
Sandown Park • United Kingdom 74 E1
Sandras Dagi • Turkey 15 J6
Sandringham • United Kingdom 7 M9
Sandur • India 106 D2
Sandvig-Allinge • Denmark 95 F16
Sandviken • Sweden 16 I6
Sandwich • United Kingdom 71 A7
Sandy Bay • Jamaica 124 C1
Sandy Bay • St Kitts & Nevis 125 G1
Sandy Cape • QL, Australia 111 F4
Sandy Hook • NJ, United States 118 H1
Sandy Lake • OT, Canada 38 M6
Sandy Point Town • St Kitts & Nevis 125 G1
Sandycove • Ireland 79 E2
Sandzak • F.R. of Yugoslavia 14 G6
Sånfjället Nat. Park **Park** • Sweden 72 [23]
Sanford • ME, United States 118 G3
Sanford • FL, United States 119 M6
Sanford, Mt • AK, United States 38 B4
Sanganer • India 105 C6
Sangar • Russian Fed. 27 K4
Sangareddy • India 106 D3
Sangatte Terminal • France 78 C4
Sangay, Parque Nac. **Heritage N** • Ecuador 60 [29]
Sangay, Volcán • Ecuador 43 B4
Sangerhausen • Germany 8 G5
Sanggau • Indonesia 32 E2
Sangha • Africa 22 H4
Sangihe • Indonesia 32 (1) C2
Sangihe, Kepulauan • Indonesia 32 (1) C2
Sangiran **Heritage C** • Java, Indonesia 63 [179]
Sangiran • Java, Indonesia 110 D7
Sangju • Rep. of Korea 30 D6
Sangli • India 106 D2
Sango • Zimbabwe 102 J4
Sangre Grande • Trinidad & Tobago 125 K4
Sangro • Italy 12 I7
Sangster, Sir Donald [Apt] • Jamaica 124 C1
Sanguem • Goa, India 105 B2
Sangüesa • Spain 10 D11
Sanguinaires, Is. • Corsica, France 85 L3
Saní • Greece 92 D1
Sanibel I. • FL, United States 119 M5
Sanjo • Japan 30 J6
Sankasia • India 105 C3
Sankt-Peterburg **Heritage C** • Russian Fed. 64 [205]
Sankuru • Dem. Rep. of Congo 23 C4
Sanli Urfa • Turkey 18 C2
Sanlúcar de Barrameda • Spain 86 B5
Sanluri • Sardinia, Italy 12 C9
Sanmenxia • China 29 E4
Sanming • China 29 F5
Sannar • Sudan 21 F5
Sannikova, Proliv • Russian Fed. 27 N2
Sanok • Poland 13 L8
Sans-Souci **Heritage C** • Haiti 62 [37]
Sansepolcro • Italy 12 G5
Sanski Most • Bosnia-Herz. 14 D5
Sanssouci, Schloß • Germany 81 F3
Sant' Agata di Militello • Sicily, Italy 12 I10
Sant Agustí • Majorca, Spain 87 H3
Sant' Andria Priu, Necropoli di • Sardinia, Italy 90 C2
Sant' Angelo dei Lombardi • Italy 91 G2
Sant' Angelo in Fórmis • Italy 91 G1
Sant Antoni de Portmany • Ibiza, Spain 87 G1
Sant Carles de la Ràpita **Beach** • Spain 68 [121]
Sant Carles de Peralta • Ibiza, Spain 87 G2
Sant Celoni • Spain 11 N3
Sant Climent • Minorca, Spain 87 F4
Sant Feliu de Guíxols **Beach** • Spain 68 [123]
Sant Feliu de Guíxols • Spain 87 D2
Sant Fransesc de Formentera • Formentera, Spain 87 G4
Sant Jaume Mediterrani • Minorca, Spain 87 F4
Sant Joan de Labritja **Beach** • Ibiza, Spain 68 [125]
Sant Joan de Labritja • Ibiza, Spain 87 G2
Sant Jordi, Golf de • Spain 11 L4
Sant Josép **Beach** • Ibiza, Spain 68 [125]
Sant Josép • Ibiza, Spain 87 G1
Sant Llorenç des Cardassar **Beach** • Majorca, Spain 68 [126]
Sant Llorenç des Cardassar • Majorca, Spain 87 H2
Sant Lluís • Minorca, Spain 87 F4
Sant Miquel de Balansat • Ibiza, Spain 87 G2
Sant Pere de Rodes • Spain 87 D2
Sant Pere Pescador • Spain 87 D2
Sant Rafael de Forca • Ibiza, Spain 87 G1
Sant Salvador, Santuari de • Majorca, Spain 87 H4
Sant Telm • Majorca, Spain 87 H1
Sant Tomàs • Minorca, Spain 87 F3
Santa Ana • El Salvador 37 D5
Santa Ana • Bolivia 44 C2
Santa Ana **Heritage C** • Argentina 62 [64]
Santa Ana • CA, United States 117 F6
Santa Barbara • CA, United States 117 F5
Santa Barbara I. • CA, United States 117 F5
Santa Catalina I. • CA, United States 117 F6
Santa Catarina • Brazil 44 G4
Santa Catarina [Adm] • Brazil 44 F4
Santa Caterina di Pittinuri • Sardinia, Italy 90 C1
Santa Clara • CA, United States 117 F3
Santa Clara • Cuba 124 D2
Santa Clara, Barragem de • Portugal 88 E2
Santa Clara Peak • NM, United States 118 J2
Santa Clara-a-Velha • Portugal 88 E2
Santa Comba • Spain 11 C1
Santa Cristina **Ski** • Italy 70 [231]
Santa Cristina Valgardena • Italy 90 B1
Santa Croce, Lago di • Italy 90 B4
Santa Cruz • Philippines 31 G4
Santa Cruz • Galapagos Is. 43 (1) A2
Santa Cruz • Brazil 43 H4
Santa Cruz • Bolivia 44 D2
Santa Cruz • Argentina 45 B6
Santa Cruz **Beach** • Madeira 68 [108]
Santa Cruz • Madeira 88 C2
Santa Cruz • CA, United States 117 F3
Santa Cruz Beach Boardwalk **Park** • CA, United States 120 [C]
Santa Cruz da Graciosa • Azores 88 B2
Santa Cruz das Flores • Azores 88 B1
Santa Cruz de La Palma • La Palma, Canary Is. 87 E5
Santa Cruz de Tenerife • Tenerife, Canary Is. 86 E1
Santa Cruz del Sur • Cuba 124 D7
Santa Cruz do Sul • Brazil 44 F4
Santa Cruz I. • CA, United States 117 F5
Santa Cruz Is. • Solomon Is. 33 H7
Santa Cruz Mtns • Jamaica 124 C3
Santa Elena • Ecuador 43 A4
Santa Elena, Cabo • Costa Rica 37 D5
Santa Eufémia, Faro di • Italy 91 F4
Santa Eufémia, Golfo di • Italy 12 J10
Santa Eugenia • Spain 11 C2
Santa Eulalia del Rio **Beach** • Ibiza, Spain 68 [125]
Santa Eulalia del Rio • Ibiza, Spain 87 G2
Santa Fé • Argentina 44 D5
Santa Fe **Ski** • NM, United States 116 [106]
Santa Fe • NM, United States 118 J2
Santa Fé • Cuba 124 D1
Santa Helena • Brazil 45 (1) C2
Santa Inês • Brazil 45 (1) C2
Santa Inés, I. • Chile 45 B6
Santa Isabel • Solomon Is. 35 (1) F2
Santa Isabel • Argentina 44 C6
Santa Lucía • Argentina 44 C5
Santa Lucía, Playa • Cuba 124 D3
Santa Luzia • Cape Verde 22 (1) B1
Santa Margalida **Beach** • Majorca, Spain 68 [126]
Santa Margalida • Majorca, Spain 87 H2
Santa Margarita, I. • Mexico 123 E3
Santa Margherita di Pula • Sardinia, Italy 90 C4
Santa Margherita Ligure • Italy 91 E6
Santa Maria • Vanuatu 35 (2) B1
Santa Maria • CA, United States 40 B5
Santa Maria • Galapagos Is. 43 (1) A2
Santa Maria • Chile 44 B6
Santa Maria • Brazil 44 F4
Santa Maria **Beach** • Azores 68 [106]
Santa Maria • Greece 71 A19
Santa Maria • Azores 88 B2
Santa Maria • Mexico 123 E2
Santa Maria, Cabo • Uruguay 44 F5
Santa Maria, Cabo de • Portugal 88 E7
Santa Maria Cápua Vetere • Italy 91 G1
Santa Maria di Leuca, Capo • Italy 12 M9
Santa Maria Mayor **Heritage C** • Argentina 62 [64]
Santa Marinella • Italy 91 F1
Santa Marta • Colombia 43 C1
Santa Marta, Cabo de • Angola 24 A2
Santa Marta, Ria de • Spain 11 D1
Santa Monica Mtns Nat. Recreation Area **Park** • CA, United States 120 [57]
Santa Pola **Beach** • Spain 68 [118]
Santa Pola • Spain 87 C1
Santa Ponça • Majorca, Spain 87 H3
Santa Rosa • Argentina 44 D6
Santa Rosa • Brazil 44 F4
Santa Rosa • CA, United States 117 F3
Santa Rosa I. • CA, United States 117 F5
Santa Rosa I. • FL, United States 119 M1
Santa Rosalia • Mexico 40 D6
Santa Severina • Italy 71 A19
Santa Teresa • NT, Australia 112 H4
Santa Teresa Aboriginal Land • NT, Australia 112 H2
Santa Teresa di Gallura **Beach** • Sardinia, Italy 68 [137]
Santa Teresa di Gallura • Sardinia, Italy 90 C2
Santa Vitória do Palmar • Brazil 44 F5
Santa's Village • OT, Canada 122 B5
Santan • Indonesia 32 F3
Santana • Madeira 88 C2
Santana da Serra • Portugal 88 E2
Santana do Livramento • Brazil 44 E5
Santander • Spain 11 H1
Santander • Colombia 43 B3
Santander **Beach** • Spain 68 [89]
Santander, Bahía de • Spain 11 H1
Santanyí **Beach** • Majorca, Spain 68 [126]
Santanyí • Majorca, Spain 87 H4
Santarém • Portugal 11 C5
Santarém • Brazil 43 G4
Santarém [Adm] • Portugal 88 A2
Santes Creus, Monestir de • Spain 87 D3
Santiago • Panama 37 E6
Santiago • Dominican Rep. 37 G4
Santiago • Bolivia 44 E2
Santiago • Brazil 44 F4
Santiago • Mexico 123 E1
Santiago de Compostela • Spain 11 C2
Santiago de Compostela **Heritage C** • Spain 64 [83]
Santiago de Cuba **Heritage C** • Cuba 62 [36]
Santiago de Cuba • Cuba 124 D8
Santiago de la Ribera • Spain 87 C3
Santiago del Estero • Argentina 44 D4
Santiago do Cacém • Portugal 11 C6
Santiago Ixcuintla • Mexico 37 (1) A1
Santiago Tuxtla • Mexico 123 E4
Santissima Trinità di Saccargia • Sardinia, Italy 90 C1
Santo André • Brazil 45 (1) B6
Santo André • Brazil 127 C3
Santo Angelo • Brazil 44 F4
Santo Antão • Cape Verde 22 (1) A1
Santo Antônio de Jesus • Brazil 44 I1
Santo Antônio de Pádua • Brazil 127 C2
Santo Antônio do Içá • Brazil 43 D4
Santo da Serra • Madeira 88 C2
Santo Domingo • Dominican Rep. 37 H4
Santo Domingo **Heritage C** • Dominican Rep. 62 [38]
Santo Domingo • Cuba 124 D2
Santo Domingo de los Colorados • Ecuador 43 B4
Santo Estevão • Portugal 88 D2
Santoña **Beach** • Spain 68 [89]
Santorini • Greece 92 D8
Santos • Brazil 127 C3
Santos Dumont • Brazil 127 C1
Santpoort • Netherlands 80 C1
Santurce-Antiguo • Spain 11 H1
Sanur • Bali, Indonesia 110 C4
Sanur Beach • Bali, Indonesia 110 C4
Sanxenxo **Beach** • Spain 68 [93]
Sanya • China 31 D3
Sanzao • Zhuhai, China 107 H3
Sanzao Dao • Zhuhai, China 107 H3
São Bartolomeu de Messines • Portugal 88 E2
São Borja • Brazil 44 E4
São Brás de Alportel • Portugal 88 E2
São Caetano do Sul • Brazil 44 G3
São Carlos • Brazil 44 G3
São Felix do Xingu • Brazil 43 G5
São Francisco • Brazil 44 G4
São Francisco do Sul • Brazil 44 G4
São Francisco [Riv] • Brazil 45 (1) C4
São Gabriel • Brazil 44 F5
São Gabriel da Cachoeira • Brazil 43 D4
São Gonçalo • Brazil 44 H3
São Gotardo • Brazil 127 C1
São João da Barra • Brazil 127 C4
São João da Madeira • Portugal 11 C4
São João del Rei • Brazil 127 C1
São Joaquim • Brazil 44 G4
São Jorge • Azores 88 B2
São Jorge • Madeira 88 C2
São Jorge I. • Goa, India 105 B2
São José do Rio Pardo • Brazil 44 G3
São José do Rio Prêto • Brazil 44 G3
São José dos Campos • Brazil 127 C3
São Leopoldo • Brazil 44 F4
São Lorenço do Sul • Brazil 44 F5
São Lourenço • Brazil 127 C3
São Luís • Brazil 45 (1) C2
São Luís **Heritage C** • Brazil 62 [59]
São Luís Gonzaga • Brazil 44 F4
São Manuel • Brazil 43 F5
São Marcos, Baía de • Brazil 45 (1) C2
São Marcos da Serra • Portugal 88 E2
São Mateus • Brazil 45 (1) C5
São Miguel **Heritage C** • Brazil 62 [64]
São Miguel • Azores 88 B1
São Nicolau • Cape Verde 22 (1) B1
São Paulo • Brazil 127 A1
São Paulo • Brazil 127 C3
São Paulo [Adm] • Brazil 44 G3
São Paulo de Olivença • Brazil 43 D4
São Pedro • Brazil 127 A1
São Raimundo Nonato • Brazil 45 (1) C3
São Roque, Cabo de • Brazil 45 (1) D3
São Sebastião do Paraiso • Brazil 44 G3
São Sebastião, I. de • Brazil 127 C3
São Teotónio • Portugal 88 E1
São Tiago • Cape Verde 22 (1) B1
São Tomé • Sao Tomé e Príncipe 22 F4
São Tomé, Cabo de • Brazil 127 C4
São Tomé e Príncipe • Africa 22 F4
São Tomé [I.] • Sao Tomé e Príncipe 22 F4
São Vicente • Cape Verde 22 (1) A1
São Vicente • Brazil 44 G3
São Vicente • Madeira 88 C1
São Vicente, Cabo de • Portugal 88 E5
Saolat, Buku • Indonesia 32 (1) C2
Saon Beach • Phuket, Thailand 109 K1
Saône • France 10 K6
Saonek • Indonesia 32 (1) D3
Saoura • Algeria 20 E3
Sapan Bay • Phuket, Thailand 109 K1
Sapanca • Turkey 15 L3
Sapele • Nigeria 22 F3
Sápes • Greece 15 G2
Saphane Dagi • Turkey 15 K4
Sapi & Chewore Safari Areas • Zimbabwe 102 J2
Sapi safari area **Heritage N** • Zimbabwe 61 [96]
Sapiéndza • Greece 15 C7
Sapo Nat. Park **Park** • Liberia 103 [18]
Saposoa • Peru 43 B5
Sappada • Italy 90 B2
Sapporo • Japan 30 K3
Sapri • Italy 12 J8
Sapudi • Indonesia 110 D4
Saqqara • Egypt 101 F1
Saquarema • Brazil 127 C4
Sar Planina • Europe 14 H7
Saraburi • Thailand 109 H2
Saragossa • Spain 71 A12
Sarai • Russian Fed. 98 B1
Sarajevo • Bosnia-Herz. 14 F6
Saramati • India/Myanmar 28 F3
Saran, Gunung • Indonesia 32 E3
Saranci • Bulgaria 15 E1
Sarandë • Albania 15 A4
Sarandí del Yí • Uruguay 127 D2
Sarangani • Philippines 31 H5
Saranley • Somalia 23 G3
Saransk • Russian Fed. 17 G4
Sarapul • Russian Fed. 17 I3
Sarasin Bridge • Phuket, Thailand 109 K1
Sarasota • FL, United States 119 M5
Saratoga Nat. Hist. Park **Park** • NY, United States 121 [319]
Saratov • Russian Fed. 17 H4
Saravan • Laos 31 D3
Sarawak • Malaysia 32 E2
Saray • Turkey 15 I2
Sarayköy • Turkey 15 J6
Sárbogárd • Hungary 13 H11
Sardarshahar • India 105 C2
Sardegna • Italy 90 C
Sardes • Turkey 92 D6
Sardinda Plain • Kenya 101 G2
Sardinia • Italy 90 C
Sarek Nat. Park **Park** • Sweden 72 [19]
Sarektjåkkå • Sweden 16 I3
Sargasso Sea • Atlantic Ocean 42 E2
Sarh • Chad 21 C6
Sarhro, Jebel • Morocco 20 D2
Sari • Iran 18 F2
Sari d'Orcino • Corsica, France 85 L3
Sária • Greece 92 D11
Sarigan • Northern Mariana Is. 33 F4
Sarigerne • Turkey 92 D9
Sarigöl • Turkey 15 J5
Sarina • QL, Australia 111 F3
Sariñena • Spain 11 K3
Sarir Kalanshiyu • Libya 21 D2
Sarir Tibasti • Libya 21 C3
Sariska Nat. Park • India 105 C2
Sariwon • D.P.R. of Korea 30 C5
Sariyer • Turkey 15 J2
Sark • Channel Is. 7 J12
Sarkad • Hungary 13 K11
Sarkand • Kazakhstan 26 M8
Sarkikaraagaç • Turkey 15 M5
Sarlat-la-Canéda • France 85 G2
Sarmi • Indonesia 32 (1) E3
Sarmiento • Argentina 45 C5
Särna • Sweden 16 G6
Sarnath • India 105 C8
Sarnen • Switzerland 89 G3
Sarnia • OT, Canada 39 O8
Sarny • Ukraine 17 D4
Saroma-Ko • Japan 30 L2
Saronic Gulf • Greece 92 D7
Saronikós Kólpos • Greece 92 D7
Saronno • Italy 12 D3
Saros Körfezi • Turkey 15 H3
Sárospatak • Hungary 13 K9
Sarot • St Lucia 125 J1
Sarova • Russian Fed. 17 G3
Sarpsborg • Norway 94 B4
Sarralbe • France 5 J5
Sarre • France 10 M5
Sarrebourg • France 10 L5
Sarreguemines • France 10 M4
Sarria • Spain 11 D2
Sarrión • Spain 11 K4
Sarstedt • Germany 8 E4
Sartène • Corsica, France 85 L3
Sarthe [Adm] • France 84 D2
Sarthe [Riv] • France 10 F5
Sárti **Beach** • Greece 69 [192]
Sárti • Greece 92 D1
Sárvár • Hungary 13 F10
Sárviz • Hungary 14 F3
Sarych, mys • Ukraine 17 E6
Sarykamysh • Turkmenistan 26 I9
Sarysu • Kazakhstan 26 K8
Sarzana • Italy 91 E10
Sasaram • India 105 C8
Sasbachwalden **Spa** • Germany 83 [184]
Sasebo • Japan 30 E8
Saskatchewan • Canada 38 K6
Saskatchewan [Riv] • MN/SA, Canada 38 K6
Saskatoon • SA, Canada 38 J6
Saskylakh • Russian Fed. 27 H2
Sasovo • Russian Fed. 17 G4
Sassandra • Côte d'Ivoire 22 C3
Sassandra [Riv] • Côte d'Ivoire 22 C4
Sassari • Sardinia, Italy 90 C1
Sassenberg • Germany 8 D5
Saßnitz • Germany 8 I2
Sasso Marconi • Italy 12 F4
Sassuolo • Italy 12 E4
Sata-Misaki • Japan 30 F9
Satan, Pointe de • Vanuatu 35 (2) B2
Satara • India 28 B5
Sater • Sweden 16 H6
Satipo • Peru 43 C6
Satna • India 28 D4
Satna • India 105 C7
Satolas [Apt] • France 85 F1
Sátoraljaújhely • Hungary 13 K9
Satpayev • Kazakhstan 26 K8
Satsunan-Shoto • Japan 31 H1
Sattahip • Thailand 109 H4
Satu Mare • Romania 14 J2
Saturn • Romania 97 D2
Saualpe • Austria 14 B3
Sauce • Argentina 44 E5
Sauda • Norway 94 C5
Saudákrókur • Iceland 16 (1) D2
Saudi Arabia • Asia 18 E5
Sauer • Germany 9 B7
Sauerland • Germany 9 C5
Saugus Iron Works Nat. Hist. Site **Park** • MA, United States 121 [349]
Saül • French Guiana 43 G3
Sauland • Norway 94 B1
Saulgau • Germany 82 J1
Saulgau **Spa** • Germany 83 [214]
Sault Ste Marie • OT, Canada 39 O7
Saum, Laem • Phuket, Thailand 109 K1
Saumarez Reef • QL, Australia 111 F4
Saumlaki • Indonesia 32 (1) D4
Saumur • France 84 D1
Saumur [Château] • France 84 D1
Saundersfoot **Beach** • United Kingdom 75 [147]
Saurimo • Angola 23 C5
Sausalito • CA, United States 117 F3
Sauternes • France 84 B3
Sauvage, Côte • France 84 C4
Sauve, la • France 85 G3
Sauveterre • France 85 J1
Sàuze d'Oulx **Ski** • Italy 70 [195]
Sàuze d'Oulx • Italy 91 E5
Sava • Europe 14 E4
Savai'i • Western Samoa 35 (2) F1
Savalou • Benin 22 E3
Savanna-la-Mar • Jamaica 124 C1
Savannah • GA, United States 41 J5
Savannah [Riv] • GA/SC, United States 41 J5
Savannakhét • Laos 31 C3
Savant Lake • OT, Canada 39 M6
Savanur • India 106 D2
Savarsin • Romania 13 L11
Savastepe • Turkey 15 I4
Save • Benin 22 E3
Save • Mozambique 24 E4
Save • Sweden 95 F6
Saverdun • France 11 M1
Saverne • France 10 M5
Savinjske Alpe • Austria/Slovenia 14 B3
Savinski • Russian Fed. 17 G2
Savognin • Switzerland 89 G4
Savoie • France 85 F2
Savona • Italy 91 E6
Savonlinna • Finland 16 O6
Savoy • France 84 A2
Såvsjö • Sweden 95 F7
Sawai Madhopur • India 105 C6
Sawakin • Sudan 21 G4
Sawakin, Jaza'ir • Sudan 21 G4
Sawankhalok • Thailand 109 G4
Sawantwadi • India 106 D1
Sawda, Jabal as • Libya 21 B2
Sawknah • Libya 21 B2
Sawqirah • Oman 18 G6
Sawtooth Nat. Recreation Area • ID, United States 117 E4
Sawu • Indonesia 34 D2
Sawu Sea • Indonesia 32 (1) B4
Saxony • Germany 81 D2
Say • Niger 20 F6
Sayan • Russian Fed. 25 K4
Sayda • Lebanon 18 B3
Sayhut • Yemen 18 F6
Saynshand • Mongolia 29 E2
Sázava • Czech Rep. 96 C2
Sázava [Riv] • Czech Rep. 96 C2
Sbaa • Algeria 20 E3
Sbeitla • Tunisia 101 E3
Scafell Pike • United Kingdom 74 C1
Scalpay • United Kingdom 75 A1
Scandinavia • Europe 16
Scandola, Réserve Naturelle **Heritage N** • Corsica, France 61 [45]
Scandola, Réserve Naturelle • Corsica, France 85 L1
Scanzano Ionico • Italy 90 A2
Scapa Flow • United Kingdom 6 I3
Scarba • United Kingdom 75 A2
Scarborough • United Kingdom 7 L7
Scarborough **Beach** • United Kingdom 75 [23-24]
Scarborough • St Kitts & Nevis 125 G4
Scarborough • Trinidad & Tobago 125 K2
Scariff I. • Ireland 79 F7
Schaalsee • Germany 8 F3
Schaffhausen • Switzerland 9 D9
Schäftlarn • Germany 82 J3
Schalksmühle • Germany 81 E4
Scharbeutz • Germany 8 F2
Scharbeutz-Haffkrug **Spa** • Germany 83 [27]
Schärding • Austria 9 I8
Scharhörn • Germany 8 D3
Scharmützelsee • Germany 8 J4
Schauinsland • Germany 82 G8
Scheffau **Ski** • Austria 70 [152]
Schefferville • QU, Canada 39 R5
Scheidegg • Switzerland 89 G2
Scheidegg • Germany 82 J5
Scheidegg **Spa** • Germany 83 [239]
Schelde • Belgium 80 A14
Schenectady • NY, United States 41 L3
Schermbeck • Germany 81 E1
Scherpenheuvel-Zichem • Belgium 80 A15
Scheveningen • Netherlands 80 C3
Schiedam • Netherlands 80 C3
Schieder **Spa** • Germany 83 [98]
Schieland • Netherlands 80 C3
Schiermonnikoog • Netherlands 80 A4
Schiltach • Germany 82 G8
Schiltigheim • France 5 K6
Schiphol [Apt] • Netherlands 80 C2
Schladming **Ski** • Austria 70 [184]
Schladming • Austria 89 H4
Schlagenbad **Spa** • Germany 83 [141]
Schlarigna • Switzerland 89 G4
Schleiden • Germany 9 B6
Schlema **Spa** • Germany 83 [314]
Schleswig • Germany 8 E2
Schleswig-Holstein • Germany 8 E2
Schleswig-Holsteinisches Wattenmeer, Nationalpark **Park** • Germany 72 [57]
Schliersee • Germany 82 J7
Schluchsee • Germany 82 G8
Schluchsee **Spa** • Germany 83 [208]
Schlüchtern • Germany 9 E6
Schmallenberg • Germany 9 D5
Schneeberg • Germany 9 H6
Schneverdingen • Germany 5 M1
Schoberpaß • Austria 14 B2
Schokland **Heritage C** • Netherlands 64 [26]
Schokland • Netherlands 80 A7
Schömberg **Spa** • Germany 83 [178]
Schönau **Spa** • Germany 83 [262]
Schönau am Königssee • Germany 82 J8
Schönberg **Spa** • Germany 83 [18]
Schönburg • Germany 82 H4

Schönebeck • Germany 8 G4
Schönefeld [Apt] • Germany 81 F4
Schöneiche bei Berlin • Germany 81 F4
Schongau • Germany 82 J6
Schönhagen **Spa** • Germany 83 [12]
Schöningen • Germany 8 F4
Schönwald **Spa** • Germany 83 [197]
Schönwalde • Germany 81 F1
Schönwalde • Germany 81 F2
Schoonhoven • Netherlands 80 C4
Schopfheim • Germany 82 G8
Schortens • Germany 8 C3
Schotten • Germany 82 G2
Schouwen • Netherlands 80 A10
Schouwen-Duiveland **Beach** • Netherlands 68 [69]
Schramberg • Germany 9 D8
Schreiber • OT, Canada 39 N7
Schröken • Austria 89 H5
Schruns • Austria 89 H5
Schulenberg **Spa** • Germany 83 [79]
Schull • Ireland 79 F7
Schultz Lake • NU, Canada 38 L3
Schulzendorf • Germany 81 F4
Schuss Mtn **Ski** • MI, United States 116 [132]
Schwabach • Germany 9 G7
Schwaben • Germany 9 F8
Schwäbisch Gmünd • Germany 9 E8
Schwäbisch Hall • Germany 9 E7
Schwäbisch Hall **Spa** • Germany 83 [174]
Schwäbische Alb • Germany 9 E8
Schwäbish-Bayerisches Alpenvorland • Germany 82 J
Schwäbmünchen • Germany 82 J2
Schwalefeld **Spa** • Germany 83 [120]
Schwalmstadt • Germany 5 M4
Schwandorf • Germany 9 H7
Schwangau • Germany 82 J6
Schwangau **Spa** • Germany 83 [245]
Schwante • Germany 81 F1
Schwarzach • Germany 9 H7
Schwarze Elster • Germany 8 H5
Schwarzenberg • Austria 89 H1
Schwarzwald • Germany 82 G8
Schwarzwaldbahn • Germany 82 G8
Schwaz • Austria 9 G9
Schwedt an der Oder • Germany 8 J3
Schweinfurt • Germany 9 F6
Schweitzer Mtn **Ski** • ID, United States 116 [69]
Schwelm • Germany 81 E4
Schwerin • Germany 8 G3
Schweriner See • Germany 8 G3
Schwerte • Germany 5 K3
Schwerte • Germany 81 E2
Schwetzingen • Germany 82 G4
Schwielochsee • Germany 8 J4
Schwielowsee • Germany 81 F3
Schwyz • Switzerland 89 G3
Sciacca • Sicily, Italy 12 H11
Scicli • Sicily, Italy 12 I12
Scilly, Isles of • United Kingdom 7 F12
Scone Palace • United Kingdom 74 B2
Sconser • United Kingdom 78 A1
Scoresbysund • Greenland 36 O2
Scorpion I. • St Lucia 125 J4
Scotland • United Kingdom 6
Scotlandville • LA, United States 118 K4
Scott [Base] • Antarctica 46 (1) V2
Scott, Cape • NT, Australia 34 E2
Scott, Cape • BC, Canada 38 F6
Scott, Fort, Nat. Hist. Site **Park** • KS, United States 121 [172]
Scott I. • Antarctica 46 (1) X3
Scottish Lowlands • United Kingdom 74 B
Scotts Bluff Nat. Mon. **Park** • NE, United States 120 [165]
Scottsbluff • NE, United States 40 F3
Scottsdale • TS, Australia 34 I8
Scottsdale • AZ, United States 118 J3
Scrabster • United Kingdom 78 B3
Scranton • PA, United States 118 H1
Scunthorpe • United Kingdom 7 L8
Scuol • Switzerland 89 G4
Scutari • Turkey 92 D3
Scutari, Lake • Albania/F.R. of Yugoslavia 14 G7
Scythopolis • Israel 98 A4
Se Mesquida de Baix • Majorca, Spain 87 H2
Sea Is. • GA, United States 41 J5
Sea Life Park • HI, United States 119 L6
Sea Palling **Beach** • United Kingdom 75 [38]
Sea View Farm • Antigua & Barbuda 125 F1
Sea World • QL, Australia 111 F6
Sea World of California • CA, United States 117 F6
Sea World of California **Park** • CA, United States 120 [J]
Sea World of Florida • FL, United States 121 C2
Sea World of Ohio **Park** • OH, United States 121 [U]
Sea World of Texas • TX, United States 119 N5
Sea World of Texas **Park** • TX, United States 121 [O]
Seaford • United Kingdom 74 E3
Seaford **Beach** • United Kingdom 75 [73]
Seaford Town • Jamaica 124 C1
Seahouses **Beach** • United Kingdom 75 [10]
Seal, Cape • South Africa 100 C7
Seal River • MN, Canada 38 L5
Seapoint **Beach** • Ireland 68 [54]
Seapoint • Ireland 79 E2
Seascale • United Kingdom 74 C3
Seaside • OR, United States 117 E1
Seaside • FL, United States 119 M2
Seaton • United Kingdom 74 F3
Seaton Carew **Beach** • United Kingdom 75 [19]
Seatons • Antigua & Barbuda 125 F2
Seattle • WA, United States 117 E1
Seaward Kaikoura Range • New Zealand 35 D6
Seaworld • Shenzhen, China 107 H3
Seba • Indonesia 32 (1) B5
Sebarok • Singapore 108 E3
Sebastiansweiler **Spa** • Germany 83 [191]
Sebes • Romania 14 K4
Sebesi • Indonesia 110 D1
Sebis • Romania 14 J3
Sebkha de Tindouf • Algeria 20 D3
Sebou • Morocco 101 D2
Sebuca, El • Egypt 101 F5
Sebuku • Indonesia 110 D1
Sécchia • Italy 91 E7
Sechura, Bahía de • Peru 43 A5
Sechura, Desierto de • Peru 43 A5
Secretary I. • New Zealand 112 L1
Secunderabad • India 106 D3
Sécure • Bolivia 44 C2
Sedalia • MO, United States 41 H4
Sedan • France 10 J4
Sedano • Spain 10 B11
Seddenga • Sudan 21 F3
Seddülbahir • Turkey 15 H3
Sedona • AZ, United States 118 J1
Sedrun • Switzerland 89 G3
Sée • France 5 B6
Seefeld • Austria 89 H2
Seeheim • Namibia 24 B5
Seelig, Mt • Antarctica 46 (1) EE1
Seeon • Germany 82 J4
Sées • France 10 F5
Seesen • Germany 8 F5
Sefrou • Morocco 101 D2
Segesta • Sicily, Italy 90 D1
Segezha • Russian Fed. 17 E2
Ségou • Mali 22 C2
Segovia • Spain 11 G4
Segovia **Heritage C** • Spain 64 [86]
Segre, el • Spain 11 L3
Séguédine • Niger 20 H4
Séguéla • Côte d'Ivoire 22 C3
Seguin • TX, United States 119 N3
Segura • Spain 11 J6
Sehlabathebe Nat. Park **Park** • Lesotho 103 [130]
Seignosse **Beach** • France 68 [86]
Seiland • Norway 16 L1
Seille • France 5 J6
Seinäjoki • Finland 16 L5
Seine • France 10 G4
Seine, Baie de la • France 10 E4
Seine, Val de • France 85 E4
Seine-et-Marne • France 85 E4
Seixal • Madeira 88 C1
Seixal • Portugal 88 D2
Sejerø Bugt • Denmark 95 F10
Sejlflod **Beach** • Denmark 68 [48]
Sekincau, Gunung • Indonesia 32 C3
Sekinchan • Malaysia 108 D3
Sekondi-Takoradi • Ghana 22 D4
Selajar • Indonesia 32 (1) B4
Selangor • Malaysia 31 C6
Selaön • Sweden 95 D3
Selaru • Indonesia 32 (1) D4
Selatan, Selat • Penang, Malaysia 108 C4
Selatan, Tanjung • Indonesia 32 E3
Selb • Germany 9 H6
Selb • Germany 13 B7
Selby • United Kingdom 7 K8
Selçuk • Turkey 15 I6
Sele • Italy 91 G4
Sele, Piana del • Italy 91 G4
Selebi-Phikwe • Botswana 24 D4
Selecka Planina • F.Y.R. of Macedonia 15 C2
Selendi • Turkey 15 J5
Selendi [Riv] • Turkey 15 J5
Selenga • Mongolia/Russian Fed. 27 G7
Selenge • Dem. Rep. of Congo 23 B4
Selennyakh • Russian Fed. 27 N3
Selenter See • Germany 8 F2
Sélestat • France 9 C8
Seletar Reservoir • Singapore 108 E1
Seleucia • Iraq 98 B4
Selfoss • Iceland 16 (1) C3
Selga • Turkey 93 G2
Selibabi • Mauritania 20 C5
Seliger, Ozero • Russian Fed. 97 E3
Selimiye • Mugla, Turkey 15 I6
Selimye • Antalya, Turkey 93 G4
Selinunte • Sicily, Italy 90 D1
Selje • Norway 94 C1
Seljord • Norway 94 B3
Seljord stavkirke • Norway 94 B3
Seljordsvatnet • Norway 94 B3
Selkirk • United Kingdom 6 J6
Selkirk • MN, Canada 38 L6
Selkirk Mtns • BC, Canada 38 H7
Selkirkshire • United Kingdom 75 A3
Sella Nevea • Italy 91 E4
Sella, Passo di • Italy 90 B3
Sellafield • United Kingdom 74 C3
Selle • France 5 F5
Sellin **Spa** • Germany 83 [280]
Selma • AL, United States 41 I5
Selous Game Reserve **Heritage N** • Tanzania 61 [93]
Selous Game Reserve • Tanzania 102 H4
Selous Game Reserve **Park** • Tanzania 103 [95]
Selsey Bill • United Kingdom 5 C4
Sélune • France 5 C6
Selva di Cadore **Ski** • Italy 70 [226]
Selva di Cadore • Italy 90 B4
Selva di Val Gardena • Italy 90 B1
Selva Gardena **Ski** • Italy 70 [232]
Selvagens, Is. • Madeira 20 B2
Selvas • Brazil 42 D5
Selworthy • United Kingdom 74 F2
Selwyn Lake • NT/SA, Canada 38 K5
Selwyn Mtns • NT/YT, Canada 38 E4
Selwyn Range • QL, Australia 34 G4
Semakau • Singapore 108 E3
Semani • Albania 15 A3
Semarang • Java, Indonesia 110 D3
Sembé • Congo 22 G4
Semeru, Gunung • Java, Indonesia 110 D8
Semey • Kazakhstan 26 N7
Semitau • Indonesia 32 E2
Semmering • Austria 13 E10
Semnan • Iran 18 F2
Semnon • France 10 D6
Semois • Belgium/France 80 A19
Semporna • Malaysia 32 F2
Sempu • Indonesia 110 D8
Sena Madureira • Brazil 43 D5
Senaja • Malaysia 32 F1
Senang • Singapore 108 E3
Senanga • Zambia 24 C3
Sénart, Forêt de • France 85 E4
Sendai • Kyushu, Japan 30 F9
Sendai • Honshu, Japan 30 K5
Sendai-Wan • Japan 30 K5
Senden • Germany 82 J1
Seneca Lake • NY, United States 122 B10
Senegal • Africa 20 B6
Senegal [Riv] • Mauritania/Senegal 20 C5
Senftenberg • Germany 8 J5
Sengata • Indonesia 32 F2
Sengwa • Zimbabwe 24 D3
Senhor do Bonfim • Brazil 45 (1) C4
Senica • Slovak Rep. 13 G9
Senigállia **Beach** • Italy 69 [163]
Senigállia • Italy 91 E12
Senj • Croatia 14 B5
Senja • Norway 16 I2
Senkaku-Shoto • Japan 29 G5
Senlin • China 30 F3
Senlis • France 85 E2
Sennen Cove **Beach** • United Kingdom 75 [121]
Senneterre • QU, Canada 39 P7
Sens • France 10 I5
Senta • F.R. of Yugoslavia 14 H4
Sentosa • Singapore 108 E4
Senyavin • Fed. States of Micronesia 25 R9
Seoni • India 28 C4
Seoul • Rep. of Korea 30 D6
Seoul **Heritage C** • Rep. of Korea 63 [158]
Sepetiba, Baía de • Brazil 127 C3
Sepik • Papua New Guinea 35 (1) C1
Sepphoris • Israel 98 A4
Sept Laux, les **Ski** • France 70 [51]
Sept-Iles • QU, Canada 123 D2
Septemvri • Bulgaria 15 F1
Sepúlveda • Spain 11 H3
Sequoia Nat. Park • CA, United States 117 F4
Sequoia Nat. Park **Park** • CA, United States 120 [53]
Serafsa Han • Turkey 93 G4
Seraing • Belgium 5 I4
Seram • Indonesia 32 (1) C3
Seram, Laut • Indonesia 35 (1) A1
Serang • Java, Indonesia 110 D1
Serangan • Bali, Indonesia 110 C4
Serangoon New Town • Singapore 108 E2
Seraya • Singapore 108 E3
Serbia • F.R. of Yugoslavia 14 H6
Serdo • Ethiopia 23 G1
Sered' • Slovak Rep. 13 G9
Sereflikoçhisar • Turkey 15 O5
Serein • France 10 I6
Seremban • Malaysia 108 D4
Serengeti Nat. Park **Heritage N** • Tanzania 61 [90]
Serengeti Nat. Park • Tanzania 102 H2
Serengeti Nat. Park **Park** • Tanzania 103 [88]
Serengeti Plain • Tanzania 102 H1
Serengeti Safaripark **Park** • Germany 73 [55]
Séres • Greece 92 D1
Serfaus **Ski** • Austria 70 [135]
Serfaus • Austria 89 H6
Sergeya Kirova, Ostrova • Russian Fed. 26 P2
Sergino • Russian Fed. 46 I3
Sergipe • Brazil 44 I1
Sergiyev Posad **Heritage C** • Russian Fed. 64 [209]
Sergiyev Posad • Russian Fed. 97 E4
Serian • Malaysia 31 E6
Sérifos • Greece 92 D7
Serífou, Stenó • Greece 15 F6
Serik • Turkey 93 G4
Sermata, Kepulauan • Indonesia 32 (1) C4
Serón • Spain 11 I7
Serov • Russian Fed. 26 J6
Serowe • Botswana 24 D4
Serpa • Portugal 11 D7
Serpent's Mouth • Trinidad & Tobago 125 K3
Serpukhov • Russian Fed. 97 E4
Serra das Divisões • Brazil 44 F2
Serra do Caiapó • Brazil 44 F2
Serra do Navio • Brazil 43 G3
Serra Orrios, Villaggio nuragico di • Sardinia, Italy 90 C2
Serrant [Château] • France 84 D1
Serrat, Cap • Tunisia 12 D11
Serre • France 5 G5
Serre-Chevalier **Ski** • France 70 [60]
Serre-Chevalier • France 85 F4
Serres • France 10 K9
Serrinha • Brazil 44 I1
Serrinha • Brazil 44 I2
Serui • Indonesia 32 (1) E3
Servion • Switzerland 89 G1
Ses Animas, Mirador de • Majorca, Spain 87 H1
Ses Figueretes • Ibiza, Spain 87 G2
Ses Salines **Beach** • Majorca, Spain 68 [126]
Ses Salines • Majorca, Spain 87 H4
Sesayap • Indonesia 32 F2
Seseh Beach • Bali, Indonesia 110 C4
Sesheke • Zambia 24 C3
Sesibi • Sudan 21 F3
Sesimbra **Beach** • Portugal 68 [99]
Sesimbra • Portugal 88 D2
Sessa Aurunca • Italy 91 G1
Sestao • Spain 11 I1
Sesto **Ski** • Italy 70 [240]
Sesto • Italy 90 B2
Sesto Fiorentino • Italy 12 F5
Sestri Levante **Beach** • Italy 68 [142]
Sestri Levante • Italy 91 E6
Sestriere **Ski** • Italy 70 [194]
Sestriere • Italy 91 E5
Set, Laem • Ko Samui, Thailand 109 J2
Setana • Japan 30 J3
Sète • France 10 I10
Sète **Beach** • France 68 [130]
Sete Cidades, Caldeiras das • Azores 88 B1
Sete Lagoas • Brazil 127 C1
Sete Quedas, Saltos das • Brazil/Paraguay 44 F3
Setesdal • Norway 94 C6
Sétif • Algeria 20 G1
Seto • Japan 30 I7
Settat • Morocco 101 D1
Setúbal • Portugal 88 D2
Setúbal [Adm] • Portugal 88 A3
Setúbal, Baía de • Portugal 11 B6
Seu d'Urgell, la • Spain 87 D1
Seul, Lac • OT, Canada 38 M6
Sevan • Azerbaijan 18 E1
Sévaré • Mali 20 E6
Sevastopol • Ukraine 17 E6
Sevelen • Germany 81 E1
Seven Springs **Ski** • PA, United States 116 [160]
Sévérac-le-Château • France 10 I9
Severn • OT, Canada 39 N5
Severn • United Kingdom 74 D1
Severn Gorge • United Kingdom 74 D1
Severnaya Dvina • Russian Fed. 17 G2
Severnaya Zemlya • Russian Fed. 26 Q2
Severnoye • Russian Fed. 26 M6
Severnyy • Russian Fed. 26 J4
Severnyy Ural • Russian Fed. 26 I5
Severnyy Uvaly • Russian Fed. 17 G3
Severo Donets • Ukraine 4 R7
Severo-Sibirskaya Nizmennost • Russian Fed. 26 R3
Severobaikalsk • Russian Fed. 97 A5
Severodvinsk • Russian Fed. 17 F2
Severomorsk • Russian Fed. 17 E1
Severoural'sk • Russian Fed. 26 J5
Sevilla • Colombia 43 B3
Sevilla **Heritage C** • Spain 64 [92]
Sevilla • Spain 86 B1
Seville **Heritage C** • Spain 64 [92]
Seville • Spain 86 B1
Seville Nueva • Jamaica 124 C2
Sevlievo • Bulgaria 97 D3
Sèvre • France 10 E7
Sèvre Nantaise • France 84 D3
Sewa • Sierra Leone 22 B3
Sewall-Belmont House Nat. Hist. Site **Park** • DC, United States 121 [294]
Seward Peninsula • AK, United States 36 A3
Sexten **Ski** • Italy 70 [240]
Sexten • Italy 90 B2
Seyakha • Russian Fed. 26 L3
Seychelles • Indian Ocean 106 F
Seydisehir • Turkey 93 G2
Seydisfjördur • Iceland 16 (1) F2
Seyitgazi • Turkey 15 L4
Seyla' • Somalia 23 G1
Seymchan • Russian Fed. 27 P4
Seymour • VI, Australia 111 G3
Seyne-sur-Mer, la • France 10 K10
Sézanne • France 10 I5
Sfakiá • Crete, Greece 93 E5
Sfaktiría • Greece 15 C7
Sfax • Tunisia 101 E4
Sfinári • Crete, Greece 93 E1
Sfintu Gheorghe • Covasna, Romania 14 M4
Sfintu Gheorghe • Tulcea, Romania 97 D2
Sha Tin • Hong Kong, China 107 H6
Shaanxi • China 107 G3
Shaba • Dem. Rep. of Congo 23 C5
Shaba Game Reserve • Kenya 101 G2
Shabelle, Webi • Somalia 23 G3
Shabla • Bulgaria 97 D4
Shache • China 26 M10
Shackleton Ice Shelf • Antarctica 46 (1) O3
Shadrinsk • Russian Fed. 26 J6
Shaftesbury • United Kingdom 74 F3
Shah Alam • Malaysia 108 D4
Shahdol • India 28 D4
Shahganj • India 105 C8
Shahjahanpur • India 105 C3
Shahpura • India 105 C6
Shahrud • Iran 18 E2
Shakhrisabz • Uzbekistan 18 I2
Shakhty • Russian Fed. 17 G5
Shaki • Nigeria 22 E3
Shala, Lake • Ethiopia 21 G6
Shaldon **Beach** • United Kingdom 75 [99]
Shaler Mtn • NT, Canada 38 I2
Shallal, Ash • Egypt 21 F3
Shaluli Shan • China 29 B4
Sham, Jabal ash • Oman 18 F6
Shama, El • Somalia 23 G3
Shamiyah • Iraq/Syria 18 C3
Shammar, Jabal • Saudi Arabia 18 C4
Shamo, Lake • Ethiopia 23 F2
Shamva • Zimbabwe 102 J2
Shan • Myanmar 31 B2
Shanagarry **Beach** • Ireland 68 [59]
Shandi • Sudan 21 F4
Shandong • China 107 G4
Shandong Bandao • China 107 G4
Shandong Peninsula • China 107 G4
Shangani • Zimbabwe 102 J1
Shanghai • China 107 J2
Shanghai [Adm] • China 107 J4
Shanghang • China 31 F1
Shangqiu • China 29 F4
Shangrao • China 29 F5
Shangri-La • Minorca, Spain 87 F4
Shangyu • China 107 J4
Shangzhi • China 27 K8
Shanjuan Cave • China 107 J1
Shanklin • United Kingdom 5 B4
Shanklin **Beach** • United Kingdom 75 [93]
Shannon • Ireland 7 D9
Shannon [Apt] • Ireland 79 F6
Shannon, Mouth of the • Ireland 79 F5
Shantarskiye Ostrova • Russian Fed. 27 M5
Shantou • China 29 F6
Shanty Creek **Ski** • MI, United States 116 [132]
Shanxi • China 107 G3
Shanzu Becah • Kenya 101 G5
Shaoguan • China 29 E6
Shaowu • China 31 F1
Shaoxing • China 107 J4
Shaoyang • China 29 E5
Shap • United Kingdom 74 C2
Shap Abbey • United Kingdom 74 C2
Shap Fells • United Kingdom 74 C2
Shapinsay • United Kingdom 75 A7
Shaqra • Yemen 18 E7
Shaqra, Ash • Saudi Arabia 18 E4
Sharafah • Sudan 23 D1
Shari • Japan 30 M3
Shark Bay • WA, Australia 34 B5
Shark Bay **Heritage N** • WA, Australia 61 [127]
Sharkiyah, Al Istiwa'iyah al • Sudan 23 E2
Sharm el Sheikh • Egypt 101 F4
Sharon • Israel 98 A3
Sharp I. • Hong Kong, China 107 H6
Sharqiyah, Ash • Oman 18 G5
Shary • Saudi Arabia 18 D4
Sharya • Russian Fed. 17 H3
Shashe • Botswana/Zimbabwe 24 D4
Shashe • Botswana/Zimbabwe 102 J3
Shashi • China 29 E4
Shasta, Mt • CA, United States 117 F1
Shati, Wadi ash • Libya 21 B2
Shatoujiao • Shenzhen, China 107 H4
Shau Tau Kok • Hong Kong, China 107 H4
Shawnee Mtn **Ski** • PA, United States 116 [169]
Shawnigan • QU, Canada 122 B4
Shâyib el Banât • Egypt 21 F2
Shaykh 'Uthman • Yemen 18 E7
Shchel'yayur • Russian Fed. 17 I1
Shchuchinsk • Kazakhstan 26 L7
Shchuchyn • Belarus 13 N4
She Xian • China 107 J3
Shebele, Wabe • Ethiopia 23 G2
Sheberghan • Afghanistan 26 K10
Sheenjek • AK, United States 38 C3
Sheep's Head • Ireland 79 F7
Sheerness • United Kingdom 74 E2
Sheerness **Beach** • United Kingdom 75 [57-58]
Sheet Harbour • NS, Canada 123 D7
Sheffield • United Kingdom 7 K8
Shek Kwu Chau • Hong Kong, China 107 H5
Shek O • Hong Kong, China 107 H6
Shekhawati • India 105 C2
Sheki • Azerbaijan 17 H6
Shekou • Shenzhen, China 107 H3
Sheksna • Russian Fed. 97 E2
Shelagskiy, mys • Russian Fed. 27 T2
Shelburne • NS, Canada 123 D7
Shelby • MT, United States 40 D2
Shelikhova, Zaliv • Russian Fed. 27 Q5
Shelley Beach • Kenya 101 G5
Shellharbour • NS, Australia 111 G2
Shelling Hill **Beach** • Ireland 68 [53]
Shelter Point • New Zealand 35 B8
Shenandoah Nat. Park **Park** • VA, United States 121 [262]
Shengsi Liedao • China 107 J4
Shengxian • China 107 J4
Shenkursk • Russian Fed. 17 G2
Shenmu • China 29 E3
Shenton, Mt • WA, Australia 34 D5
Shenyang • China 29 G2
Shenzhen • China 107 H3
Shenzhen Special Economic Zone • China 107 H3
Shepparton • VI, Australia 111 G3
Sheppey, Isle of • United Kingdom 74 E2
Sherard, Cape • NU, Canada 39 P2
Sherborne • United Kingdom 74 F3
Sherbro I. • Sierra Leone 22 B3
Sherbrooke • QU, Canada 122 B8
Sherbrooke Village • NS, Canada 123 D7
Sherda • Chad 20 I4
Sherding Shan • China 29 I1
Shere Hill • Nigeria 22 F3
Sheremetyevo [Apt] • Russian Fed. 97 E4
Shergui • Tunisia 101 E4
Sheridan • WY, United States 40 E3
Sheringham • United Kingdom 5 E2
Sheringham **Beach** • United Kingdom 75 [35]
Sherkin I. • Ireland 79 F8
Sherman • TX, United States 119 N1
Sherwood Forest • United Kingdom 5 B1
Shetland • United Kingdom 75 A7
Shetland Is. • United Kingdom 6 K1
Sheung Shui • Hong Kong, China 107 H3
Sheung Wan • Hong Kong, China 107 H5
Sheyenne • ND, United States 38 L7
Shibam • Yemen 18 E6
Shibam **Heritage C** • Yemen 63 [104]
Shibetsu • Japan 30 L2
Shibetsu • Japan 30 M3
Shibukawa • Japan 30 J6
Shibushi-Wan • Japan 30 F9
Shiel, Loch • United Kingdom 6 G5
Shihezi • China 26 O9
Shihr, Ash • Yemen 18 F7
Shijiazhuang • China 29 E3
Shikarpur • Pakistan 28 A3
Shikoku • Japan 30 G8
Shikoku-Sanchi • Japan 30 G8
Shikotan, Ostrov • Russian Fed. 27 O8
Shikotan-To • Russian Fed. 27 O8
Shikotsu-Ko • Japan 30 K3
Shilega • Russian Fed. 17 G2
Shilka • Russian Fed. 27 I6
Shilka [Riv] • Russian Fed. 27 J6
Shilla • India 28 C2
Shillong • India 28 F3
Shiloh • Jordan 98 A6
Shiloh Nat. Military Park **Park** • TN, United States 121 [229]
Shilong • China 107 H2
Shimabara • Japan 30 F8
Shimanovsk • Russian Fed. 27 K6
Shimba Hills Game Reserve • Kenya 101 G5
Shimba Hills Nat. Reserve **Park** • Kenya 103 [86]
Shimizu • Japan 30 J7
Shimoda • Japan 30 J7
Shimoga • India 106 D6
Shimoni • Kenya 101 G5
Shimonoseki • Japan 30 F8
Shin, Loch • United Kingdom 6 H3
Shindand • Afghanistan 18 H3
Shing Mun Country Park • Hong Kong, China 107 H5
Shingu • Japan 30 H8
Shinjo • Japan 30 K5
Shinoússa • Greece 92 D8
Shintuya • Peru 127 B2
Shinyanga • Tanzania 102 H1
Shio-no-Misaki • Japan 30 H8
Shipka Pass • Bulgaria 97 D3
Shipki La • China/India 28 C2
Shiprock • NM, United States 40 E4
Shiqi • China 107 H1
Shiquan He • China 28 D2
Shiquanhe • China 28 C2
Shirakami-Sanchi **Heritage N** • Japan 61 [120]
Shirakawa • Japan 30 I6
Shirakawa-Go **Heritage C** • Japan 63 [168]
Shirane • Gumma/Tochigi, Japan 30 J6
Shirane • Yamanashi, Japan 30 J7
Shiraz • Iran 18 F4
Shiren • China 30 D4
Shiretoko-Misaki • Japan 30 M2
Shiriya-Zaki • Japan 30 K4
Shirley Heights • Antigua & Barbuda 125 F4
Shishaldin Volcano • AK, United States 46 FF4
Shitou Shan • China 27 K6
Shiucheng • China 31 C1
Shiveluch Sopka, Vulkan • Russian Fed. 27 R5
Shivpuri • India 105 C6
Shivpuri Nat. Park • India 105 C6
Shiwa Ngandu • Zambia 24 E2
Shiyan Lake Hot Springs Resort • China 107 H2
Shíza • Greece 15 C7
Shizuoka • Japan 30 J7
Shkodër • Albania 14 G7
Shoalhaven • NS, Australia 111 G2
Shobara • Japan 30 G7
Shoeburyness **Beach** • United Kingdom 75 [53-54]
Shoreham-by-Sea • United Kingdom 7 L11
Shortland • Solomon Is. 35 (1) F2
Shoshone Falls • ID, United States 117 E4
Shoshone Mtns • NV, United States 117 F4
Shreveport • LA, United States 118 K1
Shrewsbury • United Kingdom 74 D1
Shri Mahalsa Temple • Goa, India 105 B1
Shri Mallikarjun Temple • Goa, India 105 B2
Shri Mangesh Temple • Goa, India 105 B1
Shropshire • United Kingdom 74 D1
Shropshire Hills • United Kingdom 74 D1
Shuangyashan • China 29 I1
Shuguri Falls • Tanzania 24 F1
Shule • China 18 K2
Shule He • China 29 B2
Shumen • Bulgaria 97 D3
Shumerlya • Russian Fed. 17 H3
Shumshu, Ostrov • Russian Fed. 27 Q6
Shunayn, Sabkhat • Libya 21 D2
Shunde • China 107 H1
Shurayk, Ash • Sudan 18 B6
Shusf • Iran 18 G3
Shute Harbour • QL, Australia 111 F1
Shuwak • Sudan 21 G5
Shuya • Russian Fed. 17 G3
Shwebo • Myanmar 31 B2
Si Racha • Thailand 109 H4
Si Satchanalai • Thailand 109 G4
Si Satchanalai Nat. Park • Thailand 109 G4
Sia • Indonesia 32 (1) D4
Siak Kecil Reserve • Indonesia 110 B4
Sialkot • Pakistan 28 B2
Sian Ka'an, Reserva de la Biósfera **Heritage N** • Mexico 60 [19]
Siána • Rhodes, Greece 93 F3
Siargao • Philippines 31 H5
Siauliai • Lithuania 13 M2
Sibay • Russian Fed. 26 I7
Sibenik • Croatia 14 C6
Siberia • Russian Fed. 25 K3
Siberimanua • Indonesia 32 B3
Siberut, Pulau • Indonesia 32 B3
Sibi • Pakistan 28 A3
Sibigo • Indonesia 110 B1
Sibiloi Nat. Park **Heritage N** • Kenya 61 [88]
Sibiloi Nat. Park • Kenya 101 G1
Sibiloi Nat. Park **Park** • Kenya 103 [74]
Sibiryakovo, Ostrov • Russian Fed. 26 M3
Sibiti • Congo 22 G5
Sibiu • Romania 14 L4
Sibolga • Indonesia 110 B4
Siboney, Playa • Cuba 124 D8
Sibu • Malaysia 32 E2
Sibut • Central African Rep. 23 B2
Sibuyan • Philippines 31 G4
Sibuyan Sea • Philippines 31 G4
Sichang, Ko • Thailand 109 H4
Sichuan • China 107 G7
Sichuan Pendi • China 107 G7
Sicié, Cap • France 85 H3
Sicilia • Italy 90 D
Sicilia, Canale di • Mediterranean Sea 12 F11
Sicily • Italy 90 D
Sicuani • Peru 127 B2
Sidári **Beach** • Corfu, Greece 69 [170]
Sidari • Corfu, Greece 92 B1
Side • Turkey 93 G4
Sideby • Finland 95 E1
Siderno • Italy 12 K10
Síderos, Akra • Crete, Greece 93 E4
Sidi Aïssa • Algeria 11 O9
Sidi Ali • Algeria 11 L8
Sîdi Barrâni • Egypt 21 E1
Sidi Bel Abbés • Algeria 20 E1
Sidi Bennour • Morocco 20 D2
Sidi Bou Saïd • Tunisia 101 E2
Sidi Daoud • Tunisia 101 E2
Sidi Ifni • Morocco 101 D5
Sidi Kacem • Morocco 101 D1
Sidi Moussa • Morocco 101 D1
Sidlaw Hills • United Kingdom 74 B2
Sidmouth • United Kingdom 74 F5
Sidorovsk • Russian Fed. 27 B3
Sidra, Gulf of • Libya 21 C1
Siebengebirge • Germany 82 G1
Siedlce • Poland 13 L5
Sieg • Germany 9 C6
Siegburg • Germany 82 G1
Siegen • Germany 82 G2
Siegerwald • Germany 9 F7
Siemiatycze • Poland 13 L5
Siemréab • Cambodia 31 C4
Siena **Heritage C** • Italy 64 [122]
Siena • Italy 91 E11
Sienne • France 5 B6
Sieradz • Poland 13 H6
Sierksdorf **Spa** • Germany 83 [26]
Sierpc • Poland 13 I5
Sierra Blanca Peak • NM, United States 40 E5
Sierra Colorada • Argentina 45 C4
Sierra Leone • Africa 22 B3
Sierra Madre del Sur • Mexico 123 E4
Sierra Madre Occidental • Mexico 40 E6
Sierra Madre Oriental • Mexico 40 F7
Sierra Nevada • Colombia 43 C1
Sierra Nevada • Spain 86 B3
Sierra-at-Tahoe **Ski** • CA, United States 116 [58]
Sierre • Switzerland 89 G6
Siesta Key • FL, United States 119 M5
Sífnos • Greece 92 D7
Sig • Algeria 20 E1
Sigdal • Norway 94 B1
Sigean, Réserve africaine de • France 85 K2
Sighetu Marmatiei • Romania 14 K2
Sighisoara • Romania 14 L3
Sigiriya **Heritage C** • Sri Lanka 63 [135]
Sigiriya • Sri Lanka 106 D15
Sigli • Indonesia 28 G7
Sigmaringen • Germany 82 J1
Signy I. [Base] • Antarctica 46 (1) A3
Sígri • Greece 92 D5
Sigtuna • Sweden 95 D2
Siguanea • Cuba 124 D1
Siguenza • Spain 71 A17
Siguiri • Guinea 22 C2
Sihuas • Peru 43 B5
Siilinjärvi • Finland 16 N5
Siipyy • Finland 95 E1
Siirt • Turkey 18 D2
Sijunjung • Indonesia 110 B4
Sikakap • Indonesia 32 C3
Sikanni Chief • BC, Canada 38 G5
Sikar • India 105 C2
Sikasso • Mali 22 C2
Sikeston • MO, United States 41 I4
Sikhote-Alin • Russian Fed. 29 J1
Sikía • Pelopónnisos, Greece 15 D7
Sikía • Halkidikí, Greece 15 E3
Sikía **Beach** • Greece 69 [192]
Síkinos • Greece 92 D8
Sikkim • India 28 E3
Siktyakh • Russian Fed. 27 K3
Sila, As • United Arab Emirates 18 F5

Silalè • Lithuania **13** L2
Silba • Croatia **14** B5
Silchar • India **28** F4
Sile • Turkey **15** K2
Silecroft **Beach** • United Kingdom **75** [232]
Sileiro, Cabo • Spain **11** C2
Silencio, Costa del • Tenerife, Canary Is. **86** E1
Silesia • Poland **13** G7
Silet • Algeria **20** F4
Silhouette • Seychelles **106** F2
Siliana • Tunisia **12** D12
Siliguri • India **28** E3
Siling Co • China **28** E2
Silistra • Bulgaria **97** D1
Silivri • Turkey **15** J2
Siljan • Sweden **16** H6
Siljan • Norway **94** B3
Silk Road • Asia **98** B4
Silkeborg • Denmark **95** F9
Sillamäe • Estonia **16** N7
Sillé-le-Guillaume [Château] • France **84** D1
Sillil • Somalia **23** G1
Sillyon • Turkey **93** G2
Siloana Plains • Zambia **24** C3
Siloso, Fort • Singapore **108** E3
Sils • Switzerland **89** G8
Sils-Maria **Ski** • Switzerland **70** [119]
Siltou • Chad **21** C4
Siluatan, Gunung • Indonesia **110** B2
Siluté • Lithuania **13** K2
Silvaplana • Switzerland **89** G8
Silvaplana-Surlej **Ski** • Switzerland **70** [120]
Silver City • NM, United States **118** J4
Silver Lake Resort • Shenzhen, China **107** H3
Silver Mtn **Ski** • ID, United States **116** [70]
Silver Star **Ski** • BC, Canada **116** [5]
Silverwood • ID, United States **117** E2
Silves **Beach** • Portugal **68** [100]
Silves • Portugal **88** E6
Silvretta **Ski** • Austria **70** [134]
Silvretta • Austria **89** H5
Sim, Cap • Morocco **20** D2
Simanggang • Malayisia **32** E2
Simareh • Iran **18** E3
Simav • Turkey **15** J4
Simav Gölü • Turkey **15** J4
Simav [Riv] • Turkey **15** J4
Simbach • Germany **82** J4
Simbirsk • Russian Fed. **17** H4
Simbruini, Monti • Italy **91** F2
Simcoe, Lake • OT, Canada **122** B5
Simei New Town • Singapore **108** E2
Simen • Ethiopia **21** G5
Simeon • Israel **98** A8
Siméto • Sicily, Italy **90** D4
Simeuluë • Indonesia **110** B1
Simferopol • Ukraine **17** E5
Sími • Greece **15** I7
Sími [I.] • Greece **92** D9
Simien Nat. Park **Heritage N** • Ethiopia **61** [78]
Simien Nat. Park **Park** • Ethiopia **103** [62]
Simla • India **28** C2
Simlångsdalen • Sweden **95** F7
Simleu Silvaniei • Romania **14** J2
Simmer • Germany **82** H3
Simmerath • Germany **5** J4
Simmern • Germany **82** H3
Simon's Town • South Africa **100** C5
Simonstorp • Sweden **95** D3
Simplonpass • Switzerland **89** G6
Simpson Desert • Australia **34** G5
Simpson Desert Nat. Park • QL, Australia **34** G5
Simpson Gap Nat. Park • NT, Australia **112** H2
Simpson Hill • WA, Australia **34** E5
Simpson Peninsula • NU, Canada **39** N3
Simrishamn • Sweden **95** F11
Simssee • Germany **82** J4
Sin Cow • South China Sea **31** E5
Sinabang • Indonesia **110** B3
Sinai • Egypt **101** F2
Sinai, Mt • Egypt **101** F4
Sinaia • Romania **96** B2
Sinaloa • Mexico **40** E7
Sincelejo • Colombia **43** B2
Sindal • Denmark **95** F6
Sindangbarang • Java, Indonesia **110** D5
Sindelfingen • Germany **9** E8
Sindh • Pakistan **28** A3
Sindirgi • Turkey **15** J4
Sinekli • Turkey **15** J2
Sines • Portugal **11** C7
Sines, Cabo de • Portugal **11** C7
Sinéu • Majorca, Spain **87** H2
Singako • Chad **23** B2
Singapore • Asia **32** C2
Singapore • Asia **108** E
Singapore City • Singapore **108** E4
Singapore Crocadilarium • Singapore **108** E4
Singapore Science Centre • Singapore **108** E1
Singapore, Straits of • Asia **108** E4
Singapore Zoological Gardens • Singapore **108** E1
Singaraja • Bali, Indonesia **110** C2
Singen • Germany **9** D9
Singh Beach • Phuket, Thailand **109** K2
Singida • Tanzania **102** H1
Singkaling Hkamti • Myanmar **28** G3
Singkarak, Danau • Indonesia **110** B4
Singkawang • Indonesia **32** D2
Singkep • Indonesia **32** C3
Singkil • Indonesia **110** B3
Singleton • NS, Australia **111** G2
Singleton, Mt • WA, Australia **34** C5
Singö • Sweden **95** D2
Singö [I.] • Sweden **95** D2
Sinharaja Forest Reserve **Heritage N** • Sri Lanka **61** [112]
Sinharaja Forest Reserve • Sri Lanka **106** D15
Sinis • Sardinia, Italy **90** C3
Siniscola • Sardinia, Italy **12** D8
Siniscóla **Beach** • Sardinia, Italy **68** [138]
Sinj • Croatia **14** D6
Sinjah • Sudan **21** F5
Sinjajevina • F.R. of Yugoslavia **14** G6
Sinnicolau Mare • Romania **14** H3
Sinoe, Lacul • Romania **97** D2
Sinop • Turkey **17** F6
Sinop **Beach** • Turkey **69** [239]
Sinp'o • D.P.R. of Korea **30** E5
Sinquerim Beach • Goa, India **105** B1
Sinsheim • Germany **9** D7
Sintana • Romania **14** I3
Sintang • Indonesia **32** E2
Sintra **Beach** • Portugal **68** [98]
Sintra **Heritage C** • Portugal **64** [99]
Sintra • Portugal **88** D1
Sintra, Serra de • Portugal **88** D1
Sinuiju • D.P.R. of Korea **30** C4
Sinzig • Germany **82** H1
Siófok • Hungary **13** H11
Sion • Switzerland **89** G6
Siouville-Hague **Beach** • France **68** [78]
Sioux City • IA, United States **41** G3
Sioux City **Park** • Gran Canaria, Canary Is. **73** [79]
Sioux City • Gran Canaria, Canary Is. **86** E4
Sioux Falls • SD, United States **41** G3
Sioux Lookout • OT, Canada **39** M6
Sipalay • Philippines **31** G5
Sipan • Croatia **14** E7
Siparia • Trinidad & Tobago **125** K3
Sipcenski prohod • Bulgaria **97** D3
Siping • China **29** G2
Sipiwesk • MN, Canada **38** L5
Siple, Mt • Antarctica **46** (1) CC2
Siple Station [Base] • Antarctica **46** (1) GG2
Siponto • Italy **71** A19
Siquijor • Philippines **31** G5
Sir Edward Pellew Group • NT, Australia **34** G3
Sir Sam's **Ski** • OT, Canada **116** [16]
Sira • Norway **16** D7
Siracusa • Sicily, Italy **90** D4
Siraf • Iran **98** B4
Sirba • Burkina Faso/Niger **20** E6
Sire, Ko • Thailand **109** K2
Siret • Romania **14** N3
Siridao Beach • Goa, India **105** B1
Sirik • Iran **18** G4
Sirik, Tanjong • Malayisia **32** E2
Sirikit Reservoir • Thailand **109** G4
Sirino • Italy **12** J8
Sirmione • Italy **91** E7
Sírna • Greece **92** D8
Sirohi • India **105** C5
Sirolo **Beach** • Italy **69** [163]
Sirolo • Italy **91** E12
Síros • Greece **92** D7
Sirsa • India **18** K4
Sirsa • India **105** C2
Sisak • Croatia **14** D4
Sisimiut • Greenland **39** U3
Sisophon • Cambodia **31** C4
Sissano • Papua New Guinea **35** (1) C1
Sisteron • France **85** H1
Sistiana • Italy **91** E4
Sistranda • Norway **16** E5
Sitapur • India **105** C3
Sitges **Beach** • Spain **68** [122]
Sitges • Spain **87** D3
Sithonía • Greece **92** D1
Sitía **Beach** • Crete, Greece **69** [215]
Sitía • Crete, Greece **93** E8
Sitka • AK, United States **38** D5
Sitka Nat. Hist. Park **Park** • AK, United States **120** [14]
Sittard • Netherlands **80** A16
Situbondo • Java, Indonesia **110** D8
Sivas • Turkey **18** C2
Sivasli • Turkey **15** K5
Sivrice **Beach** • Turkey **69** [241]
Sivrihisar • Turkey **15** M4
Sivry-sur-Meuse • France **5** I5
Sîwa • Egypt **21** E2
Siwalik Range • India/Nepal **28** C3
Six Flags AstroWorld • TX, United States **119** N4
Six Flags AstroWorld **Park** • TX, United States **121** [P]
Six Flags Fiesta • TX, United States **119** N3
Six Flags Fiesta **Park** • TX, United States **121** [N]
Six Flags Great Adventure • NJ, United States **118** H1
Six Flags Great Adventure **Park** • NJ, United States **121** [KK]
Six Flags Great America **Park** • IL, United States **121** [S]
Six Flags Magic Mtn • CA, United States **117** F6
Six Flags Magic Mtn **Park** • CA, United States **120** [D]
Six Flags over Georgia **Park** • GA, United States **121** [Z]
Six Flags over Mid-America **Park** • MO, United States **121** [Q]
Six Flags over Texas • TX, United States **119** N1
Six Flags over Texas **Park** • TX, United States **121** [L]
Six Flags WaterWorld • TX, United States **119** N4
Six Flags WaterWorld **Park** • TX, United States **121** [P]
Six Flags Wild Safari Animal Park • NJ, United States **118** H1
Six Men's Bay • Barbados **125** H1
Sixt **Ski** • France **70** [17]
Sizergh Castle • United Kingdom **74** C4
Sizewell **Beach** • United Kingdom **75** [47]
Sjælland • Denmark **95** F10
Sjenica • F.R. of Yugoslavia **14** H6
Sjöbo • Sweden **95** F11
Skadarsko jezero • F.R. of Yugoslavia **14** G7
Skadarsko jezero Nat. Park **Park** • Fed. Rep. of Yugoslavia **72** [121]
Skadovsk • Ukraine **17** E5
Skælskør **Beach** • Denmark **68** [43]
Skælsør • Denmark **95** F14
Skærbæk **Beach** • Denmark **68** [52]
Skærbæk • Denmark **95** F9
Skaftafell Nat. Park **Park** • Iceland **72** [2]
Skäfthammar • Sweden **95** D2
Skagen **Beach** • Denmark **68** [48]
Skagen • Denmark **95** F6
Skagern • Sweden **95** F3
Skaggerak • Europe **95** F5
Skagway • AK, United States **58** A2
Skála **Beach** • Greece **69** [171]
Skála • Greece **92** C2
Skälderviken • Sweden **95** F11
Skalistyy Golets, gora • Russian Fed. **27** I5
Skalitsty Golec • Russian Fed. **46** B4
Skanderborg • Denmark **95** F9
Skándzoura • Greece **92** D4
Skåne • Sweden **95** F11
Skaneateles Lake • NY, United States **122** B10
Skanès [Apt] • Tunisia **101** E4
Skånevik • Norway **94** C5
Skänninge • Sweden **95** F4
Skanör • Sweden **95** F15
Skara • Sweden **95** F3
Skaraborg • Sweden **95** F3
Skaralid • Sweden **95** F11
Skardu • Jammu & Kashmir **28** C1
Skärholmen **Beach** • Sweden **69** [21]
Skarnes • Norway **94** B2
Skarzysko-Kamienna • Poland **13** J6
Skawina • Poland **13** I8
Skeena • BC, Canada **38** F6
Skeena Mtns • BC, Canada **38** F5
Skegness • United Kingdom **7** M8
Skegness **Beach** • United Kingdom **75** [30]
Skei • Norway **94** C2
Skeleton Coast • Namibia **24** A3
Skellefteå • Sweden **16** K4
Skellefteälven • Sweden **16** J4
Skellig Michael **Heritage C** • Ireland **64** [11]
Skellig Michael • Ireland **79** F7
Skëndërbout • Albania **15** A2
Skerries • Ireland **79** E2
Skhirat-Plage • Morocco **101** D1
Ski • Norway **94** B2
Ski Acres **Ski** • WA, United States **116** [44]
Ski Apache **Ski** • NM, United States **116** [107]
Ski Beech Mtn **Ski** • NC, United States **116** [151]
Ski Dagmar **Ski** • OT, Canada **116** [24]
Ski le Chantecler **Ski** • QU, Canada **116** [30]
Ski Liberty **Ski** • PA, United States **116** [161]
Ski Morin Heights **Ski** • QU, Canada **116** [31]
Ski Roundtop **Ski** • PA, United States **116** [163]
Ski Snow Valley **Ski** • OT, Canada **116** [18]
Ski Sundown **Ski** • CT, United States **116** [187]
Ski Windham **Ski** • NY, United States **116** [182]
Skíathos **Beach** • Greece **69** [188]
Skíathos • Greece **92** D4
Skibbereen **Beach** • Ireland **68** [59]
Skibbereen • Ireland **79** F8
Skibotn • Norway **16** K2
Skidda • Algeria **20** G1
Skiddaw • United Kingdom **74** C2
Skiddaw Forest • United Kingdom **74** C2
Skien • Norway **94** B3
Skierniewice • Poland **13** J6
Skiftet Kihti • Finland **95** E3
Skilingaryd • Sweden **95** F7
Skinári, Akra • Greece **92** C3
Skinnskatteberg • Sweden **95** D1
Skipton • United Kingdom **7** J8
Skíros • Greece **15** F5
Skíros [I.] • Greece **92** D4
Skíti **Beach** • Greece **69** [189]
Skive • Denmark **95** F9
Skjærhalden • Norway **94** B4
Skjálfandafljöt • Iceland **16** (1) E2
Skjálfandi • Iceland **16** (1) E1
Skjeberg • Norway **94** B4
Skjern • Denmark **95** F9
Skjolden • Norway **94** C2
Sklad • Russian Fed. **27** J2
Sklavopoúla • Crete, Greece **93** E5
Skocjan Caves **Heritage N** • Slovenia **61** [51]
Skole • Ukraine **14** K1
Skópelos **Beach** • Greece **69** [188]
Skópelos **Beach** • Lesbos, Greece **69** [199]
Skópelos • Greece **92** D4
Skopje • F.Y.R. of Macedonia **14** I8
Skorba • Malta **93** H3
Skørping • Denmark **95** F5
Skotfoss • Norway **94** B3
Skotína **Beach** • Greece **69** [190]
Skotselv • Norway **94** B1
Skotterud • Norway **94** B2
Skoura • Morocco **20** D2
Skövde • Sweden **95** F3
Skovorodino • Russian Fed. **27** J6
Skowhegan • ME, United States **118** G4
Skrimfjella • Norway **94** B3
Skrinkle **Beach** • United Kingdom **75** [152]
Skudeneshavn • Norway **94** C5
Skuleskogen Nat. Park **Park** • Sweden **72** [21]
Sky Harbor [Apt] • AZ, United States **118** J3
Sky Lake • FL, United States **121** C2
Skye • United Kingdom **6** F4
Slagelse **Beach** • Denmark **68** [43]
Slagelse • Denmark **95** F14
Slamet, Gunung • Java, Indonesia **110** D6
Slane • Ireland **79** E1
Slaney • Ireland **7** F9
Slano • Croatia **14** E7
Slantsy • Russian Fed. **16** O7
Slany • Czech Rep. **13** D7
Slask • Poland **13** G7
Slatina • Romania **14** L5
Slave Coast • Africa **22** E3
Slave Lake • AL, Canada **122** C2
Slave Lake, Lesser • AL, Canada **122** C2
Slavgorod • Russian Fed. **26** M7
Slavjanka • Bulgaria/Greece **15** E2
Slavonice • Czech Rep. **96** C4
Slavonija • Croatia **12** L3
Slavonski Brod • Croatia **14** F4
Slavskovsky Les • Czech Rep. **96** C1
Slavyansk • Ukraine **17** F5
Slawno • Poland **13** F3
Sleat, Sound of • United Kingdom **6** G4
Sleeper Is. • NU, Canada **39** P5
Sleeping Bear Dunes Nat. Lakeshore **Park** • MI, United States **121** [163]
Slemmestad • Norway **94** B2
Slidell • LA, United States **118** K4
Slidre • Norway **94** C4
Sliedrecht • Netherlands **80** C4
Sliema • Malta **93** H4
Slieve Aughty Mtns • Ireland **79** F4
Slieve Mish Mtns • Ireland **79** F5
Slievefelim Mtns • Ireland **7** D9
Sligo • Ireland **79** F2
Sligo [Adm] • Ireland **79** F2
Sligo Bay • Ireland **79** F2
Slimbridge • United Kingdom **74** D3
Sliven • Bulgaria **97** D3
Slobozia • Moldova **14** Q3
Slobozia • Ialomita, Romania **97** D1
Slobozia • Pitesti, Romania **97** D1
Slough • United Kingdom **7** L10
Slovak karst **Heritage N** • Slovak Rep. **61** [50]
Slovak Republic • Europe **13** H9
Slovenia • Europe **12** I2
Slovensko • Slovak Rep. **13** J9
Slowinski Nat. Park **Park** • Poland **72** [90]
Slunchev Bryag • Bulgaria **97** D3
Slunj • Croatia **14** C4
Slupsk • Poland **13** F3
Slutsk • Belarus **17** D4
Sluys • North Sea **71** A7
Slyne Head • Ireland **79** F3
Småland • Sweden **95** F8
Smålandsfarvandet • Denmark **95** F14
Smålandsstenar • Sweden **95** F7
Smallwood Reservoir • NF, Canada **39** S6
Smederevo • F.R. of Yugoslavia **14** H5
Smedjebacken • Sweden **16** H6
Smeralda, Costa • Sardinia, Italy **90** C2
Smeraldo, Grotta di • Italy **91** G4
Smir-Restinga • Morocco **101** D2
Smith Arm • NT, Canada **38** G3
Smith, Cape • QU, Canada **39** P4
Smith, Fort, Nat. Hist. Site **Park** • AR, United States **121** [192]
Smith I. • MD, United States **118** H3
Smiths Falls • OT, Canada **39** P7
Smithton • TS, Australia **34** I8
Smögen • Sweden **95** F2
Smoky • AL, Canada **38** H6
Smøla • Norway **16** D5
Smolensk • Russian Fed. **17** E4
Smólikas • Greece **15** B3
Smolyan • Bulgaria **14** L8
Smorgon • Belarus **16** N9
Smugglers' Notch **Ski** • VT, United States **116** [204]
Smyadovo • Bulgaria **97** D3
Smyrna • Turkey **92** D5
Smyrna • DE, United States **118** H3
Snake • YT, Canada **38** E4
Snake • United States **40** C3
Snake River Plain • ID, United States **117** E4
Snake Temple, Penang • Penang, Malaysia **108** C3
Snasavatnet • Norway **16** G4
Sneek • Netherlands **80** A3
Sneem • Ireland **79** F7
Snettisham **Beach** • United Kingdom **75** [31]
Snezka • Czech Rep./Poland **96** C2
Snina • Slovak Rep. **13** L9
Snøhetta • Norway **94** C2
Snoqualmie **Ski** • WA, United States **116** [44]
Snow Lake • MN, Canada **38** K6
Snow Summit **Ski** • CA, United States **116** [65]
Snow Trails **Ski** • OH, United States **116** [147]
Snowbasin **Ski** • UT, United States **116** [78]
Snowbird **Ski** • UT, United States **116** [83]
Snowdon • United Kingdom **7** H8
Snowdonia • United Kingdom **7** H8
Snowdonia Nat. Park **Park** • United Kingdom **72** [47]
Snowmass **Ski** • CO, United States **116** [98]
Snowshill Manor • United Kingdom **74** D4
Snowshoe **Ski** • WV, United States **116** [154]
Snowy Mtns • NS/VI, Australia **111** G4
Snowy [Riv] • NS/VI, Australia **111** G4
Snug Corner • Bahamas **124** B4
Snuol • Cambodia **108** B1
Snyder • TX, United States **40** F5
So, Laem • Ko Samui, Thailand **109** J2
Soar • United Kingdom **5** B2
Soave • Italy **91** E7
Soba • Nigeria **20** G6
Sobaek-Sanmaek • Rep. of Korea **30** D7
Sobat • Ethiopia/Sudan **23** E2
Sobotka • Czech Rep. **96** C2
Sobradinho, Reprêsa • Brazil **45** (1) C4
Sobral • Brazil **45** (1) C2
Soc Trang • Vietnam **108** B3
Sochaczew • Poland **13** J5
Sochi • Russian Fed. **17** E6
Society Is. • French Polynesia **33** L7
Socompa, Paso • Argentina/Chile **44** C3
Socorro • Colombia **43** C2
Socorro • NM, United States **118** J4
Socorro, I. • Mexico **123** E7
Socotra • Yemen **18** F7
Sodankylä • Finland **16** N3
Söderåsen • Sweden **95** F11
Söderfors • Sweden **16** I6
Söderhamn • Sweden **16** I6
Söderköping • Sweden **95** F4
Södermanland • Sweden **95** D3
Södertalje **Beach** • Sweden **69** [20]
Södertälje • Sweden **95** D4
Södertörn • Sweden **95** D4
Sodo • Ethiopia **23** F2
Södra Kvarken • Finland/Sweden **16** J6
Soekarno-Hatta [Apt] • Java, Indonesia **110** D1
Soest • Germany **8** D5
Soest • Germany **71** A8
Soest • Netherlands **80** C2
Soeste • Germany **8** C3
Sœurs, les • Seychelles **106** F4
Sofala • NS, Australia **111** G2
Sofala, Baia de • Mozambique **24** E4
Sofia • Bulgaria **14** K7
Sofia • Madagascar **24** H3
Sofiya • Bulgaria **14** K7
Sofiysk • Russian Fed. **27** L6
Sofporog • Russian Fed. **17** E1
Sofrino • Russian Fed. **97** E4
Sogamosa • Colombia **43** C2
Soganli • Turkey **15** N2
Sogda • Russian Fed. **27** L6
Sogeri • Papua New Guinea **35** (1) D2
Sogn og Fjordane • Norway **94** C1
Sogndal • Norway **94** C4
Sognefjorden • Norway **94** C3
Sogod • Philippines **31** G4
Sögüt Gölü • Turkey **15** K6
Sohâg • Egypt **101** F4
Sohano • Papua New Guinea **35** (1) E2
Sohna • India **105** C2
Sohuksan • Rep. of Korea **30** C7
Soignies • Belgium **5** H4
Soissons • France **85** E2
Sojoson-man • D.P.R. of Korea **30** C5
Soka Beach • Bali, Indonesia **110** C3
Sokal • Ukraine **13** N7
Söke • Turkey **92** D9
Sokele • Dem. Rep. of Congo **23** C5
Sokkuram Grotto **Heritage C** • Rep. of Korea **63** [162]
Sokna • Norway **94** B1
Soko Is. • Hong Kong, China **107** H5
Sokodé • Togo **22** E3
Sokol • Russian Fed. **97** E2
Sokólka • Poland **13** M4
Sokolo • Mali **22** C2
Sokolov • Czech Rep. **96** C1
Sokolów Podlaski • Poland **13** L5
Sokosti • Finland **17** D1
Sokoto • Nigeria **22** F2
Sokoto [Adm] • Nigeria **22** F2
Sokoto [Riv] • Nigeria **22** F2
Sol, Costa del • Spain **86** B
Sol, Costa do • Portugal **88** D1
Sol y Nieve • Spain **86** B3
Sol-Iletsk • Russian Fed. **26** I7
Sola • Vanuatu **35** (2) B1
Sola • Venezuela **43** E1
Sola [Apt] • Norway **94** C5
Solapur • India **28** C5
Solda • Italy **91** E3
Sölden **Ski** • Austria **70** [137]
Sölden • Austria **89** H6
Soldier Point • Antigua & Barbuda **125** F4
Soledade • Brazil **44** F4
Solent, The • United Kingdom **7** K11
Solenzara • Corsica, France **85** L4
Solignac • France **85** G2
Solihull • United Kingdom **7** K9
Solikamsk • Russian Fed. **26** I6
Solimões • Brazil **43** E4
Solingen • Germany **81** E4
Solitude **Ski** • UT, United States **116** [82]
Solivella • Spain **11** M3
Söll **Ski** • Austria **70** [151]
Söll • Austria **89** H3
Sollefteå • Sweden **16** I5
Sollentuna • Sweden **95** D4
Sóller • Majorca, Spain **87** H1
Solna • Sweden **95** D4
Solo • Java, Indonesia **110** D7
Solo [Riv] • Java, Indonesia **110** D7
Solok • Indonesia **110** B4
Sololá • Guatemala **37** C5
Sololvin • Ukraine **14** L1
Solomon Is. • Pacific Ocean **33** H6
Solomon Sea • Papua New Guinea/Solomon Is. **35** (1) E2
Solor, Kepulauan • Indonesia **32** (1) B4
Solothurn • Switzerland **89** G2
Solovetskiye Ostrova **Heritage C** • Russian Fed. **63** [76]
Solovyevsk • Russian Fed. **27** I7
Solsvik • Norway **94** C3
Solta • Croatia **14** D6
Soltau • Germany **8** E4
Soltau **Spa** • Germany **83** [60]
Solund • Norway **94** C3
Solvang • CA, United States **117** F5
Sølvegruvene • Norway **94** B1
Sölvesborg **Beach** • Sweden **69** [15]
Sölvesborg • Sweden **95** F11
Solway Firth • United Kingdom **7** I7
Solwezi • Zambia **24** D2
Som, Ko • Thailand **109** J1
Soma • Turkey **15** I4
Soma • Japan **30** K6
Somali Peninsula • Somalia **100** A2
Somalia • Africa **23** H2
Sombo • Angola **24** C1
Sombor • F.R. of Yugoslavia **14** G4
Sombrerete • Mexico **37** (1) B1
Somerset • Australia **32** (1) F4
Somerset • KY, United States **41** J4
Somerset • United Kingdom **74** F3
Somerset East • South Africa **100** C4
Somerset I. • NU, Canada **38** M2
Somerset West • South Africa **100** C5
Somerton • United Kingdom **74** F3
Somes • Romania **14** K2
Somme • France **10** H4
Sommen • Sweden **95** F4
Sömmerda • Germany **9** G5
Somnathpur • India **106** D6
Son • Norway **94** B4
Son • India **105** C8
Son Bou de Baix • Minorca, Spain **87** F4
Son Bou, Platja de • Minorca, Spain **87** F3
Son Moll • Majorca, Spain **87** H2
Son Parc • Minorca, Spain **87** F2
Son Sant Joan [Apt] • Majorca, Spain **87** H1
Son Servera **Beach** • Majorca, Spain **68** [126]
Sonagiri • India **105** C7
Sonch'on • D.P.R. of Korea **30** C5
Sønderborg **Beach** • Denmark **68** [45]
Sonderborg • Denmark **95** F13
Sønderjylland • Denmark **95** F13
Sondershausen • Germany **9** F5
Søndervig • Denmark **95** F9
Søndre Strømfjord • Greenland **39** V3
Sondrio • Italy **91** E2
Song Shan • China **107** G3
Songea • Tanzania **102** H4
Songhua Hu • China **29** H2
Songhua Jiang • China **29** G1
Songjiang • China **107** J4
Songkhla • Thailand **31** C5
Songnim • D.P.R. of Korea **30** C5
Songo • Mozambique **24** E3
Songo Mnara **Heritage C** • Tanzania **63** [99]
Songo Mnara • Tanzania **102** H4
Sonid Youqi • China **29** E2
Sonipat • India **105** C2
Sonneberg • Germany **9** G6
Sonoma • CA, United States **117** F3
Sonora • Mexico **40** D5
Sonora • CA, United States **117** F3
Sonoran Desert • AZ, United States **118** J3
Sonsbeck • Germany **81** E1
Sonsorol Is. • Palau **32** (1) D2
Sonthofen • Germany **82** J6
Sooneck, Burg • Germany **82** H4
Soontornpoo Mon. • Thailand **109** H4
Sopelana **Beach** • Spain **68** [88]
Sopi, Tanjung • Indonesia **32** (1) C2
Sopocani Monastery **Heritage C** • F.R. of Yugoslavia **64** [160]
Sopot • Poland **13** H3
Sopot • Bulgaria **15** F1
Sopron • Hungary **13** F10
Sopur • Jammu & Kashmir **28** B2
Sør-Trøndelag • Norway **16** F5
Sora • Italy **91** F4
Sorak • Rep. of Korea **30** E5
Sorbas • Spain **11** I7
Sorel • QU, Canada **39** Q7
Sörenberg **Ski** • Switzerland **70** [102]
Sörenberg • Switzerland **89** G2
Sorfjorden • Norway **94** C4
Soria • Spain **11** I3
Sorø **Beach** • Denmark **68** [43]
Sorø • Denmark **95** F14
Soroa • Cuba **124** D1
Soroca • Moldova **14** P1
Sorocaba • Brazil **44** G3
Sorong • Indonesia **32** (1) D3
Soroni • Rhodes, Greece **93** F2
Soroti • Uganda **23** E3
Sørøya • Norway **16** L1
Sorraia • Portugal **11** C6
Sørreisa • Norway **16** J2
Sorrento • Italy **91** G3
Sorsele • Sweden **16** I4
Sorsogon • Philippines **31** G4
Sortland • Norway **16** H2
Sosan • Rep. of Korea **30** D6
Sösdala • Sweden **95** F11
Sosnogorsk • Russian Fed. **17** I2
Sosnovka • Ukraine **13** N7
Sosnowiec • Poland **13** I7
Sosva • Khanty-Mansi, Russian Fed. **26** J5
Sosva • Yekaterinburg, Russian Fed. **26** J6
Sotavento de Jandía, Playa de • Fuerteventura, Canary Is. **87** E2
Sotavento, Is. de • West Indies **43** D1
Sotkamo • Finland **16** O4
Sotra • Norway **94** C3
Sottern • Sweden **95** F4
Sotteville-les-Rouen • France **5** E5
Souahel, Boukhalef [Apt] • Morocco **101** D1
Souanké • Congo **22** G4
Soúda • Crete, Greece **93** E1
Soúda, Ormos • Crete, Greece **93** E2
Souflí • Greece **92** D2
Soufrière • St Lucia **125** J3
Soufrière Bay • St Lucia **125** J3
Soúgia • Crete, Greece **93** E5
Souillac • France **85** G2
Souilly • France **5** I5
Souk Ahras • Algeria **20** G1
Souk el Arba du Rharb • Morocco **101** D1
Soul • Rep. of Korea **30** D6
Soulac-sur-Mer **Beach** • France **68** [85]
Soulac-sur-Mer • France **85** G1
Soúnio, Akra • Greece **92** D7
Soúnion Nat. Park **Park** • Greece **72** [141]
Soûr **Heritage C** • Lebanon **64** [246]
Sour el Ghozlane • Algeria **20** F1
Soure • Brazil **43** H4
Souris • Canada/United States **38** K7
Souris • PE, Canada **123** D7
Sous • Morocco **20** D2
Sous le Vent, Is. • French Polynesia **33** L7
Sousa • Brazil **45** (1) D3
Sousse **Heritage C** • Tunisia **64** [229]
Sousse • Tunisia **101** E2
Souterraine, la • France **84** D4
South Africa • Africa **24** C6
South America cruise area • S. America **58** A3
South Andaman • India **28** F6
South Aulatsivik I. • NU, Canada **39** S5
South Australia • Australia **34** F5
South Beach • Bahamas **124** B3
South Bend • IN, United States **41** I3
South Carolina • United States **41** J5
South China Sea • Asia **31** E3
South Dakota • United States **40** F3
South Downs • United Kingdom **74** E3
South East Cape • TS, Australia **34** I8
South East Point • VI, Australia **111** G3
South Friar's Bay • St Kitts & Nevis **125** G2
South Geomagnetic Pole • Antarctica **46** (1) Q2
South Georgia • Atlantic Ocean **42** G10
South I. • New Zealand **35** B6
South I. Nat. Park • Kenya **101** G1
South Kitui Game Reserve • Kenya **101** G4
South Luangwa Nat. Park **Park** • Zambia **103** [104]
South Magnetic Pole • Antarctica **46** (1) T3
South Moll I. • QL, Australia **111** F1
South Nahanni • NT, Canada **38** F4
South Negril Point • Jamaica **124** C1
South Orkney Is. • Antarctica **46** (1) A3
South Pacific cruise area • Pacific Ocean **58** A1
South Pacific cruise area • Pacific Ocean **59** A9
South Pass • WY, United States **40** E3
South Point • Barbados **125** H4
South Pole • Antarctica **59** A10
South Ronaldsay • United Kingdom **6** J3
South Sandwich Is. • Antarctica **46** (1) C4
South Saskatchewan • SA, Canada **38** J6
South Shields • United Kingdom **7** K7
South Turkana Game Reserve • Kenya **101** G1
South Uist • United Kingdom **6** E4
Southampton • United Kingdom **7** K11
Southampton, Cape • NU, Canada **39** O4
Southampton I. • NU, Canada **39** O4
Southend • SA, Canada **38** K5
Southend-on-Sea • United Kingdom **74** E2
Southend-on-Sea **Beach** • United Kingdom **75** [55]
Southern Alps • New Zealand **35** C6
Southern Cross • WA, Australia **34** C6
Southern Indian Lake • MN, Canada **38** L5
Southern Uplands • United Kingdom **6** I6
Southland • New Zealand **112** L
Southport • QL, Australia **111** F6
Southwest Cape • New Zealand **35** A8
Southwold • United Kingdom **5** E2
Southwold **Beach** • United Kingdom **75** [45-46]
Soutpansberg • South Africa **24** D4
Sovetsk • Russian Fed. **13** K2
Sovetskiy • Russian Fed. **26** J5
Soya-Misaki • Japan **30** K2
Soyo • Angola **23** A5
Sozopol **Beach** • Bulgaria **69** [242]
Sozopol • Bulgaria **97** D3
Spa • Belgium **80** A16
Spa-Francorchamps • Belgium **80** A16
Spaandem • Netherlands **80** C1
Spain • Europe **11**
Spalato • Croatia **71** A14
Spalding • United Kingdom **7** L9
Spánda, Akra • Crete, Greece **93** E1
Spanish Town • Jamaica **124** C4

Spanish Wells • Bahamas 124 B1
Spargi • Sardinia, Italy 12 D7
Sparks • NV, United States 117 F1
Sparreholm • Sweden 95 D3
Sparta • Greece 15 D6
Spartel, Cap • Morocco 101 D1
Spárti • Greece 15 D6
Spartilas **Beach** • Corfu, Greece 69 [170]
Spartivento, Capo • Calábria, Italy 12 K11
Spartivento, Capo • Sardinia, Italy 90 C4
Spassk-Dalniy • Russian Fed. 27 L8
Speichersee • Germany 82 J3
Speightstown • Barbados 125 H1
Spello • Italy 91 E12
Spence Bay • NU, Canada 36 H3
Spencer, Cape • SA, Australia 34 G7
Spencer Gulf • SA, Australia 34 G6
Spenser Mtns • New Zealand 35 D6
Sperillen • Norway 94 B1
Sperlonga **Beach** • Italy 68 [147]
Sperlonga • Italy 91 F4
Sperone, Capo • Sardinia 12 C10
Sperrin Mtns • United Kingdom 7 F7
Spessart • Germany 9 E7
Spetsai • Greece 92 D7
Spétses • Greece 92 D7
Spétses [I.] • Greece 15 E6
Spey • United Kingdom 6 I4
Speyer **Heritage C** • Germany 64 [43]
Speyer • Germany 82 G4
Speyside • Trinidad & Tobago 125 K2
Sphinx • Egypt 101 F1
Spice Is. • Indonesia 110 A
Spiddal **Beach** • Ireland 68 [62]
Spiddal • Ireland 79 F4
Spiekeroog • Germany 8 C3
Spiekeroog **Spa** • Germany 83 [41]
Spiez • Switzerland 89 G2
Spijkenisse • Netherlands 80 C3
Spili • Crete, Greece 93 E6
Spilion Kamarón • Crete, Greece 93 E6
Spinalónga, Herson • Crete, Greece 93 E8
Spingdale • NF, Canada 123 D3
Spirit Mtn **Ski** • MN, United States 116 [110]
Spisská-Nová Ves • Slovak Rep. 13 J9
Spisské Pohradie **Heritage C** • Slovak Rep. 64 [151]
Spithead • United Kingdom 5 B4
Spitsbergen • Arctic Ocean 4 M1
Spitsbergen • Arctic Ocean 46 N2
Spittal • Austria 89 H8
Spitzingsee • Germany 82 J7
Spjelkavik • Norway 94 C2
Splendid China • Shenzhen, China 107 H3
Splendid China • FL, United States 121 C1
Split • Croatia 14 D6
Split **Heritage C** • Croatia 64 [157]
Split Lake • MN, Canada 38 L5
Splügen • Switzerland 89 G3
Spodsbjerg • Denmark 95 F14
Spokane • WA, United States 117 E2
Spoleto • Italy 91 F1
Spongeorama • FL, United States 119 M5
Spontin • Belgium 80 A15
Sporades, N • Greece 92 D4
Sportgastein • Austria 89 H8
Spotorno • Italy 91 E6
Spøttrup **Beach** • Denmark 68 [49]
Spratly Is. • South China Sea 31 E5
Spree • Germany 8 I4
Spreepark Berlin • Germany 81 F4
Spremberg • Germany 8 J5
Sprengisandur • Iceland 16 [1] D2
Spring Hill • FL, United States 119 M5
Springbok • South Africa 24 B5
Springdale • AR, United States 41 H4
Springe • Germany 8 E4
Springfield • New Zealand 35 C6
Springfield • MO, United States 41 H4
Springfield • IL, United States 41 I4
Springfield • OH, United States 41 J4
Springfield • OR, United States 117 E3
Springfield • MA, United States 118 H2
Springfield Armory Nat. Hist. Site **Park** • MA, United States 121 [340]
Springhill • NS, Canada 123 D7
Springs • South Africa 24 D5
Springvale **Beach** • United Kingdom 75 [90]
Sprockhövel • Germany 81 E2
Spruce Knob • WV, United States 41 K4
Spui • Netherlands 80 C3
Spurn Head • United Kingdom 7 M8
Squamish • BC, Canada 38 G7
Squaw Creek **Ski** • CA, United States 116 [57]
Squaw Valley **Ski** • CA, United States 116 [57]
Squillace • Italy 12 K10
Squillace, Golfo di • Italy 12 K10
Sravanabelgola • India 106 D6
Sravasti • India 105 C4
Srbija • F.R. of Yugoslavia 14 H6
Srebarna • Bulgaria 97 D1
Srebarna Nature Reserve **Heritage N** • Bulgaria 61 [57]
Srebrenica • Bosnia-Herz. 14 G5
Sredinny Khrebet • Russian Fed. 27 Q5
Sredna Gora • Bulgaria 15 F1
Srednesibirskoye Ploskogorye • Russian Fed. 26 Q4
Sredni Verecki • Ukraine 14 K1
Sredniy Ural • Russian Fed. 26 I6
Srednrusskaya Vozvyshennost • Russian Fed. 17 E4
Srednyaya Olëkma • Russian Fed. 27 J5
Srem • Poland 13 G5
Sremska Mitrovica • F.R. of Yugoslavia 14 G5
Sretensk • Russian Fed. 27 I6
Sri Lanka • Asia 106 D15
Srikakulam • India 28 D5
Srikalahasti • India 106 D7
Srinagar • Jammu & Kashmir 28 B2
Srirangam • India 106 D11
Srirangapatnam • India 106 D6
Srisailam • India 106 D3
Sroda Wielkopolska • Poland 13 G5
Staaten River Nat. Park • QL, Australia 34 H3
Stabbursdalen Nat. Park **Park** • Norway 72 [4]
Stade • Germany 8 E3
Stade de France, Paris • France 85 E1
Stadskanaal • Netherlands 5 J1
Stadtallendorf • Germany 9 E6
Stadthagen • Germany 8 E4
Staffelsee • Germany 82 J7
Staffelstein • Germany 9 F6
Staffelstein **Spa** • Germany 83 [224]
Stafford • United Kingdom 7 J9
Staffordshire • United Kingdom 75 A4
Stagnone, I. della • Italy 90 D1
Stahnsdorf • Germany 81 F3
Staigue Fort • Ireland 79 F7
Stalheim • Norway 94 C4
Stalin, Mt • BC, Canada 38 G5
Stalingrad • Russian Fed. 4 T7
Stalowa Wola • Poland 13 L7
Stamford • United Kingdom 7 L9
Stamford • CT, United States 118 H2
Stamford Bridge • United Kingdom 71 A7
Stamnes • Norway 94 C3
Stampalia • Greece 92 D8
Stamsund • Norway 16 G2
Standerton • South Africa 24 D5
Standley Chasm • NT, Australia 112 H2
Stanley • TS, Australia 34 I8
Stanley • Falkland Is. 45 E6
Stanley • Hong Kong, China 107 H6
Stanley Falls • Dem. Rep. of Congo 23 D3
Stanley, Mt • Uganda 23 E3
Stanorvoye Nagorye • Russian Fed. 27 H5
Stanovoy Khrebet • Russian Fed. 27 J6
Stansted [Apt] • United Kingdom 74 E1
Stanthorpe • QL, Australia 34 J5
Stanwix, Fort, Nat. Mon. **Park** • NY, United States 121 [318]
Star Buck • Kiribati 33 L6
Stara Zagora • Bulgaria 97 D3
Staraplanina • Bulgaria 14 K7
Staraya Russa • Russian Fed. 97 E1
Stargard Szczecinski • Poland 13 E4
Stari Ras **Heritage C** • F.R. of Yugoslavia 64 [160]
Starkenburg • Germany 82 H3
Starkville • MS, United States 118 K2
Starnberg • Germany 82 J3
Starnberger See • Germany 82 J3
Starogard Gdanski • Poland 13 H4
Start Bay • United Kingdom 74 F5
Start Point • United Kingdom 74 F5
Staryy Oskol • Russian Fed. 17 F4
Staszów • Poland 13 K7
State College • PA, United States 118 H1
Staten I. • NJ, United States 118 H1
Statesboro • GA, United States 41 J5
Stathelle • Norway 94 B3
Statue of Liberty **Heritage C** • NJ, United States 62 [12]
Statue of Liberty • NY, United States 118 H2
Statue of Liberty Nat. Mon. **Park** • NY, United States 121 [331]
Stavanger • Norway 94 C5
Stavern • Norway 94 B3
Staverton [Apt] • United Kingdom 74 D4
Stavoren • Netherlands 80 A3
Stavropol • Russian Fed. 17 G5
Stavropolskaya Vozvyshennost • Russian Fed. 17 G5
Stavrós • Thessaly, Greece 15 D4
Stavrós • Halkidiki, Greece 92 D1
Stavrós • Crete, Greece 93 E1
Stavrós, Akra • Crete, Greece 93 E3
Stavrovouni Monastery • Cyprus 93 J4
Steamboat **Ski** • CO, United States 116 [88]
Steamboat Springs • CO, United States 40 E3
Steamboat Springs • CO, United States 116 A
Steamtown Nat. Hist. Site **Park** • PA, United States 121 [315]
Stebnik • Ukraine 13 M8
Stechelberg **Ski** • Switzerland 70 [96]
Steenwijk • Netherlands 5 J2
Stefansson I. • NU, Canada 38 J2
Stege • Denmark 95 F14
Steiermark • Austria 13 D10
Steinach • Austria 89 H6
Steinau an der Straße • Germany 82 G2
Steinbeck **Spa** • Germany 83 [84]
Steinfurt • Germany 8 C4
Steingaden • Germany 82 J6
Steinhuder Meer • Germany 5 M2
Steinkjer • Norway 16 F4
Steinsel • Luxembourg 80 A20
Stella Maris • Bahamas 124 B4
Stellenbosch • South Africa 100 C5
Stëlvio • Italy 91 E3
Stelvio, Parco Naz. dello **Park** • Italy 72 [84]
Stelvio, Parco Naz. dello • Italy 91 E3
Stenay • France 10 K4
Stenbrohult • Sweden 95 F11
Stendal • Germany 8 G4
Stenga • Rhodes, Greece 93 F2
Stenhouse Bay • SA, Australia 34 G7
Stenó Andikithiron • Greece 15 E8
Stenó Elafónissou • Greece 15 D7
Stenungsund • Sweden 95 F2
Stepehnville • NF, Canada 123 D3
Stephens, Mt • Antarctica 46 [1] A1
Stephenville • TX, United States 119 N1
Sterling • CO, United States 40 F3
Stern **Ski** • Italy 70 [233]
Stern • Italy 90 B2
Sternberk • Czech Rep. 13 G8
Stérnes **Beach** • Crete, Greece 69 [212]
Sterrenberg, Burg • Germany 82 H2
Sterzing • Italy 90 B1
Stes Maries-de-la-Mer • France 10 J10
Stessor Peak • Antarctica 46 [1] I3
Stettin • Poland 13 D4
Stettiner Haff • Germany/Poland 8 J3
Stevenage • United Kingdom 7 L10
Stevens Pass **Ski** • WA, United States 116 [43]
Stewart I. • New Zealand 35 A8
Steyr • Austria 13 D9
Steyr [Riv] • Austria 9 J9
Steytlerville • South Africa 100 C7
Stikine • BC, Canada 38 E5
Stilfs • Italy 91 E3
Stilida • Greece 15 D5
Still Bay • South Africa 100 C6
Stip • F.Y.R. of Macedonia 14 J8
Stirling • United Kingdom 74 B3
Stirlingshire • United Kingdom 74 B3
Stjernøya • Norway 16 L1
Stjørdal • Norway 16 F5
Stobi • F.Y.R. of Macedonia 15 C2
Stockerau • Austria 13 F9
Stockholm **Beach** • Sweden 69 [22]
Stockholm **Heritage C** • Sweden 64 [6]
Stockholm • Sweden 95 D4
Stockholm [Adm] • Sweden 95 D4
Stockport • United Kingdom 7 J8
Stockton • CA, United States 117 F3
Stockton-on-Tees • United Kingdom 7 K7
Stoeng Trêng • Cambodia 31 D4
Stogovo • F.Y.R. of Macedonia 14 H8
Stoke-on-Trent • United Kingdom 7 J8
Stoke-sub-Hamdon Priory • United Kingdom 74 F3
Stokksund • Norway 16 F4
Stolbcy • Belarus 16 N10
Stolberg • Germany 9 B6
Stolbovoy, Ostrov • Russian Fed. 27 M2
Stolzenfels, Schloß • Germany 82 H1
Stone, Thomas, Nat. Hist. Site **Park** • MD, United States 121 [277]
Stoneham **Ski** • QU, Canada 116 [37]
Stonehaven • United Kingdom 6 J5
Stonehenge **Heritage C** • United Kingdom 64 [20]
Stonehenge • United Kingdom 74 F3
Stones River Nat. Battlefield & Cemetery **Park** • TN, United States 121 [231]
Stonington I. • Antarctica 59 A10
Stony Rapids • SA, Canada 38 J5
Stora Le • Norway/Sweden 94 B4
Stora Lulevatten • Sweden 16 J3
Stora Sjöfallet Nat. Park **Park** • Sweden 72 [19]
Storavan • Sweden 16 J4
Stord • Norway 94 C5
Stordal • Norway 94 C2
Store • Norway 94 C3
Store Bælt • Denmark 95 F14
Store Heddinge • Denmark 95 F15
Store Mosse Nat. Park **Park** • Sweden 72 [27]
Store Mosse Nat. Park • Sweden 95 F7
Støren • Norway 16 F5
Storfjorden • Norway 94 C2
Storis Passage • NU, Canada 38 K3
Storkerson Bay • NT, Canada 38 F2
Storlien • Sweden 16 G5
Storm Lake • IA, United States 41 G3
Stornoway • United Kingdom 6 F3
Storsjøen • Norway 94 B2
Storsjön • Sweden 16 H5
Storsteinfjellet • Norway 16 I2
Storstrøm • Denmark 95 F14
Storuman • Sweden 16 I4
Storuman [Lake] • Sweden 16 I4
Storvreta • Sweden 95 D2
Stöttingfjället • Sweden 16 I4
Stour • United Kingdom 5 D2
Stour • United Kingdom 5 E3
Stour • United Kingdom 74 F3
Stourbridge • United Kingdom 7 J9
Stourhead • United Kingdom 74 F3
Stourport • United Kingdom 74 D1
Stow-on-the-Wold • United Kingdom 74 D4
Stowe **Ski** • VT, United States 116 [203]
Stowe • VT, United States 118 G3
Strà • Italy 91 E7
Stradbally • Ireland 79 E3
Strakonice • Czech Rep. 96 C3
Straldzha • Bulgaria 15 H1
Stralsund • Germany 8 I2
Stranda • Norway 94 C2
Strande **Spa** • Germany 83 [15]
Strangford Lough • United Kingdom 7 G7
Strängnas • Sweden 95 D3
Strångsjö • Sweden 95 D3
Stranraer • United Kingdom 7 H7
Strasbourg • France 10 M5
Strasbourg **Heritage C** • France 64 [52]
Strasburg • PA, United States 118 H1
Strassburg • France 71 A8
Stratford • New Zealand 112 K3
Stratford-upon-Avon • United Kingdom 74 D2
Strath Earn • United Kingdom 74 B1
Strathcona Prov. Park • BC, Canada 122 C3
Strathgordon • TS, Australia 34 I8
Strathmore • United Kingdom 74 B2
Stratton **Ski** • VT, United States 116 [196]
Stratton Mtn • VT, United States 118 G3
Straubing • Germany 9 H8
Straumsjøen • Norway 16 H2
Strausberg • Germany 8 I4
Streaky Bay • SA, Australia 34 F6
Streaky Bay [Gulf] • SA, Australia 34 F6
Strehaia • Romania 14 K5
Strelka • Russian Fed. 26 P6
Stresa • Italy 91 E2
Strete Gate **Beach** • United Kingdom 75 [107]
Strezhevoy • Russian Fed. 26 M5
Strib • Denmark 95 F9
Strickland • Papua New Guinea 32 [1] F4
Strigno • Italy 90 B3
Strimonas • Greece 15 E3
Strimonikós Kolpos • Greece 15 E3
Strjama • Bulgaria 15 F1
Strómboli, I. • Italy 90 D2
Strømfjord, Nordre • Greenland 39 U3
Strømfjord, Søndre • Greenland 39 U3
Strömstad • United Kingdom 6 I3
Strömsnäsbruk • Sweden 95 F11
Strömstad • Sweden 95 F2
Strömsund • Sweden 16 H5
Stronsay • United Kingdom 6 J2
Stroud • United Kingdom 74 D3
Struer **Beach** • Denmark 68 [50]
Struer • Denmark 95 F9
Struga • F.Y.R. of Macedonia 15 B2
Struisbaai • South Africa 100 C6
Struma • Bulgaria 14 K8
Strumica • F.Y.R. of Macedonia 14 J8
Stry • Ukraine 13 M8
Stry [Riv] • Ukraine 13 M8
Stryn • Norway 94 C2
Strynsvatn • Norway 94 C2
Strzelin • Poland 13 G7
Stuart Mem. • NT, Australia 112 H2
Stuart Mtns • New Zealand 112 L1
Stubbekøbing • Denmark 95 F14
Stubbenkammer • Germany 8 I2
Stuben • Austria 89 H5
Stubice • Poland 13 D5
Studen • Switzerland 89 G2
Studenica **Heritage C** • F.R. of Yugoslavia 64 [161]
Studley Royal Park **Heritage C** • United Kingdom 64 [17]
Sturgeon Falls • OT, Canada 122 B1
Sturt Creek • NT/WA, Australia 34 E3
Sturt Desert • QL/SA, Australia 34 H5
Sturt Nat. Park • NS, Australia 34 H5
Sturup [Apt] • Sweden 95 F11
Stuttgart • AR, United States 41 H5
Stuttgart • Germany 82 G6
Stuttgart **Spa** • Germany 83 [176]
Stützerbach **Spa** • Germany 83 [306]
Stykkishólmur • Iceland 16 [1] B2
Styr • Ukraine 17 D4
Styria • Austria 89 F4
Su Nuraxi • Sardinia, Italy 90 C4
Su Nuraxi di Barùmini **Heritage C** • Sardinia, Italy 64 [135]
Suavanao • Solomon Is. 35 [1] F2
Subang • Java, Indonesia 110 D2
Subang [Apt] • Malaysia 108 D4
Subbético • Spain 11 I6
Submeseta • Castilla y León, Spain 11 F2
Submeseta • Castilla-La Mancha, Spain 11 H5
Subotica • F.R. of Yugoslavia 14 G3
Suceava • Romania 14 N2
Sucia, Bahia • Puerto Rico 125 E3
Suck • Ireland 79 F4
Suckling • Papua New Guinea 35 [1] D2
Sucre • Bolivia 44 C2
Sucre **Heritage C** • Bolivia 62 [54]
Sud, Costa del • Sardinia, Italy 90 C3
Sudan • Africa 19 H4
Sudan [Region] • Africa 22 F2
Sudbury • OT, Canada 39 O7
Sudd, As • Sudan 23 E2
Sude • Germany 8 G3
Sudeten • Poland/Czech Rep. 13 F7
Sudety • Poland/Czech Rep. 13 E7
Sudirman, Pegunungan • Indonesia 32 [1] E3
Sudong • Singapore 108 E3
Sue • Sudan 23 D2
Sueca • Spain 11 K5
Sueca **Beach** • Spain 68 [119]
Suez • Egypt 101 F2
Suez Canal • Egypt 101 F2
Suez, Gulf of • Egypt 101 F4
Suffolk • United Kingdom 7 N9
Sugar Bowl **Ski** • CA, United States 116 [53]
Sugar Loaf **Ski** • MI, United States 116 [134]
Sugar Mtn **Ski** • NC, United States 116 [152]
Sugarbush **Ski** • VT, United States 116 [201]
Sugarloaf USA **Ski** • ME, United States 116 [219]
Sugla Gölü • Turkey 93 G2
Sugoy • Russian Fed. 27 Q4
Suhar • Oman 18 G5
Suheli I. • India 106 D9
Suhl • Germany 9 F6
Suide • China 29 D3
Suihua • China 29 H1
Suippe • France 5 H5
Suippes • France 5 H5
Suir • Ireland 7 E9
Suizhong • China 29 G2
Sukabumi • Java, Indonesia 110 D1
Sukadana • Indonesia 32 D3
Sukaraja • Indonesia 32 E3
Sukhona • Russian Fed. 17 G2
Sukhothai **Heritage N** • Thailand 61 [122]
Sukhothai **Heritage C** • Thailand 63 [173]
Sukhothai • Thailand 109 G4
Sukhumi • Georgia 17 G6
Suki • Sudan 21 F5
Sukkur • Pakistan 28 A3
Sukon • Indonesia 32 [1] B3
Sukses • Namibia 24 B4
Sukumo • Japan 30 G8
Sula • Norway 94 C3
Sula, Kepulauan • Indonesia 110 A3
Sulaiman Range • Pakistan 28 A2
Sulawesi • Indonesia 32 [1] A3
Sulayyil, As • Saudi Arabia 18 E5
Sulb • Egypt 21 F3
Suldalsvatn • Norway 94 C6
Sulden • Italy 91 E3
Sulechów • Poland 13 E5
Suleskar • Norway 94 C6
Sulima • Sierra Leone 22 B3
Sulina • Romania 97 D2
Sulingen • Germany 5 L2
Sulitjelma • Norway 16 H3
Sulitjelma [Mtn] • Norway 16 I3
Sullana • Peru 43 A4
Sulmona • Italy 91 F2
Sulphur • AR/TX, United States 119 N2
Sulphur Springs • TX, United States 119 N2
Sulphur Springs • St Lucia 125 J3
Sultan Daglari • Turkey 15 M5
Sultanhani • Turkey 15 O5
Sultanpur • India 105 C8
Sulu Archipelago • Philippines 31 G5
Sulu Sea • Philippines 31 F5
Sülüklü • Turkey 15 N5
Sulz am Neckar • Germany 82 G6
Sulzbach-Rosenberg • Germany 9 G7
Sulzberger Bay • Antarctica 46 [1] AA2
Sumadija • F.R. of Yugoslavia 14 H5
Sumalata • Indonesia 32 [1] B2
Sumatera • Indonesia 32 C3
Sumatera Barat • Indonesia 110 B4
Sumatera Utara • Indonesia 110 B4
Sumatra • Indonesia 32 C3
Sumava • Czech Rep. 96 C3
Sumayh, As • Sudan 23 D2
Sumba • Indonesia 32 [1] A4
Sumbawa • Indonesia 32 [1] A4
Sumbawa Besar • Indonesia 32 [1] A4
Sumbawanga • Tanzania 102 H3
Sumbe • Angola 23 A6
Sumbing, Gunung • Java, Indonesia 110 D7
Sumbu • Zambia 23 E5
Sumburgh Head • United Kingdom 6 K2
Sumenep • Indonesia 110 D4
Sumgait • Azerbaijan 18 E1
Summerside • PE, Canada 123 D7
Summit Lake • BC, Canada 38 G5
Sumperk • Czech Rep. 13 F8
Sumter • SC, United States 41 J5
Sumter, Fort, Nat. Mon. **Park** • SC, United States 121 [237]
Sumy • Ukraine 17 E4
Sun Kosi • Nepal 28 E3
Sun Peaks **Ski** • BC, Canada 116 [4]
Sun Valley **Ski** • ID, United States 116 [72]
Sun Valley • ID, United States 117 E4
Sun Yat-sen's residence • China 107 H2
Sunak, gora • Kazakhstan 26 L8
Sunan • D.P.R. of Korea 30 C5
Sunapee • NH, United States 118 G3
Sunbury • VI, Australia 34 H7
Sunbury House and Museum • Barbados 125 H4
Sunch'on • Rep. of Korea 30 D7
Sunchales • Argentina 44 D5
Sunda, Selat • Java, Indonesia 110 D1
Sunda Strait • Indonesia 32 D4
Sundarbans • Bangladesh/India 28 E4
Sundarbans **Heritage N** • Bangladesh 61 [110]
Sundarbans Nat. Park **Heritage N** • India 61 [109]
Sunday River **Ski** • ME, United States 116 [218]
Sunde • Norway 94 C5
Sunderland • United Kingdom 7 K7
Sunderland Sound • New Zealand 112 L1
Sundern • Germany 5 K3
Sundern • Germany 9 D5
Sündiken Daglari • Turkey 15 L4
Sundown Mtn **Ski** • IA, United States 116 [116]
Sundsli • Norway 94 C6
Sundsvall • Sweden 16 I5
Sundybyberg • Sweden 95 D4
Sungai Petani • Malaysia 31 C5
Sungaiguntung • Indonesia 32 C2
Sunndalsøra • Norway 94 C2
Sunne • Sweden 16 G7
Sunnerbo • Sweden 95 F7
Sunnersta • Sweden 95 D2
Sunny Beach • Bulgaria 97 D3
Sunrise Park **Ski** • AZ, United States 116 [87]
Sunset Beach • HI, United States 119 L1
Sunset Crater Nat. Mon. • AZ, United States 118 J1
Sunset Crater Nat. Mon. **Park** • AZ, United States 120 [106]
Sunshine Coast • QL, Australia 111 F6
Sunshine Village **Ski** • AL, Canada 116 [13]
Suntar • Russian Fed. 27 I4
Suntar Khayata, Khrebet • Russian Fed. 27 M4
Sunyani • Ghana 22 D3
Suolahti • Finland 95 E2
Suomenlinna • Finland 95 E4
Suomussalmi • Finland 16 O4
Suonenjoki • Finland 16 N5
Suoyarvi • Russian Fed. 17 E2
Sup'ung-Chosuji • China 30 C4
Super-Sauze • France 85 H2
Super-St-Bernard • Switzerland 89 G6
Superbagnères • France 85 K1
Superdévoluy **Ski** • France 70 [64]
Superior • WI, United States 41 H2
Superior, Lake • Canada/United States 41 I2
Suphan Buri • Thailand 109 H1
Supiori • Indonesia 32 [1] E3
Sur • Oman 18 G5
Sur • Lebanon 98 A1
Surabaya • Java, Indonesia 110 D8
Surahammar • Sweden 95 D1
Surak • Iran 18 G4
Surakarta • Java, Indonesia 110 D7
Surat • India 28 B4
Surat • QL, Australia 111 F5
Surat Thani • Thailand 31 B5
Suratgarh • India 105 C2
Surduc • Romania 13 M10
Sûre • Luxembourg 80 A20
Surfers Paradise • QL, Australia 111 F6
Surgidero de Batabano • Cuba 124 D2
Surgut • Russian Fed. 26 L5
Surgutikha • Russian Fed. 26 O5
Surhob • Asia 18 J2
Surigao • Philippines 31 H5
Surin Beach • Phuket, Thailand 109 K1
Surin, Ko • Thailand 109 F3
Surinam Quarters • Jamaica 124 C3
Suriname • S. America 43 F3
Surrey • United Kingdom 74 E3
Surrey • Jamaica 124 C4
Surt • Libya 21 C1
Surtsey • Iceland 16 [1] C3
Surud Ad • Somalia 25 F9
Suruga-Wan • Japan 30 J7
Susa • Italy 12 B3
Susak • Croatia 14 D7
Susaki • Japan 30 G8
Susanville • CA, United States 117 F1
Susice • Czech Rep. 96 C3
Suso **Heritage C** • Spain 64 [77]
Susoh • Indonesia 110 B1
Susquehanna • PA, United States 118 H1
Sussex • United Kingdom 74 E3
Susuman • Russian Fed. 27 O4
Sütçüler • Turkey 93 G2
Sutherland • United Kingdom 75 A1
Sutherland • South Africa 100 C2
Sutjeska Nat. Park **Park** • Bosnia-Herz. 72 [114]
Sutlej • India/Pakistan 28 B2
Sutton on Sea **Beach** • United Kingdom 75 [29]
Suursaari • Russian Fed. 16 N6
Suva • Fiji 35 [2] D2
Suva Planina • F.R. of Yugoslavia 14 J6
Suvadiva Atoll • Maldives 106 E3
Suwa • Japan 30 J6
Suwalki • Poland 13 L3
Suwannee • FL/GA, United States 119 M3
Suweis, El • Egypt 101 F2
Suwon • Rep. of Korea 30 D6
Suzdal **Heritage C** • Russian Fed. 64 [210]
Suzdal • Russian Fed. 97 E4
Suzhou **Heritage C** • China 63 [153]
Suzhou • China 107 J2
Suzu • Japan 29 J3
Suzu-Misaki • Japan 30 I6
Suzuz Han • Turkey 93 G1
Svalbard • Arctic Ocean 46 N2
Svaljava • Ukraine 13 M9
Svaneke • Denmark 95 F16
Svaneti area **Heritage C** • Georgia 64 [211]
Svarstad • Norway 94 B3
Svartenhuk Halvø • Greenland 39 U2
Svärtinge • Sweden 95 D3
Svartisen • Norway 16 H3
Svatoy Nos, mys • Russian Fed. 27 N2
Svedala • Sweden 13 C2
Sveg • Sweden 16 H5
Svelvik • Norway 94 B2
Svendborg **Beach** • Denmark 68 [44]
Svendborg • Denmark 95 F14
Svene • Norway 94 B1
Svenljunga • Sweden 95 F7
Sverdrup Is. • NU, Canada 36 H2
Sveshtari **Heritage C** • Bulgaria 64 [168]
Svetac • Croatia 14 C6
Svetlaya • Russian Fed. 27 M7
Svetlograd • Russian Fed. 17 G5
Svetly • Russian Fed. 13 J3
Svetlyy • Russian Fed. 27 I5
Sviahnúkar • Iceland 16 [1] E2
Sviatoy Nos, mys • Russian Fed. 17 F1
Svihov • Czech Rep. 96 C3
Svilaja • Croatia 14 D6
Svilengrad • Bulgaria 14 N8
Svinecea Mare, Virful • Romania 14 J5
Svir • Russian Fed. 17 E2
Svishtov • Bulgaria 97 D1
Svitava • Czech Rep. 13 F8
Svitavy • Czech Rep. 13 F8
Svobodnyy • Russian Fed. 27 K6
Svolvær • Norway 16 H2
Svrljig • F.R. of Yugoslavia 14 J6
Swain **Ski** • NY, United States 116 [174]
Swain Reefs • QL, Australia 111 F4
Swakopmund • Namibia 24 A4
Swan • Honduras 37 E4
Swan Hill • VI, Australia 111 G1
Swanage • United Kingdom 74 F6
Swanage **Beach** • United Kingdom 75 [85]
Swansea • United Kingdom 7 I10
Swartberg Pass • South Africa 100 C7
Swaziland • Africa 24 E5
Sweden • Europe 14
Swedish Lakeland • Sweden 95 F3
Sweetwater • WY, United States 38 J8
Sweetwater • TX, United States 40 F5
Swellendam • South Africa 100 C6
Swetes • Antigua & Barbuda 125 F3
Swidnica • Poland 13 F7
Swidnik • Poland 13 L6
Swidwin • Poland 13 E4
Swiebodzin • Poland 13 E5
Swiecie • Poland 13 H4
Swietokrzyskie, Gory • Poland 13 K7
Swift Current • SA, Canada 38 J6
Swilly, Lough • Ireland 7 E6
Swinburne, Cape • NU, Canada 38 L2
Swindon • United Kingdom 7 K10
Swinemünde • Poland 13 D4
Swinoujscie • Poland 13 D4
Swiss Nat. Park **Park** • Switzerland 72 [81]
Swiss Nat. Park • Switzerland 89 G4
Swiss Valley **Ski** • MI, United States 116 [144]
Switzerland • Europe 4 L7
Swords • Ireland 79 E2
Sybaris • Italy 12 K9
Sydals **Beach** • Denmark 68 [45]
Sydfalster **Beach** • Denmark 68 [37]
Sydlangeland **Beach** • Denmark 68 [44]
Sydney • NS, Australia 111 G2
Sydney • NS, Canada 123 D8
Sydney Mines • NS, Canada 123 D8
Sydthy **Beach** • Denmark 68 [49]
Sykkylven • Norway 94 C2
Syktyvkar • Russian Fed. 17 I2
Sylhet • Bangladesh 28 F4
Sylling • Norway 94 B1
Sylt • Germany 8 D2
Sylt **Spa** • Germany 83 [2]
Sylt-Ost **Spa** • Germany 83 [2]
Sylvan **Ski** • MI, United States 116 [131]
Sylvensteinsee • Germany 82 J7
Symond's Yat • United Kingdom 74 D3
Syowa [Base] • Antarctica 46 [1] J3
Syr Darya • Kazakhstan 26 K9
Syracuse • NY, United States 41 K3
Syracuse • Sicily, Italy 90 D4
Syria • Asia 18 C3
Syrian Desert • Asia 18 C3
Syutkya • Bulgaria 14 K8
Syvde • Norway 94 C1
Syzran • Russian Fed. 17 H4
Szamotuly • Poland 13 F5
Szarvas • Hungary 13 J11
Szczecin • Poland 13 D4
Szczecinek • Poland 13 F4
Szczytno • Poland 13 J4
Szeged • Hungary 13 J11
Székesfehérvár • Hungary 13 H10
Szekszárd • Hungary 13 H11
Szentendre • Hungary 13 I10
Szentes • Hungary 13 J11
Szeskie Wzgórza • Poland 13 L3
Szigetvár • Hungary 13 G11
Szolnok • Hungary 13 J10
Szombathely • Hungary 13 F10
Szprotawa • Poland 13 E6
Szubin • Poland 13 G4
T'aech'on • D.P.R. of Korea 30 C5
Ta'if, At • Saudi Arabia 18 D5
Ta'izz • Yemen 18 D7
Taba • Egypt 101 F2
Tabar • Papua New Guinea 35 [1] E1
Tabarka • Tunisia 101 E1
Tabarz **Spa** • Germany 83 [301]
Tabasco • Mexico 37 C4
Tabasco y Campeche, Llanos de • Mexico 37 C4
Tabelbala • Algeria 20 E3
Taberg • Sweden 95 F7
Tabernacle • St Kitts & Nevis 125 G1
Tabla • Niger 20 F6
Tablas • Philippines 31 G4
Table Bay • South Africa 100 C5
Table Cape • New Zealand 35 G4
Table Mtn • South Africa 100 C5
Tábor • Czech Rep. 96 C4
Tabor, Mount • Israel 98 A4
Tabora • Tanzania 102 H1
Tabou • Côte d'Ivoire 22 C4
Tabriz • Iran 18 E2
Tabuaeran • Kiribati 33 L5
Tabuk • Saudi Arabia 18 C4
Tabwemasana • Vanuatu 35 [2] B2
Täby • Sweden 95 D2
Tacheng • China 26 N8
Tachilek • Myanmar 109 G2
Tachov • Czech Rep. 13 B8
Tacloban • Philippines 31 G4
Tacna • Peru 127 B4
Tacoma • WA, United States 117 E1
Tacoronte **Beach** • Tenerife, Canary Is. 68 [109]
Tacoronte • Tenerife, Canary Is. 86 E1
Tacuarembó • Uruguay 44 E5
Tademaït, Plateau du • Algeria 20 F3
Tadjourah • Djibouti 21 H5
Tadmur • Syria 18 C3
Tadmur **Heritage C** • Syria 64 [240]
Tadrart Acacus **Heritage C** • Libya 63 [90]
Taebaek-Sanmaek • D.P.R. of Korea/Rep. of Korea 30 E6
Taegu • Rep. of Korea 30 E7

Taehan-Haehyop • Rep. of Korea 29 H4
Taehuksan • Rep. of Korea 30 C7
Taejon • Rep. of Korea 30 D6
Tafahi • Tonga 35 (2) F2
Tafassasset • Algeria 20 G4
Tafers • Switzerland 89 G2
Taff • United Kingdom 10 B2
Tafí Viejo • Argentina 44 C4
Tafilalt • Morocco 101 D6
Tafiré • Côte d'Ivoire 22 C3
Tafraoute • Morocco 101 D5
Taft, William Howard, Nat. Hist. Site **Park** • OH, United States 121 [184]
Taftan, Kuh-e • Iran 18 H4
Taga Dzong • Bhutan 28 E3
Taganrog • Russian Fed. 17 F5
Tagant • Mauritania 20 C5
Tagbilaran • Philippines 31 G5
Taggia **Beach** • Italy 68 [140]
Tággia • Italy 91 E9
Tagliacozzo • Italy 91 F2
Tagliamento • Italy 12 G2
Tagomago, I. de • Ibiza, Spain 87 G2
Tagounit • Morocco 20 D3
Taguersimet • Western Sahara 20 B4
Taguish Lake • YT, Canada 38 D4
Tagus • Portugal/Spain 86 A2
Tahan, Gunong • Malaysia 32 C2
Tahat • Algeria 20 G4
Tahiti • French Polynesia 33 M7
Tahoe, Lake • CA/NV, United States 117 F3
Tahoua • Niger 20 G6
Tahuna • Indonesia 32 (1) C2
Tai • Côte d'Ivoire 22 C3
Tai Hu • China 107 J1
Tai Lam Country Park • Hong Kong, China 107 H5
Tai Mo Shan • Hong Kong, China 107 H5
Tai Mo Shan Country Park • Hong Kong, China 107 H5
Tai O • Hong Kong, China 107 H5
Taï, Parc nat. de **Heritage N** • Côte d'Ivoire 61 [75]
Taï, Parc nat. de **Park** • Côte d'Ivoire 103 [19]
Tai Po • Hong Kong, China 107 H6
Tai Shan **Heritage N** • China 61 [113]
Tai Shan **Heritage C** • China 63 [151]
Tai Shan • China 107 G4
Tai Tam Country Park • Hong Kong, China 107 H6
Taibai Shan • China 29 D4
Taibilla, Sierra de • Spain 11 I6
Taicang • China 107 J2
Taichung • Taiwan 29 G6
Taígetos, Oros • Greece 15 D6
Taihape • New Zealand 112 K4
Taimba • Russian Fed. 26 Q5
Tainan • Taiwan 29 G6
Taipa • Macau 107 H1
Taipa Village • Macau 107 H1
Taipei • Taiwan 29 G6
Taiping • Malaysia 32 C2
Taiping • China 107 J3
Taiping Ling • China 29 G1
Taisetsu • Japan 30 L3
Taitao, Península de • Chile 45 B5
Taitung • Taiwan 29 G6
Taivalkoski • Finland 16 O4
Taiwan • Asia 29 G6
Taixing • China 107 J1
Taiyuan • China 29 E3
Taizhou • China 107 J1
Taizi • China 30 C4
Taj Mahal **Heritage C** • India 63 [119]
Tajikistan • Asia 26 L10
Tajima • Japan 30 J6
Tajo • Spain 11 D5
Tajrish • Iran 18 F2
Tajumulco, Volcán • Guatemala 37 C4
Tajura • Libya 21 B1
Tak • Thailand 31 B3
Takahe, Mt • Antarctica 46 (1) DD2
Takamatsu • Japan 30 H7
Takaoka • Japan 30 I6
Takapuna • New Zealand 35 E3
Takasaki • Japan 30 J6
Take • Japan 30 F6
Take Lake • BC, Canada 38 F5
Takeo • Cambodia 108 B1
Takern • Sweden 95 F3
Takht-i-Bakhi **Heritage C** • Pakistan 63 [112]
Takijuq Lake • NU, Canada 38 I3
Takingeun • Indonesia 110 B1
Takitimu Mtns • New Zealand 112 L4
Takli Makan Shamo • China 26 N10
Taklimakan Desert • China 107 G1
Takum • Nigeria 22 G3
Takutea • Cook Is. 33 L7
Talacre **Beach** • United Kingdom 75 [204]
Talaion • Crete, Greece 93 E2
Talak • Niger 20 G5
Talamanca, Cordillera de **Heritage N** • Costa Rica 60 [24]
Talara • Peru 43 A4
Talasea • Papua New Guinea 35 (1) D2
Talata Mafara • Nigeria 20 G6
Talaud, Kepulauan • Indonesia 31 H6
Talaud, Kepulauan • Indonesia 32 (1) C2
Talavera de la Reina • Spain 11 G5
Talbot, Mt • WA, Australia 34 E5
Talca • Chile 44 B6
Talcahuano • Chile 44 B6
Talcy [Château] • France 84 D2
Taldy-Kurgan • Kazakhstan 26 M9
Talence • France 10 E9
Talgar • Kazakhstan 26 M9
Taliabu • Indonesia 32 (1) B3
Taling Ngam Beach • Ko Samui, Thailand 109 J2
Talisajan • Indonesia 32 F2
Talisman **Ski** • OT, Canada 116 [21]
Taliwang • Indonesia 32 (1) A4
Tallahassee • FL, United States 119 M2
Tallinn • Estonia 16 M7
Tallinn **Heritage C** • Estonia 64 [201]
Talmest • Morocco 20 D2
Talo • Ethiopia 23 F1
Taloqan • Afghanistan 28 A1
Taloyoak • NU, Canada 38 M3
Talpona Beach • Goa, India 105 B2
Taltal • Chile 44 B4
Tam • France 10 G10
Tamale • Ghana 22 D3
Taman Ayun Temple • Bali, Indonesia 110 C4
Taman Negara Nat. Park • Malaysia 108 A4
Tamanrasset • Algeria 20 G4
Tamanrasset [Riv] • Algeria 20 F4
Tamar • United Kingdom 74 F5
Tamarinda • Minorca, Spain 87 F3
Tamarugal, Pampa del • Chile 44 C2
Tamasag-Bulak • Mongolia 29 F1
Tamási • Hungary 14 F3
Tamatave • Madagascar 24 H3
Tamaulipas • Mexico 37 B3
Tamazunchale • Mexico 123 E2
Tambacounda • Senegal 22 B2
Tambelan, Kepulauan • Indonesia 110 A2
Tambo • QL, Australia 111 F3
Tambo • Peru 127 B4
Tambo Colorado • Peru 127 B1
Tambora, Gunung • Indonesia 32 (1) A4
Tambov • Russian Fed. 17 G4
Tambre • Spain 11 C2
Tambunan • Malaysia 31 F5
Tambura • Sudan 23 D2
Tamchaket • Mauritania 20 C5
Tamdi Surla Temple • Goa, India 105 B1
Tame • Colombia 43 C2
Támega • Portugal 11 C3
Tamegroute • Morocco 101 D6
Tamel Aike • Argentina 45 B5
Tamenghest • Algeria 20 G4
Tamerza • Tunisia 101 E3
Tamgak, Mts • Niger 20 G5
Tamgue, Massif du • Guinea 22 B2
Tamiahua, Laguna de • Mexico 123 E2
Tamil Nadu • India 106 D7
Tamlingan, Danau • Bali, Indonesia 110 C2
Tammerfors • Finland 95 E2
Tammisaari • Finland 95 E4
Tämnaren • Sweden 95 D1
Tampa • FL, United States 119 M5
Tampa Bay • FL, United States 119 M5
Tampere • Finland 95 E2
Tampereen Sarkanniemi Oy **Park** • Finland 73 [11]
Tampico • Mexico 123 E2
Tampin • Malaysia 108 D4
Tampines • Singapore 108 E2
Tamsweg • Austria 13 C10
Tamu • Myanmar 31 A2
Tamuda • Morocco 101 D2
Tamuin • Mexico 37 B3
Tamworth • NS, Australia 34 J6
Tamworth • United Kingdom 74 D2
Tan An • Vietnam 108 B3
Tan Son Nhat [Apt] • Vietnam 108 B1
Tan-Tan • Morocco 101 D5
Tana • Norway 16 O1
Tana • Kenya 101 G4
Tana, Lake • Ethiopia 21 G5
Tana [Riv] • Norway 16 N1
Tana River Primate Game Reserve • Kenya 101 G4
Tanabe • Japan 30 H8
Tanacross • AK, United States 38 C4
Tanafjorden • Norway 16 O1
Tanagro • Italy 12 J8
Tanah Lot Temple • Bali, Indonesia 110 C4
Tanah Rata • Malaysia 108 D1
Tanahbala • Indonesia 110 B4
Tanahgrogot • Indonesia 32 F3
Tanahmasa • Indonesia 110 B4
Tanami Desert • NT, Australia 34 F3
Tanami Desert Wildife Sanctuary • NT, Australia 112 H1
Tanana • AK, United States 38 A3
Tanana [Riv] • AK, United States 38 A4
Tanargue, le • France 10 J9
Tánaro • Italy 91 E5
Tanch'on • D.P.R. of Korea 30 E4
Tandil • Argentina 127 D3
Tando Adam • Pakistan 28 A3
Tanega • Japan 30 F9
Tanezrouft • Mali/Algeria 20 E4
Tanezrouft-n-Ahenet • Algeria 20 F4
Tang Kem Bay • Phuket, Thailand 109 K2
Tanga • Kenya 23 F5
Tanga • Tanzania 102 H2
Tanga Is. • Papua New Guinea 35 (1) E1
Tangalla • Sri Lanka 106 D15
Tanganyika, Lake • Dem. Rep. of Congo/Tanzania 102 H3
Tanger • Morocco 101 D1
Tangermünde • Germany 8 G4
Tanggu • China 29 F3
Tanggula Shan • China 28 F2
Tanggula Shankou • China 28 F2
Tangier • Morocco 101 D1
Tangier I. • VA, United States 118 H3
Tangkuban Perahu, Gunung • Java, Indonesia 110 D2
Tangra Yumco • China 28 E2
Tangshan • China 29 F3
Tania, la **Ski** • France 70 [35]
Tanimbar Is. • Indonesia 25 O10
Tanimbar, Kepulauan • Indonesia 32 (1) D4
Tanjung Bunga • Penang, Malaysia 108 C1
Tanjung Malim • Malaysia 108 D1
Tanjung Tokong • Penang, Malaysia 108 C2
Tanjungbalai • Indonesia 110 B2
Tanjungpandan • Indonesia 32 D3
Tanjungpinang • Indonesia 32 C2
Tanjungredep • Indonesia 32 F2
Tanjungselor • Indonesia 32 F2
Tankwa-Karoo Nat. Park • South Africa 100 C2
Tanna • Vanuatu 35 (2) B2
Tannenberg • Poland 71 A9
Tannis Bugt • Denmark 95 F6
Tannu Ola • Russian Fed. 26 P7
Tanout • Niger 20 G6
Tantâ • Egypt 101 F1
Tantallon Castle • United Kingdom 74 B4
Tanum **Heritage C** • Sweden 64 [2]
Tanum • Sweden 95 F2
Tanzania • Africa 102 H
Tao, Ko • Thailand 109 F3
Tao'er He • China 29 G1
Taormina **Beach** • Sicily, Italy 69 [153]
Taormina • Sicily, Italy 90 D2
Taos **Ski** • NM, United States 116 [105]
Taoudenni • Mali 20 E4
Taounate • Morocco 101 D2
Taourirt • Morocco 101 D2
Taouz • Morocco 20 E2
Taoyuan • Taiwan 31 G1
Tap Mun Chau • Hong Kong, China 107 H4
Tapa • Estonia 16 N7
Tapachula • Mexico 37 C5
Tapah • Malaysia 108 D1
Tapajós • Brazil 43 F4
Tapaktuan • Indonesia 110 B1
Tapan • Indonesia 32 C3
Tapanui • New Zealand 112 L4
Tapauá • Brazil 43 E5
Taphan Hin • Thailand 31 C3
Taphao Noi, Ko • Thailand 109 K2
Taphao Yai, Ko • Thailand 109 K2
Tapini • Papua New Guinea 35 (1) D2
Tapolca • Hungary 13 G11
Tappi-Zaki • Japan 30 K4
Tapti • India 28 B4
Tapul Group • Philippines 32 (1) B1
Taquara • Brazil 44 F4
Taquile, I. • Peru 127 B4
Tara • F.R. of Yugoslavia 14 G6
Tara • Russian Fed. 26 L6
Tara • Ireland 79 E1
Tara Nat. Park **Park** • Fed. Rep. of Yugoslavia 72 [117]
Tara [Riv] • F.R. of Yugoslavia 14 G6
Taraba • Nigeria 22 G3
Tarabuco • Bolivia 44 D2
Tarabulus • Libya 21 B1
Taraclia • Moldova 14 P4
Taradale • New Zealand 112 K4
Taraghin • Libya 21 B2
Tarakan • Indonesia 32 F2
Tarakan [I.] • Indonesia 32 F2
Taranaki [Adm] • New Zealand 112 K3
Taranaki Bight, North • New Zealand 112 K3
Taranaki Bight, South • New Zealand 112 K3
Taranaki, Mt • New Zealand 112 K3
Tarangire Nat. Park • Tanzania 102 H2
Tarangire Nat. Park **Park** • Tanzania 103 [92]
Taransay • United Kingdom 75 A1
Tarantaise • France 71 A13
Táranto • Italy 12 L8
Táranto, Golfo di • Italy 12 L8
Tarapoto • Peru 43 B5
Taraqua • Brazil 43 D3
Tararua Range • New Zealand 35 E5
Tarascon-sur-Ariège • France 85 K1
Tarasp-Vulpera • Switzerland 89 G4
Tarat • Algeria 20 G3
Tarata • Peru 127 B4
Tarauaca • Brazil 43 C5
Taravilla • Spain 11 I4
Taravo • Corsica, France 85 L3
Tarawa • Kiribati 33 I5
Tarawera, Lake • New Zealand 112 K2
Tarazona • Spain 11 J3
Tarazona de la Mancha • Spain 11 J5
Tarbagatay • Kazakhstan 26 N8
Tarbert • United Kingdom 6 F4
Tarbes • France 85 J2
Tarcoola • SA, Australia 34 F6
Tardienta • Spain 11 K3
Tardoki Yani, gora • Russian Fed. 27 M7
Taree • NS, Australia 34 J6
Tarentais • France 85 F2
Tarfaya • Morocco 101 D5
Tarhankut, mys • Ukraine 17 E5
Tarifa • Spain 86 B6
Tarifa o Marroqui, Punta de • Spain 86 B6
Tarija • Bolivia 44 D3
Tariku • Indonesia 32 (1) E3
Tariku-Taritatu • Indonesia 32 (1) E3
Tarim • Yemen 18 E6
Tarim Basin • China 107 G1
Tarim He • China 26 N9
Tarim Pendi • China 26 N10
Tarin Kowt • Afghanistan 18 I3
Taritatu • Indonesia 32 (1) E3
Tarko-Sale • Russian Fed. 26 M5
Tarlac • Philippines 31 G3
Tarm • Denmark 95 F9
Tarma • Peru 43 B6
Tarma • Peru 127 B1
Tarn • France 10 H9
Tarn Hows • United Kingdom 74 C4
Tärnaby • Sweden 16 H4
Tarnobrzeg • Poland 13 K7
Tarnów • Poland 13 J8
Tärnsjö • Sweden 95 D1
Taro • Italy 12 E4
Taroom • QL, Australia 111 F5
Taroudannt • Morocco 101 D5
Tarpon Springs • FL, United States 119 M5
Tarquínia • Italy 91 F1
Tarragona **Beach** • Spain 68 [121]
Tarragona • Spain 87 D3
Tàrrega • Spain 11 M3
Tarrytown • NY, United States 118 H2
Tarso Emisou • Chad 21 C3
Tarsus • Turkey 18 B2
Tart • China 28 F1
Tartagal • Argentina 44 D3
Tartu • Estonia 16 N7
Tarutau, Ko • Thailand 32 B1
Tarutung • Indonesia 110 B4
Tarxien Temples • Malta 93 H4
Tasagil • Turkey 93 G4
Tasawah • Libya 21 B2
Tash Kurgan • China 98 B2
Tash-Kumyr • Kyrgyzstan 18 J1
Tashauz • Turkmenistan 18 G1
Tashk, Daryachech-ye • Iran 18 F3
Tashkent • Uzbekistan 26 K9
Tashkepri • Turkmenistan 18 H2
Tashtagol • Russian Fed. 26 O7
Tasikmalaya • Java, Indonesia 110 D6
Tåsinge • Denmark 8 F2
Tåsinge • Denmark 95 F14
Taskan • Russian Fed. 27 P4
Tasker • Niger 20 H5
Tasman • New Zealand 112 J3
Tasman Bay • New Zealand 35 D5
Tasman Sea • Australia/New Zealand 33 H9
Tasmania • TS, Australia 34 I8
Tasmanian wilderness **Heritage N** • TS, Australia 61 [136]
Tasmanian wilderness **Heritage C** • Australia 63 [183]
Tassa Takorat • Niger 20 G5
Tassara • Niger 20 G5
Tassili n'Ajjer **Heritage N** • Algeria 61 [68]
Tassili n'Ajjer **Heritage C** • Algeria 63 [91]
Tassili-n-Ajjer • Algeria 20 G3
Tassili-Oua-n-Ahaggar • Algeria 20 G4
Tata • Hungary 13 H10
Tata • Morocco 20 D3
Tata Mailau • East Indies 32 (1) C4
Tataba • Indonesia 32 (1) B3
Tatabánya • Hungary 13 H10
Tataouine • Tunisia 101 E6
Tatarbunary • Ukraine 14 Q4
Tatarsk • Russian Fed. 26 M6
Tatarskiy Proliv • Russian Fed. 27 N7
Tatarstan • Russian Fed. 17 I3
Tateyama • Japan 30 J7
Tathlina Lake • NT, Canada 38 H4
Tathlith • Saudi Arabia 18 D6
Tatilya Turizm **Park** • Turkey 73 [87]
Tatilya Turizm • Turkey 92 D3
Tatnam, Cape • MN, Canada 39 M5
Tatry • Poland/Slovak Rep. 13 J8
Tatrzanski Nat. Park **Park** • Poland 72 [96]
Tatshenshini-Alsek Prov. Wilderness Park **Heritage N** • BC, Canada 60 [1]
Tau • Norway 94 C5
Taubaté • Brazil 127 C3
Tauberbischofsheim • Germany 9 E7
Tauchik • Kazakhstan 26 H9
Tauern, Hohe • Austria 89 H7
Tauern, Niedere • Austria 89 H8
Taufkirchen • Germany 82 J3
Taufstein • Germany 9 E6
Taumarunui • New Zealand 112 K3
Taungdwingyi • Myanmar 28 G4
Taunggyi • Myanmar 31 B2
Taungup • Myanmar 31 A3
Taunus • Germany 82 H2
Taunus-Wunderland • Germany 82 H4
Tauplitz **Ski** • Austria 70 [181]
Taupo • New Zealand 112 K4
Taupo, Lake • New Zealand 112 K4
Taurage • Lithuania 13 L2
Tauranga • New Zealand 112 K2
Tauroa Point • New Zealand 35 D2
Taurus • Turkey 15 N7
Tauysk • Russian Fed. 27 O5
Tauyskaya Guba • Russian Fed. 27 O5
Tavas • Turkey 15 K6
Tavas Ovasi • Turkey 15 K6
Tavda • Russian Fed. 26 K6
Tavda [Riv] • Russian Fed. 26 J6
Tavernes de la Valldigna **Beach** • Spain 68 [119]
Tavestehus • Finland 95 E4
Taveuni • Fiji 35 (2) E2
Taviano • Italy 12 M9
Tavignano • Corsica, France 85 L2
Tavira **Beach** • Portugal 68 [100]
Tavira • Portugal 88 E8
Tavira, I. de • Portugal 88 E8
Tavistock • United Kingdom 74 F5
Tavolara, I. • Sardinia, Italy 90 C2
Tavoy • Myanmar 31 B4
Tavropoú, Tehnití Límni • Greece 15 C4
Tavsanli • Turkey 15 K4
Taw • United Kingdom 74 F2
Tawakoni, Lake • TX, United States 119 N2
Tawangmangu • Java, Indonesia 110 D7
Tawau • Malaysia 32 F2
Tawitawi • Philippines 31 F5
Tawkar • Sudan 21 G4
Taxco • Mexico 123 E4
Taxila **Heritage C** • Pakistan 63 [113]
Taxila • Pakistan 98 B5
Taxkorgan • China 98 B2
Tay • United Kingdom 74 B1
Tay, Firth of • United Kingdom 74 B2
Tay, Loch • United Kingdom 74 B1
Tay Ninh • Vietnam 108 B1
Tayga • Russian Fed. 26 O6
Taygonos, mys • Russian Fed. 27 R4
Taygonos, Poluosatrov • Russian Fed. 27 R4
Tayinloan • United Kingdom 78 A2
Taylor • TX, United States 119 N3
Tayma • Saudi Arabia 18 C4
Taymyr, Ozero • Russian Fed. 26 R3
Taymyr Peninsula • Russian Fed. 97 A5
Taymyr, Poluostrov • Russian Fed. 26 S2
Taymyra • Russian Fed. 26 Q2
Taymyrlyr • Russian Fed. 27 J2
Tayshet • Russian Fed. 26 Q6
Taytay • Philippines 31 F4
Tayu • Java, Indonesia 110 D3
Taz • Russian Fed. 26 N4
Taza • Morocco 101 D2
Tazovskiy • Russian Fed. 4 Z3
Tbilisi • Georgia 17 G6
Tchad, Lac • Africa 21 B5
Tchien • Liberia 22 C3
Tchin Tabardem • Niger 20 G5
Tchogha Zanbil **Heritage C** • Iran 63 [107]
Tczew • Poland 13 H3
Te Ana-Au Caves • New Zealand 112 L1
Te Anau • New Zealand 112 L1
Te Anau, Lake • New Zealand 112 L1
Te Araroa • New Zealand 35 G3
Te Aroha • New Zealand 112 K2
Te Awamatu • New Zealand 112 K1
Te Hapua • New Zealand 35 D2
Te Kaha • New Zealand 35 F3
Te Kao • New Zealand 35 D2
Te Kuiti • New Zealand 112 K1
Te Puke • New Zealand 112 K2
Te Urewera Nat. Park • New Zealand 112 K2
Te Waewae Bay • New Zealand 112 L3
Te Wahipounamu-SW New Zealand **Heritage N** • New Zealand 61 [141]
Teano • Italy 91 G1
Tebay • United Kingdom 74 C4
Tébessa • Algeria 101 E3
Tebingtinggi • Indonesia 110 B2
Téboursouk, Mts de • Tunisia 12 C12
Techirghiol • Romania 97 D2
Tecka • Argentina 45 B4
Tecomán • Mexico 123 E3
Tecuci • Romania 14 O4
Tedzhen • Turkmenistan 18 H2
Tedzhen [Riv] • Iran/Turkmenistan 18 H2
Tees • United Kingdom 7 J7
Tees Bay • United Kingdom 7 K7
Tefe • Brazil 43 E4
Tefenni • Turkey 93 G1
Tegal • Java, Indonesia 110 D2
Tegéa • Greece 15 D6
Tegeh Koripan Temple • Bali, Indonesia 110 C2
Tegel [Apt] • Germany 81 F1
Tegeler See • Germany 81 F1
Tegernsee • Germany 82 J7
Tegernsee **Spa** • Germany 83 [258]
Tegernsee [Lake] • Germany 82 J7
Tegucigalpa • Honduras 37 D5
Teguidda • Niger 20 G5
Teguise **Beach** • Lanzarote, Canary Is. 68 [111]
Teguise • Lanzarote, Canary Is. 87 E3
Tehek Lake • NU, Canada 38 M4
Tehi-n-Isser • Algeria 20 G3
Tehoru • Indonesia 32 (1) C3
Tehran • Iran 18 E2
Tehuantepec • Mexico 37 B4
Tehuantepec, Golfo de • Mexico 37 B4
Tehuantepec, Istmo de • Mexico 37 C4
Teiche, la • France 85 G3
Teide, Pico de • Tenerife, Canary Is. 86 E1
Teifi, Afon- • United Kingdom 7 H9
Teignmouth • United Kingdom 74 F5
Teignmouth **Beach** • United Kingdom 75 [98]
Teisendorf • Germany 82 J4
Teith • United Kingdom 74 B1
Tejakula • Bali, Indonesia 110 C2
Tejeda • Gran Canaria, Canary Is. 86 E4
Tejo • Portugal 11 C5
Tejupan, Punta • Mexico 123 E3
Teke Burun • Turkey 15 H5
Tekeli • Kazakhstan 26 M9
Tekeze • Africa 21 G5
Tekiliktag • China 26 N10
Tekirdag • Turkey 15 I3
Tekirova **Beach** • Turkey 69 [230]
Tekirova • Turkey 93 G3
Tekke Burun • Turkey 15 H3
Tekulthili Lake • NT, Canada 38 I4
Tel 'Arad • Israel 98 A7
Tel Ashqelon • Israel 98 A7
Tel Aviv • Israel 98 A5
Tel Bet Shemesh • Israel 98 A7
Tel Dan • Israel 98 A2
Tel Lakhish • Israel 98 A7
Tel Meggido • Israel 98 A3
Tela • Honduras 37 D4
Teladgama Plateau • India 106 D3
Telavi • Georgia 17 H6
Telc **Heritage C** • Czech Rep. 64 [147]
Telc • Czech Rep. 96 C4
Telciu • Romania 14 L2
Telde • Gran Canaria, Canary Is. 86 E4
Telegraph Creek • BC, Canada 38 E5
Telemark • Norway 16 E7
Telemark Sommarland **Park** • Norway 73 [2]
Telemark Sommerland • Norway 94 B3
Telen • Indonesia 32 F2
Telén • Argentina 44 C6
Telenesti • Moldova 14 P2
Telese • Italy 12 I7
Telford • United Kingdom 74 D1
Teli • Russian Fed. 26 P7
Tell Atlas • Algeria 4 K10
Tell Deir 'Alla • Jordan 98 A6
Tell el Amarna • Egypt 101 F3
Telluride **Ski** • CO, United States 116 [101]
Telmessos • Turkey 92 D9
Telposiz, gora • Russian Fed. 17 J2
Telsen • Argentina 45 C4
Telsiai • Lithuania 13 L2
Teltow • Germany 81 F3
Teltowkanal • Germany 81 F4
Teluk Anson • Malaysia 108 D1
Teluk Bahang • Penang, Malaysia 108 C1
Teluk Bahang Forest Reserve • Penang, Malaysia 108 C1
Teluk Duyung • Penang, Malaysia 108 C1
Teluk Intan • Malaysia 108 D1
Teluk Kumbar • Penang, Malaysia 108 C3
Telukbetung • Indonesia 110 D1
Telukbutun • Indonesia 32 D2
Telukdalem • Indonesia 110 B3
Temanggung • Java, Indonesia 110 D7
Témara Plage • Morocco 101 D1
Tembeling • Malaysia 108 D2
Tembeling [Riv] • Malaysia 108 D2
Tembilahan • Indonesia 32 C3
Tembo • Angola 23 B5
Tembo, Mt • Gabon 22 G4
Teme Valley • United Kingdom 74 D1
Temerloh • Malaysia 108 D4
Temesvár • Romania 14 I4
Teminabuan • Indonesia 32 (1) D3
Temirtau • Kazakhstan 26 L7
Témiskaming • QU, Canada 122 B1
Temora • NS, Australia 111 G1
Tempelhof [Apt] • Germany 81 F4
Tempio Pausania • Sardinia, Italy 12 D8
Templar Park • Malaysia 108 D4
Temple • TX, United States 119 N3
Templemore • Ireland 7 E9
Templetown **Beach** • Ireland 68 [53]
Templi, Valle dei • Sicily, Italy 90 D3
Templin • Germany 8 I3
Templiner See • Germany 81 F3
Temuco • Chile 45 B3
Temuka • New Zealand 35 C7
Ten Degree Channel • India 28 F6
Ten Thousand Is. • FL, United States 119 M8
Tenali • India 106 D3
Ténaro, Akra • Greece 15 D7
Tenasserim • Myanmar 31 B4
Tenby • United Kingdom 7 H10
Tenby **Beach** • United Kingdom 75 [148-150]
Tendaho • Ethiopia 23 G1
Tende • France 10 M9
Tendrara • Morocco 101 D2
Ténéré • Niger 20 H5
Ténéré du Tafassasset • Niger 20 H4
Ténéré, Erg du • Niger 20 H5
Ténéré, Réserve du **Heritage N** • Niger 61 [77]
Ténéré, Réserve du **Park** • Niger 103 [5]
Tenerife • Canary Is. 86 E1
Ténès • Algeria 20 F1
Ténès, Cap • Algeria 11 M8
Tengah, Kepulauan • Indonesia 32 (1) A4
Tengrela • Côte d'Ivoire 22 C2
Tenke • Dem. Rep. of Congo 23 D6
Tenkeli • Russian Fed. 27 N3
Tenkodogo • Burkina Faso 20 E6
Tennant Creek • NT, Australia 34 F3
Tennessee [Adm] • United States 41 I4
Tennessee [Riv] • United States 41 I5
Tenojoki • Finland 94 A3
Tenryu • Japan 30 I7
Tenterfield • NS, Australia 34 J5
Teófilo Otoni • Brazil 44 H2
Teos • Turkey 92 D5
Teotepec, Cerro • Mexico 37 A4
Teotihuacan **Heritage C** • Mexico 62 [17]
Teotihuacán • Mexico 123 E2
Tepa • Indonesia 32 (1) C4
Tepic • Mexico 123 E1
Teplá • Czech Rep. 96 C1
Teplice • Czech Rep. 96 C1
Teposcolula • Mexico 123 E4
Tequila • Mexico 123 E1
Ter • Spain 87 D2
Ter Heijde • Netherlands 80 C3
Téra • Niger 20 F6
Teramo • Italy 91 F2
Terceira • Azores 88 B2
Tercero, Rio • Argentina 45 D2
Terengganu • Malaysia 31 C6
Teresina • Brazil 45 (1) C2
Teresinha • Brazil 43 G3
Teresópolis • Brazil 127 C4
Teressa • India 28 F7
Terezín • Czech Rep. 96 C2
Tergnier • France 10 I4
Terhazza • Mali 20 D4
Termas de Río Hondo • Argentina 44 D4
Terme • Italy 12 E5
Termessos • Turkey 93 G1
Termez • Uzbekistan 18 I2
Términi Imerese • Sicily, Italy 12 H11
Términi Imerese, Golfo di • Sicily, Italy 90 D1
Terminille • Italy 12 G6
Termit, Massif de • Niger 20 H5
Térmoli • Italy 12 I7
Térmoli **Beach** • Italy 69 [159]
Ternate • Indonesia 32 (1) C2
Terneuzen • Netherlands 80 A10
Terney • Russian Fed. 27 M7
Terni • Italy 91 F1
Ternopil • Ukraine 17 D5
Terpeniya, mys • Russian Fed. 27 N7
Terpeniya, Zaliv • Russian Fed. 27 N7
Terra Firma • South Africa 24 C5
Terra Nova Nat. Park • NF, Canada 123 D4
Terracina • Italy 91 F4
Terralba • Sardinia, Italy 12 C9
Terrassa • Spain 87 D3
Terre Adelie • Antarctica 46 (1) S3
Terre Haute • IN, United States 41 I4
Terre-Neuve, Bancs de • NF, Canada 39 T7
Terreiro da Luta • Madeira 88 C2
Terrell • TX, United States 119 N1
Tersakan Gölü • Turkey 15 N5
Terschelling **Beach** • Netherlands 68 [66]
Terschelling • Netherlands 80 A3
Tersef • Chad 22 H2
Teruel • Spain 11 J4
Teruel **Heritage C** • Spain 64 [75]
Tervel • Bulgaria 97 D1
Tervola • Finland 16 M3
Teseney • Eritrea 21 G4
Tésero **Ski** • Italy 70 [215]
Tésero • Italy 90 B3
Teshio • Japan 30 K2
Teshio [Mtn] • Japan 30 L2
Teshio [Riv] • Japan 30 L2
Teskraia • Tunisia 101 E1
Teslin • YT, Canada 38 E4
Teslin [Riv] • YT, Canada 38 E4
Tesovo-Netyl'skiy • Russian Fed. 97 E1
Tessalit • Mali 20 F4
Tessaoua • Niger 20 G6
Test • United Kingdom 5 B3
Test, Tizi n • Morocco 20 D2
Testa, Capo • Sardinia, Italy 90 C2
Testa del Gargano • Italy 14 D8
Teste-de-Buch, la **Beach** • France 68 [85]
Teste-de-Buch, la • France 85 G3
Testigos • Venezuela 43 E1
Têt • France 85 K2
Tetas, Punta • Chile 44 B3
Tete • Mozambique 24 E3
Teterow • Germany 8 H3
Teteven • Bulgaria 14 L7
Tétouan **Heritage C** • Morocco 64 [213]
Tétouan • Morocco 101 D2
Tetovo • F.Y.R. of Macedonia 14 H7
Tettnang • Germany 82 J5
Teulada **Beach** • Spain 68 [118]
Teulada • Spain 87 C2
Teulada, Capo • Sardinia 12 C10
Teutoburger Wald • Germany 8 D5
Tévere • Italy 12 G6
Tewkesbury • United Kingdom 74 D4
Texarkana • AR/TX, United States 119 N2
Texas • United States 40 G5
Texas City • TX, United States 119 N6
Texas Safari Wildlife Park • TX, United States 119 N3
Texel • Netherlands 80 A3
Texoma, Lake • OK/TX, United States 119 N1
Teya • Russian Fed. 26 P5
Teykovo • Russian Fed. 97 E4
Tha Chin • Thailand 109 H1
Thabana Ntlenyana • South Africa 24 D5
Thabazimbi • South Africa 24 D4
Thai Binh • Vietnam 31 D2
Thailand • Asia 31 C3
Thailand, Gulf of • Thailand 31 C4
Thailand, Peninsular • Thailand 109 F4
Thalang • Phuket, Thailand 109 K1
Thale • Germany 8 G5
Thalith, Ash Shallal ath • Sudan 21 F4
Thames • United Kingdom 7 K10
Thames • New Zealand 35 E3
Thames Estuary • United Kingdom 74 E2
Thana • India 28 B5
Thanet, Isle of • United Kingdom 74 E2
Thanh Hoa • Vietnam 31 D3
Thani, Ash Shallal ath • Sudan 21 F3
Thanjavur **Heritage C** • India 63 [129]
Thanjavur • India 106 D11
Thann • France 9 C9
Thannhausen • Germany 82 J2
Thar Desert • India/Pakistan 105 C1
Thar Ua • Phuket, Thailand 109 K1
Thargomindah • QL, Australia 34 H5
Thárros • Sardinia, Italy 90 C3
Thasi Gang Dzong • Bhutan 28 F3
Thassos **Beach** • Greece 69 [194]
Thássos • Greece 92 D1
Thássos [I.] • Greece 92 D1
Thaton • Myanmar 31 B3
Thatta **Heritage C** • Pakistan 63 [110]
Thayetmyo • Myanmar 31 B3
The Dalles • OR, United States 117 E3
The Pas • MN, Canada 38 K6
The Potteries • Barbados 125 H1
Thebes **Heritage C** • Egypt 63 [82]
Thebes • Egypt 101 F4
Thelle • France 85 E1
Thelon • NT/NU, Canada 38 K4
Theodore • QL, Australia 111 F4
Theódori, Agii • Crete, Greece 93 E1
Theológos • Thássos, Greece 15 F3
Theológos **Beach** • Rhodes, Greece 69 [211]
Theológos • Rhodes, Greece 93 F2
Thérain • France 5 F5
Thérèse, I. • Seychelles 106 F1
Thérma • Greece 15 G3
Thermaikós Kólpos • Greece 15 D3

Thermí • Greece **92** D5
Thermia • Greece **92** D7
Thermisía **Beach** • Greece **69** [184]
Thermisía • Greece **92** D7
Thessalía • Greece **15** D4
Thessaloníki **Heritage C** • Greece **64** [175]
Thessaloníki • Greece **92** D1
Thessaly • Greece **92** A1
Thetford • United Kingdom **7** M9
Thetford Mines • QU, Canada **123** D6
Thethi Nat. Park **Park** • Albania **72** [125]
Thibodaux • LA, United States **118** K4
Thief River Falls • MN, United States **41** G2
Thierbach **Ski** • Austria **70** [147]
Thies • Senegal **22** A2
Thießow **Spa** • Germany **83** [281]
Thika • Kenya **101** G3
Thillot, le • France **9** B9
Thimphu • Bhutan **28** E3
Thinalio **Beach** • Corfu, Greece **69** [170]
Thio • New Caledonia **35** (2) B3
Thionville • France **10** L4
Thíra • Greece **92** D8
Thíra [I.] • Greece **92** D8
Thirlmere • United Kingdom **74** C2
Thiruvarur • India **106** D11
Thisted **Beach** • Denmark **68** [49]
Thisted • Denmark **95** F5
Thitu • South China Sea **31** E4
Thíva • Greece **15** E5
Thiviers • France **85** G2
Thoen • Thailand **31** B3
Thoiry, Parc zoologique de • France **85** E3
Tholen • Netherlands **80** A10
Thomas, Fort • St Kitts & Nevis **125** G1
Thompson • MN, Canada **38** L5
Thompson • BC, Canada **122** C3
Thompson Sound • New Zealand **112** L1
Thomson • QL, Australia **34** H4
Thon Buri • Thailand **109** H1
Thon Buri floating market • Thailand **109** H1
Thong Krok, Laem • Ko Samui, Thailand **109** J2
Thonon-les-Bains • France **85** F2
Thorn • Poland **71** A9
Thoronet, Abbaye du • France **85** H3
Thorpe Park **Park** • United Kingdom **73** [35]
Thorpe Park • United Kingdom **74** E1
Thorpeness **Beach** • United Kingdom **75** [48]
Thorshavn • Faroe Is. **4** I4
Thouars • France **84** D3
Thrace • Greece/Turkey **14** N8
Thráki • Greece **15** H2
Thrakikó Pélagos • Greece **15** G3
Thredbo • NS, Australia **111** G4
Three Kings Is. • New Zealand **35** D2
Three Pagodas Pass • Myanmar/Thailand **31** B3
Three Points, Cape • Ghana **22** D4
Threlkeld • United Kingdom **74** C2
Thuburbo Majus • Tunisia **101** E2
Thuile, la **Ski** • Italy **70** [197]
Thuile, la • Italy **91** E1
Thuin • Belgium **5** H4
Thule • Greenland **36** K2
Thule, Mt • NU, Canada **39** P2
Thulhagiri • Maldives **106** E2
Thulusdhu • Maldives **106** E2
Thun • Switzerland **89** G2
Thunder Bay • OT, Canada **39** N7
Thuner See • Switzerland **89** G2
Thung Salaeng Nat. Park • Thailand **109** G4
Thung Song • Thailand **31** B5
Thung Yai-Huai Kha Khaeng Wildlife Sanctuaries **Heritage N** • Thailand **61** [123]
Thur • Switzerland **9** D9
Thüringen • Germany **9** F5
Thüringer Wald • Germany **9** F6
Thuringia • Germany **81** D3
Thurlestone **Beach** • United Kingdom **75** [114]
Thurn, Pass **Ski** • Austria **70** [159-160]
Thursday Island • QL, Australia **34** H2
Thurso • United Kingdom **6** I3
Thuy Duong • Vietnam **108** B4
Thy • Denmark **95** F5
Thyborøn • Denmark **95** F5
Thyborøn-Harboør **Beach** • Denmark **68** [50]
Thyon 2000 • Switzerland **89** G6
Ti Tree • NT, Australia **112** H2
Ti-n-Alkoum • Algeria **20** H4
Ti-n-Tarabiné • Algeria **20** G4
Ti-n-Toumma • Niger **21** B4
Ti-n-Zaoâtene • Algeria **20** F4
Tianbaoshan • China **30** E3
Tianjin • China **29** F3
Tianjin [Adm] • China **107** G4
Tianjun • China **29** B3
Tianmu Shan • China **107** J3
Tianshui • China **29** D4
Tiaret • Algeria **20** F1
Tías **Beach** • Lanzarote, Canary Is. **68** [111]
Tías • Lanzarote, Canary Is. **87** E3
Tib, Ras el • Tunisia **101** E2
Tibati • Cameroon **22** G3
Tiber • Italy **91** F1
Tiberias • Israel **98** A4
Tiberias, Lake • Israel **98** A4
Tibério, Villa di • Italy **91** F4
Tibesti • Chad **21** C3
Tibet • China **28** E2
Tibet, Lake • FL, United States **121** C1
Tibet, Plateau of • China **107** G1
Tibidabo, Parque de Atracciones **Park** • Spain **73** [75]
Tibro • Sweden **95** F3
Tiburón • Mexico **40** D6
Tichit • Mauritania **20** D5
Tichitt **Heritage C** • Mauritania **63** [92]
Tichka, Tizi n • Morocco **20** D2
Tichla • Western Sahara **20** C4
Ticino • Switzerland **89** G7
Ticino [Riv] • Italy/Switzerland **91** E6
Ticul • Mexico **37** D3
Tidaholm • Sweden **95** F3
Tidjikja • Mauritania **20** C5
Tidra, I. • Mauritania **20** B5
Tiefenbronn • Germany **82** G6
Tiel • Netherlands **80** C4
Tielerwaard • Netherlands **80** C4
Tielongtan • China **28** C1
Tielt • Belgium **80** B2
Tien Shan • Asia **26** N9
Tienba • Côte d'Ivoire **22** C3
Tienen • Belgium **80** A15
Tieroko, Tarso • Chad **20** I4
Tierp • Sweden **95** D2
Tierpark Friedrichsfelde • Germany **81** F2
Tierra Amarilla • Chile **44** B4
Tierra del Fuego, I. Grande de • Argentina/Chile **45** C6
Tierradentro, Parque Arqueológico Nac. **Heritage C** • Colombia **62** [44]
Tieté • Brazil **44** F3
Tiflet • Morocco **101** D1
Tifton • GA, United States **119** M3
Tiga • New Caledonia **35** (2) B3
Tigani, Hersónisos • Crete, Greece **93** E1
Tighina • Moldova **14** Q3
Tigil • Russian Fed. **27** Q5
Tignes **Ski** • France **70** [31]
Tignes • France **85** F2
Tigre • Ecuador **43** B4
Tigris • Asia **18** D3
Tihamat • Saudi Arabia **18** D6
Tijuana • Mexico **40** C5
Tikal • Guatemala **37** D4
Tikal, Parque Nacional **Heritage N** • Guatemala **60** [20]
Tikhoretsk • Russian Fed. **17** G5
Tikhvin • Russian Fed. **97** E1
Tikitere • New Zealand **112** K2
Tiksi • Russian Fed. **27** K2
Tikus • Malaysia **108** C2
Til-Châtel • France **10** K6
Tiladummati-Miladummadulu Atoll • Maldives **106** E1
Tilburg • Netherlands **80** A11
Tilbury • United Kingdom **74** E1
Tileagd • Romania **14** J2
Tilemsi, Vallée du • Mali **20** F5
Tilichiki • Russian Fed. **27** S4
Tílisos • Crete, Greece **93** E7
Tillabéry • Niger **20** F6
Tillanchong • India **28** F7
Tillberga • Sweden **95** D1
Tilleul, le **Beach** • France **68** [77]
Tillia • Niger **20** G5
Tiloa • Niger **22** E2
Tílos • Greece **92** D9
Tima • Egypt **21** F2
Timagam, Lake • OT, Canada **39** O7
Timanfaya, Parque Nac. de **Park** • Lanzarote, Canary Is. **72** [79]
Timanfaya, Parque Nac. de • Lanzarote, Canary Is. **87** E3
Timanskiy Kryazh • Russian Fed. **17** I2
Timaru • New Zealand **35** C7
Timashevsk • Russian Fed. **17** F5
Timassah • Libya **21** C2
Timbáki • Crete, Greece **15** F8
Timbédra • Mauritania **20** D5
Timber Ridge **Ski** • MI, United States **116** [143]
Timberline **Ski** • OR, United States **116** [48]
Timbuktu • Mali **20** E5
Timbuktu **Heritage C** • Mali **63** [93]
Timgad **Heritage C** • Algeria **64** [223]
Timimoun • Algeria **20** F3
Timiris, Cap • Mauritania **20** B5
Timisoara • Romania **14** I4
Timmendorf-Niendorf **Spa** • Germany **83** [28]
Timmernabben • Sweden **95** F8
Timmins • OT, Canada **39** O7
Timor • East Indies **32** (1) B4
Timor, Laut • Australia/Indonesia **25** N11
Timor Sea • Australia/Indonesia **34** E2
Timote • Argentina **44** D6
Timpanogos Cave Nat. Mon. **Park** • UT, United States **120** [79]
Timpson • TX, United States **119** N4
Timrå • Sweden **16** I5
Timucuan Ecological & Hist. Preserve • FL, United States **119** M3
Timucuan Ecological & Hist. Preserve **Park** • FL, United States **121** [219]
Tin Can Bay • QL, Australia **111** F6
Tin Fouye • Algeria **20** G3
Tin Shui Wai • Hong Kong, China **107** H5
Tinaca, Kaap • Philippines **31** H5
Tinahely • Ireland **79** E4
Tinaztepe • Turkey **93** G2
Tindari • Sicily, Italy **90** D2
Tindouf • Algeria **20** D3
Tineo • Spain **11** E1
Tinerhir • Morocco **101** D4
Tinetto, , I. del **Heritage C** • Italy **64** [119]
Tinghert, Hamadat • Libya **21** B2
Tinglev • Denmark **95** F13
Tingo Maria • Peru **43** B5
Tingsryd • Sweden **95** F12
Tinjil • Indonesia **110** D1
Tinker Field • FL, United States **121** C2
Tinnsjø • Norway **94** B1
Tino, I. del **Heritage C** • Italy **64** [119]
Tinogasta • Argentina **44** C4
Tínos • Greece **92** D8
Tínos [I.] • Greece **92** D8
Tinou, Stenó • Greece **15** G6
Tintagel • United Kingdom **74** F4
Tintern Abbey • United Kingdom **74** D3
Tipasa **Heritage C** • Algeria **64** [219]
Tipitapa • Nicaragua **37** D5
Tipperary • Ireland **7** D9
Tipperary • Ireland **7** E9
Tipperary • Ireland **79** F6
Tiracambu, Serra do • Brazil **45** (1) B2
Tiracol Fort • Goa, India **105** B1
Tiradentes • Brazil **127** C1
Tirana • Albania **14** G8
Tiranë • Albania **14** G8
Tirano • Italy **91** E2
Tiraspol • Moldova **14** Q3
Tire • Turkey **92** D6
Tiree • United Kingdom **6** F5
Tîrgoviste • Romania **97** D1
Tîrgu Jiu • Romania **14** K4
Tîrgu Mures • Romania **14** L3
Tîrgu Neamt • Romania **14** N2
Tírintha • Greece **15** D6
Tîrnava Mare • Romania **14** M3
Tîrnava Mica • Romania **14** L3
Tîrnaveni • Romania **14** L3
Tírnavos • Greece **15** D4
Tirnovo • Bulgaria **71** A15
Tirol • Austria **89** H3
Tirrénia **Beach** • Italy **68** [145]
Tirrénia • Italy **91** E11
Tirso • Sardinia, Italy **90** C2
Tirstrup [Apt] • Denmark **95** F10
Tirtha Empul Temple • Bali, Indonesia **110** C2
Tiruchirappalli • India **106** D11
Tirukalikundram • India **106** D7
Tirumala • India **106** D7
Tirunelveli • India **106** D10
Tirupati • India **106** D7
Tiruppur • India **106** D10
Tiruvannamalai • India **106** D7
Tiryns • Greece **15** D6
Tisa • Europe **14** K1
Tisnaren • Sweden **95** D3
Tissemsilt • Algeria **11** M9
Tisvildeleje • Denmark **95** F10
Tisza • Hungary **13** J11
Tiszafüred • Hungary **13** J10
Tiszakecske • Hungary **13** J11
Tiszantúl • Hungary **13** J11
Tit-Ary • Russian Fed. **27** K2
Titicaca, Lago • Bolivia/Peru **127** B4
Titisee • Germany **82** G8
Titisee **Spa** • Germany **83** [209]
Titlagarh • India **28** D4
Titov Veles • F.Y.R. of Macedonia **14** I8
Titov vrh • F.Y.R. of Macedonia **14** H8
Titovo Uzice • F.R. of Yugoslavia **14** G6
Tittmoning • Germany **82** J4
Titu • Romania **97** D1
Titus Mtn **Ski** • NY, United States **116** [185]
Titusville • FL, United States **119** M6
Titz • Germany **81** E3
Tivaouane • Mauritania **20** B6
Tiveden • Sweden **95** F3
Tiveden Nat. Park **Park** • Sweden **72** [26]
Tiveden Nat. Park • Sweden **95** F3
Tiverton • United Kingdom **74** F2
Tivoli **Park** • Denmark **73** [18]
Tivoli • Italy **91** F2
Tiwai I. Wildlife Sanctuary **Park** • Sierra Leone **103** [17]
Tiwi Beach • Kenya **101** G5
Tiya **Heritage C** • Ethiopia **63** [88]
Tizi Ouzou • Algeria **20** F1
Tiznit • Morocco **101** D5
Tjällmo • Sweden **95** F4
Tjeggelvas • Sweden **16** I3
Tjeukemeer • Netherlands **5** I2
Tjolöholm • Sweden **95** F6
Tjøme • Norway **94** B4
Tjörn • Sweden **95** F2
Tjust • Sweden **95** F8
Tlaxcala • Mexico **37** B4
Tlaxcala [Adm] • Mexico **37** B4
Tlaxco • Mexico **123** E2
Tlimsen • Algeria **20** E2
Tnahmerah • Indonesia **32** (1) F4
Toamasina • Madagascar **24** H3
Toapoon, Ko • Thailand **109** J1
Toay • Argentina **44** D6
Toba, Danau • Indonesia **32** B2
Toba, Lake • Indonesia **110** B2
Toba Range • Pakistan **28** A2
Tobago • Trinidad & Tobago **125** K2
Tobelo • Indonesia **32** (1) C2
Tobercurry • Ireland **79** F2
Tobermory • United Kingdom **6** F5
Tobi • Palau **32** (1) D2
Toblach **Ski** • Italy **70** [237]
Toblach • Italy **90** B2
Toboali • Indonesia **32** D3
Tobol • Kazakhstan **26** J7
Tobol [Riv] • Kazakhstan/Russian Fed. **26** K6
Tobolsk • Russian Fed. **26** K6
Tobruk • Libya **21** D1
Tobseda • Russian Fed. **17** I1
Tocantins [Adm] • Brazil **45** (1) B4
Tocantins [Riv] • Brazil **45** (1) B4
Toco • Trinidad & Tobago **125** K2
Tocopilla • Chile **44** B3
Tod Mtn **Ski** • BC, Canada **116** [4]
Todd • NT, Australia **112** H4
Todi • Italy **91** E12
Todo-qa-Saki • Japan **30** L5
Todos os Santos, Baía de • Brazil **44** I1
Todra, Gorges du • Morocco **101** D4
Todtmoos **Spa** • Germany **83** [205]
Todtnau • Germany **82** G8
Tödy • Switzerland **12** C2
Toekomstig Reservoir • Suriname **43** F3
Toetoes Bay • New Zealand **112** L4
Töfsingdalen Nat. Park **Park** • Sweden **72** [22]
Tofte • Norway **94** B4
Toftlund • Denmark **95** F13
Tofua • Tonga **35** (2) E2
Toggenburg • Switzerland **89** G3
Togian, Kepulauan • Indonesia **32** (1) B2
Togo • Africa **22** E4
Togwotee Pass • WY, United States **38** I8
Toi-Misaki • Japan **30** F9
Toijala • Finland **95** E2
Toisvesi • Finland **95** E2
Tok • Japan **30** F6
Tokelau • Pacific Ocean **33** J6
Tokkevatn • Norway **94** B3
Tokmak • Kyrgyzstan **26** M9
Tokoroa • New Zealand **112** K2
Tokur • Russian Fed. **27** L6
Tokushima • Japan **30** H7
Tokyo • Japan **30** J7
Tokyo-Wan • Japan **30** J7
Tol'yatti • Russian Fed. **17** H4
Tolaga Bay • New Zealand **35** G4
Tolanäro • Madagascar **24** H5
Toleant • Mexico **123** E2
Toledo • Spain **11** G5
Toledo • OH, United States **41** J3
Toledo • Brazil **44** F3
Toledo **Heritage C** • Spain **64** [88]
Toledo Bend Reservoir • LA/TX, United States **118** K1
Toledo, Montes de • Spain **11** G5
Tolentino • Italy **91** E12
Tolfa • Italy **91** F1
Tolfa, Monti della • Italy **91** F1
Toliara • Madagascar **24** G4
Tolimo • Colombia **43** B3
Tolitoli • Indonesia **32** (1) B2
Tollarp • Sweden **95** F11
Tolmezzo • Italy **12** H2
Tolmin • Slovenia **14** A3
Tolo • Dem. Rep. of Congo **22** H5
Toló **Beach** • Greece **69** [184]
Tolo Harbour • Hong Kong, China **107** H6
Tolosa • Spain **11** I1
Tolstoy, mys • Russian Fed. **27** Q5
Toluca • Mexico **123** E4
Toluca, Nevado de • Mexico **123** E4
Tom Price • WA, Australia **34** C4
Tomakomai • Japan **30** K3
Tomar • Portugal **11** C5
Tomar **Heritage C** • Portugal **64** [96]
Tomaszow Lubelski • Poland **13** M7
Tomaszów Mazowiecki • Poland **13** J6
Tombôco • Angola **22** G6
Tombouctou • Mali **20** E5
Tombstone • AZ, United States **118** J4
Tomé • Chile **44** B6
Tomé-Açu • Brazil **45** (1) B2
Tomelilla • Sweden **95** F11
Tomelloso • Spain **11** H5
Tomkinson Ranges • SA/WA, Australia **112** H3
Tommot • Russian Fed. **27** K5
Tomo • Colombia **43** C3
Tomorit • Albania **15** B3
Tomorri Nat. Park **Park** • Albania **72** [128]
Tompe • Indonesia **32** (1) A3
Tompo • Russian Fed. **27** M4
Tomsk • Russian Fed. **26** O6
Tonala • Mexico **37** C4
Tonale, Passo del • Italy **91** E3
Tonbridge • United Kingdom **74** E3
Tondano • Indonesia **32** (1) B2
Tønder • Denmark **8** D2
Tønder • Denmark **95** F13
Tonesai Falls • Phuket, Thailand **109** K1
Toney • Antarctica **46** (1) DD2
Tong Pha Phum • Thailand **31** B4
Tonga • Pacific Ocean **35** (2) F2
Tonga Trench • Tonga **35** (2) F2
Tongariro Nat. Park **Heritage N** • New Zealand **61** [140]
Tongariro Nat. Park • New Zealand **112** K4
Tongatapu • Tonga **59** A9
Tongatapu Group • Tonga **35** (2) E3
Tongchuan • China **29** D3
Tongeren • Belgium **5** I4
Tonghe • China **29** H1
Tonghua • China **29** H2
Tongjoson-man • D.P.R. of Korea **30** D5
Tongking • Vietnam **108** A1
Tongliao • China **29** G2
Tongling • China **29** F4
Tonglu • China **107** J3
Tongoa • Vanuatu **35** (2) B2
Tongtian Hel • China **28** G2
Tongue • United Kingdom **6** H3
Tongue • MT/WY, United States **38** J7
Tönisvorst • Germany **81** E1
Tonk • India **105** C6
Tonkin, Gulf of • China/Vietnam **31** D2
Tonle Sap • Cambodia **31** C4
Tönning • Germany **8** D2
Tonopah • NV, United States **117** F4
Tønsberg • Norway **94** B4
Tonto Nat. Mon. • AZ, United States **118** J3
Tonto Nat. Mon. **Park** • AZ, United States **120** [111]
Tooele • ID, United States **40** D3
Toowoomba • QL, Australia **111** F6
Top End, The • NT, Australia **111** E2
Topçam Plaji • Turkey **93** G3
Topeka • KS, United States **41** G4
Topki • Russian Fed. **26** O6
Topko, gora • Russian Fed. **27** M5
Toplita • Romania **14** M3
Töplitz • Germany **81** F3
Topol'cany • Slovak Rep. **13** H9
Topolnica • Bulgaria **15** F1
Topolovgrad • Bulgaria **97** D3
Tor Bay • United Kingdom **74** F5
Torbali • Turkey **15** I5
Torbat-e Heydariyeh • Iran **18** G2
Torbat-e Jam • Iran **18** H2
Torcross **Beach** • United Kingdom **75** [108]
Tordesillas • Spain **11** G3
Töreboda • Sweden **95** F3
Toresund • Sweden **95** D3
Torgelow • Germany **8** J3
Torgon **Ski** • Switzerland **70** [74]
Torhamn • Sweden **95** F12
Torhout • Belgium **80** B2
Tori • India **105** C8
Torino **Heritage C** • Italy **64** [108]
Torino • Italy **91** E5
Torkovichi • Russian Fed. **97** E1
Tormes • Spain **11** F3
Torne älv • Sweden **16** K3
Torne-träsk • Sweden **16** J2
Torneå • Finland **16** M4
Tornesch • Germany **8** E3
Torngat Mtns • NF/QU, Canada **39** S5
Tornio • Finland **16** M4
Tornionjoki • Finland **16** M3
Toro, Cerro del • Argentina/Chile **44** C4
Toro Muerto • Peru **127** B4
Törökszentmiklós • Hungary **13** J10
Toronto • OT, Canada **122** B9
Toropets • Russian Fed. **97** E3
Tororo • Uganda **101** G1
Toros Daglari • Turkey **15** N7
Torpa • Sweden **95** F6
Torquay • United Kingdom **74** F5
Torquay **Beach** • United Kingdom **75** [100-102]
Torralba • Portugal **88** E6
Torre Annunziata **Heritage C** • Italy **64** [128]
Torre Annunziata • Italy **91** G3
Torre de Areas • Portugal **88** E8
Torre de Carredo • Spain **11** G1
Torre de la Higuera • Spain **86** B1
Torre de Moncorvo • Portugal **11** E3
Torre del Greco • Italy **91** G3
Torre del Mar • Spain **86** B7
Torre-Pacheco • Spain **11** K7
Torreblanca • Spain **11** L4
Torreblanca **Beach** • Spain **68** [120]
Torredembarra **Beach** • Spain **68** [121]
Torredembarra • Spain **87** D3
Torredonjimeno • Spain **86** B3
Torreilles **Beach** • France **68** [128]
Torrelavega • Spain **11** G1
Torremolinos **Beach** • Spain **68** [114]
Torremolinos • Spain **86** B7
Torrens Creek • QL, Australia **111** F3
Torrens, Lake • SA, Australia **34** G6
Torreón • Mexico **40** F6
Torres de Alacala • Morocco **101** D2
Torres Is. • Vanuatu **35** (2) B1
Torres Strait • Australia **34** H1
Torres Vedras **Beach** • Portugal **68** [98]
Torrevieja **Beach** • Spain **68** [118]
Torrevieja • Spain **87** C3
Torridge • United Kingdom **74** F2
Torrox • Spain **86** B7
Torsås **Beach** • Sweden **69** [16]
Torsby • Sweden **16** G6
Torshälla • Sweden **95** D3
Torsö • Sweden **95** F3
Tortola • British Virgin Is. **58** B7
Tortona • Italy **91** E6
Tortoreto **Beach** • Italy **69** [161]
Tortosa • Spain **11** L4
Tortosa, Cabo de • Spain **11** L4
Tortuga • Venezuela **43** D1
Torugart • China **26** M9
Torun • Poland **13** H4
Torun **Heritage C** • Poland **64** [137]
Torup • Sweden **95** F7
Torver • United Kingdom **74** C4
Tory I. • Ireland **79** D1
Torzhok • Russian Fed. **97** E3
Toscana • Italy **91** E11
Toshka Depression • Egypt **101** F5
Toson Hu • China **28** G1
Töss • Switzerland **9** D9
Tossa de Mar **Beach** • Spain **68** [123]
Tossa de Mar • Spain **87** D4
Tossens **Spa** • Germany **83** [52]
Tostado • Argentina **44** D4
Tostedt • Germany **8** E3
Tosterön • Sweden **95** D3
Tostón • Fuerteventura, Canary Is. **87** E2
Totak • Norway **94** C6
Totana • Spain **11** J7
Tôtes • France **5** E5
Totma • Russian Fed. **17** G2
Totnes • United Kingdom **74** F5
Totness • Suriname **43** F2
Totora • Bolivia **44** C2
Totoya • Fiji **35** (2) E2
Tottori • Japan **30** H7
Touba • Côte d'Ivoire **22** C3
Toubkal, Jebel • Morocco **101** D5
Tougan • Burkina Faso **22** D2
Touggourt • Algeria **20** G2
Tougué • Guinea **20** C6
Toûil • Algeria **20** F2
Toukota • Mali **22** C2
Toul • France **10** K5
Toulon • France **85** H3
Toulouse • France **85** G4
Toummo • Niger **21** B3
Toungoo • Myanmar **31** B3
Touques • France **5** D5
Touquet-Paris-Plage, le • France **5** E4
Touraine • France **84** D4
Tourcoing • France **10** H3
Touriñan, Cabo • Spain **11** B1
Tourine • Mauritania **20** C4
Tourmalet, Col du • France **85** J2
Tournai • Belgium **80** A14
Touro Synagogue Nat. Hist. Site **Park** • RI, United States **121** [338]
Touroparc • France **85** F1
Tours • France **84** D2
Toury • France **10** G5
Toussoro • Central African Rep. **23** C2
Toussuire, la **Ski** • France **70** [46]
Toussuire, la • France **85** F4
Touws • South Africa **100** C6
Touws River • South Africa **100** C6
Tovdal • Norway **94** C6
Townshend, Cape • QL, Australia **111** F4
Townshend I. • QL, Australia **111** F4
Townsville • QL, Australia **111** F1
Towton • United Kingdom **71** A7
Towuti, Danau • Indonesia **32** (1) B3
Toyama • Japan **30** I6
Toyama-Wan • Japan **30** I6
Toyapakeh • Indonesia **110** C4
Toyo'oka • Japan **30** H7
Toyohashi • Japan **30** I7
Tozeur • Tunisia **101** E3
Traben-Trarbach • Germany **82** H3
Traben-Trarbach **Spa** • Germany **83** [161]
Trablous • Lebanon **18** C3
Trabzon • Turkey **18** D1
Trafalgar, Cabo • Spain **86** B5
Tragaki **Beach** • Greece **69** [172]
Tragáki • Greece **92** C3
Traighli • Ireland **79** F5
Trail • BC, Canada **122** C4
Trakai Nat. Park **Park** • Lithuania **72** [147]
Tralee • Ireland **79** F5
Tralee Bay • Ireland **79** F5
Tramore • Ireland **7** E9
Tramuntana, Serra de • Majorca, Spain **87** H1
Tranås • Sweden **95** F4
Tranebjerg • Denmark **95** F10
Tranemo • Sweden **95** F7
Trang • Thailand **31** B5
Trangan • Indonesia **32** (1) D4
Trani • Italy **12** K7
Trans-Siberian Railway • Russian Fed. **96** A3
Transylvania • Romania **14** L3
Transylvanian Alps • Romania **96** B2
Tranum Strand • Denmark **95** F5
Trápani • Sicily, Italy **90** D1
Traralgon • VI, Australia **111** G3
Trarza • Mauritania **20** B5
Trás os Montes • Portugal **11** D3
Trasimeno, Lago • Italy **91** E11
Träslövsläge **Beach** • Sweden **68** [3]
Trasvase, Canal de • Spain **11** I5
Traumland • Germany **82** G6
Traun • Austria **13** C9
Traun [Riv] • Austria **13** D9
Traunreit • Germany **82** J4
Traunsee • Austria **89** H4
Traunstein • Germany **82** J4
Travemünde • Germany **8** F3
Travemünde **Spa** • Germany **83** [29]
Travers, Mt • New Zealand **35** D5
Traverse City • MI, United States **41** I3
Travnik • Bosnia-Herz. **14** E5
Travo • Corsica, France **85** L4
Trbovlje • Slovenia **13** E11
Treasure Beach • Jamaica **124** C3
Treasure Cay • Bahamas **124** B1
Trebaluger • Minorca, Spain **87** F4
Trebbin • Germany **81** F3
Trébeurden **Beach** • France **68** [80]
Trébeurden • France **84** C1
Trebic • Czech Rep. **96** C4
Trebisov • Slovak Rep. **13** K9
Trebizond • Turkey **98** B1
Trebnje • Slovenia **13** E12
Trebon • Czech Rep. **96** C4
Trédrez **Beach** • France **68** [80]
Trédrez • France **84** C1
Treetops **Ski** • MI, United States **116** [131]
Trégastel **Beach** • France **68** [80]
Trégastel • France **84** C1
Tregosse Is. • CL, Australia **111** F2
Tréguier • France **84** C2
Treinta y Tres • Uruguay **44** F5
Treis-Karden • Germany **82** H1
Trelew • Argentina **45** C4
Trelleborg • Sweden **95** F15
Tremblade, la **Beach** • France **68** [84]
Tremblade, la • France **85** G1
Tremblant **Ski** • QU, Canada **116** [33]
Tremezzo • Italy **91** E2
Tremitti, Is. • Italy **12** J6
Tremmen • Germany **81** F1
Tremp • Spain **11** L2
Trencín • Slovak Rep. **13** H9
Trenque Lauguen • Argentina **44** D6
Trent • United Kingdom **75** A4
Trentino-Südtirol • Italy **91** E3
Trenton • NJ, United States **118** H1
Trenton • OT, Canada **122** B6
Trepassey • NF, Canada **123** D4
Tréport, le • France **10** G3
Tres Arboles • Uruguay **44** E5
Tres Arroyos • Argentina **45** D3
Três Corações • Brazil **127** C3
Tres Esquinas • Colombia **43** B3
Três Lagoas • Brazil **44** F3
Três Marias, Reprêsa • Brazil **44** G2
Tres Picos • Argentina **45** D3
Tres Puntas, Cabo • Argentina **45** C5
Três Rios • Brazil **127** C4
Tres Zapotes • Mexico **123** E4
Tresaith **Beach** • United Kingdom **75** [172]
Treska • F.Y.R. of Macedonia **15** C2
Treskavica • Bosnia-Herz. **14** F6
Treuchtlingen • Germany **9** F8
Treuer Range • NT, Australia **112** H1
Treviglio • Italy **12** D3
Trevinca, Peña • Spain **11** E2
Treviño • Spain **11** I2
Treviso • Italy **91** E8
Trevose Head • United Kingdom **74** F4
Trévou-Treguignec **Beach** • France **68** [80]
Triánda • Rhodes, Greece **93** F2
Triberg • Germany **82** G8
Triberg **Spa** • Germany **83** [197]
Tricase • Italy **12** M9
Trichur • India **106** D10
Trier **Heritage C** • Germany **64** [40]
Trier • Germany **82** H3
Trieste **Beach** • Italy **69** [167]
Trieste • Italy **91** E8
Trieste, Golfo di • Italy/Slovenia **91** E8
Trieux • France **10** B5
Triglav • Slovenia **14** A3
Triglav Nat. Park **Park** • Slovenia **72** [107]
Trigno • Italy **14** B8
Trihonida, Límni • Greece **15** C5
Tríkala • Greece **15** C4
Tríkomo • Cyprus **93** J2
Trikora, Puncak • Indonesia **32** (1) E3
Trim • Ireland **79** E1
Trincomalee • Sri Lanka **106** D15
Trindade, I. da • Atlantic Ocean **19** B7
Trinec • Czech Rep. **13** H8
Trinidad • Bolivia **44** D1
Trinidad **Heritage C** • Cuba **62** [35]
Trinidad **Heritage C** • Paraguay **62** [56]
Trinidad • Cuba **124** D2
Trinidad • Trinidad & Tobago **125** K3
Trinidad • Uruguay **127** D2
Trinidad & Tobago • West Indies **125** K
Trinidade, I. da • Brazil **127** A2
Trinitapoli • Italy **12** K7
Trinity • TX, United States **119** N4
Trinity Bay • NF, Canada **123** D4
Trinity Hills • Trinidad & Tobago **125** K4
Trinkstein • Italy **90** B2
Triomote • Japan **29** G6
Trípoli • Greece **15** D6
Tripoli • Lebanon **18** C3
Tripoli • Libya **21** B1
Tripolitania • Libya **21** B2
Tripura • India **28** F4
Tristan da Cunha • Atlantic Ocean **19** C9
Trivandrum • India **106** D14
Trnava • Slovak Rep. **13** G9
Trobriand • Papua New Guinea **35** (1) E2
Trofors • Norway **16** G4
Trogir • Croatia **14** D6
Trogir **Heritage C** • Croatia **64** [156]
Troglav • Bosnia-Herz. **14** D5
Tróia • Portugal **88** D2
Trois Fourches, Cap de • Morocco **101** D2
Trois-Rivières • QU, Canada **122** B4
Troisdorf • Germany **5** K4
Troitsk • Chelyabinsk, Russian Fed. **26** J7
Troitsk • Krasnoyarsk, Russian Fed. **26** P6
Troitsko-Pechorsk • Russian Fed. **17** J2
Trollhättan • Sweden **95** F2
Trollhaugen **Ski** • WI, United States **116** [119]
Troms • Norway **16** J2
Tromsø • Norway **16** J2
Trondheim • Norway **16** F5
Trondheimsfjorden • Norway **16** F5
Troödos • Cyprus **93** J3
Troödos Mtns • Cyprus **93** J3
Troödos region **Heritage C** • Cyprus **64** [200]
Troon **Beach** • United Kingdom **75** [1]
Tropea • Italy **12** J10
Tropical, Costa • Spain **86** B7
Trosa • Sweden **95** D4
Trossachs, The • United Kingdom **74** B1
Trostberg • Germany **82** J4
Trotus • Romania **14** N3
Troussay [Château] • France **84** D2
Trout Lake • NT, Canada **38** G4
Trout Lake • OT, Canada **38** M6
Troutbeck • United Kingdom **74** C4
Troutbeck • Zimbabwe **102** J2
Trouville-sur-Mer • France **10** F4
Trowbridge • United Kingdom **74** F3
Trowulan • Java, Indonesia **110** D8
Troy • AL, United States **41** I5
Troy • Turkey **92** D2
Troyan • Bulgaria **14** L7
Troyes • France **10** J5
Trujillo • Spain **11** F5
Trujillo • Peru **43** B5
Trujillo • Venezuela **43** C2
Truman, Harry S., Nat. Hist. Site **Park** • MO, United States **121** [173]

Trundholm **Beach** • Denmark 68 [43]
Trung Phan • Vietnam 31 D3
Truro • United Kingdom 74 F4
Truro • NS, Canada 123 D7
Truth or Consequences • NM, United States 118 J4
Trutnov • Czech Rep. 96 C2
Truva • Greece 92 D2
Tryavna • Bulgaria 97 D3
Trysilelva • Norway 16 G6
Trzcianka • Poland 13 F4
Tsabong • Botswana 24 C5
Tsambika • Rhodes, Greece 93 F2
Tsangaráda **Beach** • Greece 69 [188]
Tsarkoye Selo • Russian Fed. 97 E1
Tsau • Botswana 24 C4
Tsavo • Kenya 23 F4
Tsavo East Nat. Park • Kenya 101 G4
Tsavo Nat. **Park** • Kenya 103 [85]
Tsavo West Nat. Park • Kenya 101 G4
Tseung Kwan O • Hong Kong, China 107 H6
Tshane • Botswana 24 C4
Tshikapa • Dem. Rep. of Congo 23 C5
Tshuapa • Dem. Rep. of Congo 23 C4
Tshwaane • Botswana 24 C4
Tsiafajavona • Madagascar 24 H3
Tsim Sha Tsui • Hong Kong, China 107 H6
Tsimlyanskoye Vdkhr. • Russian Fed. 17 G5
Tsing Yi • Hong Kong, China 107 H5
Tsingy Bemaraha, Réserve du **Heritage N** • Madagascar 61 [98]
Tsiroanomandidy • Madagascar 24 H3
Tsitsikamma Mtns • South Africa 100 C7
Tsitsikamma Nat. Park • South Africa 100 C7
Tsodilo Hills • Botswana 24 C3
Tsetserleg • Mongolia 29 C1
Tsu • Japan 30 I7
Tsuchiura • Japan 30 K6
Tsuen Wan • Hong Kong, China 107 H5
Tsugaru-Kaikyo • Japan 30 K4
Tsumeb • Namibia 24 B3
Tsurugi • Japan 30 G8
Tsuruoka • Japan 30 J5
Tsushima • Japan 30 E7
Tsushima-Kaikyo • Japan 30 E8
Tsuyama • Japan 30 G7
Tua • Portugal 11 D3
Tual • Indonesia 32 (1) D4
Tuam • Ireland 79 F4
Tuamotu • French Polynesia 33 M7
Tuapse • Russian Fed. 17 E6
Tuas • Singapore 108 E1
Tuatapere • New Zealand 112 L3
Tuba City • AZ, United States 118 J1
Tubai Is. • French Polynesia 33 L8
Tuban • Java, Indonesia 110 D3
Tubarão • Brazil 44 G4
Tubayq, Jabal at • Saudi Arabia 21 G2
Tubbataha Reef Marine Park **Heritage N** • Philippines 61 [124]
Tübingen • Germany 82 G6
Tubize • Belgium 5 H4
Tubruq • Libya 21 D1
Tubuai • French Polynesia 33 M8
Tuchola • Poland 13 G4
Tucson • AZ, United States 118 J3
Tucumcari • NM, United States 40 F4
Tucupita • Venezuela 43 E2
Tucuruí, Represa de • Brazil 45 (1) B2
Tudela • Spain 11 J2
Tuen Mun • Hong Kong, China 107 H5
Tufi • Papua New Guinea 35 (1) D2
Tugela • South Africa 100 B2
Tuguegarao • Philippines 31 G3
Tugur • Russian Fed. 27 M6
Tuineje • Fuerteventura, Canary Is. 87 E2
Tuk Tuk • Indonesia 110 B2
Tukangbesi, Kepulauan • Indonesia 32 (1) B4
Tuktoyaktuk • NT, Canada 38 E3
Tukums • Latvia 16 L8
Tula • Russian Fed. 17 F4
Tula • Mexico 123 E2
Tulamben • Bali, Indonesia 110 C2
Tulancingo • Mexico 123 E2
Tulayat al Ghassul • Jordan 98 A6
Tulbagh • South Africa 100 C5
Tulcan • Colombia 43 B3
Tulcea • Romania 97 D2
Tuli, Fort • Zimbabwe 102 J3
Tulla • Ireland 79 F6
Tullamarine [Apt] • VI, Australia 111 G3
Tullamore • Ireland 7 E8
Tulle • France 85 G2
Tullow • Ireland 79 E3
Tully • QL, Australia 111 F1
Tuloma • Russian Fed. 16 Q2
Tulovo • Bulgaria 97 D3
Tulsa • OK, United States 41 G4
Tulsk • Ireland 79 F2
Tuluá • Colombia 43 B3
Tulum • Mexico 37 D3
Tulun • Russian Fed. 26 R7
Tulungagung • Java, Indonesia 110 D7
Tumacacori Nat. Mon. • AZ, United States 118 J3
Tumacacori Nat. Mon. **Park** • AZ, United States 120 [115]
Tumaco • Colombia 43 B3
Tumba • Sweden 95 D4
Tumbes • Peru 43 A4
Tumen • China 30 E3
Tumen [Riv] • China/D.P.R. of Korea 30 E3
Tumkur • India 106 D6
Tummel • United Kingdom 74 B1
Tumucumaque, Serra • Brazil 43 G3
Tun • Sweden 95 F3
Tun Chung • Hong Kong, China 107 H5
Tunapuna • Trinidad & Tobago 125 K3
Tunas de Zaza • Cuba 124 D2
Tunduma • Tanzania 102 H3
Tunduru • Tanzania 102 H4
Tundzha • Bulgaria 14 N7
Tung Ling Chau • Hong Kong, China 107 H6
Tungabhadra • India 106 D2
Tungelsta • Sweden 95 D4
Tunis **Heritage C** • Tunisia 64 [226]
Tunis • Tunisia 101 E2
Tunis, Golfe de • Tunisia 101 E2
Tunisia • Africa 101 E
Tunja • Colombia 43 C2
Tunnsjøen • Norway 16 G4
Tunxi • China 107 J3
Tuostakh • Russian Fed. 27 M3
Tupã • Brazil 44 F3
Tupanciretã • Brazil 44 F4
Tupelo Nat. Battlefield **Park** • MS, United States 121 [202]
Tupiza • Bolivia 44 C3
Tupungato, Cerro • Argentina 44 C5
Tuquan • China 27 J7
Túquerres • Colombia 43 B3
Tur'ah Jonglei • Sudan 21 F6
Tûr, El • Egypt 101 F4
Tura • Russian Fed. 26 R5
Turabah • Saudi Arabia 18 D4
Turabah • Saudi Arabia 18 D5
Turan • Russian Fed. 26 P7
Turana, Khrebet • Russian Fed. 27 L6
Turangi • New Zealand 112 K4
Turayf, At • Saudi Arabia 18 C3
Turbah, At • Yemen 21 H5
Turballe, la **Beach** • France 68 [82]
Turballe, la • France 84 C4
Turbat • Pakistan 18 H4
Turbo • Colombia 43 B2
Turda • Romania 14 K3
Turek • Poland 13 H5
Turenne • France 85 G2
Turfan • China 98 B3
Turgay • Kazakhstan 26 J8
Turgay Basin • Kazakhstan 96 A3
Turgayskoye Plato • Kazakhstan 26 J7
Turgovishte • Bulgaria 97 D3
Turgut • Turkey 15 M5
Turgutlu • Turkey 15 I5
Turia • Spain 11 K5
Turiaçu, Baía de • Brazil 45 (1) C2
Turimiquire • Venezuela 43 E2
Turin **Heritage C** • Italy 64 [108]
Turin • Italy 91 E5
Turinsk • Russian Fed. 26 J6
Turkana • Kenya 23 F3
Turkana, Lake • Kenya 101 G1
Turkestan • Kazakhstan 26 K9
Turkey • Asia/Europe 4 R8
Turkey Creek • WA, Australia 34 E3
Türkmenbashi • Turkmenistan 18 F1
Turkmenistan • Asia 26 I10
Turks & Caicos Is. • West Indies 37 G3
Turku • Finland 95 E3
Turku Archipelago • Finland 95 E3
Turkwel • Kenya 101 G1
Turnagain, Cape • New Zealand 35 F5
Turneffe • Belize 37 D4
Turner's Hall Woods • Barbados 125 H1
Turnhout • Belgium 80 A11
Turnov • Czech Rep. 96 C2
Turnu Magurele • Romania 14 L6
Turoa • New Zealand 112 K4
Turpan • China 26 O9
Turpan Depression • China 26 P9
Turquino, Pico • Cuba 124 D8
Turquoise Coast • Turkey 93 G
Turtkul • Uzbekistan 18 H1
Turtle I. • Bali, Indonesia 110 C4
Turtle I. • CL, Australia 111 F2
Turukhansk • Russian Fed. 26 O4
Turun Ja Pori • Finland 95 E3
Turunç **Beach** • Turkey 69 [233]
Turunç • Turkey 92 D9
Tuscaloosa • AL, United States 41 I5
Tuscánia • Italy 91 F1
Tuscany • Italy 90 A1
TusenFryd **Park** • Norway 73 [4]
TusenFryd • Norway 94 B2
Tuskegee Institute Nat. Hist. Site **Park** • AL, United States 121 [204]
Tuticorin • India 106 D11
Tutóia • Brazil 45 (1) C2
Tuttlingen • Germany 82 G8
Tutuala • East Indiea 32 (1) C4
Tutuila • American Samoa 35 (2) F1
Tutupaca, Volcán • Peru 127 B4
Tuul • Mongolia 27 G7
Tuva • Russian Fed. 26 Q7
Tuvalu • Pacific Ocean 33 I6
Tuvana-i-Ra • Fiji 35 (2) E3
Tuvana-i-Tholo • Fiji 35 (2) D3
Tuwayq, Jabal • Saudi Arabia 18 E5
Tuxpán • Mexico 37 (1) A1
Tuxpan • Mexico 123 E2
Tuxtla Gutiérrez • Mexico 37 C4
Túy • Spain 11 C2
Tuy Hoa • Vietnam 31 D4
Tuz Gölü • Turkey 15 O5
Tuz, Lake • Turkey 92 A3
Tuzigoot Nat. Mon. • AZ, United States 118 J1
Tuzigoot Nat. Mon. **Park** • AZ, United States 120 [108]
Tuzla • Bosnia-Herz. 14 F5
Tuzlata • Bulgaria 97 D4
Tvedestrand • Norway 95 F1
Tveitsund • Norway 94 C6
Tver' • Russian Fed. 97 E4
Tverfjellet • Norway 94 C2
Tvertsa • Russian Fed. 97 E3
Tvurditsa • Bulgaria 15 G1
Tweed • United Kingdom 6 J6
Tweedsmuir Prov. Park • BC, Canada 122 C1
Twelve Apostles, The • VI, Australia 111 G3
Twelve Bens • Ireland 79 F3
Twente [Apt] • Netherlands 80 A8
Twilight Cove • WA, Australia 34 E6
Twin Falls • ID, United States 117 E4
Twin Is. • NU, Canada 39 O6
Twin Peaks • UT, United States 116 B
Twistringen • Germany 8 D4
Two Thumb Range • New Zealand 35 C6
Twycross • United Kingdom 74 D2
Txiki **Park** • Spain 73 [77]
Tychy • Poland 13 H7
Tygda • Russian Fed. 27 K6
Tyin • Norway 94 C4
Tyler • TX, United States 119 N2
Tylösand • Sweden 95 F11
Tylösand • Sweden 95 F4
Tym • Russian Fed. 26 N6
Tymovskoye • Russian Fed. 46 A4
Tynda • Russian Fed. 27 J5
Tyndrum • United Kingdom 74 B1
Tyne • United Kingdom 7 K7
Tynemouth • United Kingdom 7 K6
Tynemouth **Beach** • United Kingdom 75 [15-16]
Tynset • Norway 16 F5
Typhoon Lagoon • FL, United States 121 C1
Tyre • Lebanon 98 A1
Tyrella **Beach** • United Kingdom 75 [241]
Tyrifjorden • Norway 94 B1
Tyrone • United Kingdom 75 A3
Tyrrhenian Sea • Mediterranean Sea 12 G9
Tysnesøy • Norway 94 C5
Tyssedal • Norway 94 C4
Tystberga • Sweden 95 D3
Tyukalinsk • Russian Fed. 26 L6
Tyulenovo • Bulgaria 97 D4
Tyumen • Russian Fed. 26 K6
Tywi, Afon- • United Kingdom 7 I10
Tywyn • United Kingdom 7 H9
Tywyn **Beach** • United Kingdom 75 [186]
Tzermiádo • Crete, Greece 93 E7

U

Uaroo • WA, Australia 34 C4
Uaupés • Brazil 43 D4
Ubá • Brazil 127 C2
Ubaitaba • Brazil 44 I1
Ubangi • Dem. Rep. of Congo 23 B3
Ubatuba • Brazil 127 C3
Ubayyid, Al • Sudan 21 F5
Ube • Japan 30 F8
Ubeda • Spain 11 H6
Ubekendt Ejland • Greenland 39 U2
Uberaba • Brazil 44 G2
Uberlândia • Brazil 44 G2
Überlingen • Germany 82 J5
Überlingen **Spa** • Germany 83 [212]
Ubin • Singapore 108 E2
Ubiña, Peña • Spain 11 F1
Ubon Rat Reservoir • Thailand 109 F2
Ubon Ratchathani • Thailand 31 C3
Ubstadt-Weiher • Germany 9 D7
Ubsu-Nur • Mongolia 26 P8
Ubud • Bali, Indonesia 110 C4
Ubundu • Dem. Rep. of Congo 23 D4
Ucayali • Peru 43 C5
Uchami • Russian Fed. 26 Q5
Uchiura-Wan • Japan 30 K3
Uchte • Germany 5 L2
Ückeritz **Spa** • Germany 83 [284]
Uckermark • Germany 8 I3
Uçpinar • Turkey 93 G2
Udachnyy • Russian Fed. 26 W4
Udaipur • India 105 C5
Udayapur • India 105 C7
Uddevalla • Sweden 95 F2
Uddjaure • Sweden 16 I4
Udgir • India 28 C5
Udhagamandalam • India 106 D10
Udine • Italy 91 E4
Udmurtia • Russian Fed. 17 I3
Udon Thani • Thailand 31 C3
Udskaya Guba • Russian Fed. 27 M5
Udupi • India 106 D6
Uebonti • Indonesia 32 (1) B3
Uecker • Germany 8 J3
Ueckermünde • Germany 8 J3
Ueda • Japan 30 J6
Uele • Dem. Rep. of Congo 23 C3
Uelen • Russian Fed. 27 X3
Uelzen • Germany 8 F4
Uetze • Germany 8 F4
Ufa • Russian Fed. 17 J4
Ufa [Riv] • Russian Fed. 26 I6
Ugab • Namibia 24 A4
Uganda • Africa 23 E3
Ugine • France 85 F2
Uglekamensk • Russian Fed. 30 G3
Uglian Pasman • Croatia 14 C5
Uglich • Russian Fed. 97 E4
Uherské Hradiste • Czech Rep. 13 G8
Uhlava • Czech Rep. 96 C3
Uig • United Kingdom 6 F4
Uige • Angola 23 B5
Uitenhage • South Africa 100 C8
Uithoorn • Netherlands 80 C2
Uithuizen • Netherlands 80 A4
Ujfehértó • Hungary 13 K10
Uji-Gunto • Japan 30 E9
Ujjain • India 28 C4
Ujung • Bali, Indonesia 110 C4
Ujung Kulon Nat. Park **Heritage N** • Indonesia 61 [125]
Ujung Pandang • Indonesia 32 (1) A4
Ukhta • Russian Fed. 17 I2
Ukiah • CA, United States 40 B4
Ukmerge • Lithuania 13 N2
Ukraine • Europe 15 E4
Ula • Turkey 15 J6
Ulā, Al • Saudi Arabia 18 C4
Ulaanbaatar • Mongolia 27 G7
Ulaangom • Mongolia 26 P8
Ulan Bator • Mongolia 27 G7
Ulan Tajga • Mongolia 26 Q7
Ulan Ude • Russian Fed. 27 G6
Ulan Ul Hu • China 28 F2
Ulanhad • China 29 F2
Ular • Singapore 108 E3
Ulàssai • Sardinia, Italy 90 C4
Ulchin • Rep. of Korea 30 E6
Ulcinj • F.R. of Yugoslavia 15 A2
Ule älv • Finland 16 M4
Uleåborg • Finland 16 M4
Ulefoss • Norway 94 B3
Ulfborg • Denmark 95 F9
Ulfborg-Vemb **Beach** • Denmark 68 [50]
Ulgiy • Mongolia 26 P8
Ulhasnagar • India 28 B5
Uliastay • Mongolia 26 Q8
Uliga • Marshall Is. 33 I5
Ullapool • United Kingdom 6 G4
Ullared • Sweden 95 F7
Ulldecona • Spain 11 L4
Ullswater • United Kingdom 74 C2
Ullung • Rep. of Korea 30 F6
Ulm • Germany 82 J1
Ulmen • Germany 82 H1
Ulricehamn • Sweden 95 F7
Ulsan • Rep. of Korea 30 E7
Ulsteinvik • Norway 94 C1
Ulster • Ireland/UK 7 E7
Ulu Watu Temple • Bali, Indonesia 110 C4
Uluabat Gölü • Turkey 92 D3
Ulubey • Turkey 15 K5
Uludag • Turkey 92 D3
Uluguru Mtns • Tanzania 23 F5
Ulundi • South Africa 100 B1
Uluru • NT, Australia 112 H3
Uluru-Kata Tjuta Nat. Park **Heritage N** • NT, Australia 61 [132]
Uluru-Kata Tjuta Nat. Park **Heritage C** • Australia 63 [181]
Uluru-Kata Tjuta Nat. Park • NT, Australia 112 H3
Ulus Dag • Turkey 15 J4
Ulva • United Kingdom 75 A2
Ulverston • United Kingdom 74 C4
Ulverstone • TS, Australia 34 I8
Ulvik • Norway 94 C4
Ulya • Russian Fed. 27 N5
Ulytau • Kazakhstan 26 K8
Uman • Ukraine 17 E5
Umánarssuaq • Greenland 39 W5
Umba • Russian Fed. 17 E1
Umboi I. • Papua New Guinea 35 (1) D2
Umbria • Italy 12 G6
Ume älv • Sweden 16 J4
Umeå • Sweden 16 K5
Umm ar Rizam • Libya 21 D1
Umm as Samim • Oman 18 G5
Umm Durman • Sudan 21 F4
Umm Lajj • Saudi Arabia 18 C4
Umpolo • Angola 24 B2
Umsini, Gunung • Indonesia 32 (1) D3
Umtata • South Africa 24 D6
Umuarama • Brazil 44 F3
Umurbaba Dagi • Turkey 15 J5
Umurbey • Turkey 15 H3
Una • Bosnia-Herz. 14 D5
Unalaska • AK, United States 36 (1) E2
Unayzah • Saudi Arabia 18 D4
Uncompahgre Peak • CO, United States 116 A
Undandita • NT, Australia 112 H1
Unden • Sweden 95 F3
Undredal • Norway 94 C4
Undu Point • Fiji 35 (2) D2
Ungava, Baie d' • QU, Canada 39 R5
Ungava Peninsula • QU, Canada 36 J3
Ungava, Péninsule d' • QU, Canada 39 Q4
Unggi • D.P.R. of Korea 30 F3
Ungheni • Moldova 14 O2
Ungwana Bay • Kenya 101 G4
União da Vitória • Brazil 44 F4
Unicov • Czech Rep. 13 G8
Unije • Croatia 14 B5
Unimak • AK, United States 36 (1) E2
Union, Fort, Nat. Mon. **Park** • NM, United States 120 [131]
Uniondale • South Africa 100 C7
United Arab Emirates • Asia 18 F5
United Kingdom • Europe 6/7
United States • N. America 36
Unity • SA, Canada 38 J6
Universal Studios Florida • FL, United States 121 C2
Universal Studios Hollywood **Park** • CA, United States 120 [E]
Universales, Montes • Spain 11 J4
Unna • Germany 5 K3
Unna • Germany 81 E2
Unst • United Kingdom 6 L1
Unstrut • Germany 9 F5
Unter Engadin • Switzerland 89 G4
Unteres Odertal, Nationalpark **Park** • Germany/Poland 72 [61]
Unterfranken • Germany 9 E7
Unterinntal • Austria 89 H3
Unterwasser • Switzerland 89 G3
Unzha • Russian Fed. 17 G3
Upata • Venezuela 43 E2
Upemba, Parc nat. de l' **Park** • Dem. Rep. of Congo 103 [59]
Upernavik • Greenland 39 T2
Upin • Indonesia 32 (1) C3
Upington • South Africa 24 C5
Uplands [Apt] • OT, Canada 122 B7
Upolu • Western Samoa 35 (2) F1
Upper Austria • Austria 89 F3
Upper Canada Village • OT, Canada 122 B7
Upper Egypt • Egypt 101 F4
Upper Hutt • New Zealand 35 E5
Upper Klamath Lake • OR, United States 117 E3
Uppsala • Sweden 95 D2
Uppsala [Adm] • Sweden 95 D2
Upshi • Jammu & Kashmir 28 C2
Uqlat as Sugur • Saudi Arabia 21 H2
Ur • Iraq 18 E3
Urakawa • Japan 30 L3
Ural • Kazakhstan/Russian Fed. 17 I4
Ural • Kazakhstan/Russian Fed. 26 H8
Urals • Russian Fed. 26 I6
Uranium City • SA, Canada 38 J5
Uraricoeral • Brazil 43 E3
Urawa • Japan 30 J7
Urbano Santos • Brazil 45 (1) C2
Urbino • Italy 91 E12
Uren • Russian Fed. 17 H3
Urengoy • Russian Fed. 26 M4
Urenui • New Zealand 112 K3
Uréparapara • Vanuatu 35 (2) B1
Urgal • Russian Fed. 27 L6
Urgench • Uzbekistan 18 H1
Urhjo Kekkonen Nat. Park **Park** • Finland 72 [30]
Urla • Turkey 15 H5
Urlings • Antigua & Barbuda 125 F3
Urnes **Heritage C** • Norway 63 [68]
Urnes stavkirke • Norway 94 C4
Urosevac • F.R. of Yugoslavia 14 I7
Urshult • Sweden 95 F12
Ursus • Poland 13 J5
Uruapan • Mexico 123 E3
Urubamba • Peru 127 B2
Urubamba • Peru 127 B2
Uruçui • Brazil 45 (1) C3
Urucurituba • Brazil 43 F4
Uruguaiana • Brazil 44 E4
Uruguay • S. America 44 E5
Uruguay [Riv] • S. America 44 E4
Urümqi • China 26 O9
Urup, Ostrov • Russian Fed. 27 P7
Uryupinsk • Russian Fed. 17 G4
Urzhum • Russian Fed. 17 H3
Urziceni • Romania 97 D1
Urzig • Germany 82 H3
US East Coast cruise area • N. America 58 A2
US Virgin Is. • West Indies 37 I4
Usa • Russian Fed. 4 W3
Usa • Russian Fed. 17 J1
Usak • Turkey 92 D6
Usambara Mtns • Tanzania 102 H2
Usborne, Mt • Falkland Is. 45 E6
Usedom • Germany 8 J3
Usedom **Spa** • Germany 83 [283]
Ushakova, Ostrov • Russian Fed. 96 A4
Ushakovskoye • Russian Fed. 27 V2
Ushkaniy, Ostrov • Russian Fed. 97 A5
Ushuaia • Argentina 45 C6
Usinsk • Russian Fed. 17 J1
Usk • United Kingdom 10 B2
Uskedal • Norway 94 C5
Uskemen • Kazakhstan 26 N7
Usküb • F.Y.R. of Macedonia 71 A14
Usküdar • Turkey 92 D3
Usküp • Turkey 15 I2
Uslar • Germany 8 E5
Usogorsk • Russian Fed. 17 H2
Usolye-Sibirskoye • Russian Fed. 27 F6
USS Arizona Mem. • HI, United States 119 L5
USS Arizona Mem. **Park** • HI, United States 120 [16]
Ussé [Château] • France 84 D2
Ussel • France 10 H8
Usseln **Spa** • Germany 83 [120]
Ussuri • Russian Fed. 27 L7
Ussuriysk • Russian Fed. 27 L8
Ust-Barguzin • Russian Fed. 27 G6
Ust-Corna • Ukraine 14 K1
Ust-Ilimsk • Russian Fed. 26 R6
Ust-Kamchatsk • Russian Fed. 27 R5
Ust-Kara • Russian Fed. 26 J4
Ust-Khayryuzovo • Russian Fed. 46 JJ4
Ust-Kut • Russian Fed. 27 G5
Ust-Kuyga • Russian Fed. 27 M3
Ust-Lyzha • Russian Fed. 17 J1
Ust-Maya • Russian Fed. 27 L4
Ust-Muya • Russian Fed. 27 I5
Ust-Nem • Russian Fed. 17 I2
Ust-Nera • Russian Fed. 27 N4
Ust-Nyukzha • Russian Fed. 27 J5
Ust-Olenëk • Russian Fed. 27 I2
Ust-Omchug • Russian Fed. 27 O4
Ust-Ordynskiy • Russian Fed. 27 F6
Ust-Pit • Russian Fed. 26 P6
Ust-Tsilma • Russian Fed. 17 I1
Ustaoset • Norway 94 C4
Ustek • Czech Rep. 96 C2
Usti nad Labem • Czech Rep. 96 C1
Usti nad Orlici • Czech Rep. 13 F8
Ustica **Beach** • Italy 69 [151]
Ustica, I. di • Italy 90 D1
Ustka • Poland 13 F3
Ustyurt Plateau • Kazakhstan 96 A2
Ustyurt, Plato • Kazakhstan/Uzbekistan 26 I9
Usu • China 26 N9
Usuki • Japan 30 F8
Usumacinta • Guatemala/Mexico 37 C4
Utah • United States 40 D4
Utara, Selat • Penang, Malaysia 108 C2
Utena • Lithuania 16 M9
Utersum **Spa** • Germany 83 [4]
Utete • Tanzania 102 H4
Utica • NY, United States 41 K3
Utica • Tunisia 101 E2
Utiel • Spain 11 J5
Utlängen • Sweden 95 F12
Utne • Norway 94 C4
Utö • Sweden 95 D4
Utö [I.] • Sweden 95 D4
Utopia Aboriginal Land • NT, Australia 112 H2
Utorda Beach • Goa, India 105 B2
Utrecht • Netherlands 80 C4
Utrecht [Adm] • Netherlands 80 A7
Utrera • Spain 11 F7
Utsjoki • Finland 16 N2
Utsunomiya • Japan 30 J6
Uttar Pradesh • India 105 C7
Uttaradit • Thailand 109 G4
Utuado • Puerto Rico 125 E1
Utvær • Norway 94 C3
Uudenmaa • Finland 95 E4
Uusikaupunki • Finland 95 E3
Uva • Russian Fed. 17 I3
Uvalde • TX, United States 40 G6
Uvdal • Norway 94 C4
Uvea • Wallis & Futuna 35 (2) E1
Uvinza • Tanzania 102 H1
Uvira • Dem. Rep. of Congo 23 D4
Uwajima • Japan 30 G8
Uwaynat • Sudan 21 E3
Uwaynat Wannin • Libya 21 B2
Uxmal • Mexico 37 D3
Uxmal **Heritage C** • Mexico 62 [26]
Uyar • Russian Fed. 26 P6
Uyedineniya, Ostrov • Russian Fed. 26 N2
Uygur Zizhiqu • China 29 A2
Uyuni, Salar de • Bolivia 44 C2
Uz • Slovak Rep. 13 L9
Uzbekistan • Asia 26 J9
Uzerche • France 85 G2
Uzhgorod • Ukraine 13 L9
Uzhur • Russian Fed. 26 P6
Uzum • Turkey 92 D5
Uzümlü • Turkey 93 G2
Uzungwa Range • Tanzania 23 F5
Uzunköprü • Turkey 15 H2

V

Vaadhu Diving Paradise • Maldives 106 E4
Vaal • South Africa 24 D5
Vaala • Finland 16 N4
Vaaldam • South Africa 24 D5
Vaasa • Finland 16 K5
Vaasa **Beach** • Finland 69 [26]
Vaasa [Adm] • Finland 94 A9
Vabbinfaru • Maldives 106 E2
Vác • Hungary 13 I10
Vacaria • Brazil 44 F4
Vaches, I. aux • Seychelles 106 F2
Vadehavet • Denmark 8 D1
Vadheim • Norway 94 C3
Vadodara • India 28 B4
Vadsø • Norway 16 O1
Vadstena • Sweden 95 F4
Vaduz • Liechtenstein 12 D1
Vadvetjåkka Nat. Park **Park** • Sweden 72 [16]
Værløse **Beach** • Denmark 68 [39]
Værøy • Norway 16 G3
Vågåmo • Norway 94 C2
Vaganski vrh • Croatia 14 C5
Vagator Beach • Goa, India 105 B1
Vågåvatn • Norway 94 C2
Vaggeryd • Sweden 95 F7
Vagnhärad • Sweden 95 D3
Vagos **Beach** • Portugal 68 [95]
Vågsfjorden • Norway 16 I2
Vågslid • Norway 94 C6
Vågsøy • Norway 94 C1
Váh • Slovak Rep. 13 I8
Vai • Crete, Greece 93 E8
Vail **Ski** • CO, United States 116 [94]
Vainguinim Beach • Goa, India 105 B1
Vaishali • India 105 C8
Vaksdal • Norway 94 C3
Val André, le • France 84 C2
Val Camónica **Heritage C** • Italy 64 [111]
Val Camónica • Italy 91 E3
Val Cenis **Ski** • France 70 [43]
Val d'Illiez **Ski** • Switzerland 70 [76]
Val d'Isère **Ski** • France 70 [32]
Val d'Isère • France 85 F2
Val d'Oise • France 85 E1
Val d'Or • QU, Canada 39 P7
Val St Come **Ski** • QU, Canada 116 [34]
Val Thorens **Ski** • France 70 [42]
Val Thorens • France 85 F4
Valahmia • Romania 14 K5
Valais • Switzerland 89 G6
Valandovo • F.Y.R. of Macedonia 14 J8
Valasské Mezirici • Czech Rep. 13 G8
Valbella • Switzerland 89 G4
Valberg **Ski** • France 70 [72]
Valcabrère • France 85 J2
Valcheta • Argentina 45 C4
Valdagno • Italy 12 F3
Valdàora **Ski** • Italy 70 [236]
Valdàora • Italy 90 B2
Valday • Russian Fed. 4 Q5
Valday • Russian Fed. 97 E1
Valdayskaya Vozvyshennost • Russian Fed. 97 E3
Valdecañas, Embalse de • Spain 11 F5
Valdeganga • Spain 11 J5
Valdemarsslot • Denmark 95 F14
Valdemarsvik • Sweden 95 F4
Valdepeñas • Spain 11 H6
Valderrama • Spain 86 B6
Valdés, Península • Argentina 45 D4
Valdez • AK, United States 46 DD3
Valdivia • Chile 45 B3
Valdosta • GA, United States 119 M3
Valdoviño **Beach** • Spain 68 [92]
Vale de Parra • Portugal 88 E6
Vale Navio • Portugal 88 E7
Vale of Trent • United Kingdom 74 D2
Valea lui Mihai • Romania 14 J2
Valença • Brazil 44 I1
Valençay • France 84 B1
Valençay [Château] • France 84 D4
Valence • France 85 F3
Valencia • Spain 11 K5
Valencia • Venezuela 43 D2
Valencia **Beach** • Spain 68 [119]
Valencia **Heritage C** • Spain 64 [74]
Valencia • Trinidad & Tobago 125 K4
Valencia, Costa de • Spain 86 A2
Valencia de Don Juan • Spain 11 F2
Valencia, Golfo de • Spain 11 L5
Valenciana, Comunidad de • Spain 11 K5
Valenciennes • France 10 I3
Valentia I. • Ireland 79 F7
Valentin • Russian Fed. 30 H3
Valentine • NE, United States 40 F3
Valera • Venezuela 43 C2
Valga • Estonia 16 N8
Valinco, Golfe de • Corsica, France 85 L3
Valjevo • F.R. of Yugoslavia 14 G5
Valkeakoski • Finland 95 E2
Valkenburg • Netherlands 80 A16
Valkenswaard • Netherlands 5 I3
Vall de Uxó • Spain 11 K5
Valladolid • Spain 11 G3
Valldal • Norway 94 C2
Valldemossa • Majorca, Spain 87 H1
Valle • Norway 94 C6
Valle d'Aosta • Italy 91 E1
Valle de Bravo • Mexico 123 E4
Valledupar • Colombia 43 C1
Vallée de Mai Nature Reserve **Heritage N** • Seychelles 61 [100]
Vallée de Mai Nature Reserve • Seychelles 106 F4
Vallejo • CA, United States 117 F3
Vallenar • Chile 44 B4
Vallendar • Germany 82 H2
Vallendar **Spa** • Germany 83 [154]
Vallensbæk **Beach** • Denmark 68 [39]
Vallentuna • Sweden 95 D2
Valletta **Heritage C** • Malta 64 [198]
Valletta • Malta 93 H4
Valley Forge Nat. Hist. Park • PA, United States 118 H1
Valley Forge Nat. Hist. Park **Park** • PA, United States 121 [307]
Valley of Fire State Park • NV, United States 117 F4
Valleyfield • QU, Canada 122 B7
Vallo della Luciana • Italy 12 J8
Valloire **Ski** • France 70 [50]
Valloire • France 85 F4
Vallorbe • Switzerland 89 G1
Valls • Spain 87 D3
Valmeinier **Ski** • France 70 [49]
Valmiera • Latvia 16 M8
Valmorel **Ski** • France 70 [44]
Valmorel • France 85 F2
Valognes • France 5 B5
Valois • France 85 E2
Valparaíso • Chile 44 B5
Valpoi • Goa, India 105 B1
Valpolicella • Italy 91 E7
Vals • Switzerland 89 G3
Vals, Tanjung • Indonesia 32 (1) E4
Valsamonero, Moní • Crete, Greece 93 E6
Váltou, Ori • Greece 15 C4
Valtournenche **Ski** • Italy 70 [200]
Valtournenche • Italy 91 E1
Valverde • Hierro, Canary Is. 87 E5
Valverde del Camino • Spain 11 E7
Valzoldana **Ski** • Italy 70 [225]
Vammala • Finland 95 E2
Vámos • Crete, Greece 93 E2
Van • Turkey 18 D2
Van Buren, Martin, Nat. Hist. Site **Park** • NY, United States 121 [320]
Van Diemen Gulf • NT, Australia 34 F2
Van Gölü • Turkey 18 D2
Van Horn • TX, United States 40 F5
Van, Lake • Turkey 92 A4
Van Rees, Pegunungan • Indonesia 32 (1) E3
Vanajanselka • Finland 95 E2
Vanavara • Russian Fed. 26 R5
Vancouver • WA, United States 117 E1
Vancouver • BC, Canada 122 C3
Vancouver, Fort, Nat. Hist. Site **Park** • WA, United States 120 [32]
Vancouver I. • BC, Canada 122 C3
Vanda • Finland 95 E4
Vandellòs i l'Hospitalet de l'Infant **Beach** • Spain 68 [121]
Vanderbilt Mansion Nat. Hist. Site **Park** • NY, United States 121 [322]
Vanderhoof • BC, Canada 122 C1
Vänern • Sweden 16 G7
Vänersborg • Sweden 95 F2
Vang • Norway 94 C4
Vangsnes • Norway 94 C4
Vangunu • Solomon Is. 35 (1) F2
Vanimo • Papua New Guinea 35 (1) C1
Vanna • Norway 16 J1
Vännäs • Sweden 16 J5
Vannes **Beach** • France 68 [81]
Vannes • France 84 C4
Vannsjø • Norway 94 B4
Vanoise, Massif de la • France 12 A3
Vanoise, Parc nat. de la **Park** • France 72 [66]
Vanoise, Parc nat. de la • France 85 F4

Vansbro

Vansbro • Sweden 16 H6
Vansittart Is. • NU, Canada 39 O3
Vantaa • Finland 95 E4
Vanua Lava • Vanuatu 35 (2) B1
Vanua Levu • Fiji 35 (2) D2
Vanuatu • Pacific Ocean 35 (2) B2
Vao, Ko • Thailand 109 K2
Var • France 85 H2
Var [Adm] • France 85 H3
Vara • Sweden 95 F3
Vara, Pico da • Azores 88 B1
Varadero • Cuba 124 D2
Varanasi • India 105 C8
Varanger-Halvøya • Norway 16 O1
Varangerfjorden • Norway 16 P1
Varano, Lago di • Italy 12 J7
Varano, Lago di • Italy 14 C8
Varazdin • Croatia 14 D3
Varberg **Beach** • Sweden 68 [2]
Varberg • Sweden 95 F6
Varca • Goa, India 105 B2
Varca Beach • Goa, India 105 B2
Vardar • F.Y.R. of Macedonia 15 C2
Varde • Denmark 95 F9
Vardø • Norway 16 P1
Varel • Germany 5 L1
Varel • Germany 8 D3
Varese • Italy 12 C3
Vårgårda • Sweden 95 F3
Varginha • Brazil 127 C1
Varkala • India 106 D14
Varkaus • Finland 16 N5
Varkiza • Greece 92 D7
Värmdölandet • Sweden 95 D4
Värmland • Sweden 16 G6
Värmlandsnäs • Sweden 95 F3
Varna **Beach** • Bulgaria 69 [243]
Varna • Bulgaria 97 D4
Värnamo • Sweden 95 F7
Varnenski Zaliv • Bulgaria 14 P6
Varósha • Cyprus 93 J4
Várpalota • Hungary 13 H10
Vars **Ski** • France 70 [67]
Vars • France 85 F4
Varzea Grande • Brazil 44 E2
Vasa • Finland 16 K5
Vasca, Costa • Spain 86 A1
Vascao • Portugal 88 E4
Vasco da Gama • Goa, India 105 B1
Vashka • Russian Fed. 17 H2
Vasiliki • Crete, Greece 93 E8
Vaslui • Romania 14 O3
Vassdalsegga • Norway 94 C6
Vassiliká • Greece 15 E3
Vassilikí • Greece 92 C1
Vassilikós • Greece 92 C3
Västerås • Sweden 95 D1
Västerbotten • Sweden 16 K4
Västerdalälven • Sweden 16 G6
Västerhaninge • Sweden 95 D4
Västerlen • Sweden 95 F11
Västermo • Sweden 95 D3
Västernorrland • Sweden 16 J5
Västervik **Beach** • Sweden 69 [18]
Västervik • Sweden 95 F8
Västmanland • Sweden 95 D1
Vasto • Italy 12 I6
Vasto **Beach** • Italy 69 [160]
Váthi • Crete, Greece 93 E1
Vathipetro • Crete, Greece 93 E7
Vathy • Greece 92 C2
Vatican City **Heritage C** • Italy 64 [124]
Vatican City • Italy 91 F1
Vatili • Cyprus 93 J4
Vatnajökull • Iceland 16 (1) E2
Vatne • Norway 94 C2
Vatoa • Fiji 35 (2) E2
Vatra Dornei • Romania 14 M2
Vättern • Sweden 95 F3
Vattholma • Sweden 95 D2
Vaucouleurs • France 5 I6
Vaughans • St Kitts & Nevis 125 G4
Vaujany **Ski** • France 70 [56]
Vava'u Group • Tonga 35 (2) F2
Väversunda • Sweden 95 F3
Vavuniya • Sri Lanka 106 D11
Vaxholm • Sweden 95 D4
Växjö • Sweden 95 F8
Vaygach, Ostrov • Russian Fed. 26 I3
Vaygach, Ostrov • Russian Fed. 96 A3
Vazon Bay **Beach** • Channel Is. 75 [244]
Vechelde • Germany 8 F4
Vechta • Germany 8 D4
Vechte • Germany 8 C4
Veckholm • Sweden 95 D1
Vecsés • Hungary 13 I10
Vedbæk • Denmark 95 F11
Veddige • Sweden 95 F6
Vedra, I. es • Ibiza, Spain 87 G3
Veendam • Netherlands 5 J1
Veenendaal • Netherlands 5 I2
Veere **Beach** • Netherlands 68 [69]
Veere • Netherlands 80 A10
Vega • Norway 16 F4
Vega Baja • Puerto Rico 125 E2
Vegår • Norway 94 C6
Veggli • Norway 94 B1
Vegoritda, Limni • Greece 15 C3
Veinge • Sweden 95 F11
Vejbystrand • Sweden 95 F11
Vejen • Denmark 95 F9
Vejer de la Frontera • Spain 11 F8
Vejle **Beach** • Denmark 68 [46]
Vejle • Denmark 95 F9
Vejle [Adm] • Denmark 95 F9
Vel Vaddo Beach • Goa, India 105 B2
Velassaru • Maldives 106 E4
Velay, Mts du • France 10 I8
Velbazdski •
Bulgaria/F.Y.R. of Macedonia 15 D1
Velbert • Germany 81 E2
Velddrif • South Africa 100 C1
Veldenz, Schloß • Germany 82 H3
Veldhoven • Netherlands 5 I3
Velebit • Croatia 14 C5
Velenje • Slovenia 13 E11
Veleta, Pico de • Spain 86 B3
Velez • Bosnia-Herz. 14 F6
Vélez-Málaga **Beach** • Spain 68 [114]
Vélez-Málaga • Spain 86 B7
Vélez-Rubio • Spain 86 B4
Velhas • Brazil 127 C1
Veligandu Huraa • Maldives 106 E4
Velika Kapela • Croatia 14 B4
Velikaya • Pskov, Russian Fed. 16 O8
Velikaya •
Magadan, Russian Fed. 27 T4
Veliki Drvenik • Croatia 14 D6
Velikiy Ustyug • Russian Fed. 17 H2
Velikiye-Luki • Russian Fed. 97 E3
Veliko Turnovo • Bulgaria 97 D3
Velikovisochnoye • Russian Fed. 17 I1
Velingara • Senegal 22 B2
Velingrad • Bulgaria 15 F1
Velino [Mtn] • Italy 12 H6
Velino [Riv] • Italy 91 F2
Vella Lavella • Solomon Is. 35 (1) F2
Velletri • Italy 91 F3
Vellinge **Beach** • Sweden 68 [12]
Vellinge • Sweden 95 F15
Vellore • India 106 D7
Velmerstot • Germany 5 L3
Velsao Beach • Goa, India 105 B2
Velsk • Russian Fed. 17 G2
Velten • Germany 81 F1
Veluwezoom, Nat. Park **Park** •
Netherlands 72 [54]
Veluwezoom, Nat. Park •
Netherlands 80 A8
Ven • Sweden 95 F11
Venaco • Corsica, France 85 L2
Venado Tuerto • Argentina 44 D5
Vence • France 85 H2
Venda • South Africa 24 E4
Vendays-Montalivet **Beach** •
France 68 [85]
Vendays-Montalivet • France 85 G1
Vendée • France 84 D3
Vendôme • France 84 D2
Véneta, Laguna • Italy 91 E8
Venetian Riviera • Italy 91 E8
Veneto • Italy 91 E7
Venézia **Heritage C** • Italy 64 [114]
Venézia • Italy 91 E8
Venézia, Golfo di •
Croatia/Italy 91 E8
Venézia-Lido • Italy 12 G3
Venezuela • S. America 43 D2
Venezuela, Golfo de • Venezuela 43 C1
Venice **Heritage C** • Italy 64 [114]
Venice • Italy 91 E8
Venlo • Netherlands 80 A12
Vennesla • Norway 95 F1
Vénnissieux • France 10 J8
Vensyssel • Denmark 95 F5
Venta • Latvia/Lithuania 16 K8
Ventadour, Château de • France 85 G2
Ventimiglia • Italy 91 E9
Ventnor **Beach** • United Kingdom 75 [94]
Ventry **Beach** • Ireland 68 [60]
Ventry • Ireland 79 F5
Ventspils • Latvia 16 K8
Ventura • CA, United States 117 F5
Venus Bay • VI, Australia 111 G3
Venus-Aurora • Romania 97 D2
Venzone • Italy 91 E4
Vera • Argentina 44 D4
Vera **Beach** • Spain 68 [116]
Vera • Spain 86 B4
Veracruz • Mexico 123 E4
Veracruz [Adm] • Mexico 37 B3
Veraval • India 28 B4
Verbània • Italy 91 E2
Verbier **Ski** • Switzerland 70 [78]
Verbier • Switzerland 89 G6
Vercelli • Italy 91 E6
Vercors • France 85 F3
Verdala Palace • Malta 93 H4
Verdalsøra • Norway 16 F5
Verde • Paraguay 44 E3
Verde, Costa • Spain 11 E1
Verde, Costa • Portugal 88 A1
Verde, Costa • Sardinia, Italy 90 C3
Verden • Germany 8 E4
Verdon • France 85 H1
Verdon, Basses Gorges du •
France 85 H1
Verdon, Grand Canyon du •
France 85 H1
Verdon-sur-Mer, le • France 85 G1
Verdun • France 10 K4
Vereeniging • South Africa 24 D5
Vérendrye, la, Prov. Reserve •
QU, Canada 122 B2
Verga, Cap • Guinea 22 B2
Vergina **Heritage C** • Greece 64 [176]
Véria • Greece 15 D3
Verin • Spain 11 D3
Veringenstadt • Germany 82 J1
Verkhneimbatsk • Russian Fed. 27 C4
Verkhnetulomskiy • Russian Fed. 16 P2
Verkhnetulomskoye Vdkhr. •
Russian Fed. 16 P2
Verkhni Kuyto, Ozero •
Russian Fed. 16 P4
Verkhoyansk • Russian Fed. 27 L3
Verkhoyanskiy Khrebet •
Russian Fed. 27 K3
Verla **Heritage C** • Finland 63 [75]
Vermeille, Côte • France 85 K2
Vermillion • SD, United States 41 G3
Vermont • United States 118 G3
Vernal • UT, United States 40 E3
Verneuil-sur-Avre • France 10 F5
Vérno • Greece 15 C3
Vernon • BC, Canada 38 H6
Vernon • TX, United States 40 G5
Vernon • France 85 E1
Vernon, Mt • VA, United States 118 H3
Vernon Valley **Ski** •
NJ, United States 116 [170]
Verona • Italy 91 E7
Versailles **Heritage C** • France 64 [59]
Versailles • France 85 E3
Versciaco **Ski** • Italy 70 [241]
Vert, Cap • Senegal 22 A2
Vertientes • Cuba 124 D7
Vertiskos • Greece 15 E3
Verviers • Belgium 80 A16
Vervins • France 5 G5
Veshenskaya • Russian Fed. 17 G5
Vesijärvi • Finland 95 E4
Vesle • France 10 I4
Vesoul • France 10 L6
Vest Agder • Norway 16 D7
Vest Sjælland • Denmark 95 F10
Vesterålen • Norway 16 H2
Vesterø Havn • Denmark 95 F6
Vestfjorden • Norway 16 H2
Vestfold • Norway 94 B3
Vestmannaeyjar • Iceland 16 (1) C3
Vestnes • Norway 94 C2
Vestvågøy • Norway 16 G2
Vésubie • France 85 H2
Vesuvio • Italy 91 G3
Vesuvius • Italy 91 G3
Veszprém • Hungary 13 G10
Vetlanda • Sweden 95 F8
Vetralla • Italy 91 F1
Vette, le • Italy 90 B4
Veurne • Belgium 80 B1
Vevey • Switzerland 89 G5
Vexin • France 85 E1
Veysonnaz **Ski** • Switzerland 70 [82]
Vézelay **Heritage C** • France 64 [55]
Vezen • Bulgaria 15 F1
Vézère • France 85 G2
Vézère, Gorges de la • France 85 G2
Vézère, Vallée du **Heritage C** •
France 64 [63]
Vezzani • Corsica, France 85 L2
Viana del Bollo • Spain 11 D2
Viana do Castelo • Portugal 11 C3
Viana do Castelo **Beach** •
Portugal 68 [94]
Viana do Castelo [Adm] •
Portugal 88 A1
Vianden • Luxembourg 80 A20
Viangchan • Laos 31 C3
Viaréggio **Beach** • Italy 68 [144]
Viaréggio • Italy 91 E10
Vibo Valentia • Italy 12 K10
Viborg • Russian Fed. 17 D2
Viborg • Denmark 95 F9
Viborg [Adm] • Denmark 95 F9
Vic • Spain 87 D2
Vicarstown • Ireland 79 E3
Vicdessos • France 85 K1
Vicecomodoro Marambio [Base] •
Antarctica 46 (1) JJ3
Vicedo **Beach** • Spain 68 [91]
Vicenza **Heritage C** • Italy 64 [112]
Vicenza • Italy 91 E7
Vichuga • Russian Fed. 17 G3
Vichy • France 10 I7
Vicksburg • MS, United States 118 K2
Vicksburg Nat. Military Park **Park** •
MS, United States 121 [200]
Vico • Corsica, France 85 L1
Vico Equense • Italy 91 G3
Vico, Lago di • Italy 91 F1
Victor Harbour • SA, Australia 34 G7
Victoria • NT, Australia 34 F3
Victoria • VI, Australia 34 H7
Victoria • Papua New Guinea 35 (1) D2
Victoria • Chile 45 B3
Victoria • Malta 93 H1
Victoria • Seychelles 106 F1
Victoria • TX, United States 119 N5
Victoria • BC, Canada 122 C3
Victoria de las Tunas • Cuba 124 D7
Victoria Falls **Heritage N** •
Zambia/Zimbabwe 61 [95]
Victoria Falls • Zimbabwe 102 J1
Victoria Falls [Waterfall] •
Zambia/Zimbabwe 102 J1
Victoria Harbour •
Hong Kong, China 107 H5
Victoria I. • NT/NU, Canada 38 J2
Victoria, Lake • Africa 23 E4
Victoria Lake • NF, Canada 123 D3
Victoria Land • Antarctica 46 (1) V2
Victoria Lines • Malta 93 H4
Victoria, Mt • Myanmar 28 F4
Victoria, Mt • Myanmar 31 A2
Victoria Nile • Uganda 23 E3
Victoria Peak •
Hong Kong, China 107 H5
Victoria River Downs •
NT, Australia 34 F3
Victoria Strait • NU, Canada 38 K3
Victoria West • South Africa 100 C3
Victory • Papua New Guinea 35 (1) D2
Vicuña Mackenna • Argentina 44 D5
Videira • Brazil 44 F4
Videle • Romania 97 D1
Vidin • Bulgaria 14 J6
Vidisha • India 28 C4
Vidöstern • Sweden 95 F7
Vidsel • Sweden 16 K4
Viechtach • Germany 9 H7
Viedma • Argentina 45 D4
Viejo • Mexico 40 D5
Viella • Spain 11 L2
Viella, Túnel de • Spain 85 K1
Vienna • Austria 13 F9
Vienna **Heritage C** • Austria 64 [107]
Vienne • France 85 F1
Vienne [Adm] • France 84 D4
Vienne [Riv] • France 10 F6
Vientiane • Laos 31 C3
Vieques • Puerto Rico 125 E4
Viernheim • Germany 5 L5
Vierschach **Ski** • Italy 70 [241]
Viersen • Germany 81 E3
Vierwald Stätter See •
Switzerland 89 G3
Vierzon • France 10 H6
Vieste • Italy 12 K7
Vieste **Beach** • Italy 69 [158]
Viet Tri • Vietnam 31 D2
Vietnam • Asia 31 D3
Vietnam Veterans Mem. **Park** •
DC, United States 121 [297]
Vieux Fort • St Lucia 125 J4
Vieux Fort Bay • St Lucia 125 J4
Vieux-Boucau-les-Bains • France 85 G3
Vigan • Philippines 31 G3
Vigévano • Italy 91 E6
Vigia • Brazil 45 (1) B2
Vigie [Apt] • St Lucia 125 J1
Vigie Beach • St Lucia 125 J1
Vigo • Spain 11 C2
Vigo **Beach** • Spain 68 [93]
Vigo di Fassa **Ski** • Italy 70 [222]
Vigo di Fassa • Italy 90 B3
Vigo, Ria de • Spain 11 C2
Vigsø Bugt • Denmark 95 F5
Vihorlat • Slovak Rep. 14 J1
Viiala • Finland 95 E2
Vijayadurg • India 106 D1
Vijayanagar • India 106 D2
Vijayapuri • India 106 D3
Vijayawada • India 106 D3
Vijfherenlanden • Netherlands 80 C4
Vijosë • Albania 15 A3
Vik • Iceland 16 (1) D3
Vikbolandet • Sweden 95 F4
Vikedal • Norway 94 C5
Viken • Sweden 95 F11
Vikersund • Norway 94 B1
Vikhren • Bulgaria 14 K8
VikingLandet **Park** • Norway 73 [4]
VikingLandet • Norway 94 B2
Vikna • Norway 16 F4
Vikos-Aóos Nat. Park **Park** •
Greece 72 [136]
Viksøyri • Norway 94 C4
Vila de Conde • Portugal 11 C3
Vila do Bispo **Beach** • Portugal 68 [100]
Vila do Bispo • Portugal 88 E5
Vila do Porto • Azores 88 B2
Vila Franca de Xira • Portugal 88 D2
Vila Franca do Campo **Beach** •
São Miguel, Azores 68 [105]
Vila Franca do Campo • Azores 88 B1
Vila Nogueira de Azeitão •
Portugal 88 D2
Vila Nova de Gaia • Portugal 11 C3
Vila Nova do Sales • Angola 23 A6
Vila Praia da Vitória **Beach** •
Terceira, Azores 68 [104]
Vila Real • Portugal 11 D3
Vila Real [Adm] • Portugal 88 A1
Vila Real de Santo António **Beach** •
Portugal 68 [100]
Vila Real de Santo António •
Portugal 88 E8
Vila Velha • Brazil 127 C2
Vilafranca del Penèdes • Spain 87 D3
Vilagarcia **Beach** • Spain 68 [93]
Vilaine • France 84 C4
Vilamoura • Portugal 88 E7
Vilanova i la Geltrú **Beach** •
Spain 68 [122]
Vilanova i la Geltrú • Spain 87 D3
Vilcabamba • Peru 127 B1
Vilcanota • Peru 127 B2
Vilcheka, Zemlya • Russian Fed. 96 A3
Vileyka • Belarus 16 N9
Vilhelmina • Sweden 16 I4
Vilhena • Brazil 43 E6
Vilija • Lithuania 13 N3
Viljandi • Estonia 16 M7
Vilkaviskis • Lithuania 13 M3
Vilkitskogo, Proliv •
Russian Fed. 26 R2
Villa Angela • Argentina 44 D4
Villa Carlos • Minorca, Spain 87 F4
Villa Constitución • Argentina 127 D1
Villa de María • Argentina 44 D4
Villa Dolores • Argentina 44 C5
Villa General Roca • Argentina 44 C5
Villa Gesell • Argentina 127 D4
Villa Hayes • Paraguay 44 E3
Villa Huidobro • Argentina 44 D5
Villa, la **Ski** • Italy 70 [233]
Villa, la • Italy 90 B2
Villa María • Argentina 44 D5
Villa Nova • Barbados 125 H4
Villa Nueva • Argentina 44 C5
Villa Romana del Casale **Heritage C** •
Sicily, Italy 64 [133]
Villa San Martín • Argentina 44 D4
Villabassa **Ski** • Italy 70 [238]
Villablino • Spain 11 E2
Villacañas • Spain 11 H5
Villach • Austria 89 H8
Villafranca del Bierzo • Spain 11 E2
Villafranca de los Barros •
Spain 11 E6
Villagarcia • Spain 11 C2
Villaggio Cóppola • Italy 91 G1
Villaguay • Argentina 44 E5
Villahermosa • Mexico 37 C4
Villajoyosa • Spain 87 C2
Villalba • Spain 11 D1
Villalon de Campos • Spain 11 F2
Villamil • Galapagos Is. 43 (1) A2
Villandry [Château] • France 84 D2
Villanueva de Córdoba • Spain 11 G6
Villanueva de la Serena • Spain 11 F6
Villanueva del Rio y Minas •
Spain 11 F7
Villaputzu • Sardinia, Italy 12 D9
Villar del Rey • Spain 11 E5
Villarcayo • Spain 11 H2
Villard-de-Lans **Ski** • France 70 [53]
Villard-de-Lans • France 85 F3
Villard-Reculas **Ski** • France 70 [57]
Villarica • Chile 45 B3
Villarreal de los Infantes •
Spain 11 K5
Villarrica • Paraguay 44 E4
Villars-sur-Ollon **Ski** •
Switzerland 70 [83]
Villars-sur-Ollon • Switzerland 89 G6
Villasimius • Sardinia, Italy 90 C4
Villavicencio • Colombia 43 C3
Villaviciosa • Spain 11 F1
Villefranche-de-Rouergue •
France 85 G4
Villefranche-sur-Mer • France 85 H2
Villefranche-sur-Saône • France 85 F1
Villena • Spain 87 C1
Villeneuve • Switzerland 89 G5
Villeneuve-les-Maguelonne **Beach** •
France 68 [130]
Villeneuve-Loubet • France 85 H4
Villeneuve-sur-Lot • France 85 G4
Villerupt • France 5 I5
Villesavin [Château] • France 84 D2
Villeurbanne • France 10 J8
Villingen **Spa** • Germany 83 [199]
Villingen-Schwenningen •
Germany 9 D8
Villingili Beach • Maldives 106 E4
Villivaru • Maldives 106 E4
Villmanstrand • Finland 16 O6
Vilm • Germany 8 I2
Vilnius • Lithuania 16 M9
Vilnius **Heritage C** • Lithuania 64 [203]
Vilppula • Finland 95 E2
Vils • Germany 9 H8
Vilsbiburg • Germany 9 H8
Vilsbiburg • Germany 82 J4
Vilshofen • Germany 9 I8
Vilvoorde • Belgium 5 H4
Vilyuy • Russian Fed. 27 I4
Vilyuysk • Russian Fed. 27 J4
Vimmerby • Sweden 95 F8
Vimperk • Czech Rep. 96 C3
Viña del Mar • Chile 44 B5
Vinarös • Spain 11 L4
Vinarös **Beach** • Spain 68 [120]
Vinarös • Spain 86 A1
Vincennes • IN, United States 41 I4
Vindeälven • Sweden 16 J4
Vinderup • Denmark 95 F9
Vindhya Range • India 28 C4
Vindö • Sweden 95 D4
Vingåker • Sweden 95 D3
Vingeanne • France 10 K6
Vinh • Vietnam 31 D3
Vinh Long • Vietnam 108 B3
Vinh Long • Vietnam 108 B3
Vinkovci • Croatia 14 F4
Vinniki • Ukraine 13 N8
Vinnitsa • Ukraine 17 D5
Vinogradov • Ukraine 13 M9
Vinslöv • Sweden 95 F11
Vinson Massif • Antarctica 46 (1) GG2
Vipiteno • Italy 90 B1
Vir • Croatia 14 C5
Virac • Philippines 31 G4
Vire • France 10 E5
Vire [Riv] • France 10 D5
Virei • Angola 24 A3
Virful Curcubata • Romania 13 L11
Virgenes, Cabo • Argentina 45 C6
Virgin • United States 118 J1
Virgin Gorda •
British Virgin Is. 58 B7
Virgin Is., UK • West Indies 37 I4
Virgin Is., US • West Indies 37 I4
Virginia • MN, United States 41 H2
Virginia • United States 41 K4
Virginia Beach •
VA, United States 118 H5
Virginia City •
NV, United States 117 F3
Virihaure • Sweden 16 I3
Virôchey • Cambodia 31 D4
Virovitica • Croatia 14 E4
Virrat • Finland 95 E2
Virsbo • Sweden 95 D1
Virton • Belgium 80 A19
Virunga • Dem. Rep. of Congo 23 D4
Virunga, Parc nat. des **Heritage N** •
Dem. Rep. of Congo 61 [84]
Virunga, Parc nat. des **Park** •
Dem. Rep. of Congo 103 [56]
Vis • Croatia 14 D6
Visayan Sea • Philippines 31 G4
Visby • Sweden 16 J8
Visby **Heritage C** • Sweden 64 [7]
Viscount Melville Sound •
NU, Canada 38 J2
Visegrad • Bosnia-Herz. 14 G6
Visegrad • Bulgaria 15 H2
Viseu • Portugal 11 D4
Viseu [Adm] • Portugal 88 A1
Viseu de Sus • Romania 14 L2
Vishakhapatnam • India 28 D5
Vishniy Volochek • Russian Fed. 97 E3
Visingsö • Sweden 95 F3
Vislanda • Sweden 95 F7
Viso, Monte • Italy 91 E5
Visoko • Bosnia-Herz. 14 F6
Visselhövede • Germany 8 E4
Vistonias, Ormos • Greece 15 G3
Vistonida, Limni • Greece 15 G2
Vitebsk • Belarus 17 E3
Viterbo • Italy 91 F1
Viti Levu • Fiji 35 (2) D2
Vitiaz Strait •
Papua New Guinea 35 (1) D2
Vitigudino • Spain 11 E4
Vitim • Russian Fed. 27 H5
Vitim [Riv] • Russian Fed. 27 I5
Vitôn • Svalbard 46 L2
Vitória • Brazil 127 C2
Vitória da Conquista • Brazil 44 H1
Vitoria Gasteiz • Spain 11 I2
Vitorog • Bosnia-Herz. 14 D5
Vitosa Nat. Park **Park** •
Bulgaria 72 [131]
Vitré • France 84 D1
Vitré [Château] • France 84 D1
Vitry-le-François • France 10 J5
Vittangi • Sweden 16 K3
Vitte **Spa** • Germany 83 [278]
Vittel • France 9 A8
Vittinge • Sweden 95 D1
Vittoria • Sicily, Italy 12 I12
Vittorio Véneto • Italy 90 B4
Vittoriosa • Malta 93 H4
Vittsjö • Sweden 95 F11
Vitznau • Switzerland 89 G3
Viveiro • Spain 11 D1
Viveiro **Beach** • Spain 68 [91]
Viver • Spain 11 K5
Vivian • LA, United States 118 K1
Vize • Turkey 15 I2
Vizianagaram • India 28 D5
Vizinga • Russian Fed. 17 I2
Vlaams-Brabant • Belgium 80 A15
Vlaanderen • Belgium 5 F3
Vlaardingen • Netherlands 80 C3
Vladikavkaz • Russian Fed. 17 G6
Vladimir **Heritage C** •
Russian Fed. 64 [210]
Vladimir • Russian Fed. 97 E4
Vladimir-Volynski • Ukraine 13 N7
Vladivostok • Russian Fed. 27 L8
Vlasic • Bosnia-Herz. 14 E5
Vlasic • F.R. of Yugoslavia 14 G5
Vlasovo • Russian Fed. 27 M2
Vlieland • Netherlands 80 A3
Vlihada, Paralia •
Crete, Greece 93 E4
Vlihó • Greece 92 C1
Vlikovo • Ukraine 14 O4
Vlissingen • Netherlands 80 A10
Vlitasaari • Finland 16 M5
Vlkolinec **Heritage C** •
Slovak Rep. 64 [150]
Vlorë • Albania 15 A3
Vlotho **Spa** • Germany 83 [92]
Vltava • Czech Rep. 96 C4
Vluyn • Germany 81 E1
Vnukovo [Apt] • Russian Fed. 97 E4
Vöcklabruck • Austria 13 C9
Vodice • Croatia 12 J5
Voerde • Germany 81 E1
Voergård • Denmark 95 F6
Vogel Peak • Nigeria 22 G3
Vogelsberg • Germany 82 G2
Voghera • Italy 12 D4
Vogtland • Germany 9 H6
Voi • Kenya 101 G4
Voiron • France 85 F3
Voitsberg • Austria 13 E10
Vojens • Denmark 95 F13
Vojvodina • F.R. of Yugoslavia 14 G4
Voknavolok • Russian Fed. 16 P4
Volary • Czech Rep. 96 C3
Volcano • HI, United States 119 L8
Volcans, Parc des **Park** • Rwanda 103 [72]
Volda • Russian Fed. 17 H3
Volda • Norway 94 C1
Volendam • Netherlands 80 C2
Volga • Russian Fed. 17 H5
Volga, Cities of the •
Russian Fed. 96 A2
Volga Delta • Russian Fed. 17 H5
Volga, Ozero • Russian Fed. 97 E3
Volga Plateau • Russian Fed. 4 T6
Volgodonsk • Russian Fed. 17 G5
Volgograd • Russian Fed. 17 G5
Volgogradskoye Vdkhr. •
Russian Fed. 17 H4
Volissós • Greece 15 G5
Völkermarkt • Austria 13 D11
Volkhov • Russian Fed. 97 E1
Volkhov [Riv] • Russian Fed. 97 E1
Völklingen **Heritage C** • Germany 64 [41]
Völklingen • Germany 82 G3
Volkovysk • Belarus 13 N4
Vologda • Russian Fed. 97 E2
Vólos **Beach** • Greece 69 [188]
Vólos • Greece 92 D4
Volovets • Ukraine 14 K1
Volta area **Heritage C** • Ghana 63 [97]
Volta Blanche •
Burkina Faso/Ghana 22 D2
Volta, Lake • Ghana 22 E3
Volta Noire •
Burkina Faso/Ghana 22 D2
Volta Redonda • Brazil 127 C3
Volterra • Italy 91 E11
Volturno • Italy 91 G1
Volubilis **Heritage C** • Morocco 64 [215]
Volubilis • Morocco 101 D1
Volvi, Limni • Greece 15 E3
Volzhskiy • Russian Fed. 17 G5
Voma • Fiji 35 (2) D2
Vóni • Crete, Greece 93 E7
Vónitsa • Greece 92 C1
Voorburg • Netherlands 80 C3
Voorne **Beach** • Netherlands 68 [68]
Voorne • Netherlands 80 C3
Voorschoten • Netherlands 80 C1
Vorarlberg • Austria 89 H1
Vordingborg **Beach** • Denmark 68 [37]
Vordingborg • Denmark 95 F14
Voré • Albania 15 A2
Vóries Sporádes • Greece 15 E4
Vøringsfossen • Norway 94 C4
Vórios Evoïkós Kólpos • Greece 15 E5
Vorkuta • Russian Fed. 26 J4
Vorma • Norway 94 B2
Vormsi • Estonia 16 L7
Vorogovo • Russian Fed. 27 C4
Voronezh • Russian Fed. 17 F4
Vorpommersche Boddenlandschaft,
Nationalpark **Park** • Germany 72 [58]
Võru • Estonia 16 N8
Vosges • France 10 L5
Vosnesensk • Ukraine 17 E5
Vosresensk • Russian Fed. 97 E4
Voss • Norway 94 C4
Vostochno Sibirskoye More •
Arctic Ocean 46 I12
Vostochnyy Sayan • Russian Fed. 26 Q7
Vostok • Kiribati 33 L7
Vostok [Base] • Antarctica 46 (1) P2
Votkinsk • Russian Fed. 17 I3
Vøtterøy • Norway 94 B4
Voukoliés • Crete, Greece 93 E1
Voúla • Greece 92 D7
Vouliagméni **Beach** • Greece 69 [185]
Vouliagméni • Greece 92 D7
Voúrinos • Greece 15 C3
Vouvray • France 84 B1
Vouvray • France 84 D2
Voúxa, Akra • Crete, Greece 93 E1
Vouziers • France 5 H5
Voyage to the Glaciers cruise area •
N. America 58 A2
Voyageurs Nat. Park **Park** •
MN, United States 121 [155]
Voyvozh • Russian Fed. 17 J2
Vrå • Denmark 95 F6
Vrådal • Norway 94 C6
Vraháși **Beach** • Crete, Greece 69 [215]
Vrahási • Crete, Greece 93 E7
Vraháti **Beach** • Greece 69 [178]
Vrakhiónas • Greece 15 B6
Vran • Bosnia-Herz. 14 E6
Vrangelya, Ostrov •
Russian Fed. 27 V2
Vranica • Bosnia-Herz. 14 E6
Vranje • F.R. of Yugoslavia 14 I7
Vranov nad Topl'ou •
Slovak Rep. 13 K9
Vrassná **Beach** • Greece 69 [193]
Vratsa • Bulgaria 14 K6
Vrbas • Bosnia-Herz. 14 E5
Vrchlabí • Czech Rep. 13 E7
Vredenburg • South Africa 100 C1
Vredendal • South Africa 100 C1
Vrindaban • India 105 C2
Vrine • Albania 92 B1
Vrissa **Beach** • Greece 69 [199]
Vrontisiou, Moni •
Crete, Greece 93 E6
Vrsac • F.R. of Yugoslavia 14 I4
Vryburg • South Africa 100 B1
Vryheid • South Africa 24 E5
Vsetin • Czech Rep. 13 G8
Vukovar • F.R. of Yugoslavia 14 G4
Vuktyl • Russian Fed. 17 J2
Vulcano, I. • Italy 90 D2
Vulkaneifel • Germany 82 H1
Vulture • Italy 12 J8
Vung Tao • Vietnam 108 B4
Vuokatti • Finland 94 A6
Vuollerim • Sweden 16 K3
Vuotso • Finland 17 D1
Vyatka • Russian Fed. 17 H3
Vyatka [Riv] • Russian Fed. 17 I3
Vyatko-Chepetsk • Russian Fed. 17 H3
Vyazemskiy • Russian Fed. 29 I1
Vyazma • Russian Fed. 97 E3
Vyborg • Russian Fed. 17 D2
Vychegda • Russian Fed. 17 I2
Vyksa • Russian Fed. 17 G3
Vym • Russian Fed. 17 I2
Vyritsa • Russian Fed. 97 E1
Vysehrad • Czech Rep. 96 C2
Vyskov • Czech Rep. 13 F8
Vyskovski • Ukraine 14 K1
Vysoké Tatry Nat. Park **Park** •
Slovak Rep. 72 [100]
Vysokoye • Belarus 13 M5
Vyssi Brod • Czech Rep. 96 C4
Vytegra • Russian Fed. 17 F2
Vyvenka • Russian Fed. 27 S4
W, Parc nat. du **Heritage N** •
Niger 61 [76]
W, Parc nat. du **Park** • Niger 103 [3]
Wa • Ghana 22 D2
Waal • Netherlands 80 A11
Waalwijk • Netherlands 5 I3
Wabasca • AL, Canada 38 I5
Wabrzezno • Poland 13 H4
Wachadima Plain • Kenya 101 G2
Wachau • Austria 89 F4
Wachtendonk • Germany 81 E1
Wächtersbach • Germany 82 G2
Wachusett Mtn **Ski** •
MA, United States 116 [193]
Waco • TX, United States 119 N3
Wad Madani • Sudan 21 F5
Waddan • Libya 21 C2
Waddan, Jabal • Libya 21 C2
Waddeneilanden • Netherlands 5 H1
Waddenzee • Netherlands 80 A3
Waddi Beach • Goa, India 105 B2
Waddington, Mt • BC, Canada 122 C3
Wadebridge • United Kingdom 74 F4
Wadi • India 106 D2
Wadi ar Ru'ays • Libya 21 C2
Wageningen • Netherlands 5 I3
Wager Bay • NU, Canada 39 N3
Wagga Wagga • NS, Australia 111 G1
Wagin • WA, Australia 34 C6
Waging • Germany 82 J4
Waginger See • Germany 82 J4
Wagrain **Ski** • Austria 70 [174]
Wagrain • Austria 89 H4

Wagrowiec • Poland 13 G5
Wah • Pakistan 18 J3
Waha • Libya 21 C2
Wahai • Indonesia 32 (1) C3
Wahat al Kufrah • Libya 21 D3
Wâhât, El • Egypt 21 F2
Wahat Jalu • Libya 21 D2
Wahat Salimah • Sudan 21 E3
Wahiawa • HI, United States 119 L5
Waialua • HI, United States 119 L5
Waianae Range • HI, United States 119 L5
Waiau • New Zealand 112 L3
Waigama • Indonesia 32 (1) C3
Waigeo • Indonesia 32 (1) D3
Waihi • New Zealand 35 F3
Waihi Beach • New Zealand 112 K2
Waikaremoana, Lake • New Zealand 112 K4
Waikato [Adm] • New Zealand 112 J2
Waikato [Riv] • New Zealand 112 K2
Waikawa • New Zealand 112 L4
Waikiki • HI, United States 119 L6
Waikokopu • New Zealand 35 F4
Wailua Falls • HI, United States 119 L4
Wailuku • HI, United States 119 L3
Wailuku River State Park • HI, United States 119 L8
Waimanalo Beach • HI, United States 119 L6
Waimangu Volcanic Valley • New Zealand 112 K2
Waimate • New Zealand 35 C7
Waimea • Kauai, HI, United States 119 L2
Waimea • Hawaii, HI, United States 119 L8
Waimea Bay • HI, United States 119 L1
Waimea Canyon State Park • HI, United States 119 L2
Wainganga • India 28 C4
Waingapu • Indonesia 32 (1) B4
Waingaro • New Zealand 112 K1
Wainiha • HI, United States 119 L2
Wainwright • AL, Canada 38 I6
Waiotapu • New Zealand 112 K2
Waiouru • New Zealand 112 K4
Waipahu • HI, United States 119 L5
Waipawa • New Zealand 112 K4
Waipio Valley • HI, United States 119 L8
Waipukurau • New Zealand 112 K4
Wairakei Thermal Valley • New Zealand 112 K2
Wairoa • New Zealand 112 K4
Waitaki • New Zealand 35 C6
Waitara • New Zealand 112 K3
Waitemata • New Zealand 35 E3
Waitomo Caves • New Zealand 112 K1
Waiuku • New Zealand 35 E3
Wajh, Al • Saudi Arabia 18 C4
Wajima • Japan 30 I6
Wajir • Kenya 101 G2
Wak, El • Kenya 23 G3
Wakasa-Wan • Japan 30 H7
Wakatipu, Lake • New Zealand 112 L2
Wakayama • Japan 30 H7
Wake • Marshall Is. 33 H4
Wakefield • United Kingdom 7 K8
Wakhan • Afghanistan 18 J2
Wakkanai • Japan 30 K2
Walachia • Romania 14 L5
Walbrzych • Poland 13 F7
Walchensee • Germany 82 J7
Walcz • Poland 13 F4
Waldbronn **Spa** • Germany 83 [179]
Waldkirch • Germany 82 G8
Waldkirch **Spa** • Germany 83 [196]
Waldkraiburg • Germany 82 J4
Waldshut • Germany 82 G8
Walensee • Switzerland 89 G3
Wales • United Kingdom 7
Wales I. • NU, Canada 39 N3
Wales, northwest **Heritage C** • United Kingdom 64 [14]
Walibi **Park** • Belgium 73 [50]
Walibi • Belgium 80 A15
Walibi Flevo **Park** • Netherlands 73 [41]
Walibi Flevo • Netherlands 80 A7
Walker Lake • NV, United States 117 F4
Walker, Maggie L., Nat. Hist. Site **Park** • VA, United States 121 [258]
Walkers Beach • Barbados 125 H1
Walkerston • QL, Australia 111 F3
Walla Walla • WA, United States 117 E2
Wallasey • United Kingdom 7 I8
Walldürn • Germany 9 E7
Wallenhorst • Germany 5 K2
Wallis & Futuna • Pacific Ocean 35 (2) E1
Wallis, Is. de • Wallis & Futuna 35 (2) E1
Wallonie • Belgium 5 H4
Wallowa Mtns • OR, United States 117 E4
Walnut Canyon Nat. Mon. • AZ, United States 118 J1
Walnut Canyon Nat. Mon. **Park** • AZ, United States 120 [107]
Walsall • United Kingdom 74 D2
Walsertal, Grosser • Austria 89 H5
Walsertal, Kleiner • Austria 89 H1
Walsrode • Germany 8 E4
Waltershausen • Germany 9 F6
Walton Heath • United Kingdom 74 E3
Waltrop • Germany 81 E2
Walvis Bay • Angola 19 F8
Walvis Bay • Namibia 24 A4
Wamba • Nigeria 22 F3
Wamba • Kenya 23 F3
Wamba • Dem. Rep. of Congo 23 D3
Wamba [Riv] • Dem. Rep. of Congo 23 B5
Wamena • Indonesia 35 (1) B1
Wami • Tanzania 23 F5
Wan • Indonesia 32 (1) E4
Wan Chai • Hong Kong, China 107 H6
Wan Hsa-la • Myanmar 109 G1
Wan Zhi • China 107 J1
Wanaka • New Zealand 112 L2
Wanaka, Lake • New Zealand 112 L2
Wanapiri • Indonesia 32 (1) E3
Wandlitz • Germany 81 F2
Wandlitzer See • Germany 81 F2
Wang • Thailand 109 G3
Wang Phetburi Mtn • Thailand 109 H3
Wang Takhrai • Thailand 109 H2
Wang Takhrai Gardens • Thailand 109 H2
Wanganui • New Zealand 112 K3
Wanganui [Riv] • New Zealand 112 K3
Wangaratta • VI, Australia 111 G3
Wangen • Germany 82 J5
Wangerooge • Germany 8 C3
Wangerooge **Spa** • Germany 83 [42]
Wangpanyang • China 107 J4
Wangqing • China 30 E3
Wanneperveen • Netherlands 80 A8
Wanshan Qundao • Zhuhai, China 107 H4
Wanxian • China 29 D4
Wanzai • Zhuhai, China 107 H1
Warangal • India 28 C5
Waratah Bay • VI, Australia 111 G3
Warburg • Germany 8 E5
Warburton • SA, Australia 34 G5
Warburton Mission • WA, Australia 34 E5
Warburton Range • WA, Australia 34 E5
Ward • New Zealand 35 E5
Wardija Point • Malta 93 H1
Wareham • United Kingdom 74 F6
Waremme • Belgium 5 I4
Waren • Germany 8 H3
Waren • Indonesia 32 (1) E3
Warendorf • Germany 5 K3
Warendorf • Germany 8 C5
Wargla • Algeria 20 G2
Warkworth • New Zealand 35 E3
Warkworth **Beach** • United Kingdom 75 [13]
Warmbad • South Africa 24 D4
Warminster • United Kingdom 74 F3
Warnemünde • Germany 8 H2
Warnemünde **Beach** • Germany 68 [33]
Warnemünde **Spa** • Germany 83 [270]
Warner Brothers Movie World **Park** • Germany 73 [57]
Warner Brothers Movie World • QL, Australia 111 F6
Warner Mtns • United States 38 G8
Warner Valley • OR, United States 117 E3
Warnow • Germany 8 H3
Waroona • WA, Australia 34 C6
Warrego • NS/QL, Australia 34 I5
Warren • OH, United States 41 J3
Warri • Nigeria 22 F3
Warrington • United Kingdom 7 J8
Warrior Reefs • Australia 35 (1) C2
Warrnambool • VI, Australia 34 H7
Warsaw • Poland 13 J5
Warsaw **Heritage C** • Poland 64 [138]
Warstein • Germany 5 L3
Warszawa • Poland 13 J5
Warszawa **Heritage C** • Poland 64 [138]
Warta • Poland 13 H6
Wartberge • South Africa 24 C6
Warth • Austria 89 H5
Waru • Indonesia 32 (1) D3
Warwick • United Kingdom 74 D2
Warwick • QL, Australia 111 F6
Warwickshire • United Kingdom 74 D2
Wasalandia **Park** • Finland 73 [10]
Wasatch Range • UT, United States 40 D4
Wash, The • United Kingdom 7 M9
Washago • OT, Canada 122 B5
Washington • United Kingdom 7 K7
Washington [Adm] • United States 117 E1
Washington, Booker T., Nat. Mon. **Park** • VA, United States 121 [252]
Washington Crossing State Hist. Site • PA, United States 118 H1
Washington DC • United States 118 H3
Washington, Fort, Park **Park** • MD, United States 121 [275]
Washington, George, Birthplace Nat. Mon. • VA, United States 118 H3
Washington, George, Birthplace Nat. Mon. **Park** • VA, United States 121 [261]
Washington, George, Mem. Parkway **Park** • VA, United States 121 [266]
Washington Mon. **Park** • DC, United States 121 [298]
Washington, Mt • NH, United States 118 G3
Washington Nat. Airport • VA, United States 118 H3
Wasilków • Poland 13 M4
Wasior • Indonesia 32 (1) D3
Waskaganish • QU, Canada 39 P6
Waspám • Nicaragua 37 E5
Wassenaar • Netherlands 80 C1
Wasserburg • Germany 82 J4
Wasserkuppe • Germany 9 E6
Wast Water • United Kingdom 74 C3
Wat Phra That Doi Suthep • Thailand 109 G1
Watampone • Indonesia 32 (1) B3
Watarrka Nat. Park • NT, Australia 112 H3
Water Cay • Bahamas 124 B2
Water Mania • FL, United States 121 C1
Waterbury • CT, United States 118 H2
Waterford • Ireland 7 E9
Waterford [Adm] • Ireland 79 D2
Waterland • Netherlands 80 C2
Waterloo • Belgium 5 H4
Waterloo • IA, United States 41 H3
Waterloo [Battlefield] • Belgium 80 A14
Watermouth Castle • United Kingdom 74 F2
Waterport • NY, United States 122 B9
Waterton Lakes Nat. Park • AL, Canada 122 C4
Waterton-Glacier Int. Peace Park **Heritage N** • Canada/United States 60 [5]
Waterton-Glacier Int. Peace Park • Canada/United States 122 C4
Watertown • SD, United States 41 G3
Watertown • NY, United States 41 K3
Waterville • Ireland 79 F7
Waterville • ME, United States 118 G4
Waterville Valley **Ski** • NH, United States 116 [213]
Waterways • AL, Canada 38 I5
Watford • United Kingdom 74 E1
Watheroo • WA, Australia 34 C6
Watrous • SA, Canada 38 J6
Watsa • Dem. Rep. of Congo 23 D3
Watsi Kengo • Dem. Rep. of Congo 22 H5
Watson Lake • YT, Canada 38 F4
Watumu Marine Game Reserve • Kenya 101 G5
Watumu Marine Nat. Park • Kenya 101 G5
Watzmann • Germany 82 J8
Wau • Papua New Guinea 35 (1) D2
Waukara, Gunung • Indonesia 32 (1) A3
Waukegan • IL, United States 41 I3
Waurika • OK, United States 119 N1
Wausau • WI, United States 41 I3
Wavre • Belgium 5 H4
Wavre • Belgium 80 A15
Waw • Sudan 23 D2
Waw al Kabir • Libya 21 B2
Waw an Namus • Libya 21 B2
Wawa • OT, Canada 39 O7
Waxahachie • TX, United States 119 N1
Wayabula • Indonesia 32 (1) C2
Waycross • GA, United States 119 M3
Waza, Parc nat. de **Park** • Cameroon 103 [42]
Wé • New Caledonia 35 (2) B3
We • Indonesia 110 B1
Weald, The • United Kingdom 74 E3
Wear • United Kingdom 7 J7
Weatherford • TX, United States 119 N1
Weda • Indonesia 32 (1) C2
Weddell Sea • Antarctica 46 (1) A2
Wedel • Germany 8 E3
Weeki Wachee Spring • FL, United States 119 M5
Weener • Germany 8 C3
Weert • Netherlands 5 I3
Weesp • Netherlands 80 C2
Weggis • Switzerland 89 G3
Wei He • China 29 D4
Wei He • China 29 F3
Weichsel • Poland 13 H4
Weiden • Germany 9 H7
Weifang • China 29 F3
Weilburg • Germany 82 H2
Weiler-Simmerberg • Germany 82 J5
Weiler-Simmerberg **Spa** • Germany 83 [238]
Weilheim • Germany 82 J7
Weimar • Germany 9 G6
Weimar **Heritage C** • Germany 64 [33]
Weingarten • Germany 82 J5
Weinheim • Germany 9 D7
Weinsberg • Germany 9 E7
Weipa • QL, Australia 34 H2
Weir Farm Nat. Hist. Site **Park** • CT, United States 121 [337]
Weiskirchen **Spa** • Germany 83 [167]
Weiße Elster • Germany 9 H5
Weissenburg • France 82 G6
Weißenburg in Bayern • Germany 9 F7
Weißenfels • Germany 9 G5
Weißenhaus **Spa** • Germany 83 [20]
Weissenhorn • Germany 82 J2
Weißensee **Spa** • Germany 83 [244]
Weißwasser • Germany 8 J5
Wejherowo • Poland 13 H3
Welbourn Hill • SA, Australia 34 F5
Welch Village **Ski** • MN, United States 116 [114]
Welchman Hall Gully • Barbados 125 H3
Welden • Germany 82 J2
Weldiya • Ethiopia 23 F1
Welel • Ethiopia 23 E2
Weleri • Java, Indonesia 110 D3
Welkom • South Africa 24 D5
Welland • United Kingdom 7 L9
Welland • OT, Canada 39 P8
Welland Canal • OT, Canada 122 B9
Wellesley Is. • QL, Australia 33 E7
Wellingborough • United Kingdom 7 L9
Wellington • NS, Australia 34 I6
Wellington • New Zealand 35 E5
Wellington [Adm] • New Zealand 112 J4
Wellington, I. • Chile 45 A5
Wells • United Kingdom 74 F3
Wells • NV, United States 117 F2
Wells Gray Prov. Park • BC, Canada 122 C4
Wells-next-the-Sea • United Kingdom 5 D2
Wellsford • New Zealand 35 E3
Wels • Austria 13 C9
Welschap [Apt] • Netherlands 80 A11
Welschnofen • Italy 90 B3
Welshpool • United Kingdom 74 D1
Welwyn Garden City • United Kingdom 5 C3
Wembley Stadium • United Kingdom 74 E1
Wembury Old Mill • United Kingdom 74 F5
Wemyss Bay • United Kingdom 78 A3
Wenatchee • WA, United States 117 E1
Wenchi • Ghana 22 D3
Wendelstein • Germany 82 J7
Wendover • UT, United States 117 F2
Wenduine • Belgium 80 B2
Wengen **Ski** • Switzerland 70 [95]
Wengen • Switzerland 89 G2
Wenlock • QL, Australia 34 H2
Wenlock Edge • United Kingdom 74 D1
Wenningstedt **Spa** • Germany 83 [2]
Wenquan • China 28 F2
Wenshan • China 29 C6
Wenshan • China 29 C2
Wentworth • NS, Australia 34 H6
Wenzhou • China 29 G5
Werda • Botswana 24 C5
Werder • Germany 81 F3
Wermelskirchen • Germany 81 E4
Werneuchen • Germany 81 F2
Wernigerode • Germany 8 F5
Werra • Germany 9 E5
Werris Creek • NS, Australia 34 J6
Wertach • Germany 82 J2
Wertheim • Germany 9 E7
Wesel • Germany 81 E1
Weser • Germany 8 E4
Wesergebirge • Germany 8 E5
Weslyville • NF, Canada 123 D4
Wessel, Cape • NT, Australia 34 G2
Wessel Is. • NT, Australia 34 G2
Wessex • United Kingdom 75 A6
West Africa cruise area • Africa 59 A5
West Bali Nat. Park • Bali, Indonesia 110 C1
West Bank • Jordan 98 A6
West Bend • WI, United States 41 I3
West Bengal • India 28 E4
West Bromwich • United Kingdom 74 D2
West Cape • New Zealand 33 H10
West Cape • New Zealand 112 L3
West Coast • New Zealand 112 J3
West Coast Nat. Park • South Africa 100 C1
West Country • United Kingdom 74 F
West End • Bahamas 124 B2
West Falkland • Falkland Is. 45 D6
West Lake • China 107 J3
West Lothian • United Kingdom 74 B4
West Midland Safari Park • United Kingdom 74 D1
West Nicholson • Zimbabwe 102 J3
West Palm Beach • FL, United States 119 M6
West Point • Falkland Is. 59 A10
West Point • NY, United States 118 H1
West Riding • United Kingdom 75 A4
West Siberian Plain • Russian Fed. 26 M5
West Virginia • United States 41 J4
West Vlaanderen • Netherlands 80 A13
West Wittering **Beach** • United Kingdom 75 [76]
West Wyalong • NS, Australia 111 G1
Westbury • St Kitts & Nevis 125 G4
Westeinder Plassen • Netherlands 80 C1
Westende-Bad • Belgium 80 B1
Westendorf **Ski** • Austria 70 [150]
Westendorf • Austria 89 H3
Westerland • Germany 8 D2
Westerland **Spa** • Germany 83 [2]
Western • NU, Canada 38 J3
Western Australia • Australia 34 D5
Western, Bukit • Penang, Malaysia 108 C1
Western Cape • South Africa 100 C6
Western Desert • Egypt 21 E3
Western Lakeland • Finland 95 E2
Western Sahara • Africa 20 C4
Western Samoa • Pacific Ocean 35 (2) F1
Westernkotten **Spa** • Germany 83 [103]
Westerschelde • Netherlands 5 G3
Westerschouwen • Netherlands 5 G3
Westerstede • Germany 8 C3
Westerwald • Germany 82 G2
Westkapelle • Netherlands 5 G3
Westland • Netherlands 80 C3
Westliche Karwendelspitze • Austria/Germany 82 J7
Westmeath • Ireland 79 D1
Westminster • United Kingdom 74 E1
Westmorland • United Kingdom 74 C4
Weston • Malaysia 32 F1
Weston-super-Mare • United Kingdom 74 F3
Weston-super-Mare **Beach** • United Kingdom 75 [141]
Westport • New Zealand 35 C5
Westport • Ireland 79 F1
Westport House • Ireland 79 F1
Westray • United Kingdom 6 I2
Westward Ho! • United Kingdom 74 F2
Westwego • LA, United States 118 K4
Wet'n'Wild • QL, Australia 111 F6
Wet'n'Wild • FL, United States 121 C2
Wetar • Indonesia 32 (1) C4
Wetaskiwin • AL, Canada 38 I6
Wethersfield • CT, United States 118 H2
Wetter • Germany 5 L4
Wetter • Germany 81 E2
Wetteren • Belgium 5 G3
Wetzlar • Germany 82 G2
Wewak • Papua New Guinea 35 (1) C1
Wexford • Ireland 7 F9
Wexford [Adm] • Ireland 79 D2
Weyburn • SA, Canada 38 K7
Weymouth • United Kingdom 74 F6
Weymouth **Beach** • United Kingdom 75 [95]
Whakapapa • New Zealand 112 K4
Whakatane • New Zealand 112 K2
Whalsay • United Kingdom 75 A7
Whampoa • China 107 H1
Whanganui Nat. Park • New Zealand 112 K3
Whangarei • New Zealand 35 E2
Wheeler Peak • NM, United States 40 E4
Wheeler Peak • NV, United States 117 F4
Wheeling • WV, United States 41 J3
Whiddy I. • Ireland 79 F7
Whipsnade Zoo • United Kingdom 74 E1
Whiskeytown-Shasta-Trinity Nat. Recreation Area **Park** • CA, United States 120 [40]
Whistler **Ski** • BC, Canada 116 [2]
Whistler • BC, Canada 122 C3
Whitburn **Beach** • United Kingdom 75 [17-18]
Whitby • United Kingdom 7 L7
Whitby **Beach** • United Kingdom 75 [21]
Whitby • OT, Canada 122 B9
White Bay • NF, Canada 123 D3
White Horse Hills • United Kingdom 5 B3
White House Bay • St Kitts & Nevis 125 G4
White House, The **Park** • DC, United States 121 [299]
White I. • NU, Canada 39 O3
White I. • New Zealand 112 K2
White, Lake • NT/WA, Australia 34 E4
White Lake • LA, United States 118 K3
White Mtn Peak • CA, United States 40 C4
White Mtns • AK, United States 38 B3
White Mtns • NH, United States 118 G3
White Nile • Sudan 23 E2
White Pass Village **Ski** • WA, United States 116 [46]
White River • YT, Canada 38 C4
White River • SD, United States 38 K8
White River Junction • VT, United States 118 G3
White Sands Nat. Mon. • NM, United States 118 J4
White Sands Nat. Mon. **Park** • NM, United States 120 [121]
White Sea • Russian Fed. 17 F1
Whitecap Mtns **Ski** • WI, United States 116 [118]
Whiteface Mtn **Ski** • NY, United States 116 [184]
Whitefish Bay • MI, United States 39 N7
Whitehaven • United Kingdom 74 C1
Whitehorse • YT, Canada 38 D4
Whitehouse • Jamaica 124 C3
Whiteman Range • Papua New Guinea 35 (1) D2
Whitemark • TS, Australia 34 I8
Whitesand Bay • United Kingdom 74 F5
Whitetail **Ski** • PA, United States 116 [162]
Whitman Mission Nat. Hist. Site • WA, United States 117 E2
Whitman Mission Nat. Hist. Site **Park** • WA, United States 120 [30]
Whitmore Village • HI, United States 119 L5
Whitney, Mt • CA, United States 117 F4
Whitsunday Group • QL, Australia 111 E4
Whitsunday I. • QL, Australia 111 F1
Wholdaia Lake • NT, Canada 38 K4
Whyalla • SA, Australia 34 G6
Wiang Ko Sai Nat. Park • Thailand 109 G4
Wichita • KS, United States 41 G4
Wichita Falls • TX, United States 119 N1
Wick • United Kingdom 6 I3
Wickenburg • AZ, United States 118 J3
Wicklow • Ireland 79 E4
Wicklow [Adm] • Ireland 79 E4
Wicklow Head • Ireland 79 E4
Wicklow Mtns • Ireland 79 E4
Wicklow Mtns Nat. Park **Park** • Ireland 72 [41]
Widgiemooltha • WA, Australia 34 D6
Widyan, Al • Iraq/Saudi Arabia 18 D3
Wied • Germany 82 H2
Wieda **Spa** • Germany 83 [81]
Wiefelstede • Germany 8 D3
Wieliczka • Poland 13 J8
Wieliczka **Heritage C** • Poland 64 [140]
Wielun • Poland 13 H6
Wien • Austria 13 F9
Wien **Heritage C** • Austria 64 [107]
Wien [Adm] • Austria 89 F4
Wiener Becken • Austria 14 D1
Wiener Neustadt • Austria 13 F10
Wieprz • Poland 13 L6
Wieringermeer • Netherlands 80 A3
Wies **Heritage C** • Germany 64 [47]
Wiesbaden • Germany 82 H4
Wiesbaden **Spa** • Germany 83 [142]
Wiese • Germany 10 M6
Wieskirche • Germany 82 J6
Wiesloch • Germany 5 L5
Wiesmoor • Germany 5 K1
Wiezyca • Poland 13 H3
Wigan • United Kingdom 7 J8
Wiggins • MS, United States 118 K4
Wight, Isle of • United Kingdom 7 K11
Wigierski Nat. Park **Park** • Poland 72 [92]
Wigtown • United Kingdom 7 H7
Wigtown Bay • United Kingdom 7 H7
Wigtownshire • United Kingdom 75 A3
Wil • Switzerland 9 E9
Wilcannia • NS, Australia 34 H6
Wild Coast • South Africa 100 B2
Wild Mtn **Ski** • MN, United States 116 [111]
Wildau • Germany 81 F4
Wildbad **Spa** • Germany 83 [257]
Wildbad Kreuth • Germany 82 J7
Wildcat **Ski** • NH, United States 116 [210]
Wildemann **Spa** • Germany 83 [79]
Wildenbruch • Germany 81 F3
Wilderness Nat. Lake Area • South Africa 100 C7
Wilderswil bei Interlaken **Ski** • Switzerland 70 [93]
Wildeshausen • Germany 8 D4
Wildhaus • Switzerland 89 G3
Wildlife Reserve • Barbados 125 H1
Wildschönau **Ski** • Austria 70 [147]
Wildspitze • Austria 89 H6
Wildwood • NJ, United States 118 H3
Wilfrath • Germany 81 E3
Wilhelmshaven • Germany 8 D3
Wilhelmshaven **Spa** • Germany 83 [49]
Wilkes Barre • PA, United States 118 H1
Wilkes Land • Antarctica 46 (1) R2
Willamette • OR, United States 117 E3
Willamette Pass **Ski** • OR, United States 116 [50]
Willamette Pass • OR, United States 117 E3
Willandra Lakes **Heritage N** • NS, Australia 61 [134]
Willandra Lakes **Heritage C** • Australia 63 [182]
Willandra Lakes • NS, Australia 111 G1
Willapa Bay • WA, United States 117 E1
Willebroek • Belgium 5 H3
Willemstad • Curaçao 37 H5
Willemstad **Heritage C** • Curaçao 62 [40]
Willeroo • NT, Australia 34 F3
William, Prince, Forest Park **Park** • VA, United States 121 [264]
Williams Lake • BC, Canada 122 C3
Williams, Roger, Nat. Mem. **Park** • RI, United States 121 [339]
Williamsburg • VA, United States 118 H3
Williamsport • PA, United States 41 K3
Williamsport • PA, United States 118 H1
Willich • Germany 81 E3
Willikies • Antigua & Barbuda 125 F2
Willingen **Spa** • Germany 83 [120]
Willis Group • CL, Australia 34 J3
Williston • ND, United States 40 F2
Williston • South Africa 100 C2
Williston Lake • BC, Canada 122 C1
Willmar • MN, United States 41 G2
Willoughby Bay • Antigua & Barbuda 125 F4
Willowmore • South Africa 100 C7
Wills, Lake • WA, Australia 34 E4
Wilmington • NC, United States 41 K5
Wilmington • DE, United States 118 H3
Wilmot Mtn **Ski** • WI, United States 116 [125]
Wilnsdorf • Germany 9 D6
Wilok • Poland 13 K8
Wilpattu Nat. Park • Sri Lanka 106 D15
Wilson • NC, United States 41 K4
Wilson Bluff • Antarctica 46 (1) L2
Wilson, Cape • NU, Canada 39 O3
Wilson's Creek Nat. Battlefield **Park** • MO, United States 121 [175]
Wilsons Promontory • VI, Australia 111 G3
Wiltshire • United Kingdom 75 A6
Wiltz • Luxembourg 80 A20
Wiluna • WA, Australia 34 D5
Wimbledon • United Kingdom 74 E1
Wincanton • United Kingdom 74 F3
Winchelsea **Beach** • United Kingdom 75 [68]
Winchester • United Kingdom 7 K10
Wind Cave Nat. Park **Park** • SD, United States 120 [152]
Wind River Range • WY, United States 38 J8
Windeck • Germany 5 K4
Windemin, Pointe • Vanuatu 35 (2) B2
Windermere • United Kingdom 74 C4
Windermere [Lake] • United Kingdom 74 C4
Windhoek • Namibia 24 B4
Window Rock • AZ, United States 118 J2
Windows of the World • Shenzhen, China 107 H3
Windrush • United Kingdom 5 B3
Windsor • OT, Canada 39 O8
Windsor • United Kingdom 74 E1
Windsor • NS, Canada 123 D7
Windward Beach • St Kitts & Nevis 125 G4
Windward Is. • West Indies 37 I5
Windward Passage • Cuba/Haiti 37 G4
Winisk • OT, Canada 39 N5
Winisk Lake • OT, Canada 39 N6
Winisk [Riv] • OT, Canada 39 N6
Winneba • Ghana 22 D3
Winnebago, Lake • WI, United States 39 N8
Winnemucca • NV, United States 117 F2
Winnfield • LA, United States 118 K1
Winningen • Germany 82 H1
Winnipeg • MN, Canada 38 L6
Winnipeg, Lake • MN, Canada 38 L6
Winnipeg [Riv] • MN/OT, Canada 38 L6
Winnipegosis, Lake • MN, Canada 38 K6
Winnipesaukee, Lake • NH, United States 118 G3
Winschoten • Netherlands 5 K1
Winsen • Germany 8 E4
Winsen • Germany 8 F3
Winslow • Kiribati 33 J6
Winston • OR, United States 117 E3
Winston-Salem • NC, United States 41 J4
Winter Gardens • FL, United States 121 C1
Winter Harbour • NT/NU, Canada 38 I2
Winter Haven • FL, United States 119 M5
Winter Park **Ski** • CO, United States 116 [90]
Winter Park • FL, United States 121 C2
Winterberg • Germany 9 D5
Winterberg **Spa** • Germany 83 [109]
Winterberge • South Africa 100 C4
Wintergreen **Ski** • VA, United States 116 [156]
Winterplace **Ski** • WV, United States 116 [153]
Winterswijk • Netherlands 80 A8
Winterthur • Switzerland 9 D9
Winton • QL, Australia 34 H4
Winton • New Zealand 112 L4
Winton Heights • Bahamas 124 B3
Wipperfürth • Germany 81 E4
Wirliyajarrayi Aboriginal Land • NT, Australia 112 H1
Wisbech • United Kingdom 7 M9
Wiscasset • ME, United States 118 G4
Wisconsin • United States 41 H2
Wisconsin [Riv] • United States 39 M8
Wisla • Poland 13 H8
Wisla [Riv] • Poland 13 I8
Wislany, Zalev • Poland/Russian Fed. 13 I3
Wisloka • Poland 13 K8
Wismar • Germany 8 G3
Wisp **Ski** • MD, United States 116 [158]
Wisseler See **Beach** • Germany 68 [36]
Witbank • South Africa 24 D5
Witjira Nat. Park • SA, Australia 112 H4
Witney • United Kingdom 7 K10
Wittdün **Spa** • Germany 83 [3]
Witten • Germany 81 E2
Wittenberg • Germany 8 H5
Wittenberg **Heritage C** • Germany 64 [32]
Wittenberge • Germany 8 G3
Wittingen • Germany 8 F4
Wittlich • Germany 82 H3
Wittmund • Germany 8 C3
Wittstock • Germany 8 H3
Witvlei • Namibia 24 B4
Witwatersrand • South Africa 24 D5
Witzenhausen **Spa** • Germany 83 [129]
Wloclawek • Poland 13 I5
Wlodawa • Poland 13 M6
Wodonga • VI, Australia 111 G3
Wodzislaw Slaski • Poland 13 H8
Woerden • Netherlands 80 C4
Wokam • Indonesia 32 (1) D4
Woking • United Kingdom 74 E3
Wolds, The • United Kingdom 5 C1
Wolf • Galapagos Is. 43 (1) A1
Wolf Mtn **Ski** • UT, United States 116 [81]
Wolf Point • MT, United States 40 E2
Wolf Trap Farm Park **Park** • VA, United States 121 [266]
Wolf, Volcán • Galapagos Is. 43 (1) A2
Wolfegg • Germany 82 J5
Wolfen • Germany 8 H5
Wolfenbüttel • Germany 8 F4
Wolfhagen • Germany 9 E5
Wolfratshausen • Germany 82 J3
Wolfsberg • Austria 13 D11
Wolfsburg • Germany 8 F4
Wolgast • Germany 8 I2
Wolin • Poland 13 D4
Wolinski Nat. Park **Park** • Poland 72 [89]
Wolkenstein **Ski** • Italy 70 [232]
Wolkenstein in Gröden • Italy 90 B1
Wollaston, I. • Chile 45 C7
Wollaston Lake • SA, Canada 38 K5
Wollaston Peninsula • NU, Canada 38 H3
Wolomin • Poland 13 K5
Wolstenholm, Cape • QU, Canada 39 P4
Woltersdorf • Germany 81 F4
Wolvega • Netherlands 5 I2
Wolverhampton • United Kingdom 74 D2
Wolverton • United Kingdom 7 L9
Women's Rights Nat. Hist. Park **Park** • NY, United States 121 [317]
Wondsorejo • Indonesia 110 C1
Wonju • Rep. of Korea 30 E6
Wonosobo • Java, Indonesia 110 D7
Wonsan • D.P.R. of Korea 30 D5
Wonthaggi • VI, Australia 111 G3
Wood Buffalo Nat. Park **Heritage N** • AL/NT, Canada 60 [3]
Woodbridge • United Kingdom 5 E2
Woodbridge Bay • Dominica 58 B11
Woodlands New Town • Singapore 108 E1
Woodlark • Papua New Guinea 35 (1) E2
Woodroffe, Mt • SA, Australia 112 H3
Woods, Lake • NT, Australia 34 F3
Woods, Lake of the • Canada/United States 38 M7
Woodstock • NY, United States 118 H1
Woodville • LA, United States 118 K4
Woodville • TX, United States 119 N4
Woodward • OK, United States 40 G4
Wookey Hole • United Kingdom 74 F3
Woolacombe **Beach** • United Kingdom 75 [137]
Woollongong • NS, Australia 111 G2
Woomera • SA, Australia 34 G6
Wooramel • WA, Australia 34 B5
Worcester • MA, United States 41 L3
Worcester • United Kingdom 74 D1
Worcester • South Africa 100 C5
Worcestershire • United Kingdom 74 D2
Wordsworth House • United Kingdom 74 C1
Wörgl • Austria 9 H9
Workington • United Kingdom 74 C1
Worksop • United Kingdom 7 K8
World's View • Zimbabwe 102 J3
Wormerveer • Netherlands 80 C2
Worms • Germany 82 H4
Wörth • Germany 5 L5
Wörther See • Austria 13 D11

Worthing - Zywiec

Worthing • United Kingdom **74** E3
Worthing **Beach** • United Kingdom **75** [74]
Worthsee • Germany **82** J3
Wosi • Indonesia **32** (1) C3
Wowoni • Indonesia **32** (1) B3
Woy Woy • NS, Australia **34** J6
Wrangel I. • Russian Fed. **27** V2
Wrangell • AK, United States **38** E5
Wrangell, Mt • AK, United States **40** (2) G2
Wrangell Mtns • AK, United States **38** C4
Wrangell-St Elias Nat. Park & Preserve **Heritage N** • AK, United States **60** [1]
Wrangell-St Elias Nat. Park & Preserve **Park** • AK, United States **120** [12]
Wrath, Cape • United Kingdom **6** G3
Wrekin, The • United Kingdom **74** D1
Wremen **Spa** • Germany **83** [53]
Wrexham • United Kingdom **7** J8
Wright Brothers Nat. Mem. • NC, United States **118** H5
Wright Brothers Nat. Mem. **Park** • NC, United States **121** [251]
Wrigley • NT, Canada **38** G4
Wrka • Poland **13** J5
Wroclaw • Poland **13** F6
Wronki • Poland **13** F5
Wrzesnia • Poland **13** G5
Wschowa • Poland **13** F6
Wu Jiang • China **29** D5
Wu Xia • China **29** D4
Wudangshan **Heritage C** • China **63** [150]
Wudaoliang • China **28** F1
Wudu • China **29** C4
Wuhan • China **29** E4
Wuhu • China **107** J1
Wujiang • China **107** J2
Wukari • Nigeria **22** F3
Wulferdingsen **Spa** • Germany **83** [94]
Wuliang Shan • China **29** C6
Wulingyuan **Heritage N** • China **61** [118]
Wulur • Indonesia **32** (1) C4
Wum • Cameroon **22** G3
Wümme • Germany **5** M1
Wun Rog • Sudan **23** D2
Wünnenberg **Spa** • Germany **83** [102]
Wunsiedel • Germany **9** H6
Wunstorf • Germany **8** E4
Wupatki Nat. Mon. • AZ, United States **118** J1
Wupatki Nat. Mon. **Park** • AZ, United States **120** [105]
Wupper • Germany **81** E4
Wuppertal • Germany **81** E4
Würm • Germany **82** J3
Wurno • Nigeria **22** F2
Wursten **Spa** • Germany **83** [53]
Würzburg • Germany **9** E7
Würzburg **Heritage C** • Germany **64** [45]
Wurzen • Germany **8** H5
Wushaoling • China **29** C3
Wusheng Guan • China **29** E4
Wusong • China **59** A8
Wustermark • Germany **81** F1
Wustrow **Spa** • Germany **83** [275]
Wutach • Germany **9** D9
Wutai Shan • China **29** E3
Wutong Shan • China **107** H4
Wuwei • China **29** C3
Wuxi • China **107** J2
Wuyi Shan • China **29** F5
Wuyiling • China **27** K7
Wuyuan • China **29** D2
Wuyuanzhen • China **107** J4
Wuzhi Shan • China **31** D3
Wyandra • QL, Australia **111** F5
Wye • United Kingdom **74** D3
Wye Valley • United Kingdom **74** D3
Wyk **Spa** • Germany **83** [4]
Wyndham • WA, Australia **34** E3
Wyndham • New Zealand **112** L4
Wynyard • TS, Australia **34** I8
Wynyard • SA, Canada **38** K6
Wyoming • United States **40** E3
Wyre Forest • United Kingdom **74** D1
Wysoczyna Ciechanowska • Poland **13** J4
Wyszków • Poland **13** K5
Wyzyna Krakowsko-Czestochowsk • Poland **13** I7
Wyzyna Lubelska • Poland **13** L6
Wyzyna Lubelska • Poland **13** M6

X

Xabia **Beach** • Spain **68** [118]
Xaghra • Malta **93** H1
Xai-Xai • Mozambique **24** E4
Xainza • China **28** E2
Xalapa • Mexico **123** E2
Xangongo • Angola **24** B3
Xanten • Germany **80** A12
Xanten • Germany **81** E1
Xánthi • Greece **92** D1
Xanthos • Turkey **92** D9
Xanthos-Letoon **Heritage C** • Turkey **64** [188]
Xanxerê • Brazil **44** F4
Xapuri • Brazil **43** D6
Xátiva • Spain **11** K5
Xeraco **Beach** • Spain **68** [119]
Xewkija • Malta **93** H1
Xi Hu • China **107** J3
Xi'an • China **29** D4
Xi'an area **Heritage C** • China **63** [149]
Xiaguan • China **29** C5
Xiamen • China **29** F6
Xiang Jiang • China **29** E5
Xiangfan • China **29** E4
Xiangshan • China **107** J4
Xiangtan • China **29** E5
Xiangzhou • Zhuhai, China **107** H1
Xiannumiao • China **107** J1
Xianqouan He • China **28** C2
Xianxia Ling • China **29** F5
Xiao Hinggan Ling • China **27** K7
Xiaobole Shan • China **27** J6
Xiaolan • China **107** H1
Xiaomeisha Beach Resort • Shenzhen, China **107** H4
Xiaoshan • China **107** J4
Xiapu • China **31** F1
Xichang • China **29** C5
Xigaze • China **28** E3
Xijir Ulan Hu • China **28** E1
Xili Lake Resort • Shenzhen, China **107** H3
Xilókastro • Greece **15** D5
Xilókastro **Beach** • Greece **69** [178]
Xilxes **Beach** • Spain **68** [120]
Ximiao • China **29** C2
Xingtai • China **29** E3
Xingu • Brazil **43** G5
Xingxingxia • China **29** B2
Xingyi • China **31** C2
Xining • China **29** C3
Xinjiang Uygur Zizhiqu • China **26** N10
Xinxian • China **29** E3
Xinxiang • China **29** E3
Xinyang • China **29** E4
Xinzo de Limia • Spain **11** D2
Xiongyuecheng • China **30** B4
Xiró • Greece **15** E5
Xisha Qundao • South China Sea **31** E3
Xisha Qundao • South China Sea **107** G7
Xitianmu Shan • China **107** J3
Xiuyan • China **30** B4
Xixabangma Feng • China **28** E3
Xizang Zizhiqu • China **28** E2
Xlendi • Malta **93** H1
Xlendi Bay • Malta **93** H1
Xochimilco **Heritage C** • Mexico **62** [21]
Xuan Loc • Vietnam **108** B2
Xuanhua • China **29** F2
Xuanwei • China **29** C5
Xuanzhou • China **107** J3
Xuefeng Shan • China **29** D5
Xun Jiang • China **29** E6
Xupu • China **31** E1
Xuwen • China **29** E6
Xuzhou • China **29** F4
Xylóskalo • Crete, Greece **93** E5

Y

Ya Men • China **107** H3
Ya'an • China **29** C4
Yabelo • Ethiopia **23** F3
Yablonovyy Khrebet • Russian Fed. **27** H6
Yabu, Laem • Phuket, Thailand **109** K1
Yabulu • QL, Australia **111** F1
Yacuma • Bolivia **44** C1
Yadé, Massif du • Cameroon/Central African Rep. **22** H3
Yaeyama-Retto • Japan **29** G6
Yafo • Israel **98** A5
Yafran • Libya **21** B1
Yagoua • Cameroon **22** H2
Yagradagzê Shan • China **29** B3
Yai, Khao • Ko Samui, Thailand **109** J1
Yai, Laem • Ko Samui, Thailand **109** J1
Yaíza **Beach** • Lanzarote, Canary Is. **68** [111]
Yaíza • Lanzarote, Canary Is. **87** E3
Yakima • WA, United States **117** E1
Yako • Burkina Faso **22** D2
Yaku • Japan **30** F9
Yakumo • Japan **30** K3
Yakushima **Heritage N** • Japan **61** [119]
Yakutat • AK, United States **38** D5
Yakutat Bay • AK, United States **38** C5
Yakutia • Russian Fed. **27** H3
Yakutsk • Russian Fed. **27** K4
Yala • Thailand **31** B5
Yala Nat. Park • Sri Lanka **106** D16
Yalgoo • WA, Australia **34** C5
Yalinga • Central African Rep. **23** C2
Yaloké • Central African Rep. **22** H3
Yalong Jiang • China **29** C4
Yalongxue Shan • China **29** C5
Yalova • Turkey **92** D3
Yalpug, Ozero • Ukraine **14** P4
Yalta • Ukraine **17** E6
Yalu • China/D.P.R. of Korea **30** D4
Yalutorovsk • Russian Fed. **26** K6
Yamagata • Japan **30** K5
Yamaguchi • Japan **30** F7
Yamal Peninsula • Russian Fed. **96** A3
Yamal, Poluostrov • Russian Fed. **26** K3
Yamarovka • Russian Fed. **27** H6
Yamaska Prov. Park • QU, Canada **122** B8
Yambio • Sudan **23** D3
Yambol • Bulgaria **97** D3
Yamdena • Indonesia **32** (1) D4
Yamma Yamma, Lake • QL, Australia **34** H5
Yamoussoukro • Côte d'Ivoire **22** C3
Yamsk • Russian Fed. **27** P5
Yamuna • India **105** C7
Yamzho Yumco • China **28** F3
Yan'an • China **29** D3
Yana • Russian Fed. **27** M2
Yanam • India **106** D4
Yanbu • Saudi Arabia **18** C5
Yanchang • China **29** E3
Yancheng • China **29** G4
Yangambi • Dem. Rep. of Congo **23** C3
Yangiyul • Uzbekistan **18** I1
Yangjiang • China **29** E6
Yangon • Myanmar **31** B3
Yangquan • China **29** E3
Yangtze • China **29** F4
Yangtze Gorges • China **107** G7
Yangzhou • China **107** J1
Yanji • China **29** H2
Yankari Nat. Park **Park** • Nigeria **103** [34]
Yankee Harbour • Antarctica **59** A10
Yankton • SD, United States **41** G3
Yano-Indigirskaya Nizmennost • Russian Fed. **27** N2
Yanqi • China **26** O9
Yanskiy Zaliv • Russian Fed. **27** M2
Yantai • China **29** G3
Yantian • Shenzhen, China **107** H4
Yantra • Bulgaria **97** D3
Yao • Chad **22** H2
Yaoundé • Cameroon **22** G4
Yap • Fed. States of Micronesia **25** P8
Yap • Fed. States of Micronesia **33** E5
Yapen • Indonesia **32** (1) E3
Yapu • Myanmar **31** B4
Yaqui • Mexico **40** E6
Yar-Sale • Russian Fed. **26** L4
Yaraka • QL, Australia **34** H4
Yaransk • Russian Fed. **17** H3
Yardimci Burun • Turkey **93** G3
Yare • United Kingdom **5** E2
Yari • Colombia **43** C3
Yariga • Japan **30** I6
Yarim • Yemen **18** D7
Yarkand • China **18** K2
Yarkant • China **98** B2
Yarkant He • China **26** M10
Yarlung Zangbo Jiang • China **28** E3
Yarmouth • United Kingdom **78** C8
Yarmouth • NS, Canada **123** D7
Yaroslavl' • Russian Fed. **97** E2
Yartsevo • Russian Fed. **26** P5
Yarumal • Colombia **43** B2
Yasawa Group • Fiji **35** (2) D2
Yashi • Nigeria **22** F2
Yass • NS, Australia **111** G2
Yatagan • Turkey **15** J6
Yateritas • Cuba **124** D8
Yatsushiro • Japan **30** F8
Yatta Plateau • Kenya **101** G4
Yau Ma Tei • Hong Kong, China **107** H6
Yauca • Peru **127** B3
Yáuco • Puerto Rico **125** E3
Yauyos • Peru **127** B1
Yavari • Brazil/Peru **43** C4
Yavero • Peru **127** B2
Yawatahama • Japan **30** G8
Yaxchilán • Mexico **37** C4
Yazd • Iran **18** F3
Yazoo • MS, United States **118** K2
Yazoo City • MS, United States **118** K2
Ydre • Sweden **95** F8
Ye • Myanmar **31** B3
Ye-u • Myanmar **28** F4
Yebbi Bou • Chad **20** I4
Yecheng • China **28** C1
Yecla • Spain **87** C1
Yedi Burun • Turkey **15** J7
Yefremov • Russian Fed. **17** F4
Yeha • Eritrea **21** G5
Yeji • Ghana **22** D3
Yekaterinburg • Russian Fed. **26** J6
Yelapa • Mexico **123** E1
Yelets • Russian Fed. **17** F4
Yelizavety, mys • Russian Fed. **27** N6
Yelizovo • Russian Fed. **27** Q6
Yell • United Kingdom **6** K1
Yellice Dagi • Turkey **15** K4
Yellow Mountains • China **107** J3
Yellow Sea • Asia **29** G3
Yellowhead Pass • AL/BC, Canada **122** C2
Yellowknife • NT, Canada **38** I4
Yellowknife [Riv] • NT, Canada **38** I4
Yellowstone • MT/WY, United States **40** E2
Yellowstone Nat. Park **Heritage N** • WY, United States **60** [14]
Yellowstone Nat. Park **Park** • WY, United States **120** [74]
Yelwa • Nigeria **22** E2
Yemen • Asia **18** E7
Yenashimskiy Polkan, gora • Russian Fed. **26** P6
Yendi • Ghana **22** D3
Yengo • Congo **23** B3
Yenice • Turkey **15** I4
Yenifoça • Turkey **15** H5
Yenisey • Russian Fed. **26** O4
Yeniseysk • Russian Fed. **27** D5
Yeniseyskiy Kryazh • Russian Fed. **26** P5
Yeniseyskiy Zaliv • Russian Fed. **26** N3
Yeo Lake • WA, Australia **34** D5
Yeovil • United Kingdom **74** F3
Yeppoon • QL, Australia **111** F4
Yerbogachen • Russian Fed. **27** G4
Yercaud • India **106** D7
Yercpótamos • Crete, Greece **93** E7
Yerevan • Armenia **18** D1
Yermak • Kazakhstan **26** M7
Yermasóyia **Beach** • Cyprus **69** [218]
Yermasóyia • Cyprus **93** J3
Yermolayevo • Russian Fed. **26** I7
Yeroskípos • Cyprus **93** J3
Yerres • France **5** G6
Yerupaja • Peru **43** B6
Yerwa • Nigeria **22** H2
Yesa, Embalse de • Spain **11** J2
Yesilbag • Turkey **93** G2
Yesilköy • Turkey **15** J3
Yesilova • Turkey **93** G1
Yessey • Russian Fed. **26** R4
Yeste • Spain **11** I6
Yeu, I. d' • France **10** C7
Yevreyskaya • Russian Fed. **27** L7
Yeysk • Russian Fed. **17** F5
Yí • Uruguay **127** D2
Yi Xian • China **107** J3
Yi'an • China **27** K7
Yialoúsa • Cyprus **93** J2
Yibin • China **29** C5
Yibug Caka • China **28** E2
Yichang • China **29** E4
Yichun • China **27** K7
Yidu • China **29** E4
Yilan • China **27** K7
Yilanli • Turkey **93** G2
Yildiz Daglari • Turkey **15** I2
Yinchuan • China **29** D3
Yingde • China **29** E6
Yingkou • China **29** G2
Yining • China **26** N9
Yirshi • China **29** F1
Yishun New Town • Singapore **108** E2
Yixing • China **107** J1
Yiyang • China **29** E5
Yläne • Finland **95** E3
Ylikitka • Finland **16** O3
Ylitornio • Finland **16** L3
Ylivieska • Finland **16** M4
Ylöjärvi • Finland **95** E2
Yngaren • Sweden **95** D3
Yoakum • TX, United States **119** N5
Yogan, Cerro • Chile **45** C6
Yogyakarta • Java, Indonesia **110** D7
Yogyakarta [Adm] • Java, Indonesia **110** D7
Yoho Nat. Park • BC, Canada **122** C4
Yoju • Rep. of Korea **30** D6
Yokadouma • Cameroon **22** H4
Yokkaichi • Japan **30** I7
Yoko • Cameroon **22** G3
Yokohama • Japan **30** J7
Yokosuka • Japan **30** J7
Yokote • Japan **30** K5
Yola • Nigeria **22** G3
Yom • Thailand **109** G2
Yonago • Japan **30** G7
Yongan • D.P.R. of Korea **30** E4
Yongdeng • China **29** C3
Yongdok • Rep. of Korea **30** E6
Yonghung • D.P.R. of Korea **30** D5
Yongju • Rep. of Korea **30** E6
Yongwol • Rep. of Korea **30** E6
Yonne • France **10** I5
York • United Kingdom **7** K8
York • WA, Australia **34** C6
York • PA, United States **118** H1
York, Cape • QL, Australia **34** H2
York, Cape, Peninsula • QL, Australia **34** H2
York I. • Antigua & Barbuda **125** F4
Yorke Peninsula • SA, Australia **34** G6
Yorkshire • United Kingdom **7** K7
Yorkshire Dales Nat. Park **Park** • United Kingdom **72** [44]
Yorkshire Dales Nat. Park • United Kingdom **75** A4
Yorkshire Wolds • United Kingdom **7** L7
Yorktown • VA, United States **118** H3
Yorton • SA, Canada **38** K6
Yosemite Nat. Park **Heritage N** • CA, United States **60** [11]
Yosemite Nat. Park • CA, United States **117** F3
Yosemite Nat. Park **Park** • CA, United States **120** [51]
Yoshkar Ola • Russian Fed. **17** H3
Yosu • Rep. of Korea **30** D7
You Jiang • China **29** D6
Youghal • Ireland **7** E10
Youghal **Beach** • Ireland **68** [59]
Youngstown • NU, Canada **39** N4
Youngstown • OH, United States **41** J3
Youshashan • China **26** P10
Youyang • China **29** D5
Yow Beach • Ko Samui, Thailand **109** J2
Ypres • Belgium **80** A13
Yquem, Château • France **85** G3
Ystad **Beach** • Sweden **69** [13]
Ystad • Sweden **95** F15
Ytre Arna • Norway **94** C3
Ytre Sula • Norway **94** C3
Yuan Jiang • China **29** C6
Yuanling • China **29** E5
Yuantouzhu • China **107** J1
Yuba City • CA, United States **40** B4
Yubari • Japan **30** K3
Yucatán [Adm] • Mexico **37** D3
Yucatán Channel • Mexico **37** D3
Yucatán, Península de • Mexico **37** D4
Yucca House Nat. Mon. **Park** • CO, United States **120** [95]
Yudoma • Russian Fed. **27** M5
Yuen Long • Hong Kong, China **107** H5
Yuendumu • NT, Australia **112** H1
Yuendumu Aboriginal Land • NT, Australia **112** H1
Yueyang • China **29** E5
Yugo-Tala • Russian Fed. **27** P3
Yugoslavia, F.R. of • Europe **14** H5
Yuhang • China **107** J4
Yukagirskoye Ploskogorye • Russian Fed. **27** Q3
Yukon • AK, United States **40** (2) F2
Yukon Flats • AK, United States **38** B3
Yukon Plateau • YT, Canada **38** D4
Yukon Territory • Canada **38** D4
Yukon-Charley Rivers Nat. Preserve **Park** • AK, United States **120** [6]
Yulara • NT, Australia **112** H3
Yulin • Shaanxi, China **29** D3
Yulin • Guangxi, China **31** E2
Yulin Jao • China **25** M8
Yulongxue Shan • China **31** C1
Yuma • AZ, United States **118** J3
Yumari • Venezuela **43** D3
Yumen • China **29** B3
Yun-Gun-Gui Gaoyuian • China **31** C1
Yunak • Turkey **15** M5
Yunan • China **107** G6
Yungas • Bolivia **44** D2
Yunkai Dashan • China **31** E2
Yunkanjini Aboriginal Land • NT, Australia **112** H1
Yunzhong Shan • China **29** E3
Yurga • Russian Fed. **26** N6
Yurimaguas • Peru **43** B5
Yurungkax He • China **28** C1
Yushan • Taiwan **29** G6
Yushkozero • Russian Fed. **17** E2
Yushu • China **29** B4
Yutian • China **28** D1
Yuxi • China **31** C2
Yuxikou • China **107** J1
Yuyao • China **107** J4
Yuzawa • Japan **30** K5
Yuzhno-Kuril'sk • Russian Fed. **27** O8
Yuzhnyy Bug • Ukraine **17** D5
Yuznho-Sakhalinsk • Russian Fed. **27** N7
Yvelines • France **85** E3
Yverdon-les-Bains • Switzerland **89** G1
Yvetot • France **10** F4
Yvoir • Belgium **80** A15

Z

Za Qu • China **28** G2
Zaanse Schans • Netherlands **80** C2
Zaanstad • Netherlands **80** C2
Zabarjad • Egypt **21** G3
Zabid • Yemen **18** D7
Zabid **Heritage C** • Yemen **63** [102]
Zabkowice Slaskie • Poland **13** F7
Zablotiv • Ukraine **14** M1
Zabrze • Poland **13** H7
Zacatecas **Heritage C** • Mexico **62** [14]
Zacatecas • Mexico **123** E1
Zacatecas [Adm] • Mexico **37** (1) B1
Zadar • Croatia **14** C5
Zadetkyi Kyun • Myanmar **31** B5
Zadi • Angola **23** B5
Zadoì • China **28** F2
Zafra • Spain **11** E6
Zagan • Poland **13** E6
Zagâzig, El • Egypt **101** F2
Zaghouan • Tunisia **101** E2
Zagora • Croatia **14** D6
Zagorá **Beach** • Greece **69** [188]
Zagorá • Greece **92** D4
Zagora • Morocco **101** D6
Zagoria • Greece **15** B4
Zagorje • Croatia **14** C3
Zagreb • Croatia **14** C4
Zagros, Kuhha-ye • Iran **18** F3
Zagyva • Hungary **13** J10
Zaháro • Greece **15** C6
Zaháro **Beach** • Greece **69** [180]
Zahedan • Iran **18** H4
Záhrada Cech • Czech Rep. **96** C2
Zajecar • F.R. of Yugoslavia **14** J6
Zakamensk • Russian Fed. **27** F6
Zakataly • Azerbaijan **17** H6
Zákinthos **Beach** • Greece **69** [172]
Zákinthos • Greece **92** C3
Zákinthos [I.] • Greece **92** C3
Zakopane • Poland **13** I8
Zakouma, Parc nat. de **Park** • Chad **103** [43]
Zákros • Crete, Greece **93** E8
Zala • Hungary **13** G11
Zalaegerszeg • Hungary **13** F11
Zalau • Romania **14** L2
Zalim • Saudi Arabia **18** D5
Zalingei • Sudan **21** D5
Zallaca • Spain **71** A16
Zaltan • Libya **21** C2
Zambezi • Zambia **24** C2
Zambezi Nat. Park • Zimbabwe **102** J1
Zambezi Nat. Park **Park** • Zimbabwe **103** [108]
Zambezi [Riv] • Africa **24** C3
Zambia • Africa **24** D2
Zamboanga • Philippines **31** G5
Zamboanga Peninsula • Philippines **31** G5
Zambrów • Poland **13** L5
Zamora • Spain **11** F3
Zamosc • Poland **13** M7
Zamosc **Heritage C** • Poland **64** [139]
Zamzam • Libya **21** B1
Zandvoort • Netherlands **80** C1
Zandvoort, Auto Circuit • Netherlands **80** C1
Zanjan • Iran **18** E2
Zante **Beach** • Greece **69** [172]
Zante • Greece **92** C3
Zanthus • WA, Australia **34** D6
Zanzibar • Tanzania **102** H2
Zanzibar I. • Tanzania **102** H2
Zaouatallaz • Algeria **20** G4
Zaozernyy • Russian Fed. **26** P6
Západné Karpaty • Europe **13** I8
Zapadno Dvina • Russian Fed. **97** E3
Zapadno Sibirskaya Ravnina • Russian Fed. **26** M5
Zapadno Sibirskoye Nizmennost • Russian Fed. **96** A4
Zapadnyy Sayan • Russian Fed. **26** O7
Zapala • Argentina **45** C3
Zapata, Peninsula de • Cuba **124** D2
Zapicán • Uruguay **127** D2
Zapolyarnyy • Russian Fed. **17** E1
Zaporozh'ye • Ukraine **17** F5
Zara • Croatia **71** A14
Zarafshan • Uzbekistan **26** J9
Zaragoza • Spain **11** K3
Zaragoza • Colombia **43** C2
Zaranj • Afghanistan **18** H3
Zárate • Argentina **127** D1
Zarautz • Spain **11** I1
Zaraza • Venezuela **43** D2
Zarco, Baia de • Madeira **88** C2
Zarechensko • Russian Fed. **16** P3
Zaria • Nigeria **22** F2
Zarnesti • Romania **14** M4
Zarqa, Az • Jordan **21** G1
Zary • Poland **13** E6
Zarzatine • Algeria **20** G3
Zarzis • Tunisia **101** E6
Zatec • Czech Rep. **96** C1
Zaventem [Apt] • Belgium **80** A14
Zawiah • Libya **21** B2
Zawiercie • Poland **13** I7
Zaysan • Kazakhstan **26** N8
Zaysan Köli • Kazakhstan **26** N8
Zayü • China **29** B5
Zdunska Wola • Poland **13** H6
Zealand • Denmark **95** F10
Zebbug • Malta **93** H4
Zebulun • Israel **98** A4
Zeebrugge • Belgium **80** B2
Zeedierenpark Harderwijk **Park** • Netherlands **73** [42]
Zeeland • Netherlands **80** A10
Zehdenick • Germany **8** I3
Zeil, Mt • NT, Australia **112** H1
Zeimena • Lithuania **16** M9
Zeist • Netherlands **80** C4
Zeitz • Germany **9** H5
Zelená Hora **Heritage C** • Czech Rep. **64** [145]
Zelenoborskiy • Russian Fed. **16** P3
Zelenodolsk • Russian Fed. **17** H3
Zelenogradsk • Russian Fed. **13** J3
Zelezná Rudá • Czech Rep. **96** C3
Zell • Baden-Württemberg, Germany **82** G6
Zell • Rheinland-Pfalz, Germany **82** H3
Zell am See **Ski** • Austria **70** [164]
Zell am See • Austria **89** H4
Zell am Ziller **Ski** • Austria **70** [144]
Zell am Ziller • Austria **89** H7
Zelzate • Belgium **5** G3
Zemaitija Nat. Park **Park** • Lithuania **72** [145]
Zembra • Tunisia **101** E2
Zembretta • Tunisia **101** E2
Zemmora • Algeria **11** L9
Zempin **Spa** • Germany **83** [283-285]
Zempoala • Mexico **37** B4
Zemst **Beach** • Belgium **68** [73]
Zemst • Belgium **80** A14
Zengfeng • China **30** E3
Zenica • Bosnia-Herz. **14** E5
Zennor • United Kingdom **74** F4
Zepce • Bosnia-Herz. **12** M4
Zepernick • Germany **81** F2
Zerbst • Germany **8** H5
Zermatt **Ski** • Switzerland **70** [91]
Zermatt • Switzerland **89** G6
Zernabatim Beach • Goa, India **105** B2
Zernez • Switzerland **89** G4
Zernsdorf • Germany **81** F4
Zestienhoven [Apt] • Netherlands **80** C3
Zetel • Germany **5** K1
Zetlands • St Kitts & Nevis **125** G4
Zeulenroda • Germany **9** G6
Zeuthen • Germany **81** F4
Zeven • Germany **8** E3
Zevenaar • Netherlands **5** J3
Zeya • Russian Fed. **27** K6
Zeya [Riv] • Russian Fed. **27** K6
Zeytindag • Turkey **15** I5
Zezere • Portugal **11** C5
Zgierz • Poland **13** I6
Zgorzelec • Poland **13** E6
Zhanagaqazaly • Kazakhstan **26** J8
Zhangbei • China **29** E2
Zhanggong Cave • China **107** J1
Zhangjiagang • China **107** J2
Zhangjiakou • China **29** F2
Zhangmutou • China **107** H2
Zhangye • China **29** C3
Zhangzhou • China **29** F6
Zhanjiang • China **29** E6
Zhanyi • China **29** C5
Zhaotong • China **29** C5
Zhaxi Co • China **28** D2
Zhejiang • China **107** G8
Zheleznodorozhnyy • Russian Fed. **17** I2
Zhen Jiang • China **107** J1
Zhengzhou • China **29** E4
Zhenhai • China **107** J4
Zhenyuan • China **31** D1
Zhi Ou • China **28** G2
Zhigalovo • Russian Fed. **27** G6
Zhigansk • Russian Fed. **27** J3
Zhijiang • China **29** D5
Zhitomir • Ukraine **14** D4
Zhitomir • Ukraine **17** D4
Zhob • Pakistan **28** A2
Zhongba • China **28** D3
Zhongdian • China **29** B5
Zhongning • China **29** D3
Zhongsha Qundao • South China Sea **107** G8
Zhongshan • China **107** H1
Zhongye Qundao • South China Sea **31** E4
Zhoukoudian **Heritage C** • China **63** [147]
Zhoukouzhen • China **29** E4
Zhoushan • China **107** J4
Zhoushan Dao • China **107** J4
Zhoushan Qundao • China **107** J4
Zhu Jiang • China **107** H2
Zhuanghe • China **30** B5
Zhuhai Holiday Resort • Zhuhai, China **107** H1
Zhuhai Special Economic Zone • China **107** H1
Zhuji • China **107** J4
Zhujing • China **107** J4
Zhuzhou • China **29** E5
Ziar • Slovak Rep. **13** H9
Zibo • China **29** F3
Zicavo • Corsica, France **85** L4
Ziegenhals • Germany **81** F4
Zielona Góra • Poland **13** E6
Zierikzee • Netherlands **5** G3
Zigong • China **29** C5
Ziguinchor • Senegal **22** A2
Zihuatanejo • Mexico **123** E3
Zijin Shan • China **107** J1
Zijing Shan • China **29** E3
Zijpe **Beach** • Netherlands **68** [67]
Zilina • Slovak Rep. **13** H8
Zillah • Libya **21** C2
Zillertal • Austria **89** H7
Zillertaler Alpen • Austria/Italy **89** H7
Zima • Russian Fed. **27** F6
Zimba • Zambia **24** D3
Zimbabwe • Africa **102** J
Zimnicea • Romania **97** D1
Zinal • Switzerland **89** G6
Zinder • Niger **20** G6
Zingst • Germany **8** H2
Zingst **Beach** • Germany **68** [32]
Zingst **Spa** • Germany **83** [277]
Zinnowitz **Beach** • Germany **69** [30]
Zinnowitz **Spa** • Germany **83** [283]
Zion • St Kitts & Nevis **125** G4
Zion Nat. Park • UT, United States **118** J1
Zion Nat. Park **Park** • UT, United States **120** [80]
Zipaqirá • Colombia **43** C3
Zippori • Israel **98** A4
Zirje • Croatia **14** C6
Zirndorf • Germany **9** F7
Zittau • Germany **9** J6
Ziway, Lake • Ethiopia **23** F2
Ziyaaraiyfushi • Maldives **106** E2
Zlatá Koruna • Czech Rep. **96** C4
Zlaté Moravce • Slovak Rep. **13** H9
Zlatijata • Bulgaria **14** K6
Zlatni Pyasutsi • Bulgaria **97** D4
Zlatograd • Bulgaria **15** G2
Zlatoust • Russian Fed. **26** I6
Zleby • Czech Rep. **96** C2
Zlín • Czech Rep. **13** G8
Zlocieniec • Poland **13** F4
Zlotów • Poland **13** G4
Znin • Poland **13** G5
Znojmo • Czech Rep. **96** C4
Zoetemeer • Netherlands **80** C3
Zoldo Alto **Ski** • Italy **70** [225]
Zoldo Alto • Italy **90** B4
Zomba • Malawi **24** E3
Zonári, Akra • Rhodes, Greece **93** F2
Zongo • Dem. Rep. of Congo **22** H4
Zongshan Hot Springs • China **107** H1
Zonguldak • Turkey **15** M2
Zonhoven **Beach** • Belgium **68** [72]
Zonhoven • Belgium **80** A15
Zonnebeke [Battlefield] • Belgium **80** A13
Zons • Germany **81** E3
Zoologischer Garten Berlin • Germany **81** F2
Zoomarine **Park** • Portugal **73** [80]
Zoorama • France **85** G1
Zorzor • Liberia **22** C3
Zossen • Germany **81** F4
Zouar • Chad **21** C3
Zourât • Mauritania **20** C4
Zrenjanin • F.R. of Yugoslavia **14** H4
Zrinska Gora • Croatia **14** D4
Zuancheng • China **107** J3
Zuari Estuary • Goa, India **105** B1
Zufar • Oman **25** G8
Zug **Ski** • Austria **70** [130]
Zug • Switzerland **89** G3
Zuger See • Switzerland **89** G3
Zugspitze • Austria/Germany **82** J6
Zuid-Beveland • Netherlands **80** A10
Zuid-Holland • Netherlands **80** A6
Zújar, Embalse del • Spain **11** F6
Zülpich • Germany **82** G1
Zumaia **Beach** • Spain **68** [87]
Zumbo • Mozambique **24** E3
Zuni • NM, United States **118** J2
Zunyi • China **29** D5
Zuoz • Switzerland **89** G4
Zuqar, Jabal • Yemen **21** H5
Zürich • Switzerland **9** D9
Zürichsee • Switzerland **89** G3
Zurmi • Nigeria **20** G6
Zurrieq • Malta **93** H4
Zürs **Ski** • Austria **70** [131]
Zürs • Austria **89** H5
Zuru • Nigeria **22** F2
Zusmarshausen • Germany **82** J2
Zut • Croatia **14** C6
Zutphen • Netherlands **80** A8
Zuurberg Nat. Park • South Africa **100** C8
Zuwarah • Libya **21** B1
Zvikov • Czech Rep. **96** C4
Zvishavane • Zimbabwe **102** J4
Zvishtov • Bulgaria **14** M6
Zvolen • Slovak Rep **13** I9
Zweibrücken • Germany **82** G3
Zweisel • Germany **9** I7
Zweisimmen **Ski** • Switzerland **70** [87]
Zweisimmen • Switzerland **89** G2
Zwettl • Austria **13** E9
Zwickau • Germany **9** H6
Zwickauer Mulde • Germany **9** H6
Zwijndrecht • Netherlands **80** C3
Zwolle • Netherlands **80** A8
Zyrardów • Poland **13** J5
Zyryan • Kazakhstan **26** N8
Zyryanka • Russian Fed. **27** P3
Zywiec • Poland **13** I8